Daniel J. Keyser, Ph.D.
Richard C. Sweetland, Ph.D.
General Editors

TEST CRITIQUES

Volume II

TEST CORPORATION OF AMERICA

Library of Congress Cataloging in Publication Data
(Revised for vol. 2)
Main entry under title:

Test critiques.

    Includes bibliographies and indexes.
    1. Psychological tests—Evaluation—Collected works. 2. Educational tests and measurements—Evaluation—Collected works. 3. Business—Examinations—Evaluation—Collected works. I. Keyser, Daniel J., 1935-　　.II. Sweetland, Richard C., 1931-
BF176.T419   1985   150'.28'7   84-26895
ISBN 0-9611286-6-6 (v. 1)
ISBN 0-9611286-7-4 (v. 2)

Printed in the United States of America

CONTENTS

ACKNOWLEDGEMENTS

The editors wish to acknowledge the special contributions of our test reviewers. They have done an outstanding job. Our thanks extend from our deep pleasure and gratitude over their participation and the quality of their work. We know many of the contributing reviewers were as "caught up" in this project as we, and are now writing additional reviews for subsequent volumes. And, thanks also go to the test publishers themselves who released information to the reviewers in an expeditious manner.

We also wish to express thanks to the staff members at Test Corporation of America who are involved in this project: Jane Doyle Guthrie, Terry Faulkner, and Barbara St. George. And our special thanks go to our colleague, Barry Hughes, Ph.D., who served as our manuscript editor. Eugene Strauss and Leonard Strauss, directors of Westport Publishers, Inc., have given freely and generously their support, encouragement, and business advice. Our indebtedness to both gentlemen is legion.

Finally, we want to express our warmest thanks to our readers. It is their use of *Test Critiques* that gives a final validity to this project. It is our sincerest desire that *Test Critiques* will have a true application for them.

INTRODUCTION

Test Critiques is a fulfillment of a goal of the editors and a continuation of a task begun with the publication of *Tests: A Comprehensive Reference for Assessments in Psychology, Education and Business* (1983) and its *Supplement* (1984). With this series, we believe we have moved into the final phase of our project—to include those vital parts that were not appropriate for our directory. With *Tests* and its supplements and the *Test Critiques* series, the reader will have a full spectrum of current test information.

When *Tests* was published, a decision was made to leave out important psychometric information relating to reliability, validity, and normative development. Normative data and questions of reliability and validity were considered simply too complex to be reduced to the "quick-scanning" desk reference format desired. It was also apparent to the editors that a fair treatment of these topics would unnecessarily burden less sophisticated readers. More learned readers were familiar with other source books where such information could be obtained. The editors were aware, however, that a fuller treatment of each test was needed. These complex issues, along with other equally important aspects of tests, deserved scholarly treatment compatible with our full range of readers.

The selections for each volume were in no way arbitrarily made by the editors. The editorial staff researched what were considered to be the most frequently used psychological, educational, and business tests. In addition, questionnaires were sent to members of various professional organizations and their views were solicited as to which tests should be critiqued. After careful study of the survey results, the staff selected what was felt to be a good balance for each of the several volumes of critiques and selection lists were prepared for invited reviewers. Each reviewer chose the area and test to be critiqued and as can be noted in each volume's table of contents, some reviewers suggested new tests that had not been treated to extensive reviews. As test specialists, some reviewers chose to review tests that they had extensively researched or were familiar with as users; some chose to review instruments that they were interested in but had never had the opportunity to explore. Needless to say, the availability of writers, their timetables, and the matching of tests and writers were significant variables.

Though the reviewers were on their own in making their judgments, we felt that their work should be straightforward and readable as well as comprehensive. Each test critique would follow a simple plan or outline. Technical terms when used would be explained, so that each critique would be meaningful to all readers—professors, clinicians, and students alike. Furthermore, not only would the questions of reliability and validity along with other aspects of test construction be handled in depth, but each critique would be written to provide practical, helpful information not contained in other reference works. *Test Critiques* would be useful both as a library reference tool containing the best of scholarship but also useful as a practical, field-oriented book, valued as a reference for the desks of all professionals involved in human assessments.

It might be helpful to review for the reader the outline design for each critique contained in this series. However, it must be stressed that we communicated with each critique writer and urged that scholarship and professional creativity not be sacrificed through total compliance to the proposed structure. To each reviewer we wrote, ''. . . the test(s) which you are reviewing may in fact require small to major modifications of the outline. The important point for you to bear in mind is that your critique will appear in what may well become a standard reference book on human assessment; therefore, your judgment regarding the quality of your critique always supercedes the outline. Be mindful of the spirit of the project, which is to make the critique practical, straightforward, and of value to all users—graduate students, undergraduates, teachers, attorneys, professional psychologists, educators, and others.''

The editors' outline for the critiques consisted of three major divisions and numerous subdivisions. The major divisions were Introduction, Practical Applications/Uses, and Technical Aspects, followed by the Critique section. In the Introduction the test is described in detail with relevant developmental background, to place the instrument in an historical context as well as to provide student users the opportunity to absorb the patterns and standards of test development. Practical Applications/Uses gives the reader information from a ''user'' standpoint—setting(s) in which the test is used, appropriate as well as inappropriate subjects, and administration, scoring, and interpretation guidelines. The section on Technical Aspects cites validity and reliability studies, test and retest situations, as well as what other experts have said about the test. Each review closes with an overall critique.

The reader may note in studying the various critiques in each volume that some authors departed from the suggested outline rather freely. In so doing they complied with their need for congruence and creativity—as was the editors' desire. Some tests, particularly brief and/or highly specialized instruments, simply did not lend themselves easily to our outline.

It is the editors' hope that this series will prove to be a vital component within the available array of test review resources—*The Mental Measurements Yearbooks*, the online computer services for the Buros Institute database, *Psychological Abstracts*, professional measurement journals, etc. To summarize the goals of the current volume, the editors had in mind the production of a comprehensive, scholarly reference volume that would have varied but practical uses. *Test Critiques* in content and scholarship represents the best of efforts of the reviewers, the editors, and the Test Corporation of America staff.

TEST CRITIQUES

William F. Chaplin, Ph.D.
Assistant Professor of Psychology, Auburn University, Auburn, Alabama.

ACTUALIZING ASSESSMENT BATTERY I: THE INTRAPERSONAL INVENTORIES

Everett L. Shostrom. San Diego, California: Educational and Industrial Testing Service.

Introduction

The construct of self-actualization was derived from the work of such human-istic scholars as Abraham Maslow, Fritz Perls, and Carl Rogers, and it has long been central to the theory and practice of humanistic psychotherapy. Indeed, the goal of such therapy is a self-actualizing person; one who is "fully-functioning," who "lives" in the present, who is aware of and can express his or her feelings, and who relies primarily on his or herself for support. The Actualizing Assessment Battery (AAB) consists of four multiscale inventories that together provide infor-mation about an individual's level of *intra*personal and *inter*personal actualization. Intrapersonal actualization is assessed by the Personal Orientation Inventory (POI) and the Personal Orientation Dimensions (POD). Interpersonal actualiza-tion is assessed by the Caring Relationship Inventory (CRI) and the Pair Attraction Inventory (PAI).

All four inventories were developed by Everett L. Shostrom who is the director of the Institute of Actualizing Therapy in Santa Ana, California and a professor of clinical psychology at the United States International University in San Diego. Shostrom received his Ph.D. in psychology from Stanford University in 1950 and has devoted most of his career to the study of self-actualization. It was his realization in the early sixties that the scientific study of this construct and the rigorous evaluation of humanistic psychotherapy required a standard measure of self-actualization that led to the development of the POI. The success of the POI, first published in 1963, and Shostrom's growing interest in actualization within heterosexual dyads, resulted in the CRI, published in 1966, and the PAI, published in 1970. The POD, published in 1976, is the newest of the inventories in the battery. It is essentially a refined and updated version of the POI.

The existence of a battery that contains all of these inventories implies that a comprehensive assessment of an individual's level of actualization should be based on the joint interpretation of the four sets of scores. However, the descrip-tion of, and interpretive guidelines for, each inventory are presented indepen-dently of the others. Moreover, although the measures of inter- and intra-personal actualization are linked at a very general level of humanistic theory, there are few specific conceptual and empirical relationships between the two pairs of invento-ries. Thus, this review will consider the measures of intrapersonal actualization;

3

the POI and the POD. A second review of the AAB, which will appear in a subsequent volume, will consider the CRI and the PAI.

Personal Orientation Inventory (POI): The POI is a 150-item inventory that assesses two global and ten specific components of self-actualization. The items use a forced-choice response format in which respondents are presented with two competing statements about values or behaviors and asked to indicate which of the two statements is most true of them. This inventory avoids one of the common problems of many forced-choice inventories by using statements that are direct antonyms. Thus, respondents are not placed in the uncomfortable position of having to endorse one of two statements, neither or both of which is agreeable to them.

The two global components of self-actualization assessed by the POI are dubbed Time Competence, the extent to which the individual "lives" in the present, and Inner Support, the degree to which the individual turns to him or herself, as opposed to others, for validation of his or her beliefs and actions. There are 23 items on the former and 127 items on the latter.

The ten specific components of self-actualization are measured by five pairs of "synergistic" scales. The first pair concerns values and consists of the Self-Actualizing Value (26 items) and the Existentiality (32 items) scales. The former assesses the degree to which the individual holds values that are compatible with self-actualization, whereas the latter concerns how flexibly (as opposed to dogmatically) the individual applies these values. The next pair concerns feelings and consists of a measure of one's sensitivity to one's own feelings and a measure of one's spontaneity in expressing these feelings. The former is called the Feeling Reactivity Scale (23 items) and the latter is called the Spontaneity Scale (18 items).

Self perception is the theme of the next two scales. The first, Self Regard (16 items), concerns the extent to which the individual recognizes his or her strengths. The second, Self Acceptance (26 items), concerns how well the individual accepts his or her weaknesses. The topic of the fourth pair of scales is general awareness. The first, Nature of Man (sic) (9 items) assesses the degree to which the individual has a positive view of people. The second, Synergy (9 items), assesses one's ability to realize that dichotomies, such as good versus bad, are not really opposites at all. (The existence of a scale called "synergy" on an inventory with a clearly antagonistic response format has given this reviewer pause. Perhaps a better way of scoring this scale would be to count the number of blank- and double-endorsed items on the entire inventory. Such responses could be interpreted as indicating dichotomies that the individual refused to accept. However, even the adoption of my new scoring key would not eliminate the contradiction between this construct and the response format). The final pair of scales concern interpersonal sensitivity. One, Acceptance of Aggression (25 items), measures the ability to accept rather than deny one's "natural" aggressiveness. The other, Capacity for Intimate Contact (28 items), assesses how well the individual can develop intimate relationships that are free from expectations and obligations.

Personal Orientation Dimensions (POD): The POD is a 260-item inventory that contains 13 scales of 20 items each. The 13 scales are grouped into four sets. The first set is called Orientation and contains the Time Orientation and the Core Centeredness scales. These scales correspond, respectively, to the Time Competence and the Inner Support scales on the POI. The next set is called Polarities. It contains the Strength, Weakness, Anger, and Love scales, which represent the major pairs of polarities that are thought to characterize interpersonal behavior. They were specifically derived from the theoretical circumplex model of Timothy Leary (1957).

The set, Integration, is made up of Synergistic Integration and Potentiation, which correspond to POI-Synergy and POI-Existentiality, respectively. The remaining five scales are grouped in a set dubbed Awareness. Being is similar to POI-Spontaneity and Trust in Humanity corresponds to POI-Nature of Man. The other three scales, Creative Living, Mission, and Manipulation Awareness have no direct POI counterparts. Creative Living assesses the ability to be effectively innovative when solving problems. Mission measures individuals' dedication to developing their potential and meeting their goals. Manipulation Awareness assesses the ability to recognize manipulative tendencies in oneself and others.

Practical Applications/Uses

The 150 items of the POI and the 260 items of the POD are presented in a reusable booklet and the individual responds on one of several answer sheets, depending upon whether the inventory is to be hand or machine scored. The directions for responding are straightforward and both inventories are essentially self-administering. The POI manual (Shostrom, 1974) reports that the test has been used successfully with high school students down to 13 years of age. Although there is no time limit the inventory is typically completed in about 30 minutes. Administration, as well as the format, of the POD is the same as the POI.

The cover sheet that accompanies the AAB indicates that it will normally be used in therapeutic sessions with couples. However, these measures can also be used with individual clients. The manuals claim that these inventories will 1) provide a starting point for open discussion between the therapist and the client, 2) eliminate the need for lengthy interviews to establish the client's strengths and weaknesses, and 3) help to ensure successful therapeutic outcome. The first of these claims is reasonable, the second may be true but should be tested, and the third is simply outrageous.

These inventories might also be used by those therapists who wish to assess how successful they are at raising their client's level of actualization. The administration of the POI or the POD before and after therapy could provide the therapists (and their potential clients if they are bold enough to share the results) some idea of their "track record" in therapy. However, a word of caution: The effect of retesting on the scores of these inventories is not well documented. Thus, any improvement may be a function of taking the test twice rather than the therapeutic intervention.

The use of these inventories as measures of actualization in basic research settings is not recommended. The division of the construct of actualization into the numerous components represented by the scales on these inventories has not been scientifically justified (see Technical Aspects section of this review). Thus, shorter, more homogeneous measures such as ideal self-ratings should be used in these contexts.

The POI may be scored either by hand or by machine. Hand-scoring is a straightforward clerical task that involves placing the appropriate scoring template over the answer sheet, counting the number of black marks showing through the holes, and recording that number on the profile sheet. Machine-scoring can also be easily accomplished by sending your answer sheets to EdITS who will score the tests and plot the profiles for a fee. Alternatively, it is a very simple matter to write your own computer program to score the tests. The advantages of this latter option are that it is cheaper and will provide you with more flexibility in analyzing your data. My recommendation is that you hand-score an answer sheet if your only interest in the data is to obtain an assessment of your client's level of actualization to use in therapy. (EdITS machine processing could also be used in this case. However, this is certainly going to mean a delay of a couple of weeks between the administration of the test and the availability of the results. If you have any interest in using your data for research, there is no substitute for doing your own scoring and analyses on a computer).

The only scoring instructions in the POD manual are to send the answer sheets to EdITS for machine-processing, but this is the least desirable scoring option for the consumer. As with the POI, this reviewer suggests hand-scoring in clinical settings where immediate feedback for the client is desired, and writing your own scoring program in research settings. Of course, the user must obtain a scoring key from EdITS in order to write a scoring program. However, a key should be obtained anyway so that the specific content of the scales is available.

The manual emphasizes that the interpretation of the POI should be undertaken only by professionals who are trained in both psychometrics and humanistic theory. Interpretation begins with the profile of twelve scale scores. The profile sheet has been constructed so that after the raw scores have been plotted they can be read as standard T-Scores. (We are only told that the standardization sample consisted of adults. We are not told how many, nor are we told how they were found.) The manual also provides a number of individual and reference group profiles to facilitate comparative interpretations. In general, T-Scores that fall between 50 and 60 are thought to be characteristic of actualizing adults, with scores below 50 indicating nonactualizing and above 60 characteristic of those individuals who are presenting a too actualized picture of themselves (presumably making them nonactualized?).

There are several interesting theoretical and psychometric implications of these interpretive guidelines that are (disappointingly) not considered in the manual. First, the hypothesized curvilinear relationship between scale scores and actualization suggests a very complicated scaling model that makes the correlations between scale scores and other measures difficult to interpret. Also, an interesting corollary of this hypothesis is that too much actualization can be a bad thing. You can test how you feel about this proposition by asking yourself if the word "overactualized" makes sense. Finally, if we assume that actualization is normally distributed in the population, about 34% of all adults are actualized. It may be the people I run around with, but his seems high to me.

Another problem with the interpretation of the POI is the use of ratio scores for the Time Competence and Inner Support scales. These scores are calculated by counting the number of actualizing responses to each scale and then counting the number of nonactualizing responses. The ratio of the responses is then obtained by dividing the number of actualizing responses by the number of nonactualizing responses. This method of scoring was developed to emphasize that actualized persons are not perfect in their time perception or inner directedness. Instead it is the *ratio* of actualization to nonactualization that is important. However, a moments reflection indicates that these ratio scales are literally pointless. The ratio score can be perfectly predicted from the scale score. For example, if individuals score 18 on the Time Competence Scale then they had 18 actualizing responses and (23-18 =) 5 nonactualizing responses for a ratio score of (18 ÷ 5 =) 3.6. Because the ratio score can be derived from the raw score and the total number of responses, the ratio score provides no new information. Moreover, the point that perfection is not the same as actualization is made as easily by the curvilinear scoring model as it is by the ratio scores. The ratio scores require much computational complexity in order to make an obvious point. This reviewer suggests you ignore them.

Yet another hinderance to interpreting the POI is the use of the same items on more than one scale. This overlap is due to the fact that 1) every item is scored once on the two global scales and again on the ten specific scales and 2) many of the items are also scored on several of the specific scales. Indeed, the only two scales that have no items in common are the Time Competence and Inner Support scales. Not only does this overlap reduce the unique interpretive value of each scale, but it also artificialy increases the interscale correlations. Thus, the components of actualization may take on an aura of homogeneity that is illusory. Certainly the convergent and divergent validation of the various aspects of self-actualization is hampered by these overworked items. Moreover, five of the items are actually scored in the opposite direction on different scales! Such psychometric synergy suggests that there is a good deal about self-actualization that is yet to be understood.

The ambiguity of the items is matched by the vagueness of the description of how they were selected. We are told 1) that the items are based on the types of value dilemmas that were faced by "troubled" clients and reported by "several" therapists over a five-year period, and 2) that the items are consistent with the principles of humanistic therapy (Shostrom, 1974, p. 23). We are not told 1) how many items formed the initial pool, 2) how the items were selected from the pool, or 3) how the items were placed on the final scales. This reviewer's guess is that the selection and placement of the items were done intuitively. Although an intuitive strategy of test construction may be acceptable for some purposes (Hase & Goldberg, 1967), it is not justified when the target construct is as theory-laden as self-actualization. In such cases it is important to use some index of content saturation such as corrected item-total correlations for placing items on scales. In addition, the use of some "differential reliability" index (Jackson, 1971) to insure the items' divergent validity from both the other scales and other general content areas, such as intelligence or social desirability is also important. The failure of the developers of the POI to use these explicit, theory-guided techniques leaves us at the mercy of their intuitions and does little to further our understanding of the construct of self-actualization.

As with the POI, the interpretation of the POD should only be undertaken by qualified professionals. Interpretation begins with a T-Score profile of the 13 scale scores. The T-Scores are based on a sample of normal adults, but we are not told how the sample was selected or even the sample size. Scores greater than 50 are considered to reflect actualization, whereas those below 50 reflect nonactualization. The POD has no scales with overlapping items and does not use ratio scores. Thus, it avoids many of the interpretive problems that plague the POI. However, particularly for the polarity scales, there is still a curvilinear scaling model that underlies the relationship between actualization and scale scores.

The POD profile sheet also includes a "flower" diagram to aid the individual interpretation of the polarity scales. The diagram has four "petals," one for each of the four polarities, which grow out of the origin and along the axes of two orthogonal dimensions. The petals indicate the optimal expression of strength, weakness, love, and anger for actualized individuals. To emphasize the importance of the balanced expression of these elements, the diagram is symmetrical. If you have EdITS score your protocols they will superimpose a red flower on the diagram so that you can show your client how close he or she is to the ideal. I find the use of a "flower" diagram on an inventory of actualization to be a bit much, but that is what they call it.

Technical Aspects

The information on the POI's reliability and validity that is presented in the manual does little to allay this reviewer's concerns about this inventory. The only reliability information is test-retest coefficients from a sample of 48 college students and a sample of 46 student nurses. These are tiny samples, and they do not even represent the normative population. For what it is worth, the test-retest reliability coefficients for the twelve scales ranged from .52 to .82 in the college student sample and from .32 to .74 in the student nurse sample. The small number of items on many of the scales may explain their poor reliability, but this explanation is not a justification. However, any conclusions about the POI's reliability must await estimates that are based on larger and more representative samples and on a variety of views of reliability such as stability across content and across forms.

The primary evidence for the validity of the POI scales comes from the comparison of the mean scores of 29 individuals nominated as actualizing by their therapists with the mean scores of 34 individuals nominated as nonactualizing. The scale means were all larger for the actualized group and, with the exception of the Nature of Man Scale, significantly so. Unfortunately, these results are not very persuasive because it was humanistic therapists who generated the POI items and humanistic therapists who generated the criteria groups. Validating intuitions with intuitions leads to serious criteria contamination. In addition, such a practice tells us little about self-actualization other than that it is something that humanistic therapists can consistently identify.

More impressive evidence would come from the demonstration that individuals' POI scores increase as a function of some treatment that is designed to increase actualization. Numerous studies in which individuals' pretest POI scores are compared with their posttest scores following their participation in encounter groups or humanistic psychotherapy are reviewed in the manual. Unfortunately the small sample sizes, different methodologies, and conflicting results of these studies preclude any definite conclusions. In addition, the absence of any independent measure of actualization in these studies leaves doubt about what was changed and what was measured. Some sort of ideal self-rating is a logical candidate for such a measure. However, this standard index of actualization is not mentioned anywhere in the manual.

Ultimately, the construct of self-actualization must be theoretically and empirically embedded in a nomological network of personality and demographic variables. The manual makes a start in this direction by considering the relationship between the POI scales and a host of scales from other personality inventories, and by presenting the POI profiles of a number of different age, occupational, and diagnostic groups. However, although the results are generally consistent with the theory of self-actualization, these scales seem to have been selected haphazardly and the work has a very inductive flavor.

The POD items were selected from a pool of 370 items, retained from item analyses of the POI and/or written to reflect advances in the theory of self-actualization. The developers submitted 338 of these items, which had endorsement frequencies of 95% or less, to a form of factor analysis called "montonicity" analysis. Thirteen factors, one for each scale, were hypothesized and extracted, and presumably (the manual is not explicit) the 20 items with the highest loadings on each factor were selected for that factor's scale. These analyses were performed on a sample of 402 college freshmen.

Although the POD's development was more psychometrically sophisticated than the POI's development there are still some problems. First, because the number of observations (402) on which the factor analysis was based is very small relative to the number of items (338) the factor solution, and thus the scales, are apt to be unstable. It is very unlikely that the same scales would appear in another sample. Second, the derivation sample (college freshmen) is not representative of the normative population (adults). It is an open question if the same factors would appear in a normal adult population. Finally, the description of the analyses is both minimal and vague. In particular we are not provided with information about the criteria used to determine the number of factors, nor are we told about the internal consistency of the items on each scale.

Information about the reliability and validity of the POD was obtained in the same way as it was for the POI. The reliability coefficients are of the test-retest variety and are based on samples of college students and one sample of alcoholics. The sample sizes ranged from 40 to 62 and the coefficients ranged from .50 to .80.

This reviewer found the mean scores on the POD scales to differ between groups nominated as actualized and nonactualized and to differ as a function of treatment. As was noted in the discussion of the POI, such results are necessary, but not sufficient for establishing construct validity.

Correlations between the POD scales and other personality measures are also reported in the manual. For example, nine of the POD scales are negatively correlated with the Eysenck Personality Questionnaire (Eysenck & Eysenck, 1975) Neuroticism Scale and the correlation between the POD scales and scales on the Clinical Analysis Questionnaire (Krug, 1971) generally make sense. However, the primary emphasis in this section is on the low level of the correlations between the

POD and other personality systems. These low correlations are taken as evidence of the discriminant validity of the POD and the uniqueness of self-actualization as a personality construct. Unfortunately, there are still very few explicit deductions from the theory of actualization that are tested in this section. Without a clear theoretical framework, the reported patterns of convergence and divergance are difficult to interpret. It is disappointing that so little was learned in the years between the development of the POI and the POD.

In addition there are some noticeable omissions in this section. No mention is made of the relationship between the POD and some ideal self-rating. This rating has long had the status of an operational definition of self-actualization, so demonstrating its convergence with the POD would be important evidence for the POD's construct validity. Also absent are the relationships between the polarity scales and other measures derived from Leary's (1957) circumplex model of inter-personal behavior. Interest in this model has been growing and it has spawned many inventories (e.g., Benjamin, 1979; Lorr & McNair, 1967; Wiggins, 1982). Because the polarity scales are central to the factor structure of the POD, it is crucial that they be validated against other inventories, which were derived from the same model.

It is not clear whether the correlations between the POI and POD scales should be viewed as validity coefficients or as alternate forms reliability coefficients. This reviewer leans toward the latter, whereas the manual seems to emphasize the former. Regardless of one's perspective, however, the correlations between many of the corresponding scales are low. For example, POD-Being and POI-Spontaneity correlate .06, POD-Trust in Humanity and POI-Nature of Man correlate .50, and POD-Core Centeredness and POI-Inner Support correlate .53. The highest correlation between corresponding scales is between POD-Time Orientation and POI-Time Competence. It is .70. The average correlation between scales that are presumably measuring the same thing is .52. When two measures of the same specific components of a construct are only moderately related there is a good deal that is yet to be understood.

Critique

The construct of self-actualization is interesting and probably useful. However, the POI is plagued by a number of serious psychometric and conceptual problems that limits its usefulness as a measure of the construct. One intriguing finding is reported in the section on the effects of dissimulation on the POI. Subjects who were instructed to try to get high scores on the scales actually obtained scores that were *below* average. This suggests that there is more to the construct of self-actualization than saying good things about oneself. Indeed, it suggests that being self-actualized means having some characteristics that are not generally viewed as desirable.

As the first effort to objectively measure self-actualization the POI is of some historical interest, but our hopes for a legitimate measure of intrapersonal actualization must be pinned to the POD.

The moderate level of convergence between the POI and the POD could be taken as a *prima facie* justification for including them both in the AAB. However, these two inventories were conceptually designed to measure the same construct: intrapersonal self actualization. Indeed, the POD is a revision of the POI and the manuals imply that one *or* the other should be used to assess this construct. Now, all this is a bit puzzling. If the POD is a revision of the POI (and in many ways it is a better inventory), why is the POI being marketed at all? Usually a revision replaces, rather than joins, the older version. Perhaps the publisher has not decided which of the two inventories is better, although the decision seems clear to me. In this reviewer's opinion—regardless of the solution to this puzzle—the users' choice is clear: If you want to measure intrapersonal actualization with one of Shostrom's inventories, order only the POD.

As an aging flower child I find the construct of self-actualization and these inventories very appealing. As a young scientist I think that the construct and inventories need a lot more work. However, it is a hopeful sign for these inventories that I endorse both these conclusions.

References

Benjamin, L. S. (1979). Use of Structural Analysis of Social Behavior (SASB) and Markov chains to study dyadic interactions. *Journal of Abnormal Psychology, 88,* 303-319.

Eysenck, H. J., & Eysenck, S. B. G. (1975). *Eysenck Personality Questionnaire.* San Diego: Educational and Industrial Testing Service.

Hase, H. D., & Goldberg, L. R. (1967). Comparative validity of different strategies of constructing personality inventory scales. *Psychological Bulletin, 67,* 231-248.

Jackson, D. N. (1971). The dynamics of structured personality tests: 1971. *Psychological Review, 78,* 358-367.

Krug, S. E. (1971). *Preliminary criterion evidence on the Clinical Analysis Questionnaire (CAQ)* (IPAT Information Bulletin No. 15). Champaign, IL: Institute for Personality and Ability Testing, Inc.

Leary, T. (1957). *Interpersonal diagnosis of personality.* New York: Ronald.

Lorr, M., & McNair, D. M. (1967). *The Interpersonal Behavior Inventory, Form Y.* Washington, DC: Catholic University of America.

Shostrom, E. L. (1974). *Personal Orientation Inventory.* San Diego: Educational and Industrial Testing Service.

Shostrom, E. L. (1977). *Personal Orientation Dimensions.* San Diego: Educational and Industrial Testing Service.

Wiggins, J. S. (1982). Circumplex models of interpersonal behavior in clinical psychology. In P. C. Kendall & J. N. Butcher (Eds.), *Handbook of research methods in clinical psychology* (pp. 183-221). New York: John Wiley & Sons.

Judith Kaufman, Ph.D.
Professor of Psychology, Ferkauf Graduate School, Yeshiva University, New York, New York.

ADOLESCENT EMOTIONAL FACTORS INVENTORY

Mary K. Bauman. Philadelphia, Pennsylvania: Associated Services for the Blind.

Introduction

The Adolescent Emotional Factors Inventory (AEFI) was developed because of the particular needs of a visually handicapped, adolescent population. Many of the tests employed in personality evaluation present visual stimuli. In addition, even those tests that do not present visual stimuli have items that might have different implications for the sighted than they do for the blind. Consequently, in 1948 the Emotional Factors Inventory (EFI) was developed especially for use with visually handicapped adults. Encouraged by its use and positive research findings the author, Mary K. Bauman, concluded that a companion scale for visually impaired adolescents should also be developed. Constructed from visually handicapped adolescents' own experiences by having a psychologist meet with them to discuss their emotional and adjustment problems and those of their visually handicapped peers. These sessions were recorded and many of the AEFI items were taken directly from the tapes using the language of these adolescents. It should be noted, however, that some of the language used in the items are no longer the language used by today's adolescent population. Additionally, items from the adult form thought to be applicable to adolescents were also incorporated.

The initial form of the AEFI contained 192 items and was administered to adolescents in residential schools for the blind and in integrated public and parochial schools. An item analysis was undertaken, utilizing the responses from 75 boys and 75 girls in residential schools and an equal number from the integrated classes. 150 items were selected which differentiated significantly between the upper and lower 27% of the scores. These 150 items make up the following AEFI scales:

Sensitivity: Examines general stability or the tendency to be fearful or easily upset, such as brooding over difficulties, responding emotionally, or feeling stress more easily than other people do.

Somatic Symptoms: Examines health difficulties, often associated with nervous tension, such as easy fatigue, headaches, stomach upsets, and nightmares.

Social Competency: Examines interest in social contacts and feelings of security and self-confidence in facing other people, especially in groups; willingness to play a leading part in a group; and ease in talking with others.

Attitudes of Distrust: Relates to EFI Paranoid Tendencies Scale; examines over-estimation and consequent suspicion of others when they do not accept the evaluation and a general lack of trust of other people and their intentions, sincerity, and honesty.

Family Adjustment: Examines the sense of belonging within a family, feelings of acceptance or rejection, and respect for parents, their judgment and guidance.

Boy-Girl Adjustment: Examines feelings of being at ease, knowing how to handle ones self, being well-liked by the opposite sex, overconcern and anxiety related to relationships with the opposite sex and dating.

School Adjustment: Examines academic self-concept, top expectations of schooling and whether these expectations are being met.

Morale: Relates to the EFI Depression Scale; examines hopefulness for future, belief that something good is likely to lie ahead as opposed to the feeling that life is scarcely worth living.

Attitudes Concerning Blindness: Examines attitudes towards blindness and problems related to loss of vision.

A Validation score, which evaluates the subjects' ability to understand the material and/or their frankness in responding, is obtained by repeating some of the same test items employing slightly modified language.

Practical Applications/Uses

The Adolescent Emotional Factors Inventory is a questionnaire developed for particular use with a visually handicapped, adolescent population. The items reflect a variety of attitudes and feelings; respondents are asked to indicate whether they agree or disagree with a given statement. Included in the 150 statements is a particular group of items that focus on feelings and attitudes associated with being blind. The test is considered to be a rough screening device, which could potentially alert mental health professionals to possible areas that might require more in-depth exploration.

The inventory consists of a single booklet of questions in large print format, to which the subject responds true or false or agree/disagree. No specific instructions for administration or scoring, are presented, but instructions for tape recording are included. The instrument is untimed and presumably administered according to the examiner's clinical practices. It would seem that the inventory be individually administered and that the client should be somewhat familiar with the evaluator, as the responses do require a degree of interaction and can be considered to be of a personal nature.

A specific age range is not specified, however the test has been normed on 13- to 18-year-olds. The test is hand-scored. As there are no right or wrong answers, interpretations of the composite scores obtained should be based on adolescent issues and require internal clinical judgment. In this reviewer's opinion, interpretations should be carried out by trained mental health professionals with an integrated theoretical orientation and grounding in adolescent psychology as well as knowledge of atypical behavior.

Technical Aspects

In examining interscale correlations, they appear to be quite low, possibly indicating that they measure relatively unique traits. However, there are only approximately 15 items on each of the scales.

Norms have been developed for the revised scale based on the responses of 140 girls and 152 boys in six residential schools and 70 girls and 80 boys in integrated public and parochial school classes (Bauman, Platt, & Strauss, 1963). In all groups the age range is from 13 to 18 years, while mean age varies from 14.87 for the nonresidential girls to 15.76 for the nonresidential boys, with the residential group means falling in between. These differences between residential and nonresidential scores are highly significant. Moreover, distributions were made to compare the 13-, 14- and 15 year-olds with the 16-, 17- and 18-year-old and no significant differences in average scores were found. In grade placement, the members of the normative groups varied from a very small number in fourth grade through 12th grade. The mean grade for the nonresidential groups was ninth grade and for residential groups eighth grade. IQs were available for only 175 students in the normative group, but there was no reason to suppose that there would be any significant difference between them and the other members of the group as they were from comparable populations. The mean IQ was 102.5 with a standard deviation of 14.3.

On all subscales except Somatic Symptoms and Boy-Girl Adjustment there is a significant difference between the mean score for the residential school girls and that of nonresidential girls; on Attitudes and Distrust there is a barely significant difference between the means for boys from residential or nonresidential schools. This of course raises some question whether separate norms should be provided for children in the two types of schools. In addition, norms are provided for boys and girls separately although on some of the scales the difference between the two is insignificant.

Only a minimum amount of information was obtained for the residential normative group and none for the nonresidential group. In one school, 50 children were rated by Q-sort procedure by a teacher-advisor who had some contact with all the children, although she did not know all equally well and admitted that some of the ratings were made with less knowledge that she would have liked (Bauman, Platt, & Strauss, 1965). In two other schools where smaller numbers of children were available a superintendent and a principal did the rating. As they had ongoing contact with the adolescents, they felt they knew them well (Bauman, Platt, & Strauss, 1963).

In each case the raters gave a single rating on global adjustment, not ratings on individual aspects of adjustment that could have been matched with AEFI subscales. Therefore, the ratings were correlated with the sum of the nine diagnostic scales, and in the case of the teacher-advisor the result is $r = .53$, and in the case of the superintendent and principal, $r = .68$.

As a further check, the ratings of the teacher were correlated with IQs, resulting in $r = -.09$ (no correlation whatever), thus indicating that the teacher was responding to qualities other than the cognitive ones measured by the Wechsler Verbal IQ. For the same 50 children, IQs were correlated with the sum of the nine AEFI subscales, $r = -.43$. This correlation is negative because the larger the AEFI score, the poorer the adjustment. This means that the qualities measured by the AEFI do relate in some small measure to those measured by the Wechsler Verbal IQ.

Critique

Associated Services for the Blind report that they are in the process of updating the norms for the inventory based on the results which have been gathered over the past several years. However, they feel that their data do not represent visually impaired populations as a whole, nor would it be possible to obtain such a highly representative population (P. G. Cautilli, personal communication, November, 1984). Additionally, they are considered carrying out a validity study that would go beyond solely face validity.

There is little published information on the AEFI. However, Associated Services for the Blind indicate that they have been using the instrument and not only keeping records of the subject scores but also following up on what adjustments the adolescents have made. General references concerning emotional screening inventory prototypes would prove helpful in order to evaluate the validity and usefulness of this particular instrument.

There is no question that tests and inventories are needed for the visually handicapped population. It must also be kept in mind that the developers of the AEFI consider the inventory only a rough screening instrument, investigating or highlighting more pervasive emotional difficulties. Counselors who have used this inventory report it as being helpful in their work (Bauman, Platt, & Strauss, 1963). The face validity of the instrument cannot be faulted. However, in this reviewers opinion, the visually handicapped adolescent is not being viewed in proper perspective. The only normative group considered is that of a visually handicapped adolescent population; a consideration of the commonality of feelings among all adolescents needs to be taken into account, irrespective of "blindness." For the most part, even in the Attitudes About Blindness subscale there are only 5 out of 15 items that can be answered only by the visually handicapped adolescent. Ten additional items appear to be attitudes about blindness and being handicapped that could also be answered by sighted individuals. The remaining 135 items apply potentially to all adolescents. Therefore, without having a sighted and/or other-handicapped group in the normative data of the inventory it is not possible to discern whether the feelings that are evoked are attributable to the condition of a visual handicap, the condition of "adolescent," or an interaction of the two. Such information would be invaluable in treating and working effectively with any adolescent population. There are analogous personality inventories already established (such as the Piers-Harris Children's Self Concept Scale) based on solid construct validity that would meet this population's needs if a visually handicapped sample included or added to existing norms.

References

Bauman, M. K. (ca. 1964). *Adolescent Emotional Factors Inventory.* Philadelphia: Associated Services for the Blind.

Bauman, M. K., Platt, H., & Strauss, S. (1963, October). A measure of personality for blind adolescents. *International Journal for the Education of the Blind*, pp.1-6.

George C. Thornton III, Ph.D.

Professor and Chair, Industrial/Organizational Psychology, Colorado State University, Fort Collins, Colorado.

ADULT BASIC LEARNING EXAMINATION

Bjorn Karlsen, Richard Madden, and Eric F. Gardner.
Cleveland, Ohio: The Psychological Corporation.

Introduction

The Adult Basic Learning Examination (ABLE) is battery of four tests designed to measure the level of general educational achievement among adults (Karlsen, Madden, & Gardner, 1967, 1971). The subtests cover vocabulary, reading, spelling, and arithmetic (including computation and problem solving). They were designed to assess educational level among adults who have not completed formal twelfth-grade education. Thus, the content of items, instructions, administrative procedures, and response format were selected to accommodate adult examinees who may be unfamiliar or uncomfortable with testing situations.

There are three levels of the ABLE. Level I covers grades 1-4; Level II covers grades 5-8, and Level III covers grades 9-12. The designated grades indicate the educational achievement levels that each test supposedly measures most reliably. For each level, there are two comparable forms of the test (A & B). These parallel forms can be used if problems arise when testing an individual examinee or if reexamination is needed to evaluate educational progress.

The content of the test covers basic competencies central to many areas of educational achievement. It does not cover specific subject matter areas, nor does it provide diagnostic information about student functioning in the areas measured.

The vocabulary test is dictated and the examinee responds in Levels I and II by making a mark in one of three positions on the test booklet or in Level III by marking the answer sheet. Thus, the test measures how well the examinee understands the meaning of words independent of the ability to read.

The reading test measures functional reading level of adults, using content appropriate to everyday life and low-level vocabulary. In Levels I and II, the examinee picks words that sensibly complete a series of sentences. In Level III the examinee reads paragraphs of increasing difficulty, then selects the word or phrase that completes sentences about the narrative.

In Levels I and II of the spelling test, words and an illustrative sentence are read to the examinees, who write their answers in the test booklet. Both words and illustrations are representative of the daily life of adults. In Level III, the examinee reads sets of four words and marks the one that is misspelled.

The computation test covers the basic arithmetic processes of addition, subtrac-

---

This reviewer wishes to acknowledge and thank Robert P. Smith II for his contributions to the preparation of this review.

tion, multiplication, and division. Examinees must complete the operation and write in the answer. A multiple-choice format is used in the problem-solving test, which presents a series of practical problems from everyday life.

At the time ABLE was originally published, Drs. Bjorn Karlsen and Richard Madden were certified psychologists in California and Dr. Eric Gardner was a certified psychologist in New York. All three had been involved in adult education, research and consulting on reading and learning, and prior test development projects. Karlsen and Madden developed the Stanford Diagnostic Achievement Test whereas Madden and Gardner coauthored the Stanford Achievement Test (SAT).

Preliminary research on the ABLE began with three forms at each level. After pilot testing, the two best forms were selected. The procedures for choosing among the Level-I and Level-II alternatives are undefined in the test manual; unspecified slight modifications to 5-10% of the items were made. For Levels I and II, the reported results are based on characteristics of the preliminary forms, thus, technically speaking, no data are presented on the exact forms of these published tests.

For Level III tests, tryouts were conducted on adult students in high-school equivalency and job-training programs in various states and on students in junior and senior high school. Item analyses (difficulty level and discrimination values) and comments by teachers were used to select the final forms. Normative data were then collected on the final forms of A and B on several additional adult samples in various academic and vocational education programs. At the same time, these latter groups were given the SAT.

Information provided to these reviewers by the senior author (B. Karlsen, personal communication, February 6, 1985) indicates that the test is currently under revision with new normative tryouts planned in late 1985. Publication of the new edition by The Psychological Corporation is expected in 1986.

The test booklet, which is used as an answer sheet in Levels I and II, is approximately 7" x 11". This departure from a normal page size was intended to limit adults' association with standard school-testing situations. Unfortunately it also causes problems in optical scan grading because the machine must be specially adjusted for this test form. For all levels a three-choice format is used for the vocabulary and reading subtests. In Levels I and II, the spelling and arithmetic computation sections require the examinee to write the correct answer in the space provided. The arithmetic problem-solving portion employs a five-answer, multiple-choice format. All answers are written on the test booklet for Levels I and II and on a special answer sheet for Level III. The examiner is required to give instructions and read the sample questions before each test. The vocabulary and spelling sections in Levels I and II must be read out loud by the examiner. This unique format provides a test of the verbal aspect of vocabulary. In undereducated adults verbal vocabulary comprehension may be much better developed than written word recognition.

Practical Applications/Uses

The ABLE is designed for group administration in a classroom setting. The examiner is advised to be completely familiar with the test instructions, but no other special qualifications are recommended. If audiotape instructions are not being used, familiarity with the correct pronunciation of the words in the vocabulary and spelling sections of the test is necessary.

One primary concern is the length of time required to administer the tests. Levels I and II require 135 minutes of testing time, which does not include a recommended minimum of four ten-minute breaks. Level III testing time is 207 minutes. The instructions state that all Level III tests should not be completed on the same day and test instructions do not specify any particular subtest sequences. Therefore, it is assumed that the subtest administration order is flexible.

The authors of the ABLE suggest that the test can be used to assess educational achievement of individual examinees and to evaluate programs to raise educational level among adults. Published research has demonstrated that the test has been successfully used for these and other purposes. Malatesta, Circo, and Smith (1977) used the ABLE as one part of a test battery to screen prisoners in a correctional institution before remedial education and vocational development. Jarmin and Stranges (1972) used ABLE to screen enrollees who needed basic education before vocational skill training. Coles, Roth, and Pollack (1978) assessed literacy skills among long-term hospitalized mental patients in order to explore the relationship among literacy, psychological, and social deficits. These applications show that the ABLE contributes uniquely to the evaluation of subjects' competencies.

Numerous evaluation research studies using the ABLE have been reported. Hutchison (1974) used the test to study improvements in vocabulary, reading comprehension, and spelling for functional illiterates trained with instructional strategies which matched their preferred styles of learning. The effectiveness of tutorials was studied by Stauffer (1972), and Lucas (1978) evaluated educational programs presented on cable TV using the ABLE. More recently, Coles et al. (1980) used the test to measure educational gains as one component of a broader domain of psychosocial and ability characteristics among 50 clients in a mental health center. These applications show that the ABLE can be used as a reliable criterion measure of program success.

More innovative uses of the ABLE by researchers include its measurement of independent, control, and dependent variables. Thorne (1975) found that the vocabulary test was the best predictor of conservation behaviors among 50 mentally retarded adults. In a study of three different methods of teaching fractions to young adults, Hector and Frandsen (1981) used the ABLE as a pretest of arithmetic computation abilities to match experimental groups. As a dependent variable, the ABLE scores have been used to study developmental patterns of cognitive abilities among less higher educated adults (Gardner & Monge, 1977) and as a standardized test against which to validate a new measure of adult basic learning (Griffin, 1971).

The tests can be hand-scored or machine-scored. For Levels I and II, the answer key for hand-scoring is designed to be compatible with the response booklet. The number of correct answers is recorded at the end of each subtest, then transferred to a profile sheet on the back of the booklet.

If a Level I or II test is to be machine-scored, an administrator must mark ovals for all correct responses to the spelling and arithmetic computation parts of the test. The remainder of the test can be machine-scored directly from the booklet, but the practice has proven problematic because the unusual size of the booklet requires adjusting the machine settings on the electrical scoring machines. Scoring services may wait to amass a significant number of answer sheets, thus delaying feedback to users.

Because respondents to Level III tests record answers on a separate sheet, which can be scored electronically, that answer sheet can also be quickly hand-scored with a stencil. Hand-scoring of the 178 items requires only a few minutes. There are no corrections for guessing, and in all subtests the raw score is simply the number correct. There are no apparent mechanical problems with the answer keys or the scoring stencils.

Machine-scoring requires the traditional care in scanning the answer sheets, packaging the material carefully, and providing certain identification information. No other unique problems are encountered for the ABLE in this regard.

Scores on the ABLE can be interpreted in one of two relatively straightforward ways: They can be transformed to norms (e.g., percentiles or stanines) or grade equivalents. The manuals for Levels I and II provide tables to convert raw scores into grade scores, which are in essence grade equivalents. These were developed by testing 1,000 school-age pupils in each grade from 1-7 in four states. The authors chose not to provide adult norms in the manuals for Levels I and II because they believed that there was no adequate way to define the population of adults at these levels in basic education programs across the United States. A few adult norms are provided in a supplementary data report (Harcourt, Brace & World, 1968). Stanines corresponding to raw scores in three research groups (1,161 adult basic education students in Connecticut; 403 basic education students in Virginia, and 1,726 men in North Carolina prisons) are shown for Level I and II subtests. These types of adult norms, plus samples more representative of the United States should be reported in the manuals.

In Level III, sets of tables of norms are provided for high-school-age students and for adult samples. The student norms enable the examiner to transform raw scores into percentiles or stanines for Grades 9-12. Adult norms for Level III tests are provided for five groups of high-school equivalency and vocational training students (samples range from 102 to 221).

Of course, individual users can develop local norms for their own settings or purposes. Although the small or occasional user may not have the resources to do this, groups, such as the Armed Forces induction centers, have compiled extensive norms for their version of the ABLE.

Technical Aspects

The subtests show uniformly high levels of internal reliability. For adult groups, the manual reports split-half reliabilities in the .80s and .90s for Levels I and II. For Level III, Kuder-Richardson reliabilities dip into the .70s for the problem-solving test. Expressed as standard errors of measurement in raw scores, an individual's score is not apt to vary more than 3 or 4 points. Seldom would such a difference change the grade equivalent more than one- or two-tenths of a grade. In terms of adult norms, a difference of 3 or 4 raw points would change a percentile rank only about .08.

In view of the fact that the test is recommended for studies of change, additional reliability estimates should be reported in terms of test-retest stability and equivalence of forms. The interpretation of developmental changes and actual educational gains would be more meaningful if the manual reported retest reliabilities over short periods (e.g., 2 weeks with no intervention) or correlations between Forms A and B at each level.

Relatively little validity data are presented in the manuals for Levels I and II and it is surprising that the manual has not been revised since 1967 to incorporate more of the research that has accumulated over the years. Correlations between the ABLE and the SAT are reported for the school groups and a group of 800 job corps participants. For Levels I and II, correlations among corresponding scales (e.g., vocabulary vs. word meaning; arithmetic problem solving vs. arithmetic applications) are substantial (in the .60s to .70s) and they are higher than correlations across different constructs (e.g., vocabulary vs. arithmetic) both within ABLE itself and across the two different tests (Karlsen et al., 1967). Such data support both the concurrent and discriminant validity of the Levels I and II subtests.

The data are not as "clean" for Level III subtests, especially for adult samples. Specifically, we see evidence that some "verbal" subtests on the ABLE correlate as highly with "quantitative" subtests on the SAT as they do with "verbal" tests. In addition, if we look at intercorrelations among ABLE subtests for adult groups, we see that the relationship among the "verbal" subtests (vocabulary, spelling, and reading) or among the "quantitative" subtests (computation and problem-solving) are often no higher than the correlations across supposedly different "verbal" and "quantitative" subtests. Such results raise many questions about the distinctiveness of the Level III subtests, especially in their ability to differentially measure separate constructs in adult individuals.

Very little validity information is presented. Conspicuously absent is validity information on adult samples, which would tell us, for example, the relationship among test scores and demographic data (e.g., age, sex, ethnicity), relationships of the same constructs measured by different methods (e.g., performance on low-verbal tests), or relationships of the tests with related cognitive and personality variables (e.g., cognitive style).

Critique

Early reviews of Levels I and II of the test were generally positive or expressed suspended judgment based on a dearth of data. Hieronymus (1972) concluded that "this is a well-conceived, well-constructed battery which should serve very well the purposes for which it was intended" (p. 5). On the other hand, Hall (1972) noted that "no empirical data regarding the published forms of the ABLE are provided" and warned that "its full capabilities cannot be assessed or realized because of inadequate empirical evidence. The most appropriate use at present may be in research regarding the effectiveness of various adult-education programs" (p. 7).

Considering the wide-spread use of the ABLE, the increase in emphasis on adult education, and the increased demand for better evaluation of all educational efforts, this reviewer finds it disappointing that the manuals have not been revised in over 15 years. It is understandable that the test itself has not been revised or that new norms have not been developed—these are expensive undertakings, but it would be relatively easy to revise the manuals to provide updated information on the reliability and validity of the test. Assuming the authors have continued to do research with the test, surely a clearer understanding of constructs measured and limitations of the tests have emerged.

The ABLE has much to recommend it. The subtests provide internally consistent measures of educational achievement among adults in verbal and arithmetic skills. The administrative procedures and exam materials are designed to minimize the anxiety felt by low-education-level adults in schoollike settings. It is one of few such tests available for adults and has enjoyed much use in adult education programs, clinics, industry, and military induction centers.

Several limitations, however, should also be noted. The test was developed before recent advances in the theory and procedures for content or domain referenced testing. Thus, item and test specifications are not as precise as we would expect from a modern educational achievement test. The samples used to develop school norms are marginally adequate and the adult norms nonexistent for Levels I and II. No test-retest or equivalent forms reliability data and very little validity data are presented in the manuals. Revision of the manuals is sorely needed and will be welcome on its anticipated publication in 1986.

References

Coles, G. S., Ciporen, F., Konigsberg, R., & Cohen, B. (1980). Educational therapy in a community mental health center. *Community Mental Health Journal, 16,* 79-89.

Coles, G. S., Roth, L., & Pollack, I. W. (1978). Literacy skills of long term hospitalized mental patients. *Hospital and Community Psychiatry, 29,* 512-516.

Gardner, E. F., & Monge, R. H. (1977). Adult age differences in cognitive abilities and educational background. *Experimental Aging Research, 3,* 337-383.

Griffin, J. Z. (1971). The relationship between behavioral objectives and measurement instruments used to evaluate student progress in an urban adult basic education program. *Dissertation Abstracts International, 32,* 1335A.

Hall, J. W. (1972). Review of ABLE. In O. K. Buros (Ed.), *The seventh mental measurements yearbook* (pp. 6-7). Highland Park, NJ: The Gryphon Press.

Harcourt, Brace & World. (1968). *ABLE* (Supplementary data rep.). New York: Author.

Hector, J. H., & Frandsen, H. (1981). Calculator algorithms for fractions with commmunity college students. *Journal for Research in Mathematics Education, 12,* 349-355.

Hieronymus, A. N. (1972). Review of ABLE. In O. K. Buros (Ed.), *The seventh mental measurements yearbook* (pp. 4-5). Highland Park, NJ: The Gryphon Press.

Hutchison, F. E. (1974). The effects of instructional strategies related to preferred interests of functionally illiterate adults. *Dissertations Abstracts International, 35,* 1946A.

Jarmin, H. R., & Stranges, R. J. (1972). Academic level of poverty program enrollees: A new look. *Journal of Employment Counselling, 9,* 175-179.

Karlsen, B. (1970). Educational achievement testing with adults: Some research findings. In *Adult basic education: The state of the art.* Washington, DC: U.S. Government Printing Office.

Karlsen, B., Madden, R., & Gardner, E. F. (1967). *ABLE handbook* Levels I and II. Cleveland: The Psychological Corporation.

Karlsen, B., Madden, R., & Gardner, E. F. (1971). *ABLE handbook Level III*. Cleveland: The Psychological Corporation.

Lucas, W. A. (1978). Spartanburg, S.C.: Testing the effectiveness of video, voice, and data feedback. *Journal of Communication, 28*, 168-179.

Malatesta, C. Z., Circo, J., & Smith, B. (1977). A discriminating, non-discriminatory test battery for a prison population. *Corrective and Social Psychiatry and Journal of Behavior Technology, Methods and Therapy, 23*, 15-17.

Stauffer, J. M. (1972). A descriptive study of a national volunteer adult literary program in the United States with an analysis of student reading grade level change. *Dissertation Abstracts International, 33*, 5461A.

Thorne, C. A. (1975). Six different types of conservation and their relation to mental age, IQ, and three areas of academic achievement. *Dissertation Abstracts International, 26*, 1405A.

David G. Ward, Ph.D.
Assistant Professor of Psychology, Fordham University, Bronx, New York.

ADULT PERSONAL ADJUSTMENT AND ROLE SKILLS

Robert B. Ellsworth. Palo Alto, California: Consulting Psychologists Press, Inc.

Introduction

The Adult Personal Adjustment and Role Skills (PARS) Scale is a 31-item rating scale designed to evaluate the community adjustment and functioning of adults who have received mental health services. Appropriate for both males and females, clinic clients or hospitalized patients, the PARS uses pre- and post-treatment ratings of the client provided by the same significant other, such as the client's spouse, parent, other relative, or friend. Thus, the PARS attempts to examine the functioning of clients outside the treatment setting as perceived by someone close to the client. Eight areas of community and home adjustment are assessed: Close Relations, Alienation-Depression, Anxiety, Confusion, Alcohol/Drug Use, House Activity, Child Relations, and Employment.

Close Relations measures the quality of social behaviors and interactions between the client and the significant other (consideration, cooperation, affection, and interest in conversation). Alienation-Depression refers to client statements of feeling treated unfairly and dominated, that no one cares, and that life is not worth living. Anxiety items deal with nervousness, restlessness, tension, and difficulty in sleeping. Confusion questions ask if the client has appeared dazed or confused, and has had poor memory. Alcohol/Drug Use refers to excessive use of alcohol or drugs, getting drunk or high, and upsetting the family. House Activity concerns the extent to which the client helps with specific household chores (e.g. housekeeping and cooking). When there are children in the home, Child Relations questions are used to rate the client's affection, dependability, and behavior toward the children. For clients who work outside the home, Employment items regard how much they earn, whether the earnings are adequate, and their attitude toward work.

The pretreatment ratings are requested at intake for clinic clients, and within a day or two after admission for hospitalized patients. The posttreatment PARS is obtained three months following intake for outpatients, and 90 days following release for inpatients. Change norms are provided to assess the degree of improvement relative to clients with the same level of pretreatment adjustment. Thus, both absolute and relative levels of adjustment may be examined, as well as the generalizability of treatment effects outside the treatment setting and over time. The PARS may be used for treatment outcome studies focusing on the individual client, as well as to evaluate the effectiveness of mental health delivery systems for program evaluation purposes.

The author and developer of the PARS, Robert B. Ellsworth, is well known for his work in clinical and community psychology and evaluation of mental health programs. Dr. Ellsworth, who received his Ph.D. in clinical psychology from the Pennsylvania State University in 1953, has served as a staff psychologist at the Veterans Administration Medical Center in Salem, Virginia. Ellsworth developed the MAAC Behavioral Adjustment Scale, Revised, which has seen considerable use with psychiatric patients. He is also the coauthor with S. L. Ellsworth of the Child and Adolescent Adjustment Profile (CAAP) Scale; the Profile of Adaptation to Life—Clinical (PAL-C) Scale; and the Profile of Adaptation to Life—Holistic (PAL-H) Scale. Both the PAL-C and PAL-H are for adults. His qualifications, based on considerable clinical experience and research, are well established.

The current PARS is based on five earlier scales developed to evaluate the community adjustment of persons receiving treatment. A guiding principle in this development is the use of significant others to provide both pre- and post-treatment ratings. The first PARS Scale (PARS-I) (1968) was for male hospitalized veterans diagnosed as schizophrenic. PARS II was an 89-item extended version of PARS I for treatment outcome studies with psychiatrically hospitalized male veterans. Subsequently, a research scale with 115 items was developed and included questions relevant to male outpatients at community clinics. Concurrently, a 120-item research form was developed for females. After item selection and factor analyses, a 57-item PARS III Scale for males and a similar 57-item version for women were developed and both scales were given to significant others of clients and patients. Whereas analyses of these ratings led to the PARS V forms, a separate PARS IV form was developed for male psychiatric patients in Veterans Administration hospitals.

The PARS V Scale saw wider use, with separate norms for clinic clients and hospital patients, as well as for men and women, based on normative data from 22 clinics and eight hospitals. However, the separate male and female versions of the PARS V were unwieldy for summary and comparative evaluation of treatment programs. Therefore, the male and female versions were combined into the PARS VI, a 50-item scale for both sexes. After use by significant others of clients in mental health centers and of patients in hospitals, item and factor analyses, and reliability and validity studies, the current PARS scale became available.

The criteria used in developing the PARS series and in selecting items were 1) item test-retest reliability (stability); 2) internal consistency (coefficient alpha); 3) significance of pre- and post-treatment ratings; 4) discriminability among clinic, hospital, and non-client populations; and 5) factor loadings. Thus, items that reflected improvement following treatment and could distinguish among outpatients, inpatients, and nonclients were retained. Finally, factor dimensions that adequately described males and females, and clients and patients were needed; the resulting eight areas of functioning contain the smallest number of items with the highest factor loadings to reliably measure each dimension.

The final standardization sample consisted of 248 outpatients and 204 inpatients. The clinic clients were most frequently diagnosed as neurotic (84%), while the hospitalized were largely psychotic (64%), versus 29% neurotic. Thirteen percent of the outpatients were diagnosed as psychotic, and the remainders in both groups were considered organic. The mean age of the outpatients was 31.0; the inpatients, 33.2. The inpatients were more likely to have never been married (49%), whereas 43% of the outpatients were married. The groups also differed in terms of their significant others; the inpatients were more often rated by a parent (58%) and the outpatients were more often rated by the spouse (41%). The outpatients averaged 5.4 clinic visits, and the inpatients' average hospital stay was 27.2 days.

The PARS is a double-sided 8½" x 11" page folded in half to form a booklet. Following background questions about the client and the rater's relationship to the client are 31 items grouped into eight areas of adjustment regarding client behavior and functioning during the preceding one-month period. Each item asks for the extent to which the individual has engaged in certain activities and expressed specific symptoms, with answer choices similar to almost never, sometimes, often, or almost always, on a 1-4 scale. The rater is asked to check the box under the answer choice alongside the question. Both the instructions and the questions seem clear, and the responses would appear to be easily and quickly made. For example, Close Relations items ask if the person has shown interest in such interpersonal activities as conversation and cooperation. Similar items assess the person's relationships with any children in the home; other questions regard the symptom areas (Alienation-Depression, Anxiety, Confusion, and Alcohol/Drug Use). Concrete questions are used to assess House Activity, and Employment.

Eight scale scores, one for each area, are obtained. The raw scores may be plotted on a profile and corresponding T-scores (mean 50, standard deviation 10) may be examined to determine a range of adjustment: poor, average, or good. Both pre- and post-treatment adjustment, and pre- to post-treatment improvement using change norms, may be profiled.

Practical Applications/Uses

There are two major uses of the PARS: 1) evaluation of a client's adjustment in home and community settings following therapy; and 2) treatment outcome studies for evaluating therapy effectiveness, especially for program evaluation and accountability purposes. Although the PARS was developed for use in community mental health centers and psychiatric hospitals, it would appear to be useful for mental health services agencies, counseling centers, and private practitioners.

The PARS was designed to measure a client's social and psychological functioning as perceived by a significant other: spouse, parent, other relative, or friend. The variables measured reflect socially relevant behaviors and attitudes and the ratees' emotional and physical well-being, as well as their relationships with others in the family or home. Thus, although the rater may not be totally detached in rating a family member or friend, such perceptions of the client's functioning are important. Because the ratings refer to activity outside the treatment facility, information may be gained regarding the generalizability of therapeutic effects, both across different settings and across time. The follow-up PARS ratings take place three months following the initial intake for clinic clients, and three months after the release for hospitalized patients. Thus, the treatment effects and the duration of effects are assessed.

Research uses of the PARS might include studies of the relationships among client self-ratings, staff ratings, and ratings of various significant others.

Although the PARS was designed for adults, it could presumably be adapted for younger persons, such as persons in their late teens. There are no questions regarding school activity, but the other items explore relevant issues, regardless of whether the person holds a job or not. Similarly, there do not appear to be any other factors, such as age, physical handicap, or diagnosis, which could limit this test's applicability. The only requirement is that there be some person who has had close contact with the client before and after treatment. Any persons receiving some form of mental health treatment may be eligible, including inpatients, outpatients, day hospital patients, and persons in group homes for the developmentally disabled. Other facilities may include substance abuse programs, correctional facilities, halfway houses, and perhaps nonpsychiatric hospitals. Due to the nature of the pre- and post-treatment ratings, there do not appear to be ways to include chronic patients recently discharged or deinstitutionalized, especially those who do not return to a significant other. Recent studies have found the PARS to be useful in examining the community adjustment of older depressives (Hyer & Collins, 1984) and of older schizophrenics (Hyer, Collins, & Blazer II, 1983).

Before administering the test the informed consent of the client should be obtained at intake for outpatients and within a day or two after admission for inpatients. The clinic secretary may obtain this, as well as the name and address of the significant other. Hospitalized patients unable to understand this request initially are contacted again four or five days after admission; if consent is not obtained within one week of admission, the patient is excluded from consideration because the rater may not be able to accurately rate the preadmission behavior of the patient. Subsequently, the pretreatment PARS is sent to the selected rater, preferably the spouse if the client is married, or to the nearest relative who has the most contact and lives with the client (e.g., a parent). Because the rater should have had close contact with the patient during the month preceding intake or admission raters of patients hospitalized elsewhere for two or more weeks are not contacted. Friends or other significant others are used only if none of the above raters are available.

The PARS is mailed (with a self-addressed, stamped envelope) to the rater with a cover letter explaining the purpose, importance, and confidentiality of the ratings. Respondents may complete the PARS at their leisure, but it is requested that the ratings be returned as soon as possible. Because the instructions are clear, directions for answering include a sample response, and there are only 31 items in addition to the background questions, the form generally takes only 10-15 minutes to complete. A second PARS form and follow-up letter are sent in about two weeks if the first PARS is not returned. To increase the return rate, it is emphasized to the client and the significant other that the ratings are used to help evaluate and improve services. Because spouses and parents have a higher return rate for both pre- and post-treatment PARS (54%) than do friends (22%), there is an emphasis on these sources over nonrelatives.

Finally, the follow-up PARS is sent to the same rater, three months after intake for outpatients and three months after release for inpatients. The three-month period was selected because the majority of clinic clients are no longer being seen after three months, and even if they are still being seen, the treatment effects would probably be apparent by then. The three-month follow-up is standardized for all cases and is designed to assess the longer-term stability and maintenance of treatment effects in the environment.

The PARS, may be scored by a clerical person; the instructions and procedures are straightforward and may be learned in a few minutes. Scoring the PARS involves noting the rating for each item and summing the ratings within each scale to obtain a total scale score. Scoring is done on the PARS form itself and can be accomplished easily and quickly by hand; there appear to be no machine-scoring procedures, nor any need for such. Procedures for missing item responses, such as prorating if one item is missing and not scoring a scale if two or more items are absent, are provided. The scale scores may also be transferred to the profile by a clerical person, but interpretation and evaluation need to be done by a graduate student or professional in the behavioral sciences. On the positive scales (Close Relations, House Activity, Child Relations, and Employment), a high score indicates good adjustment. On the symptom scales (Alienation-Depression, Anxiety, Confusion, and Alcohol/Drug Use), low scores indicate good adjustment.

Finding the pre- to post-change involves using change norms tables, one for each scale, based on previous clients' and patients' degree of improvement. A T-score for each scale is obtained from the pre-post combination and then entered on the profile. Change T-scores of 50 represent average or typical improvement, scores above 50 represent more improvement than expected, and scores below 50 show less improvement than expected. The same change norms tables are used for all subjects.

Adjustment ranges are provided on the profile: T-scores above 60 indicate good adjustment; T-scores between 40 and 60 indicate average adjustment; and T-scores below 40 indicate poor adjustment. "Average" and "good" are considered desirable, whereas "poor" indicates problem areas. Interpretation involves scanning the profile to see in which range the scale scores lie, apparently on a scale-by-scale basis, with no overall measure of adjustment, such as the average of all the scale scores. Specific items may be examined to determine particular problem areas. The symptom areas reflect maladjustment, the two relationship areas reflect both role skills and personal adjustment, and House Activity and Employment are presumed to reflect life style and role choices.

For interpretation of pre- to post-change prior work indicated that persons initially poorly adjusted tend to improve more than persons initially better adjusted. These findings have been incorporated into the change norms, so that change T-scores indicate improvement relative to persons initially manifesting the same pretreatment scores. Thus, the improvement scores are relative, depending on the pretreatment level of adjustment, and clients may be compared on relative degree of change. To find absolute levels of change, the pre- and post- T-scores may be compared directly. Some degree of clinical judgement may be required for dealing with a particular case. For institutional and program evaluation purposes, group results may be useful in terms of overall ranges of improvement in adjustment or more specific summary scale means and variances.

Technical Aspects

The face validity of the PARS appears to be quite good because the items generally refer to specific and clearly defined behaviors. A few questions may be open to some degree of subjective interpretation on the part of the rater, but nonetheless these items appear to assess clinically relevant aspects of general adjustment. The answer choices may also be open to some interpretation; for example, just how often is "often" or "sometimes"? However, that there are four choices per item may result in common interpretations of these categories.

In terms of content validity, the eight scales appear to sample important aspects of adjustment and functioning, relationships with the significant other and any children in the home, and common symptoms of disturbance. The three to four items per scale are reported to be the minimum number to reliably measure each dimension (Ellsworth, 1981).

PARS ratings by relatives are correlated with reworded, self-rated PARS for hospital patients at admission and at one- and six-month follow-ups (Ellsworth, 1981, p. 8; Fontana & Dowds, 1975, p. 226): admission ($rs = .20$ to $.76$; median of $.38$); one-month ($rs = .36$ to $.83$, median of $.61$); six-months ($rs = .35$ to $.85$, median of $.56$).

For inpatients, PARS ratings by others and self-ratings on the Brief Symptom Inventory (BSI) were more highly correlated at follow-up than at intake (Ellsworth, 1981, p. 8). For outpatients at intake six out of seven correlations were significant ($rs = .22$ to $.45$); at three months, three out of seven were significant; and at six months, six out of the seven were significant. Thus, the raters and the ratees showed significant, but not strong, agreement, especially at follow-ups.

In a validity study involving 145 clinic clients (Ellsworth, 1981), pretreatment PARS ratings by relatives were compared to client self-ratings on the Profile of Adaptation to Life (PAL-C). The patterns of correlations showed discriminant and convergent validity for the PARS scales. For example, Close Relations and Child Relations scales were significantly correlated (rs between $.55$ and $.77$). The symptom areas showed generally significant positive correlations with other symptom scales ($rs = .20$ to $.33$) and significant negative correlations with positive role skills scales ($rs = -.20$ to $-.58$). Alcohol/Drug Use was independent of other scales. Employment was negatively correlated with maladjustment (symptom) scales ($rs = -.34$ to $-.37$) and positively related to positive scales ($rs = .23$ to $.86$), with one exception: for females, Employment and Child Relations were negatively correlated ($r = -.28$). Thus, PAL-C self-ratings and PARS ratings showed substantial agreement.

The scales measuring personal adjustment (Alienation-Depression, Anxiety, Confusion) are more sensitive to the effects of therapeutic treatment for both men and women (Ellsworth, 1975, 1981), and consistent with general findings that these areas are more affected by therapy than are the role skills areas (House Activity and Employment) and social relationship areas. Both men and women showed less alcohol and drug use from pre- to post-adjustment and men also showed more improvement than did women, perhaps because men had lower pretreatment adjustment scores.

Further, the PARS also distinguishes between the pretreatment adjustment of clinic clients and hospital patients, in that the latter are more frequently diagnosed as psychotic and have higher scores on the symptom scales (Ellsworth, 1978). Male outpatients are also more apt to be married, have children, be employed, and not abuse alcohol as much as the hospitalized patients. Female clients are also more apt to be married, have children, and have better homemaking and social skills than the hospitalized women.

Because one goal of treatment is to help the client function in the community and get along with significant others, the perceptions of these other persons are important and should contribute to the social validity of this instrument. Because the PARS refers to behavior outside the treatment setting, especially in home and work-related areas, the generalizability and ecological validity of the treatment program may be examined. The extent to which relatives' ratings reflect actual behavior and adjustment of the client is reported to be acceptably valid.

Based on data collected for the earlier PARS (Ellsworth, 1975), scale test-retest reliabilities range between .80 and .98, median of .91. Scale reliabilities were somewhat lower for women than for men, apparently due to men providing less reliable ratings for females. Internal consistency estimates (coefficient alpha) of the current PARS scales range from .83 to .92, median of .86 (Ellsworth, 1981).

The eight scales were selected from the earlier PARS V scales. Because each scale score is the unweighted sum of the item ratings, and item weights were not selected so as to make the scales uncorrelated, there are some patterns among the scales. The correlation matrix is computed separately for males and females, and these do not appear to have been tested for any differences. The "factor loadings" or the correlations between the items and the scale factors indicated that items within a scale loaded highly on that factor and little on other scale factors. Thus, there was good "simple structure" in that each item measures the particular scale dimension for which it is intended and does not contribute substantially to other scale dimensions.

The aspects of personal adjustment and symptoms are moderately positively correlated with one another, although more so for men (rs = .54 to .56) than for women (rs = .31 to .49). Close Relations and Child Relations are positively related to one another (r = .54 for males and .48 for females). For women, the relationship scales and House Activity were all positively correlated. Employment was more strongly related to the other areas for men than for women. Alcohol/Drug Use was not strongly related to other scales. Overall, the scales are relatively independent and appear to be assessing different components of adjustment and skills.

The change norm tables are based on regression equations predicting post-scores from pre-scores because the pre- and post-scores are correlated; adjustment scores generally improve over the course of treatment, and the poorer the initial adjustment, the greater the improvement. The change norm scores are T-scores based on the difference between actual postscores and predicted postscores. Thus, a person whose actual and predicted postscores were the same would have a change T-score of 50. Scores above 50 indicate more than expected improvement and scores below 50 show less than average improvement. The regression equation slopes were found to describe both males and females, and clients and patients; thus, the same change norms are used for all persons.

Critique

Eichman (1978), in his review of the earlier PARS V, concludes that "the PARS is a sound and worthwhile instrument. It offers the potential of evaluating treatment effectiveness for the cost of postage, PARS materials, and clerical time" (p. 638).

Ellsworth makes a convincing case with supporting references for the importance of significant others, especially if the client and the significant other live together. The larger issues of patient-family interactions, social judgement, and social validity are all important in assessing the effectiveness of therapy. One question is to what extent different significant others, such as spouse compared to a parent, provide comparable ratings. Certainly, different significant others have different perspectives on the same client, but the cost and effort in obtaining more than one rating might be prohibitive. There do not appear to be any comparative studies of the PARS and another measure of treatment outcome with adults (e.g., the Katz Adjustment Scale), which uses ratings of relatives.

Because it may be desirable to look at each client individually and different individuals may have differential reactions to therapy there is some disagreement over the use of standardized residual scores to equate pretreatment scores, (cf., Ellsworth, 1978, 1979a; Blackman, 1979). However, because there is evidence that persons initially poorly adjusted improve more than those persons initially better adjusted, there does seem to be a need for comparing patients based on level of pretreatment adjustment in reference to some normative population. Of course, the clinician may wish to consider pre- and post-raw scores for individual treatment outcome.

There are concerns about the proportion of patients elegible for the PARS. Ellsworth (1975) reports that 59% of hospital patients met the criteria for use of the PARS. Eichman (1978) points out that numerous patients do not have a significant other before treatment, and those who do have may not return to them following treatment. There is also discrepant evidence about low follow-up return rate reflecting poorer patient adjustment. Ellsworth (1979b, cited in Ellsworth, 1981) found that patients for whom follow-up ratings were missing were as well-adjusted as those for whom follow-ups were returned, data loss being due to the rater's lack of motivation or interest. However, Penk, Uebersax, Charles, and Andrews (1981) report that subjects less well-adjusted (on the MMPI and the Brief Psychiatric Rating Scale) at pretreatment had the lowest outcome return rates (on ratings by significant others). Thus, the problems of data loss and differential return rates are not fully resolved.

There is little question that obtaining ratings by significant others by mailed questionnaire is cost-effective, being the least expensive method and adequate for most purposes (Warner, Berman, Weyant, & Ciarlo, 1983). Positive aspects of the PARS include its clear, direct questions and convenience for the rater. There are no overlapping items as in the MMPI, the PARS is quickly and easily scored, and the unit weights for the items composing scale scores may be more stable than other weights designed for other purposes. On the other hand, including more items might allow sampling a wider range of clinically and socially relevant behaviors.

Overall, the PARS appears to be a good clinical instrument and summary measure of an individual client's progress and response to therapy, and therefore useful for program evaluation and accountability purposes. Without experimental studies using control groups, patient improvement cannot be attributed solely to treatment, but as a survey instrument, the PARS Scale may provide useful information. There could be further studies of some practical concerns, such as utility of the information provided and more theoretical issues (role of support systems in maintaining mental health, patient-family interactions, person perception). No doubt, these will come along as the PARS is used more frequently.

References

Blackman, S. (1979). A comment on Robert B. Ellsworth's "The comparative effectiveness of community clinic and psychiatric hospital treatment." *Journal of Community Psychology, 7,* 179.

Eichman, W. J. (1978). Review of PARS Scale. In O. K. Buros (Ed.), *The eighth mental measurements yearbook* (pp. 988-990). Highland Park, NJ: The Gryphon Press.

Ellsworth, R. B. (1975). Consumer feedback in measuring the effectiveness of mental health programs. In M. Guttentag & E. L. Struening (Eds.), *Handbook of evaluation research* (Vol. 2) (pp. 239-274). Beverly Hills, CA: Sage.

Ellsworth, R. B. (1978). The comparative effectiveness of community clinic and psychiatric hospital treatment. *Journal of Community Psychology, 6,* 103-111.

Ellsworth, R. B. (1979a). A reply to Blackman's comment. *Journal of Community Psychology, 7,* 180-181.

Ellsworth, R. B. (1979b). Does follow-up loss reflect poor outcome? *Evaluation and the Health Professions, 2,* 419-437.

Ellsworth, R. B. (1981). *PARS Scale: Measuring personal adjustment and role skills.* Palo Alto, CA: Consulting Psychologists Press.

Fontana, A. F., & Dowds, B. N. (1975). Assessing treatment outcome: I. Adjustment in the community. *The Journal of Nervous and Mental Disease, 161,* 221-230.

Hyer, L., & Collins, J. (1984). Community adjustment among older depressives. *Journal of Clinical Psychology, 40,* 659-668.

Hyer, L., Collins, J., & Blazer, D. II. (1983). Community adjustment of older schizophrenics. *Journal of Clinical Psychology, 39,* 160-163.

Penk, W. E., Uebersax, J. S., Charles, H. L., & Andrews, R. H. (1981). Psychological aspects of data loss in outcome research. *Evaluation Review, 5,* 392-396.

Warner, J. L., Berman, J. J., Weyant, J. M., & Ciarlo, J. A. (1983). Assessing mental health program effectiveness. A comparison of three client follow-up methods. *Evaluation Review, 7,* 635-658.

Donald I. Templer, Ph.D.
Professor of Psychology, California School of Professional Psychology, Fresno, California.

AFFECTS BALANCE SCALE

Leonard R. Derogatis. Towson, Maryland: Clinical Psychometric Research.

Introduction

The Affects Balance Scale (ABS) is a self-report instrument that assesses positive affect, negative affect, and the difference or "balance" between the two.

Dr. Leonard Derogatis of John Hopkins University is an eminent psychologist who is well known for his development of other psychometric instruments such as the SCL-90-R, the Hopkins Psychiatric Rating Scale, and the Derogatis Sexual Functioning Inventory. The ABS was copyrighted by Dr. Derogatis in 1975 and is marketed by him as part of the Clinical Psychometric Research Series. Dr. Derogatis apparently views affect in a complex fashion that goes beyond a simple continuum conceptualization. In a sense, the Affects Balance Inventory is to affect as the Bem Sex Role Inventory and the associated concept of androgyny are to sex role. It should be borne in mind that Dr. Derogatis regards his instrument as one that assesses mood rather than the depressive syndrome.

The ABS consists of one sheet of 8" x 11" paper. The instructions on this 40-item adjective checklist are to indicate the degree that one experiences the 40 emotions under consideration "during the past _____ including today." (The examiner designates the time frame intended in this blank space.) The 40 emotions are each displayed with one word to which the subject indicates "never," "rarely," "sometimes," "frequently," or "always" as applied to himself or herself. Twenty of the words pertain to positive emotions and 20 to negative ones. There are five words each for the four positive affect dimensions (Joy, Contentment, Vigor, and Affection) and for the four negative affect dimensions (Anxiety, Depression, Guilt, and Hostility).

The reverse side of the answer sheet contains the scoring key, computational aids, and designated spaces for the eight individual dimension scores, the Positive Score Total, the Negative Score Total, and the Affect Balance Index (ABI).

Practical Applications/Uses

The Affects Balance Scale has considerable utility in psychological and psychiatric research in assessing the nature of various psychopathological syndromes presumed to have an affective componant and in determining affect change over time such as in response to various interventions.

32

The present reviewer proposes the concept of "total affective charge," which is the sum of the ABS Positive Score Total and the Negative Score Total. Such a concept would appear to bear some resemblance to the sum of color responses on the Rorschach and to the addition of the Depression (D) Scale T-score and the Hypomania (Ma) Scale T-score of the MMPI. An example of a person with very high total affective charge would be a patient given a diagnosis of bipolar disorder, mixed. It would appear that determining both the change in Affects Balance Index and change in total affective charge over time would prove useful in assessing emotional lability.

Currently the ABS is primarily a research instrument. It seems to have potential for clinical use, but more information such as mean scores for various patient groups would have to be provided before the prudent clinician could use it with great confidence.

The test is appropriate for adults and adolescents in both clinical and non-clinical populations. Ability to read and comprehend words at about the seventh-grade level is necessary.

The ABS can be administered by clerical personnel either individually or in a group setting. Each of the 40 emotions (words) is scored from 0 for "never" through 4 for "always." The score of each of the eight dimensions (e.g., Joy) is the sum of the score for each of the five words. The sum of the 20 words constituting the four positive dimensions is the "Positive Score Total." The sum of the 20 words constituting the four negative dimensions is the "Negative Score Total." Affect Balance Index = (Positive Score Total ÷ 20) − (Negative Score Total ÷ 20). The scoring can be carried out by clerical personnel and can be learned in a few minutes.

Technical Aspects

The ABS has excellent face validity. Norms for normal males and females may be obtained from Dr. Derogatis. A manual is currently being developed. However, there are presently no published studies regarding internal consistency and reliability over time. Nevertheless, it is difficult to fault a weapon that performs very well in the battlefield because it was not tested before combat. The research using the ABS has unquestionably established its construct validity. Sexually dysfunctional men and women were found to have higher Negative Score Totals and lower Positive Score Totals and Affects Balance Index than normal men and women (Derogatis & Meyer, 1979). Transsexual men were found to have significantly higher Negative Score Total and significantly lower Positive Score Total than the normal men (Derogatis, Meyer, & Vazquez, 1978). Cancer patients who scored in the more pathological direction on other measures exhibited more negative affect and less positive affect on the ABS (Derogatis, Abeloff, & Melisaratos, 1979).

Critique

The Affects Balance Scale is an excellent instrument for assessing various facets of affect state, individual and group affect differences, and change in affect over time. It has very fine face and construct validity. This scale is of proven value for research purposes and appears to have potential for clinical use.

References

Derogatis, L. R., Abeloff, M. D., & Melisaratos, N. (1979). Psychological coping mechanisms and survival time in metastatic breast cancer. *Journal of the American Medical Association, 242,* 1504-1508.

Derogatis, L. R., & Meyer, J. K. (1979). A psychological profile of the sexual dysfunctions. *Archives of Sexual Behavior, 8,* 201-222.

Derogatis, L. R., Meyer, J. K., & Vazquez, N. (1978). A psychological profile of the transsexual. *The Journal of Nervous and Mental Disease, 166,* 234-254.

Perry M. Nicassio, Ph.D.
Assistant Professor of Psychiatry, School of Medicine, Vanderbilt University, Nashville, Tennessee.

ANALYSIS OF COPING STYLE

Herbert F. Boyd and G. Orville Johnson. Columbus, Ohio: Charles E. Merrill Publishing Company.

Introduction

The Assessment of Coping Style (ACS) is a projective instrument that is designed to elicit responses concerning coping style in children kindergarten through twelfth grade. The ACS's authors, Boyd and Johnson (1981) define coping style as "the cognitive processes used to deal with presently occurring inter/ intrapersonal problems" (p. 7). The instrument itself consists of 20 figure drawings depicting children or youth in various school settings interacting with peers or authority figures. The assessment of coping style is determined by having the test subject describe what the child or youth in the figure is thinking, feeling, or doing by selecting one of six statements measuring different forms of coping. The coping styles assessed are externalized attack, externalized avoidance, externalized denial, internalized attack, internalized avoidance and internalized denial. The internal-external distinction, according to the authors, is based on whether the individual perceives the problem as being outside or within the self. The authors provide a detailed description of the six coping styles with examples in the test manual, but in the most fundamental sense, the coping styles refer to tendencies in children and adolescents to either attack or withdraw (avoidance, denial) from problems and frustrating occurrences.

The authors, Herbert F. Boyd and G. Orville Johnson, are professors of special education at the University of South Florida and have devoted much of their careers to the study of behavior problems of children in classroom settings. The ACS has been preceded by over 20 years of research and development before evolving into its present form.

The original version of the instrument, the School Picture-Story Test (Johnson & Neely, 1954), employed a TAT-like format in which subjects were requested to tell a story to 16 stimulus pictures depicting a "hero" figure interacting with authority figures, peers, or the impersonal school environment. The stories of subjects were evaluated by ratings of whether positive or negative attitudes were expressed and by a checklist reflecting themes in five different attitude categories.

Due to problems in scoring and the amount of time involved in evaluating the stories, the School Picture-Story Test was subsequently revised to include six statements from which subjects were to select one that most accurately described the feelings of the child in the picture. The six statements referred to feelings of adequacy-inadequacy, acceptance-rejection, and interaction-withdrawal. The

School Picture-Story Test underwent another revision in which new stimulus pictures were drawn and new attitude statements were written. The test was then renamed the School Attitude Inventory (Johnson, 1969) and is the most recent precursor to the ACS.

The ACS differs significantly from previous versions with its emphasis on coping rather than on the general assessment of attitudes in school-aged children. The ACS also represents an operationalization of a model of coping developed by the authors that is used to conceptualize children's and adolescents' behavior problems in relation to authority figures and peers and to design remedial interventions in the classroom setting.

Two forms of the ACS have been developed; Form C for use with children of elementary-school age (grades 1-8), and Form Y for use with preadolescents and adolescents of junior- and senior-high age (grades 9-12). The only difference in the two forms is that older youth are depicted in the stimulus pictures in Form Y, whereas younger children appear in Form C. The pictures themselves and the accompanying statements are identical.

The 20 pictures consist of ten figures involving interactions of a child or adolescent with school authority figures (teachers, principals) and ten others involving interactions with peers. It is clear from the pictures that the context is the school environment, however, the exact situations depicted are ambiguous. Also, facial features of the persons in the pictures have been omitted presumably to maximize the likelihood of projecting emotional content into the situation and to prevent the task from being an exercise in perceived emotion.

Practical Applications/Uses

The ACS is designed for use by guidance counselors, school psychologists, regular classroom teachers, and special education teachers, and requires minimal expertise on the part of the examiner. The test can be administered in either an individual or group format. When administering the test individually, the examiner presents each stimulus picture, instructs the subject to read the six statements (or reads them for the subject if a reading deficiency exists), and asks the subject to choose the statement that best describes what the child or adolescent in the picture is thinking or feeling. The examiner then records the response of the subject on an Individual Record Form by circling the type of coping style that the chosen statement reflects. After responses to all the pictures have been obtained and scores summarized, the examiner conducts an inquiry with the subject into those responses that are indicative of the subject's dominant coping style. During the inquiry the examiner asks the subjects to explore the reasons for their response selections to relevant picture stimuli.

The group administration of the ACS involves the presentation of the 20 pictures via transparencies with an overhead projector. Two examiners are required to conduct the group assessment: one to present the test stimuli and give instructions and the other to monitor the performance of subjects. In this format subjects select one of the six statements by marking their own record form after each picture has been projected. The authors claim that between 25 and 110 students between grades 3 and 12 can be assessed in this manner but suggest that second-graders be tested in groups of 10 to 12. The group testing of first-grade children is not recommended. Scoring templates are used to categorize the subjects' responses into the six coping styles. It is recommended that group administration of the ACS be followed by individual assessment for subjects found to have a limited coping repertoire and for greater diagnostic clarification.

Scoring of the ACS is simple and straightforward. Responses are summed separately for each of the six coping styles for authority and peer pictures. These scores are then combined to provide total scores. Eight or more responses for a particular coping style are indicative of restricted coping, and according to the authors, are suggestive of adjustment problems. It is also possible to obtain summary scores by collapsing across externalized and internalized attack, and externalized and internalized avoidance categories, although the authors do not provide guidelines as to the significance of the scores so obtained.

Thus, in its present state of development, the ACS is an easily administered, brief projective measure that may be used to achieve a better understanding of how children and adolescents cope with authority figures and peers in the school environment. However, a more thorough evaluation of the uses of the ACS will depend on the outcome of validity studies relevant to its diagnostic and clinical screening value. A discussion of the validity research on the ACS is provided below.

Technical Aspects

Content for the coping statements accompanying the 20 pictures was derived by having 23 teachers submit verbal statements made by children in their classes reflecting the six coping styles. Twenty sets of six statements were then selected for each picture and submitted to three professional judges familiar with the coping style model who were asked to classify the coping statements. The judges agreed 85% of the time in assigning the statements to the six coping categories. This constitutes favorable evidence for the content validity of the ACS.

Studies of the construct validity of the ACS have employed the known groups method (Cronbach & Meehl, 1967) and have been guided by the premise that the ACS should discriminate between students with adjustment problems placed in special education classrooms or settings and "normal" students in regular class-rooms. Boyd and Johnson have argued that children with adjustment problems have more limited coping skills and should thus demonstrate more of a tendency to rely on one coping style in their responses on the ACS than controls. Research on normal adults has shown that limited coping repertoires are associated with greater psychological distress (Pearlin & Schooler, 1978). To test this postulate, they administered the ACS in a group format to 598 children (grades 2 through 12) in a variety of public, private, and state educational settings. Of this number, 203 students had been designated as emotionally disturbed or delinquent and were participants in special educational programs.

The authors found evidence to support their hypothesis, especially in children of elementary-school age (grades 2-8). Forty-three percent of the children in special education gave eight or more responses reflecting one coping style com-pared to 18% in the control group. The criterion of eight responses also significantly discriminated between the two groups among those enrolled in secondary schools (grades 9-12), but the differences were less pronounced. Unfortunately, Boyd and Johnson do not present statistical findings on differences in mode of coping style between criterion and control groups, although they note that emotionally disturbed children tended to show a more "externalizing pattern" (p. 27).

In another validity study, Schaefer (1982) reported similar findings on the use of the ACS in discriminating between normal and emotionally handicapped children. Her data, which are based on the group administration of the ACS to 687 children in grades 2-12, revealed that the criterion of eight or more responses of one coping style differentiated between the normal and emotionally handicapped samples. Significantly fewer normal subjects (29%) used one coping styie eight or more times than emotionally handicapped subjects (43%). Sex and grade level were independent of ACS scores, but contrary to her hypothesis, students who achieved above the median on standardized tests of reading and language skill were significantly more limited in their choice of coping style than students scoring below the median. If the ACS is to be viewed as a measure of adjustment, then this finding would seem to contradict the fact that problems in psychosocial and emotional adjustment are typically associated with greater difficulties in academic performance in children.

Due to the brevity of the measure and the manner in which the ACS is scored, the authors could not adequately test its internal consistency but do provide data on its test-retest stability (Boyd & Johnson, 1981). Eighty-two students who were administered the ACS via the group format in a morning session were retested on the same day approximately three hours later. Subjects changed their pattern of responses considerably on the second test administration, showing a greater tendency to limit their coping style. The test-retest stability of the ACS is therefore in doubt. The stability of the ACS is central to the question of whether a coping style, which should have some permanence across time and situations, is being assessed by responses in the six categories.

Critique

The development of the ACS represents a novel attempt to measure coping in children and adolescents. Its semi-projective format avoids some of the artificiality and reactivity inherent in other self-report coping measures that have been developed for adults (see Folkman & Lazarus, 1980; Rosenbaum, 1980) and provides an opportunity for examining how coping may differ in relation to authority and peers. There is clearly a need to understand the coping process in younger people, and the development of valid, relevant measures is crucial to this area of inquiry.

The ACS, however, is in its infant stage of development and its validity and reliability have not been adequately established. While the measure appears to have some discriminative validity, studies have not examined its concurrent relationship with behavioral measures or standardized tests of other scales of theoretically relevant constructs. A similar question also may be raised about the construct validity of the six individual coping styles measured in the ACS and their relationship with psychological criteria and other forms of coping assessed via self-report. Demonstrating, for example, that children who have high denial scores on the ACS also tend to show this tendency on other measures or in contrived experimental situations would substantially reinforce the basic premise of the ACS that subjects are, in fact, using projection in their responses to test stimuli.

A related concern is whether the ACS is really tapping a coping style in subjects or a more situation-specific pattern of responsiveness. Some evidence exists that coping tendencies have generalizability across situations (Rosenbaum, 1980; Stone & Neale, 1984). The only reported test-retest data on the ACS, however, do not support its stability or consistency.

In view of the limited amount of validity and reliability data, the ACS should be considered an exploratory measure that may serve as an initial step in evaluating the coping process in children and adolescents in relation to the school context. Until investigators have more thoroughly evaluated the psychometric properties of the ACS, school personnel should be extremely cautious in using this measure for diagnostic or intervention purposes.

References

Boyd, H. F., & Johnson, G. O. (1981). *Analysis of coping style: A cognitive behavioral approach to behavior management.* Columbus, OH: Charles E. Merrill.

Cronbach, L. J., & Meehl, P. E. (1967). Construct validity in psychological tests. In D. N. Jackson & S. Messick (Eds.), *Problems in human assessment* (pp. 55-77). New York: McGraw-Hill.

Folkman, S., & Lazarus, R. S. (1980). An analysis of coping in a middle-aged community sample. *Journal of Health and Social Behavior, 21,* 219-239.

Johnson, G. O. (1969). *School Attitude Inventory.* Unpublished manuscript.

Johnson, G. O., & Neely, J. H. (1954). *School Picture-Story test.* Unpublished manuscript.

Pearlin, L., & Schooler, C. (1978). The structure of coping. *Journal of Health and Social Behavior, 9,* 2-21.

Rosenbaum, M. (1980). A schedule for assessing self-control behaviors: Preliminary findings. *Behavior Therapy, 11,* 109-121.

Schaefer, E. M. (1982). *Construct validation of the Analysis of Coping Style instrument.* Unpublished doctoral dissertation, University of South Florida, Tampa.

Stone, A. A., & Neale, J. M. (1984). New measure of daily coping: Development and preliminary results. *Journal of Personality and Social Psychology, 46,* 892-906.

M. Ebrahim Fakouri, Ph.D.
Professor of Educational and School Psychology, Indiana State University, Terre Haute, Indiana.

ARLIN TEST OF FORMAL REASONING
Patricia Kennedy Arlin. East Aurora, New York: Slosson Educational Publications, Inc.

Introduction

The Arlin Test of Formal Reasoning (ATFR) is designed as a group test to assess cognitive abilities associated with the formal operations stage according to Inhelder and Piaget (1958). Based on the score received on the ATFR, the student's cognitive level can be assessed as being at one of five levels: concrete, high concrete, transitional, low formal, and high formal. Since the ATFR is constructed on Piaget's theory, a short description of the stages of cognitive development, particularly the stage of formal operations, will provide a theoretical perspective for the test.

Piaget's developmental theory (1952) is based on the assumptions that thought processes during adolescence and adult life are qualitatively different from those of childhood. According to Piaget, in the course of development each individual passes through several stages toward the formal operations stage which emerges during adolescence. Piaget has proposed four major stages of intellectual development which are qualitatively different from each other: the sensorimotor stage, from birth to 18 months; the pre-operational stage, from 18 months to 7 years; the concrete operations stage, from 7 to 11 years; and the formal operations stage, from 11 years on. These age spans simply suggest a time frame during which most children are expected to show the intellectual characteristics associated with a particular stage. The sequence of the stages, however, is fixed for all individuals. Formal operational thought is logical thought, a generalized orientation toward problem solving. The person at this stage is capable of exploring all possible hypotheses and checking their validities. The adolescent who has reached this stage can organize thinking into higher order operations for finding abstract rules by which to solve not only the problem at hand but also all other similar problems. As can be seen, the formal operations stage according to Piaget's theory is the final stage of cognitive development. "Thus, this general form of equilibrium can be conceived of as a final in the sense that it is not modified during the life span of the individual . . ." (Inhelder & Piaget, 1958, p. 232). The eight specific abilities that characterize this stage of development are:

1. the combinational operations
2. proportions
3. coordination of two systems of reference and relativity of motion or acceleration
4. the concept of mechanical equilibrium

5. the notion of probability
6. the notion of correlation
7. multiplicative compensation
8. the forms of conservation which go beyond direct empirical verification

(pp. 310-329)

Piaget's approach to assessment of intellectual functioning is called *methode clinique*, a highly individualized interview technique for eliciting the reasons for an answer provided by a child or adolescent. This method requires individual attention, rapport, and a good knowledge of the foundations of his theory. Through this method both the answers given to a question or problem and the process by which the answer or solution is arrived at are assessed. On the basis of such assessment the individual's stage of cognitive development is determined.

It is evident that Piaget's clinical method is individualized and as such is very time-consuming for testing a large group. In recent years, the need for testing a large number of children and adolescents in a relatively short time has resulted in a number of attempts to develop group tests for Piagetian tasks to determine stages of cognitive development (e.g., Pinard & Laurendeau, 1970; Tuddenham, 1970). The Arlin Test of Formal Reasoning is the most recent and most improved of these tests. The items of the ATFR were selected on the basis of the eight specific abilities listed previously. The following descriptions are provided for these abilities associated with formal operations:

1. *Multiplicative compensation*—the ability to consider more than one dimension at a time and make appropriate compensation in one dimension as a result of changes in another dimension (e.g., ability for conservation of volume).

2. *Probability*—the ability to figure the odds in a game of chance.

3. *Correlations*—the ability to consider the causal relationship of two variables (e.g., supply and demand and prices).

4. *Combinatorial reasoning*—the ability to consider all possible combinations of two or more variables (e.g., considering all possible combinations for choosing a 3-member team from 5 players).

5. *Proportional reasoning*—a mathematical ability to see or make equal proportions (e.g., if 2A = 5B then 5A = ?B).

6. *Forms of conservation beyond direct verification*—the ability to deduce and imply certain conservations and infer their existence by observing their effects (e.g., when one marble hits another marble on a flat surface the momentum of the first marble is transferred to the one that was hit).

7. *Mechanical equilibrium*—the ability to coordinate two or more complimentary forms of reversibility-reciprocity and inversion (e.g., economic theories).

8. *The coordination of two or more systems or frames of reference*—the ability to co-ordinate two or more systems, "each involving a direct and an inverse operation, but with one of the systems in a relation of compensation or symmetry in terms of the other. It represents a type of relativity of thought" (Arlin, 1984, p. 10-12).

Practical Applications/Uses

According to the manual, the purpose of the ATFR is fourfold: 1) to be able to administer it to a large group for determining the stage of cognitive development;

2) to obtain specific information on each of eight abilities of formal operations; 3) to use it with other tests for screening and placement of gifted students; and 4) to assess logical reasoning separately from other intelligence and achievement test results for students with learning or reading disabilities.

The ATFR contains 32 items in a multiple-choice format. For each item four choices are given and the test taker chooses an answer and checks the response on a separate answer sheet. The instructions for the test are rather simple and clear. It is very much like multiple-choice tests with which students are familiar. The examiner has some flexibility in the administration of the test, such as answering questions regarding the vocabulary of the test or administering the test orally to those whose reading levels are below the level of the test. The required time for the test is 45 minutes; however, there is some flexibility here as well—if more time is needed, it can be given. There is one sample question provided to clarify that the test is trying to assess "thinking skills" and "thinking style." This sample question is very helpful in showing the test taker that despite similarity to other multiple-choice tests the ATFR attempts to assess the process by which the answer is obtained.

Another helpful feature is that each page of the test contains a graphic presentation of the problem relating to the items on that page. There are 14 such drawings including one for the sample item.

The test can be scored by hand or computer, with the score for each subject falling between 0 and 32. The ATFR provides two sets of scores. The first set is the total score and determines one of the five cognitive levels: concrete (0-7 points), high concrete (8-14 points), transitional (15-17 points), low formal (18-24 points), and high formal (25-32 points). The second set, the subset scores for each of the eight abilities of formal reasoning, provides a profile for the test taker indicating his or her strengths and weaknesses. If the test is scored by computer, the subtest scores are provided automatically. For hand scoring a scoring template transparency is provided. This scoring template is easy to use and provides a total score and a score for each subtest.

Technical Aspects

According to the manual, this version of the ATFR was used with more than 6,500 students, ranging in age from 11 to 19 years, as well as with adults. The majority of the students came from white, middle-class, English-speaking backgrounds. The overall readability of the test is reported to be at the sixth-grade level. Cross-validation of the test has been done by using two methods of administration. A paper-and-pencil version was given to a large group and individual clinical interviews were conducted with a sample chosen randomly from this group. However, the validity coefficients are not reported in the manual and the manual makes reference to another source (Arlin, 1982). The reader who wants to check these coefficients encounters two problems. First there is the inconvenience of looking for them in a source other than the test manual, particularly where the volume number and the page numbers of this citation are not accurately printed in the manual. Second, the validity coefficients for only six of eight subtests are reported. These coefficients are determined by calculation of degree of relationship (Kendall taus) between measures obtained for each ability by two methods, clinical and paper-and-pencil. These validity coefficients are reported to range from .55 to .74. This technique in determining validity is consistent with the recommendations of Nagy and Griffiths (1982), who have criticized all of the attempts to develop group tests for Piagetian tasks to determine stages of cognitive development. Test-retest reliabilities (8-week to 6-month intervals between the two testings) range from .76 to .89. The Hoyt estimates of reliabilities range from .71 to .89, and the Cronbach alphas for the total composites are reported to range from .60 to .73.

Critique

The Arlin Test of Formal Reasoning is a group test in which attempts have been made to retain the efficiency and economy of the paper-and-pencil group test while incorporating some of the advantages of clinical method. It is a great improvement over its predecessors and a welcome addition to assessment instruments for professionals who are engaged in educational and psychological assessment and research. Nevertheless, like all previous attempts, it has certain shortcomings.

Piaget's approach in *methode clinique* is process oriented; that is, the information obtained about the process by which the question is answered or the problem is solved is very important. The psychometric approach, particularly in group testing, is for the most part a product-oriented approach; that is, the assessment is made on the basis of the answers given.

All those who have attempted to develop a group test to assess cognitive abilities based on Piaget's theory have in one way or another acknowledged that for group testing of these abilities we cannot obtain as much information about the structural aspects of cognitive development by the use of the psychometric approach as we can by the use of clinical method. For example, Tuddenham (1970), while apologizing for his attempts to "psychometrize" *methode clinique*, "absolves" Piaget from all responsibilities in this regard. Arlin (1984) on the other hand indicates that "clearly it is not possible in a paper-and-pencil test to achieve the quality of response and explanation that the clinical method yields. But the necessity of large group testing for any practical use of cognitive levels assessment in schools requires the trade-off of response quality for efficiency and economy of administration" (p. 3).

In the construction of the ATFR, assessment of the process is not ignored. The problem presented in one item is frequently followed by a rationale included in the next item in order to assess not only the product (the answer) but also the process (rationale) by which the subject arrives at the answer. Arlin (1984) indicates that this approach "is analogous to the use of the clinical method in the use of individual interviews to assess formal reasoning" (p. 3). It should be remembered however that: 1) the items containing the rationale are also in a multiple-choice format and are not open-ended; 2) unless the test items are specifically analyzed and interpreted by looking at the answer for each item and its rationale, the information obtained will only be of psychometric value; and 3) there is no specific recommendation in the manual for this kind of diagnostic interpretation and analysis.

There are also certain other minor problems which can be eliminated in later revisions. For example, the introduction to the problem and the graphic presentation for Items 7 and 8 are not clear, in Items 9 and 10 it is not clearly stated that all children weigh 20 kilograms, and for Items 25 and 26 the description of the problem should say that weights do not fall through water. Although the manual allows the examiner to answer questions about the test's vocabulary at his or her discretion as long as doing so does not give hints for the solution of the problem, increasing the clarity of these items will reduce the questions on the part of the test takers.

All in all this is a practical, short, and efficient test in the field of assessment that was long dominated by instruments that were not based on any developmental theory. This reviewer has already introduced this test to the students in an assessment course and some of the ambiguities of the items listed previously are based in part on the reactions of the graduate students to the test. The ATFR is a new instrument; as its use in clinical assessment and research increases some other suggestions for its improvement will no doubt be made. While using the test for now, this reviewer is already looking forward to its revision.

References

Arlin, P. K. (1982). A multitrait-multimethod validity study of a test of formal reasoning. *Educational and Psychological Measurement, 42*, 1077-1088.

Arlin, P. K. (1984). *Arlin Test of Formal Reasoning.* East Aurora, NY: Slosson Educational Publications, Inc.

Inhelder, B., & Piaget, J. (1958). *The growth of logical thinking from childhood to adolescence.* New York: Basic Books.

Nagy, P., & Griffiths, A. K. (1982). Limitations of recent research relating Piaget's theory to adolescent thought. *Review of Educational Research, 52*, 513-556.

Piaget, J. (1952). *The origin of intelligence in children.* New York: International Universities Press.

Pinard, A., & Laurendeau, M. (1970). A scale of mental development based on the theory of Piaget: Description of a project. In I. J. Athey & D. O. Rubadeau (Eds.), *Educational implications of Piaget's theory* (pp. 307-317). Waltham, MA: Ginn-Blaisdel.

Tuddenham, R. D. (1970). Psychometrizing Piaget's *methode clinique.* In I. J. Athey & D. O. Rubadeau (Eds.), *Educational implications of Piaget's theory* (pp. 317-324). Waltham, MA: Ginn-Blaisdel.

Barry P. Frost, Ph.D.
Chairman, Clinical, School and Community Psychology Program, The University of Calgary, Calgary, Alberta, Canada.

ASSESSMENT OF BASIC COMPETENCIES

Jwalla P. Somwaru. Bensenville, Illinois: Scholastic Testing Service, Inc.

Introduction

The Assessment of Basic Competencies (ABC) is a battery of tests designed to assess subjects' learned skills, rather than their presumed underlying abilities and processes. The author's rationale, based on the Cumulative Learning Model of Gagne (1968), is that:

> ". . . simple associative learnings lead to other learnings, which in turn lead to generalizations, such as concepts and rules. Learning in any one area is a continuum. A process of task analysis enables one to determine where a student is located in the continuum, and what must be learned in order to achieve a particular goal" (Somwaru, 1981, p. 1).

Also of major importance is the fact that the battery is based on a latent trait model that allows criterion-referenced as well as norm-referenced assessment. There are two ways in which criterion-referenced assessment may be carried out: 1) in a diagnostic mode in which performance on skills and clusters is evaluated or 2) a developmental mode in which performance is evaluated against a developmental scale or sequence.

The rationale for the battery, following the lead of P. E. Vernon (1955, 1960) with respect to the overlap of intelligence and achievement functions, avoids the need for an ability-achievement discrepancy and suggests instead a generalized-specific learning discrepancy. According to the ABC Manual (Somwaru, 1981), the component skills of the Information Processing domain are not only more generalized than those of language and mathematics, but they overlap and strongly interact. Although the Information Processing domain seems to be central to the acquisition of other school subjects, such as mathematics and language, "it does not represent a different kind of learning" (p. 2).

Another element of major importance in this approach is that the ABC provides a single integrated system instead of several tests that differ in purpose, content, norms, and scales. The parts of this battery are logically and statistically related, have a common metric, and are normed as similar and overlapping populations. The ABC allows moving directly from assessment to recommendations for remedial instruction. In addition, the battery's equal interval scaling allows a user to assess growth over time by taking repeated measures. This is not a valid procedure with the usual ordinal, scale-based normative tests.

The system is appropriate for a wide range of children who are not coping well

45

in school, whether they are diagnosed as learning-disabled, emotionally disturbed, language-disordered, educable-mentally-handicapped, dyslexic, behavior disordered, or disadvantaged. It is not designed for those with visual, auditory, or speech impairments. Provided that the purpose of the assessment is to determine capability of coping with school learning in English, the battery may be used with bilingual students. The assessed skills are those necessary in order to function successfully in school. In general, the battery is nonbiased if the assessment's purpose is that of determining educational needs of children in the context of current educational organization and methods.

All of the battery's tests are power tests, i.e., untimed. The manual states that the ABC takes about three hours for the administration of the whole battery and about another half-hour for scoring and conversion of the scores. Diagnostic interpretation and the writing of a prescription or suggestions for instruction takes additional time.

The author, Dr. Jwalla P. Somwaru is an assessment specialist in the Division of Special Services of the Minnesota Department of Education and a post doctoral associate at the Institute for Research on Learning Disabilities at the University of Minnesota. In addition, he directs a psychoeducational clinic in Circle Pines, Minnesota.

He obtained his B.A. degree from the University of London, his M.A. degree from the University of Chicago, and his Ed.D. degree from the University of Toronto. Prior to joining the staff of the Minnesota Department of Education he was director of research and development at American Guidance Service and coordinator of research and evaluation for the Etobicoke Board of Education in Toronto. He has also had several years experience in teaching and school administration.

Dr. Somwaru was dissatisfied with the current state of the art in current assessment practice where a student may be given several tests (over a dozen in some cases), including intelligence, aptitude, achievement, perceptual and attitudinal instruments designed for a variety of purposes, scaled differently, normed on different populations, and having various degrees of relevance to classroom learning. Having noted that under such conditions diagnosticians use their art instead of science to integrate the results and suggest some relation to instruction (Manual, p. 2), he was motivated to construct a battery based on the same metric, similar or overlapping populations; capable of direct comparison of its subtests; and directly relevant to schoolwork. The battery was designed primarily for use in the United States and Canada where there is much similarity in the basic competencies that are taught and learned. The norm group included students from both countries (see Manual, Tables 58, 59) and confined norms were produced for the tests.

On the basis of the content design (see Manual, Figs. 1, 2) more than 250 items were written for each test scale. These were pilot-run on small groups of children (K-6) in Central Lutheran School, St. Paul, Minnesota, to assess the items' appropriateness for different grades and efficiency of format. The content of the Language and Mathematics domains closely followed the content of curricular materials used in Minnesota schools. The content of items for the Information Processing tests reflected Somwaru's perception in the clusters; these skills were identified to some extent by theory and research in the field of cognitive development. (Manual, pp. 154-155).

In initial field-testing, 200 items were selected for each of seven tests and 180 for each of the remaining four. The tests were administered to children preschool-grade 9 at various locales in the United States and Canada, and selected according to a stratified random sampling plan (specified in the manual's appendix). Each subtest was administered to 60-70 students at the grade level considered most appropriate for the items' difficulty level. In addition, the subtest was given to 60-70 students in grade levels immediately above and below this grade. Thus a total of 180-210 students were given the items in each subtest, resulting in a total of approximately 1,900 students responding to each of the eleven tests. The precise pattern is given in Fig. 5 in the Manual. The test administrators were selected, trained and supervised by a school psychologist, director of special education, guidance counselor, other person skilled in testing, or the author, who also visited most of the sites to make arrangements for the field testing. On the basis of these data, seven tests of 100 items each and four tests of 85 items each were constructed.

During the spring of 1977, calibration and norming data were collected across the United States and Canada from a stratified random sample. Stratification was done on the basis of geographical region, type of community, race, and sex. The American regions corresponded to the four geographical divisions used by the U.S. Census Bureau: Northeast, North Central, South, and West. The states sampled were Maine, New Jersey, New York, Illinois, Minnesota, Iowa, Florida, Tennessee, Texas, Idaho, Washington, and California. The Canadian provinces were New Brunswick, Nova Scotia, Ontario, Manitoba, Alberta, and British Columbia. Urban, suburban and rural districts were sampled. Typical schools were chosen in each district and students were selected at random, with boys and girls drawn in nearly equal proportions as classes were usually mixed and racial proportions, including Eurasian, Black and other nonwhite, balanced. Seriously handicapped students, such as TMR and visually and auditorily impaired, were excluded. Table 60 in the Manual (p. 157) gives a breakdown of the over 20,000 children involved.

The responses to the items in each subtest were scored and the items calibrated using the computer program LOGIST, which computes the values of three item parameters: an index of discrimination, an index of difficulty, and a guessing plan. Unsatisfactory items were flagged for exclusion.

The item calibration procedure resulted in the generation of three parameters for each of the 20 items in the nine to ten subtests of each scale. Linkage of the subtests was achieved by a sampling design that called for samples of students from overlapping grades to take the same subtests and by carrying out appropriate transformations of the item parameters (for details see Sympson, 1979; Manual, Figure 5).

Scoring tables were developed by means of the procedure described by Sympson in his 1980 research report (Sympson, 1980). This procedure allows users of the ABC to arrive at an estimate of ability (Level of Competence) by referring to a double-entry table with a raw score and a known test starting point. The raw score is a pseudo-number correct and is calculated by either adding the numbers of items correct between the basal and ceiling items to the index number of the basal item or by subtracting the number of errors between the basal and ceiling items from the index number of the highest item correct.

Users wishing to compare the child in question with age or grade groups can convert the Level of Competence into a Developmental Age or a Grade Equivalent. It is also possible to determine a percentile rank, based either on age or grade, and to convert the percentile rank into a Standard Score or Normal Curve Equivalent.

According to the Manual (p. 161), norms were derived from two empirically estimated regression relationships: Developmental Age from the estimated regression of ability on age and Grade Equivalent from the estimated regression of ability on grade level. The Developmental Age Scale, intended to express test performance in terms of what is typical of a child at different age levels, is particularly useful in describing functions that increase rapidly with age, whereas Grade Equivalent, intended to express test performance in terms of what is typical of a child at a given grade level, is particularly useful in describing functions known to be related to instruction in schools. The means and adjusted standard deviations were smoothed and used to generate standard scores for each possible Level of Competence for both age and grade norms. The manual gives an example of such a growth curve for the Information Processing: Observing Skills test (Figure 6) and provides tables with the means and SDs for each of the eleven tests for children from preschool (Age 3 +) through Grade 9 (Spring Norms, Table 62; Fall Norms, Table 63), and the means and SDs for ages 42-180 months (Table 64). Complete figures are given only for age 54 months onward.

The battery consists of 11 spiral-bound books and a package containing colored cube blocks, sticks, triangles, shoe laces, a pointer, and a template. It is easy to transport in a reasonably sized briefcase (not supplied). There are two recording forms: diagnostic and developmental. In the diagnostic form items are grouped in clusters and arranged in parallel strands in ascending order of difficulty. The focus is on which skills and clusters appear to be mastered and which ones are not. The number of items passed in each cluster in relation to the number of items administered in the cluster can be recorded. The substantial, 199-page manual is also spiral-bound.

Each of the eleven books corresponds to a test sampling one of the basic areas: Information Processing, Language and Mathematics. Information Processing consists of three tests: Observing Skills, Organizing Skills, and Relating Skills; Language consists of five tests: Understanding Words, Comprehending Expressions, Producing Expressions, Decoding, and Reading; and Mathematics consists of three tests: Knowing Number and Operations, Understanding Concepts, and Solving Problems.

The tests are described (Manual, pp. 3-4) and examples of typical items given as follows:

Observing Skills: Perceptual processes that enable a child to sense information. Visual-motor processes that enable a child to respond to stimuli. Organizing skills, grouping, or classifying by inclusion and exclusion; ordering in terms of spatial characteristics and time. Includes items in which the child is asked to discriminate between line drawings and reproduce geometrical figures.

Organizing Skills: Includes items in which the child is asked to discriminate between shapes and colors.

Relating Skills: Inferring and applying rules; completing analogies; identifying incongruent relations—what does not fit; solving novel problems. Includes items in which the child is asked to reproduce or match geometric figures and discern incongruencies in pictures.

Understanding Words: Words as labels for objects, descriptions, actions, categories, and ideas. Includes items in which the child is asked to relate specific actions or emotions to those presented in pictures.

Comprehending Expressions: Use of form-class words—nouns, verbs, adjectives, adverbs, and pronouns; use of function words—auxiliaries, model, copula, prepositions—and endings to indicate tense, number, possession, etc.; sentence structure and transformation of sentences; use of idiomatic language. Includes items in which the child is asked to identify pictures using the proper grammatical forms.

Producing Expressions: The same aspects of language that are tested in Comprehending Expressions. Includes items in which the child is asked to form questions and use correct grammar.

Decoding: Knowledge of letters, sounds, and sound-symbol relationship; recognition and pronunciation of phonic and sight words. Includes items in which the child is asked to pronounce letters and distinguish between certain sounds.

Reading: Literal and inferential comprehension of detail, main idea, sequence, cause and effect, etc. Includes items in which the child is asked to select a sentence that best describes an action depicted in pictorial form.

Knowing Number and Operations: Knowledge of number, the numeration system, and the four basic operations with whole numbers and fractions. Includes items in which the child is asked to count and perform arithmetic tasks.

Understanding Concepts: Understanding of mathematical sentences, measurement processes and units, symbols, sets, geometry and graphs, relational concepts, and money. Includes items in which the child is asked to discriminate between geometrical shapes and recognize mathematical concepts.

Solving Problems: Interpretation of mathematical data, determining methods of solution and carrying out solutions of practical problems in one, two, or three steps. Includes items in which the child is asked to solve word problems using mathematical data.

Practical Applications/Uses

Somwaru notes:

> The Assessment is a specialist's instrument. Its use requires adequate academic background and training. Psychologists, psychiatrists, diagnosticians, consultants, or other specialists who have had training in the use of individualized tests would be able to use the battery after a brief presentation . . . It cannot be over-emphasized that interpretation of the test results should be carried out by persons who are professionally trained, and not delegated to test administrators who may not have the background necessary to do so. (Manual, p. 7)

The battery itself is relatively easy to administer and professionals as well as others such as school counselors could readily administer it. However, interpretation should be undertaken only by a trained school psychologist. Even though the battery is designed so that each subtest can be directly compared to each of the other ten, this should not be done mechanically. This battery, like other cognitive tests, needs to be used with the usual professional precautions.

Although the ABC is clearly designed to replace tests such as the WISC-R, Stanford-Binet, or Kaufman ABC, there is much to be gained from using it or part of it in tandem with the earlier instruments. Certainly, it seems to this reviewer that the Information Processing tests complement rather than replace the WISC-R in the appropriate age group.

Currently the ABC is also clearly of more use to school psychologists than to clinical psychologists, although if sufficient research is carried out, the three information processing tests could be used more widely. The Language and Mathematics tests, though obviously of more use to school-based personnel than others, could prove of use to others. In this reviewer's opinion they are preferable to quick tests such as the WRAT (cf., Snart et. al., 1983) or ones more difficult to administer such as KeyMath (Connolly et. al., 1972).

The major purpose of the battery is to obtain scores on Information Processing, Language, and Mathematics tests that are directly comparable to each other. Other purposes are to avoid the potentiality-achievement dichotomy by means of the general-specific attainment approach and to provide power rather than timed tests and both diagnostic and developmental approaches to the achievements and deficits of the particular child.

Direct comparability is obtained via the latent trait-criterion referenced approach. According to Somwaru, IQs were designed to report individual differences in relation to the average of successive age groups, *not* for assessing growth, a purpose for which IQs were not designed. Other standard scores have percentile ranks tied to the distribution of norm groups without equal intervals along the scale (Manual, p. 114). Because the ABC scales are equal they permit the assessment of growth and can be used for assessing growth in each test area.

The system is appropriate for a wide range of children from Kindergarten through Grade 9 who are not coping well with school. According to the manual, the battery may be used with bilingual students or those using English as a second language, provided that the purpose of the assessment is to determine their capability to cope with school learning conducted in English.

The battery, designed to be administered on an individual basis by a trained professional, can be easily administered and the instructions are explicit and very clear in both the manual and in the individual test booklets. Though normally one would want to administer the Information Processing tests first, the tests may be administered in any order. However, because the items are in ascending order of difficulty their order should not be altered. In addition, although it is possible to administer every item to each student, this is inadvisable because some items may be either too easy or too difficult for some examinees. Because the test battery has been designed for adaptive use, students should be administered only those items that are within their range of ability. In order to implement this adaptive procedure, starting points given in Table 1 of the Manual and at the beginning of each test, have been determined for each grade (p. 13).

In this reviewer's experience with severely learning disabled children the Manual's suggested administration time of 2-3 hours is very much an underestimate. Four and one-half hours were taken to administer the full battery to some chidren of this type. Additionally, the scoring and conversion of scores if both diagnostic and developmental forms were used, would take approximately another one and one-half hours. Normally, as with any test, the greater the familiarity, the greater the speed.

Somwaru points out that the decision to give the battery should be based on prior information from other tests or from teachers' assessments. If such prior information is not available, a preliminary test such as the Survey of Basic Competencies (Somwaru, 1979a) may be administered. This survey consists of four short scales (Information Processing, Language, Reading, and Mathematics) that assess the same content domains as the full ABC. In addition to this survey, there is available a Test of Early Learning Skills (Somwaru, 1979b), made up of items from the ABC domains and consisting of three short scales (Thinking, Language and Number), that is appropriate for children aged 3½-5½ years.

In the present reviewer's opinion, a better strategy would be to give the three Information Processing Tests, one from the Language, and one from the Mathematics (probably Reading and Knowing Number and Operations) from the full ABC. This would give a much sounder estimate of the child's abilities than the survey which is designed as a screening instrument. Particularly in respect of learning disabled children, one wants to see if there are discrepancies between observing skills, organizing skills, and relating skills. The survey has too few items for each of these to be really useful in a diagnostic sense.

Interpretation is fundamentally based on objective scores but the full connotation of a score involves the educational and clinical skills of the examiner. The objective status of the child is clear but the etiology and the prescriptions for change based on the scores require a knowledgeable professional, preferably a school psychologist, for interpretation.

Nevertheless, the ABC provides the practitioner with a much sounder base for such decisions than does the currently widespread tactic of using an intelligence test (e.g., WISC-R) and an attainment test (e.g., KeyMath) and attempting to relate the two without any scientific data based on a regression analysis.

The manual provides six pages of suggestions on interpretation (pp. 109-114) and 27 pages on moving from diagnosis to instruction (pp. 115-141). These suggestions are concise, cogent, and specific. They are very helpful, particularly to the novice school psychologist. However, with increasing experience, the need for a cookbook lessens.

Technical Aspects

The detail given concerning the technical aspects of the ABC's development is much fuller than is commonly provided and certainly goes beyond the sophistication of the vast majority of users. In this reviewer's opinion, basing the test both on latent-trait technique and criterion-referencing was a very sound decision.

Construct validity was approached via the smallest space analysis procedure

(Schlesinger & Guttman, 1969) and led to the construction of a new model that provided the theoretical framework for the development of the test battery. In Guttman's analysis of several data sets, including the Thurstones' correlation matrices for the Primary Mental Abilities Tests, a two-dimensional space appeared to be adequate to represent the relationships among most commonly used ability, achievement, and aptitude tests. The two dimensions were *process* (e.g., analytical reasoning, recall, and application) and *language of communication* (e.g., verbal, numerical, and geometric or pictoral). Guttman, who considered this type of configuration preferable to the structures produced by conventional factor-analytic methods for the purpose of describing relationships, designed the smallest space analysis procedure to reduce correlation matrices to more meaningful configurations based on prespecified numbers of dimensions. Somwaru used this procedure (computer program TORSCA) to analyze three sets of correlation data for Grades 1-3, 7, and 12, using 23, 29, and 32 cognitive variables, respectively. According to the Manual, each of these analyses confirmed the adequacy of the two-dimensional model and the clustering of the 11 separate cognitive tests in three regions of the geometric space "with the clusters seemingly based on the language of communication, i.e., verbal, numerical, and geometric on figural modes" (p. 168; also see Figs. 1 & 2, pp. 5-6).

The final test battery, developed as noted above, was administered to two groups of children in grades 2 and 6, respectively. Construct validity was achieved when an analysis of the two intercorrelation matrices by TORSCA confirmed the structure as originally conceived (p. 168).

Being unfamiliar with the Guttman procedure, this reviewer analyzed the same correlation matrices (see Manual, Tables 66 and 67, pp. 169-170) by means of a conventional principal components and varimax rotation approach. The varimax results are given in Tables 1 and 2 of this review. This conventional approach largely confirms the Buttman technique results.

In the Grade 2 varimax matrix (based on 62 children) there is an excellent approach to simple structure, the only deviants being Relating Skills, Understanding Words, Producing Expressions and Solving Problems, in the sense that they load on two factors. However, one is not surprised, for example, to find that Solving Problems loads on both an Information Processing Factor and a Mathematics factor.

The situation is not quite so clear for the Grade 6 matrix but, as this was based on only 45 children, chance relationships could have played a big part. Clearly more work needs to be done but the basic structure as outlined by Somwaru is definitely present.

Content validity was checked by several consultants (see acknowledgements in the manual) who reviewed the items for their content and ability to assess the cluster of skills listed in the model (Manual, Figure 2). It was considered important that the items test the identified skills, and that the clusters adequately assess the defined test areas; items were dropped or modified if they did not fit the content design and some new items were added. Several professionals in Special Education reviewed the content design of the test for its appropriateness for students with special needs.

It appears to this reviewer that, at least on face value, this procedure has been

Table 1

Varimax Factors (Grade 2)*

	I	II	III
Observing Skills	78		
Organizing Skills	75		
Relating Skills	48		63
Understanding Words	60	46	
Comprehending Expressions		69	
Producing Expressions	50	62	
Reading		88	
Decoding		85	
Knowing Numbers & Operations			80
Understanding Concepts			83
Solving Problems	42		77
Eigenvalue	2.44	2.99	2.79

*Loadings .4 omitted; decimal points omitted.

successful.

To assess criterion-related validity, several investigations were carried out and these are specified in Table 68 of the manual. The figures demonstrate that magnitude was usually found to increase with increasing chronological age (Kindergarten, Grades 2, 6, 8) but the criteria themselves leave a lot to be desired, especially the WRAT (see Snart et al., 1983). Much more work needs to be done in this area as the criteria used by Somwaru (SRA Assessment Survey, WRAT, and teachers' ratings) are quite inadequate. The correlation coefficients obtained vary from .19 (Observing Skills with SRA Assessment Survey Math, Grade 2) to .85 (Knowing Number and Operations with WRAT Spelling, Grade K-8 combined). The mean coefficients for all criteria with the total Information Processing, Language, and Mathematics scores are .57, .66, and .72, respectively.

These are of the same magnitude as those typically found between cognitive tests of differing content but both the criteria used and the number of subjects (45

Table 2

	I	II	III
Varimax Factors (Grade 6)			
Observing Skills			75
Organizing Skills			85
Relating Skills		56	58
Understanding Words	94		
Comprehending Expressions	72		59
Producing Expressions			76
Reading	63	46	48
Decoding			82
Knowing Numbers & Operations		82	
Understanding Concepts		76	
Solving Problems		86	
Eigenvalue	2.42	3.09	3.77

*Loadings .4 omitted; decimal points omitted.

to 159) relegate these studies to the pilot variety.

The test-retest reliability coefficients reported in Table 65 of the manual are impressive. These vary for individual tests from .76 (Comprehending Expressions at Kindergarten level) to .96 (Comprehending Expressions at Grade 6). The mean of the three coefficients (Grade 2, Grade 6, and Kindergarten) for the average of the three scales (Information Processing, Language, and Mathematics) are .97, .92 and .93, respectively. However, again these are based on small samples (N = 41-62).

Clearly, Somwaru has demonstrated a sound statistical base for his instrument but if it is to replace other currently used tests, much more work on larger samples needs to be done. Obviously, the problem for him has been that he did not have the resources of the Psychological Corporation behind him. As this is a very new test, not at all widely known, there is no literature to report at this stage.

Critique

This new battery has a lot going for it. It is innovative and appropriate in its statistical design (latent trait-criterion-referenced base); is integrated and, due to its equal interval scaling, allows for the assessment of growth in a valid manner; is easy to administer; and is highly reliable. In addition, its construct and content validity are both sound. Best of all, it is based on a "learning skill" rather than an "underlying ability" model, which allows a generalized versus specific deficit approach rather than a "potential-specific attainment" discrepancy. Also, it allows both a developmental and a diagnostic assessment that leads to specific prescriptions. The manual is very helpful with respect to the latter.

On the negative side there are quite insufficient data with respect to criterion validity, and much more work needs to be carried out in this respect. Finally, the battery as a whole takes a long time to administer, and users will have to make some difficult decisions about how many of the eleven tests they will be able to administer in the time at their disposal. It seems to this reviewer that the particular tests chosen will depend on 1) the particular type of child being assessed and 2) the questions that need to be answered. This battery, because of its statistical and design structure, does allow the practitioner much more leeway in this respect than do conventional tests such as the WISC-R, Stanford-Binet, or Kaufman ABC.

References

Connolly, A. J., Nachtman, W., & Pritchett, E. M. (1972). *KeyMath Diagnostic Arithmetic Test*. Circle Pines, MN: American Guidance Service.

Gagne, R. M. (1968). Contributions of learning to human development. *Psychological Review, 75,* 177-191.

Schlesinger, J. M., & Guttman, L. (1969). Smallest space analysis of intelligence and achievement tests. *Psychological Bulletin, 71,* 95-100.

Snart, F., et al. (1983). Concerns regarding the Wide Range Achievement Test (WRAT). *Canadian Psychology, 24,* 99-103.

Somwaru, J. P. (1979a). *Survey of Basic Competencies*. Bensenville, IL: Scholastic Testing Service.

Somwaru, J. P. (1979b). *Test of Early Learning Skills*. Bensenville, IL: Scholastic Testing Service.

Somwaru, J. P. (1981). *Manual for the Assessment of Basic Competencies*. Bensenville, IL: Scholastic Testing Service.

Sympson, J. B. (1979, August). *The assessment of basic competencies: A new test battery*. Paper presented at the annual meeting of the American Psychological Association, New York.

Sympson, J. B. (1980). *An approach for some estimation problems in latent trait theory* (Research Rep. 80-X). Minneapolis: University of Minnesota, Department of Psychology, Psychometrics Methods Program.

Vernon, P. E. (1955). The psychology of intelligence and g. *Bulletin of the British Psychological Society, 26,* 1-14.

Vernon, P. E. (1960). The classification of abilities. *Educational Research, 2,* 184-193.

Robert G. Malgady, Ph.D.
Associate Professor of Educational Statistics, Department of Mathematics, Science, and Statistics, New York University, New York, New York.

BALTHAZAR SCALES OF ADAPTIVE BEHAVIOR II: SCALES OF SOCIAL ADAPTATION

Earl E. Balthazar. Palo Alto, California: Consulting Psychologists Press, Inc.

Introduction

The Balthazar Scales of Adaptive Behavior II: Scales of Social Adaptation (BSAB-II) was constructed as an observational system to measure the adaptiveness of social coping behaviors of emotionally disturbed and severely or profoundly mentally retarded individuals in residential, institutional settings. The test consists of 19 scales composed of items representative of a comprehensive domain of behaviors indicative of social adaptation (e.g., verbal communication, play activities, response to instructions), and is administered by a nonprofessional rater technician who records the frequency of each behavior during a designated observation period. The purpose of the BSAB-II is to evaluate individual children and adults, and to provide a system for specifying, describing, and evaluating the goals of treatment or training programs for the mentally retarded. Focused only on social skills, the BSAB-II (Balthazar, 1973) was designed as a supplement to the Scales of Functional Independence (BSAB-I) that was developed by Balthazar in 1972 to assess more basic self-care skills, such as eating/drinking, dressing/undressing, and toileting behaviors.

The BSAB-II was developed from observations of 288 severely and profoundly mentally retarded residents in nursery and infirmary wards at the Central Wisconsin Colony and Training School in Madison, Wisconsin. Based on five years of observation of these subjects, and two years additional study of mentally retarded individuals in the Northern Wisconsin Colony and the Dixon State School in Illinois, an item pool representative of a broad variety of coping behaviors was generated. The age range of the individuals under observation was 5-57 years, with a median age of 17 years. Their global IQ scores were in the profoundly to severely mentally retarded classifications, ranging from 20 to 35. Further, the subjects were multiply handicapped, although ambulatory, and according to the BSAB-I Scales of Functional Independence, were able to eat and dress independently, but experienced difficulties with independent drinking and toileting.

The BASB-II, published in 1973 by Consulting Psychologists Press, was known earlier as the Central Wisconsin Colony Scales. Factor analysis was used to distill the current version of the BSAB-II from the original Central Wisconsin Colony Scales. Behavioral definitions and examples of the behaviors were formulated with the assistance of technicians who were observing the target population from 1964 through 1971. Semantic difficulties in wording and defining items were resolved by inductive study and demonstration, and item revisions were conducted accordingly. Items were revised further on the basis of statistical analyses.

The test consists of 74 subscale items drawn from seven global behavior categories: unadaptive self-directed behaviors, unadaptive interpersonal behaviors, adaptive self-directed behaviors, adaptive interpersonal behaviors, verbal communication, play activities, and response to instructions. The subscale items in these seven categories are clustered into 19 scales, which were derived from factor analysis. In addition, there is a 9-item checklist of behaviors related to personal care, such as toileting, drinking, and clothing adjustment.

Practical Applications/Uses

The behaviors represented by the subscale items and the superordinate scales are intended to provide specific objectives for treatment and training programs for the severely and profoundly mentally retarded, either on an individual or group basis. Subjects are observed during typical activities in a residential institutional setting (e.g., state school, hospital) and are evaluated by a nonprofessional rater technician who is familiar with the subject. The BSAB-II can be administered either wholly or in part and provides a system to develop and evaluate programs and the means to obtain clinical information useful to professional staff and researchers.

The manual accompanying the BSAB-II (Balthazar, 1973) is divided into two sections: one for professional supervisors and a second for the rater technician. The first section describes the background and research implications of the instrument for professional supervisors and offers extensive information on systematic program development and evaluation. The second section describes procedures for training rater technicians, administration instructions, scoring and interpretation procedures, and presents definitions and examples of the subscale items. The test package also includes scoring sheets for the observation sessions and a summary sheet to display the social coping behavior profile.

According to the manual, rater technicians need not have a professional background to administer or score the scales. The only requisites are that the rater be articulate, alert, accurate, and thoroughly acquainted with the subscale items prior to the onset of evaluation activities. In order to minimize bias in the assessment process, it is recommended that the rater be a person independent of any training or program evaluation team. To this end, the manual provides rather detailed definitions and examples of the individual social coping behaviors represented by the subscale items, the 19 component scales, and the broad categories from which behaviors were sampled. This information should be especially helpful in improving the objectivity of the rating procedure. However, the manual does not indicate how much training is necessary to bring rater technicians to an acceptable level of interrater reliability.

In order to achieve valid ratings, the manual recommends that subjects be observed in the ward or central activity area, but not during therapy, when sick in bed, or under restraint by ward staff. The manual cautions that both ward staff members and subjects themselves may be sensitized by the rater's presence and therefore behave different from usual. A number of suggestions are offered to reduce the intrusiveness of the rater in the hope of improving the validity of observations. Videotaping, for example, is strongly recommended if institutional resources are sufficient. The manual also suggests that the rater should tell the subject to behave normally; however, with subjects in the 20-35 IQ range, this does not seem to be a realistic strategy. In order to observe a representative sample of a subject's behavior, it is recommended that ratings be conducted during different periods of the day and on different days. No more than one third of the ratings should be collected in a single day, and the entire observation period should be extended over a period of at least three days. Although it is suggested that six 10-minute rating sessions make up the standard evaluation procedure, 60 minutes of observation—despite the staggered observation schedule—may not be as representative of a subject's characteristic behavior as the manual leads one to believe.

For the purpose of scoring, the BSAB-II provides a tally sheet on which the ratings are made during the observation sessions. Scoring is accomplished by tallying the subscale items either on the basis of their frequency of occurrence throughout the 60 minutes of observation or by number of one-minute intervals during which the behavior occurred (score range 0-60). Scoring by "occurrence" is a simple frequency count of each subscale behavior each time it is observed. On the other hand, scoring by "one-minute intervals" is an attempt to record the duration of behaviors; each behavior is tallied not more than once during a given one-minute interval. The timing of observation intervals is accomplished by a stopwatch or preferably an auditory timer. The rater is alerted to the need to score multiple behaviors that the subject might exhibit simultaneously.

Tally sheets from all observation sessions ultimately are transcribed onto a Scoring Summary Sheet that constitutes the subject's social coping behavior profile. An optional Prebaseline Information Sheet provides space for recording additional information, such as the subjects' medical and social history, prescribed medications, modal behavior reported by staff, personality and IQ reports. A Program Information Sheet and Ward Supervisors and Staff Information Sheet (also optional) serve to summarize information about treatment programs for development or evaluation purposes.

Scores on the BSAB-II are interpreted in the context of the purpose for the evaluation. On an individual basis, scores yield a profile of the subject's skills and deficits in social situations. The manual reports mean subscale item scores on the standardization sample (N = 102) described earlier in this review, althogh neither percentile rank nor standard score norms are available for interpreting scores. The mean scores are of questionable clinical utility to researchers, professional supervisors, or therapists, however, because standard deviations and distributional characteristics (skew) are not reported. Despite the lack of emphasis on normative referenced interpretation of scores, the BSAB-II appears to be much like a criterion-referenced test. As such, profiles can be used much in the manner of an IEP (individualized educational plan), as mandated by PL 94-142, for structuring the treatment or training program of handicapped individuals. Alternately, the BSAB-II is a system for developing institutional goals programmatically, providing a built-in means for summative and formative program evaluation by assessing profile changes over time.

Technical Aspects

The BSAB-II manual does not present extensive information on the psychometric properties of the instrument. The author stresses the need for "serious" researchers, program evaluators, and professional supervisors to conduct their own reliability studies, especially interrater agreement and intrarater stability over time. The appendix to the manual reports the results of two interrater reliability studies conducted with an earlier version of the current scale. The subjects in these studies were ambulatory, severely and profoundly mentally retarded individuals in residential institutions and, hence, representative of the target population of the BSAB-II. There were 21 subjects in the first study and 25 subjects in the second, each independently rated by two rater trainees. The method of scoring by occurrence was used to tally behavior frequencies, based on the standard six 10-minute observation sessions conducted over a four-month interval. Because the raters in these studies were in the initial phase of training, the author maintains that the reliability estimates reported in the manual illustrate the degree of interrater agreement which can be obtained during the initial stages of training.

Interrater agreement was calculated for each subject on each subscale item as the ratio of the two independent raters' scores: lower score and higher score. The author cautions against computing either parametric or nonparametric correlations with BSAB-II data, although the rationale for this caveat is unclear. The manual reports only the mean (averaging across subjects) proportion of agreement between raters on individual subscale items. Unfortunately, therefore, in the absence of ranges or standard deviations of the agreement ratios, one loses a sense of the variability of the agreement indices as a function of individual subjects. Interrater agreement is not reported for some subscale items because the author did not have the opportunity to calculate them, and other items simply were not exhibited by the sample of subjects observed in the two studies. In addition to the scattered pattern of missing data, four entire scales are omitted in the two studies.

At first glance, the proportion of agreement figures seem impressive, ranging from .42 to .95 in the first study and from .60 to 1.00 in the second. However, the interrater reliability estimates are consistently lower in the first study, which the author neither explains or even acknowledges. This raises several questions, such as whether the discrepancies are due to possible differences between the two samples of subjects, or perhaps between the intensiveness of raters' training. The sample sizes in the two studies admittedly are small to begin with, but the number of subjects reportedly displaying each behavior is considerably smaller. Many of the highest interrater reliability estimates (above .90) are based on observers' agreement about as few as one or two subjects. Indeed, the median sample size across items in both studies is less than 10 subjects.

In summary of the reliability data reported, there is encouraging evidence of interrater agreement for a portion of the subscale items on the BSAB-II, but even this is based on very few subjects. No evidence is reported in favor of test-retest reliability (stability) or internal consistency (homogeneity). In light of the fact that only five of the 19 scales are composed of more than four items, internal consistency may pose a problem, given the well-known relationship between reliability and test length. It would appear that the author has finessed the issue, arguing that parametric and even nonparametric correlation coefficients cannot be computed with the BSAB-II. However, because the subscale item scores are sums of the number of behaviors observed, there is no sound reason why conventional item analytic strategies cannot be applied to BSAB-II data. To the contrary, elsewhere in the manual the author asserts that nonparametric statistics are particularly suited to the BSAB-II for the purpose of research or program evaluation. Thus, this reviewer wonders why BSAB-II item analyses cannot be conducted using conventional correlational methods when subscale items can be correlated in a test-retest paradigm or program evaluation of change scores.

No specific mention is made of any effort to establish content validity. From the description of the item development process, however, one might infer that the items are an adequate sample from the domain of social-coping behaviors likely to be exhibited in a residential setting. The author notes that many items will be scored "zero" (i.e., are not observed) in a typical situation for a large majority of subjects, and that this poses a problem for statistical analysis. Nevertheless, the author claims that in the interest of clinical utility, they are highly important items. Alternately, lack of occurrence of many of the behaviors represented in the BSAB-II might lead one to question the instrument's content validity. Perhaps a more prudent strategy for users of the BSAB-II would be to distinguish clinically important behaviors, which rarely occur, from items composing a psychometric instrument.

As with the Functional Scales of Independence in the BSAB-I, the author adheres to the argument that behavior observations constitute the criterion measure itself. In other words, validity is perfect! The author contends that it is not relevant to inquire if observers' judgments are valid and that one cannot question the validity of the behavioral criterion. This assumption seems highly suspect, if for no other reason, because—due to the fact that independent raters cannot agree perfectly on their observations—one must necessarily question the validity of their judgments in classifying the observed behaviors according to subscale items. In this regard, it would have been enlightening if in the interrater reliability analyses the author had reported interrater agreement about whether or not a target behavior occurred in a given instance and the pattern of misclassification of behaviors in instances when both observers chose to rate a given behavior.

Examination of the content of subscale items or the nature of the behaviors to be recorded reveals considerable room for subjective interpretation. A rater technician is called upon to judge, for example, the appropriateness or inappropriateness of the subject's response to negative peer contact, initiation of contact with staff and peers, self-directed behavior and verbalizations, to name a few. In addition, judgments must be made about the creativity of the subject's object relations, articulateness of speech, and cooperativeness, among others.

Given that subjective judgments of the extent of adaptiveness or maladaptiveness of behavior are required of the observer, researchers and professional supervisors using the BSAB-II would be wise to consider corroboration by an independent criterion of the validity of score profiles. The author employed factor analysis to develop the 19 scales, but the details are not reported in the manual. Insofar as so few items loaded on the various factors, it must be suspected that these factors (scales) are underdetermined. Despite such a concern, simply because the 74 subscale items factored into 19 clusters does not buttress any claim for the BSAB-II's validity.

In summary of the validity evidence reported, it is safest to say there simply is none. It is not unusual to encounter a test published in a rudimentary stage of development with only scant or at least promising evidence of validity, but clearly in this case the author is content with mere face validity. Perhaps other researchers or program evaluators, who choose to study the BSAB-II, will demonstrate its validity and clinical utility. However, in the absence of such evidence, unless the observation scales are conceived as the ultimate criterion, it must be concluded that the validity of the BSAB-II is dubious.

Critique

During the past decade, the increased focus of psychologists and other mental health professionals on the adaptive behavior of mentally retarded individuals has prompted the consideration of behavioral functioning, concurrent with impaired intellectual functioning, as a criterion for classification of mental retardation. This change in formal definition of mental retardation has spawned a variety of behavioral evaluation instruments to supplement traditional IQ measures. In addition, mental health practitioners and educators have faced federal and state concerns for systematic evaluation of services provided to the mentally retarded and the mandate to develop individual educational plans for the handicapped (PL 94-142). While numerous "rating scales" have been standardized and validated in the interim, the BSAB-II is probably the most systematically developed "observation scale" for such purposes. Researchers and clinical professionals wishing to conduct observational studies of the mentally retarded will find that the BSAB-II provides useful information about the social behavioral functioning of their target population.

Practitioners will find the BSAB-II appealing because it can be administered by nonprofessional personnel in a relatively short period of time; observations are collected *in vivo* in the subject's daily ambience; a comprehensive behavior profile is obtained for treatment or training on an individual basis; a broad age range of subjects can be assessed; and built-in procedures are offered for program development and evaluation. Drawbacks to the use of the BSAB-II are psychometric concerns. If the BSAB-II is viewed as a test, there is limited evidence of reliability and no evidence of validity. Rating scales, such as the AAMD Adaptive Behavior Scales, have far superior psychometric properties. If, on the other hand, the BSAB-II is viewed as an observational system, researchers and practitioners alike need only concern themselves with the problem of training observers to achieve objectivity in their ratings.

References

This list includes test citations as well as suggested additional reading.

Allen, R. M. (1978). Balthazar Scales of Adaptive Behavior. In O. K. Buros (Ed.), *The eighth mental measurements yearbook.* Highland Park, NJ: The Gryphon Press.

Balthazar, E. E. (1972a). *Balthazar Scales of Adaptive Behavior I: Scales of Functional Independence.* Palo Alto, CA: Consulting Psychologists Press.

Balthazar, E. E. (1972b). Residential programs in adaptive behavior for the emotionally disturbed and more severely retarded. *Mental Retardation, 10,* 10-13.

Balthazar, E. E. (1973). *Balthazar Scales of Adaptive Behavior II: Scales of Social Adaptation.* Palo Alto, CA: Consulting Psychologists Press.

Balthazar, E. E., & English, G. E. (1969a). *A system for classifying the social behavior of the severely retarded* (Monograph Supplement No. 4). Madison, WI: Central Wisconsin Colony & Training School Research Findings.

Balthazar, E. E., & English, G. E. (1969b). A system for the social classification of the more severely mentally retarded. *American Journal of Mental Deficiency, 74,* 361-368.

Balthazar, E. E., & English, G. E. (1969c). A factorial study of unstructured ward behaviors. *American Journal of Mental Deficiency, 74,* 353-360.

Balthazar, E. E., & Stevens, H. A. (1969). Scalar techniques for program evaluation with the severely mentally retarded. *Mental Retardation, 7,* 25-29.

Balthazar, E. E., & Stevens, H. A. (1974). *The emotionally disturbed mentally retarded: A historical and contemporary perspective.* Englewood Cliffs, NJ: Prentice-Hall.

Patricia A. Chesebro, Ph.D.
Associate Professor of Psychology and Coordinator of Women's Studies, Illinois State University, Normal, Illinois.

BASIC ACHIEVEMENT SKILLS INDIVIDUAL SCREENER

The Psychological Corporation, Measurement Division Staff. Cleveland, Ohio: The Psychological Corporation.

Introduction

Basic Achievement Skills Individual Screener (BASIS) is an individually administered achievement test for measuring the skills of reading, mathematics, and spelling. An optional writing test is included in the testing time of ten minutes. Tasks typical of classroom activities are organized in grade-referenced clusters of six to ten items with a stated criterion which must be achieved before proceeding to the next higher cluster. These clusters, ranging from Readiness through Grade 8 for Mathematics and Reading and from Grade 1-8 for Spelling, yield scores that can be expressed as norm-referenced or criterion-referenced information from Grade 1-12 and posthigh school. The raw scores can be converted to standard scores; percentile ranks; stanines, grade, age, and normal curve equivalents; Rasch scale scores; and suggested grade- or text-level placements. An optional Writing Exercise of ten minutes is included in the testing time of less than one hour. It may be compared only to average writing samples from Grades 3-8.

The developers determined which objectives were representative of mathematics curriculum for each grade by analyzing mathematics textbook series, achievement tests, state syllabi, and teacher questionnaires. Six computation problems and two dictated word problems comprise a cluster of items for each grade level. The Mathematics Readiness subtest is a cluster of 6 items sampling the basic facts of 1 to 10 (e.g., counting objects in a picture).

Reading comprehension, deemed the most valid aspect of reading for a screening instrument, is measured by the cloze technique in which the student reads a passage aloud and supplies missing words. Cloze breaks appear at the ends of sentences or passages and include equal numbers of nouns, verbs, adjectives, and adverbs. The deleted words are a grade level below that of the passage and are text dependent. The Harris-Jacobsen (1972) Basic Elementary Reading Vocabularies and the Educational Developmental Laboratories (1979) CORE Vocabularies in Reading, Mathematics, Social Studies and Science were used for guidelines in construction of passages and in grade-level placement of words.

In the Reading Readiness subtest, students are asked to identify letters of both upper and lower case, to match letter combinations, and to relate words and sentences to illustrations. Distractors were selectively chosen to aid in diagnosing reading difficulties such as reversals.

63

Spelling words were selected from the master list compiled for the development of the 1978 Metropolitan Achievement Test based on analyses of major spelling series. Inclusion of a word meant that the word had appeared on a majority of the consulted lists, and the grade placement was the median grade placement across texts. Deletions were made to avoid "tricky words," words used on other achievement tests, or spelling "demons." A panel of ten educational and research specialists reviewed the list and the final pool was checked for accuracy of grade placement against the 1982 edition of the Stanford Achievement Test.

The ten-minute writing sample is scored holistically. After reading the passage once, the examiner compares it with samples of average writing for Grades 3-8.

BASIS was standardized in the fall of 1982 using students in Grades 1-12 and a sample of posthigh-school young adults. The sample totaled 3,296 students, aged 6-0 to 18-11 years, in Grades 1-12 from 66 school systems in 23 states. The sample of students in Grades 1-8 was twice as large as the sample of students in Grades 9-12 because of the content level of the tests. Only students in mainstreamed classes were included in the standardization program and the numbers and kinds of students comprising the 4% who were disabled are carefully identified in the manual. The posthigh-school sample totaled 232, aged 18-0 to 22-11 years, from community colleges and GED/Adult Basic Education programs, and included a few U. S. Army recruits and CETA trainees.

The demographic variables used for selecting school systems were geographic regions, school system enrollments, community socioeconomic status, public vs. nonpublic schools, and ethnic representation, thus assuring that the sample paralleled the national school population.

BASIS materials include the Content Booklet, Manual, and Record Form. The Content Booklet is a reusable, spiral bound booklet of heavy manila stock containing the Mathematics Readiness, Reading Readiness, and Reading Passages subtests to which the student responds. The Record Form, a consumable booklet for both the student's work and scoring, contains summary pages for analysis of the student's performance. The Manual is composed of an orientation to BASIS, directions for administering and scoring, norm-referenced interpretation, grade-referenced interpretation, test development, and technical data.

Practical Applications/Uses

All materials are attractively packaged, easily comprehended, and compact for ease of handling. Administration does not require formal training; it is recommended that those familiar with individualized tests study the manual carefully and administer several practice tests before giving credence to their test results. Because the test is designed to assess only entry levels in math, reading, spelling, and writing, the general purpose would probably be most suitable for placement in educational settings and in planning individualized educational programs (IEPs). Because grade placements or textbook levels may be recommended only through Grade 8 +, the greatest usage of the test will probably be for elementary-age pupils. However, it is appropriate for special populations of high-school age or adults.

BASIS would also be a useful tool for program planning, assessment, evaluation, and research. It could be helpful as a measure of literacy for social agencies, rehabilitation programs, the courts, or mental health agencies. Government or industry could use it as part of a battery for entry-level employees. Because the test is so new there are few references in the literature; but as time passes, nontraditional settings may be identified to extend its use. Gerontological researchers might assess retention or loss of basic mental abilities accompanying aging or various health conditions.

The test is appropriate for students aged 6 years and above and especially helpful for populations needing the flexibility of a power test over a speed test. The record form would permit answers to be typed if physically disabled persons required this mode. Enlarged type or Braille could be used for the visually impaired, but permission must first be secured from The Psychological Corporation. For the hearing impaired, sign language might be required. The test lends itself to such modifications so students can function at their optimum levels. The manual stresses techniques for establishing rapport to obtain the best results. The relative brief testing time of less than one hour makes it a very useful measurement for persons with short attention spans. Even though it might be necessary to omit some tests, one may still obtain useful criterion-referenced information.

The appropriate setting for administering this test is a quiet, adequately lit room, with the administrator and student seated diagonally to each other at a flat table or desk. The Mathematics Readiness Test is proposed as the introductory test because it is the section most comparable to class procedures familiar to the student. The order of the presentation of the subtests may be changed or some tests omitted, but interpretations should be cautiously modified bearing in mind that the test was standardized using a particular order.

Directions for scoring are clearly stated in the manual, and the record form includes charts for easily tallying the raw scores. Raw scores can be converted to norm-referenced or criterion-referenced information by consulting tables in the manual.

Items for Mathematics, Reading Readiness, Beginning Reading, and Spelling are grouped by clusters representing the various grade difficulties. Criterion levels for the passing of each cluster are provided. The procedure calls for identifying both the lowest level at which the student achieves or exceeds the criterion (probably the entry level which is recommended to be two grade levels below the age- or grade-level of the student) and the ceiling level where the criterion score was not met. These scores are transferred to the summary sheet of the record form. For the lowest level, a base score is provided to which the number of items answered correctly on all successive grade clusters are added, thus providing a total raw score for conversion to the most appropriate interpretive data.

Interpretation is based on objective scores for mathematics, reading, and spelling. The Writing Exercise is rated Average, Above Average, or Below Average for the student's particular grade or age, or is equated with a sample for Grades 3-8. Bipolar criteria for ideas, organization, vocabulary, sentence structure, and mechanics help reduce the subjectivity inherent in evaluating any writing.

The total scoring time is approximately five minutes. The professional education, experience, and expertise of examiners will enable them to note the personality traits and test-taking attitudes observable in an individual during testing procedure. Items missed in the Mathematics Test can be compared to a checklist of objectives for a quick diagnosis of basic math deficiencies.

Technical Aspects

Reliability as assessed by the Kuder-Richardson Formula 20 was spuriously high due to scoring procedures. A subsample of students from Grades 2, 5, and 8 were administered tests two to four weeks after the original testing by the original examiner whenever possible. Test-retest reliabilities corrected for the variability of the samples for the three grades respectively for Math were .81, .83, and .88; for Reading, .91, .82, and .96; and for Spelling, .94, .90, and .94.

Content validity is obtained from the techniques and analyses utilized in the construction and selection of items. Objectives for the BASIS Mathematics Test were derived from current math texts and state department curriculum guidelines. Vocabulary for reading and spelling were selected from highly respected reference materials from reading experts.

Evidence for the validity of the clusters is provided by point biserial correlations computed for each item using data only from students whose school grade level matched the grade level of the item. Median point biserial correlations for Grades 1-8 for Math ranged from .52 in Grade 3 to .68 in Grade 1; for Reading, from .55 in Grade 7 to .74 in Grade 1; and for Spelling, from .58 in Grade 2 to .77 in Grade 7.

Concurrent validity is provided by correlations between BASIS total raw scores and report-card grades for subsamples of 185 to 300 students in Grades 2-6. Correlations between BASIS Mathematics and math grade ranged from .34 for Grade 3 to .56 for Grade 5; for BASIS Reading and reading grade, .44 for Grade 4 to .52 for Grade 2; for BASIS Spelling and spelling grade, .29 for Grade 2 to .61 for Grades 5 and 6; and BASIS Spelling and writing grade, .25 for Grade 2 to .41 for Grade 5.

Correlations between BASIS raw scores and stanine scores on national or statewide achievement tests by school-grade level 2-8 for subsamples of the standardization group (N = 24 to 270) range from .30 for BASIS Math/Problem Solving in Grade 2 to .72 for BASIS Reading/Total Reading in Grade 3.

Grade-referenced placements as derived from BASIS subtests are compared with the actual grade placements of students and provide support for criterion-referenced interpretations. These are reported as the percentage of students whose grade-referenced placement was within one grade level of actual grade placement. The percentages for Mathematics ranged from 65% in Grade 7 to 93% in Grade 2; for Reading, from 42% in Grade 4 to 80% in Grade 7 (Grade 8 is not reported because Grade 7 is the highest possible grade-referenced placement); and for Spelling, 43% in Grade 7 to 80% in Grade 2. The percentages for Grade 1 were all in the 90s.

The results of studies with special populations are reported to validate the use of BASIS with subgroups such as learning disabled, severely learning disabled, gifted, educable mentally retarded, emotionally handicapped, hearing impaired and native Americans. The studies used samples of only 25 to 35 and are meant only as guidelines for establishing local validation studies.

Critique

BASIS is a compact achievement test designed as a screener for basic mathematics, reading, and spelling skills with an optional writing test easily administered and scored in approximately one hour. It yields norm-referenced information for Grades 1-12 and posthigh school and criterion-referenced information suggesting grade level and textbook placement through Grade 8 +. Primary usage will probably be for educational decisions for elementary students and special populations of high-school age and adults. The manual is very thorough in directions for use and extensive data are provided to support reliability and validity.

Because BASIS is a newly developed achievement test, not much data has accumulated thus far; however, Fitzpatrick (1984) in the first published review regards the development effort of the publisher as "exceptional" and the test "effective and efficient."

References

Educational Developmental Laboratories. (1979). *CORE vocabularies in reading, mathematics, social studies and science.* New York: Arista Corp.

Fitzpatrick, A. R. (1984). Test review: BASIS. *Journal of Educational Measurement, 21*(3), 309-311.

Harris, A. J., & Jacobsen, M. D. (1972). *Basic elementary reading vocabularies.* New York: Macmillan Publishing Co.

The Psychological Corporation. (1982). *Basic Achievement Skills Individual Screener (BASIS).* Cleveland: Author.

Ann Booker Loper, Ph.D.
*Assistant Professor of Education, University of Virginia,
Charlottesville, Virginia.*

A BASIC SCREENING AND REFERRAL FORM FOR CHILDREN WITH SUSPECTED LEARNING AND BEHAVIORAL DISABILITIES

Robert E. Valett. Fresno, California: Robert E. Valett.

Introduction

The Basic Screening and Referral Form for Children with Suspected Learning and Behavioral Disabilities records in-class behaviors of children suspected of needing special education service. The primary purpose of the device is to "aid (1) in the early identification of possibly significant learning and behavioral disabilities and (2) in the planning of prescriptive developmental and remedial education" (Valett, 1972, p. 1). The form is filled out by a child's regular classroom teacher and then used as a basis of collaboration with auxiliary school special education personnel, such as a resource teacher or school psychologist. The instrument should not technically be considered a "test" as there are no formal scoring procedures or interpretation guidelines. Rather the device serves as a vehicle allowing teachers to record specific behaviors that are problematic in the classroom.

Robert Valett is a professor in the Department of Advanced Studies, School of Education at California State University, Fresno. He received his doctorate in counseling and educational psychology from UCLA in 1957 and is currently a Diplomate in School Psychology of the American Board of Professional Psychology. He has authored several books and tests concerning psychoeducational assessment and remediation.

Dr. Valett developed the recording form to meet what he saw as the need for an intermediate step between large-scale, group-administered screening and intensive individual testing by highly trained school personnel. The development of the form focused on selecting common specific behaviors, frequently observed by teachers, which could serve as concrete examples of school difficulties. The items were adapted from two previous works of the author (Valett, 1967; 1969). The instrument was developed over a three-year period through informal use and refinement of the instrument within the local elementary and junior high schools. There are no norms for the instrument. The author did not collect reliability or validity information concerning the device. The test has not undergone revision and there are no other forms.

The form consists of an 11-page booklet, divided into 5 subsections. There are no other materials or manuals required. The first section, "Description of the Problem," contains 5 questions that prompt the teacher to describe the basis of the problem, previous solutions, the child's view of the problem and the teacher's expectations concerning the special education consultant. The second section contains 6 simple questions on the child's educational history, e.g., "In what has this pupil been most successful in school," (Valett, 1972, p. 3). The third section requests teachers to rate children on a scale from 0 to 2 on a lengthy list of problems concerning behavior difficulties. Teachers' ratings are divided into 8 categories: conceptual-cognitive, language, visual-motor, visual, auditory, sensory-motor, and gross-motor. The instructions request teachers to rate the children and then circle any behaviors that are of prime consideration. The teachers then elaborate on circled items by describing in detail, with classroom illustrations, the basis of their judgments. The fourth section consists of an individually administered Pupil Work Sample, a collection of varying items including copying, visual discrimination, drawing, letter and word recognition, math facts, and self-statements. The final section summarizes the teachers' impressions of priority objectives and recommendations.

There is no formal scoring system. After the form is completed by the classroom teacher the interpretation as such is left to special education personnel who are assumed to be sufficiently trained to know how to use the information.

Practical Applications/Uses

This device is designed for use with school children in grades 1-12. It would be useful to special education personnel who wish to gain specific information from classroom teachers before conducting further individual testing. Depending on the structure of the school system this would probably be a special education resource consultant or a school psychologist. The instructions encourage the teacher to be quite specific in the description of the child's problematic behaviors.

The instrument is not suitable for group use. The purpose of the device is to provide a basis for screening students seen by their classroom teachers as needing special services. It is intended to be an intermediary step between group screening and intensive individual testing. Although the information gained from the test can be used by competent personnel in their own screening of students, it should be emphasized that the instrument is not itself a screening device: it does not provide a scoring method by which children are or are not targeted as being high-risk for learning disability. According to the test's author, it is best to use it in conjunction with other diagnostic and remedial materials (Valett, 1972, p. 1).

The majority of items are quite general and thus germane to any student enrolled in elementary or secondary education. The pupil work sample is composed almost exclusively of items that would be appropriate for children whose achievement level is approximately 4th-grade or less. It is quite plausible that an older LD child could successfully perform all of the items in the work sample and yet still be suitable for referral. As with the rest of the form, the decision concerning which items are and are not of priority is left to the interpreting trained personnel.

Four of the five portions of the test are filled out by the classroom teachers at their convenience. The pupil work sample would probably be collected within the regular classroom. The test is then interpreted by trained special education personnel, such as a resource consultant or psychologist; and interpretation is based entirely on their judgment. No guidelines are given, nor are norms provided suggesting typical guidelines. The length of time needed to complete the form would vary greatly depending on the child evaluated and the verbosity of the teacher filling out the form. The pupil work sample could probably be completed in 20 minutes or less in most cases.

The test assumes that those interpreting the form are able to evaluate the information presented. For competent use of this instrument, this assumption is critical. For example, errors by young children would be expected on several items of the pupil work sample (e.g., drawing, copying).

Technical Aspects

Estimates of the validity or reliability of the form have not been undertaken. To this reviewer's knowledge there have been no formal studies conducted concerning the instrument.

Critique

The Basic Screening and Referral Form for Children with Suspected Learning and Behavioral Disabilities is, as its name indicates, a form and not a test. It organizes typical referral information into easily identifiable sections and can be of value in making the initial dialogue between referring teacher and resource teacher efficient and task-oriented. A resource teacher charged with determining which referrals deserve priority for individual psychoeducational testing may benefit from efficiently gathered, detailed information from teachers.

The instrument is not a screening device in the traditional sense. It does not provide guidelines indicating which children would or would not be high-risk for learning or who have behavioral disabilities. This judgment is left to the interpreting personnel.

There is no data-based reason to assume that this instrument is any stronger psychometrically than other informal devices constructed by the individual seeking the same information. There is no reliability or validity information available or normative base for the instrument. The author presents no data-based evidence that indicates how children with learning or behavioral disabilities will typically perform or be rated using this instrument. The relevance of each item to disability is assumed.

In summary, the advantages of the device are that it is relatively inexpensive, is simply laid out, and can provide a good starting point for dialogue between referring teacher and resource personnel. However, its usefulness in screening high-risk children will depend entirely on the skill of the interpreting personnel in informally evaluating the information provided and interacting with the referring teacher. No guidelines or data-based information is provided to assist the resource personnel in this endeavor.

References

Valett, R. E. (1967). *The remediation of learning disabilities: A handbook of psychoeducational resource programs.* Belmont, CA: Fearon Education.

Valett, R. E. (1969). *Programming learning disabilities.* Belmont, CA: Fearon Education.

Valett, R. E. (1972). *A Basic Screening and Referral Form for Children with Suspected Learning and Behavioral Disabilities.* Belmont, CA: Fearon Education.

Robert G. Harrington, Ph.D.
*Assistant Professor in Educational Psychology and Research,
University of Kansas, Lawrence, Kansas.*

BATTELLE DEVELOPMENTAL INVENTORY

*Jean Newborg, John Stock, Linda Wnek, John Guidubaldi, and
John Svinicki. Allen, Texas: DLM Teaching Resources.*

Introduction

The Battelle Developmental Inventory (BDI); (Newborg, Stock, Wnek,
Guidubaldi, & Svinicki, 1984) represents a very recent addition to the area of early
childhood screening and diagnosis. The BDI is a nationally standardized, individually administered assessment battery covering five developmental skills from
birth to eight years. The five developmental domains include: personal-social,
adaptive, motor, communication, and cognitive. Two primary purposes are
served by this test. The major application of the BDI is in the identification of the
developmental strengths and weaknesses of handicapped and nonhandicapped
children in infant, preschool, and primary programs. Because the BDI also has a
screening test component it can be used for general screening of preschool and
kindergarten children "at risk" for developmental delays.

There have been several phases in the development of the BDI. A test entitled
the Children's Early Development Inventory (CEDI), developed at the Columbus
Laboratories of Battelle Memorial Institute, was the predecessor of the BDI. The
review of child development research and existing early school tests, the generation of developmental milestones, test-item development, and test adaptations
for handicapped children employed in the development of the CEDI laid the
groundwork for the BDI. The preparation of the experimental version of the BDI
developed by Jean Newborg, John Stock, and Linda Wnek of the Battelle Memorial Institute began in 1973. Subsequently, John Guidubaldi of Kent State University revised and edited the scales as well as directing the norming study and
validity evaluations. In the last stages of test development the final item-sequenc-
ing, the graduated scoring system, the BDI Screening Test, and standardization
were completed by John Svinicki and James Dickson of Applied Behavior Systems, Inc. and Anne Markley under contracts with Teaching Resources
Corporation.

The BDI consists of an examiner's manual containing the norms, tables, and six
separate test manuals, one for each of the five domains and the Screening Test.
Most of the necessary test materials are included in the test manuals or accompany the test. Other needed materials not included in the BDI can be commonly
found in preschool- and primary-level programs. All materials required to administer any particular domain are listed by age level at the beginning of each test
manual. Also contained in these test manuals is a listing of supplementary

materials useful in modifying the test items for assessing handicapped children. Thirty copies of the Screening Test protocol and 15 copies of the BDI protocol are also contained in the test kit.

Depending on the age of the child the Screening Test can be administered in 10 to 30 minutes. Three- to five-year-olds will take 20 to 30 minutes. Children younger or older than this age range will take less time, possibly 10 to 15 minutes. The Screening Test is not recommended for children under six months because of the limited number of items at this level. Likewise, children in the three- to five-year-old range can be expected to require more time on the diagnostic version of the BDI, from one and one-half to two hours. Otherwise, children under three or over five years of age can be administered the entire BDI in one hour or less. Normal children with high skill levels may occasionally take somewhat longer than these estimates. The Personal-Social and Adaptive domains take less time to administer than do the Motor, Communication, and Cognitive domains. To save time any one of the five domains may be administered separately or in combination with the total BDI. Although testing can occur over several days if necessary, best practice would require that it should be completed in as few sessions as possible.

The items contained in each of the five domains of the full scale BDI are grouped by subdomain. The 341 items contained in the full scale BDI were organized by subdomain to facilitate assessment in specific skill areas such as Body Coordination or Fine Muscle control without administering all the other subdomains in their domain. Scores are available for subdomains as well as total domain scores.

The BDI was developed on a milestone approach so that a child's development could be characterized by attainment of critical skills or behaviors in a particular sequence. The items in the subdomains were sequenced by empirically assigning each item to the age level at which approximately 75% of the children received full credit for the item. Because of this decision rule the number of items at different age levels is unequal. This may be reflective of the nonlinear pattern of normal child development. The behavioral content and sequence of the developmental milestones are claimed to be fairly compatible with the content and organization of developmentally based infant, preschool, and early primary program curricula. Descriptions of each of the five domains and their subdomains are as follows:

Personal-Social: Consists of 85 items grouped into 6 subdomains: 1) Adult Interaction, assessing the quality and frequency of child-adult interactions; 2) Expression of Feelings/Affect, assessing the child's ability to express a wide range of emotions appropriately in a variety of situations; 3) Self-Concept, assessing factors that contribute to selfconcept (e.g., self-worth, self-awareness, and interests); 4) Peer Interaction, assessing the quality and frequency of social interactions with other children of the same age; 5) Coping, assessing the child's ability to adapt to the environment including coping with aggressive peers, tolerating frustration, solving personal problems, and conforming to rules; 6) Social Role, assessing the child's ability to recognize the differences between child and adult roles, to understand the rationale for prosocial behavior, and to understand different points of view.

Adaptive: Consists of 59 items grouped into 5 subdomains: 1) Attention, assessing the child's visual and auditory attention span; 2) Eating, assessing feeding skills such as using knives and forks; 3) Dressing, assessing the child's ability to dress without help; 4) Personal Responsibility, assessing the child's ability in assuming personal responsibility for moving around the neighborhood, completing home chores, initiating play with peers, persisting with a task, and receiving satisfaction from achievements; 5) Toileting, assessing the extent to which the child can care for own sleeping, bathing, and personal needs.

Motor: Consists of 82 items grouped into 5 subdomains: 1) Muscle Control, assessing large muscle control used primarily in sitting, standing, transferring objects from one hand to the other, and other gross motor activities; 2) Body Coordination, assessing the child's ability to use large muscle systems to establish increasing body control and coordination (e.g., rolling over, kicking, throwing, catching, hopping, and doing push-ups and broad-jumps); 3) Locomotion, assessing the developmental skills involved in using large muscles to move from one place to another (e.g., crawling, walking, and running); 4) Fine Muscle, assessing the child's development of small muscle control in the arms and hands needed to pick up objects, open doors, string beads, turn pages, fold or cut paper and draw; 5) Perceptual Motor, assessing the child's ability to integrate visual-motor skills in such activities as building towers, drawing and printing.

Communication: Consists of 59 items grouped into 2 subdomains: 1) Receptive Communication, assessing the child's reception and comprehension of sounds and words as well as nonverbal information received through gestures, sign, and Braille; 2) Expressive Communication, assessing the child's ability to produce sounds, words, or gestures, and grammatically correct phrases and sentences to communicate with others.

Cognitive: Consists of 56 items grouped into 4 subdomains: 1) Perceptual Discrimination, assessing sensorimotor interactions with the immediate environment (initial items) and the child's ability to discriminate the features of objects such as size or shape, and to selectively respond to them (later items); 2) Memory, measuring the child's ability to retrieve information from short-term memory when presented with various stimuli to be recalled; 3) Reasoning and Academic Skills, assessing critical thinking skills (e.g., problem identification and resolution, analysis, and judgment of ideas) and preacademic skills required in counting, reading, writing, mathematics, and spelling; 4) Conceptual Development, measuring the child's ability to grasp concepts and draw relationships among objects (e.g., color and shape recognition, sequencing of events, and sorting skills) and to recognize perceptual distortions.

In lieu of the full diagnostic version of the Battelle Developmental Inventory a shortened screening version of the BDI, The Screening Test, may be administered. The Screening Test consists of 96 items (two per age level for each of the five domains). These items were selected from the five domains on the basis of high item-domain score correlations and 75% of the standardization sample receiving full credit for each of these items.

Twenty items each from the Personal-Social, Adaptive, and Motor domains, and 18 items each from the Communication and Cognitive domains appear on the BDI Screening Test. Both reception and expressive language skills are represented at each age level from the Communication domain. There are 9 gross-motor and 11 fine-motor items from the Motor domain. The items from the Cognitive, Personal-

Social and Adaptive domains were selected independently of their respective subdomains. Most children will actually be administered no more than six items per domain for a total of about 30 items.

Practical Applications/Uses

The BDI and its accompanying Screening Test are intended to be used by a wide range of educationally—as well as psychologically—oriented professionals. This would include infant, preschool, and primary teachers in regular or special education; psychologists; speech clinicians; adaptive physical education specialists; and clinical diagnosticians.

The BDI serves four specific purposes in assessment, educational planning and program evaluation. The most basic function of the BDI Screening Test is to identify those children at risk for developmental handicaps in need of a more comprehensive evaluation using the full scale BDI. The normative comparisons made possible by administering the full scale BDI provide the basis for decisions about whether a child may be eligible for special services. Furthermore, the full scale BDI can help specify the developmental strengths and weaknesses of these handicapped children.

A second benefit of the behavioral skills covered in the BDI is to help identify relative developmental strengths and weaknesses of nonhandicapped children who may be performing well in the regular classroom or who may be gifted. This kind of profiling and longitudinal monitoring of early developmental skills is feasible with the BDI because of its milestone approach to early childhood assessment and the multiple domains it covers.

A third use of the BDI is in the development and monitoring of instructional plans. Because items on the BDI are behaviorally specified, hierarchically sequenced, and cover a range of relevant skill areas the BDI is ideal for task analyzing a behavioral sequence of skills and for setting the kinds of short- and long-term goals and objectives required in individual education plans (IEPs). In addition, multidisciplinary teamwork and decision-making may be fostered because the independent domains and subdomains of the BDI permit professionals to assess in their own areas of expertise. For example, the school psychologist might administer the Cognitive and Personal-Social; the speech clinician, the Communication; the occupational therapist, the Motor; and the social worker, the Adaptive.

A fourth use of the BDI is in the evaluation of the effects of various educational programs on the progress of groups of handicapped children. The progress of whole self-contained classrooms, subsets of children within a classroom, or individual children with various handicapping conditions may be charted and documented to show the benefits of one form of instruction over another or that early intervention is indeed helpful.

One of the greatest obstacles examiners must confront is how to administer a test to handicapped children in a standardized manner. The BDI deals directly with this problem by providing both general and specific adaptation recommendations for items in each domain. The general adaptations may be found at the beginning of each test book and are especially useful in testing multiply handicapped children. These general adaptations describe behaviors that may interfere with obtaining reliable responses and limitations imposed by various handicaps as well as general strategies for dealing with these problems. On the other hand, specific adaptations are suggested in conjunction with specific items when appropriate so that motor, visually, hearing, and speech impaired; emotionally disturbed; and multiply handicapped children can be evaluated without changing the behaviors being assessed. In many cases, these specific adaptations involve demonstrations of what is to be done, specific positioning suggestions, or alternative testing materials. A list of these supplementary test materials is located at the front of each test book. Of course, these adaptations should be used only when the item cannot be administered to the handicapped child as originally stated in the examiner's manual. Visual, auditory, or gestural cues given to the child other than those described in the general and specific adaptations would invalidate the testing.

Unlike many other instruments, multiple types of administration procedures are employed on the BDI. These three procedures include structural administrations, observations, and interviews. One or more of these procedures is suggested in the test books for each item. Consequently, some items describe only a structured testing procedure whereas others may give instructions how only one or all three could be used.

With this test format items are administered in a standardized manner. Usually some verbal or material stimulus is presented to the child who must respond in some desired manner. Behaviorally explicit item-by-item administration procedures are given in the test books. Because the structured procedures, however, are the most explicit and defined they may be the most clearcut to administer and score, followed next by observation and then the interview approach. In addition, these latter two approaches may take more time than structured administration. Especially, the interview approach may be less reliable because of the subjectivity in scoring.

Many of the behaviors in the Motor, Cognitive, and Communication domains may be readily administered using the structured administration format. In contrast, many Personal-Social and Adaptive items are more readily observed in the natural setting of the classroom or in the child's home. Observation may be the preferred method of administration especially in those cases where particular items require that the child must demonstrate the desired behavior consistently when presented with the appropriate situation or stimulus conditions. Likewise, observation may be the most convenient procedure when the assessment is being conducted by a teacher or another professional who has the opportunity to observe the child daily.

There are two situations in which the interview may be the administration procedure of choice. First, interviews or observations should be used when the examiner is unable to reliably assess a child in a structured format because of some handicapping condition, testing fatigue, or motivational problems on the part of the child. Secondly, the parent, caregiver, teacher, or other informant may have greater opportunity to consistently observe the child's behavior during daily contacts than does the examiner. With this procedure, the knowledgeable informant is asked to describe the child's behavior under given conditions. The examiner decides whether credit should be awarded based on the informant's response. The frequency of occurrence of the behavior may be heavily weighted in deciding whether credit is given or not. The examiner's job is to look for specific evidence based on the informant's report that the child can perform the behavior in question. Behaviorally specified criteria to be applied to the responses accompany each item. The same criteria apply whether the item is administered in a structured format or through observation or interview. Examiners must decide and use the procedures that will yield the most reliable data.

Despite the fact that the domains of the BDI may be administered separately there is an advantage to administering the Personal-Social and Adaptive domains first when a child is given the full inventory. Because interviews and/or observations are the usual methods by which information on these two domains is gathered they represent excellent vehicles for building rapport with the child's parents, caregiver, or teacher. The observations and interviews conducted in assessing these two domains may also provide insights into concommitant deficits in functioning existing in the Motor, Communication and Cognitive domains to be administered next, usually in the structured format.

There are a number of requirements to be met when administering items on a standardized test such as the BDI. The testing environment should be free of auditory and visual distractions. A quiet part of a classroom may suffice but a small private testing room is preferable. Wherever the testing occurs, it should be in a place that is familiar to the child, well-lit and ventilated, and equipped with a child-size table and two chairs. Occasionally, when the child is being resistant, the parent or caregiver may administer the item to the child with the child seated in his or her lap or by using a lapboard. Parents will need coaching so that the item will be administered in a standardized manner. The examiner always does the scoring.

The instructions for administering many of the items are often presented in bold print and should be read verbatim whenever possible. If the child fails to comprehend the meaning of the directions some deviation from the exact words is permissible. This feature of the BDI is in direct contrast to most other diagnostic instruments. Examiners should be careful to modify the instructions such that they convey only their original meaning and should not include cues that would lead the examinee in responding to the question. How much information is too much and what kinds of changes are unfair are extremely difficult to answer. Without careful consideration such modifications made by individual examinees may threaten the validity of the test results. Except for these changes, no other modifications in standardized procedures are allowed. This means that no extra trials may be given to complete a task and the sequence for administering domains must be followed.

Within each domain, the items in each subdomain are sequenced developmentally from 0- through 8-years-old according to ten age categories. During the birth to age-two range when development proceeds rapidly there are half-year intervals. One-year categories are provided from two to eight years of age. The subdomains and their items should be administered in consecutive order and all subdomains should be administered unless they contain no items at the appropriate level for the child. Because the BDI is a developmental scale similar basal and ceiling rules found in other tests apply to each subdomain of the BDI. The basal is the level of item difficulty below which the examiner may assume that the child would get all of the items correct. To obtain the basal the examiner begins testing at the child's estimated developmental age level and moves down the item sequence until the child gets full credit on all items at an age level in that subdomain. The ceiling is the level of item difficulty above which the child would get a 0. The ceiling level for each subdomain is reached when the child receives a 0 on two consecutive items. Finding the item ceiling should be relatively easy since the items are empirically sequenced and grouped by age. On occasion an examiner may wish to test the limits of splinter skills beyond the basal and ceiling levels for instructional planning purposes but no credit is given for any items administered above the first ceiling level. There is only one difference between administration procedures for the full BDI and the Screening Test. The basal and ceiling rules for the Screening Test apply to each domain whereas the basal and ceiling rules for the full BDI apply to each subdomain.

Items on the full BDI and Screening Test are scored using a three-point system according to criteria presented with each item. A score of 2 is given when the child's response meets the specified criteria. A score of 1 means that the child attempted the item but did not fulfill all the criteria for a correct response. Zero points are scored when the response is clearly incorrect or when there is "no opportunity" or "no response." Items given 1-point scores may represent emerging skills and should be monitored for progress as part of an IEP. Raw scores for each domain and subdomain should be transferred to the summary profile section of the test protocol. Probability tables are provided for individual domain raw scores and the total score on the Screening Test. Instructions are provided as to how pass/fail decisions about individual domains and the whole Screening Test can be made.

Similarly, the raw scores for each of the 24 subdomains and the five total scores for each of the domains on the full BDI should be transferred to the summary profile sheet on the protocol. A total BDI raw score can also be calculated. These 29 domain and subdomain raw scores should be converted to standard scores with a mean of 10 and standard deviation of 3. A Developmental Quotient (DQ) may also be calculated, based on a composite of the separate domains to provide an index of overall developmental progress. This DQ has a mean of 100 and standard deviation of 15. Age equivalents in months are available for each of the total domain scores, the Fine Motor, Expressive and Receptive subdomains, and the BDI total score. A chart for profiling domain and subdomain standard scores is also available on the summary sheet, making the job of analyzing score comparisons for strengths and weaknesses relatively easy. These kinds of subdomain comparisons can aid in pinpointing whether the deficit is due to a general weakness in all skills areas represented by that domain or the result of a specific skill deficit. For example, a deficit in the Motor domain could be generalized to all subdomains or localized in the Fine Motor domain.

The examiner's manual presents a full chapter on interpretation strategies, and five sample case studies show how these strategies could be applied. Another chapter explains how IEP goals and objectives could be developed for four of these cases. Age-appropriate skills specified in each domain may be regarded as the goals and the items may be considered the short-term objectives that lead to the long-term goal. Instructional materials for each short-term objective may be conceptually similar to those used in the BDI assessment. The BDI scoring criteria can be used as the criteria for evaluating the accomplishment of each short-term objective. The comments column of the scoring sheet can be used to monitor and date progress in meeting short-term objectives for each item. The three-point scoring system may also be sensitive to more subtle gains in meeting these short-term goals. When the BDI is used as a pre- and post-testing instrument it can prove useful in revising IEPs, in projecting rates of progress toward projected goals, and in explaining instructional gains during parent conferences.

Technical Aspects

Norming data collection on the BDI began in December, 1982 and was completed in March, 1983. During this same period the BDI was administered to a clinical sample for comparison purposes. Eight-hundred subjects participated in the norming study. They were selected based on age, sex, race, and geographic region and subregion, according to data from the U.S. Bureau of the Census Statistical Abstract (1981) using a stratified quota sampling procedure. About 50 subjects or more were represented at each age level. The sample was divided into approximately 75% urban and 25% rural and represented a wide range of socioeconomic status. The norming sample ranged in age from newborn to 95-months-old. There were 330 white males, 341 white females, 63 minority males, and 66 minority females. The white sample represented 83.9% of the sample and the minority sample represented 16.1%. Overall, the percentages by sex were 49.1% males and 50.9% females. These percentages by race and sex are quite representative of the percentages reported by the U.S. Census Bureau.

Forty-two test administrators from a variety of settings and educational backgrounds at 28 sites in 24 states were selected to administer the BDI and its Screening Test during the standardization study. Test administrators consisted of preschool and elementary-teachers, paraprofessionals, educational diagnosticians, psychologists, and nursery and day care staff. The reason for such diversity was because the BDI was designed to be used in a variety of settings by examiners with a range of expertise in assessment procedures.

In terms of reliability, the standard error of measurement for the BDI is generally small thus offering the examiner assurance that the obtained score is close to the child's "true score." The approximate average standard error of measurement for domain scores is 1.5 and for the DQ, 3.75. The test-retest and interrater reliability coefficients for the BDI were generally in the .90 range and above, demonstrating that the BDI is a stable instrument that produces accurate scores. The internal consistency of the BDI using Cronbach's Alpha was quite high for all five domains and the total score at each age level. The average reliability ranged from .81 to .95.

The verification of BDI test items by content experts during test development helped ensure the content validity of the resulting instrument. Furthermore, the intercorrelation matrix for subdomain and domain scores showed generally high and positive correlations. This indicates that the subdomains and items are properly located in the domains, thus supporting the factorial validity of the BDI. When comparisons were made between the T-scores of adjacent age groups on all BDI components the vast majority of the comparisons were significant at the .001 level. These age comparisons provide support for the contention that the BDI is developmental in nature. In a study comparing the BDI component scores of the norming sample with a clinical sample of 160 handicapped children, all comparisons were significant at the .01 level or greater. These results provide strong support that the BDI can discriminate between clinical and nonclinical populations on the ten major components of the test.

Concurrent validity coefficients were calculated using test scores for children in the clinical sample. Correlation coefficients between the ten major BDI components and the Vineland Social Maturity Scale (Doll, 1965) and the Developmental Activities Screening Inventory (DASI) (Dubose & Langley, 1977) are quite high and significant in the .78 to .93 range. Correlations with the Stanford-Binet Intelligence Scale (Terman & Merrill, 1960) are moderate and positive in the .40 to .61 range, but then the BDI was not intended to be a measure of intelligence. Overall, the correlations between the Peabody Picture Vocabulary Test-Revised (PPVT-R) (Dunn & Dunn, 1981) and the ten BDI component scores are relatively high. The correlations are especially high for PPVT-R Receptive and Expressive subdomains and the Communication domain total as one might expect because of the similarity of constructs measured. At this point, all validity data indicate that the BDI is valid for its intended purposes. Of special interest is the fact that no statistically significant sex or social differences across ages were found on the 30 BDI scores. BDI scores appear to be valid for both sexes and for minority populations. Caution is advised in overinterpreting this finding, however, since the minority sample consisted primarily of black and Spanish-origin children.

The validity of the BDI Screening Test was evaluated by administering it to a total of 164 children in the norming and clinical samples prior to their receiving the full BDI. All of the correlations between Screening Test scores and the comparable components of hte BDI were at or above .96 except for the Cognitive domain at .92. Consequently, a child's performance on the Screening Test should be an excellent predictor of performance on the full BDI. This does not mean that the Screening Test can be used for diagnostic purposes or for instructional planning, only for referral of children needing a comprehensive evaluation, including the full BDI.

Critique

It is rare to find a developmental inventory that meets the psychometric requirements of the *Standards for Educational and Psychological Tests* (1974) as well as the letter and spirit of Public Law 94:142, the *Education for All Handicapped Children Act* (Federal Register, 1977). The Battelle Developmental Inventory and its Screening Test seem to have met both of these standards in admirable form. The BDI is a versatile test because it contains both screening and diagnostic components. Furthermore, because the BDI is a standardized developmental inventory an examiner can get both norm-referenced data useful in determining appropriate pupil placement in addition to criterion-referenced data useful in developing individual educational plans. The 5 domains and 24 subdomains give breadth and scope to profile interpretations of individual strengths and weaknesses. The Total BDI Developmental Quotient helps pinpoint overall skill development for determination of placement eligibility. The technical data provided in the examiner's manual reveal a test that is both reliable and valid for its intended purpose of identifying young handicapped children.

The age range of 0-8 allows for long-range follow-up of pupil progress. Furthermore, the behaviorally specified administration procedures and scoring criteria permit pre- and post-test data to be gathered to measure short-term individual pupil progress and to show program accountability. Because items may be answered via structured test administration, observation, or parent/teacher report the BDI fosters multisourced assessment and multidisciplinary participation as advocated by PL 94:142. Finally, the BDI is one of the very few developmental scales with adapted administration and scoring procedures to meet the special needs of handicapped examinees.

Despite the many merits of the BDI, no test is any better than its examiner, who should be aware of its limitations. In the case of the BDI, three examiner caveats are in order. First, according to the examiner's manual it is permissible for the professional experiences and educational backgrounds of BDI examiners to vary widely. Potential examiners should be careful, however, not to misinterpret this casual attitude to mean that no knowledge of measurement theory and no previous testing experience are necessary. On the contrary, the BDI may be relatively easy to administer and to score, but an unprepared examiner can invalidate test results and distort interpretations. New examiners should thoroughly familiarize themselves with the test manual and materials and seek supervised practice using the BDI before testing their first subject.

A second cautionary note may be warranted in regard to examiners who adapt administration procedures for handicapped children. Quite a bit of latitude in structuring these modifications is given to the examiner. Examiners should be reserved in their clinical judgments about how much items should be modified. Future research should address whether the reliability of standard scores is affected when examiners modify test items for the handicapped.

Thirdly, there may be danger in considering the BDI a nonbiased test for all minority groups at this time. The study that showed no racial differences on standard scores used a small sample size consisting mostly of black and Spanish children. More research needs to be conducted with an increased sample size and a greater diversity of minority representation. Until then, the same care should be applied in interpreting the results of minority examinees on the BDI as is used to interpret other tests.

Finally, the excellent sampling procedures used to standardize the BDI mirror those of the widely used Wechsler Scales. One difference is the relatively small sample size of 800 children on the BDI. Predictive validity studies need to be conducted with the BDI using an increased sample size. The BDI is a very new test and is yet to be widely disseminated and used in the field. If its excellent research base continues to expand, the full scale BDI and its accompanying Screening Test should become two of the most widely used instruments in the area of developmental assessment.

References

American Psychological Association. (1974). *Standards for educational and psychological tests.* Washington, DC: Author.

Doll, E. A. (1965). *Vineland Social Maturity Scale.* Circle Pines, MN: American Guidance Service.

Dubose, R. F., & Langley, M. B. (1977). *Developmental Activities Screening Inventory.* Hingham, MA: Teaching Resources Corporation.

Dunn, L. M., & Dunn, L. M. (1981). *Peabody Picture Vocabulary Test-Revised.* Circle Pines, MN: American Guidance Service.

Federal Register. (August 23, 1977). *Education for handicapped children. Regulations implementing education for all handicapped children act of 1975* (42474-42518).

Newborg, J., Stock, J. R., Wnek, L., Guidubaldi, J., & Svinicki, J. (1984). *The Battelle Developmental Inventory.* Allen, TX: DLM Teaching Resources.

Terman, L. M., & Merrill, M. A. (1960). *Stanford-Binet Intelligence Scale, Third Revision (Form L-M).* Boston: Houghton Mifflin Company.

U.S. Bureau of the Census. (1981). *Statistical Abstract of the United States: 1981* (102nd edition). Washington, DC: U.S. Government Printing Office.

Wechsler, D. (1974). *Wechsler Intelligence Scale for Children-Revised.* New York: The Psychological Corporation.

R. Scott Stehouwer, Ph.D.
Associate Professor of Psychology, Calvin College, Grand Rapids, Michigan.

BECK DEPRESSION INVENTORY

Aaron T. Beck. Philadelphia, Pennsylvania: Center for Cognitive Therapy.

Introduction

The Beck Depression Inventory (BDI) is a 21-item test presented in multiple-choice format which purports to measure presence and degree of depression in adolescents and adults. Each of the 21 items of the BDI attempts to assess a specific symptom or attitude "which appear(s) to be specific to depressed patients, and which are consistent with descriptions of the depression contained in the psychiatric literature" (Beck, 1970, p. 189). Although the author, Aaron T. Beck, M.D., is associated with the development of the cognitive theory of depression, the Beck Depression Inventory was designed to assess depression independent of any particular theoretical bias.

The BDI was developed by Beck and his associates at the University of Pennsylvania School of Medicine. At that time he was Professor of Psychiatry and also chief of the psychiatry section of Philadelphia General Hospital. In undertaking research on depression, Beck decided it would be useful to develop an inventory for measuring depth of depression and felt such an inventory would be particularly advantageous for research purposes.

The BDI was first developed with psychiatric patients who were drawn from routine admissions to the psychiatric out-patient department of the University of Pennsylvania Hospital and to the psychiatric out-patient department of the Philadelphia General Hospital. The test was developed over a seven-month period starting in June, 1957 with an original sample of 226 patients. A later study, which began in February, 1960, was undertaken over a five-month period with 183 patients.

The original BDI was published in 1961 (Beck, et al., 1961) and was later contained in Beck's (1970) classic work, *Depression: Causes and Treatment*. The original BDI was a 21-item multiple-choice test in which the selections for each item varied from four to seven choices. Each choice was given a weight of zero to three points. A revision was undertaken in 1974, then later in 1978, standardizing each item to four possible choices, each choice still assigned a weight of zero, one, two, or three points. Additionally, a short form of the Beck Depression Inventory has been

The reviewer wishes to acknowledge gratefully the help of Mr. Robert Nykamp in the preparation of this review.

developed (Reynolds & Gould, 1981). This short form consists of 13 items taken from the revised 21-item test.

Although Aaron Beck is credited with the development of the BDI, credit is also given to C. H. Ward, M. Mendelson, J. Mock, and J. Erbaugh for their original work in the test's development.

Each of the inventory items corresponds to a specific category of depressive symptom and/or attitude. Each category purports to describe a specific behavioral manifestation of depression and consists of a graded series of four self-evaluative statements. The statements are rank ordered and weighted to reflect the range of severity of the symptom from neutral to maximum severity. Numerical values of zero, one, two, or three are assigned each statement to indicate degree of severity. The 21 items purport to measure the following symptoms and attitudes:

1. Sadness	12. Social Withdrawal
2. Pessimism/Discouragement	13. Indecisiveness
3. Sense of Failure	14. Body Image Distortion
4. Dissatisfaction	15. Work Retardation
5. Guilt	16. Insomnia
6. Expectation of Punishment	17. Fatigability
7. Self-Dislike	18. Anorexia
8. Self-Accusation	19. Weight Loss
9. Suicidal Ideation	20. Somatic Preoccupation
10. Crying	21. Loss of Libido
11. Irritability	

Practical Applications/Uses

The BDI is designed for simple administration. A trained interviewer can read aloud each statement for the items, though usually the test is self-administered. Originally, the inventory was developed for adult and late adolescent patients, though later research indicates the BDI is appropriate for use with even young adolescents, as young as 12 years, 10 months (Strober, Green, & Carlson, 1981).

The test is very simple to administer and very simple to take. The reading difficulty level is quite low (eighth grade), the statements are easy to understand, and directions are very clear. Responses are indicated directly on the question sheet by having the subjects circle the number beside the statement they endorse. Subjects are asked to read each group of statements carefully and then select the statement from each group that best describes what they have been feeling over the past week including the day of administration. If several statements in the group seem to apply equally well, subjects are asked to circle each statement they believe fits them.

The score is obtained by taking the highest score circled for each item and adding the total number of points for all items. While the authors admit there is no arbitrary score that can be used for all purposes as a cutoff score and that the specific cutoff point depends upon the characteristics of the patients used and the purpose for which the inventory is being given, they do give the following guidelines:

0-9 Normal Range
10-15 Mild Depression
16-19 Mild-Moderate Depression
20-29 Moderate-Severe Depression
30-63 Severe Depression

The practitioner who is in need of a simple, quick, and helpful tool in gathering information about a patient's depressive state may do well to use the BDI. The BDI is particularly useful in mental health settings as a screening device since it correlates very well with psychiatric ratings of depression. In any situation where a screening device is necessary for depression, the BDI would seem to be the test of choice. The ease of administering, taking, scoring, and interpreting the BDI makes it a very attractive test. Practitioners must be aware that the BDI should certainly not be used as the sole means of determining presence or degree of depression; as indicated above, however, it can be an excellent screening and supplementary device for individual or group administration.

Individuals who are most likely to benefit from using the BDI are mental health practitioners in a variety of settings. This would include psychiatrists, psychologists, social workers, mental health counselors, school counselors, school psychologists, and industrial psychologists. In this latter case, the BDI may be very helpful as a screening measure for industry.

The Beck Depression Inventory has been used with a wide variety of populations including psychiatric in-patients, psychiatric out-patients, general university populations, and the adolescent population. It is also appropriate for subjects with a wide range of abilities. Since the test can be given orally, all that is necessary is that the subject be able to understand the words of the test. They do not have to write a response, but merely can endorse a particular answer. This makes it particularly advantageous for individuals who have a short attention span, for individuals who have difficulty reading, and for individuals who may be less compliant with a longer test.

Because of the simplicity of the BDI, it can be administered almost anywhere by a variety of individuals, with very little training. If the BDI is administered individually, it would be quite helpful for the examiner to be aware of his or her ability to provide behavior observations that may aid in the further delineation of presence and/or degree of depression.

The time required for the test varies from individual to individual but should be no more than ten minutes. Since scoring the BDI involves simple addition, the time required is therefore minimal, usually less than three minutes per inventory. The BDI is available in computer format from National Computer Systems, Minneapolis, MN.

Interpretation is based on objective scoring and is generally straightforward. Based on the total score, individuals are categorized into five levels of depression, from normal to severe depression, as indicated previously. The amount of training for interpreting the BDI varies with the use to which the inventory is put. If it is used to diagnose a patient, the examiner should have appropriate psychological training. If the inventory is used to categorize a particular individual for research purposes only, training need not be extensive.

Technical Aspects

One of the disadvantages of the BDI is that there is no manual available for its use. Perhaps it is felt a manual is not necessary because of the simplicity of the instrument; however, it is more difficult to determine such things as reliability and validity without one.

It appears that most of the studies of BDI reliability have been undertaken with psychiatric patients. Test-retest reliability has been studied in the case of 38 patients who were given the BDI on two occasions (Beck, 1970). It was discovered that the changes in BDI scores tended to parallel changes in the clinical reading of the depth of depression, indicating a consistent relationship between BDI scores and the patient's clinical state. The reliability figures here were above .90. Item analysis also demonstrated a positive correlation between each item of the BDI and the total score. These correlations were all significant at the .001 level. Internal consistency studies demonstrated a correlation coefficient of .86 for the test items, and the Spearman-Brown correlation for the reliability of the BDI yielded a coefficient of .93.

In assessing the validity of the BDI, the readily apparent face validity of the BDI must be addressed. The BDI looks as though it is assessing depression. While this may be quite advantageous, it may make it easy for a subject to distort the results of the test.

Content validity would seem to be quite high since the BDI appears to evaluate well a wide variety of symptoms and attitudes associated with depression.

Studies of the BDI have also been undertaken with regard to concurrent validity. One study demonstrated a correlation of .77 between the inventory and psychiatric rating using university students as subjects (Bumberry, Oliver, & McClure, 1978). Beck (1970) reports similar studies in which coefficients of .65 and .67 were obtained in comparing results of the BDI with psychiatric ratings of patients. Other measures of concurrent validity have been undertaken by comparing the results of the BDI with those of other measures of depression, such as the Depression Adjective Check Lists (DACL) and the MMPI. Beck (1970) reports a correlation of .66 between the BDI and the DACL and a correlation of .75 between the BDI and the MMPI D Scale. Again, this study was undertaken with psychiatric patients as subjects.

Overall, the results of reliability and validity studies strongly support the BDI as a very useful measure for assessing depression. This has been demonstrated with a variety of subjects in a variety of situations. Additionally, cross-validation research tends to support the reliability and validity findings with regard to the BDI.

Critique

The Beck Depression Inventory is a simple, perhaps deceptively and even elegantly simple, test for the presence and depth of depression. It is extremely helpful as a screening procedure and is also of value as a validation procedure for other means of determining depression. It is difficult to determine how well the BDI has been accepted in general clinical or applied practice. Certainly the Beck

Depression Inventory has become the inventory of choice for researchers in selecting depressed subjects from a larger population (Stehouwer & Rosenbaum, 1977). It has also been useful in delineating differences in depressive symptomatology between men and women (Hammen & Padesky, 1977) and between adolescents and adults (Stehouwer, Bultsma, and Termorshuizen, in press). Nonetheless, if the clinical issue is one of determining the presence and degree of depression and if the subjects are motivated to accurately reflect their emotional status, the Beck Depression Inventory would certainly seem to be the inventory of choice for clinical as well as research purposes.

References

This list includes text citations and suggested additional reading.

Beck, A. T. (1970). *Depression: Causes and treatment*. Philadelphia: University of Pennsylvania Press.

Beck, A. T., & Beamesderfer, A. (1974). Assessment of depression: The depression inventory. In P. Pichot (Ed.), *Psychological measurements in psychopharmacology: Vol. 7. Modern problems in pharmacopsychiatry* (pp. 151-169). Basel, Switzerland: Karger.

Beck, A. T., Ward, C. H., Mendelson, M., Mock, J., & Erbaugh J. (1961). An inventory for measuring depression. *Archives of General Psychiatry, 4*, 561-571.

Bumberry, W., Oliver, J. M., & McClure, J. N. (1978). Validation of the Beck Depression Inventory in a university population using psychiatric estimate as the criterion. *Journal of Consulting and Clinical Psychology, 46*, 150-155.

Hammen, C. L., & Padesky, C. A. (1977). Sex differences in the expression of depressive responses on the BDI. *Journal of Abnormal Psychology, 86*(6), 609-614.

Reynolds, W. M., & Gould, J. W. (1981). A psychometric investigation of the standard and short form Beck Depression Inventory. *Journal of Consulting and Clinical Psychology, 49*(2), 306-307.

Steer, R. A., Beck, A. T., & Garrison, B. (1982). Applications of the Beck Depression Inventory. In N. Sartorious & T. Ban (Eds.), *Assessment of depression*. Geneva, Switzerland: World Health Organization.

Stehouwer, R. S., Bultsma, C., & Termorshuizen, I. (in press). Cognitive-perceptual distortion in depression as a function of developmental age. *Adolescence*.

Stehouwer, R. S., & Rosenbaum, G. (1977, December). *Frequency and potency of reinforcing events in anxiety and depression*. Paper presented at the 17th annual convention of the Association for the Advancement of Behavior Therapy, Atlanta, GA.

Strober, M., Green, J., & Carlson, G. Utility of the Beck Depression Inventory with psychiatrically hospitalized adolescents. *Journal of Consulting and Clinical Psychology, 49*(3), 482-483.

David L. Streiner, Ph.D.
*Professor of Psychiatry, Chief Psychologist, McMaster University,
Hamilton, Ontario.*

BEXLEY-MAUDSLEY AUTOMATED PSYCHOLOGICAL SCREENING

William Acker and Clare Acker. Windsor, England: NFER-Nelson Publishing Company Ltd.

Introduction

The Bexley-Maudsley Automated Psychological Screening (BMAPS) and the Bexley-Maudsley Category Sorting Test (BMCST) comprise a set of six computer-administered tests. They are designed to assess patients, primarily chronic alcoholics, who present with "non-specific psychological deficits." The tests are to be used as a screening battery, to select patients who should be referred for individual psychological testing and/or neurological investigation. The focus is to detect deficits in nonverbal skills, including visual-spatial problems, psychomotor slowing, inaccuracy and slowing in visual-perceptual analysis, difficulties with verbal and visual-spatial memory, and abstract problem solving.

The Bexley-Maudsley is a relatively recent battery, released in England in 1982. It was developed by two clinical psychologists, Dr. William Acker and Mrs. Clare Acker, who are at the Institute of Psychiatry of the University of London and the Bexley Hospital. Their normative sample consisted of between 60 and 94 patients being treated on the Alcoholism Treatment Unit of Bexley Hospital (the sample size differed for each subtest), and between 44 and 56 normals drawn from a variety of sources. Subjects were excluded if they had a history of head injury, severe physical illness, epilepsy, or psychiatric disturbance. The groups differed significantly in the proportion of females, the number of years of education, and intelligence, with the control group higher in all three areas.

The Bexley-Maudsley battery consists of a floppy disc containing the set of six programs, which can be run on either a Commodore Pet (Models 3032, 4032, or 8032) or Apple II (models unspecified) microcomputer, and a keyboard. This latter piece of hardware clips over the user's computer keyboard, leaving only nine keys exposed. For the subtests that use fewer than nine keys, the unused ones can be blocked off with masks. After loading the programs into the computer, the examiner first selects whether to give the BMCST or the BMAPS. If the latter is used, the examiner then chooses one of the five subtests from a menu. After that subtest has been completed, the menu reappears on the screen and the examiner can then stop testing, review the results of the tests completed thus far, or select another subtest. There does not appear to be any way to run a number of subtests without returning to the menu between them. The results can be displayed on the monitor or directed to a printer, if one is available.

The first BMAPS subtest is called Visual Spatial Ability ("Little Men"; the masculine pronoun is used throughout the manual in describing this test). The test is derived from one developed by Benson and Gedye (1963) and modified by Ratcliff (1979). An outline of a person holding an object is presented to the subject in one of four positions: standing upright or on his head, and facing toward or away from the subject. The task is to determine in which hand the figure holds the object. When the figure is upside down, the message on the screen ("Is it in his right or left hand?") is also upside down and on the bottom. After four practice trials on which the subject receives feedback, there are 32 test trials. If the subject has not responded after 15 seconds, the next frame is automatically presented. For each orientation (head up or down), the test yields the number of trials correct, the average response time, and the number of omitted trials. The guideline for interpretation, though, uses only the number correct in the head-down position. An abnormal score in a patient who knows right from left is said to indicate visual-spatial deficits. There are two pictures in the manual, one supposedly showing the figure standing on his head facing the subject and other showing him standing upright with his back to the subject. However, there was nothing in the pictures to indicate that he was facing one way or the other; this may simply be a case of having put the wrong diagram in the manual or it may reflect a more serious drawback in the task. Without the software itself, it was impossible for this reviewer to tell which was the case.

The second BMAPS subtest, Symbol Digit Coding, is a variation of the Digit Symbol Substitution subtest (DSS) of the Wechsler Scales. However, instead of writing a symbol that matches a number, on this task the subject must choose a number that matches one of the nine symbols shown. As with the DSS, the key is present throughout the task. There are 60 trials, apparently without any time limit per trial. At the end, mean reaction times and total number of errors are given for each block of 20 trials. The guidelines state that performance slower than one standard deviation below the mean indicates a deficit in perceptual motor speed (it is not stated whether this applies if the person falls below this criterion on only one or two blocks of trials, or on all three).

The third subtest is called Visual Perceptual Analysis. Three geometric patterns comprised of 20 blocks each are arrayed horizontally on the screen and the subject must indicate which pattern is different from the other two (which are identical to each other). On half of the trials, the patterns differ in two of the 20 blocks; on the more difficult trials, they differ in four of the blocks. Subjects are encouraged to work as quickly as possible and feedback is given after each trial (the total number of which is not specified in the manual). The results consist of the number of correct trials and their mean response times for both levels of difficulty. The guidelines state that performance poorer than one standard deviation below the mean reflects problems with perceptual motor speed, but the manual does not state which of the four possible scores is used for this determination.

The fourth subtest, Verbal Recognition Memory, consists of two parts: memorization and recognition. During Part One, 36 "high frequency" nouns are presented serially. The instructions on the screen state that if the word is a "strong" one, the person should press Key 1; if it is a "weak" word, Key 2 should be pressed. This semantic judgment is not scored, but is designed to ensure that the subject focuses on the word. (The manual does not state whether the subject receives any feedback or, if so, how "strong" and "weak" were determined.) In Part Two, the same words are presented in the same order, but each is accompanied by two distractors; the subject's task is to select which of the three words was in the original list. Recognizing fewer than 31 words (one S.D. below the mean) is supposed to reflect problems with verbal memory.

The last subtest of the BMAPS is called Visual Spatial Recognition Memory. The subject is presented with a geometric pattern similar to one used on the Visual Perceptual Analysis subtest. After three seconds the screen goes blank for a time, and then the pattern is presented again along with two distractors; as with the previous subtest (Verbal Recognition Memory), the task is to choose the one that was previously shown. There are 12 trials with a one-second interval between initial presentation and recognition, 12 trials with a five-second delay, and 12 trials with a 10-second delay. The final score is a composite of the standardized scores for each retention interval.

The BMCST is a computerized version of the Wisconsin Card Sorting Test. In the WCST, sorting is based on three dimensions: the number of elements, the shape of the elements (square, star, triangle, and circle), and their color. Since the BMCST is designed for a microcomputer with a monochrome screen, color has been replaced by "orientation"—that is, whether a black band running across the white card is vertical, horizontal, diagonal to the upper right, or to the upper left. The original shapes have been replaced by symbols "hardwired" into the Commodore Pet: a greater-than sign, an upward-pointing arrow, an asterisk, and a solid circle. As in the card form of the test, the four target patterns are arrayed across the top of the screen, with the test pattern centered near the bottom. The patient presses one of four buttons to indicate to which category the test card belongs. After each attempt, the card is redrawn under the chosen target and the subject is told whether or not that choice was correct. After six correct trials based on orientation, the concept switches to number and then to type. If, after 24 trials the subject still has not attained the criterion of six consecutive correct answers, the sorting rule changes to the next in sequence. The test continues for two complete cycles of the three sorting rules. There are seven performance measures available, ranging from total number of categories achieved, through total number of errors, to percentage of perseverative errors. The guidelines indicate that almost any of these scores could be used to determine if the person has problems with "abstract problem solving."

Practical Applications/Uses

The cover of the manual states that the BMAPS and BMCST "provide an efficient and practical means of assessing psychological deficits in chronic alcoholic patients. Designed to be administered on a microcomputer by support staff, the tests are ideally suited to the routine screening of incoming patients." As such, it would probably be of most use in an inpatient setting that would include a large number of detoxified chronic alcoholics. The tests are not intended to diagnose deficits in nonverbal skills, but rather to select patients who show some problems in these areas so they can be referred for further neurological or psychological testing.

The tests are intended to indicate whether the patient displays any deficit in a variety of nonverbal areas: visual-spatial; perceptual motor; visual-spatial memory; abstract problem solving; and, despite its description, there is also one subtest that taps verbal memory. As previously mentioned, the only norms provided in the manual are for detoxified chronic alcoholics as compared against normals. However, since many other patients, primarily nonalcoholic organics and severely depressed individuals, evidence problems in these areas, one would expect that in the near future this test will be used with them and norms will be developed. The main users of this battery will likely be clinical neuropsychologists in a hospital or clinic setting. The normative data given in the manual are for chronic alcoholic patients and normal controls. Because of the nature of the tasks used, subjects must have good vision, a working knowledge of written English (grade level has not been specified), and at least minimal use of one finger on one hand.

The BMAPS and BMCST are individually administered tests. It appears as if each subtest takes between five and 15 minutes to administer, depending on the speed of the patient. Because the examiner must read instructions to the subject, and give directions if the person makes an error, it would be infeasible to test more than one person at a time. The examiner need not be a psychologist; as most of the test is automated, the examiner's tasks are limited to 1) initially setting up the programs to run on the microcomputer; 2) selecting the test to be administered; 3) giving some additional instructions; and 4) prompting the patient if he or she makes a mistake during the practice trials. Technicians, nurses, or secretaries, with some training, should be able to administer the battery. The instructions for administering each subtest are brief but straightforward. With a bit of practice and common sense, no problems should be encountered.

The directions for loading the programs into the computer are a bit trickier, especially for someone unfamiliar with micros. Although the tests are available for both the Commodore Pet and the Apple II, the manual addresses only the former. No mention is made at all of using the tests with the Apple—how to load the disc, run it, or correct errors. The manual also states that if an error is made while running the program, the examiner need "simply follow the instructions in the error message." However, as a sample of the test was not available, it was impossible for this reviewer to tell how easy the instructions are to follow or how successfully they rectify the problem.

Scoring is done by the computer, eliminating errors due to the examiner. At the end of the session, a list of scores is displayed on the screen or printed out.

For interpreting each of the subtests, the manual proposes between one and nine "guidelines." As the name suggests, these appear to be quite flexible and even tentative. It is suggested that the intelligence of the person be taken into account, but the manual does not state how this should be done or even what the correlation is between each score and IQ.

No provision is made for making decisions based on the results of two or more subtests together, only on the individual scores. The manual does not indicate what to do if a person scores in the abnormal range on only one of the six subtests or, for example, three of the dozen or so scores.

Technical Aspects

The most serious drawback to these tests at present is the lack of adequate reliability and validity data. While interrater agreement should be quite high, as the role of the examiner is quite structured, there are no data regarding test-retest reliabilities on any of the subtests. Similarly, no data are presented in the manual regarding practice effects or how soon a patient can be retested.

For subtest one, Visual Spatial Ability, the manual states that Ratcliff's modification of the test discriminates "neurosurgical patients with right parietal lesions" (it does not state what the other group was). However, the computerized version of the test differs in some significant ways from Ratcliff's, so the results are not directly applicable. The only study reported in the manual using the computerized version is an unpublished paper, which shows that the test "discriminates monozygotic twins discordant for alcohol consumption." The norms, though, are based on the non-computerized version. Moreover, there are no criterion-related or construct validity studies that would support the assertion that the test measures "visual spatial deficits." This claim seems to be based on the face validity of the test; the figures are rotated in space.

Subtest two, Symbol Digit Coding, has slightly more data available. It, too, discriminates between the previously mentioned monozygotic twins, and between normal controls and detoxified alcoholics. The manual reports that it correlates .57 with the WAIS Digit Symbol score, .55 with Part A of the Halstead-Reitan Trail Making Test, and .65 with Part B. However, since none of these other tests are pure measures of perceptual motor speed (especially Trails), the claim that this is what the test measures remains unproven at this point.

The third subtest, Visual Perceptual Analysis, is said to measure visual information processing and the ability to perceive differences in geometric patterns. Not surprisingly, the twins differed yet again, as did normals from detoxified alcoholics. However, what the test measures is open to argument, as there are no criterion-related or construct validity studies reported.

Verbal Recognition Memory, subtest four, discriminates between alcoholics and normal controls (30.5 words recognized vs. 33.6, respectively). It correlates .47 with the Logical Memory Story on the Wechsler Memory Test (the manual does not state whether this is based on the first or second story, or a composite score). As the authors correctly point out, only 22% of the variance is shared between the tasks.

The last BMAPS subtest, Visual Spatial Recognition Memory, discriminates between normals and alcoholics, but only at the 10-second delay (10.1 vs. 9.0 figures correctly recognized, respectively), and correlates .52 with the Benton Visual Retention Test (form and delay not specified). No other studies are reported.

Most of the validity studies reported in the manual for the BMCST are for the card version of the Card Sorting Test; as the computerized version differs along a number of dimensions (e.g., mode of presentation, absence of color, symbols used, and so forth), the applicability of these studies is questionable. Normals differed from alcoholics in the computerized version.

In summary, the reliability and validity data are quite inadequate. The fact that normals differ from alcoholics on all of the subtests does not support the claim of concurrent validity for each of them, as the manual suggests. Normals differ from alcoholics in many spheres, so these results are not surprising. What are urgently needed are studies supporting the contention that the tests are actually measuring what they claim they are; these studies are not reported in the manual. Further, footnotes to some of the tables in the manual state that "there was a significant effect of premorbid intelligence . . . The significance levels for differences between control subjects and alcoholics have been corrected for this effect of premorbid intelligence" (p. 12). The groups are also significantly different in the number of years of school completed. It is quite disconcerting, therefore, to see no data relating test results to intellectual or educational level. Further, although the normal and alcoholic groups differed in the proportion of females (more in the control group), sex differences have been found on many similar tests and the value of this test would be greatly abetted by reporting the effect of this factor.

There are also difficulties with the interpretation of the results. As indicated previously, guidelines are given for each of the subtests individually, with recommendations for referral if subjects score below a given cutoff. In almost all instances, these are set at one standard deviation below the mean. If only one guideline is used per test, then there is a 40% probability that a normal subject will have one score below criterion by chance alone. If a total of 10 guidelines are used, this increases to almost 57%. While screening tests should err on the side of overinclusiveness, this appears to be a very high false positive rate.

After establishing reliability and validity, the results of any diagnostic test must also include the sensitivity and specificity. The former is the proportion of patients having a disorder, as established by a "gold standard," who are detected by the new test (i.e., the "true positive rate"); the latter is the proportion of people who do *not* have a problem and whom the test labels as problem-free (the "true negative rate"). While mean scores may differ significantly, especially with a large sample size, these values may be so low as to render the test useless for clinical purposes; that is, for making a decision about an individual, not a group. Unfortunately, neither value is reported for these tests, individually or as a whole.

Critique

With the explosive growth in the number of microcomputers, it is inevitable that they will be used to automate some aspects of psychometric assessment. All too often, though, these machines are put to the wrong use—automating tests that can be given just as rapidly and accurately by hand, rather than designing new tests that use the unique features of the computer. The Bexley-Maudsley falls into both camps. Some tests, like the Symbol Digit Coding or the Wisconsin Card Sort, appear to have gained little through computerization, while sacrificing the validity studies which have been done on the original versions. Other subtests, like Visual Spatial Recognition Memory, seem more suited to a computer format.

Accepting the authors' choices of subtests, can the battery fulfill its stated purpose as a screening test for non-specific, nonverbal deficits with detoxified chronic alcoholics? Even with this highly restricted population, this reviewer does not feel that sufficient reliability and validity testing has been done to justify the claims made on its behalf. The normative samples are inadequately described and the normals differ from the alcoholics on some significant dimensions. No reliability data are reported at all and only on a few subtests have any criterion-related validity studies been done, yielding equivocal results. The sensitivity and specificity of the tests are not given, and this reviewer's suspicion is that there will be an unacceptably high level of false positives in actual clinical practice.

Apparently much work and time has gone into designing these tests and programming them for the computer. It is unfortunate that the same care does not appear to have been taken in proving the worth of the end product.

References

Acker, W. (1982). Objective psychological changes in detoxified chronic alcoholics. *British Medical Bulletin, 38.*

Acker, W., & Acker, C. (1982). *Bexley-Maudsley Automated Psychological Screening and Bexley-Maudsley Category Sorting Test manual.* London: NFER-Nelson Publishing Company Ltd.

Benson, A. J., & Gedye, J. L. (1963). *Logical process in the resolution of orientation conflict* (RAF Institute of Aviation Medicine Report No. 259). London: Ministry of Defence (Air).

Ratcliff, G. (1979). Spatial thought, mental rotation and the right cerebral hemisphere. *Neuropsychologia, 17,* 49-54.

Robert J. Konopasky, Ph.D.

Chairperson and Associate Professor, Department of Psychology, Saint Mary's University, Halifax, Nova Scotia.

BIPOLAR PSYCHOLOGICAL INVENTORY

Allan V. Roe. Orem, Utah: Diagnostic Specialists Inc.

Introduction

The Bipolar Psychological Inventory (BPI) is a general purpose personality inventory that has been developed for prison inmates and adults and adolescents with criminal records. The author, Allen V. Roe, constructed the inventory with the goal "that it be maximally useful for diagnosing, understanding and predicting criminal behavior" (Roe, 1974, p. 27). In addition, the BPI was designed to be useful for making corrections-related decisions, establishing therapeutic goals, and in research. However, while developed to assess criminal behavior, the inventory is intended for clients, patients, and students from the general population as well as for personnel screening and police officer selection.

The background and early history of the BPI is discussed in detail in Roe's (1974) doctoral dissertation. The BPI was developed because no personality test examined by the author could discriminate among subsets, such as recidivists and escapees, of the criminal population. Thus, "the problem was to incorporate the necessary requirements of a good psychological test and at the same time to coordinate these with the variables peculiar to the criminal population" (Roe, 1974, p. 5). Roe's objectives were threefold: 1) the scales and items of the test were to be relevant to the analysis of criminal populations; 2) test items were to be appropriate for populations of low reading ability and low frustration tolerance; and 3) the test was to be easy to administer, score, and interpret.

To develop an item pool, a panel of five psychologists decided what scales would be especially useful in assessing criminal populations and then wrote what they considered to be appropriate items for those scales. An equal number of true and false responses to items making up a scale were keyed to the pathological and non-pathological poles of each scale. In addition, items on each scale were equally divided between those referring to behavior and those referring to affect. This preliminary test of 437 items and 15 scales was given to 63 inmates at Utah State Prison. Items that did not correlate significantly with their own scale scores were discarded. In addition, a behavioral item was also discarded if it correlated more highly with the affect items of its own scale than it did with the behavioral items and vice versa.

The final BPI was administered to 576 Utah State Prison inmates and their responses were used to establish norms. Percentiles were calculated and incorpo-

---

Sections of the administration manual are reprinted in this review by permission of Allan Roe, Ph.D.

rated into the profile sheets rather than SDs because of the skewed distribution of the scores. Norms for university males and females are based on the test data collected from two Utah universities and one California college in 1974.

The BPI is a self-administered questionnaire of 300 true-false items constituting 15 rationally developed and empirically tested scales (which will be described later in this review). There are two forms of the BPI: Form A includes a Sexual Maturity Scale, but does not include the general purpose Problem Index; Form B includes the Problem Index but not the Sexual Maturity Scale.

The BPI package consists of an eight-page administration manual, five-page questionnaire booklets with semi-rigid covers, answer sheets suitable for marking with a soft pencil for Opscan data entry or hand-scoring, a set of 15 tough, crease-resistant, transparent hand-scoring templates, and a set of normed profile sheets calibrated in percentiles. The administration manual, dated 1975, contains sections on the development and rationale of the BPI, the administration of the test, the hand-scoring and machine-scoring of the test, the different uses of Forms A and B, the description of the profile norms, and a rather weak discussion of test validity. There are detailed descriptions of all the scales and test-retest reliabilities for most of the scales.

The test booklets present the items in a well-organized format. Blank lines between each question enhance the ease of reading and responding to the test. The BPI, which can be read by a population having achieved the ninth-grade level, can be successfully administered to subjects with low frustration tolerance (Roe, 1974). The test may be administered to groups and requires little participation on the part of the examiner.

There are six different profiles, marked off in percentile scores, on four scaled sheets: 1) Offender Norms, Form A, Male (there are no Form B offender norms); 2) General Norms, Form A, Male and Female; 3) General Norms, Form B, Male and Female; 4) Police norms. General Norms sheets are printed with male norms on one side and female norms on the other.

Practical Applications/Uses

The BPI has proved useful in correctional settings. Norms exist for male prison inmates and the test has been used successfully to discriminate between, for example, those convicted of violent crimes from those convicted of nonviolent crimes (Roe, 1972).

Would the test be useful for noncriminal groups? There are norms for college students in California and university students in Utah. As the test is easy to administer, read, and score, it could be administered by minimally trained paraprofessionals and interpreted by appropriately trained psychologists. However, there are few studies that indicate that the test is a valid measure of personality for these groups. Thus, while it would seem that the test is appropriate for college groups and, because of its low level of difficulty, groups in high school or even upper level primary school, the decision to use the test with these groups must await further research.

The BPI has been specifically designed for the diagnosis, prognosis, research, and therapy of criminal populations. Computerized versions of the BPI are marketed for clinical and for personnel use but neither norms nor validity studies for these populations exist. The general computerized version contains norms appropriate for police officer selection and two studies, described by Roe (personal communication, January 15, 1985) but not found, on the validity of the BPI for police officer selection exist. As norms for the BPI do not exist for general populations other than university students, and as validated inventories such as the 16PF, the California Personality Inventory, and the Jackson Personality Inventory do provide general norms, these tests should be used for general populations. Few other uses for the BPI have been reported in the literature. Scale interpretations are clear to laymen and even to subjects with little education. The BPI could be used in court assessments; judges and lawyers would have no difficulty understanding the descriptors attached to the individual scales.

The administration manual claims the BPI is suitable for all subjects at ninth-grade reading level and above. However, this reading level may prove too high for some prisoners. Norms and validity studies are supplied only for prison males; norms but not validity studies are supplied for university students and police officers. Because the BPI was specifically designed for prison males, it would seem that the BPI would be most useful for prison populations and perhaps other antisocial groups. Norms for juvenile delinquents and high school and junior high school "troublemakers" would be of value in order to ascertain the test's discriminative ability with these groups.

A simpler version of the BPI should be developed for persons whose reading ability is below the ninth-grade level. Alternatively a speech synthesis module for the computerized version of the BPI could be installed to present the questions to "illiterate" subjects orally.

The Sexual Maturity Scale includes several male-oriented items. Form B, which includes the Problem Index but not the Sexual Maturity Scale, would be more appropriate for female populations.

The BPI is self-administering and appropriate for group settings such as classrooms. Minimally trained clerical personnel could hand out the test materials (question booklet, answer sheet, soft pencil), read the instructions to the examinees, and proctor the test. Psychological personnel could administer the test orally to the blind or the illiterate, but no studies reporting on such use have been found in the literature. The computerized version of the BPI is completely self-administering. Administration usually requires 30 to 60 minutes to complete.

Scoring is straightforward and clearly described in the manual. Hand-scoring by template is so simple it could be mastered by clerical personnel in five minutes. One simply lays each of the transparent templates over the answer sheet (a clear reference point is provided on both the template and the answer sheet), counts the number of black marks enclosed by circles, and records the score on the answer sheet through a slot cut in the template. Hand-scoring should take no longer than 10 minutes per subject. Machine scoring via Opscan reader provides a printout description of summary statistics suitable for developing one's own norms. The computerized version of the BPI automatically generates a detailed interpretive report.

Profile sheets facilitate easy plotting of scale scores. Scales are named along the X axis and percentile scores are provided along the Y axis. All raw scores for all the scales are prerecorded on the profile sheet; one simply blacks out the appropriate scores and connects the points to draw the profile. Scoring and profiling require no more than 15 minutes.

An automated version of the BPI is available on disk for the Apple II or the IBM PC. The user is provided three options: 1) the test can be administered onscreen, 2) test results can be input by a Chatsworth Mark Sense Card Reader, or 3) the raw scores can be entered from the keyboard. Scoring, profiling, and interpretation are completely automatic, and a one- to two-page narrative may be generated and printed. Keyed items for each scale may be printed along with their responses. A list of test item numbers with their answers may also be printed. The programs are segmented and consequently slow running, and copy protection prevents speeding up the program by running from hard disk. Different versions of the program are available for general use, for prison populations, for clinical populations, and for general personnel selection. The police officer selection option is available on the "general" disk.

The BPI is designed to measure 15 variables considered psychologically and socially important by psychologists in both general and correctional settings. The administration manual contains clearly stated interpretations for high and low scores, determined objectively, on each of the scales and the entire procedure of test administration, scoring, profiling, and interpretation need take no more than an hour per individual tested. The 15 bipolar-dimension scales, which include a validity scale, and their interpretations as given in the administration manual follow:

Invalid-Valid
(10 Items)

High Score. Gross confusion (psychosis, brain damage, retardation), inability to read, random marking of answer sheet without reading the items, uncooperative, practical joker, or defiant individual.

Low Score. Accurate reading of items and instructions.

Lie-Honest
(13 Items)

High Score. Dishonest in test taking, exaggerates positive traits, minimizes deficiencies.

Low Score. Meticulously honest, tendency to exaggerate weaknesses.

Defensive-Open
(22 Items)

High Score. Defensive, does not like to reveal self or personal problems, keeps feelings to self, resists professional help, guarded, does not solicit feedback.

Low Score. Open, accepts help, reveals problems freely, solicits professional help.

Psychic Pain-
Psychic Comfort
(21 Items)

High Score. Psychic pain, emotional, behavioral and physical symptoms of anxiety, dissatisfaction, nervous, tense.

Low Score. Comfort, contentment, relaxed, calm, satisfied, unconcerned, controlled.

Depression-Optimism
(22 Items)

High Score. Depression, fearful of future, regret of the past, feeling of impending doom, suicidal, failure experiences, unhappy.

Low Score. Happiness, optimism, successful, satisfaction, cheerful, energetic.

Self Degradation-
Self Esteem
(22 Items)

High Score. Self degradation, self critical, inferiority feelings, dissatisfaction with self, self depreciating, poor self image, low ego strength, intropunitive.

Low Score. Self esteem, secure, self satisfied, confident, self assured, high self regard.

Dependence-
Self Sufficiency
(20 Items)

High Score. Dependent, inadequate, meek, gullible, follower, acquiescing, submissive, deferent.

Low Score. Self sufficient, independent, assertive, confident, leader, self directing.

Unmotivated-Achieving
(20 Items)

High Score. Unmotivated, underachiever, lazy, procrastinator, unassuming, slothful, irresponsible.

Low Score. Achievement oriented, competitive, aggressive, untiring, recognition seeking, academically oriented, successful, hard working, accomplished.

Social Withdrawal-
Gregariousness
(21 Items)

High Score. Social withdrawal, loner, solitary, avoids interaction and confrontation, schizoid, social avoidance, introverted.

Low Score. Gregarious, sociable, seeks companionship, outgoing, extrovertive, affiliative.

Family Discord-
Family Harmony
(22 Items)

High Score. Family discord, hatred, mutual rejection, dissension and interpersonal conflict.

Low Score. Family harmony, closeness, pride, love, acceptance and unity.

Sexual Immaturity-
Sexual Maturity
[Form A Only]
(24 Items)

High Score. Sexual immaturity, deviant tendencies, sexual anxieties, promiscuity, sexual guilt.

Low Score. Heterosexual maturity, adequacy and satisfaction, and sexual control.

Problem Index, High-
Problem Index, Low
[Form B Only]
(25 Items)

High Score. Possibly severe problems with multiple symptoms—psychotic reactions are possible. Dissatisfaction high. Many areas to explore in interview. See individual items on scoring key.

Low Score. Few problems in areas sampled by test.

Social Deviancy-
Social Conformity
(21 Items)

High Score. Social deviancy, antisocial, criminal behavior, societal conflict, anti-establishment, irresponsible, psychopathic, law breaking, rebellious.

Low Score. Social conformity, law abiding, ethical, socially sensitive, conforming, prosocial attitude.

Impulsiveness-
Self Control
(22 Items)

High Score. Impulsivity, joy seeking, narcissistic, uncontrolled, moody, erratic, changeable, unreliable.

Low Score. Self control, consistent, dependable, reliable, persistent, planful, stable.

Hostility-Kindness
(20 Items)

High Score. Hostility, anger, challenging, aggressiveness, verbally assertive, "eye-for-eye" attitude, threatening, intolerant, violent, vengeful.

Low Score. Friendliness, easy going, accepting, kind, forgiving, cooperative, peaceful.

Insensitivity-
Empathy
(20 Items)

High Score. Cruelty, insensitive, morbid, punitive, calloused, sadistic.

Low Score. Empathy, concern, sensitive to others, kind, considerate, sympathetic.

The manual clearly indicates that while the test is relatively easy to administer, score, and profile, appropriately trained psychologists must interpret the profiles. "Putting this information together in a meaningful way depends on the purposes of the evaluation, the model of human behavior used, and the skill of the examiner in integrating the findings" (Roe, Howell, & Payne, 1975, p. 8).

Technical Aspects

Payne and Roe's (1972) test-retest reliability results are claimed to be better than those of the MMPI and the CPI although the time between test and retest was only two weeks. The estimates of reliability, provided in the administration manual, are: 1) Lie-Honest .83; 2) Defensive-Open .82; 3) Psychic Pain-Psychic Comfort .90; 4) Self Degradation-Self Esteem .79; 5) Dependence-Self Sufficiency .81; 6) Unmotivated-Achieving .87; 7) Social Withdrawal-Gregariousness .90; 8) Family Discord-Family Harmony .91; 9) Sexual Immaturity-Sexual Maturity .84; 10) Social Deviancy-Social Conformity .90; 11) Impulsiveness-Self Control .85; 12) Hostility-Kindness .86; and 13) Insensitivity-Empathy .81.

Concerning validity, the administration manual claims that "face and content validity have been assured by careful test construction procedures. Construct validity has been assured in certain instances and research is continuing on the individual scales" (Roe, Howell, & Payne, 1975, p. 7). When contacted at Diagnostic Specialists Inc., Roe (personal communication, January 15, 1985) indicated that the booklet, *Bipolar Psychological Inventory Studies* (Roe, 1972), served as the technical manual and reported validity studies, summaries of which are also available in Roe (1974).

The construct validity of the BPI was investigated by factor analytic results on prison populations. Gottfredson (1972) found three main factors: the first measured neurotic traits, the second psychopathic tendencies, and the third social withdrawal tendencies. A smaller fourth factor appeared to measure validity. The first three factors are strikingly similar to those of Eysenck's EPQ: Neuroticism, Psychoticism, and Introversion (Eysenck & Eysenck, 1977).

In another factor analytic study, Oldroyd (1975) investigated both the MMPI and the BPI and found BPI scale loadings on three main factors, named by a panel of five psychologists as Intrapsychic Pain, Belligerent, and Social Withdrawal, which were similar to those reported by Gottfredson. Some MMPI scales also loaded on these three factors. Additionally, Oldroyd found two other major factors, Psychoticism and Disowned Problems, which loaded only on the MMPI. Oldroyd suggests that to measure these components, which are important in working with criminal populations, the MMPI be used to supplement the BPI. Finally, Oldroyd found three smaller factors, Sexual Identity, Young Radical, and Lie, for which there were loadings by both MMPI and BPI scales.

According to the manual, "predictive and concurrent validity is also being explored." Studies indicate that the BPI can make important discriminations among various types of prisoners. First-timer prisoners were compared with recidivists on the BPI by Roe (1973). The recidivists were lower on Psychic Pain and higher on Social Withdrawal, Hostility, and Social Deviancy. Roe, Howell, and Payne (1974) compared inmates with and without a juvenile record on the BPI. The juveniles were less motivated, more hostile, and more socially deviant. Roe (1972) found that the same three scales also differentiated inmates with prison infractions from those without infractions. The 23 items that distinguished the two groups constituted an infraction scale, but no further studies have indicated that this scale is useful in discriminating between inmates with high and low infraction records and none have indicated that the scale might be useful in predicting infraction rates.

Roe (1972) found that violent criminals showed less pathology on the Depression, Self Degradation, Unmotivated, Family Discord, Social Deviancy, and Impulsiveness Scales than the nonviolent criminals. No explanation of these results has been offered. Apparently, items have not been set aside to develop a violence scale and no further studies have reported on the successful discrimination of violent and nonviolent criminals.

Single inmates were found more pathological than married ones on the Unmotivated, Sexual Maturity, Social Deviancy, and Defensive Scales (Payne, Howell, & Roe, 1971). Tattooed inmates scored higher than nontattooed on Psychic Pain, Family Discord, Self Degradation, Social Deviancy, Impulsiveness, Hostility, and Depression (Howell, Payne, & Roe, 1971).

These studies suggest that the criminal population can be subcategorized by the BPI. Would different therapies be more effective with different subcategories? Unfortunately, the relevant research, which would vary both type of inmate and type of therapy, has not been conducted.

Can the BPI be used to make predictions of likelihood of criminal behavior? Pryor's (1971) study compared the efficiency of the BPI with the MMPI in distinguishing university students from inmates.

It was found that the MMPI had significant correlations [with being a prison inmate] on seven of its scales, four significant at the .01 level while the Bipolar Personality Inventory had significant correlations on ten of its scales, eight significant at the .01 level. Comparing the Psychopathic Deviate scale of the MMPI with the Social Deviancy scale of the Bipolar Psychological Inventory, both of which are supposed to indicate criminal tendencies, the Psychopathic Deviate scale correlated .55 with incarceration while the Social Deviancy scale correlated .63 with incarceration (Roe, 1972, p. 5).

The power of the BPI to distinguish inmates from students was also the subject of a pilot study by Walters and Roe (1973). Nine of the BPI scales significantly distinguished the students from the inmates, six at the .001 level, one at the .01 level, and two at the .05 level. But, to date, no studies have indicated that the BPI can be used to predict the likelihood of becoming an inmate.

There are few validity studies with noncorrectional populations. Dawkins, Terry, and Dawkins (1980) found users of mental health services more dependent, less motivated, and more socially withdrawn than nonusers. Gibb and Millard (1981) found the BPI did not distinguish frequent aborters from nulliparas. Gibb, Bailey, Lambirth, and Wilson (1983) examined the relationships among high and low use of video games and BPI scales but found that for females only there was a significant correlation between length of time video games were played and scores on Unmotivated. Thus, it would appear that while norms do exist for university students from California and Utah, validity studies do not.

According to Roe (personal communication, January 15, 1985) two validity studies exist for police officers but even after an extended search of the literature these studies could not be located.

Critique

The BPI is a relatively new personality inventory especially designed for criminal populations. Up-to-date and appropriate methods of test construction have been employed in developing the BPI. The scales were carefully selected, rationally developed, and empirically tested. Furthermore, the test is easy to read, administer, score, and interpret. Completely automated computer versions are available. Clients can readily understand the language used to describe high and low scores on the scales.

There are a few studies of the reliability and validity of the BPI but most are written by Roe and the co-authors of the test.

Because the BPI seems to be a worthy test it is to be hoped that the inventory will be investigated in a wide variety of settings and geographical areas. Until such time however, the BPI can only be recommended for correctional and similar settings. Even in such settings the BPI must, because it does not measure psychotic traits, be supplemented with other measures of pathology.

References

This list includes text citations as well as suggested additional reading.

Barnes, M. E., & Van der Veur, F. H. M. (1973). *An evaluation of factors utilized in inmate custody assignments at the Utah State Prison.* Unpublished master's thesis, University of Utah, Salt Lake City.

Dawkins, M. P., Terry, J. A., & Dawkins, M. P. (1980). Personality and life style factors in utilization of mental health services. *Psychological Reports, 46,* 383-386.

Eysenck, H. J., & Eysenck, S. B. G. (1977). *Psychoticism as a dimension of personality.* New York: Crane, Russak, and Co.

Gibb, G. D., Bailey, J. R., Lambirth, T. T., & Wilson, W. P. (1983). Personality differences between high and low electronic video game users. *Journal of Psychology, 114,* 159-165.

Gibb, G. D., & Millard, R. J. (1981). Preliminary findings of personality differences between nulliparas and repeated aborters along the dimensions of locus of control and impulsivity. *Psychological Reports, 49,* 413-414.

Gottfredson, D. K. (1972). *Factor analysis of the Bipolar Psychological Inventory.* Unpublished manuscript.

Howell, R. J., Payne, I. R., & Roe, A. V. (1971). Differences among behavioral variables, personal characteristics, and personality scores of tattooed and nontattooed prison inmates. *Journal of Research in Crime and Delinquency, 8*(1), 33-37.

Leak, G. K. (1980). Effects of highly structured versus nondirective group counseling approaches on personality and behavioral measures of adjustment in incarcerated felons. *Journal of Counseling Psychology, 27*(5), 520-523.

Moss, W. R. (1971). *A comparative study of trait differences among prisoners who were elementary school dropouts, high school dropouts, and high school graduates.* Unpublished master's thesis, Brigham Young University, Provo.

Oldroyd, R. J. (1975). A principal components analysis of the BPI and the MMPI. *Criminal Justice and Behavior, 2*(1), 85-90.

Oldroyd, R. J., Howell, R. J. (1977). Personality, intellectual, and behavioral differences between black, Chicano, and white prison inmates in Utah State Prison. *Psychological Reports, 41,* 187-191.

Payne, I. R., & Roe, A. V. (1972). *The test-retest reliabilities of the Bipolar Psychological Inventory.* Unpublished manuscript.

Payne, I. R., Howell, R. J., & Roe, A. V. (1971). Marital status of prison inmates as a diagnostic index of personal characteristics and personality traits. *Psychological Reports, 28,* 859-862.

Pryor, A. B. (1971). *Relationships of the Minnesota Multiphasic Personality Inventory and the Bipolar Psychological Inventory to each other and to incarceration.* Unpublished doctoral dissertation, University of Utah, Salt Lake City.

Roe, A. V. (1972). *Personality characteristics of violent offenders.* Unpublished manuscript.

Roe, A. V. (1973). *Comparison between first-timers and recidivists on behavioral, personal, and personality characteristics.* Unpublished manuscript.

Roe, A. V. (1974). *The development of the Bipolar Psychological Inventory.* Unpublished doctoral dissertation, Brigham Young University, Provo.

Roe, A. V., Howell, R. J., & Payne, I. R. (1975). *Bipolar Psychological Inventory: Administration manual.* Orem, UT: Diagnostic Specialists Inc.

Roe, A. V., Howell, R. J., & Payne, I. R. (1974). Comparison of prison inmates with and without juvenile records. *Psychological Reports, 34,* 1315-1319.

Walters, J., & Roe, A. V. (1973). *A comparison of university students and prison inmates on the behavior and affect dimensions of the Bipolar Psychological Inventory.* Unpublished manuscript.

John C. Brantley, Ph.D.

Professor of School Psychology, School of Education, The University of North Carolina, Chapel Hill, North Carolina.

BRISTOL SOCIAL ADJUSTMENT GUIDES

D. H. Stott. San Diego, California: Educational and Industrial Testing Service.

Introduction

The Bristol Social Adjustment Guides (BSAG) are designed to detect and assess observable behavior disturbances (maladjustment) in children aged 5 to 16 years within a school setting. The scale comes in two forms, one for boys and one for girls, each containing seven areas: interaction with teacher, school work, games and play, attitudes toward other children, personal ways, physique, and school achievement. Under each area the teacher, psychologist, or other knowledgeable adult marks none or as many of the phrases that apply to the child.

Items are keyed to five temperament dimensions: unforthcomingness, withdrawal, depression, inconsequence, and hostility; and to four associated groupings: peer-maladaptiveness, non-syndromic over-reaction, non-syndromic under-reaction, and neurological symptoms. Except for neurological symptoms, these dimensions are grouped together under the two main scales of the test, Under- and Over-reaction.

According to the test's author the major uses of the scale are: 1) to provide clinicians with a teacher's resport of relative adjustment and maladjustment in school; 2) to provide school counselors and social workers with information about children's adjustment and a means of insight into reasons for learning disabilities; 3) to assess the effects of particular therapies or placement in a special school or class; 4) to train teachers to recognize maladjustment and adopt an objective professional attitude toward "bad" behavior; and 5) to provide a research tool in studies of relationships between maladjustment and other variables.

The author of the BSAG, D. H. Stott, is director of the Center for Educational Disabilities and Professor of Psychology, University of Guelph, Ontario, Canada. The original 1956 Day-School edition was developed from characteristics attributed by teachers to children who were not thriving, not interacting effectively, creating bad situations for themselves, or not acting in their own best interests, together with systematic observations of behavior by trained observers within the classroom and school.

The 1970 revision updates the instrument to deal with more current theoretical constructs such as hyperactivity. An experimental version of 150 items was reduced by statistical and logical means to the 116 items in the final version. The manual states the normative sample consisted of 2,527 children ages 5 to 14 (but with a smaller proportion over 14) taken from a population attending public elementary schools in a fairly large industrial city, an adjoining rural county, and a network of parochial schools throughout Ontario.

The Guides consist of four-page lists of phrases that describe school behavior problems. The protocol states that the object of the Guide is to ". . . give a picture of the child's behavior and to help in the detection of emotional instability." The date, child's name and age, respondent, and school are noted on the record. Instructions direct the user to "Underline in ink the phrases which describe the child's behavior or attitudes over the past month or so. More than one item may be underlined in each paragraph, but do not underline any unless definitely true of the child. Items inappropriate because of age, etc., can be ignored." As an example, under *Talking with Teacher,* there are these alternatives: "can't get a word out of child/overtalkative, tires teacher with constant chatter/chats only when alone with teacher." The 16-page manual presents uses, development, and psychometric characteristics of the Guides.

Practical Applications/Uses

This scale could be useful to a variety of mental health specialists, such as counselors, social workers, and psychologists, both in and outside of school for screening school maladjustment and identifying deviant trait characteristics. An accompanying profile visually illustrates the extent of deviant traits relative to a Canadian normative sample. The Guides are more widely used in Canada than in this country in clinical and research settings and for initial recognition and classification of disturbed child behavior.

In the United States, an innovative computer-based diagnostic and classification system, the MMAC (Westphal, 1983), uses information from a number of tests including the BSAG to arrive at psychological diagnoses and to make prescriptive recommendations (McDermott & Hale, 1982; McDermott, 1980a). As a part of the MMAC procedure the BSAG appears to contribute (together with other measures) to both diagnostic and program decision-making.

Teachers are the best respondents on the BSAG because the items, which are school specific, require intimate knowledge of children. No training is needed for teachers to understand the straightforward questions and the scale is self-administered. Fifteen minutes are needed to answer the questions. Instructions for scoring are adequate, but the procedure is awkward, involving the use of a template over the answer form and the transfer of credits onto a diagnostic scoring form. Scores are then added and raw scores transferred onto a profile displaying T-score and percentile values. Fifteen to twenty minutes are needed to score and interpret the scale.

Psychologists should be able to interpret and report significant findings using the information available in the manual. Users may choose among several levels for interpreting scores: T-score = 80 (97th percentile), T-score = 70 (94th percentile), and T-score = 60 (87th percentile). Brief descriptions of the core syndromes (Unforthcomingness, Withdrawal, Depression, Inconsequence, and Hostility) and the associated groupings are provided as aids to interpretation.

Technical Aspects

The development and standardization procedures for the revised scales are only briefly described in the manual. Questions on the scale are related to the author's theory of maladaptive trait characteristics (Stott, Marston, & Neill, 1975). Logical judgment and nonparametric procedures appear to have been used to select items and assign them to cluster groupings on this version. To demonstrate internal consistency the author compared item assignments between the revised version and the original edition, finding support for some of the original syndromes and identifying new ones. It was concluded that Under- and Over-reactivity, the main types of maladjustment measured by this scale, were manifested in similar behavior over the age range of the sample. Among the comparisons made using syndrome scores, evidence was found for social class and rural-urban differences.

External validation was explored through smaller studies showing relationships between: the number of health problems reported in children and over- and under-reaction scores; increases in over- and under-reaction scores with severity of motor impairment in children; and increases in syndrome scores with progressive numbers of offenses committed by juvenile delinquents (Stott, 1970) and epidemiological predisposition (Stott, 1978).

Studies of internal consistency and construct validity have been conducted by McDermott (1980b; 1981a; 1981b; 1982; 1983; 1984) using data from the normative sample. He concluded that the under- and over-reactive adjustment scales can be used as primary measures of maladjustment across the age ranges for which the BSAG was designed and that the scales are empirically justified.

Critique

Available research suggests that the BSAG's traits have construct validity as well as etiological and prognostic correlates, but the definitive research with the BSAG has been done with normative samples in countries outside the U.S. (Canada [McDermott, 1984] and Great Britain [Buros, 1972; Davis, Butler, & Goldstein, 1972]). Since these are English-speaking populations, use of the BSAG for research and screening purposes in this country can be defended.

Research with limited samples of U. S. children illustrates the construct validity of the BSAG (Hale & Zuckerman, 1981) and suggests that the BSAG may help identify maladaptive behavior among kindergarten children (McDermott & Watkins, 1981). However, the data base identified in the present review is not adequate to support use of the BSAG, by itself, for diagnostic or placement decision-making with U. S. school children, nor is there evidence that it is valid for assessing benefits of therapy or placement in special programs. Definitive external validation with exceptional and pathological populations in this country remains to be done.

References

Buros, O. K., (Ed.). (1972). *The seventh mental measurements yearbook* (p. 22). Highland Park, NJ: The Gryphon Press.

Davis, R., Butler, N. R., & Goldstein, N. (1972). *From birth to seven: Second report of the National Child Development Study.* London: Longman and National Children's Bureau.

Hale, R. L., & Zuckerman, C. (1981). Application of confirmatory factor analysis to verify the construct validity of the Behavior Problem Checklist and the Bristol Social Adjustment Guides. *Educational & Psychological Measurement, 41*(3), 843-850.

McDermott, P. A. (1980a). A systems-actuarial method for the differential diagnosis of handicapped children. *Journal of Special Education, 14*(1), 7-22.

McDermott, P. A. (1980b). Prevalence and constituency of behavioral disturbance taxonomies in the regular school population. *Journal of Abnormal Child Psychology, 8*(4), 523-536.

McDermott, P. A. (1981a). Patterns of disturbance in behaviorally maladjusted children and adolescents. *Journal of Clinical Psychology, 37,* 867-874.

McDermott, P. A. (1981b). The manifestation of problem behavior in ten age groups of Canadian school children. *Canadian Journal of Behavior Science, 13*(4), 310-319.

McDermott, P. A. (1982). Syndromes of social maladaptation among elementary school boys & girls. *Psychology in the Schools, 19,* 281-286.

McDermott, P. A. (1983). A syndromic typology for analyzing school children's disturbed social behavior. *School Psychology Review, 12*(3), 250-259.

McDermott, P. A. (1984). Child behavior disorders by age & sex based on item factoring of the Revised Bristol Guides. *Journal of Abnormal Child Psychology, 12*(1), 15-36.

McDermott, P. A., & Hale, R. L. (1982). Validation of a systems-actuarial computer process for multidimensional classification of child psychopathology. *Journal of Clinical Psychology, 38*(3), 477-486.

McDermott, P. A., & Watkins, M. W. (1981). Dimensions of maladaptive behavior among kindergarten level children. *Behavior Disorders, 1*(1), 11-17.

Stott, D. H. (1970). *Manual for the Bristol Social Adjustment Guides (1970 ed.).* San Diego, CA: Educational and Industrial Testing Service.

Stott, D. H. (1978). Epidemiological indicators of the origins of behavioral disturbance as measured by the Bristol Social Adjustment Guides. *Genetic Psychology Monographs, 97,* 127-159.

Stott, D. H., Marston, N., & Neill, S. J. (1975). *Taxonomy of behavior disturbance.* Toronto: Musson.

Westphal, K. (1983). *Announcement for the MMAC: A computer system for classifying childhood exceptionality and designing IEPs.* Cleveland, OH: The Psychological Corporation Measurement Division.

Jacqueline V. Lerner, Ph.D.

Assistant Professor of Human Development, The Pennsylvania State University, University Park, Pennsylvania.

BURKS' BEHAVIOR RATING SCALES

Harold F. Burks. Los Angeles, California: Western Psychological Services.

Introduction

The Burks' Behavior Rating Scales (BBRS) are intended to measure areas of behavioral problems. There are two versions of the scales, with 110 items in the Grades One-Nine version and 105 items in the Preschool and Kindergarten version. Children are rated by parents or teachers and the items probe many areas of behavioral functioning; the BBRS does not assess the inner experiences of the child. The test is not suitable for the routine screening of groups of children with no obvious difficulties; rather, it is designed for use in the differential diagnosis of children who already are presenting problems. The BBRS is designed to gauge the severity of negative symptoms that children present as seen by outside persons (i.e., teachers and parents). Quantitative judgments are made by the rater indicating the degree to which each behavior is manifested by the child being rated.

The BBRS Grades One-Nine version is comprised of 19 categories of behaviors and the Preschool and Kindergarten version is comprised of 18 categories of behaviors. These categories, which will be described later in this review include such areas as poor physical strength, poor intellectuality, excessive aggressiveness, excessive anxiety, and poor sense of identity.

The author and developer of the scales, Harold F. Burks, received his doctorate in 1955 from The University of Southern California. During the development and standardization of the scales he was a school psychologist. The scales were developed over a four-year period as a preliminary device for identifying problems a child may be presenting. The 110 items were selected from a larger pool of items constructed by the author and used in a previous checklist since 1966. Additional items were chosen after meeting standards of reliability and of content, construct, and predictive validity. The current BBRS were published in 1977.

Development took place by using samples of normal elementary school children referred to guidance departments, disturbed children, educable mentally retarded children, educationally handicapped children, orthopedically handicapped children, and speech- and hearing-impaired children. Items not taken from previously developed checklists had to meet several criteria. First, these items had to distinguish between children in special classes (i.e., for disturbed pupils) and children in regular classrooms. Items were retained only if they showed a significantly greater incidence of high ratings (indicating more disturbance) for educationally handicapped children than for regular class students.

Second, the items were retained only if a high test-retest reliability coefficient was obtained and if they were judged by educational specialists to be descriptive of a specific observable behavior aspect. Last, items were retained if, using factor analytic procedures, they statistically grouped with other items to form meaningful categories of behaviors.

The rating scales for the 110-item Grades One-Nine form and the 105-item Preschool and Kindergarten form consist of a four-page booklet and profile sheet. Raters should know the child in question well, and when teachers are used as raters it is recommended that they observe the child on a daily basis for at least two weeks before rating him or her. If at all possible, ratings should be obtained from both parents and teachers. The child in question need not be present at the time of rating. The scales are designed to measure the degree of severity of behaviors emitted by the child over some length of time. In addition, raters of the child should *not* score the results to avoid a "halo" effect.

Instructions for rating the items are given on the first page of the booklet. Raters are instructed to respond by putting the number of the most appropriate descriptive statement in a box opposite each item. The statements range from 1 ("You have not noticed the behavior at all") to 5 ("You have noticed the behavior to a very large degree").

The items are clear and concise and should not be difficult for raters to understand. Both forms of the BBRS have no subtests but, as mentioned previously, the items group into 19 clusters for the Grades One-Nine form and 18 clusters for the Preschool and Kindergarten form (the Poor Academics cluster is not included in the Preschool and Kindergarten form). Raters mark their responses directly in the question booklet and then ratings are summed for each category and transferred to a profile sheet that lists the categories. A mark is placed on the line next to each category indicating the child's score and the degree of significance of that score. Marks can then be connected for a visual profile.

From factor analytic studies, the categories that have been determined are: excessive self-blame; excessive anxiety; excessive withdrawal; excessive dependency; poor ego strength; poor physical strength; poor coordination; poor intellectuality; poor academics; poor attention; poor impulse control; poor reality contact; poor sense of identity; excessive suffering; poor anger control; excessive sense of persecution; excessive aggressiveness; excessive resistance; and poor social conformity.

Practical Applications/Uses

The BBRS can be administered in a private setting to parents, teachers, clinicians, or guidance counselors who know the particular child well and it should take less than 30 minutes to complete the ratings. This test would be useful for private practitioners, clinicians in mental health settings, junior high school counselors, and school psychologists who wish to describe particular areas of a child's behavior that are problemmatic; however, it should be used in conjunction with other sources of data from people who know the child well (e.g., the child's parents). The BBRS can assist in the differential diagnosis of children who are already experiencing difficulties and should not be used routinely to screen large groups of children who are not presenting problems. The test does not appear to be suitable for adaptation for groups other than those for which it was designed. However, the author notes that the scales may be used to identify personality characteristics in other groups such as visually impaired, deaf, and mentally retarded children. The author has also developed the Burks' Behavior Rating Scales for Organic Brain Dysfunction.

Scoring should be done by someone other than the rater and usually requires less than 30 minutes. Instructions for scoring are clear. Boxes appear in columns to the right of each item where the rating for that item is made. Each column represents a category, and item scores are summed and total scores for each category are placed on the profile sheet. The test can only be scored by hand.

The interpretation of the profile is addressed in the manual. Each category is described in detail with possible causes and manifestations outlined. The meaning of high scores is indicated and possible intervention approaches are discussed. This section is thorough and presents the results of studies using the scales. To make proper use and interpretation of the BBRS, some training in child development and behavior is needed. Users without such training should be advised to consult with a child development specialist (e.g., clinician, therapist, school psychologist) to discuss the results and to make proper interpretations and conclusions.

Technical Aspects

Item reliability for the BBRS Grades One-Nine form was established using 95 disturbed children from grades 1 through 6. These children were rated and rerated after 10 days by their teachers. Significant differences in the ratings from one time to the next were found for a few items, with none being large enough to make a practical difference. Correlation coefficients for all items were between .60 and .83 with the average test-retest correlation coefficient being .705.

For the Preschool and Kindergarten form of the BBRS, 84 kindergarten children were rated and rerated after a 10-day period by their teachers. No significant differences from Time 1 to Time 2 were found for any items. Correlation coefficients for these items ranged between .74 and .96. The fact that relatively high test-retest reliability was found in these studies may present a problem for those users who may want to employ the BBRS over a period of time in order to assess changes in the rated behaviors or problem areas of some children. Because items were selected for high statistical stability, the instrument itself may be biased toward less sensitivity to change than is desirable.

In terms of validity, the items were selected from both clinical observations of children and from evidence in the literature. Extensive use of the scales indicate that they have face validity (i.e., the items make sense to the users). To assess content validity (how well the content of the items of the BBRS samples fit the behaviors about which one wishes to draw conclusions), 22 school psychologists utilized the Grades One-Nine form of the scale and acted as a jury. For the Preschool and Kindergarten form of the scale, a jury of 26 kindergarten teachers judged the appropriateness of each item for measuring child behaviors and assisted in the modification of the scale for those persons using it with young children.

The BBRS Grades One-Nine form has demonstrated its ability to differentiate between groups of referred and non-referred children. Comparisons of the differences in distributions of ratings show that the members of the referred group (153 children) are given significantly higher ratings on the BBRS than are children from regular classrooms (494 children).

To obtain information about the content of the scales the author factor analyzed the category scores derived from a study of 268 students from regular first-through ninth-grade classes. Three groupings emerged from this analysis but the author notes that across all findings from studies done with a variety of samples two streams of pathology emerge: "aggressive-hostile acting-out" conduct versus "neurotic-inhibited-anxious" behavior. Samples used in these studies were 122 primary-age disturbed children, 99 elementary-age disturbed children, 76 seventh- and eighth-grade disturbed children, 205 educable mentally retarded children, 198 educationally handicapped children, 30 orthopedically handicapped children, and 42 speech- and hearing-handicapped children for the Grades One-Nine Scale. For the Preschool and Kindergarten Scale category ratings were factor analyzed for 127 preschool and 337 kindergarten children.

The author of the scales notes that across ages factor patterns are both quantitatively and qualitatively different. For example, he notes that more factors are evident at younger ages and that an aggressive acting-out factor occurs at all ages. In addition, an immature factor is found at the primary age level and disappears at older age levels, and the neurotic factors change dimensions and seem to have different meanings from one age level to another. However, these findings should be accepted as tentative since the exact nature of the analyses performed is vague. It seems that exploratory factor analytic techniques were used with these samples and not the more conclusive hypothesis testing procedures that would have provided a more rigorous assessment of similarities and differences among the samples. In addition, the small sample sizes used in some of the analyses should lead us to be cautious about accepting the stability of parameter estimates for each population and generalizing these results to other populations. It should be noted, however, that the factors emerging from these analyses are similar to those found by other researchers.

Studies evaluating the construct validity of the BBRS (determining if the test measures the qualities it proposes to measure) indicate that children who are rated as having high levels of inner disturbance obtain ratings that indicate high levels of problem behaviors on the BBRS. Research has demonstrated the BBRS has the ability to correctly identify children who are experiencing difficulties. Researchers using the BBRS agree that it is a valuable instrument in screening children who exhibit behaviors that are predictive of future learning problems.

Critique

Overall, the BBRS is a widely employed scale designed for use by parents, teachers, and other professionals to assess children who are presenting problems. Although it should not be used alone for diagnosis, it can be a valuable tool in the differential diagnosis of children with problems when used in conjunction with other souces of information about the child. It can gauge the severity of negative symptoms presented by the child and the profile can point to areas of disturbance that should be the focus of intervention. Research with the BBRS has demonstrated its usefulness with the screening of children with behavior problems. This reviewer would recommend the use of this scale to those professionals who work with problem children and who have a need to ascertain areas of behaviors requiring remediation.

References

This list contains text citations as well as suggested additional reading.

Beilin, H. (1959). Teachers' and clinicians' attitudes toward the behavior problems of children: A reappraisal. *Child Development, 30,* 9-25.

Burks, H. F. (1968). Discipline methods employed by some teachers of neurologically handicapped children. *Psychology in the Schools, 5*(2), 141-145.

Burks, H. F. (1968). *Burks' Behavior Rating Scale for Organic Brain Dysfunction.* Huntington Beach, CA: The Arden Press.

Burks, H. F. (1970). *School Attitude Survey.* Huntington Beach, CA: The Arden Press.

Coleman, A. B. (1966). *School-related attitudes and behavior of parents of achieving adolescents.* Unpublished doctoral dissertation, University of Michigan, Ann Arbor.

Lucero, E. J., & Meyer, B. T. (1951). A behavior rating scale. *Journal of Clinical Psychology, 7,* 250-254.

Patterson, G. R. (1964). An empirical approach to the classification of disturbed children. *Journal of Clinical Psychology, 20,* 326-337.

Quay, H. C. (1963). Some basic considerations in the education of emotionally disturbed children. *Exceptional Children, 30*(1), 27-31.

Quay, H. C., Morse, W. C., & Cutler, R. L. (1966). Personality patterns of pupils in special classes for the emotionally disturbed. *Exceptional Children, 32,* 297-301.

Williams, M. (1968). *A study of structure of intellect factors as determined by the Stanford-Binet and the ratings of kindergarten boys' behavior by parents and teachers on the Burks' Behavior Rating Scale.* Unpublished master's thesis, University of Southern California, Los Angeles.

Marcia D. Horne, Ed.D.

Associate Professor of Education and Special Education Area Chair,
College of Education, The University of Oklahoma, Norman,
Oklahoma.

CALIFORNIA PHONICS SURVEY

Grace M. Brown and Alice B. Cottrell. Palo Alto, California:
Consulting Psychologists Press, Inc.

Introduction

The California Phonics Survey (CPS) is a group-administered test designed to determine the phonics adequacy of students in Grade 7-college. Its five Exercises (subtests) contain a total of 75 items, with each subtest having from 10 to 25 items. There are five choices for each item, including "None" which may be selected when none of the other choices is deemed correct. The first four subtests involve the student attempting to match a spoken stimulus with a printed form. The fifth requires the student to select which, if any, of four printed nonsense syllables represents the oral counterpart of a real word. Both real words and nonsense syllables are used as spoken stimuli and printed choices. According to the manual (Brown & Cottrell, 1963, p. 4) the "five exercises do not measure different kinds of phonic skill; each item contributes to the overall pattern of errors a student may make. The test is divided into five units largely to provide variety in the mode of presentation and to obviate any fatigue." As will be pointed out, however, the subtests do make differing, and sometimes very different, demands on the examinee. The CPS yields a total score that is used to determine the student's general level of phonic proficiency (adequate phonics, some phonic disability, serious phonic disability, gross phonic disability). No norms are provided. The errors are used to develop an individual diagnostic profile.

The CPS was developed by Drs. Grace M. Brown and Alice B. Cottrell. Dr. Brown was the director of the Remedial and Developmental Reading Program at San Francisco City College. Dr. Cottrell held a similar position at Sacramento City College. Apparently the CPS evolved from their experiences in working with college students.

The first version of the CPS appeared in 1954 and over the next 2½ years five other versions were developed. These six versions were administered experimentally to over 1,100 students, ranging in academic level from junior high school to graduate school, and a 90-item prototype was completed in 1956. There is no information as to what specific changes occurred in the test over these years. The final edition, which has 75 items, was copyrighted in 1963, and there have been no revisions since that time. Fifteen items that were usually missed by students with serious phonic inadequacy were eliminated from the prototype. Apparently these deletions were made to provide more convenience in administering the test at any scholastic level within a single class period.

The exercises are as follows:

Exercise 1 (25 items): The examinee attempts to determine which, if any, of the printed choices corresponds to the word or nonsense syllable spoken by the examiner or presented on a tape. Therefore, the ability to make sound-symbol associations is involved in the task. That is, the student must associate an oral stimulus with its printed counterpart. Each oral stimulus is pronounced in isolation three times, and the student is given five seconds to respond. Eleven of the oral stimuli are real words and, although not spelled as it would be, "drout" is also a real word (*drought*). Of these 12 items only *alone* and *through* are possible correct printed choices with the others being *None*. The 13 other oral stimuli are nonsense syllables (e.g., "bal," "salg," and "elbereth"). Twenty of the oral stimuli are monosyllabic, with most containing three or four phonemes. Thus these items should place little strain on short-term memory.

It is assumed by the test constructor that a correct choice involves comparing the component phonemes of the spoken word with the graphemes that appear in the printed choices. However, for over half of the items it is quite possible to arrive at the correct answer or to at least narrow the choice to a 50-50 chance by employing other strategies. Form 1, which is used to arrive at the diagnostic profile, is used to illustrate this point. In five (20%) of the items, none of the four printed choices begins with a grapheme that could represent the first phoneme in the oral stimulus. This assumes that the student differentiates between consonant clusters (e.g., *gl*) and single consonants (*g*) and can make the necessary sound-symbol associations. So without any other phonic knowledge, the student could select the correct answer as being *None*. In nine other items (36%) only one of the four choices begins with a grapheme that could represent the initial phoneme in the spoken stimulus. Therefore, use of this minimal cue would reduce the possibilities to either that choice or *None*. Use of the final grapheme-phoneme correspondence could further delineate the most probably correct response.

On both Forms 1 and 2, the correct response in 16 (64%) of the 25 items is *None*. So an examinee who marked all 25 items as *None* could get almost two-thirds of the items in Exercise 1 "correct." In fact, a student could get 44% of the items "correct" by marking all 75 as *None*. Of course, an alert examiner or scorer could pick this up.

The use of real words in this and the other exercises is probably an advantage for students who are skilled at word recognition and/or spelling, particularly if the word is in their lexicon (mental dictionary).

Exercise 2 (11 items): The student hears a 1-to-3 sentence context that ends with an imaginary name or term (e.g., "gozgab," "Mandarin Mansions") which is repeated in isolation two more times, with a one-second pause between each. The oral stimuli contain 2-5 syllables (only one has 5). Thus the stimuli in Exercise 2 place more demands on short-term memory than do those in Exercise 1. The oral context in 8 of the 11 items is of little, if any, value as an aid to recall.

Two items could be answered correctly by using only the initial sound-symbol associative and one other could be reduced to a 50-50 chance. For five (45%) of the items, the correct response is *None*.

Exercise 3 (10 items): Ten real words are used as the oral stimuli, with each word pronounced in isolation three times with a one-second interval between each. These oral stimuli on Form 1 range from a one-syllable word ("dirge") to four-syllable words (e.g., preservation), with eight being comprised of either three or four syllables. The printed forms and meanings of these oral stimuli (e.g., "disparate," "importune") are less apt to be known to students, especially younger students; therefore Exercise 3 appears to be more difficult than Exercises 1 and 2.

Use of the initial phoneme-grapheme relationship will reduce the odds of a correct choice to 50-50 for three items and additional use of the final symbol-sound association will do likewise for two other items. The correct answer to six of the items is *None*.

Exercise 4 (14 items): According to the manual, the task in each item is "to select the printed response that rhymes with the whole sound of the spoken stimulus words." It should be realized, however, that "rhyme" in this subtest means something different than the commonly understood definition. In this exercise, two words rhyme if they differ *only* in their initial phonemes or syllable. Thus "liver" does not rhyme with *silver*, but does with *sliver*; and "meet" does not rhyme with *seats*. The student must disregard the spellings of the printed stimuli (real words and a few nonsense syllables are used).

Some items (e.g., tree -she, who -do) appear to be easier than others. For example, "friction" rhymes with "diction" and not "section" (particularly for some dialect speakers), and "hauling" does not rhyme with "railing" (the key to the latter appears to be in making the correct symbol-sound association for *ai* or in realizing that /au/ cannot be represented by *ai*).

Unlike the first three exercises, the initial symbol-sound association is useless in making a choice. Chance correct choices are also less apt to occur, and *None* is the correct choice for only two items.

Exercise 5 (15 items): This subtest not only places considerably different demands on the student, but probably the most difficult. The skills required to perform correctly more closely approximate the decoding aspects of reading, whereas the other exercises require tasks that are related more closely to spelling ability. In each item there are four printed nonsense syllables. The task is to select which, if any, of these choices (there are 2 possible correct choices for Item 70) represents the sound of a real word (i.e., although spelled differently it can be pronounced the same way as a real word). Thus the task not only involves skills and processing similar to that required by decoding a real word which is not recognized immediately, but also requires subjects to "overlook" or "override" what they know about how these words are really spelled. It also requires that the spoken form of the real word is in the students' lexicon. (All of the choices that make real words are likely to be in the lexicons of the age group for whom the test is intended.) Examples of correct choices are *wawk* (walk), *phurst* (first), *knessed* (nest), and *celphesh* (selfish).

Some of the items may cause problems for various reasons. For example, certain dialect speakers may choose *exter* as being "extra" or *probablem* as "problem" when the correct answers are *None*. Not knowing that a double consonant marks the preceding single vowel as having its short sound could lead the student to incorrectly selecting *statted*, *nottess*, *unnit*, and *peppal* as representing real words. Similarly, the student could have to apply the final silent *e* generalization and know that a single vowel letter followed by a single consonant other than *r* usually represents its long sound to rule out such choices as *skipe* and *flate*.

A student could use an analogy strategy to arrive at the correct response rather than have to decode the printed stimulus completely as the authors assume. For instance, *wawk* could be chosen because the student recognizes that it is similar to *hawk*, and therefore deletes the *h*, makes the correct symbol-sound association for *w*, and blends it with /auk/ to obtain "walk." A similar strategy could be employed with phurst-burst, naim-maim, and knessed-dressed.

In order to completely decode the 11 choices that represent real words, a student would have to be able to make the following symbol-sound associations (the numbers in parentheses indicate the times the element appears more than once): *b, c* = /k/, *c* = /s/ (2), *d, k* (2), *l* (3), *m* (2), *n* (2), *p* (2), *r, ss* (2), *w; sh, ph* = /f/ (3), *wr* = /r/ (2), *kn* = /n/, *cks* = /ks/, *st; a* = /ă/ (2) ,*e* = /ĕ/ (4), *i* = /ĭ/ (3), *u* = /ŭ/, *u-e* = /ōo/, *ur* = /er/ (2), *er* = /er/, *aw* = /au/, *oo* = /ōo/ or /ū/, *ai* = /ā/, *ee* = /ē/; *sion* = /shun/. Few, if any, of these symbol-sound associations should cause a problem for students in Grade 7 or above, except perhaps for severely disabled readers.

The test responses may be made directly in the test booklet, on a SCOREZE (when the top sheet is removed, the bottom sheet provides an analysis of the student's responses), or on an IBM Answer Sheet.

There are two forms of the CPS, but only Form 1 can be used to develop an individual diagnostic profile. Form 2 is to be used for retesting. The same test booklets are used for both forms, but the same oral stimuli are not used for all of the items on Exercises 1-4. Nine of the oral stimuli in Exercise 1 are the same in both forms, five in Exercise 2, three in Exercise 3, and five in Exercise 4 (although the same rhyming elements appear in 10 of the 14 items on both forms). Exercise 5 is exactly the same on both forms. Therefore almost half of the 75 items are exactly the same on both forms. This is bound to influence any test-retest reliability coefficient as well as test-retest results.

A correlation of .92 between the two forms is reported for 94 eighth-graders, but this was based on one of the earlier 90-item editions. The manual also reports a correlation of .99 between a 90-item edition and the 75-item edition. This correlation may be spurious, however, because it was based on simply deleting 15 items from the 90-item test.

Practical Applications/Uses

Despite its claims as a diagnostic test, the CPS would better serve as a screening instrument. When seeking to determine if phonic disability may be contributing to weak spelling ability, only Exercises 1-3, and perhaps 4, really need to be given. When seeking to screen for possible decoding problems in reading, only Exercise 5 needs to be used. In such cases, clinical judgment would have to serve in evaluating a student's performance.

The CPS is a group-administered test that requires little expertise to administer if the accompanying taped administration directions are used. Otherwise, for Exercises 1-4 the examiner must be able to decode the nonsense syllables accurately, to recognize the real-word stimuli presented in the manual, and to enunciate these stimuli clearly. Cues to the pronunciation of many of the nonsense syllables are given in the manual. Rhyming words are provided (*bal* rhymes with *Hal*), as are diacritical marks (rŏg) and syllabication and accenting (el'ber·eth'). Most of the possibly less familiar real words are partially syllabicated and accented (hos'pitable, adven'turous). Unless the examiner knows the pronunciations of some of these words, such cues are of little help (e.g., dis'parate, adventi'tious) and may even be misleading (previ'sion in which *e* may represent /e/ or /ĭ/ depending primarily on regional dialect and not /ĕ/ as suggested by the syllabication, and the first *i* represents its short and not its long sound as suggested by the syllabication). Interestingly *sciatica* is accompanied by an incomplete pronunciation guide (si·at'-ika). Apparently the authors had some concern about the word recognition ability of some examiners. The other directions in the manual are clear, and should not pose any problems.

The quality of and enunciation of the male voice on the tape is generally good, but at times another voice in the background gives an echo quality.

Although the test is not timed, it should take about 45 minutes to administer. The taped directions take 38 minutes.

The means by which the CPS is scored to determine into which of four general categories the student's phonic ability falls will depend on the answer form used. If the answers are made in the test booklet, the answer key in the manual must be employed. If a SCOREZE is used, the scoring is relatively simple because the examiner only needs to count the number of items in which the response falls in the circle. Use of a separate answer sheet allows for machine-scoring or use of a heavy-gauge plastic overlay. Obviously, the machine-scoring is fastest, followed by use of the SCOREZE, overlay, and answer key. Similar scoring procedures can be used in developing the individual diagnostic profiles.

Four levels of general phonic adequacy are defined by the total raw score on the CPS: 1) 70 to 75 = adequate phonic ability, 2) 58 to 69 = some phonic disability, 3) 46 to 57 = serious phonic difficulty, and, 4) 0 to 45 = gross phonic disability.

According to the manual (pp. 17-19), students in the top group "can profit by most developmental reading courses"; those in the second group have "enough phonic disability to affect their spelling, and perhaps their speed of reading comprehension" but they may improve noticeably in spelling "once their specific phonics misconceptions are cleared up"; pupils in the third group generally have "considerable difficulty with phonics, probably to the extent of weakening their reading and writing skills"; those in the lowest group have "gross disability in all areas of phonics, which is likely to be accompanied by serious impairment of skill in reading and writing". Students in the two lowest groups will require "intensive and systematic retraining in phonics . . . before any significant improvement can be expected in reading, spelling, composition, or mechanics of English." The implication of such statements is that weak phonic ability or marked phonic disability is the cause—or at least a major cause—of students' low performance in the language arts. Although this may be the case for some students, such claims must be examined closely, especially when they are made in reference to junior high-school, senior high-school, and college students. The claims rest on three unproven assumptions: 1) that the four categories accurately and reliably differentiate among four levels of phonic ability, 2) that the CPS measures the skills actually needed for encoding and decoding words, and 3) that the CPS reliably identifies the specific phonic weaknesses of individuals.

Differentiation among levels of phonic ability depends heavily on the use of accurate and reliable cutoff scores. The CPS cutoff scores were established by using a very unusual procedure. In 1956, a 90-item edition of the CPS was administered to 1,652 college freshmen. According to the manual (p. 6), "In order to determine the extent of phonic disability in the population sampled, the cutting score of 80 was established on the basis of 2.7 standard errors of measurement" by subtracting 9.99 (2.7 x 3.7) from the maximum possible score (90). "For those with adequate phonic ability, ten points below a perfect score of 90 would occur only four times in 1,000 trials. All students scoring 80 and below were thus assumed to have some phonic disability". Why 80 instead of 79 was used as the cutting score is not clear because 80 would seem to fall within 2.7 SE_Ms of 90. Even more perplexing is the footnote that reveals the "scoring formula then used was the number right minus one-fourth of the number wrong. Ten points below a perfect score indicated eight actual errors for those who answered all ninety items" (p. 6). Exactly how use of statistical probability can be used to define phonic adequacy is not clear. But these fears may be moot because it seems that such a procedure was not used in establishing the cutoff points for the final 75-item edition.

"In 1958, the ninety-items phonics survey was published in a research edition. A diagnostic cutting score of two standard errors of measurement below the top was determined on the basis of testing hundreds of students (ranging in age from eight to sixty years), both in the classroom and individually. This top range identified students whose phonic skills were adequate" (p. 8). According to this criterion, those who score between 84 and 90 have adequate phonic ability. Exactly how this was accomplished or determined is not revealed, and no data are provided. A rather confusing footnote is given to "clarify" the distinction between *survey* and *diagnostic* cutting scores: "The *survey* cutting score marks the point below which there is a certainty of phonic disability. The *diagnostic* cutting score is set somewhat higher; scores below this point may include some students with merely the *likelihood* of phonic disability" (p. 8). Thus it would appear that students with a score of 79 certainly have a phonic disability, but some students who score below 83 only have the *likelihood* of a phonic disability. Somehow this logic does not make sense.

Apparently the SE_M also changed to 3.0—at least for the top group—because use of a "2 standard-errors of measurement" criterion resulted in a range of from 84 to 90 raw score points. (A SE_M of 3.0 is inferred from the data in Tabel 5, but SE_M is not reported in the manual.)

The manual does state that "Another cutting score, six standard errors of measurement from the top, distinguished between those with slight but real phonic disability and those seriously handicapped for reading and writing" (p. 8). Because this cutoff point is a raw score of 70, the SE_M must have been less than 3.0 because 90-(6 x 3) = 72.

Some data indicate a correspondence between the four "diagnostic groupings for phonics" and scores on standardized reading and spelling tests. Apart from the fact that the criterion used to establish the lowest two groups differs from what the manual suggests was done in establishing these categories, there is not real evidence of any cause-effect relationship.

"Diagnostic cutting scores, based on the same criterion used for the research edition (see p. 8), were adjusted to the seventy-five item test: i.e., within two standard errors of measurement from the top, 70-75; between six and two standard errors of measurement from the top, 58-69; between ten and six standard errors of measurement from the top, 46-57; and ten or more standard errors of measurement from the top, 45 and below" (pp. 8-9). What is the justification for eliminating 15 items that were "usually missed only by students with serious phonic inadequacy"—apparently ones that most students found easy—and still maintaining a "2 SE_M" criterion. No standard errors of measurement are reported, but either they differed from phonic level to phonic level or computation errors were made. Whereas the standard error of measurement for the two top groups apparently approximated 2.5 (e.g., 75-70 = 5; 5 ÷ 2 = 2.5 SE_M) it was apparently closer to 3.0 for the bottom group (75-45 = 30; 30 ÷ 10 = 3). Use of the standard error of measurement as establishing a cutoff score assumes, probably incorrectly, that the distribution of scores obtained by the "norming" sample (whoever they were) approximates that of the groups who take the CPS.

The SE_M is normally employed to estimate the range within which a student's real score lies (a measure of reliability) by adding and subtracting a SE_M to and from the obtained score. Thus if the SE_M were 2.5 and students correctly answered 67 items (a correction formula for guessing was not used in the 75-item version of the CPS) the odds are 2 to 1 that their true scores lie between 64.5 and 69.5 (plus and minus 1 SE_M) and 19 to 1 that it is between 62 and 72 (plus and minus 2 SE_Ms). Given the fact that the range of scores in the "phonics adequate" group is 70 to 75 and that in the "some phonics disability" group is from 58-69, it becomes apparent that the cutoff points are not as definitive as suggested. There is a high degree of probability that those scoring at the lower range of the top group and at the upper range of the second group could have their classifications reversed on another testing.

Let us now turn to the assumption that using the student's incorrect choices allows one to make a useful diagnosis of phonic problems. According to the manual, the incorrect choices may be used to plot a profile which "will often uncover previously undetected phonic deficiencies which could interfere with the student's later academic achievement. It will also indicate the type and extent of remedial work which might prove helpful in individual cases" (p. 18). The student's incorrect responses are classified into one or more of eight diagnostic categories. Not all incorrect choices have diagnostic significance, and eight incorrect choices are classified in more than one category. Placement is reportedly based on "an analysis of the specific misreadings made when the test was administered individually" (p. 19). No data regarding this statement are provided.

If a student's number of errors in one of the categories falls above the chance number of errors as indicated on the profile chart, "the likelihood is great that the student's silent reading is being contaminated by errors of a similar nature" (p. 19). No data are provided to back this claim. Although the total number of possible incorrect choices in each category range from 15 to 30 (more than one of the choices in a test item may be an incorrect choice of diagnostic significance), the "safe number of errors" range from 1 to 2. All that the manual reveals about these is that they were determined by "individual follow-ups of the actual reading patterns of students who had been tested, and . . . by analysis of the errors made by students whose total rights score was 70 or above" (p. 19). No other explanation is given.

The diagnostic profile chart also indicates for each category a maximum number of errors which students rarely exceed. Although it is not clear, it appears that if one considers the "safe zone" and the likely maximum error scores, the possible range of errors in diagnostic categories range from 4 to 7 (3 to 9 or 2 to 8, 2 to 5 or 1 to 4). This is somewhat surprising because the number of test items that contain an incorrect choice, which is designated as falling within a particular "diagnostic category," range from 11 to 20. The range of possible choices is even greater—14 to 30. If my interpretation is correct, a "diagnoses" based on so few items is open to question. Each of the diagnostic categories presented in the manual (pp. 21-23) is discussed below.

IA Long-Short Vowel Confusion (16 test items containing a total of 20 possible choices): "Errors in this category indicate confusion with regard to the rules for the pronunciation of long and short vowels." For example, if the printed choice *lick* is selected as matching the spoken word "like," it is assumed that the student incorrectly decoded the *i* in *lick* as having its long rather than short sound. This assumption does not recognize the possibility that the student selected *lick* because of an overreliance on the initial elements in words (*lick* is the only choice beginning with *l*). If the student selects *None*, even though one of the other four choices for that item is the correct response, the error is classified as a long-short vowel confusion. Thus if in response to the spoken stimulus "prane," the student selects *pran* or *None* for Item 9, either error is classified or considered to be a long-short vowel confusion. Surely there might be different reasons why a student might select one of the choices over the other, rather than *prane*.

IB Other Vowel Errors (17 test items containing a total of 20 possible choices): "Errors in this category indicate confusion with regard to any other vowel sounds, and the correct pronunciation of vowel digraphs." (Use of the term "pronunciation" is unfortunate. Almost all students produce these sounds, but they may have trouble making the appropriate sound/symbol association.) "Other vowel" errors involve such things as selecting *bole* as matching "bal," *swale* for "sarl," *None* rather than *clupe* for "cloop," *wood-peck* for "would-peck" (on which vowel(s) did the student err?), *desperate* for "disparat;" picking either *dibe, lib,* or *None* rather than *meb* as rhyming with "reb;" or opting for *None* when *wawk* represents the sound of a real word.

IIA Consonants-Confusion with Blends and Digraphs (14 test items containing 24 possibilities): "Errors in this category indicate ignorance of the correct pronunciation of consonant digraphs or of consonant blends, and confusion between single consonants and consonant blends." Examples of consonant errors include selecting *clear* to match "cheer," or *breev* or *None* rather than *briph* to match "briff," or *cyclic* or *physic* to match "psychic" when none of the printed choices do so, or *chulp, clooph,* or *croop* (b   ot *None*) rather than *clupe* to match "cloop."

IIB Consonant-Vowel Rev   ls (12 test items containing 15 possible choices): Consonant-vowel reversals indicate "a tendency to transpose vowels and consonants and therefore to pronounce the word incorrectly, by reversing the letter sounds." Thus *trit* is chosen to match "tirt" and *perseveration* to match "preservation" or, *None* is chosen in response to "liver," because one of the printed choices (*sliver*) does rhyme with "liver." Some of the error choices classified as consonant-vowel reversals do not contain the same vowel as the oral stimuli (e.g., *gulb*-"glab," *dirt*-"druut").

III. *Configuration* (22 test items containing 30 possible error choices): Configurative errors "occur because the student, instead of perceiving the printed letter combination accurately, guesses the answer on the basis of general appearance or configuration." There are two types of configuration errors. According to the manual, in Exercises 1-4, in which a letter combination must be matched to a spoken word, students may be (and often are) influenced in their choice by the sound of the word they just heard. What is meant by this is not clear and the provided examples do little to clarify it (*physic* for "psychic", *undermined* for "undetermined"). In Exercise 5 the authors claim that the silent exercise where examinees must identify a letter combination having the sound—though not the spelling—of a real word, can be influenced only by the configuration of the nonsense word. Thus they state that *instrution* may be identified from its appearance as having the sound of the word *instruction*. An equally plausible interpretation is that the student is not paying close enough attention to the letters and their sequence, and/or to the phonemes and their sequence. And, perhaps because we define "configuration" differently, it is difficult to understand why, for example, the choice of the printed word *whit* is considered to have the same configuration as would the printed form of the spoken stimulus *with*.

In Exercise 5, it appears that the incorrect printed words, which are designated as "configuration" errors, are those nonsense syllables which would be a real word if spelled correctly (e.g., *knid* = kind). Such designations apparently are based on the questionable assumption that the student has a configuration of the real word in mind, and attempts to match it with one of the printed choices. Among the reasons why certain nonsense syllables are chosen is poor spelling ability (e.g., *afriad* is chosen because the student thinks it spells "afraid").

IV. *Endings* (15 test items containing 20 possible error choices): "Ending" errors involve "misreading of suffixes." These include selecting *Easy-slimmer* for "Easy-slimming" in Exercise 2; *statistics* for "sadistic" in Exercise 3; or *seats, greeted,* or *eater* as rhyming with "meet" in Exercise 4.

The manual claims that "the diagnostic value of this category is that it identifies individuals who, in silent reading, distort or ignore the syntactically-significant endings of words. This may have a curious effect on both reading comprehension and reading rhythm". However, making such errors on words in isolation does not necessarily mean that they also will be made in context where semantic and syntactic cues are available for monitoring one's reading. Furthermore it is difficult to believe that many seventh-graders, let alone college students, would have difficulty encoding or decoding the suffixes sampled by this subtest (e.g., *ing, er, ity, y, ish, able, ed, s, ev, ful, ly*).

V. *Negatives and Opposites; Sight Words* (11 test items containing 20 possible error choices): Two error groups are combined in this category. Included in the Negative and Opposites subcategory are such errors as selecting *without* for "with." Errors in the Sight Words subcategory include selecting *thought, tough,* or *None* for "through." These two subcategories were combined "because of the small number of items in each, and because in both categories, an apparently minor error in word perception can produce a major error in the perception of meaning."

Although not indicated in the manual, an analysis of the items indicates that five items (5 possible error choices) could be classified as the Negative-Opposites subcategory, and four items (10 possible error choices) could be classified in the Sight Words subcategory. The classification of two items (5 possible error choices) would depend on the choice made. For instance choosing *don't* for "didn't" would be a "sight word" error; *did* for "didn't" a "negative" error. The only "negative-opposite" markers that sampled are *n't, un,* (oral stimuli) *in,* and *mis* (printed stimuli). The only "sight words" sampled are "ever," "on," and "didn't" (oral stimuli only); alone, through (oral and printed stimuli). It is of interest to note that the correct answer to 9 of the 11 test items is *None.*

The manual states "the confusion with sight words can be interpreted as a residue from early reading patterns; unfortunately these are often so deeply embedded as to be extremely difficult to overcome." Based on the "sight words" actually sampled, it would be very difficult for this reviewer to accept such an interpretation.

The manual also states "the confusion with regard to negatives, and the tendency to substitute a word of opposite meaning for the correct choice (as in adding or removing a prefix), is far less easy to understand. Undoubtedly there is a psychological causation, but its nature is by no means clear, although some kind of negativism would seem to be involved." Given the task demands and the range of possible reasons for errors, it is very difficult to accept such a psychoanalytic interpretation. Could making between one and four errors in this category possible mean that the student needs psychological help in order to acquire the basic sight words sampled?

VI. Rigidity (14 test items containing 14 possible error choices): Rigidity errors "seem to occur when the student is some way too tied to the visual appearance of words." According to the manual, although students may have specific instructions, they cannot dissociate auditory from visual associations in the perception of words. Thus errors are made because they rely too heavily on configuration clues and are lost without them. Although the authors claim that these errors were the only ones the students made and thus suggested the presence of "some factor other than over-reliance on configurational clues", (the exact nature of the rigidity factor remains ambiguous), the category was retained because it "shows a relationship to silent-reading comprehension." No data regarding these claims are provided.

Apparently the assumption of "rigidity" is based primarily on the choice of *None* rather than selecting the printed word that rhymes with the oral stimuli (3 items) or of selecting a nonsense syllable which when decoded has the sound of a real word (11 items). But errors on these test items could occur for other reasons. For example, a student who could not make the correct symbol-sound associations for *ph* = /f/ and *wr* = /r/ could reject four correct choices (*phurst, celphish, wrooph, wrib*). This alone could cause the student to exceed the "safe limit" of two.

Distribution of Test Items for a Diagnostic Category: It also is important to note how many classified errors occur within particular subtests. Despite the claim to the contrary, the subtests do place differing demands on the examinee. An examination of the stimuli will also suggest what specific skills are probably involved in obtaining the correct answer or why the student possibly erred. For example, the following are the number of test items in which long-short vowel confusion errors can occur in each subtest: Exercise 1 = 5, Exercise 4 = 3, Exercise 5 = 8. In Exercise 1 in which the task is to match the spoken stimulus with its printed counterpart, the oral stimuli-correct answer patterns are "like"-*None* (*lick* is a printed choice); "rog"-*rog*; "prane"-*prane* (*pran* is also a printed choice); "threep"-*None* (*trep* is a printed choice); and "frol"-*None*. Even when there are alternative printed choices to the correct printed choice, a response of *None* is classified as a long-short vowel confusion. That there are differences among the stimuli and choices in these is apparent. In Exercise 4 in which the task is to match "rhyming words" the oral stimulus-correct response patterns are "ban"-*than* (incorrect vowel choice = *pane*); "hoping"-*sloping* (incorrect vowel choices = *dropping* or *None*); and "head" = *shed* (incorrect vowel choices = *deed* or *None*). In Exercise 5, which requires the ability to decode printed nonsense words and determine which resulting pronunciations are the same as real words the correct choices are *wawk* (*skipe* but not *chass* is an incorrect vowel choice), *phurst* (*statted* but not *None* is an incorrect vowel choice), *None* (*flate* and *jeelo* are incorrect vowel choices); *naim* (*shope* is an incorrect vowel choice, but *dist* [diced] or *None* is not); *cimpul* (*notiss* is an incorrect vowel choice, *None* is not), *eckskursion* (*unnit* is an incorrect vowel choice, *None* is not), *None* (*stricking* is an incorrect vowel choice, *none* is not); *celphish* (*spile* is an incorrect vowel choice, but *physices* or *None* is not).

The distribution of diagnostic error items is shown in Table 1.

Classification of Responses as a Particular Type of Error: There is some inconsistency as to which incorrect choices are classified as indicating a particular type of error. For example, in the long-short vowel confusion category the choice of *None* when one of the four choices does match the oral stimulus is considered to be a long-short vowel error in Exercises 1 and 4, but in Exercise 5 a choice of *None* is not. Other questions, such as why isn't *chass* classified as a long-short vowel confusion (chase) when *statted* is, could also be raised. Isn't it possible that the student incorrectly decodes *wawk* as "wake" and in doing so is "commiting a vowel error"? Is it assumed that *tulk* is decoded as "talk" and is therefore classified an "other vowel error."

Some of the responses also may be chosen "correctly" for reasons other than those implied by the classification. For instance, *rog* could be selected in response to "rog" only because it is the only choice beginning with *r*, rather than because the student made the appropriate vowel sound-symbol association. Or, students could select *dared* because they can spell the word, or could reject all of the four printed choices for "on" because none of them spell "on." Why is not *warg* classified as C-V reversal on the assumption that *wrag* = "rag" and would therefore represent a real word? The same is true for turble (trouble = trouble).

The manual states that "even a very few errors will usually be significant. This is especially likely to be true if the errors are all of the same type (endings, sight words, blends, etc.) *and* if the student is well-read and in good academic standing." The diagnostic significance of "a very few errors" has already been addressed. Why would anyone want to measure the phonic ability of a student who is "well read" (the manual suggests that reading will "cure" the phonic

Table 1

Test Item Distribution

Diagnostic Category	Exercise				
	1	2	3	4	5
IA	5	0	0	3	8
IB	6	1	1	3	6
IIA	9	3	2	0	0
IIB	8	1	2	1	0
III	4	2	5	3	8
IV	0	4	4	6	1
V	6	2	3	0	0
VI	0	0	0	3	11

Possible Choices

Diagnostic Category	Exercise				
	1	2	3	4	5
IA	6	0	0	5	9
IB	6	1	1	6	6
IIA	16	5	3	0	0
III	4	2	8	4	0
IV	0	5	4	10	12
V	15	2	3	0	1
VI	0	0	0	3	11

problems) and in "good academic standing"? In fact, why would one want to measure the phonic ability of any reader except those in Grades 7-16 who are severely disabled.

The manual goes on to indicate that the lower the student's levels of verbal and academic achievement, "the less importance probably should be attached to a few scattered errors," that ten errors by a student of high verbal ability and good academic standing are more apt to imply a real phonic disability than the same amount of errors by a student with low academic standing, poor vocabulary, and little reading experience. The authors claim that the former may have obtained a high score because of "an extensive sight vocabulary and a facility for deriving right answers by 'thinking up' real words" containing some of the same elements as nonsense syllables, whereas the latter "may be less attributable to ignorance of phonic rules, in which he has a good grounding, than to lack of practice in reading" which causes him to not be "sufficiently alert to differences in letter arrangement." Apparently such a student needs to read more, which will probably improve his phonics score. "This will not occur with the first type of student". Is one to interpret this to mean that bright students should not use a compare-contrast or analogy strategy as an aid to word recognition? Why are less intelligent/verbal students more likely than the bright/verbal student to be "well grounded" in phonic rules but not be applying them? If simply "reading more" is the treatment of choice, why bother giving the CPS?

Similar questions could be raised about a number of other statements in the Interpretation of Results section of the CPS Manual, especially in regard to interpreting errors in the diagnostic categories.

Technical Aspects

Four types of validity are claimed for the CPS: construct validity, content validity, concurrent validity, and predictive validity. According to the manual (p. 5) the CPS was initially developed based on the authors' assumption that the lack of some students' competence in recognition of the written representation of sounds in the English language and resulting inability to read aloud with accuracy and meaning affected their ability to extract meaning from their silent reading. In spite of their apparent, adequate intelligence and motivation, these students failed to improve. This suggests that college students who are weak in making symbol-sound associations are likely to be weak in reading comprehension and implies that overcoming such weaknesses will result in improved reading comprehension. There is no evidence provided in the manual to substantiate such claims. In addition it is much more likely that variables other than "weak phonic skills" are contributing to any reading comprehension problems encountered by the vast majority of 12- to 18-year-old students.

A correlation of .98 is reported between the results obtained by 64 junior college students on a group and an individual test of phonic ability. This is used as a rationale for using a group test rather than testing individually. Such an assumption is based on correlational data and is not justified. Similarly, reporting correlations between various editions of the CPS and silent reading comprehension (.54, .63, .64, .65, .67) or verbal aptitude (.32, .35, .51, .62, .65). Correlations do not indicate a "cause-effect" relationship; and even if they did, the direction of that relationship would not be indicative (i.e., Which is the cause? Which is the effect?).

When the CPS scores of 1,652 college freshmen are divided into 11 levels of phonics ability, the average reading comprehension score decreases with each lower level of phonic ability (the standard deviations also decrease indicating less variability in scores). These data are also offered as evidence of the relationship between phonic ability and reading comprehension. But the range of comprehension scores within each level of phonic ability suggests that the relationship may not be as strong as implied. For instance, use of 1 standard deviation indicates the range of scores of 68% of the testees. Using the data from Figure 1 in the manual one finds that the reading comprehension scores of those in the top phonics group (CPS scores 84-90) ranged from 55 to 75, in the second level (CPS scores 77-83) from 49-67, and in the third group (CPS scores 70-76) from 45-61. Obviously, there was a great deal of overlap. Data in Figure 2 indicate a wide range of CPS scores when the college freshmen were divided into 3 levels of English instruction. For example in the State College sample, the CPS scores in the upper group ranged from 69 to 90, with regular group from 48 to 90, and in the remedial group from 28 to 90. These ranges of scores also indicate that high CPS scorers are not necessarily good at reading comprehension or English, and also that low CPS scorers may be. The manual even states "in the junior high school, some students at even low phonic levels achieved respectable reading scores" (p. 8).

Content Validity: According to the manual (p. 10), the sounds of the vast majority of English words are represented in writing by less than 100 phonograms (a phoneme or combination of phonemes—e.g., *s, sh, tion*), and phonic adequacy may be defined as adequate proficiency in the use of this code. Although the CPS was mainly constructed empirically from the study of students' errors and designed to include the more usual spellings of all the common, English-language speech sounds, it is impossible to tell how well the CPS accomplishes this because the 3,000-word list used by the authors in making their determination was not available to the reviewer. An examination of the CPS, however, reveals that students would have to make almost all of the common symbol-sound associations *if* they had to decode every choice in every test item. The following points should be noted: 1) some of the printed stimuli contain vowels that represent the schwa sound (e.g., *a*lone), are nonphonemic (e.g., *one*), and contain graphemes that represent other than their most common sounds (e.g., ag*a*in) or different sounds in different words (e.g., *s*ciatica, *s*coam); 2) some elements (e.g., 1 = /1/) are sampled much more frequently than others (e.g., *m* = /m/); 3) silent consonants (*wr*) and digraphs (ph = /f/) seem to be "over sampled"; and, 4) students must know that the same grapheme may represent various sounds (e.g., *ed* = / ed/, /t/, or /d/).

Concurrent Validity: The manual (p. 14) claims that the concurrent validity studies indicate that 1) the CPS is "a sound measure of phonic adequacy as defined by individually administered phonics tests"; 2) "phonic adequacy is an important component of scholastic aptitude and intelligence"; and 3) "phonic adequacy is particularly important for successful achievement in various aspects of the language arts."

The authors indicate that 47 seventh-graders were tested individually with 1 of 5 "nationally-recognized phonic diagnostic instruments." A rank order correlation (rho) of .89 is reported, but this appears to be based on the correlation between their CPS scores and their level of phonic ability as ranked by two remedial reading teachers who based their decisions on the "individual test" performance. At least one of the "individual" phonics tests is a group test. Administering a group test to an individual does not make it an "individually administered" test; the task remains the same whether one child or 50 children take the test. The second and third claims are based on correlations, and as such, are open to serious question.

Correlations (.23 to .74) between CPS scores and reading achievement are reported. Data on the relationships between the CPS and spelling and English proficiency are also provided.

Predictive Validity: The CPS scores of 81 eighth-graders were arranged in descending order, split into 3 equal groups, and compared with the students' spelling, English, and reading marks at the end of each semester. In general, these data indicate that the top third of the sample tended to receive the highest grades in school (e.g., 19 received As, 2 received Bs, and 2 received C or below in reading). The reading grades of the lowest third were almost equally distributed (8 received As, 9 received Bs, 10 received Cs). Again, neither phonic ability nor phonic disability seem to predict reading grades particularly well. CPS scores do appear to be better predictors of spelling and English grades. A comparison of high and low achievers on the CPS produced results which can be interpreted similarly.

A test-retest reliability coefficient of .92 is reported for 94 eighth-grade students as are 4 Kuder-Richardson reliability coefficients (measures of internal consistency)—.90, .93, .93, and .89 for four different samples. The standard errors of measurement for each of these samples ranged from 2.50 to 3.06 in raw score units. A split-half correlation coefficient of .88 and a standard error of measurement of 3.70 is also reported (under validity) for the scores of 501 college freshmen.

A Pearson product-moment correlation of .99 between a 90-item and a 75-item version of the CPS also is reported. It should be noted, however, that this extremely high r may be misleading. According to the manual (p. 10), it was "obtained by administering and scoring the 90-item test, then rescoring the sample papers [N = 228] with omission of the fifteen items that were deleted in the final version." There are no reliability data on the 75-item CPS.

Critique

For generally more favorable reviews of the CPS, refer to the review by Thomas E. Culliton in *The Sixth Mental Measurements Yearbook* and a review by Constance M. McCullough in *The Seventh Mental Measurements Yearbook*.

In this reviewer's opinion, as a diagnostic test, the CPS has little to recommend it. At best it could serve as a screening test, but even then the main question would be "Why measure the phonic ability (or whatever else is required by the CPS) of senior high-school and college students?"

References

Brown, G. M., & Cottrell, A. B. (1963). *California Phonics Survey.* Palo Alto, CA: Consulting Psychologists Press, Inc.

Culliton, T. E. (1965). Review of the California Phonics Survey. In O. K. Buros (Ed.), *The sixth mental measurements yearbook* (pp. 1100-1101). Highland Park, NJ: The Gryphon Press.

McCullough, C. M. (1972). Review of the California Phonics Survey. In O. K. Buros (Ed.), *The seventh mental measurements yearbook* (pp. 1109-1110). Highland Park, NJ: The Gryphon Press.

Sheridan P. McCabe, Ph.D.

Associate Professor of Psychology, University of Notre Dame, Notre Dame, Indiana.

CAREER ASSESSMENT INVENTORY

Charles B. Johansson. Minneapolis, Minnesota: NCS Professional Assessment Services.

Introduction

The Career Assessment Inventory (CAI) is a vocational interest inventory patterned after the Strong-Campbell Interest Inventory (SCII) but designed for a subject population that is not intending to pursue education at the college or university level. Rather this inventory is directed toward those who want immediate career entry or business school, technical school, or limited college training. It compares their interests with those of workers in occupations requiring less than a four-year college education. This inventory grew out of the research on the Strong inventory and follows a similar format and pattern. In a sense, it forms a downward extension of the SCII in terms of occupational level.

This test was developed by Charles B. Johansson at the Interpretive Scoring Systems, the publishers of this test as well as one of the primary distributors of the SCII. The preface of the second edition of the CAI manual provides a brief but interesting overview of the origins of this test. While Johansson was an undergraduate and graduate student of David Campbell at the University of Minnesota between 1961 and 1970, he worked on the revisions of the Minnesota Vocational Interest Inventory, one of the early efforts to assess the occupational interests of nonprofessional level workers. In addition, he worked on the revisions of the male and female versions of the Strong Vocational Interest Blank (SVIB) and assisted in the research that eventually resulted in combining the male and female inventories into a single inventory. This background in the role of sex differences in vocational interests has had a substantial impact on the development of the CAI.

In 1972 Dr. Johansson joined the staff of Interpretive Scoring Systems and began a project developing a computer-generated, narrative report produced by the scoring of the SCII. Upon completion of this project in 1973, he turned his attention to the development of an interest inventory for noncollege-bound individuals. The first edition of the CAI appeared in 1975 and was patterned after the SCII in both format and content. It had 6 Theme scales, 22 Basic Interest Scales, and 42 Occupational Scales. In a 1976 update 7 more occupational scales were added. The next edition (1978) had the same General Themes and Basic Interest Scales, but the number of occupational scales was increased to 89. In addition, four new nonoccupational scales were added: a Fine Arts-Mechanical scale that operated somewhat like the older M-F scales; an Occupational Extroversion-Introversion scale similar to the one on the SVIB; an Educational Orientation scale that related to interest in further education; and a Variability of Interest Scale.

The present edition of the CAI, the 1982 edition, is a revision based on the experience of the users of the earlier editions. The number of occupational scales was increased to 91; however, the major change in the test was the development of combined male-female occupational scales. The test has also been translated for use with Spanish- and French-speaking subjects. This translation has been carefully done to preserve the meanings of the items for French- and Spanish-speaking individuals in North America. The test has not been revised for use in other parts of the world.

The test booklet is a very efficiently designed, four-page booklet with the responses marked in the booklet immediately opposite the questions. The booklet and a pencil are all that are required to take the test. The first page contains space for an individual's name, age, sex and identification number. However, other than to identify the results, the requested information is not essential for scoring. The remaining three pages contain the 305 items of the test. These are divided into three sections: Activities, School Subjects, and Occupations. There is a consistent response format over all items and it provides for five response possibilities that range from "like very much" through like "somewhat," "indifferent," "dislike somewhat" to "dislike very much." This consistent format aids in the ease of taking the test. The author (1982) states that the reading level required for adequate comprehension is sixth-grade, although this assertion is not supported by use of a standard measure. The manual also states that the inventory is usually completed in about 30 minutes by most adults. The test can readily be administered in group situations.

The items for this test were written to be relevant for the subjects to whom this test was directed and, at the same time, to sample broadly from a wide range of the world of work. The author was especially sensitive to the role of bias, especially sex bias, in terms of the item content. For example, it was found that items based on activities were less subject to such bias than items involving job titles even when both dealt with the same occupation. The section on Activities, comprised of 151 items, is almost 50% of the inventory; the second section, containing 43 items relating to School Subjects, is 14%; and the final section, made up of 111 items that are job titles, is 36%. The manual points out that approximately 300 items is about the right length for an inventory to yield valid and reliable scales without disrupting the attention span and motivation of the subjects.

Although the manual does not specify the age range for which this test is appropriate, it does appear rather clearly that the test is best used with those who are about to enter the world of work or who are already employed. There is a reference in the manual to the possible utility of the test in 10th or 11th grade to assist in the process of career exploration. The author did administer the test to 6th- and 8th-grade students to evaluate the comprehensibility of the items, but utility of the test itself to such a young age group is questionable.

Practical Applications/Uses

This test is particularly useful in assessing the vocational interests of individuals who fall in the mid-range of ability and who do not plan to continue their academic education beyond high school. The manual asserts that this represents 80% of the work force. For individuals who plan careers that demand college education or require higher levels of management or artistic accomplishment, the SCII would be a more appropriate instrument. For individuals who are at the lowest end of the ability spectrum, their pattern of skills and aptitudes will probably be more important in setting appropriate career goals than will inventoried interests. However, the large majority fall within the scope of the CAI. Counselors in high schools, especially those not primarily dedicated to college preparation, as well as those who do vocational assessment for vocational rehabilitation, will find this a highly relevant and useful inventory. Counselors in technical and vocational training institutes and programs will also find the CAI to be especially valuable in assisting students to arrive at meaningful career plans. This test may have useful applications in the area of personnel selection but more research will be necessary to support this.

This test is designed to provide a comprehensive overview of an individual's occupational interests. This is done in terms of a global overview of one's expressed interests in terms of the General Themes. A more refined approach to content validity is used in terms of the results of the Basic Interest Scales. Finally, an empirically derived pattern of similarities and differences in preferences as compared to the preferences of individuals who are stable and content in their specific occupations is presented. These profiles are supplemented with scores on four nonoccupational scales and by results in terms of response bias to evaluate the adequacy of the patterns obtained. This test will prove to be particularly applicable to those who are entering the world of work for the first time, those who wish to select the most appropriate training program to prepare for such entry, or those who because of disability or other reasons need to change their career.

Although the manual indicates that the test items are pegged at about the sixth-grade reading level, this reviewer has found that frequently individuals who do not read at this level often can successfully complete the CAI. In testing such individuals, however, special care needs to be taken to ascertain that they are comprehending the items. Individuals with problems of literacy or serious visual deficits can often complete the test by having the items read to them. One of the major contributions of this test is the attention that has been paid to the issue of sex bias and steps that were taken to assure its applicability to subjects irrespective of sex. Few interest inventories enjoy this feature.

This test does not require any special training or sophistication for its administration. Once the subject understands the rather simple instructions, it is self administering. Most subjects can complete the inventory without assistance or the need for supervision. In general, adults will complete the test in about 30 minutes. Those accustomed to taking tests or completing inventories will often finish in about twenty minutes. Large group testing can be undertaken without intensive proctoring.

Like many interest inventories of this complexity and scope, this test is not suitable for hand-scoring. There are far too many scales and the presentation of the patterns of scores can be more effectively accomplished with computer scoring. It is necessary to return the answer sheets to the publisher to have them scored. There are three options in this respect: First, one can obtain a profile of the results. In this case, the results are returned printed on an attractive two color form similar to the one used with the SCII. The results include sections for the General Themes, the Basic Interest Scales, and the Occupational Scales, all color-coded according to the themes to which they relate. Both numerical scores and a graphic presentation of the results are presented. Second, a narrative report that both presents the results and a comprehensive interpretation of the results can be ordered. This is a detailed report of approximately 15 pages of single spaced type. It is less attractive than the preprinted form but no less detailed in the scores it reports. Third, rather than mailing in the answer sheets, one can submit the information electronically by use of a microcomputer or terminal with a modem directly to the mainframe computer at Interpretive Scoring Systems and receive the results immediately. Either the profile results or the more detailed narrative report can be obtained in this medium. However, the turn around time on mailed answer sheets is quite good, and in the reviewer's experience rarely did more than seven days elapse between the time the sheet was mailed and the results were in hand.

While the administration of the inventory is extremely simple, the interpretation of the results is not. The complexity of the large array of scores and the various types of interests that this inventory measures demand an informed and well-trained expert for their adequate interpretation and integration. This aspect is not immediately obvious to the user. The lengthy narrative report, which is available from the computer scoring service, is a comprehensive and technically accurate interpretation. However, too frequently the printed page does not do justice to the questions and issues that the subject brings to the testing situation. Such a report would be far more useful with an appropriate guide to assist in its use. The preprinted profile form has a detailed explanation of the results printed on the reverse side and is a masterful presentation of the meaning of the results in general terms, but it falls short of an adequate individualized interpretation. From this reviewer's perspective, justice to the richness of the results provided by this inventory can only be done through the efforts of an interpreter who is well versed in the theory and research of vocational interests and their role in vocational choice and adjustment. The manual does an excellent job of presenting the origin and development of this inventory, but it does not provide much background on the nature and assessment of occupational interests. A counselor who has a good background in vocational psychology and psychological measurement will have little difficulty in using this test well after a thorough reading of the manual. A background in vocational theory is necessary to place in perspective results such as Holland's Themes (the 6 General Occupational Themes), the role of the rationally derived Basic Interest Scales, and the implications of the results of the empirically derived Occupational Scales, especially when there is some discrepancy noted among these scales. For effective vocational counseling the relations between these various approaches to the assessment of interests as well as factors such as abilities, personality traits, and values need to be appropriately understood. In some respects, the CAI is deceptively simple in its efficient and economical presentation of a great deal of complex information.

Technical Aspects

The author of this test has had a considerable amount of experience in the development of interest inventories. He has had direct experience with data files of considerable proportions and has worked in a situation well known for its high standards of technical excellence in the field of interest measurement. The CAI manual suggests that this test grew out of this background and attention in the technical aspects of its development were directed more at such features as freedom from sex bias, the clarity, comprehensibility and internal consistency of the items, and overall efficiency, rather than on matters pertaining to external or predictive validity. Such concerns as predictive validity had already been thoroughly explored in the decades of developmental research that supports the SCII. However, the result of this is that the reader is not entirely satisfied with the treatment rendered issues, such as validity, in the present edition of the manual.

For each of the major sections of the test the approach used was to work with the items in the development of coherent scales modelled on those of the SCII. This technique yields scales with a high degree of internal consistency and have a demonstrated relationship to comparable scales of the SCII. Each of the major category of scales will be discussed individually.

The Administrative Indices were developed in this way. For the Fine Arts-Mechanical scale, a group of males and females who were in the same twelve occupations were selected and their response percentages to each of the test items were compared. Those items that differentiated these two groups were selected for inclusion on the scale. The scale was further refined by item-scale correlations, and the result was 36 items, with 19 in the Fine Arts direction and 17 in the Mechanical direction. For the Occupational Extroversion-Introversion scale, items were correlated with scores for similar scales on other inventories. This resulted in a tentative scale made up of 39 items. Again this scale was further refined by internal consistency and a final scale of 37 items was obtained. The Educational Orientation scale was empirically developed using a group of subjects and dividing them on the basis of their attending college or terminating their education at high school. Items which differentiated these groups were selected. This scale was further refined to eliminate sex bias and 42 items comprise the final scale. The Variability of Interest Scale was constructed from items which evidenced a low intercorrelation. Again only those items which appeared to work equally well for both males and females were retained resulting in a 25 item scale. In the case of all of these scales, a reference group of 750 males and 750 females was used to develop standard scores with a mean of 50 and a standard deviation of 10. The manual reports test-retest reliabilities for these scales over time intervals ranging between one week and seven years. All of these coefficients are quite respectable and indicate good stability. In the case of the first three, they range from .80 to .92 over a four- to five-year interval. The Variability of Interests scale is somewhat less stable, though still very adequate. For example, the test-retest reliability over four to five years is .74.

A rational-empirical approach was used in the development of the General Theme scales. Working definitions of each of Holland's types were used to guide the selection of items for inclusion. In addition, the entire test had been administered to a group of subjects who had also taken Holland's Vocational Preference Inventory. Each item of the test was correlated with each of the six Holland dimensions. Only those items that correlated with a single dimension and fit conceptually with the working definition of the type were included. Also, only those items that showed a small male-female difference were used. Finally, the scales were refined by means of internal consistency. The result was a set of six scales each of which contained 20 nonoverlapping items. Each of the items is weighted from +2 to −2 according to the extent to which it is liked or disliked. Thus these scales are subject to positive response set. Like the Administrative Indices, these scales are normed according to the results obtained from the 1,500 adults who made up the reference sample. The developmental approach used for these scales suggests content and construct validity. The manual also reports concurrent validity in the form of the results of subjects who belong to specific occupational groups. These groups obtain mean scores on the General Themes, which are consistent with theoretical predictions. The manual also reports test-retest reliability data for these scales. Again these results are quite acceptable. The coefficients are in .90s for intervals up to 30 days and in the .80s for intervals as long as 6-7 years.

The 22 Basic Interest Scales were developed in a somewhat different fashion. The test was administered to 866 students, and the items of the test were intercorrelated. The items were grouped into clusters such that items tended to correlate highly with items in the same cluster and with items in other clusters. Every effort was made to avoid item overlap, and the manual states that "only a few" items are found on more than one Basic Interest Scale (p. 52). Further refinement of the placement of items in clusters was based on judgments regarding the psychological meaningfulness of the item placement. The scales were then cross-validated on the reference sample of 1,500 adults. Subsequent studies of the item-scale correlations indicated that there is good internal homogeneity with correlations in the .60s and .70s. These scales were also normed based on the results of the reference sample with a mean of 50 and a standard deviation of 10. The scales were then grouped according to their relationship to the General Themes based on the correlation of each scale with the six themes. Further, Basic Interest Scales were ordered with their groups such that each scale is adjacent to the scales with which it correlates more highly.

The manual discusses content validity, construct validity, and concurrent validity. Content validity stems from the method of development of these scales. The median item-scale correlations are quite high, generally in the .60s and the .70s. Construct validity was investigated by correlating the Basic Interest Scales with similar scales on the SCII. The manual reports the results, with the correlations generally in the .70s and the .80s. Concurrent validity is supported by data presented that indicates that 91 samples of a diversity of occupations obtain scores that follow a meaningful and logical distribution of a significant range. As with the other scales of the test, the manual reports median test-retest reliability coefficients for the Basic Interest Scales. These coefficients range from .93 for a one-week interval to .77 for a six- to seven-year interval. These scales appear to measure relatively stable traits in individuals.

There are 91 Occupational Scales on the CAI. These scales are empirically derived and follow the tradition of the SVIB. Therefore, the procedures are somewhat more complex. Occupational criterion groups were obtained in a variety of ways, including mailing lists from mail-order companies, professional directories, and membership lists, through personnel managers of large companies, and in a few instances, the yellow pages of large city telephone directories. For a CAI record to be included in that of the criterion group, five criteria had to be met: the individual had to 1) be in the appropriate job, 2) have at least two years of experience, 3) indicate that he or she liked their work, 4) be less than 60 years old, and 5) in some instances have the appropriate credentials. A reference sample was developed by assembling a group of records that were derived from an equal number of men and women, with equal representation of those scoring high on each one of the six themes. Identifications were made of 100 women and 100 men who had obtained their highest score on each of the six General Themes. These 1,200 individuals then formed the reference sample. The following sequential strategy was used in the development of the Occupational Scales. Chi-square values were computed on the actual response frequencies between the criterion and reference groups separately for men and women. Those items that appeared significant for both men and women were screened further. Next, response percentages for each of the response alternatives were computed for the criterion and reference groups. Only those items that indicated a practical difference were retained. Finally, it was decided to include between 20 and 60 items on each Occupational Scale. Items with less differentiating ability, even though they met the above criteria, were eliminated to bring the scale to this size. The items were then weighted between $+2$ and -2 according to the size and direction of the response percentages between the criteria and reference groups. Norms were then constructed by converting raw scores to standard scores such that the mean of the criterion group was equal to 50 with a standard deviation of 10. In the organization or grouping of the Occupational Scales, primary consideration was given to the correlation of each of the Scales with the General Theme scales. Secondary consideration was given to the mean scores obtained by the Occupational groups on the Themes. This procedure maximizes the relationship between the more content oriented scales of the CAI and the more empirical Occupational scales.

The manual discusses the validity of the Occupational Scales in terms of their concurrent validity and their construct validity. Concurrent validity is regarded as the degree to which the scales separate the occupational criterion samples from the reference samples. Data on this are presented in the form of overlap statistics indicating the degree to which the criterion sample and the reference sample overlap. Inspection of these data suggest that concurrent validity as defined here is quite good even for combined sex scales. Construct validity is investigated by computing correlations between the Occupational Scales and the equivalent scales on the SCII. Given the differences between the two tests in terms of occupational level, the fact that the SCII has separate scores for men and women, and the differences in the reference groups used, extremely high correlations were not anticipated. Correlations were obtained from the results of 182 adult subjects on 36 occupations and are presented in the manual. The median for the male SCII score is .66 and .67 for the female. The manual concludes that these results are in the range that was predicted and are evidence of fairly good construct validity.

The manual presents test-retest reliability data on all of the 91 Occupational Scales. Again these presented for the five time intervals of one week, two weeks, 30 days, 4-5 years, and 6-7 years. The results are quite favorable suggesting that these scales represent very stable measures. They are in the same range as those of the General Theme Scales, the Basic Interest Scales, and the occupational scales from the SCII.

Critique

Although the developmental research presented in the manual is solid and reflects a sophisticated approach to test development, there is a disturbing lack of supporting research done independently of the development of the test itself. A computerized search of bibliographic data bases revealed only a few studies that utilized the CAI and in most of these the use was incidental to the primary purpose of the research being presented. The fact that the SVIB was the pacesetter for the psychometric sophistication in the assessment of interests and personality traits for many decades was in no small measure due to the excellent predictive validity that was established for this instrument.

The lack of predictive validity studies in the manual and in the literature is a cause for concern. Even though it is probably the case that the CAI is built on the tradition and the methodology established in the SVIB, supporting evidence would be helpful. The relationship between the various types of scales that make up the CAI and actual criteria of job performance, satisfaction, and persistence would also be most helpful. Much of the construct validity data presented in the manual stems directly from the developmental effort in producing the test. Confirmatory construct validity studies, perhaps utilizing multitrait-multimethod approaches, would provide further support to the utility and interpretation of the results of the CAI. The fact that this test can at present be scored only through the test publisher and at an appreciable cost probably introduces an obstacle to more independent research endeavors of this type. This test offers a highly useful and much needed resource in the vocational counseling of people seeking to enter the large and expanding job market of technical and subprofessional administrative work as well as a measure of career interests that is reasonably free of sex bias. A resource of this potential importance and value deserves to be supported by much needed independent investigation. Although the manual is well written and quite complete, it does have one rather irritating shortcoming: there are a number of citations of theoretical, historical, and research articles throughout the manual, but no reference section to enable the reader to easily locate these sources.

Despite the fact that this test fills an important need in the area of vocational assessment and seemingly works very well, there has not been a great deal of comment on it in the literature. However, Buros' *Eighth Mental Measurement Yearbook* contains two critical reviews of an earlier edition of the CAI. Both are generally positive. The first of these is that of J. L. Bodden (1978). He concludes that "The CAI is an excellent instrument and one which will probably receive wide acceptance and usage. It has an appropriate reason for being and should prove especially valuable to high school counselors in areas where a minority of students typically attend college" (p. 1548). He commends it for its careful construction and its basis in the research of Holland, Strong, and Campbell. His only major criticism is the relatively small number (32) of occupations included in that edition.

The second review by P. R. Lohnes (1978) suggests that the structure of the test might be too complicated and that it could be improved by reducing the number of major categories from six to three. It commends the manual for adequately presenting information on reliability, content, and construct validity, but takes issue with the absence of predictive validity. The reviewer concludes: "As it stands, I judge it a good addition to the collection of interests inventories in print. It should be highly competitive. I give it especially high marks for the way it is tailored to a special clientele and would choose it myself if I had to counsel an indecisive youth who had properly ruled out seeking a baccalaureate education" (p. 1550). Although these reviews were written concerning an earlier edition, the general tone of the comments continues to be pertinent. The present edition has improved on the earlier one in terms of the greater number of occupational scales and the effort to eliminate sex bias.

The CAI fills an important and longstanding need for an adequate interest inventory designed for use with individuals who are not planning to attend college and it does this very well. It is far more successful than earlier attempts to assess the career interests of this level of the world of work. It is similar to the SCII in terms of its structure, item content, and appearance. From the point of view of the user, it offers much the same information as the SCII and with an apparently similarly high utility. It appears to excel the SCII in terms of both its combined sex applicability and the internal consistency of its scales. It falls far short of the SCII in terms of the extensive research base which supports the latter test.

The manual of the CAI was clearly written for the prospective test user. The technical and developmental data on the test are presented with a view to assisting and supporting the task of interpretation. There is a great deal of information on the technical aspects of the test and it is presented in a clear and easy-to-understand text. A thorough reading of the manual provides the prospective test-user with a thorough orientation to the test and what it can offer. The format of the results is also very "user friendly." The profile report is attractive, clear, and easily understood. A great deal of information is concisely communicated. The material printed on the reverse side serves as a quick review of the more thorough discussion in the manual regarding the scores and the scales. The interpretive report is also very well designed and clearly written. It goes beyond the data from the test itself in that it lists career areas that are consistent with the test results and even indicates *Dictionary of Occupational Titles* and *Occupational Outlook Handbook* citations for particular possibilities. Although it must be scored through a scoring service, there is not a long delay between the submission of the answer sheet and the availability of the results.

On the negative side, the test is relatively expensive to score and this will probably render it less suitable for large group testing situations or for extensive research. It is not very expensive considering the quality of information it yields in individual cases in which a determination of inventoried interests is important. In one sense, the test is deceptively simple. This test provides a broad spectrum of complex information in terms of interests and career orientation, and this information needs to be properly integrated into a larger framework of considerations for effective career planning. The clarity of the results could lead individuals into a false sense of confidence about the implications of the results if they do not have a solid background of vocational psychological theory. Finally, the promise and usefulness of this test would be greatly enhanced if there were more available research data to support the findings of the test author from independent investigations.

All things considered, I would rate this as a very important test, and one which fills a significant need. The test is well developed and is engineered to be easily and appropriately used. Although it is not perfect, it appears to accomplish what it sets out to do and to do this quite effectively. Perhaps further research and development will render it even more useful and lead to its wider utilization.

References

The following list of references is not presented with a view to completeness or with the implication that they provide an important background for the use of this test. There is a notable shortage of references that provide basic research data on the CAI. The articles cited below are offered as illustrative of research applications to which the test has put or as investigations into issues of interest assessment which the CAI addresses.

Bodden, J. L. (1978). Review of the Career Assessment Inventory. In O. K. Buros (Ed.), *The eighth mental measurements yearbook*. Highland Park, NJ: The Gryphon Press.

Johansson, C. R. (1982) *Manual for Career Assessment Inventory, Second edition*. Minneapolis: NCS Interpretive Scoring Systems.

Lamb, R. R., & Prediger, D. J. (1979). Criterion-related validity of sex-restrictive and unisex interest scales—Comparison. *Journal of Vocational Behavior, 15*, 231-246.

Lamb, R. R., & Prediger, D. J. (1980). Construct-validity of raw score reports of vocational interests. *Journal of Educational Measurement, 17*, 107-115.

Lohnes, P. R. (1978). Review of the Career Assessment Inventory. In O. K. Buros (Ed.), *The eighth mental measurements yearbook*. Highland Park, NJ: The Gryphon Press.

Phillips, J. S. (1978). Occupational interest inventories: An often untapped resource. *Journal of Applied Rehabilitation Counseling, 9*, 10-12.

Prediger, D. J. (1982). Dimensions underlying Holland hexagon—Missing link between interests and occupations. *Journal of Vocational Behavior, 21*, 259-287.

Weiser, M. A., Klimek, R. J., & Hodinko, B. (1981). Career perspectives of male prison inmates in college courses. *Journal of Vocational Behavior, 19*, 36-41.

Robert B. Slaney, Ph.D.

Associate Professor of Psychology, Southern Illinois University, Carbondale, Illinois.

CAREER DECISION SCALE

S. H. Osipow, C. G. Carney, J. L. Winer, B. Yanico, and M. Koschier. Columbus, Ohio: Marathon Consulting and Press.

Introduction

The Career Decision Scale (2nd Edition) by Osipow, Carney, Winer, Yanico, and Koschier (1980) is a 19-item self-descriptive questionnaire designed to measure career indecision. More specifically, the scale measures the degree to which respondents report that individual, career-related statements describe them and their particular circumstances. In addition to 16 items describing educational and/ or vocational indecision there are two describing decisiveness and one in which subjects may write their own descriptions if none of the others apply.

The first author of the instrument, Samuel H. Osipow, is a central figure in the area of career development. He is the author of numerous articles and books on the topic and his textbook, *Theories of Career Development* (3rd Edition) (1983), is a basic resource in this area. He is a past editor of the *Journal of Counseling Psychology* as well as the first editor of the *Journal of Vocational Behavior.* Recently he edited, with Bruce Walsh, the two-volume *Handbook of Vocational Psychology* (1983). The coauthors of the scale, Clarke G. Carney, Jane Winer, Barbara Yanico, and Mary-anne Koschier, have also pursued professional careers in which the general area of career development has played a central role.

The original development of the scale apparently began in a graduate seminar directed by Osipow. The overall plan was to determine initially the basic components or antecedents of career indecision and develop items that represented them. The next step was to develop self-administered audio-cassette interventions that, together with accompanying workbook exercises, would be responsive to each of the specified antecedents. The antecedents and their items were based on the authors' experience with career clients. An article by Osipow, Winer, Koschier, and Yanico (1975) contains the plan, an early version of the Career Decision Scale, and an example of a script for one of the audio-cassettes.

The evolution of the scale from 14 to 16 to the 19 items contained in the current edition (the third revision), however, is not easily discerned. Some revisions took place, primarily by adding items, but the process is not detailed in either the article or in the Manual for the Career Decision Scale (2nd ed.) manual (Osipow, 1980). The present version of the scale, described by Osipow, Carney, and Barak (1976) contains 16 antecedent items (items 3-18), two initial items measuring the respondents' reported decidedness, comfort with, and knowledge about implementing a career choice and a college major, respectively. The final item is open-ended and allows the respondents to describe their own sources of career indecision.

The entire scale is contained on a 4-page, 7" x 8½" sheet with detailed, clear instructions on the front page for responding to the simple format. A sample question and answer are then followed by the 19 items. Opposite each item are the numbers 4, 3, 2, and 1 (4 = "exactly like me"; 3 = "very much like me"; 2 = "only slightly like me"; 1 = "not at all like me"). Respondents are asked to circle the number that most accurately describes their situation in relation to each of the items.

The measure was designed for high school and college students. Although no reading level is noted in the manual, the language is clear and simple and seems appropriate for the intended audience.

Practical Application/Uses

This scale is potentially useful to career counselors, researchers, and teachers of a variety of courses relevant to educational and vocational exploration and/or career decision-making. The scale provides an estimate of career indecision and its antecedents as well as an outcome measure for determining the effects of a variety of interventions relevant to career choice or career development. Although the scale was originally developed to relate specific interventions to particular antecedents of career indecision, this approach has not received much attention. In one study, Barak and Friedkes (1982) divided the subjects into groups based on subtypes according to their responses to the Career Decision Scale. They did not, however, attempt to match the interventions to these subtypes. In any event, for counselors it may make intuitive as well as clinical sense to examine the responses of clients to the individual items to formulate possible approaches to counseling or to identify particular issues that need attention. Generally, the treatment implications of the items seem clear. Although this is a positive virtue for counselors, researchers need to consider the possibility that simply reading the scale items may have an effect on subjects.

The Career Decision Scale can be administered in classes or large groups as well as individually. The instructions are clear and it is unusual to have questions raised about how to respond. There is no specified time limit but 10 to 15 minutes is usually enough time to complete the scale. The instructions for scoring are clear and simply involve summing the numerical values that were circled for items 3-18. This yields an objective overall score for career indecision with higher numerical values representing higher degrees of career indecision. Items 1 and 2, which indicate decidedness about the choice of a career or college major, are not included in the career indecision score and are scored in the opposite direction (i.e., higher scores on these items indicate greater decidedness). This is a possible source of confusion although the manual is clear on this point. Item 19 is not scored and may offer clues to issues that are of concern to respondents but are not covered by the other items. There is some room, perhaps, for counselor interpretations using item 19, although the published studies on the scale thus far have simply disregarded it.

Technical Aspects

The Osipow et al. article (1976) was the first published paper focusing on the current version of the Career Decision Scale. The article contains an impressive amount of data on the scale. Seven undergraduate samples (N = 737) were involved in an elaborate plan to gather data on relevant groups. The hypothesis that students requesting help in career decision-making would score higher on the scale than students not requesting such help was supported. Students requesting career counseling had significantly higher scores on the Career Decision Scale than students who did not request career counseling. The results were mixed for students in courses on educational-vocational exploration. It was also found, as expected, that the career indecision scores for two groups of students in courses on educational-vocational exploration declined significantly while the scores for introductory students and two groups of students in a course on personal effectiveness did not change significantly. Items 3-18, as expected, were almost all negatively correlated with items 1 and 2. The above results provide clear support for the construct and concurrent validity of the scale and its individual items.

Test-retest reliabilities calculated over two-week intervals on the summary scores yielded values of .90 for 56 introductory students and .82 for 59 students in a course on personal effectiveness. For the individual items, the reliabilities varied considerably. Osipow et al. (1976) also conducted a factor analysis on the 16 indecision items using the principal factors solution with test-retest reliability coefficients used as the principal diagonal estimates. Using the varimax method, four factors were rotated that accounted for over 81% of the variance. The factor structure raised the possibility that instead of 16 basic antecedents of career indecision, perhaps there were just four. Osipow et al. (1976) said the first factor seemed to have two basic elements that involved a lack of structure and confidence in approaching decision-making and choice anxiety. Both lead to avoiding a choice. The second factor was seen as suggesting a perceived or actual external barrier to a preferred choice and questions about alternative possibilities. Factor three was interpreted as representing an approach-approach conflict where the difficulty involved choosing from a number of attractive alternatives. The fourth and final factor seemed to indicate the presence of some kind of personal conflict over making the decision. One of the implications of the factor analysis was that perhaps interventions could be devised to respond to the factors that were found.

More recent studies have added to the support for the validity of the Career Decision Scale. Most notably, Slaney, Palko-Nonemaker, and Alexander (1981) divided subjects into career decided and undecided groups based on their responses to a 6-item scale on career decidedness that appeared in a study by Holland and Holland (1977). There were statistically significant differences in the expected direction for the summary scores, the factor scores, and all of the individual items. A factor analysis using principal factors and varimax rotation replicated Osipow et al.'s first factor but otherwise the factor structure was unclear. Rogers and Westbrook (1983) found clear support for the construct and concurrent validity of the scale. They factor analyzed the responses of 175 students to the Career Decision Scale using a varimax rotation. They found four factors, two of which coincided with the second and third factors found by Osipow et al. (1976). They concluded that the match of two factors obtained by using different methods of analysis and different subjects indicated "some degree of convergent validity for the CDS" (p. 84). Other recent studies have also supported the construct and concurrent validity of the Career Decision Scale (Niece & Bradley, 1979; Slaney, 1980). Slaney (1984) found that the Career Decision Scale scores of undergraduate women who changed their career choices over a two-year period were significantly higher originally (more undecided) than were the scores for women whose choices remained stable. This result not only supports the construct validity of the scale, it also attests to its potential pragmatic usefulness for career counselors. Overall, the support for the construct validity of the Career Decision Scale seems consistent and substantial. The factor structure of the scale, however, does seem to be in need of additional clarification.

Critique

The current edition of the manual provides succinct, articulate, and accurate summaries of the published and unpublished research that has been conducted on the scale. It is nicely produced and includes, in addition to the research summary, a table of contents, 39 references, a copy of the Career Decision Scale, and 53 pages of tables containing data on the measure. It is a rich source of data for potential users but perhaps even more so for researchers. There is, of course, a certain irony in the fact that because the scale has been well received and used with increasing frequency in recent years, the manual is already dated. This is likely to be even more of a problem in the future because the measure seems likely to become one of a very small number of carefully developed measures that are available for use in studies on career indecision and career interventions. Given the alternatives, the authors may consider the need for frequent revision a tolerable problem.

For the Career Decision Scale, a number of issues, mostly minor, remain unclear or in need of additional investigation. For example, the amount of information available on the initial stages of the development of the scale is minimal. How was it determined that there were 16 antecedents of career indecision? Why not more or less? What revisions took place at what points and for what reasons? A more important issue concerns the lack of clarity of the factor structure. In turn, this lack of clarity may be related to the lack of clarity that exists in some of the items. Several consist of two or three sentences that make it unclear which aspect subjects are responding to. For example, item 11 requires subjects to give one response to the following statements:* "Having to make a career decision bothers me. I'd like to make a decision quickly and get it over with. I wish I could take a test that would tell me what kind of a career I should pursue." These three statements seem at least potentially independent of each other. The need for clarifying the factor structure does seem important, especially if the future development of the

---

*Copyright © 1980 by Samuel H. Osipow. This item is reproduced by permission of Samuel H. Osipow.

scale is to involve the development of career interventions that are based on this structure. The development of such interventions was, of course, part of the original plan and the idea still seems imaginative despite numerous difficulties. Clearly one of the difficulties is that developing this plan will involve an extended effort in performing complex and time-consuming intervention studies. Whether that effort will occur remains to be seen. Regardless, the ideas do seem to merit attention.

On the other hand, if the research done thus far on the scale is predictive, there may be less need to be concerned about clarifying the individual items or the factor structure. Almost all of the studies have used the scale as a unidimensional measure of career indecision by deriving a scale score by summing items 3-18. Used in this way, the scale has received a truly impressive amount of research attention since its initial development. The fact that the research support has provided substantial support for the test-retest reliability of the instrument and for its construct and concurrent validity is even more impressive. This seems particularly true in an area where so many of the measures do not have adequate research, or for that matter, any research at all on their reliability or validity. It can be concluded that the Career Decision Scale is a brief, easily administered, valid, and reliable measure of career indecision that is also capable of measuring changes that occur over time. The early development of this measure has been impressive and this reviewer clearly recommends it for use by researchers and counselors as a measure of career indecision.

References

Barak, A., & Friedkes, R. (1982). The mediating effects of career indecision and subtypes on career-counseling effectiveness. *Journal of Vocational Behavior, 20,* 120-128.

Holland, J. L., & Holland, J. E. (1977). Vocational indecision: More evidence and speculation. *Journal of Counseling Psychology, 24,* 404-414.

Niece, D., & Bradley, R. W. (1979). Relationship of age, sex, and educational groups to career decisiveness. *Journal of Vocational Behavior, 14,* 271-278.

Osipow, S. H. (1980). *Manual for the Career Decision Scale.* Columbus, OH: Marathon Consulting and Press.

Osipow, S. H. (1983). *Theories of career development* (3rd ed.). Englewood Cliffs, NJ: Prentice-Hall Inc.

Osipow, S. H., Carney, C. G., & Barak, A. (1976). A scale of educational-vocational undecidedness: A typological approach. *Journal of Vocational Behavior, 9,* 233-243.

Osipow, S. H., Carney, C. G., Winer, J. L., Yanico, B., & Koschier, M. (1980). The Career Decision Scale (2nd ed.). Columbus, OH: Marathon Consulting and Press.

Osipow, S. H., Winer, J., Koschier, M., & Yanico, B. (1975). A modular approach to self-counseling for vocational indecision using audio-cassettes. In L. Simpson (Ed.), *Audio-visual media in career development.* Bethlehem, PA: College Placement Council.

Rogers, W. B., & Westbrook, B. W. (1983). Measuring career indecision among college students: Toward a valid approach for counseling practitioners and researchers. *Measurement and Evaluation in Guidance, 16,* 78-85.

Slaney, R. B. (1980). Expressed vocational choice and vocational indecision. *Journal of Counseling Psychology, 27,* 122-129.

Slaney, R. B. (1984). Relation of career indecision to changes in expressed vocational interests. *Journal of Counseling Psychology, 31,* 349-355.

Slaney, R. B., Palko-Nonemaker, D., & Alexander, R. (1981). An investigation of two measures of career indecision. *Journal of Vocational Behavior, 18*, 92-103.

Walsh, W. B., & Osipow, S. H. (Eds.). (1983). *Handbook of vocational psychology: Vol. 1: Foundations.* Hillsdale, NJ: Lawrence Erlbaum Associates Inc.

Walsh, W. B., & Osipow, S. H. (Eds.). (1983). *Handbook of vocational psychology: Vol. 2: Applications.* Hillsdale, NJ: Lawrence Erlbaum Associates Inc.

Gerald M. Devins, Ph.D.
Assistant Professor of Psychology, The University of Calgary, Calgary, Alberta, Canada.

Carolee M. Orme, Ph.D.
Post Doctoral Research Fellow in Psychology, The University of Calgary, Calgary, Alberta, Canada.

CENTER FOR EPIDEMIOLOGIC STUDIES DEPRESSION SCALE

Center for Epidemiologic Studies. Rockville, Maryland: Center for Epidemiologic Studies, Department of Health & Human Services, National Institute of Mental Health.

Introduction

The Center for Epidemiologic Studies Depression (CES-D) Scale is a self-report "state" measure of depressive symptomatology that was developed for research applications, initially for use in epidemiologic surveys of depression within the general (i.e., nonpsychiatric) population. It provides an index of cognitive, affective, and behavioral depressive features as well as indicating the frequency with which these symptoms have occurred. The CES-D provides a state measure of depression insofar as it indicates *present* levels of functioning and is limited in its assessment to the one-week interval preceding its administration. Its primary application involves the investigation of relationships between depressive symptoms and other variables across population subgroups. However, insofar as several of the somatic features characteristic of depression and the total duration of reported symptoms have not been included in the measure, it cannot be used for the determination of diagnoses (e.g., within standardized systems such as DSM-III; American Psychiatric Association, 1980).

The CES-D, reproduced in Table 1, is a 20-item questionnaire assessing the frequency/duration of symptoms associated with depression in the preceding week. Cognitive, affective, behavioral, and somatic symptoms associated with depression are assessed by 16 items. Positive affect is assessed by four items, which have been included for their intrinsic information value and to minimize biases attributable to response sets. For each item, respondents indicate the frequency or duration with which they have experienced a specific feature during the preceding week by circling a number between 0 and 3. The anchors assigned to these values are labelled as follows: *0* indicates that a feature has occurred

---

These reviewers would like to express our appreciation to Dr. L. S. Radloff for her generous assistance in permitting us to reproduce the CES-D in this chapter and for providing us with relevant background information regarding the scale. The writing of this review was supported by a grant to Gerald M. Devins from the Alberta Mental Health Advisory Council.

Table 1

CES-D Scale: Format for Self-Administered Use

Circle the number for each statement which best describes how often you felt or behaved this way—DURING THE PAST WEEK.

DURING THE PAST WEEK:	Rarely or None of the Time (Less than 1 Day)	Some or a Little of the Time (1-2 Days)	Occasionally or a Moderate Amount of Time (3-4 Days)	Most or All of the Time (5-7 Days)
1. I was bothered by things that usually don't bother me	0	1	2	3
2. I did not feel like eating; my appetite was poor	0	1	2	3
3. I felt that I could not shake off the blues even with help from my family or friends .	0	1	2	3
4. I felt that I was just as good as other people	0	1	2	3
5. I had trouble keeping my mind on what I was doing .	0	1	2	3
6. I felt depressed	0	1	2	3
7. I felt that everything I did was an effort	0	1	2	3
8. I felt hopeful about the future	0	1	2	3
9. I thought my life had been a failure	0	1	2	3
10. I felt fearful.	0	1	2	3
11. My sleep was restless	0	1	2	3
12. I was happy	0	1	2	3
13. I talked less than usual . . .	0	1	2	3
14. I felt lonely	0	1	2	3
15. People were unfriendly . . .	0	1	2	3
16. I enjoyed life	0	1	2	3
17. I had crying spells	0	1	2	3
18. I felt sad	0	1	2	3
19. I felt that people disliked me	0	1	2	3
20. I could not get "going" . . .	0	1	2	3

"rarely or none of the time" (less than 1 day); *1* indicates "some or a little of the time" (1-2 days); 2 indicates "occasionally or a moderate amount of time" (3-4 days); and 3 indicates "most or all of the time" (5-7 days). The possible range of total scores is, thus, from 0 to 60, with higher scores reflecting greater distress.

The instrument has been designed to require minimal involvement of the examiner and can be self-administered. Instructions are clear and readily understood. The measure, as a whole, has been accepted without difficulty by adult subjects in community samples. It is intended for all age groups older than 18.

Depression is clearly among the most prevalent of mental health problems and has long been the focus of clinical and research attention. Current estimates indicate that at any given time 4-11% of the general population may be affected by this disorder (Amenson & Lewinsohn, 1981; Costello, 1982; Lehman, 1971). Specific subpopulations are believed to evidence even higher rates—e.g., 18% among chronic illness populations (Kathol & Petty, 1981); 36% among the bereaved (Clayton, Halikas, & Maurice, 1972); 53% among women in the midst of a marital breakup (Costello, 1982). Interest in depression has been both basic and applied and has focused on questions regarding its etiology, measurement, assessment, course, treatment, prediction, and prevention. Moreover, scientists and clinicians interested in the problem have been concerned with the disorder (a) as a major mental health problem, in and of itself, and (b) as a secondary response to other physical, psychological, social, and societal problems.

Given the widespread interest in depression, there has understandably been considerable attention directed at its measurement and assessment. A variety of measurement approaches have been developed, including: 1) standardized interviews (e.g., Present State Examination, Wing, Cooper, & Sartorius, 1974; Schedule for Affective Disorders and Schizophrenia, Endicott & Spitzer, 1978); 2) psychiatric rating scales (e.g., Hamilton Psychiatric Rating Scale for Depression; Hamilton, 1967); and 3) self-report scales (e.g., Beck Depression Inventory; Beck, Ward, Mendelson, Mock, & Erbaugh, 1961). Each of these approaches, however, has been recognized to introduce its own unique set of advantages and disadvantages.

Standardized interviews, for example, are capable of yielding a rich base of information regarding a broad range of clinical conditions. Information regarding the nature and severity of a presenting complaint can be augmented by a detailed collection of relevant historical data, related symptoms, personality strengths and weaknesses, previous treatment experiences and the individual's response to past interventions. Thus, standardized interviews are particularly well suited to situations in which highly detailed information may be required (e.g., for the establishment of differential diagnoses in clinical psychology or psychiatry). This high degree of detail does not come without cost, however. In order to provide valid and reliable data, interview techniques must be administered and scored by a highly specialized individual (e.g., psychiatrist, clinical psychologist). Standardized interviews are, thus, likely to be inefficient for applications involving large numbers of individuals (e.g., screening for psychopathology, group research applications, etc.). Moreover, despite vigorous attempts to reduce the effects of interviewer expectancy effects, standardized interviews may still be subject to observer biases (Engelsmann, 1976), introducing the need for cross-validation precautions which add even further to their overall cost and inefficiency when large numbers of individuals must be assessed.

Rating scales eliminate some of the difficulties intrinsic to standardized interviews insofar as they are typically focused on a single or relatively small number of complaints (e.g., the Hamilton Scales for Anxiety and Depression; Hamilton, 1959, 1967). This narrower focus notwithstanding, rating scales must also be based on an interview (or some other standardized situation in which observations may be made) so that their administration also requires specialized personnel. Moreover, given that human judges are involved in the evaluation of observations, rating scales are also susceptible to observer biases. Unlike standardized interviews, however, the scoring of rating scales does not typically require a high level of expertise once the ratings themselves have been completed.

Self-report measures circumvent many of the problems associated with standardized interviews and rating scales. They are typically quick and easy to administer and are usually objectively scored. There is, thus, no need for highly trained professionals to be involved in their administration or scoring (such expertise is usually required for their interpretation and integration with other clinical data, however). Understandably, therefore, self-report measures have become extremely popular and widely used. A number of pitfalls must be acknowledged and avoided, however, if these measures are to contribute usefully. Perhaps the most obvious potential problem is the possibility of *distortion* by respondents. Individuals may be motivated to under- or over-represent the features assessed by a self-report scale so that the severity of symptoms is inaccurately reflected in total scores. A related issue involves the possibility that respondents may *misinterpret* one or more of the items that comprise a self-report measure and thereby reduce its information value. Regardless of the underlying motivation contributing to such biases, their results are equally damaging to the meaningfulness and ultimate utility of the test.

Some of the pitfalls associated with self-report scales are unique or especially relevant to depression. Self-report measures of depression, for example, are particularly susceptible to the biasing effects of interactions between the disorder and the assessment device: at the upper levels of severity, respondents may simply be *too depressed* to complete the scale! A more subtle and less frequently recognized pitfall involves the assessment of depression that occurs in the context of an intercurrent disorder or illness. Several of the symptoms of depression overlap with those of a variety of other conditions so that the differential assignment of symptoms to one or another diagnostic entity can be particularly challenging. End-stage renal disease (i.e., irreversible kidney failure; ESRD), for example, produces several symptoms that are identical to those of depression (e.g., fatigue, apathy, inability to concentrate, anorexia and weight loss, decreased libido, and sleep disturbances; Schreiner, 1959). However, inasmuch as ESRD does not produce these features universally in all affected individuals, their concurrence with other depressive symptoms can introduce particularly troublesome diagnostic issues even for the most expert of practitioners. As a result, the administration of a simple self-report measure in this situation could produce a dramatically inflated estimate of depression due to the misidentification of ESRD-induced symptoms as depressive in origin.

While this problem may be equally characteristic of standardized interviews and rating scales, precautions may be introduced relatively easily to reduce such biases. Insofar as these methods must be administered by a qualified individual, for example, additional specifically focused questions, tests, etc., may be selected to assist in the task of differential symptom assignment. A second possibility, more germane to research applications, involves the introduction of statistical covariance controls for other intercurrent conditions. As will be shown, the design of the Center for Epidemiological Studies Depression (CES-D) Scale has successfully circumvented this problem for a wide range of potential applications.

The CES-D was developed by the Center for Epidemiologic Studies, an agency within the U.S. National Institute of Mental Health, to measure depressive symptomatology in the community. Scale items were selected from a larger pool of items that had been selected from previously validated measures of depression (e.g., Beck et al., 1961; Dahlstrom & Welsh, 1960; Raskin, Schulterbrandt, Rearig, & McKeon, 1969; Zung, 1965). Major components of depressive symptomatology to be included in the new scale were decided on the basis of the clinical literature and factor analytic studies. The following components were ultimately retained for inclusion: depressed mood, feelings of guilt and worthlessness, psychomotor retardation, loss of appetite, and sleep disturbance (Radloff, 1977).

In its initial application, the scale was embedded within a 1-hour (300-item) interview protocol which included previously developed measures of depression (Lubin, 1967), emotional distress (Langner, 1962), positive and negative moods (Bradburn, 1969), subjective well-being (Cantril, 1965), and social desirability (Crowne & Marlowe, 1960). In addition, the protocol included measures of recent stressful life events, alcohol problems, social functioning, physical illness, and medication usage patterns, plus a variety of standard sociodemographic indices (e.g., age, sex, educational level, etc.; Radloff, 1977). Participants were identified via a probability sampling procedure in which households were randomly selected and a single adult (18 years or older) from each was asked to submit to a standardized individual interview. The entire 300-item package was administered at this time.

Two separate field surveys were performed. The first (labelled *Q1*) was conducted in two major U.S. centers—Kansas City, Missouri (response rate = 75%; final *n* = 1,173) and Washington County, Maryland (response rate = 80%; final *n* = 1,673)—between October, 1971, and March, 1973. The second survey (labelled *Q2*) took place in Washington County only, and yielded a total of 1,089 completed data files (response rate = 75%). This survey was conducted from March, 1973, through July, 1974. Each respondent to the *Q2* panel was also requested to complete and mail back a retest of the CES-D either two, four, six, or eight weeks following the original interview. This yielded a total of 419 mail-backs (response rate = 56%). Finally, two subsets (*Q3*) of the *Q1* and *Q2* samples were reinterviewed. Among the Kansas City participants, a total of 343 reinterviews were conducted approximately 12 months following the initial interview. Reinterviews were also conducted with Washington County participants. However, these were performed over a broader range of intervals: three, six, or twelve months subsequent to the initial interview (total *n* = 1,209). Psychometric characteristics were estimated on the basis of these data (cf. "Technical Aspects" section of this review). Interested readers are referred to papers by Radloff (1977; Radloff & Locke, in press) for greater detail regarding the history and background of the CES-D.

Practical Applications/Uses

The CES-D has two major practical applications: initial screening and research. As an initial screening device in settings where psychological distress is not routinely assessed (e.g., general medical practice), scores on the instrument can signal a need for further clinical investigation. Radloff and her colleagues (1977; Radloff & Locke, in press), for example, have suggested that a total score of 16 be employed as the cutoff to indicate "case" depression. Barnes and Prosen (1984) have suggested that scores of 0-15.5 be interpreted to indicate that an individual is "not depressed"; 16-20.5 to indicate "mild depression"; 21-30.5 to indicate "moderate depression"; and 31 or higher to indicate "severe depression." However, the CES-D must not be relied upon exclusively for the detection of "caseness" because of a high false negative rate (i.e., a substantial proportion of respondents who are actually clinically depressed may obtain total CES-D scores which are below suggested cutoff criteria). Similarly, it cannot be employed in the absence of additional data for diagnostic decision-making insofar as its concordance with standardized diagnostic systems (e.g., DSM-III) is only moderate (e.g., several somatic symptoms of depression are not assessed; duration of symptoms beyond one week is not assessed). Roberts and Vernon (1983), for example, reported a false negative rate of 50.7% when a cutoff criterion score of 16 on the CES-D was compared to case depression identification based on the Schedule for Affective Disorders and Schizophrenia-Research Diagnostic Criteria (Endicott & Spitzer, 1978; Spitzer, Endicott, & Robbins, 1978).

The CES-D has more often been employed for research purposes, particularly where the focus of investigation is on levels of depression or distress within a nonpsychiatric population. Its lack of emphasis on somatic symptoms of depression distinguishes the CES-D from other commonly used measures and, as indicated, renders it especially valuable for investigations involving medical patients for whom a confound may exist between symptoms associated with the disease state and these vegetative symptoms of depression. The CES-D is not recommended for research use, however, when a diagnosis of depression according to DSM-III or other standardized criteria (e.g., Research Diagnostic Criteria: Spitzer, Endicott, & Robbins, 1978) is required.

The CES-D was designed for the epidemiological study of depression and the testing of hypotheses relating it to other variables (e.g., stressful life events, social support). The measure itself assesses the respondent's current extent of depressive symptomatology by ascertaining the number of symptoms present and weighting them by their frequency or duration. It has been used most frequently in the assessment of distress among community residents and is increasingly being used in more specific nonpsychiatric populations, particularly medical samples such as end-stage renal disease and multiple sclerosis (e.g., Devins, in progress-a, in progress-b; Devins & Binik, in progress). Its users, therefore, are primarily epidemiologists and mental health researchers. As indicated, it also appears to have considerable potential for use as a screening device.

The CES-D is appropriate for use with adult populations regardless of age, sex, or socioeconomic status. Within the U.S., the scale has been demonstrated to have comparable validity among black, Caucasian, and Hispanic respondents; no data regarding such issues in non-American populations appear to have been published to date. The scale is not recommended for application within known psychiatric populations.

The CES-D can be administered under a variety of conditions and the effects of several of these have been examined. Radloff (1977) observed that CES-D scores were unaffected by administration variations in the time of day, day of the week, or month of the year. Some differences in average CES-D scores have been observed between interviewers. However, these were of borderline significance and did not affect the test's reliability or its patterns of relationships with other variables. Although no differences in scores occurred when methods of administration were varied—e.g., in-vivo interview vs. telephone interview vs. self-administration there is some evidence that higher error rates may occur under self-administration conditions (Radloff & Locke, in press).

Regardless of the method selected, administration of the CES-D is simple and straightforward. Standardized instructions appear at the top of the questionnaire and are easily understood. Completion of the scale requires no more than 10 minutes. Although the measure has been designed to measure depressive symptom levels during a one-week interval, investigators interested in obtaining estimates for a period of more than one week may do so by modifying the initial instructions to indicate the desired interval for assessment (e.g., "during the past *month*"). The effects of such modifications on the scale's reliability and validity have not yet been documented, however, so that those interested in maintaining the established reliability and validity of the measure should administer it in its standard form.

Scoring the CES-D is straightforward and requires neither training nor practice. Each symptom item is weighted by the frequency endorsed by the respondent (i.e., 0 through 3) and these are summed across the 20 items of the scale to yield a single total. The weights for the four positive-feature items (nos. 4, 8, 12, and 16) are reversed before adding them to the total score; for example, if the respondent circles 3 ("most or all of the time") for item #12 ("I was happy"), the score for this item is 0. In its initial development and field testing, total CES-D scores were not calculated (i.e., the score was considered "missing") if four or more of the 20 items were unanswered by a respondent. No machine or computer scoring is available. Certainly for individual applications, the simplicity and brevity of the scoring procedure do not require computer assistance (scoring time should not exceed five minutes). In the case of group applications, automated scoring may be accomplished very easily—e.g., via computational facilities available via widely used statistical software packages for personal microcomputers or large main-frames.

The precise meaning of elevated CES-D scores has not yet been established. However, given the scale's noncoverage of several central features, scores should not be interpreted as indicating the presence or absence of the clinical syndrome of depression. It would seem more reasonable to assert that elevated scores reflect the types of distress that may *accompany* clinical depression. Interpretation regarding specific *levels* of distress is based solely upon objective scores. However, no norms have been established.

Technical Aspects

There is considerable evidence that the CES-D is characterized by adequate psychometric properties. The initial procedures employed in item development and selection during the test's construction phase were anchored solidly in current clinical and factor analytic findings regarding the elements of "depressive symptomatology," the construct which the test was designed to measure (Radloff & Locke, in press). As a result, the CES-D provides relatively comprehensive coverage of the construct. Subsequent work has added important information regarding its reliability and validity.

A number of studies have employed the CES-D to assess depressive symptomatology among unselected community residents. These have typically employed relatively large samples (e.g., $Ns = 1,000+$), yielding relatively stable estimates of population distribution characteristics. Mean values reported for total CES-D scores among community residents have been reported to range from 7.5 to 12.7 (modal values have centered around 8.5) and standard deviations have ranged from 7.5 to 9.8 (Lewinsohn & Teri, 1982; Lin & Ensel, 1984; Radloff & Locke, in press). Barnes and Prosen (1984) reported an overall mean of approximately 13.3 among a sample of 1,250 family medicine practice attenders. With regard to the frequencies with which individual scores are observed, reported CES-D distributions have typically been positively skewed—i.e., relatively low scores have been observed much more commonly than have elevated scores. This is to be expected given that the prevalence of depressive disorders (which would be reflected in elevated total CES-D scores) is only 4-11%. Radloff (1977), for example, reported that the indices of skewness in the three panels included in the test's initial field testing ranged from 1.50 to 1.69 and that groups with higher mean scores were also characterized by higher variances. This problem does not appear to occur among groups in which depression is more prevalent (e.g., disturbed populations). The CES-D's initial field trials included a sample of 70 psychiatric inpatients who were considered to be characterized by elevated levels of depression. The distribution of these CES-D scores was considerably less skewed (skewness = .20, a value well within the limits of a normal distribution). Nevertheless, given that the scale is intended for use with nonpsychiatric populations, Radloff (1977) has pointed out that the pattern of larger means associated with higher variances characteristic of the community resident samples has the effect of rendering standard parametric significance tests (e.g., *F*-ratios calculated in the analysis of variance and covariance) inexact, so that observed probability levels should be considered simply as *approximations*.

Considerations of total score distributions have also contributed to the establishment of cutoff criteria for the differentiation of "case" versus "noncase" identity. As indicated, Radloff and her colleagues have recommended that a cutoff score of 16 be employed to differentiate "case" depression from non-cases. This suggestion is based on the results of the initial field trials in which a total CES-D score of 16 corresponded approximately to the 80th percentile of the *Q1* distribution (Radloff & Locke, in press). Barnes and Prosen (1984), however, reported that this score corresponded only to about the 67th percentile among family practice attenders. Unfortunately, few other researchers have reported this information. The question of what specific cutoff criterion maximizes this discrimination has not yet been adequately resolved (cf. below).

Considerable evidence has documented the reliability of CES-D scores. Reliability relates to the *consistency* of a test score and, as noted by Anastasi (1982), can involve several dimensions. Radloff's (1977) analyses of the original field trial data have provided an extensive examination of several facets of this issue. *Test-retest* reliability concerns the consistency with which a test can yield a measurement over the dimension of *time* (assuming that the underlying psychological construct it has been developed to measure has not changed in the interim). The data collected during the CES-D's initial field testing permitted the calculation of test-retest reliabilities for several specific intervals (this is particularly valuable insofar as values associated with different intervals between testings may vary widely). Radloff (1977) reported, however, that the CES-D is characterized by test-retest reliabilities that are quite consistent across retesting intervals. Reliabilities estimated on the basis of two- ($r_{tt} = .51$), four- ($r_{tt} = .67$), six- ($r_{tt} = .59$), and eight-week ($r_{tt} = .59$) intervals were remarkably similar. Longer test-retest intervals were also examined. These, too, yielded similar values: $r_{tt} = .48$ for a three-month interval; $r_{tt} = .54$ for six months; and $r_{tt} = .49$ for 12 months. Lin and Ensel (1984) have reported a 12-month test-retest correlation of .41 in a similar sample of community residents. While these values are slightly below acceptable limits (e.g., Nunnally [1978] has suggested that acceptable reliability levels should not fall below the .70s during the early stages of test development and that they should equal or exceed the .80s once it has been adjusted for initial limitations), this may be due to the test's focus on *state* depression—i.e., depressive features having occurred during the preceding one-week interval only.

Reliability may also involve the dimension of *item content* and the extent to which the items of a test all appear to measure the same construct. Such an index is generally regarded as more appropriate for evaluating the consistency of a state measure, such as the CES-D, insofar as the underlying construct—i.e., depressive state—may actually change dramatically from one occasion to another (e.g., pre- vs. post-treatment). This form of reliability has been termed *internal consistency* and can be estimated via a number of methods. Cronbach's *coefficient alpha* has been recognized as the most general, meaningful, and useful of these. Coefficient alpha provides an estimate of the expected correlation of a test with a hypothetical alternative form containing the same number of items. Its square root is the estimated correlation of a test with errorless true scores (Nunnally, 1982). Radloff (1977) reported coefficient alphas of .84, .85, and .90 for the CES-D in her field trial data. Barnes and Prosen (1984) reported a value of .89 for their sample of family practice attenders. Insofar as these levels clearly exceed the recommended minimum standards, the reliability of the CES-D would appear to be adequate for a wide variety of potential applications.

In its most general sense, validity relates to the issue of *what* a test measures and *how well* it does so—what can be inferred from test scores (Anastasi, 1982). As indicated, the CES-D has been purported to measure *depressive symptomatology* and a growing body of evidence has indicated that this is reflected well in test scores. A variety of tests may be employed in establishing the construct validity of a specific measure. In the following section, validity data will be presented within the context of the specific tests performed. These have been categorized as follows: 1) contrasted groups tests; 2) convergent and discriminant validation; 3) relationships with other variables; and 4) factor analytic findings.

Contrasted groups. This strategy involves establishing the degree to which a new test is capable of discriminating among groups that have been formed on the basis of previously established and independent criteria. At least three separate investigations have compared CES-D scores across groups of individuals differing in depression as identified by an independent criterion. Radloff (1977) presented some initial data comparing the CES-D scores obtained by a "psychiatric inpatient" group, unselected for diagnosis, with those reported for the $Q2$ community sample in the initial field trials and reported that the former ($M = 24.4$, $SD = 13.5$) obtained significantly higher scores than the latter ($M = 8.2$, $SD = 8.2$; $p < .05$). She also observed significant improvements in CES-D total scores pre- and post-treatment among a sample of psychiatric outpatients in treatment for depression.

Weissman et al. (1977) compared the total CES-D scores obtained by five separate psychiatric outpatient groups with the scores observed for the field trials' entire community sample ($N = 3,932$). The five psychiatric groups included: 1) acutely depressed outpatients who were currently undergoing treatment (Raskin Depression Scale scores ≥ 7; $n = 148$); 2) previously depressed individuals who had been treated successfully (Raskin scores < 7; $n = 87$); 3) individuals in treatment for opiate addictions ($n = 60$); 4) individuals in treatment for alcohol abuse ($n = 61$); and 5) schizophrenic patients ($n = 50$). In comparing CES-D scores across these groups, Weissman et al. observed that acutely depressed individuals (i.e., group 1; $M = 38.1$, $SD = 9.0$) scored significantly higher than (a) recovered depressives (group 2; $M = 14.9$, $SD = 10.1$); (b) all other psychiatric groups ($Ms = 17.1, 23.0$, and 13.0 respectively; $SDs = 10.7, 13.6$, and 13.0); as well as (c) the nondisturbed community residents ($M = 9.1$; $SD = 8.6$). Moreover, Weissman et al. also divided each of the four nondepressed psychiatric groups into "relatively depressed" and "relatively nondepressed" subgroups on the basis of Raskin scale scores ("depressed" status was determined by a score of 7 or higher). In each case, relatively depressed subgroups were characterized by significantly higher CES-D scores as compared to the relatively nondepressed (all $ps < .05$).

A careful study by Roberts and Vernon (1983) has also provided data to suggest that the CES-D is a valid measure of depressive symptomatology. A random sample of 528 community residents completed a two-stage screening procedure. In phase 1, participants completed the CES-D together with other self-report "adjustment" measures with the assistance of lay interviewers. In phase 2, they participated in a formal diagnostic interview—the Schedule for Affective Disorders and Schizophrenia-Research Diagnostic Criteria (SADS-RDC)—administered by trained clinical interviewers. Both current and lifetime diagnoses were established for major and minor depression as well as depressive personality. Results indicated that elevated CES-D scores successfully discriminated among

RDC-depressed and nondepressed individuals when cutoff scores of 16 (and 17) were employed. However, a high rate of false negatives—i.e., individuals identified as nondepressed by the CES-D but who were diagnosed as depressed by the SADS-RDC—was observed. When a CES-D cutoff score of 16 was employed, the false negative rate was 40.5%; a cutoff of 17 resulted in a rate of 40%; and a cutoff of 23 yielded a false negative rate of 60%. The false positive rates observed were substantially lower: 14.1%, 15%, and 7%, respectively. The CES-D "correctly" identified 60% of the individuals diagnosed by the SADS-RDC as having major depression, 71% diagnosed as minor depression, and 57% diagnosed as depressive personalities (59% of all depression). However, CES-D scores did not discriminate adequately among these three subtypes. Given that the scale purports to measure "depressive symptomatology" and not a specific syndrome, in particular, these findings support its construct validity. As will be discussed in greater detail, however, they also contraindicate its independent application to the formulation of clinical diagnoses.

Convergent and discriminant validation. Convergent validity relates to the degree to which the measurements provided by one test are in agreement with those provided by other tests that have been designed and demonstrated to measure the same or related constructs. Data relevant to this question have been reported in some of the contrasted groups studies cited previously. Weissman et al. (1977), for example, reported Pearson correlations between the CES-D and two other widely used depression scales—the Hamilton rating scale (*r*s = .50s to .80s across the various psychiatric groups) and the Raskin scale (*r*s = .30s to .80s). Radloff (1977) has also reported correlations between the CES-D and a number of related measures. These were calculated on the basis of data obtained during the test's initial field trials. The CES-D correlated significantly with the Lubin (1967) Depression Adjective Checklist (*r*s = .40s to .50s), the Bradburn (1969) Affect Balance Scale's Negative Affect (*r*s = .60s) and Positive Affect Scales (*r*s = .20s), the Langner (1962) scale (*r*s = .50s), and the Cantril (1965) "life satisfaction ladder" (*r* = .43). Radloff also reported correlations between the CES-D and other standard depression measures among psychiatric patients both pre- and post-treatment for depression. Pre-treatment correlations with the CES-D were .44 for the Hamilton and .54 for the Raskin scales; post-treatment correlations were .69 and .75, respectively (all *p*s < .05).

A second important dimension is *discriminant validity*—the degree to which a test measures only the construct that it is intended to assess; that is, test scores do not overlap with measures of another construct (e.g., if the CES-D is a "pure" measure of depression, scores should not also reflect other types of emotional responses, such as anger, fear, boredom, etc.). Unfortunately, the data are less supportive of the CES-D's discriminant validity as compared to its convergent validity. Although relatively limited attention appears to have been directed at this issue, the data suggest that CES-D scores reflect psychological distress in general in addition to depressive symptomatology in particular. Weissman et al. (1977), for example, noted that CES-D scores were significantly correlated with total scores on the Symptom Check List-90 (SCL-90; Derogatis, Lipman, & Covi, 1973), a general screening measure that assesses nine independent psychiatric symptoms. In addition to correlating significantly with the SCL-90's depression subscale (*r*s =

.70s to .80s across groups), it was significantly correlated with each of the remaining (nondepression) subscales, scales that assess somatization (rs = .40s to .60s), obsessive compulsive (rs = .50s to .70s), interpersonal sensitivity (rs = .50s to .80s), anxiety (rs = .50s to .80s), hostility (rs = .30s to .70s), phobic anxiety (rs = .40s to .60s), paranoid ideation (rs = .40s to .70s), and psychoticism (rs = .50s to .70s). The correlations with the global SCL-90 symptom severity score were in the .70 to .90 range. Amenson and Lewinsohn (1981) also reported a significant correlation between total CES-D scores and a "brief symptom index" that is derived from SCL-90 responses (r = .79). Thus, as suggested by Weissman et al., "the symptoms included in the CES-D Scale, although typical of depression, are perhaps the most prevalent manifestations of psychological distress [in general]" (p. 44). While the symptoms covered by the scale may reasonably be considered *depressive* in nature, these findings would suggest that they are not limited exclusively to the family of clinical syndromes entitled "depression."

Evidence has been reported, however, that the focus of the CES-D does not extend beyond emotional distress. Heusaini and Neff (1981), for example, administered the CES-D and Rotter's internal-external (I-E) locus of control scale to a sample of 713 community residents. They then combined the 20 CES-D items with those of the I-E scale and submitted the entire "package" to a principal-components factor analysis. The results indicated that the items of the two scales clearly loaded on independent factors, with the majority of explained variance attributed to the first (CES-D) factor extracted, suggesting that a negligible degree of overlap characterizes the two measures. Radloff (1977) has also reported some data pertaining to the question of discriminant validity. In the initial field trial data, the CES-D correlated significantly but only slightly with the Marlowe-Crowne (Crowne & Marlowe, 1960) social desirability scale (rs = −.20s), a measure of defensive response style. A relationship of this magnitude is to be expected, however, insofar as the differentiation of positive psychological adjustment (or the absence of difficulties) from a relatively defensive response style has not yet been accomplished (i.e., scales such as the Marlowe-Crowne cannot discriminate between nondefensive well-adjusted and defensive poorly adjusted individuals). Thus, a statistically significant but relatively low correlation between a defensive response style variable, such as social desirability, and a measure of emotional distress, such as the CES-D, is supportive of the construct validity of both tests.

Relationships to other variables. Yet another important means of establishing the construct validity of a measure is to examine the extent to which it is associated with other variables that have already been found to be related to the construct that it purports to measure. To the extent that the new measure yields a pattern of relationships that is consistent with the larger literature, one can have increased confidence in its validity. Relatively little CES-D research appears to have adopted this approach to date, although a growing number of studies have appeared in the recent literature. Initial applications of the CES-D have involved replication efforts regarding established relationships between depression and sociodemographic characteristics. A number of investigators have documented the well-established sex-difference in depression and have reported that women typically report higher total CES-D scores than do men (e.g., Barnes & Prosen, 1984). Moreover, this difference appears not to be an artifact—it does not result from differential distributions of depressive self-labelling, help-seeking tendencies, or self-presentation to an independent diagnostician (Amenson & Lewinsohn, 1981), nor is it the product of differential levels of exposure to depression-precipitating factors such as early parental loss, unemployment, economic hardships, or physical illness, among others (Radloff & Rae, 1979). Several replications have established that the CES-D is related to a number of other demographic characteristics in the same ways as is depression when measured by more established psychiatric measures. Elevated CES-D scales have been found to correlate significantly with lower levels of socioeconomic status, education, and annual income; high CES-D scores have also been found to be reported significantly more frequently by separated and divorced individuals as compared to married people (Amenson & Lewinsohn, 1981; Barnes & Prosen, 1984; Heusaini & Neff, 1981; Radloff & Rae, 1979; Warren & McEachren, 1983).

The relationships between depression and stressful life events and social support have received considerable attention. The generally accepted conclusion is that increased depression is associated with higher exposure to stressful events and decreased levels of social support (Costello, 1982; Monroe, Bellack, Hersen, & Himmelhoch, 1983). This relationship has also been observed when the CES-D has been employed to assess depressive symptomatology. Warren and McEachren (1983) administered the CES-D to a random sample of 499 adult female community residents together with a questionnaire concerning their perceived social support, among other hypothesized contributors to depression (cf. below). They observed a correlation of −.29, indicating a significant association between decreased perceived social support and increased depression. Lin and Ensel (1984) administered the CES-D together with measures of perceived social support and recent stressful life events to a community sample of 871 adults in a prospective two-wave longitudinal design (lag = 12 months). They observed that changes in depression—both in the directions of increased *and* decreased depression—were associated, as anticipated, with changes in social support and stressful events. Controlling for initial levels of depressive symptomatology (as measured by the CES-D), significant partial correlations were observed between changes in depression (i.e., CES-D_2 minus CES-D_1) and changes in (a) perceived social support and (b) exposure to stressful life events. Increases in social support and decreases in life events were associated with significantly decreased depressive symptoms; decreases in social support and increases in life events were associated with significantly higher depression.

As indicated previously, Warren and McEachren (1983) examined the relationships between depressive symptoms (as measured by the CES-D) and factors that have been hypothesized to contribute to the onset and/or maintenance of depression. Self-report measures constructed by the investigators indicated that increased CES-D scores were significantly related to 1) decreased perceived control over life, in general ($r = -.52$); 2) a decreased sense of accomplishment in life ($r = -.49$); and 3) an increased tendency to base one's sense of identity on relationships with others ($r = .33$; all $ps < .01$).

Collectively, these findings support the construct validity of the CES-D insofar as they indicate that it is related to a variety of variables in the same ways as other more established measures are.

Factor analysis. Implicit in the notion of validity is the question of what meaning can be assigned to test scores; that is, *what does the test measure?* Factor analysis can help to answer this question by identifying the underlying hypothetical constructs or influences that contribute to test scores. Anastasi (1982) has proposed the term *factorial validity* to relate to this aspect of test construction and evaluation. Radloff (1977) has submitted the 20 items of the CES-D to factor analysis in an effort to identify the patterns of interrelationship among them. Separate principal-components analyses were applied to the data obtained from the three separate panels of community residents who participated in the CES-D's initial field trials. For each analysis, four factors were extracted with eigenvalues greater than 1.0, collectively accounting for 48% of the total variance. As reported by Radloff, the varimax rotated solution in each of these cases was quite consistent. Factor interpretation was based on consideration of items with loadings of .40 and above. Factor 1 was labelled *depressed affect* and included items 3, 6, 14, and 17. Factor 2 was termed *positive affect* and included items 4, 8, 12, and 16. Factor 3 was labelled *somatic and retarded activity* and included items 1, 2, 7, 11, and 20. Factor 4 was called *interpersonal* and included only items 15 and 19. The remaining five items failed to load purely on any single factor and apparently were not included in the interpretation as a result. A factorial invariance statistic was employed to evaluate the degree of similarity across the three separate factor solutions (i.e., one for each of *Q1*, *Q2*, and *Q3*) and indicated that, in fact, they were very alike. However, given the scale's high degree of internal consistency (cf. previous discussion of reliability), Radloff suggested that a simple total score be calculated and submitted to statistical analyses rather than constructing four separate factor scores on the basis of these results. Future research involving additional populations is required before conclusions regarding the generality of the scale's underlying factorial composition can be drawn.

Critique

The CES-D scale is a most welcome addition to the measures that assess depressive symptomatology and emotional distress. It provides a reliable and valid measure of distress and can easily be administered—either by an interviewer or by respondents themselves—quickly and efficiently across a broad range of populations. Given the findings that the scale's focus is not limited exclusively to *depressive* symptomatology, however, it would seem more reasonable to assert that it provides a useful index of the more general construct of *emotional distress*. While such symptoms may frequently be associated with depressive syndromes, the findings that CES-D scores were highly correlated with symptoms of anxiety and other neurotic and psychotic conditions contraindicate their interpretation as solely depressive in nature.

Such interpretative cautions notwithstanding, the CES-D can contribute very valuably. Its focus on the types of distress symptoms prevalent among nonpsychiatric populations makes it ideal for applications in epidemiological and hypothesis-testing research concerning their determinants and concomitants among nonpsychiatric groups. Recent trends in the areas of clinical and abnormal psychology have clearly broadened the focus of interest and treatment to include the distress and suffering experienced by nonpsychiatric populations as a major priority. Recent years have witnessed a substantial increase in attention to the problems associated with a variety of significant life stresses (e.g., involuntary unemployment, chronic and life-threatening illness, marital and family dissolution, etc.) and it is precisely in such specialized populations that the CES-D is most appropriate. As a result, it is likely to appear with increasing frequency in the professional literature in years to come. Assuming a continuous as opposed to a discontinuous perspective on distress and abnormal psychological states, it may thus be worthwhile for future investigators (a) to deal in greater depth with disentangling depression-specific from nondepressive distress symptoms before they have reached pathological proportions and subsequently (b) to improve upon the present version of the measure so that it is able to assess these more precisely.

The CES-D would also apear to constitute a very promising initial screening instrument for psychological distress or dysfunction in medical, industrial, or other settings in which professional psychological or psychiatric services are not routinely available. As has been emphasized throughout this review, however, it is critically important that such scores be interpreted no further than as indicating that further psychological assessment and attention *may* be necessary and should, therefore, be sought. Under no circumstances can diagnoses of depression (or of any other disturbance) be based on CES-D scores in the absence of additional data.

Thus, the Center for Epidemiologic Studies Depression Scale is an important measure which is likely to be useful to a large number of mental health professionals. It is likely to remain in use for considerable time and to contribute valuably in both research and applied settings.

References

Amenson, C. S., & Lewinsohn, P. M. (1981). An investigation into the observed sex difference in prevalence of unipolar depression. *Journal of Abnormal Psychology, 90*, 1-13.

American Psychiatric Association. (1980). *Diagnostic and statistical manual of mental disorders* (3rd ed.). Washington, DC: Author.

Anastasi, A. (1982). *Psychological testing* (5th ed.). New York: Macmillan Publishing Co.

Barnes, G. E., & Prosen, H. (1984). Depression in Canadian general practice attenders. *Canadian Journal of Psychiatry, 29*, 2-10.

Beck, A. T., Ward, C. H., Mendelson, M., Mock, J., & Erbaugh, J. (1961). An inventory for measuring depression. *Archives of General Psychiatry, 4*, 561-571.

Bradburn, N. M. (1969). *The structure of psychological well-being.* Chicago: Aldine Publishing Co.

Cantril, H. (1965). *The pattern of human concern.* New Brunswick, NJ: Rutgers University Press.

Clayton, P. J., Halikas, J. A., & Maurice, W. L. (1972). The depression of widowhood. *British Journal of Psychiatry, 120*, 71-77.

Costello, C. G. (1982). Social factors associated with depression: A retrospective community study. *Psychological Medicine, 12*, 329-339.

Crowne, D. P., & Marlowe, D. (1960). A new scale of social desirability independent of psychopathology. *Journal of Consulting Psychology, 24*, 349-354.

Dahlstrom, W. G., & Welsh, G. S. (1960). *An MMPI handbook*. Minneapolis: University of Minnesota Press.

Derogatis, L. R., Lipman, R. S., & Covi, L. (1973). An outpatient psychiatric rating scale: Preliminary report. In W. Guy (Ed.), *ECDEU assessment manual* (pp. 320-331). Rockville, MD: U.S. Department of Health, Education, and Welfare.

Devins, G. M. (in progress-a). *Stress-related adjustment problems in end-stage renal disease*. Project supported by a grant from the Alberta Mental Health Advisory Council.

Devins, G. M. (in progress-b). *The psychosocial impact of chronic and life-threatening illnesses*. Project supported by a grant from the Alberta Mental Health Advisory Council.

Devins, G. M., & Binik, Y. M. (in progress). *Psychosocial impact of chronic life-threatening illness: Lessons from end-stage renal disease*. Project supported by a grant from Health and Welfare Canada.

Endicott, J., & Spitzer, R. L. (1978). A diagnostic interview: The Schedule for Affective Disorders and Schizophrenia. *Archives of General Psychiatry, 35*, 837-844.

Engelsmann, F. (1976). Rating scales for the assessment of depression. In J. Ananth & J. Pecknold (Eds.), *Depression prognosis and prediction of response* (pp. 27-48). Montreal: Poulenc.

Hamilton, M. (1959). The assessment of anxiety states by rating. *British Journal of Medical Psychology, 32*, 50-55.

Hamilton, M. (1967). Development of a rating scale for primary depressive illness. *British Journal of Social and Clinical Psychology, 6*, 278-296.

Heusaini, B. A., & Neff, G. A. (1981). Social class and depressive symptomatology: The role of life change events and locus of control. *Journal of Nervous and Mental Disease, 169*, 368-647.

Kathol, R. G., & Petty, F. (1981). Relationship of depression to medical illness. *Journal of Affective Disorders, 3*, 111-121.

Langner, T. S. (1962). A twenty-two item screening score of psychiatric symptoms indicating impairment. *Journal of Health and Social Behavior, 3*, 269-276.

Lehman, E. E. (1971). Epidemiology of depressive disorders. In R. R. Fieve (Ed.), *Depression in the 1970's: Modern theory and research*. Princeton, NJ: Excerpta Medica.

Lewinsohn, P. M., & Teri, L. (1982). Selection of depressed and nondepressed subjects on the basis of self-report data. *Journal of Consulting and Clinical Psychology, 50*, 590-591.

Lin, N., & Ensel, W. M. (1984). Depression-mobility and its social etiology: The role of life events and social support. *Journal of Health and Social Behavior, 25*, 176-188.

Lubin, B. (1967). *Manual for the Depression Adjective Check List*. San Diego: Educational and Industrial Testing Service.

Monroe, S. M., Bellack, A. S., Hersen, M., & Himmelhoch, J. M. (1983). Life events, symptom course, and treatment outcome in unipolar depressed women. *Journal of Consulting and Clinical Psychology, 51*, 604-615.

Nunnally, J. C. (1978). *Psychometric theory* (2nd ed.). New York: McGraw-Hill Publishing Co.

Nunnally, J. C. (1982). *Psychometric theory* (2nd ed.). New York: McGraw-Hill Publishing Co.

Radloff, L. S. (1977). The CES-D Scale: A new self-report depression scale for research in the general population. *Applied Psychological Measurement, 1*, 385-401.

Radloff, L. S., & Locke, B. Z. (in press). The community mental health assessment and the CES-D Scale. In M. Weissman, J. Meyers, & C. Ross (Eds.), *Community surveys*. New Brunswick, NJ: Rutgers University Press.

Radloff, L. S., & Rae, D. S. (1979). Susceptibility and precipitating factors in depression: Sex differences and similarities. *Journal of Abnormal Psychology, 88*, 174-181.

Raskin, A., Schulterbrandt, J., Rearig, N., & McKeon, J. (1969). Replication of factors of psychopathology in interview, ward behavior, and self-report ratings of hospitalized depressives. *Journal of Nervous and Mental Disease, 148*, 87-96.

Roberts, R. E., & Vernon, S. W. (1983). The Center for Epidemiologic Studies Depression Scale: Its use in a community sample. *American Journal of Psychiatry, 140,* 41-46.

Schreiner, G. E. (1959). Mental and personality changes in the uremic syndrome. *Medical Annals of the District of Columbia, 28,* 316-324.

Spitzer, R. L., Endicott, J., & Robbins, E. (1978). Research diagnostic criteria: Rationale and reliability. *Archives of General Psychiatry, 36,* 773-782.

Warren, L. W., & McEachren, L. (1983). Psychosocial correlates of depressive symptomatology in adult women. *Journal of Abnormal Psychology, 92,* 151-160.

Weissman, M. M., Sholomskas, D., Pottenger, M., Prusoff, B. A., & Locke, B. Z. (1977). Assessing depressive symptoms in five psychiatric populations: A validation study. *American Journal of Epidemiology, 106,* 203-214.

Wing, J. K., Cooper, J. E., & Sartorius, N. (1974). *An instructional manual for the Present State Examination and CATEGO programme.* London: Cambridge University Press.

Zung, W. W. K. (1965). A self-rating depression scale. *Archives of General Psychiatry, 12,* 63-70.

Thomas J. Huberty, Ph.D.
Assistant Professor of Education, Department of Counseling and
Educational Psychology, Indiana University, Bloomington, Indiana.

CHILDREN'S ADAPTIVE BEHAVIOR SCALE-REVISED

Richard H. Kicklighter and Bert O. Richmond. Atlanta,
Georgia: Humanics Limited.

Introduction

The Children's Adaptive Behavior Scale-Revised (CABS-R) is a measure of adaptive behavior for children aged five-ten years that assesses the areas of Language Development, Independent Functioning, Family Role Performance, Economic-Vocational Activity, and Socialization. It proposes to assess knowledge and skill development that are related to a child's ability to adapt to the demands of everyday living. The authors, Richard H. Kicklighter of the Georgia Department of Education, Atlanta, and Bert O. Richmond, Professor of Educational Psychology at the University of Georgia, used the definition of adaptive behavior proposed by the American Association on Mental Deficiency in the development of the CABS-R, which is "the effectiveness or degree with which the individual meets the standards of personal independence and social responsibility expected of his age and cultural group" (Grossman, 1973, p. 11).

The CABS-R is a revision of the Children's Adaptive Behavior Scale (CABS) (Richmond & Kicklighter, 1980) in that the manual has been revised and normative statistical data have been extended. In the CABS-R Manual (Kicklighter & Richmond, 1983) the scale is referred to as the CABS and will be referred to as such in this review.

The length of time required for the development of the CABS was not reported in the manual. The authors report the following nine-step process in the development of the scale (Manual, pp.4-5).

1. Reviewing available social, developmental, and adaptive behavior instruments;

2. Deriving and categorizing behavioral/performance indicators by skill area and age;

3. Selecting behavioral domains/skill areas on the basis of literature and authors' judgment of utility and measurement feasibility;

4. Analysis of skills, concepts, and/or knowledge in each area;

5. Development of initial item pool;

6. Having experts (school psychologists) rate trial items on a five-point scale;

7. Choosing items receiving ratings equal to or better than + 3;

8. Administering the test to the normative population; and

9. Analysis of normative data and determination of reliability, validity, and norms.

From this process the five areas listed previously are identified, defined, and retained (Manual, pp. 5-6):

> *Language Development* (16 items)—language skills used in the child's social environment in and out of school;
>
> *Independent Functioning* (30 items)—level of capability to cope with "everyday tasks in commonly encountered environments" (p. 5);
>
> *Family Role Performance* (20 items)—"effectiveness with which the child copes with the most intimate and intense behavioral demands that occur in a home (family or quasi-family) setting" (p. 5);
>
> *Economic-Vocational Activity* (21 items)—assesses the child's understanding and use of concepts that are involved in working, earning, and spending;
>
> *Socialization* (28 items)—assesses skills in relating to and cooperating with others and discriminating important from trivial social demands. Includes self and social awareness.

As an adaptive behavior measure, the CABS is rather unique in that it obtains information directly from the child. Most adaptive behavior measures, e.g., Vineland Adaptive Behavior Scales (VABS) (Sparrow, Balla, & Cichetti, 1984), the AAMD Adaptive Behavior Scale-School Edition (ABS-SE) (Lambert, Windmiller, & Cole, 1981), and the Adaptive Behavior Inventory for Children (ABIC) (Mercer, 1979) require that a knowledgeable third party evaluate the child on several dimensions, such as self-help skills and socialization. The CABS was developed on premises that observers may be biased or uninformed about a child, need elaborate or extensive instructions to complete the items properly, not have the opportunity to observe the child in particular situations, and necessitate lengthy observation periods. The authors also point out that information obtained from external observers may be limited due to the perceptiveness of the respondent.

The original normative sample of the CABS consisted of 250 educably mentally retarded (EMR) students in North Carolina and Georgia special education programs, with 50 subjects being included in each of the five age groups between six-ten years. The CABS is purported to be appropriate for children aged five-ten years, but there are no norms for the age range of 5-0 to 5-11 for the EMR sample. Although most test standardizations include data from "normal" subjects in their development, the CABS did not, thus limiting the generalizability of the test. The CABS revision includes normative data on children in regular education programs in areas considered to be representative of the population as to age and sex: southeast, northeast, midwest, and western coast (N = 969). These data also included children in the age ranges of 5-0 to 5-11 and 11-0 to 11-11. The data from the original standardization sample are included in the revised version, with no new data being reported.

The addition of the regular student norms expands the range of applicability from 5-0 to 11-11 years. Although not specifically discussed in the manual, the examiner could plot an individual child's score relative to these norms. Extended reliability data on psychometric quality and relationships to the Wechsler Intelligence Scale for Children-Revised (WISC-R) (Wechsler, 1974) are also provided. There is no discussion in the manual as to the scale's applicability to children with low-incidence handicaps or those for whom English is not the native language.

Materials needed by the examiner are the Manual, Student Record Booklet, Student Picture Book, three quarters, three dimes, three nickels, three pennies, a pair of scissors, sheet of paper, and fourteen blocks (or similar objects, e.g., chips) of one color. For the actual administration, the examiner uses the record booklet on which are printed the test items; the manual is used for determining norms.

The Student Picture Book is a spiral-bound booklet of 21 templates, 20 of which have printed monochromatic pictures, letters, or words for use in various domains, and one of which has four colored squares for use in the Language Development domain.

The Student Record Booklet contains specific instructions for each item, including questions that are to be asked verbatim. Items are not to be reworded to make them easier, but words that are difficult for the child to understand are to be noted and appropriate colloquial language used if necessary. Items are scored correct or incorrect on the answer booklet, and item raw scores are summed for each domain. The booklet also contains a profile sheet for plotting individual domain scores and a total score in the form of age equivalents.

The profile sheet is part of the Student Test Booklet and is arranged so that after raw scores are converted to age equivalents they can be plotted according to domain and total scores. The norms for profiling are for EMR students, although it is possible to compare the scores to those of the regular class students.

Practical Applications/Uses

The CABS is primarily useful in determining the level of adaptive behavior skills and helping to determine eligibility for special education placement in classes for the educably mentally handicapped. It should be administered by persons well-trained in individual psychoeducational assessment, such as school or clinical psychologists. It would probably be used most often in a public school setting, although it could be used in other settings, such as mental health centers or hospitals. It would not be appropriate to use in residential settings with its current norms, which were based upon nonresidential, ambulatory children in public school settings. There might be occasions when a child in a residential setting, however, would be considered for placement in a public school. In these circumstances the CABS norms might be useful in predicting whether a child has adequate adaptive behavior levels to function successfully in the less restrictive environment.

The test is to be administered in conditions conducive to individual assessment, e.g., a quiet, well-lighted room free from distractions. The manual describes very well the types of conditions that are likely to result in an accurate assessment. Little discussion is given to helping the examiner address unique problems presented by the child, e.g., distractibility, but the authors caution that good rapport should be established and that persons trained in individual assessment should use the CABS. They also suggest, and this reviewer agrees, that several practice administrations be conducted prior to using the CABS for an actual assessment. The sequence of administration of the domains can be altered, but the authors suggest that the "scoring and administration procedures may then be awkward" (Manual, p.11). All items of each domain are to be administered to each child, and the authors state that there is adequate "floor" and "ceiling" to assess "seriously defective" five-year-olds as well as "mildly impaired" ten-year-olds (p. 4).

The examiner begins with Language Development by asking questions that the child might know, such as "How many brothers do you have?" then asking the child to identify a picture in the Student Picture Book, write a word, or identify one of the objects that the examiner presents. All items of each domain are to be administered to each child. The test is untimed but the manual indicates that administration requires approximately 45 minutes. This reviewer would add approximately 15 minutes for scoring items and plotting profiles.

The items are easy to score right or wrong, although there may be occasions when clinical judgment will be necessary to determine the correctness of an answer. The manual offers very helpful "scoring guidelines" to aid the examiner in determining the correctness of a response in those situations.

The protocols can only be hand-scored. The examiner derives a total for each domain, as well as a total score. The raw scores are converted to age equivalents using the norms for mentally handicapped students. The age equivalents are then transposed to the profile sheet containing domain and total scores. The clinical norms are plotted in plus or minus one-half standard deviations to indicate the ranges of normalcy for each age level. For raw scores below the tabled values, the interpretation apparently would be recorded as "below six years." For the regular class norms, the plus or minus standard deviation values are not reported, but presumably could be calculated.

Interpretation is based upon comparing the child's scores to the age equivalents derived from the manual. The authors recommend comparison of the results to those obtained in a comprehensive assessment that includes the child's history, teacher and parent observations, and scores for other scales. Persons who interpret the scale should be very familiar with the concept of adaptive behavior, its relationship to achievement and intelligence, and the limitations imposed by the use of a small normative base.

Technical Aspects

The reliability of the CABS was established by the use of the Kuder-Richardson 21 internal consistency formula for the 250 children who comprised the norm group. The reported reliability coefficients were Language Development = .63, Independent Functioning = .83, Family-Role Performance = .76, Economic-Vocational Activity = .79, Socialization = .72, and Total = .93.

Test-retest reliabilities were computed on a subsample of 36 black children referred for a psychoeducational evaluation. A readministration was completed two weeks after the initial assessment for three males and three females at each of the age levels of five-ten years. None of the children had been diagnosed as mentally retarded. The correlation coefficients were .98 for the Economic-Vocational Activity and Socialization domains, and .99 for the remaining domains and the total score.

Intercorrelations among domains and the total score for a sample of 60 slow learners and 60 mildly retarded children suggest that the CABS domains tend to measure a unidimensional trait, but there is some overlap among them. The correlations ranged from .52 for Socialization and Language Development to .84 for Independent Functioning and Total Score. The reliability data should be viewed with caution due to the small sample sizes, lack of representativeness of the samples (both geographic and racial), and the fact that they were based on only a clinical sample. More reliability studies need to be conducted with regard to race, sex, geographic representation, and increased sample sizes for handicapped and normal groups.

Initial evidence for the validity of the CABS is presented in the observation that raw scores for the normative sample increased significantly with age. The normative group was established using a "modified random selection procedure" (p. 19) that was not elaborated. Scores were than evaluated with regard to intellectual level as measured by the WISC-R, and then the children were assigned to either an educably mentally retarded (EMR) (IQ = 50-69) or a slow learner (SL) group (IQ = 70-89). The criteria for determination of these categories was not discussed. CABS domains were significantly correlated with chronological age ($p < .0001$) and ranged from .43 (Socialization) to .64 (Economic-Vocational Activity) (Bailey, 1978).

An analysis of covariance using age as a covariate indicated significant differences between the groups, with the SL group receiving higher scores. Black EMR students scored higher than their white counterparts, but black SL pupils did not receive higher scores than the white SL participants. The authors state that this finding suggests that IQ scores may penalize black students more at lower than higher levels of intelligence. Consequently, adaptive behavior data should be accumulated prior to placing children in programs for the mentally handicapped rather than reliance on IQ scores alone. This point is consistent with the AAMD definition presented earlier.

Content validity, i.e., the degree to which a test contains items that measure desired areas, is presented by the observation that CABS items appear "in one form or another, in virtually all adaptive, developmental or social competence scales" (p. 22). The degree to which a test is consistent with the constructs upon which it was based, i.e., construct congruence, is supported by the fact that scores increased with increasing age at all IQ ranges sampled.

In the development of the scale, the authors assumed that there is a relationship, although not an identical one, between intelligence and adaptive behavior. The data presented indicate the presence of this relationship in that children with lower IQ scores had lower scores on the CABS. In a principal components factor analysis with varimax rotation (age adjusted) of the CABS, the WISC-R, and the ABIC three separate factors were identified (Graham-Clay, 1982). The Economic-Vocational Activity domain was the only one to load on the WISC-R factor, suggesting a moderate relationship between the two measures. The moderate correlations with the WISC-R suggests that the CABS places much emphasis upon the cognitive processes that mediate most forms of learning. The authors emphasize that cognitive processes are necessary for a child to acquire knowledge that leads to performance. Reschly (1982) has also observed that the CABS relies on the presence of cognitive processes that mediate adaptive functioning.

Concurrent validity was established by comparing the scores of the CABS and the AAMD Adaptive Behavior Scale-Public School Version (ABS-PSV) (Lambert, Windmiller, Cole, & Figueroa, 1974) for both parent and teacher ratings of a sample of 120 children. Several correlation are reported and the total correlations for teacher ratings ranged from .02 to .51 with an overall total of .42. For parent ratings, the range of correlations was .04 to .51, with a total of .42. These results suggest that there are some similar skills being measured, and that both teachers and parents view these skills similarly. Moreover, the CABS appears to measure some aspects of adaptive behavior not assessed by the ABS-PSV.

Moderate correlations between the CABS and the WISC-R suggest that adaptive functioning is dependent upon a general cognitive factor, in addition to specific skills and knowledge. This view has also been proposed by Lambert (1981) and Reschly (1982). This reviewer, while in general agreement with the authors' conclusions concerning the relationship between intelligence and adaptive ability, offers caution with regard to the CABS. These conclusions were made on a limited sample in terms of age and number, which was also not representative of a cross-section of students. Thus, evidence that the CABS assesses this relationship should be viewed with caution, pending more research data.

Estabrook and Cummings (1983) conducted a matrix sampling study comparing the CABS EMR sample to a sample of fourth-grade students in a midwestern city. There were significant differences between the variances of the samples in the Economic-Vocational and Socialization domains, and the standard deviations of the local sample were more restricted. These findings suggest that the CABS national sample is not representative of all groups of children and that local norms should be developed. These authors suggested that the multiple matrix sampling procedure may be an alternative for school systems to use in developing local norms.

Critique

The CABS is one of several adaptive behavior scales that is available for the assessment of children's skills. It is unique in that it attempts to gain information directly from the child, as opposed to gathering it from third-party respondents. It assesses many of the same areas as most of the other scales of this type and offers the potential of reducing respondent bias that could occur due to lack of information, difficulty in understanding directions, or inadequate opportunity to observe the child in a variety of settings.

In this reviewer's opinion, however, there are several limitations to the routine use of the CABS. The normative sample is a clinical one, and the child's scores are not compared to a "normal" group unless the examiner does this independently. The normative sample of 250 children from a specific region of the country does not offer the user the assurance of representativeness of the norms. In developing the norms for regular class students the authors also note that some of the data came from research studies. Thus, there is no assurance that this data is representative of "normal" students. The normative sample is much too small and non-representative to be used with confidence. Tha authors are aware of these limitations and suggest that perhaps school districts could develop their own norms. While this suggestion is generally good practice for other scales such as the CABS, the feasibility of such norming appears unrealistic for most schools, even using a matrix sampling procedure, such as the one described by Estabrook and Cummings (1983).

This reviewer is also concerned about the obvious amount of reliance that is put on the child's receptive and expressive language skills. The child must have adequate skills in these areas to be able to understand the directions and respond to them. If these skills are deficient and are not due to intellectual deficits per se, e.g., language disorders or learning disabilities, the child could be misdiagnosed on this basis. This issue is not addressed by the authors and is one worthy of consideration, both in practice and future research. Additionally, because the CABS does require the use of language skills it should not be used with children for whom English is not the native language until further research indicates its applicability for such populations. A preliminary, unpublished version for Spanish-speaking students has been developed that does contain norms (Richmond & de la Serna, 1978). The authors recommend, however, that users develop local norms when using this version.

Even though a child reports having knowledge of a concept or how to do a task, this does not assure that the task can be adequately performed. More research is needed to determine the degree of congruence between what a child demonstrates on the CABS and what can be actually performed.

The use of age equivalents are always to be used with caution because differences from one age level to another are usually not equal. Age scores do not have the same meaning at different ages, e.g., a deficit of one year at five years of age is more significant than the same deficit at ten years of age.

In conclusion, while the CABS does have merit as an adaptive behavior measure, particularly in its direct assessment of the child, it has the limitations indicated above. Consequently, caution is recommended in its use, and it should be used only as a clinical instrument in conjunction with other adaptive behavior measures having similar content. Use of the scale as the only adaptive behavior measure in a psychoeducational assessment is not recommended, pending further research and development.

References

Bailey, B.S. (1978). *Differential perceptions of children's adaptive behavior.* Unpublished doctoral dissertation, University of Georgia, Athens.

Estabrook, G. E., & Cummings, J. A. (1983). A matrix sampling study of the Children's Adaptive Behavior Scale. *Journal of Psychoeducational Assessment, 1,* 101-111.

Graham-Clay, S. L. (1982). *A critical examination of the relationship between adaptive behavior and ability measures.* Unpublished Ed.S. thesis, Iowa State University, Ames.

Grossman, H. J. (1973). (Ed.). *Manual on terminology and classification in mental retardation.* Washington, DC: American Association on Mental Deficiency.

Kicklighter, R. H., & Richmond, B. O. (1983). *Children's Adaptive Behavior Scale-Revised.* Atlanta, GA: Humanics, Ltd.

Lambert, N. M. (1981). *AAMD Adaptive Behavior Scale-School Edition. Manual.* Monterey Park, CA: Publishers Test Service.

Lambert, N. M., Windmiller, M., & Cole, L. (1981). *AAMD Adaptive Behavior Scale-School Edition*. Monterey Park, CA: Publishers Test Service.

Lambert, N. M., Windmiller, M., Cole, L., & Figueroa, R. (1974). *AAMD Adaptive Behavior Scale-Public School Version*. Washington, DC: American Association on Mental Deficiency.

Mercer, J. R. (1979). *SOMPA Technical Manual*. New York: Psychological Corporation.

Reschly, D. (1982). Assessing mild mental retardation: The influence of adaptive behavior, sociocultural status, and prospects for nonbiased assessment. In C. R. Reynolds & T. B. Gutkin (Eds.), *Handbook of school psychology* (pp. 209-242). New York: John Wiley & Sons.

Richmond, B. O., & de la Serna, M. (1978). *Escala Internacional de Conducta Adaptativa: Manual tecnico y de administracion*. (Available from Dr. Bert O. Richmond, College of Education, University of Georgia, Athens, GA 30602.)

Richmond, B. O., & Kicklighter, R. H. (1980). *Children's Adaptive Behavior Scale (CABS)*. Atlanta, GA: Humanics, Ltd.

Sparrow, S. S., Balla, D. A., & Cichetti, D. V. (1984). *Vineland Adaptive Behavior Scales*. Circle Pines, MN: American Guidance Service.

Wechsler, D. (1974). *Wechsler Intelligence Scale for Children-Revised*. New York: The Psychological Corporation.

Frank Auld, Ph.D.

Professor of Psychology, University of Windsor, Windsor, Canada.

CLAYBURY SELECTION BATTERY

T. M. Caine, O. B. A. Wijesinghe, D. Winter, and D. Smail.
Windsor, England: NFER-Nelson Publishing Company Ltd.

Introduction

The Claybury Selection Battery consists of three tests that are intended primarily for use in psychiatric clinics or hospitals. The first test, the Direction of Interest Questionnaire (DIQ), purports to measure C. G. Jung's concept of the direction of libidinal flow, i.e., introversion vs. extraversion. The second test, the Treatment Expectancies Questionnaire (TEQ), purports to measure patients' expectancies regarding psychological and psychiatric treatment, in particular whether these patients expect that they will have an active, participative role in the treatment or will be dealt with authoritatively by an expert who knows best what should be done for them. The third test, the Attitudes to Treatment Questionnaire (ATQ), is designed to measure attitudes of the staff members of psychiatric organizations toward the treatment process, in particular, whether these staff members favor a biological-directive or a psychosocial-participative approach.

The authors of these tests were four English psychologists: T. M. Caine, University College Hospital, Medical School, London; the late Brian Wijesinghe who was head of the Claybury Hospital Psychology Department; D. J. Smail, Nottingham Area Psychiatric Service, Nottingham; and D. A. Winter, Barnet Health Authority, Napsbury Hospital, near St. Albans. The authors named this test battery The Claybury Selection Battery in recognition of the fact that most of the research on which it is based was carried out at the Claybury Hospital at Woodford Bridge, Essex, in Greater London.

Although the manual to this battery does not make clear which of the authors was mainly responsible for developing each of the tests, the information provided in the manual and in a book by Caine, Wijesinghe, and Winter (1981) leads one to surmise that the DIQ was developed mainly by Caine and Smail, beginning in 1969 or earlier; that the TEQ owes most of its development to the work of Caine and Wijesinghe beginning in 1976 or earlier; and that Caine and Smail contributed significantly to the ATQ, beginning not later than 1969. The work on these tests expresses the authors' interest in making available to psychologists working in the National Health Service a means for allocating therapeutic resources more effectively. If psychologists could discover, by means of personality questionnaires, which patients are apt to do well in analytic group therapy and which ones will do poorly in that treatment but well in behavior therapy, then psychologists could add greatly to the effectiveness of psychiatric treatment. The Claybury Battery is intended to enhance such decisions on assignment to various treatments.

The DIQ, a 14-item scale, was derived from Scale C of the Kuder Preference Record, from the M scale of Cattell's 16 Personality Factor Questionnaire, and from

169

the S/N scale of the Myers-Briggs Type Indicator. The authors of the TEQ, building on previous studies of patients' attitudes toward psychological and physical approaches to psychiatric treatment, framed questions that might reflect a preference for either a psychological approach or an organic approach. Those questions that practicing therapists believed expressed an attitude favoring one approach or the other were retained in the preliminary version of the test. When the test had been given to 135 patients at a psychiatric clinic, the authors did a principal components analysis of the responses. They then retained in the test the 15 items that loaded highly on the first principal component, which produced the same selection of items as choosing the items that correlated most highly with the total score on the test would have.

In developing the ATQ Caine and Smail framed items that in their opinion expressed the attitudes that staff members and patients in an outpatient therapeutic community had revealed during open-ended interviews. They circulated this preliminary version of the test to a large number of hospitals and therapeutic communities within the United Kingdom. They had returns from 281 persons (82 patients, 79 doctors, 120 nurses). Doing separate components analyses for the three subgroups (patients, doctors, nurses), the authors selected the items that loaded on the first principal component. Because there was substantial agreement among the three analyses, the authors decided to choose just one of them—the analysis of data from the nurses—as the basis for selecting 19 items for the final version of the ATQ.

Each of the three tests is presented to the subject on a single 210 mm X 297 mm (approx. 8¼" X 11¾") sheet of paper. Instructions for the DIQ are presented on one side of the sheet, with the 14 dichotomous, forced-choice items on the other side. The items are of the form "I like mystery stories—I like romantic stories" and subjects are required to choose one or the other statement. Both the instructions and the questions for the TEQ are presented on one side of the sheet only. The 15 items are in a 4-choice true/false format, and subjects indicate their expectancies of psychological and psychiatric treatment by circling T, PT, PF, or F ("true," "possibly true," "possibly false," and "false," respectively). Like the TEQ, the ATQ presents all of the material on one page. Respondents indicate their attitudes to psychiatric and psychological treatment by circling each of the 19 items SA, A, U, D, or SD ("strongly agree," "agree," "uncertain," "disagree," and "strongly disagree," respectively).

These tests can be administered individually or in a group session, and subjects can do the test without intervention from the examiner. An adult of normal intelligence who is not mentally handicapped can understand the language of any of the three tests. The user of these tests should, however, take account the following points:

1) There are a few British expressions in the DIQ that may puzzle American readers, for example, "holiday" referring to what an American would call a "vacation."

2) The wording of the TEQ is directed toward psychiatric patients. The phrasing suits that group, for which the test was intended, but does not suit other groups.

3) The wording of the ATQ is directed toward the staff of psychiatric facilities; it suits these persons, but not others.

Practical Applications/Uses

The DIQ measures introversion-extraversion and would be of use to researchers who want to measure this important personality trait as defined by Jung originally—an inward or outward direction of interest. It differs from Cattell's second-order extraversion factor and Eysenck's scale of extraversion-introversion, which measures a somewhat different trait related to sociability. Because the DIQ measures a person's direction of interest it would be useful to any clinician who wants to measure this trait. It might also be useful in deciding what kind of vocation would be suitable for the subject.

The other two tests have a much more practical orientation: they are meant to define who prefers a psychosocial orientation to therapy, and to predict who will do well when participating in that kind of therapy. Both the TEQ and the ATQ, therefore, would be useful to a psychologist working in a psychiatric hospital or clinic.

The authors believe that the first two tests, the DIQ and the TEQ, are useful in the selection of patients for psychoanalytically oriented group therapy or for physical-medical treatment. They believe that the ATQ is useful for measuring whether staff members have attitudes appropriate to performing psychosocial or to performing biologically oriented treatment.

Any of the three tests can be administered individually or to a group of subjects and all three are self-administered. A subject should be able to complete the DIQ in about 5 minutes, and the TEQ or the ATQ in less than 10 minutes.

For the DIQ, each choice of a statement representing an outer-directed interest is scored 2; each choice of an inner-directed statement is scored 0. If the subject has checked both statements or neither, the item is scored 1.

For the TEQ, the response categories are weighted 5, 4, 3, 2, and 1, respectively; the high end of the scale is for agreement with an organic or behavioral treatment-orientation, the low end for a group psychotherapy orientation.

For the ATQ, the response categories are weighted 4, 3, 2, and 1. The high scores reflect an organic treatment approach, whereas the low scores represent a psycho-therapeutic approach.

Transparent scoring templates fit over the answer sheets, making scoring relatively easy.

Almost anyone can serve as an examiner—a clinician, secretary, or receptionist. In order to interpret the test results, however, one needs to have a level of training corresponding to that of graduate members of the British Psychological Society or members of the American Psychological Association.

Persons lacking a comprehensive clinical background should not interpret this test clinically. If examiners do use the DIQ clinically, they would do so within the framework of their training as a clinical psychologist. However, they should not make use of the DIQ score as an isolated, fragmented datum.

If the DIQ is used for vocational guidance, the examiner should have training in vocational counseling. As is the case in clinical applications, the test score should not be used as an isolated fragment in vocational counseling. An examiner could make use of the data in the test manual showing the mean scores of several occupational groups, along with the standard deviations of these groups. However, because these samples are small (ranging only from 11 to 116) one could not put a great deal of confidence in these data as defining typical scores for the groups they represent.

In the manual for the battery the authors suggest cutting points for the TEQ that are optimal for discriminating patients who do better in group psychotherapy from those who do better in bahavior therapy. According to the research reported in the manual, these cutting points worked well in the psychiatric outpatient samples from which the cutting points were originally determined. We cannot know whether the TEQ would work as well in new samples or whether the cutting points that worked well for the authors would be most effective in new samples. Users of the test would do well to develop local norms for the TEQ and to cross-validate the test by seeing whether it is predictive in their clinic or hospital before using the TEQ for prediction.

Technical Aspects

Direction of Interest Questionnaire. The authors retested 42 occupational therapy students after three months in order to assess test-retest reliability; the coefficient was .84. No data are provided about internal consistency of the scale.

The manual provides information about concurrent validity, reporting that the DIQ correlated .81 with the S/N scale of the Myers-Briggs Inventory. Because some questions from the Myers-Briggs scale have been included in the DIQ, we must consider this correlation to be partly an indication of reliability rather than of validity. The mean scores of various occupational groups, reported in the manual, are in the order that one would expect if the test is a valid measure of inward vs. outward interest. For example, psychotherapists have higher (i.e., more inward) scores than metallurgists, as one would expect. The occupational samples are, however, small and of unknown representativeness.

The DIQ does not correlate substantially with the Neuroticism, Extraversion, or Lie scales of the Eysenck Personality Inventory, as it should not if it is measuring something different. The sample in this study was small (N = 27). In another study, the DIQ was shown to correlate with the Kuder Preference Inventory scales that one would expect it to correlate with; but again, the sample was small (N = 31).

On the whole, in this reviewer's opinion, the evidence for validity is good as far as it goes, but much more research needs to be done.

The Treatment Expectancies Questionnaire. The manual provides no information about internal consistency or test-retest reliability. The method of selecting items, choosing those that loaded on the first principal component, would be expected to produce good internal consistency; one would wish, however, that the authors had done the proper calculations of internal consistency coefficients and had reported the results.

Studies of the relationship between response to treatment and TEQ score, as reported in the manual, have consistently shown a moderate relationship between TEQ score and such criterion measures as length of stay in treatment, rating of success by therapist, rating of success by patient, and a composite score of therapeutic gain based on psychological tests. The authors reported significant *t*-tests; when this reviewer transformed these into point-biserial correlations, the *r*'s were around .4.

The Attitudes to Treatment Questionnaire. When the authors retested 52 nurses after a year they obtained a test-retest *r* of .79. Another researcher with a sample of 21 student psychiatric nurses retested at three months reported an *r* of .76.

The group comparisons reported in the manual make a convincing case that professional groups expected to favor physical treatment score high (as they should), and groups expected to favor psychological treatment score low.

Although persons who are more inward according to the DIQ tend also to do better on intelligence tests, the authors argue that this fact does not damage the value of the DIQ. Within any intelligence or social-class level, they point out, the DIQ distinguishes the more inwardly oriented from the more outwardly oriented. They found no relationship of age or gender to DIQ score.

The authors found no sex differences on the TEQ. They found, however, that older patients and patients having lower intelligence-test scores, had higher (more behaviorally-physically oriented) scores on the TEQ. To some extent, then, these covariates cloud the meaning of the relationship between TEQ score and success in one or another kind of therapy. We do not know whether those scoring low on the TEQ do better in group therapy because their attitude suits them for it or because thay are younger and brighter.

The authors report no relationship between age or gender and ATQ score within samples of nurses (N = 239), psychiatric hospital staff (N = 99), and general practitioners (N = 34).

Critique

Caine and his co-workers have given us a new test, the DIQ, that measures a theoretically very interesting dimension of personality. Although we lack extensive norms for this test and much further research needs to be done to establish the test's validity as a measure of Jung's extraversion-introversion dimension, the work done so far seems sound. This test may find a place as a measure of a fundamental personality dimension.

The TEQ and the ATQ represent a different kind of test than the DIQ. They were developed to deal with the pressing, practical need to select those patients who will do best in a particular kind of psychiatric therapy (the TEQ) or to select those staff members most in tune with a particular approach to therapy (the ATQ). On the evidence provided in the manual, one would conclude that these two tests do, at least reasonably well, aid in this selection process. They are quite short and easy to administer. Do the tests tell us more than we could learn by simply asking the patients and the staff members what approach to therapy they prefer? Perhaps not. Yet there is an advantage in making such an inquiry in a systematic, quantitative way—that is, by giving a psychological test. Therefore it seems to this reviewer that the authors have made a contribution to clinical practice by devising these instruments.

References

Caine, T. M., Smail, D. J., Wijesinghe, O. B. A., & Winter, D. A. (1982). *The Claybury Selection Battery manual.* Windsor, England: NFER-Nelson Publishing Co. Ltd.

Caine, T. M., Wijesinghe, O. B. A., & Winter, D. A. (1981). *Personal styles in neurosis.* London: Routledge & Kegan Paul.

Jung, C. G. (1971). *Psychological types.* In R. F. C. Hull (Trans.), *The collected works of C. G. Jung* (Vol. 6). London: Routledge & Kegan Paul. (Original work published in 1921)

Jung, C. G. (1971). *Psychological typology.* In R. F. C. Hull (Trans.), *The collected works of C. G. Jung* (Vol. 6). London: Routledge & Kegan Paul. (Original work published in 1936)

Norman W. Mulgrave, Ph.D.
Professor of Educational Psychology, University of Pittsburgh, Pittsburgh, Pennsylvania.

CLIFTON ASSESSMENT PROCEDURES FOR THE ELDERLY

A. H. Pattie and C. J. Gilleard. Cleveland, Ohio: Distributed by The Psychological Corporation.

Introduction

This assessment procedure, consisting of the Cognitive Assessment Scale (CAS), which includes the Gibson Spiral Maze, and the Behavior Rating Scale (BRS), has been devised to assess the cognitive and behavioral competence of the elderly. The procedure is a reasonably brief method of determining the existence of impairment in mental functioning and the existence and degree of behavioral disability.

The Cognitive Assessment Scale, first published as Clifton Assessment Schedule, is a rather short test eliciting information and orientation, counting, repeating the alphabet, reading a word list, and producing a writing sample. In addition, psychomotor ability is measured by the Gibson Spiral Maze. This test can be administered to an elderly person in a rather short time (5 to 15 minutes).

The Behavior Rating Scale, on the other hand, is a shortened version of the Stockton Geriatric Rating Scale originally devised for use in the assessment of elderly hospitalized patients. This scale measures four principal areas of behavior disability: physical disability (Pd), apathy (Ap), communication difficulties (Cd), and social disturbance (Sd). This scale should be completed by a person familiar with the behavior of the elderly person to be rated. The rater is instructed to rate each item according to the person's current functioning and is advised to consider the person's behavior over the past week or two.

On the basis of the responses to the CAS and/or the BRS the Report Form is completed. This summary may be used to place an individual into one of five grades of dependency: a) no impairment/independent elderly, b) mild impairment/low dependency, c) moderate impairment/medium dependency, d) marked impairment/high dependency, or e) severe impairment/maximum dependency.

Anne H. Pattie is the principal clinical psychologist in the York Health District in the United Kingdom and her coauthor is Christopher J. Gilleard, clinical psychologist, now senior clinical psychologist at the York Health District. This assessment is the result of research projects dating back to 1973. At that time Dr. Pattie was the principal clinical psychologist at the Clifton Hospital and Christopher Gilleard was a clinical psychologist at the same institution. Their interest was in the devising of a reasonably brief method of assessing the cognitive and behavioral competence of the elderly. The Cognitive Assessment Scale, originally titled the

Clifton Assessment Scale, was described in the *British Journal of Psychology* in 1975 (Pattie & Gilleard, 1975). The Behavior Rating Scale was adapted from the Stockton Geriatric Rating Scale (Meer & Baker, 1966) and was first published as the Shortened Stockton Geriatric Rating Scale (Gilleard & Pattie, 1977). These two scales combined make up the Cognitive Assessment Procedures for the Elderly (CAPE).

The CAS was originally devised as a brief measure of psychological functioning on a chronic psychiatric patient group (Pattie, Williams, & Emery, 1975) and it was subsequently found to be of value with elderly patients (Pattie & Gilleard, 1975). The CAS was a new test that consisted of a 12-item information and orientation subtest, a brief mental abilities test, and a psychomotor performance test. Because the authors were interested in a brief cognitive and behavioral assessment procedure in place of more elaborate and time-consuming ones they found it necessary to revise and shorten the Stockton Geriatric Rating Schedule. Although this procedure has been developed for English-speaking elderly persons, there is no reason to believe that it could not be translated into other languages and used in other cultures, provided normative data is collected in those cultures and appropriate revisions made.

The Cognitive Assessment Scale is in two parts. The first part is printed on both sides of a single 8¼" x 11" x ¼" sheet of paper. This page contains the information/ orientation and mental abilities subtests of the CAS. The psychomotor subtest consists of the Gibson Spiral Maze (Gibson, 1965, 1977) printed on a 9¾" x 12" heavy paper. The information/orientation subtest of the CAS consists of personal awareness, some knowledge of general information, and current government leaders. The mental ability subtest covers ability to count, knowledge of the alphabet, simple reading, and cursive writing. The Gibson Spiral Maze provides the psychomotor score although a different scoring procedure has been devised for this population. This is an individually administered instrument in which the examiner asks the questions and records the answers. Although the examiner is permitted to rephrase the questions once or twice, no assistance or clues should be given and "excessive repetition is not recommended" (Pattie & Gilleard, 1979). The examiner is required to have a writing implement and a stop watch and should simply introduce the test with a phrase such as "There are some questions I'd like to ask you" or some other innocuous statement. The manual lists each question and next to each the rather clear and concise criteria for scoring. The information/orientation section of the test consists of 12 items and the mental ability section consists of four items; qualitative scoring is used. For certain items the faster the individual completes the item, the higher the score. Error-free answers get higher scores than those containing errors. In the psychomotor subtests, the Gibson Spiral Maze, the fewer the errors, the higher the score. A bonus is given if the maze is completed under two minutes.

The Behavior Rating Scale consists of 18 items that are answered by a person who is familiar with the elderly person's behavior. As with the CAS, all items are on a single printed page. There are six items that are added to provide the physical disability (Pd) score, five items added together to provide the apathetic (Ap) score, two items comprise the communication difficulty (Cd) score, and five items comprise the social disturbance (Sd) score. There are two items assessing hearing and vision that are uncalculated in the score. The rater is advised to rate each item according to the person's current functioning level based on observations during the past week or so. Each item is scored 0, 1, or 2 in terms of the severity of the physical disability or inappropriateness of behavior. For example, if a person needs no assistance in dressing, their score for that item is 0. If, on another item, the person is judged never willing to "help out," the score is 2. Thus, high scores indicate need for assistance and/or dependency whereas low scores indicate independence.

All answers are recorded directly on the two printed sheets and they are then transferred to the Report Form that contains the usual biographical information, a place for other "relevant background information," the subtest scores, and the total scores of the CAS and the BRS. On the reverse side of the Report Form the norms for Dependency Grade are printed. There is a space on the Report Form for a Dependency Grade for cognitive, behavioral, and overall. Nowhere on the Report Form or in the manual is there directions for calculating the overall Dependency Grade. On the basis of the total score on both the CAS and BRS one gets a dependency grade of A, B, C, D, or E. Thus a person may have no cognitive impairment if the CAS total score is between 35 and 30 but may have medium dependency if the BRS total score is between 8 and 12.

Practical Applications/Uses

This Cognitive Assessment Scale is useful for a quick evaluation of the existence and degree of impairment in mental functioning but it is not to be confused with an intelligence test and should not be considered such. The scale would be useful for professionals, psychologists, social workers, health personnel, general practitioners, occupational therapists, and others professionally concerned with care and management of the elderly. The Behavior Rating Scale is simply an overall measurement of an individual's behavioral disability level. When the CAS and BRS are combined it is possible to determine the most appropriate living arrangements or the degree of support and services necessary for the elderly client because the degree of dependence or independence of an elderly person both in terms of mental ability and behavior is determined. The CAPE has been shown to differentiate between those acute psychiatric patients who are discharged after a short period of treatment and those who are not discharged within three months. It is also useful as an instrument to evaluate the progress of an individual or groups of individuals. The brevity of the procedure enhances the CAPE as an evaluation instrument when serial assessment is necessary.

The CAS and/or BRS have been used to determine the extent and degree of cognitive impairment as an independent variable in experiments to determine the effects of chair design on mobility (Finlay, Bales, Rosen, & Milling, 1983), the effects on relatives of elderly demented patients (Greene, Smith, Gardiner, & Timbury, 1982), as a criterion measure for the Test of Reality Orientation with Geriatric Patients (Johnson, McLaren, & McPherson, 1981), and as an evaluation instrument to test the effectiveness of reality orientation among the elderly (Greene, Timbury, Smith, & Gardina, 1983). The CAPE has also been used to group elderly institutionalized clients according to degree of impairment.

The test is designed for persons 60 years of age and older, as a reasonably brief method for assessing their cognitive and behavioral competence. Many parts of the CAS could not be administered to a totally blind client but the hearing impaired should have no difficulty if it is possible to communicate with them in some fashion.

The test is individually administered. It should be given in an area that is without distraction and where the examinee is comfortably seated at a table. A well trained paraprofessional should be able to administer and score the test. Depending on the competence of the elderly person the time to administer the test could range from 5-30 minutes.

The scoring is relatively simple and accomplished on the test protocol. No extensive training is required; there is no need for machine scoring. There are no inherent problems with the scoring of the instruments, because the scoring directions are simple and clear scoring is therefore easily accomplished.

To interpret the scores one simply gets a Dependency Grade on cognitive and behavioral impairment. High scores on the CAS and low scores on the BRS indicate independence and no impairment; Dependency Grade A is defined as elderly who are comparable to those living without support in the community. Medium scores on both tests indicate moderate impairment and medium dependency or Dependency Grade C defined as elderly who are "likely to need residential care or considerable support and help if at home." Dependency Grade E, low CAS score and high BRS score, is defined as severe impairment and maximum dependency . . . "seen most often in psychogeriatric wards . . ." (Pattie & Gilleard, 1979, p. 12). The Dependency Grade can also be established using only the CAS or the BRS. The interpretation would be limited, therefore, to either the cognitive or behavioral domain.

Technical Aspects

Because the test is useful for both chronic and acute elderly psychiatric patients two reliability studies are reported using the CAS: 1) short term test-retest reliability, short term defined as retesting within three to four days, and 2) long term defined as an interval of six months. In the short term study the reliabilities of the subtests of the CAS ranged from a low of .79 on the psychomotor subtest to .87 on the information/orientation subtest on a group of 38 patients aged 65 or over. Other short-term (two- and three-month intervals) test-retest reliability studies found reliability estimates of the subtests ranging from .56 to .90. The 6-month test-retest reliabilities calculated on the subtest scores of 39 newly admitted residents to homes for the elderly ranged from .69 to .84. The authors do not provide reliability estimates for the total CAS score, which is the sum of the three subtest scores. It is this total test score that is used in determining the Dependency Grade of the elderly person and because the three subtest scores are moderately intercorrelated one would anticipate that the reliability of the total CAS would be higher than the reliabilities of the subtest scores, making the total test score a rather stable indication of cognitive impairment.

The reliability of the BRS is appropriately interrater reliability. The authors report five interrater reliability studies of the subscales of the BRS. They fail, however, to report the number of subjects in each study. The interrater reliabilities of the BRS subscales across the five studies range from a low of .54 to a high of .91. One of the subscales, communication difficulties (Cd), consists of only two items, therefore, the interrater reliabilities of this scale are low. Eliminating interrater reliabilities of the Cd scale, the reliabilities range from a low of .72 to a high of .91. Again, as with the CAS, the BRS total score is used to determine the Dependency Grade. Because the total score consists of more items than any of the subtests one would anticipate the reliability of the total score to be higher than the reliability of the subtests.

All of the subtests of both the CAS and BRS are moderately to substantially intercorrelated; a Dependency Grade based on both scales should be very reliable.

The CAPE was designed for three main functions: 1) individual assessment, 2) population surveys and screening, and 3) identifying patients for rehabilitation and for the evaluation of the effects of therapeutic intervention.

Functions 1 and 3 can be considered together as clinical applications, Pattie and Gilleard (1975, 1976, 1978) found that scores of eight and above on the CAS information subtest have generally been associated with an absence of significant cognitive deterioration, whereas scores below that are found among patients with the diagnosis of dementia or acute organic brain syndrome. The percentage of agreement between subsequent diagnosis and the score on the information subtest varied from 83% to 92% across the three studies.

A study of the association between CAS subtest performance and likely outcome was reported in the manual (Pattie & Gilleard, 1979). Using a score of less than eight on any of the subtests of the CAS classified a newly admitted, acute patient as having significant cognitive deterioration. The outcome measure used was discharge within three months. Of those who did not exhibit significant cognitive deterioration on admission, 78% were discharged within three months; of those with significant cognitive deterioration, 79% were still institutionalized at the end of three months. A discriminant function, based on the three subtests of the CAS resulted in 83% correct classification.

The validity of function 2, population and surveys and screening, can be demonstrated by a review of the normative data supplied in the manual. Norms based on several hundred elderly people ranging from independent healthy members of the community to those permanently hospitalized in long-term geriatric and psychogeriatric wards are reported. In every case the mean scores for such groups are as one would anticipate. The community, "well" group has the highest average CAS score and the lowest mean BRS score. The chronic psychiatric group, the most involved group, has the lowest CAS mean score and the highest BRS mean score.

A review of Table 4 of the manual, listing means and standard deviations of groups of elderly living in the community, in supervised apartments, in nursing homes, and acute and chronically institutionalized psychiatric patients demonstrates that those who are living in the least restrictive environments have the highest CAS score and the lowest BRS scores and those in the most restrictive environments have the lowest CAS scores and the highest BRS scores.

The authors report "comparative validity" studies with the Weschler Memory Scale and the Verbal, Performance, and Full Scale IQ scores of the WAIS. The numbers are small and the evidence less persuasive than the information cited above.

Critique

This procedure, designed to evaluate cognitive and behavioral deficit in elderly patients in the United Kingdom, appears to function well among groups of elderly persons. It is a short, brief, easily administered assessment of deficits. The BRS could be used at admission to a psychiatric unit to help determine the level of care and supervision needed. The cognitive deficit measured by the CAS could be used to predict success in therapy.

The authors of a battery, developed for the purpose of differential diagnosis of organic dementia from depression among the elderly, comment as follows:

> . . . there are now two carefully standardized procedures available, these being the revised version of the Kendrick battery, used here, and the Pattie and Gilleard's (1979) Clifton Assessment Procedures for the Elderly (CAPE) . . . The CAPE should be used when the assessment of dependency needs is required, and when management decisions must be taken . . . (Gibson, Moyes, & Kendrick, 1980).

The value of this assessment procedure probably lies in its ability to classify persons in terms of their need for services. Agencies and professionals dealing with the care, treatment, and management of the elderly will find the CAPE useful if norms are developed for use in the United States.

A shortened version of the CAPE, the Survey Version (Pattie, 1981), combines the information orientation subtest (I/O) of the CAS and the physical disability subscale (Pd) of the BRS. The survey score, which combines cognitive and behavioral deficit, is calculated by subtracting the Pd score from the I/O score giving a possible range of +12 (perfect performance on I/O and no rated Pd) to −12 (no score on I/O and maximum Pd).

Three factor analyses of the seven subscales of the CAPE (N = 400, 290, 211) revealed that the first factor accounted for 60% or more of the variance. I/O and Pd subscales had the highest loadings on the first factor for all three analyses. The correlations between the factor scores, derived from the factor analysis, and the survey score (I/O-Pd) ranged from .90 to .96. Furthermore, the survey score correlated with CAS total score .87 and with BRS total score −.87. The test-retest reliability estimates of the survey score on three occasions were .86, .88, and .82. Validity studies similar to the longer CAPE have been carried out with similar results. Those with higher survey scores survive longer, need less level of care, and have more positive outcomes. Norms for Dependency Grades are given.

The short version seems to be as reliable and valid as the longer version of the scale and may be used by persons responsible for the management of the elderly. It would be especially suitable for screening and large scale surveys.

References

Finlay, O. E., Bales, T. B., Rosen, C., & Milling, J. (1983). Effects of chair design, age and cognitive status on mobility. *Age and Ageing*, 12, 329-333.

Gibson, A. J., Moyes, I. C. A., & Kendrick, D. (1980). Cognitive assessment of the elderly long-stay patient. *British Journal of Psychiatry, 137,* 551-557.

Gibson, H. B. (1965). *Manual of the Gibson Spiral Maze* (1st ed.). London: University of London Press.

Gibson, H. B. (1977). *Manual of the Gibson Spiral Maze* (2nd ed.). London: Hodder & Stoughton.

Gilleard, C. J., & Pattie, A. H. (1977). The Stockton Geriatric Rating Scale: A shortened version with British normative data. *British Journal of Psychiatry, 131,* 90-94.

Greene, J. G., Smith, R., Gardiner, M., & Timbury, G. C. (1982). Measuring behavioural disturbance of elderly demented patients in the community and its effect on relatives: A factor analytic study. *Age and Ageing, 11,* 121-126.

Greene, J. G., Timbury, G. C., Smith, R., Gardiner, M. (1983). Reality orientation with elderly patients in the community, an empirical evaluation. *Age and Ageing, 12,* 38-43.

Johnson, C. H., McLaren, S. M., & McPherson, F. M. (1981). The comparative effectiveness of three versions of "classroom" reality orientation. *Age and Ageing, 10,* 33-35.

Meer, B., & Baker, J. A. (1966). The Stockton Geriatric Rating Scale. *Journal of Gerontology, 21,* 393-403.

Pattie, A. H. (1981). A survey version of the Clifton Assessment Procedures for the Elderly (CAPE). *British Journal of Clinical Psychology, 20,* 173-178.

Pattie, A. H., & Gilleard, C. J. (1975). A brief psychogeriatric assessment schedule—validation against psychiatric diagnosis and discharge from hospital. *British Journal of Psychiatry, 127,* 489-493.

Pattie, A. H., & Gilleard, C. J. (1976). The Clifton Assessment Schedule—Further validation of a psychogeriatric assessment schedule. *British Journal of Psychiatry, 129,* 68-72.

Pattie, A. H., & Gilleard, C. J. (1978). The two year predictive validity of the Clifton Assessment Schedule and the shortened Stockton Geriatric Rating Scale. *British Journal of Psychiatry, 133,* 457-460.

Pattie, A. H., & Gilleard, C. J. (1979). *Manual of the Clifton Assessment Procedures for the Elderly (CAPE).* Kent: Hodder & Stoughton.

Pattie, A. H., Williams, A., & Emery, D. (1975). Helping the chronic patient in an industrial therapy setting: An experiment in inter-disciplinry co-operation. *British Journal of Psychiatry, 126,* 30-33.

Scott W. Brown, Ph.D.
*Assistant Professor of Educational Psychology, The University of
Connecticut, Storrs, Connecticut.*

COLUMBIA MENTAL MATURITY SCALE

*Bessie Burgemeister, Lucille H. Blum, and Irving Lorge.
Cleveland, Ohio: The Psychological Corporation.*

Introduction

The Columbia Mental Maturity Scale (CMMS) (Burgemeister, Blum, & Lorge,
1972) is an individually administered instrument designed to assess the general
reasoning ability of children between the ages of 3 years, 6 months to 9 years, 11
months. The CMMS consists of 92 pictorial and figural, classification items
arranged in a series of eight overlapping levels. Each of the eight levels contains
between 51 and 65 items that are appropriate for a specific chronological age.

The items consist of a collection of three to five drawings printed on a 6" x 19"
card. Cards portray objects that are ". . . within the range of most American
children, even those whose environmental backgrounds have been limited"
(Burgemeister et al., 1972, p. 7). Children are asked to look at all the drawings and
select the one that is different from all the others, and indicate their choice by
pointing to it. For younger age levels, the discriminations are made on the basis of
color, size, and form. The older age levels require the child to process more subtle
and abstract differences among the drawings.

Administration of the CMMS takes approximately 15 to 20 minutes and yields
several scores: raw score, Age Deviation Score, percentile rank, stanine, and
Maturity Index. The Age Deviation Score is a standard score with a mean of 100
and a standard deviation of 16. The maturity indexes are comparable to mental
ages, although they are more global, employing the use of ranges of age rather
than specific mental ages.

Prior to 1947, the principal method for assessing the mental abilities of children
with physical and/or mental impairments was to modify available mental ability
instruments, with only limited success. In 1947, Bessie Burgemeister, Lucille
Hollander Blum, and Irving Lorge began an effort to develop an instrument
capable of assessing the mental ability of handicapped children at early ages,
namely, the CMMS. The first edition of this test was published in 1954, the second
in 1959, and the latest in 1972. The authors developed the CMMS while at Columbia University and have a well-documented list of qualifications and experience in
the area of intellectual assessment and test construction, as indicated by an
extensive list of publications. For instance, Irving Lorge's accomplishments within
the field of psychometrics are highly regarded and include the publication of
numerous journal articles and books, as well as the development of the Lorge--
Thorndike Intelligence Test.

Initial test development focused on the selection of an appropriate test format that could be satisfactorily administered to both handicapped and normal children, and yield a reliable and valid index of mental abilities. It became clear that the items must require minimal motoric and verbal response, and that the purpose of the task must be easily communicated to the child by the examiner. After some pilot testing, the pictorial classification format was selected because it met both the administration and response requirements. Also, this type of test format had been used successfully in other individual and group administered nonverbal instruments of mental ability. Subsequent exploration with handicapped and normal samples have supported the format decision.

The first edition of the CMMS (1954) provided an IQ score that was based on a mental age calculation utilizing the mental ages derived from the relationship between the CMMS scores and the mental ages from the Stanford-Binet Intelligence Scale and several other well-known known tests of mental ability. The second edition (1959) incorporated only minor changes from the earlier edition, including 17 new items and scores similar to the earlier edition. In 1968, extensive research began that culminated in the third edition (1972) of the CMMS. Although the test retained many of the features of the earlier editions, several major changes, which employed current test development and norming procedures, were made.

In the 1972 edition of the CMMS eight overlapping levels replaced the single-level approach of the earlier editions. These eight levels were designed to measure approximately an equal range of abilities. Each of the eight levels was calculated based on data collected during the standardization procedure. Through the use of the multilevel test, a more efficient use of testing time for both examiner and child was made possible. Children are administered a set of 51-65 items that are most appropriate for children of their specific chronological age. Thorough item analysis allowed for the elimination of items judged to be too easy or too difficult for children of a specific age. Use of the eight-level approach also eliminated the need for complicated procedures to determine the termination of testing that was required in the previous editions.

The norms for the third edition were collected from a sample of 2,600 children at 67 test centers spread across 25 states. A national sample of 200 children stratified on several important demographic variables was tested at each age level. Earlier editions obtained norms through calibration of the CMMS with the Stanford-Binet Intelligence Scale and other tests of mental ability. The current procedure for collecting normative data demonstrated the establishment of a sound foundation for the current edition of the CMMS.

The third edition also included two new types of derived scores: the Age Deviation Score (ADS) and the Maturity Index (MI). The abandonment of the use of the ratio IQ represents a response to the well-documented problems regarding the use of such a score. The ADS is a standard score within an age group indicating deviation from the average score of that specific age group. The MI designates the average performance of the standardization group most similar to the performance of the child, indicating developmental status that may be useful in decisions of educational placement, diagnosis, and remediation.

Additionally, this last edition included a revision of the Individual Record Form that included biographical data and descriptive test information, a major overhaul of the earlier items, and specific instructions for administering the CMMS to Spanish-speaking children. Of the 92 items on the third edition, 50 are completely new and 40 are modifications of earlier editions. All items were subjected to a complete item analysis before being included in the final form, and changes for the Spanish-speaking administration are minimal, involving only a Spanish translation of the general instructions.

The CMMS kit contains 95 cards (92 items and 3 sample items), a manual and individual record form. The items are presented on 6" x 19" cards, each of which contains 3-5 drawings. Ideally, the child is seated across from the examiner and is presented with the card. Once rapport has been established, the child is requested to point to the picture that does not belong with the others. The child does not have to verbally identify the different picture, merely point or gesture to it. Sample items are used to initiate the testing procedure, which is consistent throughout all age levels. The CMMS is a power test with no time limit for items; however, the examiner is encouraged to use good judgement in the pacing of the items.

Children are administered one of the eight age levels appropriate for their chronological age and all items within that specific age level are administered. Specific administration procedures for exceptional children (either dull or bright) are included for either further testing at a lower or higher age level with the CMMS in order to obtain a thorough assessment of their mental abilities.

The CMMS answer form is complete and easy to use, with a single form used for all age levels. The front page has space for biographical data (e.g., date of birth, last grade level completed, primary language spoken at home); personal factors (i.e., conditions or characteristics that may be useful in the interpretation of the test performance); and the final CMMS test data (i.e., raw score, ADS, percentile rank, stanine, MI, and age level administered). Below is a brief synopsis of the purpose of the CMMS, a discussion of the different scores obtained, and a table of the percentile ranks corresponding to the ADS. The next three pages contain the answer key for the items at each age level.

The answer form is designed so that the items are numbered 1-92 and the number of drawings for each test item indicated by small pink boxes where black numbers designate correct options and white numbers designate incorrect options. The examiner merely marks the box corresponding to the selection by the child. The record form indicates the starting and stopping points (also written on the back of the cards) for each age level printed next to the items to facilitate the test administration.

The raw score is the total number of correct responses by the child between the start and end of the specific age level. These raw scores are then converted easily to the ADS by using the appropriate table included in the manual. The raw score is converted to the MI through the use of a separate table. In each case, the child's score is determined through comparison with the norms of his or her own age peers. Separate tables are available for the calculation of the stanines and percentile ranks. The scores obtained are gross indications of mental abilities and are not separated into different components of mental abilities. Therefore, the scores obtained on the CMMS are indications of the general reasoning ability of the child in comparison to the normative sample for that age. No in-depth profiles of specific mental abilities are available.

Practical Applications/Uses

The CMMS is an easily administered, individual test yielding an estimate of the general reasoning ability of children aged 3½ years to 9 years, 11 months. This instrument does not require a verbal response by the child and only minimal gross motor movement, making it an appropriate screening device for children with or without verbal and/or motor impairments. Its value as a screening device for young children suspected of having problems with general reasoning and specific use with children having physical impairments (i.e., Cerebral Palsy) is well documented (Hirschenfang, Jaramillo & Benton, 1966; Kaufman, 1978; Nicholson, 1970; Petrosko, 1973; Ritter, Duffey & Fischman; 1974; Salvia & Ysseldyke, 1981). The ease of administration and good psychometric properties make the CMMS a valuable tool for psychologists and educators dealing with young children.

The CMMS is designed to assess the general reasoning ability of young children. Because one of the authors' original goals was to develop an instrument that could be quickly administered to both normal and handicapped children, the CMMS can be judged a success. The ability to use the CMMS with children having hearing loss, speech impairment, brain damage, or mental retardation makes it an extremely valuable screening instrument for the majority of children.

In addition to its use with normal and handicapped children, it is also useful for assessing children whose primary language is not English. Because, however, the items selected contain pictures of objects that should be familiar to children who have access to television, the authors caution the use of the CMMS with those from other countries and from extremely isolated environments and warn that these children may have difficulty with certain items. Studies of the CMMS have found that scores on the CMMS may be influenced by the socioeconomic status of the child (Ratusnik & Koenigsknect, 1975). This data supports the contention that the lack of exposure to the objects contained in the CMMS may lower a child's score as reported by an earlier study using the 1959 version of the CMMS. Rosenberg and Stroud (1966) found that the scores of poverty-area children increased after they had been exposed to some schooling.

The CMMS may be used with the vast majority of children, but should not be used with children having severe vision loss that may prevent them from being able to inspect the pictured objects and abstractions accurately. All other children who have been exposed to the types of objects portrayed in the pictures may be administered the CMMS.

The use of the CMMS with normal and handicapped children serves as a useful screening device for global reasoning ability. However, caution must be used in the interpretation of the CMMS scores as a component of intellectual processing and not as an IQ score.

The CMMS is individually administered by school psychologists, elementary counselors, and classroom teachers who are under the supervision of school psychologists. The examiner should sit at a table across from the child. Once rapport has been established, the examiner presents the three sample items and the appropriate age-level items to the child. The child is instructed to point to the one that does not belong with the others. The manual provides the specific step-by-step procedures for administration with suggestions for varying the prompts and procedures for specific problems that occur (e.g., the child points to more than one picture). The administration instructions in the manual are explicit and complete, including examples and suggestions that are clear and relevant. Administration takes approximately 15-20 minutes.

All children are administered the age level appropriate for their chronological age, but if they receive a raw score either above or below a specific point, they are administered another age level. The manual describes the procedure for testing at additional age levels and presents the rationale for such testing.

Procedures for obtaining the various scores are straightforward and clearly presented in a six-step process in the manual. The raw score, which can be tallied quickly by counting the black numbers marked on the record form, is the total number of correct responses by the subject within the specific age level. The ADS is then determined by locating the appropriate table for the age level of the test administered on tables 3A to 3H and using the table with the child's chronological age and raw score. The ADS may be used to determine the percentile rank and stanine using another table, and an additional table provides the MI as indicated by ranges of raw scores within each age level of the test. The total time required for scoring the CMMS is approximately 5-10 minutes, but an experienced examiner should be able to complete the scoring in just 5 minutes. The simple procedures and lack of calculations required by the examiner minimize scoring errors.

At the time of this review, the CMMS can only be scored by hand. However, because the scoring procedure is fairly simple and straightforward, computer scoring is not necessary.

The CMMS yields four scores for interpretation: percentile rank and stanine (found on almost all standardized tests of intellectual ability and achievement) and ADS and MI (particular to the CMMS). The percentile rank and the stanine of the CMMS, as with any test, provide the measure of a child's performance compared to the normative sample of the test. Because the percentile ranks and stanines are determined by first obtaining the ADS, children are compared only with their age peers. The ADS, which is similar to a deviation IQ score, is an index of the general reasoning ability of one child compared to the performance of children in the norming sample of the same age. Scores range from a low of 50 to a high of 150.

The MI, a rather unusual score yielded by the CMMS, is comparable to the use of mental age, but specifies age ranges. The MI is used to indicate the child's level of maturity that most closely matches one of the 13 age groups used in the normative sample. The MI yields scores such as 4L (indicating the level of a child 4 years to 4 years, 5 months) or 5U (indicating the level of a child 5 years, 6 months to 5 years, 11 months). The utility of the MI is probably minimal because it is such a gross measure of performance and because of the problems inherent in the use of mental age indices (Egeland, 1978; Kaufman, 1978; Petrosko, 1973; Salvia & Ysseldyke, 1981).

In addition to the scores described above, the CMMS also provides a table of interlevel standard scores. These scores are not necessary for the normal use of the CMMS but are desirable in situations where long-term growth of a child is being examined through several administrations of the CMMS across more than one age level. The interlevel standard scores are also very valuable in research studies using children of different ages and requiring a score that can be compared across age levels.

The interpretation of the CMMS is based on the ADS, MI, percentile rank, and the stanine. Because there are no profile scores beyond the index of the total performance, there is very little training or practice required by the examiner. Interpretation is limited to discussions of the child's performance on the CMMS relative to the normative sample and in relation to the child's performance on other tests or observed behaviors. Several illustrative examples of cases are provided in the manual.

Technical Aspects

The CMMS was standardized on 2,600 children stratified on the basis of parental occupation, race, geographic location, and size of residence community. A sample of 200 children were selected for each age level closely reflecting the population distribution of the above variables as indicated by the 1960 U.S. Census. With only one small exception, the standardization procedures and data are considered excellent. In a review of the CMMS, Salvia and Ysseldyke (1981) note that the figures reported for the community-size distribution indicated that approximately twice as many children from large cities were included in the sample than is true of the general population, according to 1960 U.S. Census statistics. The standardization procedures and data are otherwise excellent.

The CMMS manual reports both split-half and test-retest reliabilities. The split-half reliabilities are reported for each of the 13 age levels, with the items for each age level divided in half forming two half-tests for each age level. Items were assigned to each of the two halves so that each half-test had the same characteristics as the total test with regard to test content and item difficulty. The split-half reliabilities were derived employing the Spearman-Brown Prophecy Formula for each of the half-test correlations. The manual reports internal consistency coefficients ranging from a low of .85 to a high of .91 with a median split-half coefficient of .90 for the standardization group, indicating excellent internal consistency.

Test-retest reliability coefficients for three different age groups are reported for a group of approximately 300 children tested with an interval of 7-10 days. A median test-retest reliability of .85 was obtained for the three groups. Children gained an average of 4.6 ADS points at retesting.

Both forms of reliability reported in the CMMS manual demonstrate good internal consistency and stability over time. However, the testing interval for the test-retest reliability is very short and further studies should be conducted to provide measures of stability over longer periods such as 2-3 months, as has been suggested by Petrosko (1973).

The standard error of measurement (SEM) provides an estimate of the fluctuation around the true score of a child. The smaller the SEM, the more precise the score estimate. The SEM of the ADS is reported as approximately 5 points for children between 3½-5½ years and 6 points for children aged 6-9 years. This means that when interpreting a 109 ADS for 5-year-old children, the actual chances are about 2 out of 3 that their "true" score lies in the range of 104-114. The authors of the CMMS warn against making unwarranted differentiation between test scores differing by only a few points because of the unreliability of such judgments.

The validity of the CMMS is reported in two forms—the data based on relationship with 1) the 1964 Stanford Achievement Test (SAT) and 2) several other intelligence tests.

The CMMS manual reports correlational data between the CMMS and the subtests of the SAT for 177 students in grades 1 and 2 in a moderate-sized school district in Virginia. These data indicate that the interlevel standard scores of the CMMS correlate substantially with the various subtest scores of the SAT with a median value of .57 (.31 to .61) for all Primary I Battery subtests and a median value of .47 (.43 to .61) for all Primary II Battery subtests.

The correlation of CMMS scores and two measures of intellectual ability, the Otis-Lennon Mental Ability Test (OL) and the Stanford-Binet Intelligence Scale (SB), are reported as concurrent validity. The study relating the CMMS and OL used 353 pupils in grades 1-3 from the same Virginia school district as cited for the SAT. The ADS of the CMMS and the Deviation IQ of the Otis-Lennon correlated from .62 to .69. The Deviation IQ score of the SB and the ADS of the CMMS correlated .67 for 52 preschool and first-grade children from a large southern city.

Studies of the CMMS with different populations have generally supported the reliability and validity reported by the CMMS authors. In a study comparing the ADS of the CMMS with the Deviation IQ of the SB for children identified as EMR, mean scores were approximately equal and a correlation of .74 between the two tests was found (Ritter, Duffey & Fischman, 1974). A study of several tests, including the CMMS, by Pascale (1973) reported a test-retest reliability of .85 over a span of 7 days for the CMMS and 25% common variance between the CMMS and the Peabody Picture Vocabulary Test (PPVT), suggesting that the CMMS is reliable and is measuring more than knowledge of vocabulary and objects, as measured by the PPVT. Nicholoson's (1970) study of cerebral palsied children with the earlier version of the CMMS found that the CMMS and the Raven's Coloured Progressive Matrices (RCPM) test resulted in approximately the same scores. However, the scores of the PPVT averaged 20 points greater than the CMMS or the RCPM, yet, all three tests were significantly correlated. Nicholoson concluded that the 20-point difference in scores may have been related to the verbal nature of the PPVT.

Although most studies have supported the use of the CMMS, a study by Johnson and Shinedling (1974) reported erratic scores for a group of mentally retarded children who were administered the CMMS. They also found that the ADS of the CMMS did not correlate as highly with the scores on the Slosson Intelligence Test as they did with the scores on the PPVT. Johnson and Shinedling concluded that the CMMS yielded lower estimates of ability than some other measures of intelligence.

Critique

Research studies and test experts generally support the use of the CMMS as a screening instrument (Kaufman, 1978; Pascale, 1973; Petrosko, 1973; Salvia & Ysseldyke, 1981). The standardization procedures, manual, and administration procedures, which are all applicable to normal and handicapped children, are often cited strengths of the CMMS.

Although the majority of the test reviews and research are positive, several authors state specific concerns about the CMMS. Petrosko (1973) questions the stability of the CMMS scores over periods longer than 10 days and the lack of extensive validity data reported in the manual. The validity studies reported are either with a small number of children or based on data collected from a single school district. Kaufman (1978) notes the good test statistics and standardization procedures but expresses some concern over the guessing factor on items with 4 options or less. Salvia and Ysseldyke (1981) and Egeland (1978) state that the claim of assessing the general reasoning ability of children is really limited to two kinds of intellectual processing: discrimination and classification. Although certainly assessing an important component of general reasoning ability, they caution that the CMMS is a limited sample of general reasoning ability. Egeland also notes that there is no discussion of an underlying theory of reasoning to support the selection of items and the test format beyond the goal of making the test applicable for both handicapped and normal children. Most test reviewers and researchers note that the Maturity Index is too gross a measurement for any practical use and discourage its use.

In this reviewer's opinion, the latest revision of the CMMS is a major improvement over earlier editions of the test. The nonverbal response format, requiring only a gross-motor gesture, makes it extremely valuable in assessments of various special populations of children and normal children. The ease of administration, excellent standardization procedures, and good test reliability and validity are all recommendations for the use of the instrument as a quick screening device. Although several criticisms of the CMMS have been made throughout this review, none of the critics suggest that the CMMS should not be used. In fact, when compared to the alternative tests, it is one of the best brief screening instruments available for assessing young children. The manual's brevity and completeness, including explicit directions for administration, scoring, interpretation, and the inclusion of special procedures for administration to extreme scorers and Spanish-speaking children are exemplary. One final excellent feature of the CMMS is the annotated bibliography of CMMS research included in the manual. Even though the majority of the studies reported in the present manual are for earlier editions of the CMMS, upon purchase of the CMMS, the user is placed on a mailing list to receive all current and future information pertaining to research studies of the CMMS.

In summary, the CMMS is recommended as an instrument for screening the general reasoning ability in young children. Only further research studies examining the CMMS with various populations will delineate the full potential of this instrument.

References

Burgemeister, B. B., Blum, L. H., & Lorge, I. (1972). *Columbia Mental Maturity Scale.* Cleveland: The Psychological Corporation.

Egeland, B. R. (1978). Review of Columbia Mental Maturity Scale. In O. K. Buros (Ed.), *The eighth mental measurements yearbook (pp. 298-299). Highland Park, NJ: The Gryphon Press.*

Hirschenfang, S., Jaramillo, S., & Benton, J. G. (1966). Comparison of scores on the revised Stanford-Binet (L), Columbia Mental Maturity Scale (CMMS) and Goodenough Draw-a-Man Test of children with neurological disorders. *Psychological Reports, 19,* 15-16.

Johnson, D. L., & Shinedling, M. M. (1974). Comparison of Columbia Mental Maturity Scale, Peabody Picture Vocabulary Test, and Slosson Intelligence Test with mentally retarded children. *Psychological Reports, 34,* 367-370.

Kaufman, A. S. (1978). Review of Columbia Mental Maturity Scale. In O. K. Buros (Ed.), *The eighth mental measurements yearbook* (pp. 299-301). Highland Park, NJ: The Gryphon Press.

Nicholoson, C. L. (1970). Correlations among CMMS, PPVT and RCPM for cerebral palsied children. *Perceptual and Motor Skills, 30,* 715-718.

Pascale, P. J. (1973). Validity concerns of preschool testing. *Educational and Psychological Measurement, 33,* 977-978.

Petrosko, J. M. (1973). Review of Columbia Mental Maturity Scale. *Measurement & Evaluation in Guidance, 6(3),* 189-191.

Ratusnik, D. L., & Koenigsknect, R. A. (1975). Normative study of the Goodenough Drawing Test and the Columbia Mental Maturity Scale in a metropolitan setting. *Perceptual and Motor Skills, 40,* 835-838.

Ritter, D., Duffey, J., & Fischman, R. (1974). Comparability of Columbia Mental Maturity Scale and Stanford-Binet, Form L-M, estimates of intelligence. *Psychological Reports, 34,* 174.

Rosenberg, L. A., & Stroud, M. (1966). Limitations of brief intelligence testing with young children. *Psychological Reports, 19,* 721-722.

Salvia, J., & Ysseldyke, J. E. (1981). *Assessment in special and remedial education.* Boston, MA: Houghton Mifflin Company.

Luella Sude Smitheimer, Ph.D.
Speech and Language Pathologist, Port Washington Speech, Language and Hearing Center, Port Washington, New York.

THE COMMUNICATION SCREEN: A PRE-SCHOOL SPEECH-LANGUAGE SCREENING TOOL

Nancy Striffler and Sharon Willig. Tucson, Arizona: Communication Skill Builders, Inc.

Introduction

The Communication Screen is a tool developed for determining the speech and language skills of preschool children, aged 2 years, 10 months to 5 years, 9 months. It can be given by professionals or paraprofessionals in any field related to the care of preschool children. It can be administered, for example, by health care workers, pediatricians, nursery school teachers, or teacher's aides. The purpose of the screening tool is to serve as a quick, easily administered device to be used by nonspeech specialists or speech specialists to determine if a child should be given a complete in-depth speech/language evaluation by a qualified speech and language pathologist.

The Communication Screen was developed by Nancy Striffler and Sharon Willig. The authors are speech and language pathologists and members of the American Speech-Language-Hearing Association. In addition, Nancy Striffler is an instructor in pediatrics and director of the Communications Disorders Division at the Georgetown University Child Development Center in Washington, D.C.; Sharon Willig, is an instructor in pediatrics at the Georgetown University Child Development Center.

Based on the premise that there is a need for the early identification of potential speech and language delayed children, the authors decided to develop an instrument that could be used by nonspeech professionals and would be efficient in terms of administrative time. Moreover, they reasoned that the earlier a child with potential speech/language problems could be identified and remediation begun, the more likely the child would be able to reach the necessary communicative, social, psychological, and educational potential.

To date, there are only preliminary data findings concerned with this test. The subjects for the development of the test were preschool children selected from the Washington, D.C. metropolitan area. The target population included children,

The reviewer wishes to extend her appreciation to Catherine Holleran, Wendy Jacobson, and Karen Luper for their participation as research assistants.

aged 2 years, 10 months to 5 years, 9 months. Three age groups were sampled. They were 1) 2 years, 10 months to 3 years, 9 months; 2) 3 years, 10 months to 4 years, 9 months; and 3) 4 years, 10 months to 5 years, 9 months. The authors indicated that "operationally, the target population was defined to include only those children who were free of hearing impairment and major developmental disabilities and came from predominately English-speaking families." (Striffler & Willig, 1981, p. 19).

There are three independent screening instruments, each of which is to be used with a specific age group of children. The age groups are as follows: 1) the three-year-old group ranging from 2 years, 10 months to 3 years, 9 months; 2) the four-year-old group ranging from 3 years, 10 months to 4 years, 9 months; and 3) the five-year-old group ranging from 4 years, 10 months to 5 years, 9 months. Each screening instrument takes approximately five minutes to administer. A quiet test area with a child-sized table and two chairs is suggested. The materials required for each independent screening tool vary. Some of the materials (e.g., action pictures and pictures of familiar objects for the three-year-old group) are included in the packet. According to the manual (Striffler & Willig, 1981), materials not included can be located easily either in the nursery school or local dime stores. These materials include, for example, a small box without a lid and a block for the three-year-old group; a toy car, pencils, book, pen, blocks, and a box of crayons for the four-year-old group; and a book, pen, several crayons, blocks, and pencils for the five-year-old group.

The independent screening instruments were developed to assess the linguistic functioning of children at different age levels. According to the manual, the authors followed developmental guidelines established through research to analyze the receptive and expressive language skills of preschool children. However, the screening instruments differ in format. At the three-year-old level, for example, the authors introduce five specific components for assessment purposes. For this group of children, they were concerned with the acquisition of skills such as vocabulary, memory, and verbal expression. As a result, The Communication Screen developed for the youngest children taps the following areas: 1) comprehension of action words, 2) comprehension of prepositions, 3) naming of familiar items, 4) memory for digits, and 5) verbal expression, which includes sentence length and intelligibility.

The 4-year Communication Screen measures different skill areas and provides six areas for analysis: 1) following commands, 2) verbal imitations, 3) naming colors, 4) understanding the number two concept, 5) verbal responses to questions, and 6) verbal expression. Another way in which the 4-year-old screen differs from that of the younger children is that certain sections of the four-year-old tool contain more than one part, that is, sections one, two, and six consist of multiple parts. Section one contains two parts: 1) understanding commands using prepositions and 2) understanding two-level commands. Section two contains two parts: 1) memory for related sentences and 2) memory for digits. Both parts are repetition tasks. Section six consists of three parts: 1) sentence length, 2) intelligibility, and 3) fluency.

The Communication Screen developed for the five-year-old children contains five skill areas: 1) commands, 2) verbal imitation, 3) understanding the number three concept, 4) definitions, and 5) verbal expression. With the section on understanding commands, the five-year-old children are required to respond to slightly more complex items than those demanded of the four-year-olds. The section on verbal imitation is essentially the same as that developed for the four-year-olds, but the tasks differ because they were developed for older children. Although five-year-olds can probably respond accurately to number concepts higher than three, this screen, according to the authors, was designed to detect those children who might demonstrate difficulty with a skill that should be acquired by the age of 4 years, 10 months. The fourth section measures the child's ability to provide oral definitions of familiar items in response to the examiner's questions. Section five does not differ from the other two screens.

The criterion for each segment on each of the three communication screens and summary charts, designating the sections included, appear on the record form needed for a particular age. Criteria for referral appear on each record form as well as in the examiner's manual. For example, referral to a speech-language pathologist is suggested for three-year-olds if they fail one section or, according to the manual, if they are suspect in two parts of one section (i.e., sentence length & intelligibility). The authors indicate that children who fail the screening tool developed for their chronologic age possess speech and language skills that may be deviant and should be referred for a complete speech and language evaluation.

Practical Applications/Uses

This set of communication screens would be of use to those who work with young children and are unsure of what to look for when speech or language problems are suspected. The Communication Screen manual is particularly useful for those with no background in speech and language development. It seems to have been written for professionals who express concern about lack of knowledge but want to know more about speech and language problems. The definitions of speech and language are easily read and understood, and the authors give their rationale for the inclusion of skill areas such as verbal imitation and memory within the framework of each Communication Screen. Interpretations of the results of The Communication Screen, however, should be guarded. Professionals without prior background in normal speech and language development should be cautioned not to assume that children who pass the screening tests have normal speech and language development. In general, screening tests are not in-depth evaluations of the linguistic abilities of young children. The Communication Screen is no exception. As the authors point out, children who appear to have passed for their calculated chronologic age possess speech and language abilities "which are grossly within normal limits" (Striffler & Willig, 1981, p. 5). The fact that a child passes the "screen" does not preclude the possibility that subtle linguistic deficits might appear later during the child's developing years.

As indicated previously, The Communication Screen was designed to be used by nonspeech-language specialists. Although the authors indicate that speech-language pathologists will find the tool useful, the primary target for use of the screens appears to be paraprofessionals. Nursery school administrators, teachers, aides, and professionals concerned about possible speech or language problems can use it in nursery school settings. General physicians, pediatricians, and health care professionals who see preschoolers in their offices can use it.

The principle objective of The Communication Screen is to determine those preschoolers whose speech and/or language development may be of concern. No effort is made to differentiate or rule out the use of these screens with preschoolers from minority or ethnic groups. Although the authors do not suggest the use of The Communication Screen with those with handicapping conditions, such as the blind or cerebral palsied, it is reasonable to assume that certain categories or sections might be used with such preschoolers. It would appear, however, to be limited to those children who have some command of the English language because children whose primary language is not English might demonstrate great difficulty with the tasks included in the three individual screening instruments.

This speech and language screening instrument is administered on an individual basis. The screening instrument includes a manual, response forms, and pictures. However, objects, which are required for the elicitation of oral responses, must be gathered before contact with the child. According to the manual, the examiner should be organized and familiar with the required materials prior to administration. Additionally, the examiner is encouraged to attempt to maintain the child's motivation and interest by giving praise and support during the screening period. The authors state that one way to maintain interest and rapport with the child is to keep only those objects required for a particular section in the child's view, with the other materials out of sight. In that way, removal of objects and the introduction of new ones signal a change in activity for the child. If a child is not able to complete all sections of The Communication Screen, it is possible for the rest of the screen to be given another time.

The Communication Screen has an average administration time of five minutes, which is acceptable for screening purposes. The instructions given in the manual are clear and the structure provided on the response forms reinforce the information given. Because the purpose of the test is to have nonspeech-language specialists assist in the task of early identification of speech and language problems, the authors have developed an instrument that is easy to administer by a wide range of individuals working with children. The school nurse teacher, the secretary, or the aide working in the classroom or the doctor's office should be able to understand the manual, use the record forms, and administer the test.

Instructions for scoring are given in the manual and on each screening record form. The criterion for passing each section can also be found on each record form. For example, when a child meets the pass criterion, screening is discontinued and the examiner moves on to the next section. Passes (+) and failures (–) for each item passed or failed, respectively, are recorded on the screening form. The examiner should not have difficulty ascertaining the correct format to follow because a summary chart, indicating the passes and/or failures for each section, is located on the reverse side of the record form. Thus, the examiner can quickly determine if the child is a candidate for further testing. Performance on the Communication Screen, using guidelines based on the age by which a child should know test items, is scored as "Pass," "Fail," or "Rescreen." Although the procedure is comparatively simple, the section related to analysis of a child's verbal expression may be more difficult than the others to score. However, a separate segment can be found in the manual to help those unfamiliar with terms related to sound production and fluency. This information should be reviewed in order to understand how to record and score responses for this section. Examiners should be able to interpret the results of most of the screening sections and determine if the child interviewed should be referred for further study. As stated previously, the authors provide the criteria for referral for each of the communication screens. They suggest, for example, that four- or five-year-old children be referred for a more thorough evaluation if they fail one section or if, in spite of normal findings, the parents express concern for the child's speech and language patterns. This reviewer, however, considers this to be an unusual criterion to find within the design of a screening test. It is also suggested that the child be rescreened within a year if a failure is noted for either "memory for related sentences" or "memory for digits." Such a child would fall into the suspect category. Failure on one part of the Verbal Imitation section (not both) could indicate that the child has a mild maturational lag. Thus, the child should be monitored.

Technical Aspects

To determine validity of The Communication Screen, performance on the screening instruments was correlated with performance on a comprehensive battery designed by the authors. The diagnostic battery consisted of the use of two standard speech and language assessment tools: the Peabody Picture Vocabulary Test, Form A and four subtests of the Illinois Test of Psycholinguistic Abilities. The authors also used informal techniques to judge articulation, language, rate and rhythm of speech, and vocal quality. Statistical analyses and comparisons were based on the responses of 133 preschool children, aged 2 years, 10 months to 5 years, 9 months. The children (the sample used to establish preliminary standardization) were given an age-appropriate screening tool (3-year, 4-year or 5-year level), a hearing screening, and the diagnostic battery. The battery was given to test out the predictability of the three screening instruments. Certified speech-language specialists and graduate students trained in the field of normal and deviant speech and language development administered all the tests. Pass/Fail scores were used for The Communication Screen (3 levels) while age appropriate Pass/Fail scores were applied to performance on the tests included in the diagnostic battery. According to the manual, the Yates Adjusted Chi Formula was used for each of the screening tools to determine if there was a statistical significance. The results show, according to the authors, a highly significant finding at the .001 level of confidence, suggesting that for the population studied, the three screening levels of The Communication Screen were 95 to 100% effective. The 133 children included in the standardization procedure were from the Washington, D.C. area and were free from hearing deficits or major developmental problems; many came from English-speaking homes. One-third of the children came from middle-class families. However, two/thirds came from wide socioeconomic backgrounds, including various ethnic groups. A sample of children came from a speech clinic population. Thus, it can be assumed that because they were selected from the clinic situation they had speech and language problems. Unfortunately, however, information pertaining to the number of such subjects is not available and there is no discussion about the types of speech or language deficits found among this sample.

Reliability was established by a test-retest procedure conducted on 22 subjects seen earlier by one author and then the other author. Intertester reliability was performed at a time interval of three weeks. Using the Pass/Fail criteria, comparisons were made using percentage of agreement for each of the three screening instruments. There was, according to the manual, 100% agreement between testers for two of the screening instruments (3- and 5-year-old levels). On the 4-year-old level, there was also 100% agreement on all subtests except the "Memory for Related Sentences" subtest, which had 91% agreement.

Critique

The Communication Screen meets some of the demands required to recommend its use in the general screening of preschool children. The test gives examiners a quick estimate of speech and language development and it is easy to administer and score. A main advantage is that it is comparatively inexpensive, an important factor to be considered by potential users and administrative personnel. However, although the Communication Screen is a fine attempt to meet the needs of those who have contact with preschoolers, there are limitations. For example, no justification is provided for including some of the categories for skill assessment other than the stated intent that The Communication Screen was designed to be used by nonspeech-language specialists and that skills chosen were age appropriate and based on normal speech and language development.

As mentioned previously, one category presents a potential problem for untrained examiners. The category, Verbal Expression, is included on each of the three screening forms but in order to make accurate judgments about a child's ability to use spoken language appropriately, the examiner must be thoroughly familiar with developmental norms related to sentence length, speech sound production (intelligibility), and the rate, rhythm, and duration of speech (fluency). The Communication Screen manual includes information that is relevant to these areas and explanations related to speech and nonfluency. The authors also present a table of speech sound acquisition according to developmental ages. Despite this useful material, however, untrained examiners who rely on this information probably will be totally subjective in the evaluation of the verbal expression of preschool children. In fact, this section, unlike the other sections of the test is so open-ended and unstructured, that it is possible for trained speech-language pathologists to be wrong in their judgments of the verbal ability of young children.

Another limitation concerns the pictures used. The graphics used are not always accurate representations of reality for small preschoolers. As a result, children make errors during the identification of pictorial objects. Finally, the small sample suggests that normative data for the test are incomplete. The Communication Screen seems to provide a behavioral description of a child's mastery of specific skills when used by trained professionals. Yet, would the same results be obtained when used by unsophisticated examiners? How many children would be referred to speech and language pathologists for in-depth evaluations when paraprofessionals do the screening? The Communication Screen is unique because it provides a system for evaluating the specific language skills of the very young and it has been designed for use by nonspeech personnel. Yet, a basic question remains: How effective is The Communication Screen in the hands of untrained professionals?

References

This list includes text citations as well as suggested additional reading.

Bankson, N. W. (1977). *Bankson Language Screening Test (BLST)*. Baltimore, MD: University Park Press.

Blank, M., Rose, S., & Berlin, L. (1978). *Preschool Language Assessment Instrument (PLAI)*. New York: Grune & Stratton.

Dailey, J. T. (1977). *Language Facility Test*. Alexandria, VA: Arlington Corporation.

Darley, F. L. (1979). *Evaluation of appraisal techniques in speech & language pathology*. Reading, MA: Addison-Wesley Publishing Co.

Stiffler, N., & Willig, S. (1981). *The Communication Screen*. Tucson, AZ: Communication Skill Builders, Inc.

Toronto, A. S., Leverman, D., Hanna, C., Rosenzweig, P., & Maldonado, A. (1975). *Del Rio Language Screening Test, English/Spanish*. Austin, TX: National Educational Laboratory Publishers, Inc.

Vane, J. R. (1975). *Vane Evaluation of Language Scale*. Brandon, VT: Clinical Psychology Publishing Co., Inc.

Jack E. Edwards, Ph.D.
Assistant Professor of Psychology, Illinois Institute of Technology, Chicago, Illinois.

COMPUTER OPERATOR APTITUDE BATTERY

A. Joanne Holloway. Chicago, Illinois: Science Research Associates, Inc.

Introduction

The Computer Operator Aptitude Battery (COAB) was designed to measure three skills that might be related to the job performance of computer operators. The COAB was developed in-house under project director A. Joanne Holloway. The item content and the information in the examiner's manual is the same as it was when it originally appeared in 1974. The examiner's manual lists two uses for the COAB: "to identify those applicants with potential to succeed in the operator job" and "to be predictive of potential for promotion to the computer programmer job."

The development of the COAB followed a job-analytic approach. After directly observing operators at work, interviewing supervisors of program operators, and reviewing training manuals and other literature, Holloway developed six subtests: Sequence Recognition, Format Checking, Logical Thinking, Information Transfer, Problem Structuring, and Number Sense. Items were sought that were likely to measure aptitude both important for learning and performing the tasks of a computer operator and for identifying potential in computer programming. Only the first three subtests met these qualifications. While some of the COAB item and test development is contained in the reliability and validity sections of the examiner's manual, much of the development is not described.

Descriptions of the subtests follow:

Sequence Recognition: This speeded subtest presents 24 activities. An activity title (e.g., PREPARING CANNED SOUP), an end behavior (e.g., POURING SOUP IN A BOWL), and six preliminary steps necessary to reach the end behavior are given for each activity. The examinee must unscramble the time-sequenced behaviors. The examinee then places an "X" in one of five boxes of alternatives to indicate the proper order for the first three steps. Similarly, the examinee then chooses between five alternatives to indicate the correct sequence of behaviors for the last three steps of the sequence. The examinee is alloted 10 minutes to complete the 48 items in this subtest.

Format Checking: For this speeded, five-minute subtest, four general rules for all formats are given. In addition to the general rules, each of the eight sets of six items have zero to two specific rules for that set of six items. For each item the respondent marks "YES" or "NO" to indicate whether the general and specific rules have been followed. Each of the items contains 6 to 11 letters, numbers, or punctuation marks.

Logical Thinking: This subtest operationally defines logical thinking in terms of an individual's ability to follow a flowchart. Because this is primarily a power test, the examinee is given 30 minutes to answer 35 multiple-choice questions. Time does not appear to be as critical here as it is with the other two subtests. For each of the five flowcharts, the examinee follows the flowchart to a numbered point and then chooses the correct answer from among five alternatives.

Practical Applications/Uses

Administering and scoring the COAB should take less than one hour. It may be administered in any area that provides adequate workspace, good lighting, and freedom from distractions. Also, it may be given as either a group or individual test. In all cases, the administrator is told to answer questions by only reading the appropriate section of the instructions; under no circumstances is the examiner to give additional comments or illustrations. While the instructions are straightforward, they are incomplete. First, examinees who finish the last test early are permitted to turn in their testing materials when they finish; such a procedure may disrupt the test setting for examinees who take longer. Second, no mention is given as to whether the examinee is permitted to use scrap paper or whether all activities are to be performed purely mentally. Because the booklets are reusable and the answer sheets are carbon copy scored, some problems may result from examinees who desire to make notes. Test booklets may be ruined by examinee marks or answer sheets may be difficult to grade because of the extraneous marks. Last, no directions are given for whether an examinee should guess at unknown answers.

The answer sheet is designed to provide minimal chances for placing answers in the wrong boxes. The answer sheet is placed under and to the right of the test booklet. Because questions are well spaced and placed only on right-side pages, the examinee needs only to answer a few questions before turning to the next page of the test booklet and moving the answer sheet another column to the left. To further insure that examinees are placing answers in the correct columns, large bold page and column numbers are printed in the middle of both the test pages and answer sheets.

Tests are hand scored. Once the answer sheet is separated from a hidden, carboned, self-scoring grid, the scorer needs only to count the number of uncircled Xs contained inside boxes on the scoring grid. Determining the examinee's score for each of the three subtests and the total COAB thus requires no specialized skills and can be done in only a couple of minutes.

Technical Aspects

Holloway constructed an "alternate form" of the initial tryout test for Sequence Recognition by reversing the order of the items. Reliability coefficients of .77 and .75 ($N = 100$ and $N = 93$) were found for separately timed halves of the initial two tryout forms. At a later time, "faulty items" were eliminated. The author suggested that the .77 and .75 were possibly conservative estimates of the reliability for the final version. The total number of items eliminated is not given. Furthermore, no descriptions are given of the samples used in this study. Also, no test-retest reliability was computed for the initial or final version. Since this subtest is speeded, internal consistency reliability was not computed.

A three-week test-retest reliability coefficient of .77 was obtained for the Format Checking subtest. For that study, data were collected from 47 students enrolled in data processing courses at a junior college in the Midwest. The author noted that the stability of the coefficients calculated for each of the classes of 9 to 16 students was "rather impressive"; these individual class reliabilities, which ranged from .71 to .89, were probably inflated by a carryover effect from the short test-retest interval.

Corrected split-half and KR-20 reliabilities of .94 and .91 respectively were obtained from the Logical Thinking subtest data on 148 people employed as computer operators in five different organizations in five states. (These 148 examinees will be discussed more fully in the validation section.) Also, even though the total battery contained two speeded tests, an internal consistency reliability ($r = .95$) was reported for the data from the 148 operators.

The intercorrelations of the three subtests ranged from .48 to .54. This relationship indicates moderate, but not excessive, overlap between the potential predictors.

Two validity studies are reported. The main validity study was conducted on data from 148 operators employed in five organizations: a municipal government in California (N = 41), insurance companies in New York and Massachusetts (N = 35 and 28), and data processing services in Texas and Illinois (N = 26 and 18). The median percentages of females and minorities included in the five groups were 7% and 22%, respectively. The ranges of the five means for each subtest were Sequence Recognition, 21.5 to 30.8; Format Checking, 24.1 to 35.2; and Logical Thinking, 20.7 to 28.4. While some variability would be expected with such small samples, no explanation is given for the possible sources of the large variability of the mean scores.

In addition to providing test data, each of the five organizations supplied rank-order criterion data on their employees' computer operator ability and various demographics. Also, three of the five organizations supplied rank-order criterion data on their employees' computer programmer potential. Because of the global nature of the two criteria, both probably suffered from criterion contamination and halo errors.

Both the raw test scores and the criteria were converted to standard scores. These procedures were based on an incorrect assumption. By converting predictors to different distribution of standard scores for each location-subtest combination, Holloway was assuming that all five groups performed equally well on her test. Clearly, the large variability of subtest means show that that is not the case. Holloway was correct in her assumption that conversion to a common metric was needed on the criteria. For instance, a rank of 18 is relatively terrible if the group has only 18 employees; however, it is relatively above average if the group has 41 persons.

The correlation between the three subtests and the ability to perform as a computer operator ranged from .15 to .33. Once the relationships between the operator criterion and the various subtests had experience partialled out, the coefficients ranged from .21 to .36. As would be hoped, experience appeared to have little effect on operator performance-subtest correlation. Similar patterns emerged when the criterion data for the subsample of 87 operators were considered. The programmer potential-subtest score correlations (.26 to .42) increased (.27 to .43) when experience was partialled from them. Even though these programmer potential-subtest correlations and later multiple correlations are reported as validity coefficients, they should not be viewed as such. Programmer *potential* is not a criterion despite being predicted; instead it should be viewed as only another predictor (i.e., an estimated aptitude) in an equation to predict programmer *ability*. No court would permit a validity coefficient determined with an aptitude as its criterion. Therefore, all of the programmer potential-subtest relationships should be viewed with caution, if at all. Potential for promotion to programmer never really determines how successful someone is on the job (i.e., ability). If a user desires a programmer aptitude test, he or she should consider some other test such as SRA's Computer Programmer Aptitude Battery, which supports its claim to validity.

Three multiple regressions were computed to predict operator ability. The regressions used the total sample and two random samples ($N = 74$ each) to compute optimal weights. In no case were the optimal weights in one sample applied to data from another sample; therefore $R = .37$ for the total group and $R = .32$ and .44 for the two samples must be viewed with skepticism. Without cross-validation, no estimate can be given of the multiple correlation expected in other locations. The Pearson correlation between the total summed COAB and the operator ability criterion was $r = .33$ for the total group. Moving back to predicting programmer potential, the multiple correlation for the subsample of 87 operators was $R = .47$; the potential summed COAB correlation was $r = .44$.

A subsequent validation study was performed on 21 computer operators in an insurance company. There, "the supervisor considered intelligence, cooperation, productivity, and potential when ranking the operators." While the three correlations were higher (.33, .43, and .20) than the zero or first-order correlations obtained in the original validation group, only one correlation was significant because of the small sample size. The higher correlation in the second validation study could have been affected by several factors, such as higher true validity, not using an inappropriate conversion procedure, outlier data points, or extraneous sample characteristics.

Two sets of percentile norms were developed for the COAB. The experienced computer operator norms were developed from the data derived from the 148 examinees in the initial validation study, the 21 people in the second validation study, and 47 people who belonged to unspecified organizations in unspecified locations. In addition to the norms for the 216 experienced operators, another set of norms was developed for 66 inexperienced applicants or trainees for computer operator positions. (The trainee applicant class was not defined but probably can be assumed to include persons with very different levels of familiarity with the job of computer operator. Because the use of computers is growing constantly and the computer industry professionals have such a high turnover rate, persons who had previous positions as computer operators may be just as likely to be applying for the trainee positions as are persons with little or no experience.) The small sample sizes undoubtedly cause the norms to be very unstable. Also, the use of percentiles developed in a few companies may not be relevant or even needed in a subsequent company that uses only the raw subtest scores as predictors in a regression equation for its selection procedure validation. Because the size, type of organization, and organization locations for the applicants and trainees are listed in the same table as the experienced operators, it is impossible to describe the trainees and applicants in terms of the earlier mentioned variables. Comparisons of examinee demographics showed the following for trainee applicants vs. experienced operators, respectively: 47% vs. 7% females; 35% vs. 19% non-whites; 23.7 vs. 28.5 years of age; and 12.4 vs. 13.7 years of education.

Like most tests published by reputable firms, the manual for the COAB warns that an examinee's performance on the test should not serve as the sole decision for hiring and that localized norms collected over a long period of time might serve the test user better than the reported norms. A very brief discussion is given of the process for finding an examinee's percentile ranks for the total test and subtests; the reader who is unfamiliar with the brief discussion of true scores, standard error of measurement, and determination of cutoff scores may erroneously assume that anyone who reads the manual can utilize the information correctly.

Two sentences in the manual are devoted to telling the reader that the subtest scores and total test scores are significantly lower for the trainee group. While that may seem a given, such is not always the case. If a test were not valid there should be no difference between individuals at different levels of performance. The significantly higher scores achieved by the experienced operators suggests that the test has some construct validity. The method of contrasted groups is but one strategy for testing construct validity. It is surprising that the manual did not allude to this, especially given the validity problems cited earlier.

When the data from the 22 white operators and 19 non-white operators in one of the validation samples was examined, differences emerged. The validity coefficients for Format Checking, Logical Thinking, and COAB Total against the operator performance and programmer potential criteria were significant for the white group and ranged from $r = .42$ to $.49$. Sequence Recognition was not related to performance or potential for the white group ($r = .20$ and $.16$, respectively). For the non-white group, all of the validity coefficients were significant ($r = .53$ to $.62$) for the potential criterion and nonsignificant ($r = .22$ to $.29$) for the performance criterion. Again as stated previously, the reader is reminded that the programmer potential-COAB battery and subtest relationships are only intercorrelations among what should be thought of as predictors (and not as validity coefficients between predictors and a criterion such as ability). Also, the reader should not conclude that the nonsignificant operator ability-COAB battery and subtest correlations for the minority group indicate single-group validity. While caution must be used in such situation, small sample sizes, range restriction, and other factors undoubtedly entered into the determination of the validity coefficient.

Moving from a within-study analysis to across-samples comparisons of white and non-white performance on the COAB, a clear trend emerges. Without exception for both the trainee and experienced operator groups, significant differences

($p < .01$) were found for the white/non-white comparisons across all three subtests and the COAB Total. While some discussion is given of the possible need for separate cutoff points for whites and non-whites, the issue is much more complex than the reader may be led to believe. The short discussion may give the reader with little selection methodology background a false sense of security. Because of the possible need for separate cutoffs, an individual experienced in test or selection-system validation would need to evaluate the data.

Critique

For the most part, specific methodological concerns have been listed as the various sections were reviewed. Several serious but general questions arise when the COAB is considered for incorporation into a selection battery. Foremost in these concerns are validity issues. Both of the validation studies have problems which were cited previously. Also, the only method reported for studying validity was a concurrent, criterion-related validation strategy. More studies using different procedures (e.g., predictive validity or validity generalization) need to be added to the validity section.

The second major concern involves adverse impact. Test users may attempt to use other batteries (e.g., SRA's Computer Programmer Aptitude Battery) to avoid the problems encountered by selecting different cutoff scores for different groups: whites vs. non-whites or women vs. men. (Male vs. female comparisons are not reported.) Unless the publisher can produce data which show that the relatively poorer performance of non-whites on the COAB is related to poorer performance on the job, extreme caution should be exercised in electing to include the COAB in a selection battery. Some attempt must be made to determine why minorities perform at significantly lower levels (than do whites) on all three COAB subtests.

Last among the general concerns is the problem of small sample sizes. Even when the samples were collapsed across groups, the sample size was too small. While the 216 cases in the experienced operator norms was low but possibly acceptable for a first edition of a manual, the 66 cases in the trainee examinee group is far from acceptable. Similar sample size problems were encounterd in the development and validation phases of the COAB.

In conclusion, the publisher needs to gather additional data or incorporate data that was not made available to this reviewer and revise the 1974 version of the COAB manual.

References

Holloway, A. J. (1974). *Computer Operator Aptitude Battery.* Chicago: Science Research Associates, Inc.

Johnson, R. T. (1978). Review of Computer Operator Aptitude Battery. In O. K. Buros (Ed.), *The eighth mental measurements yearbook* (p.p. 1691-1692). Highland Park, NJ: The Gryphon Press.

Smith, N. L. (1978). Review of Computer Operator Aptitude Battery. In O. K. Buros (Ed.), *The eighth mental measurements yearbook* (pp. 1692-1694). Highland Park, NJ: The Gryphon Press.

Jack E. Edwards, Ph.D.

Assistant Professor of Psychology, Illinois Institute of Technology, Chicago, Illinois.

COMPUTER PROGRAMMER APTITUDE BATTERY

Jean M. Palormo. Chicago, Illinois: Science Research Associates, Inc.

Introduction

The Computer Programmer Aptitude Battery (CPAB) was developed by Jean M. Palormo, a project director at Science Research Associates (SRA). It is designed for selecting computer programmers and systems analysts. The battery, originally published in 1964, contains five subtests: Verbal Meaning, Reasoning, Letter Series, Number Ability, and Diagramming. Two other subtests: Ingenuity and Number Series, were eliminated during the developmental stages of the first edition of the CPAB. The CPAB Examiner's Manual was revised in 1974.

The 8-minute Verbal Meaning subtest consists of 38 items. The examinee is asked to select synonyms from sets of five alternatives. The examiner's manual (Palormo, 1974) notes that this subtest was added despite the fact that vocabulary tests have not been very useful in predicting performance in the programmer field. In an effort to make this test more meaningful, Palormo generated the CPAB items from the literature on systems engineering, mathematics, general business management, and similar fields.

The 20-minute Reasoning subtest consists of 25 items. For each item, the examinee must read a short problem and then choose among five response alternatives. Almost without exception, the alternatives are expressed as simple mathematical formulas using the arbitrary letters given in the reading problem stem. The vocabulary used in the word-problems appears to be at a sufficiently elementary level to eliminate the possibility of contamination caused by reading level.

The 10-minute Letter Series subtest consists of 26 items. Item stems consist of strings of 5 to 15 letters, which are well spaced, and five response alternatives of one letter each. The examinee's task is to discover the letter that comes after the pattern set forth in the stem.

The 6-minute Number Ability subtest consists of 28 simple arithmetic items. The test appears to assess only whether a person can add, subtract, multiply, and divide whole numbers, fractions, and decimals; compute percentages; and round numbers; only 21% of the items require the examinee to perform more than one arithmetic function of a single item.

The 35-minute Diagramming subtest consists of seven flowcharts, each of which has narrative information and five questions. Using the narrative and diagram information, the respondent must choose from five alternatives the action that would occur at a given place in the flowchart. Once again, the respondent's reading level probably will not influence the construct that is being measured because the narrative information is written on a very simple level.

During the development of the CPAB, job analyses and a review of empirical programmer and systems analyst studies identified seven hypothesized item types that had potential for predicting performance for individuals in the computer field. Enough items were generated to create two "parallel" forms, which were tested simultaneously. Although data is provided for both the CPAB and an experimental alternate form (CPST), this review will focus primarily on the CPAB because all of the final subtests were taken from the former instrument. In this reviewer's opinion, a future revision of the CPAB manual should describe the initial steps of the CPAB's development (e.g., representativeness, number of jobs samples, and major duties identified) more adequately.

For Sample 1, the CPAB was administered to 186 programmers and analysts, most of whom were employed by a major computer manufacturer. Of these 186 people, only 46 people had criterion data gathered on them. These 46 employees shared the common characteristic of being known by at least four supervisors. Using supervisory nominations, a criterion score was computed for each individual by taking the ratio of "times known" divided by "times nominated." In a second sample 18 machine operators were rated by two supervisors for their potential for promotion to the programmer classification. While reading the following discussion of the findings for Sample 2, the reader should keep in mind that even though correlations may be significant, the statistics should be reviewed with due concern. The criterion used for Sample 2 is not really a criterion (i.e., ability) in the industrial validation sense; instead, it is a predictor of future behavior.

Subtests were eliminated from the final CPAB if they added little unique variance and/or validity coefficients were anticipated to be low. As mentioned earlier, two of the initial seven tests were eliminated. Ingenuity was dropped because it had negative validity coefficients of −.22 and −.09 with the criteria in Samples 1 and 2, respectively. The Number Ability subtest was deleted because all but 19% of its variance was accounted for by other factors. A primary reason for this latter finding was the .74 correlation between Number Ability and Reasoning.

Seven of the 10 validity coefficients for the remaining five CPAB subtests were not statistically significant ($p > .05$) despite 3 of the 7 nonsignificant coefficients being .36 and above. Clearly, the small sample sizes ($N = 46$ and $N = 18$) were part of the reason for nonsignificance; however, a review of the coefficients revealed some relationships which may, in fact, be weak or near zero. For example, for Sample 1, Verbal Meaning correlated −.13 with the nomination criterion; and for Sample 2, Letter Series correlated .08 with the programmer-potential criterion/ aptitude. (Six of the validity coefficients for the CPST were of similar magnitudes [i.e., $r > .29$] but statistically significant.) Although a reader of the examiner's manual might automatically assume that the sizes ($N = 69$ and $N = 61$) of the two CPST samples were the sole reason for obtaining significance, other factors, particularly different criteria, may have provided some of the reasons for obtaining significance.

The item statistics and reliability indices reported in the examiner's manual were determined on the experimental form of the CPAB. Therefore, it is assumed that these statistics were computed on the full sample ($N = 186$) from which Sample 1 was taken.

Less than 10% of the experimental items were deleted to form the current Letter Series and Number Ability subtests. "Considerably" more than 10% of the experimental items were eliminated from each of the other three subtests. It is impossible to ascertain the exact effect that these changes had on the item and reliability measures; however, SRA suggests that only slight overestimates may have occurred. This is probably true for all subtests except Diagramming, which had an entire book of interdependent items eliminated. Like other subtests, the reliability for Diagramming after item reduction should still be sufficiently high; however, SRA should have reexamined the reliability indices for all of these subtests before it published its second edition of the examiner's manual.

Even though no information was given on the criteria for choosing which items were to be eliminated, it can probably be assumed that items with either high difficulty levels or low correlations with the subtest total score were tabbed for deletion. The median p values (i.e., probability of passing an item) for the subtests ranged from .57 to .86. Although the items were relatively easy, the reported p values were probably inflated by virtue of the fact that only experienced programmers participated in this part of the test development.

Practical Applications/Uses

Administering the CPAB should take approximately 90 minutes and should not require any specialized skills for the test examiner. It may be administered in any area that provides adequate workspace, good lighting, and freedom from distractions. It may be given to either groups or individuals. In all cases, administrators are told to answer questions by reading the appropriate section of the instructions only and under no circumstances to give additional comments or illustrations. For the most part, the instructions are simple, straightforward, and complete. For example, the test manual instructs examinees to answer questions even when they are not certain of the correct answer. The one problem that might be encountered by the administrator is that no mention is given as to whether the examinee is permitted to use scrap paper or whether all activities are to be performed purely mentally. Because the booklets are reusable and the answer sheets are carbon-copy scored, some problems might result from examinees who make notes. Test booklets may be ruined by examinee marks, and answer sheets may be difficult to grade because of extraneous marks.

The answer sheet, placed under and to the right of the test booklet, is designed to provide minimal chances for placing answers in the wrong boxes. Because questions are well-spaced and placed only on right-sided pages, the examinee needs only to answer a few questions before turning to the next page of the test booklet and moving the answer sheet another column to the left. To ensure that examinees place answers in the correct columns, large, bold corresponding numbers are printed in the middle of the test pages and answer sheets.

Tests are hand-scored only. Once the answer sheet is separated from a carboned, self-scoring grid, the scorer needs only to count the number of noncircled Xs contained inside boxes on the scoring grid. Determining the examinee's score for each of the five subtests and the total CPAB thus requires no special skills and can be completed in only a few minutes.

Technical Aspects

Internal consistency was estimated for each subtest by computing the mean correlation between individuals' item scores and in subtest total scores. Mean subtest point-biserial correlations ranged from .44 to .60, except for an underestimated mean item-total correlation (.33) for Letter Series. This underestimate was probably caused by too severe a time limit during experimental data gathering. Turning to more widely used measures of reliability, the Letter Series and Number Ability subtests were administered in separately timed halves. After scores on the corresponding halves were correlated and corrected with the Spearman-Brown prophesy formula, internal consistency was estimated to be .67 for the Letter Series and .85 for Number Ability. The KR-20 reliabilities for the other three tests were Verbal Ability, .86; Reasoning, .88; and Diagramming, .94. Finally, a total score CPAB reliability of .95 was obtained.

In a footnote (Palormo, 1974, p. 12) the CPAB author notes that she included all validity studies that had used some aspect of the CPAB, regardless of the findings. Four of the ten validity studies included in the manual used success in training (course grades) as their criteria. For the most part the Reasoning, Number Ability, and Diagramming subtest scores and the CPAB total test score predicted the criteria very well. The median validity coefficients for the subtests were in the .30 to .40 range. The CPAB Total score-criteria correlations were .52, .56, .71, .46, and .30. (Five coefficients were reported because one of the four training-criterion studies did not examine the predictive utility of the CPAB Total and another study reported coefficients for each of its three samples).

Moving to the job performance criteria studies, the results become more ambiguous. Even though studies 5 to 10 are purported to be CPAB studies, only five studies should have been included. Discussion of the results from Study 7 will not be covered because the predictor was the CPST, the supposed alternate form of the CPAB. Those results are omitted because no attempt was made to determine the coefficient of equivalences for these "alternate forms." Study 5 showed the same pattern as Studies 1-4, which had used training performance; however, the four significant validity coefficients for the five subtests and the total were generally lower—.27 to .31. A similar pattern of nonsignificant correlations was found for Study 9. There, the nonsignificance appeared to be primarily the result of a small sample of 24 hirees from an applicant pool of 86 people. Study 6 and Study 10 lead to very different conclusions about the usefulness of the CPAB in predicting job performance. Study 6 shows all near .00 correlations; whereas, Study 10 showed that all five subtests and the total predicted the criterion quite well. Study 8 added little extra information; only the CPAB Total was used as a predictor. In that study, two of the four samples yielded significant CPAB Total-criterion correlations.

In this reviewer's opinion, the validity coefficients reported in the CPAB examiner's manual appear to be sufficient to consider using it in an experimental selection battery for computer programmers. This conclusion is especially true for the prediction of success in training. Although the prediction of success in training is not the ultimate goal of a validity study, it does add support. Of the ten validity studies cited in the manual, all but one (Study 6) seemed to find Reasoning, Number Ability, Diagramming, and CPAB Total a help in the prediction of job performance. The findings from Study 6 have little generalizability. In that study, the .65 correlation between experience and performance ratings and the −.31 correlation between CPAB Total and tenure lead to questions regarding criterion contamination.

SRA (1985) also provided this reviewer with a supplement to the CPAB examiner's manual, which listed a series of post-1974 validity studies. In a study of 106 students enrolled in three computer courses: Advanced COBOL Programming, Systems Analysis, and Design I and II, students' final grades in the courses were significantly related to each of the five subtests and the CPAB total. Verbal Meaning, previously a poor predictor of the criteria, correlated higher than other subtests with both COBOL grades (.39) and a composite of each student's two systems grades (.35). One of the post 1974 validation study was quite extensive. Nearly 6,000 applicants and employees working for financial service companies participated. Two of the five subtests, Diagramming and Reasoning, were suggested to validly select entry-level computer programmers. The zero-order correlations between the sum of Reasoning and Diagramming scores and the three-month performance ratings were .22 and .27; the validity coefficients for the sum and the nine-month performance ratings were .17 and .20. Seven other post 1974 concurrent validity studies, which used employees rather than students were performed using the CPAB and various performance criteria. In almost all of the studies, a majority of the validity coefficients were quite good. The CPAB manual provides statistics for the effect of several demographic variables. Female trainees scored significantly higher (14.9) than their male counterparts (13.5) on the Letter Series subtest. The means for experienced applicants were in the opposite direction for the three differences. Male and female means were 15.2 and 12.1 for Number Ability, 28.2 and 27.4 for Diagramming, and 90.9 and 85.5 for CPAB Total respectively. When age was trichotomized to examine the subtest and total test scores at those levels, no significant difference emerged. An analysis of the effect of education showed significant differences between high-school graduates and BA/BS degree persons on each subtest and the CPAB total. Similar trends were present for the experienced applicant grade. The manual notes, probably correctly, that advanced education has improved the skills measured by the CPAB and that abler persons are more apt to continue their educations. Race is the only demographic characteristic that appears to be an obstacle in avoiding adverse impact. "All but one (Reasoning-experienced applicants) of the test score means for nonwhites are significantly lower than for whites" (Palormo, 1974, p. 17). Whites outscored nonwhites by 2.4 to 8.4 points on the subtests and by 20 points on the CPAB Total. Although this could be a very serious problem, it should not automatically cause test users to select other tests. Instead, selection procedure becomes somewhat more complicated by the probable need for more than one cutoff score. SRA alerts potential CPAB users to the possible need for separate cutoffs for whites and nonwhites in its "Use of the CPAB with Minority Applicants" section. For example, SRA notes that a CPAB Total score of 85 is at the 60th percentile for mostly white trainees; whereas the 60th percentile for nonwhites has a raw score equivalent of 67.

One major problem in using multiple cutoffs is that the nonwhite trainee norms were developed on only 66 cases. Given the seriousness of potential adverse impact and the unstability of norms developed on such a small possibly hetero-genous sample of all nonwhites, SRA should incorporate the data from some of the post 1974 studies into new norms and also develop norms for minority experienced applicants; currently the CPAB does not have norms for this latter group. Future norms for the total group ($N = 641$) should be revised to include only whites so as not to artificially lessen the differences in the norms. As it is now, total group norms are too low. These lowered total group norms are the result of including minorities (10% of the total sample) and people of undetermined race (12%). Similarly, the experienced applicant norms ($N = 299$) should have norms developed for both minorities and whites to give the CPAB user more information about the potential adverse impact for minority experienced applicants.

Other than these race-related problems, the norms appear to have a good variety in terms of the types of companies, the location of the companies, sample sizes, ages, and educational background. The only other area that should be substantially supplemented is the proportion of females included. In the 1974 manual, 25% of the trainee group and 16% of the applicant group is female. Currently, one would expect a much higher percentage of females in computer programming positions.

Critique

For the most part, the CPAB appears to be a useful instrument for selecting programmers. More numerous and more up-to-date studies are needed before a similar statement would be warranted for selecting system analysts; however, at this time there is some support. The major reason that this review is not more positive is due to the problems that revolve around the potential for adverse impact. SRA and the rest of the industrial testing industry need to avail them-selves of the item bias techniques commonly found in educational testing. Latent trait analysis, or even something as simple as the data technique, could be invaluable in identifying legally nondiscriminatory items. The current pro-cedures—total group p values and point biserial correlations—do nothing to address the item bias issue. SRA probably has sufficient archival data on the CPAB that it could begin such analyses.

Although the manual does contain a brief explanation on interpreting CPAB scores, the section should supply references for the user who is interested in obtaining more information about such concepts as the standard error of estimate. Also, SRA probably should add a disclaimer to emphasize that choosing multiple cutoffs must take into account many factors that might be known to only the experienced selection validation expert.

Even though the simple composites of multiple subtest scores have proven useful in most cases, more information is needed on statistically weighted com-posites. The 1974 manual cites only one study that used multiple regression. The samples in that study (and in one post 1974 study) were too small to determine the stability of future cross validations.

References

Palormo, J. M. (1974). *Computer Programmer Aptitude Battery manual.* Chicago: Science Research Associates.

Science Research Associates. (1985). *CPAB manual supplement.* Chicago: author.

G. Cynthia Fekken, Ph.D.
Assistant Professor of Psychology, Queen's University, Kingston, Canada.

CREATIVITY ASSESSMENT PACKET

Frank E. Williams. Buffalo, New York: D.O.K. Publishers, Inc.

Introduction

The Creativity Assessment Packet (CAP) consists of two tests measuring various components of creativity in children, plus an observational rating scale completed by parents or teachers on the same components.

The theoretical underpinnings of the CAP (Williams, 1980) derive from J. P. Guilford's Structure of Intellect model (1969). The CAP measures both divergent-*thinking* aspects of creativity, including fluency, flexibility, originality, and elaboration, and divergent-*feeling* aspects of creativity, including curiosity, imagination, complexity, and risk-taking. In addition, the CAP assesses a fifth divergent-thinking component not explicitly part of Guilford's model, namely, general verbal skills. By measuring both left-brain verbal and right-brain affective processing, the author, Dr. Frank E. Williams, claims that the test meets "hemisphericity criteria." The theoretical relevance of the components of creative behavior measured by the CAP is further underlined in Williams' (1969) three-dimensional model of creativity. Based on a content analysis of the creativity literature, the model derives the eight primary components of creative behavior by crossing subject matter (e.g., art, science) with strategies of teaching (e.g., analogies, provocative questions). Although the CAP is clearly and directly a measure of the eight primary components, neither the specific rational nor empirical criteria underlying the Williams' model are explicated in the test manual.

The CAP comprises three separate tests: The Exercise in Divergent Thinking, The Exercise in Divergent Feeling, and The Williams Scale.

The Exercise in Divergent Thinking: is made up of 12 identical frames containing complete (e.g., circle, diamond) or incomplete lines. The exercise is group administered, usually in a classroom setting, and timed at 20 minutes for upper grades (6-12) and 25 minutes for lower grades (3-5). Instructions inform the examinees that this measure of creativity requires them to draw as many colorful pictures as possible, giving each a clever title. Five raw scores, each based on an explicit rational, are obtained from these data: 1) The Fluency Score is a count of frames attempted, on the assumption that creative people are more productive than noncreative people; 2) the Flexibility Score is the number of times an individual shifts among four possible categories of pictures—living, mechanical, symbol, or view—with creative people expected to show cognitive flexibility and shift across categories; 3) the Originality Score reflects the area of the drawing on which the individual works, with the least creative person drawing outside or around the closure formed by the line, a somewhat more creative person drawing only inside the closure, and, the most creative person drawing both inside and outside the closure; 4) the Elaboration Score is based on the placement of details that make the picture asymmetrical, with creative people using more off center details; and 5) the Titles Score, an index of general verbal ability, reflects the clever and complex use of words to construct a title for each picture. Despite instructions to draw with various colors, color use is not actually scored.

The Exercise in Divergent Feeling: can be group administered, again most commonly in a classroom setting. The test is not timed but generally requires 20 to 30 minutes to complete. This exercise consists of 50 statements to which the student responds Mostly True About Me, Partly True or Untrue About Me; or Mostly Untrue (False) About Me. A fourth category, Cannot Really Decide, is also included, but respondents are actively encouraged to avoid it. Categories are subtitled: yes, maybe, no, and don't know. Why these simple, straightforward labels are not the primary category labels is not obvious. The Exercise in Divergent Feeling is objectively scored with the aid of cardboard scoring templates. For each of the four affective components—Curiosity, Imagination, Complexity, and Risk Taking—keyed responses are scored as "2" whereas "maybe" and the nonkeyed responses are scored "1" and "don't know" is scored "-1." The negative weight is explained by the notion that indecision characterizes less creative people. Assuming a cumulative measurement model, equal weights for nonkeyed and "maybe" responses are somewhat unusual, although sometimes justifiable. But why not simply use dichotomous categories, for example, "True-False" or "Yes-No"? More problematic may be the negative weights associated with "Cannot Decide" responses. Given little support for the efficacy of such a scoring procedure in the psychometric literature, the validity of corrected vs. uncorrected scores needs explicit evaluation.

The Williams Scale: consists of eight groups of six items, one group related to each of the eight modes of creativity. Either a parent or teacher rates the child on each item, using the categories, Often, Sometimes, and Seldom. In addition, four open-ended questions elicit information on the child's ability and creative potential and on the school's special program for creative children. The scoring of this scale is straightforward. Items checked Often, Sometimes, and Seldom are scored "2," "1," and "0," respectively. For the open-ended questions, items receiving a "Yes" response plus qualifying remarks are scored "1." "No" answers are scored "0" as, presumably, are "Yes" answers minus qualifying remarks.

Practical Applications/Uses

Williams developed the CAP to screen for gifted or talented children so that they might be placed in enriched educational programs. Published in 1980, the tests are now recommended for the general assessment of creative potential in school children aged 8-18 years.

Administration of the CAP could be conducted by a psychologist, guidance counselor, teacher, teaching assistant, proctor, or secretary. The objective scoring system presented in the manual is clear and well-illustrated by numerous helpful examples. Mastering the instructions for administration and scoring should not require more than an hour or two. The actual time to score a single CAP protocol is estimated at 15 to 20 minutes.

Calculating CAP scores is extremely easy; unfortunately, interpreting CAP scores is fraught with difficulties. Lack of information is the main block to adequate score interpretation. The manual provides means and standard deviations for total scores on all three CAP instruments and for the five subtests on the Exercise in Divergent Thinking and the four subtests on the Exercise in Divergent Feeling. The size and demographic characteristics of the normative sample are unreported. Further, sex and age differences in scores are unevaluated. Presumably it is appropriate to compare the scores of an 8-year-old girl and of an 18-year-old boy to the same norms. But consider, for example, that age-related changes in speed (reflected in the Fluency Score) and in vocabulary (reflected in the Titles Score) may influence CAP creativity scores. Conversely, recommendations on the Williams Scale for enriched education may favor younger rather than older children who may be perceived as having almost finished their school career. Sex differences in verbal and spatial abilities are well-documented in the psychological literature. To the extent that the CAP assesses such abilities (e.g., the Titles, Originality, and Elaboration Scores), appropriate normative data are required. An evaluation of both sex and age differences is fundamental to any argument that one set of norms is adequate.

On the ill-advised assumption that the norms in the manual are acceptable, an individual's scores may be compared to these norms using the Pupil Assessment Matrix. The Pupil Assessment Matrix, a profile sheet printed on the back of the Exercise in Divergent Feeling, permits raw scores to be plotted in terms of standard deviations from the mean. The profile depicts two standard deviations above the mean but only one standard deviation below. Also, the profile needs to be turned on its side in order to be read, something which should be clarified in the instructions. Alternatively, reorienting the profile by placing standard deviations down the far left-hand column and score labels along the top would make the profile easier to use.

Advice on how to evaluate the completed profile is largely intuitive. The manual notes that scores on the components of creative behavior should show consistency—that is, individuals should tend to score high, medium, or low on all components of creative behavior. However, the eight components measured by the Williams Scale are not outlined on the profile sheet. More problematic is the lack of discussion regarding how to establish the degree of relatedness of scores. Calculating correlations between test scores and ratings for individuals or for groups is recommended. However, if for a single student profile, the four Divergent Thinking and the four Divergent Feeling scores were correlated with the corresponding eight components rated by parents or teachers, the Titles Score calculated for Divergent Thinking would need to be omitted. Some elaboration on how to interpret these correlations is essential. For instance: What levels of significance/reliability are associated with correlations based on eight pairs of numbers? How large must a correlation be to conclude that the individual's scores are consistent? Does a low correlation suggest that the CAP scores are invalid for a student or that the Williams Scale scores are inaccurate?

Establishing the consistency of scores through group correlations involves correlating, *across* individuals, scores on each Divergent Thinking and Divergent Feeling component with corresponding Williams Scale scores. This would yield eight correlations for an entire group of individuals and bear on test or perhaps construct properties rather than on individuals. The final statement in the manual's section on score interpretation is that CAP score changes may be used to evaluate enrichment programs. Gains in creativity scores collected before and after a program are attributed to program success. To make such a statement, the onus is on the author to present evidence in the form of controlled studies that scores do not change simply as a function of retesting or of maturation, both of which are apt to occur regardless of educational program.

Technical Aspects

Lack of empirical data also makes the reliability and validity section of the manual inadequate. The 10-month, test-retest reliability coefficients for the instruments of the CAP are reported to be in the 60s for a sample of 256 students ranging from Grades 3 to 12. Whether these reliability coefficients may apply to the three CAP total scores or to the subtest scores is not clear. Estimates of test-retest reliability will be inflated to the extent that the mixed sample yields inflated variance. Even if the reliabilities are in the 60s, considerable lack of individual predictability exists for the CAP. The CAP may be useful for evaluating program effects (given earlier qualifications about the need for appropriate control groups) but may not be reliable enough to serve as a basis for making decisions about individuals. To address this issue, an examination of other reliability estimates for both CAP total and component scores and an examination of the standard error of measurement would be an excellent starting point.

The validity of the CAP is largely unexplored. The manual reports validities of .71 and .76 for the Exercises in Divergent Thinking and Divergent Feeling, respectively, but does not indicate what the criteria were. The manual also reports that "pairs of tests and parent/teacher ratings correlated significantly at .74" (p. 24). Perhaps this correlation was calculated by correlating eight group means for test scores with eight for parent/teacher ratings. Perhaps this correlation is the mean/median of eight correlations calculated by correlating test scores and parent/teacher ratings across individuals for each of the eight components. Or perhaps this is the mean/median of individual correlations calculated by correlating test scores and parent/teacher ratings across the eight components for each individual. All of these possibilities have different interpretations with regard to the validity of the CAP. Finally, the manual reports that the correlations between total scores on the Exercises in Divergent Thinking and Divergent Feeling and total parent/teacher ratings as measured by the Williams Scale were .59 and .67, respectively. These data support the hypothesis that the tests and ratings are measuring similar constructs. However, in light of the absence of empirical data on discriminant validity, the particular construct may be creativity or it may be something else, such as general intelligence. Both the convergent and the discriminant validity of the CAP need to be evaluated.

Finally, the empirical basis for conceptualizing creativity in terms of eight components is unassessed. This is most surprising given the effort that the author devotes to developing logically and theoretically the model underlying the CAP. The intercorrelation matrix based on the eight (or nine) scores yielded by the Exercises in Divergent Thinking and Divergent Feeling would indicate the degree of relationship among components. Because all scores purport to reflect a single construct, namely, creativity, a positive manifold would be predicted. To test explicitly the rational division of creativity into cognitive (Thinking) and affective (Feeling) dimensions, a two-factor confirmatory principal components analysis could be performed. Establishing the external validity of the eight CAP components is problematic by virtue of the longstanding difficulty in deriving appropriate creativity criteria. The Williams Scale parent/teacher ratings on the eight itemgroups may in fact serve as excellent validation indices. Of course, the interrater reliability of the Williams Scale must first be examined and avoidance of criterion contamination must be maintained (i.e., raters must be previously unaware of CAP scores).

Critique

In summary, the CAP is a measure of creativity that should be limited to use in research settings. The CAP may be well-conceptualized in terms of the theory of creativity, but data attesting to its psychometric properties are lacking. Ultimately, the CAO may have a role in the school setting for selecting creative (or noncreative) individuals for enrichment programs, for evaluating such enrichment programs, or for contribution to vocational guidance decisions. Further, the CAP may be useful for selecting individuals for general interest programs offered in many communities, such as art classes, creative writing, dance groups, etc. However, such potential applications must wait until empirical evidence bearing on the fundamental issues of normative comparisons, reliability, and validity are collected and evaluated.

References

Guilford, J. P. (1969). *Intelligence, creativity and their educational implications.* San Diego: Educational and Industrial Testing Service.
Williams, F. E. (1969). *Classroom ideas for encouraging thinking and feeling.* Buffalo: D. O. K. Publishers.
Williams, F. E. (1980). *Creativity Assessment Packet manual.* Buffalo: D. O. K. Publishers.

Robert G. Malgady, Ph.D.
*Associate Professor of Educational Statistics, Department of
Mathematics, Science and Statistics Education, New York University,
New York, New York.*

CULTURE-FREE SELF-ESTEEM INVENTORIES FOR CHILDREN AND ADULTS

James Battle. Seattle, Washington: Special Child Publications.

Introduction

The Culture-Free Self-Esteem Inventories (SEI) for Children and Adults are a series of self-report checklists designed to measure an individual's perception of self, independent of cultural context and psycholinguistic skills. The 60-item Children's SEI provides a measure of general self-worth, as well as more specific components of self-esteem related to peers, school, and the home. The 40-item Adult SEI yields a General, Social, and Personal self-esteem score. A short form of the Children's SEI consisting of 30 items, is available for quick administration. Both the Children's and Adult SEI contain Lie Scales signaling examinees' extent of defensiveness. Self-esteem profiles derived from SEI scores are intended for researchers studying the concept of self-esteem and mental health clinicians for diagnostic and psychotherapeutic purposes.

The Culture-Free SEI for Children and Adults were developed by James Battle, a school psychologist in Edmonton, Canada, after six years of work as a counselor of school children and as a teacher of learning disabled children. After a review of the literature of educational programs and procedures for remediation of children's learning problems, Battle concluded that interventions with academically troubled students must not only emphasize cognitive development, but also their affective needs. Hence, after a series of over 30 research studies, the Culture-Free SEI were developed and standardized to benefit diagnosticians, educators, and researchers. The instruments formerly were known as the Canadian Self-Esteem Inventories for Children and Adults.

The 60-item Culture-Free SEI for Children (Form A) was standardized on elementary school children in Grades 3-6, and junior high-school students in Grades 7-9. Additionally, it has been used with high-school students.

Separate Form A norms are provided in the manual for elementary students (Grades 3-6), based on a sizable standardization sample of N = 891, and for junior high-school students (Grades 7-9), based on a substantially smaller sample of N = 224. The short form (B) norms are based on relatively small samples of N = 212 elementary students and 274 junior high-school students. The Adult Form AD was standardized on a sample of N = 252 adults. No other characteristics of the standardization samples are reported in the manual. Although there are no significant sex differences on the three forms, separate norms nevertheless are provided for males and females. Examination of the percentile rank and T-score conversions reveals little appreciable difference between male and female norms. Examination of the percentile rank distribution suggests (although it is not reported in the manual) that the total scores for each form are negatively skewed.

The 60 items of Form A are clustered into five subscales on the basis of factor analysis: *General self-esteem items* (e.g., I worry a lot; Most boys and girls are better than I am); *Social/peer-related items* (e.g., I have only a few friends; Boys and girls like to play with me); *academics/school-related items* (e.g., I am a failure at school; I am satisfied with my school work); *Parents/home-related items* (e.g., My parents love me; I often get upset at home); and *Lie items,* indicative of defensiveness (e.g., I always tell the truth; I never do anything wrong). The 30-item short version (Form B) of the Children's scale is available for a quick assessment of self-esteem. The Adult SEI (Form AD) consists of 40 items in four categories: *General self-esteem items* (e.g., Are you happy most of the time? Do you often feel ashamed of yourself?); *Social items* (Do you have only a few friends? Do people like your ideas?); *Personal items* (e.g., Are your feelings easily hurt? Do you worry a lot?); and *Lie items* (e.g., Do you ever lie? Do you gossip at times?). The phrasing of items on the three SEI forms is balanced between positive and negative content to control for examinees' acquiescent response style.

Both the Children's and Adults' SEI are easily administered and scored in 15-20 minutes by a nonprofessional examiner, with little or no special training. The three forms are available for written or audio-cassette administration to individuals or groups in three languages (English, French, Spanish).

Practical Applications/Uses

The SEI is of practical use to professional psychologists, psychiatrists, counselors, or teachers, as a screening mechanism to diagnose individuals in need of psychotherapeutic services. According to the author, the SEI is especially useful in identifying depressed mood states, and the instrument has been shown to be sensitive to affective change induced by psychotherapeutic intervention. The Children's SEI is particularly useful for identifying students with learning disabilities. The subscale self-esteem profile will be helpful to clinicians in formulating treatment objectives, structuring therapeutic activities, and in deciding when to terminate intervention on the basis of profile changes.

In addition, the manual provides "time-tested" classifications of total and subscale scores (i.e., very high, high, intermediate, low, very low) for diagnostic purposes. The author acknowledges, however, that the score limits defining these classifications do not necessarily conform to universally acknowledged standards. It is not clear how the classifications were developed or validated, and indeed their boundaries seem quite arbitrary.

All three forms of the SEI may be administered either to individuals or groups, in written form or orally. For children below Grade 3, adults who are nonreaders, the visually impaired, or otherwise handicapped examinees individual oral administration is recommended. In group administration when the written form is administered to children and adults of average reading ability, examinees are instructed to read and follow the test directions while the examiner also reads them aloud. The examiner is permitted to answer any questions of the examinees because the test is presumably culture free. Instructions are simple and easy to follow. Examinees are instructed that, if an item describes how they usually feel, they should check the "yes" column on the answer sheet; otherwise they are to check the "no" column. The examinee is also informed that "this is not a test" and there are no "right" or "wrong" answers. Written or oral administration of any of the three SEI forms generally requires about 10-15 minutes, although handicapped individuals may require more time.

For standardized oral administration, the three forms are available from the publisher on audio-cassette tape. The instructions are similar to the written form, but 5-second intervals are interposed between items to allow for the examinee's verbal response and the examiner's recording. The pause between items can be extended, depending on the time needed by the examinee, which is particularly useful with handicapped individuals. The Form A audio-recording runs for 10 minutes; Form B for 7 minutes; and Form AD for 8 minutes. The author claims that the French and Spanish versions "can be administered, scored and interpreted with the same assurance of validity and reliability as the English protocols" (Battle, 1981, p. 20). However, the Culture Free SEI forms were standardized only in English, the manual is available only in English, and no research is reported on Hispanic or French examinees. The author also asserts that because the items do not test psycholinguistic skill, dialectic differences are not assumed to skew the results (p. 20).

The examiner may be a clinician, teacher, research assistant, or, more generally, any responsible adult. No professional skills or special training is required to administer the SEI. Except for a cassette recorder necessary for oral administration, no special equipment is required for administration.

Scoring is accomplished with a template by summing the number of items checked in the direction of high self-esteen. A separate score is calculated by tallying the number of Lie Scale items checked by the examinee. For large-scale research projects involving group administration, tests can also be machine-scored from answer sheets that are available from the publisher.

On the Children's Form A, total scores may range from 0 (low self-esteem) to 50 (high self-esteem), and 0-10 on the Lie Scale. On the Children's short form (B), scores may vary from 0 to 25, and 0-5 on the Lie Scale. On the Adult Form (AD) the range is 0 to 32 in self-esteem, and 0-8 on the lie items. Subscale scores can be derived by summing the appropriate item scores composing each subscale, as delineated in the manual's scoring instructions.

Raw scores can be converted into percentile ranks or standardized T-scores (mean = 50, standard deviation = 10) to achieve a norm-referenced interpretation of the total and subscale self-esteem scores. Subscale norms should be interpreted with caution because relatively few raw score differences are accompanied by rather dramatic percentile rank and T-score changes. On Form A, for example, a one-point raw score difference in the vicinity of the mean and upward is associated with a percentile rank change of about a decile or more, and a T-score change of about half a standard deviation unit. This is even more pronounced on the short form due to the fewer number of items composing each subscale.

Although minimal requirements are made of the examiner, only qualified professionals can interpret SEI profiles. These include psychologists, researchers, counselors, or as the manual suggests: a person "knowledgeable in measurement, psychology of adjustment, self-theory, and perceptual psychology" (Battle, 1981, p. 8).

Technical Aspects

The manual reports extensive data collected in a series of studies of the reliability and validity of the three SEI forms. Apparently all data were collected from examinees in Edmonton, Canada. Unfortunately, the test-retest interval in studies of the stability of SEI scores is not reported in most studies.

In one study of 198 elementary school students (Grades 3-6), Form A test-retest reliabilities (correlations) ranged across grade levels from .81 to .89 for the total sample, .72 to .93 for boys, and .74 to .90 for girls. Subscale reliabilities were .61 to .76 for General, .60 to .76 for Social, .26 to .71 for Academics, and .52 to .67 for Parents. In a junior high-school sample of 117 seventh- to ninth-graders, total score reliability ranged from .88 to .96 across grade levels, .89 for females and .93 for males. Subscale reliabilities were .81 to .86 for General, .78 to .84 for Social, .67 to .89 for Academics, and .70 to .82 for Parents. Hence both total score and subscale reliabilities are high for Form A, but the test-retest interval is not reported for these studies in the manual. However, another study of 75 students indicated that over a two-year interval test-retest correlations were .65 for total scores, and .63 for General, .57 for Social, .53 for Academics, and .41 for Parents subscales.

A study of the short form (B) administered to 110 students in Grades 3-6 reported test-retest reliabilities of .79 to .92 for total scores, .59 to .73 for General, .71 to .80 for Social, .49 to .72 for Academics, and .61 to .76 for Parents subscales. Thus, Form B reliabilities are comparable to the test-retest stability of the longer Form A, although the interval between testings again is not reported in the manual. Another study of 74 fifth- and 86 sixth-graders indicated that Form B correlated highly with Form A ($r = .89$ for fifth-graders, $r = .80$ for sixth-graders). But there is no information on the correlation between Forms A and B at other grade levels.

The adult form (AD) was administered to 127 college students in introductory educational psychology with a resulting test-retest reliability of .81 for the total sample, .79 for males, and .82 for females. The General subscale reliability was .82, .56 for Social, and .78 for Personal. As with Form A and B, the test-retest interval is not reported in the manual.

Although test-retest reliabilities for the children's and adults' forms are high, internal consistency reliabilities are somewhat marginal. In a study of 117 junior high-school students, Form A internal consistencies (alpha) were .71 for General, .66 for social, .67 for Academics, .76 for Parents, and .70 for Lie subscales. Subscales correlated .53 to .86 with the total score, but individual item-total and item-subscale correlations are not reported in the manual. Form AD internal consistencies were .78 for General, .57 for social, .72 for Personal, and .54 for Lie subscales. Further, subscales correlated .54 to .91 with the total score, but item analyses are not reported for Form AD. The most problematic subscales on Form AD are the Social and Lie subscales, which have internal consistency reliabilities of less than .60.

In summary of the reliability studies conducted with the Culture-Free SEI for Children and Adults, there is compelling evidence of test-retest stability, although over what period of time is unclear. Internal consistency reliability of the subscale is low to moderate, suggesting that the item composition of some subscales is not very homogeneous. The children's short form correlates acceptably with the long form. Inter-rater reliability of the SEI is not in question because the test is objectively scored.

Content validity was established by writing items "intended to cover all areas of the construct" (Battle, 1981, p. 14) of self-esteem. The 60 items composing Form A reported are the "most discriminating" from an initial pool of 150 items, and the 40 items on Form AD are the most discriminating from among an initial pool of 85 items.

In one study of concurrent validity with 198 children in Grades 3-6, Form A correlated .71 to .82 across grade levels with the Coopersmith Self-Esteem Inventory. Concurrent validity coefficients ranged from .72 to .84 for males and .66 to .91 for females. These concurrent validity correlations appear to be so high as to question what the Culture-Free SEI is measuring that the Coopersmith Self-Esteem Inventory is not. This also raises suspicion about the so-called "culture-free" nature of the SEI. If other self-esteem inventories are tainted by cultural bias, the Culture-Free SEI would not be expected to correlate very highly with such criterion-related measures.

The author attempts to adjust SEI scores to be comparable with Coopersmith scores by multiplying by "2" such that 100 is the maximum SEI total score. On this basis, the Culture-Free SEI scores generally are 3 to 5 points higher than Coopersmith scores across grade levels and genders. However, this conversion is an inappropriate attempt to equate the two inventories because the standard deviations are different. Coopersmith standard deviations are consistently larger than Culture-Free SEI standard deviations by as much as 5 points. Therefore, the transformation of SEI scores for equation with Coopersmith scores is incorrectly reported in the manual because the two tests are not standardized to a common metric.

Other criterion-related validity studies have examined the relationship of SEI scores to teacher ratings, students' perceptions of ability, intelligence, and handicapped status. The manual reports that a study of 90 students in Grades 1-8 revealed a correlation of .70 between the SEI Form A and the Student's Perception of Ability Scale. Form A correlated significantly ($r = .39$)—although not highly— with teacher ratings of males students, but not of female students. Surprisingly, the Academics self-esteem subscale did not correlate with teacher ratings. However, the author interprets this as evidence supportive of the assumption that self-esteem is multidimensional and complexly determined. Form A was found to significantly discriminate between learning disabled ($N = 90$) and successful students ($N = 97$) who were functioning at or above grade level in school. Successful students had higher SEI scores on the average by six points, which is a rather large difference. On the other hand, another study did not indicate a significant difference between brain dysfunctional and normal examinees. The SEI was correlated with 44 students' Canadian Lorge-Thorndike IQ scores to examine the relationship of self-esteem to intelligence. Results indicated that the correlation of the SEI with verbal and performance IQs were both low (.15 and .08, respectively) and not significant. This lends evidence to the construct validity of the SEI because it is not expected to correlate with intelligence.

The manual reports that a study of the relationship between depression and self-esteem was conducted by the author with 43 male and 86 female college students. Results confirmed that the adult SEI correlated significantly in the predicted direction ($r = -.55$) with Beck's Depression Inventory, and consistently so for both genders. The SEI was also correlated with 22 high-school students' scores on the Beck Depression Inventory and a short form of the MMPI depression scale. Total SEI score correlated highly ($r = -.75$) with both measures of depression as did the General and Personal subscales ($-.61$ to $-.78$); however, the correlations were somewhat lower ($-.34$, $-.42$) for the Social subscale. The magnitude of these correlations suggests that the SEI is a good predictor of depression as measured by other standardized tests.

In summary of the validity studies conducted with the SEI, evidence suggests that the children's form (A) is highly correlated with other measures of self-esteem, with students' self-perceptions, school achievement, and teachers' ratings, but not with intelligence. The adult form is highly predictive of depression in high-school and college students. Evidence of systematically established content validity is lacking in the manual, although the above criterion-related validity studies lend confidence to the clinical utility of the children's and adults' SEI.

Critique

The Culture-Free SEI for Children and Adults were developed as objective measures of self-esteem, independent of cultural context, for use in research or by mental health professionals. Apart from a global self-esteem score, items have been factored into more specific dimensions of self-esteem. The tests are easily administered as self-report checklists of feelings indicative of high and low self-worth; scoring is easily accomplished either by template or computer. The three forms of the SEI are available in three languages and in written or oral format. Psychometric studies conducted with the children's and adults' tests have yielded substantial evidence of test-retest stability, marginal internal consistency, and strong concurrent validity coefficients.

Unfortunately, there is no discussion in the manual as to how it was established that the three SEI forms are free of cultural bias. Indeed for quite some time, psychologists have abandoned the notion that psychometric measures can be constructed independent of culture, and instead have focused on either developing culturally "fair" tests or assessing ethnic differences and making the necessary score adjustments to avoid bias against minority cultures. The tests are available in two languages besides English (French and Spanish) but no evidence is available regarding the normative performance, reliability, or validity for French or Hispanic examinees. No studies are available to provide information about bilinguals' performance on alternate linguistic forms. To be sure, dialectic differences in item interpretation cannot be dismissed so readily, as suggested in the manual because the items are not void of distinct cultural meanings. Thus, cross-cultural researchers or mental health professionals working with ethnic minority clients should be wary of SEI norms, which may not be universal standards of self-esteem.

References

This list includes test citations as well as suggested additional reading.

Battle, J. (1976). Test-retest reliability of the Canadian Self-Esteem Inventory for Children (Form A). *Psychological Reports, 38,* 1343-1345.

Battle, J. (1977). The Canadian Self-Esteem Inventory for Children. *Test Collection Bulletin, 11,* 1.

Battle, J. (1977). Test-retest reliability of the Canadian Self-Esteem Inventory for Adults (Form AD). *Perceptual and Motor Skills, 44,* 38.

Battle, J. (1977). Test-retest reliability of the Canadian Self-Esteem Inventory for Children (Form A). *Psychological Reports, 40,* 157-158.

Battle, J. (1978). The relationship between self-esteem and depression. *Psychological Reports, 42,* 745-746.

Battle, J. (1979). Self-esteem of students in regular and special classes. *Psychological Reports, 42,* 212-214.

Battle, J. (1980). The relationship between self-esteem and depression among high school students. *Perceptual and Motor Skills, 51,* 157-158.

Battle, J. (1981). *Culture-Free Self-Esteem Inventories for Children and Adults.* Seattle: Special Child Publications.

R. Scott Stehouwer, Ph.D.
Associate Professor of Psychology, Calvin College, Grand Rapids, Michigan.

DETROIT TESTS OF LEARNING APTITUDE-2
Donald D. Hammill. Austin, Texas: PRO-ED.

Introduction

As I searched for the materials on the Detroit Tests of Learning Aptitude (DTLA), I soon discovered that things have changed for the DTLA. The original publisher, Bobbs-Merrill Company, no longer owns the test and in many respects the DTLA no longer exists. What does exist, however, is the Detroit Tests of Learning Aptitude-2 (DTLA-2). More than just a revision, the DTLA-2 could better be called "Son of DTLA" since in many respects it is a new test. Revisions that have taken place and the added and refined materials seem on the whole to have produced a significantly improved version of the DTLA.

In one of the more recent reviews of the DTLA, Silverstein (1978) criticized the standardization and statistical evaluation of the DTLA. Further, little material had been available regarding this standardization and evaluation. In fact, well over 40 years ago reviewers commented that the DTLA appeared to have been published before it was properly standardized and before adequate data were available regarding reliability and validity. Reviewers consistently called for remediation of this situation. The DTLA-2 is an attempt not only to correct this deficit but also to create a more useful and widely utilized test, one which holds true to the demographic characteristics of today's children and adolescents.

As the DTLA-2 is an aptitude test, it is concerned with measuring ability or capability on the part of a certain population, specifically the ability to learn new tasks. The DTLA-2 was developed by Donald D. Hammill in order to "determine strengths and weaknesses among intellectual abilities, . . . identify children and youths who are significantly below their peers in aptitude, and . . . serve as a measurement device in research studies investigating aptitude, intelligence, and cognitive behavior" (Hammill, 1985, pp. 10-11).

Donald Hammill, Ed.D. is retired from the department of special education at Temple University, and is the owner of PRO-ED, the current publisher of the DTLA-2. He has authored or coauthored a number of assessment devices in the field of special education and his background includes extensive training in education, special education, and speech pathology.

The main purpose of the DTLA-2 is to focus on intra-individual strengths and weaknesses with regard to learning aptitude. In other words, this test provides an

---

This reviewer wishes to acknowledge gratefully the help of Mr. Robert Nykamp in the preparation of this review.

opportunity to compare the individual with him- or herself on various aspects of intellectual and cognitive abilities.

The potential for the DTLA (and in essence the DTLA-2) has long been evident (Anastasi, 1938; Wells, 1949). Reviewers focused particularly on the asset of the test's ability to evaluate intra-individual strengths and weaknesses. Another asset of the DTLA was its physical layout and the relative ease of administering and scoring the test, a test that was not threatening to the children who were tested. The DTLA-2 has attempted to maintain these strengths and where possible to improve upon them. An example of this is the fact that the use of item analysis has resulted in shortening many subtests without any ill effect.

Each review of the DTLA, as indicated previously, was particularly critical of the poor standardization and lack of appropriate reliability and validity information. The last DTLA handbook (Baker & Leland, 1967) had failed to discuss such aspects as the interpretation of scores and profiles and the theoretical issues underlying the test. Another consistent criticism was the fact that demographic variables had changed a great deal from the 1930s when the test was developed and standardized. In fact, the test itself had an outdated appearance.

The DTLA-2 represents the result of a major effort to develop an appropriate level of standardization. Studies were also undertaken to establish an appropriate level of reliability and validity. The material has been extensively revised and updated, including the development of a presentation of test items that appear appropriate to the 1980s and beyond.

Consulting on the revision were 100 professionals who had used the test frequently. These professionals were asked to choose the most useful and appropriate subtests of the DTLA and they indicated a clear preference for seven of them. Although some were retitled, these subtests were retained in the DTLA-2: Word Opposites, Sentence Imitation, Oral Directions, Word Sequences, Design Reproduction, Object Sequences, and Letter Sequences. In addition, four new subtests were developed: Story Construction, Symbolic Relations, Conceptual Matching, and Word Fragments.

No other forms of this test have been developed. However, as with the DTLA, the author of the DTLA-2 recommends selecting certain subtests depending on the capabilities or physical impairments of the person to be tested. The DTLA-2 comes in a box comparable in size to the various Wechsler tests which contains the test manual, examiner record forms, student response forms, summary and profile sheets, and a spiral-bound picture book.

Because this is an individually administered test the examiner's participation is crucial. As with all such tests, the examiner sets the tone for the examination procedure. The directions are read to the child being tested and, as with all individually administered tests, the examiner is in a position not only to score the tests but also to observe the child's response to the test itself as well as to his or her successes and failures. The test is intended for persons from the age of 6 years, 0 months through 17 years, 11 months. This would include most persons from first through twelfth grade.

One real advantage of this test concerns the use of basal and ceiling scores. This format, very similar to that of tests such as the Peabody Individual Achievement Test (PIAT), not only saves a good deal of time and effort on the part of the examiner, but also saves time for the child being tested. It lessens both boredom due to overly simple items and frustration due to too many failures in any individual subtest.

As indicated, the DTLA-2 consists of 11 subtests, which yield nine composite scores. Examinee responses vary from answering questions directly to drawing pictures. The subtests and variables that each subtest is intended to measure are as follows (adapted from Hammill, 1985):

Word Opposites: A measure of vocabulary, specifically a test of antonym knowledge.

Sentence Imitation: A measure of rote sequential memory which is influenced by competence in standard English grammar.

Oral Directions: A series of complex tests that measures listening comprehension, spatial relations, manual dexterity, short-term memory, and attention.

Word Sequences: A test of short-term verbal memory and attention.

Story Construction: A verbal subtest that measures story-telling ability and that depends on creating and telling a logical story.

Design Reproduction: A measure of attention, manual dexterity, short-term visual memory, and spatial relations.

Object Sequences: A measure of attention and visual short-term memory.

Symbolic Relations: A measure of problem solving and visual reasoning.

Conceptual Matching: A measure of the ability to observe theoretical or practical relationships between objects.

Word Fragments: A measure of the ability to form closure and recognize partially presented familiar words in printed form.

Letter Sequences: A measure of short-term visual memory and attention.

The nine composite scores were developed as an aid to delineating intra-individual strengths and weaknesses. Discrepancies between the composites are particularly important in determining these. Most normal individuals will show little discrepancy. Discrepancies can be particularly useful in determining abilities on which the individual can capitalize as well as specific areas of disability that may create frustration and that the individual and significant others must address.

The nine composites (General Intelligence, Verbal Aptitude, Non-Verbal Aptitude, Conceptual Aptitude, Structural Aptitude, Attention-Enhanced Aptitude, Attention-Reduced Aptitude, Motor-Enhanced Aptitude, and Motor-Reduced Aptitude) are described as follows (adapted from Hammill, 1985):

The General Intelligence (GIQ) score represents a person's overall, global aptitude. Comprised of the standard scores of all the DTLA-2 subtests, it is considered the best predictor of achievement. Hammill also considers it the best estimate of the individual's ability to handle the intellectual demands of the environment.

In the *Linguistic Domain,* two composites are considered important: Verbal Aptitude (VBQ) and Non-Verbal Aptitude (NVQ). The Verbal Aptitude score is a measure of the examinee's ability to understand, integrate, and use spoken and written language. Non-Verbal Aptitude represents the ability to use spatial relationships and non-verbal symbolic reasoning.

The *Cognitive Domain* is determined by abilities involving conceptual meaning (abstract thinking, reasoning, and problem solving) and those which involve structural knowledge (recognition of physical properties). The Conceptual Aptitude (COQ) and Structural Aptitude (STQ) composites measure these abilities.

In the *Attentional Domain* two composites attempt to guage differences between short-term memory and attentional abilities on the one hand and long-term memory on the other. Attention-Enhanced Aptitude (AEQ) is a measure of immediate recall, short-term memory, and focused concentration. Attention-Reduced Aptitude (ARQ) measures long-term memory.

The ability to utilize particularly fine motor skills is assessed within the *Motoric Domain*. The Motor-Enhanced Aptitude (MEQ) composite is a measure of the ability to utilize complex motoric abilities, particularly hand-eye fine motor coordination. The second composite, Motor-Reduced Aptitude (MRQ), shows the examinee's ability to perform tasks that are relatively free from fine motor abilities.

The answer forms provided include the Examiner Recording Form on which the examiner notes whether an item was passed or failed. Most of the subtests are presented orally; however, a number of other subtests involve motor activity such as reproducing designs and following directions to perform certain motor tasks. These latter two items are completed on the Student Response Form.

Results of the test are transcribed to a Summary and Profile Sheet. There are five sections to this sheet: Section I contains a record of subtest scores including the raw scores, percentiles, and standard scores for each of the 11 subtests; Section II allows for a listing of other tests administered prior to or along with the DTLA-2 and for indicating the date, standard score, and the DTLA-2 equivalent of the score for each of the other tests; Section III contains a profile of subtests scores that is completed on a graph representing the subtests and the standard scores for each subtest; Section IV contains workspace for computing composite quotients; and Section V presents a profile of composite quotients and space to present a profile of the results of other tests which were administered.

Practical Applications/Uses

The DTLA-2 has a number of practical uses for persons between the age of 6 and 18 years. The Detroit Tests of Learning Aptitude have long been used in connection with school systems and in fact were developed originally with school children and their academic needs in mind. The DTLA-2's ability to test for intra-individual strengths and weaknesses and to delineate specific areas of learning ability and disability make it particularly well suited for academic planning. The results of the DTLA-2 can be very beneficial in planning an appropriate course of study and method of teaching for specific students. Realizing that a child has problems with auditory attention but is capable of using motoric ability, for example, may be particularly beneficial in developing a more "hands-on" approach to the educational experiences of this child.

The DTLA-2 can also be beneficial in vocational assessment and planning. For example, determining that an individual has strong ability in the motoric area or a strong ability in the linguistic area can be very helpful in outlining specific careers and/or training the individual might pursue.

The DTLA-2 offers a number of uses in mental health settings. In fact, this reviewer first became acquainted with the DTLA in such a setting. The DTLA has been a useful component in a battery of tests focusing on intellectual/academic/cognitive abilities or disabilities of child and adolescent patients. It was particularly well suited, for example, in determining attentional deficits children may evidence. The DTLA proved valuable in detecting auditory attention deficits, which have profound implications for a child's ability to follow directions or orders from parents. Anecdotally, the DTLA was helpful in behavior management in this regard, helping parents to understand their child's limitations in understanding verbal commands and aiding them in the development of healthier interaction and more appropriate methods of child rearing. The DTLA-2 holds perhaps even greater promise for use in mental health settings.

The DTLA-2 can be quite helpful as a neurological screening device. The DTLA has been a useful device in neurological assessment of children and presumably DTLA-2 will be better. Using the discrepancy formula of the composites, an examiner can very quickly and precisely pinpoint areas of deficit in which there may be some neurological impairment. Thus, the DTLA-2 can be helpful either as a screening device for further neuropsychological testing or as part of a neuropsychological battery for children and adolescents.

The DTLA-2 is particularly well suited for use by psychologists and educators. Persons in the fields of special education, vocational education, counseling, clinical psychology, and neuropsychology can benefit from using this test. Additionally, because the DTLA-2 focuses on grammatical and speech structure it may be potentially useful for professionals in the field of speech pathology.

The DTLA-2 can be used with persons from age 6 years, 0 months to 17 years, 11 months. It has been standardized on boys and girls from both city and rural areas in a representative sample of geographic areas in the United States. The education level of the parents in the sample varied from less than high school graduate through postgraduate training. The standardization sample included white and black children as well as American Indians and those of Hispanic and Asian ethnic backgrounds.

In terms of test administration, the DTLA-2 is to be given on an individually administered basis. Certain subtests could be appropriately administered to subjects with physical impairments (e.g., for the deaf, an examiner could select Design Reproduction, Conceptual Matching, and Letter Sequences; for the blind, Word Opposites, Sentence Imitation, and Word Sequences). The testing environment should be free from distractions, well ventilated, well lighted, quiet, private, and comfortable. Some training is necessary to administer the test. A psychometrist or technician should be easily able to master the requisite skills for administering the test. However, interpretation of the test is another matter and should be left to a trained professional. The time necessary for administering the DTLA-2 depends on the number of subtests used, though the full test should take between 50 minutes and 2 hours.

The manual for the DTLA-2 is one of the best this reviewer has ever seen for any test. It includes a thorough review of issues regarding aptitude testing, description of the test, rationale for the test, its appropriate and inappropriate uses, interpretation data as well as methods for controlling bias, sharing results, and testing the limits. These are all presented in a very readable format. Dr. Hammill is to be commended for the excellent, clear, and well-developed manual.

Scoring methods and instructions are presented clearly in the manual. Each subtest is scored differently and the procedures for each are explained. The test is for the most part very objective and scoring is therefore relatively easy to determine. The manual presents sample responses for each subtest that are quite helpful in learning how to administer and score the tests. The author suggests administering the DTLA-2 at least three times as adequate practice.

In order to shorten the testing and scoring time, basal and ceiling scores are used. Answers are checked against the manual and a designation of correct or incorrect is given for each. At the time of this writing there was no machine or computer scoring available. Because of the simplicity of the scoring procedure, few if any scoring problems should arise.

Interpretation of the test is based on the objective scoring. Though scoring is a relatively simple matter, interpreting the DTLA-2 is more difficult. Interpretation is based on the subtest scores, the total score, and the composite scores, and the use of scoring profiles eases the process. Effective interpretation depends, however, on the interpreter's qualifications, not only regarding the specific test but also in terms of what the interpreter knows about development, childrens' and adolescents' cognitive abilities, etc. This takes a relatively high degree of training and therefore interpretation is best left to individuals who are well acquainted with individually administered psychological tests in general and issues in learning abilities and disabilities, intellectual assessment, aptitude assessment, etc., specifically.

Technical Aspects

Because the DTLA-2 is in essence a new test, the only available studies of reliability and validity are those of Dr. Hammill and his associates. The results of these studies are presented in the manual.

In terms of reliability, internal consistency for test scores was analyzed for 300 subjects in six age groups ranging from six- to seven-year-olds through 16- to 17-year-olds. Coefficients ranged from .81 to .95 for the subtests and from .95 to .96 for the composites. Thirty-three subjects ranging in age from six to 17 were used in a study of test-retest reliability. Subjects were retested after a two-week interval. With a correction factor for the restricted range of the sample, all composites yielded a coefficient greater than .80 (range .80 to .93). Seven of the 11 subtests yielded a coefficient greater than .80 (range .82 to .91). Oral Directions, Object Sequences, Conceptual Matching, and Letter Sequences yielded coefficients ranging from .63 to .78.

The manual also reports studies regarding content, criterion-related (concurrent), and construct validity. For content validity, Hammill states the DTLA-2 fits well with Wechsler's (1974) verbal-performance dichotomy and Kaufman and Kaufman's (1983) sequential-simultaneous processing dichotomy. The DTLA-2 also fits well (as it should) with Hammill's taxonomy (Hammill, Brown, & Bryant, in press).

An investigation of the criterion-related (concurrent) validity of the DTLA-2 was conducted using 76 students either currently enrolled in or referred for special education programs. All subjects had received the Wechsler Intelligence Scale for Children-Revised (WISC-R) and 25 of them had also been administered the Peabody Picture Vocabulary Test (PPVT). Results were corrected for reduced reliability due to restricted variance. The subtest comparisons yielded coefficients ranging from .38 to .76 with a median of .55. The composites yielded coefficients ranging from .54 to .84 with a median of .71.

The construct validity of the DTLA-2 has been researched regarding five issues. First, the subtests have been demonstrated to relate to chronological age and to conform to developmental patterns known to exist for aptitude measures. Second, the subtests have been shown to be highly intercorrelated, suggesting they all measure a similar trait (i.e., learning aptitude). Third, the test scores correlate well with tests of academic achievement, confirming the idea that the DTLA-2 measures abilities related to academic performance. Fourth, the DTLA-2 differentiates between individuals known to be of normal learning aptitude and those of poor learning aptitude. Finally, the items of each subtest correlate highly with the total score of the subtest, suggesting the items of each subtest measure similar traits. While the results of these studies support the construct validity of the DTLA-2, studies utilizing a multitrait-multimethod matrix (Campbell & Fiske, 1967) could be most beneficial.

Taken together, these few studies suggest adequate reliability and validity for the DTLA-2. However, all of the information available on reliability and validity is found only in the test manual. These data are for the most part clearly given, but certainly need cross-validation. Also, further delineation of the subjects employed in reliability and validity testing would be helpful. The information provided on these subjects leads one to wonder whether they are representative of the larger population on which the DTLA-2 is to be employed.

Critique

Because of the very recent publication of the DTLA-2 (two months prior to the preparation of this review), other reviews are not yet available. As mentioned previously, there were numerous reviews of the DTLA—one of the major reasons for the development of the DTLA-2 was in order to deal with the identified weaknesses of its predecessor.

Personally, this reviewer found the DTLA very useful and believed it had great potential. while remaining aware of its limitations. The DTLA-2 may be in a good position to fulfill the potential of the original. It seems to address some unique issues, particularly those relative to intra-individual strengths and weaknesses. As educational planning becomes more individualized not only for students in general but specifically for those with special needs, the DTLA-2 may become even more useful. As neuropsychological assessment of children advances, the DTLA-2 may help lead the way. As clinicians seek a better understanding of the cognitive functioning of children and adolescents and as vocational planning takes on an ever-increasing importance in society, the DTLA-2 is at least potentially in a position to help guide the effort.

However, much more work is necessary in order to assess the usefulness of the new test. Research must be undertaken to cross-validate the reported studies of reliability and validity. Further research will determine whether the DTLA-2 can take its expected place in clinical, academic, and neuropsychological assessment.

References

Anastasi, A. (1938). Detroit Tests of Learning Aptitude. In O. K. Buros (Ed.), *The 1938 mental measurements yearbook* (pp. 108-109). Highland Park, NJ: The Gryphon Press.

Baker, H. J., & Leland, B. (1967). *Detroit Tests of Learning Aptitude: Examiner's handbook.* Indianapolis: Bobbs-Merrill.

Campbell, D. T., & Fiske, D. W. (1967). Convergent and discriminant validity by the multitrait-multimethod matrix. In D. Jackson & S. Messick (Eds.), *Problems in human assessment* (pp. 124-132). New York: McGraw-Hill, Inc.

Hammill, D. (1985). *Manual of the Detroit Tests of Learning Aptitude-2.* Austin, TX: PRO-ED.

Hammill, D., Brown, L., & Bryant, B. (in press). *A consumer's guide to tests in print.* Austin, TX: PRO-ED.

Kaufman, A. S., & Kaufman, N. L. (1983). *Kaufman Assessment Battery for Children.* Circle Pines, MN: American Guidance Service.

Silverstein, A. B. (1978). Detroit Tests of Learning Aptitude. In O. K. Buros (Ed.), *The eighth mental measurements yearbook* (pp. 214-215). Highland Park, NJ: The Gryphon Press.

Wechsler, D. (1974). *Wechsler Intelligence Scale for Children-Revised.* Cleveland: The Psychological Corporation.

Wells, F. L. (1949). Detroit Tests of Learning Aptitude. In O. K. Buros (Ed.), *The third mental measurements yearbook* (p. 356). Highland Park, NJ: The Gryphon Press.

Kenneth Polite, Ph.D.
Assistant Professor of Psychology, Rosemead School of Psychology,
Biola University, La Mirada, California.

THE DEVEREUX CHILD BEHAVIOR RATING SCALE

George Spivack and Jules Spotts. Devon, Pennsylvania: The
Devereux Foundation.

Introduction

The Devereux Child Behavior Rating Scale (DCB) is a paper-and-pencil test consisting of 97 questions that require the respondent to compare the behavior of the child being rated to the behavior of "normal" children of the same age. The purpose of the DCB is to describe and communicate the behavioral syndromes of atypical, latency age children, aged 8-12 years, who are emotionally disturbed and mentally retarded. The test was specifically designed to provide a profile of a child's problematic behaviors that caused an adult to decide that the child's "problems" required professional intervention.

The Devereux Child Behavior Rating Scale, first published in 1966, was developed by Dr. George Spivack and Dr. Jules Spotts at the Devereux Foundation in Devon, Pennsylvania. At the time of this instrument's development, Dr. Spivack, a Diplomate in clinical psychology, was the director of research for the Devereux Foundation, and Dr. Spotts was a research psychologist for the same institution. The Devereux Foundation is the largest nonprofit organization of residential treatment centers seeking to serve the needs of emotionally disturbed and mentally handicapped individuals in the United States.

The development of the Devereux Child Behavior Rating Scale is reported to be the result of four years of investigation (Spivack & Spotts, 1966). Spivack and M. Levine began early developmental work on the instrument with an intensive review of the literature on atypical, brain damaged, schizophrenic, and autistic children and interviews with the residential treatment staff of the Devereux Schools (Spivack & Levine, 1964). Their purpose was to develop a set of behavior rating scales that would accurately describe the symptoms common to disturbed, latency age children, and thus augment the usefulness of the then extant diagnostic nomenclature. It was felt that the scales should describe the symptom behavior of these children as that behavior is observed in a day-to-day living situation over a period of two weeks.

The search of the literature and the staff interviews produced a list of approximately 850 test items. From this list a set of 68 rating scales was devised. The scales were used by a houseparent and a supervisor at the Devereux Schools to rate 140 children. Factor analysis of the results yielded 15 factors, six of which correlated with factors found in other published studies: 1) proneness of anger,

2) autistic social unresponsiveness, 3) disinhibition, 4) negativism, 5) cognitive coherence, and 6) fear of physical harm.

Subsequent to the first study a second study was carried out by Spivack and Spotts (1965). It was aimed at replicating, refining, and expanding the previous study by Spivack and Levine. In the second study both a larger sample of children (N = 252) and a larger sample of symptom behaviors (128) were used. As a result, 20 first-order factors and six second-order factors emerged. The final form of the Devereux Child Behavior Rating Scale is based on this second study, a study of 100 retarded children from a state residential facility, and a study of 348 public school children. In its present form the DCB yields 17 scores based on the following analytically derived factors: 1) Distractibility, 2) Poor self care, 3) Pathological use of senses, 4) Emotional detachment, 5) Social isolation, 6) Poor coordination and body tonus, 7) Incontinence, 8) Messiness-sloppiness, 9) Inadequate need for independence, 10) Unresponsiveness to stimulation, 11) proneness to emotional upset, 12) Need for adult contact, 13) Anxious-fearful ideation, 14) "Impulse" ideation, 15) Inability to delay, 16) Social aggression, and 17) Unethical behavior.

The Devereux Child Behavior Rating Scale is an 8-page booklet. Although a 34-page manual is also available, the booklet is complete in itself and most users will not require the manual. The front of the booklet provides space for the child's name, sex, and birthdate, the rater's name and relationship to the child, and the date of the rating. There are eight specific guidelines provided for the rater to follow. The following five pages contain 97 questions for the rater to answer about the child's behavior. Most questions are rated on a scale of 1-5 (1 = Never, 2 = Rarely, 3 = Occasionally, 4 = Often, and 5 = Very frequently). Those questions that cannot be rated on the 1-5 scale are rated on similar, appropriate Likert scales. Page 7 is blank with the exception of a request on the last two pages space is provided for additional written comments, the same information requested on page one, and the child's IQ score. The 17 factors and scoring key for each factor are included. The raw score for each question involved in a particular factor is entered in the space provided; the total is determined; and then the total raw score for each factor is plotted on a profile of standard score units. This produces a profile that can be used to compare the behavior of the rated child with the behavior of normal children on each of the 17 factors.

Practical Applications/Uses

The Devereux Child Behavior Rating Scale was designed as a descriptive instrument and, as such, it is helpful for the mental health professional who has the responsibility of diagnosing and setting up treatment plans for children. Clinicians in private practice will find it particularly helpful because they do not need to be present while the form is being filled out.

Houseparents, childcare workers, nurses, and similar professionals who have occasion to work with children may find this instrument helpful. Although this test was initially developed for use with institutionalized children, it is also useful with children who are being seen in outpatient settings.

Any latency age child, aged 8-12 years, who is evidencing problematic behavior is an appropriate subject for the DCB. Two companion versions have also been developed: The Devereux Adolescent Behavior Rating Scale for use with disturbed adolescents, and the Devereux Elementary School Behavior Rating Scale for use by educators to identify, prevent, and remediate behavioral difficulties affecting academic performance.

Administration of the scale is extremely simple and generally takes about 20 minutes. Most individuals will require no professional supervision because the instructions printed on the front of the test are easy to follow. The scoring key is included and scoring generally takes about 5-10 minutes. Although one obtains objective standard scores, the proper interpretation of those standard scores require some clinical judgment. Many of the aforementioned professionals would be qualified to use the Devereux for screening purposes (i.e., to determine that a child's behavior requires professional intervention); however, full interpretation of the results should be left to those individuals who have been thoroughly trained in test interpretation.

Technical Aspects

The DCB manual reports interrater reliability, item reliability, and factor reliability scores. The scorer reliability is based on the initial study of 140 institutionalized children (Spivack & Levine, 1964). In that study the reliability scores ranged from a low of .77 to a high of .93, with a median score of .83.

The reported item reliability scores were determined by a one-week, test-retest study in which Devereux houseparents rated a heterogeneous group of 80 children. The raters were not aware that a retest would be performed when they filled out the first scale. The median item test-retest correlation was .83. Factor reliability data were also determined using the same data. The obtained median coefficient was .91, with a range from .80 to .99.

Although these reliability data are surely adequate, it is unfortunate that almost no research has surfaced to substantiate the validity of the 17 factors used in the Devereux Child Behavior Rating Scale. For example, is a child who obtains a high score on the "social isolation" factor really a child who is socially isolated? A study by C. Michael Nelson (1971) lends some support to the claim that the DCB does indeed measure what it purports to measure. Nelson used a direct observation technique to determine if classroom teachers' ratings on the "inability to delay" and the "social aggression" subscales of the DCB would reliably differentiate between "conduct disturbed" and "normal" children. He found that these two subscales did reliably predict those children who were "conduct disturbed."

A second study that has some indirect bearing on the validity of this scale was conducted by Forbes (1978). He compared a matched sample of 20 "hyperactive" and 20 "emotionally-behaviorally disturbed" children who had been seen in a private practice setting and who were rated by one of their parents (usually their mother). The mean scores for the hyperactive group and the emotionally-behaviorally disturbed group were compared with the mean scores of the "normals" from Spivack and Spotts standardization sample (1966). When independent two-tailed t-tests were performed for each of the 17 factors of the DCB Forbes found that the hyperactive group scored consistently higher than the emotionally-behaviorally disturbed group and both groups scored significantly higher than the normals. These data suggest that the Devereux Child Behavior Rating Scale does have some validity as a screening device to identify hyperactive children. This study seems promising, but further validity studies are needed.

Critique

Although the reliability data on this test are more than adequate, very little validity data has been forthcoming. Despite this limitation, the Devereux Child Behavior Rating Scale has proven to be a clinically useful assessment and treatment planning instrument. Perhaps its usefulness has grown out of the fact that the DCB is a descriptive system using empirically determined factors. As Dr. Alan Barclay (1972) pointed out, the factors used in the DCB seem to be similar to the kinds of behaviors reported by researchers working with the populations that the Devereux Child Behavior Rating Scale was developed to address.

The fact that this instrument was empirically and atheoretically derived seems to enhance its attractiveness to individuals from various theoretical orientations. For instance, a behaviorist might use the descriptions as is, whereas a dynamically oriented individual might use the descriptors to help them arrive at a developmental diagnosis. Viewed in the light of its ease of administration, relative low cost, and potential for providing useful information, the Devereux Child Behavior Rating Scale seems to be a helpful instrument for those working with "atypical" children.

References

Barclay, A. G. (1972). Devereux child behavior rating scale. In O. K. Buros (Ed.), *The seventh mental measurements yearbook* (pp. 67-68). Highland Park, NJ: The Gryphon Press.

Forbes, G. B. (1978). Comparison of hyperactive and emotionally-behaviorally disturbed children on the Devereux Child Behavior Rating Scale: A potential aid in diagnosis. *Journal of Clinical Psychology, 34*(1), 68-71.

Nelson, C. M. (1971). Techniques for screening conduct disturbed children. *Exceptional Children, 37*(7), 501-508.

Spivack, G., & Levine, M. (1964). The Devereux Child Behavior Rating Scale: A study of symptom behavior in latency age atypical children. *American Journal of Mental Deficiency, 68*, 700-717.

Spivack, G., & Spotts, J. (1965). The Devereux Child Behavior Rating Scale: Symptom behaviors in latency age children. *American Journal of Mental Deficiency, 69*, 839-853.

Spivack, G., & Spotts, J. (1966). *Devereux Child Behavior Rating Scale manual.* Devon, PA: The Devereux Foundation.

James R. Deni, Ed.D.
Professor of Psychology, Appalachian State University, Boone, North Carolina.

DIAGNOSTIC ACHIEVEMENT BATTERY
Phyllis L. Newcomer and Dolores Curtis. Austin, Texas: PRO-ED.

Introduction

The Diagnostic Achievement Battery (DAB) is an individually administered, paper-and-pencil instrument designed to assess children's ability in listening, speaking, reading, writing, and mathematics. Students' raw scores may then be converted to standard scores and percentile ranks for evaluating individual student strengths and weaknesses.

The DAB consists of a manual, examiner record forms, student worksheets, and a student booklet—all of which are required to administer the complete battery of twelve subtests. However, the test is designed so that the entire battery would not be required for every child because some students would only need a specific area screened or evaluated. The 75-page manual, consisting of four chapters and appendices, clearly describes the directions for administering and scoring the test. Chapter 3 provides all the specific administration and scoring information for the twelve subtests. The examiner record form includes student information and a record of scores on the front page, followed by the name of each subtest with the beginning point for children under 9 years of age, scoring instructions, and ending point on the inside. Each subtest includes numbered items, scoring space, correct responses, and child's response. Because each subtest is blocked off there is ample room for scoring and recording. The student worksheet is required for administering the Capitalization and Punctuation, Spelling, Written Vocabulary, and Math Calculation subtests. The student booklet is used by the examiner to present visual information to the student for several subtests. Standard scores and percentiles are available for ages 6 years, 0 months through 14 years, 11 months. According to the manual (Newcomer & Curtis, 1984, p. 3), the twelve subtests are aimed at achieving four major purposes:

1. To identify those students who are significantly below their peers in areas of spoken language (listening and speaking), written language (reading and writing), and mathematics and who, as a result, may profit from supplemental or remedial help.

2. To determine the particular kinds of components' strengths and weaknesses that students possess.

3. To document students' progress in specific areas as a consequence of special intervention programs.

4. To serve as a measurement device in research studies of the academic achievement of elementary school children.

The twelve subtests are as follows:

Listening consists of two subtests: 1) Story Comprehension (SC) has 35 items and requires the examiner to read aloud brief stories and the student to answer questions on the story just read. The stories get progressively longer and more difficult. This subtest requires the students to listen and comprehend what they hear read. 2) Characteristics (CH) requires the students to give a true or false answer to brief statements that are read to them. This subtest requires a high level of listening ability.

Speaking consists of two subtests: 1) Synonyms (SY) has 25 items and requires the student to supply a word that has the same meaning as the stimulus word. This subtest requires both receptive and expressive abilities. 2) Grammatical Completion (GC) has 27 items and measures the students' ability to understand and use common morphological forms in English. The examiner reads unfinished sentences and the student responds with the correct missing morphological forms in English.

Reading consists of two subtests: 1) Alphabet/Word Knowledge (A/WK) requires letter recognition at the early ages. The child is asked to call out letters in the student booklet and a few sight words. Later in the Word Knowledge portion students are required to demonstrate their visual recognition of words by reading from a word list. This test is similar to the Reading subtest on the Wide Range Achievement Test (Jastak & Jastak, 1976). 2) Reading Comprehension (RC) requires the student to read short stories silently and answer comprehensive questions about the material read. The comprehensive questions are asked by the examiner.

Writing consists of four subtests: 1) Capitalization (CA) and 2) Punctuation (PT) both of which require the student to provide the correct capitalization and punctuation found in a paragraph in the student worksheet. 3) Spelling (SP) requires the examiner to read a list of 20 words, and the student to use each dictated word in a sentence. 4) Written Vocabulary (WV) requires the student to write a story in the student worksheet after looking at three pictures that have a beginning, middle, and ending. The pictures are similar to what you might find in the Picture Arrangement subtest of the Wechsler Intelligence Scale for Children-Revised (WISC-R: Wechsler, 1974).

Applied Mathematics consists of two subtests: 1) Mathematics Reasoning (MR), at the lower levels, requires children to respond orally to pictured items; at the upper levels statement problems are read aloud orally. Students must retain the problem in their heads and solve the problem without pencil and paper. The test is similar to the Arithmetic subtest of the Wechsler Intelligence Scale for Children-Revised (WISC-R). 2) Mathematics Calculation (MC) in which the student must solve math problems presented in the student worksheet under timed conditions. The student solves the problems directly in the worksheet—similar to the Arithmetic subtest of the Wide Range Achievement Test.

Practical Applications/Uses

The DAB should be useful in a variety of applied settings where a norm referenced instrument is required to screen or evaluate achievement in listening, speaking, reading, writing, and mathematics. The DAB is an individually administered diagnostic achievement battery which can be used effectively to screen and evaluate children having learning problems. The instrument will be of particular value to psychologists, resource teachers, and other educators interested in testing students' level of academic achievement. It would also be of particular value to psychologists and other educators who are responsible for evaluating exceptional children under the guidelines of PL 94-142. It incorporates the aspects of many different diagnostic tests into a single comprehensive instrument. Although the DAB has a total battery of twelve subtests, the examiner is not required to give all twelve to every child. In fact, at the younger ages—6 and 7 years—this would not be possible with most children, especially those experiencing learning problems. In assessing Listening, Speaking, Reading, and Applied Math, each requires the administration of two subtests. In assessing Spoken Language and Writing, each requires the administration of six subtests. Therefore, examiners are free to choose particular portions required in evaluating a given child. Standard scores are also reported for administering 2, 4, 6, or all 12 subtests.

The test should be administered in a quiet area by psychologists and educators having a psychometric background. The examiner is encouraged to review the administration and scoring procedures before attempting to administer this test. Also, studying the examiner's record form, student worksheet, and student booklet would be necessary. The entire test, however, could be learned within a few hours by an experienced examiner. Others with less experience and training would require more time. The total administration time can vary—depending on the number of subtests given, the particular child, and skill of the examiner. Some of the subtests can be given in a matter of 15-20 minutes; however, the entire battery of 12 subtests could take two hours.

This test is hand-scored and no machine scoring capabilities are available. The scoring procedures are provided in the manual's chapter (3) entitled Specific Administration and Scoring Instructions. The examiner record form also provides instructions for beginning and ending each subtest as you move from subtest to subtest as well as scoring procedures. Most of the test is scored during the administration, but a few subtests (e.g., Capitalization, Punctuation, Spelling, Written Vocabulary, and Math Calculation) are scored after terminating the test.

After completing the test the examiner adds up the student's raw score for each subtest, then records them in Section I Record of Scores located on the front of the examiner's record form. The examiner then turns to the Appendices entitled Standard Scores and Percentiles for Different Ages to find the page and table number of the appropriate age for that child. Once the appropriate page for that age is found, the examiner finds the student's raw score under each subtest. The child's Standard Score is found at the far left of the page (shaded area) and the percentile rank (at the far right). The percentile rank and standard score are then entered in Section I Record of Scores. Chapter 4 in the manual, entitled Analyzing the DAB Results, provides the examiner with an easily understood sample of the scoring procedure. Also provided are subtest descriptors of the scores, which are entered into Section I. The descriptors (Superior, Above Average, Average, Below Average, Poor) provide guidelines for interpreting student subtest performance. Subtest standard scores have a mean of 10 and a SD of 3. After completing the Section I Record of Scores: Subtests, the examiner transfers the subtest standard scores to the box for Composites, the second box in Section I. The total achievement composite is the sum of all 12 subtests' standard scores. The composite of Listening is the sum of the two subtests, Story Comprehension, and Characteristics; Speaking is the sum of the two subtests, Synonyms, and Grammatical Completion; Reading is the sum of the two subtests, Alphabet/Word Knowledge and Reading Comprehension; Writing is the sum of the standard scores for four subtests, Punctuation, Capitalization, Spelling, and Written Vocabulary; Math is the sum of the two subtests, Math Reasoning and Math Computation; Spoken Language is the sum of four subtests, Story Comprehension, Characteristics, Synonyms, and Grammatical Completion; Written Language is the sum of the standard scores on six subtests, Alphabet/Work Knowledge, Reading Comprehension, Punctuation, Capitalization, Spelling, and Written Vocabulary. On Table M (last three pages in manual) the examiner finds the Quotients, which have a mean of 100 and SD of 15, for each standard score composite sum. The examiner can also find descriptors (Superior, Above Average, Average, Below Average, Poor) for the composite scores. Subtest standard scores and composite quotients in Section II DAB Profiles are then recorded on the last page of the form. The last column of the profile also allows the examiner to enter the student's cognitive ability. This is of particular advantage if an individual test (e.g., the WISC-R) was given because the mean and SD would be the same as the DAB quotients. This allows an examiner to compare the student's achievement quotient with their IQ quotient.

Technical Aspects

. The DAB was standardized on a sample of 1,534 children from 13 states (California, Washington, Missouri, Ohio, Iowa, Kansas, Kentucky, Louisiana, New Mexico, New Jersey, North Dakota, Pennsylvania, and Texas). The manual includes a table of the characteristics of the students in the standardization sample. Although the manual states, "it was possible to compare percentages based on the standardization sample with those of the United States population that are reported in the Statistical Abstracts of the United States," the Ns in some geographic areas could have been larger. However, the sample is adequate for this type of individual achievement battery.

The manual has a section on validity and discusses the three most reported types of validity for test purposes: content validity, criterion-related validity, and construct validity. The DAB does seem to have relatively good content validity as described in the item selection section. The median discriminating power for all the DAB subtests, except three, are presented in Table 2 of the manual. The Capitalization, Punctuation, and Written Vocabulary subtests would not allow statistical analysis because of the nature of the test.

The DAB's criterion-related validity was studied by correlating its scores with other similar tests. Table 10 in the manual lists the correlations with criterion tests such as the Durrell Analysis of Reading Difficulty, Keymath Diagnostic Arithmetic Test, Test of Language Development—Intermediate and Primary (TOLD-I, TOLD-P), Test of Written Language (TOWL), Wide Range Achievement Test (WRAT), and the Woodcock Reading Mastery Test. Reported coefficients range from .37-.81. Construct validity is discussed but could be more adequately covered. The DAB was also correlated with tests of intelligence: the Slosson Intelligence Test and the Otis Lennon Quick Score Test. However, the sample, done in the Philadelphia area, is small (N = 55). The subtest coefficients ranged in size from .36-.71 with the composite coefficients being higher. The DAB does seem to be correlated with intelligence, which we would expect because most intelligence tests, especially individual tests, are good predictors of school success. More research should be done using individual tests such as the Wechsler Intelligence Scale for Children-Revised.

Reliability is addressed fairly and adequately in the manual and all but one subtest (Synonyms) seem to have constantly good reliability. Reliability for most applied sittings should be at or exceed .80. In most cases the DAB meets this criteria of .80 or above in most of the subtests. The manual does point out a sampling error which probably accounts for the inconsistencies in subtest reliability coefficients at age 13 years. The authors also caution the over interpretation of the Synonyms subtest because of inconsistencies in reliability coefficients below .80 and recommend that examiners look at the composite Speaking (Synonyms and Grammatical Completion) rather than Synonyms alone. The Standard Error of Measurement for each subtest and composite is also small and is an important consideration in educational decision making concerning student achievement and, in fact, test selection.

The DAB was also administered to 55 children identified as learning disabled according to the rules and regulations governing the classification of handicapped children in Pennsylvania. The age ranges were from 6-11 years, although only 6 of the 12 subtests were administered to the 6- and 7-year-olds because they were not capable of completing all subtests. T-tests were used to estimate the difference between the handicapped and nonhandicapped groups and a significant difference (.05 level of confidence) was found in all cases in favor of the nonhandicapped groups. This is one area where additional research would be desirable because the number (N) was small and only represents a limited geographic area in one state.

In sum, this reviewer thinks that the authors did an adequate presentation of the technical aspects of the test. They also seem to be honest in presenting its limitations and call for further research where needed. A larger sample and better geographic representation would certainly help the test. This reviewer also plans to contribute to that research. In helping to get away from the misuse and interpretation of grade and age equivalent scores, normative scores are provided in percentiles and standard scores. The standard score subtest mean was set at 10 and the standard deviation at 3. However, the standard score (quotients) for the DAB components and constructs are assigned a mean of 100 and a standard deviation of 15. This makes it a good test for identifying children suspected of being learning disabled if the criteria calls for achievement tests having a standard score mean of 100 and a standard deviation of 15, which is the same mean and SD reported for the WISC-R. The manual also has a table comparing other types of standard scores (e.g., normal curve equivalents (NCE), T-Scores, Z-Scores, and stanines to percentile ranks, DAB Total Achievement Quotients and DAB Subtest scores.

Critique

The DAB is a new test which this reviewer is very excited about because of its usefulness to psychologists and educators responsible for screening and evaluating student achievement. It combines the strengths of many individual achievement tests into one achievement battery. It will also be extremely valuable in helping to identify and diagnose children with learning problems. According to the main author (P. Newcomer, personal communication, March 4, 1985) improvements are being made in the manual with each new printing. The author is also due to have the upward extension of the DAB for adolescents out in 1985. In addition, the instrument has the potential to become a very effective research tool for achievement purposes. This test is an asset to psychologists and educators responsible for educational decision making of children. However, the Capitalization, Punctuation, and Written Vocabulary subtests do have limitations of adequately assessing all children, especially younger children. These were also the three subtests identified as not allowing for statistical analysis because of the nature of the test. These three subtests should be supplemented with other screening instruments, student work samples, and teacher feedback.

References

Newcomer, P. L., & Curtis, D. (1984), *The Diagnostic Achievement Battery*. Austin, TX: PRO-ED.

Colleen B. Jamison, Ed.D.
Professor of Special Education, California State University, Los Angeles, California.

THE DYSLEXIA SCREENING SURVEY

Robert E. Valett. Belmont, California: David S. Lake Publishers.

Introduction

The Dyslexia Screening Survey (DSS), a "checklist of basic neuropsychological skills," summarizes some of the diagnostic tasks presented in the author's book, *Dyslexia: A Neuropsychological Approach to Educating Children with Severe Reading Disorders* (Valett, 1980). The DSS uses a case study approach, allowing the user to record information from reading tests, the Wechsler Intelligence Scale for Children—Revised, school records or observation, as well as direct assessment of specific skills and neuropsychological functions. This survey was developed by Robert E. Valett, Professor of Special Education, consulting psychologist, and author. His work has been highly regarded by school psychologists and special educators for many years.

The DSS is presented in a 12-page booklet, with one page devoted to the purpose, content, use, and administration of the survey, plus a definition of dyslexia. It consists of 90 items distributed under the following seven steps (factors):

1. *Functional Reading Level:* The purpose is to verify possible problems in reading; items, however, are not specific enough for programming. Because many of the skills include several parts, marking some of the items is difficult. Examiners also obtain information from school history, classroom observation, and teacher records and reports. Space is provided for recording scores from reading tests and the 20 developmental reading skills are marked "Yes," "No," or "?".

2. *Reading Potential:* The purpose is to determine the comprehension level of textbook material (Listening-to-story Grade-Level Comprehension). In addition, the examiner writes in WISC-R scores, as well as other evaluations of reading potential. This step is more of a preliminary to the next step rather than a process for acquiring specific information from the assessments.

3. *Significant Reading Discrepancy:* The purpose is to determine whether or not a "significant" discrepancy (i.e., one of approximately two or more years; see Valett, 1980a, p. 84) exists between potential ability and achievement.

4. *Specific Processing Skill Deficiencies:* A series of tasks is presented to the student in the areas of phonetic-auditory, visual, and multisensory skills. The visual stimuli presented in the survey booklet, however, are quite small and could possibly interfere with the performance of many students. Examiners are advised also to attach samples of school work that illustrate specific processing errors and possible dysfunctions, and to "supplement tasks with other items you feel would be helpful" (DSS, p. 3). Responses are recorded according to the number of correct

241

responses and the number of errors or marked "good," "fair," or "questionable."

5. *Neuropsychological Dysfunctions:* A series of tasks is presented to the student, including Tandem Walk, Finger to Nose Coordination, Standing Balance and Hop, and Stereognosis. Directions for administration are in the text. Eye, foot, and hand preference are assessed, and developmental and school history is secured in seven areas, involving parents if possible. The examiner is directed to "supplement tasks as necessary" and to "obtain medical history and information" (DSS, p. 3). Depending on their nature, items are marked yes/no, right/left, or good/fair/questionable.

6. *Associated Factors:* The purpose is to identify four factors: pupil interest and motivation in reading, current physical health, self-confidence and esteem (lack of anxiety), and adequate instruction and reinforcement of reading, with a space for other possible factors to be included. No instructions are provided except to "give particular attention to determining possible gaps in the teaching and acquisition of basic reading skills" (DSS, p.3). Factors are rated "good," "fair," or "questionable."

7. *Developmental-Remedial Strategies:* The purpose is to determine pupil strengths and weaknesses from a task analysis of the responses. The examiners carefully consider and evaluate the greatest percentage of incorrect processing skills, presumably the processing skills with the greatest percentage of incorrect responses. However, percentage is difficult to determine because all skills have a small sample of tasks presented and some are evaluated qualitatively. The examiner then ranks the highest percentage of incorrect responses and writes priority instructional objectives for the top three ranked "processing errors." For each priority objective, at least one prescriptive learning task is to be recommended. Twelve forms of special education are listed to be checked for followup consideration. This section is perhaps the most difficult to complete, given the information obtained from the survey.

Practical Applications/Uses

According to the author, the DSS is not a standardized or normative test. Nor is it a complete screening device when used by itself. The survey is a checklist of basic developmental skills or criterion tasks learned by most children in the primary grades. The author suggests that the DSS be used with "other behavioral observations, classroom task analysis, criterion evaluations, standardized psychological and language tests, and appropriate medical examinations" (p. 3).

The Survey is designed for reading-disabled students who may be dyslexic, however, an appropriate age range is not given. According to the survey, the DSS may be used by teachers and others concerned with screening children with reading disabilities for possible special education, such as special educators, remedial reading specialists, psychologists, and speech therapists.

The Survey might best be used as a case study outline by the person with primary responsibility for developing an instructional plan for a student with reading problems, preferably by a school psychologist. Although the text presents background information and special education interventions, the detail required to adequately complete the survey is not included; in fact, valid completion may require extensive training and experience of a clinical nature. The sections of the Survey, however, do remind one of the points to be included in a study prior to developing an instructional plan for a student with reading problems.

Technical Aspects

No validity or reliability data are presented in the manual.

Critique

The DSS does not include criteria for scoring, suggested age range, time estimates, nor normative information. Without more complete directions and more information regarding expected responses, the Survey is of limited use to the less experienced user. The transition from assessment to the recommendation of developmental-remedial strategies would be particularly difficult, even with the use of the author's book on dyslexia (Valett, 1980a); the book, however, does present information that is very useful to concerned educators.

References

Valett, R. E. (1980a). *Dyslexia: A neuropsychological approach to educating children with severe reading disorders*. Belmont, CA: David S. Lake Publishers (formerly Pitman Learning, Inc.).
Valett, R. E. (1980b). *The Dyslexia Screening Survey*. Belmont, CA: David S. Lake Publishers (formerly Pitman Learning, Inc.).

Robert G. Harrington, Ph.D.
Assistant Professor in Educational Psychology and Research,
University of Kansas, Lawrence, Kansas.

EARLY SCREENING INVENTORY

Samuel J. Meisels and Martha Stone Wiske. New York, New York: Teachers College Press.

Introduction

The Early Screening Inventory (ESI) (Meisels & Wiske, 1983) is a standardized, individually administered developmental screening instrument for children aged four to six years. It samples performance in the areas of speech, language, cognition, perception, and gross- and fine-motor coordination. The ESI was intended to identify those children "at risk" for academic problems in the early school grades. Such children will need to be referred for a more comprehensive diagnostic evaluation. A separate informal Parent Questionnaire accompanies the ESI. Its purpose is to assist the examiner in making clinical interpretations of ESI test results by collecting relevant case history information about the child's family background, school attendance, prenatal and postnatal medical problems, current health, and developmental skills.

The precursor of the ESI was the Eliot-Pearson Screening Inventory (EPSI) (Meisels & Wiske, 1976) developed at Tufts University in Medford, Massachusetts in 1975. Some of the items on the EPSI were developed by the authors; others were adapted from well-known diagnostic and screening measures such as the Stanford-Binet Intelligence Scale (Terman & Merrill, 1973), the Denver Developmental Screening Test (Frankenburg, Dodds, Fandal, Kazuk & Cohrs, 1975), The Illinois Test of Psycholinguistic Abilities (McCarthy & Kirk, 1978) and the Purdue Perceptual-Motor Survey (Roach & Kephart, 1966). After piloting on more than 3,000 children and preliminary reliability and validity studies, the ESI underwent four major revisions (Schlossberg, 1978). The test items retained after revision were intended to represent a broad range of developmental skills as well as some readiness skills, (e.g., color naming and counting). Administration and scoring ease, speed, reliability, cost efficiency, and child interest were also prime considerations in choosing items for the fourth and final version (Meisels & Wiske, 1976).

The ESI is divided into four sections: 1) Initial Screening Items, 2) Visual-Motor-Adaptive domain, 3) Language and Cognition domain, and 4) Gross Motor/Body Awareness domain. A Draw-a-Person task (DAP) and Letter Writing represent the two Initial Screening Items in the first section of the ESI. These two exercises are nonverbal and may be useful in developing rapport with an anxious examinee. The DAP is scored on the basis of the number of different body parts drawn and allows the examiner to observe how the child organizes an abstract form concept.

244

Letter Writing is not scored but offers another opportunity to observe eye-hand coordination and provides an informal comparison with performance on other fine-motor items on the ESI. A child's letter-writing ability itself is also a skill many early childhood educators may wish to evaluate.

Visual-Motor Adaptive taps fine motor skill, eye-hand coordination and the ability to remember visual sequences, to draw two-dimensional visual forms, and to reproduce three-dimensional visual structures. Language and Cognition items focus on language comprehension and verbal expression, the ability to reason and count, and the ability to remember auditory sequences. Gross Motor/Body Awareness items examine balance, large motor coordination used in hopping and skipping, and the ability to imitate body positions from visual cues.

The ESI takes 15-20 minutes to administer. None of the four sections of the test is meant to be administered alone. There is considerable overlap in the abilities investigated in each section. For this reason comparisons and contrasts in performance should be made across sections to identify strengths and weaknesses. Such observations should be regarded as trends, and referral or retesting decisions should be made based on the child's overall performance in conjunction with reports from parents, teachers, medical professionals, learning and vision specialists, and other informed sources.

The Parent Questionnaire, which accompanies the ESI, has five sections. The first section provides background data on the child's family (e.g., the parents' ages, educations, occupations; descriptions of problems siblings have experienced in school; the number and types of preschool or day-care experiences the child has had).

In the second section the child's medical history is covered. It addresses prenatal and postnatal developmental risk factors, the full range of childhood diseases and allergies, and a record of overnight hospitalizations.

The third section assesses the family history of birth defects and other illnesses.

The fourth section focuses on the child's health problems that may contribute to school absences or problems in learning. Questions relate to all the major body systems, including eyes, ears, nose, throat, heart, lungs, abdomen, urinary tract, extremities, and neurological functioning.

The fifth section deals with the overall development of the child. The parents' perceptions of developmental skills in eating, dressing, toileting, play, fine- and gross-motor coordination are requested. In addition, other behaviors important to school success are investigated, including activity level, ability to follow directions, emotionality, communication skills, and receptive language. It is helpful to compare the individual responses of both parents for differences in their perceptions and reactions to these questions.

Rather than a formal score, The Parent Questionnaire is intended to give perspective and possibly some insights into the etiology of a child's presenting problem or alert examiners to conditions placing a child "at risk" for normal development. For example, the questionnaire may show that the child suffered from anoxia at birth, experiences dizzy spells, and has trouble attending. By identifying developmental patterns such as this the examiner may gain greater understanding of the range factors contributing to a referral for a possible attention deficit disorder. By administering the Parent Questionnaire before the ESI it may be possible to further investigate any evidence of developmental delays or anomalies during the subsequent screening and medical exams. For example, if a parent reports on the questionnaire that the child has difficulties in hearing, the examiner should pay special attention to the child's performance on the Language and Cognitive sections of the ESI. This questionnaire is quite extensive and may take fifteen minutes or more to complete, especially if the parent elaborates on the items.

Included among the ESI test materials are the examiner's manual, cards for Copy Forms and Visual Sequential Memory tasks, ten one-inch cubes for Block Building and Number Concept tasks, and a variety of objects for the Verbal Expression task, including a small ball, a one-inch wooden cube, button, and small toy car. Examiners are obliged to supply the following materials themselves: manila paper, eight 2" x 2" squares of colored paper, a large pencil, plain white drawing paper, and an 8½" x 11" cardboard.

The score sheet for the ESI is organized into the four sections of the test. Each subtest and item is labeled with a descriptive term such as "Copy Forms" or "Number Concept." Next to each item there is a space for the screener's comments. This is an opportunity to note pertinent child behaviors, such as attitude, motivational level, spontaneous remarks, affective response to test items, and language usage, that may have affected performance on the item. The combination of item comments should assist the examiner in deciding whether the child's total score is an accurate reflection of the subject's present developmental skills. At the end of the ESI protocol the examiner may comment further in response to several questions about color-matching problems, consonant errors, and sentence usage.

The ESI is a short test and relatively easy to administer. Nevertheless, the ESI should be administered only by examiners knowledgeable of early childhood behavior and development who have received supervised practice. Research has shown that unqualified screening examiners may not reliably score certain items requiring scoring judgments such as the Draw-a-Man item (Reynolds, 1978).

Any professional who needs to screen children for developmental disabilities will find the ESI useful. This group might include early childhood teachers, school psychologists, occupational and physical therapists, speech clinicians, nurses, and physicians. A videotaped demonstration of the ESI and a discussion and interpretation of results is available for rental from Michigan Media, The University of Michigan, Ann Arbor, MI 48109.

Practical Applications/Uses

The ESI was never intended to be an intelligence test, nor is it totally a measure of school readiness or achievement. Rather, it is a developmental screening test. Screening may be viewed as the second step in a five-step sequence of procedures. This five-step sequence includes the following stages: 1) case-finding, 2) screening, 3) diagnosis, 4) educational assessment, and 5) program evaluation (Harrington, 1984). Each of these steps has a different function and purpose. Screening involves brief forms of assessment to identify those children most likely to develop learning or behavior problems and who may need special services. Readiness testing is sometimes confused with screening. Items on the ESI sample are primarily developmental milestones necessary to acquire new skills. In contrast, readiness testing focuses on a child's preparedness to benefit from a specific academic program (Meisels, 1978). If a child is suspected of certain developmental delays during screening, then that child is referred for further diagnostic assessment. During diagnosis the examiner tries to determine the exact nature of the problem and develop an appropriate treatment plan. The ESI should never be used as an entry examination for Kindergarten or the early primary grades. Instead, the ESI was designed to be used as one part of a comprehensive screening battery in school-based "child find" projects, or possibly as an efficient screening instrument for physicians seeking to identify developmental delays in their young patients.

Because the ESI is an individually administered, standardized test it should be administered in a quiet test environment, free of distractions. Instructions for administration and scoring should be followed verbatim. In general, test items are administered in the order given in the examiner's manual. Under certain circumstances the examiner has the prerogative to begin testing with the block-building items, the verbal expression/car item, or a large-motor activity. This option depends on whether the examiner judges that a particular child would be more comfortable with a verbal or motor item to start. When a child refuses to respond to a particular item that item may be repeated later except on visual and auditory sequential memory tasks. The child should be seated at a childsized chair and table across from the examiner. If more than one child is being screened in the same room, then room dividers should be erected to reduce noise and distractions. Before testing begins, the examiner should spend time establishing rapport with the child. Without this effort at rapport-building the child may become unmotivated to perform at an optimal level.

A parent will generally accompany the child to the screening session. Parents should be seated behind the child so that they can watch and support the child without interferring. Parents should be cautioned in advance to avoid intervening no matter how their children perform; such interferences will destroy the standardized administration. Young children may have had very few previous experiences with tests and may lack achievement motivation. For these reasons, the examiner should be careful to reinforce and encourage the child for working hard. Furthermore, the word "test" should be avoided. If the child appears visibly upset, the testing should be rescheduled. The examiner should note any salient aspects of the child's performance or behavior, including such features as hand preference, pencil grip, mood, ease of performance, articulation and syntax errors, and unusual remarks made by the child. The screener's comments on the score sheet should indicate whether the score appears to be an accurate reflection of the child's present abilities. At the conclusion of the screening session the examiner should confirm that every appropriate item has been administered.

Each item on the ESI is individually scored "pass," "fail," or "refuse." Every item is administered to each child regardless of whether they are aged 4 or 5 years. The total points possible for a "pass" on any particular item varies from 1 to 3; however, most items are scored on a 0-1 or 0-1-2 scale. The examiner's manual contains fairly complete directions for administration and scoring. Materials needed to administer each item are listed next to that item. Examples of "passing" and "failing" responses are given as an aid in scoring when appropriate.

No domain scores are available on the ESI. Only a total ESI score is computed. Cutoff scores are provided for each six-month age range from 4-0 to 6-0 years. Examiners should note that the cutoff scores for the age ranges of 5-6 to 5-11 years represent extrapolations from the standardization scores for subjects in the three younger age ranges. By comparing the child's total ESI score with the cutoff score one of three recommendations may be made: "OK," "rescreen," or "refer." A child's performance on the ESI is "OK" if the total ESI score is less than one standard deviation below the mean (about 16th percentile). "Rescreening" in eight to ten weeks should be the recommendation if a child's total ESI score is between one and two standard deviations below the mean (approximately 2nd to 16th percentile). If an examiner suspects a delay in a developmental domain based on observed performance that screener may recommend rescreening even when the total ESI score is in the "OK" range. Likewise, other observations such as test anxiety, unintelligible speech, or flat affect may prompt the examiner to reinvestigate at a later date using the ESI. Children with total ESI scores two standard deviations below the mean for their age range should be "referred" immediately for a more comprehensive diagnostic assessment.

The cutoff points that correspond to the "OK," "rescreen," and "refer" categories were determined by analyzing the total scores of the sample on which the ESI was standardized. An item analysis of 465 low and lower middle-class urban white children's protocols has shown that the ESI items clearly discriminate between the "OK" and "refer" groups. Out of 24 children "referred" from this sample approximately 60% failed each item, while 75% of the 441 children in the "OK" group passed each item. Unfortunately, no referral rates for the normative sample are reported in the examiner's manual; however, a table of ESI item mean scores and total ESI mean scores are given for children aged four and five years in the normative sample. The authors suggest that examiners may increase the relevance of their reference comparisons by developing their own local cutoff points because the standardization sample was restricted to low and lower middle-status urban families.

If the interpretation of developmental screening results is to amount to more than a simple "OK," "rescreen," or "refer" classification, then examiners must have a fund of background knowledge and personal experiences with young children. Otherwise, only a screening supervisor should interpret each child's protocol in collaboration with the impressions of teachers, hearing and vision specialists, and medical doctors. The Parent Questionnaire may be used quite effectively to stimulate active participation by parents on the multidisciplinary team. Furthermore, parents who observe their children's screenings are probably best able to judge whether their children's performance was typical or not. In all cases, parents should be consulted regarding whatever conclusions and recommendations are formulated. Because parents have the right to be informed, their questions both before and after screening should be answered as completely as possible. So that future ESI screeners might better understand how to interpret ESI results in the context of referral problems the examiner's manual discusses the interpretive results of three sample profiles representative of hypothetical "OK," "rescreen," and "refer" outcomes.

Technical Aspects

The normative sample for the ESI contained 465 low to lower middle-class urban children from predominantly white families. Two hundred children were included in the two middle-age ranges of 4-6 to 4-11 and 5-0 to 5-5 years. Only 50 children were in the 4-0 to 4-5 age range; and by deduction it would appear that only 13 children were included in the 4-6 to 6-0 age range.

To test the interscorer reliability of the ESI three examiners rotated the roles of tester and observer. Eleven children aged four years and seven aged five years served as subjects. Each child was individually administered the ESI and every item was scored individually by each examiner. The percent agreements between the tester and the two observers for the four subdivisions of the ESI were all higher than .80. The total score correlation was .91.

Another important form of test reliability is test-retest reliability. Test-retest reliability assesses the stability of test scores due to changes in the examinee's motivational level, test anxiety, rapport with the examiner, or answers to specific test questions. Six examiners tested a total of 28 males and 29 females, aged 4 years to 5 years, 10 months on two occasions, approximately one week apart. The test-retest reliability study showed a percent agreement of .82 for the total score on the ESI. The percent agreements for the subscales of the ESI were reported to be below .80. Neither the interscorer reliability study nor the test-retest reliability study analyzed data in terms of classification outcomes.

On the assumption that screening tests should not only detect present developmental delays, but also identify children at risk for future school achievement problems, the ESI validation studies utilized both concurrent and longitudinal criterion measures. In the concurrent validity study the General Cognitive Index (GCI) scores on the McCarthy Scales of Children's Abilities (MSCA) (McCarthy, 1972) were compared to total ESI scores based on a sample of 102 children from six different school systems in the Boston area. Subjects were stratified and matched by age, sex, socioeconomic status, and results on the ESI (i.e., "OK," "rescreen," or "refer"). Classification outcomes on the MSCA were also established by setting cutoffs on the General Cognitive Index at one and at two standard deviations below the mean of 100 (i.e., standard scores of 68 and 84, respectively) to yield three categories that correspond to the three ESI classifications. The results showed that the ESI referred 8 children who were two standard deviations below the mean on the MSCA, 9 children one standard deviation below the mean on the MSCA, and 8 children who were within normal range on the MSCA. This represents a referral/rescreen rate of 17 out of 25. Of the children classified "rescreen" on the ESI, 3 out of 12 were in the MSCA "at risk" categories. Out of 65 children identified as "OK" on the MSCA the ESI results recommended "rescreening" on only 3 and agreed with the MSCA "OK" classification on 62. The correlation between classification recommendations based on the ESI and MSCA was .73.

A short-term predictive validity study correlated the ESI scores of 472 children screened in early fall with the Metropolitan Readiness Tests (MRT) Form P, Level II (Nurss & McGauvran, 1976) prereading composite scores obtained in the late spring. For comparison purposes, the 15th percentile was chosen as the cutoff point for identification of "at risk" children on both the ESI and MRT. The resulting correlation coefficients between the ESI and MRT scores were moderate but statistically significant (i.e., children aged 4 years = .44; 5 years = .49; males = .45; females = .46; total = .45; $p < .001$. There were no significant age or sex effects. Overall agreement between the two tests was 83% indicating that the ESI is a good short-term predictor of reading readiness. Of the 66 children scoring below the 15th percentile on the MRT, the ESI referred 22, and failed to refer 44 children or 67% of those low on the MRT criterion measure. On the other hand, of the 40 children scoring above the 15th percentile on the MRT the ESI referred 38 children. In other words, the ESI incorrectly "referred" only 9% of those children who scored high on the MRT and correctly identified 369 or 91% of the high MRT scorers.

A longitudinal predictive study (Wiske, Meisels, Tivnan, 1982) compared the accuracy of ESI scores in predicting grades, referral for special educational services, and promotion vs. retention for 115 kindergarten through fourth-grade children in two elementary schools. From each grade 20 to 28 students were randomly selected. The highest and most significant correlations were between ESI scores and report-card grades in Kindergarten (.70, $p < .001$), first grade (.50, $p < .001$) and second grade (.52, $p < .001$). The correlation was also significant between ESI results and the need for special education services in first grade (.42, $p < .01$), second grade (.51, $p < .01$), third grade (.53, $p < .01$) and fourth grade (.41, $p < .05$). The correlation between ESI scores and retention vs. promotion disposition was significant only at the second-grade level (.57, $p < .001$). A multiple regression coefficient was never significant between the results of the Parent Questionnaire, medical, vision, and hearing screening and later school performance. In contrast, the regression coefficient between these screening results and the three measures of later school performance always increased when the ESI scores were added to the results of the other screening components. In the prediction of grades and referral for special educational services in the first and second grades, the inclusion of the ESI results in the regression calculation made the regression coefficient statistically significant. Such was also the case for grades and referral vs. promotion disposition in Kindergarten and second grade.

Using the 15th percentile as the cutoff score for both the ESI and the three measures of later school performance, the total percentage of children correctly classified ranged from 65% to 79%. The variation between Kindergarten and fourth grade was slight. Furthermore the false positive rate (i.e., children incorrectly referred based on the ESI score) was consistently higher than the false negative rate (i.e., children incorrectly classified as "OK" based on the ESI score). This hit and miss ratio suggests that ESI recommendations tend to be conservative as might be expected on a developmental screening test. Generally, the rates of sensitivity (proportion of children "at risk" who are correctly identified) and specificity (proportion of children "not at risk" who are correctly excluded from referral for further assessment) on the ESI are moderate to high in Kindergarten and are somewhat lower in grades three and four.

Critique

Generally, a screening regimen is developed based on consideration of the following factors (Kurtz, Neisworth, & Lamb, 1977; Scott & Hogan, 1982): 1) the kinds of assessment questions that need to be answered, 2) the types and severity of handicapping conditions to be assessed, 3) the ages of the children, and 4) the psychometric properties of available instrumentation. The ESI will be critiqued in relation to each of these factors.

Kinds of Questions to Be Answered: The ESI is a screening instrument designed to identify young children with developmental delays that may place them "at risk" in regard to later school achievement. It is not an IQ Test, a kindergarten-entry examination, or a readiness test. Rather, the ESI tests developmental skills that may be related to learning in Kindergarten through fourth grade. Before a screening team should decide to adopt the ESI they should thoroughly review its item contents to ensure its face validity for their own specific screening purposes. Screening team members must decide whether items contained on the ESI match the philosophical intent and the general curricular content of the educational programs for which they are screening the children.

The Types and Severity of Handicapping Conditions to be Assessed: Because of the paucity of psychometrically sound instrumentation an examiner needs to be very careful in selecting screening tests and especially in modifying any standardized procedures to accommodate when a child's handicap is severe (Abbott & Crane, 1977). The ESI examiner's manual contains no test administration modifications for physically, sensorially, or multiply handicapped children. This means that if children have a handicapping condition that prevents them from processing the test directions or responding to items on the ESI, another more suitable screening measure should be substituted. In this regard the Parent Questionnaire could be used effectively as a handicapped prescreening questionnaire. Based on parental reports of the child's medical and health history individual children could be selected as eligible for ESI screening or cross-referred for other forms of nonbiased assessment.

The utility and reliability of the Parent Questionnaire as a prescreening questionnaire would be greatly enhanced if it rendered formal cutoff scores instead of clinical impressions. If a child's score fell below the cutoff point, then a formal screening instrument, such as the ESI, could be administered. Otherwise, the child would not be screened, and overreferrals for screening would be reduced. The Denver Prescreening Developmental Questionnaire (PDQ) (Frankenburg & vanDoorninck, 1975) is a good example of this kind of instrument. Similar efforts should be made to formalize the scoring of the Parent Questionnaire.

The Ages of the Children: Preschool screening instruments have been normed on children of different ages. For this reason not all screening instruments will be appropriate for the target population a team may select. The ESI was intended to cover the somewhat restricted age ranges of 4-0 to 6-0 years. Consequently, the ESI may be used predominantly for prekindergarten screening. The screening team should agree that the ages they have chosen to screen represent the "best ages" for the kinds of interventions they want to perform. A general rule is that the earlier the intervention, the more potential impact the program will have on the child's development (Reynolds, 1979; Gerken, 1979). With new programs, on the other hand, the argument may be valid for screening older preschoolers first and working backwards so that a continuous program of education can be developed.

Because of certain anomalies in the ESI norming study examiners would be well advised to limit the use of the ESI norms to children in the age ranges of 4-5 to 5-5 years. Because the normative sample had a lower age limit of 4-2 years these cutoff points for children aged 4-0 and 4-1 years may be too high. Likewise, the cutoff scores for age ranges of 5-6 to 5-11 years were extrapolated from the standardization scores for subjects aged 4-0 to 4-5, 4-6 to 4-11, and 5-0 to 5-5 years. In addition, there were only 13 subjects sampled in the age ranges of 5-6 to 5-11 years and 50 subjects in the age ranges of 4-2 to 4-5 years in the norming study. These sample sizes are too small for norm-referenced comparisons. The best approach would be for screening teams to establish local norms for the age ranges of 4-0 to 4-5 and 5-6 to 5-11 years, if not the whole age range of 4-0 to 6-0.

The Psychometric Properties of the ESI: The administration and scoring of the ESI may not be as simple as it first appears. Lichtenstein and Ireton (1984) have given several examples of problems in these two areas. Some subtests such as Verbal Expression require the examiner to judge what follow-up questions should be asked based on the child's response. Inexperienced examiners may also have great difficulty in evaluating syntax and articulation errors, as instructed, following administration of the Verbal Expression subtest. On other subtests, the examiner must independently determine whether to stop or continue testing based on the child's performance on earlier items in that subtest. Other Gross Motor/Body Awareness subtests, such as the Imitate Movements and Skip subtests, may be inherently difficult to score because of confusing and/or subjective scoring criteria.

At least one of the block-building items would have been better deleted than included on the final version of the ESI (Lichtenstein & Ireton, 1984). The item requires the child to build a gate from a model by balancing a block rotated 45° between two other block towers. The examiner is advised to sand the edges of slippery block surfaces and place a sheet of manila drawing paper on the table so these surfaces will not be so slippery. These seem like extraordinary measures to take to preseve an item that may be unreliable and invalid. In fact, because the interscorer reliabilities are reported for total ESI scores only it is impossible to be sure about the scoring reliability of this particular item or any other specific item.

Another minor technical problem that examiners should consider relates to the way in which the results of the concurrent validity study with the MSCA were reported. High hit rates are reported for the "OK," "rescreen," and "refer" categories based on comparisons with MSCA classifications, but no follow-up hit rates are reported for the "rescreen" group. An examiner may be falsely led to assume that 100% of the rescreen cases will be correctly assigned to either the "OK" or "refer" group when rescreening. This is most probably an invalid assumption and actual hit rates as a result of rescreening should be reported in the examiner's manual.

In conclusion, the ESI is a valuable screening instrument to identify children suspected of developmental delays in the age ranges of 4-5 to 5-5 years. The test covers a wide range of relatively brief, but at the same time, age-appropriate developmental milestones predictive of prereading skills in the near future and of grades, referral for special educational services, and promotion vs. retention over the long term. The test should be administered, scored, and interpreted by professionals trained and experienced in working with prekindergartners. When carefully selected for its intended purpose and used in combination with the Parent Questionnaire, and medical, hearing, and vision exams, the ESI may serve as a valuable tool in an early screening and intervention program.

References

Abbott, M. S., & Crane, J. S. (1977). Assessment of young children. *Journal of School Psychology, 15,* 118-128.

Frankenburg, W. K., & van Doorninck, W. (1975). *Denver Prescreening Developmental Questionnaire.* Denver: Ladoca Project and Publishing Foundation, Inc.

Frankenburg, W. K., Dodds, J., Fandal, A., Kazuk, E., & Cohrs, M. (1975). *Denver Developmental Screening Test.* Denver: University of Colorado Medical Center.

Gerken, K. C. (1979). Services to preschoolers and children with low incidence handicaps. *School Psychology Digest, 8*(3), 246-343.

Harrington, R. G. (1984). Preschool screening: The school psychologist's perspective. *School Psychology Review, 8,* 363-374.

Kurtz, D. P., Neisworth, J. T., & Lamb, K. W. (1977). Issues concerning the early identification of handicapped children. *Journal of School Psychology, 15,* 136-140.

Lichtenstein, R., & Ireton, H. (1984). *Preschool screening: Identifying young children with developmental and educational problems.* New York: Grune & Stratton, Inc.

McCarthy, D. (1972). *Manual for the McCarthy Scales of Children's Abilities.* New York: The Psychological Corporation.

McCarthy, J., & Kirk, S. (1978). *Illinois Tests of Psycholinguistic Abilities.* Champaign: University of Illinois Press.

Meisels, S. J. (1978). *Developmental screening in early childhood: A guide.* Washington, DC: National Association for the Education of Young Children.

Meisels, S. J., & Wiske, M. S. (1976). *The Eliot-Pearson Screening Inventory.* Medford, MA: Tufts University.

Meisels, S. J., & Wiske, M. S. (1983). *Early Screening Inventory.* New York: Teachers College Press.

Nurss, J. R., & McGauvran, M. E. (1976). *Metropolitan Readiness Tests, Teacher's Manual.* New York: Harcourt, Brace, Jovanovich.

Reynolds, C. R. (1978). Teacher-psychologist interscorer reliability for the McCarthy tests. *Perceptual and Motor Skills, 47,* 538.

Reynolds, C. R. (1979). Should we screen preschoolers? *Contemporary Educational Psychology, 4,* 175-181.

Roach, E. G., & Kephart, N. (1966). *The Purdue Perceptual-Motor Survey.* Columbus, OH: Charles E. Merrill Publishing Co.

Schlossberg, B. (1978). *The development of a developmental screening test.* Unpublished master's thesis, Tufts University, Medford, Massachusetts.

Scott, G., & Hogan, A. E. (1982). Methods for the identification of high-risk and handicapped infants. In C. T. Ramey & P. L. Trohanis (Eds.), *Finding and educating high-risk and handicapped infants* (pp. 98-119). Baltimore, MD: University Park Press.

Terman, L. M., & Merrill, M. A. (1973). *Stanford-Binet Intelligence Scale.* Chicago: The Riverside Publishing Company.

Wiske, M. S., Meisels, S. J., & Tivnan, T. (1982). Development and validation of the Early Screening Inventory: A study of early childhood developmental screening. In W. J. Anastasiow, W. K. Frankenburg, & A. W. Fandal, (Eds.), *Identifying the developmentally delayed child* (pp. 203-225). Baltimore: University Park Press.

Allan L. LaVoie, Ph.D.

Professor of Psychology, Davis & Elkins College, Elkins, West Virginia.

EGO STATE INVENTORY

David G. McCarley. Chicago, Illinois: Stoelting Company.

Introduction

The Ego State Inventory (ESI) (McCarley, 1974) was rationally designed to measure ego states (Berne, 1961). The transactional analysis definition of ego states is that they are systems of feelings and behavior patterns. The ESI produces scores for five ego states: Punitive Parent, Nurturing Parent, Adult, Rebellious Child, and Adaptive Child. The five scores are interdependent and hence should be usable as scores for an egogram; that is, scores should be proportional to the amount of time spent or energy invested in each of the ego states. There is a bias towards high raw scores on Adult so the resulting profile is not strictly an egogram.

David G. McCarley devised the test as his doctoral dissertation at the University of Alberta, Edmonton, Canada, in 1971. Beginning with the basic cartoons, he developed a set of alternative responses for each. A panel of judges then selected the best or most characteristic ego state out of the five states defined by McCarley for each cartoon situation. The completed inventory consists of 52 cartoon sketches; in each cartoon one person initiates an interaction with a statement like "You've missed your train" and five response choices are given. Respondents then choose the one statement out of five that is closest to the way they would actually reply, e.g., "You should have brought me sooner."

The test is packaged in an attractive booklet with 5 scoring stencils and 100 separate answer sheets. There are simple instructions; the test is self-administering in 10 to 30 minutes and is appropriate for individuals or groups. The obverse of the answer sheet is a graph for the raw scores. Neither adults, nor adolescents will have trouble understanding the instructions or response alternatives though the latter may have problems in identifying with some of the cartoon figures.

Practical Applications/Uses

As the first quantitative measure of ego states, the ESI could be used to measure students to find the characteristics of high and low achievers; to identify inmates who are likely recidivists or good candidates for parole; to monitor the progress of clients during therapy, and many other ways. It was for these purposes that the ESI was created.

Yet despite its potential utility, the only published references to the test in the ten years after it was made available commercially are in reports of the development of competing measures of ego states Heyer, 1979; L'Abate, 1978; Thorne &

255

Faro, 1980; Williams & Williams, 1980). It may be that most users of the ESI are in private practice as is Dr. McCarley and not engaged in research.

The inventory is hand-scored using five sturdy transparent templates that fit neatly over the answer sheets. It takes only a minute to score a protocol and graph the results.

Interpretation does not work nearly so well. The graph of results can be easily read but the appearance is misleading. Everyone who volunteered to use the test in one of my classes scored very high on Adult, making it seem on the egogram that they spend most of their time in that ego state. That is an unlikely conclusion, however. Other tests suggest that college students spend roughly a third of their time in Adult. One problem with the ESI manual is that there are no norms. Further, while means are reported for five occupational groups (totaling 290 subjects), no standard deviations are given. It is impossible to specify where a particular score falls except in the crudest terms: above or below the mean. From the manual it appears that the five groups typically score twice as high on Adult as on Nurturing Parent or Adaptive Child, while the Punitive Parent and Rebellious Child alternatives are chosen roughly 6% and 6½% of the time.

In short, even for experts in transactional analysis, the results of ESI testing cannot be statistically interpreted based only on the manual. Users must develop their own data base to make adequate inferences about clients.

Technical Aspects

In terms of reliability, the internal consistency of the five scales averages nearly .76 and ranges from .36 to .98. Score stability over a seven-week interval was good, averaging .62 for the five scales on a sample of 29 undergraduates. In each case, the Adaptive Child Scale is a problem.

McCarley attempted to demonstrate validity. The five occupational groups mentioned earlier were selected so that each would score high on one scale; e.g., policemen were expected to score high on Punitive Parent. Only one of the five predictions was confirmed. Scores on the ESI were correlated with scores on various other tests such as the Dogmatism Scale and the California Psychological Inventory but results show little. Out of 50 correlation coefficients, only four were significant and none were compelling. This is barely better than chance and certainly does not indicate either convergent or discriminant validity. McCarley also found no relationships with age, sex, or education.

In summary, the ESI seems reliable, but validity remains an open question.

Critique

The ESI has been little used. No published reports of its use could be found for the ten years after it was made available commercially. Though it was developed in a rational, competent way, it fell short during its validity trials.

The manual suffers from several problems as well. There are no norms. No standard deviations are given with the sample means, so the user cannot calculate standard scores. Various grammatical errors have been left uncorrected. Further cautions against the clinical use of the ESI might properly have been included.

In this reviewer's opinion if a reliable, valid measure of ego states is needed, one of the later tests would be more suitable. For instance, the report of Williams and Williams (1980) looks especially promising. Unless and until McCarley corrects the problems outlined above, the ESI should be avoided.

References

Berne, E. (1961). *Transactional analysis in psychotherapy.* New York: Grove Press, Inc.

Heyer, N. R. (1979). Development of a questionnaire to measure ego states with some applications to social and comparative psychiatry. *Transactional Analysis Journal, 9,* 9-19.

L'Abate, L. (1978). An experimental paper-and-pencil test for assessing ego states. *Transactional Analysis Journal, 8,* 262-265.

McCarley, D. G. (1974). *Ego State Inventory: Instruction manual.* Chicago: Stoelting Co.

Thorne, S., & Faro, S. (1980). The Ego State Scale: A measure of psychopathology. *Transactional Analysis Journal, 10,* 49-52.

Williams, K. B., & Williams, J. E. (1980). The assessment of transactional analysis ego states via the Adjective Check List. *Journal of Personality Assessment, 44,* 120-129.

Robert Drummond, Ph.D.
*Interim Chairperson, Division of Educational Services and Research,
University of North Florida, Jacksonville, Florida.*

EYSENCK PERSONALITY INVENTORY

*H. J. Eysenck and Sybil B. G. Eysenck. San Diego, California:
Educational and Industrial Testing Service.*

Introduction

The Eysenck Personality Inventory (EPI) is an objective 57-item paper-and-pencil inventory that measures Extraversion-Introversion and Neuroticism-Stability. There is also a Lie (or falsification) Scale that provides for detection of response distortion. The test items are in the form of questions to which the examinee gives a "Yes" or "No" answer.

The authors of the test are H. J. Eysenck and Sybil B. G. Eysenck. H. J. Eysenck is a prominent British psychologist who has contributed significant books and tests on dimensions of personality and personality measurement, as well as having authored several personality inventories. He served as Professor of Psychology at the Institute of Psychiatry at the University of London and was director of the psychology departments at Maudsley and Bethlehem Royal Hospitals.

Sybil B. G. Eysenck also has coauthored books and tests on personality with her husband as well as having authored the Junior Eysenck Personality Inventory.

The EPI was based on the theories of research on extraversion and neuroticism that H. J. Eysenck began in the 1940s. EPI is a refinement of the Maudsley Personality Inventory (MPI) (Eysenck, 1962) used initially to measure the constructs. The EPI is similar to the MPI but improved. The items on the EPI were carefully reworded in order to make them more understandable by subjects of low intelligence and/or education. A Lie Scale was developed for the test in order to help identify subjects who put themselves in a very positive or desirable light. The MPI did not have such a scale. The construction of the test led to increased reliability and validity of the scale over the MPI.

There are three forms of the EPI, Forms A & B and an Industrial Form A1, which are also available in Spanish from the publisher. In addition, microcomputer software programs are available for Forms A & B for the Commodore PET 4000 or 8000 series.

The EPI consists of 57 questions in which the respondent is asked to mark "Yes" or "No." For example, an item might read: "Would you call yourself a calm person?" The items are presented in two columns on the back side of the test booklet. The directions are on the front side of the inventory. The test is self-administered, but the examiner can read the instructions to the examinee or group if necessary.

The test is designed for high-school and college students and adult populations.

258

The readability level is, in general, appropriate for adults but the language is somewhat dated.

There are three subscales on the test: an Extraversion-Introversion Scale consisting of 24 items, a Neuroticism Scale consisting of 24 items, and a Lie Scale consisting of nine items.

The test booklet is consumable and serves as the answer sheet. Examinees record their answers in the spaces provided under the yes/no statements by each item. There are percentile norms available for American college students. Computerized scoring is available from the publisher and scores can be compared to different age, sex, and occupational groups.

Practical Applications/Uses

Eysenck reports the use of the test in employee selection and placement, educational guidance and counseling, in clinical diagnosis, and for experimental studies. The test is short, reliable, and a valid measure of two major dimensions of personality. It is convenient to use in research studies and in undergraduate and graduate classes in personality theory or personality assessment to illustrate Eysenck's theory. Overall, this reviewer has found that other tests, such as the California Psychological Inventory or the MMPI, provide more useful information to assist diagnosis in clinical situations. Such tests as the Myers Briggs Type Indicator give a fuller picture of the extraversion/introversion dimension.

The test, however, can be used by the counselor or the psychologist as a quick screen of the two personality dimensions assessed by the inventory because it can be given and scored within 10 to 15 minutes.

The test measures Exraversion/Introversion and Neuroticism. Extraversion on the EPI refers to the outgoing, uninhibited, impulsive, and sociable inclinations of a person (Eysenck & Eysenck, 1968a, p. 5). Neuroticism on the EPI is defined as emotional overresponsiveness and liability to neurotic breakdown under stress (Eysenck & Eysenck, 1968a, p. 5). The two dimensions of personality were found to be independent of each other.

The test has been used in educational settings for guidance and research purposes. Both extraversion and neuroticism have been found to be related to academic attainment. The EPI has been used extensively for clinical diagnostic purposes and found to differentiate among different types of psychopathologies.

The EPI has been widely used in many contexts, including to study personality structure and correlates, because it is a short, reliable, and valid inventory. It has been used in schools, industrial settings, mental hospitals, and clinics by psychologists, counselors, researchers, and college professors. However, overall, this reviewer does not see any major new uses of the EPI because it is dated and has been superseded by the Eysenck Personality Questionnaire (Eysenck & Eysenck, 1975).

The EPI is appropriate for use with high school and college students and adults with normal intelligence or above, as well as those with lower educational levels. It is appropriate for use with different clinical populations. Data were collected from the EPI of different neurotic and psychotic groups and normal individuals from different occupational levels. American college students were also assessed. The test would be inappropriate for certain types of handicapped adults, such as the visually handicapped and some physically handicapped because it would have to be orally administered. Additionally, the small-sized print might cause some adults problems in reading the items.

The test can be either administered individually or in large groups. The instructions are printed in full on the front side of the questionnaire. Normally, the administrator is directed to read these directions aloud to the subjects. Because it is a personality test, it would be best administered by a psychologist or counselor, especially when questions arise in the test session. It is a simple test to administer and the directions take only a minute or two to read. If both the test and directions are read by the examiner, the administration time is roughly about ten minutes.

The test takes approximately 30 seconds to handscore. There are three hand overlay stencils for scoring purposes. They are placed on top of the answer sheet and one point is given for each blackened answer space showing through the holes. The test can also be scored on the microcomputer.

The interpretation is based on the objective scores derived from the scoring of the test. There are norms presented for American college students only. Although sex differences have been found on the EPI scales, only combined sex groups are presented. Although means and standard deviations are presented for different types of occupational and clinical groups, the number and description of these groups are limited. In order to interpret the test correctly, the EPI manual, as well as some of the other books on personality that Eysenck has written on his personality theory and assessment (e.g., Eysenck, 1952, 1970), should be read carefully. Overall, one of the major problems is the limited number of reference groups and norm tables available.

One needs to note the definitions of the constructs measured. Although many tests measure constructs such as introversion/extraversion, not all test authors define the constructs in the same way. It is important for the user to read the items belonging to each scale.

Technical Aspects

Extensive validity and reliability studies have been conducted on the EPI. Test-retest and split-half reliabilities are reported on the scale.

The test-retest reliabilities range from .84 to .94 for the complete test and between .80 and .97 for the separate scales (Eysenck & Eysenck, 1968a, p. 15). The split-half reliabilities, A vs. B for 1,655 normals, 210 neurotics, and 90 psychotics range from .74 to .91. No reliability information is presented for the Lie Scale. Eysenck suggests that if the test is to be used for individual decisions, both forms should be used, whereas, if it is to be used for experimental studies, one form would be sufficient. Overall, the Extraversion and Neuroticism Scales have fairly substantial reliability for personality tests.

Eysenck provides information on the factorial and construct validity of the test as well as the concurrent validity. Much evidence has been collected of the existence and orthogonality of the Extraversion and Neuroticism dimensions. The scales differentiate between different types of neurotics and psychotics and normals. Correlation studies were reported between the EPI and Taylor Manifest

Anxiety Scale, Cattell's IPAT Anxiety Scale, the Multiple Affect Adjective Check List, and the California Personality Inventory. The correlational studies provide some evidence of the concurrent validity of the scales on the EPI. Eysenck has conducted extensive factor analytic studies which demonstrate the independence of the Extraversion and Neuroticism diversions (Eysenck & Eysenck, 1968b).

The test has been studied by other researchers and psychologists and, in general, there is support for the validity and reliability of the scale. The manual of the EPI does not contain emperical studies comparing the EPI and the Maudsley Personality Inventory, the test from which the EPI was generated.

Critique

Lingoes (1965), Cline (1972), Lanyon (1972), and Tellegen (1978) have presented critical reviews of the EPI in editions of the *Mental Measurements Yearbooks*.

Tellegen (1978) and Lanyon (1972) question the conceptualization of the two dimensions of the test and the value of the narrow conceptualization. Lingoes (1965) and Lanyon (1972) have problems evaluating the validity and usability of the Lie Scale. Tellegen (1978) has identified problems with the dimension framework, provided by the EPI of the two constructs.

One major area of criticism is the manual. Tellegen (1978) criticizes the test for not discussing explicitly the content and conceptualization of each scale. Lanyon (1972) feels there is a deficiency in the reporting of norms for the test.

Overall, the critics feel that the EPI is psychometrically well constructed but probably of limited value to practitioners. This criticism is based partially, on the conceptualization of constructs measured and partially on the deficient information reported in the manual on the interpretation of the test. They feel that the manual ought to be updated and improved by including better normative and interpretative information as well as a more complete review of the research conducted using the EPI. The test is perceived as a gross screening device or a test that might supplement the information from other more appropriate and global measures such as the MMPI and CPI.

This reviewer has used the EPI over a 20-year period for clinical, educational, and research uses. Adults tend to have a negative reaction to the items as well as to the test format. Most of the items on the Neuroticism Scale focus on negative behaviors and this stimulates discussion and a negative reaction to the test. Examinees do not like the appearance of the test, the size of print, and the language used in phrasing the questions. The items on the Lie Scale are of questionable value. The EPI is easy to administer and score and has sufficient reliability for research purposes. The test has been a good instrument to illustrate Eysenck's theory of personality in psychology classes and to stimulate discussion on the structure of personality.

Generally in counseling I have found global measures of personality such as the 16PF, CPI, Myers Briggs, and MMPI to be more useful in diagnoses and assessment. Nevertheless, the EPI still has value as a research tool and a supplemental instrument, especially if the user reads the test manual and booklet carefully and understands the conceptualization of the constructs measure.

References

Cline, V. B. (1972). The Eysenck Personality Inventory. In O. K. Buros, (Ed.), *The seventh mental measurements yearbook* (pp. 161-163). Highland Park, NJ: The Gryphon Press.

Eysenck, H. J. (1952). *The scientific study of personality.* London: Routledge and Kegan Paul.

Eysenck, H. J. (1962). *The manual of the Mandsley Personality Inventory.* San Diego: Educational and Industrial Testing Service.

Eysenck, H. J., & Eysenck, S. B. (1968a). *The manual of the Eysenck Personality Inventory.* San Diego: Educational and Industrial Testing Service.

Eysenck, H. J., & Eysenck, S. B. (1968b). *Personality structure and measurement.* San Diego, CA: Knapp.

Eysenck, H. J. (1970). *The structure of human personality.* London: Methuen.

Eysenck, H. J., & Eysenck, S. B. G. (1975). *Eysenck Personality Questionnaire.* San Diego: Educational and Industrial Testing Service.

Eysenck, S. B. G. (1965). *Junior Eysenck Personality Inventory.* San Diego: Educational and Industrial Testing Service.

Lanyon, R. I. (1972). The Eysenck Personality Inventory. In O. K. Buros, (Ed.), *The seventh mental measurements yearbook* (pp. 163-164). Highland Park, NJ: The Gryphon Press.

Lingoes, J. C. (1965). The Eysenck Personality Inventory. In O. K. Buros, (Ed.), *The sixth mental measurements yearbook* (pp. 215-217). Highland Park, NJ: The Gryphon Press.

Tellegen, A. (1978). The Eysenck Personality Inventory. In O. K. Buros, (Ed.), *The eighth mental measurements yearbook* (pp. 802-804). Highland Park, NJ: The Gryphon Press.

James R. Caldwell, Ph.D.

Professor of Psychology, Department of Education and Psychology, Trevecca Nazarene College, Nashville, Tennessee.

FAMILY ENVIRONMENT SCALE

Rudolf H. Moos and Bernice S. Moos. Palo Alto, California: Consulting Psychologists Press, Inc.

Introduction

The Family Environment Scale (FES) is a 90-item true-false instrument designed to measure the social-environmental attributes of various kinds of families. The FES contains ten subscales which are designed to appraise these attributes and assess three underlying domains structured after Murray's beta-press concept: the Relationship dimensions, the Personal Growth dimensions, and the System Maintenance dimensions.

The Relationship dimensions are appraised by the Cohesion, Expressiveness, and Conflict subscales. More specifically, the Cohesion subscale assesses the amount of commitment, assistance, and sustenance family members contribute to one another; Expressiveness measures the degree to which family members are encouraged to express their feelings directly and to act overtly; and Conflict appraises the extent to which family members engage in aggression, conflict, and overt anger.

The Personal Growth dimensions are measured by these five subscales: Independence, Achievement Orientation, Intellectual-Cultural Orientation, Active-Recreational Orientation, and Moral-Religious Emphasis. The Independence subscale appraises the degree to which family members exhibit assertiveness, self-sufficiency, and independent decision-making; Achievement-Orientation measures the impact of activities (e.g., work and school) in casting families into a competitive or achievement-oriented frame of mind; Intellectual-Cultural Orientation assesses the amount of interest in cultural, intellectual, political, and social activities; Active-Recreational Orientation judges the amount of participation in recreational and social enterprises; and Moral-Religious Emphasis rates the amount of emphasis on religious and ethical values and problems.

The System Maintenance dimensions include the Organization and Control subscales. The Organization subscale measures the extent to which lucid organization and structure carry weight in planning family activities and responsibilities, and Control assesses the extent to which established procedures and regulations are followed in running family life.

The FES was developed by Rudolf H. Moos, Ph.D., and Bernice S. Moos at the Social Ecology Laboratory, Department of Psychiatry and Behavioral Sciences, Stanford University, and the Veterans Administration Medical Center, Palo Alto, California. The development involved utilizing several procedures. Structured interviews with members of various kinds of families yielded information from which test items were constructed. Other items were adapted from other existing social climate scales. In addition, information accruing from pretesting eventually made it possible to develop an initial 200-item Form A of the FES.

Form A was given to over 1,000 family members from 285 families. This sample was made up of diverse kinds of families including those who responded to a newspaper advertisement, those enlisted from three church groups, and those families enrolled through student contact at a local high school. A number of minority families were included in the above sample; black and Mexican-American research assistants were also able to increase minority participation. In addition the Form A sample included a number of distressed families receiving treatment at a psychiatrically oriented family clinic and families with members under parole and probation who were associated with a local correctional department.

In choosing items for Form R, five psychometric criteria were employed. First, to prevent selecting items representative of atypical families the overall item split was to be as close to 50-50 as obtainable. Second, the correlation index of each item was to have been higher with its own subscale than with any other subscale. (Each of the 90 items achieved this criterion.) Third, to control for acquiescence response set all subscales were to contain similar numbers of true and false items. Fourth, each subscale was to demonstrate low to moderate intercorrelation. Finally, each item and subscale needed to discriminate among families. According to the manual each of these five criteria was achieved in subsamples of Causasian, minority, ethnic, and distressed families.

Normative data on the subscales of Form R were compiled for 500 distressed families and 1,125 normal families. The original 285 families identified earlier were among these subsamples. The subsample for normal families involved families from all parts of the country, of all ages (from young newlyweds to older, retired persons), multigenerational and single-parent families, and ethnic minority families. In addition, the normal sample included 294 families drawn randomly from designated census tracts in the San Francisco vicinity. Since the means and standard deviations are similar for both the San Francisco subsample and the other subsamples in the normal family sample, it would seem that findings from Form R are representative of the range of normal families.

The original subsample (N = 42) for distressed families consisted of those in which one or more members were receiving treatment or some kind of rehabilitation at a psychiatric-oriented family clinic or through a local correctional facility. Additional subsamples included families of alcohol abusers (N = 220); of various psychiatric patients (N = 77); and those (N = 161) with children or adolescents in a crisis situation (e.g., a runaway, a delinquent, or a situation requiring placement in a foster home). The manual furnishes a table of subscale means and standard deviations for the distressed and normal families.

Even after statistical controls were inaugurated to control for effects of such differences as socioeconomic and family background attributes (e.g., number of children, education and age of parents), distressed families were higher on Conflict and Control and lower on Cohesion, Independence, Expressiveness, and Intellectual and Recreational Orientation than normal families. Researchers can benefit from tables in the manual's appendix in comparing their sample families to a representative group of community families because the standard score conversion table in Appendix A contains normal family data. Those researchers desiring to compare their sample with the distressed family sample may do so by computing standard scores from the means and standard deviations subscales for distressed families in Table 2.

The FES has three forms: Form R (the Real Form) was developed to measure each family member's perception of his or her family environment; Form I (the Ideal Form) was developed to assess each family member's conception of what would constitute an ideal family environment; and Form E (the Expectations Form) was developed to appraise each family member's expectations about the impact of future events on the family, such as the arrival of a new baby. Forms I and E are special forms of the FES and are not commercially available. Unless otherwise stated all references to the FES throughout this critique refer to Form R.

Practical Applications/Uses

The FES contains 90 statements about families. An examinee is requested to mark an item "true" if he or she concludes that it is true or mostly true about his or her family, and false if judged false or mostly false. The item is to be marked "true" if the statement is true of *most* family members; respondents do not assess each other family member separately, but rather give an overall assessment of their entire family.

Accompanying the reusable FES booklets are separate answer sheets, templates for scoring the answer sheets, and separate profile sheets in standard score units for interpreting performance on each of the ten subscales.

In order to develop family profiles for data interpretation, raw scores are computed first on each subscale for each family member by determining the number of correct responses for each subscale. Second, an average score is calculated for all members of each family for each subscale. Third, family averages are transformed to standard scores, using conversion tables in the appendix section of the manual. In addition to family profiles, an individual profile which would plot a single member's ten subscale scores can easily be generated from brief instructions in the appendix.

The manual suggests that the examiner read the instructions aloud while examinees follow along both in their test booklets and on their answer sheets. Each respondent is to be given a lead pencil with an eraser to avoid the use of ballpoint pens. When requested, the examiner is to clarify word meanings but guard against influencing the respondent in either direction. Examinees with indecisive tendencies may be assisted by such responses as: "Answer true if you think it is true most of the time" (or "true of most of your family on most days"). However, as a last resort the customary response is "If you are not sure, just guess."

Examinees should be encouraged to answer all items because of the relatively few items in each subscale. Test administrators are encouraged to check each answer sheet as it is turned in for unattempted items and possible incomplete identifying information.

The qualification of the examiner would vary, depending on whether the subjects are normal or otherwise. Generally, normal subjects would require little or no assistance. The time required to complete this instrument is not indicated.

An experienced clerk can easily score the FES with help from the templates. The number of Xs that appear through the template in each column (one column for each subscale) will yield the person's total raw score. An average family score for each subscale can then be calculated. Appendix A of the manual enables the scorer to convert family average subscores and individual subscale scores to standard scores.

No statement could be found in the manual to determine whether a specific minimum age requirement exists for participating family members. The manual does indicate that families of all ages, including families with preschool children and adolescents, were included in the subsample for normal families. Although each statement in the FES is short and relatively simple in content, it would appear that children would probably need to be at least ten years old to complete this instrument.

The manual does not state explicitly in the introductory sections what the authors had in mind concerning specific purposes and designed uses of the FES before Form R was fully developed. The later sections of the manual elaborate in much detail on diverse practical and research applications and findings of this instrument after it was published in final form. Hence a clear distinction between the scales' designed use and actual practical and research applications seems impossible. Generally speaking, the FES attempts to appraise the social-environmental characteristics of all kinds of families in keeping with three underlying domains—the Relationship, Personal Growth, and Systems Maintenance dimensions. These three dimensions are measured by ten different variables or subscales.

Because the ten FES subscales can be plotted on a standard score profile and because the Form R profiles have demonstrated adequate stability correlations over intervals of time up to one year, the FES has numerous practical applications, including: comparisons of family perceptions between males and females; comparisons of profiles between two kinds of families (e.g., achievement-oriented families and relationship-oriented families); comparisons between Real and Ideal Family environments (utilizing Forms R and I). The FES is particularly suitable for therapists and counselors with a family systems approach to whom the family as a unit has come for counseling. Profiles could be compared between the family at the beginning and following a series of counseling sessions. Interpretation can also be made of an individual's initial perception of his or her family versus perceptions after counseling. Parents of relatively normal families can profit from such an instrument by becoming informed of marked discrepancies between their perceptions of family characteristics and those of one of their siblings. The FES is structured to enable its user to achieve a clear focus on a person's perceptions of the present family environment.

In addition to such practical uses, the manual devotes almost 18 pages to two sections titled "Clinical and Practical Applications" and "Research Applications." The latter section alone begins by stating that the FES has been utilized in more than 100 research studies. Because of the large number of fairly extensive practical and research projects and because the primary sources were inaccessible, it is beyond the scope and power of this critique to discuss these studies in any detail. However, certain aspects of these studies provided in the manual can be introduced. First, when normal persons or families are considered, there is marked flexibility in the kinds of settings in which studies with the FES were conducted. This classification would also include "relatively" normal persons or families undergoing crises or prolonged stressful circumstances. The FES has been utilized in studying distinctive features of different kinds of normal families: 1) two-parent versus one-parent families (Reinhart, 1977); 2) multigenerational families in which an elderly parent resides with an adult offspring and spouse (Lee & Rohbock, 1979); 3) black versus Mexican-American families (Moos & Moos, 1981a); 4) families with a delinquent or runaway adolescent in a residential treatment facility (Malin, 1978/1979); 5) families with an alcoholic member (Filstead, 1979); and 6) families with a depressed member (Wetzel, 1976/1977).

The manual indicates that FES has also been utilized in other settings: 1) analyses of physical living environments, including perceptions of family members as to use of housing facilities (Melson, Inman, & Kemp, 1977); 2) study of relationships of the family environment to adult career and occupational configurations developing, for example, when a wife returns to college (Ballmer & Cozby, 1978); 3) research on family members concerning measures of self-disclosure (Beckert, 1975); 4) matched comparisons of the family environments of mothers of severely handicapped children (Saur, 1980); 5) comparisons of coping styles of policemen's wives with their family environments (Maynard, et al., 1980); 6) analysis of surviving family members of servicemen missing in action (Boss, 1977); 7) comparison of family environment and marital adjustment of repatriated prisoners of war and their spouses with a subgroup of matched families (Nice, McDonald, & McMillan, 1980); 8) relationship studies between family features and child—rearing attitudes (Schneewind & Lortz, 1978); 9) relationship research between family environment and behavior problems (language deficiencies, aggressive acts, indications of anxiety) among pre-kindergarten children (Fowler, 1980); 10) relationship investigations between family environment variables and locus-of-control orientation (Nowicki & Schneewind, 1977); 11) correlational studies involving perceived family environment and behavior and attitudes toward school (Janes & Hesselbrock, 1976); 12) comparisons between average families with a gifted adolescent and average families with an average adolescent, utilizing both Forms R and I (Tabackman, 1976/1977); 13) investigation of adults' perceptions of the social milieu of their families' origin and the correlation between that origin and the person's nuclear family environment (Penk, Robinowitz, Kidd, & Nisle, 1979); 14) study among care professionals such as nurses who need to gather pertinent information on families when caring for patients in a family setting (Eichel, 1978); 15) cross-cultural research in other countries, as the FES has been translated into Dutch, German, Hebrew, Italian, and Spanish. The German version was utilized by Engfer, Schneewind, and Hinderer (1977); a Dutch version was administered before and after psychotherapy by Geffen and Lange (1978).

The second major classification of settings would involve families undergoing counseling and families with at least one "dysfunctional" and/or psychotic member. Whereas, in the first classification a wide variety of professions utilized the

FES (including psychotherapists in a number of instances), the second classification would be heavily dependent on the professional training of psychotherapists or counselor-related professions. The manual informs the reader that the FES is used in such settings as: 1) patients in psychotherapy or counseling (Lange, 1978; White, 1978; Young et al., 1979); 2) utilization of Form R and Form I as teaching aids in a marriage and family course (Waters, 1979); 3) as a training packet for student clinicians as a procedure of evaluating family and marital systems (Cromwell & Keeney, 1979); 4) in numerous situations of family members confronting drug abuse (including alcohol), drug addiction, recovered and relapsed alcoholic states (Filstead, 1979; Moos, Bromet, Tsu, & Moos, 1979; Rassmussen, 1979/1980); 5) to appraise, in detail, activities of schizophrenic patients living in independent-community situations in order to create a framework for evaluating such patients (Paskiewicz, 1979); 6) at the outset of and during therapy to demonstrate its clinical value (Fuhr, Moos, & Dishotsky, in press); and 7) numerous studies on various kinds of patients undergoing psychotherapy or counseling to ascertain differences between the perceived family milieus of distressed families (families with at least one "dysfunctional" member) and of normal families (Lange, 1978; White, 1978; Young et al., 1979).

Technical Aspects

Regarding the technical aspects of this test, the question arises as to what extent the research studies lean toward internal clinical judgment (subjective approaches) or objective statistical analyses. Generally speaking, the emphasis is on the latter; however, certain qualifications seem in order. First, much of the research on the FES is exploratory in nature and therefore has taken place in a great diversity of settings involving many different goals. Also, some initial studies make comparisons of FES profiles between either two persons or the same person before and after counseling. Second, much of the research revolves around psychotherapy and counseling, and therefore clinical interpretations do emerge frequently. Nevertheless, one gets the impression that on the whole the researchers consistently strive toward maximizing nonsubjective research procedures wherever possible. Whenever appropriate, statistical tests of significance were utilized even though many of these initial exploratory studies did not yield significant results.

A theme arising frequently throughout the research studies is the need either to control statistically for environmental and other factors that could influence how one interpreted findings or to exercise caution in interpretations due to uncontrolled factors. The manual cites studies comparing recovered and relapsed subjects after residential treatment emphasize the need of such controls when they matched the treatment and control groups on sociodemographically related variables (Moos & Moos, 1981b; Moos, Finney, & Gamble, 1981). The exploratory investigation of relationships between family environment and background factors revealed that family size, partner's age, and education should be controlled whenever groups of families are compared. One variable identified by Eiswirth-Neems and Handal (1978) as possibly affecting family climate detrimentally are the effects of maternal occupational status. Cronkite and Moos (1980) bring out the need to monitor the relationship between increases in life stressors on alcoholic patients and corresponding increases in negative family environments.

Considerable effort has been expended in developing different representative subsamples for normal families (N = 1,125); distressed families (N = 500); single-parent families (N = 81); black families (N = 85); Mexican-American families (N = 93); families in which one of the spouses is over 60 (N = 106); different sized families (N = 446). Means and often standard deviation values are furnished for these subsamples. In addition a separate table appears in Appendix A to convert raw scores for normal family samples to standard scores. Means and standard deviations are also provided for distressed families to enable them to develop standard scores. Moos and Moos have developed a Family Incongruence Score to measure the amount of disagreement between family members. Clear and specific instructions enable the user to calculate scores objectively (Appendix B).

As indicated in the manual, research studies frequently utilize a matched or representative control group and one or two treatment groups (e.g., Steinbock, 1977/1978; Bader, 1978), and test for statistical significance between mean group performance on the FES subscales (e.g., Abbott, 1975/1976). Druckman (1979) and others have developed pretest-posttest designs for different periods during therapy. Engfer, Schneewind, and Hindered (1977) submitted their data on the German version of the FES to factor analysis and reported the emergence of three similar second-order factors. Moos and Moos (1976) employed cluster analysis to produce an empirical taxonomy of family social environments.

Cronbach's alpha was used in computing internal consistency reliability coefficients for each of the ten FES subscales. The lowest correlations were .61 and .64 for Independence and Achievement Orientation, respectively. Cohesion, Intellectual-Cultural Orientation, and Moral-Religious Emphasis each yielded correlations of .78—the highest measures of internal consistency. Conflict and Organization yielded correlations of .75 and .76, respectively. All of these subscale coefficients are satisfactory.

Test-retest reliabilities were computed for the 10 subscales for intervals of 8 weeks, 4 months and 12 months. Reliability coefficients for six subscales ranged between .76 and .89 for the 12-month interval. Coefficients for the remaining four subscales were .52, .63, .69 and .69. These coefficients were adequate.

Intercorrelations were also computed for each subscale; separate intercorrelations were calculated for 1,468 fathers and mothers and 621 sons and daughters selected from 534 normal and 266 distressed families. The subscales that are positively correlated are Organization with Cohesion and Active-Recreational Orientation with Intellectual-Cultural Orientation. The negatively correlated subscales are Control with Independence and Cohesion with Conflict.

Judging from the intercorrelations the subscales assess distinct, yet to some extent related, features of family social environments. Similar intercorrelations were found for parents and children and account for less than 10% of the subscale variance that exists in different family structures such as two-parent versus one-parent families.

Profile stability correlations were also computed for the subscales for different time intervals and demonstrated adequate stability. The average 4-month profile stability coefficient was .78, and the average 12-month profile coefficient was .71.

In addition to demonstrating adequate stability the standard score profiles also have demonstrated that they are sensitive to changes.

Critique

Traditionally, two of the approaches for measuring aspects of personality and other areas of the affective domain have included psychometric tests and projective techniques. Psychometrics is the study and application of mathematical procedures to psychological questions. Those items in psychometric tests that correlate highest empirically with a criterion measure are retained and developed into reliable scoring norms that are appropriate for everyone who takes this instrument in the same manner. The assumption of such psychometric tests is that they sample a person's typical behavioral patterns as an independent or predictor variable and that they correlate this sample of items with an appropriate dependent or criterion variable.

The FES is one of nine social climate scales developed by Moos and his co-workers. All of these scales stem from the projective approach in that they utilize key concepts employed by Murray and Morgan in the initial construction of their Thematic Apperception Test (TAT), a projective instrument. Here they clearly attempted to construct a type of shortcut method of free association, a process used by psychoanalysts. Administrators of the completed version displayed 20 pictures to subjects and requested that they tell a story about what was taking place in each picture. Interpreters then looked for recurring themes arising out of a number of these pictures and evolved a list of the most dominant themes or need-press combinations. *Press* was defined as the power that objects, including people, in the environment have to benefit or harm an individual. *Beta press* is an individual's subjective perceptions of this existing power, as opposed to *alpha press*, the objective potential in the environment for benefit or harm.

Alll of the nine social climate scales can be traced to this concept of beta press developed by Murray. The press dimensions of the FES are defined as Relationships, Personal Growth, and System Maintenance, and are the three underlying domains that have a direct influence on the choice and wording of all items in the FES. Obviously Murray's concept of press has a profound impact on the technical aspects of the FES; consequently, Moos et al. have not escaped the criticisms directed toward the TAT and other projective measures for decades (i.e., unsatisfactory predictive validity). This is not to imply that Moos is unaware of these problems, nor to suggest that he and his colleagues have not grappled with these issues. However, in consistently utilizing the beta press dimensions it would appear he has not shifted from a conceptual-theoretical emphasis to a more psychometric-methological emphasis in search of supporting empirical evidence. Despite the very extensive research studies contained in the manual, this reviewer notes a separate section on validity to be absent entirely. Sections on reliability, interrrcorrelations, and profile stability are present. Further, this reviewer found only one reference to validity (i.e., construct validity) throughout all studies reported in the manual. The words "predictive validity" appear to be absent altogether. That vital aspect of the psychometric approach is missing.

It should be pointed out that therapists and others who are involved in areas largely within the affective domain may prefer and defend conceptual-theoretical emphases rather than psychometric emphases. Certainly current psychology embodies approaches that range from the artistic, though subjective, to the scientific or positivistic approach. Regardless of one's psychological orientation, however, validity studies would lend credence to the instrument.

Because Moos begins with an a priori commitment to the three underlying beta press dimensions, however, does he not thereby delegate any later serious empirical deliberations to a minor after-the-fact role, once the initial a priori die has been cast? It is true that the FES subscale internal psychometric attributes are generally acceptable with regard to such factors as reliability, intercorrelations, and profile stability. The complex questions that must be dealt with concern the empirical evidence to support the use of FES subscales, taken separately or in combination as a dependent variable or for purposes of decision-making. External validity data for the FES are lacking.

The FES appears to have robust face validity. Generally speaking, each item seems relevant to the respondent and is expressed with clarity. Each statement tends to appear reasonable. Norms are presented in standard score units, enabling ready comparisons in some instances.

Overall impressions of the manual can be misleading. For example, the inclusion of extensive research studies should not communicate to the reader that the FES has substantial validity support and is well established as a criterion measure or some similar variable.

The manual is silent on areas that could seriously affect the resulting scores. Adequate statements are lacking concerning who is qualified to both administer and interpret the test results. The danger always exists that "common sense" is fraught with subjectivity. Second, more needs to be said about interpreting profiles between individuals as compared to groups. Confusion could be reduced if Moos had discussed implications for interpreting FES scores when the unit of measurement changes from families to individuals. Third, when groups were compared in research studies, differences often seem to be small and not significant. No tables or statements are included to indicate at what level group differences were significant. Fourth, the implications of utilizing mean values versus consensus values for families are not discussed. Fifth, the technical implications arising out of Moos' assumption that he is measuring attributes of the family environment when, in fact, the FES measures the perceptions of family members about their family should be addressed. What the family members convey about their families may be inaccurate or distorted. Also, empirical evidence is needed to investigate congruence or lack of congruence, and kinds of relationships between key family environment constructs and actual behavior of family members. To assume kinds of relationships (e.g., linear) that really do not exist can lead to serious distortions of the data.

To summarize, Moos and his colleagues at the Ecology Laboratory, Stanford University, are introducing innovative ways of advancing the frontiers of ecological psychology into different avenues and settings. In this sense their entire nine social climate scales, and the diverse applications of each scale, are opening new vistas for exploration and research. The FES can be very useful when employed with caution. It is extremely flexible and can be used in many different settings.

Within the domain of ecological psychology it has great potential for opening new areas for investigation. It is an excellent device for bringing into sharp focus factors for scrutiny within the family social milieu. It can be an effective "hunch" producer to introduce additional possibilities into individual or group deliberations.

References

This list includes the reference citations from the test manual that were inaccessible to this reviewer.

Abbott, D. (1976). The effects of open forum family counseling on perceived family environment and on behavior change of the child (Doctoral dissertation, Brigham Young University, 1975). *Dissertation Abstracts International, 36*, 8335A.

Bader, E. (1976). Redecisions in family therapy: A study of change in an intensive family therapy workshop (Doctoral dissertation, California School of Professional Psychology, San Francisco). *Dissertation Abstracts International, 37*, 2491B.

Ballmer, H., & Cozby, P. (1978, April). *Family environments of women who return to college.* Paper presented at the Western Psychological Association Convention, San Francisco.

Beckert, C. (1975). The effect of self-disclosure within a family on the perceived family environment and on individual personality traits (Doctoral dissertation, Brigham Young University, 1974). *Dissertation Abstracts International, 35*, 4714A.

Boss, P. (1977). A clarification of the concept of psychological-father presence in families experiencing ambiguity of boundary. *Journal of Marriage and the Family, 37*, 141-151.

Cromwell, R., & Keeney, B. (1979). Diagnosing marital and family systems: A training model. *Family Coordinator, 28*, 101-108.

Cronkite, R., & Moos, R. (1980). The determinants of posttreatment functioning of alcoholic patients: A conceptual framework. *Journal of Consulting and Clinical Psychology, 48*, 305-316.

Druckman, J. (1979). A family oriented policy and treatment program for juvenile status offenders. *Journal of Marriage and the Family, 41*, 627-636.

Eichel, E. (1978). Assessment with a family focus. *Journal of Psychiatric Nursing and Mental Health Services, 16*, 11-15.

Eiswirth-Neems, N., & Handal, P. (1978). Spouse's attitudes toward maternal occupational status and effects on family climate. *Journal of Community Psychology, 6*, 168-172.

Engfer, A., Schneewind, K., & Hinderer, J. (1977). *Die Familien-Klima-Skalen (FKS): Ein fragebogen zur erhebung perzipierter familienumwelten* (Research Rep. No. 16). Munich: University of Munich, ELB Project.

Filstead, W. (1979). *Comparing the family environments of alcoholic and "normal" families.* Chicago: Northwestern University, Department of Psychiatry and Behavioral Sciences.

Fowler, P. (1980). Family environment and early behavioral development: A structural analysis of dependencies. *Psychological Reports, 47*, 611-617.

Fuhr, R., Moos, R., & Dishotsky, N. (in press). Use of family assessment and feedback in ongoing family therapy. *American Journal of Family Therapy.*

Geffen, M., & Lange, M. (1978). *The effectiveness of psychotherapy with children: A comparison of symptom improvement and changes in the family.* Nijmegen, the Netherlands: Catholic University, Department of Clinical Psychology.

Janes, C., & Hesselbrock, V. (1976, September). *Perceived family environment and school adjustment of children of schizophrenics.* Paper presented at the American Psychological Association Convention, Washington, DC.

Jones, S., & Jones, D. (1977, August). *Serious jogging and family life: Marathon and sub-marathon running.* Paper presented at the American Sociological Association Convention, Chicago.

Lange, M. (1978). Some characteristics of the validity of Dutch translations of the FES and

WES. Nijmegen, The Netherlands: Catholic University, Department of Clinical Psychology.

Lee, A., & Rohbock, C. (1979). *Perceptions of home environment in multigenerational families.* Unpublished master's thesis, Brigham Young University, Provo.

Malin, N. (1979). Pathways to child placement: Parental perceptions of adolescent children in residential treatment (Doctoral dissertation, University of California at Los Angeles, 1978). *Dissertation Abstracts International, 39,* 6360A.

Martinez, M., Hays, J., & Solway, K. (1979). Comparative study of delinquent and nondelinquent Mexican-American youths. *Psychological Reports, 44,* 215-221.

Maynard, P., Maynard, N., McCubbin, H., & Shao, D. (1980). Family life in the police profession: Coping patterns wives employ in managing job stress and the family environment. *Family Relations, 29,* 495-501.

Melson, G., Inman, M., & Kemp, P. (1977, April). *Perceived environmental stress and family functioning in married student families.* Paper presented at the Environmental Design and Research Association Convention, Urbana, IL.

Moos, R. (1974a). *Combined preliminary manual for the Family, Work, and Group Environment Scales.* Palo Alto, CA: Consulting Psychologists Press.

Moos, R. (1974b). *The Social Climate Scales: An overview.* Palo Alto, CA: Consulting Psychologists Press.

Moos, R., & Moos, B. (1976). A typology of family social environments. *Family Process, 15,* 357-372.

Moos, R., & Moos, B. (1981a). *Manual for the Family Environment Scale.* Palo Alto, CA: Consulting Psychologists Press.

Moos, R., & Moos, B. (1981b). *The process of recovery from alcoholism: III. Comparing family functioning alcoholic and matched control families.* Palo Alto, CA: Stanford University Social Ecology Laboratory and Veterans Administration Medical Center.

Moos, R., Bromet, E., Tsu, V., & Moos, B. (1979). Family characteristics and the outcome of treatment for alcoholism. *Journal of Studies on Alcohol, 40,* 78-88.

Moos, R., Finney, J., & Gamble, W. (1981). *The process of recovery from alcoholism: II. Comparing spouses of alcoholic patients and spouses of matched community controls.* Palo Alto, CA: Stanford University Social Ecology Laboratory and Veterans Administration Medical Center.

Nice, D., McDonald, B., & McMillian, T. (1980). *The families of U.S. Navy prisoners of war five years after repatriation from Viet Nam.* San Diego: Naval Health Research Center.

Nowicki, S., & Schneewind, K. (1977). *Relation of family climate variables to locus of control orientation as a function of culture, sex and age.* Atlanta: Emory University, Department of Psychology.

Paskiewicz, P. (1979). *Conceptualizing the psychosocial milieu of the aftercare client: An exploratory study.* Unpublished master's thesis, Oakland University, Rochester, MN.

Penk, W., Robinowitz, R., Kidd, R., & Nisle, A. (1979). Perceived family environments among ethnic groups of compulsive heroin users. *Addictive Behavior, 4,* 297-309.

Rasmussen, R. (1980). Perceived family climate and interpersonal characteristics of alcoholic women and their husbands. (Doctoral dissertation, California School of Professional Psychology, Berkeley, 1979). *Dissertation Abstracts International, 40,* 3418B.

Reinhart, G. (1977). One-parent families: A study of divorced mothers and adolescents using social climate and relationship styles (Doctoral dissertation, California School of Professional Psychology, San Francisco). *Dissertation Abstracts International, 38,* 2881B.

Saur, W. (1980). *Social networks and family environments of mothers of multiply severely handicapped children.* Unpublished doctoral dissertation, Florida State University, Tallahassee.

Schneewind, K. (1976). *Familienklimaskalen: Ein fragebogen zur erfassung der perzipierten familienumwelt* (Research Rep. No. 10). Trier, Federal Republic of Germany: University of Trier, Project on Parental Child Rearing Attitudes.

Schneewind, K., & Lortz, E. (1978). *Familienklima und elterliche erziehungseinstellungen.* In K. Schneewind & H. Lukesche (Eds.), *Familiare sozialisation: Probleme, ergebnisse, perspektiven.* Stuttgart: Klett-Cotta.

Steinbock, L. (1978). Net-leaving: Family systems of runaway adolescents (Doctoral dissertation, California School of Professional Psychology, San Francisco, 1977). *Dissertation Abstracts International, 38,* 4544B.

Tabackman, M. (1977). A study of family psycho-social environment and its relationship to academic achievement in gifted adolescents (Doctoral dissertation, University of Illinois at Urbana-Champaign, 1976). *Dissertation Abstracts International, 37,* 6381A.

Waters, J. (1979). The Family Environment Scale as an instructional aid for studying the family. *Teaching of Psychology, 6,* 162-164.

Wetzel, J. (1977). Dependence upon unsustaining environments as an antecedent variable of depression (Doctoral dissertation, Washington University, St. Louis, 1976). *Dissertation Abstract International, 37,* 5361A.

White, D. (1978). Schizophrenics' perceptions of family relationships (Doctoral dissertation, Saint Louis University, St. Louis). *Dissertation Abstracts International, 39,* 1451A.

Young, R., Gaynor, J., Gould, E., & Stewart, M. (1979). The Family Environment Scale in a psychiatric inpatient sample. San Francisco: University of California, Department of Psychiatry.

Thelma Hunt, Ph.D., M.D.
*Professor Emeritus of Psychology, George Washington University, and
Director, Center for Psychological Service, Washington, D.C.*

FLANAGAN APTITUDE CLASSIFICATION TESTS

*John C. Flanagan. Chicago, Illinois: Science Research
Associates, Inc.*

Introduction

The Flanagan Aptitude Classification Tests (FACT) established a classification
system of aptitudes, with the development of tests for evaluating the established
aptitudes. The current edition of the test consists of 19 parts covering 16 important
aptitudes or on-the-job skills. The aptitudes are *job elements,* which distinguishes
them from the *mental factor* type of aptitudes characterizing the majority of
aptitude tests. The aptitudes cover those important in performing the duties of
many occupations.

The system of aptitude classification used in this test is supported by intensive
and systematic job analyses. Flanagan (1948) defines a job element as being
general in the sense that it may be found in a number of occupations, but specific
or unique in the sense that it measures something different from other job
elements in the test. These concepts of job elements form the rationale for the
FACT battery of tests.

In both the *Technical Report* and the *Technical Supplement,* Dr. Flanagan discusses
the advantages of the job element approach to the development of aptitude tests
as compared with the common procedures as represented by 1) the miniature job
sample and 2) the primary mental factor approaches. He sees this intermediate
procedure as avoiding the expensiveness in building and administering job simulation tests and their applicability to only one job. He sees the practical advantages
of his tests in their use and interpretation over more statistically involved interpretations of tests developed by the mental factor approach.

The Flanagan Aptitude Classification Tests are a battery of 19 relatively short
tests. They cover 16 job elements of Inspection, Mechanics, Tables, Reasoning,
Assembly, Judgment and Comprehension, Components, Arithmetic, Ingenuity,
Scales, Expression, Precision, Coordination, Patterns, Coding, and Memory. The
tests can be used separately or in combinations appropriate to the purpose for
which used.

All the tests are pencil-and-paper tests which can be given to fairly large groups
by one examiner. No separate answer sheets are required. They are self-scoring,
utilizing a unique carbon paper format in relation to the scoring. The total battery

Valuable assistance was rendered in the preparation of this report by Clyde J. Lindley.

can be given in two half-day sessions. The tests are appropriate for high school students (Grades 9 through 12) and for adults.

The FACT battery provides a valuable tool for general vocational counseling and selection. It includes the major intellectual and performance job elements that the author has identified and defined on the basis of studies of a wide variety of occupations. It does have some limitations, however. Factors in such occupations as music, dramatics, painting, and the graphic arts do not appear to be adequately covered.

Dr. John C. Flanagan, author of the Flanagan Aptitude Classification Tests, was born in 1906. He has a Ph.D. in psychometrics from Harvard University. Dr. Flanagan has been an active member of the American Board of Professional Psychology and the Society for Industrial and Organizational Psychology, is a past president of the Division of Evaluation and Measurement of the American Psychological Association, and had an academic career at the University of Pennsylvania until his retirement as Professor in 1972. He founded the American Institute for Research (AIR) and is currently the chair of its board of directors. His purpose in founding AIR was to apply the methods of psychological research that had been so successful in the U.S. Army Air Force (USAAF) to industrial, educational, and governmental problems. Dr. Flanagan has directed a number of important test projects under the aegis of AIR. Perhaps the best-known study was Project TALENT, a national survey and follow-up study of 400,000 high school students begun in 1960.

The history of the Flanagan Aptitude Classification Tests goes back to the Army Air Force Aviation Psychology Program during World War II. Dr. Flanagan directed the establishment of this program, a major accomplishment of which was the development of tests and procedures for selecting pilots, navigators, and other air-crew members. A full report of this development can be found in *The Army Air Force Aviation Psychology Research Reports No. 1,* published by the United States Government Printing Office in 1948.

With the success of the Air Force tests, Flanagan began a series of similarly patterned and developed aptitude tests for civilian occupations. These studies resulted in the publication of a 14-test FACT battery in 1953 and the 19-test FACT battery in 1958 (the subject of this review).

The self-scoring procedure involves an arrival by the student at a *raw score* for each of the 19 parts of the test, and a *stanine value*. The student brochure *Your FACT Scores and What They Mean* explains the significance of the stanines in terms of verbal descriptions of the scores from "very high," "high," through "low," "very low," and in terms of the percentage of high school seniors attaining the stanines.

FACT tests are sold in package quantities for each of the 19 tests. Each package contains 25 booklets of one test. The test booklets are not reusable. Inquiries regarding current prices should be addressed to the test publisher, Science Research Associates, Inc.

Norms on the tests were developed utilizing scores of 10,972 students in Grades 9, 10, 11, and 12 in seventeen schools throughout the country. Raw scores are converted into stanine scores for each of the separate tests directly on the self-scoring test from a conversion table. Conversion tables for occupational stanine scores are listed in the examiner manual. The technical report provides percentile norms separately for Grades 9, 10, 11, and 12. Stanine scores are recommended. The report contains this statement: "While percentile scores are useful in student counseling, the lack of equality of percentile units at various positions on the scale precludes their use in computing means or in conducting correlational analyses."

The following abbreviated definitions for the 16 job elements covered by the present FACT battery are from the Science Research Associates' catalog:

1. *Arithmetic*—ability to add, subtract, multiply, divide.
2. *Assembly*—ability to visualize an object from separate parts.
3. *Coding*—ability to code typical office information.
4. *Coordination*—ability to control hand and arm movements.
5. *Components*—ability to identify a simple figure that is part of a complex drawing.
6. *Expression*—knowledge of correct English grammar and sentence structure.
7. *Ingenuity*—ability to invent or discover a solution to a problem.
8. *Inspection*—ability to spot flaws in a series of articles.
9. *Judgment and Comprehension*—ability to read with understanding, reason logically, and use good judgment in practical situations.
10. *Mechanics*—ability to understand mechanical principles and to analyze mechanical movements.
11. *Memory*—ability to remember codes.
12. *Patterns*—ability to reproduce simple pattern outlines.
13. *Precision*—ability to do precision work with small objects.
14. *Reasoning*—ability to understand basic mathematical concepts and relationships.
15. *Scales*—ability to read scales, graphs, and charts.
16. *Tables*—ability to read two types of tables: numbers only and words or letters only.

While the test is *essentially self-scoring* with some instructions from the examiner, it is *not self-administering*. The test must be administered by an examiner, suggested in the manual in a ratio of about 1 to every 25 students. The examiner must be cognizant of the demands for good testing conditions and the necessity of accurate adherence to instructions and time limits for the tests. Yet, the FACT battery was designed for ease and simplicity of administration and attains this aim.

Each of the tests in the FACT series is published as a separate test book or pamphlet to permit flexibility in the selection of the tests and the order in which they are given.

Practical Applications/Uses

The FACT tests were originally designed without particular reference to their areas of practical application—rather to evaluate the distinct aptitudes emerging from the Air Force and subsequent civilian studies related to the tests. As indicated, the civilian FACT battery was visualized as affording an instrument applicable in high schools as its Air Force predecessor was applicable in the Air Force. In this introduction its practical use related to assistance in directing high school students into curricula and goals related to their aptitudes. In this use, the FACT battery was an early recommended vocational guidance test.

In personnel-employment use, the FACT tests have found a lasting place. They can be very useful in the functions of selection, placement, reassignment, upgrading, or reclassification. For these personnel functions, the wide variety of the 19 FACT tests permits the choice of a combination of tests that correspond to critical requirements of specific jobs. Validity and normative data for a variety of jobs are available on the tests.

Applications other than those mentioned are likely to relate to research and may cover many topics. How can the factors covered in the tests be refined? Are the 19 tests sufficiently unique? Can tests be added that cover factors not adequately covered for the more creative occupations? What is the best way to establish validity of tests developed by the FACT approach? What EEOC concerns, if any, threaten FACT tests?

Appropriate subjects for use of the Flanagan Aptitude Classification Test are high school students, or adults who can be assumed to have an elementary school education with some added experience background that might put them in the category of comparable age individuals with some high school background. Educational norms supplied for the test are for high school grades, but there are distributions of scores for a large number of occupations without respect to education.

Administration of the test does not require a psychologist or other technically trained psychometrist. A teacher, an educational counselor, an employment counselor, or an employment interviewer can administer the FACT tests. *Can administer* means *can* after thorough acquaintance with the test (its individual parts) and the detailed instructions for administration of each part. The administrator must have no other concurrent (side-line or major) responsibilities during preparation for and administering the test, and must be aware of the importance of short timings (a few minutes for some tests). Timing should be controlled by adequate devices (stopwatches controlled by an informed examiner) or other automated devices.

The tests are objective, so that no subjective judgment is involved in the scores. As already indicated, a special carbon-copy answering format permits self-scoring by mere counting of marks in indicated answer spaces.

Bases for interpretation of raw scores are furnished by the norms supplied for the 19 tests in the technical report available from the publisher. The percentile norms as stated in the report enable the student to understand his or her abilities relative to those of other individuals both in the total population and in specific occupations. These norms were achieved for the tests through a national standardization of the tests and through follow-up studies of individuals who took the tests.

Technical Aspects

In the technical report reliabilities are reported for the separate 19 tests and nine different combinations (for combined occupational scores for prediction of success in occupational groups). The median reliability coefficient for separate parts of the FACT battery as reported on ninth- and twelfth-grade students is .75. It is pointed out that the FACT tests are not designed for separate use, but in combinations. For the nine combinations reported the reliability coefficients range from .83 to .93, most exceeding .90. Ns involved in the studies are large.

Validity discussion and data are presented in studies of 1) the uniqueness of the 19 tests, 2) follow-up studies of success in relation to test scores, and 3) correlations of test scores with concurrent criteria of validity.

Uniqueness of the tests. In evaluating the validity of multifactor aptitude tests it is important to inquire into the intercorrelations of the parts (separate tests). Maximum validity would be achieved by tests that have no overlap, no correlation between them. This ideal is never attained in practical testing situations. In reported studies based on 991 ninth-grade students and 1,056 twelfth-grade students the test intercorrelations averaged .20 and .31. These are low enough to conclude adequate uniqueness for the tests. To quote from the report, "The data clearly indicate that each of the nineteen tests *is* making a unique contribution to the assessment of an individual's aptitudes, and that each test is capable of adding to predictions of success in any study of the tests' external validity" (Flanagan, 1959, p. 22).

Follow-up Studies. A major follow-up study relates stanine scores that reflect combinations of FACT tests representing stated occupational plans of high school seniors to the criteria of progress and success related to the occupation, the criteria being examined five years after the testing. For college occupations the code used for progress in the field was a combination of these two sets of values:

A. Graduated and enrolled in graduate work in this field = 4
B. Graduated from the field or still attending in this field = 3
C. Graduated from college in an unrelated field, or still attending in an unrelated field = 2
D. Entered field or a related field and dropped out = 1
E. Never entered college, or entered and dropped out of an unrelated field = 0

Average college grades were coded as follows:

A or better	= 5
B + or A–	= 4
B	= 3
C + or B–	= 2
C or grade not given	= 1
C– or below	= 0

For nine groups of college fields, correlations between the Occupational FACT Stanines and Criteria of Progress and Performance were as follows: Engineers .36; Natural Scientist (Physicist, Biologist, Chemist, Mathematician) .52; Medical Profession (Physician, Dentist, Pharmacist) .36; Social Scientist (Lawyer, Psychologist, Social Scientist, Political Scientist, Historian, and Sociologist) .65; Clergyman, Missionary, Social Worker .04; Teacher .39; Business (Accountant, Businessman, Manager) .44; Humanities Professor, Artist, Writer .38; and Nurse .42. Except for the field of Clergyman, Missionary, and Social Worker, these coefficients (significant at the 1% level) provide evidence for the predictive value of the combinations of FACT test scores proposed for the occupational group.

Similar studies, using criterion measures based on salary and promotion, were made for non-college groups. The correlation coefficients for these groups tended to be low and not statistically significant. Flanagan suggests that for the non-college occupations, factors related to motivation, personality, opportunity, and special assistance from family appear to be much more important than aptitudes of the type measured by FACT tests.

Correlations of FACT Test Scores with Concurrent Criteria. Flanagan undertook studies of the relationship of FACT test scores with grades of ninth- and twelfth-grade students. Each of the 19 FACT scores was correlated with teacher grades in English, social studies, science, and mathematics. Specific FACT tests were found with good predictive value for all four grade areas. A summary paragraph from Flanagan's report on the studies states:

> The ninth-grade and twelfth-grade studies combined indicate that Test 5—Vocabulary is generally the best predictor of high school grades. Test 4—Reasoning ranks second; Test 7—Judgment and Comprehension ranks third; Test 13—Expression ranks fourth; and Test 9—Planning ranks fifth as a predictor of high school grades (Flanagan, 1959, p. 40).

The technical report summarizes studies relating the 19 FACT scores to four separate external criteria: high school grade average, WAIS (Wechsler Adult Intelligence Scale) scores, SCAT (School and College Ability Test) scores, and Otis Higher Examination scores. Samples consisted of over 600 Colorado high school students. These studies were conducted by A. J. White (1959).

In the high school grade average study the best validity coefficient was yielded by FACT Test 4 (Reasoning), the coefficient being .66. Coefficients above .50 were yielded for the following FACT tests: Arithmetic, Ingenuity, Expression, Judgment and Comprehension, and Vocabulary.

Studies of the WAIS, SCAT, and Otis show a range of correlations between the various subtests of the three ability measures and the 19 FACT measures. In summary, Flanagan states: "If one accepts the WAIS, SCAT, and Otis instruments as representative measures of general intelligence, White's data indicate that Test 11—Ingenuity is most closely related to this construct. Test 4—Reasoning ranks second, and Test 7—Judgment and Comprehension ranks third in relating to these measures of general intelligence" (Flanagan, 1959, p. 43).

Critique

This review reveals enough favorable information on the series of aptitude tests included in the Flanagan Aptitude Classification Tests to recommend them with confidence to counselors and employment personnel who may be faced with problems of student vocational counseling or personnel problems of selection, placement, or reclassification. The tests are very much job oriented, measuring aptitudes for on-the-job skills that have been established by careful job analyses. Confidence in the opinions about the tests from a rational standpoint are enhanced by the supporting statistical studies upon an unusually large number of cases.

The cautions to be recommended for the FACT tests are not peculiar to them, but for all "aptitude *tests*." Tests for evaluation of vocational aptitudes must be supplemented by evaluation of other criteria, such as interests, personality characteristics, and appraisal of opportunities. These cautions are not criticisms of the tests, but suggest considerations that establish the FACT tests in their singular role.

References

This list includes text citations as well as suggested additional reading.

Flanagan, J. C. (1948). *The aviation psychology program in the Army air forces* (Army Air Forces Aviation Psychology Program Research Rep. No. 1). Washington, DC: U.S. Government Printing Office.

Flanagan, J. C. (1953). *Aptitude Classification Tests* (14-test edition). Chicago: Science Research Associates.

Flanagan, J. C. (1954). The critical incident technique. *Psychological Bulletin, 51,* 327-358.

Flanagan, J. C. (1957). The Flanagan Aptitude Classification Tests. *Personnel and Guidance Journal, 25,* 495-507.

Flanagan, J. C. (1959). *Flanagan Aptitude Classification Tests: Technical report.* Chicago: Science Research Associates.

Flanagan, J. C. (1984). The American institutes for research. *American Psychologist, 39*(11), 1272-1276.

Lathan, A. J. (1948). *Job appropriateness: One-year follow-up of high school graduates.* Unpublished doctoral dissertation, University of Pittsburgh.

Lindquist, E. F. (1957). *ITED manual for the school administrator.* Chicago: Science Research Associates.

Newman, L. C. (1958). *The FACT "airplane pilot" composite score as a predictor of pass-fail criterion in naval flight training.* Unpublished research report, Pensacola Naval Air Station.

Volkin, L. (1951). *A validation study of selected test batteries applied to fields of work.* Unpublished doctoral dissertation, University of Pittsburgh.

White, A. J. (1959). *A comparison of the Flanagan Aptitude Classification Tests with the Wechsler Adult Intelligence Scale, the School and College Ability Test, and three other measures of mental variables at the high school level.* Unpublished doctoral dissertation, Colorado State College, Ft. Collins.

David E. Borrebach, Ph.D.
Associate Professor of Psychology, La Roche College, Pittsburgh, Pennsylvania.

FLANAGAN INDUSTRIAL TESTS

John C. Flanagan. Chicago, Illinois: Science Research Associates, Inc.

Introduction

The Flanagan Industrial Tests (FIT) are a battery of 18 short, speeded tests designed to aid employee selection in business and industry. Like the Flanagan Aptitude Classification Tests (FACT) from which they are descended, each test in the FIT is designed to cover a separate job element or employee ability.

During World War II the tests' author, John C. Flanagan, was charged with establishing the Army Air Corps Aviation Psychology Program. The program resulted in the development of a procedure for studying and analyzing the activities and aptitudes required in various jobs. Subsequent to the war the procedure was refined and termed the critical incident technique (Flanagan, 1954). It was from a list of 21 separate job elements identified through the use of this technique that Flanagan developed the FACT, and from it the FIT.

The critical incidents technique involves determining the general objectives of the job being analyzed and collecting numerous factual incidents concerning the behavior of job incumbents. In the context of employee selection and classification, the factual incidents are clustered together into job elements and hypotheses are generated concerning the aptitudes needed for success in each of the job elements. Specific selection tests that measure the identified aptitudes are selected and then tested for validity.

The FACT battery, first published in 1953, was designed for both vocational counseling and employee selection, but acceptance in industry was hindered by the length of the tests and the length and complexity of the instructions that had to be read to the examinees. The FIT, published in 1960, was designed to overcome these problems. The tests are short and speeded, with each test requiring only 5-15 minutes for administration. Their relatedness to the FACT is emphasized by the statement "a special edition of FACT for business and industry" printed on the cover of each test booklet in the FIT series.

Each of the 18 tests in the FIT is designed for "stand-alone" use and each is printed on a separate, disposable form. The tests are hand-scored using plastic overlay stencils except for the Coordination and Precision tests, which must be scored without stencils. The first version of each test published was designated Form A, and eleven of the tests continue to be published in that original form. Seven of the tests, which were revised shortly after their initial publication, are designated Form AA.

Each test is described and its time limit given as follows:

Arithmetic, Form A (5 minutes): Covers proficiency in addition, subtraction, multiplication, and division. Because the test is organized such that questions requiring the same operation are grouped together fast examinees will demonstrate a different group of skills than slow examinees. It is unlikely that examinees whose scores fall in the bottom half of the distribution would have reached the multiplication and division questions.

Assembly, Form AA (10 minutes): Requires the visualization of how an object would appear after it is assembled from a set of separate parts.

Components, Form AA (10 minutes): Assesses ability to locate a simple geometric shape embedded in a more complex design.

Coordination, Form A (5 minutes): Assesses arm and hand coordination by having the examinee trace a path with a pencil.

Electronics, Form AA (15 minutes): Designed to assess knowledge of electrical and electronics principles.

Expression, Form A (5 minutes): Assesses an individual's knowledge of grammar and sentence structure and ability to express ideas in both speech and writing.

Ingenuity, Form AA (15 minutes): Attempts to measure inventive or creative skill and apparently requires a high degree of verbal fluency. Each problem consists of a paragraph that describes a problem situation, followed by five possible answers. Each answer is one or two words in length, with only the first and last letters of each word given and blanks substituted for middle letters. Examinees hypothesize a potential solution and match it to one of the answer choices.

Inspection, Form AA (5 minutes): Designed to measure ability to spot flaws or imperfections in articles.

Judgment and Comprehension, Form A (15 minutes): Attempts to measure reading with understanding, logical reasoning, and the ability to use good interpretative judgment in regard to the materials.

Mathematics and Reasoning, Form A (15 minutes): Attempts to measure knowledge of basic mathematical concepts and ability to translate ideas and operations into mathematical notations.

Mechanics, Form A (15 minutes): Attempts to measure knowledge of mechanical facts, symbols, and principles, and ability to understand mechanical relations.

Memory, Form AA (10 minutes—5 min. for memorizing the word list and 5 min. to answer questions about the memorized items.): Measures ability to remember the association of familiar words with unfamiliar (nonsense) words.

Patterns, Form A (5 minutes): Requires ability to reproduce simple pattern outlines with accuracy and precision.

Planning, Form A (15 minutes): Measures ability to plan, organize, and schedule through the use of questions that require a relatively high amount of verbal sophistication.

Precision, Form A (5 minutes): Attempts to measure ability to do precise work with small objects and involves making repetitive tracings of a small design.

Scales, Form AA (5 minutes): Assesses ability to read graphs, charts, and scales.

Tables, Form A (5 minutes): Attempts to measure an examinee's ability to read tables with speed and accuracy.

Vocabulary, Form A (5 minutes): Assesses knowledge of word meanings, especially of business and government, through the selection of synonyms. This test is presented in a clear manner, but the words chosen for the test are generally quite difficult.

Practical Applications/Uses

Unlike the case in most test batteries, the user of the FIT is expected to select a subset of the tests to match the specific requirements of each position for which personnel are being selected. The entire battery would rarely, if ever, be administered to one individual.

Some of the tests, such as Electronics and Mechanics, are designed to assess specialized skills; other tests, such as Judgment and Comprehension, Planning, and Mathematics and Reasoning, assess more general intellectual skills. Because of the diversity of the tests, the FIT is potentially useful in selecting personnel for a wide variety of occupations.

In addition to using job analysis techniques to aid in the initial selection of tests from the FIT battery, the potential user may wish to consult the extensive Science Research Associates (SRA) validity studies of 1972 and 1974. These studies include recommendations concerning the use of specific FIT subtests in selecting personnel for a number of predominately clerical and blue-collar occupations. For example, the Tables and Expression tests are recommended as useful in selecting general clerks and secretary-stenographers; the Ingenuity and Arithmetic tests for selecting claims auditors; and Patterns, Tables, Electronics, and Assembly (negatively weighted) for selecting electricians. In all, the SRA found various FIT subtests concurrently related to success in over two dozen different occupations.

Tests in the FIT battery are designed for adults and are described as self-administering, with directions and sample problems printed on each test booklet. Whether or not the examiner reads the instructions aloud is optional but preferred. Examiners are needed to time the tests and ensure that work ceases when time expires, but they are not required to have any specialized skills.

Not all of the tests are self-administering, however. The Coordination test requires that the examiner time the 30-second practice trial in addition to the regular time limit and read an additional brief statement not printed on the test form. On the Memory test the examiner not only reads the instructions (also not printed on the test booklet), but must time the five-minute memorizing period, the five-minute answer period, and one-minute sample test periods.

Most of the tests in the battery are clearly presented and easily scored. For example, on the Assembly test answers are clearly separated from one another and the answer space appears unambiguously to the upper left of each option. The answer stencil is easily positioned on the answer sheet and is easy to use. Some tests present problems for scoring. For instance, on the Arithmetic test, as on the Expression and Tables tests, positioning circles are omitted from the test booklet, requiring the scorer to determine the proper location of the stencil.

Another problem for scoring concerns error scores. For the Arithmetic, Inspection, and Tables tests the scoring procedure provided in the examiner's manual directs the scorer to reduce an examinee's score by subtracting a fraction of the number of incorrect answers given from the total number of items correctly answered. However, the industrial norms printed in the examiner's manual are based on scores determined by using the number correct only. Directions for scoring the Expression test, which are printed on the answer key, indicate that an error score can be obtained if desired, but no mention of an error score for the Expression test is made in the examiner's manual. These inconsistencies are, at best, problematic.

Two of the tests must be scored without stencils, a somewhat laborious procedure. The Coordination test is scored by scanning the traced diagrams to ensure that the examinee's pencil line did not cross outside the designated path and then counting the number of diagrams completed. The Precision test is scored by examining each of the tracings for errors.

Technical Aspects

Industrial norms were developed as part of the SRA validation studies in 1972 and 1974, and contain separate tables for majority- and minority-group workers as well as for all workers combined. Percentile and stanine norms are also provided for twelfth-grade students and males entering one university.

Because all 18 tests are speeded their reliability is difficult to assess, and the examiner's manual presents relatively little evidence concerning reliability. Most of the data that are presented concern correlations between corresponding FIT and FACT tests. These correlations range between a value of .28 for both the FIT and FACT Memory and Inspection tests to a high of .79 for the corresponding Arithmetic tests. The manual concludes that alternate-form reliability coefficients, if they were available, would be between .50 and .90. The manual also notes that cutoff scores, in which a single low score can mean that an applicant is not selected for a position, are inappropriate for tests as brief as these. A composite score in which individual test scores are summed is more appropriate.

With the exception of the Mathematics and Reasoning, Planning, and Vocabulary tests, the concurrent validity of the tests in the FIT battery was examined in the extensive SRA validity studies begun in 1969 (SRA, 1972; 1974). The criterion used in the SRA validity studies was the performance ranking of each employee in a job category by his or her immediate supervisor. Employees ranked in the top or bottom 25% were given an experimental test battery, and then point biserial correlations were calculated between the test scores and the criterion. For each job category a table is provided that lists each test administered in the experimental battery, its correlation with the criterion, and the raw score mean and standard deviation. When the number of minority-group workers in an occupation permitted, separate minority-group results were published. The examiner's manual (Flanagan, 1975) contains a summary of the results of the validity studies.

Also presented in the validity studies are the results of analyses designed to identify, for each job category, the subset of tests that comprise the smallest, most efficient predictive battery. When the number of subjects in a job category was sufficiently large a cross-validation analysis was performed. Many of the multiple correlations derived from the cross-validation group are similar to the values obtained in the original validation analysis, but some of the cross-validation coefficients are of a low positive or negative value. Additionally, the validation study (SRA, 1972) included the FACT Mechanics test instead of the FIT version. The FACT Mechanics test did seem to be useful in identifying positions such as successful electricians and heavy equipment operators, but the correlation between the FIT Mechanics test and the FACT Mechanics test, as reported in the FIT examiner's manual, is .59. What holds for the FACT Mechanics test may not be true for the FIT version.

Potential users are advised to read the validation data carefully and conduct their own local validation studies as soon as feasible.

Critique

A number of serious problems exist with the industrial norms. The number of examinees who took each test in the industrial validation sample varied from test to test, as did their occupations, and no norms are provided for four of the tests (Inspection, Mathematics and Reasoning, Planning, and Vocabulary). An additional problem with the industrial norms arises from the procedure used in the validation studies. Workers who ranked in the middle 50% of their job category for each company were not tested as part of the validation project. The industrial norms were therefore based only on the highest ranked 25% and the lowest ranked 25% of the workers within each job category in a company.

According to the publisher, the norms for twelfth-grade students were developed using earlier (Form A) versions of seven of the tests, although this fact is not noted in the manual. More recently collected data on twelfth-grade mean scores reported in Table 5 of the 1972 validation report often vary considerably with the score listed at the 50th percentile in the norms table. These inconsistencies underscore the manual's recommendation of the development of local norms.

There are specific problems concerning some of the tests. For instance, on both the Arithmetic test and the Scales test the answer spaces are separated from the corresponding answers; this increases the clerical and perceptual burden put on the examinees in marking the correct answer.

The Inspection test has a crowded appearance on the page. The answer space, which is always to the lower right of the object it marks, is sometimes physically closer to the next drawing in the row. As the test progresses, examinees can become confused as to which item an answer space refers and may lose time or points as a result.

Although drawings appearing on the Assembly test are clearly reproduced, letters that indicate the positioning of corresponding parts are overly reduced and are sometimes difficult to read. A similar problem exists on the Mechanics test, where the identifying letters and labels on two diagrams are also overly reduced in size, making the letters on one virtually illegible.

The Electronics test has two problems that may compromise its utility. A substantial portion of the questions on the test deal with electricity, not electronics, and the test was written prior to the advent of integrated circuits. Potential users would be advised to examine the contents of the test prior to its local adoption.

In general, the Flanagan Industrial Tests are a potentially useful battery of tests. The tests vary in quality, and the norms leave much to be desired. Nevertheless, deficiencies in the norms are mitigated somewhat by the SRA validation studies, thus giving the local user a basis for test selection and a foundation for a local validation study.

References

Flanagan, J. C. (1953). *The Flanagan Aptitude Classification Tests.* Chicago: Science Research Associates.

Flanagan, J. C. (1954). The critical incident technique. *Psychological Bulletin, 51, 327-358.*

Flanagan, J. C. (1975). *Flanagan Industrial Tests examiner's manual.* Chicago: Science Research Associates.

Science Research Associates. (1972). *Validation: Procedures and results. II. Results from SRA test validation studies.* Chicago: Author.

Science Research Associates. (1974). *Validation: Procedures and results. III. Supplementary results.* Chicago: Author.

P. G. Aaron, Ph.D.

Professor of Educational and School Psychology, Indiana State University, Terre Haute, Indiana.

THE FLORIDA KINDERGARTEN SCREENING BATTERY

Paul Satz and Jack Fletcher. Odessa, Florida: Psychological Assessment Resources, Inc.

Introduction

The Florida Kindergarten Screening Battery (FKSB) is a brief screening device that was designed to detect early learning disabilities; attempts to predict the likelihood that an individual kindergartner will manifest reading problems three years later, at the end of Grade 2; and is used to predict the reading performance of the child in Grade 5.

The authors, Paul Satz and Jack Fletcher, are well known for their large scale longitudinal study of reading disabilities in very young children. The FKSB is a by-product of the Florida Longitudinal Project which followed 497 white male kindergarten children who represented almost all kindergarten age boys in Alachua County, Florida. Results of the six-year follow-up of this study are available (Satz, Taylor, Friel, & Fletcher, 1978). The project was initiated in 1970 and the prediction studies reported in the test manual were carried out in two stages, once in 1973 when these children reached the end of Grade 2 and again in 1976, when they were in Grade 5. Even though the FKSB is primarily intended for kindergarten-aged white, male children, cross validation studies indicate that it could be successfully used with children from other backgrounds.

This is an individually administered test and takes about 20 minutes to administer. The examiner need not have any extensive training to administer the battery. The battery is made up of the following five tests:

1. Peabody Picture Vocabulary Test (Dunn, 1965)
2. Recognition-Discrimination (Small, 1969)
3. Beery Visual-Motor Integration (Beery & Butenica, 1967)
4. Alphabet Recitation
5. Finger Localization Test (Benton, 1959)

The test comes in the form of a kit that includes a small manual, recording forms, Recognition-Discrimination test and a cardboard-cloth shield for the Finger Localization test. The manual is easy to follow and a considerable portion of the manual is devoted to the description of the standardization procedures.

The battery uses the older version of the Peabody Picture Vocabulary Test (PPVT) (Dunn, 1965), and if the revised form is used, the score used for prediction should be the equivalent score for the PPVT older version. These converted scores

288

can be obtained from the PPVT-R manual. The Recognition-Discrimination task requires the child to identify a geometric stimulus design among a group of four figures, three of which were rotated and one similar in shape to the stimulus figure. The Beery Visual-Motor Integration Test is an age-normed, perceptual-motor copying task. The Alphabet Recitation task requires the child to name as many letters of the alphabet as he can, and this becomes his score, regardless of the order of recitation. The Finger Localization task represents the neuropsychological component of the battery and is made up of five subtests, such as naming the fingers touched by the examiner, identifying the touched fingers on a corresponding diagram, and recalling the number of fingers touched. The fingers are stimulated by the examiner behind a screen so that the child cannot see which fingers were touched.

The battery is administered individually in a single session. The scores obtained by the child on each of the five tests are multiplied by a weight that is provided in the manual, and the product is added to a constant. The resultant score determines in which one of the four groups of reading ability the child will fall when he will be at the end of Grade 2 or Grade 5. The four reading ability groups are: severe, mild, average, superior. The administration of the battery and the interpretation of the scores are, therefore, simple and straightforward.

Practical Applications/Uses

The battery is useful in predicting the future reading performance of children entering Kindergarten. The test is particularly helpful by providing objective data where decisions regarding the promotion or detention of the child at the end of the kindergarten year have to be made.

The FKSB was designed to create an early warning index of risk for reading disabilities. The validation studies show that this goal has been accomplished. Assuming that early identification and intervention would reduce the incidence of reading difficulties later in school, the FKSB will provide a much needed service.

But will it do a better job than the kindergarten teacher in predicting reading achievement? The authors themselves have addressed this question by asking kindergarten teachers at the end of the year to predict the future reading performance of the children in their classes. When the accuracy of teacher prediction was compared with that of the battery, it was found that the hit rates of both approaches were comparable (74 and 75%, respectively). Teacher prediction, however, failed to identify a large number of future cases of severe reading disability. This, in addition to the fact that the battery can be administered early in the kindergarten year, whereas teacher prediction has to wait several months, places the FKSB in an advantageous position. Furthermore, the potential variability among teachers in their predictive ability would make the FKSB a preferred instrument.

The FKSB serves as an early warning device and permits early detection of high-risk children. It should be mentioned, however, that this test is intended to predict only the reading performance of the child and not any other aspect of his learning ability. The FKSB is designed to be a screening device and is not intended to be used as a diagnostic instrument.

Technical Aspects

The major strength of the FKSB lies in the sound standardization procedures adopted in developing the test.

The test was standardized on a population of 497 white male boys from Florida who were entering kindergarten in 1970. With the exception of about 10%, all of the boys came from middle-class or upper-class homes. An additional 181 kindergarten white boys were utilized in 1971 for cross validation purposes. A third group of 132 children (13 black boys, 15 black girls, 54 white boys, 50 white girls) was also used for a second cross validation study.

A battery of 13 neuropsychological and cognitive tests was administered at the beginning of Kindergarten to the 497 children. Subsequently, reading achievement was assessed when these children were at the end of Grade 2 and again at the end of Grade 5. Reading achievement was derived by using two indices: 1) instructional book level, which actually refers to the book level (preprimer, primer, etc.) the child was in, and 2) IOTA word reading test (in Grade 2) or Reading Recognition, Spelling, and Arithmetic subtests of the Wide Range Achievement Test (in Grade 5). By combining these two indices, the authors classified the children into the following four reading ability groups: severely disabled, mildly disabled, average, and superior readers.

The next step in the standardization procedure was to examine the 13 variables to see which one of them correlated highly with (or predicted) reading achievement. Using multivariate statistical procedures, the authors then selected the optimal predictors and eliminated tests that correlated poorly with reading achievement. This procedure yielded five tests which, when administered as a battery at the beginning of Kindergarten were found to successfully predict 75% of reading failure cases at Grade 2 and 72% at Grade 5. These five tests constitute the current battery.

The authors have provided information on construct validity and predictive validity. Construct validity was determined by factor analyzing the scores obtained on 14 variables (the 13 neuropsychological-cognitive tests and SES). This yielded three factors which were interpreted as 1) sensori-motor perceptual, 2) verbal-conceptual, and 3) verbal cultural. According to the authors, these represent measures of language and nonlanguage factors that make up reading skill.

The authors were concerned more with predictive validity than with construct validity. Predictive validity was determined by first classifying the second-grade children into four reading ability groups and then by seeing, with the aid of Discriminant Function Analysis, how successfully the battery could separate the four reading ability groups. It was found that, at the second-grade level, the battery could correctly classify about 75% of the children according to their reading ability. The battery, however, missed 12 out of 143 below-average readers (false negatives) and misclassified 26 of the 213 average readers as high risks (false positives). At the end of Grade 5, similar results were obtained. While the battery held up fairly well at both extremes, it did not perform quite as well in correctly predicting reading achievement of slightly below-average readers.

The real test of any battery of this kind is the cross validation procedure when predictions are made on a sample that is independent of the original population on which standardization was based. This avoids the elements of circularity involved in the original validation process. The cross validation study was carried out by administering the battery to 181 white kindergarten boys in 1971, making predictions, and then seeing how accurate these predictions were regarding the reading achievement of these boys three years hence. It was found that the battery could correctly classify 74% of the children. Another cross validation study was carried out on a racially mixed group of 132 boys and girls. The hit rate again was 75%.

The reliability scores are reported independently for the five tests in the battery. All are within acceptable range with the exception of two tasks in the Finger Localization Test which showed some inconsistencies.

Critique

How does the battery compare with other instruments that are designed for similar purposes? A number of Reading Readiness tests are available but few of them are based on rigorous standardization procedures. One assessment instrument that is comparable in rigor and scope is the battery developed by DeHirsch, Jansky, and Langford (1966) and later revised by Jansky and DeHirsch (1972). The original battery assessed 53 kindergarten children (mostly lower middle-class and racially mixed) on 37 variables and followed the children through Grade 2 at which time standardized reading and spelling tests were administered. On the basis of rank order correlations obtained between the 37 variables and reading, these authors identified 10 variables that made up a predictive index. This index correctly identified 10 of the 11 poor readers (91%); there were 4 instances of false positives (8%) and 1 case of false negative (9%). The revised battery was standardized on a much larger population (401 kindergarten children). With the aid of stepwise multiple linear equation technique, Jansky and DeHirsch identified 5 tests that made up the Screening Index. The Screening Index was able to identify more than 75% of the kindergarten children who eventually failed in reading at the end of the second grade. The Jansky-DeHirsch battery also used preexisting tests such as the Bender Gestalt. Thus, in many respects, the FKSB and the Jansky-DeHirsch batteries are comparable. It is interesting to note that even though the two batteries do not have any subtest in common, both batteries tend to assess two areas: perceptual-motor and language. The Jansky-DeHirsch battery is more loaded with language ability than the FKSB. The FKSB, on the other hand, has a neuropsychological component in the form of the Finger Localization Test. Even though it is possible to arrive at a predictive index without using the Finger Localization Test, the authors suggest that its inclusion will result in improved predictions. Comparison of tables of predictive validity that were arrived at with and without the Finger Localization Test does not show substantial change in the predictive ability of the battery.

The major strengths of the FKSB include the ease of administration and the sound standardization procedures utilized in developing the test. Additionally, it also comes in the form of a packaged kit. The weakness of the test shows up in its relatively inferior performance in making accurate predictions at the mild-risk range. The test will help decision-making procedure at the end of kindergarten year to be a reasonably objective process.

References

Beery, K., & Buktenica, N. A. (1967). *Developmental Test of Visual-Motor Integration.* Chicago: Follet Educational Co.

Benton, A. L. (1959). *Right-left discrimination and finger localization: Development and pathology.* New York: Hoeber-Harper.

DeHirsch, K., Jansky, J. J., & Langford, W. S. (1966). *Predicting Reading Failure.* New York: Harper & Row.

Dunn, L. (1965). *Peabody Picture Vocabulary Test.* Circle Pines, MN: American Guidance Service.

Jansky, J. J., & DeHirsch, K. (1972). *Preventing reading failure.* New York: Harper & Row.

Satz, P., Taylor, H. G., Friel, J., & Fletcher, J. M. (1978). Some developmental and predictive precursors of reading disabilities: A six year follow-up. In A. L. Benton & D. Pearl (Eds.), *Dyslexia: An appraisal of current knowledge.* New York: Oxford University Press.

Small, N. (1969). *Levels of perceptual functioning in children: A developmental study.* Unpublished master's thesis, University of Florida, Gainesville.

David S. Goh, Ph.D.
Professor and Director, School Psychology Program, Department of Educational Psychology, Southern Illinois University, Carbondale, Illinois.

Mark E. Swerdlik, Ph.D.
Associate Professor of Psychology, Illinois State University, Normal, Illinois.

FROSTIG DEVELOPMENTAL TEST OF VISUAL PERCEPTION

Marianne Frostig and Associates. Palo Alto, California: Consulting Psychologists Press, Inc.

Introduction

The Frostig Developmental Test of Visual Perception (DTVP) is a test designed to assess visual perceptual skills in children. It provides information that includes 1) an estimation of the overall visual perception ability of the child and 2) a delimitation of the distinct visual perception difficulties in need of training. Despite some conflicting research findings, the DTVP has become one of the better known instruments in the evaluation of visual perception difficulties in young children.

The DTVP was developed by Marianne Frostig, Phyllis Maslow, Welty Lefever, and John R. B. Whittlesey. Frostig, the primary author of the test, is the founder of the Marianne Frostig School of Educational Therapy in Los Angeles. Her work in visual perception has gained national recognition. Frostig maintains that there is a positive relationship between perceptual development and school learning and adjustment. Children with perceptual impairments often show difficulties in learning. She further postulates that perceptual development necessary for academic learning takes place between the ages of 3 to 7 years. If development in visual perception during this period is hindered, cognitive deficits will result. Therefore, she maintains, tests should be developed to facilitate the early identification of problems in visual perception. Frostig also makes the assumption that after these visual perception deficits are identified by tests such as the DTVP, a specific training program should be developed to aid in overcoming these disabilities.

The actual development of the DTVP was preceded by several year's observations of children who were referred to the Marianne Frostig School of Education Therapy because of learning difficulties. Based on these clinical observations, as well as the findings of others, Frostig theorized that visual perception consists of five distinct functions that are relatively independent of one another. Accordingly, she set out to construct a test that would effectively measure these five functions

293

or abilities. The construction of DTVP test items began in 1958. Item analyses were performed to arrange items along an easy-to-difficult continuum. Two preliminary versions were prepared, before the test was published in 1961.

The DTVP was standardized based on 2,116 normal school children between the ages of 3-9 years enrolled in nursery and public school in Southern California. Between 107 and 240 children were included at each half-year interval. As the authors have candidly pointed out in the manual, this standardization sample was unselected and not representative. The sample was chosen for three main considerations: the attempt to get a stratified socioeconomic sample of children, the willingness of the school to cooperate, and the proximity to the research center. As a result, the sample was drawn from a restricted area and was predominantly middle class (93%) in nature. Children from low socioeconomic groups and generally minority groups were poorly represented with only a small number of Chicanos and even fewer Orientals included. No black children were represented. In addition to the geographical, racial, and social class restrictions of the DTVP sample, little other demographic information is presented about the sample or sampling procedures. For example, sex, grade, parental occupation, and their educational attainment for the subjects included in the standardization sample are not provided. Thus, the standardization sample represents a major weakness of the test.

Since its publication in 1961, the DTVP has seen two revisions. The test materials have not been modified since 1964, but the administration and scoring manual was revised in 1966. No other forms of the test for special handicapped groups or minority groups have been developed.

The DTVP materials included a manual that contains instructions for administration and scoring, a technical monograph that includes test construction and standardization data, and a 35-page consumable test booklet. The back cover of the test booklet serves as a scoring sheet. In addition, there are 11 demonstration cards and three transparent scoring stencils.

The five DTVP subtests are presumed to measure five distinct subareas of visual perception:

1. *Eye Motor Coordination:* consist of 16 items involving the drawing of continuous straight, curved, or angled lines between boundaries of various widths or from point to point without guidelines. This subtest assesses the ability to integrate vision with movement of the body, particularly with fine visual motor skills necessary for success with pencil-and-paper activities.

2. *Figure Ground:* consists of 8 items involving shifts in perception of figures against increasingly complex backgrounds (intersecting and "hidden" geometric forms are used). This subtest investigates the ability to select from a mass of stimuli a particular center of attention and to ignore the rest of the stimuli.

3) *Constancy of Shape:* consists of 32 items requiring the recognition of certain geometric figures presented in a variety of sizes, shadings, textures, and positions in space, and their discrimination from similar geometric figures (circles, squares, rectangles, ellipses, and parallelograms are used). This subtest assesses the ability to recognize that a figure may vary in size, texture, or position without altering its basic form.

4) *Position in Space:* consists of 8 items involving the discrimination of reversals and rotations of figures presented in a series (schematic drawings representing common objects are used). This subtest assesses the ability to distinguish a particular form from other figures as it is presented in an identical, rotated, or reversed position.

5) *Spatial Relationships:* consists of 8 items that require the analysis of simple forms and patterns consisting of lines of various lengths and angles that the child is required to copy using dots as guide points. This subtest assesses the ability to perceive the position of two or more objects in relation to oneself and to each other.

The five subtests were selected based on Frostig's contention that each of them measures a rather distinct area of visual perceptual functioning. While she acknowledges that other abilities also are involved in the total process of visual perception, Frostig maintains the five types of skills selected for the DTVP have particular relevance to school learning. Disturbance in these areas are often related to poor performance in reading, writing, word recognition, etc. Moreover, Frostig asserts that training in these areas is very frequently successful.

Practical Application/Uses

Frostig indicates that the DTVP is intended to be an individually or group administered test that provides normative age data, and differentiates various kinds of perceptual abilities and disabilities. The test is designed for children between the ages of 4 to 8 years but it can also be used for older children who appear to have visual perception difficulties or suffer from learning difficulties; for adult victims of stroke or other brain injury (although some modification of scoring procedures is necessary); and as a screening device for nursery school, kindergarten, and first-grade children. In addition, the test can be used for research purposes to explore the relationship of visual perceptual disabilities to problems of school learning and adjustment, brain damage, and other handicaps.

Although the DTVP is designed for normal children, it can be administered to hearing impaired and non-English-speaking subjects by utilizing the proper adaptation of the manual with additional demonstration items available from the publisher. Further, it may also be used with other handicapped or disturbed children, but the examiner must use clinical judgment in assessing these children. The test would not be appropriate for children with motor impairments affecting the use of their dominant hand.

The DTVP is an untimed test that can be administered to a group or individually. It should be administered by a trained and experienced individual, such as a school psychologist. The authors urge that the test not be administered by regular classroom teachers and provide formal examiner training requirements in the manual. Individual administration of the test usually requires approximately 30-45 minutes and group testing requires 60 minutes or less. The number of items given in each subtest depends on the subject's grade level. Handicapped or disturbed children should be administered the test individually. The test is fairly easy to administer. Rules for administration are provided in the manual with alternative wording enclosed in parentheses and additional explanations that can be given to the subject marked "optional." It is permissible for the examiner to repeat instructions.

Instructions for scoring are clearly presented in the manual. The test can be scored with a fairly high degree of objectivity, although there are occasional situations where clinical judgment should be exercised. Procedures for scoring and specific examples are also provided. The test is hand-scored and usually takes approximately 5-10 minutes. The scoring sheet for entering and recording scores on individual items is at the back of the test booklet. Except for subtest #2, all test items are scored 0, 1, or 2 points. Raw scores are obtained for each of the five subtests and then converted to Age Equivalents or Perceptual Ages (PAs) and Scale Scores (SSs). Raw Score conversion directions and tables are provided in the manual for these transformations. The total test results are expressed in Perceptual Quotient (PQ) and percentile rank scores.

The manual does not provide specific information regarding the interpretation of the DTVP results, except for some simple explanations of the four types of scores. PA and PQ are the most useful in interpreting the test results. While PA indicates the developmental level of children, PQ (with a median of 100 and a quartile deviation of 10) is interpreted as an index of the children's level of perceptual ability when compared to their agemates. The manual also suggests a cutoff score of 90 and that children with a PQ below 90 should receive special training. However, no further information or discussion about this cutoff score is provided.

Concerns have been raised about the various scores yielded by the DTVP. The Scale Scores are not typical standard scores with a predetermined mean and standard deviation. Rather, they represent a ratio score obtained by dividing the Perceptual Ages by the subject's chronological age and multiplying the total by 10; Scale Scores are then rounded to the nearest whole number. Because the SS is a ratio score, different means and standard deviations at various ages occur. As a consequence it can cause teachers and others much confusion (Mann, 1972). The PQ has been criticized as being too global a score, giving users the impression that it is fixed and unaffected by experience. A number of inconsistencies can also be found in the scoring procedures, which can lead to confusion. For example, it is possible for a subject who earns less than the maximum PA to have a higher score with a resulting higher PQ as compared to a subject who earns a maximum PA. Raw scores and Scale Scores can therefore be inversely related resulting in a ceiling effect (Salvia & Ysseldyke, 1978).

Technical Aspects

The authors report three test-retest reliability studies in the standardization monograph. The studies employed unspecified learning disabled students, and first- and second-graders. Sample sizes were relatively small. The reliability coefficients based on two- to three-week intervals for the total test (PQ) ranged from .69 to .98. Test-retest reliability coefficients for the subtests (SS) were lower, ranging from .29 (Subtest 1) to .80 (Subtest 3), with most coefficients falling in the .50-.60 range. Split-half reliability was also reported based on 1,459 subjects in four age groups (5 years or older). Reliability coefficients for the total test ranged from .78 (8-9 years) to .89 (5-6 years). A pattern of an inverse relationship between age and reliability exists. Coefficients for the DTVP subtests ranged from .35 to .96, with The Figure Ground subtest (2) showing the highest reliability (.91-.96) and The Position in Space subtest (4) showing the lowest reliability (.35-.70).

The authors reported two validity studies based on the 1961 standardization. Correlations between scores on the DTVP and teacher ratings of classroom adjustment, motor coordination, and intellectual functioning were .44, .50 and .50, respectively. Correlations between scores on the DTVP and the Goodenough Draw-A-Man Test ranged from .32 to .46 for Kindergartners and first- and second-graders. The authors did not perform any factor analysis on the DTVP. Factor analytic studies reported by other researchers (e.g., Corah & Powell, 1963; Ohlmacht & Olson, 1968; Sprague, 1963) have indicated that a single perceptual factor exists rather than five independent factors represented by each subtest. This suggests that the PQ is a valid overall measure of visual perception but the DTVP's ability to differentially assess specific areas of visual perception is questionable. There is also little evidence the DTVP scales predict specific reading deficits.

Further, although the authors suggest that a SS of less than 8 on any DTVP subtest or a PQ of 90 or lower necessitates the remediation of a perceptual motor deficit by special training programs, no validity evidence exists to support these cutoff points. In addition, there is no clear cause and effect relationship between DTVP performance and school achievement; there is only a correlational relationship between scores on the DTVP and teacher ratings.

Critique

The DTVP has a number of merits and limitations. In general, it can provide useful information about visual-perceptual development for children ages 4-8. The test is fairly easy to administer. The test booklet is well-organized and no other materials are needed. The instructions for administration are clear and generally adequate. For clinical evaluation, only individual administration should be used. Group administration, however, may be useful for research or program evaluation purposes. Some concerns have been raised that the required administration time might to too long for younger children (Anderson, 1965; Austin, 1965). However, this should not present a serious problem for the skilled examiner, as the subtests can be given with breaks between or at different sittings. The procedures for scoring are generally clearly presented and illustrative examples are provided. This serves to greatly reduce scoring errors and thereby increase test score reliability. The global test score, the PQ, has been shown by research as a valid measure of overall visual perception. Further, a remedial program has been developed to accompany the DTVP and provides materials to work on skills after visual perception difficulty has been diagnosed.

Several limitations of the DTVP are also noted. A major problem lies with the nonrepresentativeness of the standardization sample. This severely limits the DTVP's usefulness with minority groups, as well as other low SES or handicapped individuals. The reliability and validity data presented in the manual are insufficient and sometimes inadequate. Although the internal consistency of the DTVP is adequate, some of the reliabilities reported at the subtest level were quite low.

Further, the sample size used to derive the reliability coefficients were rather small. The authors did not present data to support Frostig's contention that the five subtests indeed measure five distinct and somewhat independent abilities. Research available in the professional literature shows that the subtests in themselves cannot be considered indicators of specific deficits. Users of the DTVP should be extremely cautious in the interpretation and diagnostic use of subtest scores as they cannot be used for differential diagnosis related to specific subareas of visual perception as suggested by the test authors. Although the accompanied remedial program places a meaningful emphasis in combining diagnosis and intervention in one continuum, the actual effectiveness of the program remains questionable. Due to the lack of validity evidence, low scores on the DTVP should not be a signal to begin perceptual training. Nevertheless, the DTVP can be useful as a part of a larger assessment battery to raise hypotheses related to the subject's overall visual-perceptual skill development.

References

Anderson, J. M. (1965). Tests and reviews. In O. K. Buros (Ed.). *The fifth mental measurements yearbook.* Highland Park, NJ: The Gryphon Press.

Austin, M. C. (1965). Tests and reviews. In O. K. Buros (Ed.). *The fifth mental measurements yearbook.* Highland Park, NJ: The Gryphon Press.

Corah, N. H., & Powell, B. J. (1963). A factor analytic study of the Frostig Developmental Test of Visual Perception. *Perceptual and Motor Skills, 16,* 59-63.

Frostig, M., Maslow, P., Lefever, D. W., & Whittlesey, J. R. B. (1961). *The Frostig Developmental Test of Visual Perception.* Palo Alto, CA: Consulting Psychologists Press.

Frostig, M., Maslow, P., Lefever, D. W., & Whittlesey, J. R. B. (1964). *The Frostig Developmental Test of Visual Perception: 1963 standardization.* Palo Alto, CA: Consulting Psychologists Press.

Frostig, M., Lefever, D. W., & Whittlesey, J. R. B. (1966). *Administration and Scoring Manual for the Frostig Developmental Test of Visual Perception.* Palo Alto, CA: Consulting Psychologists Press.

Kephart, N. C. (1972). Review of the Developmental Test of Visual Perception. In O. K. Buros (Ed.). *The seventh mental measurements yearbook.* Highland Park, NJ: The Gryphon Press.

Mann, L. (1972). Review of the Developmental Test of Visual Perception. In O. K. Buros (Ed.). *The seventh mental measurements yearbook.* Highland Park, NJ: The Gryphon Press.

Ohlmacht, F. W., & Olson, A. V. (1968). Canonical analysis of reading readiness measures and the Frostig Developmental Test of Visual Perception. *Educational and Psychological Measurement, 28,* 479-484.

Salvia, J., & Ysseldyke, J. E. (1978). *Assessment of special and remedial education.* Boston: Houghton Mifflin Co.

Sprague, R. (1963). *Learning difficulties of first-grade children diagnosed by the Frostig visual perception tests: A factor analytic study.* Unpublished doctoral dissertation, Wayne State University, Detroit.

Michael Bradley, Ed.D.

Professor of Psychology, University of North Carolina, Wilmington, North Carolina.

FULL-RANGE PICTURE VOCABULARY TEST

Robert B. Ammons and Helen S. Ammons. Missoula, Montana: Psychological Test Specialists.

Introduction

The Full-Range Picture Vocabulary Test (FRPV) is a relatively brief nonverbal assessment of word recognition. It can be used to determine the recognition vocabulary of preschool and school-aged children, adults, psychiatric patients, the mentally retarded, physically handicapped, and those with speech and communication disorders.

Robert B. Ammons and Helen S. Ammons developed the FRPV in 1948. At that time, there were no short and valid assessments of verbal ability that did not require reading, writing, or speaking. The authors believed that because vocabulary assessment correlated highly with intellectual ability there was a need for a brief method of testing this ability in specific nonverbal populations such as spastic children and aphasic adults.

Ammons and Huth (1949) prepared a preliminary set of test items using 16 stimulus plates based on the Van Alstyne Picture Vocabulary Test for Preschool Children. Out of the original 291 test items, 248 items were retained after 43 were eliminated because of ambiguity and sex differences in the responses. These 248 remaining items were then administered in a pretest validation check. Twenty-two additional items were eliminated, and the rest of the items were arranged in order of difficulty. These 226 items were then used with 589 subjects between the ages of 2-34 years. On the basis of this standardization test, 56 items were rejected because of discrimination in percent passing between successive age levels, regional bias, sex differences in difficulty, ambiguity of denotation, poor discrimination of various age levels, or duplication of words. The remaining 170 items were then divided into alternate forms A and B with each having equal length and level of difficulty (Ammons & Rachiele, 1950).

Ammons and Holmes (1949) used both forms to develop norms for preschool children 2-5 years of age, with Ammons, Arnold, and Herrman (1950) producing norms for school children. Ammons, Larson, and Shearn (1950) then developed the adult norms while Ammons and Manahan (1950) developed them for a rural population and Ammons and Aquero (1950) developed them for the school-age, Spanish-American population. Coppinger and Ammons (1952) completed the test by devising norms for black children. The only subsequent revision has been the Ammons Quick Test, which has only one plate per form and therefore fewer stimulus materials.

The stimulus materials for the Full-Range Picture Vocabulary Test, Forms A & B, consist of 16 plates, each of which contain four ink-line drawings that are similar either in subject matter or appearance. The test items are various words referring to these pictures and are arranged by plates that are presented in approximate order of difficulty. Answer sheets for each form include tables to convert the raw scores to mental ages, which are to be interpreted like Revised Stanford-Binet mental ages. Wechsler-type norms to convert raw scores to deviation IQs are also included, as well as a brief manual with instructions on administration, scoring, and interpretation.

In administering the test, the examiner converses casually with the testee in an attempt to gain rapport and alleviate any anxiety which may be present. The examinee is then asked which of the four pictures on a stimulus plate best illustrates a word given by the examiner. The examinee is asked to respond simply by pointing, nodding, or gesturing. Instructions not to guess are given and the examiner should present the same word again later in the test if guessing is suspected. The presentation of the stimulus is varied to help maintain motivation and, if necessary, easy words not actually on the test may be presented to stimulate responses. Words on a particular card are given until three levels are passed consecutively and three failed. The items answered correctly for each card are counted and passes for all cards are totaled with the resulting mental age or IQ obtained from the sheet of norms.

Practical Applications/Uses

The Full-Range Picture Vocabulary Test may be used as a screening tool of verbal ability for anyone needing such an instrument. It is particularly useful for assessing those who have communication difficulties such as the speech impaired and those with severe physical handicaps such as the cerebral palsied. The simplicity of the task directions also make it especially useful for those with limited comprehension.

The FRPV is designed to produce a rapid estimate of verbal ability of both adults and children. It is a verbal recognition test in which the response may be either verbal or nonverbal. It appears to measure receptive vocabulary, aural-visual association, and general language comprehension. Factor analytic studies indicate loadings on a vocabulary or verbal comprehension factor rather than a more abstract verbal concept formation factor (Osborne, 1964, 1965, 1966). Though originally designed as a rapid assessment of verbal ability, it soon became used as a quick measure of both verbal and general intelligence. This was an invalid and dangerous generalization as the FRPV measures a much more limited behavior sample than any measure of intelligence.

The FRPV can be used by psychologists, counselors, and educators assessing those afflicted with speech and/or physical handicaps. It has been used by psychiatrists in evaluating schizophrenics because it seems to be less affected by the deterioration process. It is used by mental health professionals, such as psychiatrists, psychologists, social workers, and counselors, as well as speech clinicians, rehabilitation counselors, and educators. However, there seems to be little potential for new uses of the FRPV due to its age and lack of revision.

There are very few populations with which this test cannot be used. It is appropriate for any subjects who can receive the stimulus words aurally or through sign language and respond orally or by simply nodding, pointing, or "eye-blink" response. This allows the test to be used with normals and almost all special populations except the blind.

The test is an individual one and can be administered by anyone able to follow the relatively simple directions, but familiarity with testing procedures in general and/or individual testing would be beneficial. There is no testing manual, only a plate with directions and accompanying forms for scoring and determining the mental ages and/or IQs. Eight journal articles are proposed as a provisional manual for the FRPV but must be obtained individually by the user or ordered as a set from the publisher. Testing time is relatively brief and would normally take about 10-15 minutes. Scoring is rather simple, and it normally takes only a few minutes to add the scores and look up the mental ages or IQs in the norms tables. Machine-scoring is not available and generally not needed. Interpretation of the test is based on objective scores that are transformed into Stanford-Binet type mental ages, then changed into ratio IQs through the $\frac{MA}{CA}$ X 100 formula. Wechsler-type deviation IQs may be found even easier by using the norms provided to transform the raw scores. Interpretation of these scores needs to be done by someone familiar with mental age and deviation IQ concepts. Care should also be taken not to overgeneralize the results because of the somewhat misleading mental age and IQ labels.

Technical Aspects

The validity of the Full-Range Picture Vocabulary Test seems to be adequate, using such measures as the Stanford-Binet, WISC, WAIS, and various achievement measures. Correlations generally run in the .70s and .80s with those for the WISC running slightly lower in the .60s and .70s. Correlations in the .40s have been found with college students, which suggests it is more suitable for those of average or below average intelligence than those of superior intelligence. Reliability studies consistently report correlation in the .70s and .80s, which indicates sufficient consistency. Dunn and Harley (1959) report a reliability of .86, which they deemed adequate to justify the FRPV's use with cerebral palsied children. Morgan (1960) reports IQ Rho's of .87 for average and high IQ groups and .80 for slow learners. All validity data, reliability data, and pertinent reports can be found referenced in Ammons and Ammons (1977a, 1977b).

Critique

The Full-Range Picture Vocabulary Test is a technically adequate test of receptive language but suffers from problems that have existed since its development. It still needs a suitable manual, the stimulus plates would be better presented in a bound arrangement, and revision, with the norms updated, should be undertaken. These changes may not have been made because the Peabody Picture Vocabulary Test seems to have become the test of choice where the FRPV was applicable. Of course, we will never know if changes in the FRPV would have reversed its demise because they never occurred.

References

Ammons, R. B., & Ammons, C. H. (1977a). Use and evaluation of Full-Range Picture Vocabulary Test: Partial summary through March, 1976: I. Published papers. *Perceptual and Motor Skills, 45,* 999-1002.

Ammons, R. B., & Ammons, C. H. (1977b). Use and evaluation of Full-Range Picture Vocabulary Test: Partial summary through March, 1976: II. Reviews, theses, reports at meetings. *Perceptual and Motor Skills, 45,* 1021-1022.

Ammons, R. B., & Aquerro, A. (1950). The Full-Range Picture Vocabulary Test: VII. Results for a Spanish-American school-age population. *Journal of Social Psychology, 32,* 3-10.

Ammons, R. B., Arnold, P. R., & Herrmann, R. S. (1950). The Full-Range Picture Vocabulary Test: IV. Results for a white school population. *Journal of Clinical Psychology, 6,* 164-169.

Ammons, R. B., & Holmes, J. C. (1949). The Full-Range Picture Vocabulary Test: III. Results for a preschool-age population. *Child Development, 20,* 5-14.

Ammons, R. B., & Huth, R. W. (1949). The Full-Range Picture Vocabulary Test: I. Preliminary scale. *Journal of Psychology, 28,* 51-64.

Ammons, R. B., Larson, W. L., & Shearn, C. R. (1950). The Full-Range Picture Vocabulary Test: V. Results for an adult population. *Journal of Consulting Psychology, 14,* 150-155.

Ammons, R. B., & Manahan, N. (1950). The Full-Range Picture Vocabulary Test: VI. Results for a rural population. *Journal of Educational Research, 44,* 14-21.

Ammons, R. B., & Rachiele, L. D. (1950). The Full-Range Picture Vocabulary Test: II. Selection of items for final scales. *Educational and Psychological Measurements, 10,* 307-319.

Coppinger, N. W., & Ammons, R. B. (1952). The Full-Range Picture Vocabulary Test: VIII. A normative study of Negro children. *Journal of Clinical Psychology, 8,* 136-140.

Dunn, L. M., & Harley, R. K. (1959). Comparability of the Peabody, Ammons, Van Alstyne and Columbia test scores with cerebral palsied children. *Exceptional Children, 26,* 70-74.

Morgan, E. F., Jr. (1960). Efficacy of two tests in differentiating potentially low from average and high first grade achievers. *Journal of Educational Research, 53,* 300-304.

Osborne, R. T. (1964). WISC factor structure for normal Negro pre-school children. *Psychological Reports, 15*(2), 543-548.

Osborne, R. T. (1965). Factor structure of the Wechsler Intelligence Scale for Children at pre-school level and after first grade: A longitudinal analysis. *Psychological Reports, 16*(2), 637-644.

Osborne, R. T. (1966). Stability of factor structure of the WISC for normal Negro children from pre-school level to first grade. *Psychological Reports, 18*(2), 655-664.

David Reinking, Ph.D.
Assistant Professor of Reading, Rutgers University, New Brunswick, New Jersey.

GATES-McKILLOP-HOROWITZ READING DIAGNOSTIC TESTS

Arthur I. Gates, Anne S. McKillop, and Elizabeth Cliff.
New York: Teachers College Press.

Introduction

The Gates-McKillop-Horowitz Reading Diagnostic Tests are designed to assess strengths and weaknesses in reading and related language skills. The entire battery consists of 15 separate tests which sample the test taker's ability to read orally, apply specific word identification skills, discriminate among letters and their sounds, spell words, and write original sentences. These tests are intended for use with children in Grades 2 through 6, although they may be appropriate for children beyond Grade 6 who are experiencing serious difficulty in learning to read. Each test in the battery must be administered individually but not all of the test need be given to every child tested. The authors encourage the test administrator to be selective in choosing only those tests that will provide useful, nonredundant information about an individual child's reading performance.

The evolution of this test can be traced to the career of its first author. The late Arthur I. Gates was a dominant force in the field of reading and his Gates Diagnostic Reading Tests represented one of the first attempts to create a formal diagnostic instrument in reading. Publication of the original test battery in 1926 and the subsequent Gates-McKillop Reading Diagnostic Tests in 1962 preceded the version reviewed here. McKillop and Horowitz both became involved with updating earlier versions of the test at Teachers College, Columbia University, where Gates spent most of his career.

Although these tests have been periodically updated, their format and content have remained largely unchanged over the years. For example, of the 15 tests available in the current version 13 are almost identical to the 1962 edition of the Gates-McKillop Reading Diagnostic Tests. In the current version a writing sample has replaced an oral vocabulary test and one test has been revised to include an untimed reading of sentences instead of a timed reading of phrases. In addition, the current version has one form instead of the two parallel forms previously available.

Test materials for this battery consists of a booklet containing items and activities presented to the child taking the tests, a pupil record book used to record the child's responses and make notations, and a manual of directions which also contains normative and interpretive information. Also included in the test booklet is a detachable card with a "window" that is used to provide a timed presentation of individual words. The pupil record book duplicates all of the stimulus material presented to the child, but provides space to record and code responses. Several checklists are also included to enable the examiner to note more subjective elements of reading performance (e.g., "Reads in a monotone."). The last two pages provide space for a written spelling test and writing sample.

The 15 tests that comprise the battery are divided into eight categories: oral reading; reading sentences; words: flash; words: untimed; knowledge of word parts: word attack; recognizing the visual forms of sounds; auditory tests; and written expression. The following skills are tested in subsections of the word attack category: syllabication, recognizing and blending common word parts, reading words, giving letter sounds, naming capital letters, and naming lower-case letters. There are two auditory tests: auditory blending and auditory discrimination. Tests for written expression include a spelling test and an informal writing sample. The individual tests in the battery are described in more detail as follows:

1. *Oral Reading.* In this test the child is asked to read a story aloud. Each of the paragraphs in the story are progressively more difficult. While the child is reading, a coding system is used to record the number and type of errors made. Reading behaviors classified as errors are hesitations (more than five seconds), omissions, additions, repetitions, mispronunciations, and self-corrections. This test is terminated if 11 or more errors are made in two consecutive paragraphs.

2. *Reading Sentences.* Oral reading errors are recorded as before while the child reads five unrelated sentences. Unlike many of the words confronted in the previous test, the words in these sentences are phonically regular.

3. *Words: Flash.* For this test the special card included with the test materials is used as a tachistoscope. The window on the card is moved quickly across words in a list so that each word is exposed for approximately one-half second. After each word has been exposed, the reader is asked to identify the word. The number of words read correctly and the nature of any errors are recorded.

4. *Words: Untimed.* A different list or words is used for this test. Unlike the previous test, as much time as necessary is allowed to identify each word, though as before words are progressively more difficult. Again, the number of words read correctly and the nature of any errors are recorded.

5. *Knowledge of Word Parts: Word Attack.* In this category six individual tests are available to assess specific, phonics-related skills. As described by the authors in the test manual, these "proceed from the largest units, words, to the smallest units, individual letters" (Gates, McKillop, & Horowitz, 1981, p. 13). They recommend that these tests be administered in the order specified and that a reader who has little difficulty with the first and second tests not be asked to complete the remaining four.

Syllabication is the first task in this section and requires the reader to pronounce multisyllabic nonsense words. In the second test, labeled Recognizing and Blending Common Word Parts, a single-syllable nonsense word is presented to the reader. Each word begins with a consonant digraph or blend (e.g., *ch* or *fl*) and ends with a phonogram (e.g., *-ight* or *-aul*). If the reader has difficulty pronouncing the word, the test materials permit the initial consonants and the phonogram to be displayed separately to help the reader pronounce and blend these word parts. Separate scores are recorded for the initial attempt to read the entire word and for subsequent attempts to blend the given word parts when the initial attempt is unsuccessful.

The third test also requires the reader to read nonsense words. These words, however, require only that the reader by aware of the primary sounds of single consonants and common spelling patterns that influence vowel sounds (e.g., the consonant/vowel/consonant/silent-"e" pattern in the word "lake"). Respectively, the remaining three tests require the test taker to complete the following tasks: give the common sound(s) represented by each letter of the alphabet and several vowel clusters (e.g., *oa*), name the capital letters, and name the lowercase letters.

6. *Recognizing the Visual Form of Sounds.* For this test the five vowels are displayed to the child. The child listens to the examiner pronounce a single-syllable non-sense word and then points to the vowel that represents the vowel sound in the word.

7. *Auditory Tests.* Two tests are included in this category. In Auditory Blending a common word is segmented into two or more component speech sounds which are then pronounced to the child. After hearing the sounds in sequence separated by slight delay (e.g., /b/-pause-/ox/), the child must attempt to say the entire word (*box*). If necessary, the child is given two trials on each word, receiving partial credit if correct on the second trial.

In the Auditory Discrimination test the child listens to the pronunciation of word pairs. Some pairs include two identical words; others are identical except for a single phoneme (e.g., *may* versus *say*). The child must classify each pair as sounding the same or different.

8. *Written Expression.* Two tests are available for assessing written expression. In the Spelling test individual words are dictated to the child until six consecutive errors have occurred or all 40 words have been attempted. The words dictated are identical to those used in the Words: Untimed test, which means they become progressively more difficult. The second test in this category is the Informal Writing Sample, in which the examinee is asked to write on any topic of interest in the space provided in the pupil record book. There are no objective criteria for scoring the writing sample; instead, the authors recommend the child's writing be examined subjectively with a general concern for writing, grammar, spelling, and handwriting skills.

Practical Applications/Uses

The purpose of diagnostic testing in an academic area like reading is to help guide instruction by determining strengths and weaknesses, usually when a learning difficulty exists. The full battery of tests reviewed here, therefore, would be of primary interest to those who regularly teach elementary school students experiencing difficulty in learning to read. Specifically, this would include reading specialists, reading clinicians, special education teachers, basic skills teachers, and similar teaching professionals. School psychometricians and other professionals who must regularly assist others make informed decisions about students' reading instruction may also wish to consider this test battery. To a lesser extent educational researchers may find one or more of the tests useful in defining populations of readers, especially if the researcher's interest is in categorizing readers on the basis of phonics skills.

Because of the level of skill required to administer and interpret many of the tests in this battery, their use may be inappropriate for anyone not well practiced in their administration or without some background in diagnosing reading problems. For example, deciding which tests in the battery to administer to a particular reader will be aided by experienced clinical judgment derived from working with children having problems learning to read. The fact that all tests are not recommended for every child taking this test also suggests that the examiner may want to have some information concerning a child's reading performance prior to administering this test.

Interpreting the results of the tests selected also requires making inferences based on understanding the relationships among the tests. The manual accompanying the battery does explicitly define some of these relationships, but this information may seem overly complex to those who are not familiar with underlying assumptions about decoding or who are not fully initiated in phonics instruction.

A related concern is the level of skill necessary to administer and score the tests. Although procedures are well documented in the test manual, many of these require considerable dexterity and expertise on the part of the examiner. In the Oral Reading test, for example, the examiner must simultaneously record and code a variety of errors while the child is reading. The authors report more than 90% agreement between two examiners scoring 50 Oral Reading test protocols. This relatively high interjudge reliability suggests, however, that these examiners may have been well practiced in using the coding system. Short of extensive practice before administering this test, the user may want to consider using a tape recorder.

Several of the remaining tests also require that the examiner exercise informed judgment when scoring responses. In the Syllabication test, for example, some of the nonsense words may have several acceptable pronunciations depending on the division of the word. Also, when the child is asked to give letter sounds, what is the correct sound for the vowel cluster *ea*? Is it the sound heard in the word *eat*, or *great*, or *death*? Or must all three pronunciations be given to be scored correct? In the Auditory Discrimination test, should dialectical differences be taken into account when asking the child to distinguish between *where* and *ware*? Although the test manual addresses some of these issues, it does not provide explicit guidance.

The latter question also suggests caution in using these tests with children who speak a non-standard dialect or with those for whom English is not the dominant language. Using the earlier Gates-McKillop version of the Oral Reading test, Lucas and Singer (1976), for example, found evidence that Spanish-language experience was related to syntactic ability in English, which in turn was significantly correlated with oral reading achievement. Research has also demonstrated that phonological variations due to dialect may affect recognition of words presented in isolation (Melmed, 1971).

The test examiner should also schedule adequate time to administer this battery. The time required will vary depending on the number of tests selected as well as the examiner's skill and experience in administering the tests. The authors suggest, however, that the average administration time is usually one hour. For some children, especially in the lower grades, more than one testing session may be required.

These constraints may preclude the use of these tests by regular classroom teachers who will not frequently have the need or opportunity to use a formal diagnostic battery with individual students. Likewise, specialists may not need to consider this test at an early stage of diagnosis. Bond, Tinker, Wasson, and Wasson (1984), in the fifth edition of their definitive text on reading difficulties, have cited the Gates-McKillop-Horowitz tests as an example of a diagnostic battery that is most appropriately considered after other survey and diagnostic tests in reading have been administered. Because this battery has a distinct phonics emphasis, the diagnostician may first need to establish that the reader's problems are primarily related to decoding.

Technical Aspects

Unlike the previous versions of this test battery, the current version does include some technical data on the norming sample and test characteristics. The latter data, however, are limited to information about the Oral Reading test.

The norming sample consisted of 600 first- through sixth-grade children in 10 different schools. Inexplicably the authors report that 65% of these 10 schools were private and 35% were public schools. Equally confusing is their location—83% are reported as being urban schools and 17% suburban or rural schools. The authors state that all of the children tested were fluent in English. Just over half of the children were male, 64% were Caucasian, 32% black, and 4% were Oriental. Spanish was spoken in the homes of 14% of the children.

No information is provided about the nature of the reading instruction to which these children were exposed. This omission is unfortunate in that it may have provided some support for the curricular validity of these tests. The orientation of this battery is centered in phonics-related decoding skills. The emphasis given this orientation in elementary schools, however, varies considerbly. The authors do report that correlation coefficients ranged from .68 to .96 when scores on the Oral Reading test and a standardized silent reading test were compared. These correlations are consistent with previous studies investigating this relationship. Nonetheless, the authors' failure to offer any evidence for the validity of the remaining tests or the entire battery is a serious technical shortcoming.

Another weakness is the lack of reliability data. A correlation coefficient of .94 was obtained when 27 children from the original sample were tested and re-tested on the Oral Reading test, but no reliability data are available for the remaining tests. Neither do the authors report intercorrelations among the individual tests in this battery. The absence of this latter information mitigates against determining the diagnostic value of each test in the battery.

The authors do supply normative data in the form of grade equivalents for several of the tests. These data become the bench mark for interpreting perform-ance on the battery; thus, they are important to the integrity of these tests. Although grade equivalents have the advantage of being easily understood, they are susceptible to a number of distortions (e.g., they may be disproportionately affected by minor variations in raw scores). Unlike many tests, this battery does not supply alternative norm-referenced scores like percentiles. Neither have the authors chosen to report measures of dispersion or standard errors of measurement. In addition, the manual recommends that a diagnostician may want to compare grade equivalents achieved on these tests to grade equivalents on other academic tests. This is a questionable practice due to differences in norming populations and in the nature of subjects taught in the elementary school.

Several of the tests in this battery, however, do not employ grade equivalents for interpretation. Instead, the examiner is encouraged to compare subjectively one child's performance to the average performance of children in the norming sample who are at the same grade level. Other than relying on the examiner's intuition, there is in most cases no guidance as to what constitutes a significant variation from these norms. In several of these tests nearly perfect performance was the norm. The diagnostic value of a reading test that produces nearly perfect scores when attempted by poor and non-readers (presumably the norming population included such children) is minimal.

Critique

As is evidenced by the previous information, the Gates-McKillop-Horowitz Reading Diagnostic Tests have notable limitations from a technical standpoint. Several less serious practical limitations have also been identified. The merit of any reading diagnostic test, however, must be judged primarily on the basis of how legitimately it encapsulates the reading process. Does it sufficiently tap essential reading skills and isolate these in a way that is meaningful for instruction?

Even a superficial examination of this battery will reveal that several important facets of reading are conspicuously absent. In addition, some of the skills tested are of questionable relevance to reading. Finally, the taks required in some of the tests conflict with what is currently considered sound reading pedagogy. The remainder of this review will focus on these objections.

Comprehension is widely accepted as the measure of reading. It is important to note that the Gates-McKillop-Horowitz tests do not specifically address reading comprehension, nor do they address meaning vocabulary. This fact may explain Bond et al.'s (1984) recommendation that the battery be considered only after other reading survey and diagnostic tests have been administered. The Gates-McKillop-Horowitz battery does focus on decoding, but predominantly from a phonics orientation. Other recognized word identification skills such as structural analysis and use of context are not specifically tested. Given the limited scope of the reading skills tested, it seems inappropriate to consider this battery a complete, formal diagnostic instrument in reading.

According to Winkley (1971), a major shortcoming of many reading diagnostic tests is that subtests aimed at assessing word recognition skills actually evaluate spelling. In other words, decoding and encoding skills have been confounded. Although related, an ability to encode (spell) is not necessary to decode (read). This error in thinking can be seen by the inclusion of a spelling test and writing sample in the Gates-McKillop-Horowitz battery. It is more subtly evident in the test that requires examinees to point to the vowel they hear in a nonsense word pronounced for them.

Several of the tests in this battery run contrary to accepted instructional practice or beliefs about teaching reading. For example, phonics principles are of limited utility for words that are not in a reader's listening vocabulary, yet in several tests children are asked to read words like "treacherous" or phrases like "sublime conceit." The timed presentation of words also does not employ words typically taught as sight words. Few teachers, for example, would consider teaching the word "illustrious" as a sight word. Also, the auditory blending activity (/b/-pause-/ox/) may be foreign and unnecessary to children taught via an analytic approach to phonics. The use of the term "errors" in the context of oral reading is also an anachronism. The current, more preferred term is "miscues," which emphasizes that some oral reading "errors" are indicative of useful and important semantic skills.

In summary, the longevity of these tests does not make them immune from the cited criticisms. In fact, because this battery has been only minimally revised since its inception, it is reminiscent of a simpler, less sophisticated era in reading and testing. Most of the major objections to this test could be overcome, however, by a simple revision of its title. Replacing "Reading Diagnostic Tests" in the title with "Informal Assessment in Phonics and Spelling" might be an improvement. Then, in the hands of the informed practitioner or clinician, this battery may be useful for a narrow range of diagnostic applications.

References

This list includes text citations as well as suggested additional reading.

Bond, G., Tinker, M. A., Wasson, B. B., & Wasson, J. B. (1984). *Reading difficulties: Their diagnosis and correction* (5th ed.). Englewood Cliffs, NJ: Prentice-Hall Inc.

Gates, A. I., McKillop, A. S., & Cliff, E. (1981). *Manual of directions: Gates-McKillop-Horowitz Reading Diagnostic Tests* (2nd ed.). New York: Teachers College Press.

Kavale, K. (1979). Selecting and evaluating reading tests. In R. Schreiner (Ed.), *Reading tests and teachers: A practical guide* (pp. 9-34). Newark, DE: International Reading Association.

Lucas, M. S., & Singer, H. L. (1976). Dialect in relation to oral reading achievement: Recoding, encoding, or merely a code? In H. Singer & R. B. Ruddell (Eds.), *Theoretical models and processes of reading* (pp. 429-439). Newark, DE: International Reading Association.

Melmed, P. J. (1971). Black English phonology: The question of reading interference. *Monographs of the Language-Behavior Research Laboratory,* 1(February).

Schell, L. M. (Ed.). (1981). *Diagnostic and criterion-referenced reading tests: Review and evaluation.* Newark, DE: International Reading Association.

Winkley, C. (1971). What do diagnostic reading tests really diagnose? In R. E. Leibert (Ed.), *Diagnostic viewpoints in reading* (pp. 64-80). Newark, DE: International Reading Association.

Roger D. Carlson, Ph.D.
Associate Professor of Psychology, Lebanon Valley College, Annville, Pennsylvania.

GESELL PRESCHOOL TEST

Gesell Institute of Human Development. Flemington, New Jersey: Programs for Education, Inc.

Introduction

The Gesell Preschool Test is designed to test the motor, adaptive, language, and personal-social behaviors of the child aged 2½-6 years.

The Gesell Preschool Test has its origins in the work of Arnold Gesell (1880-1961), who received his Ph.D. in psychology from Clark University and M.D. from Yale University. The basic philosophy from which the test has been developed is that behavior is a function of structure that develops in a patterned predictable way. The earliest versions of the test appeared in 1925, and revisions subsequently appeared in 1940, 1964-65 as the Gesell Development Tests, 1978 as the School Readiness Tests, which are the immediate predecessors of the present Gesell Preschool Test. Through the years there have been changes in subtests used; however, there remain scales originally included by Gesell. The work of Gesell continues to be carried out at the Gesell Institute of Child Development in New Haven, Connecticut.

Gesell used his tests in order to locate individuals on his developmental "schedules"—listings of behaviors typically appearing at particular ages. It is still the conviction of workers at the Gesell Institute that the maturation of behavior is not necessarily well indexed by chronological age. Thus, such tests are necessary in order to arrive at an adequate assessment of the child's development.

The test consists of a ten-page packet of materials designed to guide the examiner, to record the responses of the child, and to locate the child's performances on the Gesell Developmental Schedules. Other materials include the 70-page softcover *The Gesell Preschool Test Manual* (Haines, Ames, & Gillespie, 1980), The Cube Test (10 wooden cubes), Gesell's Copy Form Test (7 cards), a bean bag, the Binet picture vocabulary booklet, pellets and bottle, cardboard color forms, a three-hole formboard, a letters and numbers card, and a vinyl and nylon carrying case.

Subtests include the Cube Test, Interview Questions, Pencil and Paper tests, Incomplete Man Test, Discriminates Prepositions, Digit Repetition, Picture Vocabulary, Comprehension Questions, Color Forms, Action Agent, Three-Hole Formboard, Identifying Letters and Numbers, and Motor.

The tests begin with the Cube Test consisting of a series of structures to be arranged using a set of ten cubes. This test is designed to measure eye-hand coordination, motor skill, attention span, and level of functioning in a structured

310

fine motor task. The Interview Questions is a brief interview in which the examiner asks the child's name, age, sex, etc., in order to ascertain clarity of speech as well as accuracy of information. Paper and Pencil Tests consist of the child drawing a circle, cross, square, triangle, divided rectangle, and a diamond in two positions. The test reveals maturity of visual perception, of neuromuscular and eye-hand coordination, as well as general level of ability. In the Incomplete Man Test the child is presented with a figure of an incomplete man and asked to finish the drawing. Discriminates Prepositions assesses the child's understanding of some words and elementary concepts of spatial position. The child is instructed to place a cube "on," "under," "in back of," in front of," or "beside" a chair. Digit Repetition measures the ability of the child to focus attention on a task having little intrinsic meaning and to hold information in short-term memory and then to repeat the information in the order given. A series of digits is presented, and the child is instructed to repeat them. Picture Vocabulary, consisting of showing the child a picture and asking the child to give the name of the item shown, gives an effective clue to verbal intelligence. Comprehension Questions require the child to solve problems in order to measure the child's ability to work out sensible coping solutions to social problem situations. Color Forms consists of the child being requested to match cutouts with comparison shapes. Action Agent, a language comprehension indicator, requires that the child be able to give an appropriate example in response to questions such as "What scratches?" "What sleeps?" "What flies?" The Three-Hole Formboard provides the child with an opportunity to put selected blocks into the appropriate cutouts on a formboard. It measures the child's form discrimination ability, attention span, and general adaptivity. Identifying Letters and Numbers is a test of the child's ability to identify written letters and numbers with their appropriate names. Computation consists of counting and simple addition and subtraction problems. Motor tasks consist of both fine motor and gross motor activity.

The results of testing are summarized on the Gesell Developmental Schedules which describe behavior along four dimensions—motor, adaptive, language, and personal-social—as correlated with chronological age. In this way the test user can ascertain the child's "developmental age" or "behavior age" when judged against typical performances of various groups of agemates. The schedules, which are completed at the conclusion of testing, are in a checklist format.

Practical Applications/Uses

The Preschool Test can be administered by pediatricians and psychologists to determine the normality of any given infant's or child's level of development. The tests can give a parent or guardian a rather clear picture of child's individuality—both strong and weak points—and reveal the adaptability of the child. Additionally, they can help in determining proper placement of children in Kindergarten and early primary grades.

The test is used primarily for screening, early intervention, or diagnosis, depending on the qualifications of the examiner. It meets Child Find Requirements of Public Law 94-142.

The test is designed for use by early childhood specialists, educators, medical and psychiatric practitioners, psychologists, care-givers, caseworkers, nursing schools, institutions and agencies. The tests require individual administration. The paperback manual (Haines, Ames, & Gillespie, 1980) is set forth in a clear efficient format that is useful during the testing process. The time required for administration is 40 minutes.

Scoring procedures are clear and relatively easy to accomplish. Performances of children are recorded on the recording sheets (10 pages). Because the purpose of the test is to determine the child's "developmental age," norms are presented by the authors showing the typical performances of children of various ages and each sex.

Because no summary composite score, quotient, or index is obtained from the battery interpretation of scores involves a degree judgment when using the Gesell Developmental Schedules. The authors speak of the concept of the "developmental age" or "behavior age" of the *child*, however it is possible for there to be a different "developmental age" for each dimension of the schedule, as well as intradimensional tasks. "Developmental age" is then, by necessity, subjectively determined on the basis of clustering of successes.

The items on the personal-social dimension of the schedules are derived from asking the parent questions about the personal-social habits of the child and are not directly derived from items on the test.

Technical Aspects

Norms are based upon a standardization study conducted by the authors on 80 children residing in New England who were tested longitudinally. Because of the lack of a coherent *quantified* profile and the use of subjective interpretation, a direct measure of the test's reliability and validity can only indirectly be derived. A number of the subtests are identical with those of the Gesell School Readiness Tests, and since one of the uses of the Gesell Preschool Test is to determine appropriate grade placement, the reliability and validity measures described in the review of the Gesell School Readiness Tests are appropriate to infer the adequacy of the test for such a purpose.

Critique

Although the manual does not specify specialized requisite training and is designed for use by early childhood specialists, educators, medical and psychiatric practitioners, psychologists, care-givers, case workers, nursery schools, institutions, and agencies, considerable practice, experience, and/or training in both administration and summarization is probably necessary in order to use the battery reliably, efficiently, and effectively. The Broward County school district in Ft. Lauderdale, Florida, requires that teachers administering the tests have 70 to 75 hours in in-service training with 25 practice examinations before certifying them as competent (L. Coffey, personal communication, March, 1985). Another school district (the Fresno diocese in California) requires that teachers administering the tests attend a one day workshop, give six more tests which are critiqued, do additional reading, and pass an examination before they are deemed qualified by the district to administer the test (M. Spomer, personal communication, March, 1985). Training workshops that run for 4½ hours are available at the Gesell Institute to prepare one for supervised administration of the Gesell Preschool Test. Advanced workshops for those who have tested 25 or more children are also available.

The object of the Gesell Preschool Tests is to be able to aid the examiner in placing the child on the Gesell Development Schedule. Much of the schedule is based on the norms of the Institute's standardization study. The schedule is a description of the child's behavior along four dimensions—motor, adaptive, language, and personal-social—which were of concern to Gesell as early as 1925. For what it attempts to do, the tests are no doubt useful to those concerned with intervention.

The Gesell philosophy, however, is not an optimistic one. Because the prevailing assumption at the Institute is that behavior is by and large biologically unfolding, the schedule, in a sense, connotes a ceiling of current *capabilities*, based upon *current* performances. It must be remembered that current performances to stimuli presented may not be an adequate sample to generalize about current capabilities, and certainly the stimuli employed in the tests do not exhaust the range of possible stimuli that one might provide and that might be used to elicit performances superior to those displayed in the test situation.

In sum, the strengths of the test include the multidimensional specific approach to the determination of a child's performance on a wide range of tasks. Also valued is the highly individualized character of the results yielded by the test, which assists both in the formulation of individualized treatment plans, as well as aiding in parent interpretation which is often obscured by the use of the score reports of other types of instruments.

References

Haines, J., Ames, L. B., & Gillespie, C. (1980). *The Gesell Preschool Test Manual*. Lumberville, Pennsylvania: Modern Learning Press.

Ilg, F. L., Ames, L. B., Haines, J., & Gillespie, C. (1978). *School Readiness*. New York: Harper & Row.

Roger D. Carlson, Ph.D.
Associate Professor of Psychology, Lebanon Valley College, Annville, Pennsylvania.

GESELL SCHOOL READINESS TEST

Gesell Institute of Human Development. Flemington, New Jersey: Programs for Education, Inc.

Introduction

The Gesell School Readiness Test is used to measure predominantly adaptive behavior of 4½ to 9-year-old children in terms of their maturity level. Specifically, they are used to determine if children are ready to begin Kindergarten, to assess their readiness for first through third grade, and to evaluate if they are in the right grade.

The Gesell School Readiness Tests have their origins in the work of Arnold Gesell whose basic philosophy was that behavior is a function of structure that develops in a patterned predictable way. The 1964-65 Gesell Development Tests are the immediate predecessors of the present Gesell School Readiness Tests (Ilg, Ames, Haines, & Gillespie, 1978). Through the years there have been changes in the subtests; however, some of Gesell's original scales remain as part of the test. The work of Gesell continues to be carried out at the Gesell Institute of Child Development in New Haven, Connecticut. In 1950, after finding out that one third to one half of school children were placed in inappropriate school grades for the work they were capable of performing, the tests began to be applied to school readiness.

The materials used in the test include the Cube Test (10 wooden cubes) and a ten-page booklet for its administration, a packet consisting of materials designed to guide the examiner and record the responses of the child, a 238-page textbook (Ilg, Ames, Haines, & Gillespie, 1978), Jacobson's Right and Left tests (6 cards), Monroe Reading Readiness Test (16 cards), Gesell's Original Copy Form (7 cards), cylinder, and cube.

The subtests include The Cube Test, Interview Questions, Paper and Pencil Tests (Gesell's original Copy Forms Test), Incomplete Man, Jacobson's Right and Left Test, Visual One and Visual Three from Marion Monroe's Reading Readiness Test, and an item from the Binet—the naming of animals for one minute. Materials that the examiner must provide are paper, pencils, and a stopwatch.

The tests begin with an interview used to assess the child's immediate knowledge and experience (name, age, sex, birthday, etc.), as well as clarity of speech and accuracy of information, and then proceeds with the Paper and Pencil Tests. Answers to questions and performances on the various subtests have been normed by age and sex of the respondents. The Gesell Cube Test, which measures eye-hand coordination, motor skill, attention span, and level of functioning in a

314

structured fine motor task, are administered to preschoolers. The test consists of a series of structures to be arranged using the set of ten cubes, provided with the test materials. Children are then asked to write their name, last name, and address. This task, as well as the Numbers and Copy Forms tasks, reveal visual perception, neuromuscular and eye-hand coordination, and general level of maturity. The child proceeds to the Paper and Pencil Tests, which consist of the child drawing a circle, cross, square, triangle, divided rectangle, and diamond in two positions. Older children who succeed at these tests are then shown three dimensional objects—a cylinder and cube—and are asked to draw them. The Incomplete Man Test in which the child is presented a picture of an incomplete man and asked to finish drawing it is then presented. This test is said to be the most revealing of the subtests and gives clues to perceptual functioning. The examiner then proceeds to the Right and Left Test which was developed by Dr. J. Robert Jacobson and consists of naming body parts, responding to a single command (e.g., "Touch your eye"), and responding to a double command (e.g., "Touch your right thumb with your right little finger"). The Monroe Visual Tests, designed to assess the child's ability to carry out instructions as well as to hold and recall information, are administered by showing the child a visual pattern and asking the child to indicate from two alternatives the one which the examiner has displayed. The child is then presented with a Binet item, the naming of animals, for sixty seconds. This test, viewed as a language item, is an attempt to measure the child's tempo, the organization of thinking, and the capacity to range. The battery of tests is concluded with a short interview in which the child is asked about preferences in school and at home. Special attention is paid to the *way* that the child expresses himself or herself. All responses are recorded on answer forms provided in the test package.

Practical Application/Uses

The tests are designed to be used primarily in a school setting in order to answer questions about the appropriate placement and readiness of the child. It is designed for use by school psychologists, educators, early childhood specialists, and child development professionals.

The tests are designed to be individually administered and to be administered in forty minutes.

The hardcover text, *School Readiness*, although containing complete instructions, imbeds normative research findings with instructions for administration and scoring, and thus instructions for administration may be difficult for the novice examiner to follow during the examination process. Some subtests and parts of subtests are specifically recommended for particular age groups, and others are specifically deleted. The ease with which the examiner can locate such specifications within the book while testing might be less than optimal unless the examiner is well practiced in its administration.

Performances of children are recorded on the recording sheets. Because the purpose of the test is to determine appropriate grade placement based on the child's "developmental age" rather than chronological age, tables are presented by the authors indicating the percentage of children of various chronological ages and each sex who display particular performances base on a standardization study conducted by the test's authors. The study was of approximately 500 Gesell test records of children (some tested longitudinally) living near New Haven, Connecticut. No summary composite score, quotient, or index is obtained from the battery. The authors suggest that local norms be obtained for the population being tested. Therefore, unless local norms are available, the examiner is left with the problem of interpreting the performances derived. Wood, Powell, and Knight (1984) used an exact developmental criterion age for placement which the authors predicted would assure success *in the particular district in which their study was conducted.* This resulted in relatively few false positives and false negatives. The authors suggest that local norms be developed in the same way to fit the demands of the particular school district in which the child is tested.

Technical Aspects

Because of the interpretive quality of the process of determining developmental age from the tests, it is difficult to determine the reliability and validity of the tests in an exact sense. There are, however, indirect measures of reliability and validity that lend support to the integrity of the test, given the purposes for which it is used.

Reliability has been ascertained by Kaufman (1971) who, in a study of 103 kindergarten students from Long Island, New York, found a reliability coefficient (alpha) of .84 and a raw score standard error of measurement of 5.3 (on a 99 unit scoring scale developed for the study) on selected Gesell subtests. This indicated that the tests are reasonably internally consistent. For 40 of the subjects, the correlation between results of the "specially trained developmental examiner" who was a school district psychologist doing the testing in the study and those of a Gesell Institute researcher was .87.

Validity might be ascertained in a manner of ways. The scores on Kaufman's (1971) study correlated .79 with a developmental examiner's clinical total for the sample. Ilg, Ames, Haines, and Gillespie (1978) report 83% agreement between the results of the developmental examination and teacher's estimates for kindergarten subjects. Kaufman (1971) found correlations of the Gesell test scores with scores from a specially constructed Piagetian battery to be .64. Kaufman and Kaufman (1972), in a study of 80 Long Island, New York children, found that scores derived from selected Gesell tests taken in Kindergarten correlated .64 with the Stanford Achievement Test composites at the end of the first grade. Kaufman (1971) found that the scores derived from the Gesell tests correlated .50 with Lorge Thorndike IQs and .61 with Lorge Thorndike Mental ages. More recently, Wood, Powell, and Knight (1984) conducted a study of 84 Massachusetts kindergarten children in order to determine the predictive validity of the Gesell Tests. Examiners were certified to administer the Gesell School Readiness Tests by the Gesell Institute. Discriminant analysis revealed that developmental age (as determined by the examiners) by itself was significantly predictive of success or failure (Chi square = 16.3; df = 2; $p < .01$) in Kindergarten. However, because of design problems (e.g., the awkward timing of the tests' administration and other evaluations being made on the children which may have skewed the results), the authors conclude that the study, conservatively speaking, may at best be support for concurrent validity instead of predictive validity of the tests.

Critique

Rather than providing a quantified outcome, praise for the tests comes from those who use the tests as one source of information for a judgment to be made concerning school placement.

The authors speak of the concept of the "developmental age" of the *child*, however it is possible for there to be a different "developmental age" or "behavior age" for each task and performance. The percentages based on the standardization study are of some use; however, separate tables are presented for each task, and thus the examiner is left with the rather large job of summarizing the myriad of results in a narrative report. Because several age groups may comprise individuals for which over 50% are able to perform the task (the authors' criterion for "norms"), it remains unclear in which "developmental age" group any particular child should be placed.

Ilg, Ames, Haines, and Gillespie (1978) stress the importance of not confusing developmental age with intelligence. In addition to intelligence, developmental age incorporates social, emotional, and general behavior development.

Although the manual does not specify the *necessity* of having specialized training, and the tests are designed for use by school psychologists, educators, early childhood specialists, and child development professionals, considerable practice, experience, and/or training in both administration and summarization is probably necessary in order to reliably, efficiently, and effectively use the battery. Ft. Lauderdale's Broward County school district requires that teachers administering the tests have 70 to 75 hours in in-service training with 25 practice examinations before certifying them as competent (L. Coffey, personal communication, March, 1985). Training workshops that run 4½ days are available at the Gesell Institute to prepare one for supervised administration of the Gesell Readiness Test. Advanced workshops for those who have tested 25 or more children are also available. Sets of cards to which an examiner may compare a particular performance on the Gesell Copy Forms Test and the Incomplete Man Test can also be obtained in order to aid in the evaluation of a child's performance.

One weak area of the test is the lack of a scoring *system* which results in a composite profile. "Developmental age" is, in the end, subjectively determined on the basis of clustering of successes. Users of the test who find it valuable cite its effectiveness in remedial placement, thereby reducing failure in grade assignments, and by using "developmental age" as an indicator rather than chronological age. In that sense the tests reveal a kind of predictive validity. A number of school districts report significant decreases in failures after using the device as a screening instrument (L. B. Ames, L. Coffey, J. Grant, & M. Spomer, personal communications, March, 1985). However, it might be argued that *any* child would benefit from such a delay.

The question remains as to how objective the tests are; that is, how much of these judgments is due to the performance on Gesell tests, and how much is due to other factors contributing to the decision. Because the judgments made on the basis of the tests correlate highly with teachers' judgments (83% agreement according to Ilg, Ames, Haines, & Gillespie, 1978), the tests may be used in practice as quasi-objective rationale or justification for the judgments of teachers.

The Broward County school district in Ft. Lauderdale, Flordia, which has used the test extensively, reports that the "real payoff" to the Gesell is that teachers who learn to administer the tests look at children in a new way and learn to plan school activities differently—in many ways supplementing the training and experience of teachers with detailed developmental descriptions found so rarely in contemporary courses in child development (L. Coffey, personal communication, March, 1985). Still, questions remain. Is this an appropriate and efficient procedure for helping teachers to obtain such insights? And more broadly, might we re-examine what might be done to change the schools, rather than to assess the child's propensity to adapt to the system and prescribe alterations in the child's life in order to make such an adaptation? That is, what should be assessed, children or institutions? Children *are* different and the Gesell tests make an important contribution to the documentation of those differences as borne out by the testimony of users. Ironically, the development of the instrument was predicated on a kind of predictable "sameness" in the unfolding of developmental patterns. The Gesell scales seek to re-index those commonalities around the concept of "developmental age" rather than chronological age. It is perhaps most revealing that the concept of a concretely determined "developmental age" remains elusive, and the unique child, richly varied as described by the instrument, is who remains.

References

Ilg, F. L., Ames, L. B., Haines, J., & Gillespie, C. (1978a). *Gesell School Readiness Test*. New York: Programs for Education.

Ilg, F. L., Ames, L. B., Haines, J., & Gillespie, C. (1978). *School readiness*. New York: Harper & Row.

Kaufman, A. S. (1971). Piaget and Gesell: A psychometric analysis of tests built from their tasks. *Child Development, 42,* 1341-1360.

Kaufman, A. S., & Kaufman, N. L. (1972). Tests built from Piaget's and Gesell's tasks as predictors of first-grade achievement. *Child Development, 43,* 521-535.

Wood, C., Powell, S., & Knight, R. S. (1984). Predicting school readiness: The validity of developmental age. *Journal of Learning Disabilities, 17,* 8-11.

Lowry C. Fredrickson, Ph.D.

Chairman, Department of Psychology, Coe College, Cedar Rapids, Iowa.

GOODENOUGH-HARRIS DRAWING TEST

Florence L. Goodenough and Dale B. Harris. Cleveland, Ohio: The Psychological Corporation.

Introduction

The first edition of the Goodenough-Harris Drawing Test was published in 1926 by Florence Goodenough and titled the Goodenough Draw-a-Man Test. The test reviewed here is the revised edition published in 1963, constructed to measure a child's current intellectual functioning using the drawings of a man and a woman by a child or a group of children. The test yields a single score resulting from comparison with a normative group of same-age peers in the form of a deviation type IQ. Research on this test supports such an IQ measure on children between the ages of 5 to 14 years. The concrete operations measured by this test support the idea of elemental cognitive concepts which in turn logically make up more complex concepts all within a theoretical context that supports such pre-adolescent reasoning. The Goodenough-Harris Drawing Test measures the child's accuracy of observation and the development of conceptual thinking more than it measures artistic skill.

Harris (1963a), discussing the measurement of intelligence, concludes that replacing the notion of intelligence with intellectual maturity, or even conceptual maturity, is supported by both current theory and research findings. This includes: 1) the ability to perceive (i.e., make discriminations); 2) the ability to classify objects into categories (i.e., likenesses and differences); and 3) the ability to generalize (i.e., via perceived features, properties, and attributes). These functions according to Harris (1963a) ''. . . comprise the process of concept formation'' (p. 5). The Goodenough-Harris Drawing Test measures mental maturity reliably and validly within the confines of this restricted definition.

The first Draw-a-Man Test developed by Goodenough utilized research from as early as before the turn of the century up to the date of its initial publication in 1926. Much of the research on the psychology of children's drawings took place on the Continent and in America between the years of 1890 and 1910. This research served to establish the developmental character of children's drawings, but from the observations of actual freehand drawings rather than some prior theoretical frame of reference. Florence Goodenough successfully showed that a large intellectual component existed in children's drawings and that such measures were closely related to the psychometric study of intelligence. This particular emphasis persisted in America, England, and Japan up to the 1940s and has been investigated in India and South Africa (Harris, 1963a). Scholars who participated in the early work on the developmental nature of young children's drawings include Earl Barnes (1893) in America, Levinstein (1905) in Germany, Claparede (1910) in Switzerland, Maitland (1895) in America, and Schuyten (1901-1907) in the Netherlands (Harris, 1963a).

It is interesting to note that this work, especially that of Claparede, was to exert a strong influence on the thinking and research of the late Swiss epigenetic epistemologist, Jean Piaget. These studies collectively revealed that young children draw the human figure by preference but also frequently draw houses, trees, furniture, boats, vehicles, and animals. The unifying feature in all children's drawings was the consistent observation that the quality of the drawings improved incrementally with age both in terms of coherence and the presence of more fully developed detail. In the decades of 1910-1950, much work was carried out with subnormal children whose drawings were compared with normals. Harris (1963a) points out that the primary feature coming out of this period in research on children's drawings ''was this classification into sequences or stages, and thus the delineation of children's drawings as developmental in character'' (p. 17).

Goodenough, using a point-scale technique, demonstrated that children manifest more cognitive than aesthetic meaning in their drawings. In addition, Goodenough's finding that drawings ceased to show age-incremental differences by early adolescence differed from other findings of research on intellect and attracted a great deal of attention at the time. Harris (1963a) discusses numerous research studies that followed the early Draw-a-Man Test concerning norms, reliability, and validity of the instrument. Research was pursued on the influence of instructions for giving the test and the use of test results in the diagnosis of behavior disorders. Research using the Draw-a-Man Test with sensory deviates (especially the deaf), artistic talent, and sex differences was common and plentiful. This reviewer recommends Harris' (1963a) chapter entitled ''The Historical Survey of the Study of Children's Drawings'' to those interested in a scholarly comprehensive study of this time span in history.

The Goodenough Draw-a-Man Test was revised by Harris in 1963 and the name of the test was changed to the current Goodenough-Harris Drawing Test. This revised edition was lengthened from 51 items or points to 73. These items were selected from a pool of about 100 with control for age differentiation and based on group intelligence test results. The normative scores in the revised edition contain 50 boys and 50 girls at each year from 6 to 15 years. These children were taken from a larger sample tested in rural and urban areas of Minnesota and Wisconsin and were representative of the population with respect to paternal occupation. Obtained raw scores on the test were converted to standard scores with a mean of 100 and a standard deviation of 15. Harris added the Draw-a-Woman Scale and the Self-Drawing Scale, both of which are scored in a similar manner to the Draw-a-Man Test. The Self-Drawing Scale was developed as a possible projective test of personality; however, research on this type of use is not favorable, at least in terms of using objective scoring.

In addition to these changes Harris introduced a set of Quality Scale Cards to aid users of the test in scoring accuracy. This scale consists of 24 cards of standardized drawings to be used for comparison purposes with specific attention to the quality of drawing at each age level. There are 12 cards for the Draw-a-Man Test to be used for drawings by boys and 12 cards to be used for drawings by girls. The Quality Scale Cards can be useful to the sophisticated clinician who has wide experience with the point scale beforehand.

The early reviewers of Harris' revised edition of this test (i.e., Anne Anastasi, James A. Dunn, M. L. Kellmer Pringle) were all complimentary about the quality of the revised test and highly recommended it to future users at that time.

It is the simplicity of this test that lends it to extensive use by psychometricians and clinicians. The short time required to take and score the test is an attractive feature. The test protocol contains a cover page where the child's personal information is recorded. There is convenient space available for the examiner's notes concerning the test administration. Scoring is easy with a special space for recording the raw score, standard score, and percentile rank for the Point Scale and Quality Scale, respectively. The remaining three pages provide adequate space for drawing a man, a woman, and one's self. Concise instructions are provided for each drawing with a place to score each of the scorable items on all three tests. The total number of items manifesting adequate clarity and quality for a positive score are summed and constitute the raw score.

An alternative scoring method available is the set of Quality Scales. These scales can be used for quick reliable scoring by experienced users of the test after mastering the detailed point scoring. The examiner chooses one of the twelve sample drawings that most closely matches the performance level of the child's drawing and assigns the scale value of the sample card. A separate quality scale is provided for the Man and Woman drawings. This test is constructed to be used with children in the age range of 5 years through 15 years. The test can be used with older children and adults manifesting subnormal intelligence corresponding to the age range given in the test norms.

Practical Applications/Uses

The Goodenough-Harris Drawing Test is interesting to subjects at the ages where its use is encouraged, takes relatively little time, yields estimates of cognitive development, can indicate sensory-motor impairment, and has been used extensively as a personality and projective test. The test has been in continuous use for more than 50 years including the 1926 Goodenough Draw-a-Man Test. Harris' 1963 revision brought the technique up to date with alternate forms, a more exact scoring procedure, and revised norms (i.e., in 1963, based on a carefully selected sampling of children). It should be kept in mind that Harris clearly states that the "Draw-a-Man Test" is primarily a test of conceptual and intellectual maturity.

This test can be used with other screening tests for selecting children who should receive more detailed and individual attention. There is ample evidence in the literature that examiner variance has proven insignificant, as has the effect of art training on test scores.

Other reviewers have consistently claimed this test is especially useful with children manifesting hearing handicaps and neurological deficiencies (Harris, 1963a). Harris warns against using these drawings as a check for creativity, special interests, or deep psychological problems and conflicts in children because research to date does not support the validity of such use (Harris, 1963a). The primary basis for use of the drawings for personality assessment or as a projective measure only apply to highly experienced clinicians whose experience with such use relies on expert clinical judgment. There is no valid objective scoring that supports personality assessment or projective uses.

This test in the hands of a school psychologist or a certified psychometrician has the advantages of brevity, general convenience, and subject interest and motivation. However, it should be used as supplementary evidence within a battery of tests or as a screening technique for singling out children who may benefit from further in-depth testing. The manual (Harris, 1963b) clearly defines the basic scope for its use as follows: ". . . the Goodenough-Harris Drawing Test is best used as a measure of intellectual maturity and should not be used for other purposes" (p. 247).

Technical Aspects

The current Goodenough-Harris Drawing Test underwent an extensive revision by Harris in 1963 building on the earlier Goodenough Draw-a-Man Test. A great deal of specificity was brought to the new revision in the exact scoring of the test and the result is scoring criteria of an objective nature and a strong empirical basis. The norms in the revised test resulted in a much improved standardization relative to the original test. Harris revised the IQ from the outdated mental age/chronological age ratio to use of the deviation IQ measure. This allows for children to be compared to same-age peers with proper control for sex, rural/urban residence, and father's occupation within the geographical areas represented in the norms. One could certainly question if the norms in the 1963 revised edition are still adequately respresentative for the children tested today. The high increase of one-parent families, population shifts from rural to urban settings, and family/children interaction patterns all seem to support the need for more recent standardized norms.

The Goodenough-Harris Drawing Test has been compared to the Stanford-Binet, WISC, WAIS, WPPSI, the Primary Mental Abilities Test, and other ability and special aptitude tests using the Pearson *r* correlation coefficient. Most of these correlations are statistically significant and indicate the high agreement among such measures. Users of this test should consult *Drawings as Measures of Intellectual Maturity* (Harris, 1963a), Chapter 5, pp. 95-107 for objective studies reporting on the high correlations stated above.

The basic evidence concerning the validity of this test comes from the item analysis used in developing the scales. The year-by-year gain in mean raw scores from ages 5 through 14 using the point scoring system is impressive. After age 14 the difference in mean scores fall off for ages 15-16 and older, which indicates the test should not be used for children above 15 years because it does not yield valid measures at this age level.

Anne Anastasi's (1975) summary statement on norms, reliability, and validity remains pertinent still: ". . . the original Draw-a-Man test has been updated, extended and restandardized; the crude ratio IQ has been replaced with standard scores; and a parallel form has been developed in the Woman Scale" (p. 858). Basically one can correctly conclude that the Goodenough-Harris Draw-a-Person Test is technically sound and usable as a screening measure for assessing developmental levels of cognitive functioning.

The care given by Harris to objective scoring procedures in the revised edition of this test went a long way to aid the reliability of children's consistency from one drawing to another as well as scoring consistency by individual examiners administering the test. Numerous studies are reported by Harris (1963a) that establish the consistency with which scorers can, with little training, reliably score this test. Harris (1963a) reports intercorrelations between two independent scorers for boys and girls ages 8 and 10, respectively, with Pearson r correlations of .91 through .98. The reader must keep in mind that all such measures are based on groups of boys and girls (i.e., 75 of each at each age in this case). It can be justifiably stated that the evidence for the reliability of this test is good between the ages of 5 and 14 years.

There has been considerable research reported that indicates that individual examiners play a minimal role in the performance of children on this test. The simplicity and clarity of the test instructions plus the minimal involvement of the administrator would support just such a finding. Another effect frequently called to question on this test is the effect of school or other art training on test performance. There has been considerable evidence accumulated to show that prior art classes or experiences have little effect on the performances of two different groups drawing the human figure when they are compared. This also speaks to the validity of the test when it can be shown that the performance on this test by two independent groups is high regardless of art training prior to testing.

The Quality Scales offer an alternative method of evaluating children's drawing on both the Man and Woman scales. Historically early attempts using this type of assessment were developed by Thorndike (1913), the Kline and Carey (1922), and others (Harris, 1963a). The set of Quality Scale cards provide a simple, global, and qualitative measure as a substitute for the detailed point-scoring technique. From a sample of twelve drawings the examiner selects one that most clearly approximates the examinee's drawing and assigns the scale value of that sample drawing. The Goodenough-Harris Drawing Test manual (Harris, 1963b) provides instructions for using the Quality Scales. The interscorer reliabilities for the Quality Scales are mostly in the range of Pearson r correlations of 0.8 or higher. It is recommended that the Quality Scales be used only by experienced examiners who have already mastered the point-scale scoring method. In fact the Quality Scales are useful mainly because the Point Scales were previously so carefully constructed with validity indicated for each item in the point scale. The reviewer recommends to anyone using the Goodenough-Harris Drawing Test that they purchase the Quality Scales and eventually use them. Clinicians using this test as a projective personality assessment may find the pictures of the Quality Scales more meaningful and helpful than numerical point values. However, the validity for this test in personality assessment resides in the skill and experience of the clinician and not in the standardized norms provided.

Critique

This reviewer has been pleasantly surprised by the scholarly scope and clarity of Harris' book, *Children's Drawings As Measures of Intellectual Maturity: A Revision and Extension of the Goodenough Draw-a-Man Test,* even though it was published 20 years ago. Anyone desiring to use the test is encouraged to read this book prior to administration and to consult it frequently thereafter. The manual provided with the test booklets is taken from this source but is not adequate to stand alone.

Harris integrates work in developmental psychology concerning maturational stage theory into the discussion of the age scales of this test. The impact of the biological basis of behavior coming out of the work of Jean Piaget and others is presented. Harris effectively ties Piaget's four cognitive levels, which are age related in terms of maturation of the human nervous system, into a meaningful context for a better understanding of this test. Specifically he shows that the norms of this test extending from 5 years to 14 years overlap considerably with Piaget's concrete operations level of cognitive development.

The literature since 1963 on the qualitative cognitive changes among groups of children during the age span of 5 to 14 years is extensive. Add to this Lawrence Kohlberg's work on moral development with emphasis on qualitative cognitive levels over the same age span and one begins to appreciate the historical roots that work on children's drawings has provided scholars with interests in developmental cognitive processes.

This reviewer has used Goodenough-Harris Drawing scores from 5-year-old children at a local daycare center for lower socioeconomic families and correlated them with Full Scale WPPSI scores and consistently found Pearson r correlations in the range of 0.72 to 0.80.

This reviewer concurs with most prior reviewers of this test that the scores obtained by this technique do not provide objective measures valid for personality assessment. However, as stated earlier in this review, clinical use of the scales over time can become useful in a practical manner for perceptive, sensitive, and experienced clinicians.

In the last decade wide use of intelligence tests in the public schools has diminished considerably. They have been replaced by the use of recently normed standardized achievement tests. However, special services, such as those that school psychologists and vocational rehabilitation counselors offer, still find valid uses for administering intelligence tests. Interest in assessing a child's capacity for future learning as well as present achievement makes such use practical in trying to sort out attention and motivation problems from mental subnormality. It is in this context the reviewer recommends using the Goodenough-Harris Drawing Test as a supplement to an individual intelligence test. This test requires little time or effort to give and score, yet provides valid added information.

Finally, it is common knowledge that a child's drawings never portray objects exactly as they appear. Children select, modify, and add to what they perceive in an object. These outcomes result whether copying models or drawing from memory. The meaning of the object to the child guides the reproduction the child draws. In this sense language is closely related to a given child's ability to draw. Factors such as these support the claim that for the child drawing is mostly a cognitive process. Such reasoning supports the claim that the Goodenough-Harris Drawing Test is useful and valid to assess intellectual or conceptual maturity in children from the ages of 5 to 14 years.

References

This list contains text citations as well as suggested additional reading.

Anastasi, A. (1975). Review of the Goodenough-Harris Drawing Test. In O. K. Buros (Ed.), *The seventh mental measurements yearbook* (pp. 857-858). Highland Park, NJ: The Gryphon Press.

Dunn, J. A. (1975). Review of the Goodenough-Harris Drawing Test. In O. K. Buros (Ed.), *The seventh mental measurements yearbook* (pp. 858-859). Highland Park, NJ: The Gryphon Press.

Gibson, J. J. (1929). The reproduction of visually perceived forms. *Journal of Experimental Psychology, 12,* 1-39.

Harlow, H. (1949). The formation of learning sets. *Psychological Review, 56,* 51-65.

Harris, D. B. (1963a). *Children's drawings as measures of intellectual maturity: A revision and extension of the Goodenough Draw-a-Man Test.* Cleveland: The Psychological Corporation.

Harris, D. B. (1963b). *Goodenough-Harris Drawing Test, Manual.* Cleveland: The Psychological Corporation.

Hebb, D. O. (1949). *Organization of behavior.* New York: John Wiley.

Honzik, M. P. (1966, January) Review of *Children's drawings as measures of intellectual maturity. Journal of Contemporary Psychology, 11,* 28.

Hunter, C. (1965, Summer). Review of *Children's drawings as measures of intellectual maturity. Journal of Educational and Psychological Measurement,* 860.

Kellmer Pringle, M. L. (1964). Review of *Children's drawings as measures of intellectual maturity. British Journal of Educational Psychology, 34,* 338 N.

Kline, L. W. (1922). *The Kline-Carey measuring scale for freehand drawing (Part I, Representation) (Johns Hopkins University Studies in Education,* No. 5a). Baltimore: Johns Hopkins University Press.

Thorndike, E. L. (1913). The measurement of achievement in drawing. *Teachers College Record, 14*(5).

Woltmann, A. (1975). Children's drawings as measures of intellectual maturity. In O. K. Buros (Ed.), *The seventh mental measurements yearbook* (p. 860). Highland Park, NJ: The Gryphon Press.

Jack G. Hutton, Jr., Ph.D.
Educational Psychologist and Professor of Behavioral Science, College of Dentistry, Howard University, Washington, D.C.

GORDON PERSONAL PROFILE-INVENTORY
Leonard V. Gordon. Cleveland, Ohio: The Psychological Corporation.

Introduction

The Gordon Personal Profile-Inventory (GPP-I) consists of two separate but compatible paper-and-pencil, self-report instruments that together measure eight aspects of personality that are thought to be significant in the daily functioning of the normal person. The Gordon Personal Profile (GPP) measures the following four traits:

> *Ascendancy (A):* Tendency to be active, take the lead in a group, be self-assured, and be capable of independent thought and action.
> *Responsibility (R):* Tendency to show determination, perseverence, and reliability.
> *Emotional Stability (E):* Tendency to be well-adjusted and relatively free from worries, anxiety, and nervous tension.
> *Sociability (S):* Tendency to be gregarious.

In addition, these four scale scores can be summed to provide a measure of *Self-Esteem (SE)*. The manual indicates that this scale was designed primarily for use in counseling and research to identify individuals with strong feelings of inferiority or low self-regard (low scorers).

The Gordon Personal Inventory (GPI) measures the following four traits:

> *Cautiousness (C):* Tendency to exercise caution, weigh matters carefully before making decisions, and not take chances or risks.
> *Original Thinking (O):* Tendency to like difficult problems, enjoy thought-provoking questions and discussions, like to think about new ideas, and be intellectually curious.
> *Personal Relations (P):* Tendency to have faith and trust in others, and be tolerant, patient, and understanding.
> *Vigor (V):* Tendency to be active, energetic, and "alive."

Each instrument contains sets of four descriptive phrases (*tetrads*), with the GPP containing 18 and the GPI containing 20. The four phrases (or items) in each set are brief descriptions of personal characteristics and represent the four personality traits measured by the instrument. Respondents mark one item in each tetrad as being *most* like themselves and one as being *least* like themselves. Both instruments are self-administering and suitable for use with adolescents and adults. Notable attributes of these instruments are the semi-forced-choice format and their brief administration times (approximately 15 minutes for each instrument).

The author of the GPP-I, Leonard V. Gordon, received his Ph.D. degree in general psychology from Ohio State University in 1950. He was a personnel research psychologist with the U.S. Navy from 1952 to 1962, and with the U.S. Army between 1962 and 1966. Since 1966, he has been a professor of educational psychology and statistics at the State University of New York at Albany, where he has also been director of the Program for Behavioral Research and a University Exchange Scholar. He is the author of numerous publications, including several tests in addition to the GPP-I, and two books related to values and their measurement. He has served as a consultant to industry and to educational and governmental agencies in the United States and abroad. Dr. Gordon is a Fellow of the American Psychological Association in the divisions of Educational Psychology, Evaluation and Measurement, Personality and Social Psychology, and Industrial and Organizational Psychology.

The GPP was designed initially as an experimental forced-choice instrument to be compared with a traditional true-false type, self-report questionnaire in a study of the validities of the two methods of personality measurement. Results of that research encouraged the author to refine and publish the instrument. Subsequently, the GPI was designed to supplement the GPP by providing measures of additional personality traits.

Rational analysis and a form of a statistical procedure known as factor analysis were used in the development of the GPP and GPI. The intent of the author was to construct scales to measure a few basic aspects of temperament or personality (i.e., traits) and to do so in such a way that each trait would be measured relatively independently of the other traits. The author hypothesized certain dimensions of personality, or constructs, based on Cattell's research on primary personality factors (see Cattell, 1947). The author then prepared pools of items presumed to measure these constructs. The items were administered to samples of college students, and the items were factor analyzed by the relatively little-known Wherry-Gaylord iterative method (see Wherry & Gaylord, 1943). Factors representing the hypothetical dimensions emerged from the analysis that were clearly defined and had substantial item representation. Items representing different factors but having approximately equal preference values (i.e., social desirability) were then paired, and these pairs of items were combined into tetrads containing two high-preference items and two low-preference items, with each item representing a different factor or trait. Trial tetrads were combined into experimental forms that were administered to other high-school, college, and industrial samples. The resulting item analysis data were used to revise the forms—five successive revisions for the GPP and four for the GPI—in order to improve the preference value balance within item tetrads as well as the discriminating power of the scale for each trait.

The final form of the GPP was published in 1953. The final form of the GPI was published in 1956 to provide a more complete coverage of the dimensions of personality. Revisions of test materials appear to have been for the purpose of adding important new validity data (1963, 1978) and providing a combined Profile-Inventory booklet and manual (1978).

The GPP and GPI are available as separate test booklets and in a combined single booklet edition. A combined manual is designed to accompany both separate and single booklet editions. Simple directions appear on the title page of all booklets, making the instruments essentially self-administering. Most individuals in school and employment settings should be able to fill out the identification information, read the directions, and mark their responses with little or no assistance. However, the preferred procedure is to have an examiner present to 1) explain the type of test to be taken and the reason for taking it, 2) give directions for filling out the identification information, 3) read the directions on the title page aloud while the examinee(s) read(s) them silently, and 4) check to make sure that each respondent marks one *Most* and one *Least* choice for each item tetrad.

Hand-scorable answer forms are part of the test booklets. Alternatively, IBM 805 Answer Document editions of the Profile and Inventory are available. Scores are recorded directly on the answer forms, and profile sheets are not provided.

Practical Applications/Uses

The GPP-I should appeal to educators, personnel specialists, and researchers who need a brief, self-administering measure of a few widely recognized personality traits for use with "normal" individuals. The GPP and GPI have been used rather extensively in both industrial and educational settings. They have been found to have applications in personnel selection, occupational assessment, vocational guidance, personal counseling, and research, and the manual contains an excellent section on suggested uses in these fields, as well as in classroom demonstration. The GPP-I will be much less appealing to clinicians and others who seek a more comprehensive assessment of personality characteristics and/or who are not constrained by very limited testing time.

The instruments have been used with high-school, college, industrial, general adult, and certain seventh- and eighth-grade groups. Several studies have indicated that Profile and Inventory scores appear not to differ significantly across racial or ethnic groups, but caution should be exercised in using these instruments with members of minority groups because consistency of test performance apparently has not been demonstrated for them. The manual states that the Profile and Inventory have been translated into more than a dozen languages; however, no foreign-language editions are listed for sale by the publisher, and only a few such applications are mentioned in the manual.

The GPP-I can be administered by anyone capable of reading and understanding the written directions and checking to see that respondents are following those directions. Experience has shown that most individuals complete the separate forms of the Profile and Inventory in 7-15 minutes each, and the combined booklet form in 20-25 minutes.

Directions for scoring the GPP and GPI are clear and concise. Hand-scoring the booklet editions (separate and combined) is straightforward and easy, and can be learned and accomplished by clerical personnel in only a few minutes. There are separate scoring keys for the Profile and Inventory that are used with both the separate and combined booklet editions. For both, if no more than two tetrads have been omitted or improperly marked, scoring may proceed. The appropriate key is placed on the answer form contained in the booklet, and a raw score for each trait scale is recorded at the bottom of the form. Directions for hand- and machine-scoring of the IBM 805 Answer Document edition of the Profile and Inventory are provided with the keys. Machine-scoring must be accomplished locally by the user as the publisher does not provide this service for these particular instruments.

Raw scores are transferred to the front of the booklet and converted to appropriate percentile rank equivalents by using either one of the norm tables provided in the manual (separate sex norms for high-school and college students, general adult sample, and various industrial groups) or locally developed norms. There are no validity scales to detect either inappropriate or socially desirable response tendencies. Forms for profiling GPP-I scores are not provided, and configural analysis of test profiles is not discussed in the manual.

Although administration and scoring of the Profile and Inventory can be handled by a secretary or teacher's assistant, interpretation of scores should be attempted only by a qualified psychologist or counselor who has had appropriate training in testing and personality theory and has carefully studied the GPP-I manual. A GPP-I Interpretive Guide became available from the publisher in 1983, and should prove useful to school psychologists and counselors who are interested in the configural analysis of GPP-I profiles.

Technical Aspects

As mentioned previously, the Gordon Personal Profile-Inventory is a combination of two separate, but compatible, measures of some basic characteristics of personality. Essentially identical rational-factor analytic procedures were used in developing both instruments. Statistical relationships between scales measuring the various traits are reported in the GPP-I manual for male and female college students and for a sample of managers. Intercorrelations are generally low, indicating relative independence, except between Ascendancy and Sociability (.64-.68), and Responsibility and Emotional Stability (.51-.60).

A variation of the forced-choice item format was employed in constructing the Profile and Inventory in an attempt to prevent faking and/or socially desirable responding on the part of those being tested. This semi-forced-choice nature of the item tetrads results in quasi-ipsative scales insofar as traits are not measured completely independently and some artificial constraints are thereby placed on the interrelationships among different scales (e.g., very high scores are not possible on all eight scales). In a discussion of the use of the forced-choice technique in self-report inventories in the Fifth Edition of her classic textbook, *Psychological Testing,* Anastasi (1982) concludes:

> it appears that the forced-choice technique has not proved as effective as had been anticipated in controlling faking or social desirability response sets. At the same time, the forced-choice item format, particularly when it yields ipsative scores, introduces other technical difficulties and eliminates information about absolute strength of individual characteristics that may be of prime importance in some testing situations. (p. 524)

Reliability data are reported in the form of the internal consistency of the eight trait scales, and the stability of scale scores over time. Scale means, standard deviations, and standard errors of measurement are also reported. Unfortunately, these data are reported only for college students and/or three specific occupational/educational groups, whereas the instruments are said to also be appropriate for use with high-school and general adult groups. Internal consistency coefficients (split-half and coefficient alpha) are comparable to those reported for other personality tests (.82-.89). Stability coefficients of the magnitude .65 to .79 are reported over the duration of a 29-week training program for a sample of U.S. Navy enlisted men, and of the magnitude .45 to .69 over the duration of a four-year educational program for three consecutive classes of optometry students. Demographic information is not reported for any of the samples used in obtaining these indices of consistency of test performance.

Approximately 40 pages of the 1978 manual are devoted to questions of validity. Answers to the question ''What can be inferred about what is being measured by the test?'' are presented in sections: Related Factor Analyses, Relationships with Cognitive and Personality Measures, and Other Construct Validity. Answers to the question ''What can be inferred about other behavior?'' are given in sections: Research in Educational and Vocational Training Settings, Industrial or Other Occupational Research, Military Research, and Health-Related Research. The particular personality traits or factors measured by the Profile and Inventory have been demonstrated to be factorially well defined and robust. Seven of the eight scales are essentially unrelated to measures of intelligence and aptitude; the Original Thinking scale tends to show low positive correlations. Moderately high correlations have been demonstrated between scale scores on the GPP-I and 1) ratings of the same traits by peers and others, and 2) similar scales included in other self-report measures of personality. Relationships between interest measures and the Profile and Inventory scales have been found to be small in magnitude. In general, the rather extensive body of research reported in the manual (validity sections plus the reference list) relevant to criterion-related validation clearly attests to the situational specificity of personality traits, and, therefore, the importance of giving close attention to empirical validation in each user setting and the need to develop and/or use specific group norms: For example, scores on five GPP-I scales were found to discriminate between a group of highly successful and well-respected optometrists and a random sample of American Optometric Association members, whereas in another study none of the eight scales were related to either academic or clinical performance in predoctoral optometric training. In the manual, the author and publisher give generally conservative and professionally responsible suggestions for uses of the Profile and Inventory. The potential user of the GPP-I will be well rewarded by a careful reading of the 1978 manual.

Critique

The Gordon Personal Profile-Inventory (GPP-I) is a short, efficient measure of eight basic personality traits for use with ''normal'' people. It was well planned, carefully constructed, and is easy to administer and score. The 1978 manual contains a wealth of information about the test. Clearly, the author and publisher knew what they were about. They are to be commended for being responsive to at least some of the suggestions made by previous reviewers: For example, providing a single booklet edition and general population norms.

In an early review of the GPP, Fricke (1959) notes that "The method used to construct the Gordon Personal Profile will probably please those who favor the rationally and factor-analytically constructed personality tests and displease those who prefer the empirically constructed ones" (p. 127).

In a later review of the GPP, Heilbrun (1965) writes: "In summary, if there is interest in a short, convenient measure of a limited number of salient personality traits, the GPP is about as good as you can do. It is carefully conceived, reliable, adequately normed, and has received at least suggestive validation" (p. 232).

Distinguishing features of the GPP-I are 1) its combination of two separate, but entirely compatible, measuring instruments; 2) the use of a variation of the forced-choice item format as a means of attempting to prevent response distortion and bias; and 3) an unusually brief testing time. If an examiner seeks a short personality test to administer to a group of "normals" for the purpose of screening or research in an educational or industrial setting, the GPP-I is probably the best test available. However, a relatively modest increase in administration time from 30 to 45 or 60 minutes would enable the psychologist, educator, or personnel manager to consider such relatively recent models of scale construction as the Comrey Personality Scales and the Jackson Personality Inventory, or, for devotees of empirical criterion keying, the venerable California Psychological Inventory.

References

This list includes text citations as well as the most significant contributions to the study of the Profile and Inventory that are listed in the 1978 GPP-I manual.

Anastasi, A. (1982). *Psychological testing* (5th ed.). New York: Macmillan Publishing Co.

Cattell, R. B. (1947). Confirmation and clarification of primary personality factors. *Psychometrika, 12*, 197-220.

Demaree, R. G., & Neil, A. F. (1973). *Normative studies of personality measures related to adaptation under conditions of long duration, isolation and confinement* (IBR Tech. Rep. No. 73-18). Fort Worth, TX: Texas Christian University, Institute of Behavioral Research.

Fricke, B. G. (1959). Review of Gordon Personal Profile. In O. K. Buros (Ed.), *The fifth mental measurements yearbook* (pp. 127-129). Highland Park, NJ: The Gryphon Press.

Gordon, L. V. (1951). Validity of the forced-choice and questionnaire methods of personality measurement. *Journal of Applied Psychology, 35*, 407-412.

Gordon, L. V. (1978). *Gordon Personal Profile and Inventory (GPP-I)*. Cleveland: The Psychological Corporation.

Heilbrun, A. B., Jr. (1965). Review of Gordon Personal Profile. In O. K. Buros (Ed.), *The sixth mental measurements yearbook* (pp. 231-232). Highland Park, NJ: The Gryphon Press.

Wherry, R. J., & Gaylord, R. H. (1943). The concept of test and item reliability in relation to factor pattern. *Psychometrika, 8*, 247-264.

John F. Wakefield, Ph.D.

Assistant Professor of Education, University of North Alabama, Florence, Alabama.

GROUP INVENTORY FOR FINDING CREATIVE TALENT

Sylvia B. Rimm. Watertown, Wisconsin: Educational Assessment Service, Inc.

Introduction

The Group Inventory for Finding Creative Talent (GIFT) is a personality inventory designed to identify pupils in kindergarten through sixth-grade who have personality characteristics related to creativity. It is scored for three factors (many interests, independence, and imagination) and percentile ranks of the total score are used to identify pupils with these and several other characteristics of highly creative children. The primary use of the GIFT is in the selection of creatively talented pupils for admission to gifted education programs.

The original instrument was developed by Sylvia Rimm in 1975 during her doctoral research at the University of Wisconsin at Madison. The three original forms (for Grades K-2, 3-4, and 5-6) each contained 36 items. In 1980, the biographical items that assumed a two-parent family were omitted, leaving 32, 34, and 33 items at the respective grade levels (Rimm & Davis, 1980). Currently, the three forms are identified by grade level as *primary* (Grades K-2), *elementary* (Grades 3-4), and *upper elementary* (Grades 5-6).

The norm group is reported to be over 8,000 K-6 pupils from diverse cultural backgrounds (Rimm, 1980). One indication of the diversity of this group is the availability of the GIFT in Arabic, French, German, Hebrew, and Spanish. Since its appearance, the instrument has undergone surprisingly extensive cross-cultural research (Rimm & Davis, 1980).

Each set of materials contains a manual for administration, 30 copies of the inventory at the specified grade level, and an update on the new dimension scores. The manual stresses ease of administration, presents instructions for administering the inventory, and includes basic information on reliability and validity. Scoring cannot be done locally, but scores are promised within two weeks of receipt of completed materials by the scoring service (Rimm, 1984). If all 30 copies are not used during a single administration, the balance may be returned to the scoring service whenever they are completed. The charge for scoring is included in the cost of the materials.

This reviewer wishes to thank Norman Elsner, head reference librarian at the University of North Alabama, for bibliographic assistance.

The inventory can be administered in the classroom in 20 to 45 minutes, but there is no time limit. Each pupil requires a copy of the inventory and a pencil with an eraser. The teacher is required to read standard instructions aloud. The author recommends that the teacher read the entire form aloud whenever any pupil might have a problem reading the items (Rimm, 1984).

Both the teacher's instructions and the answer form direct the pupils to read each sentence and fill in the circle under YES if they agree with the statement and the circle under NO if they disagree. Examinees are told that there are no right or wrong answers and that no blanks should be left; nevertheless, the teacher should watch for blanks when the answer forms are handed in.

The items on the test are similar to "I like to ask questions" (YES scored + 1) and "I like things that are easy to do" (YES scored –1). After the inventories are sent to the scoring service, a computer printout is returned with the names of pupils, raw scores and stanines for three characteristics (many interests, independence, and imagination), total scores, percentile ranks, and normal curve equivalents (standard scores with a mean of 50 and standard deviation of 21.06). See Rimm (1984) for an illustration of a score report.

"High" percentile ranks (85-99) are noted as an indication that "the child has characteristics similar to those which are typical of highly creative children" (Rimm, 1984, p. 183). These ranks correspond to total scores greater than one standard deviation above the norm. This high-average-and-above range seems appropriate for an inventory that selects creative talent.

Practical Applications/Uses

The GIFT is specifically designed as a criterion measure to select creative pupils for gifted education programs. Rimm (1980) suggests that high scores be complemented by teacher, parent, and/or peer nominations to identify these pupils, but in no case should low GIFT scores be used to screen pupils out of a program. It would be prudent, however, to include an average to high average (100-115) IQ score as one of the criteria for identification of creative talent or "giftedness."

The instructional implications of the inventory need to be developed in the future. These implications may include planning individual study programs to suit the breadth of interests, degree of independence, and depth of imagination that each child expresses. Individual programs can range in terms of variety, structure, and fantasy, just to name three programmatic variables that appear to be related to the three dimension scores.

This inventory might also have two uses outside of gifted education programs. One potential use would be for elementary school counselors, to help identify creative pupils among those who are referred to them for guidance (Davis & Rimm, 1977). In practice, this use may be as beneficial to communities as screening better-behaved pupils for gifted programs. Early identification of creative pupils in this population may alert counselors and schools to the need to create unique opportunities and provide special support for a few individuals outside of formal programs.

A second potential use of the GIFT would be as a criterion measure for basic research on creativity in the elementary years. The problem-finding-and-solving approach to the study of creativity continues to be fruitful, but it requires alternative approaches as criteria for validation. The characteristics approach can be a reliable and valid alternative to the creative performance criterion.

Regarding the practical aspects of administration, no familiarity with research or guidance testing is assumed. The inventory can be administered in class by the regular classroom teacher. Each teacher should have a manual but otherwise requires no equipment or special training. The author requests (Rimm, 1980) that no other work take place simultaneously.

Since scoring is not done locally, there is a delay in feedback, but the manual notes that scores can sometimes be returned within a week if the completed inventories are marked "RUSH." A minimal acquaintance with educational testing is required to interpret the scores, which include means and standard deviations for each class. Normal curve equivalents may be useful for comparison of groups, but total scores or percentile ranks are sufficient for identification purposes.

The GIFT has been administered to a wide range of K-6 pupils with diverse backgrounds and abilities (i.e., heterogeneous, gifted, learning disabled, culturally deprived, lower SES, upper middle SES, rural, suburban, urban, public, private, minority, and white) and seems generally valid for the groups tested so far. The GIFT also seems generally valid for different nationalities, including American, Australian, French, and Israeli pupils.

Technical Aspects

The reliability of the inventory increases with the age of the pupil. The manual reports split-half reliabilities for the three forms of .80 (Grades K-2), .86 (Grades 3-4), and .88 (Grades 5-6). Test-retest reliability over a six-month period for 126 K-6 pupils is reported to be .56 (Rimm & Davis, 1976). Like the split-half reliability of scores, the stability probably increases with the child's age, becoming acceptable for individual identification of personality characteristics at age nine or so.

Content validity was established by using items that described the personality characteristics of creative children as researched by other investigators. The main characteristics included curiosity, independence, flexibility, perseverance, and breadth of interests. In 1982, the three dimension scores were introduced as the result of factor analysis.

As Rekdal (1977) mentions, the efforts to demonstrate criterion-related validity have been painstaking. In the initial study (Rimm & Davis, 1976), scores on a brief form of GIFT (25 core items administered to Grades 1-6) were correlated with a composite criterion consisting of teacher nominations for creative ideas and acceptably reliable ratings of short stories and pictures. The correlation for Grade 1 apparently did not reach significance, but correlations for the other grade levels did, ranging from .28 (third grade) to .42 (fifth grade). Rimm and Davis (1976) noted that GIFT validity increased with higher grade levels, a result probably due to the increased reliability of the responses.

Scores for girls seem to be somewhat more valid than scores for boys (Davis & Rimm, 1977). This sex difference may be due to the validation criteria or to differential rates of maturation. Its source should be identified in future research.

In addition to the composite criterion, scores on two divergent-thinking tests (adapted from Circles and Unusual Uses in the Torrance tests) were used as creativity criteria. Correlations between GIFT scores and scores on these tests were .03 (n.s.) and .21 ($p < .01$). Apparently, GIFT assesses an aspect of creativity that is only marginally assessed by tests of divergent thinking.

Despite more than a dozen validity studies by Rimm and Davis since 1976, the central tendencies of the validity coefficients are about the same as the values reported in the initial study. Scores on the primary and elementary forms seem to correlate modestly (.3) with the composite criterion, and those on the upper elementary form correlate with it more substantially (.4).

Little independent confirmation of the success of the upper elementary form is as yet available. In a study of problem finding in a divergent-thinking exercise (Wakefield, 1985), scores for 23 above-average pupils on the upper elementary form of the GIFT were correlated with responses to two divergent-test items invented by the examinee (an acceptably reliable measure of creative performance). The resulting value (.46, $p < .05$) offered independent confirmation of the validity of GIFT. GIFT scores were also correlated with highly reliable divergent-thinking scores and the resulting value (.33) was positive but not significant, confirming a second conclusion. The GIFT and divergent-thinking tests assess only marginally related aspects of creativity.

Questions that remain to be addressed are: 1) what is the relation of the GIFT score to intelligence? and 2) is the GIFT score a better index of creativity than an intelligence test score? Both of these questions are related to construct validity. The only evidence available to the reviewer (Wakefield, 1985) suggests that the GIFT score may be related to intelligence (e.g., WISC-R Vocabulary) but that it is also a much better indicator of creativity than is an intelligence test score.

If confirmed by larger studies or other investigators, these relationships would imply a significant advantage of GIFT over divergent-thinking tests, which indicate creativity only slightly better than do intelligence tests (see Barron & Harrington, 1981). Clearly, the GIFT has something to offer to education and research.

Critique

The GIFT is an inventory that deserves advised use both in education and in psychological research. Its assets are its ease of administration and its multicultural validity for pupils in Grades 4 through 6.

Research on creativity is possible with children in Grades K through 3, but it is unlikely that further research on the GIFT forms will result in measures that are more reliable and valid for this group. The results of research with children in Grades 4 through 6 are more encouraging. At these levels, the GIFT appears reliable and valid enough to identify pupils with personality characteristics related to creativity.

No creativity inventory or measure should be judged by the standards of intelligence or achievement tests. As they continue to be developed, they must be judged by the standards of existing creativity instruments. By these standards, GIFT has something to offer.

References

Barron, F., & Harrington, D. M. (1981). Creativity, intelligence, and personality. *Annual Review of Psychology, 32,* 439-476.

Davis, G. A., & Rimm, S. (1977). Identification and counseling of the creatively gifted. In N. Colangelo & R. T. Zaffrann (Eds.), *New voices in counseling the gifted* (pp. 225-236). Dubuque, IA: Kendall/Hunt Publishing Co.

Rekdal, C. K. (1977). In search of the wild duck. *Gifted Child Quarterly, 21,* 501-516.

Rimm, S. (1980). *GIFT: Group Inventory for Finding Creative Talent.* Watertown, WI: Educational Assessment Service.

Rimm, S. (1984). The characteristics approach: Identification and beyond. *Gifted Child Quarterly, 28,* 181-187.

Rimm, S., & Davis, G. A. (1976). GIFT: An instrument for the identification of creativity. *Journal of Creative Behavior, 10,* 178-182.

Rimm, S., & Davis, G. A. (1980). Five years of international research with GIFT. *Journal of Creative Behavior, 14,* 35-46.

Wakefield, J. F. (March, 1985). *Towards creativity: Problem finding in a divergent-thinking exercise.* Paper presented at the meeting of the Southeastern Psychological Association, Atlanta, GA.

Mary E. Procidano, Ph.D.
Assistant Professor of Psychology, Fordham University, Bronx, New York.

HOME OBSERVATION FOR MEASUREMENT OF THE ENVIRONMENT

Bettye M. Caldwell, Robert H. Bradley, and Staff. Little Rock, Arkansas: University of Arkansas, Center for Child Development and Education.

Introduction

The Home Observation for Measurement of the Environment (HOME) most recently revised in 1984, is an inventory intended to reflect the extent to which children's home environments provide adequate nurturance and stimulation relevant to cognitive development. In particular, the HOME is intended to be a screening tool to be utilized in identifying "high risk" children, that is, children at elevated risk for later difficulties especially of an intellectual nature. It is also used to investigate ways in which the home environments of particular groups (e.g., preterm infants, developmentally disabled children, or children of low income parents) may differ from others. As an outcome index, HOME has been used to assess the effects of early-intervention parent-training programs on subsequent parenting behavior and provision of environmental stimulation actually occurring in the home. In addition, it has been used to investigate home-environment correlates of cognitive performance and change, as well as relative hereditary and environmental contributions to children's intellectual attainments.

HOME is intended to be an environmental "process" measure, that is, to reflect ongoing patterns of nurturance and stimulation provided to children in their homes. It is intended by its authors to be a more useful alternative to "status" indices (Caldwell & Bradley, 1984). The latter refers to demographic attributes of parents, such as education, occupation, income, and home density (i.e., per capita space) as well as cumulative indices of socioeconomic status (SES) that have been developed to reflect meaningful environmental variation.

As a process measure, HOME involves direct observation of children's home environments. Many of the items on the inventory are scored according to what the observer sees, although some items require scoring based on the verbal self-report of the mother obtained through semistructured interviewing during the home visit. All items on the HOME are scored by the observer in binary ("yes/no") fashion, reflecting, for instance, the occurrence or nonoccurance of particular maternal behaviors, presence or absence of types of play materials, or types of in-home or out-of-home activities in which a child has or has not participated.

The inventory consists of two developed in accordance to the age of the target child. The infant and toddler form is intended for use with families of children birth-3 years and has been utilized and validated more than the form for pre-schoolers, intended for use with families of children 3-6 years. A third form for elementary school children, intended for use with families of children 6-10 years is still in an experimental stage at the time of this review.

Development of the HOME inventories was conducted by Bettye M. Caldwell and Robert H. Bradley and their colleagues. Initial development and validation began in Syracuse, New York. Most of the work was conducted subsequently at the Center for Child Development and Education, College of Education, University of Arkansas at Little Rock, where Dr. Caldwell is Donaghey Professor of Education, and Dr. Bradley is research director and professor of Educational Foundations.

Development of the HOME emerged out a growing appreciation (e.g., among educators and psychologists) to assess adequately salient aspects of people's, particularly children's, environments. The goals of environmental assessment have been multiple and include aims of complementing more traditional "within-person" approaches to account for developmental and other psychological outcomes, and providing means of identifying individuals at relatively high risk for subsequent maladjustment. Identification of high risk individuals in turn is intended to enhance the study of the development of maladjustment and indicate appropriate recipients of preventive interventions.

Within the context of inquiry regarding adverse environmental effects on development and adjustment, many studies have indicated relationships between SES or "status" measures and intelligence, as well as psychological adjustment, with lower SES membership associated with significantly lower scores on traditional IQ and achievement tests. Caldwell and Bradley (1984) have reviewed some of this literature, indicating that although social class is important in understanding parental and child behavior, it is limited in utility as a predictor of children's intellectual and school performance. That is, substantial proportions of variance of those performance measures are not accounted for by variation of class status indices. Furthermore, such indices may obscure potentially large within-class variation in parent and child behavior and in salient environmental characteristics (Malone, 1963; Pavenstedt, 1965; cited in Caldwell & Bradley, 1984). To these limitations one might add that demographic attributes alone (e.g., parental education, income, or occupation) are inadequate in identifying the pathways or nature of the association between low SES membership and lower intellectual attainment; nor do they indicate the nature or components of potentially effective preventive or remedial programs.

As an alternative, HOME was developed to provide a process measure of aspects of children's home environments believed to be associated to some degree with SES, and more importantly, salient determinants of children's development, particularly cognitive development. The contents of HOME were derived from a list of 12 environmental processes, identified by Caldwell in 1968, that "appear to show a relatively consistent relation to (optimal) development" (Caldwell & Bradley, 1984, p. 10). Briefly, these include gratification of all basic physical needs and provision for health and safety, frequent contact with a relatively small number of adults; a positive emotional climate that fosters trust of self and others; optimal need gratification; an appropriate level of varied and patterned sensory input; consistency in the physical, verbal, and emotional responses of others, so as to provide modeling and reinforcement of valued behaviors; a minimum of social restrictions on exploratory and motor behavior; an organized physical and temporal environment to allow the formation and revision of the child's expectations; provision of varied cultural experiences, interpreted by persons who share the experiences; play materials and a play environment; contact with adults who value achievement; and a cumulative programming of experiences that match the child's developmental level.

The HOME manual (Caldwell & Bradley, 1984) indicates a prior developmental history of 15 years, during which time the forms for both infants/toddlers and preschoolers were developed and frequently revised. The revision process leading to the present versions consisted of shortening the inventories by eliminating items so as to retain psychometric soundness while increasing efficiency of use.

The infant and toddler form was standardized using data from families from Syracuse, New York, and then from Little Rock, Arkansas. The standardization samples were neither random nor stratified, but overrepresented lower SES groups, compared to the general population. As indicated by Caldwell & Bradley (1984), the Little Rock Sample (N = 174) consisted of 34% welfare recipients, 29% father-absent households, approximately 66% black families, average maternal and paternal education levels of 12-13 years, and an average paternal occupation ranging from skilled labor to sales. The present version was shortened from 72 items to 45 items by means of grouping items with similar content into 23 subscales, obtaining summative subscale scores, and performing a factor analysis on those subscale scores. A varimax rotation produced seven factors, and subscales with loadings ≥ .40 were retained. Items retained were those that correlated ≥ .34 with the factor on which the relevant subscales had its highest loading. Two additional items were dropped because of their low loadings on one of the factors, and one factor dropped because it contained only two items.

The development and revision of the preschool form were similar to those of the infant/toddler form. The current version consists of 55 items, shortened from a previous version of 80 items. The same type of factor analytic procedure was utilized, based on data from 232 families in Little Rock, including 30% on welfare, 28% father-absent, approximately 66% black families, an average of 11 years of education for both parents, and average paternal occupation ranging from skilled labor to sales.

Each of the HOME inventories begins with a cover sheet with space for coding relevant identifying and demographic information and for a summary report that is completed after the inventory is scored. There is space to record subscale scores that are then transformed into broadband percentile ranges in order to allow convenient inferences regarding the relative position of a particular child's home environment separately for each subscale and for the total score.

On the following pages, items are arranged by subscale. Each item refers to behaviors in which the parent may or may not engage, types of activities that may or may not be available to the child, etc. At the end of each item is a box that the observer checks if the item is ''present'' in the environment. Boxes also are provided for coding subtotals for all subscales, and space is provided for additional comments by the observer.

The manual provides rather complete descriptions and recommendations for persons using the inventories, including arranging the home visit and establishing rapport with a child's caregiver, usually the mother. HOME is completed by the observer in the context of a prearranged, semistructured interview that occurs in the home and, importantly, while the child is awake. Scoring should be based on direct observation but if this is not possible, the mother is questioned; it is assumed that when questions are posed in a nonthreatening and appropriate manner the mother's verbal report will be valid. The test forms also serve as the answer and scoring forms. The manual provides explanations of all the items, and examples of instances calling for positive versus negative scores.

The different forms of HOME are composed of different subscales that correspond to factors obtained in the item-reduction process described previously. Examination of the items suggests, among other things, that the HOME score reflects in part the childrearing, social and emotional competence of the parent or caregiver and that some of the variance of scores *may* be accounted for by the child's own behavior. One item asks specifically about the child's interactions with the father, and another item refers specifically to both parents.

The form for infants and toddlers (ages 0-3 years) consists of the following six subscales:

Emotional and Verbal Responsivity of Parent (11 items);
Acceptance of Child's Behavior (eight items);
Organization of Physical and Temporal Environment (six items);
Provision of Appropriate Play Materials (nine items);
Parent Involvement with Child (six items); and
Opportunities for Variety in Daily Stimulation (five items).

The form for preschoolers consists of the following eight subscales:

Learning Stimulation: stimulation through toys, games, and reading material (11 items);
Language Stimulation (seven items);
Physical Environment: safe, clean and conducive to "Development" (seven items);
Pride, Affection and Warmth (seven items);
Academic Stimulation (five items);
Modeling and Encouragement of Social Maturity (five items);
Variety in Experience (nine items); and
Acceptance/Physical Punishment (four items).

The form for elementary school children, still in an experimental stage, consists of 59 items that fall into the following eight subscales:

Emotional and Verbal Responsivity (10 items);
Encouragement of Maturity (seven items);
Emotional Climate (eight items);
Growth Fostering Materials and Experiences (eight items);
Provision for Active Stimulation (eight items);
Family Participation in Developmentally Stimulating Experiences (10 items); and
Aspects of the Physical Environment (eight items).

Practical Applications/Uses

The characteristics of the HOME suggest many potential practical applications. (Its usefulness as a research tool is described subsequently.) Since norms are provided, it could be used to identify children for whom some type of preventive or remedial intervention might be appropriate. Such an intervention might include training parents in childrearing skills, providing materials for home-environment enrichment, or a school-based cultural enrichment program. HOME could be very useful as part of an assessment battery that an educator, psychologist, or social worker might use to design a therapeutic intervention for children and/or their families. Because HOME includes several subscales it could be used to identify particular strengths and weaknesses of household environments; to provide focus for ameliorative efforts; or for populations not at elevated risk to recommend specific means of enriching or enhancing aspects of children's home experience that might in turn enhance cognitive, social, or emotional maturation. In a more "parent-oriented" way, HOME could be used to evaluate the childrearing competencies and assets of parents who might be expected to be somewhat deficient in them (e.g., teenage or low-income mothers). In this case, the pattern of subscale scores could also be used to identify training needs; and a follow-up assessment could be used to assess skill acquisition. The effectiveness of psychotherapy, for example with depressed mothers, might be examined through the use of repeated administrations of HOME because it is reported to be very sensitive to changes in the home environment (Caldwell & Bradley, 1984).

As described previously, HOME is intended to reflect variations across home environments by measuring aspects of those environments that are thought to be related to and contribute to children's cognitive development. In general, maternal emotional and social responsivity to the child, play and educational materials available, and sufficient variety in the child's routine seem to be important growth-promoting aspects of the child's environment. Educators, therapists, designers of preventive interventions, and social-science researchers might find HOME useful. Most essentially, it was designed as a screening device in order to identify high-risk children. In particular, children at risk for developmental delay or intellectual difficulty have been the main focus of use for the test; however, data collected in Guatemala by Cravioto and DeLicardie in 1972 (cited in Caldwell & Bradley, 1984) suggest its potential utility in identifying children at risk for subsequent malnutrition.

The relationship of lower HOME scores to other risk indices such as low SES (see, Caldwell & Bradley, 1984), suggests its utility in describing the nature of risk in greater detail. In this context it should be noted that the HOME was standardized on nonrepresentative samples. This is certainly consistent with goals of providing a screening instrument that differentiates effectively among low-income households. At the same time, HOME scores have been found to have low variability and questionable utility in middle-class samples (Caldwell & Bradley, 1984; Karger, 1979; cf., Metzl, 1980). The HOME has also been used as an outcome measure to indicate the effectiveness of parent training programs (Gray & Ruttle, 1980; Karger, 1979; Ross, 1984).

Another very important use of the HOME is in studying the nature of children's cognitive and social development, which might be of interest to any educator or social or behavioral scientist. In this context it could be useful in identifying aspects of children's environments that could 1) be related to their cognitive performance; 2) contribute (over time) to their cognitive performance; 3) be related to other aspects of children's behavior, such as sociability; 4) be in part a function of other (antecedent) aspects of children's behavior; 5) be related to or be a function of parents intelligence, education, or other competence; and 6) serve as causal pathways between parental intelligence and education and children's cognitive performance.

By necessity, the HOME is to be administered in the child's home with adequate notice when the caregiver is available and, importantly, the child is awake. The manual does not specify any particular level of training necessary to administer the HOME. It appears that a reasonably mature, interpersonally skilled person with some training in psychology and interviewing could administer the HOME because what is required primarily is establishing and maintaining rapport, asking questions about childrearing practices in appropriate, nonthreatening ways, and coding scores for all the items.

According to the manual, administration of either form takes approximately one hour. The manual appears quite adequate in providing explanations of the meaning of items; examples of circumstances requiring positive versus negative scores; and more "process" recommendations regarding making contact, establishing and maintaining rapport, and conducting the semi-structured interview. Thus, the process of scoring seems to be straightforward. Scoring is accomplished by adding all the items that have received positive or "yes" scores. Scoring is done by hand and should not be at all time-consuming. Caldwell & Bradley (1984) report that due in part to the binary scoring system, "it is easy to obtain high levels (90% or better) of interobserver agreement after fairly brief periods of training." (p. 11-12).

Interpretation of HOME is based on the scores obtained for the total and the subscales as well as from the percentile bands that are provided on the cover sheet. The manual does not provide much detail regarding interpretation. However, means and standard deviations from the standardization samples are provided, along with cutting scores utilized in previous studies. Thus a knowledge of social-science statistics and some normative data regarding HOME scores and their correlates in the population under study should enable a user to interpret HOME scores. The raw scores are usable in correlational analyses or group comparisons.

Technical Aspects

Over the past few years Caldwell and Bradley have published a number of studies related to the reliability and validity of HOME (see Manual for references). Reliability and validity data are provided for infants and toddlers and for preschoolers, particularly the former, in the manual.

The infant and toddler version seems to be justifiably considered an internally consistent instrument, with a Kuder-Richardson 20 reliability estimate of .89 for total scores, and estimates of subscale reliabilities ranging from .38 to .89. As the authors suggest, these reliability estimates seem reasonable considering the length of the subscales. Similarly, test-retest reliabilities of subscales range from low-moderate ($r = .24$) to high ($r = .77$) over periods ranging from six months to one year. Mean scores on this form tend to increase at least two points from age 6-12 months, probably because parents increase their behavioral repertoires and provide more types of play materials. The manual presents intercorrelations among subscale scores obtained with samples of 6-, 12-, and 24-month-old children. Subscale intercorrelations range from very low to moderate, indicating that the factors measure different but somewhat related constructs. The manual also presents data regarding point-biserial correlation coefficients between individual items and their respective subscales (all above .25 with one exception) and the total score (ranging from .05 to .51). In addition, there is a difficulty index for each item that reflects the percentage of families in the standardization sample who received credit for that item. Between 30 and 80% of families tested received credit for most items. Again, the normative samples overrepresented low SES groups, and middle-income groups have been observed to obtain rather homogeneously high scores.

The infant and toddler version has been validated in a variety of ways, particularly by obtaining correlations with SES indices and mental test scores. HOME was developed to be a more meaningful, sensitive environmental index than social class and thus be capable of reflecting meaningful variation within lower SES groups. Therefore, it was expected that HOME scores would be significantly but not highly related to SES indices. Results reported by Caldwell and Bradley (1984) show a reasonable pattern of moderate, significant correlations between HOME subscales and mother and father education, father occupation, and crowding ratio, but weak relationships to mother occupation among infants of 6, 12, and 24 months.

Equally important, multiple regression analyses have shown HOME scores to be better predictors of mental test performance than SES indices, and SES indices were found not to add significantly to the variance of mental test scores. Thus, the contention that the HOME inventory provides a more sensitive and meaningful environmmental assessment than status indices appears reasonable.

Concurrent predictive validity of the HOME are supported by correlations obtained between HOME scores and concurrent and subsequent Bayley and Stanford-Binet socres. Interestingly, the pattern indicates stronger predictive than concurrent validity. Validity is also supported by correlations obtained at six and 24 months between HOME scores and language scores obtained at 37 months.

Although such data regarding simple correlations are useful, HOME was developed to serve as a screening instrument. Its validity in that regard was investigated by performing a discriminant analysis in which HOME scores were used to classify home environments obtained when infants were six months old, related to retarded versus below average versus average intellectual development at age three years. Results showed the HOME to be 71% correct in classifying children with IQ scores below 80. It was virtually as efficient in classifying above average performance (70% correct), but somewhat poor in predicting retarded development (43% correct). It should be noted that HOME has been utilized fairly often to study the environments of trainable and educable retarded children (see below). Caldwell and Bradley (1984) also reported the utility of HOME scores obtained at six months in discriminating children who increased versus decreased in mental test performance from six months (assessed by Bayley MDI) to 36 months (assessed by Stanford-Binet).

In order to investigate potentially reciprocal causal relationships of HOME scores and children's mental test performance over time, the manual reports cross-lagged correlations involving HOME subscale and Bayley MDI scores at six versus 12 months and 12 versus 24 months. Results show rather complex patterns in which

> in some cases major environmental variables are influenced by a child's early cognitive capability, whereas later developmental status is influenced by other environmental variables. Further, it seems that the relation between cognitive capability and certain environmental variables may change from the first to the second year of life. (p. 50).

Research pertaining to construct validity of the HOME emerging from both examination of the manual as well as review of the literature reveals an overall pattern of positive findings, with HOME scores related to subsequent malnutrition, language and cognitive development, school competence, therapeutic intervention, and high-risk status (summarized in Caldwell & Bradley, 1984).

Information regarding reliability and validity of the HOME inventory for use with preschool children is more limited but consistent with data presented for infants and toddlers. Kuder-Richardson 20 reliability estimates ranged from .53 to .83 for subscales and to .93 for the total score. Subtest test-retest reliabilities obtained between ages 3 and 4½ ranged from $r = .05$ to $r = .70$. Again, these reliability estimates should be interpreted bearing in mind the brevity of the subscales. As with the infant and toddler version, the subscale intercorrelations obtained for 3- and 4½-year-olds ranged from negligible to moderate.

Many nonsignificant and a few significant correlations were observed between HOME subscale scores, total scores, and SES variables, of which the mother's and father's education (but not occupation) and crowding ratio appear to be related to salient aspects of children's home environments between ages three and six. Finally, HOME scores obtained at three years, particularly Stimulation Through Toys, Games, and Reading Materials; Pride, Affection, and Warmth; and Variety of stimulation, were significantly related to IQ scores at ages 3 and 4½. Patterns of correlations between HOME scores at age five and SRA achievement test scores were complex, but do serve to support the validity of the version of the Inventory.

Critique

As mentioned previously, the HOME, particularly the infant and toddler version, has been used in several studies pertinent to its validity. An examination of literature published between 1975 and 1984 has revealed an overall pattern of positive findings regarding covariation of the HOME with other indices, and expected between-group differences on the HOME. In a series of articles Zimmerman (1981a, 1981b) questioned the interrater reliability and validity of the HOME as described by Elardo and Bradley (1981a, 1981b). In general, however, the validity of the instrument appears to be widely accepted.

In this reviewer's opinion, HOME appears to be an interesting, useful, and potentially important measure. The areas of environmental assessment and high-risk ascertainment are timely ones, with relatively few psychometrically sound instruments currently available to them. The validity data seem reasonable; the low to moderate correlations presented in that context may illustrate the multiple and complex pathways that we tend to assume exist in relation to cognitive development, but which we wish were not the case when we undertake empirical studies. The HOME shows promise as a research and clinical-educational assessment tool. As with so many other constructs currently of interest, more experimentally and longitudinally derived data with relatively large samples would be useful to investigate constructs related to important aspects of children's home environments.

References

This list includes text citations as well as suggested additional reading.

Affleck, G., Allen, D. A., McGrade, B. J., & McQueeney, M. (1982). Home environments of developmentally disabled infants as a function of parent and infant characteristics. *American Journal of Mental Deficiency, 86,* 445-452.

Caldwell, B. M., Bradley, R. H. (1984). *Home Observation for Measurement of the Environment.* Little Rock: University of Arkansas at Little Rock/Center for Child.

DeFries, J. C., Plomin, R., Verdenberg, S. G., & Kuse, A. R. (1981). Parent-offspring resemblance for cognitive abilities in the Colorado Adoption Project: Biological, adoptive, and control parents and one-year-old children. *Intelligence, 5,* 245-277.

Elardo, R., & Bradley, R. H. (1981a). The Home Observation for Measurement of the Environment (HOME) Scale: A review of research. *Developmental Review, 1,* 113-145.

Elardo, R., & Bradley, R. H. (1981b). The Home Observation for Measurement of the Environment: A comment on Zimmerman's critique. *Developmental Review, 1,* 314-321.

Gray, S. W., & Ruttle, K. (1980). The family-oriented home visiting program: A longitudinal study. *Genetic Psychology Monographs, 102,* 299-316.

Karger, R. H. (1979). Synchrony in mother-infant interactions. *Child Development, 50,* 882-885.

Landy, S., et. al. (1983). Mother-infant interaction of teenage mothers and the effect of experience in the observational sessions on the development of their infants. *Early Child Development And Care, 10,* 165-185.

Metzl, M. N. (1980). Teaching parents a strategy for enhancing infant development. *Child Development, 51,* 583-586.

Nihira, K., Mink, I. T., & Meyers, C. E. (1981). Relationship between home environment and school adjustment of TMR children. *American Journal of Mental Deficiency, 86,* 8-15.

Olson, S. L., Bates, J. E., & Bayles, K. (1984). Mother-infant interaction and the development of individual differences in children's cognitive competence. *Developmental Psychology, 20,* 166-179.

Piper, M. C., & Ramsay, M. K. (1980). Effects of early home environment on the mental development of Downs Syndrome infants. *American Journal of Mental Deficiency, 85,* 39-44.

Ramey, C. T., Mills, P., Campbell, F. A., & O'Brien, C. (1975). Infants' home environments: A comparison of high-risk families and families from the general population. *American Journal of Mental Deficiency, 80,* 40-42.

Ross, G. S. (1984). Home intervention for premature infants of low-income families. *American Journal of Orthopsychiatry, 54,* 263-270.

Zimmerman, M. (1981a). The Home Observation for Measurement of the Environment: A comment on Elardo and Bradley's review. *Developmental Review, 1,* 301-313.

Zimmerman, M. (1981b). The Home Observation for Measurement of the Environment: A rejoinder to Elardo and Bradley's comment. *Developmental Review, 1,* 322-329.

Arthur A. Dole, Ph.D.

Professor and Chair, Psychology in Education Division, University of Pennsylvania, Philadelphia.

INCOMPLETE SENTENCES TASK

Barbara P. Lanyon and Richard I. Lanyon. Chicago, Illinois: Stoelting Company.

Introduction

The Incomplete Sentences Task (IST) (Lanyon & Lanyon, 1980) is a useful screening device designed to identify junior and senior high school and college students with problems in handling hostility, anxiety, or dependency. Respondents require about 20 minutes to complete the 39 sentences, which are printed on both sides of a single sheet, working as quickly as they can. For example, the first stem, "When I am bored," is designed to measure hostility. A trained scorer then codes each written completion either 0 (*no indication*), 1 (*suggests*), or 2 (*definitely indicates*) on one of the three scales (Hostility, Anxiety, and Dependency) by following a set of coding examples in the manual. Separate percentiles for boys and girls, for the School Form (Grades 7-9 and Grades 10-12) and for the College Form are provided.

The IST was in part developed from the master's thesis and doctoral dissertation of Barbara J. Lanyon more than 15 years ago at the University of Pittsburgh. She is a clinical child psychologist and is licensed in Arizona. Her collaborator, Richard I. Lanyon, is Professor of Psychology and director of clinical training at Arizona State University. Well known for his research in clinical appraisal, he co-authored *Personality Assessment* (Lanyon & Goodstein, 1971).

Practical Applications/Uses

The authors have attempted, on the whole successfully, to comply with the American Psychological Association's (1974) *Standards for Educational and Psychological Tests* in their recommendation that those who have overall responsibility for IST use should not only be psychologists with appropriate state certification, but also should respect the limitations of projective interpretation and understand psychologists' tendency to overinterpret projective test data. In fact, the authors are so cautious, rigorous, and objective that this reviewer wonders why they do not simply convert IST to an objective personality inventory.

The authors recommend that the IST be used in the screening of student populations for counseling and in "making objective predictions and decisions." They caution against its use in situations where deliberate distortion of responses might be a major issue and against "intuitive" individual interpretation. In this reviewer's opinion, when the IST is used in school or college settings responsibility for administration and interpretation should be clearly assigned to a professional psychologist. If used as a supplement to other measures, the IST would be helpful in designing an individualized program for an emotionally disturbed child or preventing academic failure by a floundering college freshman.

Although overall this reviewer is impressed with the authors' care in developing the IST instruction manual, they would be well advised to correct a number of deficiences in future editions. The administration section lacks a paragraph on communicating to subjects why they are taking IST, why they should answer honestly and accurately, and what will be done with their replies.

Accuracy in scoring might be improved by indicating how in Figure 1 of the manual the protocol for "Jim" (a case illustration) was scored and by incorporating definitions of the three scales in the Appendix, Manual of Scoring Examples. Also, users should be apprised of the approximate time involved for scoring, which this reviewer estimates would average about six protocols per hour for a trained scorer.

Regarding the normative data, the percentiles provided for a single junior high school in Pittsburgh should be replaced with a larger and more representative sample, those for high school students with a real sample rather than contrived averages, and those for college students with a broader sample rather than volunteer introductory psychology students at Arizona State University. Norms for special groups, especially minorities and the learning and emotionally disabled, would be helpful, assuming that IST is appropriate and valid for them.

Interpretation would benefit from additional case illustrations and from further suggestions from the authors as to how to communicate findings clinically in objective, projective, intuitive, or interpretative terms without violating the authors' "warning: CAUTION." For instance, if a psychologist says to a youngster, "I wonder what you meant when you wrote here . . . ," he or she can often skillfully begin to translate the client's message in the written response.

Technical Aspects

The construction and empirical evaluation section of the manual is a model for the application of objective psychometric methods to projective materials within a behavioral framework. Less attention is paid to completions which describe the internal, private, affective world of the respondent.

The rationale for using sentence completions to assess personality characteristics related to children and adolescents is strongly documented with empirical research. Sentence stems were based as closely as possible on specific behaviors generated from psychologists, teachers, and existing rating scales. The final 39 stems survived item analyses of internal consistency, evidence of power to discriminate criterion groups, and factor analyses; there were 18 for hostility, 10 for anxiety, and 11 for dependency. The manual reports high (Mdn. .97) interscore correlations for one set of 12 items over 30 protocols. Not only should there be correlations for each complete scale but also means and standard deviations by scorer. The importance of checking out scorers after training and periodically thereafter to counter drift should be stressed in the manual.

Data on test-retest reliability are not reported. This reviewer would like to know how stable the three scale scores (Hostility, Anxiety, and Dependency) are, especially for early adolescents, some of whom may not take IST seriously.

The School Form was cross-validated on teacher criterion ratings, which were themselves verified for reliability and validity. Also, each scale was correlated (low and negative) with intelligence test scores and grade point average. The College Form was significantly (.63 to .67) related to ratings by persons who knew the students well but not to self-ratings. Evidence about predictive and clinical validity is lacking. It would be interesting to follow up a group of students screened for anxiety, for instance— do they later exhibit anxious behavior or do appropriate interventions reduce anxiety?

Critique

All in all, although further development of IST is clearly necessary, the Lanyons are to be commended for their objective and sophisticated approach. IST should be a useful tool in the hands of an experienced practitioner. It may also have merit for research; for example as a dependent measure in outcome studies of psychotherapy or in experimental studies of hostility, dependency, and anxiety.

References

American Psychological Association. (1974). *Standards for educational and psychological tests.* Washington, DC: Author.

Lanyon, B. P., & Lanyon, R. I. (1980). *Incomplete Sentences Task (IST): Instruction manual.* Chicago: Stoelting Co.

Lanyon, R. I., & Goodstein, L. D. (1971). *Personality assessment.* New York: John Wiley & Sons.

Paul Conrad Berg, Ph.D.

Professor of Education, University of South Carolina, Columbia, South Carolina.

INFORMAL READING INVENTORY

Revised by Betty D. Roe. Scarborough, Ontario: Nelson Canada.

Introduction

The Burns and Roe Informal Reading Inventory (the second edition of the Informal Reading Assessment) is designed to help teachers discover the levels of reading material that students can read with or without teacher assistance. Further, the test indicates a reading level at which students should not be asked to function, and the level at which they should be able to function based on their ability to comprehend material that is read to them. A second general purpose of the test is to help teachers diagnose some of their students' specific reading skills problems in word recognition and comprehension through qualitative analysis of student responses to the test items.

The authors and developers of this test are Paul C. Burns (deceased, 1983) and Betty D. Roe. Dr. Burns held a Ph.D. degree in elementary education and English/ mathematics from the University of Iowa. As an elementary school teacher he participated in a Fulbright Teacher Exchange Program with Great Britain and later became an elementary school principal. He was a professor at a number of universities, including the University of Kansas, Lawrence; the Ohio State University, Columbus; and the University of Tennessee, Knoxville. His special areas of teaching were language arts, reading, and mathematics, in which he also served as consultant to various school systems. He was a member of several educational organizations and was widely published. His works include twelve texts with major publishers, many monographs, convention papers, research studies, and articles that appeared in educational journals and magazines.

Betty D. Roe holds an Ed.D. in curriculum and instruction with reading instruction emphasis, and the collateral areas of elementary education and educational psychology from the University of Tennessee, Knoxville. She is currently a professor of curriculum and instruction at the Tennessee Technological University, Cookeville, where she teaches courses in reading and language arts methods.

Prior to her present position Dr. Roe was an elementary school teacher and a remedial reading diagnostician and tutor for students in Grades 1-12. She has developed and supervised special reading programs and acted as a reading consultant for school systems, educational television, and state task forces on education. She has codirected many language arts and reading conferences, acted as editor for journal and newsletter publications, and has been a member and officer of several educational organizations. Her writings, which have been extensive, have been published by major publishers and in educational journals.

The positions held and productions of both of these test authors eminently qualified them for the development of the Informal Reading Assessment. Both worked with pupils and students in developmental and remedial reading at all levels evaluated by the Informal Reading Assessment and Informal Reading Inventory. Their contribution is from many years of professional, clinical, and teaching experience.

The authors had previously worked with a number of the commercial informal reading inventories and felt that several of their features could be improved. Reading passages selected for the inventory were longer than those used in other inventories, making for greater reader response; thus more data could be collected on students' reading strategies. Instead of using specially written passages that might not parallel the material that appears in students' texts, these authors chose selections from materials that are used in schools, including basal readers and literature series. Various types of questions assessing comprehension were written to avoid the tendency, common with some inventories, to include mostly detail questions that check only literal comprehension. Opinion questions were also avoided because they may indicate little about comprehension of the writer's message. More questions per passage than are used by other inventories were included. There are eight questions for preprimer through grade-two passages and ten questions for grades 3-12 passages, whereas some inventories use only four, five, or six questions. This inventory includes all grades through Grade 12, whereas many others extend only to Grades 6, 8, or 9. Development of the inventory took two years for the first edition (1980) and an additional year for the second-edition (1985) revisions to make the material in the passages more representative of females and minorities. Passages in the first edition were deleted if students had not reacted to them positively, and questions were analyzed and revised on the basis of user responses.

The second edition was developed for two distinct purposes: 1) to teach informal reading assessment to college students and inservice teachers, and 2) to give teachers an easily administered assessment instrument to use with their students. The inventory is contained in a spiral-bound paperback book for convenient use and administration.

The first two sections of the inventory contain information on administering, scoring, and interpreting an informal reading inventory. The remainder contains two equivalent forms of graded word lists and four equivalent forms of graded passages for each reading level from preprimer-Grade 12.

Each word list contains 20 words from one difficulty level, that is, the first list has word selections from a preprimer level, the second from a primary level, the third from a first-grade level, and on through Grade 12. Administration of these lists can help the teacher make a quick approximation of a student's reading level, give an idea where testing in the graded reading passages should begin, give some insight into the ways a student attacks the pronunciation of words, and indicate a measure of the student's sight vocabulary.

The levels of the inventory's graded reading selections were identified by use of the Spache Readability Formula (1953) for selections from preprimer-Grade 3 and the Fry Readability Formula (1977) for selections from Grades 4-12. The four equivalent sets of selections are provided at each reading level to facilitate pre- and post-testing. Each of the inventory's four Forms (A, B, C, and D) also contain two separate printings of each reading selection. One set of reading selections is used by the student to demonstrate his or her reading; the companion selections of the same words are used by the teacher during testing to note the student's pronunciation strategies, miscues, etc. At the end of each reading selection sheet used by the teacher there are comprehension questions for that selection. These measure the student's comprehension of main ideas, details, sequence, cause-effect, and inference. Also on each of the teacher's sheets are directions for scoring the student's performance. Finally, each form contains a summary sheet where the student's performance in word recognition and reading comprehension are posted; a profile chart where the student's skills for word recognition miscues and comprehension skills are recorded; and a summary table for recording word recognition, oral comprehension, silent comprehension, and average comprehension in percentages.

Practical Applications/Uses

According to the authors, every student in Grades 1-12 should be administered the inventory so that the teacher can plan a carefully designed reading program for each individual. However, if time does not allow for the testing of every student, those students who have indicated reading problems, who have scored low on a reading achievement test, or those on whom the teacher has no data should be assessed.

This instrument is an individually administered, informal reading inventory. It should be administered by a classroom teacher, reading teacher, or other person who is familiar with the purpose, use, and administration of such inventories. Reading clinicians in private practice, school psychologists, and guidance counselors may find the instrument useful. Although classroom teachers or other practitioners may have had training in the use and administration of an informal inventory, practice in administering and scoring the Burns/Roe Inventory is necessary for valid results from a testing situation.

The examiner opens the testing period by setting the student at ease, then begins the testing with a graded word list at least two grades below the student's grade placement. As the student reads from the list, the teacher makes appropriate notations on his or her companion list. If the student makes one or more word recognition errors, an easier list is provided until he or she reads a list without error. This level becomes the basis on which to begin the student's reading in the graded passages later on in the sequence. The teacher introduces word lists to the student until five words are missed in a given list. The list from which only two words are missed is probably the student's independent reading level; four errors represent a probable instructional level, and five or more errors represent the level at which reading material is apt to be too difficult.

The teacher introduces the next part of the test by explaining to the student what is expected during the testing. Before each reading passage, the teacher may read a short motivational statement to the student about the selection to be read. The student begins by reading a passage orally at the level at which he or she achieved a perfect score on the graded word list. As the student reads the selections, the teacher may tape the session, making comments and notations concerning the student's reading at a later time. However, the teacher may make notations of the selection at the time of the testing, noting mispronunciations, substitutions, insertions, omissions, reversals, and refusals to pronounce a word. After the oral reading, the selection is removed, and the teacher asks the questions following the selection, marking the student's responses on the teacher's copy. The student then reads a passage silently at the same difficulty level, and the comprehension questions are asked and noted as in the previous oral reading. This process continues up through the passages until the student falls below 90% in word recognition on an oral passage or achieves below 50% comprehension on the combined passages. Beginning with an alternate form of the level at which the student failed to meet the criteria, the teacher reads aloud to the student at each successive level, asking the associated questions, until less than 75% of the questions are answered on any one passage.

Analysis of the data collected from the student's oral and silent reading helps the teacher to determine the student's independent reading level (level that can be read without aid), and instructional level (level at which the student can read, but with some aid), and a frustration level (that level at which reading is too difficult). The listening level indicates the student's capacity level, or that level at which the student comprehends oral language.

A study of the student's word recognition miscues, both in the word lists and from the reading passages, will indicate his or her use of semantic, syntactical, and graphic clues, giving the teacher information for eventual remediation as needed.

Directions for administering and evaluating the inventory are clear. Several pages of examples of test protocols are included, making scoring and evaluation relatively easy. Administration can be mastered by a teacher who has had some training and/or experience in teaching reading and several practice sessions with the Burns/Roe Inventory before actual testing. Because the inventory is informal, strict standardized procedures are not demanded of the test administrator. Thus, the test may be timed (to determine the student's reading rate) or untimed, and other modifications in administration are possible, as noted in the manual.

Directions for scoring are also clear. The teacher can make notations on the student's reading during the testing session or may use a tape recorder so that scoring and evaluation may be done after the testing session is completed. Because the nature of the resultant test protocol are notations made by the teacher, these are summarized and posted on the summary sheet at the end of each form.

There are guidelines for determining an independent, instructional, frustration, and expectancy level from the data collected furing the testing session. Perhaps more important are the notations made on the way the student attacks word pronunciation and the reasoning and thinking skills indicated in his or her answers to questions. Any reading teacher or professional reading practitioner can interpret the test results with practice.

Technical Aspects

This informal test was constructed according to guidelines set forth for such tests. One of the most important requirements for the test was that the passages be chosen so that they become increasingly difficult as the student progresses through the selections in a form. The desire was to make the passages fit each successive grade level as perfectly as possible. Use of readability formulas and field testing were the methods chosen to try to ensure this appropriateness of difficulty. The word lists, passages, and questions were field tested with students in the grade levels for which the test was intended. Each word list was field tested on approximately 90 students. The questions were analyzed by graduate students in reading before they were field tested on students in Grades 1-12. Each form of the inventory was administered to students at the appropriate grade levels until every selection had been administered to a minimum of ten students, with most of the selections being given to many more than that. Nineteen passages from the first edition were replaced in the second edition. The newer passages reflect current concerns, represent minority groups, and in general raise the overall interest level of the reading passages. The new passages were field tested on students in Grades 1-12. In both field tests, the passages were found to become increasingly difficult as the grade levels increased. Any questions that proved to cause problems because of ambiguity, alternate responses, or other factors were revised or replaced.

The inventory has no section dealing with reliability and validity that would be expected in a standardized instrument. However, decisions on setting standards for the instrument were based on other studies of like instruments. For example, the work of Harris and Sipay (1980) was cited as a basis for interpreting reading rate scores. Decisions made by the authors on setting criteria for independent, instructional, frustration, and capacity levels were from the works of Betts (1946), Johnson and Kress (1965), Powell (1970), Powell and Dunkeld (1971), and Ekwall (1974).

Critique

The Burns/Roe Informal Reading Inventory, the second edition of the Informal Reading Assessment, was developed to aid teachers in assessing the reading levels of students and to obtain qualitative information concerning students' word recognition and comprehension difficulties. No reference to this instrument was found in the literature, but the fact that an informal reading inventory can aid in these decisions has been well documented by Pikulski and Shanahan (1982). Directions for administration, including several pages of illustrative scoring and evaluation charts, make this inventory easy to administer, score, and interpret. The authors have followed the principles proven by earlier inventory developers and have made such changes as were necessary to add relevancy to reading selection content by selecting from classroom materials. They have also given greater face reliability by selecting longer passages and adding more questions, and have extended the range of the test to Grade 12. Questions asked after each reading cover a range of possible types, rather than focusing mainly on literal meaning.

This inventory is well constructed and should be a fine addition to ways teachers have available for assessing and evaluating students' instructional needs in reading.

References

This list includes text citations as well as the list of references that appear in the Burns/Roe Informal Reading Inventory that discuss the general theory and practical uses of informal inventories.

Aaron, I. (1960, November). An informal reading inventory. *Elementary English, 37,* 457-460.

Betts, E. A. (1946). *Foundations of reading instruction.* New York: American Book Co.

Brecht, R. D. (1977, October). Testing format and instructional level with the informal reading inventory. *Reading Teacher, 31,* 57-59.

Burns, P. C., & Roe, B. D. (1980). *Informal Reading Assessment.* Scarborough, Ontario: Nelson Canada.

Cunningham, P. (1977, October). Match informal evaluation to your teaching practices. *Reading Teacher, 31,* 51-56.

D'Angelo, K., & Wilson, R. M. (1979, February). How helpful is insertion and omission miscue analysis? *Reading Teacher, 32,* 519-520.

Ekwall, E. E. (1976, April). Informal reading inventories: The instructional level. *Reading Teacher, 29,* 662-665.

Ekwall, E. E. (1974, January). Should repetitions be counted as errors? *Reading Teacher, 27,* 365-367.

Farr, R. (1969). *Reading: What can be measured?* Newark, DE: International Reading Association. (ERIC Reading Review Series)

Fry, E. B. (1977). Fry's readability graph: Clarifications, validity, and extension to level 17. *Journal of Reading, 21,* 242-252.

Geeslin, R. H. (1972, January). The placement inventory alternative. *Reading Teacher, 25,* 332-335.

Gonzales, P. C., & Elijah, D. V., Jr. (1975, April). Rereading: Effect on error patterns and performance levels on the IRI. *Reading Teacher, 28,* 647-652.

Goodman, Y. (1970, February). Using children's reading miscues for new teaching strategies. *Reading Teacher, 23,* 455-459.

Harris, A. J., & Sipay, E. R. (1980). *How to increase reading ability* (7th ed.). New York: Longman.

Hollander, S. K. (1974, September). Why's a busy teacher like you giving an IRI? *Elementary English, 51,* 905-907.

Johns, J. L., Garton, S., Schoenfelder, P., & Scriba, P. (Compilers). (1977). *Assessing reading behavior: Informal reading inventories.* Newark, DE: International Reading Association.

Johnson, M. S., & Kress, R. A. (1972). Individual reading inventories. In L. M. Schell & P. C. Burns (Eds.), *Remedial reading: Classroom and clinic* (2nd ed.) (pp. 185-206). Boston: Allyn and Bacon.

Johnson, M. S., & Kress, R. A. (1965). *Informal reading inventories.* Newark, DE: International Reading Association.

Kibby, M. W. (1979, January). Passage readability affects the oral reading strategies of disabled readers. *Reading Teacher, 32,* 390-396.

Livingston, H. F. (1974, September). Measuring and teaching meaning with an informal reading inventory. *Elementary English, 51,* 878-879.

Marzano, R. J., Larson, J., Tish, G., & Vodehnal, S. (1978, March). The graded word list is not a shortcut to an IRI. *Reading Teacher, 31,* 647-651.

Pikulski, J. (1974, November). A critical review: Informal reading inventories. *Reading Teacher, 28,* 141-151.

Pikulski, J. J., & Shanahan, T. (Eds.). (1982). *Approaches to the informal evaluation of reading.* Newark, DE: International Reading Association.

Powell, W. R. (1970). Reappraising the criteria for interpreting informal reading inventories. In J. DeBoer (Ed.), *Reading diagnosis and evaluation*. Newark, DE: International Reading Association.

Powell, W. R., & Dunkeld, C. G. (1971, October). Validity of the IRI reading levels. *Elementary English, 48*, 637-642.

Roe, B. D. (1985). *Informal Reading Inventory*. Scarborough, Ontario: Nelson Canada.

Rupley, W. H. (1975, October). Informal reading diagnosis. *Reading Teacher, 29*, 106-109.

Spache, G. D. (1953). A new readability formula for primary-grade reading materials. *Elementary School Journal, 53*, 410-413.

Valmont, W. J. (1972, March). Creating questions for informal reading inventories. *Reading Teacher, 25*, 509-512.

Williamson, L. E., & Young, F. (1974, July). The IRI and RMI diagnostic concepts should be synthesized. *Journal of Reading Behavior, 5*, 183-194.

Frank Auld, Ph.D.
Professor of Psychology, University of Windsor, Windsor, Canada.

IPAT ANXIETY SCALE

Raymond B. Cattell and Ivan H. Scheier. Champaign, Illinois: Institute for Personality and Ability Testing, Inc.

Introduction

This test is intended to measure a trait that clinicians term "anxiety." The authors of the test, Raymond B. Cattell and Ivan H. Scheier, arrived at their definition of anxiety largely by considering the results of factor analyses of personality questionnaires. They found that tests believed to measure tension, guilt-proneness, emotional instability, suspiciousness, and poor integration of the personality formed a cluster (technically speaking, a "second-order factor"). This finding implies, for example, that a person experiencing tension is also likely to be emotionally unstable and suspicious. The authors chose the word "anxiety" to describe this pattern of experience and behavior.

Cattell and Scheier did not adopt a particular theory of anxiety—Freud's, for example—and build a test to fit the theory. Nor did they develop the test out of a theory of their own, even though Cattell has presented cogent views about personality structure, and Cattell and Scheier (1961) devoted a chapter of their book, *Neuroticism and Anxiety*, to an analysis of the concepts "neurosis" and "anxiety."

By factor-analyzing the scores on many personality scales, Cattell developed a taxonomy of personality—a specification of the dimensions along which persons differ in their adaptation, feeling, and thinking. Cattell proposed that there are 16 primary dimensions of personality, or source traits. These 16 traits, however, turned out not to be independent of each other. Studying the relationships among these 16 traits, Cattell defined seven second-order factors—in effect, clusters of the source traits that have some coherence and that can be plausibly interpreted as corresponding, in some instances, to a concept that clinicians believe to be important. Cattell called the second of these second-order factors "anxiety."

The IPAT Anxiety Scale developed out of the sixteen Personality Factor (16 PF) Questionnaire (Cattell, Saunders, & Stice, 1950). That test is a product of the life-work of Cattell in applying multivariate statistical methods to the study of personality. Although Cattell has thought deeply about the relationships between psychodynamic processes and the factors that emerge from factor analyzing both observations of behavior and responses of persons to questionnaires (e.g., Cattell, 1959), he seems not to claim that this present anxiety scale was derived from any theory of personality, only that it represents a second-order factor that combines five primary factors.

Born in 1905, Cattell did graduate study at the London Day Training College with the pioneer factor analyst Sir Cyril Burt, earned a Ph.D. from the University of London, and was awarded a doctor of science degree from the University in 1939. For 50 years, most of it spent at the University of Illinois, Cattell carried out research on the structure of personality, using multivariate statistical methods, especially factor analysis. Although he has devised a number of psychological tests, he is best known for the Sixteen Personality Factor Questionnaire.

The publisher asserts that the *Handbook for the 16 PF* (Cattell, Eber, & Tatsuoka, 1970) provides normative data based on testing 30,000 persons, and that supplements to the handbook provide data from 20,000 more. Cattell, however, at first explored the whole domain of personality by obtaining ratings on 171 traits for only 100 adults. Having made use of this original study to shorten the list of traits, Cattell then obtained ratings on the shortened list from 208 men. A relatively small group, therefore, led to Cattell's first specification of what the salient dimensions of personality are. Once having defined these dimensions, Cattell steadily accumulated more and more data about the brief, self-report scales that he had devised to measure these dimensions.

In the manual for the Anxiety Scale (Krug, 1976) as well as in the 16 PF handbook and other writings, Cattell and his associates have given rather skimpy descriptions of how he acquired his subjects and their backgrounds. In describing the normative samples the Anxiety Scale manual states only that the three main reference groups—normal adults, college students, and high school students—together involve a total of almost 3,000 cases. Footnotes to the norm tables give a little more information, but not much more. For example, the table for "general adults" states only that it is based on 935 cases; 530 men and 405 women, aged 18-50 years with an average age of 30 years.

The manual describes four studies in which the Anxiety Scale was correlated with ratings of anxiety, and nine in which it was correlated with other tests purporting to measure anxiety.

The Anxiety Scale manual states that in 1976 test items were "carefully updated to adjust for language changes which had taken place in the interval since initial publication" (p. 6).

The 40 questions of the IPAT Anxiety Scale are presented in a four-page, 8½" x 11" booklet, with instructions appearing on the first page; questions presented on the two inside pages; and space for recording scores, observations, and a diagnostic summary provided on the last page.

Each item has three possible answers. For example for a statement such as "I like to read books" the subject is required to mark "yes," "sometimes," or "no" directly on the booklet.

Practical Applications/Uses

The scale can be administered individually or to a group of persons in any reasonably quiet, serene setting. It should not be given to a subject to fill out at home. Almost anyone—a psychologist, receptionist, secretary—can administer the test, which only requires directing the subjects' attention to the instructions printed on the first page. After that, the subject is ordinarily expected to read the instructions, then answer the questions without help from the examiner. However, in some instances it may be necessary for the examiner to go over the instructions carefully with the subject. The test is untimed and usually takes about 10 minutes to complete.

The test is intended for persons aged 14 years or older who can read at least at the sixth-grade level.

The user of this test can obtain scores on the separate traits that Cattell and Scheier grouped together to get a measure of anxiety, namely, tension, guilt-proneness, emotional instability, suspiciousness, and low integration. Because of the small number of questions for each of these component subscales the reliability of each subscale is quite low. The user can also get two anxiety subscores, one based on the 20 questions that measure anxiety in a less obvious ("covert") way and another based on the 20 questions that measure anxiety in a more direct ("overt") way.

The norms for the test are based on samples from general population groups, presumably normal adults, college students, and high-school students. Accordingly, one knows what is usual and what is exceptional within these groups, thus helping us to know whether an examinee is unusually anxious compared to normal persons. However, we would not know how unusual such a score would be for a patient in a psychiatric hospital or for a person attending a psychiatric clinic or hospitalized with a physical illness. No doubt the test can be used in such clinical settings despite the handicap that no norms for such groups are available.

Scoring this test is easily done. There is a scoring template that fits over the circles in which subjects have marked their responses. For each item an extreme score in the keyed direction (i.e., "yes" or "no") is counted as 2 points; the in-between choice (e.g., "sometimes," "uncertain," "rarely") counts 1. It should probably take less than 5 minutes to score the test—the manual suggests about a minute.

Interpretation of scores on this test is largely a matter of transforming the raw score into a standard score by making use of one of the three norm tables: adults in general, college students, and high-school students. The standard score that one gets from any of the tables is set to have a mean of 5.5 and a standard deviation of 2. The standard—or "sten," scores are figured in integer values, ranging from 1 to 10.

Scores of 4, 5, 6, and 7 were received by the middle two-thirds of subjects in the normative group and are average for the standardization group; scores of 1, 2, or 3 were obtained by the least anxious sixth of the normative group; and scores of 8, 9, or 10 by the most anxious sixth. Only about 2% of the normative group received scores of 10.

It takes no special knowledge, therefore, to translate the raw score on this test into a sten score, or to say how unusual such a sten score would be within the normative group. Where judgment is required is 1) in deciding whether the normative group provides the proper framework in which to consider the subject's score, 2) in judging what the IPAT Scale is measuring and 3) in determining the relevance of this information to decisions concerning the subject. These questions are harder to answer than one might suppose. For example, if the subject who took the test is an adult who came to a psychiatric clinic, how well do the general adult norms apply? It is not clear that they provide the appropriate framework in which to judge the subject's score.

The test manual does not make clear what training one should have in order to interpret the scores on the IPAT Anxiety Scale. This reviewer believes, however, that the interpreter should have the qualifications of a member of the American Psychological Association, namely, a doctoral degree in psychology.

Technical Aspects

"Reliability" refers to the consistency with which a test measures what it purports to measure. Does the test produce the same results today as it did two weeks ago? Does one part of the test measure the same thing as another part?

The first kind of reliability, concerned with stability over time, is indicated by the test-retest correlations. The IPAT Anxiety Scale shows adequate reliability of this kind. When the retest was administered after a two-week period, test-retest correlations were around .86. The second kind of reliability is best measured by the Kuder-Richardson Formula 20 (or by Cronbach's alpha). The IPAT Anxiety Scale, in a study by Cattell and his co-workers, had a K-R 20 coefficient of .80, which is quite adequate.

The authors rest their proof of validity on the factor loadings of the scale in factor analyses of the IPAT Anxiety Scale and other tests, on the correlations of the Anxiety Scale with psychiatrists' ratings of anxiety, and on the correlations of the Anxiety Scale with other questionnaires that claim to measure anxiety.

There is no doubt that in factor analyses of the Anxiety Scale and other tests, the IPAT Anxiety Scale has factor loadings on the same factor as other supposed measures of anxiety. Whatever these other tests measure, the Anxiety Scale also measures. However, from the information provided in the manual, one cannot tell what other measures of anxiety were included in the five studies cited, nor can one judge whether these other supposed measures of anxiety in fact measure that trait.

Data on the correlation of the Anxiety Scale with clinical judgments of anxiety were derived from four samples in three studies. The reported correlations vary so much from one study to another—ranging from .17 to .95—that one finds it hard to believe that the four studies are all concerned with the same test and the same process of clinical judgment. Nevertheless the author of the manual averaged these four widely divergent numbers, arriving at a summary correlation coefficient, .49.

Finally, the manual reports nine studies that compared subjects' scores on the Anxiety Scale with their scores on different tests supposedly measuring anxiety. These studies show a substantial relationship (correlations averaging about .70) between the IPAT Anxiety Scale and such tests as the Taylor Manifest Anxiety Scale, Eysenck's Neuroticism Scale, and Spielberger's Trait Anxiety Scale.

Critique

Because the Anxiety Scale was derived from the 16 PF Questionnaire, expert judgments about the 16 PF indicate, to a considerable degree, what specialists in psychological testing think of the Anxiety Scale. In a review first published in *The Sixth Mental Measurements Yearbook* Maurice Lorr (1970) wrote, "Although at present it appears to be the best factor-based personality inventory available . . . the 16 PF is still primarily a research instrument" and that "more specific facts concerning the construct validity of the individual factors is needed" (p. 1173).

Cronbach (1960) states: "The [16 PF] short scales have extremely low reliability (.45-.55) and the information on norms is unsatisfactory. Not recommended for the assessment of individuals" (p. 497). Cronbach's complaint about reliability of subtests would apply to each of the five components of the Anxiety Scale, but not to the scale as a whole; as we have seen, the total test has adequate reliability.

Anastasi (1982) wrote: "There is also some question about the factorial homogeneity of items within each [16 PF] scale, as well as the factorial independence of scales . . . . Available information on normative samples and other aspects of test construction is inadequate" (p. 514). Anastasi also expressed the opinion that the IPAT Anxiety Scale and the other IPAT scales devised for clinical applications are "experimental instruments requiring further development, standardization, and validation" (p. 515).

We cannot blame Cattell and Scheier for failing to clarify for us what anxiety is, as they offered the world their Anxiety Scale. Although disappointed that they did not clarify the concept, we must be content that they have produced another test that measures about the same thing—whatever it is—that a number of other tests that claim to measure "anxiety" or "neuroticism" measure.

The IPAT Anxiety Scale is in a convenient format, with all the questions printed on the inside pages of a four-page booklet. It is easy to score. It is of adequate reliability.

The vexing questions about this test concern validity. What is it that is measured by the test? We cannot be sure that it is what clinicians are wont to call anxiety; the evidence for that is skimpy. It seems probable that the test measures people's willingness to acknowledge that they are tense, prone to guilt, and not (in their own judgment) doing too well in meeting life's challenges.

Is this test, then, ready to be applied to such tasks as screening large groups to discover those who could profit from psychotherapy, or indicating who has become less tense and more secure as a result of therapy? I have serious reservations about such uses of this test—and I would have similar reservations about all the other currently available tests of "anxiety" or "neuroticism." In my judgment, research psychologists should now be using this test and others like it, to do extensive research that will give us the capability in a few years to use the IPAT Anxiety Scale clinically with justified confidence.

References

Anastasi, A. (1982). *Psychological testing* (5th ed.). New York: Macmillan Publishing Co.

Cattell, R. B. (1959). Personality theory growing from multivariate quantitative research. In S. Koch (Ed.), *Psychology: A study of a science: Vol. 3. Formulations of the person and the social context* (pp. 257-327). New York: McGraw-Hill, Inc.

Cattell, R. B., Eber, H. W., & Tatsuoka, M. M. (1970). *Handbook for the Sixteen Personality Factor Questionnaire (16 PF)*. Champaign, IL: Institute for Personality and Ability Testing, Inc.

Cattell, R. B., Saunders, D. R., & Stice, G. (1950). *The Sixteen Personality Factor Questionnaire*. Champaign, IL: Institute for Personality and Ability Testing, Inc.

Cattell, R. B., & Scheier, I. H. (1961). *The meaning and measurement of neuroticism and anxiety.* New York: Ronald.

Cattell, R. B., & Scheier, I. H. (1976). *The IPAT Anxiety Scale.* Champaign, IL: Institute for Personality and Ability Testing, Inc.

Cronbach, L. J. (1960). *Essentials of psychological testing* (2nd ed.). New York: Harper.

Krug, S. E. (1976). *Handbook for the IPAT Anxiety Scale.* Champaign, IL: Institute for Personality and Ability Testing, Inc.

Lorr, M. (1970). The Sixteen Personality Factor Questionnaire. In O. K. Buros (Ed.), *Personality tests and reviews* (pp. 1172-1173). Highland Park, NJ: The Gryphon Press.

Rebecca Bardwell, Ph.D.

Professor of Educational Psychology, School of Education, Marquette University, Milwaukee, Wisconsin.

I.P.I. APTITUDE-INTELLIGENCE TEST SERIES

Joseph E. King. New York, New York: Industrial Psychology, Inc.

Introduction

The I.P.I. Aptitude Intelligence Test Series, consisting of 5 aptitude and personality tests and the I.P.I. Employee Aptitude Series, consisting of 3 tests (the CPF, NPF, and 16 PF), are used in different combinations to select employees in 28 job fields. These 18 individual tests and a description of each are as follow:

1. *Office Terms:* Tests ability to understand the special words and terminology used in business, industrial, and government settings, particularly routine office procedures. It aids in the selection placement, promotion, and training of clerical, administrative, office technical, sales, and office supervisory personnel.

2. *Sales Terms:* Tests ability to comprehend and understand information of a sales or contact nature. It is used in sales and other contact job fields. The score may be used to suggest applicant's overall IQ score and/or to estimate over-qualification for the job.

3. *Factory Terms:* Tests comprehension, aptitude, higher level mechanical knowledge, and information used in skilled worker, scientist, engineer, and factory supervisor job fields.

4. *Tools:* Tests comprehension and aptitude of simple tools and mechanical equipment used in mechanical jobs, and for engineer and factory supervisor positions. It requires no reading or writing to complete.

5. *Numbers:* Tests ability to work rapidly and accurately with numbers and to understand mathematical concepts that are important in a variety of tasks such as bookkeeping, accounting, billing, actuarial work, sales, and other numerical jobs. It aids in the selection, placement, promotion, and training of clerical, administrative, factory/technical, sales, and supervisory personnel.

6. *Perception:* Tests ability to perceive details in words and numbers quickly and to recognize likenesses and differences rapidly. These skills are important in a variety of tasks such as coding, checking, verifying, and other detail-oriented assignments. It is used for all clerical job fields and for certain technical and supervisor jobs.

7. *Judgement:* Tests ability to deduce solutions to abstract problems and measures aptitude to think logically, foresee, and plan. These skills are important in a variety of tasks such as supervision, technical writing, computer programming, sales, machine operator, advanced clerical, secretarial duties, and any positions requiring instructional or organizational skills.

363

8. *Precision:* Tests ability to recognize likenesses and differences of objects and pictures. This skill is necessary for some technical jobs and is an important component of mechanical aptitude, especially where inspection-type duties are involved.

9. *Fluency:* Tests ability to think of words rapidly and easily, and to write or talk without blocking or searching for the right word. It is important in a variety of jobs such as sales, clerical contact, correspondence positions, and other jobs requiring substantial speaking and writing ability.

10. *Memory:* Tests ability to remember different types of material. It consists of three subtests—Visual Memory (recognize faces), Verbal Memory (recall words), and Numbers Memory (recall numbers). These skills are used in a variety of jobs including clerical, secretarial, sales, supervisory, technical, and professional areas of work where rapid recall and recognition of information is required.

11. *Parts:* Tests ability to see the whole in relation to its parts. It measures aptitude to visualize sizes, shapes, and spatial relations of objects in two and three dimensions. It is used with two other tests (Blocks and Dimensions) to measure spatial aptitude. These skills are important in jobs such as office-machine operators, clerical positions, factory inspectors, assembly workers, technical jobs (e.g., designer, engineer, and draftsman), and supervisory positions in an office factory setting where layout, planning, and organization skills are required.

12. *Blocks:* Tests space relations aptitude and measures quantitative ability. It is used mainly for jobs where numerical type of space relations is involved.

13. *Dimension:* Tests space relations aptitude. It is the most difficult of the spatial aptitude tests and is used in certain mechanical and technical jobs, such as inspector, designer, and engineer, where a heavy amount of spatial aptitude is required.

14. *Dexterity:* Tests aptitude for fine and gross muscle control, dexterity, and coordination of eye and hand. It is used for some clerical, mechanical, and technical jobs.

15. *Motor:* Tests coordination ability, but it is a more direct measure of coordination than Dexterity. It is used for all mechanical jobs, except inspector. It is the only test in the series that requires a piece of apparatus (a board with nuts, bolts, and washers).

16. *CPF (Contact Personality Factor):* Tests extroversion vs. introversion or contact vs. noncontact personality. Information about the type of behavior to expect from employees based on their CPF rank is also included.

17. *NPF (Neurotic Personality Factor):* Tests general stability, emotional balance, and lack of neurotic tendencies. As with the CPF, expected behaviors are included.

18. *16 PF (Personality Factor):* Tests full personality in terms of 16 basic factors (i.e., participating, bright, mature, dominant, enthusiastic, consistent, adventurous, tough-minded, trustful, conventional, sophisticated, self-confident, liberal, self-sufficient, controlled, and stable). It is also possible from this instrument to compute "complex" personality scores for extroversion, stability, level of anxiety, leadership, research-creativity, and initiative-drive.

Table 1 indicates which of these 18 tests are used to judge each of 28 different job fields. The relationship between the test and the job field is a weighted relationship. That is, the tests associated with each field are ordered as to their

Table 1

Subtests Required for Specific Job Fields

Job Fields	1	2	3	4	5	6	7	8	9	10	11	12	13	14	15	16	17	18
Junior Clerk	x				x			x								x		
Numbers Clerk	x				x		x	x								x	x	
Office Machine Operator	x				x				x				x			x	x	
Contact Clerk		x			x		x	x								x		
Senior Clerk	x				x	x	x		x							x		x
Secretary		x				x	x		x	x	x					x	x	x
Unskilled Worker			x			x								x		x		
Semi-skilled Worker			x			x					x			x	x	x		
Factory Machine Oper.			x			x					x		x	x	x	x		
Vehicle Operator			x			x							x	x	x	x		
Inspector			x			x				x	x	x				x	x	
Skilled Worker	x		x	x	x	x					x				x	x	x	
Sales Clerk		x			x	x			x	x						x		
Salesman		x			x	x			x	x						x		x
Sales Engineer					x		x		x	x	x					x	x	x
Scientist	x		x		x		x	x					x	x		x	x	x
Engineer	x		x	x	x		x	x					x			x	x	x
Office Technical	x				x	x	x			x	x					x	x	x
Writer		x				x	x		x	x	x					x	x	x
Designer		x						x		x	x	x	x			x	x	x
Instructor		x				x	x		x	x	x					x	x	x
Office Supervisor	x				x	x	x		x	x	x					x	x	x
Sales Supervisor		x			x	x	x		x	x	x					x	x	x
Factory Supervisor	x		x	x	x		x		x	x	x					x	x	x
Optometric Assistant	x				x	x	x		x							x	x	
Dental Office Assistant	x				x	x	x									x	x	
Dental Technician													x	x		x	x	
Computer Programmer	x				x	x	x			x								

*1 = Office Terms; 2 = Sales Terms; 3 = Factory Terms; 4 = Tools; 5 = Numbers; 6 = Perception; 7 = Judgement; 8 = Precision; 9 = Fluency; 10 = Memory; 11 = Parts; 12 = Blocks; 13 = Dimension; 14 = Dexterity; 15 = Motor; 16 = C.P.F.; 17 = N.P.F.; 18 = 16 P.F.

importance and weighted by their importance. This allows the same tests to be used by different fields, although the same results may lead to different scores for the different fields.

This test battery was originally developed in 1947 by Dr. Joseph E. King. Though the individual tests are presented separately by the publisher and appear to have been developed separately, there is much similarity among the procedures. Thus, this discussion will consider the battery as a whole. Dr. King began his development of the test by analyzing a variety of jobs in the business world. From this he constructed a large pool of items designed to measure the knowledge required for these jobs. Through item analysis, individual items were selected to be published. The original 1947 test was revised in 1956 and a current revision which commenced in 1978 is presently underway. This most recent revision began by testing 95 high-school and college students to determine item difficulty, ambiguity, and item-total score validity. This resulted in some item changes. The revised test was then tested using 874 employees from eight different corporations across 11 job classifications. The major thrust of the revisions seems to be reducing ambiguity in the test items and making the tests more accurately represent the skills desired by the employer.

All the test forms are in English, but the individual tests are also available in both French and Spanish. The following tests are graphic, requiring no language skills: Tools, Precision, Dimension, Parts, Blocks, Dexterity, and Motor. Comparison norms for minority and nonminority persons are included.

All forms of the test are presented in individual 3- to 10-page test booklets each of which has a test examiner's manual that includes directions for administering the test, scoring procedures, normative data, and reliability and validity information. All of the tests are paper-and-pencil tests except the Motor test that requires a board with nuts, bolts, and washers. In this test the examinee is allowed two minutes to remove nuts and washers from 20 bolts and replace them on 20 other bolts. The other tests vary depending on the skill being tested. For example, the three Terms tests (Office, Sales, and Factory) use a term in a sentence or phrase and require the examinee to select one of four possible responses. Numbers requires the examinee to compute mathematical problems. Perception presents an item, such as a dollar amount, name, address, or number, and asks the examinee to select the one of four that is exactly the same. It is similar to the skills one would require for proofreading. Most of the tests are verbal tests. However, the Tools test pictures a tool and asks which tools in four other pictures belong with it. Most of the tests are timed, with the allowed time ranging from approximately two to six minutes.

A hiring summary worksheet is also included for each of the job categories. The hiring summary lists the recommended tests for a particular job, provides instructions for weighting the tests, and includes space for information from the interview.

Practical Applications/Uses

Because this is an employment aptitude test, it is meant to be used with adults. The difficulty level varies with each of the subtests, though the overall reading level seems to be appropriate for high-school students.

The test battery has broad applicability in employment for both hiring and promotion. It is not recommended for purposes other than employment. It can easily be administered and scored by an employer. The materials contained in the test include instructions for administration, scoring, and interpreting the results. Instructions for administration are written in a clear language that is appropriate for the layman. The time limit for the test battery varies because examinees in different job fields are required to take different tests. The tests are arranged in an order for each field and divided into groups so that a prospective employee might take two or three tests at an initial interview and, if called back for a second interview, might take another group of tests. An employer can also pick and choose among the individual subtests to select a battery that predicts the skills required for his particular operation.

The scoring materials are also clearly stated. The administrator can probably learn to score the tests in an afternoon by reading the individual manuals. Once learned, the scoring for an individual test will take only a few minutes. Machine- or computer-scoring is not available from the test publishers, though the scoring is such that one could write a program to score the test with relative ease.

The score interpretation materials are clear enough that one need not be trained as a psychometrician to use them, though a consultant may be needed to establish the company's norms. For each job field, score values on the individual subtests are related to qualification levels. These qualification levels are then weighted and combined to arrive at a total score. This total score would then be compared to other persons applying for the same position or in line for the same promotion. No overall norms by profession are given, thus requiring a comparison across individuals. The test publishers recognize that each employment situation will be different and suggest that an employer develop norms unique to that situation by testing the organization's present employees.

Technical Aspects

Reliability was established for the individual subtests and not for the total test score. In most cases the reliability was assessed by administering the same test to a group of about 100 workers at two different times about four hours apart. This allowed test-retest relilability and Kuder-Richardson reliability to be computed. The reported test-retest reliabilities ranged from .701 to .838 with, for example, Office Terms equal to .811, Fluency equal to .701, Memory equal to .71, and Parts equal to .735. Likewise, the Kuder-Richardson reliabilities ranged from .745 to .897, with Office Terms equal to .897 and Parts equal to .879.

Validity was assessed in a variety of settings by assessing the validity of an individual test. In all cases it was concurrent validity that was being studied. The test was given to a group of employees ranging in size from 15 to 78 and correlated with their job performance. Several different job performance criteria, such as work quality, dependability, overall performance, effective handling of special assignments, appropriate use of information sources, effective work scheduling, adherence to office procedures, and written communication skills, were used.

The correlations between the test scores and these criteria ranged from .21 to .72 with the significance levels of the correlations ranging from .10 to .01.

Critique

All of the research available (Siegal et al., 1983a; b; c) assesses the reliability and validity of the individual tests. Nowhere could information be found that assessed the total test battery. This is perhaps because the subtests can be used in any combination for different needs. This certainly has advantages in an employment setting, but what is lacking is a sense that this is a test battery. One is left with the feeling that it is merely a collection of tests.

The publisher does suggest that the test can be used to measure IQ and on some of the tables comparative IQ norms are given. This appears to be an overstatement of the test's goals. As a measure of employee effectiveness the instrument has much promise and impressive data to support it. As a measure of IQ it is inappropriately represented.

References

Cattell, R. B., King, J. E., & Schuettler, A. K. (1960). *I.P.I. Employee Aptitude Series*. New York: Industrial Psychology Inc.

King, J. E. (1947-1981) *I.P.I. Aptitude Intelligence Test Series*. New York: Industrial Psychology, Inc.

Siegel, J., Bondy, J., Yovanni, A., Tatham, J., & Nowark, M. (1983, June). *A statistical summary of validation studies in the data processing field for applications programmer, advanced applications programmer and analyst, and technical services staff.* (Available from [Industrial Psychology Inc., 515 Madison Ave., New York, NY, 10022])

Siegel, J., Stanley, B., Bondy, J., Yovanni, A., & Nowark, M. (1983, June). *A statistical summary of validation studies in the insurance industry for a variety of clerical positions.* (Available from [Industrial Psychology Inc., 515 Madison Ave., New York, NY, 10022])

Siegel, J., Stanley, B., Bondy, J., Yovanni, A., Tatham, J., & Nowark, M. (1983, June). *A statistical summary of validation studies in the banking industry for teller, clerk, and supervisor.* (Available from [Industrial Psychology Inc., New York, NY, 10022])

Calvin O. Dyer, Ph.D.
Professor of Education, University of Michigan, Ann Arbor, Michigan.

JACKSON PERSONALITY INVENTORY

Douglas N. Jackson. Port Huron, Michigan: Research Psychologists Press, Inc.

Introduction

The Jackson Personality Inventory (JPI) may be used to assess a variety of personality characteristics in normally functioning individuals to aid in counseling, personality research, and making predictions relevant for school and industry. The personality dimensions include relating to other people, alternative value orientations, and some general features of cognitive functioning. Examples of traits measured by the 16 scales are breadth of interest, conformity, responsibility, and value orthodoxy. The test has a practical orientation of predicting behavior in a variety of contexts without emphasizing psychological disturbance or deviance. It was developed to use with senior high school and college students and adults of average or above average ability.

The test was developed over a period of 14 years by Douglas N. Jackson, who has had a significant record of research and publications in the study of personality. Development was rigorous and painstaking and the results are generally praised. Jackson has participated actively in theoretical research on self-report methodology and as a result has used the most favorable rationale for the development of the test. He also capitalized on the use of computers in item development and analysis.

There is a strong interest among many research and counseling people to have a personality inventory that measures dimensions that are practical or based on common sense, do not threaten, tend not to overlap with one another, and feature clear interpretations without response biases, such as social desirability or acquiescence which tend to make interpretations ambiguous. The JPI is considered by many to succeed at these features. The JPI is not derived from any particular personality theory, however, as is the author's former test, the Personality Research Form (1965), which is an assessment of Murray's personality theory of needs. The JPI is not related to the former test in either content or goal.

The test consists of 320 true-false items printed in reusable booklets with answers marked with ''X'' on a single answer sheet. The test takes from 30 to 60 minutes to complete. It is most appropriately used for college students as well as high school students, but as norms become available, it is also appropriate for noncollege adults and younger people. The manual (Jackson, 1976) indicates the readability level is appropriate for at least junior high age students. The test is scored by hand and the scores then transcribed onto a profile sheet showing a

369

picture of the magnitude and the direction of score for each of the scales. People who administer and interpret the JPI should have an intermediate qualification level of education in psychological measurement according to the designation system of testing standards.

The 16 personality scales used in the inventory are as follows:

Anxiety	Responsibility
Breadth of Interest	Risk Taking
Complexity	Self Esteem
Conformity	Social Adroitness
Energy Level	Social Participation
Innovation	Tolerance
Interpersonal Affect	Value Orthodoxy
Organization	Infrequency

The Infrequency scale is a validity scale which indicates a tendency for careless or random responding. Each scale has 20 items; with half of the items keyed true and half keyed false in order to aid in reducing response set bias and permit positively worded interpretations for each end of the bipolar scales. Scoring by hand is convenient. The answer sheet has 32 columns so that each scale is assigned two columns of answers. A single scoring template can then be placed over the answer sheet, and marks tallied for each column, then summed for each scale. Scores on the profile sheet are converted to standard scores which are T-scores with a mean of 50 and standard deviation of 10. The T-scores were developed from the standardization sample of 2,000 males and 2,000 females from 40 American and 3 Canadian colleges and universities. The manual also reports that a sample was obtained from 400 males and 554 females for an 11th- and 12th-grade high school in Canada but separate norms are not reported.

Practical Application/Uses

Each scale has an explicit narrative definition in the manual for interpreting performance of both high and low scorers. In addition, there are corresponding sets of adjectives for describing each high and low scorer on each scale. These explicit definitions were first used as the basis for the development of the items in the scale construction. They thus become the basis for interpretation of performance on the scales and for validation studies of the scales. It is emphasized in the manual that test interpreters should adhere to these definitions rather than imply meaning to the scale from other informational sources or from their own perceptions of what the scale labels mean. The manual provides examples of profiles for several people whose results are different in one way or another, such as a leading teacher, student, nurse, and people with academic difficulty or other problems.

An "Interpreter's Guide to the Jackson Personality Inventory" (Jackson, 1978) is available as a separate book chapter and in some respects it is more informative for interpretation than the manual. In this guide the discussion for each scale begins with a sample item that is keyed true and follows with comments about research origins and rationale for the personality dimension. Characteristics for high and low scorers are then given, respectively. Evidence is also presented where gathered for the relationship of the scale with other personality scales or nontest predictions of behavior. For instance, an example for the Complexity Scale might read as follows:

I enjoy the challenge of reading a complicated novel: The scale denotes a preference for complexity rather than complex dynamics within the individual. It suggests that the examinee is likely to manifest an interest in intellectual and artistic problems that require complex analysis or thought processes. Origin of the trait is related to research on the Barron-Welsh Art Judgement scale and also the social perception research of Sechrest and Jackson, for example. Content of the scale items broadly encompasses interpersonal motives, artistic preferences, and general topics requiring analysis. People who score high on Complexity enjoy abstract thinking, pursuing topics in depth, thinking about intricate solutions to problems, and are impatient with oversimplification. These people are complex, contemplative, clever, discerning, and thoughtful. People who score low on Complexity tend to prefer concrete over abstract thinking, avoid contemplative thought, and generally avoid activities aimed at probing for new insights. These people are uncomplicated, straightforward, unreflective, and predictable.

There is also an entirely separate mode of interpretation presented in the guide which is the concept of modal profiles. Higher order constructs of interpretation and additional insights about individuals may be obtained by considering the entire configuration of their scale responses. By considering elevation, scatter, and the shape of score profiles as components of a complex data matrix, the author describes procedures for developing replicable profiles. Five male and five female modal profiles are thus defined and retained for further evaluation and research. Examples of individuals representing these profiles are given in the guide. One of the modal profile types for males, for example, shows high scores on Organization, Responsibility, and Value Orthodoxy, with accompanying low scores on Complexity, Innovation, and Risk Taking. The implication is that males with this configuration will behave in a predictable manner in, for example, occupations, teaching situations, or learning situations that reinforce or are relevant to those scale characteristics. The reverse modal profile set of responses is also possible for a male who scores high on Complexity, Innovation, and Risk Taking and low on the other three. These modal profile types represent quite different modes of interpretation than the composite of single scales because they depend on the total configuration of high and low as well as intermediate score performance. The author proposes further applications from this type of profile analysis in research to attempt matching people with careers and occupations or to study optimal teaching and learning situations.

Technical Aspects

Historically, there have been two opposing approaches to developing self-report data for studying personality. In Meehl's (1945) classic article he takes exception to the traditional approach of defining personality dimensions and content items intuitively and assuming that people's responses to items may be interpreted directly as a sample of their own behavior on that particular dimension. He proposes that responses may have meaning only as signs of behavior that are related in some pattern to some external criteria, and thus the meaning of each response is not accepted at "face value." Jackson's (1971) update highlights the importance of both approaches in using rational judgment in personality theory as well as empiricism. He proposes a number of principles for personality scale development that attend to critical issues of sources of error variance, integrity of multivariate scales, and means of convergent and discriminant validation. The enormous progress and current complexity is succinctly described by Burisch (1984) who categorizes three general approaches: external, inductive, and deductive. The external approach keys and validates the data empirically with external criteria to form the dimensions of personality. The inductive approach analyzes large amounts of data into as simple a structure and meaning as possible, and the personality scales are developed from the data themselves. The deductive approach derives the constructs to be measured from either personality theory or from significant research and practice, and the item content is rationally judged and weighed to be relevant to each of the constructs. Burisch presents impelling arguments for why current personality tests could employ all three approaches, and thus profit in construct validity, effectiveness, communicability, and economy in developing the tests. The Jackson Personality Inventory reflects the deductive approach together with features of the inductive.

A number of innovations, which are consistent with Jackson's creative research in structured personality test development, were used in the development of the instrument. The test is among those with the most elaborate procedures yet applied to personality test construction because of the attention given to developing definitions of the scales and writing items appropriate for the scales, as well as the addition of empirical procedures employed in item analysis. There were ten sequential steps in the construction. A decision was made about the constructs to be measured and carefully worded definitions were written for both poles of each construct. More than 20 people then wrote items equalling 5 or 10 times needed. A total of 1,800 edited items were next divided into seven booklets, each composed of a large pool of items for 2 to 3 different scales and in addition the items from two Social Desirability Scales. These booklets were then administered to seven trial groups of college students with a minimum of 300 students in each group. The item analysis that followed was designed to select items that had the best internal consistency and discrimination, the most normal distributions of scores, and suppression of social desirability bias. The best 40 items for each dimension were reassembled into two forms of the 15-scale inventory and administered to additional groups. An additional item analysis was performed to develop optimally independent scales by reducing item correlation with irrelevant scales and to enhance scale generalizability by reviewing the balance of number of items across all facets in each scale content. For example, to justify a broad Risk Taking Scale it was reported that items covered the following four facets: taking risks in physical activities, in monetary affairs, in social situations, and in ethical behavior. The final 20 items for each scale were assembled and used with the standardization sample of 2,000 males and 2,000 females for calculating norms, and further reliability and validity evidence.

It would be expected that internal consistency as one type of reliability would be high because there was a built-in design in scale construction using the author's differential reliability and item efficiency indices to optimize scale homogeneity and differentiation between scales. The manual, however, does not report final evidence for any of the scales. Jackson (1977) reports in a separate publication the reliability of the scales from two studies: a California sample of 36 male and 46 female college students, and a Pennsylvania sample of 146 males and 161 females. The results are favorable, showing internal consistency coefficients of .84 to .95 with a median of .93 for the California sample, and .75 to .93 with a median of .90 for the Pennsylvania sample. A Bentler theta coefficient was used in these studies because Jackson argues it is more appropriate than coefficient alpha in permitting evaluation of scale dimensions using several facets. The scales of the test showing the least favorable evidence are Tolerance, Social Adroitness, and Responsibility.

The evidence for differentiation between the scales is presented in the manual from a study of 100 males and 115 females in the standardization group. Impressively low correlations with other scales for the females are Organization, Self Esteem, Innovation, Interpersonal Affect, and Social Adroitness. For the males lowest intercorrelations are for Self Esteem, Risk Taking, Social Adroitness, and Tolerance. There are several scales that show less independence from other scales across both males and females and have correlations ranging between ± .30 and ± .58 with a third to one-half of all of the other scales. These scales are Conformity, Complexity, Energy Level, and Responsibility.

Stability of the test as a type of reliability is not reported in the manual from any studies of retesting the same samples of people over time. It is ironic that one of Jackson's (1971) principles stressed not only the importance of retest evidence for a test but of awareness of response stability that differs among people tested on different occasions, thus specifying also the reliability of samples of people when reporting evidence about the test.

Evaluating the test from the usual points of view of content, criterion related, and construct validity introduces two qualitatively different categories of judgment. One presents concrete and more obvious conclusions expected for any published instrument. The other category deals with psychometric conceptions that are abstract and may still be controversial and thus conclusions can differ depending on one's a priori reference or rationale.

One obviously unfavorable feature of the JPI is that the manual is much too brief in presenting both its empirical evaluation evidence and information on construction and interpretation of the inventory. In reference to content validity the approach used was deductive rather than external criterion keyed in defining and developing scale content. Some critics still prefer the empirical approach, but the weight of contemporary writing justifies the approach Jackson used. Nevertheless, the JPI manual does not provide elaboration of why the personality dimensions selected are viable, useful dimensions to study. The "Interpreter's Guide" (Jackson, 1978) is the first source of information about the history of research and rationale for each dimension. In reading item by item from a subjective point of view there are some items that are keyed for different scales and appear similar in content, but in general show satisfactory coherence to the particular scale definitions they are assigned.

Evidence for criterion-related validity does not meet expectations in the brief form presented in the manual. What is reported are summaries of studies correlating the JPI with other tests and types of behavior, JPI performance among different groups of people, convergent and discriminant validity of scales, and factor analyses of the scales. In the correlation studies, two types of self-ratings and peer ratings made by 6 to 10 peers for each person showed correlations with the JPI with median values of .70 and .56 for the self-ratings, and only .38 with the composite peer ratings. No information is given about sex and degree of familiarity of the peers, nor the correlations between the self-ratings and peer ratings. A second analogous study of females showed median JPI correlations of .47 with self-ratings and .25 with ratings of single peer roommates.

A factor analysis of the JPI is reported for a sample of 215 college students with results showing that 8 of the 16 scales contribute to a first factor, which may be considered close to a general factor. Four additional factors with their salient scales described account for the major 65% of the variance. An additional factor analysis is reported of multitrait-multimethod correlations composed of JPI scores and responses from two forms of self-rating and the composite peer ratings. The results do support satisfactory convergent and discriminant validity of the JPI scales by showing the predicted measures and show substantial loadings on their respective factors. However, using self-ratings to correlate with self-report inventory data as evidence for validity is vulnerable to criticism because external sources of data should be compared to show the degree of consistency across methods for measuring the trait. On the other hand, McClelland (1981) represents a divergent view from the classic interpretations from the multitrait-multimethod analysis. Lack of consistency across methods of measurement does not always have to be considered error. Peers or external raters may disagree with people's self-report inventory responses because they have sampled different aspects of their behavior and because they feel differently about them.

Wiggins (1973) emphasizes, nevertheless, that regardless of theoretical considerations or mathematical elegance of item analysis data, practical utility of the test must be assessed by showing a number of relationships and their magnitude of the test with nontest criteria. The manual reports several studies of JPI performance showing contrast among varying groups. A study of student demonstrators showed remarkably strong differences ($p < .001$) from nondemonstrators on Conformity and Value Orthodoxy in addition to four other scales that are reasonably relevant. A study of attitudes toward curriculum change by nursing education faculty showed the relevance of six of the JPI scales in contrasting their attitudes from traditional to modern approaches to change. A study of stereotyped attitudes toward ethnic groups showed that the most salient JPI scales were Tolerance, Interpersonal Affect, Responsibility, and Complexity.

Critique

The JPI, in summary, is an impressive instrument with much promise. The personality dimensions have clear popular appeal with labels that are relevant to the way we think about people; avoid negative, deviant statements about people; and suppress ambiguous interpretations from response bias. Meaningful positive statements can be made about the examinee from either pole of each scale. The development of scale definitions, writing of items, and scale construction were among the most sophisticated and elaborate procedures. Items are generally relevant to their assigned scales and a good portion of the scales are distinctive, having relatively low correlations with one another.

The delivery of the product as a practical instrument is unfortunately not up to the level of its promise. The 40-page manual is too brief and perhaps too cryptic to be educational to users. Information about procedures for reliability and validity are outlined but most of the data in evidence are not included. As a personality inventory developed primarily from the deductive approach it needs additional explanation for the viability of the personality dimensions selected. Lacking is additional criterion-related evidence for the practical clinical use of the instrument and, thus, it should be used primarily in research. Most appropriate would be studies the author suggests for showing personality correlates with particular occupations, and also correlates with particular teaching-learning situations or styles.

References

Burisch, M. (1984). Approaches to personality inventory construction: A comparison of merits. *American Psychologist, 39*, 214-227.

Jackson, D. N. (1965). *Personality Research Form*. Port Huron, MI: Research Psychologists Press.

Jackson, D. N. (1971). The dynamics of structured personality tests: 1971. *Psychological Review, 78*, 229-248.

Jackson, D. N. (1976). *Jackson Personality Inventory manual*. Port Huron, MI: Research Psychologists Press.

Jackson, D. N. (1977). Reliability of the Jackson Personality Inventory. *Psychological Reports, 40*, 613-614.

Jackson, D. N. (1978). Interpreter's guide to the Jackson Personality Inventory. In P. McReynolds (Ed.), *Advances in psychological assessment* (Vol. 4). San Francisco: Jossey-Bass.

McClelland, D. C. (1981). Is personality consistent? In A. I. Rabin et al. (Eds.), *Further explorations in personality*. New York: John Wiley & Sons.

Meehl, P. E. (1945). The dynamics of structured personality tests. *Journal of Clinical Psychology, 1*, 296-303.

Wiggins, J. S. (1973). *Personality and prediction: Principles of personality assessment*. Reading, MA: Addison-Wesley.

H. O'Neal Smitherman, Ph.D.

University of Alabama System, Tuscaloosa, Alabama.

KAHN TEST OF SYMBOL ARRANGEMENT

Theodore C. Kahn. Missoula, Montana; Psychological Test Specialists.

Introduction

The Kahn Test of Symbol Arrangement (KTSA) is a projective test designed to measure attributes of personality. A number of characteristics, however, set it apart from other projective personality measures. First, the test offers a somewhat structured, quantitative method of scoring in addition to the normal "subjective" scoring techniques used by most other projective measures. Second, the KTSA provides a novel set of stimuli on which attributes may be imposed. Third, the KTSA willingly accepts the fact of cultural bias toward the objects in the test and uses the cultural loadings in the interpretation of test results.

The KTSA is based on the assumption that human beings deal with their world symbolically. Further, it is assumed that the relationships associated with symbolic objects are generalized to other objects. The pattern of these generalizations provide information as to one's personality and presumably to one's pattern of response.

Kahn measures the symbolic relationships and the tendency to relate objects symbolically by using an interesting process. Indeed, the development of the test methodology provides valuable insights. In 1949, Theodore Kahn, a graduate student interested in symbols, noticed the apparent importance of cultural symbolism on purchases made in a Los Angeles hobby shop (Campos, 1968). He then set out to develop a test of personality attributes from objects that represent symbolic items in our culture. The first publication of this work was a manual that appeared in 1949 (Kahn, 1949). Additional work was detailed in a doctoral dissertation (Kahn, 1950) and further studies comparing normal subjects to psychotic patients (Fils, 1950) led to a revision of the manual (Kahn, 1956). This manual and the clinical manual published in the following year (Kahn, 1957) provide the basis for the current uses of the test. It appears that since these manuals were published other researchers have used the test under varying conditions (e.g., changing instructions and scoring procedures). However, these two manuals provide the most comprehensive basis for review.

During the 1950s and 1960s work on the KTSA consisted primarily of attempts to establish both the test's usefulness as a personality measure and its ability to discriminate between diverse groups of individuals (e.g., normals, psychotics, neurotics). By the 1970s and 1980s work has been applied to developmental issues and cross-cultural application. Although some researchers are still using this measure, the test has not yet been widely accepted as a primary diagnostic tool.

The KTSA consists of 16 culturally structured object symbols (Kahn, 1956) that vary in color, size, thickness, and translucence. These objects are an anchor; three hearts; three stars; two butterflies; a green, amorphous, phallic symbol; a black, equilateral cross; three dogs; a circle; and a segment of a circle. A felt strip with 15 equally spaced segments, numbered 1-15, and a recording sheet are also included. The scoring and recording procedure requires a systematic, structured approach in order to capture all of the information made available from the test.

The recording form contains space for 1) recording the responses to the six arrangement tasks, 2) indicating the subject's responses to requests to name objects, 3) indications of what each symbol represents, 4) the subject's explanation for subject's choices of liking and disliking, 5) recording subject's reasons for the items' arrangements, and 6) recording the time taken to complete tasks in the test.

The record sheet also contains the form for sketching the subject's KTSA profile, which is used to depict the outcome of the scoring components. Additionally, it presents percent scores and Sigma scores charted against raw scores in each of the following categories: (A) Bizarre, (B) No Reason/No Symbol, (C) Same as Before, (D) Naming or Function, (E) Shape Material Appearance, (F) Color, (X) Concrete Association, (Y) Tangible Abstraction, and (Z) Intangible Abstraction. In developing the profile, the raw score (the number of responses of each category) is multiplied by the weight assigned to each category.

Practical Applications/Uses

The test is appropriate for a wide range of subjects, including children through senior citizens and those with emotional makeups ranging from normal through psychotic and organic brain disorders. The test is able to measure high levels of abstraction abilities as well as the lack of symbolic interrelationships which can exist in organic brain dysfunctions and the sometimes bizarre symbolism of the psychotic disorders.

The KTSA was developed to serve as a "comprehensive evaluation which includes prediction" (Kahn, 1957, p. 98). As such, it was hoped to measure not only what an individual will do in the normal events of the day, but to also deal with the underlying processes that are tapped whenever the individual encounters novel experiences. Thus it would provide information offering insight into the complex components that guide our most basic tendencies to act.

The KTSA has been applied to numerous situations and used to address a variety of questions. The earliest works focused on the test's ability to differentiate between psychotic and normal individuals, a task believed to be a necessary prerequisite for further use (Kahn, 1957). If such gross distinctions could not be made using the test, it would be of little value for its original purpose, but the 1957 clinical manual presents many studies that demonstrate the KTSA's abilities in this area. Further, other studies have shown the tests' ability to make even finer distinctions. L'Abate and Craddick (1965) demonstrate the KTSA's ability to classify normal, neurotic, and character disordered individuals from schizophrenics and individuals with organic brain syndrome. Other studies by White and McLeod (1963) support the differentiating ability, but similar research by Hedlund & Mills (1964) yield less support for the test's classification ability.

Other research has used the KTSA to compare 1) college-aged men and women

(Theiner, 1965; Wyman, 1963); 2) children's gender differences (Kenny, 1962); 3) individuals from different cultures such as German, American, Vietnamese (Theiner & Giffen, 1963; Theiner, 1969); 4) KTSA scores to children's Mental Age scores (Fink & Kahn, 1959); 5) extreme scores among college students (Rose, 1980); 6) normal and psychotic Germans (Plaum, Maier, & Rupf-Bolz, 1980); 7) children with auditory learning disabilities and emotional disturbances (Reeves, 1980); 8) conceptual thinking abilities (Wagner, 1974); 9) cross-cultural and cross-religious differences, including Christian, Buddist, Taoist, and Islamic groups (Nakanishi, 1969); 10) high-school students (Wagner, 1969); 11) creativity (Kahn, 1968); 12) alcoholics (Shearn & Warren, 1967); 13) aggressive and nonaggressive prisoners (Craddick & Levy, 1968); and 14) habitual criminals versus normal persons (Kipper, 1971).

As can be seen from the variety of uses made of the KTSA, its potential applications are great. Although interpretive considerations might be necessary, it has been shown not to have gender, ethnic, nor cultural limitations, which might otherwise preclude its use. Even though the test has been available and researched since 1949, many options are still open and there are still numerous, possible avenues for its application. The disconcerting side of this coin is the lack of an established use of the test to define its arena of operation.

The administration of the KTSA is straightforward and relatively uncomplicated. The examiner is provided with a felt strip marked off into 15 equal sections, a set of the 16 symbolic objects, and a Scoring/Recording sheet.

In addition to presenting the objects and instructions to subjects for each trial and scoring their responses, the examiner is expected to offer encouragement as needed.

The examiner presents the objects and procedes with a specific set of instructions directing subjects through five (possibly six) separate trials in which they are asked to arrange the objects along the felt strip. The first, second, and fifth times subjects may choose any kind of arrangement; however, the third time they are asked to arrange the objects in the same order chosen during the second trial and the fourth time they are asked to arrange the objects according to their attitude towards the object (most liked to least liked). A sixth trial may be used when there is some question as to why a subject did not place objects into a ''logical'' order on previous trials.

First, the examiner presents the objects, saying: ''In this box there are a number of objects. Some people say that what we are going to do now reminds them of a game.'' The examiner then displays the objects on a table in front of the subjects and tells them that they may place the objects along the strip in any way desired. When the subjects have placed the objects on the strip, the examiner notes the occurrences on the answer sheet. Notations include 1) a code letter representing the test object and the position, (1 through 15) of the object on the strip, 2) the slant of the object as it is positioned on the strip, 3) the direction the dog symbols are facing, 4) the numerical sequence in which the objects were placed (e.g., although the heart may be the first item placed, it could be placed in position 12), 5) an indication as to whether objects are out-of-segment or overlapping into adjacent segments, 6) the direction of the arrangement, 7) the time of the test, and 8) the amount of time taken for the task.

After the first arrangement has been completed, the examiner also asks the respondents to give their reasons for arranging the objects in such a way and records their replies on the record sheet for Arrangement I (I. Reason). Leaving the items in their current position on the strip, the examiner then asks the subjects to begin in segment one and name each object and records the responses under the section labeled "I. Naming." Further, the examiner notes whether the subject pointed, touched, picked up, or held objects during the naming process. In addition, the examiner notes any of the subject's remarks, questions, or other test behavior on another sheet of paper.

The second trial follows the same procedures except that the examiner also asks the subjects to report what the objects symbolize (i.e., "Would you agree that a flag can represent a country? For example, our flag stands for the United States. Some people say that a horseshoe is a sign of good luck. A light can symbolize knowledge or freedom. Now I would like you to tell me what each of these objects can stand for, represent, or symbolize. Start with the first object and go to the end."). Some respondents, such as young children may require coaxing (e.g., "What does this make you think of?"). These responses are recorded in the section marked II. Symbolizing and any reaction times exceeding 5 seconds are recorded in the adjacent section marked Time.

One additional component of the second test involves a newly introduced Y-shaped object that subjects are to place over any one of the objects. The response is then recorded.

Prior to the third arrangement, subjects are asked to estimate how many objects they can place on the strip in exactly the same order of the previous arrangement. After the response is recorded and they have proceded with arranging the objects, they are asked how many right answers they think they have.

For the fourth arrangement, subjects are asked to arrange the objects according to how the objects appeal to them and explain why they liked or disliked each of the objects.

In the fifth arrangement subjects place eight rectangles (i.e., Love, Hate, Bad, Good, Living, Dead, Small, Large) on the paper where they think they best belong; all objects must be placed somewhere, but any rectangles may be left vacant or have several objects.

If subjects fail to give any reasons for Arrangements I, II, or V, or their responses appear to represent no symbolizing, they may be asked to complete a sixth arrangement. The purpose of this trial (called Testing the Limits) is to determine whether the lack of logical ordering or reasons is due to a lack of reasoning power or resistance to the test. Subjects are asked to arrange the objects in some logical order, and the responses are recorded.

Two scoring methods, Objective and Semi-objective, are employed. The Objective scoring involves 11 of the subjects' responses:

Recall: Accuracy in estimating how many objects they can place in the same position as in the previous arrangement and the number representing the actual number of accurate placements;

Direction: The number of times they placed objects left-to-right, right-to-left, mixed, or from the center;

Arrangement Time: The number of times they completed the task "very fast,"

"fast," "medium," "slow," or "very slow";

Position of Objects on Strip: The total number of times they slanted, inverted, overlapped objects, or placed them off the segment;

Contact: The number of times they pointed to, touched, picked up, held, or did none of these things during the naming or symbolizing tasks;

Togetherness: The number of similarly shaped objects which they placed in juxtaposition during the arrangements;

Objects Over: The associations made when transparent objects were placed over other objects on the strip (Arrangement III);

Preferences: The number of items placed within the liking or disliking categories (e.g., living, inanimate);

Reaction Time: The time they hesitated in responding to Arrangement II;

Sorting Ratios: The number of objects placed in sorting categories and the ratios that are derived from dividing one category by another (i.e., the number of emotional items, such as LOVE and HATE, divided by the number of nonemotional items, such as SMALL and LARGE); and

Naming: The number of objects for which they give names that match normative responses for their age group.

The Semi-objective scoring criteria are based on the subjects' responses that indicate what the objects symbolize and explain their likes and dislikes for the objects. The results of these responses are placed into one of nine categories: (A) Bizarre, Illogical, Inappropriate; (B) No Reason, Don't Know, No Symbolizing, Can't Do It; (C) Same as before (the reason for the arrangement); (D) Naming or Giving its Function; (E) Shape, Material, Looks, Appeal, Beauty, (if color is not mentioned) Design; (F) Color, Mention Absence of Color, Mentioning Any Specific Color; (X) Concrete Association Form Fidelity; (Y) Tangible Abstraction Freedom From Original Shape; and (Z) Intangible Abstraction, Freedom From Shape and Material Substance.

The manual includes numerous examples of the above categories and provides adequate descriptions of how to assign a subject to a category. Interestingly, the semi-objective criteria are discussed most frequently in the research articles.

Although the scoring/recording part of administering this test appears to be complicated, the method can usually be mastered after a few administrations.

Interpretations can be based on any of the objective measures, the profile of measures, the semi-objective measures, or a combination of all of them. Many of the research articles emphasize the semi-objective ratings, but if this interpretive system is used, a high level of sophistication in psychological testing and a degree of experience with the KTSA is required.

Technical Aspects

Numerous studies have been conducted using the KTSA. Most of these provide some evidence regarding its utility. However, some of the strongest support comes from the clinical manual (Kahn, 1957) and the administration manual (Kahn, 1956). These documents present normative data from studies over a seven-year period. As reported in Campos (1968, p. 499), these studies reflect scores for "453 men and 47 women, aged 17-87 years, with a mean educational level of 10 years, and IQ of 103." These data were used to develop a psychodiagram, which continues to be widely used.

Both test-retest and interrater reliability have been reported for the KTSA. Interrater estimates presented by Kahn (1950) and Kahn et al. (1957) show high overall reliability (.97-.99).

Test-retest figures also show adequate stability in the early studies, .95 (Kahn, 1950) and .66 (Kahn et al., 1957), as well as in later studies (Kelly, 1972).

It is difficult to determine validity of this instrument because it is not clear precisely what it purports to measure. Kahn (1957) suggests that the best tests will allow one to predict an individual's responses to novel situations. Indeed, the KTSA may perform such a task, but the research focuses on the more traditional type of predictive validity. Numerous studies have demonstrated the KTSA's ability to differentiate between various groups of individuals. For instance, Kahn (1957) reports the test's ability to discriminate between psychotics and non-psychotics, normals from schizophrenics, epileptics from nonepileptic children, normal individuals from a variety of syndromes, and paranoid schizophrenics from brain damaged psychotics.

Critique

The studies cited in this review demonstrate to some degree the KTSA's utility in personality research. However, even with all of the work that has been done and the great interest that has been shown to this test, it has not become established as a clinical tool. Refinements are still necessary in the specific steps to be used in classification systems and in the cutoff points to be used for classification.

The KTSA is an intriguingly creative effort to measure constructs that are difficult to define, much less measure. The developer has demonstrated a willingness to go the extra mile in establishing his instrument, and further work may fulfill his desires. At this stage, however, the KTSA should still be considered a valuable research instrument but unproven as a clinical tool.

References

Campos, L. P. (1968). Other projective techniques. In A. I. Rabin (Ed.), *Projective techniques in personality assessment*, (p. 461-520). New York: Springer Publishing Co.

Craddick, R. A., & Levy, G. (1968). Note on the categorization, recall and preference of KTSA objects by "aggresive" and "non-aggressive" prisoners. *Perceptual and Motor Skills, 27,* 26.

Fils, D. H. (1950). *Comparative performance of schizophrenics and normals on an object symbol arrangement test.* Unpublished doctoral dissertation, University of Southern California, Los Angeles.

Fink, H. H., & Kahn, T. C. (1959). A comparison of normal and emotionally ill children on the KTSA. *Journal of Educational Research, 53,* 35-36.

Hedlund, J. L., & Mills, D. H. (1964). Cross validation of the KTSA with psychiatric population. *Journal of Clinical Psychology, 20,* 100-103.

Kahn, T. C. (1950). *Comparative performance of psychotics with brain damage and non-psychotics on an original symbol arrangement test.* Unpublished doctoral dissertation. University of Southern California, Los Angeles.

Kahn, T. C. (1953). *Manual for the Kahn Test of Symbol Arrangement.* Beverly Hills: Western Psychological Service.

Kahn, T. C. (1956). Kahn Test of Symbol Arrangement: Administration and scoring. *Perceptual and Motor Skills* (Supplement No. 4), 6, 299-334.

Kahn, T. C. (1957). The Kahn Test of Symbol Arrangement: Clinical manual. *Perceptual and Motor Skills* Supplement No. 1), 7, 97-168.

Kahn, T. C. (1968). Signs of creativity on the Kahn Test of Symbol Arrangement. *Perceptual and Motor Skills, 26,* 1065-1066.

Kahn, T. C., Harter, H., Rider, P., & Lum, M. D. (1957). *Reliability and validity of the KTSA as a technique in screening schizophrenics, psychotics with brain damage, and non-psychotics.* Unpublished manuscript.

Kelly, W. L. (1972). Reliability assessments of the group Kahn Test of Symbolic Arrangement. *International Journal of Symbology, 3,* 22-34.

Kenny, J. A. (1962). *Maladjusted children: A comparison of 216 normal and maladjusted children on the basis of their performance on psychological tests.* Unpublished doctoral dissertation, Johannes Guttenberg University, Mainz, Germany.

Kipper, D. A. (1971). Identifying habitual criminals by means of the Kahn Test of Symbol Arrangement. *Journal of Consulting and Clinical Psychology, 37*(1), 151-154.

L'Abate, L., & Craddick, R. A. (1965). The Kahn Test of Symbol Arrangement (KTSA): A critical review. *Journal of Clinical Psychology, 21,* 115-135.

Nakanishi, N. (1969). Symbol perception of the Kahn Test of Symbol Arrangement among four cultures. *International Journal of Symbology, 1,* 20-24.

Plaum, E., Maier, T., & Rupf-Bolz, E. (1980). The Kahn test of Symbol Arrangement (KTSA) as a method for determining pathological thought processes: An investigation with German speaking patients. *Zeitochrift fur Klinische Psychologie, Forschung und Praxis, 9,* 210-218.

Reeves, W. H. (1980). Auditory learning disabilities and emotional disturbance. Diagnostic differences. *Journal of Learning Disabilities, 13,* 199-202.

Rose, A. (1980). Characteristics of extreme KTSA scorers. *Perceptual and Motor Skills, 50,* 553-554.

Shearn, C. R., & Warren, S. L. (1967). Performance of hospitalized male alcoholics on the Kahn Test of Symbol Arrangement. *Perceptual and Motor Skills, 25,* 705-710.

Theiner, E. C. (1965). Differences on abstract thought processes as a function of sex. *Journal of General Psychology, 73,* 285-290.

Theiner, E. C. (1969). Current approaches to symbolization: The Kahn Test of Symbol Arrangement. *International Journal of Symbology, 1,* 52-58.

Theiner, E. C., & Giffen, M. B. (1963). A comparison of abstract thought processes among three cultures. In R. E. McKenzie (Ed.), *Proceedings of the Fourth Annual Conference of AF Clinical Psychologists.* Brooks AFB, Texas: USAF SAM.

Wagner, R. F. (1969). Levels of symbolization in adolescent adjustment patterns. *International Journey of Symbology, 1,* 67-74.

Wagner, R. F. (1974). Dyssymbolia as a specific learning disability. *International Journal of Symbology,* 22-30.

White, P. O., & McLeod, H. W. (1963). A multiple discriminant analysis comparing psychotic, neurotic, and character disorder patients on the Kahn Test of Symbol Arrangement. *Ontario Psychological Association Quarterly, 26,* 1-5.

Wyman, B. A. (1963). *The effect of sex differences, masculine-feminine interests, and opposite sex roles on performance on the Kahn Test of Symbol Arrangement.* Unpublished master's thesis, New Mexico State University, Las Cruces.

Jeanette M. Reuter, Ph.D.
Professor of Psychology, Kent State University, Kent, Ohio.

KAUFMAN INFANT AND PRESCHOOL SCALE
Harvey Kaufman. Chicago, Illinois: Stoelting Company.

Introduction

The purpose of the Kaufman Infant and Preschool Scale (KIPS) is to provide a means of measuring higher-level cognitive functioning in infants and children under four years of age and in older mentally retarded persons who function at cognitive levels below 48 months of age. The KIPS author, Harvey Kaufman, believes that "lower cognitive functions" as measured by the motor and self-help items on traditional developmental assessment instruments falsely inflate cognitive level estimations for delayed children and infants and lead to inappropriate programming and expectations (Kaufman, 1979).

The KIPS examiner determines which of 86 cognitive tasks an infant or child is able to perform successfully. These tasks are grouped on the basis of content into three preacademic areas: General Reasoning (20 tasks), Storage (32 tasks), and Verbal Communication (34 tasks). Almost all of the tasks and their age norms, which are presented in an age-ordered sequence, were taken from published research. Procedures for determining a child's preacademic function age (PAFA) and preacademic functioning quotient (PAFQ) from the number of tasks successfully demonstrated are described in the test manual. The number of tasks accomplished, weighted for the age span covered, yield the PAFA that is then used to calculate the PAFQ, a ratio score based on chronological age.

The KIPS was administered to a research sample of 304 children, aged 1-48 months, but neither the average age of passing a task nor the average number of tasks passed by an age group were determined from this sample. However, the stated goal of the author was not to provide a clinical tool for diagnostic or comparative purposes but to provide a "curricular" instrument, "in that all items assessed are maturational prototypes, samples of the type of item that can be taught to enhance maturation." (Kaufman, 1979, page 1).

The KIPS was preceded by the Kaufman Development Scale (KDS) published by the Stoelting Company in 1975. However, the KDS was not seen as being able to discriminate between the high level cognition components and the general developmental components of overall maturation. Therefore, research began in 1976 to develop an instrument to measure high-level cognition only. As a result, the KIPS, designed to meet that need, was published in 1979. The Scales' author, Dr. Harvey Kaufman, is assistant clinical director of the Mental Health Center of Fond du Lac, Wisconsin, and has worked in child neuropsychology extensively.

The contribution of Linda Jones, B.A., Kent State University, in the preparation of this review is gratefully acknowledged.

The test components, which are packaged in a briefcase, consist of test objects, a test manual, and a scoring booklet. The test objects used to present the test tasks include: a bell, flashlight and extra battery, doll, nine small plastic figures in three colors, toy car, blocks of different sizes and colors, four wooden balls, and a spiral notebook containing 21 picture cards. The manual contains sections on theoretical perspectives, test development and description, research information, administration and scoring directions, and a case illustration. The scoring booklet contains a page for recording the tasks successfully completed by the child from the General Reasoning, Storage, and Verbal Communication areas at each of five age stages: Infancy Stage Phase I (birth to 6 months) and II (6-18 months), Early Childhood Stage Phase I (18 months-3 years) and II (3-4 years), and the Play Age (4 years +). The scoring booklet also contains aids for calculating the PAFA and PAFQ, and a scatter analysis form and profile form to display the functional age levels for the three areas.

Practical Applications/Uses

The KIPS would be most useful as a structured play interview of infants or preschool children to assess in a general way how their cognitive skills compare with those of their age peers. The age range for which the scale is applicable—1 month to 48 months for normal children—is unique in that it covers both infancy and early childhood. Other tests for infants, such as the Bayley Scales, or tests for preschool children, such as the early years of the Stanford-Binet, cover only part of this age range. Agencies where young children and infants who are at risk, disadvantaged, or disabled are assessed would find a test covering this age range useful.

Because the scale was not designed to meet the standardization criteria for tests of the American Psychological Association, social workers, teachers or therapists who work in Head Start centers, well-child clinics, and pediatricians' offices would be more comfortable using the test than psychologists. The author emphasizes the utility of the 86 tasks for programming and cognitive habilitation. Therefore, the scale would be particularly useful to those professionals who have continuing contact with the infants and children they assess with the KIPS.

The manual describes the use of the KIPS with 91 mentally retarded persons ranging in age from 1-55 years who were clients at two rehabilitation centers. If a person's age level of cognitive functioning were below four years of mental age, the scale would provide a series of tasks that could help ascertain cognitive skills and contribute to programming.

The lack of empirical norms make it inappropriate for legal or diagnostic developmental assessments of infants or young children. The test would not be useful, without adaptation, for assessing the higher cognitive functioning of blind, deaf, or cerebral palsied children because of its heavy loading of items dependent on vision, hearing, and fine-motor coordination.

A well-trained professional should administer the tasks to infants or children beginning with items appropriate for their chronological age. The examiner should establish a basal below which it can be assumed that the child would be able to perform all of the tasks on the age-ordered sequence. A ceiling is similarly established. It is recommended that the basal and ceiling settings be made following the failure or successful accomplishment, respectively, of an entire age-stage sequence of tasks. It is permissible to credit a child with successful perform-ance on a task based on the report of a parent or significant other person, but it is preferable to observe the child's performance directly. This may necessitate more than one testing session.

The manual has two lists containing directions for administering each task or item. One list orders the 86 tasks by age within the three preacademic areas, i.e. General Reasoning, Storage, and Verbal Communication. A second list presents the item, its preacademic area, and the same one or two sentence task instructions ordered by age only. The instructions for administering an item are not precise or detailed enough to allow a novice examiner to work from the manual alone. Training in administration of the test by the author, either on videotape or directly, would be necessary in order for an examiner to reliably measure what the author intends. The inclusion in the test kit of the toys and objects necessary to administer the test is helpful (with few exceptions) in this regard, but not helpful enough. For example, the instructions for a General Reasoning item from the Infancy State, Phase I section of the test labelled "Secondary Circular Reaction" state: "Child repeats responses which provide results, such as kicking legs to produce swinging of toy over crib, or knocking down pillow to watch it fall." (Kaufman, 1979, p. 20). However, it would be difficult to know what is permissible for the examiner to do to elicit the secondary circular reaction and what essential behaviors are necessary for an infant to achieve credit for a successful performance.

Each task that is successfully performed or reported as successfully performed by a significant other person is entered on the appropriate page of the age-ordered sequence of tasks in the scoring booklet. Ten tasks are eligible for half credit if the examinee is at the mid-point of skill maturation. Each item is given a weighted score, 1.71 down to ½, depending on the number of tasks covering the age range of the stage. Thus, because there are 20 tasks in the Infant Stage, Phase I, which covers an age range of 6 months, each task performed is given .30 months credit. The total number of months credited is the PAFA expressed in months. The PAFA divided by the chronological age of the infant or child and multiplied by 100 yields the PAFQ. When a PAFA exceeds 4-0 years, a quotient (PAFQ) should not be calculated.

When the PAFQ is calculated from the PAFA of a mentally retarded adult the chronological age used should not exceed 192 months (16 years), and should disregard the actual chronological age of the examinee.

Pages are provided in the scoring booklet to record the age scatter of successes and the profile of successes by the preacademic areas (General Reasoning, Stor-age, and Verbal Communication).

The author's position is that the 86 tasks provide the items needed to design "an appropriate curriculum." For this purpose, the manual provides charts called the "Intercorrelation Matrix for High Level Cognitive Maturation." (pp. 8-12). The tasks are displayed graphically by age sequence in the three assessment areas in sections corresponding to the five age periods. And, as the author states: "From a practical standpoint, the professional using this scale should be able to find commonalities in tasks between the three modalities, at appropriate stages, and to use these common threads in the preparation of an appropriate curriculum'' (Kaufman, 1979, p. 8).

There are no guidelines in the KIPS manual for what constitutes significant delay on this test for an infant or young child. Presumably, the PAFQ is a standard score similar to the IQ or DQ (Development Quotient) and can be interpreted in the same way. In order to interpret the PAFQ of the mentally retarded, a table that gives the PAFQ ranges for levels of retardation (borderline, mild, moderate, severe, and profound) is provided. In addition, for a given chronological age and PAFQ, the table classifies and predicts developmental ages and school grades corresponding to each of these retardation levels. No empirical bases or literature citations document any of the interpretive guides. The author's clinical experience must be the source of the information provided and it would be risky for anyone with less experience with the KIPS and its use with infants, children, and mentally retarded persons to rely on these interpretive guidelines for the PAFQ.

Technical Aspects

The KIPS was administered to a sample of 304 Caucasian children from two midwest medical clinics. The age range was 1-48 months. None of the children had been previously identified as mentally handicapped. Children who received PAFQs lower than 75 were dropped from the statistical analysis. The proportion of males and females was about equal so the sexes were combined for the analyses.

The mean PAFQ for this sample was 108.24 with a standard deviation of 15.24. The odd-even reliability coefficient corrected by the Spearman/Brown Formula for the total test was .98. The standard error of measurement is 2.15. According to Kaufman (1979, p. 5), the ''method of using standard error of measurement in this context, is to consider the probable true score range at evaluation time and not as a prediction for the future.''

The intercorrelations of the PAFQs derived from the General Reasoning, Storage, and Verbal Communication areas calculated separately for four age groups ranged from .59 to .87, but the manual expresses a need for caution when speaking of specific area strengths or deficits.

In order to study the validity of the KIPS, a method of arriving at validity by inference was adopted. The mean IQs (derived from the Otis-Lennon or the Academic Aptitude test) for one first-grade and four second-grade samples drawn from the same midwest geographic area as the KIPS research sample, varied from 105 to 110. The KIPS, therefore, is seen as ''congruous,'' yielding evidence for the validity of the KIPS' PAFQ.

A second validity study that used a sample of 80 children aged 6-18 months is described, with PAFQs in the full range from 55-145. The mean PAFQ was 102 with a standard deviation of 18.02, an odd-even reliability coefficient of .95, and a standard error of measurement of 4.18. The author assumes that the KIPS will provide a mean quotient of approximately 100 with a normal population and that this is clearly shown through the study of this age group.

The KIPS was also administered to a mentally handicapped sample of 91 persons who were from two rehabilitation centers in the same geographical area and whose chronological ages ranged from one month to 55 years. The sample was grouped into three age groups: 1-48 months, 48-72 months, and 19-55 years. The mean PAFQ, the standard deviation, the odd-even reliability coefficients, and the standard error measurement are displayed in a table. As expected, all PAFQ means were below 75, and standard deviations were smaller than those for the more heterogeneous normal sample. The odd-even reliabilities ranged from .90-.99 and the resultant standard errors of measurement from .71-2.89.

Critique

The statistical studies performed on the KIPS did not address the age placement of the items nor did they describe the number of tasks completed by the infants and children of the normal sample. The achievement of mean PAFQs close to 100 with standard deviations of about 15 for this sample does not satisfy requirements for standardization or empirical norming. The reliability studies are confined to tests of internal consistency. No child was given two KIPS over time by two examiners in order to demonstrate test-retest or interjudge reliability of the KIPS as it is published. No validity coefficients were published. The "congruity" of means between the KIPS research sample and that of a sample using different tests and different aged children does not demonstrate validity for the KIPS. Therefore, the standardization of the KIPS and the technical studies on the reliability and validity of its scores remains to be measured.

Until the above work is done, the KIPS is not a test to measure the cognitive functioning of infants, young children, and severely mentally retarded adults. It is a structured inventory of cognitive tasks around which cognitive habilitation curricula can be built. The tasks on the inventory are the distillation of years of experience observing infants and children solving problems and developing cognitive competence. As such, it should provide information and structure for curricula for infant stimulation and early childhood special education programs.

References

Kaufman, H. (1975). *Kaufman Developmental Scale.* Chicago: Stoelting Company.
Kaufman, H. (1979). *Kaufman Infant & Preschool Scale, Instruction Manual.* Chicago: Stoelting Company.

Michael D. Franzen, Ph.D.
Director, Neuropsychology, West Virginia University Medical Center, Morgantown, West Virginia.

KENDRICK COGNITIVE TESTS FOR THE ELDERLY

Don C. Kendrick. Windsor, England: NFER-Nelson Publishing Company, Ltd.

Introduction

The Kendrick Cognitive Tests for the Elderly (KCTE) (Kendrick, in press), previously known as the Kendrick Battery for the Detection of Dementia in Elderly, was designed to aid in the diagnosis of dementia in aged subjects. The name of the test was changed because of the effect of the name of the test on subjects. Subjects who saw the former test name with the word "Dementia" in the title became unduly alarmed. The Kendrick Tests are composed of two separate tests: the Object Learning Test (OLT) and the Digit Copying Test (DCT). A third component test, the Kendrick Numbers Test, is currently in development. The present form of the KCTE is a revised version of the earlier form developed by Andrew J. Gibson and Don C. Kendrick (1979).

The original Kendrick Battery was composed of the DCT and the Synonym Learning Test. However, criticisms of the battery (Skelton-Robinson & Telford, 1982) have resulted in certain changes (Kendrick, 1982). For example, the Synonym Learning Test was judged to be too stressful to subjects. Its immediate feedback of a response of "correct" or "incorrect" resulted in some subjects refusing to complete an examination. The Synonym Learning Test was replaced by the OLT. The intent of the KCTE is to screen for organic brain disorders and provide information regarding changes in level of functioning in serial testing situations. The KCTE was specifically designed for use with aged subjects.

The rationale behind the KCTE involves a two-arousal system hypothesis in normal brain function (Routtenberg, 1968). The first arousal system is a function of the reticular activating system. It is largely involuntary and is related to the reticular system and to concepts of drive. The second system is a function of higher cortical areas and is partly voluntary. Level of arousal in the second system is a function of the limbic system and is related to concepts of motivation and incentive.

Kendrick (1972) postulates that these two systems are differentially affected by dementia and depression. He states that dementia is associated with decrements in both arousal systems and that depression is associated with decrements only in the second system. The DCT is posited as a test of sensorimotor performance, sensitive to changes in both systems. The OLT is posited as a test of intermediate memory, sensitive to changes in the second arousal system. Dementia is hypothesized to result in decrements in performance on both the DCT and OLT. Pseudodementia associated with depression is hypothesized to result in decrements in performance only on the OLT.

The OLT consists of four cards, each of which is divided into 25 equal sections. There are ten line drawings of objects on the first card, 15 on the second, 20 on the third, and 25 on the fourth. Six of the objects are repeated across the four cards. The cards are exposed for 30, 45, 60, and 75 seconds respectively, after which time the subjects are asked to name as many of the objects as he or she can remember.

The DCT uses a sheet of paper on which are printed a series of 100 numbers. The subject is asked to copy the numbers in the space directly below each number. Two minutes are allowed to complete the task. If the subject finishes before the time is up, the score is the time elapsed until completion. If the subject does not finish the task in the allotted time, the score is an extrapolation from the number of items finished to the time it would have taken to finish all 100 numbers. In all, the KCTE requires 10-15 minutes to administer.

Practical Applications/Uses

The KCTE is most useful in evaluating aged subjects, between the ages of 55 and 85. The manual states its applications as being in the diagnosis of dementia, in charting changes in function over time, and in research comparing the relative functioning of different groups of aged subjects. In particular, treatment with neuroleptics or antidepressants may obscure the difference between normal and depressed subjects (Kendrick & Moyes, 1979). The author warns that when used in an inpatient setting, assessment should occur in the first three weeks following admission. Anxiety and arousal will influence the results. Lastly, the results of the test are questionable in subjects with a Verbal IQ of less than 70 and in institutionalized subjects.

The KCTE is a promising instrument, but more information regarding its validity and reliability in different populations will increase the utility of the instrument in clinical settings. Standardized score transformations need to be derived on a much larger sample than was used in the original study.

The original validation study used only eight subjects of each sex in each group. Subsequent research has tended to support the validity of the instrument (Kendrick, 1982; Gibson, 1981; Cowan et al., 1975; Searle, 1984) but more research is needed before unequivocal conclusions can be reached. Further, the diagnostic efficiency of the instrument has been evaluated only in a situation where the base rate of organicity was known. Information from the test data was combined with the base rate information in order to determine the diagnosis. Because not all situations will have the same base rate characteristics of the experimental sample and because the diagnostic efficiency of the instrument will vary as a function of the base rate, it is desirable to know the diagnostic accuracy of the instrument in a situation with unknown base rate prevalence.

Technical Aspects

In order to provide standardized, age corrected scores for the DCT and OLT, the KCTE was administered to 11 depressed, 32 normal healthy group home residents,

28 normal healthy independent-living subjects, and 22 demented subjects. Standardized T-scores were derived for each of the three age groups of 55-64, 65-74, and 75-84 years. The very small number of subjects in these age groups (about 30 each) necessitates the recalculation of the standardized scores on a larger sample. To date this research has not been conducted.

Using subjects drawn from the same settings as above, Kendrick et al. (1978) obtained data on 102 individuals tested twice across an interval of six weeks, the recommended time to allow optimum efficiency in diagnosis. From this group of subjects, 48 individuals were divided into three groups of 16 subjects each (8 females and 8 males) matched for group mean age. The three groups consisted of depressed, demented, and normal subjects. Scores on the two subtests were visually inspected in order to provide cutoff points for the diagnosis of demented versus not demented as well as to examine changes across time. Information from the cutoff points was combined with the base rate information using Bayes' theorem (Bayes, 1763) in order to evaluate the probability of membership in the demented or not demented group. This resulted in 100% agreement with independent psychiatric diagnoses. This evaluation was completed on the remainder of the sample with similar results. Kappa coefficients were computed for the 2 X 2 contingency table where the contingencies were demented versus not demented and psychiatric diagnosis versus diagnosis using the KCTE. The values of the coefficients ranged from 0.92 to 0.98.

A further set of analyses was carried out on the same set of subjects. This time there were three possible diagnoses: normal, depressed, and demented. In a 3 X 3 contingency table, there was a 79% agreement overall. When the data from both the test sessions were used, the agreement dropped to 73%. Cowan et al. (1975) found improvement in the DCT but not in the OLT over time for depressed subjects. These results indicate that the KCTE may have reasonable concurrent validity; however, replication and cross-validation is needed.

Interpretative suggestions require two test administrations with an interval of six weeks in order to assess changes. For that reason, the KCTE exists in two alternate forms. In order to assess the alternate form reliability, Kendrick, Gibson, and Moyes (1979) administered the KCTE to 80 subjects, each of whom was over the age of 55. Administration occurred twice with an interval of 24 hours. The subjects were divided into four groups of ten females and ten males each. Groups 1 and 2 received the alternate forms in counterbalanced order. Group 3 received Form A twice, and Group 4 received Form B twice. There was a significant practice affect for each of the two forms. There were no significant differences between the two forms. The correlation between the two forms was 0.92. The subjects in this study were a heterogeneous group of healthy and impaired subjects in independent living, group home, and medical and psychiatric settings. It may be that different characteristics of the subjects influence the reliability values, and research to address this point is needed.

Critique

In summary, the KCTE holds promise to be a useful instrument in the differential diagnosis of dementia and depression in the aged. There has been more published research relevant to the original version, some of which has addressed the above points (Kendrick, 1967, 1972; Kendrick & Post, 1967). To date, the small number of studies that have examined the revised KCTE have provided favorable results. However, more research specifically investigating the revised version is needed before the battery can be unequivocally recommended for use as the solitary instrument in a clinical setting. For the present, clinicians would be well advised to use the KCTE in conjunction with other more established instruments.

References

Bayes, T. (1763). Essay toward solving a problem in the doctrine of chance. *Philosophical Transactions, 53,* 370-418.

Cowan, D. W., Copeland, J. R. M., Kelleher, M. J., Kellett, J. M., Gouraly, A. J., Smith, A., Barron, G., De Gruchy, J., Kuriansky, B., Gurland, B., Sharpe, L., Stiller, P., & Simon, R. (1975). Cross national study of diagnosis of the mental disorders: A comparative psychometric assessment of elderly patients admitted to mental hospitals serving Queens County, New York, and the former borough of Camberwell, London. *British Journal of Psychiatry, 126,* 560-570.

Gibson, A. J. (1981). A further analysis of memory loss in dementia and depression in the elderly. *British Journal of Clinical Psychology, 20,* 179-185.

Gibson, A. J., & Kendrick, D. C. (1979). *The Kendrick Battery for the Detection of Dementia in the Elderly.* Windsor, England: The NFER-Nelson Publishing Company, Ltd.

Kendrick, D. C. (1967). A cross-validation study of the use of the SLT and DCT in screening for diffuse brain pathology in elderly subjects. *British Journal of Medical Psychology, 40,* 173-178.

Kendrick, D. C. (1972). The Kendrick battery of tests: Theoretical assumptions and clinical uses. *British Journal of Social and Clinical Psychology, 11,* 373-386.

Kendrick, D. C. (1982). Administrative and interpretative problems with the Kendrick Battery for the Detection of Dementia in the Elderly. *British Journal of Clinical Psychology, 21,* 149-150.

Kendrick, D. C. (in press). *The Kendrick Cognitive Tests for the Elderly.* Windsor, England: The NFER-Nelson Publishing Company, Ltd.

Kendrick, D. C., Gibson, A. J., & Moyes, I. C. A. (1979). The Kendrick Battery: Clinical studies. *British Journal of Social and Clinical Psychology, 18,* 329-340.

Kendrick, D. C., & Moyes, I. C. A. (1979). Activity, depression, medication, and performance on the Revised Kendrick Battery. *British Journal of Social and Clinical Psychology, 18,* 341-350.

Kendrick, D. C. & Post, F. (1967). Differences in cognitive status between healthy, psychiatrically ill, and diffusely brain-damaged elderly subjects. *British Journal of Psychiatry, 113,* 75-81.

Routtenberg, A. (1968). Two-arousal hypothesis: Reticular formation and limbic system. *Psychological Review, 75,* 57-80.

Searle, R. T. (1984). A community based follow-up of some suspected cases of early dementia: An interim report. *Bulletin of the British Psychological Society, 37,* 20-21.

Skelton-Robinson, M., & Telford, R. (1982). Observations on the Object Learning Test of the Kendrick Battery for the Detection of Dementia. *British Journal of Clinical Psychology, 21,* 147-148.

Mark Stone, Ed.D.

Associate Professor of Psychology, Forest Institute, Des Plaines, Illinois.

KOHS BLOCK DESIGN TEST

S. C. Kohs. Chicago, Illinois: Stoelting Company.

Introduction

The Kohs Block Design Test was designed as a standardized measure of intelligence. The test's author, S. C. Kohs, citing Binet, states that all "intelligent" operations involve three essential activities; 1) attention to the problem presented, 2) a conscious attempt on the part of the subject to complete an adequate adaptation to the situation, and 3) the exercise of autocriticism in order to determine effectively and efficiently the adaptability level in problem solving. Kohs argues that the block designs clearly demonstrate attention, adaptation, and autocriticism in the successful accomplishment of each problem. The point at which a person begins to fail could be a rough measure of the development of the ability to attend, adapt, and critically survey accomplishment. Kohs continues his argument by saying that if intelligence involves the mental operations of analyzing, combining and pairing, deliberating, completing, discrimination, smudging, criticizing and deciding, then his block design test may be said to call upon the functioning of intelligence and, hence, is a measure of that mental capacity.

The current designs of the test were developed from a larger sample. These items were subjected to preliminary pilot studies and from the original 35, all but 17 were eliminated. However, details for their elimination are not provided in the manual. The remaining 17 designs are graded in difficulty in the following manner: 1) The use of full colors, 2) the use of diagonal sides, 3) the use of all diagonal sides, 4) turning the design on one of its corners, 5) eliminating the outside boundary line, 6) increasing the number of blocks to be used, 7) increasing asymmetry in the designs, and 8) decreasing the number of different colors used in the design.

The test materials consist of a 20-page manual, an answer sheet, and 16, 1" x 1" cubes, having each side painted either red, blue, white, yellow, blue and yellow at the diagonal, or red and white at the diagonal. Users of the Wechsler Scales will note the similarity of these designs, especially evident because of Wechsler's adaptation of this test into his own scales. The test is administered in a similar manner to the Block Design subtest of the Wechsler Scale. The designs themselves are centered on semigloss, white 3" x 4" cardboards and are 1/4 the size of the actual designs to be made by the cubes.

The test is administered by first introducing the subjects to the blocks, the arrangement of their colors on the sides, the designs, and a demonstration. When the task is sufficiently understood by the subject the other designs are presented. There are time limits to the test and the answer sheet provides these details for

392

facilitating scoring. To examiners unfamiliar with the Kohs Block Design Test, an additional aspect of the scoring and a very important one is the recording of moves so that in this test both moves and time are critical observations. Hence, the examiner records the total time and the number of individual moves. A move is counted when a block is given a separate and distinct change in position. Moves are counted from the point when a block is given its initial position on the table. Each change in position is counted as a separate move. This produces a total point value for each design based on the amount of time taken and the number of individual moves of blocks in completing a design. The answer form is contained on a single sheet with ample space for recording the moves, a summary of the total moves, the total time and the score for each design. These score values are summed producing a total score, the maximum of which is 131 points.

Practical Applications/Uses

Kohs Block Designs have probably seen less use since their adaptation for the Wechsler Scales. However, they do represent one valuable adjunct to the mental examiner's list of available tools. The recording of individual moves in problem solving is an essential aspect of scoring that has been observed by every examiner using the Wechsler Scales. Some subjects make deliberate and purposeful moves with surety of purpose and clear problem-solving intent. Other individuals move blocks aimlessly, use trial-and-error methods, or repeatedly make the same moves. This element of qualitative analysis in test performance is not recorded and does not affect the score of the Wechsler Scales, but it has a specific impact when scoring the Koh's Block Designs. Actually, the examiner will want to provide qualitative and narrative description of test behavior in problem solving, but the counting of moves in completing the design is an indispensible element of the task in order to differentiate intellectual performance and problem solving ability.

This test should find appropriate use with all individuals from preschool through adulthood. The lack of verbal responses in completing the test makes it appropriate for non-English-speaking individuals, those with difficulties in expressive language, and deaf and hearing impaired persons. The simplicity of the directions and the intuitive enjoyment of such a task make the designs very appealing to subjects.

Although the instrument has utility over the entire age range of persons, normative data are specifically provided for ages 5-18. For persons older than the normative data provided, the instrument still serves to judge the adequacy of an adult performance and the skill with which it is demonstrated.

The test must be administered individually. Examiners who are already trained and familiar with the Wechsler Scales will have no difficulty accommodating themselves to Kohs Block Design Test. Because there is a need for more careful observations in the recording of individual moves persons not trained in the administration of individual tests of ability should first seek to develop these skills and leave the administration of the Kohs Block Design Test to a trained person. The amount of time taken to administer this test is approximately 30 to 40 minutes. The longest time required is probably an hour, and very able persons can complete all the designs in 15 to 20 minutes. The manual provides clear and specific instructions for scoring. The answer sheet, as described earlier, has clear indications for all responses. The quality of the materials is excellent. For example, the blocks of 16 cubes are contained in a sturdy box and both the manual and answer sheet are without fault.

Use of the Kohs Block Design Test will require interpretative insight with respect to the norms as well as clinical judgement. The manual (pp. 5-7) provides normative mental age equivalents for the score values to a mental age of 19-11. The norms in the manual were based on a sample of 285 persons, and more up-to-date norms are needed.

Technical Aspects

The Kohs Block Design Test appears to describe an adequately developed variable as demonstrated by an increase in scores year by year with respect to age and ability against an increase in the difficulty of the designs. The test manual itself has not been updated with any current normative information. This is a serious fault and an impediment to its potential use. The correlation between the Binet and Kohs Block Design Test for 300 students was .80. Correlations using the Binet and the Block Design Test for samples involving mentally handicapped and other school age samples range from a low of .66 to a high of .81.

Critique

Aside from inadequate norms, Kohs' test remains useful. After all it was adapted by Wechsler for his scales. Examiners should consider using the test and useful local norms could easily be developed.

References

This list includes text citations as well as suggested additional reading.

Arthur, G. (1943). *A point scale of performance tests*—Chicago: Stoelting Co.

Kohs, S. C. (1919). *Kohs Block Design Test*. Chicago: Stoelting Company.

Kohs, S. C. *Intelligence measurement*. New York: Macmillan Company.

Matarazzo, J. D. (1972). *Measurement and appraisal of adult intelligence*. Baltimore: Wilkins Co.

Saunders, D. R., & Giffinger, J. W. (1968). Patterns of intellectual functioning and their implications for the dynamics of behavior. In M. M. Katz, (Ed.), *Classification—Psychiatry and psychopathology* (USPHS#1584) (pp. 307-390). Washington, DC: U.S. Government Printing Office.

Wechsler, D. (1974). *Wechsler Intelligence Scale for Children-Revised*. New York: Psychological Corporation.

Wechsler, D. (1981). *Wechsler Adult Intelligence Scale-Revised*. New York: Psychological Association.

Witkin, H. A. et al. (1962). *Psychological differentiation*. New York: John Wiley.

Jole A. Williams, Ph.D.
Unit Director, Maplewood, Grafton North Dakota State School, and Assistant Professor of Counseling, University of North Dakota, Grand Forks, North Dakota.

John D. Williams, Ph.D.
Professor and Chair, Department of Educational Measurement and Statistics, Center for Teaching and Learning, University of North Dakota, Grand Forks, North Dakota.

KUDER GENERAL INTEREST SURVEY, FORM E

Frederic Kuder. Chicago, Illinois: Science Research Associates, Inc.

Introduction

The Kuder General Interest Survey-Form E (KGIS) is a 168-item interest inventory that catalogues measured interests—as opposed to claimed or expressed interests—of adolescents. It consists of eleven scales, ten of which reflect broad areas of interest to be measured: Outdoor, Mechanical, Computational, Scientific, Persuasive, Artistic, Literary, Musical, Social Service, and Clerical; the eleventh scale is the Verification Scale, designed to determine the sincerity of the responses.

The survey has a forced-choice triad format and is partially ipsative in character. The limited sense in which it is ipsative is that some triads are scored for more than one scale. The KGIS-Form E is designed for use with grades 6-12. It requires only a sixth-grade reading level.

G. Frederic Kuder, author of the KGIS-Form E, was born in Holly, Michigan in 1903. He received an A.B. in 1925 from the University of Arizona; an M.A. in 1929 from the University of Michigan; and a Ph.D. in psychology in 1937 from Ohio State University.

Kuder's professional experience includes: membership on the Illinois Board of Exams, 1936-1940; personnel methods consultant, Social Security Board, 1940-1942; chief of test construction and review unit, U.S. Civil Service, 1942-1943; chief of civilian studies section, information and education division, U.S. War Department, 1943-1945; consultant, 1945-1947; professor of psychology, Duke University, 1948-1963; president, Personnel Psychology, Inc. 1948-present. Concurrently Kuder was editor of *Educational and Psychological Measurement*, 1940-1970, and *Personnel Psychology*, 1948-1952, 1958-1964 and 1971.

The Kuder General Interest Survey has evolved from a series of Kuder vocational interest inventories published over a period of more than forty years. Its various forms, versions, and editions may be regarded as a family of related instruments that approach the measurement of interests from different perspec-

395

tives and are designed for somewhat different purposes. Data from each part of the long series of experimental and published inventories became part of the foundation for later inventories. The earliest and the best known of these inventories is the Kuder Vocational Preference Record.

The first Preference Record, Form A published in 1939, was a vocational interest inventory constructed to yield seven relatively independent scores on the following scales: Literary, Scientific, Artistic, Persuasive, Social Service, Musical, and Computational.

The earliest experimental form was a vocational interest blank of 40 items, each consisting of descriptions of five activities that the subjects ranked in order of preference, comparing each with every other in the group. Preferences were indicated by 500 students at the Ohio State University who filled out the blank in the academic year 1934-35. The blanks were then scored tentatively for preferences for several types of activities. For example, comparisons that provided the opportunity to indicate a preference for mechanical over other kinds of activities were scored as mechanical preferences, a scoring procedure that was followed in each of the interest areas.

Because the experimental blank was constructed to represent as wide a variety of activities as was feasible, it did not include many activities in any one field. Consequently the reliabilities of the resulting scores were relatively low.

During the development of the first Preference Record's seven scales the Prestige Scale was dropped because it was difficult to develop new scales that were uncorrelated with it and at the same time build satisfactory reliability. Scales in the areas of athletics, religion, finance, politics, and annoyances were also dropped from the final form.

Experience with the first Preference Record suggested that the clerical and mechanical interest areas should be represented more adequately in subsequent forms. When items for the second form were compiled, comparisons involving activities in these areas were included.

College students who had previously filled out the first Preference Record were administered the experimental edition of Form B, and the correlations between each item and each of the seven scores obtained from the first form were computed. These correlations were the main basis for including an item in the new form's scales. Although only a limited number of items would be tried out in the experimental editions, there was little overlap in seven of the nine scales.

The construction of the second vocational Preference Record (Form B) was complicated by attempting to include more items without increasing the time required to fill out the form. Mechanical and Clerical Scales were added, and it was considered desirable to construct scales of higher reliability in the areas covered by the first Preference Record. Instead of increasing the number of choices in each scale, a triad form of item was used where the subject was asked to indicate which of three activities would be most liked and which would be least liked. The triad process allowed cutting the apparent length in half. Form C, published in 1948, was constructed because many users of Form B expressed a need for a measure of interest in agricultural and related outdoor activities. After a lengthy tryout period, Kuder developed the Outdoor Scale. Experience with Form B also indicated the need for a process to identify subjects who have answered carelessly or without understanding. A Verification Scale composed of responses that most subjects select was developed. It was found that groups of subjects who were diligent obtain scores on this scale ranging from 38 to 44, while subjects who deliberately answered carelessly generally obtained much lower scores.

Form E evolved from the realization that an interest inventory for younger people was not just a matter of putting Form C into simpler language. Because the responses of younger students tend to be less reliable it was thought necessary to construct longer scales in order to achieve greater reliability.

Through the years, Kuder received suggestions for revised and new items from several sources (e.g., graduate students wrote sets of easier items). All items above fifth-grade difficulty were scheduled for revision. Items were also considered from the standpoint of whether they were likely to change in meaning as children grew older. For example, occupational titles were avoided because a young person's impressions and knowledge of specific occupations are subject to change over time.

Revised items often showed little resemblance to their counterparts in Form C. The items used were those that were reliable with adults and distinguished those who answered sincerely and carefully from those who answered less diligently. It was still necessary, however, to check the items at a lower level, particularly because some of them had to be cast in simpler language.

An experimental edition of 197 items was given twice with four weeks between administrations to approximately 2,000 seventh-grade students. During the second administration some subjects were asked to try to give answers that they thought would make a good impression even if they did not reflect their interest. The reliabilities (test-retest) for each response to each item were obtained for 500 boys and 500 girls separately. The subjects were asked to answer sincerely both times—that is, without trying to make a good impression. An index of relationship of each response with scores on tentative keys for all ten areas was also generated by sex; keys were subsequently developed on the basis of these data. The objective was to develop in each subtest reliable scales that would have relatively low correlations with the other scales. Intercorrelations and reliabilities were obtained for a set of revised scales, and these scales were successively revised until the length of the form was reduced to the current 168 items.

Practical Applications/Uses

The KGIS, a revision and downward extension of the Kuder Vocational Preference Record, was developed in response to a need for an instrument to tap the measured interests of young people, particularly at the junior high level. Designed for grades 6-12 it employs simpler language and an easier vocabulary than the earlier form, and requires only a sixth-grade reading level.

The younger people are, the less stable their interests are likely to be; nevertheless, in the seventh grade and sometimes even earlier they should begin to make some decisions about their junior high and high school courses of study. Those decisions—which cannot be postponed—will tend to influence their eventual occupational choices.

The school counselor can use the results of the KGIS and data on abilities, achievement, and home environment to develop discussions with students and their parents to select appropriate educational and vocational goals. Supplementary information may also be needed to develop a complete picture of a student. A student's pattern of interests as shown in the Kuder profile may seem in conflict with other relevant information about him or her.

In the seventh or eighth grade KGIS results help students to decide what electives to take in junior high school; determine the kind of high-school curriculum to choose (e.g., college preparatory, vocational, business, commercial, or general); plan programs of reading and other activities around their principal interest areas; and explore new experiences that might lead to the discovery of new interests.

In the ninth or tenth grade the survey's results help students to reexamine their interests and if they have been measured earlier, to see which of their pronounced preferences have persisted or become even more pronounced, which ones have diminished, and in what areas new peaks have shown up on their profile. They also help them to plan high-school courses of study if they are in a junior high school; see the relation between interests and various part-time jobs, summer jobs, and other experimental experiences; relate their preferences to the high-school extra-curricular program; and encourage them to consider, not specific occupational choices, but a broad exploration (e.g., individual investigation, related reading, field trips, films, and interviews) of jobs in the areas of their most pronounced interests. In addition they help them with immediate vocational choice if they are determined to leave high school before graduation.

In eleventh or twelfth grade the results help students to make tentative vocational choices if they are planning to go to work or into job-training programs immediately after high school graduation, and aid college-bound students in outlining their general objectives.

Even though the Kuder General Interest Survey most typically would be used by school counselors and classroom teachers working with grades 6-12, and very little research has been done on the KGIS, studies looking at use with a variety of populations would seem to be of interest. Some potential new applications might be 1) successful use with the developmentally disabled population—clients with mild to moderate levels of retardation—because of the simple language and easy vocabulary; and 2) use in rehabilitation counseling with a client population— usually those who have experienced change in physical and/or mental functioning— and are in need of thorough exploration of interests to reassess what is of interest to them in relation to what they are presently capable of performing.

Although the intended use of the Survey includes sixth-grade students, more than reading level should be considered. Data suggests that sufficient maturity to attain an acceptable Verification (V) score is necessary. Test-retest correlations developed separately for each grade for students with acceptable V scores, as well as the correlations obtained for superior sixth-graders indicate that reliability at the sixth-grade level may be high enough to warrant use of the instrument with such students. General use of the KGIS with average sixth-graders, however, may be a waste of time and money because of the likelihood of a sizable proportion of unacceptable V scores. It is hoped that in time research will yield a more precise way of identifying sixth-graders whose interests can be measured reliably.

The survey can be administered on a group or classroom basis; it is untimed but the manual (Kuder, 1975) indicates that students generally complete it in 45-60 minutes. However, untimed tests are somewhat problematical for classrooms where students may only be scheduled for 45-50 minutes; also even if enough time is available for the slower students, providing appropriate activities for the faster ones may often be less than optimum.

A classroom teacher can administer the test; no specialized skills are required but familiarity with the manual surely would be helpful. Form E has both a hand-scoring and machine-scoreable version. The directions for the two tests differ slightly, principally because the hand-scored version uses pins and corrugated paper. One possible area of difficulty in this version is the changing of answers, which is more cumbersome with pins than erasers. Students are told that if they want to change an answer, they must punch two more holes as close as possible to the undesired answer, then punch the new answer in the usual way. The novel use of the pin and difficulty of instructions might intimidate a sixth-grader (if not an adult), resulting in several unchanged, but inaccurate, answers.

Another problem area can be the hand-scoring: it is suggested that the actual scoring be done by the students under the direction of the teacher. Scoring directions are given in the answer section of the survey; they are not reproduced in the manual. Scoring amounts to counting the number of circles with pin pricks through them, not including those with three pin pricks (changes). While this process is fairly routine, it may be too much of a challenge for younger examinees. Where it is financially feasible the machine-scoring version would seem to be preferable.

Scores are profiled into ten interest areas together with a V Scale. When machine-scored, each student receives a copy of the results; hand-scored surveys could also be profiled in the same way. The V score (Verification score) may be problematical for some users; if a V score exceeds 15, the manual is less than definitive as to how to interpret the scores. Determining the level of difficulty in interpreting the results is itself a task. On the other hand, rather simplistic interpretations are readily available; putting the Kuder results in an overall gestalt of career choice may be a more demanding task. The sophistication required to interpret the scores would not seem to be too high; many classroom teachers with no special training might do well at this task. However, those teachers who tend toward dogmatic interpretations rather than flexible interpretations might be less than helpful to young students. Thus, though it is not recommended by Kuder, specific workshops on the KGIS would be helpful to the survey's appropriate use.

Technical Aspects

Because the Kuder interests tests in their many forms have been around since 1939, the research literature is replete with studies involving one or another form. Due to the newness of Form E, however, the studies reported in the manual are those done by the research staff. In all, they tested 9,819 students in grades 6-12, reporting information by socioeconomic level, region, and sex. Test-retest correlations and KR 20 reliabilities are reported for grades 6-7. Also, test-retest correlations are separately recorded for grades 6-8 and grades 9-12, together with means and standard deviations by sex. Although all (except one) correlations and reliabilities for the ten subscales ≥ .70, generally the older students show somewhat higher correlations on a test-retest basis. The Persuasive Scale may be somewhat problematical for younger students, showing test-retest relationships of .69 and .73 respectively for boys and girls in grades 6-8 on a six-week retesting. Overall, however, the KR 20 reliabilities would seem acceptable to many users; in grades 6-8, KR 20 measures were between .72 and .89 for boys and .76 to .90 for girls. For grades 9-12, KR 20 reliabilities were between .86 and .92 for boys and between .80 and .90 for girls. Also reported are grade-by-grade reliabilities on each test.

A four-year followup study yielding stability measures has been completed on Form E for three different intelligence groups: Group I, intelligence scores ≥ 120; Group II, intelligence scores between 100 and 119; and Group III, below 100. The stability measures tend to be higher for those with higher level intelligence scores, though this outcome is not uniform. The mean stability coefficient is .50, though the lowest is only .19 for lower intelligence scoring subjects on the Clerical Scale. Because clerical jobs might be more probable for Group III than other groups this low a stability coefficient would bring into question usefulness of the form for this group.

In general, the manual is very complete regarding reliability data; however, two points should be brought out in this regard: the very completeness might seem confusing to a person unaccustomed to the different reported reliabilities; reliabilities are reported variously for four-week, six-week and four-year intervals. This poses no problem for sophisticated users but may be confusing to beginning counselors. A more important point is that they do not have a separate section on validity; the manual reports studies that clearly fall under this rubric, but users looking for a specific section on validity will find the manual wanting in this regard. Also, problems on validity have been addressed by earlier reviewers of other versions of the Kuder (Arnold, 1959; Clendenon, 1965; Layton, 1965).

Critique

If one conceptualizes future occupational success as a combination of interest, ability, and opportunity, it is clear that many measures of the first two constructs exist and that the Kuder measures are among the most respected for measures of interest. In addition, many different types of measures exist to measure many different aspects of ability. But given interest and ability, what if there is no *opportunity?* Careers cannot be made out of interest and ability alone.

Put another way, for those specifically looking for a measure of interest, the Kuder is definitely an acceptable measure. But interest is only one prong in the triumvirate of interest-ability-opportunity. The most important prong, opportunity, has generated the least psychometric interest. That this would be so is not surprising. Opportunity is by far the hardest construct to define, but those who deal in career counseling should never ignore it, regardless of the difficulty in measurement and definition.

References

In addition to the 44 references in the *manual* these reviewers has found reviews of earlier Kuder interest measures useful. This list includes the most accessible of these as well as text citations.

Anastasi, A. (1976). *Psychological testing.* New York: Macmillan Publishing Company.

Arnold, D. L. (1959). Review of Kuder Preference Record-Personal. In O. K. Buros (Ed.), *The fifth mental measurements yearbook.* Highland Park, NJ: The Gryphon Press.

Clendenon, D. M. (1965). Review of Kuder Preference Record-Personal. In O. K. Buros (Ed.), *The sixth mental measurements yearbook.* Highland Park, NJ: The Gryphon Press.

Dolliver, R. H. (1972). Review of Kuder Occupational Interest Survey. In O. K. Buros (Ed.), *The seventh mental measurements yearbook.* Highland Park, NJ: The Gryphon Press.

Harmon, L. W. (1978). Review of Kuder Preference Record-Vocational. In O. K. Buros (Ed.), *The eighth mental measurements yearbook.* Highland Park, NJ: The Gryphon Press.

Kuder, G. F. (1975). *General Interest Survey (Form E)-Manual.* Chicago: Science Research Associates.

Layton, W. L. (1965). Kuder Preference Record-Personal. In O. K. Buros (Ed.), *The sixth mental measurements yearbook.* Highland Park, NJ: The Gryphon Press.

Sweetland, R. C., & Keyser, D. J. (Eds.). (1983). *Tests: A comprehensive reference for assessments in psychology, education and business.* Kansas City, MO: Test Corporation of America.

Walsh, W. B. (1972). Review of Kuder Occupational Interest Survey. In O. K. Buros (Ed.), *The seventh mental measurements yearbook.* Highland Park, NJ: The Gryphon Press.

Mary A. Hudak, Ph.D.
Assistant Professor of Psychology, Allegheny College, Meadville, Pennsylvania.

LEARNING STYLES INVENTORY

Joseph S. Renzulli and Linda H. Smith. Mansfield Center, Connecticut: Creative Learning Press, Inc.

Introduction

The Learning Styles Inventory (LSI) by Renzulli and Smith (1978) clearly falls within the individualization school of thought in education. The underlying assumption is that students differ with respect to "style" in the learning process and these individual differences should be respected. This translates into gearing instructional mode to preferences of students. The claim is that when students are matched with their preferred instructional mode, achievement and satisfaction with learning will be enhanced. This matching model of instruction focuses on nine teaching modes: projects, drill and recitation, peer teaching, discussion, teaching games, independent study, programmed instruction, lecture, simulation.

The rationale and construction of the LSI was developed in Linda Smith's (1976) dissertation, under the direction of Dr. Joseph Renzulli, Professor of Educational Psychology at the University of Connecticut. Despite the fact that several learning style inventories had already been developed (e.g., Dunn & Dunn, 1975; Kolb, 1974), Renzulli and Smith argued for the need of an instrument that avoided abstract levels of analysis. Hence, their LSI deals directly with common instructional techniques, such as lecture vs. independent study formats. There is no attempt to infer the underlying explanations (such as cognitive styles) for alternative learning-format preferences. The advantage of this concrete approach is that assessment results can be readily translated into practice by teachers.

The preliminary version of the LSI consisted of 54 items describing classroom situations (e.g., panel discussions) assumed to be related to specific categories of instruction. Content validation was by categorization of items into teaching modes by "expert judges" in the field of education. This 54-item version of the LSI was administered to a sample of junior high students (N = 698). Principal component analysis resulted in 14 factors, 9 of which were considered "psychologically meaningful" (congruent with prior conceived categories of instruction). Based on loadings of .35 or better, 38 of the original 54 items were retained for the revised version of the LSI. Internal consistencies for items by factor/subscale proved inadequate; hence, 27 items were added, based on estimation of increase in reliability via the Spearman-Brown formula. Thus, the revised version consists of 65 items.

The LSI is a paper-pencil survey. Each of the 65 items is evaluated on a 5-point

Likert Scale, ranging from "very unpleasant" to "very pleasant." Subjects are given the standard "there are no right or wrong answers" instructions, typical of attitude scales. The LSI is claimed to be appropriate for grades 4-12. Users are advised that administration to primary students may require two sessions and the examiner should consider reading test items to students in small groups (Renzulli & Smith, 1978).

Although the LSI is primarily for determining instructional preferences among students, there is a parallel form for teachers. The aim is to evaluate the existing profile of class activity for comparison with activities preferred by students. Parallel examples are: (Student Form) "Having other students who are experts on a topic present their ideas to the class"; (Teacher Form) "Have students who are experts on a topic present their ideas to the class" (Renzulli & Smith, 1978). The teacher form also employs a 5-point Likert Scale. Teachers respond according to how frequently a particular instructional situation occurs in the class being tested; response range is from "very infrequently" to "very frequently."

Both the student and teacher forms of the LSI are presented on optical scanning sheets, appropriate for computer scoring and analysis. Analyses include individual and average group preferences for students, and a profile of the frequency of alternate teaching techniques used in the class being tested.

Practical Applications/Uses

The aim of the administration of the LSI is to optimize the outcome of the learning experience. In theory, learning is enhanced when instruction preference and practice are congruent. The foremost application is the straightforward analysis of individual preferences for classroom instructional practices and the complementary analysis of instructional practices that typify the teaching in a particular class. Such an analysis would be appropriate in virtually any class situation. A more particular example of this application would be the analysis of a gifted class or program. In point, there is some suggestion (Stewart, 1981; Wasson, 1980) that gifted vs. average/normal students differ in instructional preferences (and by inference, in needs).

Any "failed" educational situation—gifted or other—may profit from a learning-style preference analysis. A school principal or counselor might cooperatively engage such an analysis in concert with teachers who have difficult students and/or classroom situations.

Other applications of the LSI might logically include "special needs" groups, such as learning disabled, deaf, and adult education groups. Other learning-style instruments have been used with some success with these groups (e.g., Dowaliby, Burke, & McKee, 1980; Price, 1982). Although the learning style instruments used in these studies deal with different levels of generality, there are no obvious reasons why the Renzulli-Smith instrument should not be useful in specific-needs contexts.

Although the authors recommend the inventory for grades 4-12, there is no apparent reason why it would not also be appropriate at the college level. Ristow and Edeburn (1983) surveyed college students with the Renzulli-Smith LSI. Although this study is descriptive of college student preferences rather than a validity study, internal consistency reliability coefficients were calculated and showed slight improvement on projected reliabilities based on Renzulli and Smith's junior-high validating sample.

On the younger age end, the authors of the LSI suggest the feasibility of use with primary students if adjustments in the test-giving format are instituted. However, a more important factor and a contraindication may be that younger students lack the experience in the educational system necessary to make meaningful evaluations of preferences.

The LSI variables—projects, drill and recitation, peer teaching, discussion, teaching games, independent study, programmed instruction, lecture, simulation—constitute attitude targets. Analysis of LSI results reveals positive or negative attitudes for these targets. While it is apparently likely for a student to have a mixture of positive and negative attitudes, a particular student may be positively disposed to every teaching technique represented or to none. Such extremes would be of interest in relation to overall attitudes toward school and/or attitudes toward self as a learner.

Although the LSI authors make explicit efforts to maintain a concrete connection between learning style and teaching strategy, the notion that the process of learning may be ultimately tied to differences in cognitive "styles" and/or stages remains as a logical inference. Hence, an interface with cognitive developmental variables may be of both theoretical and practical interest. For example, how do preferences for learning style change with age and the development of abstract-thought capacity? Research with both the Renzulli-Smith LSI (Stewart, 1981; Wasson, 1980) and Dunn's LSI (Price, Dunn, & Dunn, 1977) suggests that grade level is related to learning-style preferences.

Administration of the LSI requires no special skills; however, completing the Teacher Form prior to administering the inventory to students is recommended by the authors. The instructions for administration in the testing manual are clear and straightforward. Survey time is approximately 30 minutes, but there is no time limit.

Although the LSI is presented on optical scanning sheets for computer scoring and analysis, it could also be easily scored by hand. All responses are scored in one direction (no reverse scoring). Items are evaluated on a 1 to 5 scale (1 = very unpleasant, 2 = rather unpleasant, 3 = neither pleasant nor unpleasant, 4 = rather pleasant, 5 = very pleasant). The authors' scoring model is for items to be summed and averaged for each learning-style dimension. Thus, each student has an individual score on each learning-style dimension, which potentially can range from 1 to 5. The computerized output lists individual scores, as well as class averages and standard deviations for each learning-style dimension.

In addition to the individual scores, the computerized output provides a number of additional analyses. The first of these is a reference sheet that indicates the two most preferred and the two least preferred learning styles for each student. This is a simple ranking procedure that does not take into account strengths of preferences. A second subsidiary analysis is a listing of students whose scores indicate a positive attitude toward particular learning styles; i.e., average scores falling within the "pleasant" range, defined as ≥ 3.51, where $3.0 =$ neutral. Teachers can use this analysis for planning group sessions, which make use of differential instructional modes. A similar listing is output for students whose scores indicate a negative attitude toward particular learning styles; i.e., average scores falling with the "unpleasant" range, defined as ≥ 2.49.

The remainder of subsidiary output consists of graphs that provide visual profiles of individual students, the class as a whole, and current teaching practices. The individual-student profiles are simply horizontal bar graphs of individual scores by learning style dimension. The class profile, derived from class averages on each dimension, is also a bar graph; individual variation is cancelled and the class is considered as a whole. A final bar graph plots frequency of the teacher's use of alternative instructional options. This output can be compared with students' individual and group preferences.

Interpretation of test results is based on objective scores, hence, perfectly straightforward. No expertise is required to read the output, other than understanding of means, standard deviations, rank ordering, and bar graphs.

Technical Aspects

The rationale for the LSI falls within the so-called aptitude-treatment interaction (ATI) research domain (Cronbach & Snow, 1969). In this domain individual differences (aptitudes) are theorized to be key variables and to interact differentially with alternate types of teaching (treatment). In any ATI-model research attempt, the burden of validation falls on the demonstration of the significance of the interaction—individual characteristics x teaching characteristics. In Renzulli and Smith's model, this hypothesized interaction is that matching student preferences with types of teaching will lead to enhanced educational outcomes. "The impetus behind the development of the LSI was the supposition that if learning style preferences can be identified and if students are permitted to learn through the method(s) of their choice, then school achievement, motivation and interest in subject matter would be enhanced" (Renzulli & Smith, 1978, p. 19).

At this stage, apparently the only study that addresses the validity of this matching hypothesis is the research undertaken in the origination of the LSI (Smith, 1976). This research focused on just three of the nine learning style dimensions—lecture, discussion, and simulation. A social studies unit for 7th-graders was developed for each of the three instructional modes. Each of these alternative "treatments" was presented in three consecutive class meetings. Subjects were pretested with the LSI, then assigned to conditions such that each of the three teaching-type treatment groups contained a mixture of subjects whose attitudes toward that type of instruction ranged from negative to positive ($N = 30$ per group). Posttesting included measures of achievement (test based on material presented), motivation (*Junior Index of Motivation*, Frymier, 1965), and interest (*Gable and Roberts Attitude Toward School Subjects*, Gable and Roberts, 1972). Interest was also assessed with the following single-item measures: 1) "I liked the way the unit was taught," 2) "I would like to learn other school subjects this way" (Renzulli & Smith, 1978, p. 20).

Learning style data was scored in three ways: 1) the standard individual scores described earlier (items summed and averaged); 2) ranked scores, calculated by ranking individual/average scores on each dimension; and 3) z scores, calculated in order to assess each individual's learning style preferences in relation to other students.

In order to assess the relationship between learning style and achievement, motivation, and interest, data were analyzed with a series of multiple stepwise regressions. The learning style scores (individual, ranked, and z scores) for the dimension under treatment served as predictor variables for scores on achievement, motivation, and the three measures of interest (5 separate regression analyses). Results indicate that LSI scores contributed significantly to the variance in each of the criterion variables ($p < .05$ or better), with the exception of motivation. These results indicate that higher scores (or greater preference) on the learning style the subject is allowed to pursue tend to be associated with higher scores on achievement and interest; and lower scores, with lower achievement and interest. This tends to support the matching hypothesis. It should be noted, however, that R values are moderate, ranging from .22 (Item 1) to .38 (achievement). R^2 for achievement, the strongest criterion variable and the variable of most interest, indicates only 14% "explained" variance. A counterpoint is that the variance in achievement is understandably related to factors other than learning style, such as IQ.

A second series of regressions included IQ and prior achievement as predictor variables, together with learning style scores. With IQ and prior achievement scores entered first, learning style scores still contributed significantly to the variance in achievement and interest variables. In the analysis with achievement, prior achievement entered with a simple r of .32. Multiple R remained at .32 with the inclusion of IQ; the inclusion of learning style scores raised R to .53, $p < .01$. This result further enhances the validation of the matching hypothesis, by suggesting that the prediction of achievement can be improved with the addition of learning-style to the known predictors of prior achievement and IQ.

In the analyses with interest, learning style significantly improved prediction with all three interest measures; Rs ranged from .25 to .33. These results indicate that being taught in a preferred manner correlates with higher interest. Since interest is a positive outcome, these results also favor the matching hypothesis.

In all analyses, motivation failed to significantly relate to learning style. Renzulli and Smith (1978) suggest that this failure may be due to the scale used. Because motivation is a critical educational-success variable further research with this variable appears most desirable.

Although the validation study reported above does provide some tentative support for the LSI and its intended objective—justification for the matching hypothesis—it includes a number of limitations. In the authors' own words, the study "was only an initial exploratory attempt to examine the educational effects of matching instruction to learning style preferences as determined by the LSI" (Renzulli & Smith, 1978, p. 21). Limitations relate to both treatment and analysis. The treatment was a contrived short-term experience vs. a standard semester-long class and included only three of the nine learning styles. Content area was limited to a social science. Type of content may be of considerable relevance in matching-hypothesis testing, as suggested by Tallmadge and Shearer (1969). The age limitation (7th-graders) also appears significant, especially since the LSI is claimed appropriate for grades 4-12. There may very well be important differences between 4th-graders and 7th-graders with respect to the meaning of LSI scores. In terms of analysis, two points are relevant. Although the regression analysis is both interesting and appropriate, additional studies that directly compare achievement scores of students matched on instruction type and learning style with students who are mismatched appear desirable. With regression analysis alone, the nature of the somewhat large amount of unexplained variance is unclear; it could be due either to some percentage of students for whom the matching hypothesis did not hold or to variance that is left to be explained by yet other variables (e.g., socialization, success expectancies). In favor of regression analysis, it makes use of the interval-level quality of the LSI. This relates to the second point of contention with the validation analysis. The interval-level-data advantage is partially lost by the LSI authors' scoring system. Ristow and Edeburn (1983) correctly point out that the practice of averaging item scores for each learning-style type leads to needless elimination of variance. This practice was no doubt instituted to make learning-style type scores numerically comparable because subscales contain different numbers of items. Although this is acceptable for teacher use, non-averaged raw scores should be maintained for statistical data analysis. Finally, the use of the three learning-style scores (standard individual scale scores, ranked scores, and z scores) in the validation analysis is puzzling at best. No meaningful pattern emerged from the inclusion of these multiple entries of learning style.

Evaluation of construct validity was based on the previously mentioned initial-study sample of 698 junior high students (7th- and 8th-graders). Principal component analysis with oblique rotation resulted in a 14-component solution. Nine of the 14 factors were representative of the theorized learning-style types. These nine factors accounted for 37.3% of the total variance, leaving somewhat sizeable unspecified variance. The percent of total variance accounted for by the named factors ranged from 3.1 (peer teaching) to 5.5 (projects). Intercorrelations among the nine factors of interest were negligible.

Internal consistency reliabilities were calculated for the nine factors (subscales) of interest. Only one factor met a .70 criterion (projects = .77). As previously mentioned, 26 items were added and the Spearman-Brown formula was employed to estimate increase in reliabilities. Reliability coefficients were projected to increase values ranging from .50 to .77, to values ranging from .66 to .77. With this projected improvement, one factor still falls below the .70 criterion (independent study = .66). Test-retest reliabilities were not conducted.

Taken together, the construct validation and internal consistency analyses suggest that confidence in the stability of the LSI constructs is somewhat tentative at this stage. Future research that includes principal-component and reliability analyses on different age groups are also considered important. Reliabilities may vary by age, as suggested by Ristow and Edeburn's (1983) stronger LSI reliabilities with college-age subjects.

Although learning-style theorists emphasize individual uniqueness, hence may disfavor the concept of standardizing by groups, it may be useful to establish norms for different groups, including age groups. There is certainly related evidence that particular groups of students profit from differences in teaching approach.

Critique

In keeping with the individualization movement in education, learning style theory rests on the assumption that students retain unique attributes that are highly relevant to the learning process. These individual differences are presumably enduring characteristics that should be taken into account by providing correspondingly-appropriate learning experiences. The idea that individuals have distinct "styles" of learning is closely tied to the earlier-theorized construct of cognitive styles. Witkin (1965) suggested that knowledge of a student's cognitive style would allow for more effective educational planning. A review of learning style/cognitive style literature reveals wide-ranging conceptualizations at different levels of generality for the meaning of "style." More recent work has attempted to sidestep the abstract levels of analysis characteristic of cognitive style and of learning style theories such as Kolb's (1974) conceptual modes. The Renzulli-Smith LSI is an example of this so-called operational-definition solution to the problem of learning styles.

At this stage of research, the most crucial concern with any measure of learning style is construct validity. An operational-definition model that focuses on stated preferences and disregards the explanation for *why* an individual prefers a particular style of learning must still demonstrate that the construct "learning style" has reality and relevance. The fundamental supposition that students should be matched on teaching-type and learning-style preferences has significant implications. Dunn, Dunn and Price (1977) go so far as to imply that student psyches may suffer if educators fail to live up to this responsibility. Other theorists have argued that learning styles are not equally adaptive and deliberate mismatching may enhance educational success. Two research examples that support this view are Hunt's (1971) findings with regard to the development of conceptual complexity and Yando and Kagan's (1968) findings with regard to reflective/impulsive characteristics. While these examples are at more abstract levels of analysis, it is quite possible that alternative types of instruction, similarly, have adaptive benefits for students mismatched with respect to preference. In support of this idea, Kolb (undated, cited in Pigg, Busch & Lacy, 1980) has presented evidence that suggests that instructional preferences are related to underlying learning style characteristics (e.g., lecture with reflective observation). Another possibility is that matching, as is the case with mismatching, is important for some vs. all students.

Confirmation of the validity of the learning-style dictum—individual characteristics should be matched with appropriate educational experiences—requires more evidence than has been advanced to date. Research on the matching hypothesis, including the whole gamut of definitions of learning style, has produced mixed findings. Operational-definition models, such as the Renzulli-Smith LSI, must also deal with the problem of whether stated preferences for learning style converge with underlying individual characteristics, which may indeed profit from particular instructional techniques. A rigorous test would be to apply the matching solution to underachieving students with a criterion of post-test achievement gain.

In this view, conclusions based on research in learning style tend to be over-stated and/or of little value in gaining confidence in the validity of the learning-style construct. For example, studies that describe small average differences among groups (e.g., gifted, gender) provide very weak evidence for the existence and/or relevance of learning styles. Those studies that deal with the preference/treatment interaction tend to emphasize the statistical significance of an interaction, with disregard for strength of association. James (1962) has been cited as support for the validity of the matching hypothesis due to his obtained significant interaction. However, closer examination reveals that subgrouping of matched vs. unmatched students produces no difference on the criterion measure of achievement.

With specific regard to research with the Renzulli-Smith LSI, four studies have tested the relevance of this approach to the learning-style problem: Smith's (1976) validation study provides some support for the matching hypothesis. Research by Ristow and Edeburn (1983), Stewart (1981), and Wasson (1980) are descriptive of learning style correlates among specific groups, rather than direct tests of the matching hypothesis.

Attempts at integration among different approaches to learning style have been sparse and equivocal. Ferrell (1983) correctly questions the rapid rise in learning-style instrument popularity despite inadequate theoretical formulation and corresponding evidence for the validity of the construct. However, in spite of the tentative state of the art, the concept of learning styles is intuitively appealing and holds promise for an advance in educational psychology. In the reviewer's view, learning style may not be as simple and global as apparently hoped, thus, future research would do well to continue work on validation by including multiple variables and controls, and taking into account developmental processes.

References

Cronbach, L. J., & Snow, R. E. (1969). *Individual differences in learning ability as function of instructional variables.* (USOE Final Rep., No. OEC4-6-061269-1217), Palo Alto: Stanford University, School of Education.

Dowaliby, F. J., Burke, N. E., & McKee, B. G. (1980, April). *Validity and reliability of a learning style inventory for postsecondary deaf individuals.* Paper presented at the annual meeting of the American Educational Research Association, Boston.

Dunn, R., & Dunn, K. (1975). *Educator's self-teaching guide to individualizing instructional programs.* West Nyack, NY: Parker Publishing Co.

Dunn, R., Dunn, K., & Price G. E. (1977). Diagnosing learning styles: A prescription for avoiding malpractice suits. *Phi Delta Kappan, 58,* 418-420.

Ferrell, B. G. (1983). A factor analytic comparison of four learning-styles instruments. *Journal of Educational Psychology, 75,* 33-39.

Frymier, J. R. (1965). *JIM Scale Student Questionnaire.* Columbus, Ohio: The Ohio State University, College of Education.

Gable, R. K., & Roberts, A. D. (1972). *The development of an instrument to measure attitudes toward school subjects.* Paper presented at the Northeast Regional Educational Research Association, Boston.

Hunt, D. E. (1971). *Matching models in education: The coordination of teaching methods with student characteristics.* Ontario: Ontario Institute for Studies in Education.

James, N. E. (1962). Personal preference for method as a factor in learning. *Journal of Educational Psychology, 53,* 43-47.

Kolb, D. (1974). On management and the learning process. In D. Kolb, I. Rubin, & J.

McIntyre (Eds.), *Organization psychology: A book of readings* (2nd ed.). Englewood Cliffs, NJ: Prentice-Hall.

Pigg, K. E., Busch, L., & Lacy, W. B. (1980). Learning styles in adult education: A study of county extension agents. *Adult Education, 30,* 233-244.

Price, G. E. (1982, March). *Relationship between learning style and students with learning disabilities.* Paper presented at the National Meeting of the American Education Research Association, New York.

Price, G. E., Dunn, R., & Dunn, K. (1977, April). *Summary of research on learning style based on the Learning Style Inventory.* Paper presented at the annual meeting of the American Educational Research Association, New York.

Renzulli, J. S., & Smith, L. H. (1978). *Learning styles inventory: A measure of student preference for instructional techniques.* Mansfield Center, CT: Creative Learning Press, Inc.

Ristow, R. S., & Edeburn, C. E. (1983, October). *An inventory approach to assessing the learning styles of college students.* Paper presented at the annual meeting of the Northern Rocky Mountain Educational Research Association, Jackson Hole, WY.

Smith, L. H. (1976). *Learning styles: Measurement and educational significance.* Unpublished doctoral dissertation, University of Connecticut.

Stewart, E. D. (1981). Learning styles among gifted/talented students: Instructional technique preferences. *Exceptional Children, 48,* 134-138.

Tallmadge, G. K., & Shearer, J. W. (1969). Relationships among learning styles, instructional methods, and the nature of learning experiences. *Journal of Educational Psychology, 60,* 222-230.

Wasson, F. R. (1980). *A comparative analysis of learning styles and personality characteristics of achieving and underachieving gifted elementary students.* Unpublished doctoral dissertation, Florida State University.

Witkin, H. A. (1965). Some implications of research on cognitive style for problems of education. *Archivio Di Psicologia Neurologia E Psichiatria, 26,* 27-54.

Yando, R. M., & Kagan, J. (1968). The effect of teacher tempo on the child. *Child Development, 39,* 27-34.

Thomas P. Petzel, Ph.D.

Professor of Psychology, Loyola University of Chicago, Chicago, Illinois.

LEITER ADULT INTELLIGENCE SCALE

Russell G. Leiter. Chicago, Illinois: Stoelting Company.

Introduction

The Leiter Adult Intelligence Scale (LAIS) is an individually administered test of adult intelligence that yields scores parallel to those of the standard measure of intelligence, the Wechsler Adult Intelligence Scale-Revised (WAIS-R) and its predecessor the WAIS. It is scored for Verbal, Performance, and Full Scale deviation IQs. The LAIS manual (Leiter, 1972) does not provide definitions of these three types of IQ scores, but does imply that they are similar to the Wechsler IQ scores.

The manual states that this test has several advantages over the Wechsler tests: it takes less time to administer and score than the WAIS-R, giving a time savings of approximately 35 minutes; it may provide purer measures of verbal and/or performance skills, a conclusion drawn from the author's reported evidence that LAIS verbal-performance correlations are lower; it is more useful at the lower and upper levels of the socioeconomic hierarchy because, according to the author, the LAIS yields lower and higher IQ results at the respective ends of the hierarchy; and the LAIS is the test *par excellence* for use in disability determination because "it does not overrate the cognitive and physical capacities of the psychologically disabled (p. iii).

The LAIS was developed by Russel Graydon Leiter in its present form in 1955 because of his dissatisfaction that WAIS results did not reflect the true lack of "industrial competitiveness" of disabled populations. Based on his description of intelligence as "a measure of one's ability to compete with one's fellows" (Leiter, 1972, p. vi), Leiter advocated comparing the score of an individual with the scores made by "men" between the ages of 18 and 34, rather than with chronological age cohorts as do the Wechsler tests.

The LAIS was developed from the Leiter-Partington Adult Performance Scale (see Partington, 1949; Leiter & Partington, 1950), which was a measure of performance skills. A version of the Leiter-Partington test was used as the performance portion of the Army Individual Test of General Intelligence (Adjutant General's Office, 1944) which was standardized on a group of 256 unselected male war veterans between the ages of 19 and 36.

Without restandardization, the Army Individual Test was made available for civilian use under the name Leiter Adult Intelligence Scale (1951). The LAIS took its present form of three verbal and three performance subtests in 1959. A revised manual was published in 1972.

411

The three subtests of the Verbal Section are 1) Similarities-Differences requiring test takers to explain how pairs of words are alike and different, 2) Digits Forward and Backward requiring repeating number sequences, and 3) Free Recall-Controlled Recall requiring the repetition of a narrative paragraph to measure free recall followed by responses to specific questions on the paragraph to measure controlled recall.

The three Performance Section subtests are 1) Pathways in which examinees draw lines to connect numbers in sequence (Part I) and connect numbers and letters alternately (Part II), 2) Stencil Designs requiring reproducing nine designs resembling military shoulder patches by arranging pieces of circular paper, and 3) Painted Cubes in which examinees arrange one-inch colored cubes to reproduce pictures on cards.

The test comes in kit form with test manual, 400 8½" x 11" Pathways Test sheets, 9 designs and 19 stencils for the Stencil Design Test, 3 model cards and 24 colored cubes for the Painted Cubes Test, and 100 record forms. The LAIS is available from the Stoelting Company.

Practical Applications/Uses

The manual (1972) provides detailed instructions for use in administration. Alternate instructions for pantomime for the three Performance subtests, eliminating the need for spoken directions or responses if the situation warrants, are also included. In addition, the manual contains tables of adult IQ norms for each subtest, for the Verbal and Performance Sections, and for the total score. Intercorrelations among subtests, and correlations with other tests are reported, but reliabilities are not reported. Data are presented on LAIS and WAIS scores for a hierarchy of six groups of varying degree of socioeconomic sufficiency, which reveal increasingly lower mean LAIS IQ scores than WAIS IQ scores, the lower the groups are in the "hierarchy."

The test is designed to be a general purpose test of adult intelligence. It takes less time to administer and score than the WAIS-R, but yields less information because of its fewer subtests. Thus, it is suited to situations where time economy is important or when general estimates of verbal, performance, or full scale IQ are sufficient. Because the LAIS standardization norms are apparently limited to young adult males, the test may be most useful for vocational/occupational assessment purposes or for evaluation of deterioration. The extended range of the LAIS IQ distribution suggests that the test has usefulness for refined discrimination among persons at the upper and lower ends of the IQ spectrum. The author of the test suggests that Pathways and Stencil Design (other versions have been labeled Trail Making and Shoulder Patches, respectively) are useful in evaluating brain injury. The LAIS is stated to be applicable to adults but no age range is recommended and raw scores of persons of any age are converted into IQ scores from the same table. Elsewhere, Leiter (1973) wrote that the LAIS is suitable for persons as young as 15 years even though the youngest age of the normative group was 19 years.

The pantomime instructions for the Performance Section makes that part suitable for non-English-speaking or hearing-impaired persons, and the non-language responses required for that section make it adaptable to persons with speech deprivation or problems.

The LAIS is individually administered most appropriately in a quiet room with a table or desk on which to work. The manual suggests that a 24" x 19" light-brown desk blotter and a stopwatch (not provided) be used. The test is probably most appropriately given by a psychologist or educator trained in intelligence test administration and interpretation, although elsewhere (Leiter, 1973, p. 33), it is suggested that skilled technicians can be trained to administer the test.

Administration and scoring instructions are presented in an easy-to-read and detailed manner. Three tables allow easy conversion of raw scores into IQ scores. However, these normative tables for subtests do not include the highest possible raw scores which can be earned. For example, a person can earn 76 points on Digits Forward and Backwards but receive maximum credit for only 60 points. On the other hand, raw score points above the maximum for individual subtest conversion are included in conversion to Verbal, Performance, or Full Scale IQ. For example, the maximum total raw scores that can be used to convert each individual subtest to IQ scores sum to 227 points (which would convert to a Full Scale IQ of 146), although there are actual raw score totals up to 251 on the table (which convert to an IQ of 160). The inconsistency is exacerbated by the fact that a perfect performance on the total test would attain 257 points, but the best performing subjects reach a ceiling at 251 raw points, which convert to 160 IQ points. As a final example, if a person earns the exact maximum convertible raw score on each of the six subtests, the average IQ of those six is 158, yet following the assumed, though not specified, procedure of summing those raw scores and converting that total gives a Full Scale IQ of only 142 according to the conversion tables.

Technical Aspects

Evidence for the psychometric soundness of the LAIS is weak. The manual provides very little psychometric information. For instance, there is no information given on the standardization sample. The sample norms on which standard IQ scores are computed are apparently from the original 256 unselected male veterans. Subsequent research has found gender differences on the LAIS but these are not taken into account on the IQ conversion tables. Reliability estimates are not reported in the manual but are reported by Leiter (1951) based on the original sample to be as low as .65 for Digits Forward and Backwards. Despite a marked range of reliabilities, the manual recommends converting subtest raw scores into individual IQ deviations to compare high and low subtests. Such a conversion may mislead the unsophisticated test user into interpreting subtests as equally reliable.

Originally, evidence for LAIS validity consisted of intercorrelations among subtests and Sections and correlations with the Stanford-Binet test giving a total correlation of .88. The revised manual reports data on "138 individuals applying for vocational rehabilitation services . . . between 1958 and 1968" (p. iii). In this sample, the LAIS correlated .91 with the WAIS (taking an average of 40 and 75 minutes to administer the two tests, respectively). Using this same sample, the manual reports a Verbal correlation of .34 and Performance correlation of .58 with the Porteus Maze test.

Critique

Dr. Leiter concludes the Preface to the current manual with an assessment of his own test which conveys the "flavor" of his approach to the LAIS development and suggested uses. He states, "My feeling upon completing 28 years of work with this scale is similar to that of Toscanini who, as he finished conducting Beethoven's 9th for the last time said, 'After studying and conducting Beethoven's 9th for 50 years this is as near as I can come to what Beethoven had in mind.' The Leiter Adult Intelligence Scale is as near as I can come to producing a valid instrument for measuring general intelligence and, it follows, a fair measure of the mental capacity of all adults to whom it is applied" (Leiter, 1972, pp. vii-viii).

On the other hand, M. R. Goldsamt (1969) in a review of the LAIS writes: "As a hypothesized measure of general adult intelligence, the LAIS apparently contains flaws which limit IQ interpretation, fails to provide unique information not supplied by other intelligence scales and may not even measure adult intelligence per se." (p. 969).

Very little research has been published on the LAIS since the 1970s, and what has been published, was generally in the late 1940s and 1950s. Furthermore, throughout the years much of the technical and psychometric information on the LAIS not available in the manual was published in *The Psychology Service Center Journal*, founded and edited by Leiter.

This reviewer does not think that the advantages of the LAIS outweigh the dated normative data and the limited published evidence for reliability and validity. The LAIS has not become sufficiently widely used to generate close scientific scrutiny by a broad spectrum of the psychological community. Finally, sophistication in psychometric techniques and advancements in professional standards for assessment have improved since the LAIS was developed and have greatly outpaced those applied to it.

References

This list includes text citations as well as suggested additional reading.

Adjutant General's Office Classification and Replacement Branch. (1944). The New Army Individual Test of General Ability. *Psychological Bulletin, 41.* 532-538.

Crawford, P., & Snyder, W. (1966). Differentiating the psychopath and psychoneurotic with the LAIS. *Journal of Consulting Psychology, 30,* 178.

Davis, P. C. (1965). Leiter Adult Intelligence Scale. In O. K. Buros (Ed.), *Sixth mental measurements yearbook.* Highland Park, NJ: Gryphon Press.

Goldsamt, M. R. (1969). An evaluation of the Leiter Adult Intelligence Scale (LAIS). *Perceptual and Motor Skills, 28,* 959-971.

Jex, F. B. (1965). Leiter Adult Intelligence Scale. In O. K. Buros (Ed.), *Sixth mental measurements yearbook.* Highland Park, NJ: Gryphon Press.

Leiter, R. G. (1951). The Leiter Adult Intelligence Scale. *Psychological Service Center Journal, 3,* 1-52.

Leiter, R. G. (1972). *Examiner's manual for the Leiter Adult Intelligence Scale*. Chicago: The Stoelting Company.

Leiter, R. G. (1973). The Leiter population: A psychological model for mental illness. *The Psychological Service Center Journal, 13,* 1-38.

Leiter, R. G., & Partington, J. E. (1949). Manual for the Leiter-Partington Adult Performance Scale. *The Psychological Service Center Journal, 1,* 139-171.

Leiter, R. G., & Partington, J.E. (1950). *The Leiter-Partington Adult Performance Scale*. Portsmouth, OH: Psychological Service Center Press.

Luber, S. A., & Walker, R. E. (1969). Sex differences on the Free Recall-Controlled Recall test of the Leiter Adult Intelligence Scale. *Journal of Clinical Psychology, 25,* 412-413.

Partington, J. E., & Leiter, R. G. (1949). Partington's Pathways Test. *The Psychological Service Center Journal, 1,* 9-20.

Shaffer, L. F. (1965). Leiter Adult Intelligence Scale. In O. K. Buros (Ed.), *Sixth mental measurements yearbook*. Highland Park, NJ: Gryphon Press.

David T. Morse, Ph.D.
Associate Professor of Educational Psychology, Mississippi State University, Mississippi State, Mississippi.

LIFE SKILLS: FORMS 1 & 2

Kenneth Majers and Dena Wadell. Chicago, Illinois: The Riverside Publishing Co.

Introduction

Life Skills: Forms 1 and 2, are tests of functional competencies in reading and mathematics. They are multiple-choice, paper-and-pencil tests of academic achievement that measure skills in reading and mathematics commonly used by high-school students or adults in daily life. Suitable for group administration, Life Skills measures four subareas in each subtest (reading and math). Each subarea is comprised of from two to six specific skills, each of which is represented by one to four items. The reading and math subtests contain 48 and 50 items, respectively. Suggested administration time is 40 minutes per subtest. An administrator is required, though no special training is necessary. Norms tables are given for Grades 9-12, adult education, and inmates from penal institutions.

Available materials and services include 1) alternate forms of the test (Forms 1 & 2); 2) examiner's manual; 3) technical supplement; 4) examination set (includes a. and b.); 5) self-mark answer sheets; 6) MRC answer sheets; 7) basic scoring services, including classroom, school, and district summaries; and 8) optional scoring services, including school frequency distribution, student response analysis, and item analysis.

Life Skills, copyrighted in 1980, is a relatively young test with the norming taking place during the fall of 1978, and alternate forms reliability data collected during the Spring of 1979. According to the statement of rationale, Life Skills was developed by Kenneth Majers and Dena Wadell to assist schools in the measurement of how well learners can apply fundamental reading and math skills to daily problems and in the identification of those who are deficient in either area. The need for such a test, based on the rationale, stems from the increasing public concern that high schools may be graduating students who lack vital, fundamental skills in reading and math.

According to the examiner's manual, a pool of 160 reading items and 192 math items were administered in May, 1978 to about 4,600 students. On the basis of this tryout, 96 reading and 100 math items were chosen for the standardization versions of Forms 1 and 2. Approximately 10,000 students in Grades 9-12 from 434 school districts participated in the norming study conducted during Fall, 1978. In addition, about 2,000 inmates from penal institutions in 22 states participated. Finally, about 1,000 adult education students were also included in the norming study, though nothing is said as to how these examinees were selected.

416

The last study prior to the test's publication was that of alternate forms reliability, the data for which were collected during spring, 1979 from about 400 students in Grades 11-12 in five school districts. The criteria used for item selection during the tryout process are not mentioned in the examiner's manual or technical supplement. The test is organized by a rational rather than empirical grouping (e.g., factor analytic) of items; according to the examiner's manual, each item tried was related to one of the specific skills. No special forms of the test (e.g., Spanish or Braille editions) are listed in the publisher's catalog.

The Life Skills test consists of a reusable booklet containing the reading and math subtests and one of three types of disposable answer sheet.

The Reading subtest measures specific skills in the following subareas:

1. Follow directions: (12 items measuring four skills). Types of stimuli include illustrations of warning labels, drug containers, appliance use directions, and phone book or pay phone directions.

2. Locate references: (12 items measuring three skills). Stimuli include a phone book, catalog, and car owner's manual.

3. Gain information: (16 items measuring five skills). Item stimuli include illustrations of want ads, public notice, time card or payroll card, utility bill, and lease contract.

4. Understand forms: (8 items measuring two skills). Stimuli include installment purchase agreement and tax forms.

The Mathematics subtest measures specific skills in the following subareas:

1. Compute consumer problems: (12 items measure four skills). The types of stimuli include illustrations of mileage logs, want ads, advertisements, check register, time cards, and word problems. The items measure the basic operations using integers, money amounts, and decimal fractions.

2. Apply principles of percent, interest, and fractions: (12 items measure four skills). Item stimuli used include time cards, advertisements, bills, shaded figures, and regular word problems.

3. Identify, estimate and convert time, currency, and measurements: (16 items measure six skills). The types of item stimuli include clocks, recipes, money combinations (coin and currency), and word problems.

4. Interpret graphs, charts, and statistics: (10 items measure five skills). Stimuli used include line and pie charts, sales receipts, thermometer, line drawings, and word problems.

For both subtests, the stimulus (e.g., checkbook register) is usually presented, followed by items which depend on the stimulus. In most cases, the stimulus and matching questions comprise the measures of a specific skill. The arrangement of stimuli and items is logical and uncrowded. Examinees should have no trouble determining which items relate to a given illustration.

All items are four-alternative, multiple-choice questions. In the math subtest, the last choice is "None of these." Alternatives are only rarely listed in a logical order (e.g., ascending or descending for numeric alternatives).

If machine-scorable (MRC or NCS 7010) answer sheets are used, two sample items are given on the test for the examinees. Otherwise, there are no practice or sample items.

An examiner is required to pass out and collect materials, read directions to examinees, and time each subtest. No special training is required for administration, which could be accomplished by clerical personnel.

The intended age range for this test includes Grades 9-12 and adult learners.

In the main, the test is easy; questions are usually straightforward and require elementary skills in reading and math of the sort typically mastered by average students long before the ninth grade. Item difficulties given for the norming samples are more frequently .70 and above (i.e., 70% or more of the group answered the item correctly) than below. The math test, based on the norm groups' performance, is slightly more difficult than the reading test, and each subtest on Form 2 is slightly more difficult than their Form 1 counterpart.

Three types of answer forms are available: self-mark; MRC; and NCS, type 7010. The examiner's manual gives separate administration directions for each. The publisher's scoring services are available only if the MRC sheets are used. The MRC sheet requires that the teacher's name, grade, and test form be entered for proper machine scoring and reporting. Each type of answer sheet contains spaces for the choices on all 98 items on a single sheet.

No profile is available, but the publisher's basic scoring services include a classroom summary (R-W record by item for all students in a class as well as average percentages correct); school summary (average percentages correct on each skill for each class); and district summary (same as school summary, only by school). Optional services include school raw score frequency distribution (frequency distribution and local percentile ranks for each school); student response analysis (alternatives selection by student); and item analysis summary (counts and percents of students choosing each alternative).

Practical Applications/Uses

Life Skills has considerable potential for use in education settings; as a relatively brief, easily-scored instrument which may be administered to groups, it provides reasonably quick and low-cost information on a student's general level of achievement in basic reading and mathematics skills. The plausible context of most of the items should help to hold an examinee's attention during the test better than straight word problems. The principal users of this test would probably be high school, adult, community education instructors, or school counselors who need a rapid screening or placement device for commonly-used, fundamental skills in reading or mathematics.

Thus, the strengths of the Life Skills test include low-cost, rapid administration and scoring, potentially interesting item stimuli, and the capability of serving as a quick "dipstick" of student performance in reading and math. However, there are applications in which the test will clearly *not* perform well.

In its present form, the Life Skills test would very likely fail to match closely the specific objectives that an individual teacher, school, or district may establish for students. For this reason, the test would be ill-suited as an indicator of mastery of locally set objectives, for purposes of comparing teachers, schools, or similar "accountability" applications. Likewise the selection of skills and very light sampling of items for each skill would make Life Skills a poor device for the identification of specific skills on which a learner was in need of assistance, or for identification of learning disabilities. None of these uses is suggested or implied in the publisher's materials.

According to the examiner's manual, the purpose of Life Skills is to provide a means by which schools can assess students' ability to perform common "life skills" which require reading or math skills. Such an instrument can aid in the identification of students deficient in these areas as well as help in gauging the degree to which such skills are being (or have been) taught.

The test itself measures fundamental skills in reading and math. In the reading subtest, most of the items appear to measure literal comprehension—answering factual questions about the item stimulus—whereas fewer items require some sort of manipulation of that information. The math subtest sticks to the basic four operations (using integers, fractions, percents, money amounts, and the rare decimal fraction) and throws in a few other skills requiring understanding of certain units of measurement, charts or graphs, and a lot of reading.

The stimuli for the items (e.g., a tax form or product label) should not be considered the focus of the measurement—the skills just enumerated more accurately represent the types of behavior which the test measures. As such, the Life Skills test covers skills that, paradoxically, would probably be considered important for a graduating high-school student to possess yet would seldom, if ever, be taught in the regular 9-12 curriculum. Adult education or GED programs might well incorporate some instruction on these skills.

Some ways in which this test might be used include:

1) As a placement or screening tool for adult education, community education, or GED programs;

2) For special remediation programs aimed at high-school or adult students, as a rough-and-ready means of gauging progress (the two forms permit pre- and post-instructional assessment);

3) As a practice test for students and as an early-warning system for teachers in schools that have implemented some sort of competency-based promotion or graduation test;

4) As a correlate for schools or states that are attempting to develop competency-based tests of promotion or graduation (assuming a sufficient match of skills, of course); and

5) As a screening device for counselors to use in evaluating students who might be in need of special remediation programs or who have transferred from a school in another district.

Some uses for which the test would *not* be well-suited include:

1) Determining which students possess the skills necessary for "survival in the real world." (The notion of "essential" or "survival" skills, while appealing, is almost impossible to establish on an absolute basis);

2) Diagnosis of learning disabilities, or of physical or emotional handicaps;

3) Identification of specific skills on which remediation may be needed. (While an instructor could gain a fair amount of insight by examining the individual items and a student's responses, the skills are too vague to suffice as instructional objectives and the sampling of items is too spare to permit skill-by-skill judgments on individual students. The examiner's manual correctly warns the user against such an application.);

4) Construction of meaningful profiles of an examinee's strengths and weaknesses (only the subtests yield reliabilities sufficient for such use.);

5) Comparison of teachers, schools, or districts in effectiveness of teaching these basic skills. (Without some credible method of equating groups for preexisting differences in ability and achievement as well as an assurance that the test's skills are completely congruent with those of a local program, it would be foolhardy to use the test as a benchmark of teaching success.); and

6) Identification of students who should or should not be promoted or receive a high-school diploma. (Such a use would imply that the test represents precisely those skills deemed necessary by a local system while omitting none, that a plausible and defensible cutting score or rule had been established, and that the test reflected the instructional program at that grade or in that system. It is unlikely that each of these conditions would be met.)

Life Skills is designed to be used in Grades 9-12 and for adults such as those enrolled in adult education programs. The test would be inappropriate below Grade 9 for regular students because its skills would not match well with those normally taught at a single grade level. As a college placement or screening examination, the test would also be inappropriate; deficiencies on the skills measured would be manifested in other indicators, such as SAT or ACT scores or high-school grades.

As long as examinees can indicate their own choice of response, there should be no limitations imposed by physical handicaps in taking the test. The one exception would be for blind or low vision examinees; Life Skills items depend on being able to read the stimuli and require rather fine visual discrimination skill on occasion (e.g., choosing the correct telephone number from a list) as to make the test useless.

Life Skills may be administered to a single student, class, or large group. The physical requirements are sufficient work space; pencils with erasers; one sheet of scratch paper per examinee; one test manual and answer sheet per examinee; a watch, and an examiner's manual for the administrator. The examiner's manual contains all of the information needed for administration of the test; no special training is needed.

Instructions given the examiner are generally clear and straightforward. Only a few possibilities for confusion might be encountered. First among these is the difference in answer sheets. The publisher makes three types of sheets available. The examiner's manual gives directions separately for each type of sheet, but a careless examiner might not notice the heading for the proper set of directions. The second potential source of confusion involves timing. A suggested time limit of 40 minutes per subtest is given, although the manual suggests that permitting examinees to try every question is more important than "adherence to a rigid time limit." The problem is that no indication is given as to how departure from the suggested times might affect the validity of the published norms.

Suggested schedules are given for one- or two-day testing. All told, 100 minutes is the recommended time for a one-day session, whereas 110 minutes may be required if the test is given in two days. These times include distribution of materials, filling in forms, and break period. The manual says nothing concerning the administration of the subtests out of order.

Overall, the administration procedure is simple.

There are three possible scoring methods. First, the publisher provides machine scoring with various reporting options only if the MRC answer sheets are used. If a school has a sheet scanner capable of reading the MRC or NCS 7010 sheets, then a simple scoring program could be used for local machine scoring. Finally, any of the types of answer sheets available could be hand-scored.

Whether by hand or machine, scoring consists of right-wrong (R-W) marking of each multiple-choice item. Hand scoring of both subtests could easily be accomplished by clerical personnel in five minutes or less per student. Looking up standard scores or percentile ranks would add a few moments to the process. Because both are determined by total rights on each subtest, this is a simple procedure. No formula scoring or correction for guessing is involved.

The advantage of choosing the publisher's test-scoring service lies in the variety of reports available, though for an additional charge beyond the scoring fee for some. Curiously, an item analysis summary or a student response analysis are among the extra-cost options.

No scoring template for hand-scoring is available from the publisher. Answer keys are given in the examiner's manual for both Forms 1 and 2. Fabricating such a template could be easily accomplished by the user, though the publisher could just have easily offered one.

If interpretation is limited to derivation of standard (T-scores) scores, percentile ranks, or both, interpretation is simple and rapid and could be performed by clerical personnel. The technical supplement gives a reasonably good description of percentile ranks, a more terse summary of T-scores, and little hint of what to do beyond obtaining these scores. The publisher's materials are a bit confusing on this point. On the one hand, the supplement suggests that only normative information (in the form of percentile ranks) permits meaning to be derived from the examinee's performance. Yet, on the other hand, only one of the six types of reports available from the publisher includes even local normative information, in the form of percentile ranks. Virtually all other information is in the form of percent of items correct, inviting skill-based interpretation. Thus, the intended interpretation is not clear.

A skill-by-skill interpretation of the results would call for an instructor who was experienced in both the teaching of the skills and in working with students like the examinee(s) to review the test item by item in order to make any kind of informed decision. Even with this, decisions would be tenuous at best for individual students. Decisions about larger groups, such as classes, schools, or districts could plausibly be made on the subareas (e.g., interpret graphs, charts, and statistics).

Technical Aspects

The technical data provided by the publisher includes detailed data for certain aspects of the test and only scanty information for others. Among the most glaring omissions is evidence of the validity of the Life Skills test. For tests that are designed or expected to yield competency-based interpretations it is critical that a thorough description of the content universe or domain be included with a discussion of how items were sampled from that domain (Linn, 1979; American Psychological Association, 1974). Such documentation, necessary for establishing the content validity of an instrument, is absent from the examiner's manual and technical supplement. Similarly, criterion-related validity is neither mentioned nor supported by data in the publisher's documentation. According to the *Standards for Educational and Psychological Tests* (APA, 1974), these omissions violate several essential standards (specifically A2, regarding the specifications followed in writing items; B5, evidence of validity to support suggested use for test; E1, limits of generalizability of validity information; E6-E8, conduct of validity studies; and E12, description of content universe and sampling procedures).

Reliability information given is uncomplicated and fairly complete. Internal consistency reliability estimates (KR-20) are reported by level (Grades 9-12, correctional inmates, adult learners), by sex and by ethnic group (Native American, Asian, Black, Hispanic, White, or No Ethnic choice) for subtest and total as well as for each subarea of the subtests. Standard errors of measurement are provided by level on subtest in T-score units and by level for subarea in raw score units (curiously, these are reported with four decimal places, which seems optimistic with regard to the precision of these estimates). These data are based on the principal norming group.

Overall subtest KR-20 reliabilities range from .85 to .92 by level for Form 1 reading, and from .79 to .89 for Form 2 reading. The math reliability estimates range from .89 to .93 by level for Form 1 and from .89 to .92 for Form 2.

In a separate study based on 393 students in Grades 11-12, the alternate forms reliability was estimated as .77 for reading, .79 for math, and .83 for total test. Contrary to the examiner's manual, Forms 1 and 2 are alternate, not parallel forms (see Lord & Novick, 1968 for an explanation of the difference).

The reliabilities of the subtests are adequate for typical use; subarea reliabilities, though, are considerably less (usually .60s or .70s for KR-20 estimates with the exception of graphs, charts, and statistics in math that were usually in the low .80s) and therefore would yield less dependable information about either an examinee or group than would the subtest score. Reliabilities of individual skills are given in the examiner's manual and range from .01 to .50 with median values of .26 for reading skills and .34 for math skills. These are far too low to use as subscores, as the examiner's manual correctly notes.

Total test score (R + M) KR-20 reliability estimates were in the low .90s. One limitation of the reliability data given is that it is all rank- or normatively based. That is, the reader cannot deduce what proportion of examinees would consistently perform with respect to some arbitrary level, such as 85% on the test. This sort of decision-making consistency (e.g., what proportion of examinees would be classified consistently as masters or nonmasters—(see Swaminathan, Hambleton, & Algina, 1974) is likely to more closely reflect the types of uses to which the test would be put in an educational setting. However, few authors or publishers of educational tests bother to check this type of consistency.

The norming of the Life Skills test, conducted during the fall of 1978, included about 10,000 examinees from Grades 9-12, about 2,000 inmates in state penal institutions, and about 1,000 adult education program students. The description of the sampling procedure suggests that a geographically stratified, proportional sampling procedure was followed, though the description is very terse. No mention is made of what procedures may have been followed to assure representativeness within school systems that agreed to participate in the study. No information is given as to how the adult learners were selected. The assignment of form to examinees is not discussed; though the number of examinees taking Form 1 of the test was about five to six times as large as the number who took Form 2. Thus, the statistics reported for Form 2 are probably less stable than those for Form 1.

Item means (proportion answering an item correctly) and discriminations (point-biserial correlations of item score and subtest score) are included by item for each level, sex, and ethnic subgroup for Forms 1 and 2. It is not clear whether the item-total correlations included or excluded the item from the subtest total; item-total correlations in which the item has been subtracted from the total are sometimes called "corrected" correlations because failure to exclude the item will inflate the observed correlation. In addition, average difficulties are given by subarea and level for both forms. With this wealth of information, it is surprising that no formal investigation of possible item bias (e.g., differential response patterns for identifiable subgroups such as ethnic group) is reported. Similarly, means and standard deviations should have been provided by level, sex, and ethnic subgroup.

Forms 1 and 2 were equated using the equipercentile method. In this method, scores on two tests are considered equivalent if they correspond to the same percentile rank for the same (or similar) examinees. For example, if on test A the median raw score is 42, while the median raw score on test B is 47, these scores would be considered equivalent (e.g., a score of 42 on test A is as good or as high as a score of 47 on test B, and vice versa). The equipercentile method is serviceable and works reasonably well even when two tests have a nonlinear relationship (Angoff, 1971), but in recent years, much attention has focused on the use of latent trait models for equating tests (see Holland & Rubin, 1982).

Norms given include raw to T-scores (a standard score having a mean of 50 and standard deviation of 10) for each subtest and form, followed by a T-score to percentile rank conversions for each level of examinee. Because the T-scores were determined from all examinees and the percentile ranks are given by grade/level, some minor discrepancies arise. For instance, one would expect a T-score of about 73 (2.3 SDs above the mean) to correspond with the 99th percentile; for most of the groups T-scores of 63 to 66 represent the 99th percentile. A more serious problem is that the given norms are applicable for individual examinees; no norms are given for groups (e.g., classes or schools), contrary to standard D7 in *Standards for Educational and Psychological Tests* (APA, 1974).

One more technical point deserves mention. The math subtest is weighted more heavily in the composite (total) score than is the reading subtest. The reason is that the variability—specifically the standard deviation—of the math subtest is about 60% larger than that of the reading subtest. The actual weight of a subtest is directly proportional to its standard deviation. Thus, the scheme of generating a total score by simply adding the reading and math subtotals yields a score in which the math total is weighted considerably more than the reading total. For this reason, subtest scores would probably be more meaningful than the total score.

A search of *Current index to journals in education* (those journals catalogued under the ERIC system) from 1979 through 1984 yielded no direct references to the Life Skills test. Specific topic areas searched were Test Construction, Test Reliability, Test Reviews, and Test Validity.

Critique

Measures of essential, life, survival, functional literacy, or other "critical" skills have certainly become quite popular in recent years, owing to the increase in local- and state-level accountability movements in education. Fabricating such a beast, though, is no mean task. The test developer faces some problematic obstacles.

First among these pitfalls is the difficulty in defining or identifying essential skills. Suffice it to say that at least one person can be found who is not capable of performing any given skill and yet can manage to function as a law-abiding citizen. The skills selected therefore represent some individual's or group's perception of important or frequently used skills. As such, any test of this type will measure an arbitrary collection of skills that may or may not match those deemed essential in a different venue. For example, whether the skill of "identifies consumer package shapes" is really an essential skill is doubtful, yet it is among the skills measured in Life Skills.

A second problem is that of fidelity. It is next to impossible for a paper-and-pencil, multiple-choice test to have high fidelity with any task as it would be performed naturally. For example, if a driver reads and follows an automotive maintenance checklist, he or she will *never* ask "Which of the following is NOT on my maintenance checklist?" Yet, Life Skills includes this type of unrealistic question.

A third problem arises from the spread of specific skills tested within a given skill. One example from the Life Skills test should help to clarify this point. One skill in the math subtest is "calculates perimeter and area." One form of the test contains a single item requiring the examinee to sum the lengths of the sides of a triangle (perimeter). On the other form, the examinee calculates the area of a square and performs a second operation to solve the given problem. That's too large a difference for the items to be considered interchangeable (which is implied by the alternate forms).

A fourth problem is that of impurity; the reading subtest items can require math skills, whereas the math items certainly require reading skill. An example from Life Skills is an item in the reading subtest that asks the examinee to figure out how many pills per day are prescribed if the given dosage is repeated every four hours. This overlap is reflected in the test by the fact that the reading-math subtest correlations are nearly as high as the alternate forms reliabilities.

These problems make it difficult indeed to generate a test that possesses high technical quality, is easy to administer and score, and has strong content-relevance to a variety of educational settings. Although Life Skills is certainly easy to administer and score, its general weaknesses stem from a lack of evidence of validity. Some other specific criticisms should also be mentioned.

Many items include numeric or very similar alphanumeric alternatives, which could be more easily differentiated if placed in some logical order (e.g., ascending or alphabetic). The scrambling of alternatives seems to serve no useful purpose on a test such as this.

There is a slight bias in the frequency with which each response position (A-D) is used as the correct response. On the reading subtest, choice C is slightly favored (14 of 48 items). Choice B is substantially favored on the math test (17 of 50 items), while choice D ("None of these") is seldom used (5 of 50). A chi-square goodness of fit test yields a probability of less than .10 for this discrepancy from equal frequencies on the math test.

A third point is the difference between the answer keys for Forms 1 and 2. All but two items are keyed the same across forms; it is not apparent why such a trivial difference should be present. On the one hand, two of 98 items is not a big enough difference to prevent examinees from recalling response patterns and thereby possibly inflating their scores. Yet, the user (or the publisher, for that matter) has to have a separate key or scoring program for each form, which makes the process of scoring more cumbersome. Further, one has to be certain of which form was used or else the scores might be incorrect.

Finally, some of the items differ markedly across forms. Form 2 is, according to the given norms, a bit more difficult than Form 1.

In sum, the Life Skills test is not so much a measure of "essential" skills as it is a measure of frequently used academic skills in reading and mathematics using item stimuli that are, in the main, plausible applications adapted from life situations. Potential users would do well to avoid use of subscores more specific than total reading or total math scores and to examine the types of reading and math skills actually measured (instead of the item stimuli used) to judge whether the test matches well enough what they wish to measure. If an easily administered and scored, reusable test of this sort is needed, if group norms are not required (though local norms are available as an extra-cost option from the publisher's scoring service), and if the lack of documentation on the validity of the test for specific applications is not a major concern, then Life Skills could reasonably fill the bill.

References

American Psychological Association, American Educational Research Association, & National Council on Measurement in Education (1974). *Standards for educational and psychological tests*. Washington, DC: Author.

Angoff, W. M. (1971). Scales, norms and equivalent scores. In R. L. Thorndike (Ed.), *Educational measurement* (2nd ed.). Washington, DC: American Council on Education.

Holland, P. W., & Rubin, D. B. (Eds.). (1982). *Test equating*. New York: Academic Press.

Linn, R. L. (1979). Issues of validity in measurement for competency-based programs. In M. A. Bunda & J. R. Sanders (Eds.), *Practices and problems in competency-based assessment*. Washington, DC: National Council on Measurement in Education.

Lord, F. M., & Novick, M. R. (1968). *Statistical theories of mental test scores*. Reading, MA: Addison-Wesley.

Majers, K., & Wadell, Dena (1980). *Life Skills: Forms 1 and 2*. Chicago: The Riverside Publishing Company.

Swaminathan, H., Hambleton, R. K., & Algina, J. (1974). Reliability of criterion-refernced tests: A decision-theoretic formulation. *Journal of Educational Measurement, 11*, 263-267.

Paula Lee Woehlke, Ph.D.
Associate Professor of Educational Psychology, Southern Illinois University, Carbondale, Ilinois.

THE LOLLIPOP TEST: A DIAGNOSTIC SCREENING TEST OF SCHOOL READINESS

Alex L. Chew. Atlanta, Georgia: Humanics, Ltd.

Introduction

The Lollipop Test is an individually administered measure of school readiness that is intended as a substitute for or supplement to the Metropolitan Readiness Tests (MRT) in assessing a child's behavioral maturity.

Alex L. Chew, Ed.D., developed the test as his doctoral dissertation at the University of Mississippi (1977). After a complete review of the literature, Chew included in the test those items found to be common to individual readiness tests and readiness assessment batteries that were most predictive of end of first-grade achievement. In addition, the test met the criteria of being short in length, easy to learn to administer, made up of stimulus items familiar to all children, interesting to children, useful for diagnosis, and amenable to local norming.

A developmental and interpretive manual for the Lollipop Test (Chew, 1981b) completely describes the test, with sections on the concept and theory of readiness, design, development, and validation of the test, interpretation and use of scores, a thorough explanation of how to develop local norms, and an extensive bibliography. One booklet contains seven stimulus cards: the first deals with identification of colors and contains pictures of lollipops in six different colors; the second requires identification of shapes, using six geometric figures; the third involves picture description and position of objects in a line drawing of a cat and kittens; card four tests spatial recognition via pictures of red lollipops of various sizes; the fifth assesses identification of numbers and shows ten Arabic numbers in large type; card six tests counting, using four boxes with red, green, yellow, or orange lollipops in various quantities; and the seventh card requires identification of letters via the presentation of 15 capital letters in large type. This booklet is made of heavy card stock, and the figures on the cards are clear and easy to see. The administration and scoring manual (Chew, 1981a) gives precise instructions for administering and scoring the test and contains space for noting clinical observations plus a summary sheet of the child's performance. Also included in the test materials is a prepublication copy of the original test validation study.

The test is intended as a criterion-referenced readiness test or screening device for preschoolers prior to their admission to first grade. It is individually administered, and the testing process itself requires that the examiner possess no special psychometric skills. Its emphasis is on behaviors that first-grade teachers expect their incoming pupils to have mastered but that are teachable, such as knowing and appropriately using words relating to position, shape, color, and numbers. It is short and responses required of the examinee include such simple actions as pointing, oral responding, and copying figures. Its difficulty level is pitched so that children who are ready for school will find it relatively easy. However, no norms are available as yet to help one to interpret individual pupils' readiness.

Practical Applications/Uses

The test would be useful to early childhood educators, kindergarten teachers, first-grade teachers, and school psychologists who must screen children for learning difficulties that might hinder their progress. Because of the newness of the test, it remains to be seen what other applications might arise for it.

Although the validation sample for the test consisted of northern Mississippi children who would be eligible for first grade the following year, the content of the test should be appropriate for younger children as well. However, because of the visual nature of the test stimuli and the requirement that some responses be made orally or by using a pencil, it would be difficult to adapt it for some types of handicaps. For example, it would not be appropriate for children with severe visual handicaps or for those with poor motor control of the hands.

The test requires the use of stimulus cards and individual interaction between pupil and examiner and is thus not appropriate for group administration as presently validated. Although no special skills are needed to give the test, a skilled examiner or teacher would probably elicit richer and more informative responses and provide better interpretation of test performance. Because the test takes only 15 to 20 minutes, it is probably usable in most educational settings.

Scoring is straightforward; instructions in the administration and scoring manual give the number of points to be assigned for each correct response on each subtest. For the subtest involving copying of shapes, examples are provided of efforts that should receive credit.

According to the administration and scoring manual, primary attention should be paid to deficit areas rather than to total or subtest scores. However, the manual suggests that children who score below 50 or who show a marked deficit on any subtest should be referred for further psychological evaluation; no reasons for this recommendation are given. It is also suggested that local norms be used to interpret scores, and, as noted earlier, the developmental and interpretive manual gives directions for establishing local norms. However, given the mobility of our population, the sole use of local norms seems shortsighted, and better national norms than the suggested score ranges given in the developmental and interpretive manual are necessary. This manual also suggests that a teacher prepare a list of items passed or failed by a pupil for each subtest and provide remediation for the latter, but specific suggestions are lacking. Because the test is described as "criterion-referenced," a skilled teacher or examiner of preschoolers is required for adequate use and interpretation of test data; the test does not explain how one would certify attainment of the criteria tested, and presumably an experienced teacher or examiner would be knowledgeable enough to estimate the level of performance necessary for successful first-grade completion.

Technical Aspects

Although The Lollipop Test is listed in *Tests in Print III* (Mitchell, 1983), at the time of this writing this reviewer could find no recent literature concerning its use. Thus the only validity data available are those provided by the original test validation. That study focused on the concurrent validity and the internal consistency reliability of the test. Data were obtained from 69 children who were eligible to enter kindergarten in the fall of 1977; the children came from five schools in four northern Mississippi counties and had a mean age of 69.94 months. Approximately half of the sample was female and half male, and half of each sex was white and half nonwhite. Scores on the test were compared with those on the MRT and teacher ratings of pupils' readiness skills. The total score was correlated .86 with MRT total score, and .58 with teacher ratings. Correlations between MRT subtests and Lollipop subtest scores ranged from .26 to .89, with a median of .52, while Lollipop subtest scores correlated between .37 and .61 with teacher ratings. In addition, Lollipop subtest scores were substantially correlated with the total score (.72 to .89). KR 20 reliability of the total test was .93. A factor analysis of The Lollipop Test revealed four factors, with all but three of the 49 items loading on one of the factors, that were labeled visual-perceptual abilities, numerical ability, color recognition and/or visual discrimination, and position and spatial recognition.

Critique

Although the validity and reliability data on The Lollipop Test are minimal, it was the only short diagnostic screening test of school readiness that could be used for both normal and exceptional children listed in *Tests in Print III* (Mitchell, 1983). Its strengths are its ease of use, familiar yet interesting tasks provided for the examinees, and brevity. Unfortunately, the latter characteristic is probably also its greatest weakness; although no reliability data were provided for the subtests, it is unusual for such short subtests to provide highly reliable data. In addition, the high correlations of subtest and total scores and the large KR 20 total reliability make it doubtful that any one subtest is tapping only one trait. However, the total score appears to possess adequate reliability and probably provides enough information to judge school readiness of an examinee. This reviewer would like to see additional studies that attempt to establish the validity and reliability of the test on diverse populations and using different indices of reliability and validity. National norms for interpreting total scores with respect to school readiness are also needed, as is more information on how the test can be used as a criterion-referenced instrument.

References

Chew, A. L. (1977). *The design, development, and validation of an individually administered school readiness test.* Unpublished doctoral dissertation, University of Mississippi.

Chew, A. L. (1981a). *Administration and scoring manual for The Lollipop Test: A diagnostic screening test of school readiness.* Atlanta, GA: Humanics, Ltd.

Chew, A. L. (1981b). *Developmental and interpretive manual for The Lollipop Test: A diagnostic screening test of school readiness.* Atlanta, GA: Humanics, Ltd.

Mitchell, J. V., Jr. (Ed). (1983). *Tests in print III.* Lincoln, NE: The Buros Institute of Mental Measurements.

E. Philip Trapp, Ph.D.

Professor of Psychology, The University of Arkansas, Fayetteville, Arkansas.

LOUISVILLE BEHAVIOR CHECKLIST

Lovick C. Miller. Los Angeles, California: Western Psychological Services.

Introduction

The Louisville Behavioral Checklist (LBC) is a parent-report checklist designed to cover the entire range of emotional behaviors indicative of child psychopathology. It is designed to differentiate between children with psychopathology and children in the general population, as well as to provide for the clinician descriptive information on a child's social assets and problematic behavioral areas. The LBC consists of a four-page, reuseable questionnaire with 164 true-false statements and a one-page response sheet. It requires a sixth-grade reading level, can be filled out by the child's parents, guardian, and/or teacher, and takes approximately a half hour to complete.

The LBC is available in three forms. Form E1 is normed for children aged 4-6 years, Form E2 for ages 7-12, and Form E3 for adolescents aged 13-17 years. Form E1 and E2 have the following scales in common: Infantile Aggression, Hyperactivity, Antisocial Behavior, Aggression, Social Withdrawal, Sensitivity, Fear, Inhibition, Immaturity, Normal Irritability, Severity Level, Prosocial Deficit, Rare Deviance, Neurotic Behavior, Psychotic Behavior, Somatic Behavior, and Sexual Behavior. In addition, Form E1 has the scales Intellectual Deficit, Cognitive Disability, and School Disturbance Predictor; and Form E2, the scales Academic Disability and Learning Disability. Thus, Form E1 has a total of twenty scales; Form E2, nineteen scales. Form E3 has the following thirteen scales: Egocentric-Exploitive, Destructive-Assaultive, Social Delinquency, Adolescent Turmoil, Apathetic Isolation, Neuroticism, Dependent-Inhibited, Academic Disability, Neurological or Psychotic Abnormality, General Pathology, Longitudinal, Severity Level, and Total Pathology.

Norms are provided for both males and females. Clinical norms are provided for all the scales; general population norms are provided for only the scales in Forms E1 and E2.

The LBC can be scored either by hand or computer. Templates are available for hand-scoring. The raw scores can be converted into standard scores with the use of conversion tables in the manual. A behavioral profile may be charted on the back of the response sheet. A special template for scanning the thirty most deviant

---

The reviewer is indebted to Mr. Dan Green for his invaluable assistance in the preparation of this review.

behaviors is provided for each form. While this allows for an overall view of the child's problematic behaviors, it does not provide comparative information. Also, visual scanning of the items ending with the digit "5" (three expections) furnishes evidence on the child's positive assets. Computerized administration, scoring, and report writing programs are available for microcomputers (IBM PC or XT, and Apple II or IIe). Western Psychological Services provides a computerized scoring and report service.

The original pool of items for developing the LBC came from previous checklists, Kanner's 1948 text on child psychiatry, and randomly drawn case histories from the files of the Louisville Child Guidance Clinic. They represented twelve categories of socially deviant behavior. The items that were retained discriminated between a group of children at the Guidance Clinic and a group of children in the general population, thereby indicating predictive validity for the items. The resulting checklist was administered to 263 parents of children ages 6-12 who applied to the clinic for services. The checklist was factor analyzed and eight first-order factors emerged. Refactoring produced three second-order factors. From this, a total of eleven scales was constructed; the first-order factors were associated with narrow-band syndromes, and the second-order factors with broad-band syndromes. Subsequent research showed that the broad-band syndromes (Aggression, Inhibition, Learning Disorder) had the highest reliability.

Since the initial appearance of the LBC in the one form with eleven scales, a series of revisions has occurred. This is reflected in the current designation of "E," indicating that Forms A, B, C, and D have preceded it. One major development has been the age extension on both ends (i.e., lowering the age level to four at the bottom and raising it to seventeen at the top). The insertion of age-specific behaviors for both the younger children and the adolescents to insure a comprehensive coverage of deviant behaviors for all the ages covered instigated the need for three forms (E1, E2, E3). The new 21 age-specific items in E1 came primarily from the Minnesota Child Development Inventory (Ireton & Thwing, 1972). There was no mention of the source of the 46 new items for E3. The fact that 97 of the original 164 behavior items are age-nonspecific means that there is high overlap among the three forms, which allows for cross-age comparisons and longitudinal evaluations.

Another major change was the inclusion of additional scales. Nine new scales were added to E1 and eight to E2. All of these new scales were nonfactorial, constructed entirely from face validity. The E3 items, however, were factor analyzed with nine scales emerging. The remaining four scales (General Pathology, Longitudinal, Severity Level, Total Pathology) were also constructed from face validity and designed primarily for clinical and research purposes.

The remaining changes were of a less substantive nature and included such things as scale refinements, item rewording, response modification (from "Yes-No" to "True-False"), and more sophisticated scoring devices (computerized scoring).

Standardization for all three forms involved children and parents from Louisville, Kentucky. General populations norms for E1 and E2 were developed from the responses to mailed questionnaires (N = 287 and 227, respectively). Clinical norms were developed with a clinical population that represented those children typically referred for psychological services (N = 124 for Form E1, N = 370 for Form E2). Only clinical norms were developed for Form E3 (N = 272). Tarte, Vernon, Luke, and Clark (1982) compared Las Vegas, Nevada subjects to the original Louisville, Kentucky standardization sample on Forms E1 and E2 and obtained highly similar results, providing support for the representativeness of the norms in urban communities.

Practical Applications/Uses

The primary usefulness of the LBC is to the service provider and the researcher. Miller (1984) states that the LBC is designed to help "parents to search their memories and to record behaviors characteristic of their children. This recording also provides the mental health worker with an overview of a child's deviant behavior" (p. 1). Thus, Miller recommends that it be used as an initial diagnostic screening tool. He further stresses that its use be restricted to professional mental health workers trained in child psychopathology and used in conjunction with other diagnostic procedures. From these remarks, the LBC would be most appropriately used as a supplemental measure during the initial intake process. The use of the clinical norms could be helpful in the differential diagnosis of disorders within a clinical population.

Research applications involve the LBC as a criterion measure of emotional and behavioral disorders. It has been used as a measure of psychosocial adjustment in children and/or siblings of children with a physical disorder (Drotar, Doershuk, Stern, Boat, Boyer & Matthews, 1981; Lavigne & Ryan, 1979). Sandler and Block (1979) correlated economic and life-events stressors with LBC scores of children in welfare and nonwelfare families. Several researchers, including Jacobson (1978a; 1978b) have used the LBC as a measure of adjustment in assessing the effects of divorce and separation. Other research applications include differentiating groups on a dimension measured by the LBC (such as Dependence-Inhibition; Mackin, 1982) and comparing them on a familial variable such as birth order. It has good potential as an outcome measure in therapy.

Technical Aspects

Spearman-Brown split-half reliability coefficients are reported for all three forms (Miller, 1984). All of the coefficients are above .70 with the exceptions of Sexual Behavior (.60), Neurological or Psychotic Abnormality (.63), and Adolescent Turmoil (.69). Most of the coefficients are above .80 with Severity Level, an overall measure of pathology, the highest (.97) on Forms E1 and E2. Test-retest means and standard deviations are reported for the LBC for a 3 month period (Miller, Hampe, Barrett, & Noble, 1972). Parents of 103 children, ages 7-12, completed a second LBC three months after participating in a normative study (Miller, Barrett, Hampe, & Noble, 1971). With few exceptions, the scores were stable.

Miller (1984) cites five studies (Miller, 1967b; Harpenau & Kimberlin, 1975; Fuchs, 1971; Hampe, 1975; Tarte et al., 1982) lending support for criterion validity of Forms E1 and E2. In each, the LBC differentiated those displaying some form of psychopathology from the general population. Parents of children in treatment centers report approximately three times the amount of deviant behaviors as compared with parents of children in the general population. Construct validity is supported by the factor analytic construction of the scales. Miller (1984) cites three studies (two by Block, 1971; Miller 1976b) that provide other evidence for the construct validity of Forms E1 and E2. The two studies by Block examined the relationship between teacher-rated behavior in the classroom and parent ratings in the home for two different age groups (4-6 and 7-12). The results showed a positive but low correlation between home and school behavior with two exceptions. Aggression at home correlated significantly with Total Disability at school for both age groups, and Learning Disability recognized at home correlated significantly with Total Disability at school for the older age group. Miller's study compared the standard scores of a random sample of general population children to those of a group of children from the general population whose aggression at school fell at or above the 85th percentile on the School Behavior Checklist. Although expected elevations did occur on certain scales, the major statistical analysis did not discriminate between the groups on the LBC. The weak supporting findings of these construct-validity studies suggest the clear-cut need for further research to strengthen child-psychopathological criteria.

Critique

The LBC, as a screening instrument, appears to fulfill its objective in that it does significantly discriminate children with emotional and behavioral disorders from children in the general population. On the average, roughly three times more pathology appear on the profiles of the disturbed children. Because these studies have been conducted on group differences, the practitioner must exercise appropriate caution in interpreting individual profiles. The LBC, however, does offer the clinician comprehensive, descriptive data about the child's behavior and can provide important insights into family dynamics. Its economy in terms of administration and scoring should be attractive to the practitioner.

In a review of parent-report measures, Humphreys and Ciminero (1979) conclude that the LBC "came much closer to meeting the appropriate standards [for a measure of child behavior] than the others" (p. 62). Additional studies can now be added to further substantiate the claim, particularly the study by Tarte et al. (1982), which supports the representativeness of the original standardization sample. However, insufficient psychometric data are available on the more recently developed E1 and E3 forms. Clinicians should be mindful of this in their use. E3, in particular, needs to be standardized on the general population.

Miller chose the dichotomous "True-False" response format over the more common "rating-scale" format on the basis of impressionistic data. With the former format less difficult to the respondents, he surmised it would lead to increased reliability and validity. Although this may be true, he could have made a stronger case with empirical data, which seems always in order when one departs from the more usual psychometric practices.

In general, parent-report inventories are a two-edged sword. On the one hand, they can provide highly relevant information to aid the clinician in the assessment process and in the formulation of treatment plans. The information is of essence for family therapy. On the other hand, studies have frequently demonstrated the low correlation between parent ratings of pathology and the ratings of trained observers. Even the unusually sensitive, experienced clinician is hard pressed to separate out of parents' perceptions the distortions caused by their pathology and by their self-serving ends. Miller and his associates do directly address this problem. One of the scales, Normal Irritability, is an index of internal validity. Parents who tend to understate pathology are more than likely to score low on this scale, and parents who tend to overstate or scapegoat are more than likely to score high. Miller provides some rules of thumb for profile interpretation when this condition prevails. However, aware of the need for more research on false positives and false negatives, he emphasizes that the checklist should always be used in combination with other assessment measures. It was never intended primarily for classifactory purposes and has never been validated against DSM-III.

All factors considered, in the opinion of this reviewer, the LBC is the best of its kind on the market. Its current form is the result of 27 years of actively involved research. Dr. Miller, in a personal communication (January 10, 1985), states that he has just completed a major cross-validation study and is in the process of writing it. The salient findings are that the original factors stood up well, and that two factors, a psychotic factor and sex-behavior factor, which did not appear in the original sample, have emerged. He attributes this to the inclusion of hospitalized children in the cross-validation study. Thus the evidence continues to accrue that if the LBC is interpreted according to the guidelines and cautions set forth in the manual, it can be a valuable addition to the assessment battery of children's behavior.

References

This list includes text citations as well as suggested additional reading.

Achenbach, T. M., & Edelbrock, C. S. (1978). The classification of child psychopathology: A review and analysis of empirical efforts. *Psychological Bulletin, 85,* 1275-1301.

Bloch, J. P. (1971). *Agreement between parents' and teachers' ratings of childhood emotional adjustment.* Unpublished master's thesis, University of Louisville.

DeSimone-Luis, J., O'Mahoney, K., & Hunt, D. (1979). Children of separation and divorce: Factors influencing adjustment. *Journal of Divorce, 3,* 37-42.

Drotar, D., Doershuk, C. F., Stern, R. C., Boat, T. F., Boyer, W., & Matthews, L. (1981). Psychosocial functioning of children with cystic fibrosis. *Pediatrics, 67,* 338-342.

Fuchs, W. L. (1971). *A quantitative study of autistic/retarded children.* Unpublished paper, Bellarmine College, Louisville, KY.

Hampe, E. (1975). Parents' and teachers' perceptions of personality characteristics of children selected for classes for the learning disabled. *Psychological Reports, 37,* 183-189.

Hampe, E., Miller, L. C., Noble, H., & Barrett, C. L. (1973). Phobic children one and two years posttreatment. *Journal of Abnormal Psychology, 82,* 446-453.

Harpenau, C. W., & Kimberlin, D. (1975). *Bingham Child Guidance outpatient population, ages 7-13, 1973.* Unpublished manuscript.

Humphreys, L. E., & Ciminero, A. R. (1979). Parent report measures of child behavior: A review. *Journal of Clinical Child Psychology, 8,* 56-63.

Ireton, H. R., & Thwing, E. J. (1972). *Manual for Minnesota Child Development Inventory.* Minneapolis: Interpretive Scoring Systems.

Jacobson, D. S. (1978a). The impact of marital separation/divorce on children: II. Interparent hostility and child adjustment. *Journal of Divorce, 2,* 3-19.

Jacobson, D. S. (1978b). The impact of marital separation/divorce on children: III. Parent-child communication and child adjustment, and regression analysis of findings from overall study. *Journal of Divorce, 2,* 175-194.

Kanner, L. (1948). *Child psychiatry.* Springfield, IL: Charles C. Thomas.

Lavigne, J. V., & Ryan, M. (1979). Psychological adjustment of siblings of children with chronic illness. *Pediatrics, 63,* 616-627.

Mackin, M. (1982). *Birth order and adolescent psychopathology: An expansion in the use of the Louisville Behavior Checklist.* Unpublished master's thesis, University of Louisville.

Miller, L. C. (1967a). Dimensions of psychopathology in middle childhood. *Psychological Reports, 21,* 897-903.

Miller, L. C. (1967b). Louisville Behavior Checklist for males, 6-12 years of age. *Psychological Reports, 21,* 885-896.

Miller, L. C. (1976). *School Behavior Checklist.* Los Angeles: Western Psychological Services.

Miller, L. C. (1980). Dimensions of adolescent psychopathology. *Journal of Abnormal Child Psychology, 8,* 161-173.

Miller, L. C. (1984). *Louisville Behavior Checklist manual—Revised.* Los Angeles: Western Psychological Services.

Miller, L. C., Barrett, C. L., Hampe, E., & Noble, H. (1971). Revised anxiety scales for the Louisville Behavior Checklist. *Psychological Reports, 29,* 503-511.

Miller, L. C., Hampe, E., Barrett, C. L., & Noble, H. (1971). Children's deviant behavior within the general population. *Journal of Consulting and Clinical Psychology, 37,* 16-22.

Miller, L. C., Hampe, E., Barrett, C. L., & Noble, H. (1972). Test-retest reliability of parent ratings of children's deviant behavior. *Psychological Reports, 31,* 249-250.

Sandler, I. N., & Block, M. (1979). Life stress and maladaptation of children. *American Journal of Community Psychology, 7,* 425-440.

Tarte, R. D., Vernon, C. R., Luke, D. E., & Clark, H. B. (1982). Comparison of responses by normal and deviant populations to Louisville Behavior Checklist. *Psychological Reports, 50,* 99-106.

William R. Merz, Sr., Ph.D.
*Professor and Coordinator, School Psychology Training Program,
California State University, Sacramento, California.*

MAKE A PICTURE STORY

*Edwin S. Shneidman. Cleveland, Ohio: The Psychological
Corporation.*

Introduction

The Make A Picture Story (MAPS) technique devised by Edwin S. Shneidman
is a projective method designed to measure psychosocial aspects of fantasy.
Shneidman's article "Schizophrenia and the MAPS Test" (1948) served as the first
manual for the technique. Eleven other uses are listed in both the 1948 manual and
the revised manual (1952). In his introduction to the 1948 manual Klopfer (1948)
states that the technique is a variation of the TAT with two changes: 1) loosening
the structure of stimulus materials by separating figures from backgrounds, and 2)
requiring expressive action to accomplish test tasks.

The method was developed by Shneidman at the University of Southern
California as part of his doctoral dissertation; he investigated characteristic psychosocial aspects of schizophrenic fantasy and provided objective norms for both
schizophrenic and normal groups. The instrument was tested and normed on
samples obtained at the Veterans Administration Neuropsychiatric Hospital, Los
Angeles. The norm group consisted of 50 psychotic and 50 nonpsychotic hospitalized patients; all were male World War II veterans. The revised manual illustrates interpretations of productions of children, adolescents, and adults. Nothing
could be found on changes or up-dates except for this revision of the initial
manual.

MAPS consists of 67 cut-out figures and twenty-two 11" x 8½" backgrounds.
There is a figure location sheet to record which figures were used and their
location on the background. The technique itself is intriguing. It presents an
interesting set of tasks that require subjects to place figures against a background
and account for their choices by telling a story or acting it out with the figures. The
tasks are inherently appealing to children and adolescents. This method allows
for the narration of stories with content important to the therapeutic process.
However, as a psychometric tool the MAPS is woefully lacking in scoring, interpretation, and technical aspects. A figure identification card assists the administrator in labeling the figures properly on the figure location sheet.

The initial version (1948) was scored quantitatively for ten signs or classifications: figure number, figure repetition, figure placement, figure selection, figure
interaction signs, figure activity, figure meaning, figure chronology, background,
and time. The author subdivided each of the signs into 4 to 29 categories from his
thematic analysis of the stories obtained from the test group. Thirteen qualitative

436

indicators for schizophrenia were interpreted from these ten signs: intergroup variability, self-identification, variability of identification, social isolation, over-inclusion, inappropriateness, symbolization, desire for environmental simplification, inhibition of fantasied violence, punitive conscience, lack of identification with male role, religiosity, and debasement of women.

The revised manual (1952) suggests scoring by five approaches: normative, hero-oriented, intuitive, interpersonal, and formal. With any of these five one might make a story-by-story analysis using the following report areas:

1. Pressures; forces; press
2. Motivations; goals; drives
3. Outlooks; attitudes; beliefs
4. Frustrations; conflicts; fears
5. Affects; feelings; emotions
   General—other than hostile
   Hostile feelings
6. Sexual thought and behavior
7. Psychosexual level and development
8. Super-ego; values; ego ideal
9. Self control; ego strength; ego capacity
10. Self concept; insight into self
11. Personality defenses and personality mechanisms
12. Reality contact; orientation
13. Interpersonal relations and object relations
    General—other than with Parents
    Relationships with Parents
14. Quality of perception, fantasy, language, style, and thought
15. Intellect; abilities; intellectual attainments; information
16. Symptoms; diagnoses
17. Etiology
18. Prognoses; predictions; treatment
19. Postdictions
    Factual biographical data
    Psychological biographical data (Shneidman, 1952, pg. 16)

No scores are derived in this process; it is essentially a thematic analysis of the stories presented by the examinee. From this analysis comments are directed to each of the report areas, making this a guideline for reporting rather than a protocol for scoring the thematic productions.

Practical Applications/Uses

Shneidman (1948, 1952) indicates the following 12 uses for the MAPS: aid to diagnostic labeling, basis for psychodynamic interpretations, technique with children, technique with adolescents, tool for studying prejudice, tool for studying psychology of minority groups, measure of psychiatric improvement, prognostic indicator of readiness for therapy, index of impaired intellectual efficiency, using the figures as a sorting task, supplement to psychodrama, and therapeutic device.

The initial purpose of the MAPS (see Manual, 1948) was to identify characteristic psychosocial aspects of schizophrenic fantasy with the signs and interpretations presenting a remarkably narrow set of categories. Although the types of analysis presented in the 1952 manual present a much wider range of interpretive possibilities, there are no normative data available. In addition, the directions for administering and scoring are so broad that the technique becomes more of an art form than a systematic data collection procedure.

Using the MAPS as a therapeutic tool rather than a psychometric measure shows much more promise. This reviewer has found it extremely helpful in therapy with abused children and adults. It has also been valuable as an adjunct to therapy for other trauma. For example, the medical office background presents an interesting approach to individuals with medical problems or fear of medical and dental procedures. However, difficulties can occur with some subjects. The 67 figures may present an overwhelming number of selections for children or individuals with problems choosing among alternatives; the number of unclothed figures may be disconcerting to adults and children who are body shy; and age-conscious adolescents and young adults may balk at working with cut-out figures, which may be referred to as paper dolls.

In one review Strother (1953) indicates that the test is appropriate for adolescents and adults; in a later review, however, Jensen (1965) indicates its appropriateness for ages six and over. In this reviewer's opinion, the technique is remarkably adaptable to adults, adolescents, and children.

The initial 1948 study in which the procedure was normed employed two groups of male World War II veterans, making generalization to females, nonveteran males, or other age groups impossible. Thus, the norms are inadequate. The 1952 manual gives illustrations of interpretations for individuals six years of age or older but provides no norms or quantitative information.

The MAPS is administered individually, requiring from 45 to 90 minutes, plus additional time for scoring. Notes on the placement of figures are made on the figure location sheet and a verbatim account of the story and other verbal interchange recorded.

In the initial manual Shneidman (1948) suggests that 11 background pictures be used—ten from a standard set consisting of a living room, street scene, medical scene, bathroom, dream, bridge, bedroom, blank, forest, and closet, and the eleventh selected by the subject from the remaining twelve.

The 1952 manual makes slight changes in administration. First, side-by-side seating at a table is suggested where no earlier recommendation had been made. This is quite similar to the side-by-side seating employed for Rorschach administration. A ten-background battery is recommended and the forest and closet backgrounds are left off the standard list with the last two selected by the examinee. In addition, the later manual describes an abbreviated four-to-six-background battery to be used when the ten-background battery might be less desirable.

Jensen (1965) indicates that the protocol is most often interpreted in a holistic impressionistic manner, although complicated scoring systems have been suggested. Shneidman et al. (1951) describe a more complex thematic analysis similar to that illustrated in the 1952 manual (Shneidman, 1952). Fine (1955) presents a general scheme for scoring projective techniques which rely on story telling. It is a way to categorize themes within the stories. The sign approach presented in the 1948 manual is cumbersome. The five approaches suggested in the 1952 manual lack a reasonable set of norms and have no reliability or validity studies presented. Shneidman et al. (1951) simply present a thematic approach like that included in the 1952 manual; Fine (1955) simply amplifies on the thematic approaches without providing a set of quantitative strategies for scoring.

Using the signs to make an interpretation along the dimensions defined by Shneidman (1948) provides relatively little information. Holistic scoring provides information useful to the individual administering the technique but provides little in terms of reliable and valid scoring data. Jensen (1965) indicates that clinicians would develop subjective norms based on their own extensive use of the instrument; this, of course, is inadequate for a psychometric technique.

Technical Aspects

Jensen's review of MAPS (1965) provides a comprehensive assessment of reliability and validity studies. He finds them clearly inadequate. The only types of reliability addressed may be labeled interrater or interrating; that is, how well scorers agree or how well scorers maintain their scoring over time. Average correlations for these interrater reliabilities range from .16 to .77. There appear to be no studies of validity. The only study involving MAPS subsequently was by Neuringer (1969). This work examined social withdrawal represented by the type of figure in the test. Neuringer found no difference in social withdrawal scores of normals and schizophrenics.

Critique

Rabin (1953) in his review found the MAPS to be of limited use. He found that it offered little new to a clinician at its level of development in 1948. Strother (1953) found it more difficult to administer than the TAT but found that this disadvantage was outweighed by the stimulating nature of the MAPS tasks. Reviewers have discussed consistently inadequacies in norming. Jensen (1965) states that the MAPS contributes little new knowledge to data that can be collected with other better researched techniques. The earlier hope that the technique would yield a significant body of research (Holt, 1950) has not materialized.

This reviewer first became familiar with the MAPS in 1966, some 14 years after Shneidman's initial effort. As a psychometric technique, it has not provided what the Rorschach, MMPI, or other better researched devices have. As a therapeutic technique it has been a valuable tool in work with traumatized and withdrawn individuals.

The ambitious list of uses provided by Shneidman (1948, 1952) presents a notion of the major weakness of the technique as a psychometric device. No measurement tool can do everything for everyone. Its ready acceptance in early review articles indicates a naivete on what might be done with psychometric techniques. As a therapeutic tool, the technique holds much more promise. Narrative techniques such as the MAPS lend themselves to therapeutic intervention more easily than to psychometric evaluation.

The desire for global, holistic interpretation defeats the strategy of psychometric measurement. It does fit in well with the goals of psychodynamic interpretation of therapeutic intervention. Thus, although MAPS cannot be recommended as a test, it can be recommended as a technique for therapeutic intervention.

References

Fine, R. (1955). A scoring scheme for the TAT and other projective techniques. *Journal of Projective Techniques, 19,* 306-309.

Holt, R. R. (1950). Make a Picture Story. *Journal of Personality, 18,* 385-387.

Jensen, A. R. (1965). Review of Make a Picture Story. In O. K. Buros (Ed.), *The sixth mental measurements yearbook* (pp. 468-470). Highland Park, NJ: The Gryphon Press.

Neuringer, C. (1969). Clinical psychologists' ratings of MAPS figures along a social withdrawal scale. *Journal of Projective Techniques and Personality Assessment, 33,* 30-33.

Rabin, A. I. (1953). Review of Make a Picture Story. In O. K. Buros (Ed.), *The fourth mental measurements yearbook* (pp. 113-114). Highland Park, NJ: The Gryphon Press.

Shneidman, E. S. (1948). Schizophrenia and the MAPS test. *Genetic Psychology Monograph, 38,* 145-223.

Shneidman, E. S. (1952). Manual for the Make a Picture Story method. (Projective Techniques Monographs No. 2) Burbank, CA: The Society for Personality Assessment, Inc.

Shneidman, E. S., Joel, W., & Little, K. R. (1951). *Thematic analysis.* New York: Grune & Stratton, Inc.

Strother, C. R. (1953). Review of Make a Picture Story. In O. K. Buros (Ed.), *The fourth mental measurements yearbook* (pp. 113-114). Highland Park, NJ: The Gryphon Press.

Gwyneth M. Boodoo, Ph.D.
Associate Professor of Educational Psychology, Texas A&M University, College Station, Texas.

MARTINEZ ASSESSMENT OF THE BASIC SKILLS

David Martinez. Portland, Oregon: ASIEP Education Co.

Introduction

The Martinez Assessment of the Basic Skills is designed to assist special educa-tion and classroom teachers in diagnosing mildly handicapped children in grades K-9 in six areas: Primary Language Concepts, Counting and Numerals, Time Telling, Spelling, Arithmetic, and Reading. A separate subtest measures each area. The test was developed by David Martinez, Ed.D., and was published by the ASIEP Education Company in 1983. It is also available in a Spanish form.

The criteria used to develop this criterion-referenced tool are clearly stated by the author in detailed behavioral objectives for each item of each test. No informa-tion is supplied regarding the choice of these criteria. The author simply states in the introduction: "Criterion-referenced tests have been developed to assist spe-cial education and classroom teachers in the diagnostic testing of handicapped children in the basic skills. Criterion-referenced tests of six basic skill areas are contained in this test package" (Martinez, 1983, p. 1). In a later discussion on content validity, however, a comparison of the test items in each of the six areas is made with instructional programs used in grades K-6 and with other commercially available skill inventories. The test is currently being edited by ASIEP to eliminate typographical errors that appear in its current printing.

The Martinez Assessment of Basic Skills is intended for "mildly handicapped students." This, the author explains, includes students identified as learning disabled as well as other underachievers. The test itself consists of six subtests. The specific grade for which each item is suitable is clearly stated in the admin-istration manual.

The Diagnostic Primary Language Concepts Test is intended to assist the teacher in identifying basic receptive skills that have not yet been mastered. It consists of 24 items which range in difficulty from grades K through 1. Each item (called a criterion test or subtest by the author) measures a different concept. This is so, the author explains, since "each of these language concepts . . . . must be explicitly and separately taught. That they must be explicitly and separately taught suggests that they must be explicitly and separately tested, each with one test item" (Martinez, 1983, p. 4).

The Diagnostic Counting and Numerals Test consists of 14 subtests with items ranging in difficulty from grades K-2. This test measures students' beginning mathematical skills.

The Diagnostic Time Telling Test contains 14 items, each measuring a different skill. Five optional items are included to assess time-telling on a digital clock. The items are suitable for grades 1-6.

The Diagnostic Spelling Test primarily measures competency with symbols and sounds, particularly the student's ability to convert symbols to sounds (decoding). The test is divided into three levels ranging from Level I (simple skills) to Level III (difficult skills), such that later skills measured in each level build upon previous ones. Each level also contains an optional section on sentence dictation. Level I contains 12 subtests with items ranging in difficulty from grades 2-3. Level II is made up of 4 subtests with items ranging in difficulty from grades 2-3. Level III contains 8 subtests with items ranging in difficulty from grades 2-6. Each subtest contains from 4 to 30 items.

The Diagnostic Arithmetic Test measures the following seven skill areas: Addition, Subtraction, Multiplication, Division, Fractions, Decimals, and Percents. The skills are arranged in order of difficulty with the easiest (Addition) first. Within each skill area, different subtests measure various computational subskills, each consisting of at least 2 items. Items across all seven skill areas range in difficulty appropriate to the grade levels in which the skills are taught. Thus, Addition items vary in difficulty from grades 2-5, while items on Percents are at grade 6-7 levels only.

The final test, the Diagnostic Reading Test, is divided into four parts: Readiness and Levels I, II, and III. Each part consists of different subtests each containing many items. This test measures competency in symbols and sounds (encoding), with the exception of the Readiness subtests and word study skills of Level III.

The administration manual includes an overview of the test as well as the separate subtests themselves and instructions for their administration. There is a separate section for each test. A separate Student Response and Record Booklet is used to record the responses of each student on each test. In addition, a student profile form may be completed which shows the subskills a student has mastered or those requiring further instruction.

Practical Applications/Uses

The Martinez Assessment of the Basic Skills is a fairly new test. It appears to be very thorough with respect to the subskills measured on each test and should be helpful to teachers in identifying basic skills that children have not mastered in each of the areas tested. The tests could be used as both pre- and post-tests for different units of instruction and for diagnostic purposes with underachievers. They should not be used to assign students to a grade level (see Martinez, 1983, p. 7) or to assess students' maximum performance in any of the six curricular areas. The latter may be better accomplished by norm-referenced tests or criterion-referenced tests with many more discriminating items and items of greater difficulty. Using this test to assess what a student *can* achieve could result in a large ceiling effect for normals or overachievers. Because of the lack of empirical studies (discussed later in this review) regarding the usefulness of this tool, care should be taken in interpreting students' responses at this time.

All of the tests are untimed, although responses correct per minute may be recorded by the teacher. However, in order to record such responses a form would need to be developed since one is not supplied by the test publishers. The author gives the approximate time a student takes to complete each test as ranging from 10 minutes (Primary Language Concepts, Time Telling) to 45 minutes (Spelling, Reading, Arithmetic). Some subtests and items are individually administered in all tests while the remainder may be group administered. Oral responses to some items are given in the Primary Language Concepts, Time Telling, Spelling, and Reading tests. All other items require written responses.

The test may be administered in a school or clinical setting. No special qualifications are required for administration and separate administration instructions for each test are included in the administration manual. For each test the materials needed, directions for where to begin testing, and the procedure for administering subtests are clearly described and easy to follow. The behavioral objective corresponding to each item is given at the end of the administration instructions so the teacher can match the test items with objectives taught and also develop individual education programs for each child if desired. The tests themselves contain some printing errors which the publishers are presently in the process of correcting.

Instructions for scoring each test are clearly presented and simple to follow. The administrator simply marks a "/" for an item answered correctly, or 0 for an incorrect item. In those cases where more than one item measures a subskill, the author indicates the number of correct answers for mastery. However, these numbers may also be supplied by the teacher. The answers can be scored directly on the Student Response and Record Booklet for each test and then transferred to a Student Profile form. The entire process should take *no longer than* five minutes after testing a child for each of the six tests. No machine scoring is available and, given the diagnostic nature of the test, does not appear necessary unless one wishes to use the test in a large-scale study.

By examining a student's responses on each test, a teacher can identify skills that a child has or has not mastered. Those skills not mastered need further instruction which may be followed by retesting. Martinez (1983) states that three of the tests contain content that may be directly taught: Primary Language Concepts, Time Telling, and Counting and Numerals. This, he states, is because these tests "measure skills that have no specific implications for learning other skills in the same general skill classification" (p. 5). To the extent that such skills are directly taught using the actual test content, scores should be interpreted as representing mastery with caution even for the "mildly handicapped."

Technical Aspects

Content validity was evaluated by comparing the test items in each of the six areas with instructional programs used in grades K-6 and with commercially available skill inventories such as the Boehm Test of Basic Concepts, Pre-School Math Inventory, Inventory of Early Development, and the Inventory of Basic Skills. The author states that such a comparison revealed substantial compatibility, but no supporting data are given. The actual instructional programs examined are not stated, nor are variables given that could describe them with regard to geographical region, socioeconomic status, or the like. Furthermore, those areas in which the Martinez Assessment of Basic Skills is most like/dislike the other tests are not discussed. Detailed behavioral objectives are clearly stated for each item on the test, thus allowing an examination of the objective and item to assure that they match a teacher's testing or teaching objective.

Each of the six tests (areas) contains a differing number of items. It is disconcerting that the Primary Language Concepts Test uses only one item to measure each skill and the author's justification, as cited previously in the Introduction of this review, is rather lame (Martinez, 1983, p. 4).

No empirical validity studies have been conducted using this test, so the jury is still out regarding the usefulness of this test in assessing the mastery of specific skills by a mildly handicapped student.

One reliability study was conducted to measure item response consistency using 20 non-handicapped students (K-8), and five handicapped (mentally retarded and learning-disabled) students ranging in age from 7-13 in a self-contained classroom. Three procedures were used. Test-retest was conducted on the Primary Language Concepts and Time Telling Tests with immediate retest. For each of the seven computational areas of the Arithmetic test, a second procedure was used which generated percentage of agreement across items in each computational area. For the Counting and Numerals, Reading, and Spelling tests an odd-even analysis of the items was carried out to measure the percentage of agreement. Percent of agreement for items across all tests varied from 81% to 100%. These measures of consistency, especially in the case of the Spelling and Reading tests, fail to take into account consistency for the subskills measured in each level of the test, since a measure of agreement is reported at each level only. Moreover, the sample on which these measures are based (N = 25) is much too small for any generalization to be made regarding the consistency of the test. Also, the percentages given are averages across grade levels and across both non-handicapped and handicapped children. This renders such statistics meaningless.

Critique

With the passage of PL 94-142 (Education for All Handicapped Children Act, 1975), it is important that there are good, psychometrically sound diagnostic tools to identify and track the development of those skills in which students are underachieving. To this end, tests like the Martinez Assessment of the Basic Skills are useful provided their development is carefully described and documented. Although the test appears to be carefully constructed, the manual supplied to this reviewer by the publishers contained no test development information. The detailed list of objectives which define each item is indeed laudable, as are the carefully documented administration procedures and scoring criteria and materials. However, these do not compensate for a lack of developmental information. The same is true with respect to validity and reliability issues. No studies of any kind have been reported except for the poor study done on percent of agreement averaged across items. Before any test can be properly used good validity and reliability evidence should be proferred in a test manual. It is indeed true that criterion-referenced tests require different reliability measures than those that are norm-referenced, and some measures that can be used may be found in the references following this review.

One further concern this reviewer has is with the teaching of test content. Taking the Primary Language Concepts test as an example, surely other resources can be used in a classroom to teach the concepts *over, under,* etc., without using the actual items on the test. It may be that because of the nature of the first three tests (Primary Language, Time Telling, Counting and Numerals), some of the test content may overlap with instructional materials; however, this should be a random, unplanned occurrence. Otherwise, the test would not be measuring a primary language concept per se but only a specific isolated application of that concept.

In summary, the Martinez Assessment of Basic Skills shows great promise if the areas of test development, validity, and reliability are more firmly addressed. In these areas, the test does not adhere to the *Standards for Educational and Psychological Tests* (American Psychological Association, 1974) and appears to have been prematurely published. If these areas can be addressed properly, the Martinez Assessment of Basic Skills could be a very valuable tool in the assessment of basic skills for both normal and mildly handicapped children.

References

American Psychological Association. (1974). *Standards for educational and psychological tests.* Washington, DC: Author.

Berk, R. A. (1980). *Criterion-referenced measurement: The state of the art.* Baltimore, MD: The Johns Hopkins University Press.

Hambleton, R. K. (Ed.). (1980). Contributions to criterion-referenced testing technology [Special issue]. *Applied Psychological Measurement, 4,* 421-581.

Martinez, D. (1983). Martinez Assessment of the Basic Skills. Portland, OR: ASIEP Education Co.

Popham, W. J. (1978). *Criterion referenced measurement.* Englewood Cliffs, NJ: Prentice-Hall.

Timothy Z. Keith, Ph.D.
Assistant Professor of School Psychology, University of Iowa, Iowa City, Iowa.

McCARTHY SCREENING TEST

Dorothea McCarthy. Cleveland, Ohio: The Psychological Corporation.

Introduction

The McCarthy Screening Test (MST) is designed to identify young children (ages 4 through 6½) at risk for educational failure. It is essentially a much shorter version of the excellent McCarthy Scales of Children's Abilities (McCarthy Scales; McCarthy, 1972), borrowing six of its 18 tests and the relevant McCarthy Scales standardization data. It is short, easily administered by a variety of school personnel, and provides a reasonable method for determining children to follow or refer for additional assessment.

Because the MST borrows so heavily from the McCarthy Scales, this earlier instrument will be discussed briefly. Authored by Dorothea McCarthy and published in 1972 by The Psychological Corporation, these Scales were designed as an individually administered measure of cognitive ability (intelligence, although McCarthy avoided the term) for children ages 2½ to 8½. The instrument consists of 18 short mental and motor tests grouped into five scales: Verbal, Perceptual-Performance, Quantitative, Memory, and Motor, with the first three further combined into the General Cognitive Index, similar to an overall IQ. The standardization of the test was excellent: approximately 50 girls and 50 boys were included at each of 10 age levels, with the sample stratified based on age, sex, color, geographic region, and father's occupation.

Six tests were chosen for inclusion in the 1978 MST, with the selection based on the tests' content (tests were chosen so as to be representative of various McCarthy Scales and because they were felt to be useful in identifying children with learning disabilities or perceptual handicaps), level of difficulty (appropriate for the 4 to 6½ age range), time required (the entire test takes about 20 minutes), and ease of administration and scoring (the MST is designed to be given by teachers or paraprofessionals). *Right-Left Orientation*, given only to children age five and above, is designed to test knowledge of right and left. Children are asked to demonstrate knowledge of right and left on their own bodies ("Which is your left ear?") and on a picture of a boy. In *Verbal Memory* the child is required to repeat a series of words and later, sentences, after the examiner. For the *Draw-A-Design* subtest, the child copies a series of designs ranging from very simple (a circle, a straight line) to fairly complex. The examiner draws the first three designs for the child to copy, while the others are on a printed model; all designs are drawn in a drawing booklet. *Numerical Memory* is a simple digit-recall task, including digits forward (part 1) and digits reversed (part 2). *Conceptual Grouping* is an interesting logical classification and selection task. The child is presented with 12 blocks that vary in color (3 colors), shape (circle and square) and size (large and small). The items start simply (e.g., when shown a large red circle and a large red square, the child is asked to point to the square one and then the round one), but quickly require classification along more than one variable at a time. In the last three items, the child discovers and applies classification rules. For example, when shown four blocks the child is asked to find two more that "go with" those four. The last test on the MST is *Leg Coordination*, in which the child is asked to perform gross motor tasks such as walking backwards, standing on one leg, and skipping. It should be noted that while the subtests included in the MST may be representative of the McCarthy Scales as a whole, only two of the six (Conceptual Grouping and Draw-A-Design) are consistently among the best measures of general intelligence (g) for normal children in this age range (Kaufman & Dicuio, 1975; Kaufman & Hollenbeck, 1973). On the other hand, Draw-A-Design and the second part of Numerical Memory (digits reversed) generally appear among the best measures of g for exceptional children (Keith & Bolen, 1980a, 1980b; Naglieri, Kaufman, & Harrison, 1981).

The MST, as noted previously, was not separately standardized, but was normed using the relevant standardization data from the McCarthy Scales for ages 4, 4½, 5, 5½, and 6½. Thus, the standardization for the MST is generally excellent, although two caveats are needed. First, it is unclear the extent to which the much shorter length of the MST might affect its norms, although such an effect is likely minimal. Second, although the McCarthy Scales were not standardized on six-year-olds, norms are provided for the MST for this age group; the norms were interpolated from the 5½ and 6½ age groups. While this same procedure is used on the McCarthy Scales and other intelligence tests, it seems slightly less defensible for the MST when applied to these short tests rather than composite scores.

The MST manual, while short, is well organized and describes the test, its purpose, development, standardization, administration, and scoring, quite well. The section on establishing rapport and general testing guidelines is especially well written and should prove helpful in teaching the MST to novice examiners. Similarly, the materials provided with the test kit are attractive and functional, and the record forms are easy to follow. The carrying case, on the other hand, is flimsy, and the test kit, at $55.00, is overpriced.

Practical Applications/Uses

The MST, as its name implies, is designed as a quick individual screening device for preschool and early-school-aged children. It is probably most often used in conjunction with mass preschool screening programs, and its ease of use, clarity of directions, and quick administration time seem well suited for this purpose. The tests chosen for the MST are relatively easy to give and the administration directions good, so that it would seem appropriate for use by teachers, other professionals, or even paraprofessionals. However, all such groups will require some training in test administration, preferably under the direction of a psychologist. The test can also be used in other situations when a quick, educationally oriented screening test is needed, but it should be remembered that the MST is a screening, not a diagnostic, instrument; it is not appropriate for making important educational (e.g., placement) decisions about individual children.

The MST is supposedly designed to identify children "at risk" for educational difficulty or failure so that these children can be followed over time or further assessed with a complete diagnostic battery. This purpose seems clear enough, and would seem to include screening for a number of potential problems, such as learning disabilities, mild mental retardation, or even general low achievement. (The MST is not intended, nor is it appropriate, for screening for visual or auditory acuity deficits. There are other, better instruments designed for these purposes.) Yet except in its statement of purpose, the MST manual virtually ignores any deficits other than learning disabilities. Such confusion of purpose is especially evident in the discussion of how the tests were chosen, but appears throughout the manual (e.g., in the discussions of research with the MST).

This confusion of purpose also seems implicit in the scoring system used for the MST. Instead of summing raw scores on the MST subtests and converting such scores to a composite, scaled score, each test is scored in a dichotomous, pass/fail fashion. The manual provides several levels of passing scores (the 10th, 20th, or 30th percentiles), depending on how inclusive or restrictive the screening is meant to be. The number of failed subtests is then summed to place the child in another dichotomous category: "at risk" versus "not at risk" (again, the examiner can decide the criteria—one, two, or three tests failed—to use in making this categorization). Although somewhat confusing, the process is reasonably well explained in the manual, along with the implications of various combinations of pass/fail and at risk/not at risk levels.

At best, this process of scoring is cumbersome. It is also clearly designed to screen for learning disabilities rather than any other type of problem. Indeed, in discussing the scoring system, the manual states: "It is common for children with learning disabilities and perceptual difficulties to perform poorly on some kinds of tasks and to perform at an acceptable or even superior level on other tests" (p. 20). No other types of problems are mentioned. Perhaps this method of scoring was also devised to discourage using the overall score as an IQ estimate, yet other types of scaled scores, such as T-scores, would perform this purpose equally well. As is, valuable information is lost by converting continuous scales into dichotomies and by ignoring any total score. Further, with the present scoring system, the test would appear much less useful in screening for more general cognitive problems than for children with problems in specific areas.

At the subtest level, most subtests are fairly easy to score. Draw-A-Design, however, can be difficult to score and requires some practice even for experienced examiners.

Technical Aspects

The MST manual reports some evidence of the MST tests' reliability, again using data derived from the McCarthy Scales. Internal consistency estimates are reported for the Draw-A-Design, Conceptual Grouping, and Leg Coordination tests, and range from .41 (Conceptual Grouping, age 6½) to .80 (Draw-A-Design, ages 4½ through 5½). Twelve of the 15 values reported are above .65, which seems adequate for a screening test of this type. None of the tests, however, are particularly reliable at the 6½-year age level. Stability coefficients are not as flattering; coefficients reported in the manual for 40 5- to 5½-year-olds retested after 3 to 5 weeks ranged from .32 (Right-Left Orientation) to .69 (Numerical Memory). In addition, such coefficients apply to the MST tests in their *continuous* form rather than the pass/fail dichotomies actually used in scoring. And while a composite score would be more reliable than the individual tests, the MST does not use such a composite, so no statistics are reported.

Scant validity evidence is reported in the MST manual. One study comparing the MST with the McCarthy Scales in identifying children with known learning disabilities and behavior problems found that 88% would be classified as "at risk" by the McCarthy versus 67% by the MST, using similar criteria. However, no normal children were included in this study, and it is not reported whether the *same* children were classified by both tests. Evidence of predictive validity (for a similar measure) is shown in another study in which the MST tests correlated moderately well with similarly named Metropolitan Readiness Tests given several months later. Unfortunately, no studies correlating the MST with later *achievement* are reported in the manual.

Independent researchers have provided additional evidence of the MST's validity. Naglieri and Harrison (1982) found substantial correlations between the MST (using a composite score) and the Peabody Individual Achievement Test ($r = .66$ between total tests). There is also evidence to support the predictive validity of the MST for achievement (Metropolitan Achievement Tests), even when using the at risk/not at risk categories (Harrison & Naglieri, 1981). However, these same authors also found another short form of the McCarthy Scales, one developed by Kaufman (1977), to provide generally more accurate prediction than the MST.

Critique

The MST is a short, easy to administer, individual screening test for children ages 4 to 6½. Designed to identify children at risk for educational difficulty, the MST may be especially appropriate for large, preschool screening situations, especially if accompanied by auditory and visual acuity screening. It is well standardized, there is evidence to support its reliability and validity, and it should be relatively easy for most school personnel to learn. Its scoring system, however, is clumsy. And while the scoring system does have its virtues, it should be at the very least supplemented by overall standard scores of some type, if not completely reworked. In addition, systems and psychologists with access to the McCarthy Scales might consider using Kaufman's proposed short form (Kaufman, 1977; Kaufman & Kaufman, 1977) of the Scales as a cheaper, and perhaps better, alternative to the MST.

References

Harrison, P. L., & Naglieri, J. A. (1981). Comparison of the predictive validities of two McCarthy short forms. *Psychology in the Schools, 18,* 389-393.

Kaufman, A. S. (1977). A McCarthy short form for rapid screening of preschool, kindergarten, and first grade children. *Contemporary Educational Psychology, 2,* 149-157.

Kaufman, A. S., & Dicuio, R. F. (1975). Separate factor analyses of the McCarthy Scales for groups of black and white children. *Journal of School Psychology, 13,* 11-18.

Kaufman, A. S., & Hollenbeck, G. P. (1973). Factor analysis of the standardization edition of the McCarthy Scales. *Journal of Clinical Psychology, 29,* 519-532.

Kaufman, A. S., & Kaufman, N. L. (1977). *Clinical evaluation of young children with the McCarthy Scales.* New York: Grune & Stratton.

Keith, T. Z., & Bolen, L. M. (1980a, April). *Factor structure of the McCarthy Scales of Children's Abilities.* Paper presented at the meeting of the National Association of School Psychologists, Washington, DC.

Keith, T. Z., & Bolen, L. M. (1980b). Factor structure of the McCarthy Scales for children experiencing problems in school. *Psychology in the Schools, 17,* 320-326.

McCarthy, D. (1972). *McCarthy Scales of Children's Abilities.* Cleveland: The Psychological Corporation.

McCarthy, D. (1978). *McCarthy Screening Test.* Cleveland: The Psychological Corporation.

Naglieri, J. A., & Harrison, P. L. (1982). McCarthy Scales, McCarthy Screening Test, and Kaufman's McCarthy short form correlations with the Peabody Individual Achievement Test. *Psychology in the Schools, 19,* 149-155.

Naglieri, J. A., Kaufman, A. S., & Harrison, P. L. (1981). Factor structure of the McCarthy Scales for school-age children with low GCIs. *Journal of School Psychology, 19,* 226-232.

J. Mark Wagener, Ph.D.

Clinical Psychologist, Mental Health Clinic-Student Health Center,
Oregon State University, Corvallis, Oregon.

MEMORY-FOR-DESIGNS TEST

Frances K. Graham and Barbara S. Kendall. Missoula,
Montana: Psychological Test Specialists.

Introduction

The Memory-for-Designs Test (MFD) is an instrument designed to screen for impairment of brain functioning by measuring the ability to copy simple geometric designs from immediate memory. It is meant to be used as a tool to behaviorally assess the presence of central nervous system impairment in children and adults. The ability to perceive geometric shapes, retain these perceptions in memory, and reproduce them manually has long been considered to be related to the intactness of brain functioning.

In the MFD the subject is requested to draw a reproduction of each of 15 designs immediately after it has been presented for five seconds. The quality of the reproductions is then evaluated according to standards presented in the test manual. A scoring system is used to categorize performance levels into critical, borderline, and normal classifications of functional intactness. Raw scores can be modified to control for variation associated with age and vocabulary level. The test is used to differentiate individuals with cerebral dysfunctions from normals and from those with psychiatric dysfunctions.

This test was developed by Frances K. Graham and Barbara S. Kendall in order to test the assumption that perceptual motor memory was impaired by brain damage. It was the result of the first well-developed attempt to scientifically demonstrate the relationship between these functions and brain damage. The authors wished to develop a highly reliable instrument that could differentiate brain-damaged subjects from others on the basis of empirical criteria. It was originally designed as a research instrument in the 1940s (Graham & Kendall, 1946; Kendall & Graham, 1948). Since then it has come into widespread clinical use as a simple method of screening for brain damage.

The 15 most promising designs from a group of 40 were selected in a preliminary study to be used in the validation procedure. A group of 70 mixed brain-disordered patients and a group of 70 controls were matched for age, education, and occupation. Various types of drawing errors were weighted to reflect the frequency with which they occurred in the brain-disordered group as compared to the controls. The scoring was then cross validated by use of an additional group of 33 brain-disordered and 168 control subjects. Additional normative data are presented in the most recent manual (Graham & Kendall, 1960). The test remains in its original form with little change in the scoring procedure other than incorporation of the new normative data.

The test materials consist of fifteen 5″ x 5″ white cardboard squares, each of which is printed with a black design. All of the designs are made of straight lines and are oriented squarely with the card. The client is presented with a pencil with an eraser and a sheet of 8½″ x 11″ paper. Clients are told that the cards will be presented individually for a 5-second interval and that they are to draw the design from memory after the card has been removed from sight. Clients are prevented from copying the design directly and are not encouraged to guess or complete partially remembered designs.

Each design is scored using an empirically derived scale from 0 to 3, with higher scores reflecting types of errors most indicative of brain damage. Satisfactory reproductions, including omitted or incomplete drawings, are given a score of 0, while those with rotation errors are given the maximum score. Specific verbal scoring criteria and sample scoring of examples of drawings are available in the manual. Scores are then totaled for the fifteen drawings in order to obtain a performance rating. The authors recommend that clients obtaining raw scores of 12 and above be placed in the brain-damaged category, 5-11 be placed in a borderline category, and 4 and below be considered normal.

The authors provide tables for conversion of raw scores into difference scores in order to partial out the effects of age and vocabulary level. This provides a means of relating performances among groups of varying age and verbal ability levels. The use of this difference score is necessary for children as well as for adults of low intelligence or those of advanced age. Although the use of difference scores was originally recommended for all, research has suggested that it is unnecessary with adults of normal intelligence and may even slightly reduce the effectiveness of the test (Hunt, 1952).

Practical Applications/Uses

The task involved is easy for most children and adults. The test is considered to be appropriate for individuals 8.5 through 60 years of age. Recently, normative data have become available for subjects over 60 years (Kendall, 1962; Riege, Kelly, & Klane, 1981). Performance levels of children less than 8½ years have been found to be too variable to make this a useful clinical tool with them.

This test is intended to be used by professionals interested in screening individuals for possible brain damage. It is likely to find its greatest usage in clinical settings where in- or out-patients are exhibiting symptoms of impaired functioning that may be the result of cerebral dysfunction. It also may be useful in educational settings as part of a diagnostic workup for students demonstrating learning disabilities or other cognitive impairments. Its simplicity of administration and nonintrusive nature make it quite appealing as a first-step procedure for gathering information in order to make a decision about referral for more extensive neurological evaluations.

This test was designed to measure the presence or absence of disorder associated with impairment of cerebral brain tissue function. The test authors indicate that they presume that completion of the MFD requires the ability to perform a sequence of behaviors. These include the attending to and perceiving a patterned visual stimulus, retaining the perception in memory briefly, and reproducing the stimulus by executing a relatively complex motor act. They also assume that success is related to the ability to inhibit drawing when memory is imperfect. The test was designed to be a global measure of organic impairment, rather than to be used to localize lesions.

The MFD has been used primarily in psychiatric settings. It is frequently used in an attempt to distinguish between organic brain damage and functional conditions. Its greatest potential usefulness lies in identifying individuals with relatively mild organic impairment rather than those with gross deficits, which could obviously be demonstrated by other means.

The administration of this test should take place on an individual basis in a setting without distractions. The instructions and procedures are clear, and anyone trained in individual psychological test administration could be expected to administer it without difficulty. It is important to attend to the orientation of the presentation of the designs so that rotation errors can be appropriately scored. The total administration time varies from 5 to 10 minutes. Since it is a simple, short-term task, modification of standard testing procedure should be unnecessary.

Since the instructions for scoring are clearly presented and numerous examples are provided, learning to score appropriately is not difficult. Though scoring judgments must be made, neophyte scorers typically do not demonstrate significant errors. Designs are scored individually by comparing the client's drawing with the standards described in the manual. It is important that the scorer be familiar with the general principles of scoring and supplement these with the examples provided.

Technical Aspects

Research data indicate that interrater reliability of the scoring of the MFD is very strong. The authors reported a correlation of .99 between the total raw scores they independently assigned for the 140 original validation subjects. Because they had devised the scoring system together, one would anticipate high agreement. However, other investigators consistently report interrater reliabilities ranging from the upper .80's to mid .90's.

A significant level of sophistication is required in order to interpret the meaning of the scores. Highly conservative cutoff points were deliberately chosen by the authors in order to minimize the possibility of false-positives. Use of the suggested cutoff scores provides results that are highly indicative of brain damage when the scores fall into the critical area, but they are not indicative of the absence of brain damage when they fall below the critical scores. Therefore, the actual hit rate (true-positive and true-negative categorizations) is substantially lower than would be the case for a "best fit" cutoff score. An appreciation of the relative cost involved from a false-positive as opposed to a false-negative is necessary to choose the optimal cutoff scores. Contrary to the authors' choice of minimizing false-positives, some writers such as Krug (1971) have suggested that it is much less desirable to diagnose an organic patient as functional than vice versa. Heaton, Boode & Johnson, (1978) make the point that particularly in acute treatment settings, most clinicians would probably find the cost of an unproductive neurologic workup much more acceptable than the consequences of misdiagnosing brain disease and treating it as if it were a functional disorder.

Extensive reliability and validity data are available. The index of reliability using the split-half method was 0.92 for the original subjects. The authors reported test-retest reliabilities in the 0.80's. Researchers typically report improvement in scores in a test-retest situation, indicating that there is a practice effect. The data indicate that there is a trend for the improvement to be greater with organic subjects than nonbrain-damaged subjects.

The manual lists a total of 535 control subjects and 243 brain-disordered subjects derived from a variety of groups used for validation. The brain-disordered groups included both acute and chronic conditions for which there was clear evidence of tissue damage. Control groups included psychotics, psychoneurotics, personality disorders, adjustment reactions, somatic disorders, and a small number of normals. Also included was a group of idiopathic epileptics (whose scores, incidentally, placed them in the normal category).

The authors employed a multiple regression technique to arrive at difference scores which partialed out the effects of age and vocabulary, thus making it unnecessary to equate groups. The difference scores of the combined controls and combined brain-disordered groups clearly discriminated. Using a difference score cutoff of 6.5, 46.5% of the brain-disordered subjects were correctly diagnosed, while 5% of the control subjects were categorized as brain-damaged. While 75.7% of the controls were placed in the normal category, 31.3% of the brain-disordered subjects were placed in the normal category. The remainder of the subjects fell into the borderline area.

Other studies provided evidence of the MFD's ability to discriminate between organic and non-organic psychiatric patients. Shearn, Berry & Fitzgibbons, (1974) found that MFD scores obtained when patients initially were hospitalized predicted more accurately eventual psychiatric diagnosis of suspected brain disorder than did initial psychiatric impressions. McManis (1974) found that 20 brain-damaged psychiatric patients scored significantly higher than 20 nonbrain-damaged psychiatric patients. He found that he could improve his hit rate by dichotomizing on a raw score cutoff of 6.5. With this cutoff, he accurately categorized 89% of his female and 82% of his male subjects.

In addition to the question as to whether a test discriminates between diagnostic groups, an important practical consideration is how well this is done in comparison to other tests designed to make similar distinctions. In studies in which the MFD was used along with other organic screening instruments, the MFD generally compares favorably, particularly when a "best fit" cutoff score was used. Pullen and Games (1965) found no significant difference between the Bender Gestalt and MFD accuracy rates in classifying 60 first admissions to a state mental hospital. However, they recommended the use of the MFD over the Bender, particularly when used by relatively inexperienced clinicians, due to its higher interrater reliability. Korman and Blumberg (1963) administered a battery of organicity screening instruments to a group of 40 cerebral-damaged subjects matched with 40 undamaged subjects. They found the MFD to have the highest accuracy of all of their measures. The reported hit rate of 90% for the MFD is very impressive, and higher than those typically found for organicity screening measures. Thus, though there are some exceptions, the literature indicates that the MFD not only significantly discriminates between diagnostic categories, it does this as well as other measures available.

Investigators have explored some nontraditional uses of the MFD with mixed results. No clinically significant relationship has been demonstrated between MFD drawing styles and personality traits, nor has it been shown to correlate with delinquency. It also has not differentiated consistently between good and poor readers.

Though the norms indicate only a relatively low correlation between intelligence and MFD scores, the MFD may be reflective of intelligence in a highly selected group. Ong and Jones (1982) found a correlation of −0.96 between the MFD and WISC full scale IQs in a class of educable mentally retarded children. They suggested that the MFD may be used as a supplement to other ability measures in the placement of these children. However, the sample in this study was quite small and the high correlation was found among students already placed in this class. Additional data demonstrating the ability of the MFD to discriminate between educable retarded students and normal students would be necessary before it could be used as a placement tool in classroom settings.

Critique

There is much to be said in favor of the MFD as a screening device to make global decisions regarding the presence or absence of cerebral damage. It is quickly and easily administered. The manual is well written, and procedures for administering and scoring the instrument are clearly elaborated. Interrater reliability is quite high for an instrument of this nature, and test-retest reliability is acceptable.

Studies generally demonstrate that it discriminates well between brain-damaged and nonbrain-damaged groups. This remains the case in situations where the brain damage is not readily apparent and where psychiatric conditions of comparison groups make distinctions difficult. Most studies indicate that scores on the MFD can discriminate as well or better than other global measures of organicity.

The MFD is also one of those rather rare psychological instruments that requires subjects to perform the same task and uses the same criteria for scoring for all individuals from age 8 through adulthood. Using difference scores, which control for age and vocabulary level variance, allows comparisons along an exceptional age range. This feature could be useful in future longitudinal studies.

Although the test is easy to administer and the scoring can be mastered fairly quickly, sophistication is required in choosing the appropriate cutoff scores. Acceptance of the authors' suggested cutoff will result in minimizing false-positives and maximizing false-negatives. Most studies indicate that reducing the adult raw score cutoff by approximately 5 points and eliminating the borderline category results in the most accurate overall classification. In a clinical setting the examiner must take into account the relative cost to the patient of over-diagnosing as well as under-diagnosing the probability of brain damage.

While the MFD clearly is most useful as a clinical tool, continued research may demonstrate its utility in educational settings. There is some suggestion that the MFD may measure the intellectual ability of educable mentally retarded students. Attempts at relating reading ability to MFD performance have produced mixed results, and this does not appear to be a particularly promising area for the use of this test.

References

Graham, F. K., & Kendall, B. S. (1946). Performance of brain-damaged cases on a Memory-for-Designs Test. *Journal of Abnormal and Social Psychology, 41,* 303-314.

Graham, K. F., & Kendall, B. S. (1960). Memory-for-Designs Test: Revised general manual. *Perceptual and Motor Skills, 11,* 147-188. (Monograph Supplement 2-VII)

Heaton, R. K., Boode, L. E., & Johnson, K. L. (1978). Neuropsychological test results associated with disorders in adults. *Psychological Bulletin, 85,* 141-162.

Hunt, H. F. (1952). Testing for psychological deficit. In D. Brower & L. E. Abt (Eds.), *Progress in clinical psychology. Vol. 1.* New York: Grune and Stratton.

Kendall, B. S. (1962). Memory-for-Designs performance in the seventh and eighth decades of life. *Perceptual and Motor Skills, 14,* 399-405.

Kendall, B. S., & Graham, F. K. (1948). Further standardization of the Memory-for-Designs Test on children and adults. *Journal of Consulting Psychology, 12,* 349-354.

Korman, M., & Blumberg, S. (1963). Comparative efficiency of some tests of cerebral damage. *Journal of Consulting Psychology, 27,* 303-309.

Krug, R. S. (1971). Antecedent probabilities, cost efficiency, and differential prediction of patients with cerebral organic conditions or psychiatric disturbance by means of a short test of aphasia. *Journal of Clinical Psychology, 27,* 468-471.

McManis, D. L. (1974). Memory-for-Designs performance of brain-damaged and non-damaged psychiatric patients. *Perceptual and Motor Skills, 38,* 847-852.

Ong, J., & Jones, L., Jr. (1982). Memory-for-Designs, intelligence, and achievement of educable mentally retarded children. *Perceptual and Motor Skills, 55,* 379-382.

Pullen, M., & Games, P. (1965). Comparison of two tests of brain damage. *Perceptual and Motor Skills, 20,* 977-980.

Riege, W. H., Kelly, K., & Klane, L. T. (1981). Age and error differences on Memory-for-Designs. *Perceptual and Motor Skills, 52,* 507-513.

Shearn, C. R., Berry, D. F., & Fitzgibbons, D. J. (1974). Usefulness of the Memory-for-Designs Test in assessing mild organic complications in psychiatric patients. *Perceptual and Motor Skills, 38,* 1099-1104.

Helen W. Loeb, Ph.D.

Professor and Head, Education Department, Eastern College, St. Davids, Pennsylvania.

MERRILL-PALMER SCALE

Rachel Stutsman. Chicago, Illinois: Stoelting Company.

Introduction

The Merrill-Palmer Scale is an individually administered mental test for young children ages 24-63 months with emphasis given to performance tests rather than verbal measures. This test is particularly suitable for use with young children who cannot be examined using more verbal instruments and gives a global estimation of whether a young child's performance is significantly below average, average, high average, or superior.

Dr. Rachel Stutsman developed this test at the Merrill-Palmer Nursery School in 1931. Professor L. L. Thurstone and Dr. Lewis M. Terman acted as her advisors on test development and statistical analysis. In addition, Dr. Terman wrote the Editor's Introduction to Dr. Stutsman's test manual.

The scale was designed to add to the Merrill-Palmer school's child development studies and was standardized there. A total of 631 preschool children, 300 boys and 331 girls, ranging in age from 18 months to 77 months were represented in the final norms. The sample was obtained from 20 different sources including the Detroit public schools, the Merrill-Palmer school waiting list, child care agencies, and health clinic clients. The test results of the children attending the Merrill-Palmer school were excluded from the standardization sample because it was felt that, due to the extremely enriched environment to which they were exposed at the school, they were not typical preschoolers. The children in the standardization sample were classified into age groups at six-month intervals, beginning with 18 months and ending with 77 months.

The test has not been revised and there are no other forms available. The performance nature of most of the tests makes it possible to administer many of the items through pantomime so that deaf or non-English-speaking children could be evaluated, at least globally. Stutsman's book, *Mental Measurement of Preschool Children* (1931), devotes a chapter to how to deal with "Children with Special Difficulties."

The Merrill-Palmer Scale consists of 38 different tests divided into groups of 3 to 14 test items within each six-month age period from 18 months to 6 years. There are 10 or more items at each level except ages 60-65 months and 66-71 months. A few verbal items are included but the majority of the tests are performance based. The materials are packaged in brightly colored boxes which are piled up on the testing table so that the subject may choose the one he or she wishes to open. Since the items may be used in any order, the examiner has a great deal of flexibility in structuring how the more difficult or less attractive items are to be

457

included. The materials come packed in a convenient carrying case which includes all test materials, a manual (consisting of a reprint of Part Three, pages 139-262, of *Mental Measurement of Preschool Children*), and 50 record blanks. The clinician planning to use this test should make every effort to obtain the original Stutsman (1931) book as it contains much useful information on preschool children, including a review of other mental tests, a discussion of the criteria for the selection of tests, a guide for personality observations, and suggestions for dealing with children with special difficulties.

The individual items that comprise the test are:

Verbal Tests: comprised of the Woodworth-Wells Association Test, in which the child is asked "What runs?", "What cries?", etc.; and the Stutsman Language Test, which asks, "What does a doggie say?", "What does a kitty say?", etc. and requires the child to repeat simple words and phrases such as "kitty," "nice doggie," etc.

Series of All-or-None Tests: consists of Obeying Simple Commands, Throwing a Ball, Building a Tower, Crossing Feet, Standing on One Foot, Folding Paper, Making a Block Walk, the Stutsman String and Stick Test, Identification of Self in Mirror, Cutting With Scissors, the Stutsman Color Matching Test, Moving Fingers and Thumb, and the Stutsman Copying Test.

Form Boards and Picture Tests: consists of the Seguin-Goddard Formboard, the Pintner Manikin Test, the Stutsman Picture Formboards (1-3), the Decroly Matching Game, and the Mare-Foal Formboard.

Other Tests of Motor Coordination: consists of the Wallin Pegboards (A and B), a box of sixteen color cubes for The Kohs Block Design Test, the Stutsman Nested Cubes, the Stutsman Pyramid Test, the Stutsman Little Pink Tower Test, and the Stutsman Buttoning Test.

The manual provides careful directions for the examiner, including what to expect of a preschool child in a test situation, how to proceed with each task, and how to score and record the results. Helpful suggestions are also given on how to evaluate the personality of the preschool child being tested.

According to the manual the test is intended for children ages 18 months to 6 years, however the author does not recommend that it be administered to children below the age of 24 months. There is also evidence that above the age of 3 years-10 months only below-average children with serious verbal difficulty should be examined with this instrument.

An answer form is provided on which the examiner records the child's replies as fully as possible as the test is given. The profile can be given in three different ways: as a mental age, a sigma value or a percentile rank.

Practical Applications/Uses

This test would be most useful with young children who cannot be evaluated using more verbal instruments. It is highly attractive to young children and there is rarely a problem of motivation. Careful interpretation is essential and therefore the scale is most appropriately given by a skilled, trained clinician. Various individual items may be used by a skilled diagnostician to test visual-motor perception, eye-hand coordination, etc. Developmentally delayed older children who have verbal difficulty may also be evaluated by a skilled clinician.

The test was designed as an alternative for, or supplement to, the Stanford-Binet Intelligence Test. It has been used in clinical settings for the evaluation of young children and in developmental research. Early childhood intervention centers find it useful for a global assessment of whether a child falls within the very low, average, high, or superior ranges of development. Individual items may be used for assessment of specific areas of difficulty.

As stated previously, the test is most appropriate for young children ages 24 months to 3 years-6 months and for the global assessment of developmentally delayed older children who have verbal difficulty. It is less appropriate for normal children who are past the age of 54 months because of statistical problems. The standard deviations of the mental ages do not increase with age beyond 3 years-6 months so that IQs cannot be computed. The results tend to be skewed at both ends and a young above-average child may appear superior due to the relatively small number of tasks that must be passed. On the other hand, an older child who scores as borderline on similar measures may appear very low on this instrument.

The test should be administered by a trained examiner and interpreted by someone with a thorough knowledge of statistics. It is an individually administered test and is best given in a comfortable testing room away from any distractions. The test manual gives no information on how long the test takes to administer. Much depends upon the child's response and interest.

One of the most helpful aspects of this test is the book written by Dr. Stutsman (1931). It is thorough and helpful, instructions are clear and advice is given for testing young children that would be valuable to any clinician who works with this age group.

Scoring instructions are complete, but careful interpretation is needed. Thus, it is essential that examiners be thoroughly trained and supervised as they begin to evaluate children using this instrument. The test is scored by hand on the answer sheet. The examiner enters a "plus" (+) for success on an item, a "minus" (–) for failure, an "O" for omitted, or an "R" for refused. There is provision in the scoring system so that children are not penalized for omitted or refused items.

The manual provides tables for interpreting the final corrected score in three ways: 1) by finding a mental age; 2) by finding the standard deviation value of the score; or 3) by finding the percentile value of the score. Clinical judgment is needed to assess the child's answers, to obtain the final score, and to use the tables. A degree of statistical sophistication is needed to interpret the test results. Dr. Stutsman herself recommended that interpretation of the score by standard deviation, in terms of score value or mental age value, and interpretation by percentile rank are preferable to interpretation in terms of the intelligence quotient.

Technical Aspects

Dr. Stutsman did not report the reliability of the scale in her manual. Validity was judged by the following criteria: 1) each item seemed to differentiate between nursery school children of the same age who were evaluated by other criteria as bright or dull; 2) there was a high correlation between chronological age and test score; 3) items showed progressive differentiation between age groups; 4) items showed ability to differentiate normal children from those who were feeble-minded; and 5) the test as a whole demonstrated a high correlation with the Stanford-Binet. Later researchers, however, have not found the same high correlation with the Stanford-Binet that Dr. Stutsman reported.

M. P. Honzik (1975) discusses a study by Ebert and Simmons (1943) which reports that the correlations between the Merrill-Palmer and the Stanford-Binet for two-, three-, and four-year old children were in the .60s. Prediction of later Stanford-Binet IQs from the Merrill-Palmer given between the ages of two and four years "fluctuates within the rather narrow range from .39 to .54" (p. 58).

Critique

The problems and advantages cited by previous reviewers are still pertinent. The Merrill-Palmer Scale items are extremely attractive to preschool children and there is rarely a problem with motivation. The examiner has much flexibility in that the items need not be administered in any specific order. The test contains few verbal items and there is provision in the scoring for refusals and omissions so that the child is not penalized for these. The test is useful, when given by a skilled examiner, for global evaluations of the functioning level of young children or older slow children who have verbal difficulty. The manual is very thorough and the suggestions for observing and/or testing preschool children are useful for anyone who plans to work with this age group.

Areas of concern include: the lack of demonstrated predictive ability common to most preschool measures; the low correlations with the Stanford-Binet, which suggest that something else is being tested; the test's limited usefulness for children older than 63 months and younger than 24 months; the lack of grouping of items into specific areas of functioning, making this the interpreter's responsibility; the inappropriate use of timed items, so that slow-moving, thoughtful preschoolers are penalized; and the fact that the standard deviations of the mental ages do not increase in proportion to chronological age throughout the age range for which the test is designed (18 to 66 months) making interpretation extremely difficult. In addition, the materials needed to administer the test are expensive, thus limiting its availability.

References

This list contains text citations as well as suggested additional reading. There are also excellent reviews of the Merrill-Palmer Scale by Nancy Bayley, B. M. Castner, Florence L. Goodenough, and Florence M. Teagarden in Buros' *Intelligence Tests and Reviews* (1975). The researcher is referred to these for more information.

Allan, M. E., & Young, F. M. (1943). The constancy of the intelligence quotient as indicated by retests of 130 children. *Journal of Applied Psychology, 27,* 41-60.
Bristol, H. (1936). An English norm for the Merrill-Palmer performance tests: Based on a

study of 530 children between the ages of two and six years. *British Journal of Educational Psychology, 6,* 250-266.

Buros, O. K. (Ed.). (1975). *Intelligence tests and reviews.* Highland Park, NJ: The Gryphon Press.

DeForrest, R. (1939). *A study of the prognostic value of the Merrill-Palmer Scale of Mental Tests and the Minnesota Preschool Scale.* Unpublished master's thesis, University of Pittsburgh.

Durojaiye, M. O. A., & Such, M. (1971). Predicting educational suitability of children in an assessment unit. *Journal of Experimental Education, 40*(2), 27-36.

Ebert, E., & Simmons, K. (1943). The Brush Foundation study of child growth and development: I. Psychometric tests. *Monographs of the Society for Research in Child Development, 8*(2, Serial No. 35).

Goldman, J. (1977). Reflections of personality functioning in psychological testing of disadvantaged three to five year olds. *Journal of Personality Assessment, 41,* 39-42.

Gordon, R. G. (1933). The Merrill-Palmer Scale of intelligence tests for preschool children applied to low-grade mental defectives. *British Journal of Psychology, 24,* 178-186.

Gould, J. (1977). The use of the Vineland Social Maturity Scale, the Merrill-Palmer Scale of Mental Tests (non-verbal items), and the Reynell Developmental Language Scales with children in contact with the services for severe mental retardation. *Journal of Mental Deficiency Research, 21,* 213-226.

Haines, M. S. (1954). Test performance of preschool children with and without organic brain pathology. *Journal of Consulting Psychology, 18,* 371-374.

Harris, D. B. (1947). An item analysis and evaluation of the Merrill-Palmer Scale of Mental Tests for preschool children. *American Psychologist, 2,* 302.

Honzik, M. P. (1975). The Merrill-Palmer Scale of Mental Tests. In O. K. Buros (Ed.), *Intelligence tests and reviews.* Highland Park, NJ: The Gryphon Press.

Hurst, J. G. (1960). A factor analysis of the Merrill-Palmer with reference to theory and test construction. *Educational and Psychological Measurement, 20,* 519-532.

Keir, G. (1966). The Merrill-Palmer test with the children from the island of Tristan da Cunha. *Journal of Child Psychology and Psychiatry* (England), *7,* 133-142.

Magrab, P. Burg, C. Scribanu, N. (1976). Stability and comparability of intellectual measures for cerebral-palsied preschoolers. *Physical Therapy, 56,* 553-558.

Mowrer, W. M. (1933). Intelligence scales for preschool children. *Child Development, 4,* 318-322.

Mowrer, W. M. (1934). Performance of children in Stutsman tests. *Child Development, 5,* 93-96.

Oberlin, D. S. (1937). Verbal and manual functions at the preschool level. *Delaware State Medical Journal, 9,* 95-98.

Roe, K. (1977). Correlations between Gesell scores in infancy and performance on verbal and non-verbal tests in early childhood. *Perceptual Motor Skills, 45,* 1131-1134.

Stott, L. H., & Ball, R. S. (1966). Infant and preschool mental tests: Review and evaluation. *Monographs of the Society for Research in Child Development, 30*(3, Serial No. 101).

Stutsman, R. (1931). *Mental measurement of preschool children.* New York: World Book Co.

Stutsman, R. (1934). Factors to be considered in measuring the reliability of a mental test, with special reference to the Merrill-Palmer Scale. *Journal of Educational Psychology, 25,* 630-633.

Takacs, C. P. (1971). Comparison of mental abilities between lower socioeconomic status five-year-old Negro and white children on individual intelligence measures. (Doctoral dissertation, Kent State University, Kent, Ohio). *Dissertation Abstracts International, 32,* 3806A.

Walsh, R. (1954). *The prognostic value of the Merrill-Palmer Mental Tests and the Nebraska Test of*

Learning Aptitude for Pre-School Deaf Children. Unpublished master's thesis, University of Buffalo.

Wellman, B. L. (1938). The intelligence of preschool children as measured by the Merrill-Palmer Scale of performance tests (University of Iowa Studies, New Series Number 361). *Studies in Child Welfare, 15*(3), 150.

George R. Bieger, Ph.D.
Assistant Professor of Education, Bucknell University, Lewisburg, Pennsylvania.

METROPOLITAN READINESS TESTS

Joanne R. Nurss and Mary E. McGauvran. Cleveland, Ohio: The Psychological Corporation.

Introduction

The Metropolitan Readiness Tests (MRT) are the principal component of a four-part program designed to evaluate a child's readiness for school and to develop the skills necessary for school success. The tests themselves assess the readiness for formal school learning of kindergarten to early first-grade pupils.

The concept of readiness used in the MRT can be defined as the extent to which a child has acquired the knowledge and skills considered as prerequisites for profitable formal instruction. The tests are intended to determine the pupil's current level of skill development in several broad skill areas that are related to broad curricular areas and, thus, are intended for use in determining the appropriate level of instruction for each pupil.

The MRT was first published in a single form in 1933 by the World Book Company of Yonkers, New York. The authors of the 1933 edition of the MRT were Gertrude Hildreth and Nellie Griffiths. The first edition of the MRT, designed to measure both reading and number readiness of first-grade entrants, was comprised of the following subtests: Perception (Similarities), Perception (Copying), Vocabulary, Sentences, Numbers, Information, and, optionally, Draw-A-Man. Scores were reported as percentile ranks for the total test and for each subtest and "readiness cutoff scores" were indicated.

In 1949, the MRT underwent its first revision by Hildreth and Griffiths. This edition of the tests included two forms (R & S) which were comprised of the following subtests: Word Meaning, Sentences, Information, Matching, Numbers, Copying, and, optionally, Draw-A-Man. Scores were reported as percentile ranks for the total test and according to five letter levels for Reading and Number Readiness and for the total test score.

The MRT was revised again in 1965 by authors Hildreth and Griffiths and their colleague, Mary McGauvran. Again, two forms (A & B) of the tests were published and included the following subtests: Word Meaning, Listening, Matching, Alphabet, Numbers, Copying, and, optionally, Draw-A-Man. Scores were reported as percentile ranks and stanines for the total test score, according to five letter levels for the total test score and each subtest, and as quartiles for each subtest. For the third edition (1965), the relationship between readiness score and achievement was illustrated by providing cumulative distributions of achievement (reported as grade equivalent scores) at the end of first grade for each letter

463

level of the MRT that had been administered at the beginning of first grade. Tables that indicated end of first-grade achievement stanines for each beginning of first-grade MRT stanine were developed.

The most recent revision of the MRT in 1976 was authored by Joanne Nurss and Mary McGauvran and is published by The Psychological Corporation. For the first time in its history, two levels of the MRT were introduced, each level consisting of two forms (P & Q). Level I is designed primarily for use in the first half of the kindergarten year or for pupils for whom Level II is too difficult or otherwise inappropriate. Level II is designed for pupils at the end of Kindergarten or the beginning of first grade.

The 1976 revision of the MRT began in 1971 and was undertaken for several reasons. First, the concept of school readiness had been refined since the 1965 revision and it was felt that the MRT should be revised to reflect those changes. For example, the recognition that auditory skills are important for school learning prompted the inclusion of tests in that area. Secondly, the overall level of skill development of entering first-graders had increased since the previous revision, thus inflating MRT rankings based on 1965 norms. Finally, it was felt that there was a need for an instrument to test the school readiness of pupils earlier in the kindergarten year, thus promoting the development of a second level of the test.

The 1976 edition of the MRT reflects the authors' view that school readiness is not an "either/or" issue but a question of determining the level of instruction for which a student is ready. The authors assert that "the purpose of the test is not to determine 'ready or not,' but rather 'ready for *what?*' under the assumption that all children are ready for some kind of instruction at some level of skill development" (Nurss & McGauvran, 1981a, p. 4).

There are two levels of the MRT, each of which has two alternate forms and both of which are administered orally and require the pupil to make simple marks in the test booklet. Prior to the administration of the test, pupils are given a practice booklet that familiarizes them with the materials and procedures used in the test. The tests are usually administered by the classroom teacher and a two-part teacher's manual is included in the test materials. (Part I of the manual provides directions for administering the MRT and Part II provides information related to the interpretation and use of the test results.)

In addition to the tests themselves, the practice booklet, and teacher's manual, the test kit includes parent-teacher conference reports for both Level I and Level II, a technical handbook, and a class record and class analysis chart for each level of the test.

Level I tests were designed for pupils early in the kindergarten year and older students for whom the Level II tests are too difficult or inappropriate. These tests measure auditory, visual, and language skills and are comprised of the following subtests:

1. *Auditory Memory:* Measures pupils' recall of a series of words spoken by the teacher. They listen with closed eyes as the teacher names several objects. They then open their eyes and mark the one of four pictures that depicts the objects named by the teacher.

2. *Rhyming:* Measures pupils' ability to hear and discriminate among medial and final sounds in a rhyming context. Pupils look at four pictures, each depicting

a different object, as the teacher names each object. They then mark the picture that depicts the object the name of which rhymes with a word spoken by the teacher.

3. *Letter Recognition:* Measures pupils' ability to recognize upper- and lower-case letters. The pupils look at four upper- or lower-case letters and mark the one named by the teacher.

4. *Visual Matching:* Measures pupils' skill in matching series of letters, words, numerals, and other symbols. Pupils look at a row of five pictures, the one on the left being set in a red box. They then mark the picture that matches the symbol depicted in the red box.

5. *School Language and Listening:* Measures listening comprehension by requiring the pupils to integrate and reorganize information presented orally. Pupils look at three pictures and mark the one that depicts the situation described by the teacher.

6. *Quantitative:* Measures pupils' knowledge of fundamental quantitative concepts, such as size, shape, and number-quantity relationships. Pupils look at a row of five pictures. The picture on the left is the stimulus item and the remaining four are response choices. The pupils put a mark on the response choice that satisfies the criterion stated by the teacher. For example, the first item consists of a row of five boxes each containing a picture of a rabbit. The box on the left is red and the pupils are told to mark the rabbit that is BIGGER THAN the rabbit in the red box.

An optional subtest, *Copying*, measures pupils' visual-motor coordination by requiring them to copy their first names from a model provided by the teacher.

The administration of the practice booklet requires approximately 15 minutes and the administration of the six subtests requires approximately 80 minutes. The tests are administered in the order listed above except that the Copying subtest, if administered, can occur at any time. The subtests are generally administered in seven or eight separate sessions, including the practice session, each lasting about 15 minutes.

The Level I tests yield a total Pre-Reading Skills Composite Score that is reported as a raw score, a percentile rank, a stanine, and a performance rating (low, average, or high). In addition, each subtest yields a raw score and a performance rating, and a raw score, stanine, and performance rating is given for Visual Skills and Language Skills.

Level II tests are intended for use with pupils at the end of the kindergarten year or the beginning of the first-grade year. In addition to auditory, visual, and language skills (measured using the Level I tests), the Level II tests have been designed to measure quantitative skills if desired. These tests are comprised of the following subtests:

1. *Beginning Consonants:* Measures pupils' ability to discriminate among the initial sounds of words. The pupils look at pictures of four objects while the teacher names each object. The pupils then mark the picture of the object the name of which begins with the same sound as a word spoken by the teacher.

2. *Sound-Letter Correspondence:* Measures pupils' ability to identify letters corresponding to specific sounds in words. The pupils look at a row consisting of a picture followed by four letters. The teacher names the object depicted in the

picture and the pupils mark the letter that corresponds to the initial sound in the object's name.

3. *Visual Matching:* Measures pupils' visual-perceptual skill in matching letters, words, numerals and other symbols. The pupils look at a row of five symbols, the one on the left being set in a green box. The pupils then mark the symbol that matches the one in the green box.

4. *Finding Patterns:* Measures pupils' ability to locate formations of letter-groups, words, numerals, and other symbols that are embedded in larger groupings of similar symbols. The pupils look at a row of five symbols, the one at the left being set in a green box. The pupils then mark the one of the large groupings of symbols that includes the symbol(s) in the green box.

5. *School Language:* Measures pupils' understanding of grammatical structures of standard American English. The pupils look at three pictures and mark the one that depicts the situation described by the teacher.

6. *Listening:* Measures pupils' ability to integrate and reorganize information, draw inferences, and analyze and evaluate information presented orally. The pupils look at four pictures and then mark the one that satisfies the criterion stated by the teacher. For example, the four pictures depict a pair of shoes, a pair of sneakers, a pair of sandals, and a pair of boots, respectively. The teacher says that it was raining and cold outside so David put on his coat, boots, and hat, then asks the pupils to mark what David put on his feet before he went outside.

7. *Quantitative Concepts:* Measures pupils' knowledge of basic mathematical concepts, such as size, shape, position, quantity, etc. The pupils look at a row of pictures and mark the one that satisfies the criterion stated by the teacher.

8. *Quantitative Operations:* Measures pupils' skill in using basic mathematical operations, such as counting and simple addition and subtraction. The pupils look at a row of four or five boxes and mark the box that satisfies the criterion stated by the teacher.

An optional subtest, *Copying,* measures pupils' visual-motor coordination. The pupils write their names on a sheet and then copy a sentence from the model shown on the sheet.

The total time for administration of all 8 Level II subtests is approximately 90 minutes, (including the optional tests) plus 15 minutes for the administration of the practice booklet. The tests are administered in the order listed above and are usually given in five sessions, including the practice session.

The Level II MRT yield a raw score, a stanine, and a performance rating (low, average, high) for each skill area (Auditory, Visual, Language, and Quantitative). In addition, a raw score, percentile rank, stanine, and performance rating is given for a Pre-Reading Skills score, which is a composite of the auditory, visual and language skill areas.

Practical Applications/Uses

One conception of school readiness refers to whether or not a pupil is "ready" to begin school (Weiner & Stewart, 1984). The notion of readiness adopted by the authors of the MRT assumes that every child of kindergarten or first-grade age is ready for some type of instruction. Thus, the MRT is useful in helping school administrators, teachers, and parents design an instructional program for a pupil that is best suited for that pupil's current level of skill development.

The MRT are designed to measure the extent to which a child has developed the skills considered necessary for reading and mathematics instruction. Such information about individual students can help classroom teachers form working groups based on ability for reading and mathematics instruction. Used in such a way, the MRT serve as a placement test. The MRT can also help the teacher decide on the amount and kind of "readiness" activities needed prior to beginning formal reading and/or mathematics instruction. In this way, the MRT serve as a tool for curriculum planning.

The Early School Inventory, which is one of the support components of the MRT, can be used for monitoring pupil progress in kindergarten, and when used with the Class Record and Class Analysis Chart, the MRT can provide useful information for the formative and summative evaluation of the kindergarten program.

The MRT are easily administered in group settings of up to ten pupils by a classroom teacher without special training. The tests can also be administered individually. The teacher's manuals provide clear, detailed, and complete instructions for administration of the tests. Included in these instructions are lists of needed materials, recommendations for scheduling, and suggestions regarding preparation for testing. This information, along with an examiner's checklist, greatly facilitates the testing process and substantially reduces, if not eliminates altogether, problems or pitfalls.

The MRT can be scored either manually or by machine. A scoring key and scoring instructions are provided for manual scoring, and clear instructions are provided for preparing and handling the machine-scorable editions.

Because of the young age of those taking the test, the nature of machine-scored responses is very important. Many five- and six-year old children would have difficulty with conventional machine-scored response sheets that require darkening a small circle or oval. The MRT machine-scoring system permits the pupil to mark directly on the response option by making an approximately diagonal line across the response box with a black pencil. The use of the machine-scored edition requires greater attention by the teacher to the students as they mark responses.

The method of score reporting and the breakdown of score reports by skill area makes interpretation of the MRT objective and relatively straightforward. Because scores are reported as performance ratings, percentile ranks and stanines, minimal training or sophistication is required to interpret the MRT results accurately. The teacher's manual (Part II) provides sufficient background information and examples to permit someone with almost no prior knowledge of test interpretation to understand the MRT score reporting scheme.

The issue of test interpretation as it relates to making professional judgments about instructional programs for students is less straightforward. The translation of MRT results into pedagogically sound curricular programs requires substantial knowledge of early childhood skill development. The teacher's manuals provide some guidelines for assisting school professionals in making such judgments; however, these guidelines would be of little use without a solid background in early childhood development and education.

Technical Aspects

In order to determine the validity of any test, it is important to know first what it is that the test claims to measure. The authors of the MRT claim that they measure the level of development of skills necessary for worthwhile engagement in formal school instruction. This suggests that the MRT's validity is contingent on the extent to which the skills that they measure are in fact the skills related to school success.

Assessing the validity of the MRT can be done in any of three ways. First, one can consider the nature of preschool reading and mathematics skills and examine the content of the MRT to determine whether they include items in all of the relevant specific skills. The authors of the MRT have done a comprehensive analysis of the skills needed for beginning reading and mathematics instruction. There are, however, some specific skills that may be relevant for school readiness and are not included in the MRT. For example, one might consider skill in word recognition and/or sound blending relevant for prereading. Neither of these skills are measured by the MRT. One might argue that these skills are part of the content of reading instruction and not prereading skills at all. Overall, the content of the MRT reveals an adequate representation of readiness skills and items to measure those skills.

A second way to evaluate the validity of the MRT is to examine the relationship between MRT performance and some criterial measure of performance. Because one use of the MRT is to predict readiness for school, the criterion-related (predictive) validity of the MRT can be determined by computing the correlation between MRT scores for a group of pupils and scores on an achievement test for that same group of pupils at some point in the future. The authors of the MRT have conducted such studies and computed correlations between MRT scores and achievement test scores for each of the subtests, the skill area scores, and the composite or total test scores for both levels of the tests and all forms of the tests.

When the coefficient of correlation is computed, the value of the coefficient can fall between −1.0 and +1.0. In the case of predictive validity, a correlation of 1.0 would mean that the test was a perfect predictor of subsequent achievement; a correlation of 0.0 would mean that there is no relationship at all between test performance and subsequent achievement.

The authors computed correlations between the MRT Level I and the Metropolitan Achievement Tests (MAT) for 719 pupils in 25 school districts. The correlation coefficients between subtest scores and achievement scores ranged from .41 to .64. The correlations between the skill area scores and achievement scores ranged from .58 to .68. The correlations between the Level I Pre-Reading Skills Composite score and Reading achievement were about .70.

For the Level II tests the authors selected 4,000 first-grade students, who had taken the MRT in the early fall of their first-grade year, and measured their achievement in the spring of first grade using either the MAT or the Stanford Achievement Test (SAT). The correlations between the MRT subtests and the achievement subtests ranged from .38 to .65 for the MAT and from .37 to .63 for the SAT.

The correlations between the MRT skill area scores and the MAT and SAT total

Reading and Mathematics scores were, except for one subtest, all above .50. (The Language Skill Area score had a correlation of .48 with the SAT Total Reading score.)

The correlations between the Pre-Reading Skills Composite score and Total Reading achievement scores were .70 for the MAT and .69 for the SAT. When the two quantitative subtests were used and added to the Pre-Reading Composite score, the correlations between the resulting Battery Composite score and Mathematics achievement score were .73 for the MAT and .69 for the SAT. The SAT also provided an overall measure of achievement. The correlation between the SAT total Basic Battery score and the MRT Battery Composite score was .78.

The data summarized above provide considerable evidence that the predictive validity of the MRT is high, especially when one uses the Battery Composite or the Pre-Reading Skills Composite scores as the predictor variables. The predictive validity of the individual subtests and the skill area scores is somewhat lower.

The third way that the validity of the MRT can be established is to compare the relationship between performance on the MRT and performance on other tests that claim to measure school readiness. Such a comparison was done between the MRT and the Clymer-Barrett Pre-Reading Battery (Clymer & Barrett, 1967). The correlations between skill area scores on the two tests ranged from .50 to .73, and the correlations between the Pre-Reading Composite and Battery Composite scores of the MRT with the Clymer-Barrett scores were .80.

The validity of the MRT is demonstrably high, although it is important to note that if a school district's kindergarten or first-grade program stresses skill areas that differ substantially from those skills measured in the MRT, the validity may be lower for that district. Where there is considerable agreement between the skills taught and those measured by the MRT, the MRT provide a valid way of measuring school readiness.

Reliability refers to the degree of consistency in measurement, and, therefore, indicates the amount of confidence that can be placed in the obtained scores. The reliability of a test can be ascertained in any of several ways. One can compare the results from two administrations of the same items (Test-Retest), compare the results from the administration of two different forms of the test (Alternate-Forms), and/or examine the consistency of results among the items or subtests from a single administration of the test (Internal Consistency). The methods used to determine the reliability of the MRT were Alternate-Forms after a two-week interval and Internal Consistency.

Reliability coefficients can vary from 0.0 to 1.0 with a coefficient of 0.0 indicating no reliability whatsoever and a coefficient of 1.0 indicating that the results are perfectly consistent. For the Level I tests, reliability measured as Internal Consistency (using the Kuder-Richardson 20 formula) ranged from .69 to .88 for the various subtests. The reliability of the skill area tests ranged from .82 to .90 and the reliability of the Pre-Reading Skills Composite score ranged from .92 to .94. The results of the reliability studies were comparable for both forms of the tests. Computations of Alternate-Forms reliability yielded coefficients of reliability ranging from .64 to .81 for the subtests and from .78 to .84 for the skill area scores; reliability was .90 for the Pre-Reading Skills Composite score.

For the Level II tests, the coefficients of reliability (KR 20) ranged from .53 to .90

for the subtests and .71 to .93 for the skill areas. The Internal Consistency was .94 for the Pre-Reading Skills Composite and .95 for the Battery Composite. The Alternate-Forms reliability coefficients ranged from .54 to .84 for the subtests and from .68 to .87 for the skill area scores. The Alternate Forms reliability of the Pre-Reading Skills Composite scores was .89 and .91 for the Battery Composite scores.

The results of the reliability studies are reported in the teacher's manuals (Part II) as reliability coefficients and as standard errors of measurement for each subtest, skill area, and for the composite scores. These data indicate that the MRT are highly reliable, especially when one considers the composite scores. As such, they can be used with the confidence that the obtained test results have a high level of consistency.

The norms for interpreting the results of the MRT were obtained from studies conducted during the 1974-75 school year. The standardization sample included students in public and parochial schools who were representative of the United States school population. The sample was randomly selected in a stratified fashion in order to achieve representativeness of the population with respect to size and type of school system, socioeconomic composition (including ethnic background and gender), and geographic region. For the Level I tests a sample of 68,997 students was employed and for the Level II tests the sample size was 66,254.

In addition to the national norms, the standardization process resulted in the publication of norms for large city school systems as well as norms for school district means that enable an entire district to be compared to the school districts that took part in the standardization study. The standardization process was thorough and complete and the norms are clear and direct.

Critique

The MRT battery is a well-standardized readiness test that is easy to administer, score, and interpret. The materials that accompany the tests include readable manuals, clear scoring and conversion charts, and effective and accurate directions for interpreting test results. In addition, the support components for the MRT recognize that standardized testing is only one part of a comprehensive and accurate assessment process.

Because readiness tests are generally administered to pupils who are often naive with respect to test-taking (the MRT are probably the first test experience for many children) and whose span of attention is often short, care must be taken that the test results present an accurate picture of the child. The MRT can minimize these problems, especially if support components are used, such as the Early School Inventory, which provides a systematic method for recording observations of children's skill development in the course of their day-to-day activities. The practice booklet and the short multiple testing sessions also help reduce differences in test performance due to attention or unfamiliarity.

The MRT battery is a reliable, valid, and well-designed instrument that can provide useful information to school administrators, teachers and parents. Used with other methods of observation, the MRT can be a valuable part of a comprehensive program for assessing a child's level of skill development.

References

This list includes text citations as well as suggested additional reading.

Anastasi, A. (1982). *Psychological testing* (5th ed.). New York: Macmillan.

Brown, F. G. (1983). *Principles of educational and psychological testing* (3rd ed.). New York: Holt, Rinehart & Winston.

Clymer, T., & Barrett, T. (1967). *Clymer-Barrett Pre-Reading Battery.* Columbus, OH: Personnel Press.

Goldman, J., Stein, C. L., & Guerry, S. (1983). *Psychological methods of child assessment.* New York: Brunner/Mazel.

Hildreth, G. H., Griffiths, N. L., & McGauvron, M. E. (1965). *Metropolitan Readiness Test: 1965 Edition.* Cleveland: The Psychological Corporation.

Mehrens, W. A., & Lehmann, I. J. (1984). *Measurement and evaluation in education and psychology* (3rd ed.). New York: Holt, Rinehart & Winston.

Nitko, A. J. (1983). *Educational tests and measurement: An introduction.* New York: Harcourt Brace Jovanovich, Inc.

Nurss, J. R., & McGauvran, M. E. (1976). *Metropolitan Readiness Tests.* Cleveland, OH: The Psychological Corporation.

Nurss, J. R., & McGauvran, M. E. (1981a). *Readiness and its Testing* (Metropolitan Readiness Tests, Technical Report No. 1). Cleveland, OH: The Psychological Corporation.

Nurss, J. R., & McGauvran, M. E. (1981b). *MRT norms and related information* (Metropolitan Readiness Tests, Technical Report No. 2). Cleveland, OH: The Psychological Corporation.

Nurss, J. R., & McGauvran, M. E. (1981c). *Validity information* (Metropolitan Readiness Tests, Technical Report No. 3). Cleveland, OH: The Psychological Corporation.

Nurss, J. R., & McGauvran, M. E. (1981d). *Reliability and related information* (Metropolitan Readiness Tests, Technical Report No. 4). Cleveland, OH: The Psychological Corporation.

Rubin, R. A. (1974). Preschool application of the Metropolitan Reading Tests: Validity, reliability, and preschool norms. *Educational and Psychological Measurement, 34,* 417-422.

Weiner, E. A., & Stewart, B. J. (1984). *Assessing individuals.* Boston: Little, Brown & Co.

Robert C. Colligan, Ph.D.
Head, Section of Psychology, Department of Psychiatry and
Psychology, Mayo Clinic, Rochester, Minnesota.

MINNESOTA CHILD DEVELOPMENT INVENTORY

*Harold Ireton and Edward Thwing. Minneapolis, Minnesota:
Behavior Science Systems, Inc.*

Introduction

The Minnesota Child Development Inventory (MCDI) is a 320-item questionnaire that provides information about the developmental status of a preschool
child, based on observations reported by the child's mother or primary caretaker.
The packet of MCDI materials includes a user's manual; a 6-page, 320-item
inventory booklet and answer sheet for the respondent; scoring templates; and
profile forms. The MCDI is appropriate for use with children from ages 1 to 6 or
older persons functioning within this developmental range. The MCDI yields a
profile of the child's development in the following eight areas: general development, gross motor, fine motor, expressive language, comprehension-conceptual
(receptive language), situation comprehension, self-help, and personal-social.

The authors of the MCDI, Dr. Harold Ireton, Associate Professor of Psychology,
Department of Family Practice and Community Health, University of Minnesota
Medical Center, and Dr. Edward Thwing, a licensed consulting psychologist in
private practice (now deceased) initiated work on the MCDI to 1) provide a
systematic method for obtaining, summarizing and interpreting child-develop-
ment information obtained from parents, and 2) reduce the amount of professional interviewing time necessary to do so. However, the MCDI was not intended
to be a substitute for parental interview but an additional source of information of
particular use when questions of developmental delay have been raised.

The first step in constructing the MCDI was a survey of the child development
literature and a review of the content of existing assessment materials for preschool children. Statements describing developmental changes in behavior from
children age 1 month to 6½ years of age were used to establish an initial item pool
of more than 2,000 statements. Redundant items were then excluded and the
following criteria were used to select items for an experimental inventory: 1)
representation of a developmental skill, 2) observability, 3) descriptive clarity, and
4) potential age-discriminating power. These criteria yielded 673 trial statements,
the age discriminating power of which was then evaluated from mothers'
responses in a sample of 441 boys and 446 girls, aged 1 month to 6½ years.

Age-discriminating power for each statement was determined by the increase in the percentage of children passing the item. Items showing no systematic relationship to age were excluded. Age levels were assigned to each item based on the age at which at least 67% of the mothers had answered yes to the item. These procedures were carried out separately for each sex and yielded 320 age-discriminating items.

These 320 items were then rationally grouped into seven scales representing specific areas of importance in a child's development. None of the scales were derived by factor or cluster analytic techniques. In addition, an eighth scale (General Development) composed of the most age-discriminating items from the other seven scales was created to provide an overall index of developmental status.

A description of each scale follows:

Gross Motor (GM): consists of 34 items measuring locomotion, strength, balance, and coordination, e.g., #160 (30-month level). Does a forward somersault.

Fine Motor (FM): consists of 44 items measuring varying degrees of visual motor coordination, e.g., #84 (36-month level). Draws or copies circles.

Expressive Language (EL): contains 54 items measuring expressive communication, extending from simple gestures to complex language, e.g., #313 (27-month level). Tells what action is going on in pictures—for example, "Kitty is eating."

Comprehension-Conceptual (CC): contains 67 items that measure receptive language, ranging from simple comprehension (e.g., responding to one's own name) to the formulation of concepts, e.g., #172 (53-month level). Talks in the past tense correctly—for example, says "went" rather than "goed," "did" rather than "do," "bought" rather than "buyed."

Situation Comprehension (SC): consists of 44 items that measure nonverbal understanding of and interaction with the child's environment through use of observation, discrimination, imitation, and motor behavior, e.g., #78 (45-month level). Dresses up in parents' old clothes and "playacts."

Self Help (SH): has 36 items measuring self-care ability in eating, toileting, and dressing, e.g., #198 (18-month level). Takes off shoes and socks.

Personal-Social (PS): contains 34 items reflecting initiative, independence, social interaction, and concern for others, e.g., #66 36-month level. Goes to a playmate's house alone.

General Development (GD): consists of 131 of the most age-discriminating items from the other seven scales and provides an overall index of development.

Subsequently the MCDI was then cross validated on a separate sample of 395 boys and 401 girls, aged 6 months to 6½ years. These 796 children in the total sample were obtained from 796 separate families in Bloomington, Minnesota, a Minneapolis suburb. Households containing children of appropriate age were identified through a suburban directory, and mothers were contacted by telephone with 85% of those contacted agreeing to participate and 88% of this group participating in the study.

Socioeconomic data indicated that mothers in the sample had a mean of 13.1 years of education, with 43% of the fathers described as having professional or managerial occupations. Later, 24 children, described by their parents as being handicapped, were excluded, and 21 others were excluded because three or more items on the answer sheet were not scorable. Extensive tables describing the sample are provided in the manual, but the general ages of the children included in the normative sample were 71 aged 6-12 months, 139 aged 12-24 months, 132 aged 2-3 years, 132 aged 3-4 years, 133 aged 4-5 years, 133 aged 5-6, and 56 aged 6-6½ years. Numbers of boys and girls were nearly equal at all age ranges; however, the authors point out that the normative group should not be considered a representative sample of white, preschool children in general (Ireton & Thwing, 1974, p. 3). In addition, they state that the norms should not be used for children from families of lower socioeconomic status or other ethnic backgrounds and they encourage the development of local norms for such groups. Some work in this regard has been done by others (e.g., Miller, Salsgiver, & Murray, 1976). A Spanish version of the MCDI is also being prepared and the preliminary work is available from the test authors.

The 28-page manual reviews the development of the MCDI, provides graphs depicting the systematic increase in scores by age for each of the seven developmental scales and the general development scale, includes statements regarding reliability and validity, instructions for scoring and interpretation, and appendices that include the developmental sequence of items by age level for each of the developmental scales.

A MCDI inventory booklet and answer sheet are provided to the parent. The booklet's front cover contains instructions for responding. The items themselves are relatively brief, behavioral in nature, and require approximately an 8th-grade level of reading comprehension for reliable completion. A casette tape containing the items and directions for completing the MCDI is available. The items are listed in random order, and are not grouped by scale or by developmental level.

The answer sheet requires the parent to indicate the items that describe the child's behavior by marking yes or no in the appropriate column of circles on the answer sheet. There are additional spaces for the child's name, sex, birthdate, date of completion of the form, an internal identification number, and a section requesting other information about the family. This includes education and occupation of each parent as well as the parents' description of any handicapping conditions carried by their child.

Nine transluscent plastic templates are included, one for each scale, and an infant-item template to be used with children 2 years of age or older patients functioning above that developmental level. The infant template is used to ensure that the child's mother has endorsed all of the infant items such as babbling, crawling, etc., which have been superceded by higher levels of functioning and which should be credited to persons functioning at a 2 year age level or above.

The profile sheets, on which responses are plotted after scoring, are printed on 8½" x 11" paper; there are separate forms for each sex. The profile (Figure 1) has the initial appearance of a bar graph. Chronological age in months or years and months is printed on the left side of the page beside the vertical axis. Lines on which to record the raw scores for each of the eight scales are printed along the bottom on the horizontal axis. The name of each scale is printed at the top of the form. The cumulative raw scores for each scale are printed vertically on each of the scales of the profile and correspond to the chronological ages printed on the vertical axis. After the raw scores for the 8 scales have been determined they are plotted by finding the appropriate raw score value on the column of numbers representing the range of scores for that scale. These points are subsequently connected by a line to yield a profile. A shaded band is printed on the profile form to indicate the age span for which each scale is considered reliable. Thus, clinicians are alerted immediately when scores fall outside this band of confidence and can be appropriately cautious in interpreting scores from those scales.

Figure 1.
Minnesota Child Development Inventory Profile

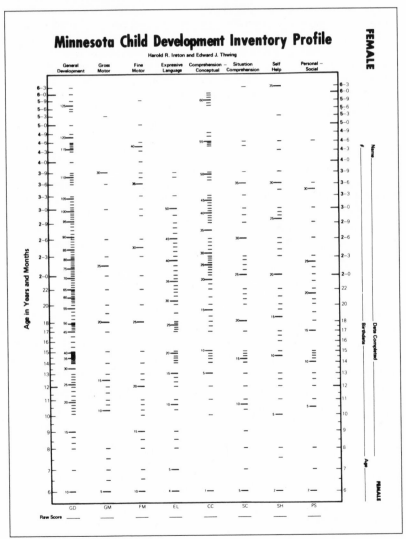

Practical Applications/Uses

The MCDI is appropriate for use by professionals concerned with the evaluation of preschool children between the ages of 1 and 6 years. This could include special educators, psychologists, pediatricians, or family practitioners, social workers, public health nurses, or others who are involved with screening young children for developmental problems.

Frequently, formal or direct assessment, even of the screening variety, can be marred by extraneous factors, such as fatigue, lack of suitable rapport, illness, or frank negativism to a degree that significantly compromises the results of the evaluation. The MCDI questionnaire is particularly helpful in such circumstances, requiring about 30-50 minutes for completion by the child's primary caretaker, usually mother, with scoring and profiling requiring an additional 5-10 minutes of clerical or secretarial time. Information obtained from parents is usually thought of as an integral part of assessment procedures with preschool children. While the MCDI should not be a substitute for parental interview, it provides an opportunity to obtain developmental information in a uniform and systematic manner allowing one to focus more closely on issues of concern during the interview time spent with parents. In addition, results of the MCDI can also be profitably used during subsequent follow-up sessions with parent or teacher when results of assessment are reviewed. The MCDI correlates well (Colligan, 1977; Gottfried, et al., 1983) with the results of formal psychometric assessment (e.g., Stanford-Binet Intelligence Scale, Catell Infant Intelligence Scale, Bayley Scale of Mental Development, McCarthy Scales of Children's Abilities). The use of the developmental age scores, based on information from the MCDI profile derived from parent observations, can be helpful in discussing learning or management expectations with the child's caretakers.

The answer sheet should be reviewed to ensure that all identifying information has been included. The child's sex, birthdate, and date the MCDI was completed are necessary for scoring. A profile form for the appropriate sex is selected and the spaces on the reverse side are used to calculate the child's age. The response section of the answer sheet should be scanned for omitted or unscorable items. The authors suggest that if three or more responses are not scorable, the results should be considered of questionable validity (Ireton & Thwing, 1974, p. 12). A horizontal red line should be drawn through the nonscorable responses and they should not be counted.

The plastic templates are placed over the top of the answer sheet, and after careful alignment the items marked on the template for that scale are counted as endorsed. The raw score for each scale is the number of items on that scale marked yes. For some scales there are a few items that are scored only for one sex, but the template includes a note to alert the scorer to such items. As each scale is scored the raw score for that scale is written on the answer sheet. After all of the scores have been obtained they are transcribed to the bottom of the profile form.

Computerized administration, scoring and interpretive services are available from the publisher.

After the score for each developmental scale has been recorded the scores are plotted on the scales and the points connected to produce the profile. The authors recommend that three lines of significance should then be drawn on the profile (Ireton & Thwing, 1974, p. 12). The first, a black line, is drawn across the profile at the point representing the child's current age in years and months. Next, a green line is placed at the age interval which is 20% below the child's current age. Finally, a red line is drawn across the profile at a point which is 30% below the child's age. A table providing these values for the ages for which the MCDI is appropriate is provided on the back of the profile.

Interpreting the results of the MCDI is relatively straightforward although some experience and knowledge of psychological assessment is required if information from the profile is to be integrated with the results of additional psychometric data. First, interpretation of severity or amount of delay is based on the degree to which the score on any given scale falls below age expectations. Second, the number of scales indicating developmental delay is noted. Finally, scores are inspected to determine whether or not they fall within the shaded band of reliability for that scale.

The General Developmental Scale, because it is the longest and most reliable, is the first to be evaluated. One then proceeds across the profile to see if there are patterns of strengths or weaknesses present among the other scales. For example, a language disabled or hearing-impaired child may have satisfactory scores in gross and fine motor functioning but be significantly weak in expressive language and conceptual comprehension (receptive language). Scores falling near the 20% below-age line are described in the manual as only suggestive of a delay, whereas those between the 20-30% line indicate a borderline but significant delay and those below the 30% line suggest apparent developmental retardation.

The authors note that scores which fall above age level should be interpreted conservatively as their experience with the normative sample suggested that they could reliably be viewed as signs of accelerated development (Ireton & Thwing, 1974, p. 17).

Technical Aspects

The validity of each scale is based upon the power of mean cumulative scores to discriminate among children of different age groups. Such discrimination among different age groups requires increases in mean score with increases in age. Graphs for each scale providing mean score by age and sex are provided as evidence for validity. Inspection of these curves indicates that there is considerable variability in the age range for which valid and reliable interpretation can be made. A table reporting the incidence of below-age performance (20-30% and > 30% below chronologic age) is also provided for Ss in the normative group.

Internal consistency of each scale was determined by measures of split-half reliability; in the following discussion range and median reliability is reported for the usable age range of each MCDI scale.

To summarize the information provided in the manual, the longest of the eight scales, General Development, appears to be a satisfactorily valid age-discriminating measure of overall development from ages 1 through 6 years (reliability range = .87-.93; median = .90). The Gross Motor scale has items sampling the first three years very satisfactorily, but there are only six items beyond age 3. This limitation is reflected in the shaded band, which the test authors have provided on the profile sheet (reliability range = .65-.94; median = .77). Coordination skills on the Fine Motor scale are well sampled up to age 2 and also from years 4 to 5, but caution should be used in interpreting scores between the ages of 2 and 4 where a relative plateau is encountered (reliability range = .40-.88; median = .71). The expressive language scale appears to be satisfactory for the first 3 years but there are only four additional items above this age (reliability range = .75-.92; median = .88). The Comprehension-Conceptual scale (receptive language) appears to be valid from 1 through 6 years (reliability range = .79-.93; median = .89). The Situation Comprehension scale is the least reliable of the eight scales but samples the first 3 years of life very satisfactorily (reliability range = .59-.80; median = .68). The Self-Help scale appears to be valid for ages 1 to 5 (reliability range = .68-.84; median = .78). The Personal-Social scale is satisfactory for the first 3 years, but has only four items above that point (reliability range = .55-.86; median = .80).

Critique

Speaking as a clinician and researcher, I am enthusiastic about the value of the MCDI in assessing young children.

The questionnaire and answer sheet are not bulky and can be sent through the mail to the child's caretaker for completion and either returned for scoring in advance or at the time of the child's appointment. The manual is brief but thorough in its treatment of all practical and technical aspects of the MCDI. Most clinicians would agree that an interview with the primary caretaker of the preschool child is an absolute necessity for thorough evaluation, supplementing formal psychometric data, observations of nursery or preschool teacher, pediatrician, or other medical specialist. Use of the MCDI can shorten the preliminary interview allowing the clinician to focus more specifically on areas of parental or clinician concern. We have found the MCDI to be well calibrated for the types of clinical referrals received in our center and it has been particularly useful when meeting with parents to review the results of their child's assessment, especially if they have observed the evaluation session. The pattern of strengths and weaknesses noted on the developmental scales of the profile are very understandable to parents. The profile of information also lends itself well to integration with other data. In addition we have found a very high correlation between the score from the General Developmental scale and the test age earned on the Bayley, Catell, or Binet.

Although the authors are appropriately cautious in pointing out the limits of utility for each of the scales, we have found that nearly all are usable and interpretable above the shaded band of confidence, provided that other information is known about the child. This advantage would not be present if the MCDI were being used alone as a screening instrument. In addition, two recently developed supplemental scales (knowledge of letters, numbers) were found useful in the assessment of kindergarten readiness (Colligan, 1976, 1981). Subsequently, this research was incorporated into the Minnesota Preschool Inventory, a questionnaire designed specifically to assess kindergarten readiness.

In addition to the Minnesota Preschool Inventory, the MCDI has two other companion instruments, the Preschool Development Inventory (a 60-item questionnaire for screening 3-5½ year olds) and the Minnesota Infant Development Inventory (a 75-item booklet for infants up to age 15 months).

The authors also caution users regarding the validity of the MCDI when more than three items are left blank. We have found, however, that inspection to determine the nature of the items that have been omitted may allow them to be understood and fairly scored by the examiner. This procedure requires some additional knowledge of the child's functioning, of such as that available from teacher observation or medical record. Typically, in our setting these items have been left blank because of an apparent lack of opportunity for the child's caretaker to observe that aspect of the child's behavior. Further information usually indicates that most blank items should be scored in the negative direction, a finding noted by others as well (Sturner et al., 1982).

Although the authors indicate the MCDI should not be used with children having demographic parameters different from the normative group, such a statement seems excessively conservative. Rather, I would suggest the development of local cutoff points or local norms; some work in this regard has already been done with a sample of Appalachian children (available from the publisher).

While I am supportive of the MCDI and encourage its use, some caveats are also in order. The directions to the child's caretaker on the front of the MCDI questionnaire are excessively long. Usually three or four sentences paraphrasing the intent of these directions is sufficient for the parent to begin. There is an insufficient number of items at the upper-age levels of most of the scales, an addition that would considerably enhance the usefulness of the MCDI. The MCDI is not appropriate for infants or toddlers under 12-15 months of age; in such circumstance the parent questionnaire of choice would be the Kent Infant Development Scale.

In summary, the MCDI is a well constructed and well standardized parent-report questionnaire which should be part of every child clinician's assessment armamentarium. It is appropriately used with children aged 1 to 6 years or with older persons functioning in that range. Reliability and validity are very satisfactory.

References

This list includes text citations as well as suggested additional reading, illustrating the type of clinical and research applications in which the MCDI has been found useful.

Colligan, R. C. (1976). Prediction of kindergarten reading success from preschool reports of parents. *Psychology in Schools, 13,* 304-308.

Colligan, R. C. (1977). The Minnesota Child Development Inventory as an aid in the assessment of developmental disability. *Journal of Clinical Psychology, 33,* 162-163.

Colligan, R. C. (1981). Prediction of reading difficulty from parental preschool report: A 3-year followup. *Learning Disability Quarterly, 4,* 31-37.

Dean, R. S., & Steffen, J. E. (1984). Direct and indirect pediatric screening measures. *Journal of Pediatric Psychology, 9*(1), 65-77.

Eisert, D. C., Spector, S., Shankaran, S. et al. (1980). Mothers' reports of their low birth weight infants subsequent development in the Minnesota Child Development Inventory. *Journal of Pediatric Psychology, 5*(4), 353-364.

Garrity, L. I., & Servos, A. B. (1978). Comparison of measures of adaptive behaviors in preschool children. *Journal of Consulting and Clinical Psychology, 46*(2), 288-293.

Gottfried, A. W., Guerin, D., Spencer, J. E., & Meyer, C. (1983). Concurrent validity of the Minnesota Child Development Inventory in a nonclinical sample. *Journal of Consulting and Clinical Psychology, 51*(4), 643-644.

Gottfried, A. W., Guerin, D., Spencer, J. E., & Meyer, C. (1984). Validity of Minnesota Child Development Inventory in screening young children's developmental status. *Journal of Pediatric Psychology, 9*, 219-230.

Ireton, H., & Thwing, E. (1974). *Manual for the Minnesota Child Development Inventory.* Minneapolis: Behavior Science Systems, Inc.

Lichtenstein, R., & Ireton, H. (1984). *Preschool screening: Early identification of school problems.* New York: Grune & Stratton.

Miller, B., Salsgiver, J., & Murray, K. (1976, August). *The development of rural Appalachian norms for the Minnesota Child Development Inventory.* Paper presented at the annual meeting of the American Psychological Association, Washington, DC.

Sturner, R. A., Funk, S. G., Thomas, P. D., & Green, J. A. (1982). An adaptation of the Minnesota Child Development Inventory for preschool developmental screening. *Journal of Pediatric Psychology, 7*(3), 295-307.

Ullman, D. G., & Kausch, D. F. (1979). Early identification of developmental strengths and weaknesses in preschool children. *Exceptional Children, 46*(1), 8-13.

Philip G. Benson, Ph.D.
Assistant Professor of Psychology, Auburn University, Auburn, Alabama.

MINNESOTA IMPORTANCE QUESTIONNAIRE

Work Adjustment Project. Minneapolis, Minnesota: Vocational Psychology Research, University of Minnesota.

Introduction

The Minnesota Importance Questionnaire (MIQ) was developed to measure an individual's vocational needs and values. Essentially, the authors of the MIQ suggest that adjustment to work involves satisfactoriness (i.e., the ability of the worker to perform the job adequately) and satisfaction (i.e., the worker's feeling of reward resulting from job performance). Within this framework, the MIQ measures those aspects of work that are especially salient reinforcers for an individual; by matching such needs with the reinforcers found in an occupation, a better match of worker and job will result.

Development of the MIQ has taken place over a number of decades and has involved the input of a number of researchers as part of the Work Adjustment Project conducted at the University of Minnesota. Various parts of the project can be identified with either the Department of Psychology or the Industrial Relations Center at the university. The following individuals have been especially notable in their contributions to the MIQ and the Work Adjustment Project:

Rene V. Dawis: Dr. Dawis received his Ph.D. in vocational psychology from the University of Minnesota in 1956. Since that time, he has been on the faculty at the university, first in the Industrial Relations Center and then, since 1968, in the department of psychology. He is the director of both the Work Adjustment Project and the university's Counseling Psychology Graduate Program.

George W. England: Dr. England received his Ph.D. in industrial/organizational psychology from the University of Minnesota in 1968. He served on the faculty of the university from 1956 until 1979, when he became director of the Center for Economics and Management at the University of Oklahoma.

Lloyd H. Lofquist: Dr. Lofquist received his Ph.D. in general psychology from the University of Minnesota in 1955, and has been a faculty member of the psychology department there since 1956. He currently serves as the chair of the department.

David J. Weiss: Dr. Weiss received his Ph.D. in counseling psychology from the University of Minnesota in 1963. Since that time he has remained on the faculty, specializing in measurement and psychometrics. Dr. Weiss is the editor of the journal *Applied Psychological Measurement.*

Numerous other individuals, however, have been involved in various aspects of this project. The following list, while not necessarily all inclusive, reflects the broad involvement of many individuals in the development of the MIQ and in the Work Adjustment Project: Fred H. Borgen, Fanny M. Cheung, Kenneth Doyle, Raina E. Eberly, Brian E. Engdahl, Peter L. Flint, Rosemary T. Fruehling, Evan G. Gay, Darwin D. Hendel, George A. Henley, Charles C. Humphrey, Cynthia Marsh, Stuart D. Rosen, James B. Rounds, Jr., Deborah J. Seaburg, Elaine B. Sloan, Kenneth D. Taylor, Howard E. A. Tinsley, and Patricia Martin Woolf.

The Work Adjustment Project first identified the lack of a proper, integrative theory of work adjustment and then developed such a theory. First published in 1964 (Dawis, England, & Lofquist), the theory has since been revised or extended in 1968 (Dawis, Lofquist, & Weiss) and 1969 (Lofquist & Dawis). Additional changes have been incorporated in journal articles and technical reports, and recently an updated review of the theory has been published (Dawis & Lofquist, 1984).

The researchers in the Work Adjustment Project first generated a 48-item questionnaire with 12 scales to measure work values. This form was called the N-Factors Questionnaire, but it suffered from insufficient reliability, insufficient variability of scores, and failure to tap certain dimensions of work adjustment. For these reasons, the MIQ was developed, although the N-Factors Questionnaire was the basis of later developments.

The first form of the MIQ consisted of 20 five-item scales, utilizing a Likert format. However, scale scores were still both skewed and intercorrelated, and thus the decision was made to adapt the measure to a pair-comparison format.

The first pair-comparison form of the MIQ was released in 1965. For each of the 20 dimensions of the MIQ, the item with the strongest correlation with the scale score was selected as typifying the work value measured. These 20 items were paired in all possible combinations (190 pairs), and then paired again in reverse sequence. Thus, the 1965 form consisted of 380 pairs of items. This form of the MIQ showed no loss of scale reliabilities (range of .73 to .94), but did result in lower scale intercorrelations and increased variability of scale scores. The altered scale intercorrelations produced a somewhat changed factor structure from the Likert-format MIQ. However, the 1965 revision did have two important drawbacks: 1) it possessed ordinal scale properties, making comparisons across time or individuals difficult; and 2) it had an administration time of about one hour, which was felt to be excessive. Thus, another revision was made in 1967.

To improve anchoring of responses, the 1967 revision of the MIQ added 20 absolute judgments of work value importance. On the basis of responses to these 20 items, each individual's responses were scaled to a "zero point," which gave a basis for comparisons across individuals or across scales within individuals.

Secondly, the 1967 revision was substantially shortened; the 380 pairs were reduced by half to 190 pairs. To assess consistency of responses, the 1967 revision relied on measures of triadic inconsistency, essentially a logical assessment of the reasonableness of a set of responses. A circular triad occurs when an individual chooses one work value as more important than a second value, chooses the second value as more important than a third value, but then chooses the third value as more important than the first. In a pair-comparison procedure, such a pattern of responses is considered an indication of response error or unreliability. Essentially, test takers who commit large numbers of such intransitivity errors are noted in the scoring of the MIQ and results for such individuals are assumed invalid. For more detail on this issue, refer to Hendel and Weiss (1970).

In 1975, a new "edition" (as opposed to "revision") of the MIQ was released. The technical manual (Gay, Weiss, Hendel, Dawis, & Lofquist, 1971), however, predates the latest edition, and thus changes are difficult for the casual user to determine. Basically, the current edition differs only in the removal of sexist language from several items. Clearly, the change is worthwhile, but supporting material should clarify the purpose of the 1975 changes. The changes are in fact quite minor and likely do not have an impact on the psychometric properties of the MIQ.

As noted previously, the MIQ can be used in either of two forms (paired or ranked). In either form, the questionnaire assesses the importance of the following 20 work needs:

Ability Utilization: the use of self-perceived skills and talents on the job.

Achievement: the pride that results from the accomplishment of productive tasks.

Activity: the requirement of some tasks that the individual maintain a fairly constant high level of energy.

Advancement: the opportunity for advancement through recognition of excellence in work-related tasks.

Authority: the opportunity to decide work methods and impose those decisions on other workers (not to be confused with authority over non-employees, as in law enforcement).

Company Policies and Practices: a job environment that has explicit, definitive guidelines, which are consistently practiced.

Compensation: the performance of tasks that provide compensation based on quantity and quality of work, paid equitably in comparison to other workers performing similar tasks.

Co-workers: the presence of other workers who are friendly and interested in positive interpersonal relationships.

Creativity: the opportunity to conceive and perform innovative tasks independently.

Independence: an environment in which one can work alone.

Moral Values: the performance of tasks that neither conflict with one's personal moral standards nor involve wrong doing.

Recognition: an environment in which rewards are given for exceptional personal job performance.

Responsibility: the performance of tasks that allow one to be autonomous and personally accountable.

Security: an environment that allows one to expect continuing employment and compensation.

Social Service: the perception that job performance will lead to benefits for the welfare of others.

Social Status: the performance of tasks that result in respect and social esteem from others.

Supervision—Human Relations: a job environment in which supervisors create and maintain mutual respect and personal investment among individuals in the workplace.

Supervision—Technical: a job environment in which supervisors are competent and effective.

Variety: the performance of tasks that are characterized by a range of possible activities.

Working Conditions: a job environment that is characterized by pleasant physical conditions.

In addition, factor analyses have been done, resulting in the reduction of the 20 scales into six underlying dimensions. These underlying values, and their component subscales, are as follows: 1) Achievement (Ability Utilization, Achievement); 2) Comfort Value (Activity, Independence, Variety, Compensation, Security, Working Conditions); 3) Status Value (Advancement, Recognition, Authority, Social Status); 4) Altruism Value (Co-workers, Social Service, Moral Values); 5) Safety Value (Company Policies and Practices, Supervision—Human Relations, Supervision—Technical); and 6) Autonomy Value (Creativity, Responsibility). According to the test manual (Rounds, Henly, Dawis, Lofquist, & Weiss, (1981), these dimensions can be described in psychological terms as values or in terms of the environmental reinforcement systems that relate to the worker's values.

The paired form requires the examinee to indicate which of two job characteristics is more important to him or her in an idealized job. In addition, each of the 20 job characteristics is rated on a dichotomous, absolute scale of importance ("Yes" or "No") in an idealized job.

The ranked form consists of 21 groups of five work value statements. Each group ("item") requires the test taker to rank order the importance of the five values included. Twenty-one additional items are included at the end of the ranked form and are dichotomously rated in terms of their importance in an idealized job. The addition of one item more than the paired form is necessary for the use of a multiple-rank-order format.

For either form of the MIQ, test booklets are reusable. Answer sheets are available from the publisher and are the only part consumed in testing. While hand-scoring is possible, it is extremely time-consuming, and thus the machine-scoring available from the publisher is recommended.

The MIQ is untimed and self-administered, which requires a minimum of input from the examiner (e.g., ensuring that instructions are clear, that examinees are responding appropriately, etc.). Typically, the paired form requires 30-40 minutes to complete, in contrast to approximately 20 minutes for the ranked form.

The MIQ is generally appropriate for use with adult populations, although the technical manual (Gay et al., 1971) reports that readability of the MIQ is at the fifth-grade level. Given the nature of the questions asked and the potential use of the MIQ in career counseling, it is unlikely that the test would ever be given to examinees younger than high-school age. The test manual (Rounds et al., 1981) gives norms for males and females aged 18-70 years, in three groups (18-25, 26-45, and 46-70), suggesting that the developers of the MIQ view it as appropriate for all adult age groups.

Each test taker responds directly onto a computer-scorable answer sheet; two forms exist, corresponding to the two forms of the MIQ. When scored by the publisher, the result is a profile of scores across each of the 20 MIQ needs.

The MIQ profile begins with the examinee's name, date of testing, and a logically consistent triad (LCT) score. If the LCT score indicates substantial response inconsistency, the MIQ is not scored and a note of the reason why is printed. When the LCT score is sufficiently questionable to void an administration of the MIQ, a report is given of LCT percentages for each of the 20 need scales.

If responses are sufficiently consistent, the report continues with a listing of the 20 needs, grouped into six values, and the scaled scores for each need and each value are then plotted (i.e., 26 scores). The second page of the report includes 90 occupations grouped into six clusters and an index of the degree of match between the examinee and the occupation. This match is based on the Occupational Reinforcer Pattern (ORP) for each occupation; ORPs are discussed in greater detail later in this review. Finally, the report gives a prediction of whether the examinee would be satisfied, likely satisfied, or not satisfied in each of the 90 occupations.

Practical Applications/Uses

According to the manual (Rounds et al., 1981), the MIQ can be used to advantage in three areas; these include vocational counseling, career planning, and job placement. As a counseling tool, the MIQ can help an individual identify his or her particularly salient psychological needs as manifested in work settings. By matching work environments with such needs, greater satisfaction should result for the counselee.

In career planning, the MIQ can identify the types of occupations that have reinforcer systems especially congruent with the examinee's needs. This is done largely by comparing the individual's need profile with the reinforcers typically found in selected occupations. These Occupational Reinforcer Patterns (ORPs) have been described for 148 benchmark occupations (Borgen, Weiss, Tinsley, Dawis, & Lofquist, 1972; Rosen, Hendel, Weiss, Dawis, & Lofquist, 1972), and additional ORPs are reportedly being developed.

As a job placement test, the MIQ is recommended as a means of maintaining employees' job satisfaction. It is suggested (Rounds et al., 1981, p. 3) that this should maximize productivity and minimize turnover, absenteeism, tardiness, accidents, and injuries.

The primary purpose of the MIQ appears more theoretical than practical. As an integral part of the theory of work adjustment, the MIQ is one of several key measures developed by the Work Adjustment Project. Others include the Minnesota Job Description Questionnaire, the Minnesota Satisfaction Questionnaire, and the Minnesota Satisfactoriness Scales.

It is likely that the clearest applications of the MIQ are to be found in vocational psychology and rehabilitation, especially in counseling individuals regarding their future work plans. The test could be used with individuals who are entering the workplace for the first time (i.e., new high school graduates) or with individuals who are of necessity or choice changing careers/occupations later in life (e.g., the vocationally disabled). Other applications, and research uses, are likely found in such diverse fields as industrial/organizational psychology, industrial sociology, industrial relations, and business management.

The MIQ has largely been administered to working adults. While designed as a paper-and-pencil test, it seems that the MIQ could be individually administered to handicapped examinees (e.g., the visually impaired or those unable to write responses on answer sheets). Such adaptation should not hamper the validity of the test and would extend its application, especially in vocational rehabilitation.

Many administrative details have already been discussed, but a few issues warrant special comment. Qualifications for administering the MIQ include "a thorough grasp of the technical nature of the instrument and a competence in reading and interpreting research studies on the MIQ" (Gay et al., 1971, p. vii). In general, a doctorate in psychology, educational measurement, or a related field seems appropriate, although the test manual (Rounds et al., 1981, p. 9) suggests that a master's degree may be sufficient.

The MIQ should be thought of as machine-scored only. While hand-scoring is possible and instructions are given to do so, the time required would be excessive.

Scoring is objective and results can be interpreted in a mechanical fashion. However, in counseling and rehabilitation use it is likely that the MIQ would be given in conjunction with other clinical assessment methods. Such interpretation requires a clear understanding of the MIQ, as well as a general background in psychometrics and assessment.

Technical Aspects

The clearest single review of MIQ reliability and validity studies can be found in the technical manual (Gay et al., 1971). Reliability data are presented in terms of the internal consistency of scales, the temporal stability of scales, and the temporal stability of profiles. Given that two forms of the MIQ exist (paired and ranked forms), information regarding alternate-form reliability would be useful; however, such data are not presented in either the test manual (Rounds et al., 1981) or the technical manual (Gay et al., 1971).

Internal consistency reliability is reported in the form of Hoyt reliability coefficients (Hendel & Weiss, 1970). In nine samples (Ns ranging from 27 to 283, with a median of 73) and across 20 scales (i.e., 180 correlations), the range of values was from .30 to .95; within each of the nine samples the median reliability was determined, and these medians ranged from .77 to .81. The technical manual does not give detailed reliability information for each individual scale, but does conclude that internal consistency is acceptably high.

Scale stability was assessed through test-retest correlations, ranging from immediate to ten-month intervals (Hendel & Weiss, 1970). The same groups were used as for the internal consistency results cited previously and the correlations obtained ranged from .19 (at nine months) to .93 (immediate). Medians ranged from .48 (six months) to .89 (immediate). Again, the technical manual fails to list reliability data for each of the 20 scales.

Hendel and Weiss (1970) also reported profile stability coefficients, as summarized in the technical manual. The reported correlations ranged from −.44 to .98; medians ranged from .70 to .95. Again, intervals ranged from immediate retest to ten months, and the same raw data were utilized as in the previously discussed reliability reports.

Finally, Hendel and Weiss (1970) analyzed MIQ stability for examinees with high and low total circular triad (TCT) scores. In general, they found that highly consistent individuals had greater test-retest reliabilities, indicating the usefulness of triadic inconsistency as a reliability measure for the MIQ.

The technical manual (Gay et al., 1971) summarizes the validity data for the MIQ in three ways. First, structural validity (i.e., content and discriminant validity) is reported. Second, indirect validity evidence for the pre-1967 form of the MIQ is reported. Finally, indirect evidence of validity is reported for the 1967 edition of the MIQ.

Based on factor-analytic data, Gay et al. (1971) argue that the MIQ subscales are sufficiently distinct to be treated as separate dimensions. In addition, the correlations between the MIQ and abilities measures (viz., the General Aptitude Test Battery) are uniformly low, while correlations with the Strong Vocational Interest Blank are moderately strong. The technical manual suggests that this supports the convergent and discriminant validity of the MIQ, albeit this alone is not sufficient evidence of validity.

Using the Likert (i.e., pre-1967) form of the MIQ, studies by the MIQ's authors show group differentiation between disabled and non-disabled workers, white collar workers and pre-employment college students, and among various occupational groupings. In each case, observed differences were consistent with the theory of work adjustment. In addition, a number of experimental hypotheses were confirmed with the Likert-format MIQ (e.g., satisfaction scores are more variable for individuals high in related needs than for those individuals low in related needs, suggesting that needs do in fact moderate worker reactions to job characteristics). Considering all of the results summarized by Gay et al. (1971), it is reasonable to conclude that the early MIQ was indeed at least a minimally valid measure of work-related needs.

A number of validity studies are reported for the 1967 edition (Gay et al., 1971), and in general validity is again supported. The technical manual, however, only reports data for concurrent validation designs, although other, later studies do support the predictive usefulness of the MIQ (e.g., Stulman & Dawis, 1976).

Data are presented indicating that all 20 MIQ scales discriminate among nine occupational groupings; while some scales differentiate more strongly than others (e.g., Supervision—Human Relations is most significant, while Co-workers and Ability Utilization are least significant), in fact all scales were statistically significant.

In addition, demographic variables were compared across the 20 MIQ scales and the TCT score within the four largest subsets of respondents (Ns = 1,897; 1,621; 578; and 317). To avoid inclusion of spurious relationships, only those variables that replicated in at least one other group (i.e., significance for two or more of the four comparisons) were interpreted as meaningful. Using this procedure, sex was found related to 15 MIQ scales and the TCT score, age was related to 11 MIQ scales, education was related to seven scales and the TCT score, marital status was related to three MIQ scales, and tenure was related to one MIQ scale. Gay et al. (1971) suggest these differences are consistent with expectations, and thus support the validity of the MIQ by showing its ability to differentiate among meaningful groups of respondents.

An important key to understanding the MIQ is the extensive use of Occupational Reinforcer Patterns (ORPs) in its interpretation (Borgen et al., 1972; Rosen et al., 1972). To develop ORPs, the researchers of the Work Adjustment Project developed the Minnesota Job Description Questionnaire (MJDQ). The MJDQ parallels the ranked form of the MIQ; however, instead of responding in terms of personal needs, individuals must rate the relative presence or absence of the reinforcer in a given job. To date, Borgen et al. and Rosen et al. report ORPs for a total of 148 different occupations, although one stated intent of the Work Adjustment Project is to continually develop more ORPs.

To further substantiate the validity of the MIQ, data are presented to compare obtained profiles to ORPs for four occupational groupings (Gay et al., 1971). The rank-order correlations of the 20 values in the MIQ and the ORPs were found to be .48 (Retail Trade Worker, Sample I), .58 (Retail Trade Worker, Sample II), .60 (Vocational Rehabilitation Counselor), and .62 (High School Counselor). Such data suggest some degree of validity for the MIQ.

Stulman and Dawis (1976) administered the MIQ to 284 college students and selected 68 individuals based on their Creativity and Independence scale scores. They then constructed tasks that were high or low in creativity and independence, and found that preferences for tasks were related to measured MIQ needs. Such results further support at least these two scales of the MIQ.

Other studies have examined job satisfaction as a result of the correspondence between MIQ scores and reinforcers available from a job. According to the theory, such correspondence should lead to greater satisfaction. Again, support for such a proposition has been found (e.g., Elizur & Tziner, 1977).

Overall, validity data for the MIQ appears to be adequate. After several decades of systematic research, the MIQ has been shown to have reasonable empirical support.

Critique

In an early review of the MIQ, Lake, Miles and Earle (1973) suggested the MIQ "should not be used for individual counseling or prediction" (p. 168). However, this assessment is based on the Likert-format MIQ and the relative paucity of early validation studies. Given more recent work on the MIQ, it now seems more reasonable to use it in application. Certainly, further research is warranted.

The MIQ is a reasonable measure of work values and needs; however, a few criticisms can in fact be raised. First, casual interpretation of scale names is potentially misleading. Certainly, users of any test should always read the supporting material for that test, but several MIQ dimensions are not what many would guess from scale titles. For example, Authority refers to a worker's relationship to other workers and not to the nature of the work; a police officer thus has relatively little authority in work reinforcers. Likewise, Compensation refers to the extent to which pay is directly contingent on performance and not the absolute level of pay available on a job; an entrepreneur who earns substantial income but is highly dependent on rather unpredictable sales demand would have a job low on this reinforcer. Again, such information is clearly pointed out in the supporting material, but casual use of the MIQ should be discouraged.

It is not clear that ORPs, as developed from MJDQ responses, are as strongly related to occupational groupings as the MIQ manuals would have one believe.

Most ORPs are based on a minimum of 20 responses by supervisors and/or job incumbents (usually supervisors), although in some cases as many as 142 raters are used; a large proportion use 50 or fewer raters. With such small samples, it is not clear that the ORPs have fairly summarized an entire occupational grouping. This problem is exacerbated by the likelihood that, for some scales, organizational variations can lead to wide divergence within an occupation. For example, the literature on salary administration makes it clear that the extent to which pay is tied to performance can vary tremendously between organizations, even within a single occupational group. It would be good practice for users of the MIQ to develop similar profiles for known local organizations and not to rely blindly on the published ORPs.

ORPs also are likely to change over time. For example, the published ORP for a Certified Public Accountant is based on an all-male sample of raters, but many women have entered this profession in recent years. Caution in interpretation is again recommended.

The technical manual for the MIQ should be thoroughly updated. At present, no single source gives a detailed and comprehensive treatment of the MIQ, which makes use difficult. The 1981 test manual lacks the necessary technical detail to fill this void.

Finally, the MIQ, for good or ill, is clearly tied to a specific theoretical orientation. While generally to be commended, such theoretical ties lead to questionable scale utility if the supporting framework is gradually rejected. At least one reviewer of the most recent statement of the theory has suggested that it is dated, lacking an integration with recent work in the area of career development (Saxberg, 1984).

Overall, the MIQ is a very good measure of work needs and values. Given the above caveats, its use is recommended.

References

This list contains text citations as well as suggested additional reading.

Betz, E. (1969). Need-reinforcer correspondence as a predictor of job satisfaction. *Personnel and Guidance Journal, 47,* 878-883.

Borgen, F. H., Weiss, D. J., Tinsley, H. E. A., Dawis, R. V., & Lofquist, L. H. (1972). *Occupational reinforcer patterns: I.* Minneapolis, MN: Vocational Psychology Research, University of Minnesota.

Dawis, R. V., England, G. W., & Lofquist, L. H. (1964). A theory of work adjustment. *Minnesota Studies in Vocational Rehabilitation, 15.*

Dawis, R. V., & Lofquist, L. H. (1976). Personality style and the process of work adjustment. *Journal of Counseling Psychology, 23,* 55-59.

Dawis, R. V., & Lofquist, L. H. (1978). A note on the dynamics of work adjustment. *Journal of Vocational Behavior, 12,* 76-79.

Dawis, R. V., & Lofquist, L. H. (1984). *A psychological theory of work adjustment: An individual-differences model and its applications.* Minneapolis: University of Minnesota Press.

Dawis, R. V., Lofquist, L. H., & Weiss, D. J. (1968). A theory of work adjustment (a revision). *Minnesota Studies in Vocational Rehabilitation, 23.*

Elizur, D., & Tziner, A. (1977). Vocational needs, job rewards, and satisfaction: A canonical analysis. *Journal of Vocational Behavior, 10,* 205-211.

England, G. W. (1967). Personal value systems of American managers. *Academy of Management Journal, 10,* 53-68.

England, G. W., & Lee, R. (1974). The relationship between managerial values and managerial success in the United States, Japan, India, and Australia. *Journal of Applied Psychology, 59,* 411-419.

Fisher, S. T., Weiss, D. J., & Dawis, R. V. (1968). A comparison of Likert and pair comparison techniques in multivariate attitude scaling. *Educational and Psychological Measurement, 28,* 81-94.

Gay, E. G., Weiss, D. J., Hendel, D. D., Dawis, R. V., & Lofquist, L. H. (1971). Manual for the Minnesota Importance Questionnaire. *Minnesota Studies in Vocational Rehabilitation, 28.*

Hendel, D. D., & Weiss, D. J. (1970). Individual inconsistency and reliability of measurement. *Educational and Psychological Measurement, 30,* 579-593.

Lake, D. G., Miles, M. B., & Earle, R. R., Jr. (1973). *Measuring human behavior: Tools for the assessment of social functioning.* New York: Teachers College Press, Columbia University.

Lofquist, L. H., & Dawis, R. V. (1969). *Adjustment to work.* New York: Appleton-Century-Crofts.

Lofquist, L. H., & Dawis, R. V. (1975). Vocational needs, work reinforcers, and job satisfaction. *Vocational Guidance Quarterly, 24,* 132-139.

Lofquist, L. H., & Dawis, R. V. (1978). Values as second-order needs in the theory of work adjustment. *Journal of Vocational Behavior, 12,* 12-19.

Rosen, S. D., Hendel, D. D., Weiss, D. J., Dawis, R. V., & Lofquist, L. H. (1972). *Occupational reinforcer patterns: II.* Minneapolis, MN: Vocational Psychology Research, University of Minnesota.

Rounds, J. B., Jr., Dawis, R. V., & Lofquist, L. H. (1979). Life history correlates of vocational needs for a female adult sample. *Journal of Counseling Psychology, 26,* 487--496.

Rounds, J. B., Jr., Henly, G. A., Dawis, R. V., Lofquist, L. H., & Weiss, D. J. (1981). *Manual for the Minnesota Importance Questionnaire: A measure of vocational needs and values.* Minneapolis, MN: Vocational Psychology Research, University of Minnesota.

Saxberg, B. O. (1984). [Review of R. V. Dawis & L. H. Lofquist, *A psychological theory of work adjustment: An individual-differences model and its applications.*] *Personnel Psychology, 37,* 756-758.

Shubsachs, A. P. W., Rounds, J. B., Jr., Dawis, R. V., & Lofquist, L. H. (1978). Perception of work reinforcer systems: Factor structure. *Journal of Vocational Behavior, 13,* 54-62.

Stulman, D. A., & Dawis, R. B. (1976). Experimental validation of two MIQ scales. *Journal of Vocational Behavior, 9,* 161-167.

Taylor, K. D., & Weiss, D. J. (1972). Prediction of individual job termination from measured job satisfaction and biographical data. *Journal of Vocational Behavior, 2,* 123-132.

Thorndike, R. M., Weiss, D. J., & Dawis, R. V. (1968). The canonical correlation of vocational interests and vocational needs. *Journal of Counseling Psychology, 15,* 101-106.

Thorndike, R. M., Weiss, D. J., & Dawis, R. V. (1968). Multivariate relationships between a measure of vocational interests and a measure of vocational needs. *Journal of Applied Psychology, 52,* 491-496.

Wiener, Y., & Klein, K. L. (1978). The relationship between vocational interests and job satisfaction: Reconciliation of divergent results. *Journal of Vocational Behavior, 13,* 298-304.

Paula Lee Woehlke, Ph.D.
Associate Professor of Educational Psychology, Southern Illinois University, Carbondale, Illinois.

MODIFIED VIGOTSKY CONCEPT FORMATION TEST

Paul L. Wang. Chicago, Illinois: Stoelting Company.

Introduction

The Modified Vigotsky Concept Formation Test, the 1984 revision of the Kasanin-Hanfmann Concept Formation Test (Vigotsky Test), is an individually administered test of problem-solving approach and ability to learn from errors. It consists of the presentation of 22 wooden blocks differing in width, height, shape, and color that are to be sorted according to four sets of instructions. These instructions involve problems graded in terms of difficulty and are administered twice: first for convergent thinking and then for divergent thinking. Although the original usage of the instrument was to determine concept formation ability in schizophrenics, the Kasanin-Hanfmann has recently been used to study the development of concept formation in children and to assess cognitive functioning in the elderly.

This test was first used in 1934 by the Russian psychologist Vygotsky in a study of concept formation ability in schizophrenics (Vygotsky, 1934); since that time, it has been used as a clinical instrument to study concept formation and attitudes in other groups as well. Kasanin and Hanfmann modified the method of administration in 1940, and the test has been used in that form for numerous studies. However, the Kasanin-Hanfmann format has been criticized for the lack of norms or ratings and for the need for standardization of administration. Thus, a revised version of the test that attempts to remedy these deficiencies was introduced in 1984. Paul L. Wang, a Canadian psychologist, modified the method of administration (based on tests of 300 subjects) so that problems are presented in sets graded according to difficulty, standardized feedback is provided to subjects, a coding system is available for analyzing a subject's approach to solving the problems, and divergent as well as convergent thinking can be studied (Wang, 1984). The basic apparatus of the test has remained the same (the 22 blocks in five colors, coded with four different nonsense labels and differing in shape, height, and width), but Wang has introduced a form that permits recording of exact subject responses.

As noted previously, continuing criticisms of the 1940 Kasanin-Hanfmann version of the test are its lack of standardization and norming. The test has been viewed consistently as a research or clinical tool. Its primary use has been with samples of schizophrenics, to study language development in normal and language-delayed children, and, more recently, to assess changes in concept formation in the aged.

491

The examiner's materials for the test consist of an instruction manual, examiner's manual, recording form, and a box of 22 wooden blocks. The blocks are five different colors (blue, green, orange, yellow, and white); six different shapes (square, triangle, circle, half-circle, quadrilateral, and hexagon); two heights (high and low); two widths (wide and narrow); and imprinted with one of four nonsense syllables (cev, lag, bik, and mur).

The examiner first asks the subject to select all of the "cev" blocks; because the categorization on which the nonsense names are based has to do with height and width rather than shape or color, the examiner's task is to provide cues and probe for the principle used by the subject in categorization. The same procedure is used in forming the "lag," "bik," and "mur" categories. The second part of the test involves divergent (rather than convergent) thinking, and the subject is presented with all 22 blocks and asked to find new ways to group them (i.e., by shape, height, width, curvature, volume, whether the block will roll or not, and number of sides).

Because the materials and tasks presented in the test are appropriate for all ages, the test has been used with subjects at all levels of language ability and cognitive functioning. Examples are provided in the instruction manual of the completed recording forms of ten subjects; these include two normal subjects, seven with brain damage in various areas, and one with Parkinson's disease. These subjects range in age from 21 to 63 years; studies reporting the performance of primary school children and the elderly have also been published.

The test consists of two subtests: the Convergent Thinking Test that is scored for total errors and perseveration errors, and the Divergent Thinking Test, on which points are assigned for each principle that is correctly identified. Subject responses are recorded on a six-page answer form that provides a separate page for each of the four categories in the Convergent Thinking Test, one page for Divergent Thinking Test performance, and a cover sheet that summarizes subject characteristics and test performance.

Practical Applications/Uses

There are two primary uses of this test. The first is as a clinical instrument to diagnose the difficulties experienced by patients with brain damage or psychiatric problems. This was the use for which the test was designed. The second use is to explore the development of concept formation and language throughout the lifespan of normal individuals. Thus, the test is appropriate in clinical settings and in research, but is not appropriate for mass screenings or group testing.

Because the purpose of the test is to assess concept formation and its expression through language, it has been used recently in the fields of language acquisition and speech and language pathology to explore the origins or various problems. Because of its obvious clinical uses, it is used primarily in individual assessment by physicians, psychologists, educational psychologists, and speech pathologists.

The test is appropriate for language-using subjects of all ages. It is not appropriate for subjects who cannot use either oral or written language because it would not be possible to determine the reasons for their responses. It also cannot be used with subjects who have severe visual deficits. Although originally designed for schizophrenics, the test is useful for assessing cognitive functioning in normal individuals as well as those with affective or physical problems other than schizophrenia.

The test should be presented in a quiet room where the blocks are spread out over a flat, neutral-colored surface and the subject is asked to perform the various convergent and divergent thinking tasks. The examiner should be an experienced psychologist, psychometrist, or other clinician who is comfortable with individual testing and skilled in probing for responses and interpreting nuances in behavior. Because it is an individual test, administration procedures are less rigid than those of a group test, but the instructions provided in the instruction manual and its three-page examiner manual should be sufficient for a skilled examiner to follow. As is usual with an individual test, the examiner is left free to explore subject responses if it is deemed necessary, and the time required to administer the test will depend on the examiner and examinee; however, it should not exceed an hour.

Methods of scoring differ for the Convergent Thinking Test and for the Divergent Thinking Test. For the former, the number of errors is counted as the number of incorrect blocks selected for each of the three trials in each set of blocks (cev, lag, bik, and mur); there is total possible error score of 72. In addition, perseveration errors are counted as three consecutive characteristics, which are erroneously selected within a block of trials or in transition from one block of trials to another. Examples of perseveration errors are provided in the scoring instructions to aid in their identification. In addition, the manual stresses the importance of the ten case samples provided in Appendix II in learning to score the Convergent Thinking Test correctly. As in the case of individual intelligence tests, practice is required before an examiner can confidently score this aspect of performance. Scoring of the Divergent Thinking Test is easier because it simply requires the examiner to ascertain which of the eight different principles for sorting the blocks have been used. Test scoring must be done by the examiner, preferably immediately following the test administration.

Substantial knowledge of language functioning, development, neurology, psychology, psychiatry, or other specialization is required to interpret test scores adequately. Although the revised (1984) scoring protocol yields numbers amenable to statistical analysis for groups of scores, this is not the primary purpose of the instrument. Identification of a subject as exhibiting characteristics of schizophrenia, Parkinson's disease, or other problems requires experience with such individuals and familiarity with their language and conceptual performance.

Technical Aspects

As has been noted in previous evaluations of the test, no data are available on its reliability; validity data concern its construct validity in terms of the theories of schizophrenia espoused by Vygotsky (1934) and later by Hanfmann and Kasanin (1942). Because it has been designed as a clinical instrument, its users generally have been content to rely on its apparent usefulness in the clinical setting.

Critique

Previous reviews of the 1940 Kasanin & Hanfmann revision (e.g., Zangwill, 1949; Kogin, 1953) indicate that although the test is useful as a clinical instrument because of the ingeniousness of the task and the insights it affords into the thinking processes of the subject, it is not adequate for more rigorous uses. In addition to problems with the original scoring method used, the lack of reliability data and paucity of information concerning validity are also noted. Although the most recent version of the test (Wang, 1984) is an attempt to provide a scoring system amenable to reliability and validity analyses, no data exist to date to indicate whether the attempt has been successful.

The 1984 version of the Concept Formation Test appears to be a moderately successful attempt to overcome the shortcomings of the previous two versions of the instrument, although relevant data are still lacking. The improved standardization of administration instructions and the added sections in the instruction manual pertaining to scoring and identification of perseveration errors, as well as the assigning of scores to test performance, should make it more useful for research. Perhaps the latest version will lead to attempts to assess the reliability of the instrument as well as its validity for uses other than the study of schizophrenics. However, the new version does not destroy the usefulness of the instrument as a clinical tool, for which it has long been praised. The insights that can be gained when the test is used clinically are perhaps its greatest strength; one would not like to see this feature destroyed in an attempt to gain it favor for traditional measurement uses.

References

Hanfmann, E., & Kasanin, J. (1942). Conceptual thinking in schizophrenia. *Nervous and Mental Disease Monographs 67.*

Kasanin, J., & Hanfmann, E. (1940). *Concept Formation Test.* Chicago: Stoelting Co.

Kogin, K. (1953). Concept Formation Test. In O. K. Buros (Ed.). *The fourth mental measurements yearbook* (p. 35). Highland Park, NJ: The Gryphon Press.

Vygotsky, L. (1934). Thought in schizophrenia. *Archives of Neurology and Psychiatry, 31,* 1063-1077.

Wang, P. L. (1984). *Modified Vygotsky Concept Formation Test.* Chicago: Stoelting Co.

Zangwill, O. L. (1949). Concept Formation Test. In O. K. Buros (Ed.), *The third mental measurements yearbook* (pp. 58-59). Highland Park, NJ: The Gryphon Press.

Lawrence Allen, Ph.D.

Professor and Chair, Department of Psychology, University of South Alabama, Mobile, Alabama.

MOONEY PROBLEM CHECK LIST

R. L. Mooney and L. V. Gordon. Cleveland, Ohio: The Psychological Corporation.

Introduction

The Mooney Problem Check List by R. L. Mooney was developed during the early 1940s to help students express their personal problems. The Problem Check List should not be viewed as a test, but rather as an instrument for enhancing communication between students or adults in a noneducational setting and counselors, teachers, or other professionals about the subjects' problems. The four forms of the Problem Check List are composed of lists of common problems, and subjects are asked to underline the problems that are of concern to them, circle ones of most concern, and write a summary of their chief problems in their own words. The Problem Check List also provides space for subjects to indicate if they would like to talk to someone about their problems. The four current forms of the Problem Check List are the Junior High School Form, the High School Form, the College Form, and the Adult Form. All four forms have a 1950 copyright date and are published by the Psychological Corporation.

Ross L. Mooney originally developed the Problem Check List because he wanted to systematize his methods of discovering the problems of young people. As an administrator and educational and psychological counselor, he felt a need for more efficient group methods of identifying problems. He developed the first published editions of the three educational forms in 1941 and 1942, and two other forms for "Students in Schools of Nursing" and for "Rural Youth" were published in 1945 and 1946.

The items for the pre-1950 editions of the forms were selected and developed from a master list of over 5,000 items from 1) experiences of the author as counselor and administrator, 2) analysis of case records and counseling interviews with school and college students, 3) review of the literature on student problems, 4) analysis of paragraphs written by 4,000 high school students describing their personal problems, 5) intensive analyses of expressed problems of 250 students in grades 7 through 12, and 6) review of 5,000 cards itemizing the "personal-educational" needs expressed by 950 students in grades 6, 9, and 12.

Selection and phrasing of the particular items used in the Problem Check List were based on the following criteria. The items were to be 1) in the language of the students, 2) short enough for rapid reading, 3) self-sufficient as individual phrases, 4) common enough to be checked frequently in large groups of students or serious enough to be important in an individual case, 5) graduated in

495

seriousness from relatively minor difficulties to major concerns, 6) vague enough in "touchy" spots to enable the student to check the item and still feel that he can hide his specific problems in later conferences if he chooses to do so, and 7) centered within the student's own personal orientation rather than in general social orientation.

An additional aim was to select items that would secure a naive, rapid "feeling" response from the student. Spontaneous rather than deliberate reaction was sought.

Using these criteria for the selection of items, judges assisted in the selection of items for the first edition of the College Form, which contained 370 items. This edition was administered and an analysis was made of the results obtained from 200 students of a small college, and a second edition of 320 items was prepared. This edition was then administered to students in remedial study classes and in mental hygiene courses at Ohio State University and to selected groups of students in other colleges. On the basis of an analysis of these results, a third edition containing 330 items was prepared and published in 1941 by the Ohio State University Press.

A similar procedure was used in developing the High School Form, with 370 items tried out on 200 students. On the basis of the results the number was reduced to 320 items in a second edition. This edition was then administered to 110 students in a rural school and to 237 students in a city school. On the basis of these results a third edition of 330 items was prepared and published in 1941 by the Ohio State University Press.

For the Junior High School Form, 225 items were first tried out on 684 pupils in four junior high schools in a large Ohio city. Of these students, 337 were girls and 347 were boys; 302 were in the seventh grade, 203 were in the eighth grade, and 179 were in the ninth grade. In addition, a modified form of 124 items was tried out with 650 fifth- and sixth-grade pupils in three school systems.

On the basis of these studies a third edition of 210 items was prepared, and after conferences with teachers and use in a school, more revisions were made so that a fourth edition was finally printed and published in 1942 by the Ohio State University Press. The use of forms at the fifth- and sixth-grade levels was practicable in the sense that the students could read and understand the items, but their attitude toward their problems was found to be so different from that of junior-high-school students that it is generally advisable not to use the lists below the seventh grade.

The 1950 revisions fo the three educational forms used the data from the preliminary editions and data from subsequent studies. Detailed analyses of responses of 1,200 college students were evaluated for use in the revision of the College Form, and responses of 12,522 students in grades 8-12 from 75 schools were analyzed for use in the revision of the High School Form. Revision of the Junior High School Forms used additional data from 3,854 students in 20 schools.

The Adult Form of the Problem Check List was developed principally by L. V. Gordon during the period he and Mooney were revising the educational forms. The Adult Form was developed for use with late adolescents and adults who are principally of nonstudent status. The items were developed from originally problem surveys, suggestions from experienced counselors, a review of adult problem literature, write-in statements made by married and employed students on the

College Form, and thousands of problem items accumulated in the development of the other forms of the check list series.

While developing and selecting the items for the Adult Form as well as for the educational forms, categories (i.e., problem areas) for the items were set up according to the following criteria: 1) The categories should cover the range of problems collected; 2) the number of items should be few enough for convenience in administration and summarization; 3) the areas should be pragmatic in pointing the data as much as possible in directions that would suggest practicable programs of action; and 4) the areas should present a homogeneity of problem content that would facilitate meaningful interpretation by the counselor.

Using these criteria, a first preliminary Adult Form was developed, consisting of 14 areas and 490 items. This preliminary form was submitted for critical appraisal to a group of experts in the field of adult counseling. From criticisms and suggestions made, items and areas were revised and a second preliminary form consisting of 12 areas and 420 items was developed. This form was put to actual survey use, and the present form constructed from an analysis of the data obtained.

Each form of the Problem Check List is printed on a six-page folder that is easy to mark by the subject and easy to summarize by the counselor or other professional. The Problem Check List is self-administering, and all the directions needed are on the cover page. The language is simple and can be readily understood by individuals of varying educational backgrounds. Usually about two-thirds of a group will finish the checking in 35 minutes and practically everyone will finish in 50 minutes. Instructions suggest, however, that individuals who are slower should be given an opportunity to finish because these persons might be the ones most deeply involved in their problems.

As mentioned earlier, while developing and selecting items for the various editions of the forms, categories for the items were also developed. The College and High School Forms have eleven categories. They are health and physical development (HPD); finances, living conditions, and employment (FCE); social and recreational activities (SRA); social-psychological relations (SPR); personal-psychological relations (PPR); courtship, sex, and marriage (CSM); home and family (HF); morals and religion (MR); adjustment to college (school) work (ACW); the future: vocational and educational (FVE); and curriculum and teaching procedure (CTP).

The Junior High School Form has seven categories. They are health and physical development (HPD); school (S); home and family (HF); money, work, the future (MWF); boy and girl relations (BG); relations to people in general (PG); and self-centered concerns (SC).

The Adult Form has nine categories. They are health (H); economic security (ES); self-improvement (SI); personality (P); home and family (HF); courtship (C); sex (S); religion (R); and occupation (O).

Practical Applications/Uses

The Problem Check List can serve as a valuable aid for counselors, teachers, psychologists, and other professionals who are interested in identifying and classifying the problems of individuals either in group or individual settings. The Problem Check List may be used as a counseling aid without assuming any single counseling technique. The data obtained from the check list are useful in counseling that is short and necessarily limited, in counseling that is deeper and more therapeutic, and in counseling with directive or nondirective orientation.

Mooney and Gordon (1950) state that several advantages will accrue from having the counselee complete the check list prior to the counseling situation itself:

1. The check list will prepare individuals for the interview by giving them an opportunity to review and summarize their own problems and to see the full range of personal matters that might be discussed with the counselor.
2. Time is saved by providing the counselor with a quick review of the variety of problems which are the expressed concern of the counselee.
3. The check list may be used to "break the ice." The problems marked may serve as a basis for initial discussion.
4. Counselors have a "green light" for discussion of the problems marked. They have reasonable certainty that little resistance will be encountered in bringing up these problems because the counselee has already indicated a willingness to admit them.
5. From the pattern of problems marked, the counselor may obtain some insight into the interrelationships among the counselee's problems.
6. The counselee may gain insight through filling out the check list.

It should be remembered that the Problem Check List is not a test and does not yield scores on traits or permit any direct statements about the adjustment status of the person who makes the responses. "Scoring" the check list is a simple process and is described fully in the manual. The checked problems are counted and summarized very easily because of the format of the check list and the arrangement of items.

According to the manual, when interpreting data from the check list, the interpreter should keep in mind that 1) the items marked by the subjects should be considered as symbols of their individual experiences and situations (their "problem world"), not the "problem world" itself; 2) Even though subjects mark the same problem or an identical pattern of problems, their problem world is not identical because of their diverse inclinations toward unique experiences; 3) Although some problems dealing with concrete situations may be marked only vaguely, others may be marked very clearly in reference to specifics; 4) problems marked are not of equal significance, with some indicating a more substantial blockage than others marked by the same subject; 5) a subject's problem could be considered "bad," "good," or "neutral" in one case and the opposite in another, depending on whether it signifies a point in progression toward growth or one of imbalance toward excessive frustration; 6) subjects who cannot recognize their problems or those who fear to express them may be in a worse situation than those who recognize or express them freely; and 7) an observer may see subjects' problems more clearly than they do themselves.

Additionally, because subjects check only those problems they are willing to acknowledge under the specific circumstances given in the check list they will limit their answers. They may be afraid the data will not be treated fairly, become confused by some distraction during the administration, not understand what they are to do with the check list, or misinterpret how the data are going to be used.

Although extensive education and training is not necessary to evaluate and interpret the Problem Check List results, it is important to realize that integration of all data about the counselee with check list data will give the best strategy for determining the direction that the counseling situation should most profitably take. The Problem Check List should be viewed as an aid to the counseling process and not as a substitute for gathering other important data about the counselee.

Technical Aspects

Reliability assessment is a problem for instruments like the Problem Check List, and the manual does not report any reliability coefficients for use of the instrument on an individual case basis. The manual states that internal consistency methods are inappropriate and that test-retest estimates are subject to error because of the rapid changes in the nature of the problems of individuals and in the way they perceive them. The authors do report reliability coefficients from two studies where data were used for survey purposes. The results of these studies appear to indicate considerable stability of pooled results for groups.

The manual states that if the Problem Check List had been developed as a personality test designed to predict definite patterns of behavior, the validation strategy would be to determine the extent to which the predicted behavior patterns corresponded with actual behavior as judged by other criteria. Because the Problem Check List is not a test and the "scores" obtained from the instrument only represent a count of the problems which individuals have identified as matters of concern to them, the manual emphasizes that a single over-all index of the validity of the Problem Check List would be meaningless.

Critique

Since its publication, the Problem Check List has been extensively researched with a number of studies attempting to validate the Problem Check list for use in specific settings. For example, several studies have attempted to use the Problem Check List as a predictor to differentiate college students who seek counseling from those who do not. (Doleys, 1964; Domino & DeGroote, 1978; Palladino & Domino, 1978; Tryon, 1983). Although such studies have some merit, this reviewer feels that users of the Problem Check List would do well to use the Problem Check List within the guidelines established in the manual.

In summary, the popularity and widespread use of the Problem Check List are well deserved. Counselors and other professionals can use the Problem Check List in the ways suggested by the authors with confidence.

References

Doleys, E. J. (1964). Differences between clients and non-clients on the Mooney Problem Check List. *Journal of College Student Personnel, 6*, 21-24.

Domino, G., & DeGroote, M. W. (1978). A comparison of counseling seekers and non-seekers on the Mooney Problem Check List. *Journal of College Student Personnel, 19,* 33-36.

Mooney, R. L., & Gordon, L. V. (1950). *The Mooney Problem Check List Manual.* New York: Psychological Corporation.

Palladino, J. J., & Domino, G. (1978). Differences between counseling center clients and non-clients on three measures. *Journal of College Student Personnel, 19,* 497-501.

Tryon, G. S. (1983, August). *Validity of a 42-item Mooney Problem Check List Scale for Counseling.* Paper presented at 91st annual convention of the American Psychological Association, Anaheim, CA. (ERIC Document Reproduction Service No. ED 237873).

Philip A. Vernon, Ph.D.
Assistant Professor of Psychology, The University of Western Ontario,
London, Canada.

MULTIDIMENSIONAL APTITUDE BATTERY

Douglas N. Jackson. Port Huron, Michigan: Research
Psychologists Press, Inc.

Introduction

The Multidimensional Aptitude Battery (MAB) is a newly developed, multiple-choice test of intelligence and mental abilities patterned quite closely after the Wechsler Adult Intelligence Scale-Revised (WAIS-R). Like the WAIS-R, the MAB consists of two subscales, Verbal and Performance, each comprising five subtests, and is scored to provide Verbal, Performance, and Full Scale IQ scores. It is designed to be used with adolescents and adults ranging in age from 16 to 74 years of age.

The author of the MAB, Douglas N. Jackson, has been involved with measurement, psychometrics, and test development for much of his career. In addition to the MAB, he has developed the Personality Research Form (Jackson, 1967), the Jackson Personality Inventory (1976), and the Jackson Vocational Interest Survey (1977), and has authored over 100 articles and book chapters on the subjects of personality assessment and psychometrics.

In the introductory chapter of the MAB manual, Jackson (1984) makes it clear that he admires the pioneering work of David Wechsler in the development of his series of intelligence tests. The most positive features of the Wechsler tests, according to Jackson, were their incorporation of a diversity of tasks, allowing an assessment of a wide variety of verbal and nonverbal abilities; their inclusion of items appropriate for persons of different ages; their recognition of the potential influence of certain personality characteristics and/or brain damage on intelligence test performance; their extremely careful and thorough standardization; the high quality of their psychometric properties; and their substantial construct and predictive validity, as assessed by large numbers of research studies.

A major drawback of the Wechsler scales, which provided the impetus for the development of the MAB, is that the former must be administered individually and that both administration and scoring must be conducted by a specially trained professional. Jackson (1984) recognizes that individual administration of an intelligence test may often provide additional valuable information to a clinician but argues that for the majority of persons for whom an estimate of intelligence is required, individual testing is costly, time-consuming, and unnecessary. In addition, a test that can be group-administered and machine scored could be of considerable value in pure research applications. He began his work on the MAB, them, with the goal of investigating the extent to which it would be possible to incorporate the positive features of a test such as the WAIS-R into an instrument that also allowed group administration and convenient hand or machine scoring.

The MAB underwent several revisions prior to its publication, which extended over a period of some 10 years. It was designed to be similar to the WAIS-R, in terms of its scales and subtests, but all of its items are original. The first version of the MAB was administered to samples of male and female university students and extensive item analyses were undertaken to provide a basis for the selection, revision, or deletion of items, and the writing and inclusion of new items. Subsequently, successive revisions of the MAB were subjected to three additional evaluations and item analyses with samples of high school and university students, psychiatric patients, prison inmates, and probationers. At each stage, items were selected, revised, or deleted on the bases of their difficulty level, their discriminatory power, the appropriateness or efficiency of their distractors or incorrect alternatives, and their contribution to the reliability of each subtest. As is described in more detail later in this review, the revisions resulted in a test that has excellent psychometric properties and that provides a valid assessment of a person's level of intellectual functioning.

Practical Applications/Uses

Jackson (1984) states that the MAB is designed to measure not only the *extent* of a person's knowledge or problem-solving skills, but also the degree to which the person can apply his or her knowledge and skills *quickly* and *efficiently*. To tap each of these aspects of intellectual functioning, the items within each of the 10 subtests of the MAB are arranged in order of increasing difficulty, starting with questions and problems that most adults would find quite simple and extending up to items that are difficult or require complex problem-solving. In addition, test takers are allowed only seven minutes to work on each subtest, thereby ensuring that the MAB comprises elements of both power and speed.

The five Verbal and Performance subtests appear in separate test booklets. Test takers are also provided with answer sheets (one for each scale), pencils, and blank paper. The examiner must have a stopwatch. According to the manual, each scale requires approximately 50 minutes for administration, including instructions. The Verbal Scale should normally precede the Performance Scale, and subtests should be administered in the order in which they appear in the test booklets. The two scales can be given on separate days or with a short break between them.

Detailed instructions for administering the MAB are presented in the manual. Brief instructions and practice items also appear before each subtest in the subjects' test booklets. If desired, the examiner's instructions can be presented by a cassette tape available from the publisher. It is recommended that one test proctor be present for each 25 examinees. The examiner's duties include reading the instructions, timing the subtests, and announcing when subjects should start and stop working on each subtest.

Every item in the MAB has five answers from which to choose. Subjects are instructed to select the one answer that they think is correct and to record their responses on the answer sheet by blackening the circle containing the letter (A to

E) corresponding to their answer. There is no penalty for guessing and subjects are encouraged to try to respond to every item in the seven minutes allowed for each subtest. Each item is scored 1 or 0. The 10 subtests of the MAB, in the order they appear in the test booklets, are as follows:

VERBAL SCALE:

1. *Information:* a 40-item test of general knowledge and information.

2. *Comprehension:* a 28-item test measuring a person's understanding of various social situations and conventions, and why things are done the way they are.

3. *Arithmetic:* a 26-item test, ranging in difficulty from simple addition and subtraction to complex problems involving fractions, percentages, and numerical reasoning. Examinees are provided with a sheet of paper on which to perform computations.

4 .*Similarities:* a 34-item test in which subjects must decide in what way pairs of words are alike. The items range in complexity from concrete to relatively abstract associations.

5. *Vocabulary:* a 46-item test in which subjects select words that have the same meaning as the test items.

PERFORMANCE SCALE:

1. *Digit Symbol:* a 35-item test. At the top of each page, a coding chart is printed in which the digits 1 to 9 are matched (or coded) with different symbols (e.g., a cross or two parallel lines). In each item of the test, a combination of the coded symbols appears (from 1 to 9 symbols in length) followed by five strings of digits. Only one of the digit strings completely matches the order of the symbols and it is the subjects' task to select the correct digit string.

2. *Picture Completion:* a 35-item test in which pictures of common objects are presented, each missing one important part or component. Below each picture are the first letters of five possible missing parts and the subjects' task is to select the correct letter. For example, if a dog without a tail was shown, one of the five letters below the picture would be a "T."

3. *Spatial:* a 50-item test that, besides the absence of digit span, is the only MAB subtest that does not directly conform to those in the WAIS-R. In this subtest—the MAB's alternative to Block Design—subjects must perform spatial rotations of figures and select one of five possible rotations presented as their answer. Only rotation is involved (i.e., figures do not have to be "flipped over") but many of the later items are very complex and demanding.

4. *Picture Arrangement:* a 21-item test in which subjects must mentally rearrange cartoon panels so that they tell a sensible story. The panels are numbered and the subjects' task is to select the correct sequence of numbers that conforms to the order in which they think the panels should be arranged.

5. *Object Assembly:* a 20-item test in which numbered silhouetted parts of common objects appear in the wrong order. Subjects must first identify the objects and then mentally rearrange their parts into the correct order. As in the previous test, they select a sequence of numbers that conforms to the order they have decided on.

Once the MAB has been administered, color-coded templates are provided for convenient hand-scoring of each scale's subtests. With practice, it should take no longer than 5 or 10 minutes to score the entire test. Answer sheets can also be scored by computer: the addresses to which they should be sent (in the U.S.A. and in Canada) appear on the sheets. Subjects' raw scores on each subtest are recorded on a record form as the total number of correct responses; no points are deducted for incorrect answers. Raw scores are then converted to standard (T) scores, with a mean of 50 and a standard deviation of 10, by means of a conversion chart on the record form. The subtest standard scores are summed to yield Verbal and Performance scaled scores, and the sum of these yields a Full Scale scaled score. Provided at least three Verbal or Performance subtests have been administered, scores on these can be prorated to provide an estimate of the total Scale and Full Scale scores.

Tables are provided in the manual to convert Verbal, Performance, and Full Scale scaled scores into IQ scores, for different age groups ranging from 16-17 to 70-74 year-olds. Separate tables are consulted for Verbal, Performance, and Full Scale IQs. Another set of tables is provided to convert raw scores to standard (T) scores, which are scaled by age-relevant norms for nine age groups between 16 and 74. These standard scores are *not* used for subsequent conversion to IQ scores. Their purpose, rather, is to provide profiles of standard scores that can be interpreted in reference to the performance of persons of the same age as the examinee. These profiles may appear rather different from those obtained from the conversion chart on the record form, particularly for the youngest and for the older age groups. Testers should be careful to use those tables that are appropriate for their respective purposes.

If answer sheets are sent for computer scoring, they will be returned with a table of raw scores and standard scores and a graphic representation of the subject's profile of age-relevant standard scores. Another profile depicts subject's Verbal, Performance, and Full Scale standard scores. An example of profile appears in Figure 1. The returned profile also provides brief descriptions of the abilities measured by each subtest and scale. Profiles should be interpreted with care: the manual notes that substantial differences should exist between scaled scores before these are subjected to psychological interpretation.

Technical Aspects

Various samples were employed to evaluate the psychometric properties of the MAB. Internal consistency reliability coefficients for each subtest, Scale, and Full Scale scores are reported in the manual for samples of males and females at each year level from 15 to 20. The sample sizes within each age range from 32 (15-year-olds) to 134 (17-year-olds). The total sample comprised 230 males and 285 females. Subtest reliabilities (KR-20) range from .70 to .96 which, while satisfactorily high, are probably somewhat overestimated because the individual subtests are timed. The reliabilities of the Verbal, Performance, and Full Scale scores range from .94 to .98 in different age groups and, being comprised of separately timed composites of different subtests, are valid estimates. Clearly, the Scale and Full Scale scores have very high internal consistency reliability.

Figure 1.

Example profile from the Multidimensional Aptitude Battery.*

```
NAME:    M.J. CASE              SEX:   FEMALE        TEST DATE:    AUG  8, 1984

ID:      000000001             AGE:   25            BIRTH DATE:   MAR  1959

                        MULTIDIMENSIONAL APTITUDE BATTERY
                                  RECORD FORM


                                 SCALED SCORES
                                    AVERAGE
                        -SCORE-   20   30   40   50   60   70   80
                        RAW  SS    .    .    .    .    .    .    .
. . . . . . . . . . . . . . . . . . . . . . . . . . . . . . . . . .
INFORMATION              30   58   XXXXXXXXXXXXXXXXXXXXXXXXX

COMPREHENSION            26   63   XXXXXXXXXXXXXXXXXXXXXXXXXXXXX

ARITHMETIC               17   57   XXXXXXXXXXXXXXXXXXXXXXXX

SIMILARITIES             23   54   XXXXXXXXXXXXXXXXXXXXX

VOCABULARY               44   78   XXXXXXXXXXXXXXXXXXXXXXXXXXXXXXXXXXXXXX
. . . . . . . . . . . . . . . . . . . . . . . . . . . . . . . . . .
DIGIT SYMBOL             26   57   XXXXXXXXXXXXXXXXXXXXXXXX
PICTURE
  COMPLETION             31   68   XXXXXXXXXXXXXXXXXXXXXXXXXXXXXXXXXX

SPATIAL                  40   66   XXXXXXXXXXXXXXXXXXXXXXXXXXXXXXX
PICTURE
  ARRANGEMENT            16   68   XXXXXXXXXXXXXXXXXXXXXXXXXXXXXXXXXX

OBJECT ASSEMBLY          15   57   XXXXXXXXXXXXXXXXXXXXXXXX
. . . . . . . . . . . . . . . . . . . . . . . . . . . . . . . . . .


                                   SUMMARY

                            STANDARD SCORES   (ST)
                        -SCORE-  200   300   400   500   600   700   800
                        SUM  ST    .     .     .     .     .     .     .
. . . . . . . . . . . . . . . . . . . . . . . . . . . . . . . . . .
VERBAL                  311  527   XXXXXXXXXXXXXXXXXXXXXXXXXXX
. . . . . . . . . . . . . . . . . . . . . . . . . . . . . . . . . .
PERFORMANCE             317  700   XXXXXXXXXXXXXXXXXXXXXXXXXXXXXXXXXXXXXXX
. . . . . . . . . . . . . . . . . . . . . . . . . . . . . . . . . .
FULL SCALE              628  600   XXXXXXXXXXXXXXXXXXXXXXXXXXXXXXXXX
. . . . . . . . . . . . . . . . . . . . . . . . . . . . . . . . . .
EXPLANATION OF SCORES
    Your Raw Score for each test indicates the number of questions you
    answered correctly.  Your Scaled Scores (SS) compare your results
    with people in general.  Your Summary Profile compares your results
    with other people your age.  The average standard score is 500 with
    2/3 of people's scores falling between 400 and 600.
```

*Reproduced with permission of the publisher.

Test-retest stability data were computed from two administrations of the MAB (on average, 45 days apart) to a sample of 52 hospitalized psychiatric patients. Subtest stability coefficients range from .83 to .97, while Verbal, Performance, and Full Scale stability coefficients are .95, .96, and .97, respectively. On average, subtest mean scores increased by less than one point across testings, indicating minimal practice or memory effects at least for this population.

A third table reports split-half (odd-even) reliability coefficients for subtest, Scale, and Full Scale scores, obtained from separately timed administrations of the scales to 71 high school students aged 16 to 18 years. Subtest reliabilities (corrected by the Spearman-Brown formula) range from .55 to .87, with a median of .77, and Verbal, Performance, and Full Scale corrected reliabilities are .92, .94, and .95, respectively. Again, these estimates indicate that the MAB has highly satisfactory reliability.

Three sources of information pertaining to the construct validity of the MAB are provided in the manual. First, tables report the intercorrelations between subtest raw scores and the results of a principal components factor analysis of the correlations, based on data obtained from 3,121 male and female high school students between the ages of 16 and 19. All correlations are positive, ranging from .24 to .73, and there is a tendency for Verbal subtests to be more highly associated with other Verbal subtests and for Performance subtests to be more highly associated with other Performance subtests. This trend is revealed more strongly in the factor analysis, which yielded two orthogonal factors after the first general factor. All subtests have moderate to high first-factor loadings (ranging from .53 to .82), indicating that the MAB has a strong general intelligence (or g) factor underlying it. The two rotated factors are clearly identifiable as Verbal and Performance factors, providing good justification for the use of separate scales in the test. Unfortunately, the manual does not report the actual correlation between Verbal and Performance Scale scores. However, a second factor analysis, based on a separate sample of 516 high school students, also yielded two distinct Verbal and Performance factors that had congruence coefficients greater than .99 with the factors extracted in the first analysis.

A second source of validity data for the MAB is its correlation with the WAIS-R. The MAB and the WAIS-R were administered individually or in small groups to a heterogeneous sample for 145 subjects, comprising university students, senior high school students, hospitalized psychiatric patients, and persons on probation from prison, ranging in age from 16 to 35 years. One hundred three were male, 42 were female. The order of presentation of the MAB and WAIS-R was counter-balanced. Correlations between the tests' subtests (the MAB Spatial test was correlated with Block Design on the WAIS-R) range from .44 (Spatial/Block Design) to .89 (Arithmetic and Vocabulary), with a median of .78. Verbal, Performance, and Full Scale MAB scaled scores correlate .92, .79, and .91 with the respective IQ scores on the WAIS-R. These correlations can be compared with those between the WAIS-R and WAIS, which are reported in the MAB manual from studies by Smith (1983) and Wechsler (1981). The average WAIS/WAIS-R subtest correlations reported in these studies (based on samples of 70 and 72, respectively) range from .33 to .84 (median = .55). In 7 out of 10 cases, the correlations between the MAB and WAIS-R subtests are higher than those between the same WAIS-R and WAIS subtests. WAIS/WAIS-R Verbal, Performance, and Full Scale IQ correlations, averaged across the two studies, are .82, .82, and .87; with the exception of Performance, slightly lower that those between the corresponding scales of the MAB and the WAIS-R. Clearly, the MAB and the WAIS-R are highly related. Insofar as the WAIS-R is accepted as a standard against which the validity of other tests of intellectual functioning can be evaluated, the MAB performs extremely well.

The third source of information pertaining to the validity of the MAB was reported by Stockwell (1984). He extracted Verbal and Performance factors from intercorrelations among the WAIS-R subtests (excluding Digit Span, for which there is no comparable subtest on the MAB) reported in the WAIS-R manual. Coefficients of factor congruence between the WAIS-R factors and factors extracted from the MAB were .97 and .96 for Verbal and Performance, respectively. Considering that the factor rotations for the two tests were completely independent of one another and that as a result no attempt was made to maximize congruence, these coefficients are very high. They indicate that the patterns of abilities measured by the MAB and the WAIS-R are very similar, notwithstanding such differences between the two tests as their content, administration, and response formats.

Since the MAB was published in 1984, no studies have been conducted to assess its predictive validity. Given the close correspondence between the abilities measured by the MAB and the WAIS-R, however, and the high correlations between these tests' Scale and Full Scale scores, it may be anticipated that the MAB will prove to have approximately the same predictive validity as does the WAIS-R in a variety of situations. Naturally, it is to be hoped that this conjecture will be subjected to empirical test and that relevant results will be included in later editions of the manual.

Given the high correlation between the MAB and the WAIS-R, Jackson (1984) decided to undertake an equating of the two tests, rather than obtaining standardization or normative data for the MAB itself. The advantage of this procedure is that it avoids problems associated with attempts to compare test scores from two (or more) tests standardized at different times and using different sampling theories in the selection of their normative samples.

MAB/WAIS-R equating was conducted on the basis of scores on the two tests obtained from a heterogeneous sample of 160 subjects. A standard linear equating formula was adopted after the absence of any curvilinear component to the relationship between the tests had been established. Equating was then performed for both the subtests and for the Verbal, Performance, and Full Scale Scores. It was on the basis of these equatings that the tables for obtaining Verbal, Performance, and Full Scale IQ scores on the MAB were developed. A test of the validity of the equating was made by administering the MAB to over 5,000 Canadian high school students, whose mean IQ, based on the WAIS-R-equated MAB norms, was found to be 103. As the manual points out, this is very close to the value of 100 that would be expected in a representative sample of the general population, and the slight overestimation is probably attributable to the fact that the sample consisted of high school students rather than a more diverse segment of the population.

Critique

The MAB would appear to be a carefully constructed test that provides a reliable and valid measure of a broad range of intellecutal abilities. It enjoys many of the advantages of the WAIS-R (such as the diversity of its subtests, the range of age of persons to whom it may be administered, and its sound psychometric properties) and has the additional advantages of being easy to administer and to score. The manual makes it clear that the MAB should not be employed as the sole means for diagnosing mental deficiency but the test does contain items spanning a wide range of difficulty from simple to hard. Indeed, according to the manual, the MAB has a higher ceiling than does the WAIS-R and may thus provide better discrimination than the WAIS-R among persons at the upper levels of intellectual ability.

More generally, the MAB is an appropriate instrument for the measurement of adult intelligence that can be used whenever an individual assessment is considered not necessary. It does not require a trained professinal for its administration or its scoring, although, of course, psychological interpretations of its score profiles—like those of the WAIS-R—require the expertise of a qualified clinician. The MAB may prove to be of particular value in research settings, allowing the testing of large numbers of subjects in a relatively short period of time and could also be of considerable use in a counseling or vocational context. Its high correlation and equating with the WAIS-R make the MAB a very attractive alternative to that test when individual administration is not required.

References

Jackson, D. N. (1967). *Personality Research Form*. Goshen, NY: Research Psychologists Press.

Jackson, D. N. (1976). *Jackson Personality Inventory*. Goshen, NY: Research Psychologists Press.

Jackson, D. N. (1977). *Jackson Vocational Interest Survey*. Port Huron, MI: Research Psychologists Press.

Jackson, D. N. (1984). *Multidimensional Aptitude Battery manual*. Port Huron, MI: Research Psychologists Press.

Smith, R. R. (1983). A comparison of the Wechsler Adult Intelligence Scale and the Wechsler Adult Intelligence Scale-Revised in a college population. *Journal of Consulting and Clinical Psychology, 51,* 414-419.

Stockwell, R. G. (1984, August). Factor structure comparisons between the MAB and the WAIS-R. In L. J. Stricker (Chair), *The Multidimensional Aptitude Battery (MAB): A new group intelligence test*. Symposium conducted at the meeting of the American Psychological Association, Toronto, Canada.

Wechsler, D. (1981). *Manual for the Wechsler Adult Intelligence Scale-Revised*. Cleveland, OH: The Psychological Corporation.

Howard E. A. Tinsley, Ph.D.
Professor of Psychology, Southern Illinois University, Carbondale, Illinois.

MY VOCATIONAL SITUATION

J. L. Holland, D. C. Daiger, and P. G. Power. Palo Alto, California: Consulting Psychologists Press, Inc.

Introduction

The My Vocational Situation (MVS) is a brief test, the underlying assumption of which is that the majority of career decision-making difficulties fall into one or more of the following categories: 1) problems of vocational identity, 2) lack of information or training, 3) environmental or personal barriers, or 4) no problem (Holland, Gottfredson, & Power, 1980b, p. 1191). The MVS provides information about respondents' vocational identity, need for occupational information, and perception of barriers to their chosen career. The test's authors, Holland, Daiger, and Power (1980a), believe that this information can be used to determine the type of vocational assistance needed by respondents, thereby allowing differential assignment of clients to counseling interventions based on their MVS scores. Use of the MVS in this manner, it is argued, will increase the effectiveness of the total counseling services offered by an agency and/or an individual counseling psychologist (Holland et al., 1980a).

John Holland, principal author of the MVS, is the author of the Vocational Preference Inventory (VPI) (Holland, 1978), the Self-Directed Search (SDS) (Holland, 1979), and a major theory of career development (Holland, 1985). Holland worked as a military induction interviewer (1942-1946) and college counselor (1950-1953) before completing his Ph.D. at the University of Minnesota in 1952. He subsequently worked with psychiatric patients at the Perry Point VA Hospital (1953-1956) before moving to the National Merit Scholarship program (1957-1963) where he turned his attention to test construction. Holland's work during this period involved large scale surveys of highly talented college-bound students. The information he obtained from samples of more typical undergraduate students while at the American College Testing program (1963-1969) was useful in expanding his theory of vocational choice and in developing the VPI and SDS. Holland began work at Johns Hopkins University in 1969 where he remained until his retirement in 1980.

Holland's contributions to the field reflect three general concerns. His experiences as a counselor sensitized him to the frustration experienced by practitioners in attempting to understand the complex world of work. Holland perceived the massive, complicated occupational classification schemes in use at that time and the complex scoring systems used with the leading assessment devices as important contributions to this sense of frustration. These experiences were instrumen-

509

tal in the formation of Holland's commitment to developing a simplified, usable occupational classification scheme and assessment devices which reflected it and were easy to administer and score.

Holland's earlier work illustrates the model followed in the development of the MVS. The research literature contained numerous examples of efforts to develop a simplified occupational classification scheme. Holland noted considerable consistency in the results of these earlier studies and concluded that occupations could be organized according to the relatively few dimensions that seemed to account for the variation in vocational interests. In a similar manner, the MVS is an outgrowth of Holland's attempt to integrate three streams of research: 1) earlier attempts to develop a counseling diagnostic scheme; 2) more recent research on career indecision; and 3) experimental investigations of the effectiveness of counseling interventions (e.g., workshops, interest inventories, career counseling programs).

Holland's emphasis on simplicity as the *sina qua non* of classification systems and tests is apparent in the MVS. Holland analyzed the early diagnostic schemes suggested for counseling and concluded that attempts to distinguish among intrapsychic problems had been largely unsuccessful. (See Rounds & Tinsley, 1984, for a review of vocational diagnostic schemes and of empirical work on the subject.) In particular, Holland et al. (1980a) concluded that systems for classifying subjects into categories representing different patterns and degrees of maladjustment had been unreliable. The authors collapsed those problems into a single category (viz., Vocational Identity) and suggested the four-category diagnostic system described in the introduction.

The development of the MVS has not been described in detail. The general impression is that the MVS began as a research questionnaire, was used in several studies, and evolved into the MVS without any systematic program of test development having been undertaken. This strategy of test development is vintage Holland (see Weinrach, 1980).

An unpublished monograph by Holland, Gottfredson, and Nafziger (1975) included some items which ultimately were retained in the MVS. The Identity (ID) and Vocational Decision-Making Difficulty (VDMD) scales used by Holland and Holland (1977) in an investigation of the correlates of vocational indecision, however, were cited by Holland et al. (1980b) as the immediate predecessors of the Vocational Identity (VI), Occupational Information (OI), and Barriers (B) scales. The VDMD Scale was derived from the responses of high-school and college students to open-ended and multiple choice questions about their career indecision, obtained from early surveys of Holland (1962, 1969). The ID Scale was developed from an Identity Scale used earlier by Greenberger and Sorensen (1974) and Greenberger, Josselson, Knerr, and Knerr (1975). Review of the pattern of results reported by Holland and Holland (1977) and analysis of the correlations among the scales for samples of high-school boys (N = 203) and girls (N = 322) (Power, Holland, Daiger, & Takai, 1979) led the authors to conclude that the ID and VDMD were measuring opposite poles of the same construct.

Holland et al. (1980b) lengthened the ID and VDMD scales to 20 and 41 items, respectively, to increase their reliability. Similar scales (cf., Osipow, Carney, & Barak, 1976) were reviewed during this process. The expanded scales were administered to a new sample of 577 high-school sophomores (345 girls, 232 boys) along with a 7-item Interpersonal Competency (IC) Scale and the SDS. The pattern of convergent (i.e., item-total score) and discriminant (i.e., item-IC) correlations was examined and a principal-components analysis was performed. Based on these data, the Vocational Identity and Occupational Information scales were formed. The Barriers Scale was developed by selecting items which had a low correlation with the ID and VDMD scales, the content of which "appeared to be a sign of an environmental barrier or a clear psychological limitation" (Holland et al., 1980b, p. 1194).

Holland et al. (1980b) described the Vocational Identity Scale as comprised of 23 items; at least three of the investigations reported in the literature involving the MVS used the 23-item version of the VI Scale. Holland et al. present reliability data for this scale, which was reduced to 18 items by eliminating "five redundent items" (1980a, p. 6). The length of the OI and Barriers scales was not reported.

The MVS is printed on the front and back of a single 8½" x 11" sheet of paper. The front page contains spaces for basic identifying data (e.g., name, date, gender, age, education completed), 12 blanks for respondents to list the occupations they are considering now, and 18 sentences: the VD Scale. Respondents are instructed to answer these items "true" or "false" in terms of how descriptive they are of their thinking about their present job or their plans for an occupation or career.

The reverse side of the MVS contains questions 19 and 20 and space for additional comments or questions. Question 19, the OI Scale, consists of four items about types of information the person may need. Question 20, the Barriers Scale, consists of four items about possible difficulties the individual may be experiencing. In both cases, the respondent is to answer "yes" or "no." Space is also provided following questions 19 and 20 for the respondent to use in providing additional information.

Practical Applications/Uses

The MVS is self-administering and can be completed individually or in groups; the manual suggests that clients complete the MVS while waiting to see a counselor. No special instructions regarding the administration of the test are given, but the minimal instructions provided on the test appear adequate. The test administrator needs no special training. Responses to the items are recorded on the questionnaire itself; alternative forms and answer sheets for the MVS are not available and a profile for the MVS has not been developed.

The age range for which the MVS is appropriate is not stated in this manual. Validity information appearing in the manual describes the use of the test with respondents, aged 16-69 years, from high school, college and business settings. Holland et al. (1980b) describe its use with 14-year-old respondents. The education level of respondents described in the validity studies varied from a high-school freshman to Ph.D.s in engineering and the social sciences. The MVS would be most appropriate for normal persons and those experiencing anxiety or difficulty regarding career concerns. The test may be used with a clinical population provided the respondents are experiencing some career concerns.

The MVS is designed for hand-scoring; other scoring services are not available. The total score of the first 18 items, the VI Scale, is the number of "false" responses. The OI Score is obtained by summing the number of "no" responses to the four statements appearing in Item 19. The Barriers Score is obtained by summing the number of "no" responses to the four statements appearing in Item 20.

High scores on all three scales are in the favorable direction. The VI Scale indicates the extent to which the respondents' knowledge of their goals, interests, personality, and talents are clear. Persons high on this scale are believed by Holland et al. (1980a) to have confidence in their ability, make good decisions in the face of environmental ambiguities, and be relatively untroubled in their decision making. The OI Scale indicates the extent to which respondents need vocational information, and the Barriers Score indicates the extent to which they perceive external barriers to their chosen occupation goals.

The test manual (Holland et al., 1980a) provides means and standard deviations, by gender, for samples of high-school students, college students, full-time workers, and graduate students and faculty. No additional information is provided to assist in the interpretation of the three scale scores. Given this lack of normative information, accurate interpretation of the MVS will be exceedingly difficult. Most users of the MVS will find it necessary to develop local norms, a strategy recommended in the test manual.

Holland et al. (1980a) suggest examining the responses to the open-ended questions appearing on the MVS, and analyzing the occupations listed in terms of the number listed, their consistency or diversity, and the occupation level. They purport that this information will shorten the time required for counseling by identifying areas which need to be discussed.

The MVS is intended to be used as a screening device with persons of high school age or older. The test may be used with clients seeking counseling to determine the most appropriate counseling intervention. Alternatively, the test could be used with large groups (e.g., the entire freshman class of a high school) to identify persons who might need services or who might benefit from special programs. According to Holland et al. (1980a) the real advantage of the MVS is that it allows the assignment of some potential clients to interventions such as workshops, printed matter, films, tapes, or other instructional media. This frees counseling psychologists to provide individual counseling to clients who most need those services.

Holland et al. (1980a) claim that scores on the VI, OI, and Barriers scales can be used in assigning clients to treatment, but these ideas appear sketchy. Clients with a poor sense of identity are said to be most in need of experience, and will benefit most from experiential activities such as career seminars, personal counseling, printed literature, and interviews with employers. In contrast, clients with a clear sense of identity primarily need information and reassurance, therefore, they might use the counseling psychologist more as a consultant than as a counselor. Other clients may need a combination of these treatments.

The Barriers Scale provides information regarding respondents' perceptions of external barriers to their career choices (Holland et al., 1980a). The counselor should assess the realism of the client's perceptions. If realistic, the counselor needs to help the client develop strategies to overcome or circumvent the barriers. Unrealistically perceived barriers suggest the need to help the client obtain more accurate information and develop self-confidence.

The MVS can be used in a general screening program to identify persons in greatest need of services (Holland et al., 1980a). The authors suggest the use of the MVS in research concerning vocational identity, career stability, and the effectiveness of career development programs.

Technical Aspects

The author located 11 investigations in which some form of the MVS or its predecessor scales had been used, but the current (i.e., 18-item) form of the VI Scale was used in only three of these investigations. Consequently, information on the reliability and validity of the MVS comes primarily from Holland et al. (1980b) as reported in that manuscript and repeated in the test manual (Holland et al., 1980a).

Both the Holland et al. (1980b) and test manual (Holland et al., 1980a) summaries of the reliability and validity of the MVS are deficient. Important information about sampling procedures and statistical analyses are omitted and in some instances it is difficult to determine on which sample of respondents an analysis was performed.

It appears that three separate samples of data were obtained. In one investigation the MVS was administered to 824 persons in high school, college, and business settings, and information was obtained about the respondents' age, gender, educational level, and number and variety of occupational aspirations. The data of a portion of this sample was evaluated by students who used a 5-point rating scale to indicate the extent to which persons appeared to be 1) well organized, 2) at loose ends, 3) self-confident, 4) tense and uncomfortable, and 5) competent to handle their life well. Hypotheses were formed regarding the correlations expected between scores on the MVS and the other data available. Holland et al. (1980a, 1980b) concluded that the hypotheses were supported, thereby indicating the validity of the MVS. The authors failed to note that the large sample size allowed rather small correlation coefficients to achieve statistical significance. In general, the typical correlation between MVS scales and the criteria were in the range of .20 to .30, indicating that only a small proportion of the variance was accounted for.

Holland et al. (1980b) reported that they analyzed the relationship between scores on the MVS and educational level, occupational status, and type of vocational interest or work. Means and standard deviations are reported for eight groups of respondents, but no statistical analyses were reported so it is difficult to tell whether statistically significant differences occurred. Scores on the current 18-item version of the VI Scale were reported for this sample by Holland et al. (1980a). In general, the VI Score increased from high-school students to college students to full-time workers to graduate students and faculty. Again, however, the authors did not report statistical analyses, so it is unclear whether the differences were statistically significant.

A short form of the VI Scale was administered to 2,343 high-school students along with a scale measuring the number of concerns with which the students would like help. The negative correlations (−.23 for females, −.29 for males) differed significantly from zero. Although the correlations are in the expected direction, only a small proportion of the variance in the students' expressed desire for help was accounted for by the MVS.

Finally, two-person teams interviewed 50 male and 50 female college students about their thoughts as they responded to the 18 VI items of the MVS. The authors concluded that the "explanations and rationalizations of responses indicated that students usually responded directly to the content of an item" (Holland et al., 1980b, page 1198). No information is provided about the training given to the interviewers or whether the interviewers were naive to the hypotheses under investigation, the method used in classifying respondents' answers, the interrater reliability of that classification or how the data were analyzed.

No data is available regarding the test-retest reliability of the MVS. Internal consistency reliability coefficients were reported for the high-school students (N = 496) and college students and workers (N = 592) used in the development of the scales. The data indicated an acceptable degree of reliability for the VI Scale (.86 to .89). Subsequently, Holland et al. (1980a, p. 6) report that those data were for the a 23-item version of the VI Scale, but that the reliability of the 18-item version of the scale is approximately the same.

The internal consistency reliability of the OI and Barriers scales was about .40 and .23, respectively, for high-school students and about .78 and .45 (males) and .65 (females) for college students and workers, respectively. Interpretation of this reliability data is difficult because the theoretical rationale underlying the traits has not been stated clearly by Holland et al. (1980a, 1980b). The authors conclude that the OI and Barrier scales "should be regarded as useful checklists or borderline scales. They do not generally function as homogeneous scales" (Holland, 1980a, p. 7). This distinction misses the point. If the constructs being measured are regarded as factor complex, a high internal consistency reliability should not be expected. Moreover, if each item on the OI and Barrier scales measures an independent dimension of the underlying construct, the practice of summing the items to obtain a total score is questionable.

Critique

It is important to distinguish between the potential and the current status of the MVS. The MVS may ultimately prove to be useful in research on career development and occupational decision making, and in applied settings. Given the information currently available about the MVS, however, the instrument can be recommended for use only in research. Indeed, the use of the MVS in research entails a calculated risk until the validity of the instrument has been more firmly established. Given the time and expense involved in conducting an investigation, researchers would be well advised to incorporate alternative measures of the constructs measured by the MVS so that the fate of an entire investigation does not rest on the information provided by this relatively untested instrument. Use of the MVS in applied settings at this time is premature.

These conclusions stand in contrast to those of Holland et al. (1980a, 1980b), who were much less restrained in advocating the use of the MVS in research and applied settings. Numerous unsubstantiated assertions were made regarding the value of the MVS. For example, "clinical experience indicates that these lists may be helpful . . . Clients often fill in the blank spaces with emotionally significant and vital information that they may not easily bring up in interviews" (Holland et al., 1980a, p. 7). Holland et al. advocate use of the MVS in assessing clients' needs for vocational assistance and in making differential assignments of clients to counseling interventions. Furthermore, they advocate use of the MVS as a screening device in high schools and colleges, and with adults. Given the scant information available regarding the reliability and validity of the MVS, however, it appears that use of the MVS in this manner would be at variance with the standards for educational and psychological tests adopted by the American Psychological Association (APA, 1974).

At least three areas need attention in furthering the development of the MVS. First, the current test manual is inadequate, failing to provide several types of information that are regarded as essential by APA standards. These include failure to "provide the information required to substantiate any claims made for its use" (APA, 1974, pp. 9-10), failure to "describe fully the development of the test . . . and the procedures and results of item analysis" (p. 11), and failure to "warn against common misuses of the test" (p. 13). More careful attention to APA standards would be helpful in future revisions of the MVS test manual.

The norms provided by Holland et al. (1980a) are based on 824 high school students, college students, full-time workers, and graduate students and faculty. The normative data consists of the means, standard deviations, and sample size for these four groups, reported by gender. This is inadequate; essential information such as the standard error of measurement (APA, 1974, p. 50) and the stability of MVS scores (p. 54), and percentiles or standard scores for appropriate reference groups (APA, 1974, p. 22) has not been provided.

Little validity information is available on the MVS, and the test manual fails to point out that the validity of most of the suggested uses of the MVS has not been investigated (p. 31). The manual does not "provide information on the . . . limits of the generalizability of validity information" (p. 35) and the quality of the criterion measures used in validating the MVS (pp. 33-34).

In summary, the MVS may have promise but the present data do not allow one to determine whether the test is valid. The available validity information is based almost exclusively on the simple, easy to obtain type of data researchers use to determine whether they are on the right track. The results reported by Holland et al. (1980a, 1980b) could be interpreted as encouraging further investigation of the MVS. Inclusion of the MVS in research as an experimental measure can be justified on the basis of the existing validity data, but not the use of the MVS in applied settings.

References

American Psychological Association. (1974). *Standards for educational and psychological tests.* Washington, DC: Author.

Greenberger, E., Josselson, R., Knerr, C., & Knerr, B. (1975). The measurement and structure of psychosocial maturity. *Journal of Youth and Adolescence, 4,* 127-143.

Greenberger, E., & Sorensen, A. B. (1974). Toward a concept of psychosocial maturity. *Journal of Youth and Adolescence, 3,* 229-258.

Holland, J. L. (1962). *National Merit Student Survey.* Chicago: National Merit Scholarship Corporation.

Holland, J. L. (1969). *A descriptive study of two-year college students.* Unpublished manuscript, Johns Hopkins University, Department of Social Relations, Baltimore.

Holland, J. L. (1978). *Manual for the Vocational Preference Inventory.* Palo Alto, CA: Consulting Psychologists Press.

Holland, J. L. (1979). *The Self-Directed Search: Professional manual.* Palo Alto, CA: Consulting Psychologists Press.

Holland, J. L. (1985). *Making vocational choices: A theory of careers.* Englewood Cliffs, NJ: Prentice-Hall.

Holland, J. L., Daiger, D. C., & Power, P. G. (1980a). *My Vocational Situation.* Palo Alto, CA: Consulting Psychologists Press.

Holland, J. L., Gottfredson, G. D., & Nafziger, D. H. (1975). Testing the validity of some theoretical signs of vocational decision-making ability. *Journal of Counseling Psychology, 22,* 411-422.

Holland, J. L., Gottfredson, D. C., & Power, P. G. (1980b). Some diagnostic scales for research in decision making and personality: Identity, Information, and Barriers. *Journal of Personality and Social Psychology, 39,* 1191-1200.

Holland, J. L., & Holland, J. E. (1977). Vocational indecision: More evidence and speculation. *Journal of Counseling Psychology, 24,* 404-414.

Osipow, S. H., Carney, C. G., & Barak, A. (1976). A scale of educational-vocational undecidedness: A typological approach. *Journal of Vocational Behavior, 9,* 233-244.

Power, P. G., Holland, J. L., Daiger, D. C., & Takai, R. T. (1979). The relation of student characteristics to the influence of the Self-Directed Search. *Measurement and Evaluation in Guidance, 12,* 98-107.

Rounds, J. B., & Tinsley, H. E. A. (1984). Diagnosis and treatment of vocational problems. In S. D. Brown & R. W. Lent (Eds.), *Handbook of counseling psychology* (pp. 137-177). New York: John Wiley & Sons.

Weinrach, S. G. (1980). Have hexagon will travel: An interview with John Holland. *The Personnel and Guidance Journal, 58,* 406-414.

Russell H. Lord, Ed.D.
Associate Professor of Psychology, Northwest Missouri State
University, Maryville, Missouri.

NEUROLOGICAL DYSFUNCTIONS OF CHILDREN

James W. Kuhns. Monterey, California: CTB/McGraw-Hill.

Introduction

The Neurological Dysfunctions of Children (NDOC) test is intended to serve as that part of a comprehensive psychological evaluation which will identify those children between the ages of three and ten who should be referred on for neurological evaluation. It is planned for use by a diverse group of individuals with or without "specialized training," under the supervision of either a school psychologist or nurse, in an attempt to contribute to differential diagnoses of learning disabilities and to eliminate unnecessary referrals while also detecting neurological impairments that might go unnoticed without the use of the NDOC. The NDOC is an attempt to put the power of neurological assessment and referral into a "cookbook" format, wherein decisions are made simply on the basis of the individual child's profile on certain "interpretation clusters," without requiring expertise on the part of the examiner. The test consists of four major components or sections: 1) 16 behavioral tasks that the child is asked to perform, 2) a measurement of head circumference, 3) historical data collected from a parent ("preferably the mother"), and 4) "further information gathered from examiner observations and health records of a child."

The NDOC was developed by James W. Kuhns and published in 1979 by Publishers Test Service, a service of CTB/McGraw-Hill. The tasks included on the NDOC are a selected sample from the much larger number of tasks normally included in a neuropsychological battery used specifically with learning-disabled children (Rourke, 1981) or a more diffusely defined population of children needing neurological assessment (Matthews, 1981). Neither revisions of the NDOC nor alternate forms are referenced. The normative population upon which the reported reliability of the NDOC rests consisted of 19 "normally functioning children three through twelve years old," stratified for Grades 1, 2, and 3 in a university campus school (apparently at James Madison University in Virginia). Two graduate students in the School Psychology Program at James Madison University administered the NDOC in a test-retest design, having a three-week interval between test dates, and they "reversed administrations for half of the subjects during the second administration." The 19 children chosen for the normative base were "randomly selected" with no control for gender, but this "random" selection was drawn from a very small group evidencing many potential biases such as campus as opposed to public school. This normative base poses many questions and, since it leaves most of those questions unanswered, causes problems for the normative basis of the NDOC.

As already noted, the NDOC uses four major components (though they are not so identified by the author) by which it organizes the data that are recorded on the *Screening and Referral Chart*. The child is rated on a "YES-NO" dichotomy for 1) each behavioral task (Items #1-16), 2) each deviation of head circumference by more than ± 2 SD (Item #17), 3) any "significant deviations from normal development" (Item #18), and 4) examiner judgment regarding normality of head shape, skin coloration on the face, head, and neck, speech patterns, visual acuity, and auditory acuity (Interpretation Clusters #3-6). Then the child's *Referral Indication* is used "to determine whether no referral is indicated or whether the child should be referred." This Referral Indication consists of 13 Interpretation Clusters, each of which is, in turn, comprised of one or more items from the four major components on the NDOC. An item-by-item description of the NDOC, organized into the major components used on the test itself, follows:

1. *Behavioral Tasks:* The 16 behavioral tasks that the child is asked to perform begin with Hand Kicking (Item #1). The child sits so that the feet are off the floor (with shoes and socks removed) and gently kicks the examiner's hand (held directly in front and alternately to each side of body midline) with the left then the right foot. Gross motor functioning, muscle strength and tonus, leg coordination, and discrepancy possibly "related to dominance" are to be evaluated.

Item #2 requires the child to "walk along" a conspicuously designated line on the floor "for about 20 paces" and return, after the examiner has demonstrated the task. Assessment is based on the number of times that the child steps to one side of the designated line (related to age on a chart), but the child is not required to place one foot directly in front of the other foot and instructions do not indicate to the child that scoring is based on the number of "errors" counted each time he or she steps to one side of the line. Muscle tension, gross motor functioning, lateral coordination, and interference by involuntary or spasmodic movements are evaluated in Item #2.

In the third item, the child is asked to walk on tiptoe for approximately 20 continuous paces and return. Again the examiner is to demonstrate this task for the child (and count to 20 for 3-year-olds?), and performance is subjectively adjusted (no chart is provided) for the child's age on the basis of "associated movements." These associated movements "do not include ordinary slight swinging of the arms" but are "most clearly seen in the arms and face," where arms and hands extend, teeth clench, the tongue is stuck out, and fists clench (but this last movement only counts if the arms are also extended). Again, gross motor functioning, muscle tonus, and lateralization problems are to be evaluated.

Walking on Heels (Item #4) is very similar to Item #3 (Walking on Tiptoe), measures basically the same skills, and is administered and scored in the same manner as Item #3. However, the "associated movements" are permitted for an extra two years (up to ages nine or ten) without counting against the child, and "partially rotated feet" are also judged.

item #5 requires the child to stand on one leg for at least 20 seconds, starting with the child's preferred leg and ending with the non-preferred leg. Again the task is demonstrated by the examiner, and lasped time is judged according to the child's age, but a chart matching ages with lapsed times is provided. This task measures basically the same skills as measured in Items #1-4, with the additional claim that cerebellar or sensory dysfunction is also assessed.

In Item #6, the child hops first on the preferred leg, then on the other, 20 times. While "hopping on the spot is preferable," children under 7 years of age are allowed to move forward if necessary to keep their balance (how far forward is not stated). As with several preceding items, this is demonstrated to the child, and scoring is based on a chart giving ages and corresponding expected number of hops. This item evaluates the same areas as Items #1-5, and together they all comprise Cluster #11 of the Interpretation Clusters. The author adds to his description of this item, however, that poor performance may be "related to central nervous system functioning or to skeletonal structure problems," with "pain from a different area of the body" also possibly interfering with the child's performance.

Foot Stimulation Reflex is Item #7, and it involves "one of the superficial reflexes, called the *plantar reflex*," which is "elicited by stimulation of surface receptors in the skin." The child removes shoes and socks and sits on a desk, table, or chair so that the feet are off the floor. The examiner then explains to the child that first the left foot, then the right foot, are going to be gently scratched by the examiner. Babinski's method for eliciting the reflex is then briefly outlined for the examiner to follow, with the caution that prior practice is required if the examiner is to conduct this procedure correctly. With only the provided instructions, it seems reasonable that untrained examiners may fail to achieve a standardized administration of Item #7. A brief explanation of the flexion (or downward curling) which should replace the extension of the great toe (and associated fanning of the small toes) observed in children up to age 5 is given in the interpretation section of the manual, but the scoring for Item #7 has no age criteria established. Little background is given as to what Item #7 provides in the way of neurological information, except to state that "asymmetries may be of significance and require further detailed investigation," and then Item #7 is placed all by itself into Cluster #12 of the Interpretation Clusters.

Item #8, Posture with Arms Extended, requires the child to stand with feet together, looking straight ahead, and to extend the arms forward at shoulder level, palms down, for 20 seconds. As with earlier items that follow one in which the shoes and socks had to be removed, it is not stated whether the child is to replace shoes and socks prior to the administration of Item #8. Children six or older respond with their eyes closed, all children repeat the procedure with palms up, and the examiner demonstrates the task prior to its start. Scoring is based on any lateral or vertical deviations from body midline and the position of the hands relative to the wrist joints. While "a slight horizontal deviation is common in children under the age of six years," no age-related criteria are given for scoring. Item #8 is intended to evaluate cerebellar functions, sensorimotor stimulation, and "local disorders of specific muscles or joints."

For the ninth item (Finger to Nose), the child is instructed to put the tip of the index finger slowly on the tip of the nose. The examiner demonstrates this task also. The task is to be repeated three times with each hand, and no mention is made relative to beginning with the preferred or non-preferred hand. Children aged five or more may be asked to repeat the task with the eyes closed, but there are no instructions for scoring such performance. Response evaluation occurs on the basis of both quality ("smoothness of movements and signs of muscular tremor") and adequacy ("success in placing the fingertip on the nose"). General guidelines for these judgments are provided, but they again fail to be the precise, unambiguous, objective standards one expects in standardized tests. When the eyes are closed, this task tests proprioceptors in addition to cerebellar function (it would seem that the same muscle, tendon, and joint receptors are involved regardless of the eyes being open or shut). It is stated that overshooting or undershooting in this task (missing the tip of the nose by being respectively long or short of the tip) is the result of disequilibrium of muscular contractions due to errors in the stimulation of the movement inductor-resistor paired muscle contractions that arrest movement. Difficulty performing the task also "may be an early manifestation of a progressive cerebellar disease."

The tenth item (Fingertip Touching) requires the child to put the tip of his or her finger on the tip of the examiner's finger three times with each hand, first with the child's eyes open and then with them shut. The position of the examiner's finger remains constant during the procedure and the examiner stands close enough that the child's elbow must be flexed. While in Item #9 the manual warns against asking children under age five to touch their index fingers to their own nose with eyes closed due to likely distress on the child's part, children aged three perform Item #10 with eyes closed. Again, both quality and adequacy of response are judged, using the same guidelines used in Item #9. With eyes open, "both cerebellar and proprioceptive sensory systems are involved" (not the visual?), and with eyes closed "it is mainly a test of proprioception." Here the manual explains that "older children, on the whole, should perform better."

Item #11, the Finger Opposition task, is for "most children six years of age and older" although "some agile five-year olds are also able to perform this task smoothly." While no age-based scoring chart is given and explicit directions are missing, it seems that children five years of age and younger would not receive a "negative" evaluation on this item if they were to fail to perform it adequately. The task requires that the child consecutively touch the fingers of one hand on the thumb of the same hand, starting with the index finger, in the sequence 2, 3, 4, 5, 4, 3, 2, 3, 4, 5, etc. Five sequences from the index finger to the little finger and back again are required first with one hand, then the other (no hand order is mentioned). After a demonstration by the examiner, the child practices five times prior to evaluation. This task is evaluated for "smoothness of movement and transition" and "mirror movements" (associated movements in the opposite hand). The manual claims that "cerebellar coordination" is specifically sampled by Item #11, but specific explanations regarding the neurological structures and functions involved in finger opposition are lacking.

In Visual Positioning, Item #12, the examiner uses a small card to cover first one of the child's eyes and then the other while the child looks at an object that is at least 15 feet (or 5 meters) away. The examiner evaluates the child's response on the basis of any shift that occurs in the uncovered eye as the other eye is covered. The manual's discussion of Item #12 deals with Cranial Nerves III, IV, and VI, diplopia, manifest strabismus, heterotropia, alternate monocular vision, amblyopis, and the anatomy and physiology of the human eye—all of which seem very advanced and well beyond the grasp of examiners without any "specialized training," the individuals for whom the NDOC is intended.

Item #13, Visual Fixation, continues the evaluation of the child's visual performance begun in Item #12 (and continued through Item #15). Here the child is asked to fixate on an object (such as the point of a pencil) held in front of his or her eyes for a period of 15 seconds and at a distance of about 12 inches. The examiner is to evaluate this task "for deviation of one or both eyes, rhythmic or jerky movements of both eyes . . . and deviation of one eye from the point of visual focus." The manual states that interpretation of this item is similar to the interpretation for Item #12, but latent strabismus is now mentioned in the discussion and the examiner is informed that Item #13 is designed to detect nystagmus by one's recognizing "horizontal, vertical, rotary, or mixed" oscillations of the eyes.

Visual Pursuit (Item #14) has the examiner move a small object (such as a pencil eraser) horizontally and vertically in front of the child, who is asked to follow the object with his or her eyes without moving the head. Evaluation of the child's response is based on the range and quality of ocular movements, with special attention to whether the eye movements are "smooth, uncoordinated, or rhythmically deviant from each other." Along with Item #15, this item is specifically supposed to evaluate the child's ability "to aim the visual axes to any point within the field of vision," and interpretation is indicated as similar to that for Item #12.

Item #15, the last of those focusing on visual performance, is Involuntary Eye Movements. In this task, a small object (the same pencil eraser perhaps) is to be held about 20 inches in front of the child. The child is instructed to follow the object with his or her eyes while keeping the head completely stationary (the examiner may hold the child's chin if necessary). The object is to be moved slowly 45 degrees to the left of the child's body midline and held in place for about 10 seconds; the procedure is then repeated for the right side. The examiner is to note the extent of slow or rapid eye movements and any other asymmetries in order to judge nystagmus. The manual briefly refers to pendular nystagmus, spontaneous nystagmus, and directional nystagmus in its "clinically significant interpretations" discussion of Item #15, but does not explicate the kinds of straightforward, basic, and simple relationships between behaviors and neurological functioning that it would seem are required if examiners having no specialized training are to evaluate a child for nystagmus in less than a minute.

The final behavioral task, Tongue movements (Item #16), has the examiner carefully note any occurrence of involuntary movements in the child's tongue while the child 1) sticks out his or her tongue and keeps it as still as possible for an unspecified time (apparently at least 10 seconds duration); 2) moves the tongue from side to side, touching the corners of the mouth an unspecified number of times; and finally 3) protrudes the tongue as far as possible. The examiner demonstrates before beginning the tasks. Evaluation by the examiner rests upon "involuntary movements or twitchings of the edges or subareas of the tongue, difficulty or slowness when moving the tongue from one corner of the mouth to the other, and inability to protrude the tongue about one-third of its visible length." Though the manual states that a child over the age of seven or eight years should be able to perform the requested tasks smoothly and fully, no age-related basis for recording or evaluating the child is provided. The examiner is supposed to correctly distinguish "ripples along the edge and on the surface of the tongue" from normal contractions of muscle fibers, making the judgment on quite subjective bases. The manual briefly explains the action and innervation of the genioglossus muscles and relates Item #16 to genioglossus functioning in a general fashion.

2. *Head Circumference:* Item #17 instructs the examiner to obtain the largest head circumference measurement of the child by taking the average of three measurements from above the eyebrows to the rear of the head. The child's head circumference measurement is then compared with composite graphs from 1968 in order to determine if the child deviates by more than 2 SD from the mean (incorrectly labeled 50%). This evaluation is refreshingly objective and does not call upon the examiner to make the type and number of subjective decisions required in so many of the other items preceding it.

3. *Developmental History:* Item #18 consists of "a recommended outline" (actually 35 quite specific questions) touching on several major aspects of the child's early development. The examiner is urged to attempt to include the outline items in the conversation "with a parent, preferably the mother" about the child's early development. Supportive reference by the parent to some form of permanent record is desired whenever possible. The questions address pregnancy, the perinatal period, developmental milestones (age when first sitting unsupported, etc.), developmental disorders (such as bed-wetting past age three and temper tantrums), a medical history (loss of consciousness due to head injury, fainting, etc.), and the child's present status (primarily relative to physical status). The coverage seems more reasonable than does the expectation that the untrained examiner collecting this data will be able to "gradually weave into the conversation items that are not spontaneously offered" relevant to the child's developmental history, and correctly record and evaluate the less than perfect responses that all researchers experienced with interview schedules know occur. Little explanation about developmental history is given under "interpretation of item responses" (p. 27), especially when contrasted with the extensive information provided concerning "cranial nerves and associated functions" (pp. 28-32). It seems that the examiners to whom the NDOC is ostensibly aimed would be better able to understand more detail about the effects of events in every child's developmental history than the technical functioning of cranial nerves and the structures they innervate.

4. *Body and Skin Abnormalities, Speech Patterns, Visual Acuity, Auditory Acuity:* Gathered from examiner observations and health records, these data constitute nearly one-third (4 of 13) of the Interpretation Clusters making up the Referral Indication section of the Screening and Referral Chart "used to determine whether no referral is indicated or whether the child should be referred for a visual, audiological, pediatric, speech, or pediatric-neurological evaluation." Evaluation of body and skin abnormalities relies upon examiner decisions concerning "discolorations on the face, head, and neck" or "any other malformations of the head." Decisions as to the normality of the child's speech patterns also rests on examiner judgments about substitutions, inversions, perseverations, use of

language, verbal responses to toys and pictures which the examiner may have available, dysarthria, dysrhythmia, and aphasia.

That untrained examiners could be expected (required?) to accurately make such judgments seems untenable. Several factors combine to exacerbate the problems inherent in having untrained examiners "evaluate the child's speech patterns for aphasia (difficulty in understanding sounds of language)" when "aphasia is generally assessed by means of a battery of subtests which are designed to cover comprehensively the major aspects of language function" (Beaumont, 1983, p. 141). Aphasia refers to a much more generic deficiency than "difficulty in understanding sounds of language"; it is more often defined as "defect or loss of power of expression by speech, writing, or signs or of comprehending spoken or written language due to injury or disease of the brain" (Kolb & Whishaw, 1980, p. 474). Dysarthria is also more generally conceived broadly as "difficulty in speech production caused by incoordination of speech apparatus" (Kolb & Whishaw, 1980, p. 477) instead of Kuhns' more specific definition of it as "faulty pronunciation of consonants." Additionally, no explanations or definitions are given of "substitutions, inversions, or perseverations." The already overwhelming judgments placed on an untrained examiner would seem to be further impaired rather than facilitated by such definitions and omissions. Evaluations as to whether the child's visual acuity and auditory acuity warrant referral, while not explicitly outlined in the manual, apparently are to be gathered directly from the child's health records. Without substantiation by cited source, the manual states that "the school nurse often evaluates the visual acuity of a child, and the data is [sic] usually included in the student's health records." Certain questions related to confidentiality and accessing private information seem neglected in view of the intended users of the NDOC, and guidelines for obtaining data on the child's visual acuity from alternate sources when the school nurse does not have such information are noticeably missing. Even more evident by their absence are guidelines relevant to auditory acuity—apparently no one such as the school nurse routinely assesses auditory acuity. Since nearly one-third of the Interpretation Clusters come from these examiner observations and health records, it would seem that more accurate definitions, detailed guidelines for data collection and analysis, and well-developed explanations and rationales for the resultant evaluations should be provided.

Practical Applications/Uses

The aim of the NDOC to enable untrained examiners to effectively "screen" children between the ages of three and ten for either "no referral" or referral for full neurological assessment after a minimum of just two practice administrations, combined with the incomplete normative basis for the test, and the subjective, insightful judgments required of the examiner, pose serious problems for determining the most appropriate users of the NDOC. Professionals involved in neuropsychological assessment, "an area of increasing interest and concern to the psychoeducational assessment practitioner" (Helton, Workman, & Matuszek, 1982, p. 134), should certainly have (or obtain) the specialized training required to use more sophisticated (hence more powerful) assessment procedures available.

On the other side of the coin, however, it is questionable whether anyone actively engaged in neuropsychological assessment can recommend that nonprofessionals, lacking the appropriately complete "background in physiological psychology" (Obrzut, 1981, p. 332) required to conduct neuropsychological evaluation, complete just such evaluations. Perhaps, under the careful scrutiny and supervision of a skilled neuropsychologist who directs all phases of the assessment program, nonprofessionals might be able to appropriately use the NDOC to provide the neuropsychologist with initial, preliminary data that could serve as a starting point for the actual assessment of the child.

As for its usefulness in "differential diagnosis of a learning disability," the NDOC encounters the same problems mentioned concerning its more generalized use. The qualified professional would presumably rely upon tests requiring greater examiner expertise and having more substantiated normative data while the untrained examiner would again seem to be in a difficult and tenuous position making the judgments required of him or her by the NDOC.

The NDOC does assess some of the variables measured in standard pediatric-neurological evaluations, but it consists of a small, selected sample of the larger set of items employed in comprehensive, professional neuropsychological evaluations. The author states that "neurological evaluation is often stressful" and use of the NDOC "will eliminate unnecessary referrals" while it also accurately identifies those children actually needing referral. These rationales and purposes are clearly stated, but no equally clear reasons are provided to explain the selection decisions that led to inclusion and sequencing of these particular items, and no reasons are supplied to show how or why examiners having neither specialized training nor background knowledge in neuropsychology can be expected to use these familiar tasks in a less stressful but equally useful manner than a trained examiner.

Though not stated explicitly, it appears that the NDOC is intended for use with "normal functioning" children who have been referred principally due to school-related difficulties ("learning disability") which may be "primarily due to neurologically related problems." Adaptations for other populations, such as the blind, are not discussed in the manual, and given the untrained examiners supposedly using the NDOC additional demands placed on them to appropriately adapt evaluation procedures seem unreasonable.

The environment in which the NDOC should be administered is the usual setting, a physically comfortable room with a sturdy table and two chairs, enough room to walk 20 paces, and above average lighting (preferably natural light from a window which the child faces). Since the manual indicates that interruptions should be avoided, perhaps the test is to be administered only as a whole.

School psychologists or nurses are recommended as qualified to supervise use fo the NDOC by classroom teachers. It is difficult to determine the source of neuropsychological expertise under such circumstances, yet "unlike standard psychometric assessment, neuropsychological assessment must be flexible. This clearly makes interpretation difficult and requires extensive training in fundamental neuropsychology and neurology as well as in neuropsychological assessment" (Kolb & Whishaw, 1980, p. 450).

Time required to administer and score the NDOC is not discussed in the manual, and it seems difficult to estimate how long untrained examiners would take. Acquiring the developmental history, waiting as younger children take off and put on shoes and socks at least a couple of times, and obtaining permission to access the child's health records would add considerable time to test completion for all examiners. Perhaps estimation of administration time was omitted due to difficulty in predicting it because of these and similar variables.

Scoring the NDOC would appear not to take very long, since there are only 18 items requiring YES-NO responses. However, there are actually 47 YES-NO decisions to be recorded, and several of those are so ambiguously explained that scoring them may be extremely difficult in some cases, not just time-consuming. For example, Item #18 is the child's developmental history. This contains 35 questions to be answered by the child's parent, but the examiner must give *one* YES-NO response on the scoring sheet, based on no criteria beyond the statement "Significant deviations from normal development reported in record." Are 3 "significant?" Or, does it take 13 to be "significant"? Several other items require the examiner to give a YES-NO in circumstances that are also highly ambiguous and must be subjectively determined.

Related to the scoring, "a YES rating indicates that the child is not able to perform the task adequately." This may not confuse users of the NDOC. However, to score a subjectively determined "mild to moderate impairment" as a YES, and then explain that "the greater the number of items scored YES, the greater the degree of neurological impairment for the child" begs several serious scaling issues. For instance, how does the dichotomy merge into "degree"? Will all subjective judgments by different examiners be along the same scale and in the same scale units? These are important problems in the scoring of the NDOC.

Interpretation is, at first glance, based strictly on Section III (Referral Indication) of the Screening and Referral Chart where the various Interpretation Clusters (Section II) are related to specific referral decisions. The manual lacks explicit guidelines as to the number of "clusters" that are minimal for making a referral, and supposedly all 9 (of only 13 total) clusters related to the Neurologist Referral do not have to be "positive" before referral is made. Additionally, interpretations have actually been made at numerous stages during the NDOC—every time the examiner had to rely upon personal, subjective decisions as to the presence or absence of "mild impairment" in performance or about the "quality" of performance.

Another significant problem with interpretation of the NDOC arises when the examiner is informed that "when a child's response ratings do not conform to one fo the interpretation clusters, it is necessary to evaluate the ratings on the individual items." While this is an accepted, integral aspect of professional neuropsychological assessment (and a point of contention between it and traditional psychometrics), what place do such judgments have in the hands of examiners not required to have any specialized training? The manual continues by informing the examiner that "Several items will have similar interpretations. Hypotheses for further evaluation will need to be formulated from the individual item interpretations." Where is the examiner's background for such hypothesis formulation and subsequent testing? Certainly it is not in the curricula of the teachers, nurses, or occupational therapists the author refers to as the intended users of the NDOC. Its historical presence, even in doctoral clinical psychology programs, has often been "patchworked from unique local arrangements between departments of psychology and neuropsychology laboratories in medical schools" (Meier, 1981, p. 754). How can such expertise be expected from untrained examiners and then used to form an integral component of the screening decisions they make? Far more expertise seems prerequisite, even for screening decisions.

Technical Aspects

The manual's claim that "the data suggest that NDOC is highly reliable when used with children in the indicated age range" seems vastly overstated at best. Only 19 "normally functioning children three through twelve years old," all of whom "were attending a university campus school," hardly seem sufficient basis for claims that one's test is highly reliable. In fact, the questions related to why normally functioning 3- and 12-year-olds were in Grades 1, 2, or 3 are overshadowed by reliance on only 19 children, all from a possibly selective, non-public campus school as the sole support for the test's reliability. Actually, in the upper age range, only six children were tested—how many 12-, 11-, 10-, 9-, or 8-year-olds were tested in establishing this reliable test for use with such aged children? Since the number of children was so small, why were several examiners not used so that the same behaviors were rated by different examiners?

The impressive agreement reported between both the test-retest administrations and the examiners can easily mislead the unsophisticated reader. In this situation, agreement was not reached across a great diversity of choices, since each item offers only a YES or NO response. In fact, since all 19 sample children were normally functioning, how often were there really even two choices? Would not such normally functioning children be expected to "pass" all items, effectively producing agreement since nearly all children would successfully perform nearly all items? Contrary to the author's assertion that the data from those 19 children "indicated a sufficiently high level of reliability characteristics for inclusion of the NDOC in the evaluation battery," the reliability data reported in the manual are inadequate to recommend the clinical use fo the NDOC at this point in time.

Reliability (the extent to which a test consistently measures whatever it does measure, free from extraneous error) is a necessary but not sufficient condition for validity (the accuracy with which the test measures that which it is claimed to measure, providing support for inferences from the test). That is, if test results are due in large part to extraneous sources of error, thus producing different results unrelated to any "real" differences, how can that test be assessed for its accuracy in measuring its purported variable(s) and what confidence should be placed in the inferences based on it? In such a situation, variability in test scores can always be interpreted as due to the error in the test (i.e., as reflecting differences due to the test itself rather than to actual or "real" differences in the person being tested).

The validity data provided in the manual are inadequate support for the author's recommendation that the NDOC "be included in the comprehensive battery for use with children in the preschool and elementary grade range." The two "empirical validity" studies reported in the manual are small, methodologically flawed, and presented in an unclear manner.

"Clinical face validity" is an impressive way to say that the test looks like it measures what it is supposed to measure. The manual states that the "NDOC was critically reviewed by medical specialists" in neurology, ophthalmology, pediatrics, and family practice, but fails to disclose the number of these specialists. Neuropsychologists were surprisingly absent from the author's list of specialists. Such expert opinion or reliance upon authority is an unstable foundation for establishing the validity of a test. Face validity is adequate when one "assumes that the measures have meaning themselves and that no other generalizations are necessary" (Kaplan & Saccuzzo, 1982, p. 118). It does not seem that the NDOC is intended for "no other generalizations"; indeed, each individual item is explicated for interpretation (read *generalization*) on its own as well as part of a cluster of items.

The "empirical validity" for the NDOC is empirically flawed in several ways. The chi-square statistic ($x2$) used in both reported studies is a popular nonparametric procedure, and as such is one of those techniques that "will usually be relatively low-powered as compared with parametric tests," which produces "more risk of a Type II error" and necessitates that the researcher use a "larger sample size" (Hays, 1981, p. 575). In lay terms, that means that with a total number of only 28 in one study and only 28 children receiving the NDOC in the other study (though total number = 66), there is an increased chance of finding "significant" results than the reported level. Since the NDOC is claimed to function as a screening instrument and not a diagnostic one, why not compare it directly with results from comprehensive neuropsychological assessments in a situation where the NDOC examiners are unaware of the comprehensive assessment results? In the study involving 66 children "referred for evaluation," 38 were not given the NDOC, and of the 28 who were, 24 were "referred to specialists for a more comprehensive evaluation." Of those 24, 22 children had their NDOC screening results "corroborated" and the other 2 went on from the "indicated specialist" to neurologists. Some obvious questions arise here. What decision-making process preceded the NDOC and was so successful that it identified 28 children (out of 66), of whom 24 needed treatment for "significant problems"? (Maybe it should be used instead of the NDOC.) Does the NDOC always refer such a high percentage? Were the "indicated specialists" who corroborated the NDOC results aware of those screening results or properly "blind" to them? It is also unclear if "random cases" is really a proper designation for a sample of "children referred for evaluation."

In general, this reviewer disagrees vigorously with the author's statement that the NDOC "is a sufficiently valid and reliable instrument." Based on the presented technical data, the NDOC should not be used for clinical purposes, though further research work might prove beneficial.

Critique

Since the "consequences of failure to appreciate the complexity of brain-behavior relationships, while serious at any age, are particularly severe when dealing wiht children" (Boll & Barth, 1981, p. 419), the NDOC represents a potentially hazardous instrument beacuse it may understate or lead others to underestimate that "complexity." Some related problems (in addition to those covered previously in this review) deal with misleading statements that dominance "suggests that one hemisphere of the brain is superior to the other in controlling motor function" (Manual, p. 25) and also that "when preference is consistent, it would seem reasonable to speak of dominance" (Manual, p. 25). Such statements are erroneous and the untrained examiner preparing to use the NDOC and interpret items and item clusters has no background from which to identify such misstatements. Actually, motor control is contralateral (right side of the motor cortex controls the left side of the body and vice versa) and "knowing the handedness of a patient does not allow us to infer his speech lateralization" (Beaumont, 1983, p. 128).

It is also disturbing that the NDOC manual reprints virtually the entire "Modified Halstead-Wepman Aphasia Screening Test" (Boll, 1981, p. 591), omitting only some fo the instructions included on the original and without any well-developed rationale or explicit role for it explained in the NDOC manual. Such reproduction of an entire screening test seems most inappropriate.

Set off by bold-face type in a separate paragraph, "Body Sensory Receptor Systems" is mentioned in a very brief discussion of "this area of evaluation" which includes superficial and deep sensory modalities, pain perception, temperature discrimination, swaying tests, and pressure stimulation using various shapes. Again, however, it is unclear to the examiner just exactly what is to be done with this information. Such indeterminate information seems inappropriate in a manual for untrained examiners.

It must also be noted that the examiners involved in establishing the normative and technical data for the NDOC were graduate students in school psychology and a "consulting psychologist." These hardly seem like untrained examiners and should reasonably be expected to produce "better" psychometric results than the future intended users of the NDOC.

Administration, scoring, and referral procedures are sufficiently ambiguous and subjective that standardized assessment, producing consistent results across examiners and children, seems very unlikely. The reported reliability and validity data also fail to establish that such prerequisite standardization occurs in the use of the NDOC. The normative data are severely limited and inadequate in a test intended for clinical use. Clear operational definitions are missing from item procedures and response evaluations describing the NDOC items, thereby requiring extensive "judgment" as to both the psychometric procedures and the neurological evaluations. All of these dozens of necessarily insightful, neuropsychologically sophisticated, psychometrically sensitive, and potentially very powerful (relative to the child) judgments must be made by examiners having *no specialized training*. Such demands and expectations are inappropriately placed on untrained examiners and subject the children being evaluated with the NDOC to undesirably naïve use of test items "selected from standard medical evaluation procedures that make up the pediatric-neurological examination procedure." That such items, occurring as they do in the context of the NDOC, should be administered and interpreted by untrained examiners is very inadvisable. Such a situation, in order to be justifiable, would require 1) absolutely clear instructions for every phase of the test, 2) virtually no subjective decision-making, and 3) thoroughly documented normative-technical data showing that the items produce the desired results in the actual intended context instead of just what they produce in standardized medical evaluations conducted by highly trained professionals. Since the NDOC does not evidence these characteristics, it can not be recommended for clinical use.

References

Beaumont, J. G. (1981). *Introduction to neuropsychology.* New York: The Guilford Press.

Boll, T. J. (1981). The Halstead-Reitan Neuropsychology Battery. In S. B. Filskov & T. J. Boll (Eds.), *Handbook of clinical neuropsychology* (pp. 577-607). New York: Wiley-Interscience.

Boll, T. J., & Barth, J. T. (1981). Neuropsychology of brain damage in children. In S. B. Filskov & T. J. Boll (Eds.), *Handbook of clinical neuropsychology* (pp. 418-452). New York: Wiley-Interscience.

Hays, W. L. (1981). *Statistics* (3rd ed.). New York: Holt, Rinehart & Winston.

Helton, G. B., Workman, E. A., & Matuszek, P. A. (1982). *Psychoeducational assessment: Integrating concepts and techniques.* New York: Grune & Stratton, Inc.

Kaplan, R. M., & Saccuzzo, D. P. (1982). *Psychological testing: Principles, applications, and issues.* Monterey, CA: Brooks/Cole Publishing Co.

Kolb, B., & Whishaw, I. Q. (1980). *Fundamentals of human neuropsychology.* San Francisco, CA: W. H. Freeman and Co.

Kuhns, J. W. (1979). *Neurological dysfunctions of children.* Monterey, CA: CTB/McGraw-Hill.

Matthews, C. G. (1981). Neuropsychology practice in a hospital setting. In S. B. Filskov & T. J. Boll (Eds.), *Handbook of clinical neuropsychology* (pp. 645-685). New York: Wiley-Interscience.

Meier, M. J. (1981). Education for competency assurance in human neuropsychology: Antecedents, models, and directions. In S. B. Filskov & T. J. Boll (Eds.), *Handbook of clinical neuropsychology* (pp. 754-781). New York: Wiley-Interscience.

Obrzut, J. (1981). Neuropsychological assessment in the schools. *School Psychology Review, 10,* 331-342.

Rourke, B. P. (1981). Neuropsychological assessment of children with learning disabilities. In S. B. Filskov & T. J. Boll (Eds.), *Handbook of clinical neuropsychology* (pp. 453-478). New York: Wiley-Interscience.

Ira Fischler, Ph.D.
Associate Professor of Psychology, University of Florida, Gainesville, Florida.

NON-LANGUAGE MULTI-MENTAL TEST

E. L. Terman, W. A. McCall, and I. Lorge. Montreal, Canada: Institute of Psychological Research, Inc.

Introduction

The Non-Language Multi-Mental Test (NLMMT) is intended to estimate general intelligence through the ability to educe perceptual and abstract relationships among sets of pictorial symbols. These symbols include line drawings of both natural objects and geometric forms. The test consists of two forms, each of which has 60 problems; each problem presents five line-drawn figures, and the task is to recognize which of the five figures does not belong with the others. The use of pictorial rather than verbal symbols and the inclusion of pantomimed instructions as an alternative to verbal ones allows the testing of individuals who are illiterate, who cannot communicate with the examiner verbally, or whose linguistic ability is suspect.

The NLMMT, first described in E. L. Terman's doctoral dissertation (Terman, 1930), was developed by Terman in the late 1920s under the direction of W. A. McCall at Teachers' College of Columbia University. Its original purpose was to allow testing of intelligence of large groups in international settings (in this case, China), where there may be no common language between the examiner and the individuals being tested. It was derived from McCall's Multi-Mental Scale (McCall, 1925), which used an identical task with problem sets of words. The NLMMT was available for some years through the Teachers' College, but was acquired in 1967 by and is now available from the Institute of Psychological Research in Montreal. Apparently no revisions or special versions of the NLMMT have been developed since its original publication.

In a WPA program in New York City an initial set of 200 problems was given to 149 adults who were also given the Otis Self-Administering Test of Mental Ability, Higher Examination. The overall correlation of the problem set with the Otis test was .60. The final 120 items were selected based on individual standardized scores that had significantly nonzero correlations with the criterion score. These items were then divided into two Forms, A and B, of equivalent mean difficulty.

Forms A and B were administered to 2,531 children in Grades 3-8 at three public schools in New York City. Mental age for students in this normative group, obtained from various group intelligence examinations available at the schools, served as a criterion measure of intelligence (Terman, et al., 1942), and scores corresponding to mental ages above 177 months and below 75 months were extrapolated. The mental age equivalents for scores on the NLMMT are presented in the NLMMT test manual.

530

Both Form A and B have the same format: Each form consists of a four-page pamphlet, the first page of which includes brief instructions and four sample problems. Each of the remaining pages contains 20 problems. The pages are balanced in difficulty, but within a page problems are presented in increasing order of difficulty.

Each problem consists of five line-drawn figures presented in a horizontal row. The examinee indicates directly on the problem which figure does not match the others. The relationships that form the basis of exclusion include similarity and opposition, seriation, part-to-whole, and whole-to-part. The relevant dimension may be perceptual (e.g., a curved figure among angular ones) or more abstract (e.g., an edible object among nonedible ones). The use of five figures and of abstract dimensions for solution creates some difficulty to examinees because the figures may be classified in a number of ways. For instance, an object could be classified according to its size, shape, orientation, composition, completeness, texture, number, or function. Another source of difficulty is that the four items that are not excluded may share no common relation, but merely can be paired off successfully, leaving one odd figure. On the other hand, use of a limited set of relations or rules allows one to solve a given type of problem; for example, when parts are presented with a whole, the whole figure is always the correct one to exclude.

The test is designed to be administered individually or in group settings. After the examiners communicate the instructions and demonstrate sample problems to the examinees, they do not interact further with the examinees. Despite the availability of normative data for Grades 3-8 only, the test is intended to be used for preschool through adult; the lowest mental age presented in the manual is 33 months.

Practical Applications/Uses

The NLMMT would be appropriate for providing a rough estimate of an individual's reasoning ability in cases where language skill or communication is a problem. The manual specifically cites ''deaf or deafened'' individuals as appropriate subjects. These individuals are not apt to be illiterate or without language skill, but because the reading level of deaf persons tends to lag substantially behind that of nonhearing-impaired persons (see Trybus & Karchmer, 1977), it is important to include some nonverbal assessment of intelligence in their evaluation. The NLMMT may also be useful in clinical settings to assess the intactness of intellectual abilities in aphasic patients, supplementing the more commonly used Progressive Matrices and other, less formal diagnostic procedures. Because the NLMMT has not been widely adopted, and little evaluative work has appeared in the literature, it would be of limited value as a research tool without preliminary exploratory work relating the test to more recent efforts concerning the components of intelligence (e.g., Sternberg, 1984). Some alternative tests that have similar intentions include the Chicago Non-Verbal Examination (see Brown, 1940), and the Snijders-Ooman Non-Verbal Scale (see Snijders & Snijders-Ooman, 1959; Lavos, 1954).

Use of the test for ages not included in the normative sample is appropriate, but the wide range of ages the NLMMT purports to assess may make it relatively insensitive to smaller differences within age groups, especially at the extremes of adult and preschool. A difference in two items correct can correspond to a difference of ten points in estimated IQ. As Whitmer (1975) states: "A 30-minute test composed of 60 items which purports to differentiate mental age from 33 months to 236 months assumes almost miraculous discriminative power" (p. 273).

Either a group or individual setting is appropriate. The examiner can be a professional, secretary, or clerk; no expertise is required for administration, but in cases where pantomimed instructions are necessary some practice in presentation is recommended.

The manual includes step-by-step instructions to be read or mimed. About five minutes are required to relate the instructions and work through the four sample problems with the examinees. These procedures are straightforward and should present no difficulty. The vagueness about the relevant dimensions of the figures and the types of relations involved may create some confusion during the test; therefore, the examiner should be prepared to make it clear to examinees before they begin the test that no further clarification or hints will be provided. Also, because of the variety of ways that individual figures can be classified, an examinee may derive both the nominally correct solution to a given problem and an arguable basis for excluding a different figure. This may raise some questions during the testing.

Although the manual suggests a maximum time of 30 minutes to complete the test, it can usually be completed in less, and the manual does indicate that 15 minutes is adequate for grade-school children. In addition, it is advised that both Forms A and B be administered to improve reliability, but for younger children this may pose a problem because their attention spans are limited.

The key for scoring both forms is presented in the manual. The key completely specifies a single correct response for each problem, and no training is needed for scoring. One form can be scored in about a minute with practice. The test is hand-scored, but for older examinees it could be automated by using machine-readable answer forms. Younger children, however, might find the correspondence between test item and a machine-scored response form difficult, which could selectively impair their scores.

The normative mental age equivalents are derived directly from the number correct out of 60 for each form, and a conversion to IQ is straightforward. Interpretation of this measure is subject to the same kinds of guidelines that are advised for any single measure of intelligence derived from a particular test. In view of the wide range of mental age involved, the extrapolation beyond the normative sample, the particular nature of the task, and the modest size of the correlation of test scores in the normative sample with the schools' measure of IQ (average about .50), small differences within an age group on the NLMMT should be interpreted very cautiously.

Technical Aspects

Aside from the original evaluation of the NLMMT, this reviewer found no studies specifically addressed to the reliability or validity of the NLMMT. For the normative sample, reliability was estimated by the Kuder-Richardson reliability formula to be .94 for the combined Forms A and B. Within a grade the correlation between Forms A and B averaged .71. Validating the scores in the normative sample to scores on the schools' measures of intelligence produced an average correlation across Forms of .66 with mental age, and .40 with IQ.

Since the NLMMT task was identical to that of McCall's Multi-Mental Scale, evaluative studies including the latter test would offer some information about the reliability and validity of the NLMMT (see Lauderbach & Hause, 1932; Witty & Taylor, 1929).

Despite the term, "multi-mental" in the title of the test, it is formally equivalent to some specific tasks used by others in the subsequent study of intelligence to reveal particular factors or skills within the broader construct of intelligence. Guilford (1967) has used a Figure Exclusion Test in his investigations of intelligence structure that was intended as a measure of inductive reasoning. According to Guilford (1976, p. 79) inductive reasoning is defined as "forming and trying out hypotheses that will fit a set of data," the task being to identify perceptual relations and exclude one of five geometric figures. A similar test, called Figure Grouping, was used by Canisia (1962). However, the specific type, number, and abstractness of the relations defining the exclusion in these tests and the NLMMT vary. For instance, the pattern of factor loadings for the Figure Exclusion Test in Guilford's reports—largely on what he terms Cognition of Figural Classes and less so on Cognition of Semantic Classes—would probably not be identical for the NLMMT. Nonetheless, the NLMMT is best seen as involving skill in identifying and reasoning about classes on which objects or events can be discriminated. As an easily administered instrument that can be used in the nonliterate and/or nonlinguistic populations of concern, it can provide a fast, but probably gross estimate of this aspect of intellectual ability.

References

Brown, A. W. (1940). The development and standardization of the Chicago Non-Verbal Examination. *Journal of Applied Psychology, 24*, 36-47, 122-129.

Canisia, Sister M. (1962). Mathematical ability as related to reasoning and use of symbols. *Educational and Psychological Measurement, 22*, 105-127.

Guilford, J. P. (1967). *The nature of human intelligence.* New York: McGraw-Hill.

Guilford, J. P. (1976). *Manual for kit of factor-referenced cognitive tests.* Princeton, NJ: Educational Testing Service.

Lavos, G. (1954). Interrelationships among three tests of non-language intelligence administered to the deaf. *American Annals of the Deaf, 99*, 303-313.

Lauderbach, J. C., & Hause, E. (1932). On the reliability and validity of derived scores yielded by the McCall Multi-Mental Scale. *Journal of Applied Psychology, 16*, 322-323.

McCall, W. A. (1925). The Multi-Mental Scale. *Teachers College Record, 27*, 109-120.

Snijders, J. T., & Snijders-Oomen, N. (1959). *Non-verbal intelligence tests for deaf and hearing subjects: Snijders-Oomen Non-Verbal Scale, S.O.N.* Groningen, Netherlands: J.B. Wolters.

Sternberg, R. J. (1984). Facets of human intelligence. In J.R. Anderson & S.M. Kosslyn (Eds.), *Tutorials in learning and memory* (pp. 137-165). San Francisco: Freeman.

Terman, E. L. (1930). *The development and application of national education survey techniques, with special emphasis on criteria for measuring intelligence internationally.* Unpublished doctoral dissertation, New York University.

Terman, E. L., McCall, W. A., & Lorge, I. (1967). Non-Language Multi-Mental Test. Montreal: Institute of Psychological Research, Inc.

Trybus, R. J., & Karchmer, M. A. (1977). School achievement scores of hearing impaired children: National data on achievement status and growth patterns. *American Annals of the Deaf, 122,* 62-69.

Whitmer, C. A. (1975). Non-Language Multi-Mental Test. In O.K. Buros (Ed.), *Intelligence tests and reviews* (pp. 273-274). Highland Park, NJ: The Gryphon Press.

Witty, P. A., & Taylor, J. F. (1929). Some results of the Multi-Mental Test. *Journal of Educational Psychology, 20,* 299-302.

Barbara J. Yanico, Ph.D.

Associate Professor of Counseling Psychology, Southern Illinois University, Carbondale, Illinois.

OCCUPATIONAL ENVIRONMENT SCALES, FORM E-2

Samuel H. Osipow and Arnold R. Spokane. Columbus, Ohio: Marathon Consulting and Press.

Introduction

The Occupational Environment Scales (OES), Form E-2 is a brief paper-and-pencil measure of the level and sources of stress individuals report experiencing from work. More specifically, the OES measures the extent to which they experience specific work conditions generally agreed in the literature as stressful. The OES provides an index of the overall amount of stress at work as well as indices of the degree of stress from six specific aspects of work.

Dr. Samuel H. Osipow, the senior author of the scale, is a psychology professor and chairman of the psychology department at Ohio State University, past president of the American Psychology Association's Counseling Psychology division, and former editor of the *Journal of Counseling Psychology*. He has authored numerous books and articles, including a recent writing concerning the counseling psychologist's role in occupational mental health. Dr. Arnold R. Spokane, the second author, is also a counseling psychologist and on the faculty of the Counseling and Personnel Services program at the University of Maryland. Both authors are known for their work in vocational psychology.

The scale was developed for two primary reasons: 1) to develop a "generic" instrument that would be valid, reliable, and measure stressors that cut across different occupations and occupational levels (existing scales measuring stress at work and studies of work stress focus mainly on stressors in a limited number of specific occupations); and 2) to develop an integrated theoretical model linking sources of stress in the environment, the strains (symptoms) experienced by the individual as a result of the stress, and the person's available coping resources to reduce the strains. Osipow and Spokane subsequently developed three instruments to measure each aspect of the model; the OES measures the stress component.

The authors began their development of the OES with a review of the literature on occupational stress to identify frequently mentioned sources of work stress. From their review they identified and defined six common stressors predominantly associated with work roles, identified underlying facets of each stressor and generated items to tap each facet. Items were selected from this initial pool based on their perceived content validity; these items formed the first version of the scale, the OES, Form E-1, published in 1980. Form E-1 was administered to an initial sample of 201 adults employed in a variety of occupations. Psychometric analyses of these responses and feedback from the respondents were used as the basis for revision of the items. Items that were low in internal consistency or that caused difficulties in responding ''were edited, revised, deleted or substituted'' (Osipow & Spokane, 1983, p. 14). The authors also state that the response format was simplified, although they do not identify how. The remaining items were then analyzed based on the responses of 549 additional workers and form the present version of the OES, published in 1981. The first manual for the scales, published with Form E-2 in 1981, contained norms for a sample of 212 adults from 49 occupations. A revised manual (Osipow & Spokane) was published in 1983. The major changes in the second manual are psychometric data on the OES based on larger samples, an expanded norm group of 425 men and women working in 103 occupations, separate norm tables for men and women, and information on additional research testing the validity of the scale. Osipow (personal communication, October 30, 1984) reports that the authors have accumulated subsequent additional research and normative data. Thus, a third revision of the manual should be forthcoming.

The OES consists of 60 items in a four page, 7" x 8½" nonreuseable test booklet. The front page contains brief instructions and space for demographic information. The next three pages contain 60 statements about the conditions of work (e.g., working under time pressures, feeling too qualified for the job, exposure to a high level of noise). Examinees indicate their degree of agreement with each statement by circling a number on a 5-point Likert Scale printed to the right of each statement. The answer scale ranges from 1 (rarely or never) to 5 (most of the time). The reading difficulty level of the OES has not been determined, but the manual recommends that the scale be used with employed adults.

The OES consists of six subscales, each of which contains, 10 items. The subscales are as follows (Osipow & Spokane, 1983, p. 14):

Role Overload: Measures the extent to which the demands of the job exceed the resources of the worker and the resources provided by the workplace as well as the extent to which the worker can complete the amount of work expected.

Role Insufficiency: Measures how well workers' training, education, skills, and experience match their work.

Role Ambiguity: Measures the clarity of work instructions, priorities, and evaluation criteria.

Role Boundary: Measures the extent to which the respondent is experiencing conflicting demands and loyalties at work.

Responsibility: Measures the degree to which the worker feels responsible for others' performance and/or their welfare.

Physical Environment: Measures the amount of exposure to negative physical conditions including environmental toxins.

Each instrument includes a profile sheet for plotting the respondent's subscale scores. A single form provides places for plotting scores not only from the OES but from all three instruments. Raw scores are converted to standard percentile scores by consulting the appropriate norm table.

The 61-page manual is generally clear and well written and provides a great deal of information on the development, use, and technical aspects of the OES. The authors explore some very creative ideas for possible future applied uses of the scale, after further research more firmly establishes its validity and reliability, and the normative base is expanded.

At present, the same manual covers all three related instruments developed by Osipow and Spokane: the OES, the Personal Strain Questionnaire, and the Personal Resources Questionnaire. The manual includes a discussion of the theoretical underpinnings and development of each instrument; information on administration, scoring, and interpretation; brief summaries of research using the instruments; 32 pages of tables; 3 pages of references; a copy of each instrument; and a profile sheet. Discussion of the three instruments and tables of supporting data for each are intermixed throughout the manual. Given that the three instruments were developed concurrently to measure three components of a theoretical model and that they share data bases for initial psychometric analyses, this arrangement makes sense and saves space. It is also a useful arrangement of information for the test consumer who is using all three instruments as an integrated package. If you are using only the OES, however, you have to search through the manual for those portions of the text and those tables that are relevant. This reviewer did not find the table of contents very helpful for locating or relocating specific information. The addition of a separate list of the location of specific tables would be useful. Also, as the development of each instrument continues and diverges, and as the data base of each grows, separate sections of the manual devoted to each scale or separate manuals might be more preferable, even at the cost of some redundancy.

Another difficulty with the manual is that some of the technical information, particularly information on the samples used in various analyses and that comprise the norm groups, is sketchy. There are also some unexplained discrepancies in numbers that are minor but confusing. For example, the text states that internal consistency analyses were based on samples of N = 201 for Form E-1 and N = 549 for Form E-2, a combined total of 750 respondents. However, a table of the occupational distribution of this combined sample shows a total of N = 848. This reviewer hopes that future editions of the manual will deal with these problems of clarity in some of the technical information.

Practical Applications/Uses

The OES' original purpose was for research use to test the authors' theoretical ideas concerning work stress. Research is still the primary recommended use of the instrument, but the authors recommend cautious applied use of the scale. In addition to researchers, the OES would be useful to consultants to business and industry, managers, employee assistance counselors, or occupational health/medical personnel. In applied settings, the OES could be used to assess the sources of stress experienced by a group of workers; this information could then be used to design individual or institutional stress reduction interventions. The scale could also be used as an evaluation measure of the effectiveness of such interventions. The instrument could be used in similar ways by private practitioners or other mental health workers whose clients complain of workrelated problems. For example, discussion of scale scores or individual items might help in identifying stressors that clients possibly could change or aid the practitioner in helping clients work on coping techniques to deal with stressors that are inevitable and out of their control.

Because the OES is designed to be a "generic" measure, it should be useful for any level of work, in any occupation, and in any workplace. As emphasized in the manual, the scale should be administered only to individuals who want to take it and who have been informed of its purpose and how the results will be used. The scale should not be used to screen employees or to identify stressors in environments other than a workplace.

The OES is self-administered and is appropriate for groups or individuals either at home or in a structured testing situation. The only requirements for setting are that respondents have a place relatively quiet and free from distractions. There is little role for an examiner, except to provide the test booklet and information about why the respondent is being asked to complete the scale. The instructions for the OES are clear and complete as well as brief. The format is simple and should not create problems for respondents. The OES takes approximately 10 minutes to complete.

The manual outlines the scoring system in a table that indicates which items go on which subscales and which items are reverse-scored. Scores are simply the sum of ratings for the 10 statements that make up each subscale. A full-scale, grand total is also calculated. Subscales are relatively simple to keep track of because the items on the OES appear in subscale order, (i.e., items 1-10 make up subscale 1, Role Overload, etc.). To discourage response sets, items are worded so that 23 of the 60 items must be reverse-scored. This necessity to reverse-score some items is probably the major inconvenience and source of possible error in the scoring.

The manual does not provide information on the time it takes to hand-score the OES. This reviewer found that a single test takes about 10 minutes and that familiarity and practice can probably shorten the time. Although it would be relatively easy to make a template for each page of the OES to identify reverse-scored items, it would be a convenient addition if this were provided by the publisher. Machine- or computer-scoring is not available; however, it would be relatively easy, with slightly altered instructions, to have respondents answer on computer answer sheets and to write your own simple program for scoring. This certainly would be time-saving if the OES were being administered to a large number of respondents.

The scores on the OES are objective, therefore their interpretation does not require a great deal of training or sophistication. Some knowledge of norm groups and of what percentile scores mean would be the minimal knowledge necessary to understand the results.

There is some possibility for confusion in the interpretation of scores because the manual fails to describe what constitutes a "high" or "low" score. The manual cautions that "high and low score determinations should be made only using the appropriate normative samples" (p. 19). A table in the manual also provides summary descriptions of the endorsements of "high scorers," but there is never a concrete statement of the criterion for a high score. The profile sheet has horizontal lines dividing the profile into quartiles. This reviewer assumes, therefore, that this defines high and low cutoff points for the subscales (i.e., at the 75th and 25th percentiles, respectively). However, this is merely implied and might be a source of confusion, particularly for the relatively unsophisticated user.

Technical Aspects

The authors provide internal consistency data for the OES based on analyses of the responses of 549 adult workers in a variety of occupations. More detailed information about the sample is not provided. Chronbach alpha = .89, for the full scale and from .71 (Responsibility) to .90 (Role Insufficiency) for the subscales. This sample is certainly large enough and the coefficients high enough to suggest the OES and its subscales have adequate internal consistency.

Two-week test-retest reliabilities are reported, but only for Form E-1 based on a small sample (N = 31) of employed adults. For the original form, full scale reliability was .90. Correlations for the subscales ranged from r = .74 (Role Ambiguity) to r = .91 (Role Insufficiency). Thus, the original form of the OES demonstrated good reliability for a restricted sample over a relatively brief time period. With the type of modifications made on the second form it seems improbable that the scale's reliabilities would be altered drastically. However, additional test-retest data for Form E-2 based on a larger sample would reinforce confidence in the instrument's reliability.

Validity data for the OES comes from two sources: factor analysis and studies that correlate the OES with variables to which, theoretically, it should be related.

The authors subjected the OES to a factor analysis with varimax rotation to confirm empirically the logically derived subscales of the instrument. The data came from the 549 adult workers used in the analyses of internal consistency. Results revealed six factors accounting for a total of 87% of the variance. The manual concludes that "the factor structure provides confirmatory evidence for the subscales as postulated in the model" (p. 38). For the most part, this is the case. However, the analysis did reveal a factor, labeled "confusion" by the authors, that was a combination of items from the Role Boundary and Role Ambiguity subscales. There was also a separate factor labeled "Ambiguity." These results suggest that the Ambiguity and Boundary subscales are not "pure" and overlap. The item loadings from the factor analysis indicate that three subscales—Overload, Insufficiency, and Physical Environment—held up well. However, the other three subscales—Ambiguity, Boundary, and Responsibility—all have five or six of their ten items loading more highly on other scales than on the one to which the items are supposed to belong. Thus, further item revision is probably needed to strengthen these scales.

The authors also report on four correlational studies of the relationship between the OES and other theoretically relevant variables. These studies are difficult to evaluate because they are all unpublished works, and the information on them in the manual is sketchy. However, in general, it appears that expected relationships were found, and the construct validity of the OES was supported. Baldwin (1981) found that the overall level of stress was negatively related to the time it took to complete a master's degree, subsequent self-reported job satisfaction, and supervisors' ratings of performance in a sample of newly graduated counselors. Kramer (1983) found a strong relationship between job uncertainty and the level of stress reported by federally employed middle-level managers, but an expected relationship between stress level and absenteeism was not found. Forney (1982) found expected relationships among the level of stress reported and measures of strain and coping, as well as several indices of job burnout in a sample of career development professionals. Finally, Cowell (1983) found strong positive relationships between the Role Overload and Role Ambiguity subscales of the OES and a self-report measure of physical symptoms. To date, there have been no treatment studies reported that have used the OES.

A strong point for the OES is that preliminary normative data are available for it and that the authors are continuing their collection of data to expand the norm samples. It is rare for measures of work stress to have norms.

As previously mentioned, there are separate preliminary norms for men and women based on samples of 168 men and 257 women working in 103 occupations. There are some difficulties in evaluating these normative samples. No information is provided about the demographic characteristics of the samples except for gender. Also, it is impossible to determine, based on information in the manual, what occupations are represented in the norm samples and whether the occupations are similar for men and women. The manual does contain a table showing a frequency distribution of the occupational titles of the combined sample of respondents (N = 848) whose data were used for the psychometric analyses of either Form E-1 or Form E-2. Presumably, the normative samples are a part of this total, although this is unclear. The table does indicate a diverse range of 159 occupations represented, and most titles are represented by one or two respondents. There is also a preponderance of the psychometric sample representing a limited number of occupations. Five categories account for nearly 30% of the sample: career development professionals (11%), airline reservation agents (6%), counselors (5%), park rangers (4%), and teachers (3%). Unfortunately, another 36% of the sample is listed as "occupation unspecified." The samples on which the technical, presumably including normative, data are based are composed primarily of professional, technical, and managerial workers. Thus, support for the "generic" nature of the OES is tentative at this point. The consumer should use the norms of the OES cautiously until more normative data become available. The norm groups are relatively small and it is difficult, given available information, to evaluate their representativeness.

A final question this reviewer has about the norms is that the authors do not explain their decision to develop separate norms for men and women, a major change between the first and second editions of the manual. Although this decision is intuitively appealing, the authors do not explain their rationale and/or present any empirical justification for this development. The one study using the OES and comparing men and women in the same occupation found no gender differences (Forney, 1982).

On the positive side, the OES is in an early stage of development; in the manual the authors do repeatedly emphasize the tentative nature of their data and show an encouraging commitment to the OES's continued development, including the accumulation of additional data for the necessary expansion of the scale's norms.

Critique

The OES has a number of advantages. It provides a global measure of work stress, but also identifies the degree of stress experienced from specific aspects of work. It is based on a model derived from the theoretical and empirical literature on work stress; related instruments have been developed to measure other components of this model so that the OES can be used as part of an integrated package of instruments. It is designed to be a "generic" instrument for use with any worker in any work setting. Other advantages are the scale's brevity, clarity, general ease of use and interpretation, and the attention of the authors to establishing the instrument's reliability and validity.

Although the instrument is still in the process of development, preliminary reliability and validity data are promising. These data suggest that the OES has adequate stability as well as promising enough content and construct validity to recommend it for research use and for cautious clinical use. Possible applied uses at present are for individual or institutional assessment and/or stress reduction treatment evaluation. As previously discussed, factor analytic results suggest that several of the subscales may need further item revision; however, in general, the results support the validity of the logically derived subscales. Although correlational studies generally support the construct validity of the instrument, it should be noted that the OES has only been used in a limited amount of reported research at this point.

Some weaknesses in the normative groups and the samples that form the data base for early psychometric analyses were discussed previously. Nevertheless, the OES is one of the only available work stress measures that has even preliminary norms. The authors' commitment to the continued development and revision of the OES make it one of the most promising measures in this area.

Another very important advantage of the OES is that it has minimal competition. There is not a similar, competing brief questionnaire measure of work stress that can claim better reliability or validity. Work stress measures generally tend to suffer from a lack of even minimal reliability and validity data. In their review of organizational stress diagnostic procedures, Quick and Quick (1984) state: "Most of these measurement devices are ad hoc inventions of individual authors, designed as much to stimulate and challenge the subject of the measurement as to provide an objective or verifiable measure of stress" (p. 112).

Based on Quick and Quick's review, only two other self-report, paper-and-pencil instruments appear to provide direct competition to the OES. The Stress Diagnostic Survey (SDS) (Ivancevich & Matteson, 1980) is a similar, slightly longer instrument. The SDS provides a more detailed breakdown of stressors and has 15 subscales. Its construct validity is based on factor analysis. External validation is minimal. The range of internal consistency coefficients reported for the SDS is wider than for the OES, though generally the figures are comparable. Although the SDS has a larger data base than the OES for its psychometric analyses, the sample is very restricted, having been drawn from just five professional and managerial occupations, and there are no norms. The other instrument is the Michigan Stress Assessment (French & Kahn, 1962). This scale measures the degree of stress experienced from seven aspects of work, several of which appear to be similar to the OES subscales. Construct validity of the subscales is based on factor analysis. The authors report reliabilities comparable to the OES, but there are no norms for this measure either. Quick and Quick report that the Michigan measure has probably been the most widely used, but that "like the SDS, the external validation of these scales has been limited" (p. 119).

Thus, although the OES compares favorably with other similar instruments it appears to not yet be widely known or used. In their brief survey chapter, Quick and Quick review nine assessment devices in some detail and briefly mention five others. The OES is neither reviewed nor mentioned. Given its strengths, this instrument deserves more attention and wider use. With continued research and development, the OES has the potential to become the best instrument of its type—that is, a brief self-report questionnaire measure of stress at work.

References

Baldwin, A. M. (1981). *The relationship between graduate admissions variables and professional performance satisfaction and stress in master's level counseling graduates.* Unpublished master's thesis, University of Maryland, College Park.

Cowell, A. M. (1983). *Relationship of role overload and ambiguity to physical symptoms.* Unpublished master's thesis, University of Maryland, College Park.

Forney, D. S. (1982). *Sex and age and the evidence of reported stress, strain and burnout among career development professionals.* Unpublished master's thesis, University of Maryland, College Park.

French, J. R. P., Jr., & Kahn, R. L. (1962). A programmatic approach to studying the industrial environment and mental health. *Journal of Social Issues, 18,* 1-47.

Ivancevich, J. M., & Matteson, M. T. (1980). *Stress and work.* Glenview, IL: Scott, Foresman, and Company.

Kramer, G. (1983). *Relationship of occupational stress, uncertainty, job involvement and coping to absenteeism among mid-level federal managers.* Unpublished master's thesis, University of Maryland, College Park.

Osipow, S. H., & Spokane, A. R. (1981). *The Occupational Environment Scales, Form E-2.* Coluumbus, OH: Marathon Consulting and Press.

Osipow, S. H., & Spokane, A. R. (1983). *A manual for measures of occupational stress, strain and coping* (Form E-2). Columbus, OH: Marathon Consulting and Press.

Quick, J. C., & Quick, J. D. (1984). *Organizational stress and preventative management.* New York: McGraw-Hill.

Jeffrey Gorrell, Ph.D.
*Professor of Educational Psychology, Southeastern Louisiana
University, Hammond, Louisiana.*

ORDINAL SCALES OF PSYCHOLOGICAL DEVELOPMENT

*Ina C. Uzgiris and J. McVicker Hunt. Champaign, Illinois:
University of Illinois Press.*

Introduction

The Ordinal Scales of Psychological Development (Uzgiris & Hunt, 1975) are observational measures that use six scales to assess the level of cognitive and perceptual development in seven different areas of infant interaction with the environment. The overriding principle governing these scales is that there exists an invariant sequence of behavioral landmarks, not linked with specific age, that characterizes the infant's abilities to manipulate and organize interactions with the environment. Based upon Piagetian principles of cognitive development, the scales are used in research studies to determine the competencies attained by children in the sensorimotor stage of cognitive development. The theoretical ground for these tests, then, rests upon now-classic conceptions of the child's interactions as becoming increasingly organized and complex as the child gains experience in physically and mentally manipulating the external world.

Uzgiris and Hunt, psychologists at Clark University and the University of Illinois at Urbana-Champaign, respectively, began construction of the ordinal scales along Piagetian principles at the University of Illinois during the spring of 1963. Their belief that early cognitive development could not be assigned simple age correlates, but should be understood in terms of the eliciting situations that provide for perceptual and cognitive advancement, led to the development of the six scales. Early development of the scales occurred in three phases that progressively narrowed and refined the observation instrument to its formal, final state.

An original series of *eliciting situations,* based on Jean Piaget's observations on the development of his own children, and specifically named *critical actions* on the part of the targeted children formed the exploratory study (first phase) of 42 male and female infants. Refinement of the scales in the second phase with 23 infants led to the development of a third version of the scales, which was presented to 84 infants during the fall of 1963 and all of 1964. The authors and four other examiners worked in pairs in examining infants from one to 24 months of age in the children's homes. Interobserver agreement, computed in the paired observers' codings of the behaviors of the children, was notably high in this phase of the development of the instrument. For most eliciting situations high degrees of

543

interobserver agreement and high levels of stability in the children's behaviors were found from session to session. A final revision of the instrument enumerated more fully than earlier versions the possible infant reactions to eliciting situations, omitting those in which little observer agreement could be found, that were too dependent on motivation or quality of the infant's mood, that were difficult to structure, and that had little or no apparent relevance to the child's developing ability.

Children tested in the development of the instrument were children of professors and graduate students at the University of Illinois who had responded to requests for volunteers in the devising of the scales. Because the original intent of the scales was to develop a series of precise eliciting situations that could be used as ordinal scales of development, related conceptually to a different set of assumptions than those found in typical tests, norms for the population-at-large were not sought. Appropriately, the authors refer to the provisional nature of this scale when proposing its uses and describing the sample on which it is based.

The Uzgiris-Hunt ordinal scales involve careful presentation of objects and eliciting situations to infants in six scales (scale 3 is divided into two subscales), each of which contain a variety of specific activities that constitute steps in development. The scales that comprise the complete instrument are 1) The Development of Visual Pursuit and the Permanence of Objects, 2) The Development of Means for Obtaining Desired Environmental Events, 3) The Development of Vocal and Gestural Imitation, 4) The Development of Operational Causality, 5) The Construction of Object Relations in Space, and 6) The Development of Schemes for Relating to Objects. The authors consider each scale to be independent from the others and capable of being used independently in assessing infant abilities, depending on the objectives of the examiner.

A 34-item list of suggested material to be used in presenting the eliciting situations accompanies the authors' scales. Most of the items can be obtained or constructed easily by any individual who desires to use the scales. Items include aluminum foil, ball, bell, blocks, bottle, box, toy car, cardboard, checkerboards, container, cotton, cup, doll, jumping jack, mechanical toy, multicolored ring, musical clown, musical rattle, necklace, pillow, pinwheel, plastic animals, plastic flower, pull-toy, rattle, screens, shoe, slinky, spool, stacking rings, stick, string, stuffed animal, and walking toy. Specifications of the desirable or essential characteristics of these items are provided. However, substitutions for the recommended objects may be made as long as they fulfill the rationale for each situation.

Instructions for each eliciting situation include a description of the location for the activity, the objects to be used, directions for providing the activity, and how often to repeat it. In addition, a list of possible infant reactions (including specification of the action that is considered to be critical for achievement of a step in a scale) is provided. The first step in scale one (The Development of Visual Pursuit and the Permanence of Objects) serves as a good example of the information provided:[1]

---

[1]From *Assessment in Infancy: Ordinal Scales of Psychological Development.* Copyright © 1975, by the University of Illinois Press. These materials are reproduced here by permission of the University of Illinois Press.

Following a Slowly Moving Object Through a 180-degree Arc

Location:	The infant may be supine on a flat surface, in an infant seat, or sitting up by himself.
Object:	Any bright object that attracts the infant's attention, but does not make a sound when moved, e.g., the multicolored ring.
Directions:	Hold the object about 10 inches in front of the infant's eyes, until he focuses on it. With a young infant it may be necessary to shake the object lightly in order to attract attention or to vary its distance from the infant's eyes, to find the optimal focal distance. If an older infant tends to focus on the examiner rather than the object, stand behind the infant. Once the infant has focused on the object, move it slowly through a lateral arc of 180 degrees.
Repeat:	3-4 times.
Infant Actions:	a) Does not follow object.
	b) Follows object through part of arc with jerky accommodations.
	c) Follows object through part of arc, with smooth accommodations.
	*d) Follows object through the complete arc smoothly.

An asterisk (*) indicates the critical action that reveals attainment by the infant.

There is some degree of latitude provided to the examiner in determining the best way to test a particular infant. This latitude is provided under the recognition from experimental settings that the infant activities elicited are robust and not dependent upon a single way of presenting stimuli.

The examiner is responsible for arranging a setting, preferably in the infant's home, that is conducive to the infant's interest and cooperation in the activities. Guidelines are provided for establishing an appropriate level of cooperation and for minimizing the negative effects of being a stranger to the infant. It is made clear that the eliciting activities as well as particular toys utilized are meant as guidelines only. The presence of two observers who are trained in coding the child's responses is important, particularly if the scales are being used for research purposes. The examiner, while presenting the stimuli to the infant, may be one of the observers. Activities are easy for the examiner to understand and to present. Sensitivity to the behavior of infants would be a clear advantage for the examiner and observers, however.

Examination record forms, designed to be used during the observation of an infant, provide concise, but highly usable descriptions of each of the eliciting activities, the number of repetitions that are recommended, and brief descriptions of the infant actions that may be noted. This checklist requires only minimal concentration and practice to be used effectively in the course of the examination. Sample summary record forms for each of the scales are also provided in order to provide a quick evaluation of the development level achieved by an infant who is tested.

The ordinal scales present information about the specific developmental level achieved in each of the six scales; therefore, there are not standard scores to be reported at the conclusion of the examination. The nature of the behavior being observed and the provisional character of the scales make such observations more meaningful if they are not scaled in traditional fashion. Thus, the checklist and specific, additional observations made by the observers form the basis for developing a profile of an infant. Some familiarity with sensorimotor development and with Piagetian principles of cognitive development may be helpful to the examiner in constructing a well-formed picture of the infant's development. Background in Piagetian theory, however, is not critical.

Practical Applications/Uses

This instrument is used in highly specific contexts with a restricted age range of subjects: infants who are developmentally normal or abnormal. It is not an intelligence test in the ordinary sense of the term, but it can be used to compare children in terms of their advancement or retardation in the various developmental areas. The scales may also be used to determine what kinds of environmental circumstances or specific encounters with the world speed up the course of perceptual-cognitive development. Researchers and practitioners who are engaged in infant training programs may find the scales useful as indices of advancement. Practitioners will not find this test a useful one for determining treatment of infants.

The Ordinal Scales provide a clear-cut, developmentally accurate set of infant scales that can be used to assess the specific attainments of infants in the sensorimotor stage of development. Variables tested are encapsulated in the six separate scales described above. Within each scale there is a sequence of activities presented that are linked in ascending order from simple to more complex. Attainment of a skill at one of the higher levels on any of the scales implies successful attainment of earlier skills. For example, if a child can track an object through a 180° arc, it is suggested that the child can also track a moving object through a lesser arc.

Subjects are infants up to about 24 months of age with intact visual and auditory senses or older mentally retarded children. The nature of the tasks typically precludes use with blind or extremely auditorily impaired children, but adaptation of the scales for the sensory and motor impaired have been suggested by some researchers (Robinson, 1981). All ranges of intellectual ability of infants may be tested; a number of studies indicates that the scales are reliable for severely and profoundly retarded children (Kahn, 1976).

Each scale is used with only one child at a time, preferably in the child's home in order to establish a cooperative relationship. It can be used in other settings, however, if the child can be made to feel comfortable in that setting. The examiner should be familiar with the procedures and guidelines presented in the instructions; formal training in psychology or any other academic field is not essential, although some knowledge about Piagetian principles of development and infant sensorimotor responsiveness would be helpful in presenting the eliciting situation.

Administration procedures are clearly described in the authors' instructions. There is leeway in the order of presentation of the activities and in the physical arrangement of the setting. It is recommended that the tests be given only as long as the child is interested and cooperative, which can range from a few minutes to two hours. Testing can be done on more than one occasion without jeopardizing the validity of the scales.

A revised set of record forms (Uzgiris & Hunt, 1982) provides clear explanations of the preferred method of scoring the instrument. Scoring occurs by means of a sample checklist that incorporates the possible actions of the infant, including specification of the critical action that reveals attainment of a particular developmental landmark. The highest level attained by a child on a scale can be thought of as the score but, as the authors point out, what is more meaningful is the understanding of a particular infant responses in the context of ordinal development. For each situation on each scale infant actions, which have been observed in the course of the authors' observations, are listed, as well as condensed descriptions of those actions. Critical actions are indicated in italics on the form. In appropriate situations, provision is made for recording actions that are not listed on the form. Also provided is a sample record form, already filled out.

An observer of the infant interactions can record actions simply and efficiently on the record forms without significantly disrupting the examination of the infant. The authors point out that simplification of the record forms may be done if the examiner's purpose is to study the range of behaviors in a particular setting. It also may be expanded to indicate clearly all of the behaviors elicited by the stimuli, not just those provided for in the record forms. Again, it is pointed out that the goal of this type of assessment is to characterize an individual child accurately and fully in various domains, not to derive a scaled score that can be compared to norms.

Instructions for scoring are clearly presented. Basically, it involves recording specific behaviors and the number of eliciting situations that were presented to the child. It takes a fairly high degree of sophistication in the basis of the instrument and familiarity with the instrument as a whole to be able to use the record forms. If two observers are used in scoring the child's actions, the usual concerns for interobserver reliability will need to be confronted. Well-trained observers, however, may be able to reach high levels of interobserver reliability without too much difficulty.

Summary record forms are intended for use following the examination. They are less detailed but provide useful summations of overall levels of development in each of the six areas. Because this summary record form lists situations and critical actions by number and letter only complete familiarity with the scales is necessary to use it without reference to the examination record forms. These summary forms allow quick perusal of the highest level attained by an infant on each of the scales and the convenient noting of patterns across scales. They are most useful in research studies where observations of infants need to be transformed into salient indicators of levels of development.

Interpretation of the scales is relatively objective because the record forms merely record infant responses. The examiner is encouraged to describe in available spaces on the form infant behavior that does not coincide with the behaviors listed. Knowledge about sensorimotor development and Piagetian theory may enable the examiner to place the child's behavior in a larger context of cognitive development. The construction of the ordinal scales is firmly tied to the assumption of invariant sequences of perceptual and motor development, and the examiner is presumed to accept that orientation in the initial decision to utilize the scales. Actions of the infant, therefore, are easily related to the underlying philosophy by someone who is versed in it.

Technical Aspects

Children used in developing the scales were chosen so that at least four infants represented each month of age from one to 24 months. The instrument is offered by the authors as provisional and not as the final word on testing sensorimotor development.

The scales are organized around ordinal principles that logically relate the accomplishment of one task to the accomplishment of prior tasks. Successful attainment of a particular activity implies the attainment of simpler activities. Thus, the authors argue that the scales have what Robert Gagne (1965) calls *intrinsic validity*. In these types of scales, comparisons of performances against norms are not meaningful ways of establishing validity. Instead, the tasks in each scale are subjected to empirical testing to determine whether, in fact, an invariant sequence of attainments does exist.

The authors' studies using the instrument support the overall validity of the scales, particularly the ones which are composed of very small steps in the sequence of activities. In those sequences of activities where a clear progression of critical actions exists with regard to the same stimuli, high confidence may be assigned to the invariant nature of the sequence. However, where the progression depends upon differing eliciting situations to bring out a sequence of critical actions there is the possibility that extensive experience with a particular activity may in itself be enough to enable the child to perform appropriate actions. In that case, later actions in the sequence would not necessarily be affected by the attainment of the prior competency; thus, the invariant nature of the hypothesized sequence would be suspect. The authors point out that their confidence in the sequences of the scales, based upon intersession stability, is high for all but scales two and six, which may be subject to the limitation mentioned above.

Reliability, as determined through interobserver agreements on the elicited actions, is notably high overall, ranging from 93.0% to 98.5% from scale to scale. Intersession stability is less strong, but still respectable in most cases; for scale one through six, the levels of stability found were 83.8%, 75.5%, 70.0%, 71.2%, 84.6%, and 79.0%, respectively.

A few studies have attempted to assesss the reliability and validity of some or all of the scales in a variety of contexts. King and Seegmiller (1973) found that a sample of 51 black, firstborn male infants obtained comparable results as those of Uzgiris and Hunt. Siegel (1981) found that many subscales, particularly the means, schemes, conceptual ability, and space scales correlated highly with the Bayley Scales of Infant Development. She also found that the Uzgiris-Hunt scales are significantly correlated with language development and that they differentiate between infants who are delayed at two years of age and those who are not. Silverstein, McLain, Brownlee, and Hubbel (1976) used cluster analysis and factor analysis to determine that the contention of Uzgiris and Hunt that the scales are independent of each other is valid. Kahn's (1976) scalogram analysis indicated that the scales are ordinal in nature with severly and profoundly retarded children. Uzgiris and Hunt point out, however, that the ordinality of the scales is lower for mentally retarded adults and motorically impaired children.

A few limitations have been observed by researchers. Seigel (1981) found that the scales are most predictive below eighteen months of age, and not very predictive from 18 to 24 months. Silverstein, Brownlee, Hubbell, and McLain (1975) found a possible ceiling effect in the object permanence scale and low levels of internal consistency in the spatial relationships scale, suggesting heterogeneity of content in that scale. Overall, however, the scales stand up as reliable and valid measures of specific developmental landmarks.

Critique

The Ordinal Scales of Psychological Development is a successful attempt to provide independent scales that assess the perceptual and cognitive developmental landmarks of infancy. An extensive body of research has demonstrated the strength of the authors' contentions regarding the invariant sequences of certain sensorimotor abilities of infants. Empirical evidence for the robustness of the eliciting situations has been gathered in the ten years since the publication of the completed scales. In may ways, the scales and the methods employed in deriving them are excellent representatives of the contemporary, practical measures that have been built around Piaget's research and theory. Possibly the strongest challenge to these scales lies in the burgeoning body of research that contradicts some essential assumptions of invariant sequence in cognitive development. Although infant development appears to be less vulnerable to contemporary revisions of Piagetian theory, some caution is appropriate in considering whether to utilize the scales as sole measures of infant development.

References

This list includes text citations as well as suggested additional reading.

Fieber, N. M. (1977). *Sensorimotor cognitive assessment and curriculum for the multihandicapped child.* Unpublished manuscript. Nebraska University Medical Center, Meyer Children's Rehabilitation Institute, Omaha.

Gagne, R. M. (1965). *The conditions of learning.* New York: Holt, Rinehart & Winston.

Holdgrafer, G. (1976). Assessment in Infancy: Ordinal Scales of Psychological Development. *Mental Retardation Bulletin, 4* (1), 36-39.

Hunt, J. McV. (1973, August). *Utility of ordinal scales derived from Piaget's observations.* Paper presented at the annual meeting of the American Psychological Association, Montreal, Canada.

Kahn, J. V. (1976). Utility of the Uzgiris and Hunt scales of sensorimotor development with severely and profoundly retarded children. *American Journal of Mental Retardation, 80* (6), 663-665.

King, W. L. & Seegmiller, B. (1973). Performance of 14- to 22-month-old black firstborn male infants on two tests of cognitive development: The Bayley Scales and the Infant Psychological Development Scale. *Developmental Psychology, 8,* 317-326.

Robinson, C. C. (1981). *A strategy for assessing motorically-impaired infants.* Unpublished manuscript. Nebraska University Medical Center, Meyer Children's Rehabilitation Institute, Omaha.

Siegel, L. S. (1981). Infant tests as predictors of cognitive and language development at two years. *Child Development, 52* (2), 545-547.

Silverstein, A. B. McLain, R. E., Brownlee, L., & Hubbell, M. (1976). Structure of ordinal scales of psychological development in infancy. *Educational and Psychological Measurement, 36* (2), 355-359.

Silverstein, A. B., Brownlee, L., Hubbell, M. & McLain, R. E. (1975). Comparison of two sets of Piagetian scales with severely and profoundly retarded children. *American Journal of Mental Deficiency, 80* (3), 292-297.

Uzgiris, I. C., & Hunt, J. McV. (1975). *Assessment in infancy: Ordinal scales of psychological development.* Urbana, IL: University of Illinois Press.

Uzgiris, I. C., & Hunt, J. McV. (1982). *Record forms for the Uzgiris-Hunt scales.* Urbana, IL: University of Illinois Press.

Allan P. Jones, Ph.D.

Associate Professor of Psychology, University of Houston, University Park, Houston, Texas.

THE ORGANIZATIONAL CLIMATE INDEX

George Stern and Associates. Syracuse, New York: Evaluation Research Associates.

Introduction

The Organizational Climate Index (OCI) is one of a set of indices developed by George Stern and his associates. This set of indices, entitled the Stern Personality and Environment Indexes, was developed to measure both the personality needs of the individual and the psychological character of the environment. The OCI is a measure of the environmental character of an institution or organization. The title, Organizational Climate Index, however, does not describe the particular area that is to be measured or the type of measurement technique that was adopted. Organizational climate has been defined in many ways and approached from a variety of theoretical perspectives. To understand the nature of the OCI and its possible uses, it is necessary to know the broader theoretical perspective that led to its development and to touch briefly on the focus of other tests in the Stern Indexes.

The Stern Personality and Environment Indexes are based on the theories of Henry Murray (1938, 1951) who stressed that behavior was an outcome of the relationships between an individual and the environment. The primary element of interest in regard to the individual was the concept of *psychological needs.* Its situational counterpart was the concept of *press.*

As discussed by Stern (1970b) in the book that details the development and validation of the Stern Personality and Environment Indexes, psychological needs are the tendencies that give unity and direction to an individual's behavior. Stern notes that a listing of needs "is essentially a taxonomy of the objectives that individuals characteristically strive to achieve for themselves" (p. 6). He formally defines needs as a "taxonomic classification of the characteristic spontaneous behavior manifested by individuals in their life transactions." (p. 7). In other words, needs must be inferred from individual preferences about behavior. Thus, The Stern Activities Index (Stern, 1972) is a questionnaire that seeks to identify a person's needs in terms of "like" or "dislike" responses to 300 items. Each item describes routine activities or feelings. The responses to these items are then translated into scores on 30 need scales.

Press describes the conditions that represent obstacles to the expression of a

---

This reviewer wishes to acknowledge the assistance of Daniel Turban and Stephen Fox in the preparation of this review.

need or make such expression easier. However, the concept of press is further differentiated. *Beta press* refers to the unique and private interpretation that each person places on the events in which he or she takes part. *Consensual beta press* refers to the fact that people who share a common ideology also tend to share common interpretations of events. Stern acknowledged that participants are apt to view events in terms that might differ from those used by detached observers. Thus, he suggested that it was also necessary to consider the concept of *alpha press*. This latter term refers to the situational climate—permissible roles, relationships, and other interpretations of events that would be described by a detached observer. The OCI, which is designed for administration to members of an organization, measures those members' interpretations of events or beta press. When group scores are developed from the OCI, such scores might also provide an index of consensual beta press.

This distinction between the private psychological interpretation arrived at by the participant and the more objective situation identified by a detached observer has become common in the literature on climate, where it has been suggested that the term "psychological climate" should be used to describe the individual's private interpretation of the environment.

Although the OCI publishers indicate that OCI is a general instrument that can be used to characterize the psychological climate of a wide variety of work settings, the OCI is a direct outgrowth of previous instruments that were intended for application only to academic settings. The initial instrument in the sequence, the College Characteristics Index (CCI) (Stern, 1970a) developed in 1957, was intended to parallel as closely as possible the 30 need scales of Stern's Activities Index. The original version was administered to upperclassmen and administrators in five schools. This initial study was described by Pace and Stern (1958). Later versions, described by Stern (1970b), have been administered to more than 100,000 students in more than 100 colleges.

The CCI was followed by two additional instruments—The High School Characteristics Index (HSCI) and The Evening College Characteristics Index (ECCI)—designed to measure high-school characteristics and developed on samples of students at Syracuse University.

The OCI grew out of these instruments and represents an attempt to make such previous instruments more general in their application. The OCI measures the environment in terms of 30 scales, each of which is directly complementary to one of the need scales. Thus, the OCI represents a questionnaire-based measure of the individual's psychological interpretation of conditions and events in the organizational environment that render it easier or more difficult to engage in various need related behaviors. An initial version (Form 662) was prepared and subsequently revised to become Form 1163, the one reviewed here. Comparison data for this form were obtained from samples of enrollees in 65 Peace Corps training units in 48 college training programs and from 223 engineering, technical, and clerical employees at three remote industrial sites in Alaska, the Near East, and the United States. As was the case for the preceding indices, however, the primary sources of validity information were academic institutions.

George G. Stern was the major architect for these different indices. Stern received his Ph.D. in social psychology from the University of Chicago in 1949. In

1953, he joined the faculty at Syracuse University where he remained until his death in 1974. From 1953 to 1974, he was head of the psychological evaluation and assessment laboratory, Psychological Research Center at Syracuse. It was during this period that most of the work on these instruments took place. However, many others, including C. Robert Pace, Carl R. Steinhoff, and Joel Richman, contributed to these efforts (see Stern, 1970b).

The OCI-1163, the long form, consists of 300 statements. A short form version, OCI-375SF, was developed later by Stern, Steinhoff, and Richman (1975). The 80 items in the shortened version all appear in the longer 300-item set. In both forms, each statement is answered true or false on an accompanying answer sheet, which is computer scorable through the use of optical scan (OPSCAN) equipment. According to the Form 1163 test booklet (Stern & Steinhoff, 1963), a statement is to be rated "True" if the respondent feels that it is "generally true or characteristic of the organization, is something which occurs or might occur, is the way people tend to feel or act" (p. 1). Alternatively, the statement is to be rated "False" if the respondent feels that it is "not characteristic of the organization, is something which is not likely to occur, is not the way people typically feel or act" (p. 1). Thus, the respondent is forced to make a categorical assessment of the applicability of each statement according to whether the statement is probably true or false. The booklet also contains explicit instructions to answer every item.

The statements are descriptive in focus. The respondent is instructed to indicate what the institution is like, *not* what it should be. The test may be administered individually or in group sessions in any environment that provides appropriate space to write responses. Ideal environments would be classrooms or offices.

The instructions are clear and self-explanatory so that the test could be self-administered by anyone with reasonable literacy skills. In addition to ensuring that the answer sheets are marked with a soft-lead pencil, the test administrator might be required to give a verbal explanation of procedures and a review of specific sample items if examinees have limited reading ability or limited experience with computer-scorable answer sheets.

Although the test is described as general in its focus, the wording of the items and the content of the 30 dimensions seemingly make it more appropriate for settings, such as offices and research or similar white collar environments, rather than heavy industry or manufacturing environments. Questions such as "Many people here enjoy talking about poetry, philosophy or religion" or "There is considerable interest in the analysis of value systems and the relativity of societies and ethics" may be viewed with disbelief in many work settings.

The authors of the test suggest that the OCI is appropriate for all persons above age 12. However, the reading level required to understand the various questions is relatively advanced and is perhaps most appropriate to settings that attract individuals with reading comprehension skills nearing a college-entry level. The authors also suggest that the average respondent will complete the short form in 20 minutes or less. Extrapolation from this figure would require approximately 80-90 minutes for the 300-item version, although the manual suggests that 40 minutes is sufficient. My personal experience with similar instruments suggests that this estimate is optimistic. In many work settings, two hours may be a more realistic estimate for the longer version.

Practical Applications/Uses

Although the OCI might be helpful in a variety of tasks, the primary uses appear to be as an instrument for individual counseling and as a possible tool for organizational diagnosis and intervention. In the former application, a counselor might wish to combine the OCI with data from the Activities Index (AI) to derive information as to how well a student or employee conforms to a particular environment. For example, a high-school counselor might combine a student's AI data with OCI group data, describing various colleges, in order to suggest schools that are appropriate for that applicant. In the second application, an organizational manager or personnel specialist might use the average score from several members' OCI responses to draw conclusions about possible changes that might be needed in that organization.

In either of these applications, the user of the OCI must keep in mind certain concerns about the nature of the data provided. First, the responses describe individual perceptions of the organization. Thus, interventions must consider the effect of changes in events upon these perceptions. Second, an attempt to change conditions requires information about the causes of these conditions and the effects of various climate profiles on the attitudes and behaviors of persons in the organization. Such information is not contained in the scoring manual but must be acquired elsewhere, such as in Stern (1970b) or in other articles and books on organizational change or climate, if the OCI is to be used as an instrument to guide change. Finally, the OCI's development history and the population used for its validation have a significant impact on the final product. As noted earlier, the manner in which questions are phrased, the reading level, and the content of OCI seem more suited for academic, administrative, research, or technical organizations than for organizations whose tasks are related to manufacturing or heavy industry. Such conclusions appear consistent with the published norms (almost all of which are referenced to academic or training institutions) and the ensuing literature. The citations of the OCI in the professional literature are almost exclusively within the educational journals. Given these patterns and the presence of several alternative climate indices that are more industrial in focus (and perhaps correspondingly less appropriate to the educational setting), it seems safe to suggest that the OCI will remain within its current well-established educational niche unless it is substantially revised and revalidated within these other settings.

The computer-scorable answer sheet makes scoring a simple task for the user who wishes to take advantage of the commercial scoring and statistical services offered by Evaluation Research Associates. This agency also sells technical manuals containing detailed instructions for hand-scoring the test as well as forms that allow one to plot scores on preprinted normative profiles.

Instructions for hand-scoring are quite clear and generally easy to follow. Scores for each of the 30 press scales are created by use of a key. This key lists the items in each scale (10 items per scale for the longer form) and indicates whether each item should be true or false. The respondent receives "1" for each answer that matches the True/False indicator and "0" for each answer that does not match. The resulting score for the scale is the sum for the 10 items. The 30 raw scores reflected in these sums form the basis for calculating the six factor scores that worksheets make it equally easy to calculate. The OCI short form provides scores for only the six factors and not for the 30 press scales.

A caveat is in order, however. The technical manual notes that the factor structure differs across different types of organization. For example, the manual describes a factor structure for school work environments that is different from the one presented for college work environments. Thus, selection of the appropriate key is essential. Similarly, the need for different scoring keys makes it difficult to use and interpret the OCI in settings that are not academic. The relative lack of information about generalizability into different environments is currently a serious limitation for broader use of the OCI.

Finally, the hand-scoring sheets reveal that six of the 30 press scores are included in the calculation of more than one of the six factor scores. The absence of differential weighting for thse scales greatly simplifies the calculation of the factor scores. On the other hand, when unit weights are given to these scales they may contribute twice as much variance to the final profile as is contributed by other scales that are assigned to a single factor. This practice also leads to substantial and somewhat artificial correlations among the factor scores. A more accepted practice would be to assign each press scale to only one factor based on the highest factor loadings for that scale. However, this step would also require the recalculation of normative data for ease of interpretation.

OCI scores are generally straightforward and easy to understand. A higher score on a scale signifies an environment that supports a particular type of activity. Similarly, the scale names generally convey well the type of environment that is represented by the score. For example, a high score on Nurturance describes an environment that welcomes newcomers, provides help and assistance readily, and leaves no one feeling excluded.

Each scale is fully described in great detail. Similarly, full descriptions are provided for the six factors and for two higher-order scores derived from the six factors. Thus, it is not difficult for even an unsophisticated user to comprehend what type of environment is being described by the score obtained from the OCI.

As noted earlier, however, the scores and the accompanying descriptions do not translate readily to specific actions or interventions that would permit the user to alter the profile of an organization. For example, one of the six factors identified for the college-work environment sample was "Intellectual Climate." The manual suggested that colleges with high scores on this factor might be described as conducive to scholarly interests in the arts, humanities, and sciences, with a general work atmosphere that is characterized by intellectual activities and pursuits. Although many colleges might desire an atmosphere that was rated high on this dimension, a review of the items contained in the scale does not identify courses of action to achieve it. Unfortunately, this comment cannot be applied only to the OCI or to the other indices developed by Stein and his colleagues. It must apply equally to a majority of climate-related instruments.

A similar concern regards the use of the published norms. While such norms convey clearly where one stands relative to an average individual or institution, they convey little about what it means to differ from these norms. Scores above the norm may be desirable if one wishes to achieve certain outcomes, whereas scores at the norm or below may be better for other outcomes. Thus, the translation of such scores to statements of "good" or "bad" or to actions or outcomes requires a breadth of theoretical perspective and supporting information that goes well beyond the OCI itself.

Technical Aspects

The majority of the validation effort that led ultimately to the development of the OCI was conducted with the CCI. Thus, instead of the full-scale effort that would be required to establish the psychometric properties of an entirely new instrument, the primary focus of the studies conducted on the OCI was to establish that the properties of the previous instrument were not lost in the translation effort. However, in spite of the previous work on the CCI, the validation of the OCI was extensive enough to stand by itself.

In the validation of the CCI, the scores on the 30 press scales were subjected to principal components factor analyses followed by an equamax rotation procedure. These analyses produced 11 factors and two second-order factors. OCI responses from three samples (931 public school teachers, 2,500 Peace Corps trainees, and 223 industrial technicians) were analyzed by a similar strategy.

The OCI analyses yielded only six factors compared to the 11 found for the CCI. However, Stern (1970b) reported that five of the six factors generalized across all three samples and were compatible with all 11 CCI factors. Second-order factors were also similar.

While no statistical comparisons (e.g., coefficients of congruence) were provided to verify such assertions, factor loadings from each sample are presented and appear supportive. Stern cautions, however, that the inclusion of more heterogeneous organizations in the analyses might yield a greater number of factors than he reported. In spite of this caveat, an increasing number of empirical studies using a variety of instruments argue that these dimensions or ones very much like them are common to most factor analytic studies of climate.

Reliability assessments of the OCI scales are reported in terms of KR 20 estimates of internal consistency. According to conventional values, these estimates are somewhat low when calculated on the 30 press scales. For example, reliabilities on the press scales obtained from the 931 public school teachers range from .23 to .87, with a median of .61. Similar ranges for the Peace Corps' sample were .39 to .76 (median = .54), while values for the industrial sites were .12 to .77, (median = .60). Such values suggest that scores on these 30 scales should be treated with a certain amount of caution because of possible attenuation of relationships due to low reliability.

Reliability data reported for the six factor scores are higher and are consistent with general acceptance practices. These values range from .67 to .98 for the sample of public school teachers and .74 to .97 for the Peace Corps trainees. Thus, the factor scores seem to provide indicators that possess sufficient internal consistency for some level of confidence in their reliability.

The primary source of validity information on the OCI has been in the form of significant differences among the average press scores in different settings. Stern (1970b) provides extensive evidence of this nature. Correlations of OCI factors or profiles with other criteria are also provided but are less frequent. For example, Intellectual Climate Scores were negatively related to attrition and positively related to high overseas field evaluations for Peace Corps trainees (no values were reported). Similarly, culture scores produced by multiplying AI and OCI scores yielded significant relationships with absenteeism and performance. A composite score that combined four AI variables with two OCI factors (Supportiveness and Orderliness) to form an index that reflected constricted teachers and a structured environment was positively related to pupil achievement ($r = .97$ with socioeconomic level controlled) and to teacher turnover ($r = .75$). Other studies have established significant relationships between OCI scores and satisfaction.

Critique

Unfortunately, to this reviewer's knowledge, neither evidence of the criterion-related validity of the test nor any form of multitrait, multirater matrix that would allow one to clearly establish exactly what is measured by the OCI scores and their effects on external criteria has been systematically assembled or presented. For such evidence, one must rely somewhat on the growing research evidence regarding other climate instruments, the items of which are similar to many of those contained in the OCI (e.g., Jones & James, 1979; Litwin & Stringer, 1968; Schneider & Bartlett, 1968; Taylor & Bowers, 1972).

The evidence suggests that the OCI is a useful and valid index of the way that individuals perceive the educational environment. There is also evidence that these perceptions are related to a variety of attitudes and behaviors in predictable but very complex ways. Because of such complexity, the OCI is most useful when the person receiving the scores is also provided with a set of corresponding data from need-based instruments, such as the AI, and with a level of organizational understanding or training that will permit those scores to be paired with appropriate recommendations for organizational change or development. Thus, especially in educational or academic settings, the OCI appears to be a valid and valuable tool for the types of uses discussed earlier.

References

The reader who wishes greater insight into the theoretical background for the OCI or the quantitative basis for the scales is directed to the following books and articles. A number of unpublished technical reports are also available from the test publishers.

Jones, A. P., & James, L. R. (1979). Psychological climate: Dimensions and relationships of individual and aggregated work environment perceptions. *Organizational Behavior and Human Performance, 23,* 201-250.

Litwin, G., & Stringer, R. (1968). *Motivation and organizational climate.* Cambridge, MA: Harvard University Press.

Murray, H. A. (1938). *Explorations in personality.* New York: Oxford University Press.

Murray, H. A. (1951). Toward a classification of interaction. In T. Parsons & E. A. Shils (Eds.), *Toward a general theory of action* (pp. 434-464). Cambridge, MA: Harvard University Press.

Pace, C. R., & Stern, G. G. (1958). An approach to the measurement of psychological characteristics of college environments. *Journal of Educational Psychology, 49,* 269-277.

Schneider, B., & Bartlett, C. (1968). Individual differences and organizational climate: I. The research plan and questionnaire development. *Personnel Psychology, 21,* 323-334.

Stern, G. G. (1970a). *College Characteristics Index.* Syracuse, NY: Evaluation Research Associates.

Stern, G. G. (1970b). *People in context: Measuring person-environment congruence in education and industry.* New York: John Wiley & Sons.

Stern, G. G. (1972). *Stern Activities Index.* Syracuse, NY: Evaluation Research Associates.

Stern, G. G., Steinhoff, C. R., & Richman, J. (1975). *Organizational Climate Index: Short Form.* Syracuse, NY: Evaluation Research Associates.

Taylor, J., & Bowers, D. G. (1972). *The Survey of Organizations: A machine scored standardized questionnaire instrument.* Ann Arbor, MI: Institute for Social Research.

Philip Himelstein, Ph.D.

Professor of Psychology, The University of Texas at El Paso, El Paso, Texas.

PARENT ATTACHMENT STRUCTURED INTERVIEW

Samuel Roll, Julianne Lockwood, and Elizabeth Jaffe Roll. Albuquerque, New Mexico: Samuel Roll, Ph.D.

Introduction

The Parent Attachment Structured Interview (PASI) was developed to provide an interview format for use with children that would assess the child's attachment to significant adults. While these significant adults can usually be expected to be parents, life situations may cause other adult figures to become the major focus of attachment. The PASI is designed to measure the strength of attachment and to identify the attachment figures.

The PASI consists of 50 questions designed to obtain information indirectly regarding the attachment target-persons. For example, the child might be asked, "Who do you ask for money to go to the movies?" or "Who tells you that you can't watch television?" Questions deal with four different aspects of attachment and follow in a systematic order on the interview schedule. These aspects are Responsiveness (who wants to be engaged with the child in pleasant or neutral activities), Confidence (who is useful to the child in difficult situations, Security (who provides a supportive and permanent affective relationship), and Hostility (who is involved in hurtful or frustrating situations). A fifth category consists of distractor items (who fixes the car when the car won't go?), designed to overcome boredom or anxiety that the interview might generate.

The examiner's role is to present each question to the child and record responses on an answer sheet. The interviewer has the freedom to modify questions according to the child's age or level of comprehension.

According to the manual (Roll, Lockwood, & Roll, 1981), the test has been successfully administered to children ranging from 6 to 12 years of age. Since questions can be modified as the clinician sees fit, there should be few if any problems dealing with a difficulty level beyond the comprehension of a typical child of six, or even younger. It would seem, from the nature of the questions, that the PASI would not lose anything in translation if used with non-English-speaking children.

The first column of the answer form consists of the 50 questions arranged (by content) in a fixed, repeating order (R, S, C, H, and D, from the aspects of attachment described previously). To the right of the questions are columns labelled "mother," "father," and "other" (with space provided for listing the other figures). Under each of these figure headings are the letters R, S, C, H, D, and the questions are arranged in this order for the entire set. If the child responds

559

to the first question with "mother," for example, the R is tallied under the mother column. This is simplified for the interviewer by the fact that the letter R (and the others as well) is printed in the appropriate space. All the clinician must do is draw a line through the letter corresponding to the attachment dimension under the figure named by the child.

A scoring booklet is also provided, which accommodates biographical information, a brief case history, scoring data, and examiner comments on qualitative observations, possible reasons for blank items, items for investigation, and recommendations.

Practical Applications/Uses

The PASI is designed for use in child custody cases where one of the issues in awarding custody is the identification of the parent to whom the child is most attached. Roll (1983) has pointed out the problems raised when a child is asked directly with whom he or she would rather live. The PASI provides an indirect and nonthreatening way to elicit this information. The manual (Roll et al., 1981) suggests that the PASI should be administered by a psychologist trained in the assessment of children and as part of a complete assessment battery. The manual also recommends that, in child custody cases, it is best to give half of the questions when one parent brings the child and the other half when the other parent brings the child. Even when only one parent brings the child to the testing session, the manual recommends that only one half be given in any one session.

The test is simple to administer, requiring only reading each question aloud and recording the child's response by a slash mark. Scores under each attachment figure for each of the five dimensions can then be summed. For each of the parents, or other figures as the case may be, a positive attachment score can be determined by adding the scores on Responsibility, Security, and Confidence, and negative attachment score by summing the Hostility dimension.

Interpretation can be based entirely on the quantitative scores and comparing the totals summed for each of the parents. Additional interpretive material can be gleaned by paying attention to the number and identity of attachment figures other than the parents. There are no norms to guide the clinician in interpreting the quantitative data collected. The examiner must be careful not to overinterpret score differences for mother and father. In the presentation of mean scores for boys and girls in the standardization sample, the mother received a higher score from both sexes than did the father on all attachment dimensions except for Hostility (S. Roll, personal communication, February 17, 1984). How large a difference must the mother have before she can rightfully claim to be the parent with the degree of bonding that the court has to consider in child custody cases? Can a difference score that corrects for normal bonding to the primary caregiver be developed? Hopefully, Roll and his associates will develop an interpretive manual to accompany the next edition.

Technical Aspects

There are no reported studies dealing with validity or reliability. These are tasks awaiting the test authors before the PASI is offered to the profession. This will be a considerable chore. What would the non-test criteria be for validating a scale that purports to measure aspects of the attachment process? Perhaps playroom situations can be designed to offer a child the choice between mother and father in an intact family. Also to be addressed in future research is the placement of interview questions in one of four attachment domains. This was apparently accomplished on the basis of item inspection, but this leaves unanswered questions dealing with the independence of the four factors. Do Responsiveness, Confidence, Security, and Hostility independently measure aspects of bonding, or is there overlap between these factors?

Critique

The PASI provides both an objectively administered series of interview questions if the format is rigidly followed and quantitative scores concerning attachment figures. This will certainly be of value to the psychologist or other professional who must provide support for views stated in a courtroom setting.

The PASI appears to have tremendous potential for the forensic psychologist in family court. In my own use of the instrument, this reviewer has found it much easier to use than writing up a description of the procedure. Much remains to be done in the way of validity and reliability studies, however, before this interview schedule can meet the stern test that acceptance by the profession entails.

References

Roll, S. (1983, September). Ties that bind. *Psychology Today*, pp. 6-7.
Roll, S., Lockwood, J., & Roll, E. J. (1981). *Preliminary manual: Parent Attachment Structured Interview (PASI)*. Albuquerque, NM: Author.

Luella Sude Smitheimer, Ph.D.
Speech and Language Pathologist, Port Washington Speech,
Language and Hearing Center, Port Washington, New York.

PATTERNED ELICITATION SYNTAX TEST

Edna Carter Young and Joseph J. Perachio. Tucson, Arizona:
Communication Skill Builders, Inc.

Introduction

The Patterned Elicitation Syntax Test (PEST) uses a distinctly different strategy for assessing the oral expressive language of young children. It is based on an analysis of the grammatic rules underlying the expressive abilities of normal developing children. The test, designed for children aged three years to seven years, six months, uses an unusual delayed imitation technique. The technique makes it possible to examine linguistic errors that may occur during the testing period. The primary purpose of the PEST is to measure the overt grammatic language skills of children and determine if those skills are age appropriate.

The PEST was developed by Edna Carter Young and Joseph J. Perachio. The authors are speech-language pathologists, members of the American Speech-Language-Hearing Association (ASHA), and each holds a Certification of Clinical Competence, issued by ASHA. Edna Carter Young, holds a master's degree in speech pathology and has worked as a speech/language diagnostician and clinician for hospitals, university clinics, schools, and day-care centers. She is assistant director of speech and language services at St. Christopher's Hospital for Children in Philadelphia, an instructor in pediatrics at Temple University Medical School, and her articles have appeared in professional journals. Joseph J. Perachio also earned a master's degree in speech pathology and has worked professionally as a diagnostician, clinician, and consultant. In addition to his interest in the grammatic functioning of small children, Mr. Perachio is an expert on the diagnosis and treatment of stuttering.

According to the manual (Young & Perachio, 1983) the PEST was developed initially as a criterion-referenced tool in 1981. The purpose was to use the tool as a means of providing a systematic analysis of possible deviant grammatic components in the language of small children. Experimental versions of the test appeared in the field, and with extensive field use modifications were made. Standardization procedures followed and the present edition of the test is the result of those revisions and modifications. The authors believe that, in addition to determining linguistic deficits, the test in its present (1983) form, can be used for planning appropriate treatment procedures when linguistic deficits are found.

The reviewer wishes to extend her appreciation to Catherine Holleran, Wendy Jacobson, and Karen Luper for their participation as research assistants.

The PEST is an individually administered tool intended to screen children who may have grammatic deficiencies. Grammar refers to the arrangement of words (and parts of words) in sentences. The PEST contains 44 items developed to assess the child's production of sentences containing various grammatic structures. Each grammatic structure is also examined, through the use of a laminated plate that contains three pictures. The examiner reads three sentences depicted by the drawings, then points to each picture, and the child is required to repeat the sentences read by the examiner. Thus, it is necessary for the children to retain, recall, and repeat the information given for each item included in the tool. The response form, which accompanies the test, contains a linguistic description for each structure under evaluation and the sentences that are to be read. Although the test was designed for children aged 3 to 7½ years, according to the manual it can be used for older children with expressive language problems.

Practical Applications/Uses

According to the authors, the PEST can be given and interpreted by professionals from many fields. They suggest that, in addition to the speech-language pathologist, the tool be used by hearing specialists, reading teachers, educational diagnosticians, and learning disabilities specialists. They indicate that the use of the test will provide important information to those who are concerned with the relationship between oral expressive grammatic knowledge and academic achievement. They purport that examiners will be able to use and interpret the results of the PEST without extensive experience in testing or in linguistic theory. However, they remind the potential user that the PEST taps only one linguistic aspect—oral expression—and should be used in combination with other language tests. They stress that the potential user should have information about the child's receptive knowledge of grammatic structures, vocabulary level, mean length of utterance based on analysis of a spontaneous language sample, and auditory memory skills because those skills are related and may influence the child's performance.

The PEST, designed to serve as a screening tool, is based on 44 grammatic features found in the English language. In addition to providing age-referenced norms, it can be used to obtain information on the type and frequency of linguistic errors found in children with oral expressive language disabilities. The examiner can delineate errors according to linguistic category and a separate chart for analysis is provided for this purpose. The 44 items contained in the final version of the test range from simple three-word phrases to eight-word complex sentences. According to the manual, the PEST provides for the examination of 34 linguistic structures (e.g., negation, possessive pronoun, plural, articles). The remaining sentences, on the other hand, have been included to assess the ability of children to produce more complex utterances, such as conjoined and embedded syntactic structures. Thus, the test becomes a clinical tool for obtaining descriptive information about a child's use of specific linguistic structures. When children with linguistic delays have been determined it is possible to use this information to establish targets for remedial training.

Although the test was standardized on a normal sample of English-speaking children, the authors state that it is possible to use it with those who speak Black English or for whom English is a second language. They posited that when applied as a clinical criterion-referenced tool, rather than an age-referenced one, the PEST will give information about the presence or absence of linguistic features. Young and Perachio also mention that they have been collecting data with children who speak Black English and have found that the test is useful as a criterion-referenced tool in that area.

Young and Perachio stress that there are important prerequisite linguistic skills to be considered in the selection of the subjects for the test. A child who is able to initiate two- to three-word utterances would be considered an appropriate candidate but one who is at the single-word stage of linguistic development would be an inappropriate candidate.

The PEST is to be given individually in a well-lighted room. The child and the examiner should be seated so that both can see the plates and be able to point to the test pictures. The authors indicate that examiners do not require extensive experience in testing or in linguistic theory. From this statement, it can be assumed that nonprofessionals or paraprofessionals would be acceptable examiners. However, before administration the examiner should be familiar with the test and its objectives. It is also important that the examiner understand the grammatic structures to be tested. The manual provides information for administration and includes the test plates. The Response Sheet contains the 44 linguistic structures and descriptions for the structures to be tested, all of the sentences or phrases to be read to the child, and space to note changes the child may make during the production of the structures. The use of a tape recorder for recording purposes is suggested, but only if a fine-quality recorder is available. However, the authors do not recommend that examiners rely solely on the tape recording because many linguistic features might not be clearly reproduced on the audio tape.

According to the manual, the sentences should be read exactly as they appear on the Response Sheet. The examiner is to begin with the demonstration plate, which shows three drawings. Then, the child is asked to look at the pictures while being told something about each one. The examiner tells the children that they will have a turn to give the same information. The examiner then points to each picture while saying the sentences. Young and Perachio indicate that it is important for the examiner to use normal rate and inflection while presenting the sentences and/or phrases. They suggest that the examiner read the three test sentences as a series with a slight pause between each one. Longer pauses between sentences tend to cause the child to repeat or answer the stimulus before hearing all three sentences. Stimuli should be repeated if the child is unable to repeat any of the test sentences, but it is important to repeat all three sentences/phrases because they are judged as a unit.

Basal and ceiling information is provided in the manual. For example, the starting point for three-year-old children is Item 1, and the test is to continue until the child has failed six consecutive items. Children who are four years of age and older can start at Item 11 and continue until six consecutive items have been failed. However, after starting with item 11, if the child fails the first six items (11 to 16), the examiner should administer the first 10 items. Young and Perachio point out "that the first 10 items in the PEST were developed to assess the earliest acquired grammatical structures . . .these items represent those that were most frequently passed by children in all age groups'' (Young & Perachio, 1983, p. 8).

Despite the fact that the administration of this test seems, on the surface, to be comparatively simple, this reviewer, during testing interactions with pre-schoolers and kindergartners, found varied individual behaviors that are not accounted for in the manual. When, for example, the test was administered to a four-year-old child and that child immediately failed Items 11, 12, and 13, this reviewer gave the child the benefit of doubt and a chance to be successful by turning back to Items 9, 8, 7, etc. until a true basal was established. The child was then asked to repeat Items 14, 15, and 16 etc. until a true terminal point was determined. This was done so that the child would not show frustration with the test items.

Another problem occurred with certain children who could not repeat the questions contained in the test. Although the manual gives a technique to follow when question forms are to be introduced, unfortunately, it is buried within the body of the administration procedures. When that technique did not work, this reviewer found that the children became distressed, reacted negatively, and wanted to stop the test. Moreover, there is no information to the effect that children with language deficits may have difficulty imitating questions.

According to the manual, the test is untimed and should take approximately 20 minutes to administer. Because it is untimed it is possible to give the child breaks during the session or continue testing another day. However, testing should be completed within a two-week period.

The manual instructions for scoring are explicit. The examiner gives a plus or zero for each response the child repeats. However, only the third response in each unit is used to obtain the final raw score. The raw score is derived by adding the plus responses for the 44 target structures. The total raw score is used to obtain the children's percentile by comparing it to norms established for their age group. Their performances on the remaining 88 sentences/phrases can be analyzed by using the Interpretation of Errors by Structure Analysis Form, which accompanies the Response Sheet.

Scoring time for the user/professional with knowledge of linguistic theory and test administration could be 30 to 40 minutes. Scoring will take longer when judgments based on varying behavior must be made. The authors advise the scorer to compare the child's response to the bold italicized element in each sentence. The bold italicized element is clearly delineated for each sentence on the Response Sheet. The elements included on the Response Sheet are, indeed, the desired target structures. But what judgment will the scorer make when, for example, the desired target element is ''can talk'' and the child produces ''could talk''? In this instance, the target linguistic structure is ''modal + verb'' and the child produced a ''modal + verbal'' response. But because the child's response differed from the italicized words on the Response Sheet, the unsophisticated examiner could have difficulty scoring the response.

A child's performance on this test, according to the manual, can be judged in two ways. One way uses the test as a criterion-referenced tool (i.e., determining which items were used correctly and which were not). The errors can be transferred to the Analysis Form and the pattern of the errors can be used to determine which additional testing measures to apply or which ones help the clinician to establish goals for remediation. The second way uses the test as an age-referenced tool (i.e., interpreting the total raw score in order to either compare the scores of children of similar ages by locating the percentile score or to find the mean score achieved by children of the same age group and compare performance to determine if the child deviates from the mean established for his or her age level).

When using the age-referenced measure, the child's percentile rank provides important information about the child's linguistic standing in relation to the standardized sample. If children achieve a score that would place them at the 50th percentile, they are considered average. If, however, children achieve a score that places them below the 10th percentile, there is cause for concern because their performance is judged to be below the normal range. If, on the other hand, children score between the 10th and 25th percentile, the authors suggest further evaluation because they are placed at the lower end of the continuum for normal performance.

Technical Aspects

The PEST was standardized on 651 children, aged three years to seven years, six months. There were 327 female and 324 male children selected from nursery schools, day-care centers, public and parochial schools in Pennsylvania, New Jersey, Tennessee, and New York. According to the manual, the majority of the children came from urban, suburban, exurban, and rural middle-class homes where standard English dialects were spoken. The children tested had no identified handicap, which would have affected normal language development.

Two measures of reliability are cited in the PEST manual to support the contention that the test is reliable. The first measure concerns temporal stability or the test-retest method of ascertaining that a test will yield similar results when given another time. Within two weeks after the initial test period 106 children from the original normative group were retested by the same examiner. The authors report a Pearson Product Moment correlation of .94 indicating excellent temporal stability. However, test-retest data for different examiners are not reported. The second measure concerns internal consistency. Internal consistency of the test for all children in the standardization sample ranged from .93 to .99 using the split-half Spearman-Brown Formula, with each test scored twice, using odd-numbered items and then even-numbered items.

The three specific validity studies reported in the manual are concerned with: 1) item validity, 2) content validity, and 3) predictive validity. The item validity study was performed by arranging the test items included in the PEST in a hierarchy of difficulty based on the performance of the 651 subjects included in the normative group. T-tests of group means by age levels showed statistically significant differences at each age level. By analyzing the performances of the children at each of nine age groups (six-month intervals), the authors determined that growth of competence for this test is a function of age.

Content validity was established by analyzing the extent to which children's performance on the PEST would reflect their spontaneous use of the grammatical structures under observation. During initial field testing, the performances of 10 normal-speaking and 30 language impaired children were compared. The language impaired children were evaluated and diagnosed as having expressive language deficits in spite of normal receptive abilities and normal hearing. Language samples containing at least 200 utterances were collected for the 40 children. Each sample was analyzed and considered adequate when target linguistic structures included in the PEST occurred in the sample at least five times. The PEST was then administered to the 40 subjects. According to the authors, the results of performance on the PEST was compared to a subject's spontaneous use of the same target structures in the language sample. A Pearson Product Moment correlation of .88 was obtained for the language impaired group and a correlation of .86 for the normal group, suggesting a high degree of correlation between children's performance on the PEST and their ability to produce the target linguistic structures in spontaneous speech.

Predictive validity was obtained by using 35 language impaired children judged to have expressive linguistic disabilities. These children not only received full batteries of diagnostic language tests administered by speech-language pathologists, but were also given the PEST. The purpose of this study was to determine if the PEST would provide information similar to that already within each child's clinical record. The results indicate that 34 of the subjects achieved scores below the 10th percentile suggesting either enrollment for therapy or further evaluation. The remaining child achieved a score between the 10th and 25th percentile indicating that there may be cause for concern, and that this performance warranted further study. Thus, the authors believe that the PEST is a valid tool for screening deviant linguistic performance from that of normal development.

Critique

The PEST is, in theory and design, a test that holds considerable promise for the linguistic assessment of children to determine those with oral expressive deficits. However, it lacks some necessary technical characteristics to make it adequate for use by paraprofessionals or nonspeech-language specialists. Until the test includes more information and modifications, its use must be restricted to experienced speech-language pathologists and should be considered experimental. One technical factor that needs recognition is that paraprofessionals will require background information concerned with linguistic terms and linguistic theory. More examples or illustrations of possible errors should be included under scoring procedures. Another technical aspect that requires modification refers to the size of some of the norm groups. There are, as mentioned previously, nine groups. The number of children in each age group varies from 51 and 54 (3.0-3.5; 3.6-3.11; 4.0-4.5) to 80, 89, 92, and 100 (7.0-7.6; 4.6-4.11; 6.6-6.11; 5.6-5.11). Thus, the size of some of the standardization groups are small.

Another problem concerns the assumption underlying the use of imitation tasks to determine a child's linguistic competence. The PEST is, according to the manual, a screening device intended to assess the competence of children in the production of various linguistic forms. A major theory behind the design of the

PEST is that imitation or repetition tasks can be used to gain a representative sample of a child's grammatical performance in an efficient and reliable manner. This theory is based on early child development research findings suggesting that children's repetition of sentences will closely approximate the manner in which they produce the sentences in spontaneous speech. Language sampling techniques have been criticized as tedious and time-consuming (Note that language samples were collected for 40 subjects in a validity study conducted by the authors of the PEST). As a result, other tests that use the imitation technique have appeared on the market. They too, however, have been criticized. To their credit, Young and Perachio point out the disadvantages and criticisms of imitation tests: "The use of immediate imitation is questioned on the basis of the effects of short-term memory, lack of communicative intent in a repetition task, and loss of contextual cues that help a speaker structure his remarks" (Young & Perachio, 1983, p. 2). Yet, the authors assure the user that the design of the PEST differs from the usual technique found in tests that employ the repetition method. The Young and Perachio test "is based on a process called linguistic slot-filling" (p. 2). According to the authors, their delayed imitation method incorporates a chunking technique used to teach grammatic structures to the hearing impaired. This technique is based on the premise that a child will hold strings of linguistic phrases/sentences in memory if they are meaningful. The technique also assumes that if a child has internalized the necessary linguistic rules, those rules will be used. If, on the other hand, the child never acquired a specific linguistic rule, it will not be used. More research is required concerning the efficacy of this assessment approach with young children.

The PEST is a relatively inexpensive test which has some shortcomings. One shortcoming, for example, is that it does take longer than 20 minutes to administer. Another shortcoming is the age-referenced measure, useful only for children who speak standard English. It cannot be applied to those who speak English as a second language or with a black dialect. A third shortcoming became evident during this reviewer's observations of the PEST when it was administered to children who require speech/language therapy. With one specific child, for instance, the test did not predict consistency of grammatic use in spontaneous speech. The child did not perform correctly on two of the "prompt sentences" included for assessing a specific linguistic rule, but did score correctly for the final sentence (the one to be scored). Therefore, the fact that the child performed correctly on one sentence and incorrectly on two does not mean that the child has internalized the linguistic rule, yet he received credit for it.

It is strongly recommended by this reviewer that speech and language pathologists use or contemplate using the PEST because it does show promise. However, its limitations need to be recognized and caution should be exercised with respect to interpretation of findings.

References

This list includes text citations as well as suggested additional reading.

Carrow, E. (1974). *Carrow Elicited Language Inventory (CELI)*. Boston: Teaching Resources Corporation.

Lee, L. L. (1971). *Northwestern Syntax Screening Test (NSST)*. Evanston, IL: Northwestern University Press.

O'Connor, L. (1982). Critique of the Patterned Elicitation Syntax Screening Test (PEST). *Journal of American Speech-Language Hearing Association*, 24(7), 491-492.

Young, E. C., & Perachio, J. J. (1983). *Patterned Elicitation Syntax Test*. Tucson, AZ: Communication Skill Builders, Inc.

Zachman, L., Huisingh, R., Jorgensen, C., & Barrett, M. (1977). *The Oral Language Sentence Imitation Screening Test (OLSIST)*. Moline, IL: LinguiSystems, Inc.

Robert D. Rothermel, Jr., Ph.D.
Post-Doctoral Fellow in Clinical Neuropsychology, University of Nebraska Medical Center, Omaha, Nebraska.

Mark R. Lovell, Ph.D.
Post-Doctoral Fellow in Clinical Neuropsychology, University of Nebraska Medical Center, Omaha, Nebraska.

PERSONALITY INVENTORY FOR CHILDREN

Robert D. Wirt, David Lachar, James E. Klinedinst, Philip D. Seat, and William E. Broen. Los Angeles, California: Western Psychological Services.

Introduction

The Personality Inventory for Children (PIC) is a 600-item inventory constructed by empirical and rational methods. It aims to describe current broad and narrow patterns of behavior in children aged 3 through 16 on the basis of a parent's responses to true-false questions. The inventory provides summary scores on validity, cognitive, clinical, and factor scales. The empirical development of the inventory and subsequent research have produced an instrument that provides information extending beyond the simple, face-valid responses by the parent to individual questions to reveal empirically derived, high-probability statements about a child's behavior.

The development of the PIC began in the late 1950s at the University of Minnesota where the MMPI had been developed 15 years earlier. Robert Wirt and William Broen were responsible for writing the original 600 items, and subsequent doctoral dissertations by various authors produced the 33 scales as well as reliability and validity data. The original normative sample consisted of 2,390 subjects obtained primarily from the Minneapolis public school system from 1958 through 1962. Since the original publication of the PIC (1977) a large data pool has been gathered at a separate university from which subsequent validation research has been derived. The test has been translated into Italian and Spanish for use within these ethnic populations.

The original format of the test consists of a booklet with 600 questions and a separate, two-sided answer sheet for recording true or false responses. Inventory items were written with language and vocabulary that require a sixth- to seventh-grade reading level for comprehension. The inventory is hand-scored using cardboard templates. Automated scoring services are not available for the original format of the inventory. Results are plotted for 16 separate scales on a separate Profile Form with opposite sides used for either sex of the child (profiles for children aged 3-5 are plotted on a separate form). A recent revision in format (1982) allows the clinician to choose between shortened versions of the inventory

570

depending on the information desired. The first section of the revised booklet consists of 131 items from which four broad factor dimensions and one validity scale can be scored. If the parent responds to the first 280 items, shortened versions of all clinical scales (including the original 16 profile scales) plus the new factor scales are obtainable. The first 421 items will provide all of the original scales in complete form plus the factor scales. The entire 600-item set yields all clinical and research scales. The revised format requires scoring with a separate set of templates. Graphing of the scales must be performed on revised profile forms unless the entire inventory is administered (again opposite sides of the profile form are used depending on the child's sex and age). Research has demonstrated a high concordance between the original and shortened scales in both clinical and normal samples.

Regardless of which format is chosen, administration of the test requires minimal participation by the clinician and in fact can be accomplished by a trained technician. Brief instructions to the parent describing the correct place to mark answers and encouraging that all questions be answered are necessary but these are also duplicated on the cover of the inventory booklet.

The inventory is divided into 12 clinical scales, 3 validity scales, 1 screening scale, and 4 factor scales (only the revised format provides templates for scoring the factor scales). The clinical scales assess areas of achievement, intellectual skills, development, somatic concern, depression, family relations, delinquency, withdrawal, anxiety, psychosis, hyperactivity, and social skills. Validity scales assess the respondent's tendency to underreport or exaggerate child behavioral symptoms or to respond randomly. The factor scales assess broad dimensions of childhood psychopathology, including externalizing behavior, internalizing behavior, social incompetence, and cognitive dysfunction. The screening scale screens for any type of psychopathology.

Practical Applications/Uses

The revised manual (1984) for the PIC outlines its potential usefulness for academic counselors, private clinicians, therapists, diagnosticians, and other specialists who are concerned with the mental health of their clients. Because it provides screening scales it can be used for identification of children in need of further diagnostic testing, special programs, or treatment within early intervention programs. Specifically, the manual describes use of the test for screening intellectual and general psychological adjustment by professionals in varied settings. Within a clinical setting the PIC assesses current status of the child with regard to clinical syndromes, the presence of emotional disturbance, and specific concerns of the respondent about the child. This information is useful for determining need for more specific diagnostic assessment and for outlining treatment programs or remedial strategies. The manual also notes that the PIC can be used to assess change in adjustment status. Research currently in progress attempts to use the inventory as an alternative classification system of childhood psychopathology.

The PIC can be validly used to assess any child between the ages of 3 and 16 because normative data are provided for each sex separately within this range. At the time of this review the normative data for preschool children (aged 3-5) are based on only 192 protocols, and research has suggested the need for caution when using the test with this population. The original normative sample was obtained from a limited geographic area and was not specifically stratified according to race or socioeconomic status. Although the manual reports that the distribution approximates census data on dimensions of economic, social, and educational status, no data are given. Data on a subset of the cases (N = 600) are reported and suggest adequate representation of different socioeconomic groups. No data on the racial composition of the normative sample are given. However, minority subjects were adequately represented in subsequent validation studies.

The PIC can be easily administered by any professional or paraprofessional with a minimum of training. The only requirement is that the clinician or technician be familiar with a few simple instructions and be able to communicate them to the parent. Similarly, scoring can be done easily by a technician with little training. The manual clearly outlines the procedures necessary for both these tasks. There is no clinical judgment necessary for scoring, which involves simply counting the number of responses made in the scorable direction on items of a given scale. Computer scoring and reporting of results can be performed for a fee through a scoring service or can be done on a microcomputer using scoring disks purchased separately. These options are available only for the revised format. Because of the ease of administration and scoring, the PIC can be included as a part of an assessment or screening battery at little cost in clinical time or effort.

The authors of the PIC caution against interpretation of the inventory by unskilled, nonprofessionals or by professionals who are limited in their understanding of the inventory's psychometric properties. Overly simplistic interpretation of the inventory is a cogent danger with the PIC because of its apparent simplicity, face-valid scale names, and resemblance to other psychometric instruments with similar format and structure (e.g., MMPI). The manual clearly states that appropriate professional interpretation of the inventory can be accomplished only by a trained professional who fully understands issues of the inventory's reliability and validity. The problem of interpretation of the PIC depends on the purpose for which it is being interpreted. Paraprofessionals can use objective criteria to establish the need for professional evaluation and diagnosis. By using the objective criteria, empirical correlates, and interpretive guidelines, professionals can obtain more valid and reliable information about the child with less effort than could be obtained from more subjective forms of personality assessment. The nomothetically-based, interpretive statements easily obtained from the test manuals and supplements must be integrated within the context of the individual case. The ready availability of empirical correlates does not substitute for thorough knowledge of the test's capabilities and limitations.

The manuals (1977, 1982, 1984) for the PIC adequately describes the rigorous psychometric methods used in constructing the original 16 scales and the 4 factor scales. Seven scales (Defensiveness, Adjustment, Achievement, Intellectual Screening, Delinquency, Psychosis, and Hyperactivity) were empirically derived by selecting items that correlated highly with criterion group membership. A first approximation scale was then successively refined by adding new items that accounted for additional unique variance in predicting the criterion. Second or third iterations duplicated the process, further refining the scales so that the maximum correlation was achieved between the group of items and the criterion. The Frequency Scale consisted of the items that were endorsed infrequently in the normative sample. Eight scales were constructed by a rational method (Lie, Development, Somatic Concern, Depression, Family Relations, Withdrawal, Anxiety, and Social Skills) in which items from the 600 item pool were nominated by three of four judges as reflective of a certain content area (e.g., depression). These scales were refined by examining the item-total correlations. Factor analysis of the items constituting the clinical scales resulted in the four broad-band factor scales that are included in the revised format. Two of these scales showed systematic age effects (Intellectual Screening and Factor IV: Cognitive Development) and are normed according to the child's age. The finding of significant sex effects for 18 scales resulted in separate norms for each sex. Subsequent research found no significant sex differences in T-scores of clinical scales. Racial differences were found only for one of the original profile scales (Frequency) with blacks scoring higher than whites. Several significant sex and race effects were found for the experimental scales. Examination of a clinical sample found that 5 of the 16 profile scales were related to sex, 9 were related to age, and 6 were related to race. In describing these differences the authors report that the differences were consistent with prior literature or theory. They also note that black children in the clinical sample actually scored lower on four scales and higher on only one.

Technical Aspects

Three forms of reliability of the PIC have been researched and are discussed at length in the manuals: internal consistency, test-retest stability, and interrater agreement. Within a heterogeneous clinic sample (N = 1,226), alpha coefficients (internal consistency) for profile scales ranged from –.03 to .86 with a mean of .74. However, only three scales achieved alpha coefficients below .60: Defensiveness (–.03), Intellectual Screening (.57), and Depression (.57). Little change in values was achieved when using the shortened versions of these profile scales (revised format). Slight improvement in internal consistency occurred despite shortening of scale length due to item selection criteria for the shortened scales. The four factor scales achieved alpha values of .81 to .92 (only Factor IV was less than .90). The internal consistency of the experimental scales is not reported in any of the manuals.

Test-retest stability of the individual scales was examined in three studies using samples of clinic-referred and normal children over varying intertest intervals. In a mixed clinical sample, an average scale correlation of .86 was achieved between first and second test administration. The interval period of 4 to 72 days included no formal treatment of pathological conditions. The Defensiveness Scale achieved the lowest correlation (.46), which may have reflected change in response set. The shortened scales of the revised format had comparable values in this study. Stability of the factor scales in this sample was indicated by correlations of .82 to .93, and the experimental scales earned correlations ranging from .45 to .93.

Within a normal sample (N = 46) over a comparable interval, test-retest correlations were lower for all types of scales than they had been in the clinical sample.

For the profile scales the values ranged from .39 to .89 with a mean scale reliability of .71. Comparable values were obtained for revised (shortened) scales (range: .43 to .90). The factor scales (range: .70 to .89) and the experimental scales (range: .34 to .91) achieved lower values. In contrast, highest test-retest correlations were achieved in a normal population (N = 55) over a short intertest interval (two weeks). The reliability of profile scales averaged .89 with a range of .70 to .93., and values of the shortened scales were roughly comparable although lower in some instances (range: .54 to .94). Correlations for each factor score in this study were at least .90 with a range of .90 to .97 indicating that they were highly stable. The range of correlations for experimental scales was .68 to .96.

The correlation of scale scores produced by different raters provides an estimate of the reliability of parental report. This important psychometric property indicates the extent to which behaviors can be reliably measured by different observers. A study examined the relationship of PIC scales obtained from each parent of normal (*n* = 146) and clinical (*n* = 84) children. Correlations of the clinical profile scales were higher within the clinical sample (average correlation = .69) than within the normal sample (average correlation = .57). The validity profile scales achieved considerably lower correlations in both the clinical (average correlation = .36) and the normal (average correlation = .33) samples. Interrater agreement of the experimental and factor scales is not reported in any of the manuals. Clinical significance of the differences between father and mother profiles was also addressed. Half of the profile scales achieved greater than 75% agreement between parents of normal children when agreement was defined as achieving T-scores within one standard deviation (10 points) of each other. Parents of clinic children obtain less agreement. Only two profile scales achieved greater than 75% agreement by this criterion.

Rank order correlations provide an index of agreement about the relative importance of different pathological conditions measured by the inventory. In a sample of autistic children (N = 26) the rank order correlation between mother-derived profiles and father-derived profiles was .99 and was significant at *p* ≤ .01. This type of analysis was not reported for the normal or mixed clinical sample, but would prove interesting.

The reliability data reviewed above is discussed in greater detail in the three test manuals. Most impressive results were obtained in the test-retest study that used normal children and a short intertest interval. This study also provides the closest approximation to measuring the same subjects under the same conditions. Studies using clinical samples or longer intertest intervals indicate adequate reliability values under conditions that allow real change to contaminate results. That is, lower correlations may reflect reliable measurement of change, which is more likely with clinical samples and over longer time intervals. The internal consistency values are adequate in most cases and are comparable to values achieved within the personality assessment field. A notable exception to this occurs with the Defensiveness Scale. Given its construction methodology using contrasting groups of low and high defensive respondents, the alpha coefficient of −.03 indicates a grouping of items generally unrelated to the unitary construct of defensiveness.

Numerous validity studies regarding the effectiveness of the PIC within different populations and in different settings have been conducted. These studies, many of which were conducted by independent researchers and are published in professional journals, are thoroughly described in the manuals for the inventory. As a whole, the PIC has been validated by numerous correlative studies that are reported in the interpretive guide and indicate that scale elevations correlate with report of problem behaviors and symptoms by teachers and clinicians (in addition to parents). Scales also correlate with behavioral dimensions created through the factor analysis of checklist information completed by teachers, clinicians, parents, or reviews of medical charts. These data indicate that parent report correlates most highly with PIC scales, and that behavioral data reported by professionals correlate more highly than data reported by teachers. This is probably due to the limited domain of behaviors on which teachers were reporting and does not detract from the important point: PIC scales correlate with behavioral observation of independent observers reporting within their own area of knowledge. The data document the concurrent validity of the inventory and serve as interpretive guidelines for its valid use.

Other data demonstrate that the PIC can be validly used to screen for cognitive dysfunction. Research has shown that the inventory's "cognitive triad" (Achievement, Intellectual Screening, and Development) correlate with standard measures of intelligence (WISC-R, WPPSI, and Stanford-Binet), with achievement test scores (PIAT Mathematics and Reading Recognition; WRAT arithmetic, reading, and spelling), and with comparable measures from other behavioral checklists (Child Behavior Checklist: School Activities and Hyperactivity subtests). Correlations are significant for all three scales of the PIC but are higher for the Achievement and Development Scales and are higher for verbal measures and reading subtests than for performance measures and mathematics subtests. The Intellectual Screening Scale correlates higher than the others in younger (preschool) populations using the WPPSI as the criterion, and the Development Scale correlates higher than the others with performance measures and freedom from distractibility factor of the WISC-R. Scales of the cognitive triad successfully identify poor achievers (92% hit rate) and retardates (95% hit rate) in cross validation studies. Scores within this triad were also found to be elevated in a population of brain-injured children. Scores on the Factor IV Scale (Cognitive Development) were found to be significantly higher in a sample of retardates than in other psychiatric samples.

The Adjustment Scale was designed to screen for the presence of psychopathological conditions which necessitate professional assessment or treatment. Established cutoff criteria correctly identified about 89% of a sample of children with mixed psychiatric disorders while misclassifying about 15% of normals and children with medical problems. High scores on the Adjustment Scale were obtained within several homogeneous samples of children representing different clinical syndromes. This attests to the scales sensitivity to a variety of clinical syndromes and to its validity as a screening measure provided the cost of the 15% false-alarm rate is determined to be relatively low.

The assessment of externalizing behavioral pathology (e.g., delinquent acting out or hyperactivity) can be validly accomplished using several of the PIC scales. Elevated scores on the Delinquency Scale have been correlated with self-report measures of delinquent activity and with self-report personality measures associated with antisocial behavior (MMPI: Psychopathic Deviate and Hypomania). The Delinquency Scale also significantly correlated with other parent-report measures of child behavioral pathology (Child Behavior Checklist: Delinquency, Aggression, and Social Withdrawal). Within a hyperactive sample, cutoff criteria correctly classified 85% of the hyperactive sample (versus a normal control sample) although statistical classification with discriminant function correctly classified 96% of the cases. The Hyperactivity Scale in combination with the Anxiety Scale correctly identified 74% of hyperactive children who responded to medication treatment from those who did not respond. Higher scores on the Factor I Scale (Undisciplined/Poor Self-Control) occurred in a group of hyperactive children over other psychiatric groups.

Scales reflecting internalizing pathology (Somatic Concern, Depression, Anxiety, and Psychosis) have been validated by several studies conducted by the test authors and their colleagues and by independent researchers. The Somatic Concern Scale was found to differentiate between a sample of children who exhibited stress-related physical complaints and a sample of diabetic children. It correlated with self-report measures in adolescents (MMPI: Hypochondriasis Scale) and with other parent report measures (Child Behavior Checklist: Somatic Complaints). This scale obtained few actuarial correlates in a large heterogeneous sample and obtained a high frequency of clinical elevations among preadolescents. Both the Depression and the Psychosis Scales correlated with comparable self-report measures (MMPI: Depression and Social Introversion, and MMPI: Schizophrenia and Social Introversion, respectively). The Depression Scale also obtained a significant relationship with the Child Depression Inventory (self-report) and with the teacher report of passivity.

These scales also have been correlated with comparable self-report measures (e.g., MMPI Depression and Schizophrenia), with other parent-report measures (e.g., Child Behavior Checklist: Somatic Complaints, Depression, and Social Withdrawal), and with clinician ratings (e.g., Psychosis with a factor dimension labeled Disorganized, Poor Reality Testing). The internalizing scales have been shown to successfully differentiate somatisizing children (Somatic Concern Scale), children diagnosed as depressed by DSM III criteria (Depression Scale), and psychotic children (Psychosis Scale). The validity of the Anxiety Scale has received less support. Research reported in the manual indicates that preadolescents in a clinical sample frequently scored in the clinical range on this scale. The Factor III Scale (Internalization/Somatic Symptoms) differentiated a group of somatisizing children from other psychiatric disorders.

Children with social relationship problems can be validly assessed using three PIC scales (Social Skills, Withdrawal, and Factor II). Again significant correlations with self-report measures (MMPI: Social Introversion), parent-report measures (Child Behavior Checklist: Social Withdrawal), clinician ratings of social withdrawal, and peer-acceptance measures support the construct validity of these scales. High scores occur among groups of retarded, psychotic, and minimal brain-injured children. Validation of the Social Skills Scale was also indicated by significant correlations with measures of moral judgment and perspective taking.

Much concern has been expressed regarding the susceptibility of the PIC to respondent bias. The manual reports that the PIC provides high probability statements about the child's behavior based on empirical correlation and not simply face-valid statements about the parent's perception of the child. The authors of the manual recognize that response bias occurs and report that the PIC handles this problem in two ways. First, response bias, being a systematic source of variance, is taken into consideration in the empirical development of each scale. Second, the PIC provides scales that allow the clinician to evaluate the presence and type of respondent bias that occurs. The test authors have researched the relationship of parental pathology (indicated by the MMPI) and parental report of child pathology (PIC) and found few significant correlations. Additionally it was determined that parents who had obtained pathological scores on the MMPI produced PICs that predicted external criteria as well as PICs from parents without pathological MMPI scores. Independent research has demonstrated that differences occur in the mean elevation of several scales when the response set is experimentally manipulated (i.e., subjects are instructed to fake bad or good). However, cutoff criteria applied to the Frequency Scale correctly identified 93% of the subjects who "faked bad." The Lie Scale correctly identified 86% of subjects who "faked good." The Defensiveness Scale was less successful and produced many false negative assignments. In a clinical sample, profiles of parents who were judged to be either defensive or exaggerating of their childrens' problems were not identified with as much accuracy. Other profile or experimental scales actually performed better. The manual reports research that demonstrates that the validity scales change in the expected direction when parents in a clinical sample are directed to fake bad or good. It also reports that additional research is in progress. Finally, the numerous validity studies reported in the manual made no attempt to eliminate protocols that were invalid or suggested a problem with response bias. To the extent that such bias was present in the samples studied, the empirical approach to validation partially controls for that bias.

The manual reports research on the differences between father- and mother-produced PIC profiles. The data indicate significantly different elevations and different patterns of predictiveness and actuarial correlations with behavioral criteria. The authors conclude that father-produced profiles have limited validation.

Research currently in progress examines profile code types. These have been related to different clinical syndromes (e.g., autism, delinquency, learning disability) in an attempt to further develop profile analysis of the inventory.

Critique

Achenbach (1981) reviewed the PIC and stated several criticisms of the inventory. He argued that the scales were constructed using old personality theories and that the inventory therefore has little relevance to behavioral approaches to diagnosis and treatment. He also argued that respondent bias was a major problem for the PIC. Dreger (1982) reported that the PIC was the most carefully constructed parent report, child personality inventory and that it had a sound empirical foundation. Other authors have criticized the inventory for the excessive length of its original format (Breen & Barkley, 1983) and for its small

normative sample for the preschool ages (DeMoor-Peal & Handal, 1983).
The PIC was originally constructed in the MMPI tradition using sound empirical methods. Subsequent research has used newer statistical and methodological procedures that have further developed the inventory's psychometric foundation. The manuals clearly present procedures for test administration as well as data relevant to scale construction, validation, and psychometric evaluation. Empirical interpretative guidelines represent a strength of the inventory. As with all parent-report inventories, the PIC is subject to the problem of respondent bias influencing the validity of its results. Relevant research has begun to address this problem, but it remains a concern that needs further study. Statements by Achenbach (1981) exaggerate this difficulty and seem to incorrectly imply that it is unique to the PIC. The application of newer statistical methodologies and profile analysis of the PIC will provide additional applications and interpretative information, which will expand the inventory's clinical relevance. This inventory has limitations that the authors recognize and discuss in the manuals. Its reliability and validity are sufficiently documented for professional, clinical use.

References

Achenbach, T. M. (1981). A junior MMPI? *Journal of Personality Assessment, 45*, 332.

Breen, M. J., & Barkley, R. A. (1983). The Personality Inventory for Children (PIC): Its clinical utility with hyperactive children. *Journal of Pediatric Psychology, 8*, 359-366.

DeMoor-Peal, R., & Handal, P. J. (1983). Validity of the PIC with four-year-old males and females: A caution. *Journal of Pediatric Psychology, 8*, 261-271.

Dreger, R. M. (1982). The classification of children and their emotional problems: An overview-II. *Clinical Psychology Review, 2*, 349-385.

Lachar, D. (1982). *Personality Inventory for Children (PIC) revised format manual supplement.* Los Angeles; Western Psychological Services.

Lachar, D., & Gdowski, C. L. (1979). *Actuarial assessment of child and adolescent personality: An interpretive guide for the Personality Inventory for Children.* Los Angeles: Western Psychological Services.

Wirt, R. D., Lachar, D., Klinedinst, J. K., & Seat, P. D. (1977). *Multidimensional description of child personality: A manual for the Personality Inventory for Children.* Los Angeles: Western Psychological Services.

Wirt, R. D., Lachar, D., Klinedinst, J. K., & Seat, P. D. (1984). *Multidimensional description of child personality: A manual for the Personality Inventory for Children revised 1984.* Los Angeles: Western Psychological Services.

Norman D. Sundberg, Ph.D.

Professor and Director of Clinical/Community Psychology Program, University of Oregon, Eugene, Oregon.

PORTEUS MAZES

Stanley D. Porteus. Cleveland, Ohio: The Psychological Corporation.

Introduction

The Porteus Maze Test is a nonverbal test of performance intelligence, which tells the psychologist more than just intelligence. It is a graded set of paper forms on which the subject traces the way from a starting point to an exit; the subject must avoid blind alleys along the way. There are no time limits. The mazes vary in complexity from simple diamond shape for the average three-year-old to intricate labyrinths for adults. There are three sets of mazes: the original (the Vineland series), and two supplements, the Extension and the Supplement. The latter two start with the design for year seven and are intended to provide parallel or more difficult forms than the original series. The test materials and Porteus' book (1965) explain the test and summarize the early literature. They are available from the Psychological Corporation; there is no separate test manual.

The Porteus mazes yield two major kinds of scores: 1) The Test Age is based on the highest level of maze successfully completed and the number of trials to solve each one. It is converted into a Test Quotient by using the subject's chronological age in a manner similar to that for obtaining the IQ and tables are available for that conversion. 2) The Qualitative (Q) score is derived from specified errors in crossing lines, lifting the pencil, and general lack of carefulness in tracing one's path through the maze. In addition, Porteus (1965) presents a rudimentary introduction to a score of the subject's style in drawing the mazes; this is called the Conformity-Variability (C-V) score and is supposed to be an indicator of personality characteristics. However, the C-V score has received little attention and will not be discussed further.

The Porteus mazes first appeared in 1914 in Melbourne, Australia, where Porteus worked with the schools. The original series was published in 1915. As with E. K. Strong and the Vocational Interest Inventory, Stanley Porteus (1883-1972) concentrated most of his professional life on one test. The original impetus came from a major problem in the *Zeitgeist* of the first decades of the 1900s—the need for schools to identify the mentally retarded (''feeble-minded'' or ''morons'' and ''idiots'' as they were called). In his 1965 book Porteus combined autobiography and opinion with a historical account of the test. Starting with the need to find a measure that was not so dependent on verbal skills as the Binet tests, Porteus found that the tracing of mazes was simple and interesting in obtaining performance from children. The early work showed that the mazes were correlated with other intelligence tests and were practical to use with children having less than the usual facility with language. The success of his test led to Porteus' appointment in 1919 to the Vineland Training School in New Jersey, then the foremost center for research and treatment of the retarded. The mazes were also incorporated in the Point Scale of Performance Tests by Grace Arthur in 1930. Later mazes of a similar sort were added to the Weschler intelligence tests for children (WISC and WPPSI).

Although Porteus' initial concern was with detection of low intelligence and application to school situations, often as a supplement to the Binet tests, he began to put emphasis on the test as a measure of planfulness and foresight. At first he thought that the Test Age score would help identify delinquents, but later found that a new score he introduced in 1942, the Qualitative or Q score, was useful by itself in distinguishing delinquents from nondelinquents. When psychosurgery, or the lobotomy, for intractable psychosis and other severe psychiatric disorders was introduced into the United States in the mid-1940s, some psychologists were surprised to find that there was little decrement in general IQ as measured by the Weschler or Binet, after the procedure. However, the Porteus Mazes test did show a significant and lasting drop. Because the frontal lobes, which were affected by psychosurgery, are believed to be the site of planning Porteus' theory about the test was supported.

Throughout his long career in clinical psychology and especially after his appointment to the University of Hawaii in 1922, Porteus also applied his test in cross-cultural studies. His 1965 book goes beyond the test itself and gives interesting observations of cultural characteristics and differences particularly with aborigines in central and western Australia and the bushpeople in the Kalahari Desert in what is now called Namibia. The maze Test Ages were uniformly low among the "primitive" peoples, but there was considerable variation, which led to speculation about differences in cultural patterns, acculturation, and environment.

The Porteus mazes, now over 70 years old, have intrigued a number of psychologists, and a persistent stream of application and research still flows today, as one will notice in the *Psychological Abstracts* and major books on testing. There are over 300 publications on the Porteus Maze Test and it occupies a small but special niche in testing in many places in the world.

Practical Applications/Uses

The Porteus mazes are usable with subjects from three years to adulthood who can see and use a pencil to draw. Even people of low intelligence and of different cultural backgrounds can understand what is expected through the use of demonstrations or practice forms. There are specific verbal instructions, but the test is essentially nonverbal. The administration, however, is not simple enough to give without considerable study of Porteus' instructions (1965) and practice. For instance, a common mistake in administration is to allow the person to go beyond the entrance of a blind alley when the subject should be stopped and given another copy of that particular maze. The scoring, although simple once learned, also needs practice. With trained people, the interscorer reliability is high.

In psychological work in clinics and schools, the Porteus mazes have probably been used most frequently for cases in which nonverbal measurement is necessary or as a supplement to the commonly used intelligence tests, such as the Stanford-Binet. In a 1982 survey of test usage in 221 clinical settings in the United States, Lubin, Larsen and Matarazzo (1984) found that the Porteus Mazes ranked 23rd among tests mentioned. However, in 1935 before the advent of the Wechsler tests and many other tests of intelligence, the Porteus was the second most used test, next after the Stanford-Binet.

Many cases would involve decisions about mental retardation in which the Porteus Mazes might be able to bring out skills and cognitive processes that would not be shown on verbal tests. Children who are speech-handicapped or from different cultural backgrounds would often be tested with the Porteus.

Another clinical usage of the Porteus mazes has been with cases of delinquency in which the investigation concerns ability to think ahead. The test requires control of impulsiveness and attention in going through the mazes, and the presumption is that poorly socialized youngsters are inadequate in seeing the consequences of their acts.

The test has been used a great deal for research on a variety of problems. At least one of the reviews in the Buros yearbooks (Horn, 1972) has recommended that the Porteus be limited to research usage or researched settings, but this restriction is unrealistic. Too much clinical experience and lore and too much general research information about the test exists to keep it out of clinical and other applied usage.

Technical Aspects

First, let us consider information about the mazes as a test of cognitive ability as indicated by the Test Age and its derivative, the Test Quotient. What is the reliability of Test Age? This question is not clearly presented in Porteus' book. Doctor in his review in Buros (1972) comments on the low parallel form reliability for Test Age scores (a correlation of about .50). Horn, in his Buros review (1972), reasons that we can assume that the reliability of the Porteus score is at least .75 because it correlates that amount with the Knox Cubes. Porteus says there are practice effects on Test Age, and in a review, Riddle and Roberts (1978) report an average effect of 1.25 years on second application and an additional .7 year on the third.

In regard to the validity of the Porteus Test Age score as an ability test, many early studies of correlations with other intelligence tests ranged widely from moderate to high coefficients. Because the Porteus is a nonverbal performance test, one does not expect a high correlation with purely verbal tests, but the correlation should be at least moderately positive. Riddle and Roberts (1977) note that a correlation coefficient of .50 is representative of studies with other IQ tests. Correlations with intelligence tests involving spatial abilities, such as the Kohs Blocks and Knox Cubes, are particularly high. One important finding would be correlations between Porteus results and WISC performance scores, especially the maze section, but there seem to be no easily available analyses. Porteus (1965) reports that a combination of the Binet and Porteus was more predictive of school ratings in early studies than either one alone. Recent studies of predictive validity are not available, and because schools have changed a great deal, it is questionable how generalizable the early studies are.

The extensive studies of psychosurgery have been mentioned earlier. In a review since Porteus' book, Riddle and Roberts (1978) reanalyzed the data taking into account the practice effects. They found that the magnitude of the changes on the Porteus Test Age score depends on the site of the surgery and the length of time between surgery and testing. There is greater loss when the cut in the frontal lobes is more posterior than anterior, and losses appear to be permanent.

The second kind of score is the Q or Quantitative score. Riddle and Roberts (1977) report that Q is relatively independent of Test Age and IQ, and they estimate a -0.2 as a reasonable correlation. The Q score depends on such maze-drawing behavior as cutting corners, waviness of lines, crossing lines, and lifting the pencil, the last one receiving the heaviest loading according to a factor analytic study. The scoring shows high interrater reliability, but the test-retest reliability appears to be rather low (.51, after three days with a sample of psychiatric patients.)

In his book Porteus (1965) presents much evidence that some cultural groups as well as delinquents score low on Q. In recent studies, Gow and Ward (1982) have found with retardates and normal high-school students significant correlations between Porteus scores and measures of reflection/impulsivity. Bell, Munday and Quay (1983) found a change on the Q score toward less impulsiveness when training sessions were given to impulsive boys. Riddle and Roberts (1977) reviewed many research studies and found the Q score (but not Test Age) specifically identifies delinquents; the differences from normals are significant and consistent. For a cutting score on the Vineland version, a score of 29 for males resulted in a hit rate of 70% correct when the numbers of delinquents in the studies are roughly equal to nondelinquents; when base rates are different, there would be different efficiencies in the cutting score. For females, the appropriate cutting score was 32. Riddle and Roberts (1977) report studies showing that a Q score of 22 would be better for differentiating delinquents in Great Britian. There are somewhat different reports from the different series of the Porteus mazes, but the general results are consistent in revealing that high Q scores are indicative of delinquent or impulsive criminal activity.

Critique

Certainly, the Porteus mazes present an interesting sequence in the history of testing and assessment. As do most reviewers, this reviewer concludes that the mazes are tapping important psychological functions. Porteus' claim for plan-fulness as an important component seems convincing, but the whole operation of responding to the test is complex, and future studies need to unravel how this test relates to work on information processing and cognitive styles. There is no other test quite like it and Porteus has certainly left his mark in the field.

However, despite its long history, there are many deficiencies in the Porteus Mazes. For one thing, there is not an adequate manual. Porteus' book (1965) is a partial manual, but it does not bring all the information together in a usable way, and now it needs updating. Administration and scoring are covered, but should be clearer. Direct suggestions for interpretation are scanty and poorly organized, and some case illustrations would be helpful. The psychometrics are not directly covered. The test awaits application of the APA guidelines for test manual presentation.

The big needs now for the advancement of the test are the following: 1) to review the over 300 publications and clarify what further information is needed, 2) to perform the needed psychometric studies, 3) to systematize the Porteus into the growing theory and research in cognitive science and neuropsychology (especially relating it to planning, impulsiveness, and attentional factors), and 4) to write a practical manual that will clarify the accumulated psychometrics and provide interpretation aids for the test. After its 70 years of impressive service to the psychological community, it would be a great service if someone would bring the information about the test into a clear, utilitarian, whole. Seventy years of effort and intriguing findings deserve more than what is now available for the Porteus Mazes.

References

Bell, C. R., Mundy, P., & Quay, H. C. (1983). Modifying impulsive responding in conduct-disordered institutionalized boys. *Psychological Reports, 52,* 307-310.

Doctor, R. F. (1972). In O. K. Buros (Ed.), *The seventh mental measurements yearbook* (pp. 751-753). Highland Park, NJ: The Gryphon Press.

Gow, L., & Ward, J. (1982). The Porteus Maze Test in the measurement of reflection/impulsivity, *Perception and Motor Skills, 54,* 1043-1053.

Horn, J. L. (1972). In O. K. Buros (Ed.), *The seventh mental measurements yearbook* (pp. 753-756). Highland Park, NJ: The Gryphon Press.

Lubin, B., Larsen, R. M., & Matarazzo, J. D. (1984). Patterns of psychological test usage in the United States: 1935-1982. *American Psychologist, 39,* 451-454.

Porteus, S. D. (1915). Mental tests for feeble-minded: A new series. *Journal of Psycho-Asthenics, 19,* 200-213.

Porteus, S. D. (1965). *Porteus Maze Test: Fifty years' application.* Palo Alto, CA: Pacific Books.

Riddle, M., & Roberts, A. H. (1977). Delinquency, delay of gratification, recidivism and Porteus Maze Tests. *Psychological Bulletin, 84,* 417-454.

Riddle, M., & Roberts, A. H. (1978). Psychosurgery and the Porteus Maze Tests: Review and reanalysis of data. *Archives of General Psychiatry, 35,* 493-497.

Patricia A. Kearney, Ph.D.
Professor of Education, John Carroll University, University Heights, Cleveland, Ohio.

A PROCESS FOR THE ASSESSMENT OF EFFECTIVE STUDENT FUNCTIONING

Nadine M. Lambert, Eli M. Bower, and Carolyn S. Hartsough. Monterey, California: CTB/McGraw-Hill.

Introduction

A Process for the Assessment of Effective Student Functioning is a three-component battery of nonintellectual measures to be used in screening school populations to identify children whose social or affective behavior may handicap their school functioning, and to help assess selected aspects of these behaviors in order to prescribe individualized programs to meet specific educational needs. Designed for use in classroom settings with pupils from kindergarten through seventh-grade levels, the battery yields data from teacher-, peer-, and self-ratings which may be combined to detect potentially dysfunctional behavior and plan intervention strategies.

A Process for the Assessment of Effective Student Functioning is based on a broad foundation of theoretical speculation and empirical tryout and revision. The authors bring impressive credentials and extensive, varied experience to the task of developing the component instruments. Nadine M. Lambert, Professor and Director of the School Psychology Training Program at the University of California, Berkeley, is a Fellow of the American Psychological Association, and a Diplomate in School Psychology; she received the Association's Distinguished Service Award in 1980. She has been a consultant to the state departments of education in California, Georgia, and Florida, as well as to the California Department of Justice, a member of the Joint Commission on Mental Health of Children, and a member of the Panel on Testing the Handicapped of the National Academy of Science. Lambert has been active for over two decades as a research principal investigator, journal consultant and editor, and author of numerous articles and reports concerned with children's adaptive behavior, the identification of educational handicaps, and compensatory education programs.

Eli M. Bower, Professor and Director of the Joint Doctorate Program in Special Education at the University of California, Berkeley, is a Fellow and past president of the American Orthopsychiatric Association, as well as a Fellow of The American Association on Mental Deficiency, and the American Psychological Association. A former deputy director of the California State Department of Mental Hygiene, he has been a consultant to the National Institute of Mental Health, California State Department of Education, and the White House Conference on Children and Youth. Like his coauthor, Lambert, he has long been active in editing and contributing to professional journals and in conducting research in mental retardation, affective training, and related fields.

Coauthor Carolyn S. Hartsough is Associate Research Editor at the School of Education at the University of California, Berkeley. She is a member of the American Psychological Association and the American Educational Research Association. A specialist in educational research, measurement, and evaluation, she has conducted research on scaling, test validity, compensatory education, and related issues. Her research reports have appeared in *American Journal of Orthopsychiatry, Educational and Psychological Measurement, Journal of School Psychology*, and others.

The components of A Process for the Assessment of Effective Student Functioning were developed to aid in the early detection of potentially educationally handicapping behavior, and to spur efforts to assist handicapped pupils. Each of the five instruments in the present battery has an individual developmental history, described in detail in a technical report prepared by the authors; however, some generalizations may be made about the battery as a whole.

Instruments in the present battery represent the third or fourth versions of scales developed by the authors. Copyrights on scale items have been obtained in 1955 and at many other times since then; items have been in continuous use and development by the authors since the 1950s. A major impetus to scale development was a three-year research program, begun in California in 1957 and supported by the State Legislature. The findings and recommendations of this project not only resulted in legislation concerning the identification of and provision for special education of children with educational handicaps, but also laid the foundation for work on the battery. In 1961-62, the California State Department of Education and Educational Testing Service distributed A Process for In-School Screening of Children with Emotional Handicaps, by Lambert and Bower, for research purposes only. In publishing this experimental package—consisting of one teacher-rating, three peer-rating, and three self-rating scales, to cover grade levels from kindergarten through 12th—the authors invited other researchers in the field to share results of investigations using the instruments in order to make them more effective.

Tryout and revision continued throughout the 1960s and 70s. A series of studies by the authors and their associates provided data concerning reliability, validity, and procedural details which enabled them to delete, add, and revise items; simplify methods of administration and scoring; refine scaling; incorporate the findings of contemporary research; and improve the format of each instrument. In 1973, a major norming project (to be described later) involving all five instruments was carried out. The Education for All Handicapped Children Act (PL 94-142) was passed in 1975; standards for its implementation were established in 1977. Lambert, Bower, and Hartsough gave consideration to the implications of this legislation for their evolving battery, and incorporated suggestions for use of their instruments to meet key provisions of the act in the manual for the forthcoming edition. In 1979, the present battery was published by Publishers Test Service.

In its present form, A Process for the Assessment of Effective Student Functioning continues to combine information from teacher-, peer-, and self-ratings. Five instruments are provided to achieve this over the span of grade levels from

Kindergarten to Grade 7: The Pupil Behavior Rating Scale, The Who Could This Be Game, A Picture Game (separate versions for girls and for boys), and The School Play: Parts I and II.

Teacher rating is accomplished for all grade levels by means of the Pupil Behavior Rating Scale (PBRS) and the accompanying PBRS Group Record Chart. After entering the names of all students on the chart, the teacher is guided by instructions in the spiral-bound PBRS booklet from broad groupings to precise ratings of all students on 11 behavioral attributes shown to be related to classroom success. The teacher rates each child along a continuum from 0 (does not exhibit the attribute) to 3.0 (exhibits the attribute to a high degree) for each attribute. Statements descriptive of behavior at selected points along each continuum serve as anchors to help clarify teacher judgments and increase objectivity of ratings. Ties in rankings are avoided by use of a score adjustment system described in the introductory section of the PBRS booklet.

Peer ratings are obtained through use of The Who Could This Be Game (Grades K-3), or Part I of The School Play (Grades 3-7). The Who Could This Be Game consists of 11 picture sheets, throughout which 20 situations are depicted. In the situations portrayed, boys and girls are equally represented as are instances of negative behavior and those of positive or neutral behavior. The instrument is administered individually to each pupil by the teacher or other examiner who shows the pictures (bound together in a reusable booklet) to the pupil one at a time. The pupil is asked to name the classmate who most resembles the child in a given pictured situation; these responses are recorded on the accompanying Recording Form by the examiner.

Part I of The School Play is used to obtain peer ratings for pupils in third through seventh grade. (Obviously, there is an overlapping of peer-rating instruments at the third-grade level; if at least 75% of pupils in a third-grade class are reading at or above grade level, The School Play may be used; otherwise, the authors recommend that The Who Could This Be Game be used.) To use this instrument, each pupil is asked to pretend to be a director who will "cast" classmates for parts in an imaginary class play. Each child is then given a consumable booklet in which the name of the boy or girl who best fits a given role is to be written next to a statement describing the role.

Self-ratings for children in Grades K-3 are elicited through use of The Picture Game. Each child receives an appropriate form (boys' or girls') of the test booklet, containing two sample pictures (to illustrate "happy" vs. "sad"), 10 practice pictures (clearly representing happy or sad situations, and used to check understanding of procedures), and 60 test pictures. The test pictures represent neutral situations; the child responding indicates his or her perception of the situation by circling with a pencil or crayon either the happy face or the sad face drawn next to each test picture.

Part II of The School Play yields self-ratings for third- through seventh-grade pupils. (Here again there is overlapping of instruments for third-graders: see the previous comment regarding overlapping peer-rating instruments.) In Part II, the 14 hypothetical roles from Part I are rearranged in 24 different sets of 4; the child is asked to indicate (by making an X) preferred and least preferred roles, and roles in which teachers or classmates might or might not cast her or him.

Practical Applications/Uses

Administration, scoring, interpretation, and use of the results of A Process for the Assessment of Effective Student Functioning represent a team effort, requiring skill, commitment, investment of time, and cooperation on the part of all concerned. Although the classroom teacher completes the Pupil Behavior Rating Scale, and the teacher—or a trained aide—administers the other instruments, a school psychologist, comparably trained administrator, or other specialist is required to supervise and assist the teachers involved and serve as liaison with concerned parents. Once screening has been completed, teachers, school psychologists, administrators, and other specialists must pool their expertise, insights, and competencies to diagnose specific difficulties of children identified by the screening process and plan individualized remediation.

Although each instrument in the battery may be administered independently of the others, it is advisable to use all three components for greatest accuracy and usefulness. Teacher ratings should be administered before the others, but only after enough time has elapsed for the teacher to become thoroughly familiar with the pupils and they with each other; the authors suggest a minimum of two months after a semester has begun. Before attempting to use any of the instruments, the teacher and all others who will participate in the process need to familiarize themselves with the underlying rationale and procedures. The *Administration and Use Manual* that accompanies the battery is thorough, well organized, and clear; however, it must be read carefully, and the procedure rehearsed, before actual administration is attempted. A resource person experienced in the techniques to be used should conduct at least one training session and remain available thereafter to answer questions and provide other assistance as needed. The time required to prepare for administration will vary with the individuals involved; approximately two or three hours might be "typical."

Detailed instructions are given in the manual for the administration and scoring of each instrument, together with practical suggestions for modifying procedures to suit individual situations and for dealing with problems that may arise (i.e., misunderstood directions, reading difficulties). All scoring and recording are done by hand, but these procedures are straightforward and guided every step of the way by clear instructions in the manual and by the layout of related recording forms.

No time limits are given for completing the Pupil Behavior Rating Scale; the time required will vary widely depending on the class size and on the teacher's familiarity with the pupils to be rated and with use of the scale itself. After all pupils have been rated on each scale, the sum of each pupil's scores on all 11 scales is found. An example of a completed PBRS recording form is presented in the manual to aid teachers' visualization.

The individually administered Who Could This Be Game requires approximately 15 to 20 minutes per pupil according to the manual; administration sessions for an entire class may be spaced over a period of one month. After all children have participated, the teacher tallies on the recording form the number of times any individual has been chosen, then finds the percentage of negative selections for each pupil.

A Picture Game, group administered, requires approximately 30 minutes for an entire class to complete. To score, the teacher records the number of pictures labeled "sad" for each pupil.

Group administered, Parts I and II of The School Play together take about 35 to 45 minutes to give to an entire class. Part I is scored by tallying pupils' responses, summing the number of nominations for each individual, and determining the percentage of negative perceptions for each. Part II is scored by recording the number of choices checked by each child, then determining the percentage of negative self-ratings.

No estimates are given of times required to score the peer- and self-rating instruments or to complete screening and other procedures described below. As in the case of the PBRS, time requirements will depend on class size and other pupil and teacher variables.

To complete screening, scores from teacher-ratings, peer-ratings, and self-ratings are combined according to step-by-step instructions in the manual. An example of a completed Class Screening Summary form is given to help clarify the procedure. Teachers are asked to identify the five students receiving the highest ratings on the Pupil Behavior Rating Scale, the five receiving the highest percentages on the peer-rating scale, and all those with extreme scores on the self-rating instrument. Pupils receiving two or three negative notations are marked for further study and referral. An individual Pupil Record Folder may also be filled out for each student, whether screened for further action or not, to become part of the individual's cumulative record.

To assist in assessment of targeted students (or others, if so desired), eight tables of norms are presented in the manual, one for each grade level from kindergarten through seventh grade. The tables report standard scores and percentile ranks together with summary descriptive statistics for appropriate subscales and total scores on each of the rating instruments (PBRS) only, for Grade 7).

Although advanced training and clinical experience (expertise such as one would expect of a master's level school psychologist) are needed for interpretations of scores as part of the diagnosis of specific handicapping conditions and planning of intervention strategies, two lengthy and thought-provoking sections especially for teachers are included in the manual. The first of these is designed to sharpen teachers' perceptions of potentially dysfunctional behavior on the part of pupils and to suggest how the underlying dynamics of such behaviors may be reflected by rating scales. The second section presents suggestions to help teachers be effective contributing members of a team planning an Individualized Education Program for pupils, as required by PL 94-142.

Technical Aspects

Only brief mentions are made in the *Administration and Use Manual* of data related to the instruments' reliability, validity, and norms—perhaps intentionally, to avoid burdening the intended classroom teacher user with technical details. However, detailed information is presented in the 151 pages and 27 tables of a manuscript technical report made available by the publishers to researchers.

Since each of the instruments in A Process for the Assessment of Effective

Student Functioning has a long and unique developmental history, it follows that reliability, validity, and norms data for each are based on somewhat different— although sometimes overlapping—groups of studies conducted at different times. (It is relevant to note in this connection that the authors offer convincing evidence, based on patterns of intercorrelations among scores on the separate instruments for primary and elementary pupils, that the instruments tap different variables and thus make relatively independent contributions to the battery as a whole.)

The Pupil Behavior Rating Scale was normed in 1973 on more than 5,500 pupils in randomly selected kindergarten through eighth-grade classrooms in San Francisco area public and private schools. This norm group was highly heterogeneous with respect to social, cultural, and educational characteristics.

Internal consistency, interrater, and stability estimates of reliability are provided for the Pupil Behavior Rating Scale. The former, indicators of relative homogeneity of content, were calculated from the scores of 4,818 girls and boys in Grades K through 5 tested in 1973; total score values ranged from a low of .89 to a high of .92. Interrater reliability estimates, indicating agreement in rankings for two raters, were based on ratings of a total of 83 third- and sixth-grade pupils; coefficients varied from .23 to .93 on individual scales (most values in the .80s), and from .84 to .95 on total scores. Rater agreement was highest for ratings of third-graders; there were no significant differences between reliability of ratings for boys and girls. Stability coefficients were reported for 4-, 8-, and 12-month intervals for a total of 1,370 primary and elementary pupils. Total score coefficients for the group as a whole were .87, .70, and .66; the values decreased progressively over time, as one would expect, indicating higher stability over a short time interval than over a longer one.

Several different lines of evidence have been pursued to explore the validity of the Pupil Behavior Rating Scale, each represented by groups of studies throughout the developmental lifetime of the instrument. Factor analyses were carried out to investigate the structure of attributes the scales purported to measure. Appropriate statistical tests of significance were performed to determine if ratings differentiated screened from unscreened pupils. Correlations of teacher ratings of 150 second- and 150 fifth-graders with clinical judgments produced after intensive study of the children and their families by social workers, a clinical psychologist, and a psychiatrist were used to explore concurrent validity, as were correlations with other measures of educational functioning (such as course marks, achievement test scores, and scholastic aptitude test scores). Predictive validity was studied by following up pupils rated after they had reached high school and correlating original ratings with such criteria as number of guidance referrals and successful graduation. All of these analyses were conducted on adequately large, appropriately selected groups of children, and give evidence of high standards of psychometric practice. The results, reported in five tables, present a somewhat mixed picture, but overall demonstrate evidence of promising validity.

The Who Could This Be Game was normed in 1973 on approximately 2,500 Kindergarten through Grade 3 children who had been rated on the Pupil Behavior Rating Scale. Retest reliability estimates were based on data collected during administration of earlier versions of the instrument. Coefficients for all grade levels combined were .75 (total selections) and .82 (negative selections). Internal consistency coefficients ranged from .43 (first-grade girls) to .77 (second-grade boys); the authors recognized the problem of item heterogeneity in interpreting obtained coefficients. Concurrent validity was assessed by correlating second-grade peer nominations (percentage of negative nominations) with former (first-grade) teacher ratings, and independently with clinical criteria for the 150 second-graders mentioned in the earlier discussion of PBRS validity. The teacher-peer coefficients were .31 and .32 respectively for girls and boys; the multiple R between total peer ratings and 9 clinical factors was .57. Seven- and 10-year follow-ups of second-graders to permit correlations of primary peer ratings with measurements collected in high school (multiple R of .54), and examination of differences in mean ratings by those later judged "successful" and "unsuccessful," provided evidence of predictive validity.

Norming for A Picture Game was carried out on the same children to whom The Who Could This Be Game was administered in 1973. Retest reliabilities, calculated from scores of 600 children tested with earlier versions of the instrument ranged from .52 to .72; for all grades (K-3) combined, the coefficient was .75. Internal consistency estimates ranged from .78 to .89. Data gathered on the 150 second-graders who were subjects in validity studies of the PBRS and The Who Could This Be Game also provided information concerning validity of A Picture Game. To study concurrent validity, pupils' self-ratings were correlated with teacher ratings, scholastic aptitude test scores, clinical adjustment ratings, and several other measures. The resulting coefficients ranged from .10 to .45 and—with only two exceptions (girls' math marks and teacher ratings) out of 11 values reported— were reportedly statistically significant. Predictively, 7-year and 10-year follow-up studies of the second-graders yielded significant correlations between second-grade self-rating and such later criteria as number of guidance referrals and graduation from high school.

It will be recalled that Part I of A School Play is a peer-rating instrument for Grades 4 through 7, while Part II is a self-rating instrument; as one might therefore expect, the technical histories of these subtests parallel those of the corresponding primary instruments. Thus, A School Play: Part I was normed in 1973 on nearly 1,800 fourth- and fifth-graders who had been rated on the PBRS. Retest reliabilities, determined for earlier versions, were .88 (total selections) and .90 (negative selections) for all fourth-, fifth-, and sixth-grade scores combined. Internal consistency coefficients ranged from .50 (fifth-grade girls) to .60 (fifth-grade boys). Concurrent and predictive validity were assessed by the same methods used for The Who Could This Be Game, except that 150 fifth-graders were the subjects, and a 10-year follow-up was not possible. Girls' negative peer nominations correlated .09 with teachers' ratings; boys' correlated .48; a combined multiple R with four clinical factors was .38 (the latter two reportedly significant). The seven-year follow-up showed a multiple R of .38 between A School Play: Part I ratings and high school criteria; once again, differences between mean ratings of "successful" and "unsuccessful" high school students were significant, this time at the .01 level.

A School Play: Part II was also normed in 1973, using the same subjects as Part I. Unlike its primary self-rating counterpart, A Picture Game, no retest reliabilities are reported for Part II of A School Play; internal consistency coefficients based on data from subjects using earlier versions ranged from .86 (fourth-grade boys) to .88 (fifth-grade boys). Estimation of concurrent and predictive validity paralleled methods used with A Picture Game, but using 150 fifth-grade pupils, and having no 10-year follow-up. Correlations of self-ratings with five concurrent measures ranged from .01 to .35; multiple R with seven clinical factors was .49. No specific values are reported for predictive validity estimates; the authors report patterns of 7-year follow-up correlations (when students were in the 12th grade) consistent with those of the 10-year follow-up on 12th-graders who had taken A Picture Game as second-graders.

As in the case of the teacher ratings, methods of data collection and analysis for the peer-rating and self-rating instruments follow accepted principles of good psychometric practice, and results lend support to the authors' contentions that these instruments make independent and useful contributions to the battery as a whole. It is to be hoped that further studies will be conducted with the battery in its present form to illuminate issues of reliability and validity, and to extend the applicability of the published norms. Given the conscientiousness of the authors' past efforts and their invitation to battery users to cooperate in its development, such studies seem highly probable. A condensed and clarified technical report should be made commercially available so that potential users may judge for themselves whether or not the instruments and related norms suit local requirements.

Critique

To study, administer, score, interpret, and apply the results of A Process for the Assessment of Effective Student Functioning requires much time and effort; one cannot simply glance over the materials, stroll into a classroom, and wrap up the project in half an hour! Nor should its use be undertaken casually, without a clear purpose and the cooperation of parents, teachers, and other professionals. But it can be a flexible, useful tool if used with thorough preparation, careful administration, and creative clinical judgment by competent, insightful professionals. It complements, but does not replace, such other types of measures as scholastic aptitude and achievement tests.

As the authors stress, the battery may be used to help meet federal, state, or local requirements for locating, evaluating, and assisting behaviorally handicapped children. Its use has also been explored in the identification of educable mentally retarded and gifted children (Hartsough, Elias, & Wheeler, 1983).

A classroom teacher could put the component instruments to good use exploring the dynamics of any class. The scales can reveal pupils' perceptions of themselves and of each other, of which the teacher may be unaware and which may be in agreement or at variance with the teacher's perceptions. Results may bring into focus the quiet, well-behaved pupils one tends not to notice in a bustling classroom. Reflection on emerging patterns may help in day-to-day planning and organizing of class activities.

The *Administration and Use Manual* provides much to think about—material which can enhance a teacher's professionalism or even serve as a springboard for inservice development activities. For example, as the authors point out, being "different" is not the same as being "handicapped"; labeling is not a substitute for action. (The manual's "Further Reading" list needs to be updated, however.)

Careful, thoughtful use of the instruments and related materials can not only sharpen teacher perceptions, alert him or her to new ideas, and suggest new avenues of professional development, but can inspire a mutually enriching team effort as well. Just as other professionals need to support the teacher through preparation and administration phases of activity, so the teacher needs to remain involved in diagnosis and follow-up as an active participant rather than remaining simply a collector of data for "the experts."

The developmental history of component instruments, as well as the apt title of the battery, reflect its tentative, dynamic nature. What we see here is a *process*, not a product, and all—pupils, parents, teachers, and other educational professionals alike—are invited to be partners in the endeavor.

References

Bower, E. M. (1960, 1969). *Early identification of emotionally handicapped children in school.* Springfield, IL: Charles C. Thomas.

Bower, E. M., & Lambert, N. M. (1966). In-school screening of children with emotional handicaps. In N. M. Long & R. Newman (Eds.), *Conflict in the classroom* (pp. 128-133). Belmont, CA: Wadsworth Publishing Co.

Bower, E. M., Tashnovian, P. J., & Larson, C. A. (1958). *A process for early identification of emotionally disturbed children.* Sacramento: California State Department of Education.

Hartsough, C. S. (1973). *Classroom adaptation of elementary school children varying with respect to age, sex, and ethnic status* (Project Report, The Stress of School Project, Grant No. MN 14605, National Institute of Mental Health). Berkeley, CA: University of California.

Hartsough, C. S., Elias, P., & Wheeler, P. (1983). Evaluation of a nonintellectual assessment procedure for the early screening of exceptionality. *Journal of School Psychology, 21,* 133-142.

Lambert, N. M. (1963). *Development and validation of a process for screening emotionally handicapped children* (U.S. Office of Education, Cooperative Research Project No. 1186). Sacramento: California State Department of Education.

Lambert, N. M. (1964). The high school drop out in elementary school. In *Guidance and the school drop out* (pp. 40-65). Washington, DC: American Personnel and Guidance Association, National Education Association.

Lambert, N. M. (1972). Intellectual and nonintellectual predictors of high school status. *The Journal of Special Education, 6,* 247-259.

Lambert, N. M. (1981). The clinical validity of the Process for Assessment of Effective Student Functioning. *Journal of School Psychology, 19,* 323-334.

Lambert, N. M., Bower, E. M., & Hartsough, C. S. (1979). *A Process for the Assessment of Effective Student Functioning: Technical report.* (Available from Publishers Test Service, CTB/McGraw-Hill, 2500 Garden Road, Monterey, CA 93940.)

Lambert, N. M., & Hartsough, C. S. (1973). Scaling behavioral attributes of children using multiple teacher judgments of pupil characteristics. *Educational and Psychological Measurement, 33,* 859-874.

Lambert, N. M., & Hartsough, C. S. (1980). Validity issues surrounding Title I ESEA eligibility criteria. *Educational Evaluation and Policy Analysis, 2*(3), 25-32.

Lambert, N. M., Hartsough, C. S., & Bower, E. M. (1979). *A Process for the Assessment of Effective Student Functioning: Administration and use manual.* Monterey, CA: Publishers Test Service, CTB/McGraw-Hill.

Lambert, N. M., Hartsough, C. S., & Zimmerman, I. L. (1976). Comparative predictive efficiency of intellectual and nonintellectual components of high school functioning. *American Journal of Orthopsychiatry, 46,* 109-122.

Lambert, N. M., & Nicoll, R. C. (1977). Conceptual model for nonintellectual behavior and its relationship to early reading achievement. *Journal of Educational Psychology, 69,* 481-490.

Lambert, N. M., Sandoval, J. H., & Sassone, D. M. (1978). Prevalence of hyperactivity in elementary school children as a function of social system definers. *American Journal of Orthopsychiatry, 48,* 446-463.

Lambert, N. M., & Urbanski, C. (1980). Behavioral profiles of children with different levels of achievement. *Journal of School Psychology, 18,* 58-66.

Fredric M. Wolf, Ph.D.
Assistant Professor, Department of Postgraduate Medicine and Health Professions Education, University of Michigan, and Associate Director of Educational Development and Evaluation, Michigan Diabetes Research and Training Center, Ann Arbor, Michigan.

Nancy Palchik Allen, Ph.D.
Instructor, Department of Postgraduate Medicine and Health Professions Education, University of Michigan, and Assistant Director of Education and Evaluation, Michigan Multipurpose Arthritis Center, Ann Arbor.

PROFILE OF ADAPTATION TO LIFE: CLINICAL AND HOLISTIC FORMS

Robert E. Ellsworth. Palo Alto, California: Consulting Psychologists Press, Inc.

Introduction

The Profile of Adaptation to Life-Clinical (PAL-C) and Holistic (PAL-H) inventories comprise two of a set of four scales in the Ellsworth Adjustment and Adaptation Profiles series. These simple, self-report scales each can be completed in 20-30 minutes, are easily scored and profiled, and are designed for reliable program evaluation. The Clinical form (PAL-C) was designed to reliably and validly evaluate the treatment adjustment of adults receiving counseling and health services. A unique aspect of the PAL-C is the assessment of positive adjustment and adaptation as well as maladjustment, the latter is more typically assessed in measures of this kind. Psychological well-being, income management, close interpersonal relations, and child relations comprise the four elements of positive adjustments; negative emotions, physical symptoms, and alcohol/drug abuse comprise the three elements of maladjustment measured.

The Holistic form (PAL-H) was designed for use by mental health agencies, counselors, ministers, and other health professionals to assist in life-style counseling. It contains all seven of the PAL-C scales along with five life-style scales:

These reviewers would like to thank Lynne Robins, M.A., for assistance with the review of literature and Deborah Patt, B.A., for technical assistance in preparation of the manuscript. This work was supported in part by grant number NIH 5 P60 AM 20572 to the Michigan Diabetes Research and Training Center and by grant number NIH 5 P60 AM 20557 to the Michigan Multipurpose Arthritis Center from the National Institute of Arthritis, Diabetes, and Digestive and Kidney Diseases.

594

Social Activity, Self-Activity, Nutrition and Exercise, Personal Growth, and Spiritual Awareness. The other two inventories in the series are the Child and Adolescent Adjustment Profile (CAAP) and the Adult Personal Adjustment and Role Skills (PARS). In contrast to the PAL-C and PAL-H, both the CAAP and the PARS are rating scales that are completed by individuals other than the individual being assessed (e.g., by parents, spouses, teachers, probation officers, etc.).

Development of the PAL inventories began in 1975 with the development of the research version (PAL-R) by Robert E. Ellsworth. The work began in response to a request for a method to measure the effects on participants of a personal growth program and was designed to ascertain the essential life-style charactertistics of emotional and physical health (Ellsworth, 1981a). Ellsworth received his Ph.D. in psychology in 1954 from Pennsylvania State University. He began a 16-year career with the Veterans Administration Hospital (VAH) system as an intern in 1953 and rose to the position of chief of research at several VAHs before entering Unity Ministerial School in 1979. Since 1981, Ellsworth has been a practicing minister in Vancouver, Washington.

The current PAL inventories are the result of revision of the preliminary PAL-R version which contained 154-items (Ellsworth, 1981a). The original items were designed to reflect a wide range of functioning and adjustment. A sample of 1,738 individuals completed the PAL-R between 1975 and 1978 during this instrument development phase. Of these respondents, 678 were mental health clinic clients, 96 were community college students, and 843 were from one of three subsamples that were either interested in psychic experience (responders to a *National Enquirer* article) or altered states of consciousness (participants in either a training program or invited conference). The test manuals state that this large heterogeneous sample insured a wide range of life-styles and adjustment levels (Ellsworth, 1981a, 1981b).

Forty-one of the original items were retained in the PAL-C based on three criteria: 1) sensitivity to treatment change at three-month follow-up from baseline as a result of such interventions as counseling in community clinics or training in Transcendental Meditation; 2) ability to distinguish between groups known to differ in adjustment; and 3) the salience of the item in measuring an adjustment domain for both sexes and for both clinical and non-clinical subjects as determined by a factor analysis. Sixteen of the original items were retained for the five life-style scales of the PAL-H based on statistically significant ($p < .01$) correlations with the four primary scales of good adjustment that comprise the PAL-C (i.e., low negative emotions and physical symptoms scores and high psychological well-being and close relationships scores).

As noted earlier, the Profile of Adaptation to Life-Clinical Form (PAL-C) contains seven scales comprised of a total of 34 items. In addition, there are seven additional items that comprise a list of Problem Codes corresponding to each of the seven scales, thus, 41 items comprise the complete PAL-C inventory.

The PAL-C is designed for self-administration by subjects with minimal involvement by the test examiner. It can be given to clients by a secretary or clerk before the first visit or completed in a telephone interview of the client. While it was designed for use with adults, it has also been used with teenagers (Ellsworth, 1985). It is relatively straightforward, uses simple language, and is designed for clients in a variety of settings, from mental health services to inpatient, day treatment, and outpatient settings.

Each of the items on the seven PAL-C scales is answered by checking on a 4-point Likert-type scale how frequently the item was experienced by the client during the past month. The rating scale for 1) Negative Emotions, 2) Psychological Well-Being, 3) Income Management, 4) Close Interpersonal Relationships, and 5) Child Interpersonal Relationships are rated on a scale of 1= never, 2 = rarely, 3 = sometimes, and 4 = often. The 6) Physical Symptoms Scale and 7) Alcohol/Drug Use employ ratings ranging from 1= not once, 2 = 1-2 times per *month*, 3 = 1-2 times per *week*, and 4 = almost daily. Descriptions of each of the seven scales and the Problem Codes follow:

1. *Negative Emotions Scale:* This factor is regarded as representing a combination of such psychological states as anxiety and depression, and is comprised of items that measure feeling worried, gloomy, tense, uneasy, troubled, and unhappy. Higher scores are indicative of poorer adjustment in this domain.

2. *Psychological Well-Being Scale:* This factor represents the degree to which people experience a sense of self-esteem and enjoyment in their lives, with higher scores reflecting greater positive adjustment to life. Items measure how much people enjoy other people, their work, and being involved in things, as well as how much they trust other people and feel useful and needed.

3. *Income Management Scale:* This scale reflects the degree to which respondents have had enough money during the month to cover both their unexpected expenses and their bills and how much they worry about their debts. The scale varies from the typical approaches that measure work activity and money earned and instead focuses on how well people manage the money available to them. Higher scores reflect better income management.

4. *Close Interpersonal Relationships Scale:* This scale is to be completed only be persons who are living with another adult (i.e., spouse, parent, etc.). It reflects such issues as discussing important matters, talking through angry situations, enjoying things together, feeling close, etc. Higher scores indicate better relationships.

5. *Child Interpersonal Relationships Scale:* This scale is completed only if children live with the individual. Its content is similar to that for the preceding close interpersonal relationships with adults scale, where higher scores suggest better relationships.

6. *Physical Symptoms Scale:* This scale is designed to measure "illness consciousness," the frequency with which individuals focus on their physical problems. The physical problems listed, such as headaches, fevers, dizziness, and nausea, are those often associated with "psychosomatic" illness. Higher scores reflect poorer functioning and adjustment.

7. *Alcohol/Drug Use Scale:* This is a measure of the self-reported frequency of alcohol/drug use and the degree to which it causes problems with family members or with thinking clearly. Higher scores reflect poorer adjustment.

Problem Codes: These seven items are not used to obtain adjustment scores, but can be used at the initial stages of interaction with clients to identify which of the formally assessed seven areas clients believe are major problems. These items are typically rated on 3-point scales from 1= no problem, 2 = some problem, and

3 = serious problem.

The Profile of Adaptation to Life-Holistic form (PAL-H) contains the same 34 items comprising the seven scales of the clinical form plus 18 additional items that comprise five additional scales. The seven-item Problem Codes for the PAL-C are not included in the PAL-H.

The format of the five additional scales of the PAL-H is similar to those on the PAL-C. Each scale asks respondents to rate the frequency of each item during the past month on a 4-point Likert-type scale. It is administered in the manner described previously for the PAL-C. The five additional scales that in conjunction with the seven PAL-C scales comprise the PAL-H are: 8) Social Activity, 9) Self-Activity, 10) Nutrition and Exercise, 11) Personal Growth, and 12) Spiritual Awareness. These life-style activities and beliefs were reported to be related to good health and adjustment according to the research study reported by Ellsworth in the PAL-Holistic Scale manual (1981b).

Ellsworth states that the PAL-H will be useful to counselors or ministers when attempting to assist clients to examine and incorporate health-related activities into their lives and assume more responsibility for maintaining or improving their own physical health and psychological well-being. Descriptions of these five life style scales follow:

8. *Social Activity Scale:* This scale includes items concerned with attending civic or organization meetings and social affairs, and spending time with or entertaining friends at home. Each of the four items is rated on a scale ranging from 1 = not once, 2 = 1-2 times per *month,* 3 = 1-2 times per *week,* and 4 = almost daily. Higher scores indicate greater social activity.

9. *Self-Activity Scale:* Items concerned with time spent alone, outdoors, or meditating comprise this scale. Each of the three items is rated from 1 = never/rarely, 2 = 1-2 times per *week,* 3 = 3-5 times per *week,* and 4 = each day. Higher scores indicate greater self-activity.

10. *Nutrition and Exercise Scale:* Items on this scale are concerned with eating fresh fruit and natural foods and doing physical activity. Each of the three items is scored on a 4-point rating scale similar to that of the Self-Activity Scale. Higher scores are interpreted to represent greater nutrition and exercise.

11. *Personal Growth Scale:* Items on this scale reflect time spent reading something about personal psychological growth or mystical/spiritual things, or participating in a study group. The rating scale is similar to that used for the Self-Activity and the Nutrition and Exercise Scales. Higher scores are thought to be reflective of greater personal growth.

12. *Spiritual Awareness Scales:* Five items that correlated most highly with good adjustment on the PAL Negative Emotions, Physical Symptoms, Psychological Well-Being, and Close Interpersonal Relationships Scales were included in this scale. These items relate to "belief in the effectiveness of psychic or spiritual healing, the reality of ESP and 'out of body' experiences, the view that problems are opportunities to grow, and that people create their own reality by the thoughts they hold" (Ellsworth, 1981b).

Once the PAL-C or PAL-H questionnaires are completed and scored, the scores for each scale may be transferred to a separate form that allows a profile for individuals to be developed. Each person's score for each scale is translated into an equivalent standardized T-score derived from the norming sample. For the seven scales that appear on both the PAL-C and PAL-H, T-scores greater than 40 are considered indicative of "adjustment" and those less than 40 (one standard deviation belows the average T-score of 50) are considered to be indicative of "poor adjustment." "Adjustment" can be subdivided into "below average" (40-45), "average" (45-55), and "above average" (55 and above).

For the five additional scales on the PAL-H (Social Activity, Self-Activity, Nutrition and Exercise, Personal Growth, Spiritual Awareness), scores ranging from 45-55 are considered "average," scores above 55 are considered "above average" and scores below 45 are considered "below average." Several case studies are provided in the Holistic form manual to illustrate how these scales can be used in life-style counseling (Ellsworth, 1981b).

If the clinical scales are used in a pre-post intervention context, Change Norms tables are provided for each of the seven scales for interpretive purposes. Change Norms are not provided for the five holistic scales. These norms were based on the combined results obtained from two samples, one comprised of individuals receiving mental health services and the other comprised of individuals receiving meditation training. Change scores greater than 50 are interpreted as more improvement than usual, and those below 50 are interpreted as less improvement than usual. According to Ellsworth (1981a, 1981b), these change scores represent a new approach to evaluating the impact of treatment for a given client. These norms are used to determine whether a person has improved more or less than other people with similar pretreatment scores and control for the effects of initial differences in subjects' adjustment levels. This is important because people with lower pretreatment adjustments scores in relation to people with higher adjustment scores tend to show greater changes in posttreatment scores. Thus these Change Norms "reflect the amount of change typically found for both initally well adjusted and poorly adjusted people" (Ellsworth, 1981b).

Practical Applications/Uses

The PAL inventories have been used primarily in clinical settings such as in mental health, drug, alcohol, and health counseling (S. Ellsworth, personal communication, January 11, 1985). They have also been used in growth enhacement programs such as Transcendental Meditation. Ellsworth (1981a) suggested the feasibility of using them to evaluate these types of programs and even for evaluating the effectiveness of individual counselors, trainers, or therapists.

Administration of both clinical and holistic PAL inventories is relatively straightforward. An examiner could administer either form with minimal training, in either an individual or group setting. However, a counseling-type setting would probably be most typical. The shorter clinical inventory can be completed in approximately 15-20 minutes and the longer holistic inventory in approximately 20-30 minutes. Both PAL inventories are pencil-and-paper instruments, thus, administration time will vary somewhat with the reading level of the subject.

Specific procedures for administering the inventories are not included in the testing manuals. However, the PAL-H manual suggests that the client complete this scale just prior to the first interview if the scale is going to be used to identify potential areas for therapeutic intervention. Although the testing manuals assume that the PAL inventories will be administered in their entirety, there is nothing in the administration, scoring, or interpretation of the inventories to preclude a user from selecting and administering particular scales of either test.

A strength of both of the PAL inventories is the relative ease with which they are scored. Instructions for scoring the scales are clearly presented in the testing manuals and the user can learn the scoring procedures with little difficulty. Only a short period of time (5 to 10 minutes) is required to hand-score either test. Items on both PAL invnetories are presented in a forced-choice format. Subjects respond to each item by choosing one of four options, scored from 1 to 4. Subjects receive a scale score for each of the seven areas that make up PAL-C and for each of the 12 areas that make up PAL-H. Each of the scale scores consists of the sum of the individual item scores for that scale. If a subject leaves one question on a scale blank, the average (rounded off to the nearest whole number) of the remaining item scores for that scale is inserted for the missing value to obtain a total scale score. The manuals recommend not computing a total score for a scale if two or more questions on a given scale are left blank. Although the test would usually be scored by hand, some agencies have developed software to permit computer scoring (S. Ellsworth, personal communication, January 11, 1985).

All of the total scale scores can be transferred to a Profile Sheet. Using the profile, the scale scores are compared to norms based on the scores obtained from 435 persons who completed and returned the PAL-R inventory in response to a *National Enquirer* article on psychic experiences. According to the test manuals, the author considered this *National Enquirer* norm group to be relatively well adjusted and representative of a broad range of educational, age, and geographic characteristics. In constructing the profile, the norm group scores for each scale were converted to standard scores with a mean of 50 and a standard deviation of 10. A Profile score below 40 (one standard deviation below the norm group mean) is considered to be in the "Poor Adjustment" range.

As mentioned previously, the PAL manual also includes Change Norm tables for PAL-C scales. These can be used in pretest-posttest comparisons to determine whether a person changed more or less than other persons with the same pretreatment scores. Change Norms were based upon differences between pretreatment scores and posttreatment scores (obtained after a three- to four-month interval) of individuals receiving mental health services or training in meditation.

Technical Aspects

The information on the reliability and validity of the PAL scales reported in this section has been taken from the author's testing manuals. To our knowledge, no independent studies on the reliability and validity of either PAL inventory has been undertaken. The 154-item PAL-R, however, was used by investigators at the Menninger Foundation in a series of studies on out-of-body experiences (Gabbard, Twemlow, & Jones, 1981, 1982; Twemlow & Gabbard, 1984; Twemlow, Gabbard & Jones, 1982). In these studies, the PAL scale was one of two questionnaires sent to 700 individuals who, in response to a *National Enquirer* interview, reported having had an out-of-body experience (an experience in which the individual thought his or her consciousness was separated from his or her physical body). Of these 700 individuals, 420 people returned valid questionnaires and of these individuals 339 reported out-of-body experiences. The investigators report that according to PAL meaures, the 339 respondents who reported an out-of-body experience were significantly healthier than a group of psychiatric inpatients and outpatients, and somewhat healthier than a group of college students. However, it is unclear how the PAL-R form was scored for determining the relationships in these studies. The PAL inventory was also used in a study of aftercare clients in a community mental health setting (Ellsworth, 1982).

Items on the original PAL-R form of the PAL inventory were selected from an initial item pool administered to individuals in an alcohol treatment program on two separate occasions, one week apart. Only items having a test-retest reliability of .80 or higher were retained in the PAL-R form of the scale. The 154 items of the PAL-R were factor analyzed to identify dimensions of adjustment common to all groups. The analyses were conducted separately for various subgroups (i.e., males, females, clinic, and non-clinic populations) and for all groups combined. Based on these analyses, seven factors were found to be common to all groups: Negative Emotions, Psychological Well-Being, Income Management, Physical Symptoms, Alcohol/Drug Use, Close Interpersonal Relationships, and Child Interpersonal Relationships. These seven factors make up the seven scales of the PAL-C form. Factor analyses of the items that comprise the five scales added to the PAL-H form of the test are not reported. According to the PAL-H manual (Ellsworth, 1981b), the items related to health and adjustment were grouped into these five scales according to similarity of content. Internal consistency (alpha) coefficients of PAL factor scores were .90 or higher for three of the clinical scales (Negative Emotions, Close Interpersonal, and Child Interpersonal), and at least .80 for the remaining four PAL-C scales (Physical Symptoms, Psychological Well-Being, Income Management, Alcohol/Drug Use.). Alpha coefficients are not reported for the five PAL-H scales.

Discriminant validity of the PAL-C scales was assessed by looking at the ability of the seven scales to differentiate among groups expected to differ in adjustment. Six groups were compared in the study: 1) clinical clients (N = 678); 2) people entering training in Transcendental Meditation (TM) (N = 121); 3) community college students (N = 96); 4) persons responding to a *National Enquirer* article on psychic experiences (N = 435); 5) persons learning conscious control of internal states through guided imagery (N = 366); and 6) participants invited to a conference on higher states of consciousness (N = 42). The author suggested that inclusion of these six groups insured a wide range of adjustment levels and lifestyles. One-way analyses of variance for each scale across the six groups of subjects were all statistically significant ($p < .001$), with PAL scores on the Negative Emotions, Psychological Well-Being, and Physical Symptoms Scales differentiating best among the six groups. Comparison of group means showed the clinic client group to be the least well adjusted in five areas, with participants in the conference on higher consciousness states the most well adjusted. When the initial scores of clinical client and TM training groups were compared with scores obtained after a three-month interval following intevention, significant improvements were obtained for all but Income Management and Alcohol/Drug Use for the clinic clients, and all but Close Interpersonal Relationships and Child Interpersonal Relationships for the TM training group. The pretreatment PAL scores of 145 of the clinic clients also showed mild to moderate agreement with ratings on a Personal Adjustment and Role Skill scale (PARS) completed by a relative of the client.

As was noted previously, items comprising the five life-style scales of the PAL-H inventory were selected for inclusion on the instrument because they wre found to correlate with good adjustment and functioning as measured by four PAL clinical scales: Negative Emotions, Physical Symptoms, Psychological Well-Being, and Close Interpersonal Relationships. Items were grouped into scales of the PAL-H with the four clinical scales were low to moderate, ranging from.19 to .47. This provides some modest support for the concurrent validity of the holistic scales.

Critique

The Profile of Adaptation to Life consists of a set of simple self-report scales designed to assess dimensions of positive adjustment as well as maladjustment. A strength of both PAL inventories is the inclusion of positive as well as negative dimensions of psychological health, as well as their relatively simple, straightforward format that allows for ease of administration and scoring. An interesting method for profiling individual client's scores for each of the scales is provided, although caution should be used in drawing inferences from the norm group from which these profiles are derived. While the author maintains that the sample of persons responding to a *National Enquirer* article on psychic experience is relatively well adjusted and representative, this sample may not be reflective of all individuals for whom these scales may be used. These reviewers encourage users of these scales to develop their own set of norms that may be more appropriate for their client populations. Caution should also be exercised in considering the use of the Change Norms for evaluating the effectiveness of individual counselors, trainers, or therapists, a use the author suggests. While evidence of the reliability and validity of the clinical scales summarized in the manual is adequate for the norming group used, additional studies with other populations would be helpful. Reliability and validity information concerning the holistic scales is less adequate and the content of these scales is somewhat value laden. Potential users should carefully examine the holistic scales for appropriateness of content to their clientele. Even considering these limitations, the Profile of Adaptation to Life Scales merit consideration for use in clinical and counseling settings when an easily obtained assessment of the dimensions they assess is desired.

References

This list includes text citations as well as suggested additional reading.

Ellsworth, R. B. (1978a). The comparative effectiveness of community clinic and psychiatric hospital treatment. *Journal of Community Psychology, 6*, 103-111.
Ellsworth, R. B. (1978b). Utilizing consumer input in evaluating mental health services. In

E. J. Posavac, (Ed.), *Impacts of program evaluation on mental health care*. Boulder, CO: Westview Press.

Ellsworth, R. B. (1979). Characteristics of effective treatment settings: A research review. In J. A. Gunderson, O. A. Will, Jr., & L. R. Mosher (Eds.), *The principles and practices of milieu therapy*. New York: Jason Aronson, Inc.

Ellsworth, R. B. (1981a). *PAL-C Scale: Profile of Adaptation to Life Clinical Scale manual*. Palo Alto, CA: Consulting Psychologists Press.

Ellsworth, R. B. (1981b). *PAL-H Scale: Profile of Adaptation to Life Holistic Scale manual*. Palo Alto, CA: Consulting Psychologists Press.

Ellsworth, R. B., Finnell, K. C., & Leuthold, C. (1978). Community treatment for young psychiatric patients: A case study in program evaluation. *Evaluation and the Health Professions, 1,* 66-80.

Ellsworth, S. (1982). *Premature termination by aftercare clients: Causes and consequences*. Ann Arbor, MI: Washtenaw County Community Mental Health Center.

Gabbard, G. O., Twemlow, S. W., & Jones, F. C. (1981). Do near death experiences occur only near death? *Journal of Nervous and Mental Disease, 69,* 374-377.

Gabbard, G. O., Twemlow, S. W., & Jones, F. C. (1982). Differential diagnosis of altered mind body perception. *Psychiatry, 45,* 361-369.

Twemlow, S. W., & Gabbard, G. O. (1984). The influence of demographic/psychological factors and preexisting conditions on the near-death experience. *Omega: Journal of Death and Dying, 15,* 223-235.

Twemlow, S. W., Gabbard, G. O., & Jones, F. C. (1982). The out-of-body experience: a phenomenological typology based on questionnaire responses. *American Journal of Psychiatry, 139,* 450-455.

Sterling Gerber, Ph.D.
Professor of Psychology, Eastern Washington University, Cheney, Washington.

PROVERBS TEST

Donald R. Gorham. Missoula, Montana: Psychological Test Specialists.

Introduction

The Proverbs Test is an assessment device for estimating abstract thinking ability. Its results correlate moderately with several intelligence tests, but not sufficiently to consider them as sampling the same domain. In practice, the major strength of this test is in eliciting responses from hospital subjects, notably schizophrenics, from which clinical assessments can be derived.

Proverbs cannot be considered as authored, inasmuch as they represent culturally evolved truisms. The original forms were developed in the early 1950s by Donald R. Gorham while at Baylor University and the Veterans Administration Center at Waco, Texas.

Dr. Gorham collected 150 proverbs and selected 40 items that through an item analysis process proved to have the greatest discrimination power. Item analyses were based on responses by 100 high school students and 100 army reenlistees. The free-answer form was first published in 1954; the Best Answer Form followed in 1956. No modifications have been made subsequent to publication, however considerable research has been generated.

The Proverbs Test employs 40 somewhat standard proverbs in two formats. The free-answer format is presented in three equivalent forms each of which consists of twelve items scaled for difficulty. Subjects are instructed to write out the meanings (or to verbally state the meanings if clinical nature of subject requires) to each of the test items. An alternate format lists all 36 of the free-answer items plus four additional items (also scaled for difficulty) to make the 40-item, multiple-choice Best Answer Form. While the free-answer form lends itself to individual assessment, the author reports using it in a group administered setting. The multiple-choice format was created for survey and screening purposes and was intended to be used in group testing.

Administering either of the two formats is relatively easy. The Best Answer Form is virtually self-administering; the free-answer forms require/permit a little more rapport-building in the process of obtaining subject involvement. Proverbs seem, however, to elicit ready participation from a wide variety of people. Scoring and interpreting this test require a high level of psychological sophistication.

Norms are available for educational levels from grade five through college juniors and seniors as well as for clinical samples, notably schizophrenics. Subjects younger than eleven years of age or who function intellectually at a level lower than average fifth-graders are likely to experience difficulty in generating usable responses. Results of either format are presented as raw scores and as percentile equivalents in two categories: abstract (Ab) and concrete (Co).

Practical Applications/Uses

The two formats make the Proverbs Test potentially very useful in that a variety of client types can be assessed; formative as well as summative measures are facilitated by the three forms of free answer and the best answer form, all of which correlate reasonably well with each other. As a psychometric device, the best-answer format is easy to use and score, but two major drawbacks are readily apparent to this approach. The first is the relative difficulty in defining the construct "abstract thinking." The second is a limitation of the test in poorly differentiating scores, particularly at the higher levels; several skips of five percentile units result from a difference of only one raw score point. Another problem seems to be a relatively restricted range for measuring subjects in higher intellectual levels.

Although abstract thinking is a difficult construct to manage, the test does measure some intellectual factor quite reliably. Continued use of this test or some form of the proverb item in research on thinking or abstract thinking is very warranted. In addition some promise has been shown for its use singly or in combination with other tests (Phillips et al., 1980) for initial screening of hospital admissions; however, any appropriate application of this test outside of the hospital, clinic, or experiment setting is unlikely.

By far the most justified use to date has been in generating verbal output from schizophrenic patients from which diagnosis or formative assessment of therapeutic progress can be made. The construction and initial use of this test, directed at evaluating schizophrenic patients, remains the most appropriate use. Until practical use is demonstrated for other populations, research is the only other warranted use.

In its most appropriate use, this test should be administered individually by a psychologist, the primary therapist. A competent psychometrist can administer, record, and score the free-answer forms, particularly if the subjects are writing their responses.

The Best Answer Form can be administered and scored by any reasonably intelligent person. Interpretation requires sophistication and so the use of the test should be restricted to qualified psychologists.

There is no time restriction in taking the test. Most subjects will finish within 30 to 40 minutes depending on the form of the test and on the subject's age and clinical condition.

The Best Answer Form is easily and quickly scored. Scoring consists of overlaying a punched key and counting correct responses. There are two keys, one for the abstract score and one for the concrete score. The free-answer forms require a judgment as to whether the response is incorrect, a one-point response, or a two-point response. For anyone who is trained in individual intelligence testing, this process is familiar and readily accomplished. The manual (Gorham, 1956a) provides guidelines and sample responses to facilitate scoring judgments.

Two conclusions are derived from performance on the Proverbs Test. The first is whether or not the subject demonstrates thinking disturbance and if so, is that disturbance typical of a schizophrenic disorder. The second relates to the subject's abstract thinking ability. Both of these conclusions are made and interpreted only on the basis of considerable training and experience in psychology. Use of the test in a research context requires specialized knowledge in addition to that of the applied specialist.

Technical Aspects

Reliability coefficients, based on parallel form and split-half comparisons as reported by the author (Gorham, 1956) range from .72 to .92. The reliability studies and much of the normative data were based on large numbers of Air Force enlistees. It may be important to note that Air Force enlistees during the early 1950s were most likely a select population due to effects of the military draft and the Korean conflict. Considering the norms to be "people in general" is inaccurate.

Validity data, also presented by the author (Gorham, 1956) are of two types. The first consists of correlations with established tests; namely, Air Force Tests, Otis, Henmon-Nelson, and the WAIS. Correlations ranged from .50 to .80 with most near .60. The other data are from applied studies of differentiating schizophrenics from normals. The Proverbs Test had a "hit rate" of 77%. In another source (Phillips et al., 1980) the proportion of correct discriminations was increased to 81.4 in combination with the Whitaker Index of Schizophrenic Thinking.

Additional norms, including some for organic patients, male schizophrenic patients, and male Air Force recruits, are furnished by the author (Gorham, 1963).

Critique

For many people, the proverb is an intriguing and involving statement. It has shown up in many assessments of mental status. In Gorham's test, this form of item is presented in two practical test formats, which are convenient to use and provide a compounding of whatever the proverb measures. The illusiveness of the construct "abstract thinking" is problematic but the usefulness of the test in identifying schizophrenic thought disorders transcends whatever label is affixed.

Perhaps the nature of proverbs, which elicits verbal production from schizophrenics, is a potential problem. It is likely that the entrancing form of the item and the disarmingly simple form of the test will attract unsophisticated users who will measure abstract thinking and as a result draw unwarranted conclusions.

Other critics have found the Proverbs Test to be useful in eliciting analyzable responses from schizophrenics (Harrow & Prosen, 1978); inneffective as a screening device for psychosis in a general clinical setting (Smith, 1971); useful as a progress measure in therapy (Shimkunas, 1970); and the technique with the greatest individual hit rate (Phillips et al., 1980). In this reviewer's opinion this test has demonstrated usefulness as a rough screen for identifying schizophrenic disorders, as a measure of therapeutic progress, and as an instrument for assessing dependent variables in research. It has a place in the clinical and research testing repertoire.

References

This list include text citations as well as suggested additional reading.

Gorham, D. R. (1956a). *Clinical manual for the Proverbs Test.* Louisville, Ky.: Psychological Test Specialists.

Gorham, D. R. (1956b). A proverbs test for clinical and experimental use. *Psychological Reports, 2,* 1-12. (Momogr. Suppl. 1-V2).

Gorham, D. R. (1956c). Use of the Proverbs Test for differentiating schizophrenics from normals. *Journal of Consulting Psychology, 20,* 435-440.

Gorham, D. R. (1963). Additional norms and scoring suggestions for the Proverbs Test. *Psychological Reports, 13,* 487-492.

Harrow, M., & Prosen, M. (1978). Intermingling and disordered logic as influences on schizophrenic 'thought disorders.' *Archives of General Psychiatry, 35,* 1213-1218.

Phillips, W. M., Phillips, A. M., & Shearn, C. R. (1980). Objective assessment of schizophrenic thinking. *Journal of Clinical Psychology, 36,* 79-89.

Shimkunas, A. M. (1970). Reciprocal shifts in schizophrenic thought processes. *Journal of Abnormal Psychology, 76*(3), 423-425.

Smith, R. C. (1971). Use of the Proverbs Test for the identification of psychotic disorder. *Journal of Clinical Psychology, 27*(2), 227.

Watson, C. G., Plemel, D., & Burke, M. (1979). Proverb Test deficit in schizophrenic and brain-damaged patients. *Journal of Nervous and Mental Disease, 167,* 561-565.

Raymond G. Johnson, Ph.D.
*Professor and Co-Chair, Department of Psychology, Macalester
College, St. Paul, Minnesota.*

PSYCHOTIC INPATIENT PROFILE

*Maurice Lorr and Norris D. Vestre. Los Angeles, California:
Western Psychological Services.*

Introduction

The Psychotic Inpatient Profile (PIP) is designed to measure the ward behavior
of adult psychotic inpatients as rated by nurses and psychiatric aides over a three-
day period. There are 74 items that describe overt behavior and 22 additional
statements that describe the content of the patient's speech. These four-point
ratings are combined on twelve scales intended to measure "syndromes of
currently observable psychotic behavior" (Lorr & Vestre, 1968).

For over thirty years, Maurice Lorr has attempted to objectify and quantify
behavioral ratings made on the basis of the mental status interview and on the
basis of ward observation. He set a goal of finding syndromes of psychopathological behavior that would represent basic psychological dimensions, be
uncorrelated, be objectively measured and quantifiable, have a high correlation
with external criteria of change or improvement, and possess comparable units
for common populations so that pattern similarity can be compared (Lorr, 1953;
for a review of early rating scales see Lorr, 1954). He and his associates have
constructed a series of instruments that are designed to assess syndromes of
psychotic behavior. The PIP is a direct descendant of two of these devices: The
Psychotic Reaction Profile (PRP) and the Inpatient Multidimensional Psychiatric
Scale (IMPS).

The PRP (Lorr, O'Connor, & Stafford, 1960) contains 85 items to be rated by
psychiatric nurses and aides on the basis of extensive observation of the patient in
the hospital setting. The initial 400-item pool was compiled after consulting
published inventories, factor analytic studies of rating scales, and several psychiatric texts. On the basis of factor analytic studies several dimensions or syndromes
were postulated. The hypothesized dimensions were Resistiveness and Motor
Disturbances, Withdrawal vs. Sociability, Perceptual Distortions, Conceptual
Disorganization, Melancholy Agitation, Paranoid Projection, Hostile Belligerence, Lack of Interest in Self or Others, and Dominance vs. Submissiveness. It
was found, however, that these scales were too highly intercorrelated. Second-
order constructs were hypothesized and scales that were considered sufficiently
independent were derived. The four scales that comprise the PRP are Withdrawal, Thinking Disorganization, Paranoid Belligerence, and Agitated
Depression.

The IMPS is a set of ratings made on the basis of a diagnostic or mental status

607

interview. The construction and use of the IMPS is discussed extensively in Lorr, Klett, and McNair (1963). This instrument was derived most directly from the Multidimensional Scale for Rating Psychiatric Patients (MSRPP) as well as from examination of the work of previous factor analysts such as Degan, Guertin, and Wittenborn. On the basis of such earlier work, ten dimensions or syndromes were hypothesized and 75 statements were devised to assess interview behaviors which comprise these syndromes.

The PIP represents a revision and expansion of the PRP, but with dimensions that are intended to be analogous to the IMPS dimensions. Most of the PIP items are new; only 41% came from the PRP. New items were written for the new dimensions of Grandiosity, Disorientation, Care Needed, Excitement, Perceptual Distortion, and Depressive Mood. The PRP Withdrawal Scale was refactored into the PIP Retardation and Seclusiveness Scales. The PRP Paranoid Belligerence Scale was split into the PIP Excitement and Hostile Belligerence Scales. The PRP scales Withdrawal and Thinking Disorganization were overly long, so some items were dropped. Factor analyses of the PIP using oblique rotations and hypothesized syndromes based on earlier work led to twelve dimensions, ten of which are given the same names as IMPS syndromes (Lorr & Vestre, 1969; Vestre & Zimmerman, 1970).

The PIP consists of 74 ratings of ward behavior and 22 ratings of verbal output. The ward behaviors are rated on a four-point scale based on frequency of occurrence over a three-day period. Sample items include "Talks in a loud voice," "Looks worried and nervous," "Demands the attention of the doctor," and "Makes no answer when questioned." The items that require verbal responses from the patient include five gauging the patient's orientation and 17 related to the patient's speech content, such as "Says he wants to die or wishes he were dead," and "Reports that he cannot concentrate or remember things." The interview-based items are rated as True or Not True.

According to the manual (Lorr & Vestre, 1968), the rater is asked to observe and talk with the patient over a three-day period after having studied the content of the PIP. Ratings are to be based only on that three-day period.

Scores on the twelve syndromes are obtained by summing the ratings on the items that make up each syndrome. Each item is scored on only one syndrome. The syndromes are as follows:

1) Excitement (7 items)
2) Hostile Belligerence (8 items)
3) Paranoid Projection (9 items)
4) Anxious Depression (7 items)
5) Retardation (8 items)
6) Seclusiveness (13 items)
7) Care Needed (8 items)
8) Psychotic Disorganization (14 items)
9) Grandiosity (4 items)
10) Perceptual Distortion (6 items)
11) Depressive Mood (7 items)
12) Disorientation (5 items)

In every scale but one high scores or ratings of True are in a pathological direction.

The Seclusiveness dimension is based on positive ratings of sociability that are then reversed by multiplying with minus one and adding a constant. A T-Score sheet allows the user to draw a profile over the dimensions. Separate norms are provided for patients who are drug-free and drug-treated, males and females.

Practical Application/Uses

The authors suggest a number of potential uses for the PIP, recognizing that not all are supported by research evidence. They are a standardized description of a patient prior to treatment, evaluation of a patient during and after treatment, description of withdrawn and mute patients, evaluation of treatment program, comparison of patients with norm groups, and training of mental health personnel to improve their observational and evaluative skills.

Several studies have used the PIP as a dependent variable in the evaluation of drug treatment (Dehnel, Vestre, & Schiele, 1968; Growe, Crayton, Klass, Evans, & Strizich, 1979; Hall, Vestre, Schiele, & Zimmerman, 1968; Nestoros, Nair, Pulman, Schwartz, & Bloom, 1983; Prien, Caffey, & Klett, 1972a, 1972b). The best designs are the double-blind studies used by Dehnel et al. (1968), Hall et al. (1968), and Prien et al. (1972a, 1972b) in comparing effects of two drugs.

Several studies have used the PIP to evaluate the effects of psychological or behavioral treatment: implosive therapy (Boudewyns & Levis, 1975), structured learning therapy (Magaro & West, 1983), independent living program (Barry & Mercer, 1983), modeling vs. instructing in social behavior (Jaffe & Carlson, 1976), and token economy and general milieu treatment (Mishara, 1978).

Some researchers have used the PIP as a screening device to select subjects for a study (Berman, 1972; Jones, 1973). The PIP scales have been correlated with suggestibility (Ham, Spanos, & Barber, 1976), the MMPI Pa scale (Vestre & Watson, 1972), body type (Watson, 1972), ward atmosphere (Alden, 1978), criterion measure for a mood scale (Luria, 1975), and type of nursing care needed for psychiatric geriatric patients (Haddad, 1981). Several studies have used modifications of the PIP. For example, Blackburn (1979) used selected items. One unusual modification was to have patients "fill out" the Seclusiveness scale to screen patients for a study (Lindsay, 1980).

In few of these studies is there any concern for the effects of rater expectancy. Reliability is seldom seen as an issue. Training programs for raters range from what the manual requests to none at all.

The PIP was designed to describe the behavior of functional psychotic adults at an inpatient facility prior to treatment. It has generally been used at installations for the chronically mentally ill, but has also been used on a service for relatively short term treatment (e.g., Young & Pandi, 1978) and with nursing home residents (Shadish, Bootzin, Koller, & Brownell, 1981).

According to the manual, the inventory should be used by "experienced nursing hospital personnel," and that for reliability "only the more intelligent, competent and conscientious" (p. 1) staff should be selected. The manual emphasizes that each rater should have sufficient opportunity to observe and interact with the patient being rated. The authors feel that such personnel need only a brief training session to use the PIP appropriately. They suggest that users complete the inventory on one or two patients whom they know in common and then discuss their ratings and attempt to resolve discrepancies and misunderstandings. An observer rating several patients is advised to keep notes during the observation period.

The scoring sheet lists each item to be rated; on the same line is a box in which to place the rating. The boxes are in separate columns according to the syndrome in which the item is scored. When raters are finished, the columns are summed to obtain the syndrome scores.

The T-Score sheet has a layout similar to an MMPI profile. The side columns contain T-Scores; in between are columns of raw scores for each syndrome. The scorer circles the raw scores and then draws a profile. There are four columns for each syndrome: drug-free males, drug-free females, drug-treated males, and drug-treated females.

The manual suggests that the profile may be interpreted "to provide insights into the patient's central disturbance and suggest the corresponding psychiatric disturbance" (p. 3). It also states that a supplement to the manual describing subgroup profiles was in preparation, but such a supplement has not appeared.

The PIP norms are based on over a thousand cases diagnosed as functional psychotics in almost a dozen psychiatric units ranging from state hospitals to university hospitals and clinics. A drug-free sample of 412 cases (277 women; 135 men) was rated within a week of admission and prior to drug treatment. Approximately a quarter were diagnosed as depressed, a quarter as paranoid schizophrenics, and half as nonparanoid schizophrenics. A drug-treated sample of 604 cases (368 women; 236 men) on mild or moderate dosages of tranquilizers was rated "shortly after hospitalization." About half were diagnosed as paranoid schizophrenics, over a third were nonparanoid schizophrenics, 15% had affective disorders.

Technical Aspects

The interrater reliabilities (intra-class r) for the PIP syndromes reported in the manual range from .74 to .99 with a median of .865. These figures are based on a sample of 57 state hospital patients.

Kavanaugh and Auld (1977) used the PIP as a criterion measure to validate a personality inventory. They checked the interrater reliability on one-tenth of their sample (17 out of 177) and found a median reliability of .83. The reliability of the Grandiosity Scale was only .45; the next lowest scale, unnamed, was .69. No other reliability coefficient was reported, so this study is omitted from Table 1. Mishara (1978) in a study of 70 state hospital patients had two raters complete the PIP on ten of the patients. They found "few disagreements" but did not quantify the reliability.

Table 1 shows that some other studies have not obtained satisfactory reliabilities.

Median reported reliabilities across all PIP scales from all the studies reporting such statistics (Table 1; Kavanaugh and Auld, 1977) are .865, .830, .715, .600, .600, .585, .425, and .330.

Table 1

Interrater Reliabilities for the PIP[1]

Sample

Scale	a[2] (57)[3]	b1 (91)	b2 (80)	b3 (59)	c1 (207)	c2 (207)	d (85)
EXC	80	50		57	76	80	65
HOS	88	41		53	71	72	55
PAR	87	46	59	60			64
GRN	99	35		81			52
PCP	74	36		-03	14	36	59
DPR	89	17		01			40
ANX	86	44		26	50	58	42
RTD	81	59		28	57	73	60
SEC	81	65		35	63	84	73
DIS	89	04		-02			
CAR	88	68		31	72	71	84
PSY	84	16	58	40	49	68	66
Mdn	865	425	585	330	600	715	600

[1]Decimals not shown. Blanks indicate scale not rated.
[2]Samples:
    a: Lorr and Vestre, 1968.
    b1, b2, b3: Knight and Blaney, 1977.
    c1, c2: Farrell and Mariotto, 1982. The c1 ratings were done by aides;
        the c2 by "professional observers."
    d: Shadish et al., 1981.
[3]N

Rosenzweig and Harford (1970) reported reliability problems with the PRP. They obtained interrater reliability coefficients of .25 and .34 for the Withdrawal and the Agitated Depression Scales, while the PRP manual reported reliabilities of .90 and .65 for these scales. In a PRP validation study, Vestre (1966) obtained .84 and .70 and argued that the shortness of the latter scale, five items, limited its usefulness. The raters used by Rosenzweig and Harford were a psychologist and an occupational therapist rather than typical ward personnel. The behavior samples encountered by these raters were considerably different and may have led to the low reliabilities.

An excellent discussion of the reliability problems of ward rating scales is given by Hall (1974). He points out that compared with the interview, the ward situation has poorer control of subject behavior, lesser sophistication of the rater, poorer degree of continuous observation possible, less ability to clarify uncertain responses, variable physical proximity of rater to subject, and frequent necessity for the rater to retain information for a period of time before rating.

Some causes of unreliability of ward scales are listed by Hall as follows: 1) The observer has other responsibilities on the ward and sees ratee in selective situations. 2) Raters may be on different shifts or have different roles so see ratee in different settings. Some behavior may relate to time of day or to setting and lead to apparent rater unreliability. 3) Scale construction—some items are written so presence of a behavior is rated as normal or abnormal; some are written such that absence of a behavior is normal or abnormal. If a patient is moved to a ward with a better staff-patient ratio, it is more likely that a rater will observe relevant behavior. Depending on the makeup of the scales the patient's scores may be more normal or more deviant. He notes that typical measures of interrater reliability, typically correlation of percentage agreement, require assumptions that scores are distributed normally, "agreement" is meaningful, chance agreement is negligible, total scores are meaningful, and mean scores of both raters are similar. Seldom are these assumptions justified. Hall proposes that Cohen's weighted kappa would provide a more assumption-free measure of reliability.

Rating scales have long been plagued by reliability problems. Guilford (1954, p. 290) cites Symonds as using "the empirical fact that the average of inter-rater correlations is in the region of .55-.60." Increased reliabilities may be obtained with statements that emphasize behavior rather than inferred characteristics and with an appropriate number of categories per item. The PIP statements do emphasize observable behavior and the four-point scale should be preferable to the two-point scale of the PRP.

The most important part of measurement error comes from the rater. Guilford (1954, p. 278 f f.) lists a number of rater errors, most of which may affect PIP scores: severity or leniency, central tendency (giving everyone average ratings, perhaps because the rater was uncertain or had not observed enough), halo effect (the rater's overall reaction to the subject affects other ratings), and logical error (traits that are seen as logically related are similarly rated).

Halo effect and logical errors may be enhanced by the format of the rating sheet. All of the boxes that make up a given syndrome are in the same column so the rater is immediately aware which ratings are combined. If interrater reliabilities are found to be low, then raters should be instructed about these potential errors as well as trained in consistent use of the device.

Personal factors in the history of the rater may contribute to unreliability. Gunderson (1965) had 35 psychiatrist-psychologist pairs rate 700 Navy volunteers for Antarctic research duty. Consistency in ratings was found to be related to factors such as most recent professional experience (such as hospital, training center, administration) and to the raters' agreement on the importance of the trait to the criterion. Raskin and Sullivan (1963) found interrater discrepancies on the IMPS related to clinical experience, age, experience with personal therapy, weekly time spent with the patient, contact with the patient's family or friends, frequency of discussion with the patient, opinion of the efficacy of tranquilizers, and time to complete the form.

Workers in behavioral assessment have been concerned with the reliability of their observations. O'Leary in a series of studies has had raters observe a child for twenty seconds and record for ten seconds over a 12.5 minute period. Even with behaviorally defined categories consistency of ratings was a problem. The reliability of raters when they knew they were being compared to another rater was .7 but when there seemed to be no other rater the reliability dropped to .4 (Romanczyk, Kent, Diament, & O'Leary, 1973). They found that without feedback raters may tend to "drift" toward idiosyncratic definitions of what is being rated. When given feedback reinforcing certain ratings, raters tend to rate in the reinforced direction (O'Leary, Kent, & Kanowitz, 1975). Such results also point up the need for blind raters when assessing treatment effects. Shadish et al. (1981) reported PIP drift among their raters. Observers tended to rate nursing home residents as more healthy the more ratings they had completed.

Knight and Blaney (1977) suggest two ways to improve reliability. One is systematically to select the most reliable raters. Another is to develop more rigorous training of raters using a standardized videotape with criterion ratings. Such a procedure would make mean ratings more comparable across locations, allow one to select the best raters, as well as be used as a training device.

While the title of the instrument, the manual, and the scoring sheet encourage the drawing of profiles, only one study reports reliability information regarding profiles. Shadish et al. (1981) found the reliability of PIP profiles to be .66.

Issues of validity with a multivariate instrument such as the PIP which has many potential uses are most complex. Validity studies must be concerned with the question of reliability. Without information on reliability, low validity coefficients are impossible to interpret.

A strong attempt was made by the PIP authors to write items that are unipolar and unidimensional; by inspection they seem to be so. The PIP dimensions arose as a result of a series of factor analyses with oblique rotations guided by hypotheses that the dimensions would be largely isomorphic with those of the IMPS. Factoring and item clustering should ensure that the syndromes are unidimensional.

As with many factored scales, the label which describes the dimension may be inadequate to represent the scale content. An obvious attempt has been made by Lorr and Vestre to keep the scale labels at a low level of abstraction. A reading of the items by scale indicates that in general they seem to represent the domains indicated by the syndrome names. But consider Paranoid Projection: the title of this scale represents a conceptual leap from the uncooperative and negativistic behaviors of many items (resists treatment, refuses to help, is sarcastic, irritable, complaining). The Excitement Scale contains the item, "Demands special privileges." With these exceptions the scales appear to have content validity.

To assess convergent and discriminant validity of the IMPS and the PIP Lorr and Hamlin (1971) obtained ratings on 125 functional psychotics from five hospitals. In addition they obtained multiple measures of social behavior, psychomotor speed, cognitive efficiency, speech, and social content. Their first step was to factor the IMPS and the PIP. Most scales correlated appropriately with their hypothesized dimension, except that the PIP Paranoid Projection score loaded more highly on the Hostile Belligerence factor (.72) than on the Paranoid Projection factor (.29) and the PIP Anxious Depression Scale loaded more highly on the Paranoid Projection factor (.41) than on the Anxious Depression factor (.30). They continued on to factor a multimethod-multitrait correlation matrix. Loadings from three methods gave evidence of convergent validity for the PIP scales of Excitement, Grandiosity, Retardation, and Conceptual Disorganization. Two methods defined Hostile Belligerence, Paranoid Projection, Anxious Depression, and Disorientation. Each of the scales except Hostile Belligerence had objective behavioral measures associated meaningfully with them. Some expected relationships did not appear; for example, psychomotor speed measures did not relate to Conceptual Disorganization or to Retardation.

The PIP has been used effectively in some studies of drug treatment. A between-groups evaluation showed haloperidol led to improvement on PIP Seclusiveness and Perceptual Distortion compared with fluphenazine (Hall et al., 1968). PIP Seclusiveness also was affected more by perphenazine than by clopenthixol (Dehnel et al., 1968). In a double-blind study, Prien et al. (1972a) found ten of the twelve PIP scales differentiated excited schizo-affectives treated with chlorpromazine from those treated with lithium carbonate.

Vestre and Zimmerman (1970) found that every scale except Seclusiveness differentiated between closed and open ward patients. They compared new admissions with patients being discharged and found that nine of the twelve scales had significant differences. The Retardation and Depressed Mood Scales did not differentiate these groups. The Disorientation Scale mean for the admission group was too low to be sensitive to any change. Some scales such as Disorientation may not be appropriate for a given subject population because the base rates of the behavior may be too low.

Watson and Klett (1972) attempted to validate the PIP against the MMPI. The sample consisted entirely of schizophrenic males at a VA hospital. Forty percent of the sample was eliminated for having invalid MMPI profiles (L and F greater than 7 and 16, respectively). The authors do not report PIP reliabilities. One group of PIP dimensions—Excitement, Grandiosity, Hostile Belligerence, Paranoid Projection, and Psychotic Disorganization—had a pattern of positive correlations with the MMPI Ma Scale, and negative correlations with D, Pt, and Sie. These PIP dimensions tended to have low, insignificant, but negative correlations with the Sc Scale. The PIP Seclusiveness, Retardation, and Care Needed Scales were all negatively correlated with the MMPI Pd Scale. With this sample the PIP Perceptual Distortion and Disorientation Scales had such low scores (modes of zero) as to be unusable. The Anxious Depression and Depressed Mood Scales were not related to any MMPI scales. The study raises more questions than it answers. Was unreliability a factor? At about this time researchers at the same hospital found extremely low reliabilities for the PIP (Knight & Blaney, 1977). Were raters sufficiently motivated? Is the sample too homogeneous to show relationships? Are the raters only responding to psychotic activity on the one hand and social withdrawal on the other? Can a schizophrenic sample be used to assess mood scales? How great a relationship should one expect between ratings of ward behavior and MMPI (presumably K-corrected) scores?

O'Neil and Calhoun (1975) found that pooled ratings on the PIP Psychotic Disorganization Scale were not correlated with objective measures of sensory defect in geriatric patients. A mental status evaluation was positively correlated with both the objective measures and with this PIP scale.

Jaffe and Carlson (1976) compared modeling and instructions in eliciting social behavior from chronic patients. Among the dependent measures were the PIP Care Needed, Seclusiveness, and Retardation Scales. The Retardation Scale showed no differences, but the other two were sensitive to some treatment effects.

Kavanaugh and Auld (1977) used the PIP as a criterion measure to evaluate the validity of the Jackson and Messick Differential Personality Inventory (DPI). Of the 161 suitable patients rated on the PIP only 60 agreed to participate in the study. A discriminant function using the PIP classified the cooperative and uncooperative groups with 88% accuracy. The cooperative patients received higher ratings on Grandiosity and on Perceptual Distortion and lower scores on Excitement, Seclusiveness, and Care Needed. They hypothesized five relationships between the PIP and the DPI and found support for four of these. Significant correlations (.23-.30) were found between DPI Depression and PIP Anxious Depression, DPI Depression and PIP Depressed Mood, DPI Cynicism and PIP Paranoid Projection, and DPI Psychotic Tendencies and PIP Seclusiveness.

Haddad (1981) found that state hospital geriatric patients needing skilled, intermediate, or psychiatric nursing care were differentiated by the Care Needed, Seclusiveness, Psychotic Disorganization, Retardation, and Disorientation Scales.

Farrell and Mariotto (1982) compared PIP ratings with the Time-Sample Behavioral Checklist (TSBC) (Power, 1979) with professional observers rating certain behaviors every waking hour for a week. Reliabilities for TSBC indices ranged from .93 to .99. For those scales on the two devices which seemed to be measuring similar dimensions, correlations ranged from -.75 (PIP Seclusiveness and TSBC Interpersonal Interaction) to -.03 (PIP Care Needed and TSBC Self-Maintenance) with a median of .3. Farrell and Mariotto also used a competitor of the PIP, the Nurses' Observation Scale for Inpatient Evaluation (NOSIE-30). PIP ratings tended, to the extent that scales were comparable, to be in agreement with the NOSIE-30 ratings.

Psychiatric scale ratings as represented by the PIP and the NOSIE appear not to be as behaviorally based as many have assumed. Such ratings represent clinical judgments summarizing a great deal of behavior, often based on inconsistent amount of observation, and processed by the cognitive set of the rater. Farrell and Mariotto argue that such judgments are important and necessary and have social validity, but for the purpose of delineating dimensions of psychotic behavior, making cross-cultural comparisons, or examining biochemical correlates, more behaviorally oriented devices are needed.

No validity data has been published regarding PIP profiles. Lorr, Klett, and McNair (1963) discuss profile types using the IMPS with similarly named dimensions.

Another way of combining scores is to solve for higher-order constructs, something Lorr has done in abundance in his attempt to find the basic dimensions of psychosis. Lorr eschews neologisms but is then forced to use word combinations to describe his constructs.

From the IMPS Lorr has derived six groups: Disorganized Hyperactivity,

Schizophrenic Disorganization, Paranoid Process, Psychotic Depression, and Hostile Paranoia (Lorr, 1971, p. 203). The four dimensions of the PRP, which were seen by Lorr as higher order constructs, were Thinking Disorganization, Withdrawal, Paranoid Belligerence, and Agitated Depression. Lorr and Vestre (1969) on an earlier version of the PIP found seven homogeneous and mutually exclusive subgroups: Excited, Hostile Paranoid, Hostile Belligerent, Anxious Depressed, Retarded-Seclusive, Retarded-Disorganized, and Excited-Disorganized. Looking at the ward behavior scales and ignoring the interview-based PIP scales for a drug-free sample yielded five groups: Seclusive, Excited, Depressed-Retarded-Seclusive, Anxious-Depressed, and Retarded-Depressed. These batches of terms are confusing and do not stimulate confidence that we are approaching great insights concerning the basic dimensions of psychopathology.

A scheme presented by Lorr, Klett, and McNair, (1963, p. 93) that makes more clinical sense is that schizophrenia has three subsyndromes: Excitement vs. Retardation, Disorganization, and Paranoid Process. They also present the Psychotic Syndrome Circle and discuss how it relates to the IMPS scales:

Excitement

Conceptual
Disorganization

Motor
Disturbance

Disorientation

Grandiose
Expansiveness

Paranoid
Projection

Anxious
Intropunitiveness

Retardation
and Apathy

A more straightforward approach is taken by Young and Pandi (1978). They had nurses rate 99 consecutive admissions on the PIP both at intake and at discharge at an adolescent and adult psychiatric unit in a university hospital. They also had psychiatrists rate these patients with the Brief Psychiatric Rating Scale (BPRS). A factor analysis of all the scores yielded three factors which accounted for 40% of the total variance. Factor I (19% of the variance) included PIP dimensions of Psychotic Disorganization, Care Needed, and Paranoid Projection. They termed this factor thought disorder. Factor II (12% of the variance) included PIP dimensions of Depressive Mood and Anxious Depression. They termed this factor mood disorder. The third factor was unique to the BPRS, but the first two factors are closer to the basic dimensions of the standard psychiatric nosologies of psychosis from Kraepelin to DSM-III.

Critique

Hall (1980) examined about thirty scales designed to rate the behavior of chronic psychiatric patients. He set several minimal criteria for acceptability: some scale refinement and preselection of items, specification of the observation period, evidence for reliability and for validity, and norms. Only four of the scales, including the PIP, met these basic standards. In particular Hall notes the difficulty for PIP observers of rating frequencies of behaviors which have different base rates, such as assaultive behavior (low base rate) and looking tired and worn out (a continuing state).

Gleser's review of the PIP in Buros' *The Seventh Mental Measurements Yearbook* (1972) bemoans the paucity of information in the manual. Gleser feels that more data should have been provided regarding internal consistency of the dimensions and also about the variation between raters. Gleser also notes that the norm group on drugs had scores higher than the non-drug group; thus the non-drug sample may represent a truncated sample.

In a subsequent review Weckowicz (1978) strongly criticizes the manual as "inadequate . . . , sketchy, not very clearly written and poorly laid out" (p. 655). In particular he mentions that the factor analyses on which the syndromes are based are referred to but are not described, and that more and better data are needed on the validity, interrater reliability, and internal consistency of the scales. While useful to asess group differences, he feels that the PIP "should not be used for making clinical decisions about individual patients."

In both clinical assessment and in research an instrument such as the PIP is needed to assess the ward behavior of psychotic patients. The PIP has an advantage over similar devices in that its scales are designed to be isomorphic with those of an interview-based rating measure, the IMPS. The PIP has been shown to have some validity in discriminating higher from lower functioning psychotic groups and to be somewhat sensitive to differential drug treatments.

The interpretation of many studies is clouded because of uncertainty about interrater reliability. Hall (1974) reports that most researchers who use ward rating scales show no concern about reliability. His observations are confirmed by a reading of the PIP literature. Another factor that contaminates many studies is that raters are not blind to treatment variables and to what outcomes are desired or expected. Some studies even do without control or comparison groups.

No good study or clinical evaluation is possible without first obtaining consistent data. In the PIP manual, Lorr and Vestre are far too sanguine about interrater reliability. Virtually no other study has obtained reliability coefficients similar to their results. Users of the PIP must study the reliability of their raters. In addition users should select raters systematically, provide extensive and intensive training, ensure that raters have adequate interaction with target patients, monitor raters and make raters aware that they are being checked, and give raters sufficient time and motivation to do the ratings. Obtaining good ratings is not a casual or inexpensive procedure.

For training, to prevent drift and to obtain consistent results both within and between settings, some standardized television cassettes should be distributed by the authors or publisher.

More information about individual scales is needed by the prospective user. Measures of internal consistency, such as coefficient alpha, should be published. Detailed information about individual items, such as item-total correlations should be made available.

It is difficult to know how to interpret the PIP norms. Patient populations especially in state hospitals have changed dramatically over the past couple of decades. Comparing a current group with patients from the 1960s may be of interest but inferences must be guarded.

There seems little reason for most researchers—and perhaps clinicians—to use the entire PIP. Use of all the scales may suggest a shotgun approach rather than an attempt to test a specific set of hypotheses. Single scales may be selected for their intrinsic interest and to answer definite questions. Strong designs will have multiple measures of the same construct. Scales dealing with rare behaviors should be dropped. Shadish et al. (1981) make some of these as well as other recommendations.

What do the clusterings represented by the PIP and IMPS scales mean? Do they show the basic behavioral syndromes of psychosis? Perhaps, but only Lorr and his colleagues seem to think of them that way. The PIP is used in the literature as a convenient instrument but it has not engendered any theoretical discussion. To what extent do the clusterings show the conceptual schemata or semantic space of the raters? The cognitive activity of the rater is an area which deserves study in its own right. The PIP organizes subjective impressions of ward personnel. To examine fundamental behavioral syndromes will require a more explicit behavioral approach with time sampling of systematic observations.

If used in a sophisticated way, the PIP may aid the researcher and perhaps the clinician, but the user who assumes that it will be sufficient simply to hand the rating sheet to nurses and ask them to rate patients they have seen around the ward is certain to be disappointed.

References

Alden, L. (1978). Treatment environment and patient improvement. *Journal of Nervous and Mental Disease, 166,* 327-334.

Barry, N. J., & Mercer, J. A. (1983). Chronic patients' response to a community-based training program in independent living. *Perceptual and Motor Skills, 57,* 126.

Berman, A. L. (1972). Videotape self-confrontation of schizophrenic ego and thought processes. *Journal of Consulting and Clinical Psychology, 39,* 78-85.

Blackburn, R. (1979). Psychopathology and personality: The dimensionality of self-report and behavior rating data in abnormal offenders. *British Journal of Social and Clinical Psychology, 18,* 111-119.

Boudewyns, P. A., & Levis, D. J. (1975). Autonomic reactivity of high and low ego-strength subjects to repeated anxiety eliciting scenes. *Journal of Abnormal Psychology, 84,* 682-692.

Dehnel, L., Vestre, N. D., & Schiele, B. C. (1968). A controlled comparison of clopenthixol and perphenazine in a chronic schizophrenic population. *Current Therapeutic Research, 10,* 169-176.

Farrell, A. D., & Mariotto, M. J. (1982). A multimethod validation of two psychiatric rating scales. *Journal of Consulting and Clinical Psychology, 50,* 273-280.

Gleser, G. C. (1972). Review of Psychotic Reaction Profile. In O. K. Buros (Ed.), *The seventh mental measurements yearbook.* Highland Park, NJ: The Gryphon Press.

Growe, G. A., Crayton, J. W., Klass, D. B., Evans, H., & Strizich, M. (1979). Lithium in chronic schizophrenia. *American Journal of Psychiatry, 136,* 454-455.

Guilford, J. P. (1954). *Psychometric methods* (2nd ed.). New York: McGraw-Hill.

Gunderson, E. K. E. (1965). Determinants of reliability in personality ratings. *Journal of Clinical Psychology, 21,* 164-169.

Haddad, L. B. (1981). Utilizing rating instruments for evaluating behavioral characteristics differentiating elderly patients selected for skilled, intermediate, and psychiatric care. *Journal of Gerontology, 36,* 583-585.

Hall, J. N. (1974). Inter-rater reliability of ward rating scales. *British Journal of Psychiatry, 125,* 248-255.

Hall, J. N. (1980). Ward rating scales for long-stay patients: A review. *Psychological Medicine, 10,* 277-288.

Hall, W. B., Vestre, N. D., Schiele, B. C., & Zimmerman, R. (1968). A controlled comparison of haloperidol and fluphenazine in chronic treatment-resistant schizophrenics. *Diseases of the Nervous System, 29,* 405-408.

Ham, M. W., Spanos, N. P., & Barber, T. X. (1976). Suggestibility in hospitalized schizophrenics. *Journal of Abnormal Psychology, 85,* 550-557.

Jaffe, P. G., & Carlson, P. M. (1976). Relative efficacy of modeling and instructions eliciting social behavior from chronic psychiatric patients. *Journal of Consulting and Clinical Psychology, 44,* 200-207.

Jones, G. (1973). Predictions of locus of control from performance on a perceptual recognition task. *Perceptual and Motor Skills, 36,* 99-102.

Kavanaugh, P. B., & Auld, F. (1977). Evidence for validity of the Differential Personality Inventory. *Journal of Clinical Psychology, 33,* 456-459.

Knight, R. A., & Blaney, P. H. (1977). The interrater reliability of the Psychotic Inpatient Profile. *Journal of Clinical Psychology, 33,* 647-653.

Lindsay, W. R. (1980). The training and generalization of conversation behaviors in psychiatric inpatients: A controlled study employing multiple measures across settings. *British Journal of Social and Clinical Psychology, 19,* 85-98.

Lorr, M. (1953). The classification problem in psychopathology. *Journal of Clinical Psychology, 9,* 143-144.

Lorr, M. (1954). Rating scales and check lists for the evaluation of psychopathology. *Psychological Bulletin, 51,* 119-127.

Lorr, M. (1971). Dimensions and categories for assessment of psychotics. In P. McReynolds (Ed.), *Advances in psychological assessment* (Vol. 2). Palo Alto: Science and Behavior Books.

Lorr, M., & Hamlin, R. M. (1971). A multimethod factor analysis of behavioral and objective measures of psychopathology. *Journal of Consulting and Clinical Psychology, 36,* 136-141.

Lorr, M., Klett, C. J., & McNair, D. M. (1963). *Syndromes of psychosis.* New York: Macmillan Publishing Co.

Lorr, M., O'Connor, J. P., & Stafford, J. W. (1960). The Psychotic Reaction Profile. *Journal of Clinical Psychology, 16,* 241-245.

Lorr, M., & Vestre, N. D. (1968). *Psychotic Inpatient Profile manual.* Los Angeles: Western Psychological Services.

Lorr, M., & Vestre, N. D. (1969). The Psychotic Inpatient Profile: A nurse's observation scale. *Journal of Clinical Psychology, 25,* 137-140.

Luria, R. E. (1975). The validity and reliability of the Visual Analogue Mood Scale. *Journal of Psychiatric Research, 12,* 51-57.

Magaro, P. A., & West, A. N. (1983). Structured learning therapy: A study with chronic psychiatric patients and level of pathology. *Behavior Modification, 7,* 29-40.

Mishara, B. (1978). Geriatric patients who improve in token economy and general milieu treatment programs: A multivariate analysis. *Journal of Consulting and Clinical Psychology, 46,* 1340-1348.

Nestoros, J. N., Nair, N. P., Pulman, J. R., Schwartz, G., & Bloom, D. (1983). High doses of diazepam improve neuroleptic-resistant chronic schizophrenic patients. *Psychopharmacology, 81,* 42-47.

O'Leary, K. D., Kent, R. N., & Kanowitz, J. (1975). Shaping data collection congruent with experimental hypotheses. *Journal of Applied Behavior Analysis, 8,* 43-51.

O'Neil, P. M., & Calhoun, R. S. (1975). Sensory deficits and behavioral deterioration in senescence. *Journal of Abnormal Psychology, 84*, 579-582.

Powers, C. T. (1979). The Time-Sample Behavioral Checklist: Observational assessment of patient functioning. *Journal of Behavioral Assessment, 1*, 199-210.

Prien, R. F., Caffey, E. M., & Klett, C. J. (1972a). A comparison of lithium carbonate and chloropromazine in the treatment of excited schizo-affectives. *Archives of General Psychiatry, 27*, 182-189.

Prien, R. F., Caffey, E. M., & Klett, C. J. (1972b). A comparison of lithium carbonate and chlorpromazine in the treatment of mania. *Archives of General Psychiatry, 26*, 146-153.

Raskin, A., & Sullivan, P. D. (1963). Factors associated with interrater discrepancies on a psychiatric rating scale. *Journal of Consulting Psychology, 27*, 547.

Romanczyk, R., Kent, R. N., Diament, C., & O'Leary, K. D. (1973). Measuring the reliability of observational data: A reactive process. *Journal of Applied Behavior Analysis, 6*, 175-184.

Rosenzweig, S. P., & Harford, T. (1970). Correlates of the Psychotic Reaction Profile in an outpatient psychiatric sample. *Journal of Consulting and Clinical Psychology, 35*, 244-247.

Shadish, W. R., Bootzin, R. R., Koller, D., & Brownell, L. (1981). Psychometric instability of measures in novel settings: Use of psychiatric rating scales in nursing homes. *Journal of Behavioral Assessment, 3*, 221-232.

Vestre, N. D. (1966). Validity data on the Psychotic Reaction Profile. *Journal of Consulting Psychology, 30*, 84-85.

Vestre, N. D., & Watson, C. G. (1972). Behavioral correlates of the MMPI Paranoia Scale. *Psychological Reports, 31*, 851-854.

Vestre, N. D., & Zimmerman, R. (1970). Validation study of the Psychotic Inpatient Profile. *Psychological Reports, 27*, 3-7.

Watson, C. G. (1972). Psychopathological correlates of anthropomorphic types in male schizophrenics. *Journal of Clinical Psychology, 28*, 474-478.

Watson, C. G., & Klett, W. G. (1972). A validation of the Psychotic Inpatient Profile. *Journal of Clinical Psychology, 28*, 102-109.

Weckowicz, T. E. (1978). Review of the Psychotic Inpatient Profile. In O. K. Buros (Ed.), *The eighth mental measurements yearbook*. Highland Park, NJ: The Gryphon Press.

Young, R. C., & Pandi, G. R. (1978). Common factors in two methods for assessing psychiatric inpatients. *Journal of Clinical Psychology, 34*, 693-694.

Gurmal Rattan, Ph.D.
*Director, School Psychology Clinic-Educational Psychology, Ball State
University, Muncie, Indiana.*

Raymond S. Dean, Ph.D.
*Associate Professor of Psychology-Educational Psychology, Director of
Doctoral Programs, Ball State University, Muncie, Indiana.*

QUICK NEUROLOGICAL SCREENING TEST

*Harold M. Sterling, Margaret Mutti, and Norma V. Spalding.
Novato, California: Academic Therapy Publications.*

Introduction

The Quick Neurological Screening Test (QNST) is an individually administered
screening device offered as a method of identifying children and adolescents with
learning disorders. The QNST is strictly a screening instrument and is not sufficiently detailed to justify a diagnosis of "neurologically handicapped" nor does it
replace a thorough neurological or neuropsychological assessment. The items of
the measure were adapted from pediatric neurological examinations and from
neuropsychological and developmental scales.

The QNST was developed by Harold M. Sterling, Margaret Mutti, and Norma
V. Spalding (1978) to provide users with a "quick" method to determine if neurological problems were adversely affecting learning ability. The current version
of the QNST represents a minor revision of a 1974 Experimental Edition. The only
changes in the current measure are in the administration and scoring criteria for
the Palm Form Recognition and Sound Pattern subtests. These revisions would
seem to allow for simpler administration and less rigorous scoring to reflect
normal neurodevelopmental trends.

The QNST consists of 15 subtests and is intended for use with students in
grades K-12 and adults. Each subtest involves a task completed by the subject and a
list of behavioral statements which if observed during performance, are scored 1
(mild dysfunction) or 3 (severe dysfunction). The subtest scores are added to yield
a total score. A "high" score (exceeding 50) is suggestive of learning difficulty in
the classroom, and the authors argue in favor of a further neurological or neuropsychological assessment. Possible neurological or developmental problems concomitant with learning problems are thought to be indicated by a "suspicious"
score (26-50). A score of less than 25 is seen as "normal" and thus the individual is
not anticipated to have any learning disorders.

Directions for the administration, scoring, and interpretation of the QNST,
along with technical information, are contained in a 76-page manual. In addition,
the manual contains a review of research relative to the educational and medical
relationships between neuropsychological factors and learning disorders. Also

621

provided with the kit are twenty 5½″ X 8½″ cue cards that contain directions for administering and scoring each subtest. The protocol consists of a six-page booklet which clearly details the procedures for scoring and calculating the total score. The only materials required other than those provided in the kit are a pencil and a ball point pen.

The QNST purports to measure the functions of large and small muscle performance, motor planning and sequencing, sense of rate and rhythm, spatial organization, visual and auditory perceptual skills, balance and cerebellar-vestibular functions, and attentional factors. The associated subtests used to measure the above skills are 1) Hand Skills, 2) Figure Recognition and Production, 3) Palm Form Recognition, 4) Eye Tracking, 5) Sound Patterns, 6) Finger to Nose, 7) Thumb and Finger Circle, 8) Double Simultaneous Stimulation of Hand and Cheeks, 9) Rapidly Reversing Repetitive Hand Movements, 10) Arm and Leg Extension, 11) Tandem Walking, 12) Stand on One Leg, 13) Skip, 14) Left-Right Discrimination, and 15) Behavioral Irregularities. As noted earlier, the examiner observes the subject performing the above tasks and scores behaviors inconsistent with neurological integrity according to the stated criteria.

Scoring instructions for the most part seem to be adequately presented, with several subtests providing pictorial illustrations. On several subtests, however, the scoring criteria is subjective and open to interpretation. For example, on the Eye Tracking subtest the subjects are required to visually follow a pencil and are scored points for "slight jerkiness." Similarly, on the Figure Recognition and Production subtest, the subjects are scored if any of the geometric figures that they are required to reproduce are drawn with "extreme rapidity" or "unusually slowly." The examiner is not provided with sufficiently detailed criteria to prevent bias or subjective scoring decisions. The authors also do not consider that a child's fast or slow responses to the above subtest may be indicative of an impulsive or reflective response style rather than being a pathological indicator.

In addition, there are theoretical problems inherent in the scoring criteria. For example, on the Figure Recognition and Production subtest, the subject receives a three-point score for poor angle execution on a figure such as a diamond. However, children are not developmentally mature enough to produce such a figure until at least age six (Dean, in press). Thus, the normal five-year-old child could unduly receive a score in the abnormal range. Similar problems may be noted with the Left-Right Discrimination subtest in which the subject is scored for left-right confusion as noted previously from their performance on Finger to Nose, Thumb and Finger Circle, and Stand on One Leg subtests. No consideration has been given to the fact that this confusion from children younger than eight years of age is due more to a lack of neurological development than a specific disability (Dean, 1982).

According to the authors, individuals receiving scores in the high range will need further assessment in the neurological and neuropsychological areas to delineate the extent of the deficit and subsequent implications in learning. Those individuals scoring in the suspicious range may pose a diagnostic problem. The manual states these individuals demonstrate a "mixture of slow development, organic damage, birth defects, sensory disorders . . ." (p. 40) and require an additional assessment using more refined techniques in order to develop suitable remediation strategies. Finally, the authors state that individuals scoring in the normal range are not expected to have any significant neurological problems which may threaten their learning capabilities. The classification of subjects in the high and suspicious levels appears to be based upon a tenuous assumption that individuals with learning disorders will evidence neurological signs without specific structural abnormalities. Not all learning disabled children experience neurological deficits, nor is neurological dysfunction a necessary concomitant factor in learning disorders (Dean, 1981). Consequently, the validity of the QNST is suspect.

Practical Application/Uses

According to the authors, the QNST is intended to screen children for potential learning problems, and as such its primary use would be in educational settings. Other places where the QNST may be utilized are child development centers, pediatric hospitals, and health centers.

Tasks on the QNST were designed to correspond to motoric and psychological processes with the assumption that by examining the nature of the deficits a remediation program could hopefully be developed. For example, deficits on the Hand Skill subtest, which assesses eye-hand coordination and motor planning, would adversely affect the ability to utilize a pencil or pen. Deficits in the Thumb and Finger Circle subtest, which assesses "order and sequence," would adversely affect order of letters and spelling skills.

The authors suggest that the QNST be administered by trained psychologists or other school personnel, such as remedial specialists, school nurses, educators, and volunteers who have been involved in at least 25 test administrations prior to administering the QNST by themselves. This is due, in part, to the subjective criteria used to score responses. Although the authors do not consider a background in neuropsychology or neuropsychological assessment a necessary component, it would recommend such a background in order to understand what the tasks purport to measure. Given that the QNST is strictly a screening instrument and does not require the examiner to make diagnostic classifications, such as neurologically impaired, an individual trained or supervised by an experienced clinician may be adequate.

The administration and scoring time as reported by the authors may range from 20 minutes for an experienced examiner to 30 minutes for a new examiner. A more realistic administration and scoring time, however, may exceed 40 minutes for an experienced examiner (Hynd, 1981). This may make the QNST prohibitive as a screening instrument.

Technical Aspects

The QNST was "standardized" on a sample of 2,239 children between the ages of under six years to over 17 years in the state of California. Two groups, a learning disabled (LD) and a normal group, were formed based on arbitrary criteria. The LD group consisted of 1,008 children currently placed in special education programs and children referred for diagnostic study, while the normal or undifferentiated group consisted of 1,231 children placed in regular classrooms. Although the sample size appears to be adequate for a screening instrument, several problems are evident. First, the authors fail to give any descriptive statistics of the sample such as the mean age, SES, and gender. Therefore, the researcher is unable to rule out a demographic contaminant. Additionally, the derived sample may not be representative of children in the United States since geographical and social factors as reported by the authors may be confounding variables. They state in the manual that "Our experience indicates that there are very strong geographical and social factors influencing the ability of groups of children to succeed on neuromotor tasks, . . ." (p. 40).

A more critical concern, however, exists with the sampling distributions with regard to age. The normal or undifferentiated and LD samples are radically skewed in opposite directions. Moreover, the sample size of children below eight years of age in the undifferentiated group consists of 814 children whereas there are only 81 children in the same age range for the LD group. At the higher age range, however, the skewness is reversed, with 125 children between 14-17+ years in the undifferentiated group and 805 children in the same age range for the LD group. Thus, when the authors assert that poor performance on subtests, such as Figure Recognition and Production, Rapidly Reversing Repetitive Hand Movement, Thumb and Finger Circle, Sound Pattern, and Leg Extension, is the most characteristic of the LD population, this differential performance may simply be an artifact of the sampling distributions. In general, the standardization procedure and the consequent assignment of subjects into the high, suspicious, and normal categories seem to be based upon tenuous parameters.

The reliability as reported in the manual is based upon a master's thesis conducted by Yamahara (1972). In this study a one month test-retest reliability estimate for a group of 33 LD children yielded a correlation coefficient of .81. It should be noted, however, that a single examiner was used and this intra-rater agreement may be a function of examiner bias. When two examiners were used, a one month test-retest reliability coefficient of .71 was noted. Yamahara also found that eye preference (see Eye Tracking subtest) had the lowest test-retest reliability of .41 compared to hand preference (see Hand Skill subtest) which had a coefficient of .93. Overall, the procedures used to establish reliability appear to lack the rigor expected of psychometric instruments.

The validity of the QNST seems to be based upon a single investigation carried out by one of the authors (Spalding, 1972, p. 57). This study as reported in the manual involved 88 children identified as LD and 88 identified as normal (reading at or above grade level). Moreover, the two groups ranging in age from 6 years, 5 months, to 18 years, 3 months, were matched on age, sex, SES, and intelligence. The pairs were then divided into three age groups: under 9 years; 9 years, 1 month, to 11 years, 11 months; and 12 years to 18 years, 3 months. A multiple discriminant analysis was performed to determine which subtests best discriminated between the two groups. Only 13 subtests were used in the above analysis, with the Left Right Discrimination subtest omitted and the Stand on One Leg and Skip subtests combined into a single measure.

Results from the above analysis showed that the Finger to Nose subtest was the best discriminator between the two age groups across all age levels. Conversely, subtests which did not significantly discriminate between the LD and normal groups at any age level were Hand Skill, Palm Form Recognition, and Double Simultaneous Stimulation of Hand and Cheek. Additionally, the Sound Pattern subtest did not discriminate between the above groups for the middle and older age levels, whereas the combined Stand on One Leg and Skip subtests and the Behavioral Irregularities did not discriminate for the older age group.

The above results suggest that slightly less than 25% of all the subtests provided no useful information in discriminating between LD and normal subjects at any age level whereas more than 45% of the subtests had similar characteristics for children 12 years and older. One needs to exercise extreme caution when interpreting the results, especially with older children, because the QNST is far less sensitive in discerning differences between normal children and those with possible learning disorders.

It is interesting to note that the authors do not report any cross validation studies with other neuropsychological measures as a means of establishing concurrent validity. This may not be suprising given that the dependent measures and research conducted by the authors focus on learning disabilities. As such, QNST may be a misnomer, being more a measure of learning disorders than of neurological dysfunctions.

Critique

In summary, the QNST makes an attempt to provide a quick screening instrument to detect possible neurological deficits in children or adults with learning disorders. The plethora of research articles cited and the overall structure and organization of the instrument attempt to establish a rationale for the use of this instrument. However, given its theoretical and conceptual weaknesses and the inadequate empirical base used in establishing standardization procedures, reliability, and validity, this instrument is less than satisfactory and cannot be recommended. Concomitantly, the time required to administer this instrument may not justify the tenuous results obtained. Further research and refinement will be required in order to meet standards set for psychometric instruments.

References

Dean, R. S. (1981). Cerebral dominance and childhood learning disorders: Theoretical perspectives. *School Psychology Review, 10*, 373-380.

Dean, R. S. (1982). Neuropsychological assessment. In T. Kratochwill (Ed.), *Advances in school psychology (Vol. 2)*. Hillsdale, NJ: Lawrence Erlbaum.

Dean, R. S. (in press). Foundations and rationale for neuropsychological bases of individual differences. In L. C. Hartlage & C. F. Telzrow (Eds.), *The Neuropsychology of individual differences: A developmental perspective*. New York: Plenum Publishing.

Hynd, G. W. (1981). Book reviews. *School Psychology Reviews, 10*, 399-401.

Spalding, N. V. (1972). *The validation of a neurological screening test for learning disabilities.*

Unpublished doctoral dissertation, University of California, Berkeley.

Sterling, H. M., Mutti, M., & Spalding, N. V. (1978). *Quick Neurological Screening Test (Revised Edition)*. Novato, CA: Academic Therapy Publications.

Yamahara, G. (1972). *A reliability study of the Quick Neurological Screening Test*. Unpublished master's thesis, California State University, San Jose.

Raymond H. Holden, Ph.D.
Professor of Psychology, Rhode Island College, Providence, Rhode Island.

READING-FREE VOCATIONAL INTEREST INVENTORY-REVISED

Ralph L. Becker. Columbus, Ohio: Elbern Publications.

Introduction

The revised Reading-Free Vocational Interest Inventory (R-FVII) developed by Ralph L. Becker was published by Elbern Publications in 1981. It is a nonreading, vocational preference test for use with mentally retarded and learning disabled persons from age 13 through adult. Pictorial illustrations with occupational meaning are presented in forced-choice format for selection by the subject. No verbal symbols or written statement is required of the subject.

Concern over vocational choices for selected populations goes back to the 1940s when Abel (1940) studied a group of mentally retarded girls who were successfully adjusted socially and vocationally. Ammons, Butler & Herzig (1949) produced the first of a series of pictorial representations of vocational choice in *The Vocational Apperception Test*. Following their lead, Becker developed *The Vocational Picture Interest Inventory* (1967), which was utilized by the American Association on Mental Deficiency in an experimental version in 1975, using separate formats for males and females. The current instrument is a revised version of this latter instrument, but with an integrated format for both males and females.

The R-FVII was devised to provide systematic information on the range of interest patterns of the exceptional male and female who are diagnosed as mentally retarded or learning disabled. The interest patterns furnish information for these persons engaged in a wide range of occupations and job tasks at the unskilled, semiskilled and skilled levels. Identifying areas and patterns of interest yields information that aids vocational counselors in the occupational planning and job placement of individuals. The instrument thus provides scores in eleven interest areas for males and females. The areas are 1) Automotive, 2) Building Trades, 3) Clerical, 4) Animal Care, 5) Food Service, 6) Patient Care, 7) Horticulture, 8) Housekeeping, 9) Personal Service, 10) Laundry Service, and 11) Materials Handling.

All items included in the inventory represent the kind and type of occupation in which mentally retarded and learning disabled persons are productive and proficient. A total of 165 illustrations arranged in triads comprise the test booklet. All pictorial items used in preparing the scoring keys were developed empirically through a series of item analyses conducted on mentally retarded and learning disabled persons.

The inventory is available as a consumable test booklet for hand-scoring and includes an individual profile sheet as an aid in the interpretation of inventory results. The amount of training required of the examiner to properly administer, interpret, and use the results of the inventory is considered to be Level B (individuals who have completed an advanced testing course at an accredited university) as defined by the test standards of the American Psychological Association. The R-FVII may be administered and scored by a trained clerical assistant, but decisions with regard to vocational planning, training, and placement should be made by personnel trained as vocational counselors, work-study teachers or coordinators, and psychologists who have knowledge of guidance and counseling practices.

The inventory may be administered easily within a 45-minute class period, including distribution of test booklets, reading of instructions, selections by examinees, and collection of test materials. The average amount of time to complete the inventory is 20 minutes or less.

Practical Applications/Uses

The most useful application of this instrument is the discovery of vocational interests of adolescents and young adults who have great difficulty in reading. The picture format is very suitable, with simple line drawings of persons engaged in a wide variety of occupations: pumping gas, serving a tray of food, sweeping the floor, driving a tractor, folding laundry, etc. The short administration time is appropriate for those who have a short attention span.

The R-FVII is self-administered and has no time limit. It is easily adaptable to either individual or group administration. The examiner explains how to use the test booklet, by circling one of the three pictures in each row, stating, "Here are three pictures. Find which job you like the best and put a circle on that picture" (Becker, 1981, p. 9). After the examinee has finished the booklet it should be checked for completeness.

Each item in the inventory has been keyed on its appropriate scale on the scoring sheet. After transferring all of the examinee's selections onto the scoring grid, the booklet may be discarded. After all scores have been totaled, the examiner converts each raw score into its corresponding T-score and percentile rank by using the appropriate norm table (e.g., EMR Males, ages 13-16; Public School LD Females, ages 16-19).

The Individual Profile is a chart for profiling the percentile ranks of the subject. The lines can be connected to form a graphic representation of the subject's interest profile, much like a WISC-R profile of scores.

Scores above the 75th percentile are considered high, those below the 25th percentile are considered low and those in between are considered average. High scores alert the counselor and student to particular vocational areas that can be helpful in occupational planning, training or job placement of the subject. Naturally, other factors, such as level of intellectual ability, personality characteristics, and particular occupational skills should be considered in decision-making.

Technical Aspects

The R-FVII was administered on a nationwide basis during the 1980-81 school year to samples of educable mentally retarded (EMR) and learning disabled (LD) males and females in grades 7-12, and to samples of mentally retarded adults in sheltered workshops and vocational training centers. School districts throughout the country were given quotas of pupils to be drawn at random from urban, rural and inner-city school systems. Workshop centers were selected from state directories of special education, and quotas were drawn at random.

Public school norms are based on 2,132 EMR males, 2,163 EMR females, 2,034 LD males, and 1,967 LD females in 30 states. Adult norms are based on 1,121 MR males and 1,106 MR females from 36 sheltered workshops in 17 states, affording a geographical representation of the country.

Test-retest reliabilities over a two-week interval were predominantly in the .70s and .80s and at levels of significance in all groups. Generally high correlation coefficients were found in the LD samples. Sample sizes, however, were small ranging from 55 to 92 cases in each group. Standard errors of measurement, indicating how closely raw scores approximate true scores, were quite satisfactory in terms of reliability.

Validity was assessed by three methods: content validity, concurrent validity, and occupational validity. Content validity is assumed because various study teams agreed on classifications of the pictures in eleven occupational groups—not a very convincing argument. Concurrent validity was much more appropriately handled by comparing correlations between the R-FVII and the *Geist Picture Interest Inventory* (GPII) (Geist, 1964). A random sample of the test-retest group of subjects was also administered the GPII at the initial testing period. Product moment correlations were significant at or beyond the .05 level for 36 of 45 correlations in the groups of mentally retarded males (N = 154), and for 38 of 45 correlations in the groups of mentally retarded females (N = 148) (Becker, 1981, p. 45). This is an appropriate representation of validity.

Occupational validity was studied by comparing the highest scores of mentally retarded males and females and sheltered workshop clients in each of eleven occupational groups (e.g., Laundry Service, Materials Handling, Food Service, etc.). Scoring of the R-FVII showed that each group of workers scored highest on their own actual occupation. For example, food service workers scored highest in the area of Food Service (Becker, 1981, p. 22). No data is given in the manual to support this claim.

Critique

Two reviewers, Esther E. Diamond and George Domino, provided an evaluation of the original form of the R-FVII in the *Eighth Mental Measurements Yearbook* (Buros, 1978). Both reviews were generally favorable, pointing to the need being filled by such an instrument as this. However, Domino particularly found fault with the status of the test's validity, and criticized the approach to vocational choice as more psychometric than humanistic. He urged that subjects be *asked* what their vocational preferences are. Reliability was considered adequate and well documented. The task itself is relatively easy, but do the mentally retarded subjects always know what the line drawings of jobs really represent?

The present reviewer generally agrees with the previous evaluations of the original test. The format of the revised instrument has not been changed, but the national norms are improved and one booklet for both males and females has replaced two booklets, one for each sex. Other changes include all eleven interest areas scored for both sexes instead of the previous eight areas for males and six for females. I consider this to be a decided improvement in the instrument.

It might be helpful to consider developing reusable test booklets because the cost of disposing of the present booklets is high if large groups are involved. However, considering the populations for which the test was developed, this may not be a feasible task. Having used this test over the past years in a vocational rehabilitation workshop setting, I have found this instrument to be greatly helpful with the many adolescents and young adults who have limited ability to read. This is its greatest usefulness. Further studies of its predictive validity are, of course, strongly recommended.

References

This list includes text citations as well as suggested additional reading.

American Association on Mental Deficiency. (1975). *Reading Free Vocational Interest Inventory.* Washington, DC: Author.

Abel, T. M. (1940). A study of a group of subnormal girls successfully adjusted in industry and community. *American Journal of Mental Deficiency, 40,* 66-72.

Ammons, R. B., Butler, M. N., & Herzig, S. A. (1949). *The Vocational Apperception Test.* Missoula, MT: Psychological Test Specialists.

Becker, R. L. (1967). *Vocational Picture Interest Inventory.* Columbus, OH: Columbus State Institute.

Becker, R. L. (1973). The Reading-Free Vocational Interest Inventory: Measurement of job preference in the EMR. *Mental Retardation, 11,* 11-15.

Becker, R. L. (1981). *Revised Reading-Free Vocational Interest Inventory Manual.* Columbus, OH: Elbern Publications.

Buros, O. K. (Ed.). (1978). *The eighth mental measurements yearbook.* Highland Park, NJ: The Gryphon Press.

Darley, J. G., & Hagenah, T. (1955). *Vocational interest measurement.* Minneapolis: University of Minnesota Press.

Diamond, E. E. (1978). Review of AAMD-Becker Reading Free Vocational Interest Inventory. In O. K. Buros (Ed.), *The eighth mental measurements yearbook* (pp. 1535-1536). Highland Park, NJ: The Gryphon Press.

Domino, G. (1978). Review of AAMD-Becker Reading Free Vocational Interest Inventory. In O. K. Buros (Ed.), *The eighth mental measurements yearbook* (pp. 1536-1538). Highland Park, NJ: The Gryphon Press.

Geist, H. (1964). *Geist Picture Interest Inventory.* Beverly Hills, CA: Western Psychological Services.

Kuder, G. F. (1951). *Kuder Preference Record Vocational.* Chicago: Science Research Associates.

Layton, W. L. (Ed.). (1960). *The Strong Vocational Interest Blank: Research and uses.* Minneapolis: University of Minnesota Press.

Strong, E. K., Jr. (1943). *Vocational interests of men and women.* Stanford, CA: Stanford University Press.

Strong, E. K., Jr. (1951). *Vocational Interest Blank.* Stanford, CA: Stanford University Press.

Super, D. E. (1954). The measurement of interests. *Journal of Counseling Psychology, 1,* 168-73.

Carl G. Willis, Ed.D.

Counseling Psychologist, University of Missouri, Columbia, Missouri.

REID REPORT/REID SURVEY

Reid Psychological Systems. Chicago, Illinois: Reid Psychological Systems.

Introduction

The Reid Report (RR) and the Reid Survey (RS) were designed to predict only one kind of behavior—theft. In another sense, the RR and RS can be viewed as a general measure of integrity or honesty. Because the target group of users is comprised of business establishments and public agencies where loss of money and/or merchandise can and does occur, the ability to assess the proneness to theft by job applicants or current employees is of paramount importance in a firm's profit margin.

The Reid Report and Reid Survey are paper-and-pencil tests. Due to both 1) the design of the instruments as assessments of theft proneness or honesty and 2) the author's belief that the best method to employ, retain, or promote honest employees is to query them concerning their beliefs on their dishonesty and their own likelihood of dishonest behavior, the instruments have received extensive usage in the marketplace. Brodsky (1978, p. 1025) reported a paradox in that ". . . the test itself seeks honest responses about personal dishonesty. Nevertheless, individuals apparently do report sufficiently honestly (or see mild amounts of dishonesty as being normal and common) . . ." Although the tests were designed based on Mr. Reid's observations of human behavior, there appears to be an implicit suggestion of a two-factor theory for the construct of honesty. Two subscales, punitive and projective, are summed with equal values to provide a total score. Ash (1975) reports a .56 correlation between the two scales. Sackett and Harris (1984) suggest that little is known about the nature of either the honesty construct or the criterion, theft or other counterproductive behavior.

The development of the Reid Report and accompanying materials extends back to 1947 when John E. Reid, a pioneer in the field of the detection of deception, established his own polygraph firm. Mr. Reid, a graduate of DePaul University School of Law, joined the Chicago Police Crimes Laboratory in 1940. Through his development of polygraph techniques, he began to observe behavior symptoms of lie detector subjects. These observations led to the "discovery that persons verified through polygraph as telling the truth answer questions in a certain manner. Those verified as lying answer differently" (Reid, undated, p. 7). Through this process, thousands of questions were considered in terms of their value in assessing attitudes toward honesty. In 1951 Reid published his first paper-and-pencil test, which was correlated with polygraph results.

Mr. Reid was coauthor of three texts in the field of polygraph and criminal interrogation, as well as author and coauthor of numerous articles in professional journals. He cofounded the American Academy of Polygraph Examiners, which merged with other polygraph organizations in 1963 to form the American Polygraph Association. The Reid-authored polygraph licensing law, a model for other states, went into effect that same year in Illinois.

To the present time, 20 versions have evolved through continual efforts to improve the reliability and validity of the Reid Report. During the years of development, the RR for job applicants and the RS for current employees were logical instruments with marketing potential. Each instrument has the basic 90-item "Yes-No" format, including three subsets of items. The basic 90-item instruments are the same; however, the Reid Report has an additional section of biographical data and 68 questions concerning previous or current behavior, whereas the RS has an additional section of biographical data and 40 questions concerning behavior and attitudes for current employees. The number of items on the many versions has varied from 80 to 150, all directed at some aspect of honesty. Both the Report and the Survey are also published in Spanish, Portugese, French, Italian, and Polish.

Althought the RR and RS both have a common set of 90 "Yes-No" items, the scoring and processing of these instruments can vary in format. Both instruments can be scored by returning the answer forms to Reid Psychological Systems (RPS) for machine scanning and reporting of the results. However, when the urgency of the test results are a determining factor for an immediate employment decision, the second page (card portion) of the answer can be separated by the administrator to obtain information for summarization. All items are marked on a top sheet of NCR forms with the responses and processing directions on the second sheet. A set of subscores and answers to specific questions can be summarized for a telephone call to RPS. This summary information allows a quick response to the user firm. In addition, a separate set of guidelines directs the use of the telephone scoring process. There is a separate answer form for the RS. The second section of both instruments is answered in the test booklet.

Within the common set of 90 items there are three sets of items. The first set of 35 items is a measure of punitiveness reflecting attitudes toward punishment of crimes ("Do you believe there are some special cases where a person has a right to steal from an employer?" "An employer discovers that a long-service, trusted employee has been taking a few dollars out of the cash register every week. Should the employer have him arrested?") (Ash, 1971, p. 162). The second set of 35 items is a projective measure of the person's own attitude and behavior relating to theft ("Did you ever think about committing a burglary?" "Are you too honest to steal?") (Ash, 1971, p. 162). The third set of 20 items is research items which currently are not scored.

The second section of the RR consists of 68 questions that contain a detailed biographical data blank covering the previous employment, education, social history, financial history, and admissions lists of previous defalcations and previous thefts. There are two supplemental sections which may also be administered. The first supplement is a sheet requesting agreement or disagreement about the administration of a polygraph examination before, during, or at termination of employment. The second supplement queries the applicant on the use of drugs and alcohol during the previous 12 months.

Included in the second section of 86 items in the RS is a biographical data blank relating the applicant's experiences with theft while currently employed, especially experience and/or perceptions of theft, and a set of questions on drug and alcohol abuse during current employment.

Practical Applications/Uses

The test is intended for use with employment situations; therefore, generally no one less than 15 or 16 years of age would attend an administration. Although an examiner must be in charge, his/her role is minimal. No information is provided on the reading or educational level necessary to complete the instrument.

In general, the administration of the RR and RS should be an easy task. There are printed administration guidelines that can easily be followed whether testing one person or a group. In the case of current employees, the administration guidelines seem clear. However, some of the specified purposes listed in the administration guide for the Survey (e.g., "Gives an indication of the employees' contentment, disgruntlement", "Indicates the employees' propensity to drug and alcohol use") do not seem justified or supported with any validation. Although job applicants and current employees are both told that about 40 minutes are needed, at least one hour should be allowed. Examples for marking the answer sheets are included in each test booklet.

When an applicant has completed the RR, the booklet and answer form are transmitted to RPS for analysis. On the basis of the item score, plus evaluation of responses to the bio-data and admissions to defalcations and theft questions, an applicant is either recommended or not recommended for employment. Norms exist for the item score alone, but the bio-data are considered in the final recommendation to the employer. For example, Ash (1971) indicates that a score in the lower recommendation range ". . . may be reversed by a bad debt history, work instability, or numerous admissions. Incredible as it may seem, applicants in significant numbers do admit to practically every crime in the books" (p. 161).

Scoring information for the item scores and guidelines for evaluating the more subjective second sections are considered proprietary information by RPS. Therefore, the actual scoring and item statistics are unavailable for critique. One study (N = 1853) by Ash (1970), on a 114-item version of the RR, found a 78-item set with approximately zero correlation with race and with item-criterion correlations of .11 or better on the sample. Use of the 78-item set provided total score validities near .4 for each race-age subgroup.

Technical Aspects

In a January 1984 correspondence, Ash summarizes some reliability information on the RR across several studies with values from .57 on black college students to .92 on black males on the KR 20 or 21 formulas. The median reliability coefficient reported was .87. The Cronbach Alpha reliabilities for a larger sample of diverse job applicants (N = 1230) was .92. Within this sample, white males (N = 797) had

.93 estimate, black males (N = 233) a .92, white females (N = 146) a .91, and black females (N = 54) a .93. Ash reports an overall reliability of .92.

Several types of validity information are available. At least three studies by Ash (1970; 1971; 1972) have used polygrapher recommendations as the criterion for RR scores. The larger samples allowed validation by race and sex with validity coefficients from .36 to .62. Today, the question of discrimination on racial or sex grounds is an important factor in developing employee selection programs. "The Reid Report does not seem to discriminate on either basis" (Ash, 1975, p. 143). When considering test performance and race, the "data overwhelmingly show that neither the test nor the criterion (polygraphs) are discriminatory against blacks" (Ash, 1970, p. 579). In terms of a predictive study, Ash (1975) found a .06 relationship with theft after employment; however, that only two employees of 140 were dismissed due to theft should be considered a criterion problem, not the RR.

Another attempt (Ash, 1974) to establish validity of the RR was a comparison of scores by convicted felons (N = 187) with male employment applicants (N = 1030). When the felons were compared with the recommended and not recommended employment applicants, only 1 in 100 of the applicants scored as low or lower than the felons.

Considerable data is presented in various materials on the RR's core 90-item test. Several statistical comparisons noted elsewhere in this review are targeted specifically at the legal concept of adverse impact. In fact, the resources and experts at RPS are promised as part of the services if needed in court. In a recent text, Inbau, Aspen, and Spiotta (1982, p. 171) indicate that in a time period from 1968 through 1981 over 1.5 million individuals were tested with the RR; "fewer than 12 of them filed charges before federal or state agencies alleging that the test was unlawfully discriminatory or illegal in other respects." No charges were sustained and through early 1982 there had been no appeals.

Only one study is available relating the RR to other psychological instruments. The 16 Personality Factor Test (16PF) was administered with the RR to applicants for employment at United Airlines. Kochkin (1982, p. 1) reports that applicants with high scores on the RR have higher ego strength, less anxiety, more socially desirable behavior, more control of their impulses, and are apt to be more successful leaders. Applicants failing the RR had 16PF profiles similar to those "of general neurotics, alcoholics, convicted criminals, narcotic addicts, and anti-social personalities . . ." However, Kochkin also reported a correlation between the RR and the 16PF faking good scale of .42, indicating that those applicants giving socially desirable responses do well on the RR.

Critique

As a proprietary test of theft proneness or honesty, the Reid Report and Reid Survey in one version or another have been available for almost 34 years. The technical knowledge of the developers in polygraph, psychometrics, and law have produced a very presentable test with much supportive material. There are appropriate research reports in the professional literature, probably more than any other similar test.

Yet there are some features that a careful reader or business owner should know.

At the writing of this review, there is no published test manual—just a collection of reports, materials, and testimonials. The research reports available for this review related to applicant testing, not current employees. Thirty-five firms have allowed RPS to print their names, a contact person, and a telephone number as an indication of their willingness to discuss their experiences with the RR and RS. There seems to be a plethora of positive but subjective evaluations by users. No published research articles in professional journals since 1976 could be found, although many firms might view their own research results as business property not to be made available to the public or competitors.

One troublesome concern lies in the basic validation with the polygraph. In part, some of the development of paper-and-pencil tests of honesty as surrogates to the polygraph examination may be due to the many state laws preventing use of the polygraph for employment purposes. According to Kleinmuntz and Szucko (1984, p. 774), in a review article on polygraphy, an "examination is based on the simplistic assumption that suspects are aware of their lying and will experience more arousal to relevant questions if they are deceptive than if they are truthful." In our contemporary times, the public tends to believe that lying provides a unique set of physiological responses which may be measured. Kleinmuntz and Szucko (1984, p. 767) again assert that this "belief, however, has no empirical basis. Quite the contrary. Lying emits no known distinctive pattern of physiological activity . . ." In general, conclusiveness on the effectiveness of polygraphy is not yet available.

Another concern for the RR is the possibility of an applicant faking the results in a positive direction. This result seems possible. Since much of the reliability and validity data reported has been on versions with varying lengths and differing item pools, there has been no disclosure of data to ascertain the applicability of the earlier data to the current test forms.

Based on all of the materials that were reviewed and on brief visits in small firms with experience with the RR/RS, there appears to be a global view that the theft proneness or honesty test of RPS serves a satisfied clientele.

The major unanswered question for this reviewer is not whether the RR/RS helps in the employment setting, but "Why?" Maybe with a public of job applicants who believe the polygraph or the honesty test, they respond from a fear that their dishonesty will be discovered.

References

Ash, P. (1970). Validation of an instrument to predict the likelihood of employee theft (Summary). *Proceedings of the 78th Annual Convention of the American Psychological Association, 5,* 579-580.

Ash, P. (1971). Screening employment applicants for attitudes toward theft. *Journal of Applied Psychology, 55,* 161-164.

Ash, P. (1972). Attitudes of work applicants toward theft. *Proceedings of the XVIIth International Congress of Applied Psychology,* 985-988.

Ash, P. (1974). Convicted felons' attitudes toward theft. *Criminal Justice and Behavior, 1*(1), 21-18.

Ash, P. (1975). Predicting dishonesty with the Reid Report. *Journal of the American Polygraph Association, 5,* 139-145.

Brodsky, S. L. (1978). Reid Report. In O. K. Buros (Ed.), *The eighth mental measurements yearbook* (pp. 1025-1026). Highland Park, NJ: Gryphon Press.

Inbau, F. E., Aspen, M. E., & Spiotta, J. E. (1982). *Protective security law.* Woburn, MA: Butterworth Publishers.

Kleinmuntz, B., & Szucko, J. J. (1984). Lie detection in ancient and modern times, a call for contemporary scientific study. *American Psychologist, 39,* 766-776.

Kochkin, S. (1982). *Personality correlates of a measure of honesty.* Chicago, IL: United Airlines Human Resources Department.

Reid, J. E., & Associates. (n.d.). *The first 30 years.* Chicago: John E. Reid and Associates.

Sackett, P. R. & Harris, M. M. (1984). Honesty testing for personnel selection: A review and critique. *Personnel Psychology, 37,* 221-245.

Michael D. Franzen, Ph.D.
Director, Neuropsychology, West Virginia University Medical Center,
Morgantown, West Virginia.

REITAN EVALUATION OF HEMISPHERIC ABILITIES AND BRAIN IMPROVEMENT TRAINING

Ralph M. Reitan. Tucson, Arizona: Reitan Neuropsychology Laboratory.

Introduction

The Reitan Evaluation of Hemispheric Abilities and Brain Improvement Training (REHABIT) is a collection of evaluation and training procedures which were brought together in order to attempt a cohesive effort at retraining cognitive abilities that have been impaired as the result of brain injury. Not all of the procedures are used with each of the subjects, and REHABIT is therefore better conceptualized as a program rather than as a battery. REHABIT was designed by Ralph Reitan (1983), the eminent clinical neuropsychologist whose work with the Halstead-Reitan Neuropsychological Test Battery (HRNTB) (Reitan, 1979) was extremely influential in fostering the standardized approach to neuropsychological assessment.

The REHABIT program is still in the early stages of its development, but the pressing need for a technology for retraining brain-impaired individuals enhances the potential importance of the program.

REHABIT is comprised of three parts. The first part involves evaluation of the subject using the age appropriate form of the HRNTB. Following this evaluation, the second part involves training deficient skills areas identified by the HRNTB using those sections of the HRNTB on which the subject demonstrated deficits. For instance, if the subject demonstrated deficits on the Tactual Performance Test, then training on that section is provided by giving feedback during practice sessions with the Tactual Performance Test. Finally, the third part involves training in more complex, largely academic skills oriented areas using materials that were designed by independent individuals for their own specific purposes. These training procedures were chosen in much the same way that the subtests of the HRNTB were chosen, by reviewing already extant materials and selecting those that were judged to be most useful.

There is no central manual; materials used in the third part of REHABIT consist of 143 procedures which are published by seven different companies. These materials must be ordered separately from the publishing companies. Purchasing the entire REHABIT program, including the HRNTB and the 143 sets of training materials, can therefore be quite an expensive endeavor. Another consequence of the heterogeneity of publishers is that decisions to publish and distribute are made individually by the companies involved. For example, Wieser Educational Publishing Company has decided to discontinue the Flip-Chex, a component of the central training track.

The training procedures in the third part of REHABIT are divided into five tracks conceptually arranged in a symmetric fashion. The central track involves relatively pure abstraction skills; the two tracks that are on either side of this track involve verbal abstraction skills, and visual-spatial and manipulatory abstraction skills, respectively. On either side of this triptych are a track involving elementary language skills and a track involving elementary visual-spatial and manipulatory skills.

The materials used in the tracks are as follows:

Track A (simple verbal skills): These materials involve practice in associating letters and words with pictures, sequencing letters into words, auditory verbal comprehension, and number recognition, as well as practice in mathematical concepts and processes. The 14 procedures in this track are at the simple skill level.

Track B (verbal abstraction skills): This track involves practice in right-left orientation, reasoning with the use of language, mathematical processes, categorization of pictures, quantitative relationships, and immediate memory. The 11 procedures in this track utilize skills that are on a gradient from simple to complex.

Track C (relatively pure abstraction): This track involves practice in classification and organization, concept formation, matching, reasoning, and associative and simple visual-perceptual skills. The 28 procedures in this track also exist on a gradient from simple to complex.

Track D (visual-spatial abstraction skills): This track involves practice in visual-spatial relations, matching and organizing visual stimuli, picture arrangement, recent memory, and planning. The 27 procedures in this track are graded from simple to complex levels.

Track E (visual-spatial skills): This track involves practice in visual matching, form perception, drawing, picture arrangement, motor coordination, sequential arrangement of pictures, auditory sequencing, form perception, and visual-spatial manipulation. The 63 procedures in this track are arranged from simple to complex levels of skill.

Practical Applications/Uses

In an unpublished manuscript, Reitan (1983) states that REHABIT is appropriate for both children and adults. However, he does not provide the upper and lower age limits for which the program is intended. The rationale for using parts of the HRNTB to train deficient skill areas is based on a simple logical premise. The subtests of the HRNTB were chosen as the best available methods to assess fundamental brain functions by requiring the subject to perform activities that require use of those functions. Through practice, it is hoped that the subject gains increased facility in the successful use of these functions. Using the actual subtests as practice material vitiates their usefulness as instruments for the assessment of changes. Therefore, Reitan's neuropsychological laboratory has developed alternate forms of the HRNTB subtests to use as training materials. The alternate forms are as yet unpublished and are unavailable except through attendance at one of Dr. Reitan's workshops.

All of the procedures in the third part were originally designed for use in training children in academic and cognitive skills. The stimuli used in the procedures are meant to attract and hold the attention of children, usually young children. As a result, there is the possibility that an adult who maintains moderate self-evaluative and social-evaluative skills may feel that the procedures are beneath him or her and that the cognitive skills therapist is being condescending. For example, use of the Peabody Language Development Kit, used in Track B, utilizes two hand puppets. Some brain-impaired adults may be reluctant to use these stimuli.

As an example of how the materials listed in the REHABIT program need further work before they can be used with adult brain-impaired subjects, let us further examine the Peabody Language Development Kit-Revised (PLDK-R) which is part of Track B. The PLDK-R originally developed to aid in the group instruction of retarded children in language usage. It does not attempt to teach grammar or diction. Instead, it attempts to encourage retarded children to produce understandable speech. As such it would seem a good choice as an instrument to increase the verbal production of aphasic adults. However, there are some problems that need to be addressed before it is used with adult subjects.

As well as using the hand puppets mentioned previously, the PLDK-R has a manual (Dunn, Dunn, & Smith, 1981) that assumes group administration to children. The instructions as printed in the manual might therefore seem condescending to adults. The instructions are easily changed to reflect both the adult population and the individual administration that would be more common in the cognitive rehabilitation setting, but this needs to be specified in a corrolary manual in order to ensure standard administration. The current manual for the PLDK-R reports the results of research investigating the effectiveness of the battery in training retarded children. The effect of three years of training using the PLDK-R impressively consists of gains in scores on the Illinois Test of Psycholinguistic Ability, in IQ as measured by Stanford-Binet, and in school achievement as measured by the Metropolitan Achievement Tests. However, this research needs to be conducted on adult subjects with acquired brain impairment before claims can be made regarding the effectiveness of the PLDK-R in this population.

As another example, the Motor-Free Visual Perception Test or MVPT (Colarusso & Hammill, 1972), which is part of Track E, is intended as an assessment instrument, and its use as a training instrument is not described in the manual. One would need to attend one of the workshops conducted by Dr. Reitan in order to learn how to use the MVPT in this capacity. Some of the other instruments, such as the Developmental Program in Visual Perception (Frostig, 1972) have fewer components, which might be objectionable to adult subjects, but there is a lack of research in the appropriate subject population.

Another possible shortcoming of the test is in its dependence upon a practice model for rehabilitation. Certainly, training will likely result in some gains in performance on the test. However, depending on the nature and severity of the injury, some subjects may benefit more from an attempt to provide them with alternate methods of performing the behavior, rather than conducting numerous training sessions resulting in frustration. For example, in a severely spatially impaired individual, providing color-coded strings of yarn that connect to various rooms (e.g., red yarn leads to the kitchen) may eventuate in more satisfactory results than training in paper-and-pencil spatial tasks. Conversely, the opposite may be true for individuals with moderate spatial deficits.

Technical Aspects

Due to the nascent state of REHABIT, there is currently no published research looking at the validity of these instruments in cognitive retraining of adults. The MVPT, for example, has been normed on children. It appears to possess reasonable reliability and validity in this population, but its psychometric properties in adult populations is unknown.

In addition, due to the heterogeneity of the development of these procedures, it is likely that validity is differential for the 143 different procedures. An important point needs to be raised here. Training using these procedures is essentially training to perform on the tests. As in all cases of training, the primary consideration of the validity is the degree of generalizability of the gains reflected by the subject. This is a more important consideration for the second part of REHABIT than it is for the third. Training on alternate forms of the subtests of the HRNTB may affect performance on the original subtests without affecting performance in the open environment. In essence, it is possible that the subject is being trained to take the test rather than to improve their skills in the measured area.

Critique

All of the instruments used for the REHABIT are aimed at the practice of basic skills. It is important to ask if this approach is cost-effective in adults or if it might be better to train the subjects in the areas identified as deficient in a functional analysis of the ability of the subject to meet the demands of the environment.

Finally, the therapist would need to be conversant with all of the instruments in order to decide which one to use in a given case. A major consequence is that the training required of a therapist would involve huge amounts of time, effort, and money. Perhaps that is necessary and should be accepted as a given. However, the promise of this exciting new program needs to be realized in the context of empirical investigations of its reliability, validity, appropriateness, and cost-effectiveness.

References

Colarusso, R. P., & Hammill, D. D. (1972). *Motor Free Visual Perception Test manual.* Novato, CA: Academic Therapy Publications.

Dunn, L. M., Dunn, L. M., & Smith, J. O. (1981). *Peabody Language Development Kit-Revised,* Circle Pines, MN: American Guidance Service.

Frostig, M. (1972). *The Developmental Program in Visual Perception-Revised*. Cleveland: Modern Curriculum Press.

Reitan, R. (1979). *Halstead-Reitan Neuropsychological Test Battery*. Tucson: Reitan Neuropsychological Laboratory.

Reitan, R. (1983). *Reitan Evaluation of Hemispheric Abilities and Brain Improvement Training*. Unpublished manuscript.

Norman D. Sundberg, Ph.D.
Professor and Director of Clinical/Community Psychology, University of Oregon, Eugene, Oregon.

ROGERS PERSONAL ADJUSTMENT INVENTORY—UK REVISION

Patricia M. Jeffrey. Windsor, England: NFER-Nelson Publishing Company Ltd.

Introduction

Resurrection from the dead is a rare event, but it appears to have happened with a test published by Carl Rogers in 1931. Over 50 years later, Patricia Jeffrey, a British educational psychologist at the Tayside Regional Council, Scotland, has revised, simplified, and applied psychometric studies to resuscitate the old test. Originally it was called the Test of Personality Adjustment, but in 1961 the American publisher renamed it the Personal Adjustment Inventory and re-issued it without change or use of additional research. Now, in honor of its originator, Jeffrey has christened her revision the Rogers Personal Adjustment Inventory, or RPAI (Jeffrey, 1984).

The RPAI is intended for the assessment of adjustment of children between 9 and 13 years old—adjustment to their environments, peers, families, and selves. Jeffrey revised it by making it somewhat shorter, changing items that were peculiarly American and/or old-fashioned. She also simplified instructions and improved the scoring. The RPAI itself consists of a 12-page booklet on which the child writes his or her answers. The forms for boys and girls have a few differences in content, but are now more closely matched in length and items and have the same scoring procedures. The test form has ample spacing and clear printing and layout. There are six sections involving the following activities: 1) making a cross in boxes that list 9 occupations; 2) putting a cross in boxes beside 12 wishes, e.g., "to be bigger and stronger"; 3) writing the names of 3 people whom the child would like to take to a "desert island"; 4) choosing whether one is like or unlike a child of ones's own sex who is briefly described on 16 items, e.g., "Bob is the cleverest boy in the class," and also choosing whether one would want to be like that child; 5) choosing among multiple choices on 20 items about such concerns as wanting many or few friends or wishing to be good-looking; and 6) by use of additional pieces of paper on which the child writes names, ranking 10 family members and friends as to one's preferences. In addition, there are some open-ended questions, which are not scored, but provide qualitative information.

Five objective scores are derived from the inventory: Personal difficulties (P), Social difficulties (S), Family difficulties (F), Daydreaming (D), and a Total difficulties score. Jeffrey has changed the names slightly from those used 50 years ago to avoid the attribution of maladjustment to the individual. (Whether the intended shift will occur is questionable!) The 16-page manual (Jeffrey, 1984) gives rather

642

detailed descriptions of the changes made from the old American test and the procedures for administering and scoring. It also provides considerable technical detail, which will be discussed later.

Practical Applications/Uses

A purpose of the RPAI is to help in the assessment tasks of psychologists working in schools, clinics, and hospitals. It can be administered individually or in small groups; Jeffrey recommends no more than 15 children at a time. It might be used for identifying children who need special psychological assistance or for research purposes.

Jeffrey states in the manual that the administration takes approximately 30 minutes. The only instructions that might be confusing are in Section 4, where the child is told to mark a cross on "Yes" or "No" or in between. Some children may interpret this as "crossing out" the given response rather than choosing it; it would have been better to have them make a cross beside the preferred answer. Jeffrey reports that the scoring takes about 1 1/2 minutes, presumably after considerable practice using the handy templates to be superimposed on the answer sheet.

It is an interesting anomaly that Carl Rogers, who in mid-career wrote passionately against the use of tests and diagnosis, should have published a test in his early child guidance days and has now allowed its revision. He must have had some qualms. Jeffrey (1984, p. 12) quotes him from the early test manual: "It should be kept in mind that at its best, a score is only a numerical summary, and although valuable in many ways, gives a less accurate picture of an individual than a study of the individual's responses." Both Rogers and Jeffrey make the point that one cannot automatically interpret results, but one must aim at a fuller clinical understanding of each child. Rogers helped show how the inventory could be used individually by presenting cases in his original manual.

Jeffrey unfortunately does not present cases, but she does discuss interpretation in some detail. For instance, in discussing Section 4, she advises noting the similarities and differences between the self and ideal-self responses. She points out that those children high on both may be braggers, and others may show their inferiority feelings and self-deprecation. She notes that very shy and cautious children avoid extremes. It is obvious that she has had experience with children, and it would be interesting to have more of her ideas on the rationale for the items. The reasoning behind the scoring of some is unclear to this reviewer.

Technical Aspects

The 11 tables in the RPAI manual (Jeffrey, 1984) provide a quite fairly extensive account of the nature of the test. The statistics are based, however, on only 210 children attending schools in the region of Tayside, Scotland. (This number is larger than the Ns reported by Rogers!) Jeffrey says that the children's backgrounds represent both working and middle-class people and rural and urban situations, but no evidence is given. The subsamples break down to between 30 and 40 girls and the same number of boys for each of three ages—9, 11, and 13. On some of the tables with age and sex breakdowns, the numbers get to be quite small. There is no evidence of sampling in other places, and one wonders how generalizable the findings are beyond Tayside. Is Tayside even representative of Scotland?

Half of the sample was given Rogers' original and the revised form one month apart. The correlations range from .42 (for F) to .53 (for P) in the subscales, and the correlation for the total score is .63. One would not expect a perfect correspondence, but it is surprising that the correlations are as low as they are; perhaps there are real cultural differences between the two forms, or perhaps the old test is less clear to the Scottish children. The test-retest reliability data with another half of the total sample (N = 107) are a little higher, ranging from .53 (F) to .75 (D) with a respectable correlation of .78 for the total scores on both administrations of the RPAI.

Jeffrey used two procedures to examine the validity of the RPAI: another self-report inventory, the California Test of Personality (CTP) and teachers' ratings on Rutter's Children's Behaviour Questionnaire (CBQ), Scale B. With both, results are available on 207 children. Strangely, Jeffrey does not give correlations, but she does break the group down into subgroups on the basis of the criterion tests and gives RPAI means and standard deviations for the subgroups. A large number of these breakdowns do not show significant differences from each other. The RPAI does discriminate between extreme levels better than between levels of moderate difference, as might be expected. At the uper age levels, the grouping of CBQ ratings into a zero category versus an above-zero category results in significantly different RPAI means.

Jeffrey also investigated age and sex differences in her sample. The average total score for 9-year-olds was 27, a score significantly higher than the one for 13-year-olds, 24. Since a lower score indicates less difficulty, it appears that problems decrease with age, but the difference is still within one standard deviation, which is roughly 4, suggesting much overlap. Sex differences also appear, with boys scoring slightly higher (25.2) than girls (24.8) but again, the overlap is very great. The correlation between subscales is quite low, ranging from .01 to .19. Social difficulties (the S score) appear to have the largest influence on the total score, the correlation being .65. No correlation is given with measures of school ability or intelligence, and apparently there have been no studies of application of the RPAI to clinical populations. Earlier publications about the original Rogers test would seem to have dubious applicability because of the rather low correlation between it and the new test.

Critique

When I did a review of the earlier Personal Adjustment Inventory for *The Sixth Mental Measurements Yearbook* (Buros, 1965), I was impressed with the clinical sensitivity shown in the test, as other reviewers were, and I sent a copy of my review to Carl Rogers. I wrote that it was a shame that such an interesting procedure had not been updated and improved. He wrote back encouraging me or someone else to do just that. I am very pleased that Patricia Jeffrey has undertaken that project; it was a test that deserved professional attention. The combination of objective and open-ended, projective, verbal responses on the RPAI makes it richly amenable to clinical usage. It also is of interest to children and simple to administer and score. It, of course, needs to be supplemented by other kinds of tests for children, and its relations with many other tests of children need to be explored.

Certainly, the RPAI is much better than the original. The total score reliability is good, though the subscales tend to be less consistent. The validity is unclear, though Jeffrey's reports suggest positive results of a moderate nature. The test is too recently published to provide the needed studies by other people in other places. One big question is whether this British revision with Scottish data will hold up well on the return trip across the Atlantic. There are a few terms like "postman," "mum" (for mother), and "desert island" that are not now commonly used in America. I suspect that the reading level will be difficult for the average American third-grader, though Jeffrey checked readability in Scotland. There are also some ticklish questions from the standpoint of many American parents; in one section, children are asked to rank their liking for their parents and others— "Who (*sic*) do you love the most?" Some parents might see that kind of question as an invasion of privacy.

The RPAI has other limitations. There is no report on correlations with intelligence and many other tests to elucidate convergent and discriminant validity. It probably is quite fakable by a bright and suspicious child. Unfortunately, item anlyses and factor analyses were not done, and it may be that items do not group together to achieve what the test developers wanted. The scoring involves an acceptance of Rogers' 1931 judgments as to the meaning of the items. The test also has limited coverage of clinical problems. There is no investigation of important questions like drug usage, conduct problems, child abuse, and boredom and discouragement with school, etc. It would be interesting, too, to have cases presented in the manual which might relate to realistic school and clinical problems and suggest questions about the environment and conditions and treatment of the children.

The RPAI is a "born again" test, and we need to have a lot more information on it before we will know if it follows a "straight" path toward helping in psychological work. It should be used with caution in clinical settings and only in conjunction with other familiar tests until more research and experience are available.

References

Buros, O. K. (Ed.). (1965). *The sixth mental measurements yearbook*. Highland Park, NJ: The Gryphon Press.

Jeffrey, P. (1984). *Rogers Personal Adjustment Inventory: Revised*. Windsor, England: NFER-Nelson Publishing Company Ltd.

Barbara B. Schoenfeldt, Ph.D.
Assistant Professor of Education, Sul Ross State University, Uvalde Study Center, Uvalde, Texas.

ROSWELL-CHALL DIAGNOSTIC READING TEST OF WORD ANALYSIS SKILLS: REVISED AND EXTENDED

Florence G. Roswell and Jeanne S. Chall. La Jolla, California: Essay Press, Inc.

Introduction

The Roswell-Chall Diagnostic Reading Test of Word Analysis Skills: Revised and Extended (RCDRT) is a short, individually administered, standardized test of fundamental phonic (decoding) and word recognition skills. It is designed for children or adults reading at approximately first- to sixth-grade levels and is available in two forms for test-retest purposes. The skills measured include:

1) sight-word recognition of high frequency words;

2) ability to name the sounds of all the single consonants (except for q and x);

3) naming the sound of three different consonant digraphs presented in isolation;

4) the ability to pronounce nine consonant blends presented in words;

5) pronunciation of the short vowel sounds presented in consonant-vowel-consonant (CVC) words;

6) short and long vowel sounds in isolation;

7) the silent e rule;

8) vowel digraphs presented in words;

9) diphthongs and r controlled vowels in words;

10) ability to read (decode) eight multisyllabic and compound words;

11) naming of 14 capital and 19 lower case letters;

12) spelling (encoding) of the first consonant heard in an orally presented word; and

13) encoding of five phonically regular CVC words.

The RCDRT can be scored by using quantitative criteria to determine instructional need (as a criterion referenced test) or by comparison with the standardization sample (pupils in Grades 1-4 at the beginning of the school year). The latter procedure allows one to estimate whether pupil or class scores are "at," "above," or "below" average for grade placement on various skills.

The authors of the RCDRT are renowned and highly experienced in the fields of reading education and reading disability. They are both authors of well known texts (Chall, 1967; Roswell & Natchez, 1977). Roswell is Professor Emeritus of City College, CUNY, and Chall is a professor at Harvard University.

The selection of both the test items and their order of presentation was based on their inclusion and order of presentation in most of the widely used basal reading programs, as well as the wide clinical experience of both authors. The standardization results of the original Roswell-Chall Test (1959) indicated that the order of the subtests corresponded to their difficulty level.

The RCDRT was first published in 1959, with reliability and validity data cited in an article by Chall (1958). Although the original test was widely used in classrooms, reading centers, and research, it was revised in 1978 to further improve it (Roswell & Chall, 1978). A technical supplement (Roswell & Chall, 1979) is also available for the revised and extended revision.

The changes include a sight word test to add information regarding "sight recognition of high frequency words and as a means of comparison with the subtests which assess knowledge of phonic elements and skills in decoding and encoding" (Roswell & Chall, 1978, p. 10). Other changes on the test include an extended evaluation section. Two of the new tests permit testing on a lower skill level than the original edition (i.e., Naming Capital Letters and Naming Lower Case Letters). The subtests of Encoding of Single Consonants and Encoding Phonically Regular CVC Word tests were also added to provide additional information about the pupils' ability to apply their phonic knowledge. All four of the subtests are given only to those students who meet, or fail to meet, specified criterion the first part of the test. The other changes in the new edition were described as relatively minor, involving some separation of subtest sections and a different format on the Consonant Blends task.

The RCDRT consists of a four-page, 8 1/2" x 11" paper record booklet. The booklet has three pages of test items and a summary of results page. A separate manual is available. Both the test and the manual are printed in light blue. During testing the student is given a copy of the record booklet to read and all the results are recorded on another. Reading items from the test booklet may be a problem for younger students who are apt to find the print difficult to read and the format distracting because of the large number of words on each page. To correct this the words for each section could be rewritten on cards.

The examiner is directly responsible for both administering the test and determining sections to be included or excluded. The first two parts of the test instructs students to read the words or letter sounds; the last two parts require students to write either the letter representing the first sound heard in a word or to spell a word. Several of the subtests include directions to discontinue after a certain number of errors, but some hints (e.g., how to pronounce the multisyllable words) to students and the quick teaching of some skills (e.g., the rule of silent *e*) are permitted. Unless evidence is needed for test-retest assessment purposes the manual suggests that testing be stopped at the point where the examiner determines the student's need for help in a particular area.

The RCDRT covers many of the word analysis skills taught in the grades 1-4. The test can be used for any student whose reading ability is fourth-grade level or below or whose skills in decoding or basic word recognition are suspect.

The Words section consists of 35 familiar high frequency words, with a graded difficulty level of preprimer to third grade. The words selected were based on their inclusion on widely used word lists. Seventy high-frequency and largely phonically irregular words were identified as being on the preprimer to third-grade level, they were then randomly assigned by level to the two forms, the purpose of this subtest being to determine whether a sample of frequently used words in print can be read at sight.

The first-grade level subtests measure the ability to give the regular phonetic sounds of 1a, 19 consonant letters including the two sound values for *c* and *g*; 1b, three consonant digraphs; and 1c, 12 consonant blends. Only part 1c presents the letters to be sounded in words. Although 15 consonant blends and digraphs are presented, many equally important consonant combinations, such as *wh*, *bl*, *tr*, and *sm*, are omitted.

The second- and third-grade level subtests assess knowledge of vowel sounds and vowel-sounding rules. They include 2a, the five short vowel sounds presented in words; 2b, the short and long vowel sounds presented in isolation; 2c, the rule of silent e presented as pairs of words with and without a silent e; 3a, regular vowel digraphs (first vowel, long; second vowel, silent); and 3b, common diphthongs, r controlled vowels, and the /au/ sound. Except for 2b all sounds are presented in real words so that a child with a large reading vocabulary can pronounce all the words correctly without knowing either the sounds or the rules.

The fourth-grade level subtest, Syllabication and Compound Words, consists of eight rather difficult multisyllabic words. The student is instructed to divide each word into its syllables and sound it out if he cannot recognize the word immediately. However, division of the word into syllables is not required for the item to be considered correct. If the purpose of this section is to determine how the child attacks unknown words, it is only effective with children who do not already know the words presented.

The Extended Evaluation section has four parts, at least one of which is given to all students. The first part (W), Letter Names, given only if the child scores 10 or less on subtest 1a, Single Consonant Sounds. It requires the child to read the 14 capital letters that are "appreciably different from their lower case forms." The second part (X) requires the child to name 19 lower case letters. The third part (Y), Encoding Single Consonants, is for students scoring 11 or above on test 1a, Consonant Sounds. The students are given the examiner's test booklet and instructed to write or print the letter that represents the first sound heard in 14 dictated words. The fourth part (Z), Encoding Phonically Regular CVC words, is given only to students who score 11 or above on test 1a and five or higher on 2a, Short Vowel Sounds. The words are dictated, along with a short sentence containing each word. The students write their answers on the test booklet. The last two sections are included to determine if students can apply their phonic skills. Because some very easy real words are used children who have had practice with spelling them could obtain perfect scores without needing to apply any phonic knowledge.

All answers are recorded on the test form/record booklet. The fourth page includes space for identifying data, a summary of results table for raw scores of each subtest, and an instructional needs interpretation (mastered, review indicated, or systematic instruction indicated), as well as two lines which can be used to write remarks.

Practical Applications/Uses

The RCDRT is intended for use in the classroom and in the reading clinic. It is designed to give estimates of a student's strengths and weaknesses on beginning-level word analysis skills. It can be used to help develop appropriate instructional programs, as well as for assessing program effectiveness (using the two forms for test-retest purposes). The authors also suggest it can be used for research purposes by comparing individual subtests with other tests. Besides the instructional interpretation, tests scores may be compared to the standardization sample to determine relative standing to a comparable normative group. Educational diagnosticians, school psychologists, learning disability and remedial reading teachers, and classroom teachers could use the test results for diagnosis and educational planning. Researchers may be able to take advantage of the standardized nature of the test.

The RCDRT is appropriate for students with word recognition skills between first- and fourth-grade levels. It can be used to test either developmental or remedial students. As there is no age limit on its use and its design is not juvenile, the RCDRT would be appropriate for diagnoses of older remedial students on their word recognition skills. However, older students are more apt to know the words used on the test than are the younger children.

The RCDRT must be individually administered. No special training is required for examiners familiar with word analysis skills. According to the manual, the test requires only those examiner skills needed in most individual testing situations.

Both the testing manual and directions for administration are easy to follow. The major deficiency in the manual is that there is no phonetic sound key. Persons who are not reading experts, therefore, might have difficulty scoring letters presented in isolation and in marking errors with their phonetic equivalents.

Instructions for scoring are clear, and a professional should only take several minutes to learn how to score the test. All scoring is done by hand, but once mastered, scoring should take less than five minutes per test. Scoring involves counting correct responses on each subtest, placing this number on the test booklet, and then determining instructional need level by use of criteria, which is based on the percentage of correct items. These criteria are 1) Mastered—86%; Review Indicated—50-85%; and Systematic Instruction Indicated—0%-49%. No overall score or reading level can be obtained. Separate tables are required to compare the obtained raw scores on each subtest with an appropriate normative group. There is, however, no designated place to put this information.

Although interpretation of the RCDRT is based on objective scores, the criteria set for determining instructional needs have been subjectively determined. The scores can also be interpreted in terms of the standardization sample, although this information has little if any practical utility. When interpreting the test results one must also keep in mind that for some of the students (especially older ones) the scores obtained may be falsely exaggerated.

Technical Aspects

The RCDRT has better evidence of validity and reliability then most tests of its type. Three types of reliability were established. The first was alternative form reliability. The correlations obtained were extremely high (.89 to .99) for most of the subtests when all items were combined. Thus, one form of the test may be used in place of the other or as a pretest and posttest.

Test-retest reliability was also established for both forms of the test. The correlations were also very high (.94 to .99 for all items combined), indicating that either form of the test is apt to yield similar scores if readministered after a relatively short interval. The third form of reliability assessed was Alpha. The results indicated that the internal consistency of the test was very high (.98) and that, therefore, the test was measuring a common trait.

The validity of the RCDRT was analyzed by comparing it to related tests. First-grade correlations indicated a positive relationship (.50 to .70) with the Metropolitan Readiness Test (Hildreth, Griffiths, & McGanvran, 1964) and high correlations (.66 to .79) were found for the second- and third-grade populations between the RCDRT and the Metropolitan Achievement Test (Durost et al., 1971). Lower fourth-grade correlations were explained as the result of the low variance of scores in that group (95% of the items were correctly answered by the fourth-graders). The correlations of the clinic population scores to some of the achievement test sections and to the total reading score tended to be even higher than some of the school population correlations (especially for fourth-graders). This is probably because the RCDRT would tend to be more difficult for remedial students (and therefore have more variance). The correlations between the Gray Oral Reading Test (Gray, 1967) scores and the RCDRT scores were even higher than that of the achievement tests (.64 to .88). This can be explained by the fact that the Gray, like the RCDRT, requires word recognition and analysis.

The normative sample of the revised edition consisted of two different populations. The first was a school population drawn from a medium-sized, northeastern, suburban school district. This sample included 203 students in grades 1-4. The average age was from 6-4 years in Grade 1 to 9-4 years in Grade 4. A clinical group of 46 children was the second population. It was drawn from the reading clinics of two northeastern universities. The age range of this group was from 7-0 years to 19-8 years and the grade placement was from 2.2 to 10.2. All testing for both populations was done at the beginning of the school year.

The school population was found to be, on the average, at the appropriate grade placement for their age. The IQs were average to slightly above average. While both the silent reading and spelling abilities of this group were slightly above average, their oral reading level was average. The clinic population, in comparison with the school population, had a wider range in age, IQ, and reading ability. While their mean IQ was normal, they had average silent reading, oral reading, and spelling scores of from one to two years below their mean grade placement.

Critique

Aaron (1965), in a review of the original version of the RCDRT, stated that the use of this "test alone gives insufficient information to evaluate effectively the word recognition skills of a child" (p. 1116). His major concern was the fact the ''only way to check functional use of word attack skills is to confront children with unknown words'' (p. 1117), but that many of the words on the test are likely to be known by most of the children taking the test.

Betts (1965) felt that the RCDRT ''suffers in comparison with both extant inventories and tests of word perception skills offered by publishers of basic textbooks in reading, and teacher-made informal inventories of phonic skills recommended by authors of textbooks on method'' (p. 1117).

The RCDRT can accurately diagnose a students knowledge of word attack skills. However, classroom and remedial reading teachers have many other standardized and informal (teacher-made) tests that could do just as well if not a better job. These tests could provide information on a wider range of phonic skills then the RCDRT and provide it more validity by using nonsense (made-up) syllables instead of real words.

The other problems connected with using the RCDRT include the type color, the fact that students must read from the protocol, and that there is no phonic key. It is therefore recommended that the items to be read by the children be copied on separate cards for each subtest, and a phonic key be provided for those requiring it.

The RCDRT may be most valuable when it is used as a standardized test. It has, however, a fairly low ceiling so that it would have limited use for test-retest purposes for older or more advanced students who are likely to score near the upper range of the test. Although the RCDRT has more evidence for its reliability and validity than many of its comparable counterparts, comparing individual subtests to other similar tests (as suggested in the manual) might be questionable in light of the small number of items and low reliability of many of the subtests.

The standardization data allows one to estimate whether a pupil or class score is at, above, or below average for grade placement. This information, however, is obtainable in many other more useable ways (with more comprehensive tests), and it has no practical value for the teacher or clinic in terms of providing appropriate treatment.

In summary, the RCDRT has little to recommend it over teacher-made tests in a classroom or clinic setting. Its high reliability and validity indicate that the RCDRT might be appropriately used as a short, easy to administer, standardized diagnostic test for research uses if its deficiencies (use of real words, failure to include several important word analysis skills, etc.) are kept in mind.

References

Aaron, I. E. (1965). Review of Roswell-Chall Diagnostic Reading Test of Word Analysis Skills. In O. K. Buros (Ed.), *The sixth mental measurements yearbook* (pp. 1116-1117). Highland Park, NJ: The Gryphon Press.

Betts, E. A. (1965). Review of Roswell-Chall Diagnostic Reading Test of Word Analysis Skills. In O. K. Buros (Ed.), *The sixth mental measurements yearbook* (p. 1117). Highland Park, NJ: The Gryphon Press.

Chall, J. S. (1958). The Roswell-Chall Diagnostic Reading Test of Word Analysis Skills: Evidence of reliability and validity. *The Reading Teacher*, 2, 179-183.

Chall, J. S. (1967). *Learning to read: The great debate*. New York: McGraw-Hill.

Durost, W., Bixler, H., Wrightstone, J., Prescott, G., & Balow, I. (1971). *Metropolitan Achievement Tests, Primary I.* New York: Harcourt Brace Jovanovich.

Gray, W. S. (1967). *Gray Oral Reading Test.* Indianapolis: Bobbs-Merrill.

Hildreth, G., Griffiths, M. A., & McGanvran, M. (1964). *Metropolitan Readiness Test.* New York: Harcourt Brace Jovanovich.

Roswell, F. G., & Chall, J. S. (1959). *Diagnostic Reading Test of Word Analysis Skills.* La Jolla, CA: Essay Press.

Roswell, F. G., & Chall, J. S. (1978). *Roswell-Chall Diagnostic Reading Test of Word Analysis Skills: Revised and Extended.* La Jolla, CA: Essay Press.

Roswell, F. G., & Chall, J. S. (1979). *Technical supplement: Roswell-Chall Diagnostic Reading Test of Word Analysis Skills: Revised and Extended.* La Jolla, CA: Essay Press.

Roswell, F. G., & Natchez, G. (1977). *Reading disability: A human approach to learning.* New York: Basic Books.

Merith Cosden, Ph.D.
Special Education Program, Graduate School of Education, University of California-Santa Barbara, Santa Barbara, California.

ROTTER INCOMPLETE SENTENCES BLANK

Julian B. Rotter. Cleveland, Ohio: The Psychological Corporation.

Introduction

The Rotter Incomplete Sentences Blank (RISB) is a projective test in which examinees are asked to complete forty sentence "stems" to create statements that reflect their feelings about themselves and others. The test is designed for use with adolescents and adults. Unlike many other sentence completion tasks the RISB has both qualitative and quantitative scoring procedures, with the goal of assessing the types of stressors and level of adjustment experienced and reported by the examinee.

The RISB was revised from a form that was used by Rotter and Willerman in the army and that had been a revision of a variety of then extant sentence completion blanks (Rotter & Rafferty, 1950). The RISB was designed to provide specific "projective" information while also being economical to administer and score. Rotter and Rafferty intended the instrument to serve a purpose similar to that of a lengthy structured interview. Although the major function of the test was not seen as "exposing" deep layers of personality, the test is frequently used to obtain information which examiners feel could not be as well obtained through direct interview.

Three similar RISB forms—High School, College, and Adult—have been developed. These forms can be objectively scored by assigning an empirically derived numerical value to each completed sentence. Responses are scaled on the basis of the level of conflict or adjustment reflected in each statement. The test can also be subjectively interpreted through qualitative analysis of the needs and dynamics projected into the subjects responses.

Practical Applications/Uses

The RISB, like other sentence completion forms, is a projective test that is structured to identify areas of personal adjustment and maladjustment. By placing some "distance" between the examinee and the examiner the test format allows the examinee to respond more freely than might be expected through direct interview. At the same time, the structure of the test, i.e., its direct inquiry into different areas of functioning, makes it possible for the examiner to use test responses at face value and rapidly develop at least a surface understanding of some of the psychological issues facing the individual.

Unlike many other sentence completion tests, the RISB has a standardized scoring system that allows the examiner to synthesize responses and assess the general level of adjustment presented by the individual. Thus, the RISB provides an efficient method for obtaining information about the individual's adjustment. This method of assessment allows the individual to respond rather directly to specific issues while eliciting more projective material than would be expected through direct interview.

This test, frequently used with adult clients in the early stages of an assessment, was found in a 1961 review of clinical assessments (Sundberg, 1961) to be the 13th most frequently used clinical test instrument and the 2nd most used test for group personality instruments. It is popular partly because it can be easily administered and quickly interpreted at "face value" as well as through more in-depth analysis of dynamic patterns.

Although many see the purpose of the test as serving as a projective device for gathering information that could not be as well obtained through direct interview, there have been questions raised about the level of projective information obtained through sentence completion methods. The RISB provides a relatively direct type of inquiry in comparison to other projective devices. Further, there is empirical evidence to suggest that individuals respond in a qualitatively different manner to this type of test than to a less structured projective test, such as the Thematic Apperception Test (TAT). Newmark and Hetzel (1974), for example, found that subjects experienced significantly greater levels of state anxiety after unstructured tests such as the Rorschach and TAT than after more structured tests like the RISB or Minnesota Multiphasic Personality Inventory (MMPI). Additionally, Murstein and Wolf (1970), in a study of the effects of different "levels" of stimulus structure, found the predicted inverse relationship between pathology and stimulus structure for normal subjects but not for psychiatric subjects using the RISB as an example of a relatively structured projective measure. This study suggests that, at least for normal subjects, less pathology would be expected to emerge on the RISB than on more unstructured projective tests, while psychiatric subjects could be expected to project as much pathological material on this type of test as on other projective devices.

Related to the issue of the "depth" of the projective information elicited by this test is the question of whether subjects' responses reflect conscious or unconscious processes and whether or not subjects can control their responses. Of specific concern is the extent to which responses reflect the underlying needs and dynamics of individuals, or the conscious attempts of the individuals to present themselves in a given manner. Clinical criticisms of this type of test describe the more conscious response process tapped by this procedure, arguing that this same information could be obtained through direct interview. Goldberg (1965), however, in his review of sentence completion tests, notes that the reliability and validity of test information inversely varies with the depth of level of the assessment. Thus, although the RISB might provide less projective information than other types of projective devices, the reliability and validity of that information can be viewed as more stable.

The RISB can be administered to any size group of examinees. The instructions are simple, i.e., the examiner asks the subjects to respond to all items, to express their real feelings, and to make complete sentences. The examiner is advised not to present the sentence stems in any but the designated format as this would disrupt use of the standardized scoring system. Altering the response context by increasing the space provided to complete sentences, for example, would prohibit the effective use of that part of the scoring system which differentiates unusually long responses from other responses. Studies have noted that changing the complexity or structure of sentence stems can have a significant effect on subject responses (Cromwell & Lundy, 1965, Turnbow & Dana, 1981). Other factors being equal, Meltzoff (1951) reported that the tone of instructions as well as the stimuli can have a strong impact on responses. Although the emotional tone of the instructions may have a significant impact, emphasizing speed (Cromwell et al., 1965) or administering items verbally (Flynn, 1974) have not been found to alter written output.

Test administration itself requires little experience or training. The test can be administered in approximately thirty minutes but is self-paced and there is no time limit.

The scoring systems for all three forms of the RISB are based on the scaled responses of college freshmen used to develop the Incomplete Sentences Blank-College Form. Although this form was later adapted to create the High School and Adult Forms through modification of the wording of certain RISB stems to make them more appropriate for their target populations, no additional normative data were collected. The manual places the responsibility on "competent clinical workers" to make the necessary transitions to appropriately use the college school scoring system with high school and adult populations. Given the broad nature of the questions, however, there is at least strong "face validity" to utilizing the scoring system with all three populations.

The information obtained through sentence completions can be summarized or "reduced" for purposes of interpretation through both qualitative and quantitative procedures. Both approaches are detailed, with case examples, in the manual. (Rotter & Rafferty, 1950, pp. 14-50).

In the objective scoring system each completed sentence receives an "adjustment" score. To obtain this score, the examiner assigns each sentence one of four possible categorical codes: 1) omission (no response after the sentence stem or a response too short to provide a meaningful sentence), 2) conflict response (a response that reflects hostility or unhappiness), 3) positive response (a statement which reflects positive or hopeful attitudes), or 4) neutral response (a simple declarative statement which does not imply either a positive or negative affect). Both conflict and positive statements are given a weight (1-3) that reflects the degree of sentiment expressed by the response. The manual provides examples for each scoring category, with responses for men and women listed separately.

Each code is scaled from 0-6, with higher values given to more negative responses. A summative adjustment score with a possible range of 0-240 is obtained in this manner. The average adjustment score reported in the manual is 127 with a standard deviation of 14. A cutoff score of 135 is frequently used to differentiate subjects who are "maladjusted" (i.e., in need of psychotherapy) from those who are well adjusted. The effectiveness of this cutoff score is discussed in the Technical Aspects section of this review.

The coding system is relatively simple, with a limited number of exclusive categories to be considered. Nevertheless, wide response variations are anticipated on a projective test of this sort, mandating reliance on the manual and its coding exemplars to ensure high reliability. The manual does not state the time needed for scoring each protocol but this reviewer has found the scoring time to be approximately 45 minutes depending on the length and complexity of the protocol.

A comprehensive but dated review of sentence completion forms by Goldberg (1965) notes that the two distinguishing characteristics of the RISB are its quantified scoring system and its single variable method of analysis. Test interpretation based on quantitative analysis of the level of adjustment reflected in one's responses is fairly straightforward. Each statement is scored and summed to provide a measure of that individual's overall adjustment. This system is touted by investigators both as the test's strength, i.e., it provides an efficient and reliable manner for interpreting test scores, and as its weakness, i.e., it limits the scope and depth of test interpretation to one variable. Goldberg summarizes these findings by concluding that the RISB sacrifices scope for efficiency in its scoring system.

Other methods for coding the RISB have been explored with some success. Rogers (1978) conducted a computerized content analysis of the words used in the RISB. Using five content categories, he was able to predict more accurately certain types of deviant behaviors than was possible with regular RISB scores. Albert (1970), on the other hand, tested a method for scoring response differences in the RISB over time. He was able to show that difference scores in this system predicted therapeutic gains. Neither of these models, however, have been advanced in the literature.

Qualitative analysis of subject responses, although allowing for a greater range and scope of interpretations, relies solely on the clinical expertise and knowledge of the test user for its reliability and validity. The manual suggests content analysis of the RISB in a manner similar to that utilized in analyzing the TAT. This procedure carries with it the problems found in all subjective analyses of projective materials, i.e., questionable reliability and validity of test interpretations. While little research has been conducted to validate the use of this type of interpretive procedure, Starr and Katkin (1969) found that subjective interpretation of the RISB was subject to the same "illusory correlations" between responses and patient symptoms as were other projective devices. That is, test users are likely to posit stronger relationships between certain types of statements on the RISB and behavior patterns than is warranted by observations of these relationships.

Technical Aspects

Reported reliability coefficients for the RISB are high. In the normative sample, Rotter, Rafferty, and Schachtitz (1965) reported interscorer reliabilities of .96 for the women tested in their sample and .91 for the men. Split-half reliability coefficients were found to be .83 for women and .84 for men. Although these reliability coefficients were obtained from researchers trained by the test developers, other investigators have reported similar high reliabilities. Churchill and Crandall (1965), for example, found interscorer reliabilities of .94 to .95 using assistants with minimal psychological expertise who were trained using the manual. While Lah and Rotter (1981) continue to report high interrater reliabilities, they also note that current student scores differ significantly from those obtained in the initial sample.

A number of studies have assessed the validity of the RISB as a screening device using a "maladjustment" cutoff score. A cutoff score of 135 has been found to correctly identify delinquent youths 60% of the time while screening nondelinquent youths correctly 73% of the time (Fuller, Parmelee, & Carroll, 1982); to identify students scoring low in manifest anxiety defenses 86% of the time and pinpoint those high in defenses 75% of the time (Milliment, 1972); to identify students in counseling 54-66% of the time and differentiate those not in counseling 64% of the time (Churchill et al., 1965); and to identify severe drug users 80-100% of the time (Gardner, 1967). These validation studies suggest that the maladjustment cutoff score does successfully screen those in crisis from those not in crisis on more than a chance basis, but the screen may not be sufficiently high to utilize alone without fear of missing too many other individuals in need of psychological help.

The subjects in the above studies had been identified in need of services prior to administration of the RISB, with the RISB administered to test its effectiveness in detecting their problems. The RISB has also been used to evaluate stresses when this information was not immediately available through other sources. Scores on the RISB have been shown to correlate with the level of difficulty experienced by individuals going through new vocational experiences during mid-life career changes (Vaitenas & Wiener, 1977). The RISB has also been successful in identifying depression in adult clients even when depression was not initially evident in overt behaviors (Robbins, 1974). There have been moderate correlations found between RISB scores and both anxiety (Richardson & Soucar, 1971), and disparities in one's self-image (De Mann, 1983). The RISB has also been used to identify students with high levels of physical complaints as measured by utilization of medical facilities (Getter & Weiss, 1968).

The RISB has been used to assess a wide range of anxiety and depressive disorders. It does not, however, appear effective in assessing psychological adjustment over short periods of time as measured by pre- and post-test differences (e.g., Krouse & Krouse, 1981; Rosenheim & Dunn, 1977). Albert (1970) found significant adjustment differences as a function of therapeutic progress on pre- and post-test RISB administrations using his own scoring system. The RISB has also had equivocal results in screening for drug use, with only heavy drug users scoring significantly in the maladjusted range (Cross & Davis, 1972; Gardner, 1967; Pascale, Hurd, & Primavera, 1980).

The validity of the RISB as an adjustment index has been questioned by some on the basis of its high loading on social desirability. Some investigators (e.g., Janda & Galbraith, 1973) feel that adjustment scores may reflect awareness of socially desirable responses rather than a lack of disorder. Janda and Galbraith argue that the high correlations between the social desirability of responses and their adjustment scores confound the direct interpretation of the RISB. Other investigators

(Banikiotes, Russell, & Linden, 1971; McCarthy & Rafferty, 1971), however, report low to moderate linear relationships between social desirability and adjustment as measured by the RISB. These investigators do not believe that adjustment scores on the RISB can be as easily interpreted as social desirability scores; rather, they posit a more limited and complex relationship between social desirability and adjustment, acknowledging that some stems on the RISB tap self-concept that, in turn, is related to social desirability.

Critique

The RISB is a relatively structured projective instrument designed for use with high school and college students and adults. It differs from other incomplete sentence blanks in that it allows both qualitative and quantitative assessment of responses. This assessment provides information on the types of stressors and level of adjustment experienced and reported by the individual. The extent to which this test taps conscious processes (i.e., attempts of the individual to provide the investigator with certain types of information) or unconscious processes (i.e., underlying needs and dynamics that the individual is not aware of expressing) is yet unclear.

As discussed by Goldberg (1965), it is the structure of the test that is both the test's strength and weakness. On the one hand, the test provides a relatively fast, efficient method for obtaining direct information on how individuals are functioning in many different aspects of their lives. Use of the empirical scoring system further allows the examiner to quickly synthesize information and obtain a picture of how well the individual is functioning overall. By the same token, this type of format may not provide the same sort of rich information obtained through other projective techniques. For some subjects it may not provide much more information than would be obtained through direct interview. Further, to the extent that this information reflects the conscious processes of the individual it is subject to the same types of bias as other self-report measures, and interpretation has to take into consideration what the individual wants the examiner to know.

The RISB is probably most effective in the early stages of an assessment with adults who are either having a difficult time defining their problems or who need some minimal distance from the examiner in order to express themselves more openly. In this way, the test can be used to help clarify for the examiner the specific areas in which individuals are feeling stressed as well as indicate the general extent of their problems and their level of adjustment.

References

Albert, G. (1970). Sentence completions as a measure of progress in therapy. *Journal of Contemporary Psychology, 3,* 31-34.

Banikiotes, P. G., Russell, J. M., & Linden J. D. (1971). Social desirability, adjustment and effectiveness. *Psychological Reports, 29,* 581-582.

Churchill, R., & Crandall, V. J. (1965). The reliability and validity of the Rotter Incomplete Sentences Test. In B.I. Murstein (Ed.), *Handbook of Projective Techniques* (pp. 873-882). New York: Basic Books.

Cromwell, R. L., & Lundy, R. M. (1965). Productivity of clinical hypothesis on a sentence completion test. In B.I. Murstein (Ed.), *Handbook of projective techniques* (pp. 883-890). New York: Basic Books.

Cross, H., & Davis, G. (1972). College students' adjustment and frequency of marijuana use. *Journal of Counseling Psychology, 19*, 65-67.

De Man, A. F. (1983). Self image disparity and adjustment in young adult females. *Psychological Reports, 52*, 78.

Flynn, W. (1974). Oral vs. written administration of the incomplete sentences blank. *Newsletter for Research in Mental Health and Behavioral Sciences, 16*, 19-20.

Fuller, G. B., Parmelee, W. M., & Carroll, J. L. (1982). Performance of delinquent and nondelinquent high school boys on the Rotter Incomplete Sentence Blank. *Journal of Personality Assessment, 46*, 506-510.

Gardner, J. (1967). The adjustment of drug addicts as measured by the sentence completion test. *Journal of Projective Techniques and Personality Assessment, 31*, 28-29.

Getter, H., & Weiss, S. (1968). The Rotter Incomplete Sentences Blank adjustment score as an indicator of somatic complaint frequency. *Journal of Projective Techniques and Personality Assessment, 32*, 266.

Goldberg, P. (1965). A review of sentence completion methods in personality assessment. In B.I. Murstein (Ed.), *Handbook of projective techniques* (pp. 777-822). New York: Basic Books.

Janda, L., & Galbraith, G. (1973). Social desirability and adjustment in the Rotter Incomplete Sentences Blank. *Journal of Consulting and Clinical Psychology, 40*, 337.

Krouse, H. J., & Krouse, J. H. (1981). Psychological factors in postmastectomy adjustment. *Psychological Reports, 48*, 275-278.

Lah, M. I., & Rotter, J. B. (1981). Changing college student norms on the Rotter Incomplete Sentences Blank. *Journal of Consulting and Clinical Psychology, 49*, 985.

McCarthy, B. W., & Rafferty, J. E. (1971). Effect of social desirability and self-concept scores on the measurement of adjustment. *Journal of Personality Assessment, 35*, 576-583.

Meltzoff, J. (1951). The effect of mental set and item structure upon response to a projective test. *Journal of Abnormal and Social Psychology, 46*, 177-189.

Milliment, R. (1972). Support for a maladjustment interpretation of the anxiety-defensiveness dimension. *Journal of Personality Assessment, 36*, 39-44.

Murstein, B., & Wolf, S. (1970). Empirical test of the "levels" hypothesis with five projective techniques. *Journal of Abnormal Psychology, 75*, 38-44.

Newmark, C., & Hetzel, W. (1974). The effects of personality tests on state and trait anxiety. *Journal of Personality Assessment, 38*, 17-20.

Pascale, R., Hurd, M., & Primavera, L. (1980). The effects of chronic marijuana use. *Journal of Social Psychology, 110*, 273-283.

Richardson, L., & Soucar, E. (1971). Comparison of cognitive complexity with achievement and adjustment: a convergent-discriminant study. *Psychological Reports, 29*, 1087-1090.

Robbins, P. R. (1974). Depression and drug addiction. *Psychiatric Quarterly, 48*, 374-386.

Rogers, G. (1978). Content analysis of the Rotter Incomplete Sentences Blank and the Prediction of Behavior Ratings. *Educational and Psychological Measurement, 38*, 1135-1141.

Rosenheim, H. D., & Dunn, R. W. (1977). The effects of rational behavior therapy in a military population. *Military Medicine, 142*, 550-552.

Rotter, J. B., & Rafferty, J. E. (1950). *Manual for the Rotter Incomplete Sentences Blank: College Form.* New York: The Psychological Corporation.

Rotter, J. B., Rafferty, J. E., & Schachtitz, E. (1965). Validation of the Rotter Incomplete Sentences Test. In B.I. Murstein (Ed.), *Handbook of Projective Techniques* (pp. 859-872). New York: Basic Books.

Starr, B. J., & Katkin, E. S. (1969). The clinician as an aberrant actuary: illusory correlation and the incomplete sentences blank. *Journal of Abnormal Psychology, 74*, 670-675.

Sundberg, N. D. (1961). The practice of psychological testing in clinical services in the United States. *American Psychologist, 16,* 79-83.

Turnbow, K, & Dana, R. (1981). The effects of stem length and directions on sentence completion. *Journal of Personality Assessment, 45,* 27-32.

Vaitenas, R., & Wiener, Y. (1977). Developmental, emotional, and interest factors in voluntary mid-career change. *Journal of Vocational Behavior, 11,* 291-304.

Howard Tennen, Ph.D.
Associate Professor of Psychiatry, University of Connecticut School of Medicine, Farmington, Connecticut.

Glenn Affleck, Ph.D.
Associate Professor of Psychiatry, University of Connecticut School of Medicine, Farmington, Connecticut.

Sharon Herzberger, Ph.D.
Associate Professor of Psychology, Trinity College, Hartford, Connecticut.

SCHEDULE OF RECENT EXPERIENCE

Thomas H. Holmes. Seattle, Washington: University of Washington Press.

Introduction

The Schedule of Recent Experience (SRE) is a questionnaire designed to assess the occurrence and frequency of 42 stress-producing events within a given time period of a person's life. Included in the questionnaire are desirable and undesirable events that involve change in one's life circumstances and lead to adaptive behavior. The SRE is most frequently used as a self-report measure, but it can be completed by others on behalf of an individual (by a spouse or parent, for example). It can also be used in conjunction with a structured interview with an interviewer soliciting the desired information.

The SRE was developed by Thomas Holmes, who is a physician at the Department of Psychiatry and Behavioral Sciences at the University of Washington School of Medicine. The instrument evolved from Adolf Meyer's Life Chart (1919), which catalogued biological, psychological, and sociological events, the individual's emotional response to the events, and their relationship to illness. Events selected for the SRE preceded the onset of illness or other clinical symptoms. The events could be termed "stressful," although the meaning of each event varies from person to person, and some events would be considered positive by most people. Nonetheless, each event indicated a change in life circumstances and necessitated adaptation.

Previous versions of the SRE required respondents to note whether some of the events occurred at all within a given time period; the present version requests frequencies of each event. Earlier versions also summed the number of life changes. The current version allows more precise measurement of stress-pro-

---

Special thanks to Juanita Pike of University of Washington Press for her assistance in preparing resource material.

duced change by weighing each event by the estimated amount of change and adaptation required. Specific predictions about the likelihood of incurring illness or other changes in health were derived using samples of physicians and medical students (Holmes, 1970; Rahe, 1969). Those who experienced more frequent and more severe life changes were more likely to experience illness during the following one- or two-year interval.

The SRE consists of 42 simply described events (e.g., "trouble with in-laws," "death of a close friend," "major change in working hours or conditions"). The events cover positive and negative changes in one's own life situation (e.g., "outstanding personal achievement," "divorce") and changes in the life situation of close friends or relatives that necessitate one's own adaptation (e.g., "major change in the health or behavior of a family member").* Alterations of family composition, job situation, finances, relationship with spouse, and residence are included, as are changes in personal habits.

In its current form, single events may be counted twice (e.g., "pregnancy" and "gaining a new family member"; "major change in living"; and "change in residence"), and no instruction is provided for avoiding such duplication or handling respondents' inquires regarding this issue. In addition, one item refers to a "wife's" employment situation. It is unclear whether female respondents should answer the item for themselves or reword the item to refer to their husband's employment.

Many response scales exist for the SRE and samples are provided in the test manual (Amundson, Hart, & Holmes, 1981). It is easy to adapt the SRE to fit the needs of the test administrator. Respondents can be asked, for example, to note how frequently an event has occurred within the last year, within the last five years, during each month of the last year, or each day. Respondents can also be asked to note the frequency of occurrence prior to and following a given significant event (e.g., an operation, a pregnancy).

The SRE was designed for adult samples but it can be used for children. A parent should complete the SRE for children younger than 13 years of age. Because many of the items are irrelevant to child respondents those interested in studying life events of childhood are better directed to a scale developed by Coddington (1968).**

Practical Applications/Uses

The SRE is useful for research, diagnosis and evaluation, and preventive efforts. It provides a means of understanding the occurrence and timing of previous or current illnesses and assessing the likelihood of future health problems. The SRE has stimulated research on means of coping with stressful events and on the relationship between stress and physical and emotional health.

---

*These items have been reproduced with the publisher's permission and may not be further reproduced without written permission from the publisher.

**Other forms of the test have been prepared specifically for, among others, college students (Marx, Garrity, & Bowers, 1975), the military (Rahe, 1975), and college athletes (Bramwell, Masuda, Wagner, & Holmes, 1975).

Holmes suggests using the SRE for preventive purposes as well by helping individuals to recognize important life events and prepare for the behavioral adaptation necessitated by change. The test could be usefully applied by medical and mental health professionals, college counselors, retirement specialists, child-birth educators, the clergy, and other professionals who work with people who are in transition from one role to another. Because the test is easy to administer to large groups or individuals and requires no special training for administration or scoring its potential for use is unrestricted.

Scoring procedures for the SRE are objective and clearly outlined in the manual. The scorer sums across events the weighted averages derived by multiplying the number of times the event occurred by the Social Readjustment Scale (SRRS) value associated with the event (Holmes & Rahe, 1967). The SRRS values, which are included in the manual, were derived from a sample of almost 400 subjects who estimated the amount of change and adaptive behavior required by each life event.

Because the frequency of each event is determined by each respondent there is no upper limit to the score. However, the higher the score, the more likely it is that the individual will become ill in the following two years. The manual predicts that 80% of those who receive scores of over 300 "Life Change Units" (LCUs) will become ill in the ensuing two-year period, with lower percentages predicted among those with lower scores. The manual, however, fails to define illness and thus provides no assistance in determining whether a health change indeed transpired within the predicted time frame.

A template is available for hand scoring the SRE, and the manual provides clear instructions as well as mean values for the items. To hand score the SRE, one multiplies the number of times each event occurred by the mean value provided for that event, and then computes a total score. The manual also provides instructions for computer scoring.

Technical Aspects

Reliability: The reliability of the SRE has been subjected to more scrutiny than other life event measures. Nevertheless, in view of the importance of reliability as a precursor of a measure's validity, surprisingly few reliability studies have been conducted.

Neubegauer (1981) categorizes available reliability studies as those using a test-retest design and those employing a paired subjects design. The test-retest design requires a group of respondents to complete the SRE at two different times. For both administrations, the participant reviews the same time period. In a paired-subjects design, two people complete the inventory separately and simultaneously. Both individuals are required to make ratings concerning the life events experienced within a given time frame by one member of the pair. Typically, the target person and his or her spouse complete the inventory and their responses are compared for level of agreement.

Casey, Masuda, and Holmes (1967) report one of the first test-retest studies of the SRE. On two occasions, nine months apart, 54 resident physicians completed the SRE. These respondents rated life events for the same 8-year period for each

SRE administration. The obtained time 1- time 2 correlations for event ratings of three different years was .67, .64, and .74. These findings led the authors to conclude that for the SRE, time may not affect recall.

In 1972, McDonald, Pugh, Gunderson, and Rahe assessed the test-retest reliability of the military version of the SRE. Respondents made their life event ratings on two occasions, separated by six months. In each instance they made ratings for the preceding 30-month period, which led to a 24-month overlap period between the two ratings. A test-retest correlation of .61 was obtained for the more recent overlapping year, and r = .52 for the earlier overlapping year.

Thurlow (1971) reports two test-retest studies of the SRE. In one study employees of a brewery completed the SRE on two occasions separated by 24 months. On each occasion subjects recorded events for the last five years. The correlation for the overlapping period was only .26. In the second study 21 college students completed the SRE on two occasions separated by two weeks. On both occasions participants made ratings for the past five years. The obtained score correlation was .78.

Both Neugebauer (1981) and Monroe (1982) note that a correlation coefficient is not a sensitive method for determining consistency of recall unless the mean and standard deviation of the scale scores are nearly equal on both administrations. Monroe recommends that investigators assess the percentage of change in event reporting over time. Jenkins, Hurst, and Rose (1979) used this statistical approach and found that when air traffic controllers rated life events on the SRE for a single six-month time period on two occasions separated by nine months, there were considerable differences in time 1 and time 2 reports.

Two reliability studies have been reported using the paired-subject method. Rahe, Fløistad, Bergen, Ringdal, Gerhardt, Gunderson, and Arthur (1974) studied a group of survivors of acute myocardial infarction (MI) and had spouses serve as coinformants. Life events were measured using an interview form of the SRE which covered the preceding two years. For those individuals who had a recent illness other than MI the score correlations were .75 and .51 for the earlier and most recent year, respectively. For those who had no other recent illness these correlations dropped to .07 for the most recent year and .49 for the earlier year. In another study using the paired subject method, Yager, Grant, Sweetwood, and Gerst (1981) had psychiatric patients, nonpatients, and their spouses (who made ratings on the index person) complete the SRE for three continuous three-month periods. While some of the items had high levels of agreement, index persons and their spouses generally demonstrated a good deal of disagreement in their ratings of the life events occurring for the index person.

In summary, test-retest and paired-subject designs have yielded moderate reliability estimates of the SRE. However, limitations in design and statistical analyses suggest that further work is needed to address the SRE's reliability. It is possible that the true association between life events and the onset of physical or emotional illness is even stronger than is currently believed, but the moderate reliability of the SRE and similar scales may have attenuated their observed relationship (Neugebauer, 1981).

Validity Studies: The range of populations sampled in validation studies of the SRE is impressive. These include normative community samples (e.g., Masuda &

Holmes, 1978; Mueller, Edwards, & Yarvis, 1977; Zautra & Beier, 1978; Zautra & Simons, 1979), college students (e.g., Clinard & Golden, 1973; Suls, Gastorf, & Witenberg, 1979), military personnel (e.g., Rahe et al., 1974; Rahe, Biersner, Ryman, & Arthur, 1972; Rubin, Gunderson, & Arthur, 1972), and members of certain occupational groups (e.g., Carranza, 1974; Pardine et al., 1981), as well as groups contending with unusual strains. The latter includes people who are physically ill (e.g., De Araujo, Van Arsdel, Holmes, & Dudley, 1973; Schonfield, 1975), mentally ill or emotionally disturbed (e.g., Aponte & Miller, 1972; Evans, 1981; Yager, Grant, Sweetwood, & Gerst, 1981), substance abusers (e.g., Dudley, Roszell, Mules, & Hague, 1974; Mules, Hague, & Dudley, 1977; Skinner & Lei, 1980), surgery patients (e.g., Cohen & Lazarus, 1973; Stevenson, Nasbeth, Masuda, & Holmes, 1979), rape victims (e.g., Ruch, Chandler, & Harter, 1980), survivors of natural catastrophes (Janney, Masuda, & Holmes, 1977; Melick, 1978), child-abusing parents (e.g., Conger, Burgess, & Barrett, 1979; Justice & Justice, 1982), and parents of ill or handicapped children (e.g., Mink, Nihira, & Meyers, 1983; Tittler, Friedman, Blotcky, & Stedrak, 1982; Townes, Wold, & Holmes, 1974).

Masuda and Holmes (1978) summarized findings from a large normative sample and reviewed other evidence pertaining to the effect of sociocultural and demographic variables on the perception and frequencies of life events contained in the SRE. Several conclusions about the effects of sociodemographic factors on SRE scores in general community populations can be drawn from this work. First, there is a moderately high concordance in the rank-orderings of the severity of life events in cross-national comparisons and across cultural subgroups in this country. Second, the role of gender, race, social class, and education as correlates of life events ratings or frequencies is ambiguous, with some investigations showing differences in SRRS weightings and life event frequencies associated with these factors and others failing to find associations. Third, effects of age and marital status have consistently been demonstrated. Being married and older appear to reduce not only the accumulation of life events but the perception of their severity. There is some suggestion, however, that the relationship between age and life events may be curvilinear, with greater numbers of events experienced by young and elderly adults (Uhlenhuth, Lipman, Balter, & Stern, 1974). Such a finding would be consistent with the expectation that middle age is commonly a time of relative stability. As Masuda and Holmes (1978) also show, however, these conclusions may not apply to special populations, such as those who have experienced adverse outcomes that may be more likely in the presence of stressful life events.

Content Validity: Content validity refers to the adequacy with which an instrument represents the universe of items that are candidates for inclusion (Nunnally, 1978). According to the test manual (Amundson et al., 1981), the 42 events listed in the SRE were selected for "their observed occurrence prior to the onset of illness or clinical symptoms" (p. 3). Holmes and Masuda (1974) note that the SRE contains life events "whose advent is either indicative of, or requires a significant change in, the ongoing life pattern of the individual" (p. 46). The items selected were also thought to have "maximal validity" for persons between the ages of 25 and 55 years. Accordingly, some investigators have modified the SRE, adding and deleting life events to construct more content-valid instruments for use with college-age (Marx, Garrity, & Bowers, 1975), high school age (Tolor, Murphy, Wilson, &

Clayton, 1983) and elderly (Amster & Krauss, 1974) populations. The SRE has also been adapted for studying military personnel (Rahe, 1975) and athletes (Bramwell, Masuda, Wagner, & Holmes, 1975).

SRE items have been subjected to factor analysis in a normative sample (Masuda & Holmes, 1978) and to cluster analysis in samples of military personnel (Rahe, Pugh, Erikson, Gunderson, & Rubin, 1971). Masuda and Holmes identified three factors, encompassing 12 SRE items, which account for nearly 30% of the variance in overall scores. The most robust of these factors included seven items related to changes in personal and social activities. The other two factors were related to loss of a loved one and change in marital status. One cluster of items from the Rahe et al. study labeled "personal and social" included the items contained in the Masuda and Holmes factor of personal and social activities. Overall, the results of the Rahe et al. analysis suggest greater interdependence among SRE events than is indicated by the Masuda and Holmes study.

The selection of life events for inclusion in the SRE has been criticized on the grounds that many items could easily refer to consequences rather than causes of stress-related outcomes (see Dohrenwend & Dohrenwend, 1981; Hudgens, 1974; Shroeder & Costa, 1984). Hudgens (1974) argued that well over half of the SRE events could be considered symptoms or sequelae of illness. Hence, the meaning of correlations of SRE scores with manifestations of underlying psychological or physical disorders may be nearly impossible to interpret from the standpoint of causal inference. This presents the greatest problem in the case of illnesses with an insidious onset in which the temporal priority of events and symptoms is difficult to establish (e.g., most psychological disorders).

Construct Validity: Critical evidence of the SRE's construct validity lies in research on the association of SRE scores with physical illness, emotional disturbance and psychological adjustment, and other stress reactions. Contributions to this literature have used various research designs. One approach is the retrospective, "case-control" design in which a case group of individuals are compared with an appropriate control group in the frequencies of previous life events. Investigators using this methodology have found that control respondents report fewer life events than child-abusing parents (Conger, Burgess, & Barrett, 1979; Gaines, Sandgrund, Green, & Power, 1978; Justice & Justice, 1982), insomniacs (Healey et al., 1981), pediatric cancer patients (Jacobs & Charles, 1980), psychiatric inpatients (Schless, Teichman, Mendels, & Digiacomo, 1977), and mothers who had delivered prematurely (Williams, Williams, Griswold, & Holmes, 1975). However, Jones (1978) found that women who had experienced complications of labor reported *fewer* life events than mothers who had normal deliveries.

Another retrospective design used in validity studies of the SRE examines the extent to which life changes precede an aversive outcome, but without the benefit of a control group. Holmes and Masuda (1974) summarized several such investigations showing a positive relationship between accumulating life change units and myocardial infarction, fractures, and other health changes. Increasing life change has also been related to surgery for duodenal ulcer (Stevenson, Nasbeth, Masuda, & Holmes, 1979), prison incarceration (Masuda, Cutler, Hein, & Holmes, 1978), and hospital admission for treatment of substance abuse (Dudley, Roszell, Mules, & Hague, 1974). Wyler, Masuda, and Holmes (1971) reported a significant association of life change units over a two-year period with ratings of disease severity in 232 patients. However, this relationship did not obtain for patients suffering infectious diseases of acute onset.

Yet another retrospective methodology examines life changes as presumed risk factors in the reported incidence of prior illness and health changes. Positive findings have been reported in college students (Klein & Cross, 1984; Stuart & Brown, 1981). Mattila and Salokangas (1977) failed to replicate these findings in a survey of the health status of employees of a large workplace in Finland. Similar investigations have attempted to predict psychological adjustment rather than health change. Prior life changes were found to correlate with work strain in managers (Pardine et al., 1981), psychological distress in a community sample (Zautra & Beier, 1978; Zautra & Simons, 1979), and mood disturbance in college students (Constantini, Braun, Davis, & Ivervolino, 1973). Ruch, Chandler, and Harter (1980) found a curvilinear relationship between SRE scores and adjustment following rape, indicating that victims who experience relatively few or relatively many prior life events may have the greatest coping difficulty.

Results from these retrospective studies are subject in varying degrees to the criticism that the recall of life events may be biased by the experience of an adverse outcome (see Critique). Simply, individuals who have become ill or experienced other threatening states may differentially recall life events because of their greater salience or meaning (Dohrenwend & Dohrenwend, 1981; Parsons, 1975). Completely prospective studies in which life events and outcomes are measured longitudinally in a cohort have rarely been reported in the literature. Garrity, Marx, and Somes (1977) followed 314 college freshmen to determine the relationship between changes in life events and health over a nine-month period. Correlations between life change and health change increased over the period, particularly for more serious illnesses. Several investigators have used "ambispective" designs involving retrospective measurement of life events at entry into the study and prospective ascertainment of illness events. A few such studies, conducted with military personnel, showed that previous life events did predict subsequent illness (e.g., Rubin, Gunderson, & Arthur, 1972; Rahe, Biersner, Ryman, & Arthur, 1972). Casey, Thoresen, and Smith (1970) found that life change scores did not predict illness occurrence, but did predict level of health care utilization by military cadets. Totman, Kiff, Reed, and Craig (1980) exposed subjects to rhinoviruses and monitored evidence of infections. Those who had accumulated greater numbers of life events involving change in level of social activity exhibited infections of greater magnitude. Ambispective designs have also been used in studying the prediction of other stress-related outcomes from knowledge of SRE scores. Popkin et al. (1976) found that lower life change units in the previous year predicted better performance by competitors in a prolonged, stressful contest (a long distance Alaskan sled race). Cohen and Lazarus (1973), however, showed that recovery from surgery was unrelated to life events measured during the preoperative period.

Several investigators have attempted to shed light on the differential validity of alternative approaches to scoring the SRE and similar instruments. It appears that not all categories of life events are equally predictive of certain illnesses or disorders; consequently, using the total SRE score may obscure significant results (see

Caplan, 1975, for a review). For example, Paykel, Myers, Dienelt, Klerman, Lindenthal, and Pepper (1969) reported that depression was associated with employment, health, and marital events but not with other family or legal events. In addition, they found that depressed patients could be discriminated by the experience of undesirable but not desirable events. Dohrenwend and Dohrenwend (1981) comment on the use of simple life event counts, normed weights (Social Readjustment Rating Scale), and subjective weights in scoring the SRE. Despite evidence that simple counts and normed weighting procedures yield scores that are highly correlated (on the order of .90; Yager et al., 1981; Skinner & Lei, 1980), Dohrenwend and Dohrenwend suggest that researchers retain both procedures and test whether either method possesses superior predictability. Joe, Miller, and Joe (1979) endorse an additional scoring dimension for the SRE—the perception of control over experienced events. They found that psychiatric symptoms were significantly related only to uncontrollable life changes in a sample of college students.

Critique

The SRE represents a pioneering effort in the study of life stress and the association between life events and subsequent illness and emotional disturbance. There are, however, significant problems which remain unresolved. These problems fall into three general categories: 1) the search for meaning and its effect on life event ratings; 2) the effect of mood state memory; and 3) the limits of memory for life events.

A large proportion of the studies using the SRE have investigated the association between life events and subsequent illness. As noted in this review, there does appear to be a link between subsequent illness and life events as reported on the SRE. Leaving aside the possibility that susceptibility to illness and the occurrence of certain life events are both due to the influence of a third factor, there is growing evidence that when faced with serious illness, people search for causes so as to bring meaning to their suffering (Taylor, 1983). Bartlett (1932) described this process as "effort after meaning." Brown (1974) describes the "emergence of meaning" in these situations, and Wong and Weiner (1981) label this process "attributional search."

The potential effects of attributional search on a person's self-report of life events is demonstrated in a recent study by Affleck, Allen, Tennen, McGrade, & Ratzan (in press) who found that mothers who perceived their child's illness as more severe derived more causes for the illness. This study and others (e.g., Stott, 1958) suggest that the search for meaning following illness and its manifestation in attributional search may very well lead to increased reports of prior life events among the seriously ill.

Even when certain aspects of meaning are taken into account, for example, by asking respondents to rate how important each endorsed SRE item was for them one must distinguish between the meaning ascribed to an event *after* a person has experienced it and has become ill or depressed or in some other way distressed from the event's meaning *before* it occurred or at least before it has been associated with distress (Dohrenwend & Dohrenwend, 1981).

Another complexity emerges in using the SRE to investigate the relationship between life events and emotional disturbance. Briefly stated, there is now considerable evidence that mood state affects memory (e.g., Bower, 1981) such that one is better able to recall events that occurred when the same mood state existed. If, for example, the investigators are concerned with the link between life events and subsequent depression (Paykel et al., 1969), they must take into account that being depressed may systematically influence the recall of recent life events.

Yet another methodological problem for the SRE and similar instruments is the reliability of recall of life events (see *Reliability*). A series of recent studies (Jenkins, Hurst, and Rose, 1979; Uhlenhuth, Haberman, Balter, & Lipman, 1977; Yager, Grant, Sweetwood, and Gerst, 1981; Monroe, 1982) demonstrate that life event scales such as the SRE are susceptible to considerable distortion in event reports due to underreporting of events. Monroe (1982), for example, found that as much as 60% of events may be underreported, even when participants are asked to recall events of the last four months. Desirable events may be even more susceptible to memory effects. The retrospective assessment strategy, which is prevalent in the study of life events, is particularly susceptible to both the effects of mood state on memory and to the strong tendency to underreport recent life events. Prospective studies, in which the meaning and incidence of life events are assessed *before* the onset of illness or emotional distress, will reduce some of this variance. But in many situations, retrospective accounts represent the only practical approach to studying the association between life events and illness or emotional distress (Brown, 1974; 1981).

References

Affleck, G., Allen, D., Tennen, H., McGrade, B. J., & Ratzan, S. (in press). Causal and control cognitions in parent coping with a chronically ill child. *Journal of Social and Clinical Psychology.*

Amster, L. E., & Krauss, H. H. (1974). The relationship between life crises and mental deterioration in old age. *International Journal of Aging and Human Development, 5,* 51-55.

Amundson, M. E., Hart, C. A., & Holmes, T. H. (1918). *Manual for The Schedule of Recent Experience (SRE).* Seattle: University of Washington Press.

Aponte, J. F., & Miller, F. T. (1972). Stress-related social events and psychological impairment. *Journal of Clinical Psychology, 28,* 455-458.

Bartlett, F. (1932). *Remembering: A study of experimental and social psychology.* Cambridge: Cambridge University Press.

Bower, G. (1981). Mood and memory. *American Psychologist, 36,* 129-148.

Bramwell, S. T., Masuda, M., Wagner, N. N., & Holmes, T. H. (1975). Psychological factors in athletic injuries: Development and application of the Social and Athletic Readjustment Rating Scale (SARRS). *Journal of Human Stress, 1,* 6-20.

Brown, G. W. (1974). Meaning, measurement and stress of life events. In B. S. Dohrenwend & B. P. Dohrenwend (Eds.), *Stressful life events: Their nature and effects.* New York: John Wiley & Sons.

Brown, G. W. (1981). Contextual measures of life events. In B. S. Dohrenwend & B. P. Dohrenwend (Eds.), *Stressful life events and their contexts.* New Brunswick: Rutgers University Press.

Caplan, R. D. (1975). A less heretical view of life change and hospitalization. *Journal of Psychosomatic Research, 19,* 247-250.

Carranza, E. (1974). Life changes and teacher performance. *California Journal of Educational Research, 25,* 73-78.

Casey, R. L., Masuda, M., & Holmes, T. H. (1967). Quantitative study of recall of life events. *Journal of Psychosomatic Research, 11,* 239-247.

Casey, R. L., Thoresen, A. R., & Smith, F. J. (1970). The use of the Schedule or Recent Experience Questionnaire in an institutional health care setting. *Journal of Psychosomatic Research, 14,* 149-153.

Clinard, J. W., & Golden, S. B. (1973). Life-change events as related to self-reported academic and job performance. *Psychological Reports, 33,* 391-394.

Coddington, R. D. (1972). The significance of life events as etiologic factors in diseases of children. I. A survey of professional workers. *Journal of Psychosomatic Research, 16,* 7-18.

Cohen, F., & Lazarus, R. S. (1973). Active coping processes, coping dispositions, and recovery from surgery. *Psychosomatic Medicine, 35,* 375-389.

Conger, R. D., Burgess, R. L., & Barrett, C. (1979). Child abuse related to life change and perceptions of illness: Some preliminary findings. *Family Coordinator, 28,* 73-78.

Constantini, A. F., Braun, J. R., Davis, J., & Iervolino, A. (1973). Personality and mood correlates of schedule of recent experience scores. *Psychological Reports, 32,* 1143-1150.

De Araujo, G., Van Arsdel, P. P., Holmes, T. H., & Dudley, D. L. (1973). Life change, coping ability and chronic intrinsic asthma. *Journal of Psychosomatic Research, 17,* 359-363.

Dohrenwend, B. S., & Dohrenwend, B. P. (1981). Life stress and illness: Formulation of the issues. In B. S. Dohrenwend & B. P. Dohrenwend (Eds.), *Stressful life events and their contexts.* New Brunswick: Rutgers University Press.

Dudley, D. L., Roszell, D. K., Mules, J. E., & Hague, W. H. (1974). Heroin vs. alcohol addiction: Quantifiable psychological similarities and differences. *Journal of Psychosomatic Research, 18,* 327-335.

Evans, W. (1981). Stress and psychoticism. *Personality and Individual Differences, 2,* 21-24.

Gaines, R., Sandgrund, A., Green, A. H., & Power, E. (1978). Etiological factors in child maltreatment: A multivariate study of abusing, neglecting, and normal mothers. *Journal of Abnormal Psychology, 87,* 531-540.

Garrity, T. F., Marx, M. B., & Somes, G. W. (1977). The influence of illness severity and time since life change on the size of the life change—health change relationship. *Journal of Psychosomatic Research, 21,* 377-382.

Healey, E. S., Kales, A., Monroe, L. J., Bixler, E. O., Chamberlin, K., & Soldatos, C. R. (1981). Onset of insomnia: Role of life-stress events. *Psychosomatic Medicine, 43,* 439-451.

Holmes, T. S. (1970). *Adaptive behavior and health change.* Unpublished medical thesis, University of Washington, Seattle.

Holmes, T. H., & Masuda, M. (1974). Life change and illness susceptibility. In B. S. Dohrenwend & B. P. Dohrenwend (Eds.), *Stressful life events and their contexts.* New Brunswick: Rutgers University Press.

Holmes, T. H., & Rahe, R. H. (1967). The Social Readjustment Rating Scale. *Journal of Psychosomatic Research, 11,* 213-218.

Hudgens, R. W. (1974). Personal catastrophe and depression: A consideration of the subject with respect to medically ill adolescents and a requiem for retrospective life event studies. In B. S. Dohrenwend & B. P. Dohrenwend (Eds.), *Stressful life events: Their nature and effects.* New York: John Wiley & Sons.

Jacobs, T. J., & Charles, E. (1980). Life events and the occurrence of cancer in children. *Psychosomatic Medicine, 42,* 11-24.

Janney, J. G., Masuda, M., & Holmes, T. H. (1977). Impact of a natural catastrophe on life events. *Journal of Human Stress, 3,* 22-23, 26-34.

Jenkins, C. D., Hurst, M. W., & Rose, R. M. (1979). Life changes: Do people really remember? *Archives of General Psychiatry, 36,* 379-384.

Joe, V. C., Miller, P. M., & Joe, J. K. (1979) Uncontrollability and psychiatric symptoms. *Psychological Reports, 45,* 333-334.

Jones, A. C. (1978). Life changes and psychological distress and predictors of pregnancy outcome. *Psychosomatic Medicine, 40,* 402-412.

Justice, B., & Justice, R. (1982). Clinical approaches to family violence: I. Etiology of physical abuse of children and dynamics of coercive treatment. *Family Therapy Collections, 3,* 1-20.

Klein, S., & Cross, H. J. (1984). Correlates of the MMPI L B Scale in a college population. *Journal of Clinical Psychology, 40,* 185-189.

Marx, M. B., Garrity, T. F., & Bowers, F. R. (1975). The influence of recent life experience on the health of college freshmen. *Journal of Psychosomatic Research, 19,* 87-98.

Masuda, M., Cutler, D. L., Hein, L., & Holmes, T. H. (1978). Life events and prisoners. *Archives of General Psychiatry, 35,* 197-203.

Masuda, M., & Holmes, T. H. (1978). Life events: Perceptions and frequencies. *Psychosomatic Medicine, 40,* 236-261.

Mattila, V. J., & Salokangas, R. K. (1977). Life changes and social group in relation to illness onset. *Journal of Psychosomatic Research, 21,* 167-174.

McDonald, B. W., Pugh, W. M., Gunderson, E. K. E., & Rahe, R. H. (1972). Reliability of life change cluster scores. *British Journal of Social and Clinical Psychology, 11,* 407-409.

Melick, M. E. (1978). Life change and illness: Illness behavior of males in the recovery period of a natural disaster. *Journal of Health and Social Behavior, 19,* 335-342.

Meyer, A. (1919). The life chart and the obligation of specifying positive data in psychopathological diagnosis. In *Contributions to medical and biological research* (Vol. II). New York: Paul B. Hoeber.

Mink, I. T., Nihira, K., & Meyers, C. E. (1983). Taxonomy of family life styles: I. Homes with TMR children. *American Journal of Mental Deficiency, 87,* 484-497.

Monroe, S. M. (1982). Assessment of life events: Retrospective vs concurrent strategies. *Archives of General Psychiatry, 39,* 606-610.

Mueller, D. P., Edwards, D. W., & Yarvis, R. M. (1977). Stressful life events and psychiatric symptomatology: Change or undesirability? *Journal of Health and Social Behavior, 18,* 307-317.

Mules, J. E., Hague, W. H., & Dudley, D. L. (1977). Life change, its perception and alcohol addiction. *Journal of Studies on Alcohol, 38,* 487-493.

Neugebauer, R. (1981). The reliability of life-event reports. In. B. S. Dohrenwend & B. P. Dohrenwend, (Eds.), *Stressful life events and their contexts.* New Brunswick: Rutgers University Press.

Nunnally, J. C. (1978). *Psychometric Theory* (2nd ed.). New York: McGraw-Hill.

Pardine, P., Higgins, R., Szeglin, A., Beres, J., Kravitz, R., & Fotis, J. (1981). Job-stress worker-strain relationship moderated by off-the-job experience. *Psychological Reports, 48,* 963-970.

Parsons, O. A. (1975). Life events, stress and depression. *Biological Psychology Bulletin, 4,* 143-151.

Paykel, E. S., Myers, J. K., Dienelt, M. N., Klerman, G. L., Lindenthal, J. J., & Pepper, M. P. (1969). Life events and depression: A controlled study. *Archives of General Psychiatry, 21,* 753.

Popkin, M. K., Stillner, V., Pierce, C. M., Williams, M., & Gregory, P. (1976). Recent life changes and outcome of prolonged competitive stress. *Journal of Nervous and Mental Disease, 163,* 302-306.

Rahe, R. H. (1969). Life crisis and health change. In. P.R.A. May & R. Whittenborn (Eds.), *Psychotropic drug response: Advances in prediction.* Springfield, IL: Charles C. Thomas.

Rahe, R. H. (1975). Epidemiological studies of life change and illness. *International Journal of Psychiatry in Medicine, 6,* 133-146.

Rahe, R. H., Biersner, R. J., Ryman, D. H., & Arthur, R. J. (1972). Psychological predictors of illness behavior and failure in stressful training. *Journal of Health and Social Behavior, 13,* 393-397.

Rahe, R. H., Pugh, W. M., Erikson, J., Gunderson, E. K., & Rubin, R. T. (1971). Cluster analyses of life changes: I. Consistency of clusters across large navy samples. *Archives of General Psychiatry, 25,* 330-332.

Rahe, R. H., Fløistad, I., Bergen, T., Ringdal, R., Gerhardt, R., Gunderson, E. K. E., & Arthur, R. J. (1974). A model for life changes and illness research: Cross-cultural data from the Norwegian Navy. *Archives of General Psychiatry, 31,* 172-177.

Rubin, R. T., Gunderson, E. K., & Arthur, R. J. (1972). Life stress and illness patterns in the US Navy: VI. Environmental, demographic, and prior life change variables in relation to illness onset in naval aviators during a combat cruise. *Psychosomatic Medicine, 34,* 533-547.

Ruch, L. O., Chandler, S. M., & Harter, R. A. (1980). Life change and rape impact. *Journal of Health and Social Behavior, 21,* 248-260.

Schless, A. P., Teichman, A., Mendels, J., & Digiacomo, J. N. (1977). The role of stress as a precipitating factor of psychiatric illness. *British Journal of Psychiatry, 130,* 19-22.

Schonfield, J. (1975). Psychological and life-experience differences between Israeli women with benign and cancerous breast lesions. *Journal of Psychosomatic Research, 19,* 229-234.

Schroeder, D. H., & Costa, P. T. (1984). Influence of life event stress on physical illness: Substantive effects or methodological flaws? *Journal of Personality and Social Psychology, 46,* 853-863.

Skinner, H. A., & Lei, H. (1980). Differential weights in life change research: Useful or irrelevant? *Psychosomatic Medicine, 42,* 367-370.

Stevenson, D. K., Nasbeth, D. C., Masuda, M., & Holmes, T. H. (1979). Life change and the postoperative course of duodenal ulcer patients. *Journal of Human Stress, 5,* 19-28.

Stott, D. H. (1958). Some psychosomatic aspects of casualty in reproduction. *Journal of Psychosomatic Research, 3,* 42-55.

Stuart, J. C., & Brown, B. M. (1981). The relationship of stress and coping ability to incidence of diseases and accidents. *Journal of Psychosomatic Research, 25,* 255-260.

Suls, J., Gastorf, J. W., & Witenberg, S. H. (1979). Life events, psychological distress and the type A coronary-prone behavior pattern. *Journal of Psychosomatic Research, 23,* 315-319.

Taylor, S. (1983). Adjustment to threatening events: A theory of cognitive adaptation. *American Psychologist, 38,* 1161-1173.

Thurlow, H. J. (1971). Illness in relation to life situation and sick role tendency. *Journal of Psychosomatic Research, 15,* 73-88.

Tittler, B. I., Friedman, S., Blotcky, A. D., & Stedrak, J. (1982). The influence of family variables on an ecologically-based treatment program for emotionally disturbed children. *American Journal of Orthopsychiatry, 52,* 123-130.

Tolor, A., Murphy, V. M., Wilson, L. T., & Clayton, J. (1983). The high school social readjustment scale: An attempt to quantify stressful events in young people. *Research Communications in Psychology, Psychiatry, and Behavior, 8,* 85-111.

Totman, R., Kiff, J., Reed, S. E., & Craig, J. W. (1980). Predicting experimental colds in volunteers from different measures of recent life stress. *Journal of Psychosomatic Research, 24,* 155-163.

Townes, B. D., Wold, D. A., & Holmes, T. H. (1974). Parental adjustment to childhood leukemia. *Journal of Psychosomatic Research, 18,* 9-14.

Uhlenhuth, E. H., Haberman, S. J., Balter, M. D., & Lipman, R. S. (1977). Remembering life events. In J. S. Strauss, H. M. Babigian, and M. Roff (Eds.), *The origins and course of psychopathology: Methods of longitudinal research.* New York: Plenum Press.

Uhlenhuth, E. H., Lipman, R. S., Balter, M. B., & Stern, J. (1974). Symptom intensity and life stress in the city. *Archives of general psychiatry, 31,* 759-764.

Williams, C. C., Williams, R. A., Griswold, M. J., & Holmes, T. H. (1975). Pregnancy and life change. *Journal of Psychosomatic Research, 19,* 123-129.

Wong, P., & Weiner, B. (1981). When people ask "Why" questions, and the heuristics of attributional search. *Journal of Personality and Social Psychology, 40,* 650-653.

Wyler, A. R., Masuda, M., & Holmes, T. H. (1971). Magnitude of life events and seriousness of illness. *Psychosomatic Medicine, 33,* 115-122.

Yager, J., Grant, I., Sweetwood, H. L., & Gerst, M. (1981). Life event reports by psychiatric patients, nonpatients, and their partners. *Archives of General Psychiatry, 38,* 343-347.

Zautra, A., & Beier, E. (1978). The effects of life crisis on psychological adjustment. *American Journal of Community Psychology, 6,* 125-135.

Zautra, A., & Simons, L. S. (1979). Some effects of positive life events on community mental health. *American Journal of Community Psychology, 7,* 441-451.

Martin Heesacker, Ph.D.
Assistant Professor of Psychology, Southern Illinois University,
Carbondale, Illinois.

SCHOOL INTEREST INVENTORY
William C. Cottle. Chicago, Illinois: The Riverside Publishing
Company.

Introduction

The School Interest Inventory (SII) is a paper-and-pencil measure intended to be used in the early detection potential high-school dropouts (Cottle, 1966). Respondents answer 150 true-false items, 90 of which comprise a single scale for males and 86 of which comprise a single scale for females. Additionally, 49 items, which are experimental, are not scored for males or females.

William C. Cottle, the test's developer, taught, counseled, and administered in public schools over a fifteen-year period. Subsequently he taught and counseled at Syracuse University (where he received his Ed.D. in 1949), was a member of the Kansas University faculty in 1947, Professor and Director of Boston College's Counselor Education and Counseling Psychology program in 1961, and president of The American Psychological Association's Division 17 (Counseling Psychology) in 1965. (Cottle, 1966).

The SII, first developed by Cottle in 1953, was based on his reading of research on factors associated with high-school dropouts (Epps & Cottle, 1958), with part of the test's first validation based on Havens' 1955 research (Herrman & Cottle, 1958). The 180-item instrument was administered to 1,834 eighth- and ninth-graders in an urban area of Kansas. A year and a half later, 61 boys and 53 girls from the sample had dropped out of school. Dropouts and an equal number of randomly sampled stay-ins were compared, and a total of 90 items discriminated the two groups at the .10 significance level (28 common items, 32 items for males, 30 for females). A cross-validation study was performed on dropouts and stay-ins from another part of Kansas.

Another validation study, based on Herrman and Cottle's (1958) first sample, compared stay-ins with students who dropped out *after* the dropouts used in the Herrman-Cottle research. The SII also discriminated between these two groups, but with fewer items discriminating than in the Herrman-Cottle research (Epps & Cottle, 1958). They also suggested that a cutoff score could be developed for the SII.

After 25,000 students from ten states were administered the SII in 1963 inspec-

Preparation of this review was supported in part by a grant from the Office of Research and Development Administration, Southern Illinois University, to Martin Heesacker, who wishes to express his appreciation to James P. Steyaert for his assistance in preparing this review and to Heather A. Tatten for her comments on an earlier draft.

tion of school records indicated that 1,300 of the respondents dropped out within a two-year period following the test (Cottle, 1966). According to the manual, items consistently discriminating dropouts from stay-ins across various states and schools were retained to form the current SII.

The SII has not undergone any formal revisions subsequent to Cottle's 1966 edition. The test manual (Cottle, 1966) mentions no other forms of the SII, but several different scoring schemes and subtests were uncovered in a review of relevant literature (e.g., Cottle, 1962; Davenport, 1971; Foley, 1972; Uber, 1970).

The SII consists of two standard-sized pages printed on both sides, with the first side serving as a cover page. Beginning with the second side spaces are provided for name, date, grade, gender, and score of the examinee, followed by inventory instructions, the 150 items, and the remaining items, respectively. Items are arranged in two columns on each page. Each item is a numbered, declarative statement with two circles, one of which contains a "T" and one of which contains an "F." Respondents darken the "T" circle for true and the "F" circle for false. Statements range in length from 5-19 words and cover such diverse areas as number of family members, the respondent's general affect, leisure and work preferences, and enjoyment of school.

According to the manual, examiners perform three major functions: 1) They read the directions aloud in a "pleasant and reassuring" manner, using a "distinct voice" (p. 5); 2) They instruct individuals how to respond to inappropriate items (e.g., items about siblings for a person without siblings) by having them omit a response or respond to an altered version of an item (e.g., answering an item about a deceased parent as if the item referred to when the parent was alive); and 3) They reduce false responding by instilling confidence in the respondents regarding the examiner and convey the value of the inventory.

The test is intended for junior high- and high-school students. Using procedures by Forbes and Cottle (1953), O'Shea (1970) found that the SII was written on a seventh-grade reading level. One factor that may contribute to dropping out of school is serious reading difficulty. Because the inventory makes no provision for detecting nonreaders, people prone to dropping out for this reason will probably go undetected by the SII. The SII appears to be easily adaptable to a vocal administration for nonreaders or the visually impaired.

The manual makes no provisions for scoring subtests or additional scales, although it, as well as other authors (e.g., O'Shea, 1970), discusses additional scales in the process of development. No separate answer forms are provided; the SII booklet also serves as the answer sheet. Because the SII yields only a single score, no profile is rendered.

Practical Applications/Uses

The primary use for the SII, according to Cottle (1966), involves the identification of students who are at risk of dropping out of school in order that school guidance personnel can take action and thus help these students to remain in school. The SII might also be used by community agencies to identify groups of students needing special attention by the community. Counseling or clinical psychologists might administer the SII to young clients whose educational future is of concern. The SII might be helpful in these settings because Cottle (1966) provided evidence that scores over 30 were associated with increased likelihood of dropping out of school.

Unfortunately, problems regarding the test curtail its usefulness in both educational and community settings. First, although the SII renders a dropout score, it provides users no information about what specific problems might trigger students to drop out of school or what specific measures might reduce the likelihood of their dropping out. Second, it is not clear that the SII is superior to predictors based on such characteristics as truancy, grades, and family size. Several SII items address information that could probably be obtained through school records. Perhaps these data would predict dropout as well as the SII. Similar concerns were expressed by Glass (1972), Goodwin (1969), and Gordon (1972).

The SII may be administered either to individuals or groups, although the examiner's instructions are worded as if addressing a group. No stipulations are mentioned regarding the examiner's qualifications except for the emphasis placed on the examiner's familiarity with the test's administration and scoring procedures prior to administration.

After the students receive the inventories they are instructed on how to complete the necessary demographic information on the form. There are separate administration instructions for the examiner, depending on whether the inventory is to be hand-scored or machine-scored. When the examiner has read the inventory instructions to the students, informing them that the questions in the inventory are constructed to find out how they feel about school, and that their responses will aid the school faculty in making their school experiences more valuable for them (Cottle, 1966, pp. 6-7), the examiner directs them to begin the inventory.

The manual is clearly written, with instructions that are easily comprehended and conducive to a quick, problem-free administration. According to the manual, the inventory usually requires 20-30 minutes to complete, but there is no time limit.

Instructions for scoring the SII are also clearly presented in the manual, with scoring procedures and materials seemingly quite adequate. The examiner is given the option of hand-scoring the test (using scoring masks) or having it sent to the Riverside Publishing Company for machine-scoring (F. L. Finch, personal communication, January 4, 1984). The form required to obtain machine-scoring (#9-79620) is not included in the test materials, but is available from the publisher on request.

The inventory user should be able to hand-score the instrument after one reading of the scoring instructions and, although the manual does not indicate any length of time required for hand-scoring, this reviewer's experience suggests that unweighted scores can be generated in a few minutes per respondent. The hand scoring procedure entails inspecting each booklet prior to calculating scores and eliminating items with both response choices marked. Raw (unweighted) scores are obtained by aligning a scoring mask with the test items and then counting the marked responses that match the mask's holes. Separate masks are used to score the inventories of females and males. For each gender, the mask may be used to obtain either weighted or unweighted scores, but weighted scores provide little benefit over unweighted scores because the manual indicates that the two correlate .96 or higher. Goodwin (1969) found similar correlations. Weights ranging from 1 to 9 have been assigned to each of the test items. For deriving a weighted score by hand, the weights are printed on the masks next to the appropriate item slots. The user is cautioned that any answer sheets with more than 15 omitted or ambiguous responses should be considered invalid.

Interpretation of SII scores differs from that of most standardized tests. For instance, there are no tables of normative data available. Scores are interpreted only in comparison to previously obtained scores from students attending the same school, so that an individual student's position or rank is determined relative to the positions of his or her peers at the school. For a typical school, only those students scoring 30 or above are identified as being at high risk of dropping out of school. Cottle (1966) recommended that SII scores be interpreted in conjuction with other available information, such as school records of academic achievement, attendance, teachers' opinions, and age relative to school grade. Because local norms are suggested and SII data are to be interpreted in the context of other information, interpretation of an SII score may be difficult.

Technical Aspects

No internal consistency data were found for the SII in its published form. However, in several studies SII items that discriminated dropouts from stay-ins in a particular sample were retained to form a scale on which internal consistency data were computed, using the KR-20 Formula (Cottle, 1962; Davenport, 1971; Foley, 1972; Uber, 1970). Although not ideal, these data provide the best available estimate of the SII's internal consistency. The higher the KR-20 score, the more individual SII items are related to each other. This reviewer suspects that these scores underestimate the internal consistency of the standard SII because these scales have fewer items. The number of items included in the four studies ranged from 48 to 81 and KR-20 scores ranged from .68 to .90, suggesting sufficient internal consistency.

Test-retest reliability refers to the correlation between examinees' scores from the instrument on one occasion and their scores on another occasion. Higher scores indicate higher correlation. Across 8 groups of seventh- to ninth-grade boys and girls test-retest reliability over a 1-2 week period ranged from .78 to .92, suggesting adequate test-retest reliability (Cottle, 1966).

Because the purpose of the SII is a accurate prediction of who will drop out and who will stay in school, the most important validity to assess is criterion validity. Criterion validity is an indication of how well an instrument predicts either present or future behavior. In this case, it is essential to determine how well the SII predicts future dropout behavior. Because the SII was created by determining which of many items discriminated students who dropped out from those who stayed in school, it might first appear that there is no need for additional criterion validity research. However, the procedures used to determine which items discriminated dropouts from stay-ins increased the likelihood that some items were wrongly retained in the final scale (Glass, 1972). To determine the predictive accuracy of the SII, data from other research must be reported. The test manual indicates that across 17 + schools from several states, with both males and females, the SII scores of seventh- to ninth-grade future dropouts and stay-ins were statistically different. This was true regardless of whether the dropping out occurred as soon as legally possible or later on. Using a single cutting score, the SII accurately predicted dropout behavior in 81% of the cases for males and 72% for females.

The most stringent test of predictive validity would assess the extent to which the SII *adds* to prediction over and above other predictors already available. In general, insufficient data have been published on this point, particularly given how many SII items appear to assess such easily accessed facts as truancy and family size. However, Goodwin (1969) has contributed to this area by comparing the predictive power the SII and the students' teachers. Goodwin suggested that both predictors were reasonably accurate, but that teachers "were even more impressive [than the SII] in identifying possible dropouts correctly" (p. 201). Unfortunately, insufficient data were provided to assess this claim independently.

Other research has shown that high achievers scored significantly lower on the SII than low achievers (O'Shea, 1970; Patros, 1970). High scorers on the SII had lower IQ scores, lower grade point averages, less vocational maturity (Das, 1963), and more negative attitudes toward school and were "rated by teachers as less well adjusted" than low scorers on the SII (Renfrow, 1969, p. 449A). Higher SII scores are associated with dropping out.

Critique

Besides Cottle, author of the SII, there may be no SII expert. However, two competent reviewers (Glass, 1972; Gordon, 1972) express concern about the SII being constructed from no theoretical base and about the possibility that the SII would not predict dropout better than a few simple facts such as "a pupil's race, family income per family member, welfare status, father's occupation, and personal educational aspirations" (Glass, 1972, p. 134).

This reviewer's overall evaluation of the SII's reliability and validity is that they are sufficient even though, as some critics have suggested, more validity data would be helpful and the manual somewhat overstates the validity data that are available. Perhaps the major concern this reviewer has about the SII involves practicality. Several practical issues seem important.

First, no evidence is provided to indicate that the SII is superior in predicting dropout over simply finding out (perhaps through school records) about such areas as student absences, family size, and parent education level. If such information predicted dropout just as well, the practical use of the SII would be reduced. Second, the SII provides no subscales to pinpoint specific etiological or treatment factors that guidance personnel and psychologists would find helpful. Third, students are asked to answer 49 items (33% of the SII) that have no function. Initially they were included to facilitate the development of additional scales, but in the 19 years since the SII was first published, no scales have been added. Fourth, Cottle (1966) advocated the use of local norms rather than a cutting score for predicting dropouts. Local norming would be a very expensive procedure and, perhaps, impossible in many cases. Fifth, machine-scoring allows for items to be weighted differently, but weighting does not appreciably improve the SII's predictive ability. The SII is easily handscored without weighting and the cost of a scoring service adds appreciably to the expense of administering the SII. Sixth, 20 of the scored items do not have universal applicability. Items referring to siblings, for example, do not apply to everyone. This lack of applicability could easily lead respondents to leave these items blank, which might be satisfactory except that the test manual states, "if more than fifteen items have been omitted, the test should be considered invalid for that student" (Cottle, 1966, p. 7). Children living with their mother, and no brothers or sisters and having little contact with their father could easily omit 18 scored items because of their inapplicability. The manual's provisions for this problem rely on the respondent initiating a discussion with the examiner during the taking of the inventory. Many respondents would not do this and those who did would disrupt other respondents. Instructions to the examiner concerning respondents' questions about inapplicable items appear to be inadequate for insuring systematic reinterpretations of items.

Despite these practical issues, the SII seems to be a useful instrument in detecting students with a high dropout potential. Several of the practical problems could easily be overcome with relatively minor revisions in the instrument and the manual, making the SII a more helpful tool in guidance, counseling, and psychotherapy.

References

Cottle, W. C. (1962). Dropout, delinquent and other scales of the School Interest Inventory. *National Council on Measurement in Education Yearbook, 19,* 94-96.

Cottle, W. C. (1966). *Examiner's manual for the School Interest Inventory.* Chicago: The Riverside Publishing Company.

Das, A. K. (1963). The effect of counseling on the vocational maturity of a group of potential drop-outs from high school. *Dissertation Abstracts, 23,* 2788.

Davenport, C. M. (1971). A study of the feasibility of developing a delinquent girl scale for the School Interest Inventory. *Dissertation Abstracts International, 31,* 215A.

Epps, M. W., & Cottle, W. C. (1958). Further validation of a dropout scale. *Vocational Guidance Quarterly, 7,* 90-93.

Foley, P. M. (1972). Differences between delinquents and nondelinquents on the School Interest Inventory. *Dissertation Abstracts International, 32,* 1851A-1852A.

Forbes, F. W., & Cottle, W. C. (1953). A new method for determining readability of standardized tests. *Journal of Applied Psychology, 37,* 185-190.

Glass, G. V. (1972). [Review of the School Interest Inventory]. In O. K. Buros (Ed.), *The seventh mental measurements yearbook* (pp. 316-317). Highland Park, NJ: The Gryphon Press.

Goodwin, W. L. (1969). School Interest Inventory. *Journal of Educational Measurement, 6,* 200-201.

Gordon, L. V. (1972). [Review of the School Interest Inventory]. In O. K. Buros (Ed.), *The seventh mental measurements yearbook* (pp. 317-319). Highland Park, NJ: The Gryphon Press.

Havens, N. H. (1955). *A study of the answers, one year in advance, to the Life Adjustment Scale by students who drop out or remain in four Kansas high schools.* Unpublished master's thesis, University of Kansas, Lawrence.

Herrman, L., & Cottle, W. C. (1958). An inventory to identify high school dropouts. *Vocational Guidance Quarterly, 6,* 122-123.

O'Shea, A. J. (1970). Low-achievement syndrome among bright junior high school boys. *Journal of Educational Research, 63,* 257-262.

Patros, P. G. (1970). An investigation of the relationship between certain non-intellective factors and academic performance of academically bright junior high school girls. *Dissertation Abstracts International, 30,* 3734A-3735A.

Renfrow, O. W. (1969). Dropout prone and non-dropout prone high school boys: A study of differences. *Dissertation Abstracts, 29,* 449A-450A.

Uber, T. B. (1970). Delinquency prediction with the School Interest Inventory. *Dissertation Abstracts International, 30,* 3742A-3743A.

Patricia Ashton, Ph.D.
Associate Professor of Educational Psychology, University of Florida, Gainesville, Florida.

SCHOOL READINESS SCREENING TEST

Gesell Institute. Flemington, New Jersey: Programs for Education, Inc.

Introduction

The School Readiness Screening Test (SRST) was developed by the Gesell Institute of Human Development (formerly the Gesell Institute of Child Development) and is published by Programs for Education, Inc., Flemington, NJ. The SRST is a shortened version of the School Readiness Test: Complete Battery for children, ages 4½ to 9 years. The SRST is intended for use in determining whether children ages 4½ to 5 years are ready to begin kindergarten.

The Gesell Institute advocates that children should begin school and be promoted on the basis of developmental age rather than chronological age or IQ scores. Developmental age (DA) refers to the age at which the child is functioning as a total organism. It represents a composite of the child's social, emotional, intellectual, and physical development. According to Gesell Institute staff, "possibly as many as fifty percent of school problems could be prevented or remediated by correct placement" (Ilg, 1982, p. 1). The SRST was developed to provide a quick assessment of the child's developmental functioning to determine if the child is ready to enter kindergarten.

The SRST is the product of an on-going process of development that was begun by Arnold Gesell. The preschool tasks that form the basis for the Gesell School Reading Test (GSRT) are described in his book *Infancy and Human Growth* (1928). Gesell continued work on the tests until his death in 1961. They were further refined and published as the Gesell Developmental Kit for children, ages 5 to 10, by Ilg and Ames in 1964. The test tasks were described, and normative responses were presented in their text, *School Readiness* (Ilg and Ames, 1964). A sample of 80 children aged 3 to 4½ years were added to the standardization group and data on their performance were included in the 1978 revision of *School Readiness*. The Gesell School Readiness Screening Test, a shortened and revised version of the Developmental Kit, was published in 1978.

Arnold Gesell was born in Alma, Wisconsin, in 1880. He was awarded the Ph.D. in psychology at Clark University, Worcester, Massachusetts, in 1906. In 1911 he obtained the position of assistant professor of education on the faculty at Yale where he founded the Yale Clinic of Child Development. In 1915 he obtained a doctorate in medicine. For 37 years he directed the Yale Clinic and conducted studies of the behavior of infants and children from which he and his colleagues created detailed descriptions of typical behavior and growth trends of children at

34 age levels from birth to age 10. Following Gesell's retirement and the termination of the Yale Clinic in 1948, Gesell's coworkers, Frances Ilg, Louise Bates Ames, and Janet Learned founded the Gesell Institute of Child Development to continue the developmental research and service begun by Gesell in 1911. In 1964, Ilg and Ames published the first edition of *School Readiness,* the text that presents the institute's philosophy that children's school placement should be based on developmental age rather than chronological age. Dr. Ilg, the late director of the Gesell Institute, received her medical degree from Cornell Medical School. Before becoming Director of the Institute, she served as a visiting pediatrician, research assistant, and assistant professor of child development at Yale. Dr. Ames, currently associate director of the Institute, earned the Sc.D at the University of Maine and the Ph.D at Yale. She was a research assistant to Dr. Gesell and an assistant professor at the Yale Clinic. She has also served as director of research at the Institute. Drs. Ilg and Ames coauthored *Youth: The Years from Ten to Sixteen* (1956) with Gesell, and after Gesell's death, they continued their collaboration, publishing among other books a series of books on each age from one through six years (e.g., *Your One Year Old,* 1982; *Your Six Year Old,* 1979). Their *School Readiness* text (Ilg & Ames, 1964) was revised in 1978 (Ilg, Ames, Haines, & Gillespie, 1978), and preschool norms for a standardization sample of children aged 3 to 4½ years were included. The SRST, a shortened version of the developmental battery described in *School Readiness* (1964, 1978) was published in 1978 for use as a quick assessment of children's readiness for kindergarten.

The SRST consists of five subtests: Cube Test, Interview Question, Pencil and Paper Tests, Incomplete Man, and Animals and Interests. The Cube Test, a structured fine-motor task intended to assess eye-hand coordination, the ability to follow directions, and attention span, requires children to build block structures demonstrated by the examiner. Interview Questions, a short initial interview designed to place children at ease and give the examiner insight into their language development and organizational ability, requires children to answer questions about themselves and their family. The Paper and Pencil Tests, intended to indicate the children's general maturity level and provide specific evidence of visual perception and neuromuscular and eye-hand coordination, requires children to write their name and numbers and to copy forms from a model. The Incomplete Man, used to measure perceptual-motor functioning, requires children to complete an unfinished figure. Animals and Interests measures children's verbal expressive abilities and is intended to give indications of their attention span, speed of response, and organization of thinking. For instance, the Naming Animals task requires the child to name as many animals as possible in 60 seconds, and Interests requires the child to describe home- and school-activity preferences.

The first answer-sheet page has lines on which to record personal information about the child, including name; birth date; age; school; class; birth weight; pregnancy term; present health; any physical problems; and the name, age, and health of siblings. The examiner and test date are also recorded, and a space is indicated for a photo.

On the first test page, the "Face Sheet," the child's name and age are recorded and a summary of the child's behavior during the test, the group for which the child is recommended, a total impression, summary, and teacher comments are noted. On the recording sheet for the Cube Test each design is pictured, with space to the right for the examiner to reconstruct the sequence and arrangement of the child's construction and space to the left to record comments the child makes in response to the examiner's questions. The interview is recorded on the following test page where each of the child's responses are recorded verbatim. Next, the children's responses to the Paper and Pencil Tests are recorded, and space is provided to also record their comments, facial expressions, and feelings, note their hand dominance, and indicate the direction of their strokes in copying the forms. They are then given a sheet with the figure of a man to complete. A description of the children's response to the question, "What does this look like to you?" is recorded, and the order in which they draw body parts and any other comments by them are noted. Space for recording the animals the children name, their home and school interests, teeth eruption, and physical characteristics is provided on another page. On the last page the examiner records physical data, and notes behaviors regarding the child's separation from mother, activity level, posture, manner of following directions, physical activity, speech, language, personality, and use of results. Pages designated for recording Right and Left and Visual I and III tests are used only for the GSRT, and not for the SRST.

Practical Applications/Uses

For many years the staff of the Gesell Institute have advocated the use of developmental placement programs that require examination of children prior to their age of eligibility for kindergarten. Children who appear immature would be placed in a prekindergarten, followed by kindergarten the next year. In addition, a prefirst-grade class would be made available for children who have finished kindergarten but are not yet ready for first grade. The SRST is designed to guide school staff in the proper placement of children in their first years of school. The Institute contends that "as many as 50% of school problems could be prevented or remedied if all boys and girls could be placed in the grade for which their behavior makes them suited" (Ames, 1982, p. 23). The SRST is being used in school systems around the country to guide school placement decisions. Brevard and Broward county school districts are among a number of school districts in Florida that are using the SRST as part of their kindergarten assessment program.

The standardization sample reported in *School Readiness* (1964/1965) was comprised of children aged 5 to 9 years in two school districts in North Haven, Connecticut. Over a 4-year period, September, 1958 to May, 1962, 65 boys and 65 girls at each age level were examined. Most children were examined at more than one age, yielding 700 examinations from 301 children. After incomplete records were eliminated, the standardization group consisted of 50 boys and 50 girls at each age level. The average IQ of the children in the standardization sample was 117.4 on the California Mental Maturity Scale (CMMS). The average score on the Wechsler Intelligence Scale for Children (WISC) administered to a subsample of 25 girls was 104.8 and 106 for a subsample of boys. On the basis of the difference in scores obtained on the CMMS and WISC, it was suggested that the CMMS probably overestimated the children's IQ by at least 10 points (Ilg, Ames, Haines,

& Gillespie, 1978). An estimate of the socioeconomic level of the sample based on the 1961 U.S. Government Scale indicated that 34% of the subjects' fathers were professional and 13% semiprofessional or managerial. An estimate based on the Minnesota Scale of Parental Occupations placed 27% of the fathers in these two groups and the majority (40%) in the clerical, skilled labor, or retail business classification. The 1978 revision of *School Readiness* included a younger standardization group comprised of 40 girls and 40 boys, each of whom were tested at ages 3, 3½, 4, and 4½ years, within one month of their birth date or of their half-year birth date. The children lived in New England and were selected on the basis of their fathers' occupations to represent the 1970 U.S. Census distribution of occupations of employed men. Approximately 8% of the sample was black and 92% was white. Because of the select and limited nature of the Gesell standardization group, there is a need to develop more representative norms for the SRST. As Ilg, Ames, Haines, and Gillespie (1978) conclude: *"Obviously, for good developmental placement, there are no norms quite as useful as those which apply to the exact population with which one is working"* (p. 218.)

The SRST is administered individually and usually requires about 20 minutes to administer. The directions for administration described in the *Scoring Notes* (Ilg, 1965, 1982) are clear and easy to follow. The *School Readiness* textbook (Ilg, Ames, Haines, & Gillespie, 1978) presents normative data on all of the SRST tasks except for the Cube Test, which is described in the Cube Test direction booklet. The performance of the standardization group is described, and the percent of children performing at each developmental age level is indicated. The discussion of normative data is extended and not easily followed as a scoring guide. Normative guidelines for scoring each task are more succinctly presented in the *Scoring Notes* (Ilg, 1982).

However, no guidelines are presented in either the *School Readiness* text or the *Scoring Notes* for determining the overall developmental age of the child. As Ilg (1982) explains in the *Scoring Notes*:

> The concept of development age is perhaps more a qualitative than a quantitative concept. It is not numerically derived, not cut and dried, not as neat and tidy as an achievement score or intelligence quotient or a simple chronological age. (p. 2)

This clinical approach to scoring is unsatisfactory for psychometric study of the instrument. Inasmuch as use of the clinical approach to scoring requires familiarity with typical responses at each developmental age level, the Gesell Institute recommends administration and scoring of a minimum of 20 to 50 practice tests before the examiner is considered proficient with the examination. Examiners are trained by Gesell staff members or by individuals who have participated in the Gesell training workshops. The Institute staff offers a three day workshop for individuals interested in learning to administer and interpret the SRST, and a qualification workshop for those interested in becoming "Qualified Gesell Examiners."

Once mastered, the scoring of the SRST requires only a few minutes beyond the actual time required to administer the examination. Because the developmental

age is based on the examiner's clinical assessment of the child's overall performance, the SRST cannot be machine scored.

Interpretation of the SRST is based on internal clinical judgment. According to
Ilg (1982), developmental evaluation, where there is no right or wrong response, is
quite different from obtaining a score or end product. On a developmental exam,
such as the SRST, one must consider "the processes, the organization, the
method, the overt behaviors, and verbalization, as well as the end product, to
determine the child's overall developmental age" (p. 2).

Technical Aspects

The Gesell Institute has not published any formal studies of the reliability or
validity of the SRST. However, several research studies have been conducted that
suggest that further study of the test is warranted to determine its appropriate
uses. Wood, Powell, and Knight (1984) examined the predictive validity of the
SRST. All children (N = 84) in a semirural, lower-middle class, predominantly
white New England school district who were eligible for kindergarten in 1980-81
were given the SRST. Between September and December of 1980, children who
were having difficulty adjusting to the district's kindergarten program were
designated as having "special needs." Discriminant analysis revealed that the
Gesell developmental age was a significant predictor of special needs status.
Chronological age was not predictive of special status. No child designated as
"special needs" was less than 5 years in chronological age, but all of the special
needs children were less than 5 years in developmental age. On the basis of the
discriminant analysis, the authors concluded that for the school district, a critical
developmental age of 57.6 months would yield the fewest prediction errors. Using
that age, one-third of the children who were chronologically eligible for kindergarten would be required to delay entrance into kindergarten. Two important
limitations of the study were noted by the authors. First, the study was actually an
investigation of the concurrent validity of the SRST rather than its predictive
validity. The measures of developmental age were made in December and January
after most of the special needs assessments had been made. An estimate of
predictive validity requires assessment of developmental age prior to determination of the special needs diagnosis. Second, the discriminant analysis suggests a
finer discrimination in developmental age than can be made given the current
practice of clinical scoring.

A study by May and Welch (1984), which included 223 children, examined the
relationship between early school retention based on the SRST and the children's
subsequent academic achievement. Children whose scores on the SRST were 4.5
or below were considered developmentally immature and were recommended by
the school's staff to "Buy a Year" by taking an extra year before second grade.
Those children (N = 62) whose parents agreed to let them take the extra year were
designated as "Buy a Year" (BAY) children and those children (N = 59) whose
parents refused were designated as overplaced (OP) children. The third group of
children (N = 102) scored in the range considered developmentally mature and
were placed in a typical kindergarten along with the OP children. The children
who were retained a year had the lowest scores on the third-grade New York State

PEP Tests in reading and mathematics and on the Stanford Achievement Test (SAT), even though they were almost a year older than the other two groups of children when the PEP and SAT tests were administered. There are some weaknesses in the design of this study. The BAY and OP groups were both assessed as immature on the SRST, but the mean developmental age of the OP group was higher than that of the BAY group. However, this is an important study because it calls into question the claim made by the Gesell Institute staff that developmental placement of children will enhance their future academic performance. Clearly, more studies of this type are needed.

Two other studies shed some light on the psychometric nature of the SRST; however, they were not conducted on the entire set of tasks included in the SRST. The Cube Test and Interests were not included. In the first study, Kaufman (1971) examined the interrelationships among the SRST tasks. The sample was comprised of 103 Caucasian kindergarten students (59 girls and 44 boys) from one elementary school in Long Island, New York. They tended to come from middle-socioeconomic level homes. The median correlation of the tasks with the total score was .58, indicating substantial consistency among tasks, although the mean correlation among the tasks was only .34. Kaufman subjected the tasks to a factor analysis to learn more about the underlying structure of the abilities measured by the tasks. He identifies three factors underlying performance on the tasks: 1) Paper-and-pencil coordination, reflected most strongly by four Copying Forms tasks (considered by Ilg and Ames to be the most reliable indicator of children's behavioral maturity); 2) awareness of part-whole relationships, of which the Incomplete Man task was most representative; 3) academic achievement, reflected most strongly by the writing tasks, Name and Numbers. Kaufman explains his labeling of this factor by stating that for kindergarten students writing is heavily dependent on specific instruction. Kaufman concludes that the presence of the paper-and-pencil factor that was reflected across all the tasks offers support to Ilg and Ames's contention that the Gesell tasks measure one basic construct—behavioral maturity. Kaufman adds that his analysis suggests that performance on the Gesell tasks was made up of "two parts behavioral maturity (factor I), one part abstract intelligence (factor II), and one part experience (factor III) "though he conceded that this characterization is admittedly rough and is certainly not complete" (p. 1358).

In the second study, Kaufman and Kaufman (1972) studied the effectiveness of the SRST battery to predict first-grade achievement. At the end of first grade 80 children, who were tested in kindergarten with the SRST tasks, a battery of Piaget's, and the Lorge-Thorndike Intelligence Tests, were given the SAT. The correlations of the Piaget and Gesell batteries were each .64 with the composite score on the SAT. The correlations between the Gesell and the Arithmetic, Spelling, and Reading subtests were .61, .56, and .63, respectively. Of the Gesell tasks, writing name and numbers was the best predictor of the SAT composite ($r = .61$). The Kaufmans divided the children into three developmental age groups on the basis of their scores on the Gesell tasks. Children with a DA of 5 were placed in the middle group; those with a DA of less than 5 were placed in the lowest group, and children with a DA above 5 were placed in the most mature group. Children in the most mature group (presumably ready for first grade) scored in the upper 75% of the sample on the SAT; 66% of the lowest group (those presumably unready) scored in the lowest 25% of the sample.

Critique

The Gesell Institute has not published any formal studies of the reliability and validity of the SRST (Ames, 1982). However, the small amount of research that has been conducted emphasizes the need for further study. For example, a recent study by May and Welch (1984) calls into question the Gesell Institute's claim that developmental placement will enable children to overcome their learning difficulties. The research that has been published on the tasks that are included on the SRST has been conducted primarily with children from white, middle-socioeconomic backgrounds. Therefore, the extent to which the tasks measure the construct of behavioral maturity in other socioeconomic level groups and the tasks' usefulness in guiding placement decisions with children of other backgrounds are unknown.

Although, according to Kaufman and Kaufman (1972), their study clearly shows that the GSRT is closely associated with first-grade performance, they caution that the results "should not be construed as offering complete support for Ilg and Ames's theory and educational practices" (p. 534). They believe the GSRT to be an excellent predictor of achievement but caution that their study was not designed to ascertain whether or not low-scoring children should be placed back into kindergarten or into transitional classes. Instead, they suggest that the test "be used to assess how well kindergarten children might achieve in first grade," and the results perhaps used "as an aid to grouping within first grade" (p. 534).

Further, if the test is employed for grade placement, they recommend that it be used cautiously until further objective research has been done with the battery. It should also be noted that in both of the studies (Kaufman, 1971; Kaufman & Kaufman, 1972) a special scoring system was devised for the tasks because the "unsystematic clinical method" used by the Gesell Institute staff was considered "not suitable for a rigorous psychometric analysis" (Kaufman & Kaufman, 1972, p. 524).

Many practitioners in early childhood education find the *School Readiness* (1978) philosophy appealing, as evidenced by the increasing use of the SRST as a guide to developmental placement in many school districts. This trend emphasizes the urgent need for research that examines the psychometric properties of the test, especially its reliability and validity in making placement decisions and its usefulness with diverse student groups.

References

Ames, L. B. (1982). Preliminary research supports Gesell School Readiness Test findings. *Academic Psychology Bulletin, 4,* 23-27.

Ames, L., & Ilg, F. (1979). *Your six year old: Defiant but loving.* New York: Delacorte Press.

Ames, L., Ilg, F., & Haber, C. (1982). *Your one year old: The fun loving, fussy 12-to-24-month old.* New York: Delacorte Press.

Gesell, A. (1928). *Infancy and human growth.* New York: Macmillan Publishing Co.

Gesell Institute (1978). *School Readiness Screening Test.* Flemington, NJ: Programs for Education, Inc.

Ilg, F. (1965). *Scoring notes: The developmental examination.* New Haven, CT: Gesell Institute of Child Development.

Ilg, F. (1982). *Scoring notes: The developmental examination.* New Haven, CT: Gesell Institute of Human Development.

Ilg, F., & Ames, L. (1964). *School readiness: Behavior tests used at the Gesell Institute.* New York: Harper & Row.

Ilg, F., Ames, L., & Gesell, A. (1956). *Youth: The years from ten to sixteen.* New York: Harper.

Ilg, F., Ames, L., Haines, J., & Gillespie, C. (1978). *School readiness: Behavior tests used at the Gesell Institute* (rev. ed.). New York: Harper & Row.

Kaufman, A. (1971). Piaget and Gesell: A psychometric analysis of tests built from their tasks. *Child Development, 42,* 1341-1360.

Kaufman, A., & Kaufman, N. (1972). Tests built from Piaget's and Gesell's tasks as predictors of first-grade achievement. *Child Development, 43,* 521-535.

May, D., & Welch, E. (1984). The effects of developmental placement and early retention on children's later scores on standardized tests. *Psychology in the Schools, 21,* 381-385.

Wood, C., Powell, S., & Knight, R. C. (1984). Predicting school readiness: The validity of developmental age. *Journal of Learning Disabilities, 17*(1), 4-11.

Giselle B. Esquivel, Psy.D.
Assistant Professor of Psychology, Graduate School of Education,
Fordham University at Lincoln Center, New York, New York.

SEARCH: A SCANNING INSTRUMENT FOR THE IDENTIFICATION OF POTENTIAL LEARNING DISABILITY

Archie A. Silver and Rosa A. Hagin. New York, New York: Walker Educational Book Corporation.

Introduction

SEARCH is a scanning instrument for the identification of young children who are vulnerable to learning disabilities, developed on the basis of the authors' extensive clinical work with children and their experimental validation of a model preventive program. SEARCH is administered as the first stage in the process of identifying children with deficits in perceptual areas that form the basis for beginning reading skills. Children considered vulnerable are given further comprehensive evaluations to diagnose and clarify their problems. TEACH, the intervention program linked to SEARCH, is then provided, consisting of a series of psychoeducational tasks to stimulate specific weak perceptual areas as a means of preventing reading failure (Silver, Hagin, & Beecher, 1978).

SEARCH is an untimed test which takes approximately 20 minutes to administer. It is administered individually to children between 63 and 80 months of age in kindergarten or first grade. The test is applicable to both sexes since no significant differences were found in terms of incidence or characteristics for this age group. The test was standarized on a multiethnic population of children from inner cities, suburban neighborhoods, and rural areas.

The 10 SEARCH subtests were developed on the basis of clinical and statistical studies which indicated that visual spatial orientation and temporal sequencing are the two basic perceptual components critical in the development of beginning reading. There are three tests of visual perception, two auditory tests, two intermodal tests, and three body image tests. Test reliability is fairly high. The predictive validity of SEARCH is particularly strong and well substantiated. Cross-cultural validation attempts include an adaption (BUSQUEDA) for children in Puerto Rico and one for use with Portugese-language dominant children (BUSCA).

SEARCH was developed by Archie A. Silver, M.D. and Rosa A. Hagin, Ph.D. Dr. Silver is a psychiatrist who is currently Professor of Psychiatry and Chairman

This reviewer wishes to acknowledge Rosa Hagin and Henrietta Kreeger for historical facts and other technical information.

of Child and Adolescent Psychiatry in the University of Florida Medical School. Dr. Hagin is a school psychologist who is Professor in the Graduate School of Education at Fordham University and Research Professor of Psychology at New York University Medical Center.

In the late 1940s Dr. Silver, as chief of the Children's Outpatient Services at Bellevue Hospital, was involved in the psychotherapeutic treatment of children referred for emotional and behavioral problems. It became evident from his work with these children that, in addition to having adjustment problems, many of them were severely retarded in reading. Dr. Silver was convinced that children with these adjustment and school learning problems could be helped through the use of psychoeducational procedures rather than by psychotherapy alone. As a result, funds were secured from the Field Foundation to begin a tutorial reading program in which educational procedures were adapted to clinical practice. In 1949, at Dr. David Wechsler's suggestion, Dr. Hagin joined the program in the capacity of teacher until 1951.

Ten years later, in 1961, a follow-up study was conducted to assess the progress made by the children who had participated in the program and to trace the effects of maturation on their early perceptual problems. Results of this study showed that the children with learning problems formed a heterogeneous group. They differed not only in terms of clinical characteristics but also in terms of their later life adjustment and academic development. In particular, a group of children whose perceptual problems had a neurological basis failed to improve perceptually and continued to evidence greater problems in learning and impulse control than other subgroups in the sample. These children could be considered vulnerable or at risk of learning failure (Silver & Hagin, 1964).

The findings of this study supported the assumption that the basis for learning disabilities may vary, that it is a long-term and tenacious problem for some children, and that using conventional remedial teaching methods would result in an unfavorable prognosis for the vulnerable ones. Moreover, the study suggested the need to devise new teaching procedures to enhance the maturation of lagging perceptual functions as a means of preventing learning failure.

From 1964 to 1968 a controlled study funded by the Carnegie Corporation was undertaken to develop and validate teaching methods to improve specific perceptual problems directly and to see what impact such improvement would have on beginning reading skills. The techniques employed involved the direct perceptual stimulation of weak perceptual functions in order to induce neuropsychological maturation as the basis for learning. This formed the basis for the development of TEACH as an intervention component (Hagin, Silver, & Kreeger, 1976). It was found that the 7- to 12-year-old boys treated in the clinic for defects in spatial and temporal orientation improved with training. Moreover, this improvement resulted in better oral reading and reading comprehension skills (Silver & Hagin, 1976).

In an attempt to begin applying this clinical knowledge to the prevention of learning problems and their emotional consequences, the study moved from the clinic into the schools. In 1969, a clinical battery was developed including various measures of perceptual functioning associated with beginning reading skills. This battery formed the basis for SEARCH as a scanning measure. The test was developed from data collected on 168 first-grade children in a midtown Manhattan elementary school called the "Kips Bay School" to preserve its anonymity. The ages of the children ranged from 5.8 to 7.8 with a mean age of 6½ and 7. The ethnic composition of this sample was 79% white (including Hispanics), 15% black, and 9% other, including Chinese, Filipino, Japanese, and Asian Indian.

During the two successive years of 1969 through 1970 and 1970 through 1971, intensive interdisciplinary examinations were conducted to assess these children (Silver & Hagin, 1972). It was found that 1/3 or 30% of the children assessed with SEARCH could be considered clinically vulnerable, independent of chronological age, sex, intelligence, and socioeconomic background. The data from these examinations were factor analyzed in order to define the major components that were being measured. Two perceptual factors involving auditory association and visual spatial skills were found. This supported previous clinical findings (Silver, 1950) that linked reading failure to a group of symptoms involving difficulties in orienting symbols in space (spatial orientation) and ordering of sounds in time (temporal orientation). Disorientation in these areas could be detected, for example, in immature visual discrimination and recall of asymmetric figures, inability to distinguish embedded patterns clearly, directional confusion, and body image disorientation (Silver & Hagin, 1960). Those perceptual tests that made the strongest contribution in measuring these components were selected for inclusion in the battery.

A preliminary version of the test, called SEARCH$_8$, was administered to 447 children comprising all pupils in the first grades of four schools in the lower east side of Manhattan during the 1971-1972 and 1972-1973 school years. Children were placed into broad categories ranging from those for whom normal progress was predicted to those who were vulnerable to learning failure. Clinical predictions were quantified by setting cutoff scores for each of the subtests of SEARCH$_8$ at approximately the lowest one-third of the distribution of raw scores on each subtest, consistent with the level of incidence found. The validity of the predictions was determined by comparing total SEARCH$_8$ scores with measures of oral reading.

In 1973 SEARCH was standardized on a sample of 2,319 kindergarten children in 31 schools of inner cities in lower Manhattan, middle-class neighborhoods in Brooklyn, and small semi-rural towns of Western North Carolina. The ethnicity of the total sample consisted of 59.8% white (including Hispanics), 17.9% black, and 22.4% other, including Oriental, Asian Indian, Arabian, and Filipino. The ages of the children ranged from 63 to 80 months with an approximately equal distribution by sex and ethnic background at each age level. Subsequent adaptations of SEARCH were made for children in Puerto Rico (BUSQUEDA) and for Portuguese-language dominant children (BUSCA). Other local norms are in the process of being developed.

SEARCH is currently published by Walker Educational Book Corporation in New York City. The testing kit this reviewer received included an expanded SEARCH manual (1981), published as a second edition (following a 1975 preliminary version and a 1976 first edition). The manual is well organized, thorough in its content, and presented in a manner that is easily understood. It includes an introductory section with background information, standardization procedures, directions for administration and scoring, interpretation of results, and new developments on the implementation of the instrument.

Also included in the manual is a list of tables with the statistical analysis of component variables for each subtest and how these were derived. There is a clear description of samples and their characteristics, normative data for children between 63 months and 80 months of age, and specialized norms for specific groups (inner city, suburban, and rural) within the same age range. Thorough information is provided in terms of reliability and predictive validity studies. Descriptive research and case studies help to further enhance the understanding of the instrument as part of a preventive approach. The TEACH manual (1976) is also available, describing the intervention tasks that are linked to SEARCH.

SEARCH test materials include 12 small toy objects used in an auditory discrimination subtest, selected because they were found to be more easily identified than pictures by very young children. These toys are colorful and appealing and fairly updated in terms of their design. SEARCH Record Blanks are used for identifying information, recording raw scores and stanines, and charting profiles. A form is included for making observations on pencil grip and for recording visual motor reproductions. A series of stimulus cards (Lamb Chops) are used for a subtest on visual discrimination and recall of figures.

Practical Applications/Uses

SEARCH consists of 10 subtests developed to measure basic neuropsychological components critical in the development of reading. There are three tests of visual perception (discrimination, recall, and visual motor control), two auditory tests (discrimination and rote sequencing), two intermodal tests (articulation and intermodal dictation), and three body image tests (directionality, finger schema, and praxis).

The 10 SEARCH subtests measuring the basic component variables are the following:

1. *Lamb Chop Matching* consists of shapes resembling a lamb chop chosen on the basis of studies on axial rotations and reading disability (Wechsler & Hagin, 1964). The test measures the ability to discriminate asymmetric figures.

2. *Lamb Chop Recall* measures immediate recall, attention, and concentration.

3. *Designs* is a test of visual motor skills which offers the first opportunity to observe pencil grip and hand dominance.

4. *Rote Sequencing* is a verbal test that taps both visual-neurological factors and auditory and directional components.

5. *Auditory Discrimination* assesses the ability to recognize similarities and differences in sounds through the use of toys and nonsense syllables.

6. *Articulation* requires reproducing sounds of common words.

7. *Initials* is an intermodal dictation task assuming exposure to the written form of first names.

8. *Directionality* assesses spatial orientation.

9. *Finger Schema* measures the ability to perceive and localize tactile stimuli as one aspect of body image.

10. *Pencil Grip* is used to rate the extent of maturity in performing a fine-motor task.

SEARCH is an untimed test which takes approximately 20 minutes to administer. The test is administered individually to children. The examiner may be a teacher, clinician, psychologist, or counselor. However, although most educators are able to administer the instrument, they need to be thoroughly trained as examiners and familiar with all materials and procedures.

General guidelines for test administration are provided in the manual as well as very specific procedures to follow for each of the subtests. Moreover, particular emphasis is given to the kind of relationship that needs to be established between child and examiner. This is especially valuable given the inattentive nature of very young children and the difficulties encountered in assessing them formally. The authors provide information as to the type of observations to make, how to engage children in the tasks, how to organize and present materials, the amount of modeling and opportunities for practice allowed, and the extent of flexibility that may be used in the process. Ascertaining that task requirements are well understood helps to insure that performance on the test is reflective of the child's actual ability.

The scoring process is relatively simple and facilitated by the specific directions that are presented in the manual. Step-by-step instructions are given for recording responses on each of the subtests. Both descriptive and objective scoring standards are provided. Criteria for passing or failing include illustrative samples when necessary. For example, various forms of pencil grip and design reproductions are depicted. In addition, the authors advise of cultural factors to consider in scoring, such as exceptions regarding Chinese children who were taught a special grip for brush-pen writing.

A checklist of procedures recapitulates the steps needed for scoring and the clerical tasks requried of the examiner. These include selecting raw scores that are indicative of vulnerability (VAB Scores), converting raw scores into stanines for profiling strengths and weaknesses on each subtest, and obtaining a Total SEARCH Score (based on the number of subtests that indicate vulnerability).

Several possibilities for the selection and use of appropriate norms are given. Age norms allow for comparisons of individual children with a broad representative sample of children of the same chronological age. However, since a large-sized sample may obscure characteristics of children within specific groups, specialized norms are available for children from inner cities, suburbia, and rural areas. The authors encourage the development and use of local norms, which allow for peer group comparisons, and provide instructions for the development of such norms.

Regarding its interpretation, one must bear in mind that SEARCH was developed as a scanning instrument to determine primarily if a child is vulnerable to learning failure. The *level* attained provides a basis for helping to predict vulnerability in basic perceptual functions associated with beginning reading. Children whose total score falls between 0 and 3 have the greatest neuropsychological and educational needs. Children scoring between 4 and 5 may have developmental problems that also need remediation. Some children whose scores fall between 6 and 7 tend to exhibit social/emotional problems requiring attention. Although

SEARCH is not a screening instrument in the sense that it can provide a clinical diagnosis, it does offer clues which can then be explored further through more intensive examinations. SEARCH individual subtest scores may be interpreted in terms of a *profile* of strengths and weaknesses. Deficits consist of those scores for individual tests that fall below the 1-/-3 cutoff point designated empirically as the criterion for vulnerability. Assets are represented by scores above that point, particularly those between 9 and 10, because fewer children attain scores at that level. In addition, specific *patterns* may be observed regarding relative strengths and weaknesses in auditory versus visual motor modalities. This kind of analysis is important for specific instructional planning and to guide educational intervention through the use of TEACH (Hagin, Silver, & Kreeger, 1976).

In general, SEARCH results need to be interpreted from a holistic perspective that goes beyond an analysis of quantitative scores. An understanding of the total child includes such factors as early stimulation, educational opportunities, possible sensory or language-processing deficits, and migration factors. Therefore, interdisciplinary involvement is an integral part of SEARCH and of the total preventive program. The use of SEARCH with groups of children in the schools requires the same kind of interpretation.

Technical Aspects

Three types of reliability measures were used on SEARCH: internal consistency, test-retest reliability, and standard errors of measurement. Internal consistency was assessed using Kuder-Richardson Formula 21 for all subtests except for those like Pencil Grip, which did not lend themselves to such analysis. For Pencil Grip, intertest agreement was found to be 90%. Internal consistency, or the extent to which each subtest component measured the same variable, ranged between .23 for Designs and .95 for Initials. In general, greater reliability was found for auditory than for visual motor tests, primarily because the latter have less items. Test-retest reliability consisted of a 14-day interval between test administrations to a randomly selected subsample of 50 children from Kips Bay School. Stability coefficients ranged from .28 on Directionality to .97 on Initials. The test-retest reliability was .80 for the Total SEARCH Score. Using standard errors of measurement, the expected band of error for a given individual on the components ranged from .72 to .80 raw score units, with a Total SEARCH of .89 raw score units (Silver & Hagin, 1981). In general, the test shows fairly high reliability given the sporadic and fluctuating nature of very young children's development.

The content validity of SEARCH is partly based on careful selection of items suitable for young children and item revision over the years to adjust to cultural and linguistic variations. Factor analytic studies have also yielded high loadings of subtests on the specific perceptual functions the test purports to assess. Construct validity is supported by clinical studies which show that these perceptual components bear a relationship to beginning reading skills.

The predictive utility of SEARCH was measured against educational criteria in a study with 52 children from no-intervention control schools at the end of first and second grades. Children's earned scores in SEARCH correlated significantly with reading scores on the Wide Range Achievement Test. All children identified as vulnerable by SEARCH, or between 0 and 3, fell below the mean in reading for the two successive years. Between 82% and 87% of those scoring between 8 and 10 were successful readers.

The measurement of predictive criteria against clinical diagnosis was determined by individual neurological and psychiatric examinations done independently of SEARCH for 71 children from Kips Bay School and 100 at Soho schools. Total SEARCH Scores could be categorized on the basis of clinical diagnosis. For example, children with 0-3 scores showed consistent neurological or pervasive health problems; those scoring 4-5 had specific language disabilities; those with 8-10 scores could be characterized as healthy. Thus, a relationship between SEARCH scores and clinical profiles was established.

The predictive validity of SEARCH was further assessed through prediction-performance comparisons of false negatives and false positives. False negatives indicated those children for whom SEARCH predicted normal progress, but who failed to achieve. False positives indicated those for whom SEARCH predicted failure, but who did not fail to achieve. The incidence of false negatives was determined by comparing children's Total SEARCH Scores with subsequent scores in reading one or more years after SEARCH administration. Data on false positives were collected on two untreated samples. Percents of false negatives ranged from 5 to 10%. Percents of false positives were 3% and 9% of the two samples, respectively. Overall, 83 to 87% of children were correctly identified by SEARCH in terms of false negatives and false positives.

Cross-validation with a different set of clinical measures, including neurological, psychiatric and psychological examinations, showed an incidence of only 1% false negatives for a sample of 124 children, out of a group of 494 who were designated as vulnerable (Silver & Hagin, 1981).

Critique

As a test instrument, SEARCH has made a significant contribution to the fields of neuropsychology, psychiatry, and education. It has led to greater understanding of learning disabilities in young children of both sexes and to illuminating the relationship between neuropsychological functioning and learning. It has further clarified the heterogeneity of learning-disabled children as a group and the need for interdisciplinary approaches to assessment and treatment. Theoretically, it has helped to reconcile the two extreme traditional positions that attributed learning disabilities to either psychogenic or organic factors alone.

Foremost, SEARCH has been of practical value in the school setting. It is in keeping with a philosophy of mainstreaming supported by recent legislation on handicapped children (Public Law 94-142) and current educational thinking. As part of a preventive program, it has been a forerunner in the early identification of perceptual problems that lead to learning failure and its emotional consequences. According to Abrams (1984) the usefulness of this type of evaluation ''is dependent upon its ability to point out specific areas of dysfunction and to give leads at least to the best modes of intervention'' (p. 28).

In general, SEARCH is a reliable instrument with strong predictive validity and cross-cultural application. Its adaptations and emphasis on the development of local norms are consistent with the need to find alternative viable means of assessing culturally and linguistically different children. Future applications of SEARCH lie in its continued standardization on various groups, extension to older children and adolescents, and possible use in the identification of gifted early readers. Efforts to study possible relationships between neuropsychological functioning and other academic areas such as math are also implications for the future. SEARCH should continue to play a major role in the areas of learning failure prevention and research.

References

Abrams, J. C. (1984). Interaction of neurological and emotional factors in learning disability. *Learning Disabilities, 3*(3), 27-37.

Hagin, R. A., Silver, A. A., & Kreeger, H. (1976). *TEACH: Learning tasks for the prevention of learning disabilities.* New York: Walker Educational Book Corporation.

Silver, A. A. (1950). *Neurological and perceptual survey of children with reading disability.* Paper presented at Section of Neurology and Psychiatry, New York Academy of Medicine.

Silver, A. A., & Hagin, R. A. (1960). Specific reading disability: Delineation of the syndrome and relationship to cerebral dominance. *Comprehensive Psychiatry, 1,* 126-134.

Silver, A. A., & Hagin, R. A. (1964). Specific reading disability: Follow-up studies. *American Journal of Orthopsychiatry, 34,* 95-102.

Silver, A. A., & Hagin, R. A. (1976). Specific reading disability: Teaching by stimulation of deficit perceptual areas. *American Journal of Orthopsychiatry, 37,* 744-752.

Silver, A. A., & Hagin, R. A. (1972). Profile of a first grade: A basis for preventive psychiatry. *Journal of the American Academy of Child Psychiatry, 11,* 645-674.

Silver, A. A., & Hagin, R. A. (1981). *SEARCH: A scanning instrument for the identification of potential learning disability.* New York: Walker Educational Book Corporation.

Silver, A. A., Hagin, R. A., & Beecher, R. (1978). Scanning, diagnosis and intervention in the prevention of reading disability. *Journal of Learning Disabilities, 11,* 437-439.

Wechsler, D., & Hagin, R. A. (1964). The problem of axial rotation in reading disability. *Perceptual and Motor Skills, 19,* 319-326.

N. Jo Campbell, Ed.D.

Associate Professor of Applied Behavioral Studies, Oklahoma State University, Stillwater, Oklahoma.

THE SELF-DIRECTED SEARCH

John L. Holland. Palo Alto, California: Consulting Psychologists Press, Inc.

Introduction

According to the author, John L. Holland, the Self-Directed Search (SDS) (1977) is designed to be a self-administered, self-scored, and self-interpreted guide for students and adults needing vocational planning assistance. Although it is not intended as a substitute for vocational counselors, the use of the instrument can supply a valuable vocational counseling experience for the majority of people who either do not have the opportunity or do not want to work with a vocational counselor. The SDS can be used in the completion of a systematic study of one's own personal interests and expertise. The results of this study are then used to relate the self-assessment to 500 occupations listed in a component of the SDS, the Occupations Finder (Holland, 1978).

The SDS, based on Holland's theory of career choice, was developed using the hypothesis that the vocational choice process should involve a consideration of several characteristics of the individual in addition to vocational interests. These characteristics include competencies, preferred activities, and self-ratings of abilities. Six types of cognate personality orientations and environmental models have been identified by Holland in his research focusing on his theory of vocational choice. The six types—realistic (R), investigative (I), artistic (A), social (S), enterprising (E), and conventional (C)—serve as the basis for relating one's self-assessments of abilities and interests to appropriate occupations. The importance attached to the relationship between an individual's characteristics and a work environment is grounded in the premise that individuals are more likely to find greater success, stability, and satisfaction in occupations if the work environment suits their personalities. Therefore, the SDS vocational counseling tool is designed to facilitate a person's identification of an appropriate career choice content.

Holland has experience as a vocational counselor in a variety of settings, including educational, military, and clinical, and is a Professor Emeritus at Johns Hopkins University. He constructed and published the Vocational Preference Inventory (VPI) in 1958 and has published extensively for over 25 years. His theory of career choice has served as the central focus for much of his writing, and his instruments, the VPI and the SDS, have been widely used by researchers and counselors. The SDS consists of the Assessment Booklet, an occupational classification booklet; the Occupations Finder; and an interpretative booklet "Understanding Yourself and Your Career" (1979). A Counselor's Guide (1982) and the SDS Professional Manual (1979) are also available.

The Assessment Booklet, a self-assessment booklet, includes six scales of 11 to 14 items per scale in each of three categories: activities, competencies, and occupations. The booklet also contains two self-ratings in six personal trait areas where each trait area corresponds to a personality type identified in Holland's theory of career choices. The scoring procedures designed to yield a three-letter summary code of the user's resemblance to the six personality types are also described in the self-assessment booklet. The summary code is subsequently used to identify appropriate occupational options listed in the Occupations Finder. Suggestions for how the user can gather further information potentially valuable in making vocational decisions and safeguards designed to decrease the possibility of undesirable results due to use of the SDS are included in the final section. A duplicate summary page is provided so that the user can prepare a copy for the appropriate counselor's or administrator's files. The last page lists 10 books that provide information regarding vocational choices and work environments.

The Occupations Finder, revised in 1978, lists 500 occupations in which about 99% of the employees in the United States are engaged. These 500 occupations are arranged by personality type and subtypes. The occupational subtypes are further arranged according to the level of general educational development required as indicated in the *Dictionary of Occupational Titles* (DOT) (Department of Labor, 1977), which is found in most libraries and employment and counseling offices. Out of the 500 occupations listed, all but approximately 3% of the entries are listed with the current DOT number that indicates the classification of the occupation in the DOT scheme.

The interpretive booklet "Understanding Yourself and Your Careers" is designed to encourage the self-directed use of the SDS. It contains an explanation of the typology serving as the base for the SDS along with information relative to some commonly found problems in interpretation of results. The user is encouraged to investigate further the jobs identified as appropriate by the results of the SDS and to view those jobs as only suggestions. Consulting with a counselor is advised for the user who is not satisfied with the occupations indicated by the summary code. Suggested sources of information relative to the problems of vocational life are printed on the last page of the interpretative booklet.

The Counselor's Guide is made up of selections of material published in the more lengthy SDS Professional Manual. The most important features of the SDS are discussed in the 14-page guide. Included are discussions of the purposes and characteristics of the SDS, the typology developed by Holland that served as the basis for the development of the SDS, descriptions of the SDS booklets and accessory materials, directions for administering and scoring the SDS, suggestions for potential uses of the SDS to serve a variety of needs, information relative to the technical quality of the SDS, and a discussion of the procedures followed in an attempt to eliminate discrimination on the basis of sex of the user.

The Professional Manual, as mentioned previously, presents the information found in the guide, plus a comprehensive section regarding the interpretation and use of scores on the SDS, and approximately 24 commonly asked questions with Holland's answers regarding the development and use of the SDS. A training program to provide competencies in the use of the SDS for counselors is also described, and a self-test for counselors is contained in an appendix. Other information contained in appendices include an alphabetic index for occupational classifications and codes, directions for translating Holland codes into DOT codes, descriptions of norms for both SDS scales and codes, and scoring procedures for individuals' decision-making ability scores and norms for interpreting those scores.

The first edition of the SDS was published in 1970. Revisions in the format and wording of items on the SDS and in the text of the Assessment Booklet were made prior to the 1977 edition. The changes in the suggested actions were made in an attempt to point out that scores on the SDS are affected by society's differential career expectations of men, women, certain ethnic groups, and children of parents employed in various occupations. The current edition (1977) is similar to the earlier edition but has been revised to update the materials. Most of the revisions were minor, but three major changes are evident. The scoring procedure has been greatly simplified from the original weighted-score procedure. The Counselor's Guide reports that the simplified system has greatly reduced college students' scoring error rate which has been an expressed concern of counselors and researchers for some years. In addition, a total of 50 job titles have been added to the Occupations Finder in order to make the list more reflective of current occupations. The Occupations scale has also been revised so that it now lists the occupational titles contained in the seventh revision of the Vocational Preference Inventory rather than those listed in the sixth revision.

Minor changes were made in an attempt to diminish sex differences in responses to the scale by altering selected items on that scale. This revision was at least partly due to the controversial issue of sexist bias in the SDS. Furthermore, the directions in the scales were altered so that respondents can now indicate changes in their interests. The suggested readings list has also been updated to include more current information relative to careers and vocational planning.

SDS, Form E (Easy) (1979), developed for use by adolescents and adults having limited reading abilities, was first published in 1970 and revised in 1973 and 1979. The reading level of Form E is several grade levels below that of the standard form. The scoring procedures yield two- rather than three-letter codes. Form E's "Occupations Finder"—titled Job Finder—has been modified so that the two-letter codes derived in scoring Form E can be used to identify appropriate occupations. This modified booklet also has easily comprehendable directions. Another feature of Form E not in the standard form is a short explanation provided for each occupational title. Form E is further simplified by the reduction of the number of items from 228 to 203.

The Spanish translation of SDS, Form E and the Jobs Finder is available from Consulting Psychologists Press, Inc., as is a Vietnamese translation of the standard SDS and the Occupations Finder. Research conducted by Barker, White, Reardon, and Johnson (1980) indicate that the SDS can be adapted through the use of an audio tape, braille, and a wooden board constructed to eliminate the requirements of writing to produce an effective career planning instrument for use by the blind.

Because the SDS is designed to be self-administered by adults, it requires little intervention by an examiner. Revision of the scoring procedures has simplified the scoring process the individual taking the test must follow, but this reviewer has not been able to locate research investigating the effects of the simplified procedures on scoring error rates, other than that reported in the manual. This research involved college students and high school students, and the reported results imply that the simplified process actually results in a large reduction in the high error rates in scoring previously reported for the SDS. The manual advises that the scores on the SDS should always be checked due to the potential of scoring errors being made by any user.

The manual recommends that monitors be provided for groups larger than 25 to 30 and more supervision is recommended if the instrument is used with students having low reading levels or with junior high school students. The SDS, estimated to have seventh- and eighth-grade reading levels, is intended to be used by high school and older populations having at least average reading abilities. People who have low reading abilities or education levels less than ninth grade will benefit from the use of Form E, estimated to have a fourth-grade reading level.

Although the SDS does not have what are generally considered subtests, it does have the following five sections in the self-assessment booklet:

1. Occupational Daydreams: the users list both careers they have daydreamed about and careers they have discussed with others. These careers are then located in the Occupations Finder and converted into three-letter codes that are combinations of the R, I, A, S, E, and C categories that indicate the six personality types and environmental models identified in Holland's theory.

2. Activities: the users mark "like" or "dislike" for activities such as "keep your desk and room neat" and "sell something." Each activity has been categorized under one of the six categories.

3. Competencies: the users mark those activities they feel they can perform competently and those they either cannot perform well or have never attempted. As in the Activities section, each activity is categorized under one of the six categories.

4. Occupations: the users respond to a list of occupations by marking those that interest them and those they dislike. The occupations are also grouped under the six categories.

5. Self-Estimates: the users rate their own abilities and skills in 12 areas using a seven-point scale. Each of the six categories are represented by two ability or skill areas. This part is treated as two sections.

The users score their own responses, which are recorded in the booklet, by summing the total occurrences of each letter (R, I, A, S, E, or C) from the Activities, Competencies, Occupations, and two Self-Estimates sections. The Occupational Daydreams responses are not used in the scoring process. The three letters out of the six possible (R, I, A, S, E, or C) having the highest frequency of occurrence indicate the summary code or profile for the user. Directions are given for the procedure to follow in the event that two letters receive equal frequencies and are also among the letters having the three highest frequencies.

The users then refer to the Occupations Finder to identify occupations which have summary codes similar or identical to the summary codes received by the users. These occupations are ones that presumably require patterns of interests and competencies that are consistent with the users' special patterns of self-estimates of skills and interests.

Practical Applications/Uses

This instrument can be used by individuals who wish to identify with minimal assistance occupations in which they have the greatest chances of satisfaction, stability, and success. It should not be made available to individuals unless some type of counseling assistance is available to the user who may experience problems in using the instrument. The SDS can help people who cannot or will not take advantage of the expertise of vocational counselors to make an intensive systematic search of their personal abilities and interests and use the information gathered to make better informed vocational decisions than would be made without that information. It can serve as an effective vehicle for the user attempting to achieve a clearer focus regarding self-estimates of interests and skills and to identify occupations having work environments congruent with the user's personality orientation.

The SDS is recommended for use with individuals or small groups of 15 to 25 persons. This reviewer cannot endorse the suggestion in the manual that the SDS be distributed by mail followed by a group meeting to discuss the result and provide additional information regarding vocational choices. The assumption that all respondents can score the SDS and arrive at an accurate summary code is not supported by research. Those users who might make scoring errors when completing the SDS in an unsupervised situation and derive an incorrect summary code may also choose not to attend the group meeting where the scoring errors might possibly be observed. These people then would have incorrect information on which they might base vocational decisions, resulting in more negative consequences than making a vocational choice without the type of information the SDS can provide. Also, there is the possibility that the users may receive summary codes which do not correspond to ones listed in the Occupations Finder. This reviewer believes the SDS should only be used under the supervision of a counselor or a psychologist. This type of supervision should protect the users from making vocational choices based on incorrect summary codes or from arriving at the misconception they are "weird" because their summary codes do not match the lengthy list of codes in the Occupations Finder. Although neither situation should occur if the users carefully read and follow the directions supplied on the instrument, in reality both situations have a high probability of occurring.

The chief functions of the SDS have included the provision of personal data, which can be used by counselors to help individuals deal with vocational problems, organize occupational files to maximize the files' usefulness, and to assist in the interpretation of interest inventories. Researchers have also found the components of the SDS to be valuable in the conduction of behavioral research.

Potential new applications of this instrument have implications for the counselor, psychologist, and researcher, but there is a need for determining how the SDS actually affects the user. Information relative to increasing the positive effects of completing the SDS would benefit both the user and the counselor. It would be of further value to complete more comprehensive validation studies of the SDS, including studies of cross-cultural differences in distributions of the six types of cognate personality orientations identified in Holland's theory of careers.

Reports indicate the settings in which the SDS has been used are many and varied. Form E has been used with young children and with prisoners who were still incarcerated. The standard form has been used by males and females ranging in age from high school to adult, including blacks, Caucasians, Spanish-Americans, and American Indians. Researchers and counselors have also reported successfully using the SDS in foreign countries, such as Australia, Canada, England, Nigeria, and Israel.

The professions which have used the SDS include vocational counseling, school counseling, personnel management, business employment consulting, and behavioral research. It is not recommended as an employment screening instrument or as a predictor of vocational success.

Although not specifically designed for use with subjects having vision problems, Barker, White, Reardon, and Johnson (1980) report research in which they adapted the SDS for use by the blind. They found their adapted version of the SDS to be an effective vocational guidance instrument for blind persons.

For optimal use, it is recommended that the SDS be completed in a quiet setting where the person can work uninterrupted. The manual reports that the instrument has been used effectively by individuals working in groups of 30 or fewer.

Even though the manual describes the SDS as a self-administered test, it is clear to this reviewer that effective use of the SDS requires that the examiner or user be thoroughly familiar with Holland's typology, which served as the foundation of the development of the SDS. Professional training as a psychologist is not required for effective use of the SDS.

The major problems encountered in the use of the SDS results from scoring errors made by the users. Even college students may not score their responses accurately. The omission from the Occupations Finder of 48 summary codes which may be derived from the self-assessment booklet can be confusing and anxiety provoking for the naive user. The instructions are clearly presented, however, as the manual states, "users do make errors" (p. 9). Therefore, the scoring procedures should be checked by a counselor or at the very least by a proctor trained to score the SDS. The test is not difficult to administer but, as mentioned previously, close attention to the directions is essential to the derivation of a valid summary code.

The process of completing the SDS takes about 30-60 minutes. This should be followed by a session with a counselor to clarify any questions the user has regarding the process or the identified occupations.

Technical Aspects

The reliability and validity of earlier versions of the SDS have been extensively researched and reported in the professional literature. One deficiency noted repeatedly in studies described in the manual and other published studies is the use of incidental samples. The internal reliability (corrected split-half) estimates of the summary scale of the 1977 edition of the SDS range from .83 (females) and .84

(males) to .91 (females) and .95 (males) (Holland, 1979). The internal reliability estimates for the subscales are generally much lower than those for the summary scale. Test-retest reliabilities computed using a very small sample (N = 30) range from .90 for the Realistic type on the Competencies subscale to .56 for the Conventional type on the Occupations subscale and cluster in the .70s for all six types on summary and subscales of the SDS (Holland, 1979).

The counselor using the manual is cautioned by Holland regarding the larger error present in the test-retest reliability estimates due to the use of a small sample. More data regarding the reliability of the scales of the 1977 version should be provided. Even though the SDS is claimed to be useful from age 15 and older, there are no high school students included in the reliability studies using the standard form of the SDS. This is of particular concern since high school students' assessments are likely to change more than those of the older subjects included in the reliability studies. Internal reliabilities calculated for Form E using a sample of 236 seventh-graders range from .63 (females) and .56 (males) to .91 (females) and .92 (males) (Holland, 1979). It would also be valuable to have reliability estimates reported for various ethnic groups of high school students, college students, and adults.

Predictive validity estimates of the SDS are reported in the manual. In a study using occupational choices of men and women collected three years after the administration of the SDS during the freshman year of college as the criterion variable and scores on the SDS as the predictor, Gottfredson and Holland (1975) report that 43% of the males and 66% of the females made occupational choices consistent with their high-point SDS codes. Gottfredson and Holland also report that the new, simplified scoring system has not affected either the predictive validity or the high-point SDS codes received by users when the old and the new scoring methods were compared. McGowan (1982) reports evidence of predictive validity of the SDS for career choices of vocationally undecided high school seniors. He found that 73% of the 84 subjects in his study had received primary or secondary summary codes on the SDS that predicted their occupational choices four years later.

It seems reasonable that the validity and reliability studies based on the 1970 version of the SDS are also pertinent when one examines the technical characteristics of the 1977 version of the SDS. The manual reports extensive information regarding research investigating those characteristics of the instrument. The internal consistency coefficients and test-retest reliability coefficients are similar to those reported for the 1977 version of the SDS. The subjects utilized in the reported reliability studies of the 1970 version included only high school and college students.

The validity studies reported both in the manual and in other literature sources are so numerous that the volume is overwhelming. The SDS was developed using a well-established theory based on Holland's hexagon which is claimed to order and represent the correlations among the six types of cognate personality orientations and environmental models. Research, such as that reported by Rachman, Amernic, and Aranya (1981), seems to support the hexagonal model. However, this reviewer is confused by the claim in the manual that the lengths of the sides and diagonals of the hexagon represent distances between occupational classes and are inversely proportional to the size of the correlations calculated between the classes when the model presented in the manual is equilateral even though the correlations between adjacent classes are not equal. For example, the distances between E and C and between C and R are equal even though the correlations between E and C and between C and R are .71 and .51, respectively. Crites (1978) implies that Holland's model is not correctly represented as a hexagon but may possess three-dimensional characteristics. Even though Holland acknowledges that the hexagon resulting from actual data collected using the SDS is likely to be less than perfect, the diagram of his model in the manual does not reflect his reservations about the use of a perfect hexagon to represent his model.

The predictive and concurrent validity estimates of the 1970 edition of the SDS indicate that career codes on the SDS have been found to either match current occupations or to accurately predict future occupations for about 35 to 45% of the males and about 55 to 65% of the females (Holland, 1979). These hit rates are consistent with those found using similar types of instruments. Validity estimates for Form E are not reported; however, Holland states the validity of Form E should be approximately the same as for the standard form because of the similarity of the items.

Validity and reliability information is presented without a coherent explanation of how the estimates are determined for the SDS. It would be helpful if exact procedures used were discussed more fully, along with the provision of jargon-free definitions of measurement terms used in the discussion.

Measurement terms utilized in this review include:

Reliability—the degree to which the results yielded by an instrument are consistent, stable, and relatively free from measurement errors.

Internal reliability—degree of relationship among items on an instrument, that is, whether each item measures the same characteristic as every other item.

Split-half reliability—a type of internal reliability estimated by calculating the correlation between scores on one half the test with scores on the other half. Usually the two halves are comprised of the odd-numbered items and the even-numbered items. The correlation coefficient is corrected by using the Spearman-Brown formula to adjust for the doubled length of the entire test.

Test-retest reliability—a type of reliability estimate obtained by administering the same test to a group of individuals on two occasions with a short time interval between the two test administrations and then correlating the two sets of scores.

Validity—the extent to which the results of an instrument serve the specific purposes for which they are intended to serve.

Concurrent validity—the extent to which results of an instrument correlate with a criterion measure collected at the time the instrument is administered.

Predictive validity—the extent to which results of an instrument predict some specified criterion.

Critique

Reviews of the SDS (1970, 1977) written by Dr. John O. Crites, Research Professor at Kent State University, were published in the *Eighth Mental Measurements Yearbook* (1978) and in *A Counselor's Guide to Vocational Guidance Instrument* (1983).

Dr. Crites indicates that he believes the use of the SDS without the supervision of a trained counselor is not advisable in spite of the claims made in the manual. He does endorse the use of the instrument by counselors to determine career-choice content of clients who desire to explore appropriate career choices.

According to Cutts (1977), the benefits gained through use of the SDS exceed the negative aspects of the instrument. She does express a concern regarding the use of the SDS with females whose work histories in clerical positions may be reflected in higher Conventional scores when their vocational interests and plans may lie in other professional areas for which they are preparing while working in the clerical positions.

The SDS was constructed using a well-established career theory, Holland's theory of career choice, as the basis. The SDS has many actual and potential uses but the efficacy of the results of some of the uses of the SDS are questionable. One reason for this is the scoring errors made by unsupervised users. It is imperative that clerical monitoring be provided during the test administration and that counselors be available to discuss aspects of Holland's theory and to encourage the users to explore the career possibilities indicated by the results of the SDS.

Another deficiency this reviewer identified in the SDS is that the developmental aspects of career choice are for the most part not addressed. The sole allusion to this important contemporary topic in vocational psychology occurs in the manual in the form of a suggestion that the SDS be used to obtain periodic information regarding appropriate career choices. However, a positive aspect of the SDS is the wide variety of alternative occupational choices included in the instrument. This can be very useful to counselors who must be concerned with helping individuals make appropriate occupational plans in an everchanging world of work.

Holland has developed a simple framework by which the personal information individuals possess regarding themselves can be used to provide matches with appropriate careers. Using the results of the SDS counselors can supply helpful information for users who wish to make career decisions based on both a systematic search of their own personal interests and skills and a knowledge of the relationship between their personal characteristics and congruent work environments.

The SDS is most appropriately used in either a small group or individual counseling environment and as a means through which the users can clarify their perceptions of careers and the process by which career choices are made. The contributions the SDS can make as a career counseling tool when used in an appropriate manner should not be overlooked by either the professional counselor or the individual desiring assistance in exploring appropriate career options.

References

This list includes text citations as well as suggested additional reading.

Barker, S., White, P., Reardon, R., & Johnson, R. (1980). An evaluation of the effectiveness of an adaption of the Self-Directed Search for use by the blind. *Rehabilitation Counseling Bulletin, 23*(3), 177-182.

Benninger, W. B., & Walsh, W. B. (1980). Holland's theory and non-college-degreed working men and women. *Journal of Vocational Behavior, 17*, 81-88.

Crites, J. (1978). Review of The Self-Directed Search. In O. K. Buros (Ed.), *The eighth mental measurements yearbook* (pp. 1608-1611). Highland Park, NJ: The Gryphon Press.

Crites, J. (1983). Review of The Self-Directed Search. In J. T. Kapes & M. M. Mastie (Eds.), *A counselor's guide to vocational guidance instruments* (pp. 88-91). Falls Church, VA: The National Guidance Association.

Cutts, C. C. (1977). Review of the Self-Directed Search. *Measurement and Evaluation in Guidance, 10*(2), 117-20.

Doty, M. S., & Betz, N. E. (1979). Comparison of the concurrent validity of Holland's theory for men and women in an enterprising occupation. *Journal of Vocational Behavior, 15*, 207-216.

Gottfredson, G. D., & Holland, J. L. (1975). Some normative self-report data on activities, competencies, occupational preferences, and ability ratings for high school and college students, and employed men and women. *JSAS Catalog of Selected Documents in Psychology, 5*, 192. (MS No. 859)

Holland, J. L. (1958). *Vocational Preference Inventory.* Palo Alto, CA: Consulting Psychologist Press.

Holland, J. L. (1970, 1973, 1979). *Self-Directed Search for Educational and Vocational Planning: Form E.* Palo Alto, CA: Consulting Psychologists Press.

Holland, J. L. (1977). *Self-Directed Search: A guide to educational and vocational planning.* Palo Alto, CA: Consulting Psychologists Press.

Holland, J. L. (1978). *The occupations finder: For use with the Self-Directed Search* (rev. ed.). Palo Alto, CA: Consulting Psychologists Press.

Holland, J. L. (1979). *The Self-Directed Search professional manual.* Palo Alto, CA: Consulting Psychologists Press.

Holland, J. L. (1985). *Making vocational choices: A theory of vocational personalities and work environments.* Englewood Cliffs, NJ: Prentice-Hall, Inc.

McGowan, A. S. (1982). The predictive efficiency of Holland's SDS summary codes in terms of career choice: A four-year follow-up. *Journal of Vocational Behavior, 20*, 294-303.

Prediger, D. J. (1981). A note on Self-Directed Search validity for females. *Vocational Guidance Quarterly, 30*, 117-129.

Rachman, D., Amernic, J., & Aranya, N. (1981). A factor-analytic study of the construct validity of Holland's Self-Directed Search test. *Educational and Psychological Measurement, 41*, 425-437.

U.S. Department of Labor. (1977). *Dictionary of occupational titles* (4th ed.). Washington, DC: U.S. Government Printing Office.

Walsh, W. B., Bingham, R., Horton, J. H., & Spokane, A. (1979). Holland's theory and college-degreed working black and white women. *Journal of Vocational Behavior, 15*, 217-223.

Walsh, W. B., Hildebrand, J. O., Ward, C. M., & Matthews, D. F. (1983). Holland's theory and non-college-degreed working black and white women. *Journal of Vocational Behavior, 22*, 182-90.

Patricia R. McCarthy, Ph.D.
Associate Professor of Psychology, Southern Illinois University, Carbondale, Illinois.

SELF-ESTEEM QUESTIONNAIRE

James K. Hoffmeister. Boulder, Colorado: Test Analysis and Development Corporation.

Introduction

The Self-Esteem Questionnaire (SEQ-3) is a 21-item, self-report inventory that measures two aspects of an individual's view of the self: 1) self-esteem—feelings of personal competence, worth, success, and importance to others; and 2) self-other satisfaction—the degree to which an individual is satisfied with the level of self-esteem achieved.

The author of the SEQ-3 is Dr. James K. Hoffmeister, president of the Test Analysis and Development Corporation in Boulder, Colorado. This company is engaged in designing and implementing evaluation systems for business, industry, government, and education. Dr. Hoffmeister is a social psychologist; he received his Ph.D. from the University of Colorado, specializing in measurement and statistics. He developed the SEQ-3 in 1970 while he was director of testing in the Department of Research of the Jefferson County school system in Colorado. Hoffmeister designed the SEQ-3 to respond to the administration's concern with the affective functioning of its student body, particularly self-esteem (J.K. Hoffmeister, personal communication, January 2, 1985). He also wanted to address some of the methodological problems inherent in other self-esteem measures, such as poor reliability and validity and ambiguous questions. One of his major purposes was to develop a test that generalizes across age groups.

Hoffmeister has had numerous experiences with test development. He is the author of Course Evaluation Questionnaire (1971a) which assesses the teaching effectiveness of college professors and has been used at universities in Colorado and New Mexico. He is also the author of the School Atmosphere Questionnaire (1971b) and the Classroom Atmosphere Questionnaire (1972). He co-authored the Conceptual Systems Test (Harvey & Hoffmeister).

The initial item pool for the SEQ-3 was rationally derived by the author by samples of the populations for which the questionnaire was targeted. Hoffmeister (1976) developed items from personal experiences and by studying other self-esteem measures. He then had groups of students and adults critique these items, making clarifications and modifications, and suggesting alternative items. He attempted to word items as simply as possible in order to make his test appropriate for a young population. He found that students with less than a 4th-grade reading level could not complete the SEQ-3 unless the questions were read to them and interpreted by the test administrator.

Hoffmeister then administered the items to groups of 4th-, 5th-, and 6th-grade students in a large Colorado school system. The students were told the purpose of the questionnaire and were asked to indicate any ambiguities in the items and response scale. This procedure was conducted on six groups of students, yielding substantial modifications that made the items and response scale as easy to understand as possible.

Hoffmeister next administered the items to two groups of junior-high students from the same Colorado school system, who similarly responded to issues of clarity, until 55 questions were developed. He then conducted an empirical evaluation of these questions, administering them to about 300 4th-, 5th-, and 6th-grade students; to 260 junior-high students; 100 high-school students; and to about 800 Air Force cadets and other adults. He conducted a cluster analysis on this data and found that the items grouped around two distinct factors: self-esteem and self-other satisfaction. Items, the oblique coefficient factors of which ranged from .51 to .70, were included in these two scales. The correlation between the self-esteem and the self-other-satisfaction factors ranged from .17 to .60, with the lowest correlations for children and the highest correlations for adults.

The SEQ-3 makes a distinction between an individual's self-*description* as positive or negative (Self-Esteem subscale) and the person's *emotional response* to the self as either upsetting or satisfying (Self-Other-Satisfaction subscale). The questionnaire has not been revised since its publication in 1971. At present, there are no published forms of the SEQ-3 adapted for special populations, such as Spanish-speaking individuals or the visually impaired.

The SEQ-3 is a 21-item, self-report measure. Twelve of the items measure self-esteem and 9 items measure self-other satisfaction. Each item is responded to on a 5-point Likert Scale, where 1 = Not at all, 2 = Only a little, 3 = Depends or not sure, 4 = Pretty much, and 5 = Yes, very much. The items and the response scale are printed on the same computerized form. Respondents must use a #2 pencil to give their answers. Scores on Self-Esteem subscale range from 12 to 60 and from 9 to 45 on Self-Other-Satisfaction subscale. A mean score for each subscale is calculated for each respondent. Lower scores indicate less self-esteem and less self-other satisfaction, respectively.

Examples of items on the Self-Esteem subscale are: "I feel sure of myself" and "Most of my friends accept me as much as they accept other people." Responses to three of the questions on Self-Esteem and to all of the questions on the Self-Other Satisfaction are reversed for scoring. Thus, the tendency for response bias is reduced. Nine of the self-esteem questions are followed by the same self-other-satisfaction question, "Does the situation described in number [previous item] upset you?". The SEQ-3 provides space for a respondent's identification number, location, and gender.

Hoffmeister (1976) states that the examiner should be moderately to highly involved in the testing process. The examiner should explain the exact nature of the variables being assessed; should encourage respondents to ask questions, for example, for clarity; encourage them to answer items, while allowing them to refrain from responding; and provide feedback about respondents' scores if requested. Hoffmeister encourages a dialogue, partly because the SEQ-3 was developed to be helpful to the respondent. This approach should help to encourage respondent cooperation and facilitate validity.

The SEQ-3 is appropriate for individuals ranging from Grade 4 through adulthood. As mentioned earlier, it has been developed at a 4th-grade reading level. The two subscales assess related, but different, aspects of the self. Self Esteem measures the degree to which an individual feels competent, confident, and accepted by others. Self-Other Satisfaction assesses how much emotional upset individuals feel with respect to their self-perceived esteem. Thus, the subscales provide a profile of how positively or negatively individuals define themselves and how distressing or negatively individuals define themselves and how distressing this view is to them.

Scores on each of the subscales are reported as either "high" (+), "low" (–), "situational" (middle), or "review test—results unclear" (inconsistent). High scores range from 3.75 to 5.00; low scores range from 1.00 to 2.24; situational scores range from 2.25 to 3.74; and "results unclear—review test" means that an individual has responded in an inconsistent manner.

Practical Applications/Uses

The SEQ-3 has wide potential for use. It would be appropriate for psychologically normal or neurotic populations with normal intelligence. It would not be appropriate for a psychotic population. It has been found to be a useful diagnostic tool with elementary- and secondary-school students, potential child abusers, individuals with Alzheimer's disease, and unemployed Hispanic women (J.K. Hoffmeister, personal communication, January 2, 1985). It has been used as an outcome measure to assess the effects of a weight-loss program for obese individuals (Murray, 1973). It has potential as a diagnostic tool for therapy clients, as an outcome measure for individual and group therapy, and it could be employed in validation studies of other, related measures. The SEQ-3 could be used in combination with other personality measures, e.g., the Personal Orientation Inventory (Shostrom, 1962), the Tennessee Self-Concept Scale (Fitts, 1964), to develop personality profiles.

The SEQ-3 can also be used for diagnostic purposes, e.g., to indicate the need for psychological services; as an outcome measure of the effectiveness of treatments; and for descriptive purposes, e.g., to assess the impact of sociological events such as unemployment. The SEQ-3 might be used with individuals currently experiencing major life crises (e.g., separation, divorce, cancer) to study their effects on self-esteem. Such issues as severity of the crises and availability of social support on changes in self-esteem and self-other satisfaction could be assessed. In addition, the SEQ-3 has potential use for school psychologists; clinical, counseling, and educational psychologists; elementary, secondary, and college guidance counselors; social workers; sociologists, health psychologists; and gerontologists.

The SEQ-3 can be administered either individually or in group settings, such as classrooms. A proctor or unskilled person can administer the SEQ-3, especially when the objective is to obtain nomothetic data (such as group norms). More idiographic data, e.g., within the context of counseling, might best be obtained by a skilled clinician who is familiar with the respondent and with the construction of the questionnaire and has some theoretical knowledge of the construct of self-esteem.

The SEQ-3 is easily administered requiring about 15 minutes to complete. Depending on the amount of dialogue between the respondent and the test administrator, this time could expand to about 45 minutes to an hour.

Responses are made on a computerized form that is available from the author. Computerized scoring is done by the author. There is a manual (Hoffmeister, 1976) that describes the development and interpretation of the SEQ-3 and is available from the author.

Hoffmeister (1975) developed a program called Convergence Analysis to score the SEQ-3 whereby a response distribution for each respondent is established. Scores on each scale are obtained by calculating a mean for each respondent. Only items that fall around the central response distribution are included in these calculations. A skilled interpreter must determine which items to include in the analyses and how to interpret the response distribution. Hoffmeister (personal communication, January 2, 1985) uses a general algorithm: If at least 70% of the items in the Self-Esteem subscale are concentrated around 1-3 adjacent response categories he discards those items not included in this group when calculating the score. If less than 70% of the items are concentrated in from 1-3 adjacent response categories, the response distribution is called "non-convergent" and no score is assigned for the subject on the scale.

Based on the mean and response distribution, individuals may receive a label of "situational" (middle), suggesting that across all situations (items) they sometimes feel adequate and sometimes inadequate. This is different from a bi-modal profile in which the individual feels positively on some items and negatively on others. A "results unclear—review test" (inconsistent) label suggests that the individual has answered quite inconsistently across all items, i.e., scores on individual items do not concentrate around the same score (e.g., around 2 and 3). If less than about 70% of the answers are around the same score, Hoffmeister marks the profile "results unclear—review test" and prints out the individual's responses for each item. Because of the difficulty in determining these scores, the SEQ-3 should be scored only by the computer program developed by the author.

Interpretation of scores on the SEQ-3 can be made according to objective data if they are high, low, or situational. This could be done by a psychometrician familiar with the questionnaire. The following normative data have been reported by Hoffmeister (1976): Students in grades 4-6 have means on the Self-Esteem subscale of around 3.65; junior-high and senior-high students score around 3.85; the mean is about 4.00 for adults. Scores on the Self-Other-Satisfaction subscale average around 4.50 for all of these populations. As expected, scores for junior- and senior-high students with a history of reading failure were somewhat lower, means = 3.40 and 3.70, respectively. Elementary students with reading failure averaged 3.40 on the Self-Esteem subscale.

A group of 50 adults who were receiving psychological services from a clinic for a variety of psychological problems averaged around 3.70 on the self-other satisfaction scale. Hoffmeister has found no significant differences in scores on either scale as a function of gender or race of the respondent. In one study, Murray (1973) found that obese subjects beginning a weight-loss program scored significantly lower on the Self-Esteem subscale than nonobese individuals. He further found that the self-esteem scores of the obese subjects increased with reduction in weight.

Interpretation of a profile scored as "results unclear—review test" must be interpreted using clinical judgment. This type of interpretation should be made by someone with at least a master's degree in school, clinical, or counseling psychology, or a related discipline. Furthermore, familiarity with the respondent would be useful.

Technical Aspects

Hoffmeister (1976) measured the test-retest reliability of the SEQ-3 for a group of 250 4th- through 6th-grade students from one suburban elementary school in Denver. Reliability for a two-week period was about .70 for both scales. Furthermore, he reports that about 70% of the students had scores in the same range at the second testing, i.e., low, middle, high, or inconsistent. Alpha coefficients ranged from .80 to .96 for both scales.

Hoffmeister (1976) conducted a comparison of the SEQ-3 with the Coopersmith Self-Esteem Questionnaire short form (Coopersmith, 1981). He administered both inventories to a group of 225 5th-grade students from a suburban elementary school in Denver. Over 50% of the students responded in an inconsistent fashion on the Coopersmith, while less than 10% responded inconsistently on the SEQ-3. These data suggest that the SEQ-3 has a high degree of internal consistency and test-retest reliability. Individuals are fairly constant in their responses over short intervals. Furthermore, he reports Cronbach coefficient alphas of .80 to .95 on the Self-Esteem subscale and from .85 to .96 on the Self-Other-Satisfaction subscale. Test-retest reliability for a group of unemployed Hispanic women in the San Francisco area was .94 (df = 94). Again, placement of individuals on the scale from low to high was similar at the second testing ($X^2 = 74.77$, df = 9).

Theoretically, self-esteem should improve with age; an examination of Hoffmeister's (1976) normative data indicates this trend, thus offering support for the validity of his measure. The questionnaire appears to have good face validity. In his comparison of the SEQ-3 with the Coopersmith Self-Esteem Questionnaire, Hoffmeister (1976) found that the Self-Esteem subscale and the Self-Other-Satisfaction subscale correlated with the Coopersmith at the .61 level and the .40 level, respectively. Its comparison to the Coopersmith suggests that the SEQ-3 has adequate construct validity. The correlation of .60 between Self-Esteem and the Coopersmith indicates that both measures are assessing similar constructs. The .40 correlation between Self-Other-Satisfaction and the Coopersmith suggests that Self-Other-Satisfaction is a related, but distinct variable.

In other studies, the correlation between scores on the Self-Esteem subscale and parent and teacher ratings of 500 elementary and junior-high students' self-esteem was about .30. The correlations between Self-Esteem Self-Other-satisfaction and IQ, as measured by the Otis-Lennon Mental Ability Test (Otis & Lennon, 1967) were .20 and .10, respectively, for a group of 300 elementary students. Hoffmeister (1976) reports that these scales correlate around .35 with the Classroom Atmosphere Questionnaire (Hoffmeister, 1972) and the School Atmosphere

Questionnaire (Hoffmeister, 1971b). He also reports low correlations between self-esteem and school achievement as measured by a standardized achievement test for 4th- through 7th-grade students. These results suggest that the scales are measuring different variables; thus discriminant validity has been obtained. But they correlate in the expected direction, thus providing predictive validity.

Critique

The SEQ-3 has been developed through rational and empirical methods to measure the personality construct of self-esteem. Its theoretical roots are compatible with humanistic theory, e.g., Abraham Maslow's (1954) self-esteem construct and Carl Roger's (1959) self-concept and positive regard. The SEQ-3 is phenomenologically oriented; the Self-Esteem subscale asks respondents about self-perceptions and relationships with others. The Self-Other-Satisfaction subscale asks for a report of feelings about one's self-esteem level. The SEQ-3 appears to have been carefully constructed to provide items that have a high level of readability. The items allow some room for subjective interpretation. This is a particular strength of the questionnaire because it can facilitate dialogue between the respondent and test administrator, e.g., between a student and guidance counselor. This potential is diminished, of course, in large testing settings.

The SEQ-3 can be easily administered and completed quickly, and scoring is done by computer. The questionnaire assesses global perceptions of the self. It is unique in that it measures two separate aspects of the self: 1) self-confidence and acceptance by others and 2) the individual's emotional response to that level of self-and other-acceptance. Test-retest reliability and internal consistency seem adequate, as does face and construct validity. There is some evidence that the SEQ-3 has predictive validity. However these data need to be supplemented with additional research on the reliability and validity of the measure.

One potential problem with the SEQ-3 involves the scoring of a respondent's answers. When the answers are generally inconsistent, the profile is scored "results unclear—review test." At present about 1 to 5% of respondents receive this rating (Crandall, 1978). This appears to be partially related to the age of the respondents, i.e., younger subjects are more likely to have non-convergent response distributions. Possibly the items are less valid or meaningful for younger respondents, and/or their feelings of adequacy, competence, etc., are not yet congruent. Furthermore, for other respondents, any items that are discrepant from the central point in their response distribution are eliminated from the analysis. This means that individual's scores are based on different items and different numbers of items. This may be problematic when the objective is to obtain nomothetic data. It is less of an issue when the objective is to obtain idiographic data. This technique makes error of measurement specific to an individual's response and not to a "group" characteristic.

The SEQ-3 is an appropriate measure for a variety of populations and for a number of objectives, including diagnostic descriptive purposes, and as an outcome measure to assess the effectiveness of different treatments, such as assertion-training, social skills training, psychotherapy, and special education programs (e.g., developmental reading). It can be used to gather both individual and group data. It seems particularly useful in applied settings where the opportunity exists to establish a relationship between the test administrator/interpreter and the respondent.

References

Coopersmith, S. (1981). *Coopersmith Self-Esteem Inventories*. Palo Alto, CA: Consulting Psychologists Press, Inc.

Crandall, R. (1978). Review of Self-Esteem Questionnaire. In O. K. Buros (Ed.), *The eighth mental measurements yearbook* (p. 672). Highland Park, NJ: The Gryphon Press.

Fitts, W. H. (1964). *Tennessee Self Concept Scale*. Los Angeles: Western Psychological Services.

Hoffmeister, J. K. (1971a). *Course Evaluation Questionnaire*. Boulder, CO: Test Analysis and Development Corporation.

Hoffmeister, J. K. (1971b). *School Atmosphere Questionnaire*. Boulder, CO: Test Analysis and Development Corporation.

Hoffmeister, J. K. (1972). *Classroom Atmosphere Questionnaire*. Boulder, CO: Test Analysis and Development Corporation.

Hoffmeister, J. K. (1975). *Convergence analysis: A clinical approach to quantitative data*. Boulder, CO: Test Analysis and Development Corporation.

Hoffmeister, J. K. (1976). *Some information regarding the characteristics of the two measures developed from the Self-Esteem Questionnaire (SEQ-3)*. Boulder, CO: Test Analysis and Development Corporation.

Maslow, A. H. (1954). *Motivation and personality*. New York: Harper & Row.

Murray, M. E. (1973). *An investigation of the relationship between obesity and self-esteem*. Unpublished master's thesis. University of Minnesota, Duluth.

Otis, A. S. & Lennon, R. T. (1967). *Otis-Lennon Mental Ability Test (OLMAT)*. Cleveland, OH: The Psychological Corporation.

Rogers, C. R. (1959). A theory of therapy, personality, and interpersonal relationships as developed in the client-centered framework. In S. Koch (Ed.), *Psychology: A study of science* (pp. 184-256). New York: McGraw-Hill Publishing Co.

Shostrom, E. L. (1962). *Personal Orientation Inventory*. San Diego: Educational and Industrial Testing Service, Inc.

Kathryn J. Smith, Ph.D., CCC-SP
*Assistant Professor of Speech, Speech and Hearing Clinic, Butler
University, Indianapolis, Indiana.*

SEQUENCED INVENTORY OF COMMUNICATION DEVELOPMENT-REVISED

*Dona L. Hedrick, Elizabeth M. Prather, and Annette R. Tobin.
Seattle, Washington: University of Washington Press.*

Introduction

The Sequenced Inventory of Communication Development-Revised (SICD-R)
by Dona L. Hedrick, Elizabeth M. Prather, and Annette R. Tobin, published in
1984 by the University of Washington Press, is an improved and expanded
version of the original inventory published in 1975 and first revised in 1977. The
SICD, as described by the authors, was originally developed to assist speech-
language pathologists in overall assessment and remediation of children ages 4
months to 4 years who were experiencing language development deficits. It also
addressed the language needs of low functioning children. Results from administration of the test were intended to provide help in planning the general
objectives or areas of focus for a language remediation program. In both the SICD
and the SICD-R, receptive and expressive skills are assessed independently.
While the first version of the test did not stress the determination of a specific
communication age derived from test scores, the authors indicate that the SICD-R
can be used to assign a Receptive Communication Age (RCA) and an Expressive
Communication Age (ECA) as well as to provide directions for intervention.

Each author of the SICD and SICD-R holds the Certificate of Clinical Competence in Speech-Language Pathology from the American Speech-Language and
Hearing Association. Dona L. Hedrick currently chairs the Department of Communication Disorders at the University of Central Florida. Elizabeth M. Prather is
a professor in the Department of Speech and Hearing Science at Arizona State
University. Both Drs. Hedrick and Prather have been honored as Fellows of the
American Speech-Language and Hearing Association in recognition of their
professional contributions to the field. Fellows in the Association have been active
members and have a record of achievment in one of three areas: 1) original
contributions to the field; 2) distinguished educational, professional, or administrative activity; and 3) outstanding service to the Association. Annette Tobin is a
communications disorders specialist employed by the Seattle, Washington
School District.

The SICD was originally developed in 1975 to provide a general diagnostic tool
for assessment of the language of young children. Test item construction was
based on the adaptation of selected language skills noted at varying age levels by
experts in the fields of general child and language development (Gessell, 1940;

714

Frankenberg & Dobbs, 1967). Items were also generated by the authors of the SICD based on their clinical expertise. During the nine years that followed, research was conducted with the instrument and it was used by speech-language pathologists in various settings including hospitals, clinics, and public preschool programs. Feedback regarding use of the SICD resulted in the identification of its strengths and weaknesses and led to subsequent publication of the SICD-R in 1984. The primary areas defined as weaknesses in the original version and addressed in the revision, included developing further standardization, enlarging the pages and changing the type in the *Instruction Manual*, offering additional suggestions for test interpretation, and providing more complete explanations for establishing basal and ceiling scores. Some objects in the original test were replaced with more appropriate and durable items. Additionally, to further support current directions in the field, a second theoretical model is presented in the SICD-R that allows for interpretation of the test using both behavioral and processing models of communication development.

With the research leading to the publication of the SICD-R, other forms of the test were added. Through the work of Lillian Rapport Rosenberg, a bilingual-bicultural speaker of Spanish (Cuban) and English who is employed at Miami's Children's Hospital, a Spanish translation of the SICD has been included in the revised manual. Forms are also available for scoring the test when administered in Spanish. Minor revisions in test items were necessary due to morphological and phonemic differences in the languages with only one item omitted from the test. While the translation is now available, it has not yet been standardized with normally developing, monolingual Spanish-speaking subjects.

The work of several authors has also provided instructions and uses for the SICD with special populations. Prather et al. (1979) modified and standardized the SICD for Yup'ik Eskimo Children while O'Reilly (1981) and Tominac (1981) conducted research using the SICD with "difficult-to-test" and autistic children. Osterkamp (1983) discussed use of the SICD with hearing-impaired children. These studies are described in the revised manual.

As a part of a study to develop a language screening test, further standardization of the SICD was conducted by Doris V. Allen and Lynn S. Bliss. The results from their study (Allen & Bliss, n.d., National Institute of Neurological and Communication Disorders and Stroke Grant No. 1-NS-6-2353, 1976-80) are in the SICD-R manual and included 609 preschool children ages 30-48 months from the metropolitan Detroit area. Subjects represented lower and middle socioeconomic classes as well as both black (276) and white (333) children. Normative data from this study generally indicated that socioeconomic status and race affected the mean scores for the children tested in varying degrees.

The original standardization study for the SICD was conducted with only 252 children representative of the general population of Greater Seattle. Twelve age levels at four-month intervals between 4 months and 4 years were represented by 21 children at each level. Children were equally well distributed between the upper, middle, and lower socioeconmic classes and were all white. Gender was not controlled; however, 124 males and 128 females were included in the sample. Hearing acuity for all of the sample children was determined to be normal. No child with ear pathologies within six weeks prior to testing or with obvious physical or mental abnormalities was included in the study. Only children with language development judged to be normal by parents and from monolingual English-speaking homes were included. Results from the standardization are reported for both the receptive and expressive scales as means and standard deviations at each age level. Additionally, each item on the test is reported in months for one or more of four percentage classifications. For example, the Receptive Item #13a (points to parts of body—ears) was passed by 50-74% of children at 20 months, and by 90+% of children at 28 months. Items were assigned to specific age intervals in months based on the age at which 75% of the children passed the item.

The SICD-R is contained in a molded plastic carrying case which contains two movable shelves and a compartmentalized bottom allowing for easy storage and accessability to all test items. With the exception of six objects (an 8½" x 11" piece of paper, four coins, and a child's picture book), all necessary items are included in the test box. A complete list of test items is included in the box. All test items are either actual three-dimensional objects (i.e., blocks, toy cars, balloons, etc.) or small replicas (i.e., chair, shoe, etc.), with the exception of 18 line-drawings that are printed on 5" x 7" cards and categorized into divided subtest items. Receptive and Expressive scoring forms are included as well as two additional forms for interpretation of each subtest's results.

All test items are administered either directly to the child or through parent reporting. Careful and detailed instructions are provided in the manual for each item and include utterances to be directed toward parents or children and directions for manipulation of test objects. Parent and direct observation items are carefully coded, as they are interspersed throughout the test. All receptive items (understanding of language) are administered first, followed by the administration of all expressive items (use of language). Items are scored as "yes" or "no" based on parent reporting or child performance. In addition to the receptive and expressive items, the SICD-R requires the collection and analysis of a 50-item language sample as a part of the test. Directions for eliciting and scoring this sample are included. Supplemental articulation testing is also suggested but is not included in the administration or interpretation of the test.

As each item is administered, it is scored "yes" or "no" on the receptive (white) scoring form and subsequently on the expressive (yellow) scoring form. Following completion of the test as well as analysis of the language sample, four supplemental profile forms are available. Two receptive and two expressive profiles support the two theoretical models presented in the SICD-R. Receptive and expressive models and items are analyzed as follows:

Receptive Behavioral Profile (green): Awareness (Sound, Speech); Discrimination (Sound, Speech); and Understanding (Words + , Words).

Expressive Behavioral Profile (buff): Expressive Behaviors—Imitating (Motor, Vocal, Verbal), Initiating (Motor, Vocal, Verbal); Responding (Vocal, Verbal); and Expressive Measures—Verbal Output (Quantitative, Descriptive).

Receptive Processing Profile (light green): Semantic; Syntactic; Pragmatic; and Perceptual.

Expressive Processing Profile (gold): Semantic; Syntactic; Pragmatic; and Phonologic.

The profiles when complete allow for ease in visually determining patterns of development and deficit as well as interpretative assignment of the RCA and ECA.

Practical Applications/Uses

The SICD-R is an individualized test designed to be used by speech-language pathologists in a variety of settings such as clinics, hospitals, and public preschools. Users of the test should thus be highly familiar with normal language development and the process of language testing for young preschool children, including language sampling and analysis. Examination of clients should be conducted in a relatively quiet setting. The children in the standardization sample were tested in a sound-treated room while children in the field test (Allen & Bliss, n.d.) were tested in a quiet room in the day-care center.

Revisions were made in the manual for the SICD-R which clarified specific items as well as provided for a more flexible format. The size of the SICD-R manual allows for easy use during administration. Bold type alerts the examiner to the exact wording of items administered to parents/children. Item titles are printed in red for easy location in the manual. Directions are provided in detail regarding manipulation and use of materials. Modification in order of administration of items is allowed to facilitate ease in presentation of items. Simultaneous manipulation of materials, administrating and scoring items, as well as parent/child interaction necessitate significant practice and expertise on the part of the examiner to administer the test effectively. Team testing, as performed with the standardization population, allows for maximum efficiency in administration. Total testing time varies depending on the age of the child, extending from 30-75 minutes.

All items on the SICD-R are scored as "yes" or "no" on the Receptive and Expressive forms with the exception of the language sample, which requires transcription and analysis using the examiner's own materials. Complete instructions for transcribing, scoring, and interpreting the sample are included in the manual. Specific requirements allowing items to be scored as "yes" are listed in the manual beside each item. Transfer of data from the score sheet to the receptive and expressive profiles requires minimal time and allows for visual examination of areas of strength and deficit and determination of an approximated RCA and ECA. Assignment of communication age scores requires significant interpretation of item level scores by the examiner; however, multiple examples for assigning the communication ages in the test manual provide for some control of variation in examiner judgment. All scoring and interpretation is completed by hand. Interpretation necessitates examiner subjective and objective judgments. In order to make appropriate interpretations, knowledge in the areas of testing as well as normal language development are required.

Technical Aspects

When studying validity and reliability of this test, at least four areas should be considered regarding validity and at least three areas regarding reliability.

When reviewing the SICD and SICD-R, one is able to examine the areas of content, construct, and concurrent predictive validity. Content validity (appropriate items for the area to be measured) was demonstrated through careful selection of items for the SICD from previously cited and recognized sources in the specific areas of normal child and language development as well as from the joint clinical expertise of the authors. The construct validity (items measure construct presented) of the test appears to be less evident through analysis of data presented for the standardization populations. Though items have been assigned to four-month intervals based on the percentage of items passed by each subject group at each level, all standard deviation scores for both receptive and expressive scales, with the exception of one receptive interval, exceed the preassigned four-month interval for subjects above 24 months. Likewise, in the Allen and Bliss (n.d.) Detroit field study, both black and white children ages 32 to 48 months exceeded the first standard deviation interval for both the Receptive and Expressive Scales. However, for children ranging from 4 to 24 months, the four-month interval appears to be appropriate and lends support to the construct validity of the SICD for children within this age range.

A secondary issue related to construct validity for the SICD is the lack of or limited number of items found at some age levels or in some of the interpretative categories that measure both receptive and expressive language skills. For example, when using the receptive processing profile for age level scores, the total number of items at any age level ranges from 1 to 14. Regarding interpretive categories across all age levels for the same profile, semantic skills are measured by 50 items, syntactic skills by 2 items, pragmatic skills by 23 items, and perceptual skills by 25 items. This uneven pattern appears for all four interpretative profiles (see Table 1). The Expressive Behavioral Profile shows the most even distribution of items into categories and appears to most appropriately represent the construct presented. Though construct validity appears to be an issue for the SICD, if scale intervals and interpretive categories are used for general rather than fine interpretation of test scores, the test may indeed serve its intended purpose.

Concurrent validity (relationship to other measures of similar skills) of the SICD has been addressed in the original standardization study when scores from the SICD were correlated with other measures of language development. When scores from the SICD were correlated to the Peabody Picture Vocabulary Test (PPVT), the Mean Length of Response (MLR) and Structural Complexity Score (SCS) correlations reached a level of significance of .001 and ranged from .75 to .80. When correlating the Receptive and Expressive Scales of the SICD, the scores reached a level of significance of .001 and were correlated at the .9477 level. The authors of the test concluded that the high level of correlation of these scales as well as the closeness of the receptive and expressive communication ages to chronological age support the validity of the test since all children in the test population were considered normal users of language. Data correlating expressive scores (ECA) to known receptive and expressive tests are provided; however, receptive scores (RCA) are correlated only to the ECA and PPVT. It would be more desirable to see the RCA also correlated to other standardized expressive measures to determine correlations both between and across categories. If all such correlations were provided, the concurrent validity would be stronger.

Table 1

Number of Items Used to Measure Interpretative Profiles

Interpretative Profile	Item Type/Quantity	
	Semantic	50
RECEPTIVE PROCESSING	Syntactic	2
	Pragmatic	23
	Perceptual	25
	Awareness	
	Sound	5
	Speech	3
	Discrimination	
RECEPTIVE BEHAVIORAL	Sound	7
	Speech	12
	Understanding	
	Words +	9
	Words	64
	Semantic	54
EXPRESSIVE PROCESSING	Syntactic	31
	Pragmatic	29
	Phonologic	4
	Expressive Behaviors	
	Imitating	
	Motor	10
	Vocal	8
	Verbal	19
	Initiating	
EXPRESSIVE BEHAVIORAL	Motor	2
	Vocal	6
	Verbal	11
	Responding	
	Vocal	4
	Verbal	37
	Expressive Measures	
	Verbal Output	
	Quantitative	MLU
	Descriptive	21

The authors of the test did not provide data regarding the predictive validity (behavior to be measured can be predicted by the outcome of the test) of the SICD. Rather, they indicated in the revised test manual that the SICD has been used with a variety of types of children known to demonstrate delayed or disordered language and that "in all instances, scores were significantly below normal means" (p. 47).

Another estimate of predictive validity may be gleaned from the Allen, Bliss, and Timmons (1981) study in which the relationship between clinical judgment and test scores was determined for three standardized language tests including the SICD. Children in the study were deemed delayed in language if their scores were 12 months or more below their chronological age. When using the SICD, 9.9% of the 182 white subjects (ages 36-47 months) were judged language impaired. Clinician judgment identified 15.2% of those same children. When examining the relationship between children identified by clinician judgment and test results, it was noted that 61.5% of the children identified by clinicians as language impaired were judged normal by the SICD. Likewise, 50% of the children judged as impaired by the SICD were judged normal by clinicians. It appears that for children known to demonstrate language delays/disorders, the SICD is a useful predictive measure; however, for children with less definitive problems, the predictive validity of the test seems less certain. When reviewing the reliability of the SICD and SICD-R one is able to obtain estimates of interexaminer and test-retest reliability for administration of the test. Again, as reported from the standardization sample, 16 subjects across age levels were randomly selected to establish interexaminer reliability. All estimates were reported to be above 90% with a mean across examiners of 96% agreement. Test-retest reliability was determined across 10 subjects using the same examiner and was reported to range from 88.0% agreement to 98.6% agreement with a mean of 92.8%. A third measure of reliability was determined for the subjective assignments of RCA and ECA for individual subjects. Again, agreement was high, 90.48%, as reported for the standardization sample. Second estimates of reliability were also reported in the Detroit field study with interexaminer reliability reported at a mean of 90% and intraexaminer reliability reported at 90% or greater. Though estimates of reliability from both sources remain high, the small number of subjects used in these estimates indicate that caution should be used in the interpretation of these reliability data.

Critique

Five reviews fo the SICD were found in the literature and are generally supportive of it as a measure of young child language development. Authors cite the current nature of a broad view of language development, particularly as it relates to the pragmatic and cognitive elements of language acquisition which is demonstrated by the test. The broad base of items selected from multiple areas of language development strongly support the use of the SICD. It has received favorable review as a general measure of language development, as a tool useful for identifying children with language deficits, and as a vehicle for identifying areas in need of remediation. Suggestions for revision and criticisms of the original version of the SICD made by these writers and other users of the test were taken into consideration by the authors of the test when the SICD-R was developed. The primary areas noted as deficiencies in the SICD, which have been addressed in the SICD-R, are:

1. expansion of the standardization population to include more children as well as including black and urban children;
2. use of the test with other groups of children in addition to the standardization populations;
3. separation of the *Instruction Manual* and *Test Manual* and changes in the *Instruction Manual* for easier and more productive use;
4. translation of the test into Spanish with specific directions and scoring forms available for use with Spanish speakers;
5. revision of specific items, directions, and scoring guidelines.

In the opinion of this reviewer, the SICD-R provides a useful clinical tool for speech-language pathologists who serve very young children (4 months to 4 years of age) or severely language-delayed children who have receptive or expressive language disorders. As currently revised, the test serves as a broadly based analysis of both receptive and expressive language skills in a number of areas that are congruent with current theories of language development and remediation. The profiles used in the interpretation of test results provide an easily visible outline of a child's areas of strengths and weaknesses and thus a useful basis for remediation. The test is attractive, durable, and provides complete testing materials with the exception of a few easily obtainable items; however, the administration of the test is somewhat complex and should be administered only by an experienced examiner or team of examiners.

The expansion of the SICD-R to include a Spanish edition as well as information regarding use of the test with a variety of disordered populations definitely strengthens the test and adds to its practicality and uses. At the same time, the addition of this information will necessitate further investigation and standardization for use of this test with added populations.

Related to the reliability and validity issues addressed earlier, four specific recommendations emerge. First, as the scores noted for the Detroit field study differed from those cited for the original standardization population, it is strongly recommended that consistent users of the SICD-R consider the development of local norms. When this is not possible, users should consider the type of population they are testing and compare their test populations to the closest group of the three now listed in the test manual: 1) the original standardization population, 2) white children in the Detroit field study, and 3) black children in the Detroit field study. As the SICD-R is further used, broader-based normative data should be provided by the authors or publisher to strengthen the construct validity of the test. Second, as the SICD-R receives more use, an attempt should be made to further examine the construct validity of the test by closer examination of the four-month test interval with possible expansion of that interval to six months. This interval appears to be more appropriate from the two standardization studies for children 24-48 months of age. This change could possibly relieve the problem of the limited number of test items at some age intervals and interpretative categories as well. Third, studies of predictive validity need to be undertaken. Finally, due to the subjective nature of the assignment of the RCA and ECA, examiners should make consistent efforts to check their reliability in assignment of these scores with others, as well as to periodically check their intratest and intertest reliability.

Clinically, this reviewer finds the SICD-R a useful and excellent way to establish both a knowledge base for language intervention and a good working relationship with very young clients and their parents.

References

This list includes text citations and suggested additional reading.

Allen, D. V., Bliss, L. S., & Timmons, J. (1981). Language evaluation: Science or art. *Journal of Speech and Hearing Disorders, 46*, 66-68.

Compton, C. (1980). *A guide to 65 tests for special education.* Belmont, CA: Fearon Education.

Frankenberg, W. K., & Dobbs, J. B. (1967). Denver Developmental Screening Test. *Journal of Pediatrics, 71*, 181-91.

Gesell, A. (1940). *First five years of life.* New York: Harper & Row.

Lamberts, F. (1978). Review of a test for communication behaviors. *Journal of Learning Disabilities, 11*, 28-29.

Lynch, L., & Tobin, A. (1973). The development of language training programs for post-rubella hearing-impaired children. *Journal of Speech and Hearing Disorders, 38*, 15-24.

McLean, J. E., & Snyder-McLean, L. K. (1978). *A transactional approach to early language training.* Columbus, OH: Charles E. Merrill Publishing Co.

McLean, J. E. (1979). *SICD.* In F. L. Darley (Ed.), *Evaluation of appraisal techniques in speech-language pathology* (pp. 68-70). Reading, MA: Addison-Wesley Publishing Company.

Miller, J. F. (1981). *Assessing language productions in children.* Baltimore: University Park Press.

Nation, J. E., & Aram, D. M. (1977). *Diagnosis of speech and language disorders.* St. Louis, MO: C. V. Mosby.

O'Reilly, R. (1981). *Language testing with children considered difficult-to-test.* Unpublished master's thesis, Arizona State University, Tempe.

Osterkamp, K. (1983). *Performance of hearing impaired children on a developmental language test.* Unpublished master's thesis, Arizona State University, Tempe.

Peterson, H. S., & Marquardt, T. P. (1981). *Appraisal and diagnosis of speech and language disorders.* Englewood Cliffs, NJ: Prentice-Hall.

Prather, E., Hedrick, D. L., & Kern, C. A. (1975). Articulation development in children aged 2 to 4 years. *Journal of Speech and Hearing Disorders, 40*, 179-191.

Prather, E., Reed, I., Foley, C., Somes, L., & Mohr, R. (1979). *Yup'ik Sequenced Inventory of Communication Development.* Anchorage: Rural Alaska Community Action Program.

Tominac, C. A. (1981). *The effect of intoned versus neutral stimuli with autistic children.* Unpublished master's thesis, Arizona State University, Tempe.

Winkler, S. J. (1979). Materials review in ASHA (August). *Journal of the American Speech-Language-Hearing Association, 21*, 622-623.

Christopher Matey, Ed.D.
Assistant Professor of Educational Psychology, Miami University, Oxford, Ohio.

SMITH-JOHNSON NONVERBAL PERFORMANCE SCALE

Alathena J. Smith and Ruth E. Johnson. Los Angeles, California: Western Psychological Services.

Introduction

The Smith-Johnson nonverbal Performance Scale (SJNPS) is an assessment tool comprised of representative tasks reflecting developmental skills from ages 2 to 4 years. There are 65 items taken from eight well-standardized tests of mental ability. These 65 items are grouped into 14 categories and are sequenced in terms of difficulty within each category. Although the scale yields no global score, it is possible to compare a child's performance in each of the 14 categories to the performance of both hearing and hearing-impaired children in the standardization sample.

Alathena Smith began work on the Nonverbal Performance Scale (NPS) (Smith, 1960) in 1955 following her work as a school psychologist and special services coordinator in Wisconsin. The development of the scale occurred primarily at the John Tracy Clinic, an agency that provides diagnostic and treatment services to hearing-impaired children. Dr. Smith served as psychologist at the clinic for over 25 years, during which time the scale was refined for use with both hearing and hearing-impaired children. Dr. Smith's original impetus for developing the scale was that there were no assessment instruments which had been standardized on young hearing-impaired children. Her dissertation in 1960 (Smith, 1960) represented the first effort in this direction. Her work in collaboration with Dr. Ruth Johnson (Johnson, 1974) culminated in the publication of the Smith-Johnson Nonverbal Performance Scale in 1977.

In constructing the Scale, Smith was guided by a number of specific criteria, the most important of which was that items "should be those which have already been shown to have high correlations with acceptable criteria of intelligence or learning ability as judged by previous studies" (Smith & Johnson, 1977, p. 17). As a result, in assembling the preliminary form of the Nonverbal Performance Scale Smith chose to select items from already existing tests of mental ability (i.e., Arthur Point Scale of Performance Tests, Arthur, 1947; Bayley Scales of Infant Development, Bayley, 1969; Gesell Developmental Schedules, Gesell & Armatruda, 1947; Hiskey-Nebraska Test of Learning Aptitude, Hiskey, 1966; Leiter International Performance Scale, Leiter, 1948; Merrill-Palmer Scale of Mental Tests, Stutsman, 1931; Ontario School Ability Examination, Amoss, 1936; Randall's Island Performance Series, Poull, Bristol, King, & Peatman, 1931; and

723

Stanford-Binet Intelligence Scale, Terman & Merrill, 1937, 1960. Another important criterion was that items had to be capable of being administered using only gestural or pantomimed instructions. Additional criteria included high interest to preschool children, ease of objectivity of scoring, ability to maintain a young child's attention, breadth of abilities tapped, ability to discriminate between age levels, and lack of time constraints. A large group of items was assembled based on the above criteria and constituted the preliminary form of the scale, which was administered from 1955 to 1959 to 350 children aged two to six at the Tracy Clinic. As an outgrowth of this work, the 65 items that comprise the current scale were chosen to be used in the 1960 standardization study.

The 1960 standardization was conducted with 602 two- to four-year-old normal children who lived on the West Coast of the United States. Approximately 50 children were selected from nine ages between 2 and 4 years, three months apart. Children were selected from child care facilities and, unfortunately, reflected "the elevated educational and socioeconomic levels of families which patronized nursery schools" (Smith & Johnson, 1977, p. 18). In addition, the sample was entirely Caucasian. In this reviewer's opinion it would have been helpful if the authors had included more information regarding the socioeconomic status of the sample, given that it was unrepresentative of the population.

In 1973, a sample of 632 hearing-impaired children was selected from the evaluations that had been done at the Tracy Clinic between 1960 and 1970 using the same 1960 standardization study scale. The group was comprised of an equal number of boys and girls between the ages of 2 and 4 years and were again selected at nine age levels, three months apart. There were 32 to 115 children at each age level with the greatest representation from 27 to 36 months. In terms of hearing loss, 36% of the children had a profound hearing loss and 64% were classified as being hard of hearing. The hearing loss of 32% of the children could be attributed to maternal rubella, whereas the other 68% represented a variety of diagnoses. This sample of hearing-impaired children constituted what Smith and Johnson refer to as the 1973 standardization sample.

Several comments regarding the 1973 standardization are in order: 1) There is no information regarding the socioeconomic status of these children and as a consequence it is difficult to determine to what groups the scale might apply. 2) The large number of children whose mothers had rubella would suggest that a separate analysis of these childrens' performance is warranted because many rubella children have additional handicapping conditions. 3) There are two age levels (45 and 48 months) where there were only 34 and 32 children, respectively; these are very small samples which to base conclusions regarding a population's abilities.

The SJNPS is comprised of 65 items in 14 categories with two to nine items per category. The 14 categories and the number of items in each are Formboard (3), Block Building (6), Pencil Drawing (8), Bead Stringing (5), Knot Tying (2), Color Items (6), Scissors (2), Paper Folding (4), Cube Tapping (9), Form Discrimination (4), Completion Items (2), Manikin (6), Block Patterns (4), and Sorting (4). All materials essential for administration of the test are included in the test kit with the exception of a stopwatch (Bead Stringing), paper (Paper Folding), and coins (Sorting). In assembling test items, the authors appear to have been successful in selecting materials that have been shown to appeal to children.

Practical Applications/Uses

The SJNPS is appropriate for use with normal and hearing-impaired children aged 2 to 4 years. Its purpose is to assess a variety of nonverbal abilities considered important in the developing child. It would be appropriate to use as a supplement to other measures of mental ability, such as the Bayley Scales of Infant Development (Bayley, 1969), Leiter International Performance Scale (Leiter, 1948), or Hiskey-Nebraska Test of Learning Aptitude (Hiskey, 1966) that yield global scores. The SJNPS has the distinct advantage over the aforementioned scales of having been standardized on hearing-impaired children. Its limitations (discussed later) and disadvantages result in its being most appropriate as a supplemental measure.

The SJNPS should be administered in a well lit room free from background distractions and equipped with tables and chairs designed for preschool children so that materials will be readily accessible to them. The test may be administered by a psychologist, speech and hearing therapist, or teacher, all of whom should be trained in the individual administration of standardized tests, familiar with the SJNPS test materials, and have had fairly extensive experience in assessing preschoolers.

The directions for administration of test items are clear and easy to follow. There are pictures illuminating administration procedures that need clarification. Administration procedures also include provisions for teaching children how to respond to the items. These provisions are especially important in administering tests to hearing-impaired preschoolers who have a difficult time understanding what is expected of them. In addition, all items are administered nonverbally, using gestures, pantomime, and demonstrations. With the exception of only one category of items—Bead Stringing—the child is permitted as much time as is needed to complete the test, thus placing little demand on the preschool child's limited attention span.

In the event that a child's attention is difficult to maintain, the authors give two suggestions. First, it is possible to vary the order of test administration in order to maintain the child's interest. Second, it is possible to take a break and return to testing later. Although it is possible to vary the order of administration of the various categories, the tasks within each category, must be administered in the prescribed order because they are sequenced in terms of difficulty. It is also permitted to finish the testing on another day.

With the exception of the Formboard and Sorting categories, the examiner should discontinue testing in a category if the child misses two consecutive items. On the Formboard tasks if the child fails the first item, the examiner should proceed to the next category; otherwise, all three items should be administered. For the Sorting category all tasks should be administered regardless of failure.

Scoring of each item is objective and clearly explained in the manual. It is highly unlikely that any questions will be raised as to whether or not a child passed an item, given the clarity of the criteria provided. These objective scoring criteria facilitate standardized administration but do not result in any global scores or overall indices of ability. Interpretation of the child's performance on the SJNPS is based on a less objective, more clinically oriented approach described below.

The authors present four tables that constitute the basis for interpretation of a child's performance on the SJNPS. A table is provided for each of the four groups of children from the 1960 and 1973 standardization groups: normally hearing girls, normally hearing boys, hearing-impaired girls, and hearing-impaired boys. Each table gives the percentages of children at one month intervals passing each item from ages 2 to 4 years. Items are grouped in the tables according to the 14 categories. To interpret a child's performance the examiner focuses on the highest item passed within each category. It is then possible to determine whether a child's performance in a category is average, above average, or below average compared to the norm group. The authors recommend the following criteria for making these determinations: if 25 to 75% of the child's age (the norm group) passed the item the child's performance is rated average; if more than 75% of the norm group passed the item the child's performance is rated below average; if less than 25% of the norm group passed the item, the child's performance is rated above average.

After the child's performance in each category is rated using the above approach the examiner should consider 1) the number of categories on which the child's performance is either above or below average for children that age, 2) whether the child is consistently above or below average, or 3) whether variations occur only on a particular type of task. The authors provide interpretive guidelines and caution that interpretation should acknowledge the variable performance of preschoolers and care should be taken in interpreting categories on which the child was rated below average.

Technical Aspects

One study dealing with test-retest reliability was conducted with 299 children from the 1960 standardization (Smith, 1960) with the retest occurring approximately one week after the initial testing. The reliability coefficients ranged from .27 to .81 with all but ten of the coefficients being larger than 50. Although the coefficients are somewhat low, they must be interpreted in the light of preschool children's more variable performance over time.

Only one study examining the validity of the SJNPS has been done (Smith, 1960) and this study used a preliminary form of the scale. In a comparison with the Leiter International Performance Scale (Leiter, 1948) using 27 children aged three to six years, a Pearson product moment correlation of .73 was obtained. Clearly additional investigation and study of the reliability and the validity of the SJNPS is needed.

Critique

There are a number of problems with the SJNPS that need to be addressed so that users of this instrument will be aware of its limitations. The tables for normally hearing boys and girls are derived from the performance of children in the 1960 standardization sample. These children were selected based on their being within seven days of the following nine ages between 2 and 4 years: 24, 27, 30, 33, 36, 39, 42, 45 and 48 months. The tables showing the percent of children passing show increases between age where there were no children in the sample based on the authors' report of their subject selection process. For example for item five, 3-Block Chair, 23% of the 25-month-old children passed the item and 27% of the 26-month-old children passed the item. Based on the authors' description of the subject selection criteria, there were no 25- and 26-month old children because children these ages could not have been within seven days of one of the nine ages previously listed. This discrepancy needs to be resolved in order that test users can more confidently use the tables that constitute the basis of the interpretive process.

An additional concern is the limited number of items and the restricted range of ability tapped by some categories. The specific examples that follow are taken from the 1960 norms for girls but are representative of the kinds of problems evident for all four groups. 1) There are three categories in which there are only two items: Knot Tying, Scissors, and Completion Items. 2) There are four categories that tap a range of less than one year's growth: Formboard, Knot Tying, Scissors, and Form Discrimination. 3) There are three categories in which the child could pass all items and still be rated below average at some ages: Formboard for ages greater than 2-5 (i.e., 2 years, 5 months), Scissors for ages greater than 3-1, and Form Discrimination for ages greater than 3-11. 4) There are seven categories where it is not possible to score above average for some ages: Formboard at all ages, Scissors for ages greater than 2-0, Paper Folding for ages greater than 3-5, Form Discrimination for ages greater than 2-10, Completion Items for ages greater than 3-8, Manikin for ages greater than 3-10, and Sorting for ages greater than 2-9. As can be seen, the limited number of items and the restricted range of abilities tapped result in a variety of problems in using the interpretive approach recommended by the authors.

Given these limitations, an alternative approach to interpretation should be explored. The 14 categories could be combined into superordinate groupings. Four such possible groups are 1) Fine Motor: Pencil Drawing, Bead Stringing, Knot Tying, Scissors, Paper Folding; 2) Memory: Block Building, Bead Stringing, Cube Tapping; 3) Visual Perceptual: Form Discrimination, Completion Tasks, Formboard, Color Items, Block Patterns, Manikin; and 4) Sorting: Sorting.

As can be seen, some categories involve abilities that cut across category groups, e.g., Bead Stringing involves both Fine Motor and Memory tasks. The above category groups may facilitate interpretation by providing a larger number and a more adequate range of items on which to base judgments about a child's strengths and weaknesses. Of course, statistical investigations of the factor structure of the SJNPS would be necessary to establish the meaningfulness of these category groups.

The SJNPS can contribute to the clinical profile of the hearing-impaired child's nonverbal abilities. It would be useful as a supplement to tests that yield more global scores but have not been standardized on two- to four-year-old hearing-impaired children. A combination of the SJNPS with these other measures might yield the most valid evaluation of a hearing-impaired child's abilities, given the instruments available today.

References

Amoss, H. (1936). *Ontario School Ability Examination.* Toronto: Ryerson.

Arthur, G. (1947). *Arthur Point of Scale of Performance Tests.* Chicago: Stoelting Company.

Bayley, N. (1969). *Manual for the Bayley Scales of Infant Development.* New York: The Psychological Corporation.

Gesell, A. J., & Armatruda, C. (1947). *Developmental diagnosis, normal and abnormal child development* (2nd ed.). New York: Hoeber-Harper.

Hiskey, M. S. (1966). *Hiskey-Nebraska Test of Learning Aptitude.* Lincoln, NE: Union College Press.

Johnson, R. E. (1974). *A nonverbal performance scale for children aged two to four presented in pantomime.* Unpublished master's thesis, Pepperdine University. (University Microfilms No. M006784)

Leiter, R. G. (1948). *Leiter International Performance Scale.* Chicago: Stoelting Co.

Poull, L., Bristol, A. S., King, H. B., & Peatman, L. B. (1931). *Randall's Island Performance Series.* New York: Columbia University Press.

Smith, A. J. (1960). *Performance of subjects aged two to four on nonverbal tasks presented in pantomime: A phase in the development of a test for the appraisal of hypacoustic and other language-impaired children.* Unpublished doctoral dissertation, Ohio State University. (University Microfilms No. 60-6422)

Smith, A. J., & Johnson, R. E. (1977). *Smith-Johnson Nonverbal Performance Scale.* Los Angeles: Western Psychological Services.

Stutsman, R. (1931). *Merrill-Palmer Scale of Mental Tests.* New York: Harcourt Brace & World.

Terman, L. M., & Merrill, M. (1937). *Measuring intelligence.* Boston: Houghton Mifflin.

Terman, L. M., & Merrill, M. (1960). *The Stanford-Binet Intelligence Scale.* Boston: Houghton Mifflin.

Michael G. McKee, Ph.D.
Head, Biofeedback Section, Department of Psychiatry, Cleveland Clinic, Cleveland, Ohio.

STANFORD HYPNOTIC SUSCEPTIBILITY SCALE

Andre Weitzenhoffer and Ernest R. Hilgard. Palo Alto, California: Distributed by Consulting Psychologists Press, Inc.

Introduction

The Stanford Hypnotic Susceptibility Scales (SHSS) consist of three forms: A, B, and C. All three forms are intended to test hypnotic susceptibility as defined and measured by how often the subject acts in the manner of a hypnotized person in response to standard presentation of hypnotic suggestions following a standard hypnotic induction. Therefore, each scale constitutes a sample of the subject's hypnotic behavior as evaluated in a standardized testing situation.

Forms A and B are intended mainly for assessment of hypnotic susceptibility with previously untested subjects. Two forms enable repeat testing, i.e., before and after investigations of changes in hypnotic susceptibility secondary to changed conditions or experiences, such as intervening treatment, changed beliefs about hypnosis, or changed desire to be hypnotized. Form A is intended to be administered first, with the directions phrased for someone who is being hypnotized for the first time, whereas Form B is intended for repeat administration.

Forms A and B have items that are quite similar. The differences are sufficient enough that exact recall would not contaminate retesting and such that the hypnotist would not feel awkward and uncomfortable because of verbatim repetition.

Form C is intended for testing after the initial test session. It has some items in common with Forms A and B, but, unlike Forms A and B, it samples a wider variety of hypnotic experiences and has items that are arranged in order of difficulty.

The scales developed out of earlier work by Friedlander and Sarbin (1938) and a significant debt is owed to these pioneers. The authors of the Stanford Scales, Andre Weitzenhoffer and Ernest R. Hilgard are themselves pioneers in clinical and research uses of hypnosis and are highly salient in the field.

Weitzenhoffer has published leading texts on hypnosis as well as coauthoring these scales. He received his Ph.D. in physiological psychology from the University of Michigan and later in Oklahoma worked with the Veterans Administration and was professor of psychiatry and behavioral science. Before going to Oklahoma he spent four years at Stanford where he and Hilgard developed the

729

SHSS. Weitzenhoffer has received many honors in hypnosis and psychology and has been recognized by the ABPP and ABPH examinations in clinical psychology and clinical hypnosis. Hilgard, received his Ph.D. in experimental psychology from Yale. His extraordinarily distinguished career in psychology includes being a past president of the American Psychological Association, the Society for the Psychological Study of Social Issues, the American Psychological Association's division of Psychological Hypnosis, and the International Society of Hypnosis. He has authored and coauthored many landmark texts in the psychology of learning as well as texts especially related to hypnosis (1965, 1975, 1977). In addition, he has carried out joint research in hynosis since 1937 with his wife, Josephine Hilgard, who received her Ph.D. in child psychology from Yale and a M.D. degree from Stanford.

Forms A and B of the SHSS, first published in 1959, developed out of long-term interest and investigation of individual differences in hypnotic susceptibility, the studies begun by Weitzenhoffer at Michigan and later continued at Stanford where the Hilgards have worked for years. A major goal of developing and publishing the Hypnotic Susceptibility Scales was to enable comparability of hypnotic study in different laboratories such that factual data concerning hypnosis and theories on hypnosis would have a sounder basis in science.

Publication of the SSHS was a landmark event in the checkered but persistently robust history of hypnosis. These scales enabled investigation of the hypnotic phenomena based on standardized assessment of hypnotic susceptibility, a significant step in establishing hypnotic phenomena as having legitimate scientific standing. That standing frequently has been at best problematic ever since the beginnings of hypnosis as we now know it with Frans Anton Mesmer (1734-1815). Mesmer, who plagiarized much of his dissertation from the work of Richard Mead, had an influential, colorful, and controversial career. His unorthodox work and his attribution of the effect of his work to animal magnetism, coincided with the early stages of rigorous scientific inquiry such that his work was subjected to investigation by one of the first blue ribbon commissions that included many notable scientists of that time including Benjamin Franklin, Lavosier, and Bailly. The commission concluded that "the repeated action of the imagination for the purpose of producing crises can be harmful" and that "all public treatment in which magnetism is used can only have, in the course of time, dangerous effects" (Pattie, 1967).

Weitzenhoffer and Hilgard are characteristic of the highly reputable and competent clinicians and academicians who have been and are involved in the use and investigation of hypnosis, helping sort out the conflicting claims for, interpretations of, theories about, and suggestions for use of hypnosis. They followed the SHSS A and B Forms with Form C in 1962 because it was felt that the first two scales did not have enough range and variety in the hypnotic behaviors and experiences that were sampled. Form C is considered more appropriate when assessing for advanced skill in hypnotic behaviors, when different forms of induction are employed, or (because of the way it is constructed) when it is desirable to have a test with items arranged in order of difficulty.

Forms A and B have also been revised by Shor and Orne (1962) into a group form (The Harvard Group Scale of Hypnotic Susceptibility—HGSH) that is frequently cited in studies involving initial assessment of hypnotic susceptibility. Because of the economy of group assessment this scale, basically a self-report version of the SHSS Form A, is employed in many research studies. It, like SHSS:A, is often used as a screening measure in an effort to identify subjects who can be tested on a more advanced scale such as SHSS:C. It is an adequate predictor of hypnotic susceptibility when the criterion measure is SHSS:C (Farthing, Brown, & Venturino, 1983).

All forms of the Stanford Scales consist of 12 items that are samples of hypnotic experience. The first item on the SHSS Form A is head falling, substituting for postural sway because in postural sway the examiner must break the fall of the subject. The next items in order of presentation are eye closure, hand lowering, immobilization, finger lock, arm rigidity, hands moving, verbal inhibition, hallucination, eye catalepsy, post-hypnotic suggestion, and amnesia. These also are the items on SHSS:B and the HGSHS:A.

Form C, on the other hand, samples a wider range of hypnotic experience, the items (in order) being hand lowering, moving hands apart, mosquito hallucination, taste hallucination, arm rigidity, dream, age regression, arm immobilization, anosmia to ammonia, hallucinated voice, negative visual hallucination, and posthypnotic amnesia.

The examiner is actively involved in the testing process, starting with spending several minutes establishing rapport before the initial induction session. For the actual induction and for the test items, the examiner reads from the manual, as it is essential that the induction and the test items be administered in the same way for all subjects. The scales are intended for adolescents and adults.

Answer forms are available in which observation notes as well as scores can be recorded. For some items it is essential to get almost a verbatim recording. Scores are simple, each item plus or minus, one or zero, the total scale score range from 0 to twelve representing the number of items that are passed, i.e., the number of items in which the subject acted as hypnotized persons act. The range of scores is very similar in Forms A, B and C, approximately 25 to 30% scoring in the high range (scores 8-12), 27 to 39% scoring in the medium range (scores 5-7), and 45 to 54% scoring in the low range (scores 0-four).

A shortened form of the SHSS, the Stanford Hypnotic Clinic Scale (SHCS), has also been developed by the Hilgards (1975) with five items that were altered from the items in the earlier scales. The SHCS thus yields scores of 0-five, having half the range of Forms A, B, and C. This scale is described at length in Hilgard and Hilgard's *Hypnosis in the Relief of Pain*. The length of the original scales was considered a shortcoming in some clinical uses as was also the amount of muscular effort and mobility required of the subject. These features made them difficult to use with some hospitalized persons. While the original scales, those reviewed here, were intended for research purposes, the SHCS is intended more for clinical use but is also correlated highly enough with Forms A, B, and C to be useful in research studies. The shorter form samples hypnotic behaviors and processes that are common in psychotherapy and is also not likely to tire the subject because of the length of the testing session and because of the demands made by the test items. The short scale overlaps with Form C in recognizing that special skills, skills in addition to general hypnotic susceptibility, may influence scores and response in treatment when hypnosis is used. The special skills include capacity to experience and gain pleasure from regression in age and to respond posthypnotically, and the readiness and richness of imagery in various sensory modalities. If one is testing patients who are very tired, very sick, have limited movement or strength, the shortened form, which correlates well with the longer forms (.7 to .8) may be more appropriate.

Practical Applications/Uses

The Stanford Hypnotic Susceptibility Scales are useful in clinical and research settings. Both the individual forms and the group forms have been widely used in research settings, but the manuals have not been significantly updated since their initial publication. In the research setting, many studies on hypnosis have been flawed by subjecting a sample representative of the general population to hypnotic induction and comparing the results of their response to hypnotic suggestion with that of unhypnotized people. Because the general population includes less than half, by standardization norms of these scales, who are highly responsive to hypnosis, such studies significantly underestimate hypnotic effect. Thus, any study intending to investigate the effect of hypnotic suggestion on some other phenomena (e.g., experience or pain or capacity at a given task) or any study that wants to investigate the influence of some other variable (e.g., attitude or motivation) upon hypnotic performance must take into account differences in hypnotic susceptibility. The Stanford Scales, as well as the Harvard Group form or the shortened Stanford Clinical Scales, are most useful for these purposes.

In the clinical setting, it is not as common to engage in formal testing of hypnosis. Clinicians as a group tend to be more convinced than researchers that hypnotic susceptibility can be increased if the rapport is good between therapist and patient. Furthermore, the ways clinicians use hypnosis often do not require high responsivity in the true hypnotic sense but instead capitalize on suggestibility, imagination, and placebo effect within the context of a good personal relationship. Despite the difference between clinical and research needs, this reviewer has found the Stanford Scales helpful in a clinical setting, although the tendency is to use the shorter form because it is less tiring and time consuming, samples a wider range of hypnotic experience than SHSS:A or B, is more easily used with some patients limited in motion or strength, and is less authoritarian in tone.

This reviewer's conviction is that assessing hypnotic susceptibility prior to embarking on hypnotic treatment increases the effective use of hypnosis, avoiding unnecessary and continued attempts to induce hypnosis in someone who simply is not very likely to respond. On the other hand it also enables identification of highly hypnotically susceptible individuals who might not otherwise have been identified, due to the scarcity of reliable indicators of hypnotic susceptibility. The lack of reliable indicators is the reason that these scales and their offspring employ a work sample approach. Actually going through the hypnotic induction and samples of hypnotic suggestion is the best way to measure to what extent a person is hypnotically susceptible.

Who should use these scales? The general instructions for Form A and B state it well:

Hypnotism is a technique to be used for serious purposes exactly as any other scientific technique is used, and the practitioner should have`appropriate training to keep its use in proper context. While anyone can learn how to use a stethoscope, administer drugs, or give a psychological examination, we have come to recognize that these tools or techniques belong in the hands of those whose training goes beyond the specific techniques. We shall assume that the user of these hypnotic scales knows what he is about, that he perceives hypnosis as but one among a number of interpersonal methods, that he is aware of the social and ethical responsibilities when he asks a subject to relinquish control to the degree required in hypnosis. Beyond these considerations, he need have no special experience with a hypnotic technique itself, although training under an experienced and qualified hypnotist is highly desirable. (Weitzenhoffer & Hilgard, 1959)

Before the test is administered, it is necessary to have an appropriate physical arrangement, appropriate equipment, and to establish rapport. In the Stanford work contributing to the development of these scales, the subject was typically seated in a comfortable and high-backed armchair. The rooms were similar to small clinical rooms where there was outside noise (e.g., voices, running water), such that the results should be generalizable to the common clinical setting.

For Scales A and B, not much equipment is needed. Because timing ten-second intervals is required for some of the tests, a stopwatch or a darkroom timer is used, the darkroom timer recommended because of quiet and because it returns to the start point after the ten-second interval. A thumbtack is put in the ceiling above and in front of the subject. It is a fixation point about six feet from the subject's eyes. The subject can wear glasses but not contact lenses.

Scale C requires more in the way of equipment: a small screwtop bottle containing household ammonia is needed for the item testing anosmia to ammonia and three small colored boxes (e.g., as red, white, and blue) about 2" x 3" x 1/2" are needed for the negative hallucination item.

Administering the scales is fairly easy, because after the initial establishment of rapport and the explanation of hypnosis, which should be memorized but not necessarily given verbatim, the examiner reads the induction and the test items from the manuals. The first items on eye closure involve options depending on how soon the eyes are closed, such that the manual has to be studied beforehand in order not to stumble while selecting and implementing the options. In Forms A and B the scoring is generally easy and objective. There is not likely to be much disagreement in scoring the items, except perhaps on items such as hallucination where the criterion involves recognizing "any movement, grimacing, or acknowledgement of effort" or the posthypnotic item where "any partial movement response" is required to meet the criterion.

Form C, on the other hand, is more difficult to score and more recording is required during the administration. The dream and age regression and hallucination items are perhaps particularly likely to cause some difficulty in scoring. The dream, for example, is scored plus if the subject "dreams well" (i.e., not just vague, fleeting experiences or feelings/thoughts without imagery, but an experience comparable to a dream. It is possible to obtain a plus score, even though the subject may insist it was not a real dream, provided the hypnotist notes that the imagery and action are not under volitional control). The age regression item is scored plus if there is "a clear change in handwriting between the present and one of the regressed ages."

These scales take approximately 45 minutes to administer, including about five minutes in establishing rapport, a half-hour for the induction and testing, and a final inquiry of about ten minutes. Typically, 50 minutes are plenty of time for administering the scale. Rarely is a subject disturbed by having taken the scales, but a small percentage (perhaps two or three) do feel a bit disturbed, and an unusual subject or two may experience a headache or other symptoms, the scale having a risk of reviving bad childhood experiences and causing stress. The manual cautions that it cannot safely be assumed that participating in this scale is not a significant experience, and some people may experience it as a significant intrusion. Therefore, anyone administering the scale should be prepared to deal with unusual consequences. Indeed, in this reviewer's setting there have been individuals presenting with clinical problems who required significant assistance in managing feelings and symptoms brought about by the hypnotic testing.

Technical Aspects

The normative populations for the scales were Stanford students, Forms A and B using 64 men and 60 women, Form C employing 101 men and 102 women.

The normative data presented in the manuals are from the studies on Stanford students leading to development of the scales. Although other normative data are available (particularly for the Harvard group scales) these are not reported in the manuals. The reported standardization data indicated no differences between sexes in scoring in hypnotic susceptibility, with a quarter to a third scoring high, approximately a third scoring in the middle, and about a half scoring low. Forms A and B are quite comparable. When there was testing on two occasions separated by one or two days and the order varied from A to B to B to A, there were no significant differences in scores. This overall finding should not be interpreted to mean that some subjects do not change. A few subjects changed six points or more on this twelve-point scale in which a six-point change could move a subject's score from low to high susceptibility.

The correlations between testing on two different days are basically retest reliabilities and of the order of .8 to .9 indicating high reliability. Form C tends to correlate about .8 to .9 with Forms A and B, suggesting that basically it is tapping the same dimensions of hypnotizability. However, Form C varies from Forms A and B in having items administered in order of difficulty, such that the test can be shortened or stopped after a subject has failed three items, and in having more varied item content, thus sampling more dimensions of hypnotizability.

Validity is a more complex matter than reliability. Data from studies such as those reported in *Hypnosis in the Relief of Pain* tend to be most compelling in demonstrating validity to the scales, with highly hypnotically susceptible subjects clearly responding significantly more as predicted for hypnotized subjects than subjects low in hypnotizability.

Critique

The Stanford Hypnotic Susceptibility scales can be used in a clinical setting to evaluate a client's hypnotizability when hypnosis is indicated as part of the treatment program. Form C further assists in suggesting the kinds of hypnotic experiences that are likely to be clinically useful. The scales are valuable in the research study of hypnotic process and outcome, such as in the effect of hypnosis in pain. Such research usually needs to take into account subject differences in hypnotizability, and these scales are well standardized and widely used in such research.

Structural analyses of HGSHC, Form A (McConkey, Sheehan, & Law, 1980) indicate multifactorial composition including a challenge factor, an ideo-motor factor, and a cognitive factor. Comparison of Barber's Creative Imagination Scale (Wilson & Barber, 1978) and HGSHS, Form A (McConkey, Sheehan, & White, 1979) suggest that imagination alone is not likely to account for a subject's ability to react with compliance to the items on test scales such as the Stanford and Harvard hypnotic scales. Hilgard's work (1977) indicates that dissociation may be an important dimension added to imagination in determining performance on the hypnotic scales, that dissociation is particularly important in determining how well one performs on the cognitive-delusory items, items which are major contributors to the factorial complexity of the Stanford and Harvard scales.

Hypnosis, the phenomenon being assessed, remains subject to much debate (Is it an altered state of consciousness? Is hypnotizability a trait?) There is disagreement in the field whether hypnotizability is a genuine phenomenon to be measured at all (Orne & Hammer, 1974). These scales do help in resolving the theoretical debates, and this reviewer has also found them clinically helpful.

References

Farthing, G. W., Brown, S. W., & Venturino, M. (1983). Involuntariness of response on the Harvard Group Scale of Hypnotic Susceptibility. *International Journal of Clinical Experimental Hypnosis, 31,* 178-181.

Friedlander, J. W., & Sarbin, T. R. (1938). The depth of hypnosis. *Journal of Abnormal Social Psychology, 33,* 281-94.

Hilgard, E. R. (1965). *Hypnotic susceptibility.* New York: Harcourt, Brace and World.

Hilgard, E. R. (1977). *Divided consciousness: Multiple controls in human thought and action.* New York: John Wiley.

Hilgard, E. R., & Hilgard, J. R. (1975). *Hypnosis in the relief of pain.* Los Altos, CA: William Kaufmann.

McConkey, K. M., Sheehan, P. W., & Law, H. G. (1980). Structural analysis of the Harvard Group Scale of Hypnotic Susceptibility: Form A. *International Journal of Clinical Experimental Hypnosis, 28,* 164-175.

McConkey, K. M., Sheehan, P. W., & White, K. D. (1979). Comparison of the Creative Imagination Scale and the Harvard Group Scale of Hypnotic Susceptibility, Form A. *International Journal of Clinical Experimental Hypnosis, 27,* 265-277.

Orne, M. T., & Hammer, A. G. (1974). Hypnosis. *Encyclopaedia Britannica* (15th ed.) (pp. 133-140). Chicago: Benton.

Pattie, F. A. (1967). A brief history of hypnotism. In J. E. Gorden, (Ed.), *Handbook of Clinical and Experimental Hypnosis* (pp. 10-43) New York: Macmillan.

Shor, R. E., & Orne, E. C. (1962). *Harvard Group Scale of Hypnotic Susceptibility, Form A*. Palo Alto, CA: Consulting Psychologists Press.

Weitzenhoffer, A. M. (1953). *Hypnotism: An objective study in suggestibility.* New York: John Wiley.

Weitzenhoffer, A. M. (1957). *General techniques of hypnotism.* New York: Grune & Stratton.

Weitzenhoffer, A. M., & Hilgard, E. R. (1959). *Stanford Hypnotic Suggestibility Scale. Forms A and B.* Palo Alto, CA: Consulting Psychologists Press.

Weitzenhoffer, A. M., & Hilgard, E. R. (1962). *Stanford Hypnotic Susceptibility Scale: Form C.* Palo Alto, CA: Consulting Psychologists Press.

Wilson, S. C., & Barber, P. X. (1978). The Creative Imagination Scale as a measure of hypnotic responsiveness: Applications to experimental and clinical hypnosis. *American Journal of Clinical Hypnosis, 20,* 235-249.

Oliver C. S. Tzeng, Ph.D.

Professor of Psychology and Director of the Osgood Center for Cross-Cultural Research, Purdue University, School of Science at Indianapolis, Indianapolis, Indiana.

STRONG-CAMPBELL INTEREST INVENTORY

E. K. Strong and D. P. Campbell. Stanford, California: Stanford University Press.

Introduction

In measuring an individual's interest in different types of occupations, educational disciplines, personality associations, and recreational activities, one of the most prominent instruments in the history of psychometrics is the Strong-Campbell Interest Inventory (SCII), the current edition of the Strong Vocational Interest Blank (SVIB). Historically, the SCII represents the culmination of over 50 years of scientific endeavors that involved hundreds of thousands of people in diverse occupations. Since the publication of the initial work by Strong in 1927, the SCII and its earlier editions have enjoyed vast popularities not only in career counseling and personnel selection, but also in scientific research communities. Literally over one thousand articles have been published on the inventory, and countless master's and doctoral dissertations have used it as the major source. Therefore, it seems almost impossible to conduct an exhaustive review of all relevant materials in this critique. For this reason the focus will be on the evaluation of its theories and psychometric properties.

As its name suggests, the SCII is intended to measure an individual's interest, not aptitude or intelligence, in various occupations. The theoretical foundation for developing the SCII is from typology and trait psychology. That is, individuals in the same occupation will display similar interests and personality characteristics, whereas people in different occupations will display different types of interests and personality characteristics. Based on the nature of homogeneity within the same occupation and heterogeneity across different occupations, the following inferences of trait attribution become the basic assumptions in the development and application of the SCII: 1) Each occupation has a desirable pattern of interests and personality characteristics among its workers. The ideal pattern is represented by successful people in that occupation. 2) Each individual has relatively stable interests and personality traits. When such interests and traits match the desirable interest patterns of the occupation the individual has a high probability to enter that occupation and be more likely to succeed in it. 3) It is highly possible to differentiate individuals in a given occupation from others-in-general in terms of the desirable patterns of interests and traits for that occupation.

The SVIB was first published in 1927 with 420 items in differentiating male certified accountants from other occupational groups (Strong, 1927). Since the first

737

distribution of the manual in 1928, the SVIB has undergone many major revisions and expansions: 1) The publications of the women's SVIB in 1933 and its manual in 1935; 2) major revision of the men's form in 1938; 3) revision of the women's form in parallel with the men's form in 1946; 4) first publication of modern SVIB manual by Consulting Psychologists Press in 1959; 5) major revisions of the men's form in 1966 with 399 items; 6) major revision of the women's form in 1969 with 398 items; 7) the publication of the handbook for the SVIB by Campbell in 1971; 8) publication of the 1974 edition of the SVIB, designated as the SCII (Form T325) that includes the merging of the men's and women's forms into a single booklet and the introduction of a theoretical framework to guide the organization and interpretation of scores (Campbell & Hansen, 1981); 9) publication of the 1984 user's guide for the SVIB-SCII (Hansen, 1984).

For the present review, the major focus will be on three contemporary sources that are vital for application of the SCII: the 1971 handbook, the 1981 SVIB-SCII manual (Form T325), and the 1984 user's guide.

The basic materials for the SVIB-SCII include three parts: the inventory booklet (Form T325) and answer sheet, a profile form, and an interpretive report.

The inventory booklet and answer sheet contain 325 items grouped under the following seven domains of measurement:

Occupations: (131 items). Respondents indicate how they would feel about doing a particular kind of work by marking each occupation (e.g., Actor/Artist, Advertising executive, Architect) as either "Like" (L), "Indifferent" (I), or "Dislike" (D).

School Subjects: (36 items). Respondents indicate their interest in each subject (e.g., Agriculture, Algebra, Arithmetic) even though they may not have studied it by marking each item L, I, or D.

Activities: (51 items). Respondents indicate their interest in a number of diverse activities that include individual behaviors (e.g., cooking, living in a city), social interactions (e.g., discussing politics, contributing to charities), and work-related functions (e.g., operating machinery, interviewing job applicants) by marking each item L, I, or D.

Amusement: (39 items). Respondents indicate their interest in nonwork-related, leisure activities (e.g., golf, fishing, concerts) by marking each item L, I, or D.

Types of People: (24 items). Respondents indicate how they would feel having day-to-day contact with each type of people (e.g., babies, aggressive people, musical geniuses) by marking each item L, I, or D.

Preference Between Two Activities: (30 items). Respondents express their preference between two "opposing" activities or occupations (e.g., taxicab driver vs. police officer, reading a book vs. watching TV or going to a movie) by marking their preference "R" if it is on the right side, "L" if it is on the left side, or " = " if they like or dislike both equally or if they are undecided.

Your Characteristics: (14 items). Respondents show what kind of person they are, according to whether or not various statements (e.g., win friends easily, put drive into an organization) describe them, by marking each item "Y" if it does, "N" if it does not, or "?" if they are undecided.

Answers to all 325 items will yield raw scores for each respondent from which various scale scores were derived by combining different items into various organizational groups (scales). The results of such derived scores are entered by computer on the profile form that contains the following five types of scale scores:

General Occupational Themes: (6 themes). Holland's (1973) six occupational types—Realistic, Investigative, Artistic, Social, Enterprising, and Conventional—were adopted to derive six theme scales. Each theme was measured by 20 marker items that were selected based on the descriptions given by Holland (1966). The raw scale score on each theme is a simple summation of the individual item scores across the 20 markers (e.g., $L = 1, I = 0, D = 1$). The respondent's raw scale score on each theme is further transformed to a standard T-score with respect to the general reference sample of 600 adults of both sexes. Such a standard score becomes the theme scale score printed on the profile for interpretation. The scores on the six themes provide a parsimonious view of the respondent's interests with respect to both the total life style and the global occupational environment.

Basic Interest Scales: (23 scales). Based on the analysis of inter-item correlations across all items, 23 clusters were obtained and identified as the Basic Interest Scales. Each scale has 5 to 24 marker items. Psychometrically, the items within each cluster are more homogeneous than the items across different clusters in representing one specific area of activities. Therefore, a respondent's score on each scale is further transformed into standard T-scores for comparisons with the general reference sample. For example, a high score on a given scale would indicate the consistency of answering "Like" to the activities in that area. These 23 scales are further clustered on the profile into the six General Occupational Theme categories. That is, the Realistic Theme contains Agriculture, Nature, Adventure, Military Activities, and Mechanical Activity; the Investigative Theme contains Science, Mathematics, Medical Science, and Medical Service; the Artistic Theme contains Music/Dramatics, Art, and Writing; the Social Theme contains Teaching, Social Service, Athletics, Domestic Arts, and Religious Activities; the Enterprising Theme contains Public Speaking, Law/Politics, Merchandising, Sales, and Business Management; and the Conventional Theme contains Office Practices.

The Occupational Scales: (162 items). The Profile carries 77 common occupations for both sexes and eight specific occupations, four for males and four for females. For example, the common occupations include Air Force Officer, Farmer, and Chemist; the four male-specific occupations are Agribusiness Manager, Skilled Crafts, Investment Fund Manager, and Vocational Agriculture Teacher; and the four female-specific occupations are Dental Assistant, Dental Hygienist, Home Economics Teacher, and Secretary. Each scale contains between 50 to 70 marker items, and each item has maximal discriminability (large response-percentage differences) between the reference group (people-in-general) and the criterion groups ("successful" employees of a specific occupation). For each scale, the respondent's answers to the markers are checked against the sex-normal keys (either "Like" or "Dislike"). A congruent response is scored as +1, whereas an incongruent response (e.g., a subject's "Like" vs. the norm group's "Dislike" key) is scored as –1. Summing over such comparison scores across all markers yields an Occupational Scale Score for each of the 85 occupations which is further transformed to the standard T-score with reference to the mean and standard deviation of the respective criterion groups (males and females). As a result, each respondent's standard scores, in the range of –44 to +96, on all 85 Occupational Scales for each sex are entered in the Profile.

For facilitating interpretation, such standard scores are further broken down into seven categories, from very dissimilar (standard score of 12 or below), dissimilar (13-21), moderately dissimilar (22-27), mid-range (28-39), moderately similar (40-45), similar (46-54), to very similar (55 or higher). A high score will indicate the respondent's interests are similar to the interests of people in that occupation (i.e., the criterion group).

In addition, the 162 occupational scales of both sexes are coded by the six General Occupational Themes based on the response scores of the criterion samples on the six themes. These codings provide easy integration of the General Occupational Themes, Basic Interest Scales, and Occupational Scales (Hansen notes in the user's guide and in a personal communication [January 18, 1985] that in the 1985 revision, the Occupational scales will contain about 207 items that will include scales for female investment managers and vocational agriculture teachers, and both female and male carpenters, etc. The new 1985 manual by Hansen and Campbell will be available July 1, 1985. The major changes and features of the 1985 revision can be found in Hansen, in press).

Special Scales (Academic Comfort and Introversion-Extroversion): The Academic Comfort Scale (AC) is designed to serve as an indicator of 1) degree of comfort in an academic setting, 2) degree of interest in intellectual endeavors, and 3) degree of persistence toward either investigative and/or artistic vocations (high scores) or toward organizational and/or action-oriented problems (low scores).

The same procedure used for constructing the Occupational Scales was used in developing the Academic Comfort Scale: 1) A large sample of college students at the University of Minnesota's College of Liberal Arts was categorized into two groups (good students vs. poor students) based on the combination of their GPA's and achievement test scores. 2) By treating these good vs. poor student groups as two criterion samples, the SCII items differentiating the two samples were then used as the marker items to construct the AC scale. 3) The respondent's endorsements of the marker items emphasizing the interests in Investigative and Artistic Themes are scored positively (+ 1s), whereas the endorsements of the marker items in the interests of Enterprising and Realistic themes are scored negatively (–1s); each respondent's AC score (in the range of –14 to 92) is the sum of weighted scores on all marker items. 4) The AC scale, normed across 198 Occupational Samples, will reflect a hierarchical relationship between the educational backgrounds of the individuals in various occupations and their AC scores (Ph.D.s score about 56 to 65; professional degrees (e.g., lawyers, dentists, optometrists) score about 50 to 55; master's and bachelor's degrees about 45 to 55; associate or vocational/technical 2-year degree about 35 to 44; and high-school diplomas about 34 or lower. 5) The AC scale is also normed so that for both bachelor's and master's degrees, occupations with Investigative or Artistic interests score higher (50-55) than those with interests in the Social or Enterprising themes (45-50). Both in the 1981 manual and 1984 user's guide, mean scores on the AC Scale for a variety of occupational samples are listed for counseling purposes, for example, Biologist (female) with a mean of 65, Chemists (male) with a mean of 62, etc.

The Introversion-Extroversion (I-E) Scale is designed to discriminate between people-oriented and nonpeople-oriented occupational interests. Low scores on the I-E Scale are earned by extroverted individuals who enjoy working with others, especially in social-service settings, whereas high scores are earned by introverted individuals who would prefer to work with ideas and things. This scale is developed under the same procedure used in developing the AC Scale: 1) A large sample of University of Minnesota students who scored in either the extroverted or introverted direction on the Minnesota Multiphasic Personality Inventory (MMPI) was categorized into two criterion (extroverted and introverted) groups. 2) The SVIB-SCII items that differentiated these two criterion groups were used as the markers for the I-E Scale. 3) Items emphasizing working with ideas or things are scored in the introverted direction (+ 1, high scores); items emphasizing working with people are scored in the extroverted direction (–1, low scores). 4) Each respondent's I-E Scale score, in the range of 18 to 94, is the sum of individual introverted or extroverted scores on all marker items. 5) The I-E Scale is normed so that the entire scale score range is trichotomized into three successive categories: scores of 45 or below reflect the extroverted direction, scores between 46 and 54 reflect a balance between extroverted and introverted interests, and scores of 55 or higher reflect the introverted direction. In the manual and user's guide, I-E mean scores for 200 occupational samples are listed for counseling purposes.

The Administrative Indexes (3 statistics): The Administrative Indexes (AI) are routine computer analyses of each respondent's answer sheet on all 325 items. Three types of indexes are reported on the profile: The Total Response, Infrequent Response, and Relative Frequency Distribution on Response Alternatives.

The Total Response Index indicates the total number of item responses read by the computer from the answer sheet. If every item was answered by the respondent and correctly read in by the computer, the Total Response Index printed on the profile should be 325. Less than 325 indicates that either omissions of item responses by the subject or mechanical problems in computer data processing have occurred. When the index drops below about 310, the answer sheet should be checked before accepting the resulting profile.

The Infrequent Response Index is a general check of subject response validity. Based on prior analyses of item-response percentages of two General Reference Samples, along with several other samples, unpopular (infrequent) items, each with 6% or less of endorsement (e.g., "Like") from all respondents were identified. As a result, the maximal numbers of infrequent responses are 6 for women and 11 for men. These numbers are used as the base line for computing each respondent's score on the Infrequent Response Index. That is, for each endorsement of the unpopular items, 1 point is subtracted from this base line. Therefore, the maximal scores of 6 (for female respondents) and 11 (for males) on this index would indicate no endorsement of any unpopular items. (Note, in the 1984 user's guide, the marker items for this Index include several popular items such as taking responsibility. Under such circumstances, the computation method will include the subtraction of the number of rejecting popular items from the base line.) Generally speaking, a very low (especially negative) score on this index would indicate a potential problem of the respondent in answering the SCII items (e.g., misunderstanding the instructions, or lack of cooperation).

The Relative Frequency Distribution on Response Alternatives contains 24 numbers. As indicated earlier, the 325 items in SCII are categorized in the test booklet under seven sections of measurement. For all items, a common three-step response format is used: the Like-Indifferent-Dislike format for the first five sections, the Left-Neutral-Right format for the measurement of Preference Between Two Activities, and the Yes-Undecided-No format for checking personality characteristics. Within each section, frequency distribution of items on these three response alternatives is computed for each respondent and converted into percentages for reporting on the profile. In addition, across all seven sections, an overall frequency distribution of the 325 items is also obtained and reported in percentage form. As a result, a total of 24 numbers is reported on the profile. These figures are intended to reveal the respondent's response style in filling in the inventory. For example, an excessively high response percentage (60% or higher) on the first alternative ("Like," "Left," and "Yes") will result in high score on all six General Occupational Themes and most of the Basic Interest Scales: people with high percentages on the second alternative tend to be indecisive, apathetic, or confused about their future occupations.

Furthermore, the indexes of Total Responses and Infrequent Responses are used to check the accuracy of the scale scores on the profile prepared by various commercial scoring series. It was reported that these checks have reduced mechanical inaccuracies in computing profile scale scores and increased the consistency and reliability of profile reporting (Hansen, 1982).

Finally, on the issue of faking (invalidity) in responses, it was concluded that most people answer the SCII items honestly even in highly competitive selection situations. However, in order to check a possible faking, the recommendation was made in the manual to check the inconsistencies between scores on the Basic Interest Scales and on the Occupational Scales, and to follow the check-and-balance system provided by using homogeneous and heterogeneous scales.

In addition to the basic, graphic profile form on which the respondent's scores can be printed directly, a descriptive form, the Interpretative Report (or Interpretative profile) is generated and printed directly by the computer. Each report includes scale scores and interpretations of each score for the individual respondent. Such a computer-interpretive profile is useful for one-to-one interactions between the examiner and examinee in various education/counseling situations.

Practical Applications/Uses

The SCII 132 items are easy to administer and can be given individually or in groups, in person or by mail. The respondent needs only a place to write, a computer-scored test booklet, and a dark lead pencil. It will take an average of 25 to 35 minutes to complete the entire test, including five demographic items.

The prospective subjects who will benefit from taking the SCII include high-school and college students, and adults seeking guidance on job entry or continued education. Therefore, the SCII is appropriate for individuals in a life span of 50 years or more. Because most students' interests have not developed enough to be differentiated before the eighth grade (ages 13-14), the SCII is not recommended for application below high school level.

The SCII items are written at about the sixth-grade level to ensure the understanding of all prospective subjects, including the slower readers with eighth- and ninth-grade education backgrounds. When a few items (e.g., calculus, botany) are unfamiliar to some respondents, the administrator is encourged to offer definitions or explanations such that respondents can estimate accurately their preference to the items.

Before administration of the SCII, pretest orientation is needed for all respondents, including such concepts as 1) career-planning is a life long activity, 2) the SCII is a measure of interest, and 3) the inventory is to help the organization of existing interests, rather than to provide solutions to occupational problems.

Completed answer sheets are normally sent to one of the commercial scoring agencies for scoring. Currently, there are three commercial agencies that will handle scoring and distribution of the SCII materials. They are CPP (P.O. Box 60070, Palo Alto, California, 94306), CPP (5100 No. Roxboro Rd., Durham, North Carolina, 27703), and CPP (P.O. Box 944, Minneapolis, Minnesota, 55440).

The SCII is reported to have diverse applicabilities. The common applications can be summarized into three broad areas: 1) counseling the individual student or employee for such purposes as high-school and college curriculum-planning, mid-career evaluation and change, occupational rehabilitation, and leisure counseling; 2) conducting field research on groups for such purposes as studying characteristic interests of particular occupations, studying indigenous cultural characteristics and cross-cultural influences; 3) conducting basic research programs that will identify interpersonal homogeneity in various social interactions, investigate the nature and process of career development, study the impacts of similar interests on human relationships (e.g., marital, sibling, and parent-child relations), and apply scientific knowledge for various occupational improvements.

For these applications, a variety of professionals who will conduct the above studies or who are in the position of assisting clients can use the SCII.

Both the manual and user's guide devote a chapter, as well as other space, to the description of procedures for interpreting the SCII results to the respondent. These procedures include 17 steps in sequence and each step is explained in detail.

Many case studies are also included to provide the foundation necessary for an understanding of the psychometric principles of the SCII and its applicational mechanisms.

Technical Aspects

The utility of a psychological measurement inventory depends on the psychometric evidence of reliability and validity at the levels of items, scales, and the entire test as a whole. This section of the review focuses on the evaluation of such psychometric properties of the SCII and its earlier edition, the SVIB especially at the item and scale levels.

Three types of statistical analyses at the item level are reported in the manual. The first type is item-response distribution for all of the SCII items. That is, for each item, the percentages of "Like" responses from 438 occupational samples were plotted in an item-response distribution. The distributions of all 325 items were then used to assess various psychometric properties, such as the differentiality across various occupations, the relationship between the content of each item and the occupations endorsing the item, the stability of distributions over time (some over four decades), and the identification of sex differences. (These distributions are available in the computer-accessible storages at the University of Minnesota.)

The second type is between-group comparisons on item-response percentages. That is, for each item, the "Like" percentages from two groups (the occupational criterion and general reference samples) were compared. The differences on all 325 items were rank-ordered, and the items that exhibited large response differences were then selected as the markers (in an average of 60 items) for that occupation in the Occupational Scales.

The third type is inter-item correlations. That is, for the selection of marker items for the 23 Basic Interest Scales, intercorrelations between the 400 items of the SVIB were calculated for the men's and women's booklets separately. Based on frequency distributions of the correlations, a cutoff point of .25 was used to select the marker items for each of the Basic Interest Scales. In the SCII scales, the male and female SVIB sets were merged by combining the parallel scales of both sexes.

Using scale scores as basic units in analyses at the scale level three types of statistics are reported: The first type is inter-group mean differences. That is, the mean scores on a given Occupational Scale were compared between the reference sample and a new respondent sample, and also between different occupational samples. The minimal differences were established as criteria to evaluate mean differences for psychometrical significance (concurrent validity). In addition, the SVIB has a long history of validity study in predicting occupational choices. Detailed information can be found in the handbook and the manual.

Concurrent validity of the Basic Interest Scales was supported by numerous comparisons among people currently in different occupations. However, the predictive validity was found not as good as concurrent validity, due to both interscale and interpersonal differences (some scales and persons are less predictable than others).

The second type of analysis is on the relationship between the Basic Interest Scales and the Occupational Scales. The manual reports that about 20% of the SVIB profiles had one or more apparent inconsistencies between these two types of scales (e.g., mathematics vs. mathematician). Such discrepancies are due to the different procedures involved in selecting their respective marker items.

The third type involves test-retest correlations for the Basic Interest Scales over various time intervals and for various age samples. The test-retest correlations and the stability of the means were also computed for the Occupational Scales. In general, the correlations are reasonably high, ranging from .60s to .90s, demonstrating that the SCII scales are quite stable over time (especially over short periods).

Critique

It should be noted that in assessing the above psychometric properties of the SCII items, not a single test of statistical significance has been used and reported in the manual. Instead, Campbell (1974) emphasized magnitude and replicabilities of differences and consistency of trends. This reviewer readily agrees with Campbell that, in many cases, statistical significance does not automatically imply psychological significance. Numerous studies that involve between-group comparisons in means or between-item correlations within such content areas as human intelligence, implicit personality theories, and semantic differential ratings have been tricked by the notion of "statistical significance" (Tzeng, 1982; Tzeng & Tzeng, 1982; Tzeng, Powers, & Schliessmann, 1984).

The approaches used in the SVIB and SCII have many desirable characteristics, but also bear many weaknesses.

There are five major strengths about the development and presentations of the SVIB-SCII:

1) The development of the seven item-response contents includes diverse occupations, school subjects, activities, amusements, important-others, preferred activities, and personality characteristics. This approach guarantees the comprehensiveness of measurement issues and concerns that are directly and indirectly related to the development of individual occupational interests and preferences. In this regard, the vision of Strong in the 1920s encompasses all four personality research paradigms that were prevalent during the last 50 years: typology, trait psychology, situationism, and interactionism.

2) The handbook provides complete documents on the theories, methods, and procedures for the development and revision of the SVIB-SCII, and the manual and user's guide synthesize very well the materials that are necessary for the users and interpreters of the test.

3) The uses of means, standard deviations, percentages, correlations, and standard scores as the major statistics are easy to understand by average researchers and prospective users.

4) Extensive studies are presented on three types of validity—concurrent validity, predictive validity, and postdictive validity—within and across various forms. Also, extensive studies on reliability (mostly test-retest) are reported.

5) The two interpretation materials—the graphic profile and the descriptive interpretation report—are easy to understand and are complementary to each other. The combination of these two will provide a comprehensive picture of a respondent's occupational interests and preferences.

Regarding the measurement properties of the SCII and its earlier edition, there are several issues that have never been assessed. As a result, the lack of such information generates many unexplainable properties of scale profiles that are interpreted as "special properties" of the SCII in the manual and user's guide. These issues are centered around the measurement concept of construct validity for the development of three types of derived measures: six General Occupation Themes, 23 Basic Interest Scales, and 162 different Occupational Scales.

Throughout the 325 SCII items, a uniform response format with trichotomous options (Like/Indifferent/Dislike, Left/ = /Right, Yes/?/No) is used. Psychometrically, the response on each item should represent an isomorphic mapping (quantification) between the empirical response continuum of the three steps and the underlying trait continuum to be measured (e.g., extroversion/introversion) (cf. Tzeng, 1983). However, the trichotomous format is qualitative (rather than quantitative) in nature, and it can detect neither the relative differentiations between two endorsed items on the same construct, nor the true relative saturations of the two constructs (both with 100% Like responses) for a single respondent. Under such circumstances, the equal number of endorsed items for an individual on two different scales does not necessarily indicate an equal interest level on these two psychological constructs. Similarly, the equal numbers of endorsed items for two persons on the same scale do not automatically imply an equal occupational interest to both individuals. Therefore, improvement of such a trichotomous response format would seem necessary in order to establish the quantitative evidence of construct validity in the future. (For detailed discussions and illustrations of comparative results across different response formats see Tzeng, 1983.)

Psychometric assessment of construct validity. The organizations of the six General Occupational Themes and the 23 Basic Interest Scales from the same 325 items are hierarchically inclusive in the theoretical postulations for the 1974 version of the SVIB. However, in the actual process of constructing the marker items, these two types of scales were initially obtained by two separate procedures, and only later linked by computing the correlations between their scale scores. Given the availability of these correlations (see Manual, Table 5-3), the assignment of the 23 Basic Interest Scales into the six General Themes was still rather arbitrary. The obvious problems include 1) the treatment of multiattributions of many individual Basic Interest Scales as a single, isolated attribution (e.g., Mathematics has apparent coattributions under the Realistic, Investigative, and Conventional Themes, but is clustered under the Investigative Theme only); 2) The use of inconsistent criteria to cluster individual Basic Interest Scales (e.g., the high correlation coefficients of .57 [male] and .64 [female] did not warrant the inclusion of Business Management under the Conventional Theme, whereas the low correlations of .28 [male] and .40 [female] were used to include Medical Service under the Investigative Theme); 3) the repeated reference in the manual to the psychometric concepts of "factors" and "clustering" in identifying markers for different scales. However, the various multivariate techniques that will perform the designated purposes of identifying factors and clusters were never used in the empirical treatment of the data. Therefore, partial and/or biased assignments of the marker items become inevitable.

To illustrate the third point, the two matrices of intercorrelations between the 23 Basic Interest Scales obtained from the two General Reference Samples of both sexes (see Manual, Table 5-2) were factor analyzed by this reviewer. The results of three to eight dimensions were rotated through Varimax criterion. The six-dimensional solutions should in theory recapture completely the categorizations of the 23 Basic Interest Scales into the six General Occupational Themes.

Table 1 presents the factor structures of both sexes with only the salient loadings being presented in the table. Generally speaking, the present results provide only partial support for the construct validity of heirarchical organizations between the Interest Scale level and the General Occupation Theme level.

Specifically, in the table the present factor solutions suggest the following: 1) For both male and female groups, six empirical factor solutions seem reasonable and each accounts for over 89% of the respective total input variance. 2) In comparisons between male and female structures, there appears roughly a one-to-one correspondence across all six factors. 3) Based on salient loadings, especially those coded with asterisks, the SCII clusterings of Basic Interest Scales into the six General Themes are not totally supported. In fact, only the five Basic Interest Scales under the Enterprising Theme appear to be relatively homogeneous and "simple" (uniquely loaded on two dimensions) for the male reference group. 4) There exist important sex differences in interrelationships between various Basic Interest

Table 1

Rotated Factor Structures for Male and Female General Reference Groups[a]

General Themes	Basic Interest Scales	Male Factor Structure						Female Factor Structure					
		I	II	III	IV	V	VI	I	II	III	IV	V	VI
Realistic	Agriculture	—[b]	-.70*	.58	—	—	—	-.30	-.76*	—	—	—	—
	Nature	-.44	-.50*	—	.43	.48	—	-.40	-.68*	—	—	.48	—
	Adventure	—	—	—	—	.48	-.92*	—	—	—	—	—	.86*
	Military Activities	.52*	—	.49	—	—	—	—	—	.46	-.81*	—	.73*
	Medical Activities	—	-.76*	—	-.43	—	—	-.30	—	—	—	—	—
Investigative	Science	-.60	—	—	-.62*	.33	—	-.50	—	—	.74*	.40	—
	Mathematics	—	-.37	—	-.89*	—	—	-.31	—	.37	-.83*	—	—
	Medical Science	-.47	—	—	—	.77*	—	-.33	—	—	-.30	-.84*	—
	Medical Service	—	—	—	—	.93*	—	—	—	.45	—	.70*	—
Artistic	Music/Dramatics	-.42	.36	-.70*	.34	—	—	—	.31	-.87*	—	—	—
	Art	-.48	—	-.69*	.37	—	—	—	—	-.94*	—	—	—
	Writing	-.45	.55	-.60*	—	—	—	—	.37	-.88*	—	—	—
Social	Teaching	.44	.61*	—	—	.37	—	—	.70*	-.32	.75*	—	—
	Social Service	—	.73*	—	.48	.30	—	—	.49	—	—	—	—
	Athletics	—	—	.82*	—	—	—	—	—	.60*	—	—	.48
	Domestic Arts	—	—	-.41	.58*	.50	—	—	—	.43	.71*	—	—
	Religious Activities	—	—	—	.34	—	.77*	-.31	-.31	.52	.59*	—	—
Enterprising	Public Speaking	—	.91*	—	—	—	—	.54	.65*	-.42	—	—	—
	Law/Politics	—	.92*	—	—	—	—	.48	.67*	-.42	—	—	—
	Merchandising	.91*	—	—	—	—	—	.88*	—	—	.35	—	—
	Sales	.91*	—	—	—	—	—	.87*	—	—	.31	—	—
	Business Management	.90*	—	—	—	—	—	.88*	.32	—	—	—	—
Conventional	Office Practices	.79*	—	—	—	—	.50	.35	—	.81*	—	—	—

[a]Correlation matrices, reported in the 1981 SVIB-SCII Manual (p. 37), were analyzed separately for males and females through prinicipal components analysis with varimax rotation.

[b]Factor loadings with an absolute value below .30 were not reported in this table. For each Basic Interest Scale, its highest loading was coded with an asterisk (*) for interpretation purposes.

Scales. For example, to females, the interests of Military Activities and Athletics were found to be highly congruent with the interest of Adventure. For males, on the other hand, Military Activities were not related to Adventure, but rather related to popular occupations for general male adults (i.e., Sales, Merchandising, Business Management, Office Practice, and Teaching as opposed to Science, Medical Science, and Artistic interests). 5) The salient interests on the six empirical factors suggest that Holland's six general themes may not be apropriate for assigning the six distinctive "clusters" from the 23 Basic Interests. For example, the third factor of the male structures indicates the dimensional nature with two opposite characteristics in behavioral contexts—overall body functions (Athletics, Agriculture, and Military Activities) vs. fine mental activities (Music, Art, Dramatic Arts, and Writing).

Psychometrically, the derivation of the 23 Basic Interest Scales and identification of their respective markers can be and should be obtained from simultaneous assessment (e.g., factor analysis) of the intercorrelations among all 325 items. Unfortunately, such intercorrelations are not available in the handbook for psychometric verification of the clusterings. Unless such analysis is completed, many unexplainable problems will remain a mystery in the literature of the SCII (e.g., only one Basic Interest Scale, Office Practice, fits into Holland's Conventional category (cf. Manual, p. 37).

The method for selecting marker items for each Vocational Scale, was based on the relative between-group discriminabilities among items. This strategy bears several potential difficulties in the context of construct validity. First, from the sheer mathematical rule of combinations, 60 items were selected from the same 325 item pool for some eighty different occupations. It would be inevitable to generate a lot of overlapping marker items for different occupation scales, thus yielding many equally appealing occupations for each respondent. Secondly, in the contemporary society individuals tend to exhibit gender interests and involvements in various activities, amusements, interdisciplinary school subjects and occupational skills, etc. As a result, it is highly probable for a respondent to be characterized as having high interests in many and diverse occupations. Under both conditions, construct validity of the SCII and its power for predicting an individual's future occupational choice will be arbitrarily inflated.

Critique

In addition to the above weaknesses many other issues have been raised by various reviewers of the SCII and reported in the *Mental Measurements Yearbooks* (Buros, 1972, 1978). Among them, the major criticisms include 1) the application difficulty of the SCII to the respondent who is either a "yes sayer" or "nay sayer"; 2) the inconsistency between the Basic Interest and Occupational Scales; 3) the sex-restrictive nature of the SCII, due to separate sex scoring keys for the common Occupation Scales, and separate sex norms for the homogeneous scales; (It should be noted that although the SCII is sex-restrictive, it meets all of the NIE guidelines on sex-fairness for interest inventories. In addition, data in the manual [chap. 7] indicate that separate-sex scales are less restrictive than combined-sex scales in the new development of interests of women and men. Also, the combined-sex norms are available for homogeneous scales in the manual.) 4) the omission of the report of marker items for individual SCII scales in the manual; 5) the omission of the report of means and standard deviations for each occupational criterion group on all Occupational Scales and the omission of the report of intercorrelations among the Occupational Scales for both sexes.

It should be noted that many of these and related issues have been discussed in depth by various scholars. Unfortunately, no consensus has been reached. The basic reason underlying such controversies seems to center around the lack of rigorous scientific studies on construct validity of the SCII at the item, scale, and profile levels. Therefore, unless all psychometric properties are thoroughly evaluated and documented in the manual or handbook, the utilities and interpretabilities of the SCII will probably continue to be questioned by some critics.

Overall, the new SCII is well constructed from the revision of its preceding edition, the SVIB. It appears to be one of the best vocational interest inventories available and is widely used for educational guidance and vocational counseling. The 1971 handbook, 1981 manual, and 1984 user's guide provide complete information for all individuals who might be interested in using the SCII either for practical purposes or for research work by or with this inventory. Generally speaking, the users should be cautious about many unique aspects of the SCII construction in interpretation of scale scores and profiles. The researchers, epecially those who plan to employ the SCII scores as indexes for prediction and/or discrimination purposes, should take into consideration many unexplainable and uncertain properties of the SCII scales (i.e., interdependence and confounding influences of individual scales that are within and/or across the three types of scale scores reported on each profile). Finally, as far as the perfection of the inventory is concerned, there is still some room for improvement, especially in the area of scientific evidence of its construct validity.

References

Buros, O. K. (1972). *The seventh mental measurements yearbook* (Vols. 1 & 2). Highland Park, NJ: The Gryphon Press.

Buros, O. K. (1978). *The eighth mental measurements yearbook* (Vols. 1 & 2). Highland Park, NJ: The Gryphon Press.

Campbell, D. P. (1971). *Handbook for the SVIB*. Stanford, CA: Stanford University Press.

Campbell, D. P., & Hansen, J. C. (1981). *Manual for the Strong-Campbell Interest Inventory* (3rd ed.). Stanford, CA: Stanford University Press.

Hansen, J. D. (1982). *Scale score accuracy of the 1981 SCII*. Unpublished manuscript, University of Minnesota, Center for Interest Measurement Research, Minneapolis.

Hansen, J. C. (1984). *User's Guide for the SVIB-SCII*. Palo Alto, CA: Consulting Psychologists Press.

Hansen, J. C. (in press). Strong Vocational Interest Blank/Strong-Campbell Interest Inventory. In W. B. Walsh and S. H. Osipow (Eds.), *Advances in vocational psychology: The assessment of interest*.

Holland, J. L. (1966). *The psychology of vocational choice*. Waltham, MA: Blaisdell.

Holland, J. L. (1973). *Making vocational choices: A theory of careers*. Englewood Cliffs, NJ: Prentice-Hall.

Strong, E. K., Jr. (1927). *Vocational Interest Blank*. Stanford, CA: Stanford University Press.

Tzeng, O. C. S. (1982). The artificial dispute over implicit personality theory. *Journal of Personality, 50,* 251-260.

Tzeng, O. C. S. (1983). A comparative evaluation of four response formats in personality ratings. *Educational and Psychological Measurement, 43,* 935-950.

Tzeng, O. C. S., Powers, K., & Schliessmann, R. (1984, November). *Cross-measurement and cross-statistical comparisons on studies of person perceptions: Measuremental fantasy vs. Statistical ghost.* Paper presented in Seventh Midwest Psychometric Conference. Bloomington, IN.

Tzeng, O. C. S., & Tzeng, C. (1982). Implicit personality theory: Myth or fact? An illustration of how empirical research can miss. *Journal of Personality, 50,* 223-239.

Grant Aram Killian, Ph.D.
Assistant Professor of Psychology, Nova University, Fort Lauderdale, Florida.

STROOP COLOR AND WORD TEST

Charles Golden. Chicago, Illinois: Stoelting Company.

Introduction

The origins of the Stroop Color and Word Test date back to 1883 and the beginnings of experimental psychology when Wilhelm Wundt suggested that his student James Cattell investigate, in his doctoral research, the time required to name objects and colors and read the corresponding words. Although some of the first experimental studies with color-word testing were carried out by Cattell (1886) who recognized that color-naming required more time than word-naming, the test as it is known today originated in the laboratory of Erick Rudolf Jaensch (1929).

The Stroop Test itself was introduced into American psychology by John Stroop when he was working at George Peabody College under the direction of Joseph Peterson. Peterson, who was interested in individual differences in the speed of color-naming and word-reading, stimulated Stroop to do his doctoral dissertation with interference in serial verbal reactions. The Color-Word Interference Test was an outgrowth of that doctoral dissertation (Stroop, 1935; 1938). To date the test remains as inconspicuous as it did over a hundred years ago, despite more than a hundred studies showing its reliability, validity and ease of administration since it was originally developed by Stroop in 1935.

The Stroop Test (1935) and all current variations consist of three cards: a *word* (W) card, a *color* (C) card, and a *color-word* (CW) card. The word card is a list of words for colors (e.g., red, green, yellow, and blue) printed in black ink; the color card is a series of color patches or asterisks in the same colors listed on the word card; and the color-word card is a list of those same color words printed in conflicting colors (e.g., the word "red" might be printed in the color "yellow" or "green" and the subject is requested to ignore the word and state the color of the ink.). The test is given in three parts, and the subject is asked to read all three parts as rapidly as possible. The subject's task on the word card is to read aloud the color words, on the color to name the colored patches or asterisks, and on the color-word to name the colors of the ink, ignoring the printed color word.

Currently, there is a standardized version (available from Stoelting Co.), which has been carefully refined by Golden (1978). However, several versions are used within the field that have differed on 1) the colors used, 2) the number of colors used, 3) the type of stimuli used to present the color patches, 4) the reading of the items across rows or down columns, and 5) the method of scoring (for an excellent review, see Jensen & Rohwer, 1966).

The original Stroop Test (1935) consisted of the three basic cards using five colors: red, blue, green, brown, and purple. The words were printed in 14-point

Franklin lower-case black ink on white paper and were arranged in a 10″ x 10″ matrix of evenly spaced rows and columns. The words were arranged randomly and each of the five colors occurred twice in a column and row, but no word was allowed to follow itself. This version is now out of print.

Thurstone and Mellinger (1953) developed a modification of the original Stroop and also used the three basic cards. However, Thurstone used a black background overlayed by photostatic negatives instead of white paper and only four colors: red, green, yellow, and blue. The colors and color-words were tinted in photographic watercolors, and the color patches were ⁵⁄₁₆″ circular dots, which were more striking over the black background than the original white background. The words and dots, like Stroop's, were arranged in a 10″ x 10″ matrix, and each card had a single row of ten practice items to insure that the subject understood the test requirements.

Another modification used by Lazarus et al. (1957), Broverman (1960) and Comalli et al. (1962), according to Jensen and Rohwer (1966), was developed at Clark University. In this modification, the items were in a 10″ x 10″ matrix; the color card consisted of rectangular patches ⁵⁄₁₆″ x ²⁄₁₆″; and only three colors—red, blue and green—were printed on a white background. Like Thurstone's version, at the top of each card was one row of practice items.

Gardner et al. (1959) developed a version similar to Thurstone's except that the words and colors were printed on a white background and the color cards consisted of a set of colored asterisks.

Jensen (1965) developed a set of cards that could be placed on an easel at eye level. The cards were 18″ x 25″ with colored dots ⁵⁄₈″ in diameter, the letters were ⁵⁄₁₆″ high, and five colors—red, green, orange, blue, and yellow—were used.

The current standardized version revised by Golden (1975) consists of three cards listing 100 items each presented in a 5″ x 20″ matrix. Golden (1975) compared the performance of subjects, using three, four, or five colors and found no significant differences between the three versions. Consequently, because all versions were equally reliable the simplest version using only red, green, and blue over a white 8½″ x 11″ background was adopted. Unfortunately, in this version the colors BLUE and GREEN are not clearly distinct and tend to blend into a blue-green color, which may contaminate the interference score and lower the color (C) score. This problem could have been easily avoided if a bolder print or more ink was used by the printer.

Card I (W) consists of 100 words (RED, GREEN, and BLUE) printed in black ink on a white sheet and arranged randomly with no word allowed to follow itself in a column.

Card II (C) consists of 100 colors (written as XXXX) printed in either red, green, or blue on a white sheet with no color allowed to follow itself in a column or match the corresponding word on card I. That is, none of the words on card I match in position the colors of card II.

Card III (CW) consists of 100 colored-words on a white sheet. On this card the order of the words from card I are printed in the order of the colors from card II. For example, word 1 on card 1 is printed in color 1 on card II to produce the color-word 1 on card III. Using this procedure, no word for a color matches that particular color.

During the test the examiner's participation is minimal and involves only reading the brief instructions and stopping the subject after 45 seconds has elapsed from the start of each card.

Although no study has offered definite norms for children on the Stroop, Golden (1978) has provided preliminary age norms. Essentially any literate child who can recognize the words "red," "green," and "blue" can be administered the test. At all ages above seven years the raw color-word score should be lower than the raw color score that should be lower than the raw word score. To date, the Stroop has been used with children as young as six years (Rand et al., 1963) and with adults up to age 80 (Broverman, 1960). Because the difficulty level is minimal the test is appropriate for ages 6 and over and can be used with all populations except the visually impaired or those unable to recognize the words for the colors. Numerous researchers have investigated Stroop scores with subjects having significantly below-average intelligence, and results of the scores seem to depend on the reading level of the retarded group (Das, 1969, 1970; Leisman, 1971; and Wolitzky et al., 1972).

In most studies females have a slight advantage in color naming (Brown, 1915; Ligon, 1932; Stroop, 1935; Jensen, 1965), however, this efficiency seems to disappear when the interference score (the time required to read the third card) is used (Golden, 1974). Consequently, Golden (1978) concluded that "the differences between the groups are slight, even when significant, and are generally of no importance in clinical or experimental work" (p. 8).

The Stroop Color and Word Test requires few materials and minimal space; any quiet setting with adequate illumination where the subject can be comfortably seated with sufficient room to read on a flat surface is appropriate. The test can be administered in an individual or group format.

For individual administrations the subjects are given all three pages with card W on top, followed by card C, then card CW. The three cards are placed in front of the subjects on a flat surface. They are allowed to rotate the cards only 45° in either direction but may not lift the cards off of the flat surface. They are given 45 seconds to read as many items on the three cards yielding three basic scores. After the subjects are given the three cards, the examiner reads the following instructions to card W (Golden, 1978):

> This is a test of how fast you can read the words on this page. After I say begin, you are to read down the columns starting with the first one until you complete it and then continue without stopping down the remaining columns in order. If you finish all the columns before I say "Stop", then return to the first column and begin again. Remember, do not stop reading until I say "Stop" and read out loud as quickly as you can. If you make a mistake, I will say "No" to you. Correct your error and continue without stopping. Are there any questions? Ready? Then begin. (After 45 seconds) Stop. Circle the item you are on. If you finished the entire page and began again, put a one by your circle. Turn the page" (p. 4).

For card C the instructions are identical except that the subjects are told to name the colors on the page. For card CW the subjects are instructed "to name the color of the ink the words are printed in, ignoring the word that is printed in each item" (p. 4) and given examples.

For group testing the same materials are used as with individual testing. Empirical studies are scant comparing the two methods (Jensen, 1966) and in most cases investigators have used different forms for both individual and group administrations. Consequently, comparisons of the two methods from study to study are extremely limited (Kipnis & Glickman, 1959, 1962; Uhlmann, 1962; Podell, 1963). In the current standardized version, Golden (1978) recommends that the group administration and the individual administration be similar, except that the words "out loud" be replaced by "to yourself." As with the individual administration, instructions should be given for each page to insure understanding and should not be utilized with psychiatric or brain-damaged populations.

Problems seldom occur with the administration of the Stroop Color and Word Test. However, sometimes a subject will cover up all but one letter on card CW in order to read the color easily. This strategy, as well as rotations of the cards in excesses of 45° should be stopped immediately.

The testing procedure is simple and straightforward; a trained psychologist is not necessary to administer the separate phases of the test and either a secretary, aide, teacher, or mental health counselor can be quickly trained to administer the test. In general, because subjects are given only 45 seconds per card the entire administration rarely requires more than 5 minutes to complete, even when administered to psychiatric populations.

Practical Applications/Uses

Research on the Stroop Color and Word Test has established that the test assess psychological processes and functions that effect cognition in normal, neuropsychological, and psychiatric populations. Stroop scores have been associated with cognitive flexibility, attention deployment, resistance to interference from outside stimuli, creativity, defense structures, and cognitive style and complexity. Moreover, the Stroop is a reliable, efficient and effective clinical test for evaluating psychopathology and brain dysfunction and can be utilized as a screening test or as part of a general test battery for making a differential diagnosis. Its short administration time, reliability, validity, and ease of administration make the Stroop a valuable test which can be successfully used in numerous settings. For example, a junior high school counselor could use the Stroop to assess efficiency of attention deployment and cognitive flexibility, a psychopathologist could use the Stroop to assess responsiveness to psychotropic medication (Killian et al., 1984), and a private practitioner could use the test to evaluate brain dysfunction.

The Stroop has not yet become part of the psychological test battery, but could easily serve as an introductory test in the battery by providing a minimally threatening and maximally absorbing beginning to psychological assessment. Serving as an easy bridge to the psychological examination with minimal contact with the examiner, the subject is not intimidated by specific questions concerning intelligence or threatening inkblots, which may disturb unconscious conflicts.

As a screening instrument for the detection of brain dysfunction, the Stroop has numerous advantages: it requires only elementary education, can be translated into foreign languages without difficulty, and requires only 5 minutes to administer. Either simple cutoff points or patterns of Stroop scores can be identified and be diagnostically useful (e.g., normal W, low C, and CW, or all low scores) in brain dysfunction (Perret; 1974, Golden, 1978).

In terms of psychopathology, Wapner and Krus (1960) found that schizophrenic patients had a significant loss of speed on all cards of the Stroop. Along similar lines, Weiss and Sherman (1962) found a significant correlation between the Manifest Anxiety Scale and poor performance on the Stroop among chronic schizophrenics but not among acute schizophrenics. Peixotto and Rowe (1969) compared schizophrenics with normals and found significant differences between the groups on all three cards. Golden (1976) and Killian et al. (1984) also found significant differences between normals and psychiatric patients on all Stroop measures.

Lichtenstein (1961) was the first to find that on the Minnesota Multiphasic Personality Inventory (MMPI) constricted subjects were more conventional and defensive. In an attempt to determine the specific aspects of personality and psychopathology that were affected by the Stroop, Golden and Golden (1975) administered the Stroop to three groups of normal subjects, categorized by high scores obtained on particular MMPI scales: 1) high scores on D and Sc; 2) high scores on Hs, Hy, Pt and Ma; and 3) high scores on Pd, Mf, Pa and Si. A one-way analysis of variance revealed significant differences among the three groups: group 1 scored worst, group 3 showed the best performance, and group 2 fell in between.

Bush (1975), also using the MMPI in normal males and females, examined the relationship between psychoticism (i.e., scales F, Sc, and Pz) in males and defensive rigidity (i.e., scales L, R, and Ec-5) in females. The Stroop significantly correlated with the psychoticism index for females ($p = .01$) and defensive rigidity for males ($p = .01$). Killian (1981) also found that of 19 cognitive measures only the Stroop inference score (CW) successfully discriminated between those schizophrenic and depressed patients who responded to psychotropic drugs from those who were classified as nonresponders.

Traditionally, there have been many scoring formulas since Stroop's (1935) original work. Jensen and Rohwer (1966) reviewed 16 scores derived from the three basic time scores on cards W, C and CW, and presented a comprehensive analysis of scores into three classes: 1) basic time scores and derived scores, 2) error scores, and 3) serial scoring. The complexities of these formulas are avoided in the revised Stroop manual which clearly and simply presents four scores based on the three cards. The Word Score (W), the Color Score (C), the Color-Word score (CW), and a predicted CW score are all based on the items completed on each card. Errors are not counted because the subject is made to repeat each incorrect response, lowering the overall score. In order to reduce the redundancies of the derived scores and assess which formulas yielded additional unique information, Golden (1978) performed a factor analysis on eight major scores which yielded three basic factors: speech, color difficulty, and interference. The presence and item loadings on these three factors were consistent with Jensen and Rohwer (1966). The one exception occurred on the speed factor in which Jensen (1965) found that the W score correlated .97 while Golden (1978) found that only W ÷ C correlated .98 with the speed factor and W correlated −.67.

The appendix in the test manual provides the user with age corrected scores, and T-scores for W, C, CW and the predicted Interference score. Because these scores are derived from the number of items completed on each card, are easily calculated, and take only a few minutes to learn, computer scoring and transparencies are unnecessary. Interpretation of these four scores is objective and not based on subjective clinical judgment. The test manual, however, is scant concerning rules or criteria for interpreting either raw- or T-score patterns and profiles. The actual meaning of certain configurations is thus left to the experience of the users and their familiarity with previous Stroop research.

Technical Aspects

Jensen (1965) found that test-retest reliabilities of basic and derived scores with intervals of three minutes, one day, and one week showed no appreciable differences. Moreover, reliability of the Stroop scores is highly consistent across different versions of the test (Golden, 1978). However, Jensen (1965) found that derived scores that utilize differences and ratios have somewhat lower reliabilities. For the three basic raw scores W, C, and CW Jensen (1965) reported reliabilities of .88, .79, and .71 respectively (N = 436). For the same scores Golden (1978) reported reliabilities of .89, .84, and .73 respectively (N = 450) for group administrations; .86, .82, and .73 respectively (N = 30) for individual administrations; and .85, .81, and .69 respectively (N = 60) for subjects administered both the individual and group forms.

Hollingworth (1915) was the first to assess the effects of practice on color-naming and found that during 100 administrations over a period of 10 to 40 days 19 subjects had a 30% improvement in speed of color-naming (C). Stroop (1935) found that with practice effects of 8 trials subjects had the most improvement on card CW and the least improvement on card W. Jensen (1965) found similar practice effects that were in agreement with both Hollingworth (1915) and Stroop (1935) and found when subjects (N = 50) were tested every day for 10 days they had a 36% improvement in speed of color-word-naming (CW), a 23% improvement in speed of color-naming (C), and a 15% improvement in the speed of word-naming (W) from the first trial (day 1) to the last trial (day 10). Most of the practice effects (Jensen, 1965) occur within the first four trials for CW (13%, 10%, 5%, and 3% improvement), within the first three trials for C (7%, 7% and 3% improvement), and within the first three trials for W (3%, 4% and 1% improvement). Smith and Nyman (1959) also found that the performance on the three basic scores became asymptotic after five trials. Despite improvement with practice, individual differences do not seem to interact with practice effects, thus, subjects tend to maintain the same rank order during stages of improvement (Gates, 1922).

Critique

The Stroop is a highly reliable and valid objective test which seems to have relevance for the practicing clinician and the experimental psychopathologist. Unlike some tests, used in the psychological test battery, that may lack reliability and fail to differentiate processess and functions, (e.g., House-Tree-Person, Killian, in press), the Stroop provides reliable and significant information about various disorders (Golden, 1976; Killian, 1984). The Stroop, which is as inconspicuous today as it was during its development, is of considerable importance and interest for the following reasons: 1) it provides reliable and stable measures on apparently three simple basic aspects of cognitive-perceptual functioning; 2) despite individual differences, rank orders are maintained even with significant practice effects (Jensen, 1966); and 3) it has been significantly correlated with a variety of instruments, populations, traits, and disorders. What is most unfortunate is that this simple reliable test with many uses has not been included in the standard psychological test battery. To quote Golden (1978), "We strongly believe that we have only touched on a few of the possible uses of the Stroop in our investigations to date, and that future research will identify more important areas (p. i)."

References

Broverman, D. M. (1960). Dimensions of cognitive style. *Journal of Personality, 28,* 167-185.

Brown, W. (1915). Practice in associating color-names with colors. *Psychological Review, 22,* 45-55.

Bush, M. (1975). Relationship between color-word test interference and MMPI indices of psychoticism and defense rigidity in normal males and females. *Journal of Consulting and Clinical Psychology, 43,* (6), 926.

Cattell, J. M. (1886). The time it takes to see and name objects. *Mind, 11,* 63-65.

Comalli, P. E., Wapner, S., & Werner, H. (1962). Interference effects of the Stroop Color Word Test in childhood, adult and aging. *Journal of Genetic Psychology, 100,* 47-53.

Das, J. P. (1969). Development of verbal abilities in retarded and normal children as measured by the Stroop test. *British Journal of Social and Clinical Psychology, 8,* 59-66.

Das, J. P. (1970). Changes in Stroop test response as a function of mental age. *British Journal of Social and Clinical Psychology, 9,* 68-73.

Gardner, R. W., Holzman, P. S., Klein, G. S., Linton, H. B., & Spence, D. P. (1959). Cognitive Control: A study of individual consistencies in cognitive behavior. *Psychological Issues, 1,* 1-185.

Gates, G. S. (1922). Individual differences as affected by practice. *Archives of Psychology, 8,*(58), 1-74.

Golden, C. J. (1974). Sex differences in performance on the Stroop color and word test. *Perceptual and Motor Skills, 39,* 1067-1070.

Golden, C. J. (1975). A group form of the Stroop color and word test. *Journal of Personality Assessment, 39,* 386-388.

Golden, C. J. (1976). The diagnosis of brain damage by the Stroop test. *Journal of Clinical Psychology, 32,* 654-658.

Golden, C. J. (1978). *Stroop Color and Word Test: A Manual for Clinical and Experimental Uses,* Chicago: Stoelting Co.

Golden, C. J., Golden, E. E. (1975). Resistance to cognitive interference as a function of MMPI profile. *Journal of Consulting and Clinical Psychology, 43,* 749.

Hollingworth, H. L. (1915). Articulation and association. *Journal of Educational Psychology, 6,* 99-105.

Jaensch, E. R. (1929). Grundformen menschlichen Seins. Mit Berucksichtigung ihrer Beziehungen zu Biologie und Medizin, zu Kulturphilosophie und Padagogik. Berlin: Otto Elsner.

Jensen, A. R. (1965). Scoring the Stroop test. *Acta Psychologia, 24,* 398-408.

Jensen, A. R., & Rohwer, W. D. (1966). The Stroop color word test: A review. *Acta Psychologia, 25,* 36-93.

Killian, G. A. (1981). *The Effects of psychotropic medication on cognitive control measures.* Unpublished doctoral dissertation, University of Chicago.

Killian, G. A., Holzman, P. S., Davis, J. M., & Gibbons, R. (1984). Effects of psychotropic medication on selected cognitive and perceptual measures. *Journal of Abnormal Psychology, 93,* (1), 58-70.

Killian, G. A. (in press). The House-Tree-Person (H-T-P) Technique. In D. Keyser & R. Sweetland, (Eds.), *Test Critiques* (Vol. I, pp. 338-352). Kansas City, MO: Test Corporation.

Kipnis, D., & Glickman, A. S. (1959). Validity of non-cognitive tests at nuclear power school. *U.S.N. Bur. Naval Personnel Technical Bulletin,* No. 59-6.

Kipnis, D. & Glickman, A. S. (1962). The prediction of job performance. *Journal of Applied Psychology, 46,* 50-56.

Lazarus, R. S., Baker, R. W., Broverman, D. M., & Mayer, J. (1957). Personality and psychological stress. *Journal of Personality, 25,* 559-577.

Leisman, G. (1971). Cognitive interference in spastic-hemiplegic children on the Stroop color word test. *British Journal of Social and Clinical Psychology, 10,* 379-382.

Lichtenstein, E. (1961). The relation of three cognitive controls to some perceptual and personality variables. *Dissertation Abstracts, 22,* 2467.

Ligon, E. M. (1932). A genetic study of color naming and word reading. *American Journal of Psychology, 44,* 103-121.

Peixotto, H., & Rowe, A. (1969). Effects of cognitive interference on performance in relation to psychopathology. *Perceptual and Motor Skills, 29,* 523-527.

Perret, E. (1974). The left frontal lobe of man and the suppression of habitual responses in verbal categorical behavior. *Neuropsychologia, 12,* (3), 323-330.

Podell, H. A. (1963). Note on successive dimensional analysis applied to affective, cognitive, and personality traits. *Psychological Report, 13,* 813-814.

Rand, G., Wapner, W., Werner, H., & McFarland, H. (1963). Age differences in performance on the Stroop color word test. *Journal of Personality, 31,* 534-558.

Smith, G. J. W., & Nyman, G. E. (1959). Psychopathologic behavior in a serial experiment. *Lunds Universitets Arsskrift,* N.F. Avd. 2, *56,* 5. Lund: Gleerup.

Stroop, J. R. (1935). Studies of interference in serial verbal reactions. *Journal of Experimental Psychology, 18,* 643-662.

Stroop, J. R. (1938). Factors affecting speed in serial verbal reactions. *Psychological Monograph, 50,* (5), 38-48.

Thurstone, L. L., & Mellinger, J. J. (1953). The Stroop test. *The Psychometric Laboratory,* University of North Carolina, No. 3.

Uhlmann, F. W. (1962). Test of color recognition (Form DE x-27-61). Detroit: The Detroit Edison Co.

Wapner, S., & Krus, D. M. (1960). Effects of lysergic acid diethylamide and differences between normals and schizophrenics on the Stroop color word test. *Journal of Neuropsychiatry, 2,* 76-81.

Weiss, R., & Sherman, M. (1962). Anxiety and interfering responses in college students and psychiatric patients. *Newsletter of Research Psychology, 4,* 35-40.

Wolitzky, D. L., Hofer, R., & Shapiro, R. (1972). Cognitive controls and mental retardation. *Journal of Abnormal Psychology, 79,* 296-302.

Daniel J. Mueller, Ph.D.
Associate Professor of Educational Psychology, Henry Lester Smith Center for Research in Education, Indiana University, Bloomington, Indiana.

SURVEY OF INTERPERSONAL VALUES

Leonard Gordon. Chicago, Illinois: Science Research Associates, Inc.

Introduction

The Survey of Interpersonal Values (SIV) measures six psychological constructs, described in the manual as "values involving relationships between people" (Gordon, 1976, p. 1). These constructs are characterized as follows:

Support: being treated with understanding; receiving encouragement from other people; being treated with kindness and consideration.
Conformity: doing what is socially correct; following regulations closely; doing what is accepted and proper; being a conformist.
Recognition: being looked up to and admired; being considered important; attracting favorable notice; achieving recognition.
Independence: having the right to do whatever one wants to do; being free to make one's own decisions; being able to do things in one's own way.
Benevolence: doing things for other people; sharing with others; helping the unfortunate; being generous.
Leadership: being in charge of other people; having authority over others; being in a position of leadership or power. (Gordon, 1976, p. 1)

The SIV was first published in 1960. In 1976 the manual was republished, with additional norms and validity data.

In a 1975 monograph, which served as a supplement to the 1960 manual, Gordon has elaborated his theory of values. He explains that values are "constructs representing generalized behaviors or states of affairs that are considered by the individual to be important" (Gordon, 1975, p. 2). Gordon divides the entire value domain into three distinct value systems: personal, interpersonal, and social. The SIV measures interpersonal values. Personal values are assessed by Gordon's Survey of Personal Values (see subsequent review in this volume), but he has not developed an instrument to measure social values.

The SIV was constructed by factor analysis. Gordon hypothesized 10 categories of interpersonal values, based on reviews of "relevant" literature. Using this model, 210 items were constructed, administered to college students, and factor analyzed. This analysis produced seven factors, six of which became the scales of the SIV. The seventh factor, labeled *aggression,* was rejected due to its "projected low reliability" (p. 2). No technical details of this factor analysis procedure are supplied.

759

Gordon has not indicated how many interpersonal values he believes there are nor how comprehensive the SIV is in representing the whole of this domain. In his 1975 monograph he mentions several interpersonal values that were purposely excluded from the SIV (Gordon, 1975, p. 20).

There are 90 items in the SIV. Each scale consists of from 13 to 16 items. The items are arranged in sets of three, each from a different scale. Within each triad respondents must rank the items from "most" to "least" important. For example, in one triad respondents are to choose among the importance of: 1) being the leader in their group (Leadership Scale); 2) having people admire what they do (Recognition Scale); and 3) being independent in their work (Independence Scale).

According to Gordon, the items in each triad have been "equated as far as possible for social desirability through a matching on preference value indices" (Gordon, 1976, p. 1). The use of a forced-choice item format and the matching of items within each triad are designed to reduce social desirability response set and "willful distortion" (p. 1). No details of the item matching are supplied, and the author's description seems somewhat equivocal regarding the success of this equating process.

Practical Applications/Uses

The SIV is designed for use with adolescents and adults. It is self-administering, may be given to individuals or groups, and administration time is about 15 minutes. Scoring is performed by hand with an overlay stencil. Within each triad, the item judged most important receives two points, the least important item zero points, and the unmarked item one point.

In addition to research and classroom demonstration uses, Gordon suggests use of the SIV in industrial personnel decisions, vocational guidance, and personal counseling. He is appropriately cautious in stating that local predictive validity must be established before using the SIV scores in industrial selection, and that SIV scores should be supplemented with other psychological and demographic data in vocational guidance.

Also described in the manual are seven typological profiles which Gordon has derived from specific combinations of the six SIV scales. For instance, the "Bureaucratic Subordination" profile has high Conformity and low Independence scores. This profile is exemplified by information clerks, assembly-line workers, and military enlisted men. Gordon characterizes these groups as "concerned with adhering to the rules, regulations, and approved standards of behavior" (Gordon, 1976, p. 49). Examples of other typologies are "Institutional Service" (high in Conformity and Benevolence and low in Recognition, Independence, and Leadership) and "Welfare of Others" (high in Benevolence and low in Recognition).

This effort toward practical application of the SIV in vocational counseling and selection is in a very early stage, as noted by LaVoie (1978). The number of profiles identified thus far is small, yet several are characterized, in part, by the appearance of Conformity at one polar extreme and either Independence or Leadership at the other. Nor does the manual indicate specifically how the typological application of scale scores is to be accomplished. The theory and development of typologies is described in greater detail in the manual supplement (Gordon, 1975), but this monograph is no longer sold by the publisher and is not readily available. (This reviewer was able to procure a copy only through interlibrary loan.)

Technical Aspects

Internal consistency reliabilities (KR 20) for the six scales ranged from .71 to .86 in a sample of college students, and from .75 to .89 in a sample of high school students. Test-retest reliabilities averaged .85 in a college student sample. These reliabilities are quite good for the measurement of six affective constructs in 15 minutes. Over longer periods of time (12 to 15 weeks) the coefficients dropped somewhat, as would be expected. In most samples the Recognition Scale had the lowest reliability (average KR 20 equals .73).

Scale intercorrelations are mostly negative, as would be expected in an ipsative inventory. The Support and Recognition Scales appear to be substantially related, however, with a median correlation of .40 in three student and adult samples (relatively high correlations, considering the ipsativity of these scales). Otherwise, the SIV scales appear to be substantially independent.

There are a wealth of validity data presented in the SIV manual. These data can be categorized into four types: 1) correlations of SIV scales with other tests; 2) known-group differences; 3) developmental differences (changes due to intervention); and 4) criterion validity studies.

In general, the SIV scales correlate in logical patterns with measures of similar and dissimilar traits, including the scales of the Allport-Vernon-Lindzey Study of Values, the Edwards Personal Preference Schedule (EPPS), the FIRO-B, the Guilford-Zimmerman Temperament Survey, and Gordon's own Survey of Personal Values. SIV correlations with the EPPS are particularly strong, with one or more EPPS scales correlating .45 or higher with every SIV scale.

More than two dozen studies reporting group mean differences on the SIV scales are reported in the manual. Statistically significant differences are noted. Many of these mean differences support validity; some do not. In general, there is too much such data reported, with no clear validity hypotheses proffered. indeed, some of the studies seem to have no relevance to validity whatsoever. As remarked by one reviewer, "one wonders how many readers will be interested in the mean scores of male students from three regions of Italy, or the means of Filipino rookie policemen vs. experienced patrolmen" (Black, 1978, p. 1108).

The SIV manual also contains a substantial number of predictive validity coefficients. Since vocational decision-making using SIV scores appears to be one of Gordon's primary goals, these are highly appropriate. In all of these studies the criterion is some measure of job performance—usually ratings. The positions studied include clerical, sales, managerial, and military. The significant correlations are highlighted in a large table, arranged alphabetically by job. These coefficients seldom go above .40, and are mostly in the teens and twenties. Sample sizes range from over 300 to merely 12. Since these results are arranged by job type rather than by scale, it is difficult to assess the relative validity of each scale. Upon close inspection one finds that fully two-thirds of the significant coefficients involve the values Leadership and Conformity.

Some other "validity" coefficients reported in the manual seem less useful. Would validity hypotheses derived from a theory concerning SIV values necessarily predict that Conformity would be significantly correlated (negatively) with college grades, but that none of the other SIV values would be? And is it instructive to discover that the value scores of Support, Recognition, and Benevolence for mothers and fathers of overachieving college students are highly correlated, whereas for underachievers the significantly correlated values of parents are Conformity, Independence, and Benevolence?

Another validity question regards social desirability response set. The manual presents data that indicate that four of the SIV scales are significantly (albeit modestly) correlated with the Marlowe-Crowne Social Desirability Scale. There is also indication that significant differences in mean scores occur under different motivational conditions. As with all personality inventories, the most honest responses can be expected when respondents do not expect their SIV scores to result in rewards or punishments. This limits the potential of the SIV in making personnel decisions.

Norms are available by sex for the following groups: ninth-grade vocational students, high school students, junior college (vocational) students, college students, and adults. Each of the student norm groups is larger than 1000, with the exception of female junior college students (N = 587). The adult samples are very small: 213 males and 212 females.

The manual states that all of the student samples are based on "planned sampling" (which seems to have no clear meaning). We are shown that the "Eastern," "Central," and "Western" regions of the country are about equally represented in these norm groups, and minority representation ranges from 17% to 30%. But the norm samples are otherwise not completely representative of their respective national populations. The high school students tested are all eleventh- and twelfth-graders. The college students are all freshmen and sophomores in liberal arts (at moderately to highly selective institutions). The high school samples are overwhelmingly urban. And the 212 adult females are almost all housewives. While these norm samples are clearly flawed, they are better than no norms at all, better than the norms in the 1960 manual, and better than the norms for some other personality inventories.

Also included are means and standard deviations for 81 specialized groups (e.g., Peace Corps volunteers, graduate students, criminally insane individuals, priests) and for 37 foreign student groups. Some of these samples are too small for reliable comparison (several below 10).

Critique

When the strengths and weaknesses of the Survey of Interpersonal Values are summed up, this inventory comes out about average among personality inventories. Reliability coefficients are quite good, and most of the scales appear substantially independent. (When Gordon [1976] factor analyzed the six scale scores he found "four typological vectors" [p. 47].)

Validity data are overwhelming in quantity, but only fair in quality. The incorporation of criterion validity coefficients is a real plus in the manual of a personality inventory. The relatively low correlations with criterion measures and the absence of an a priori validity hypothesis, however, diminishes the practical and theoretical usefulness of these data.

Social desirability response set is a minor problem for non-decision-making uses, but a potentially serious problem in decision-making applications. (This is a standard commentary on personality measures.) Gordon's use of a forced-choice item format is an attempt to overcome socially desirable responding. This in turn introduces the psychometric problem of ipsativity.

Ipsative scales are causally interdependent. This occurs because opting for one item in a forced-choice triad (or diad, etc.) assigns points to one scale, while at the same time *precluding* those points from the scale(s) represented by other items in the triad. This causes scores of psychologically independent constructs to correlate negatively at the following level: $-1 \div (n-1)$, for n scales (with equal variance). Thus, on the average, the SIV scales would be expected to correlate $-.20$ simply as a function of their ipsativity. High scores on some scales, therefore, necessarily result in low scores on others.

Ipsativity also affects the correlation of scale scores with criterion measures and with other tests. It further causes problems in interpersonal comparison on a single scale. Two individuals with the same rank-ordering of the six values will receive the same or similar scale scores on the SIV, whether or not their absolute levels of these values are the same. Intra-individual interpretation (comparison of the six scores for one individual) is not problematic, and the normative comparison of group means, on any or all scales, seems not seriously affected by ipsativity.

Whether or not the SIV measures *values* is a theoretical or definitional issue. Gordon makes frequent reference to Murray's manifest need system in his discussion of values (especially in the 1975 monograph). This, and the relatively high correlations of SIV scales with EPPS scales (which are based on Murray's need theory), makes it clear that Gordon's definition of values is much akin to Murray's definition of needs.

Because of the similarity of these two instruments it is necessary to ask whether the SIV is really needed among the ranks of personality measurement instruments. This question was raised in an early review by Siegel (1962) and is reinforced when we learn that self-ratings by college students on a five-point scale for each of the SIV values correlated between .47 and .73 (median = .655) with their counterpart SIV scale scores. In the female sample four of the six correlations were above .70, which is *very* high when we consider the limitations on correlation imposed by the combined reliabilities of the ratings and the scales and by the ipsative nature of the SIV.

References

Black, J. D. (1978). Review of the Survey of Interpersonal Values. In O. K. Buros (Ed.), *The eighth mental measurements yearbook* (pp. 1107-1108). Highland Park, NJ: The Gryphon Press.

Siegel, L. (1962). Review of the Survey of Interpersonal Values. *Journal of Counseling Psychology, 9*, 92-93.

LaVoie, A. L. (1978). Review of the Survey of Interpersonal Values. In O. K. Buros (Ed.), *The eighth mental measurements yearbook* (pp. 1108-1110). Highland Park, NJ: The Gryphon Press.

Gordon, L. V. (1976). *Survey of Interpersonal Values: Revised manual.* Chicago: Science Research Associates.

Gordon, L. V. (1975). *The measurement of interpersonal values.* Chicago: Science Research Associates.

Robert D. Dugan, Ph.D.
Associate Professor and Coordinator, Industrial/Organizational Psychology Program, University of New Haven, West Haven, Connecticut.

SURVEY OF ORGANIZATIONS

Rensis Likert Associates, Inc. San Diego, California: University Associates, Inc.

Introduction

The Survey of Organizations (SOO) is an instrument for measuring employee perceptions of organizational practices and job satisfaction. However, it is not an "off the shelf" questionnaire that an organization can buy and administer to its employees, referring only to a manual of instructions for guidance in its use. It is rather an instrument that is the focus of an organizational intervention which is guided by interaction with the professional staff of the developing organization— Rensis Likert Associates, Inc. (RLA). The guided intervention is "built in" to the process of purchasing and using the survey. If one orders the SOO from University Associates, Inc. (the listed publisher), there is an immediate referral to RLA for prices, manuals, and procedures.

The 1980 instrument and intervention is the current revision of a survey-guided development process begun in 1966 by the Center for Research on Utilization of Scientific Knowledge of the Institute for Social Research at the University of Michigan headed by Rensis A. Likert. David G. Bowers, president of RLA, has been intimately involved with the SOO since 1966. Since then, there have been six different but very similar instruments as predecessors to the current version. The 1980 SOO and organizational intervention is the result of an orderly evolutionary process that began with Likert's theories about management and organizational effectiveness (Likert, 1961; 1967) and developed over a period of 25 years through the translation of theory into an action research program that used the survey in a wide variety of organizations as a central part of an organizational change process. The result is that the RLA professional staff has had extensive experience with its use, interpretation, research efforts, and application in organizational interventions.

The 1980 survey contains 120 items that measure employees' perceptions of organizational climate, supervisory leadership, peer relations, group functioning, job characteristics, and satisfaction. There are an additional five demographic questions: sex, tenure, age, education, and job level combined with broad categories of job location (production, technical, sales, clerical). There is provision for

---

The reviewer wishes to thank Jane Delaney at RLA and Daniel W. Murray for their assistance.

the user organization to add 75 additional questions of its own. Each item is answered by responding to a five-point scale. The survey is machine processed by RLA and interpretation of results relies on using the normative data and professional staff input from RLA.

Items in the survey are formed into indexes which comprise the various organizational domains they describe. For example, Item #5, ''Is the information your work group gets about what is going on in other departments or units adequate?'', is combined with Items 6 and 7 to produce the first level category called *Communication Flow*. Communication Flow is one of four categories subsumed under *Guidance System*. Guidance System is one of five categories that comprise *Organization Climate*. Percentiles are reported for Items 5, 6, and 7 and for Communication Flow but are not given for Guidance System or Organization Climate. There are 18 items that are not combined in any first-level scale but are designated as *Non-Index Questions* for a higher order scale. Percentiles are shown separately for each of these items.

The complete classification system looks like this:

I. Organization Climate

1. Guidance System
   (1) Communication Flow   Scored—3 items
   (2) Decision-making Practices   Scored—2 items
   (3) Concern for People   Scored—3 items
   (4) Influence and Control   Scored—3 items

2. Job Design
   (1) Job Challenge   Scored—4 items
   (2) Job Reward   Scored—3 items
   (3) Job Clarity   Scored—3 items
   (4) Non-Index Questions   —— 2 items

3. Shape
   (1) Organization of Work   Scored—4 items
   (2) Absence of Bureaucracy   Scored—3 items
   (3) Coordination   Scored—3 items

4. Coordination Moderators
   (1) Work Interdependence   Scored—2 items
   (2) Emphasis on Cooperation   Scored—2 items

5. Organization Climate: Non-Index Questions   —— 7 items

II. Supervisory Leadership

   (1) Support   Scored—3 items
   (2) Team Building   Scored—2 items
   (3) Goal Emphasis   Scored—2 items
   (4) Work Facilitation   Scored—3 items
   (5) Encouragement of Participation   Scored—3 items

1. Perceived Causes of Supervisory Leadership

(1) Interpersonal Competence	Scored—3 items
(2) Involvement	Scored—2 items
(3) Administrative Scope	Scored—2 items

2. Supervisory Leadership: Non-
   Index Questions   —— 6 items

III. Peer Relationships

(1) Support	Scored—3 items
(2) Team Building	Scored—3 items
(3) Goal Emphasis	Scored—2 items
(4) Work Facilitation	Scored—3 items

IV. End Results

(1) Group Functioning	Scored—6 items
(2) Goal Integration	Scored—2 items
(3) Satisfaction	Scored—7 items

V. Miscellaneous Non-Index Items   —— 3 items

There are 99 items included in this system. 21 items in the areas of Supervisory Leadership and Peer Relationships have one stem and two questions for each stem— "How it is *now?*" and "How I would *like* it to be?" For instance, Item 24 has the stem "How friendly and easy to approach is your supervisor?" Item 24 is "This is how it is *now.*" Item 25 with the same stem is "This is how I'd *like* it to be." The sample printout sent to the reviewer does not show the "How I would *like* it to be" items. However, the *Supervisors' Handbook* which accompanies the packet of materials sent by RLA gives guidance to the supervisor about their use.

The cover of the 1980 survey carries the notation that it is derived from the 1974 edition of the Survey of Organizations and the 1976 edition of the Organization Survey Profile. This latter instrument was the name given by RLA to the Institute for Social Research-developed Survey of Organizations. The announcement of the 1980 SOO from RLA states that both instruments contained a virtually identical core of questions. However, of the 115 questions in the 1967 version, 85 are in the 1980 SOO. Ten of these were written "negatively" in 1967, but changed to a "positive" or "neutral" presentation in later versions. Sixty-four of the 85 1967 items are identical in the 1980 edition or have slight word changes (i.e., the word "Overall" was substituted for "All in all" in four items). Twenty-one of the 85 items have more substantive changes and the meaning could be affected.

Of the 125 questions in the 1980 SOO, 89 were present in the 1969 version. Seventy-one of these were the same or had minor changes and 18 had significant changes in wording.

The 1980 SOO, then, is the current version of an instrument that has evolved through a succession of pragmatic applications to real-life organizational settings. In addition, it has had the advantage of periodic research efforts directed toward understanding and improving its psychometric properties.

Practical Applications/Uses

The SOO can only be used by involving the professional staff of RLA. This involvement could be minimal if the user organization has either an internal or external consultant who is experienced in the application of survey methodology to organizational interventions. The consultant should also be comfortably familiar with the assumptions about organizational effectiveness that underlie the SOO approach. The RLA staff involvement would be limited to establishing schedules of administration, providing computer printouts of results, a supervisor's manual, and other background material for management people in the user organization. They would also furnish minimal guidance in planning and executing the project.

The results of the SOO are presented in percentiles for each item and index, for each item for the entire population, and for predesignated sub-unit work groups. Mean responses and a percentage distribution of item responses are also given. In addition, percentile scores are given for each item and scale for comparable work groups in the RLA data bank as well as for other work groups in the organization. There is also provision for giving scores from a previous administration of the SOO. The direction and magnitude of the change that has occurred are given in this case.

This basic service is designated "Level A" by RLA. The cost is based on the number of questionnaires processed as follows:

Quantity	Total Price
100	$ 1,500
101- 200	$ 1,500 + $10.00 each over 100
201- 500	$ 2,500 + $6.20 each over 200
501-1,000	$ 4,360 + $5.70 each over 500
1,001-2,000	$ 7,210 + $5,20 each over 1,000
2,001 +	$12,410 + $4.70 each over 2,000

There is a Level B service with the same components as Level A that additionally includes a comprehensive report which gives an organization-wide diagnosis in narrative form, with emphasis on specific strengths and weaknesses of the organization. The cost of Level B service is:

Quantity	Total Price
100	$ 3,575
101- 200	$ 3,575 + $19.00 each over 100
201- 500	$ 5,475 + $7.50 each over 200
501-1,000	$ 7,725 + $6.85 each over 500
1,001-2,000	$11,150 + $6.20 each over 1,000
2,001 +	$17,315 + $5.50 each over 2,000

Any use of the SOO will involve an organizational intervention of some magnitude. Even if the organization's management is only interested in getting a "reading" of the perceived climate, supervisory leadership, and other measures produced by the SOO, the initiation of the survey and minimal feedback will require careful implementation which will include obtaining management and employee support and understanding.

The materials that RLA has developed for the prospective user clearly imply that the intervention will be more long range and more complex than just a "reading." The supervisor's handbook assumes that there will be a series of group meetings chaired by the supervisors in which they will feed back the survey data, assist their groups in identifying organizational problems, and lead them to suggested solutions to the problems.

Also included with the materials this reviewer received from RLA was a document titled "An Introduction to Survey-Guided Development," containing a time chart that covers such activities as Internal Resource Person Training, Concepts Training, Systematic Diagnosis and Resource Allocation, Intermediate Interviews, and Second Questionnaire Administration and Interviews. All of the listed activities are scheduled to take 11 months.

This reviewer contacted a staff member at RLA and determined that RLA will provide a one-week training program for the Internal Resource Person. The cost of this training was not specified but said to vary depending on location of training and number of people trained. If a potential user organization does not have access to someone who is skilled in survey and intervention techniques, it is essential that this training option be used.

The RLA staff member also mentioned that, if an organization wants to undertake a complete Survey Guided Development activity, professional staff are available to work with the user on a consulting basis. No cost figures were given.

Apparently, RLA offers two additional levels of involvement beyond the published Levels A and B. The first provides training to one or more people who represent the user and the second furnishes a complete consulting service in organizational intervention, development, and change with the SOO as the diagnostic instrument.

Technical Aspects

Research with the 1967-1970 antecedent versions of the 1980 SOO is reported in Taylor and Bowers (1972). This publication is described as a manual for the 1967-1974 versions of the SOO and was reviewed in Buros (1978) by three reviewers. All three of the reviewers raised questions about the adequacy of various aspects of the research effort but two of the three praised the undertaking as unique among survey instruments and a laudable attempt. The third reviewer (Motowidlo, 1978) concluded, "In my opinion there is little evidence that SOO scales included in the core questionnaire yield much information about specifically *what* may be wrong, and therefore it is probably less useful for guiding efforts toward particular features of organizations that may need to be changed" (p. 1530).

Can one generalize from the research conducted on the earlier versions of the 1980 SOO? Undoubtedly purists would say "no." But, given the amount of item overlap mentioned above and the lack of more current information, this reviewer is willing to do so. Here are some conclusions that seem warranted:

1. The reliability of the instrument is probably acceptable.

2. The validity of the individual scales should be investigated further, but there is evidence that the content does represent Likert theory. It is reasonably content valid. Reported studies of construct and criterion-related validity lead to the conclusion that the 1980 SOO probably has some, if the studies were replicated.

3. The negative reviewer based his case on the high intercorrelations among items included in what this reviewer has designated as third-order scales. At the least it seems clear to me that this is sufficient evidence to allow for the reporting of percentile scores for second- and third-level scales. Whether this tactic would improve the organization's understanding of the results is a practical question. It is difficult to believe that providing more quantitative data could hurt.

In his review of the 1980 SOO, Golembiewski (1981) states that RLA has a user's guide and a revised edition of the technical monograph (Taylor & Bowers, 1972) in preparation. Neither of these materials is mentioned in the information recently (1984) supplied by RLA, nor did the staff representative mention them in conversations with this reviewer. Although both would be helpful to a reviewer, the group at RLA is apparently convinced that neither is necessary for current users. Presumably, information that could be contained in a user's guide is relayed to the user during the various personal interactions with RLA staff that must take place in planning and executing an intervention with the 1980 SOO.

It would be reassuring if the 1980 SOO were researched in the detail presented in Taylor and Bowers (1972). Not that the work there should be slavishly replicated, but current studies of the validity and reliability of the SOO categories would give added insight into the 1980 SOO as a measuring instrument.

The most needed additional analysis of the 1980 SOO, in this reviewer's opinion, concerns a determination of the underlying factor structure of the instrument. The high intercorrelation among items in the earlier versions reported in Taylor and Bowers (1972) were the basis for the negative conclusion reached by Motowidlo (1978).

It must be at least 20 years since some of the data underlying the studies were collected. Organizations and employees' perceptions of them may have changed markedly in the interim. It would be surprising if they had not, particularly as the intent of the SOO intervention was organizational change. Given the computational ease with which it is now possible to perform a factor analysis, it would be a relatively easy job for RLA to do so with the data from some of its recent organizational clients who have used the 1980 SOO. Different organizations may well have different factor structures. The use of the technique with current clients could give insights about which variables are relevant for feedback and problem-solving activities. If nothing else, such an investigation should demonstrate the feasibility of using percentile scores with second- and third-level scales, or perhaps provide a different way of looking at combinations of items or present scales.

Because the SOO scales embody an integral part of Likert's theoretical base and because a large data base has amassed during the history of their use in organizations, it may not be desirable (or even possible) to abandon them should a factor analysis yield a different structure. Undoubtedly, experience with the present scales in a number of different organizations have given the professionals at RLA a sense of the subtleties and complexities of what the scales' practical meanings are and how they can be used in a specific organizational context.

The preceding discussion exemplifies the differences between using the instrument as a device for rigorous measurement purposes and using it as a stimulus for group discussion that is intended to lead to problem identification and solution in a unique "here and now" organizational situation. In the latter case the responses to a single item may be the impetus for a significant instance of problem-solving and change in a particular organization. However, no statistician would be willing to use a single item, standing alone, to measure anything across a number of organizations. Nevertheless, precise psychometric analysis can give the professional additional insights into the instrument's use as a stimulus for problem identification.

Critique

Two reservations about the earlier 1967-1974 SOO discussed by Fitzpatrick in his Buros (1978) review are also relevant to the 1980 SOO. The first concerns the reading difficulty of the items. As Fitzpatrick said, "The items of this survey seem more complex and less down-to-earth than those in other surveys" (p. 1527) and "The ideas contained in the Likert theory, and hence the SOO, are sophisticated. Do workers at all levels have a common understanding of what it means to 'suppress' or 'work through' a disagreement?" (p. 1528). Although there is some evidence presented in Taylor and Bowers (1972) that hourly workers' misunderstandings were minor and a staff member at RLA insisted this was not a problem, this reviewer's experience with a number of traditional attitude surveys in several organizations suggests otherwise.

In one organization the hourly workers in manufacturing, who had, at best, a bad high school education, had great difficulty in reading and understanding a survey with much less difficult items. However, these workers would have had even more difficulty with a feedback-problem identification session as described in the supervisor's manual for the 1980 SOO. It may be that the complexity of the ideas and process is such that, whether hourly workers or not, the surveyed population must have a minimum education-experience level.

The second criticism raised by Fitzpatrick (1978) was that there is no provision for write-in comments by respondents. Again, this reviewer's experience is that these comments can be helpful in interpreting the objective data. One can certainly get a feeling for the affect of employees as well as specific descriptions of the organization and its people that the standard items miss from these responses, which can serve in much the same way as interview data and are much easier to collect. Should an organization want to include such an option there is no reason that it could not, as there is provision for including an additional 75 items to be prepared by the user.

Should an organization consider using the 1980 SOO-RLA intervention? Many organizations or parts of organizations could benefit and many others have already benefitted from the undertaking. To quote Fitzpatrick (1978) again, "The content and wording of the items in a survey imply something about the values of the organization involved. The SOO implies that workers at all levels should be given opportunities to discuss decisions before they are made, that cooperation and teamwork are quite important, that rewards should be based on performance, that disagreements are necessary and desirable if they are worked through, etc. Most of us would agree that these are good values, but they are not necessarily desirable for all organizations'' (p. 1528).

Although there may be an implication that these good things are implied for *all* workers, there are organizations where the implication is accurate for some organizational units and levels but not others. The 1980 SOO would be appropriate for use in those parts of an organization that bear out its assumptions; it would not work in a thorough-going Theory X organization, whether desirable or not.

Organizations that *do* have the values implied in the Fitzpatrick quote and who want help in realizing them are very fortunate to have the 1980 SOO available. The years of practical, professional and scientific involvement and dedication in the development of the instrument, the creation of a large data base from many organizations, plus the ready availability of the product and guidance for its use make the 1980 SOO unique.

If a potential user is not sure whether the 1980 SOO intervention is an appropriate strategy or not, consultation with the staff at RLA can be very helpful in reaching a decision.

References

Bowers, D. G. (1973). OD techniques and their results in 23 organizations: The Michigan ICL study. *Journal of Applied Behavioral Sciences, 9*(1), 21-43.

Bowers, D. G., & Franklin, J. L. (1977). *Survey-guided development I: Data-based organizational change.* San Diego, CA: University Associates, Inc.

Fitzpatrick, R. (1978). Review of Survey of Organizations. In O. K. Buros (Ed.), *The eighth mental measurements yearbook* (pp. 1527-1528). Highland Park, NJ: The Gryphon Press.

Golembiewski, R. (1981). Instrumentation—A review of Survey of Organizations—1980 Edition. *Group and Organization Studies, 6*(2), 247-255.

Hausser, D. L., Pecorella, P. A., & Wissler, A. I. (1975). *Survey-guided development: A manual for consultants.* Ann Arbor, MI: Organizational Development Research Program, Institute for Social Research, University of Michigan.

Likert, R. A. (1961). *New patterns of management.* New York: McGraw-Hill.

Likert, R. A. (1967). *The human organization.* New York: McGraw-Hill.

Motowidlo, S. J. (1978). Review of Survey of Organizations. In O. K. Buros (Ed.), *The eighth mental measurements yearbook* (pp. 1528-1530). Highland Park, NJ: The Gryphon Press.

Taylor, J. C., & Bowers, D. G. (1972). *Survey of Organizations.* Ann Arbor, MI: Institute for Social Research.

Toplis, J. (1973). Review of the Survey of Organizations. *Occupational Psychology* (England), *47*(3-4), 260-261.

Daniel J. Mueller, Ph.D.
Associate Professor of Educational Psychology, Henry Lester Smith Center for Research in Education, Indiana University, Bloomington, Indiana.

SURVEY OF PERSONAL VALUES

Leonard V. Gordon. Chicago, Illinois: Science Research Associates, Inc.

Introduction

The Survey of Personal Values (SPV), a twin value measurement instrument to the Survey of Interpersonal Values (SIV) (see preceding review, p. 759) was first published in 1964. The manual was published in 1967 (Gordon, 1967) and republished with additional technical data and norms in 1984 (Gordon, 1984).

In the 1967 SPV manual the surveys' author, Leonard Gordon, calls values "basic motivational patterns," explaining that value systems of individuals influence both their immediate decisions and life goals.

In Gordon's value theory, values fall into three major categories: interpersonal, social, and personal. Interpersonal values (six of which are measured by the SIV) involve direct interaction with others; social values (for which no instrument has been published by Gordon) represent behaviors or states of affairs that an individual considers to be important in others; and personal values (six of which are measured by the SPV) do not necessarily involve one's interaction with others or their behaviors. Personal values represent behaviors that an individual values in his personal day-to-day activities (Gordon, 1984, p. 2).

The six values measured by the SPV are described in the 1984 manual (pp. 1-2) as follows:

Practical Mindedness: High scores typify those who are materialistically oriented and who prefer doing things that are practical, immediately useful, and/or economically advantageous.

Achievement: High scores are made by those who value accomplishment and growth. Such individuals enjoy challenging work, particularly of the type that allows for personal initiative and in which individual effort can pay off.

Variety: High-scoring individuals prefer not to narrow the focus of their activities. They like to deal with new and different situations and enjoy work that does not develop into the routine.

Decisiveness: High-scoring individuals tend to value their own opinions and their ability to think things through for themselves. They enjoy jobs in which decision-making is an integral part of their work activities.

Orderliness: High scores are made by those who tend to be well organized and systematic in their approach to work, irrespective of the nature of the work or the level at which they are operating. These individuals prefer to have their activities scheduled or routinized as far as possible.

Goal Orientation: High scoring individuals prefer jobs in which the requirements or objectives have been clearly defined or specified. They tend to be task-oriented and to limit the span of their activities toward that end. (Gordon, 1984, pp. 1-2).

As in the case of the SIV, SPV scales were constructed by factor analysis. Following a review of value and interest categorization studies by other researchers, including some factor analytic studies, Gordon hypothesized the existence of seven personal value constructs. A total of 175 items were written to represent these constructs. Although one factor analysis based on the responses of a college student sample supported Gordon's seven-factor hypothesis, one factor, *understanding*, was not utilized because it had too few items. Scales were constructed for each of the other six factors. Unfortunately, the SPV manual supplies no technical information about this factor analysis procedure—not even sample size.

Practical Applications/Uses

The SPV is a self-report, group-administered, paper-and-pencil instrument, appropriate for administration to adults and high-school-aged youths. The SPV may be self-administered. When administered to groups it is recommended that the administrator read the instructions aloud. The testees' task is clearly explained, and procedures for responding are unambiguous. There is no time limit. According to Gordon, most respondents finish in about 15 minutes.

As with the SIV, the SPV contains 90 items arranged in triads. Each triad contains items from three of the six value scales. Respondents rank the three statements by selecting the "most" and "least" important value statement. For instance, from one triad respondents would select which they consider to be least important and to be most important: experiencing the unusual (*Variety*); always getting their money's worth (*Practical Mindedness*); or working on a difficult problem (*Achievement*).

Scoring is done by hand with an overlay stencil and can be accomplished in a few minutes. For each triad, the item designated "most" important receives 2 points, the "least" important receives 0 points, and the middle-ranked (unmarked) item receives 1 point. If the scoring is done accurately, the sum of each respondent's scores from all scales will total 90. Respondents answer directly on the test booklet, thus test booklets are not reusable.

The author suggests uses of SPV scores ranging from counseling to research, to selection and promotion in industrial settings. The inclusion of vocationally oriented and occupationally specific norm groups is further indication that Gordon intends this inventory to be used in personnel selection and in vocational decision-making. But no data are presented in the manual supporting predictive or concurrent validity. There is no direct evidence that workers in certain occupations or types of occupations who have high scores on particular SPV scales, are necessarily better at or happier in their jobs than are workers with low SPV scores. (This problem is a bane of all affective scales intended for use in vocational counseling.) Some of the differences in group means presented in the manual supply a modicum of support for such conclusions, but surely not enough to legitimate vocational decision-making on the basis of these scores. To his credit, in the 1984 manual Gordon moderates his suggestions for decision-making applications of the SPV with such phrases as: "experimental inclusion" (p. 29) in industrial selection batteries; "after being [locally] validated" (p. 29); and "should be interpreted in conjunction with other available test, biographical, and interview information" (p. 29).

Gordon also suggests that SPV scores relate to respondents' manner of coping with problems of everyday living (p. 1). No data, whatsoever are supplied to support this claim.

Technical Aspects

In a sample of 114 college students, internal consistency (alpha) coefficients for the six scales ranged from .77 to .87, with a median of .825. Test-retest coefficients in three adult and college samples, over periods ranging from one week to three months, averaged .81. The Variety Scale consistently exhibited the highest reliabilities, with a median of .885. The Decisiveness Scale had the lowest reliabilities, with a median of .765. These are very respectable levels of reliability for such short affective scales.

Among high-school students, in a one-year retest, the reliability coefficients ranged from .38 to .74, with a median of .59. These are very low coefficients, although a one-year test-retest seems an unusually stringent test of reliability.

Nearly half of the SPV manual is devoted to presenting validity data. These data fall into two categories: 1) correlations of SPV scales with scales on other psychological inventories and tests, and 2) group differences. In addition, the manual dicusses intercorrelations among SPV scale scores, fakability, and social desirability response set. These are also validity concerns.

Not surprisingly, most correlations among SPV scales are negative. The forced-choice response format results in causally interdependent, or *ipsative*, scales. This response format tends to depress positive relationships and enhance negative relationships among scales. (An inventory with six ipsative scales will have average scale intercorrelations of –.20 when the constructs being measured are completely independent.) The highest *positive* SPV correlations are between Orderliness and Goal Orientation (.30, .31, and .33 in three separate samples). Achievement and Decisiveness are also consistently found to be moderately positively correlated. The highest *negative* correlations are between Goal Orientation and Variety, Orderliness and Variety, Achievement and Practical Mindedness, and Decisiveness and Practical Mindedness. These correlations vary somewhat by sex and age, but many are at or greater than –.50.

Based on this pattern of scale intercorrelations, Gordon has developed a typological model that reduces all SPV scales to two dimensions. One axis combines Orderliness and Goal Orientation at one pole, with Variety at the opposite pole. The other dimension combines Achievement and Decisiveness at one pole, with Practical Mindedness at the opposite pole. Gordon goes on to show that certain personality traits, assessed by other personality measures, are associated with these collapsed SPV dimensions. For instance, authoritarianism, dogmatism, acquiescence, and cautiousness are associated with the Achievement-Decisiveness combination, and conformity, bureaucratic orientation and self-disciplined are associated with the Orderliness-Goal Orientation combination.

I have two criticisms of this theoretical model: 1) Based on a pattern of moderate intercorrelations among scale scores, Gordon has forced the six SPV scales into two dimensions. There is no empirical basis for this extreme collapsing of dimensions. 2) It is not at all clear what is to be done with the two-dimensional model. In fact, immediately after presenting the model, Gordon specifically states that "interpretations are to be made at the individual scale level . . ." (Gordon, 1984, p. 6). It seems to me that Gordon has entered a paradox. To the extent that the six SPV scales are independent, the two-dimensional model is meaningless. To the extent that the model appropriately represents reality, the six scales must be seriously redundant.

In general, the SPV scales do not correlate significantly with cognitive measures. Of 72 correlations between SPV scales and subtests on four aptitude measures, only three were significant at the .05 level. This is positive validity data.

Gordon also correlated the SPV scales with several other value and personality inventories, including the Survey of Interpersonal Values (Gordon, 1960), the Allport-Vernon-Lindzey Study of Values (SV) (1960), and the Sixteen Personality Factors (16 PF) (Cattell, 1949). The highest *positive* correlations between SPV and SIV scales were: Orderliness and Conformity (.57), Variety and Independence (.56), Practical Mindedness and Support (.39), Decisiveness and Independence (.31), and Goal Orientation and Conformity (.31). The highest *negative* SPV/SIV correlations were: Variety and Conformity (−.54), Achievement and Support (−.42), Orderliness and Independence (−.40), and Orderliness and Leadership (−.33). Most of these correlations seem intuitively appropriate, and thus are supportive of construct validity. Without the benefit of a priori validity hypotheses, however, these validity conclusions must be considered tentative.

Of 36 correlations between SPV and SV scales, six were statistically significant. SV Economic correlated significantly with four SPV scales: Practical Minded (.41). Achievement (−.33), Variety (−.40) and Orderliness (.37). SV Economic correlated significantly with SPV Variety (.44) and SPV Goal Orientation (−.37). I would have predicted some, but not all of these correlations, based on the scale definitions. it seems curious that the SV Economic Scale correlates significantly with four of the six SPV scales.

The highest SPV correlations with 16 PF scales were: Variety and Conscientious (−.46), Variety and Self-disciplined (−.40), Orderliness and Conscientious (.34), Decisiveness and Dominant (.32), Achievement and Apprehensive (−.31), and Goal Orientation and Self-disciplined (.29). All of these correlations are statistically significant. Most seem theoretically appropriate.

A number of studies reporting differences or changes in group means are also reported in the 1984 manual. For example:

Parochial high-school students, both male and female, scored significantly higher than did public high-school students on Goal Orientation, and significantly lower on Variety. In addition, the parochial school males (but not the females) scored higher on Orderliness and lower on Decisiveness.

Nursing-school faculty members scored significantly higher on Achievement than did graduate-nursing students, whereas the students scored significantly higher on Practical Mindedness.

Peace Corps volunteers, both male and female, scored significantly higher on Achievement and on Decisiveness than did same age college students. The college students, again of both sexes, scored higher on Practical Mindedness and on Orderliness.

After participating in group guidance sessions "designed to help the students look at themselves in terms of their interests and values and to explore the world of occupations" (p. 19), eighth-grade students scored significantly higher on Achievement and Decisiveness and lower on Practical Mindedness and Orderliness than prior to participating in these sessions. Students were self-selected for participation.

Japanese college students, both male and female, scored significantly higher on Orderliness and Goal Orientation, and significantly lower on Practical Mindedness, Achievement, and Variety than did American college students.

These studies typify the type and quality of Gordon's known-group difference validity data. Some of the mean differences seem fairly clearly to support validity. Others seem irrelevant, or even contrary to intuitive validity expectations. Unfortunately, as with the SPV correlations with other value and personality inventories, no a priori validity hypotheses were proffered. Thus, as is proverbial with beauty, validity is largely "in the eyes of the beholder."

Faking and social desirability response set are notorious problems in all self-report affective measurement. Gordon makes two major points regarding this concern: 1) Within each triad he has equated the items "as far as possible" for social desirability (Gordon, 1984, p. 1, and 2) research shows that with a forced-choice item format "response differences in the direction of making a more favorable impression are either slight or non-significant" (p. 10).

The first argument is insubstantial. Gordon supplies no technical data regarding the preciseness of this equating process, and indeed his weak statement in this regard gives little assurance of its success. (In the 1967 manual he makes an equally equivocal statement: "Within each triad . . . the three statements . . . were equated, to a large extent, for social desirability") (Gordon, 1967, p. 1).

Gordon's second argument is more sound. While there is evidence that personality measurement, generally, is adversely affected by social desirability response set, there is also evidence that this source of invalidity accounts for a relatively small proportion of total score variance—especially in counseling and research situations where there is no reason for respondents to believe that "faking good" will improve their life condition. Further, in a forced-choice response format it is impossible for respondents to manipulate their scores positively on all scales. At best they could affect high scores on some scales at the expense of high scores on other scales.

An interesting aside is that in his 1967 manual Gordon presents evidence that some of his scales are significantly correlated with the Crowne-Marlow Need for Approval Scale (Gordon, 1967, p. 6), but he has deleted this data from the 1984 manual. Nonetheless, Gordon ends this discussion with sage advise. The validity of the SPV (and for that matter, of all psychological measures) should be judged on the basis of validity data in particular application situations, rather than by more indirect focus on possible sources of invalidity.

In the 1984 manual, norms based on samples ranging from 587 to 2,311 cases (in most instances over 1,000) are reported by sex for the following groups: ninth-grade vocational students, high-school students, vocational-college students and college students. There are also norms for "workers in routinized jobs" and for "managers," both based on samples of over 1,000. These norms represent an improvement in both size and diversity over those presented in the 1967 manual, and in the case of both the vocational college and regular college groups, are based upon a "planned sampling . . . from all major geographic regions of the country" (Gordon, 1984, p. 8). Significant proportions of minority group members are included in these norm groups.

In addition, means are reported for several dozen smaller samples, in particular occupational groups (e.g., civil engineers, clinical psychologists, order clerks, secretaries, and high-school teachers). These norms are sex specific.

Critique

The Survey of Personal Values has very good reliability, especially for relatively short affective scales. Coupled with its quick and easy administration, it constitutes an efficient measure of six relatively independent affective constructs. Its validity is no better and no worse than that of many comparative affective inventories. There is moderate support for construct validity, but little or no evidence of predictive validity. Because of the lack of validity for specific applied purposes, scale scores must be interpreted and used with caution. Norms are adequate but not strong.

Two other issues, which loom large in the evaluation of the SPV, are the ipsativeness of scale scores and the nature of the value construct. Ipsativeness is caused by the forced-choice item format and results in the interdependence of scale scores. This is a somewhat common psychometric characteristic in value and interest inventories, and occurs in some personality inventories as well. Some value theorists argue that values do, indeed, compete with one another in peoples' value systems, and that a forced-choice item format is therefore appropriate. The psychometric problem, though, is that normative interpretation of individual scale scores from ipsative instruments is inappropriate.

The question of whether the SPV is truly measuring *values* is difficult to answer. It is an entirely theoretical question, which hinges on one's definition of value. One of the most accepted value definitions throughout the social sciences is by Clyde Kluckhohn: "A value is a conception, explicit or implicit, distinctive of an individual or characteristic of a group, of the *desirable* [italics added] which influences the selection from among available modes, means, and ends of action" (Kluckhohn, 1951, p. 395). Judged by this definition, and based upon extensive research and study in the area of value measurement, it is the judgement of this reviewer that the Survey of Personal Values does not measure values, but personality traits. (Some personality theorists would say it measures needs.) Whether this constitutes a problem depends on the purpose of the users and on their definition of value.

References

Allport, G. W., Vernon, P. E., & Lindzey, G. (1960). *Study of Values* (3rd ed.). Chicago: The Riverside Publishing Co.

Cattell, R. B. (1949). *Sixteen Personality Factor Questionnaire*. Champaign, IL: Institute for Personality and Ability Testing, Inc.

Glass, G. V. (1978). Review of Survey of Personal Values. In O. K. Buros (Ed.), *The eighth mental measurements yearbook*. Highland Park, NJ: The Gryphon Press.

Gordon, L. V. (1960). *Study of Interpersonal Values*. Chicago: Science Research Associates.

Gordon, L. V. (1967). *Survey of Personal Values: Examiner's manual*, Chicago: Science Research Associates.

Gordon, L. V. (1984). *Survey of Personal Values: Examiner's manual*, Chicago: Science Research Associates.

Kluckhohn, C. (1951). Values and value-orientations in the theory of action. In, T. Parsons & E. A. Shils (Eds.), *Toward a general theory of action* (pp. 388-433). New York: Harper & Row.

Mark E. Troy, Ph.D.
Evaluation Researcher, Center for Development of Early Education,
Kamehameha Schools, Honolulu, Hawaii.

TEST OF COGNITIVE SKILLS

CTB/McGraw-Hill. Monterey, California: CTB/McGraw-Hill.

Introduction

The Test of Cognitive Skills (TCS) is an instrument designed to assess a student's aptitude on certain cognitive abilities that are considered important for academic success. The list of abilities includes problem solving, discovering relationships, evaluating, and remembering. It is not billed as a test of intelligence or mental ability because the domain of abilities it measures is more modest in scope than those designations imply. The scope of the test is limited by its emphasis on abilities that contribute to school success. The test was intended for group administration by a teacher in a classroom.

The Test of Cognitive Skills was developed and published by CTB/McGraw-Hill of Monterey, California. Published in 1983, the TCS is a relatively new test, but it has several predecessors among ability tests. In fact, the TCS is a major revision of the Short Form Test of Academic Aptitude (SFTAA), which itself is a revision of the California Test of Mental Maturity (CFMM). For a brief review of the SFTAA, see Lennon (1980).

Both the TCS and the SFTAA have four subtests at each of five levels. The SFTAA subtests are Vocabulary, Memory, Sequences, and Analogies. The test publishers claim that a conceptual ambiguity could arise from including vocabulary items in an aptitude test as these are commonly found in achievement tests. Therefore, the Vocabulary subtest of the SFTAA was replaced in the TCS with a Verbal Reasoning subtest with items similar to reasoning items found on other ability tests. The SFTAA Memory subtest was completely revised in the TCS and new items were developed for the Sequences and Analogies subtest as well.

Probably the most important distinction between the TCS and the SFTAA is in the use of Item Response Theory (IRT) in the selection and scaling of TCS items. IRT, also called Item Characteristic Curve (ICC) Theory, is at the leading edge of psychometric theory and practice (Lord, 1980). The testing industry is turning more and more to the application of IRT models in the scaling of items of new or revised tests. For readers who may be familiar with IRT, a very brief summary follows; a fuller treatment of the topic can be found in Hambleton's (1983) *Applications of Item Response Theory.*

IRT is the basis of several statistical models for analyzing test data. The three-parameter model used in scaling the TCS assumes that the probability of correctly answering a particular item can be expressed by a logistic function, the shape of which is determined by three parameters—the discrimination parameter, the location parameter, and the guessing parameter. The *discrimination* parameter refers to an item's power to differentiate between examinees of high and low ability on the trait being measured. The *location* parameter represents the item's difficulty level in terms of the examinee's ability at the level at which the item discriminates best. If an item's difficulty level is too far below the examinees' ability level, the item will have no discrimination power because everyone will pass it. The *guessing* parameter is an estimate of the probability of answering a question correctly with little or no ability on the trait being measured.

The IRT parameters are derived from empirical data in an iterative procedure. First the student's ability on the trait is estimated from the raw data, then the parameters for each item are derived from the student's estimated ability. Having obtained the three parameters, an improved estimate of the student's ability can be computed. This is used to estimate new item parameters, which in turn are used to estimate ability again. The process continues until the system stabilizes.

The TCS is divided into five levels for use at Grades 2 through 11. Each level of the TCS includes four subtests: Sequences, Analogies, Memory, and Verbal Reasoning. A measure of general ability may be obtained by averaging the scaled scores of the four subtest.

The *Sequences* subtest requires a student to analyze a pattern among the elements of an item and then select the part that would complete the pattern. Being able to recognize patterns and progressions, apply a principle or rule of operation, and combine parts into a whole are required for success on Sequences items.

The *Analogies* subtest requires a student to comprehend the relationship between two pictures and then choose another picture that is related to a third in the same way that the first two are related. Students must be able to compare and contrast, understand degree and proportion, and recognize numerical, quantitative, or spatial relationships.

The *Verbal Reasoning* subtest requires students to identify relationships between pictures or words, recognize the essential features of objects or concepts, and draw logical conclusions. The items at Level 1 are primarily pictorial in nature. At Levels 2 through 5, the item responses are words or sentences. The rationale underlying this subtest is that tasks are related to general learning ability and achievement in basic skills.

The *Memory* subtest requires the student to recall material that was learned previously. At Level 1, the items to be learned consist of picture pairs; at all other levels the items consist of obscure words and their definitions. This type of content, according to the test manual, should facilitate associative learning. All material to be learned is presented at the beginning of the test. Approximately 10 minutes are allotted for learning. Recall of the material is tested approximately 15 minutes later at Level 1 and 25 minutes later at Levels 2 through 5 following the Sequenses and Analogies subtests. Thus, the Memory subtest is intended to measure the strength of a student's associations and the resistance of associations to decay and interference.

Going from picture pairs at Level 1 on the Memory subtest to obscure words and definitions at the other levels is not merely a change in item difficulty, but quite possibly changes the construct validity of the subtest. Research on associative learning and memory indicates that information can be represented in memory in two distinct forms, imaginal and verbal, and that the format of the stimuli has an effect on the form of representation (Paivio, 1970). Unfortunately, there is not a simple relationship between the form of the stimuli and the form of representations; pictorial stimuli can be represented verbally in memory and sentences or words can be represented imaginally. The form of representation, however, has important consequences for learning (Wittrock, 1977). Thus, the Memory subtest should include both verbal and pictorial stimuli at all levels.

The unusual practice of choosing obscure words and their definitions as items raises a few questions concerning the criteria by which the words were selected. Even nonsense syllables differ in the number of associations they generate. Are these words equal in associative value? Some of the words, although unknown to this reviewer, generated associations that led to correct guesses without having studied the learning materials. Are the words equally obscure? Students who have studied state birds might recognize the state bird of Hawaii in one of the items.

Practical Applications/Uses

Test booklets for Levels 1 and 2 are available in machine-scorable, non-reuseable form or in non-machine-scorable form. Students may use the non-machine-scorable booklets with answer sheets, in which case they are reusable, or they may record their answers directly in the booklets for hand scoring. Test booklets for Levels 3, 4, and 5 are reusable and inteded for use with either machine-scorable or hand-scorable answer sheets. Each test booklet contains a separate Memory Learning Materials booklet which contains sample items and learning materials for the Memory subtest. The Memory Learning Materials must be administered at the beginning of the test session and then collected.

The TCS comes with a practice test for use at all five levels. Its use is optional but strongly recommended by the publisher as it was administered to all students during the standardization.

The examiner's manual is comprehensive and well-written. All material to be read aloud to the students is printed in color and boldface. All information necessary for administering the test and processing the materials may be found in the examiner's manual.

Detailed information about the test can be found in three additional publications. The *TCS Test Coordinator's Handbook and Guide to Interpretation* is attractive, informative, and easy to read. The sections on organizing a testing program and interpreting scores should be very valuable to anyone charged with administering a testing program. The *TCS Norms Books* provide the information necessary for scoring the test. The *TCS Technical Report*, in addition to describing the norming and equating procedures, gives a good introduction to Item Response Theory.

Scale scores for each of the subtests are obtained by either the IRT method or the number correct method. The IRT method may be used if the tests are machine-scored. In IRT scoring, a computer applies an iterative procedure directly to the student's item responses to obtain a scale score. The number-correct scoring, a simpler method, is used when the test is hand scored. In number-correct scoring, the conversion tables in the norms books are entered with the number correct to obtain the scale score. The number-correct method is somewhat less accurate than the IRT method.

Percentile ranks on both age and grade norms have been established. The age percentile indicates the student's rank with respect to students of the same age regardless of grade in school. The grade percentile indicates the student's rank with respect to other students in the same grade regardless of age. The former should be most useful in predicting achievement at some future time; the latter should be of value in helping teachers work with a classroom of varying ability levels. A stanine score on grade norms is also available for each child.

The Cognitive Skills Index (CSI) is an age-normed measure of general academic aptitude. Like the age percentiles, it indicates the student's overall level of ability relative to chronological age, regardless of grade. The CSI, with a mean equal to 100 and a standard deviation of 16, has statistical properties similar to an Intellegence Quotient. CSI is the preferred term, however, to avoid the misunderstandings frequently associated with IQ.

One type of score that is lacking is the group mean percentile. The classroom summaries obtained from machine-scoring report a percentile associated with the group mean scale score. A comparable value can be obtained in hand-scoring the test by entering the grade percentile table with the mean scale score. An error occurs because the grade percentile table is based on individual norms but the classroom scale score is a mean. The percentile associated with the group mean should be based on group mean norms. Failure to provide norms for evaluating group means is a serious oversight on the part of the test publisher. There is every reason to believe that the TCS results will be used to evaluate groups in addition to individuals. In such cases, normative data based on group statistics should be available. The National Council for Measurement in Education *Standards for Educational and Psychological Tests* are very clear on this point: "Where it is expected that a test will be used to assess groups rather than individuals (i.e., for schools or programs), normative data based on group summary statistics should be provided" (Brown, 1980, p. 79).

The consquence of using individual norms to evaluate a group mean is that the mean will be overvalued if it is below the norm mean and it will be undervalued if it is above the norm mean, the reason being that the variability among individual scores is much greater than the variability among means. The test manual warns the user of this problem but goes on to suggest that the mean percentile can be interpreted as the percentile rank of the most typical child. However, most users who calculate a mean do so because they are interested in seeing how the group performs relative to other groups; the grade percentile reported on the TCS is unacceptable for this purpose.

The *Test Coordinator's Handbook and Guide to Interpretation* provides a handy list of the applications for which the publisher believes the test is useful. In general, the TCS is useful for purposes of instruction, administration, and evaluation. Teachers should find that the test can be used to group students for instructional purposes, plan instruction and instructional materials to match the range of abilities of the students, and serve as a basis for parent-teacher conferences among other uses. School administrators should find the TCS useful in planning for remedial or enrichment programs by providing information about the range and distribution of cognitive abilities in the school. Finally, results of TCS testing can be used in development and evaluation of an educational program at the level of a district or school.

As with many other such instruments, the TCS is most useful when used in conjunction with information from other sources, especially achievement test data. In fact, teachers and administrators who use the test as the sole means of classifying students run a risk of making errors, the consequences of which can be very serious. This point is raised at several places in the coordinator's handbook, but it cannot be stressed enough to the test user.

Another recommendation found in the coordinator's handbook is that, in addition to measuring cognitive skills, the TCS can be used as a framework for class discussions of reasoning strategies in order to help students understand the ways in which they themselves solve problems. Unfortunately, the handbook provides the teacher with no help in using the test in such a manner. There is a lack of discussion in the TCS publications of the relationship between the cognitive abilities being measured and the four tests that measure them. Does each subtest measure a unique ability each with its own set of appropriate strategies? Or do the four subtests measure the same set of abilities and strategies in four different ways? The handbook suggests that, as an example, the steps to be followed in solving analogies are encoding, inferring, mapping, applying, justifying and responding. This analysis was derived from Sternberg's (1977) theory of intellgence and is presented with no guidelines for incorporating it into instruction or discussion. Teachers are left on their own to decide if the same steps can be applied to solving problems in the Sequences, Memory, and Verbal Reasoning subtest. Until the broad classes of reasoning strategies and their exemplars are made explicit, this application of the TCS will have doubtful utility.

Technical Aspects

Because the TCS measures some of the abilities necessary for learning, it should serve as a useful predictor of school success. The test user should be cautioned, however, that tests with different names do not necessarily measure different traits. There appears to be some overlap in the traits measured by the subtests. For example, it seems evident from inspection of the items that reasoning by analogy is an important part of some tasks on the Sequences and Verbal Reasoning subtest in addition to being the trait measured by the Analogies subtest. Whatever the skills measured by the TCS, they are primarily verbal in nature. Most of the items on the Analogies subtest, although pictorial in form, describe relationships that could be expressed as effectively in words. In fact, restating the item verbally is often necessary for uncovering the relationship. In general, the Sequences, Analogies, and Verbal Reasoning subtests seem to measure similar if not identical traits. Of the four, only the Memory subtest seems to be distinct. Intercorrelations between Sequences, Analogies, and Verbal Reasoning range from .35 to .68 with a median of .60. Correlations between Memory and each of the other three subtests range from .10 to .52 with a median of .40.

Despite the doubtful validity of the separate subscales, the TCS gives a good measure of general ability. The construct validity of the TCS was established by correlating it with the SFTAA. Correlations of the Cognitive Skills Index with the SFTAA Total IQ range from .69 to .83 with a median of .81. The SFTAA Total IQ has been found to have a correlation of .73 with the WISC-R Full Scale IQ (Wikoff & Parolini, 1982). No studies directly correlating the TCS with WISC-R have been found.

The TCS is a good predictor of academic achievement as indicated by the correlations between the California Achievement Tests and the TCS. The correlations for CAT Total Battery and TCS Total Scale Score range from .61 to .86 with a median of .82.

Two indicators of reliability are reported in the *TCS Technical Report*. The Kuder-Richardson formula 20 (KR 20) coefficients of internal consistency range from .72 to .90 with the median being .81. The KR 20 coefficients are based on number-correct scoring of the TCS.

Standard errors of measurement (SEMs) are reported for each scale score available on each level. A set of SEMs was estimated using IRT scoring and another set was estimated using number-correct scoring. The latter method is used for comparison with other tests scaled according to tradition methods. Calculating an SEM for each scale score is a departure from traditional practice in which one SEM is calculated for the entire test. Examination of the SEMs confirms the fact that, for any particular level of the test, achievement of students with the lower and the higher scale scores is measured less reliably than achievement of students with scale scores near the median. SEMs of extreme scale scores tend to be five to eight times larger the SEMs of the median scale scores. Examination of SEMs also indicates that all SEMs estimated from the IRT scale scores are lower than those estimated from number correct scores, thus verifying the greater accuracy of IRT scaling.

The techical report gives a greater wealth of detail about the standardization procedure and the characteristics of the norm sample of 83,000 children than this reviewer has found with other group administered tests. The norm sample was partitioned into types of district (public, Catholic, private), geographic region (four), community type (urban, suburban, rural), size of community (large or small), and a demographic index based on district performance on achievement tests (high, medium, low, not available). There were 86 cells. A questionnaire was sent to all participating schools to obtain background information. The results are summarized in the technical report. The contents of items were reviewed for bias by male and female educators from various ethnic groups. In addition, empirical comparisons of item performance across ethnic groups were made and biased items eliminated.

Critique

The Test of Cognitive Skills is an excellent test from a technical point of view. In the opinion of this reviewer, CTB/McGraw-Hill has, with one exception, set laudable technical standards for other test publishers to imitate. The norming, scaling, and elimination of bias has been done thoroughly and competently; the data have been reported clearly and informatively. The directions for administration are clear and easy to follow. The one exception, discussed previously, is the failure to provide group norms.

But despite the technical quality, there is a vexing concern about what the test measures. It appears, at first look, to be a test of four different cognitive skills, as specified by the subtest; however, on closer inspection, the differences between the subtests blur and disappear. No correlations with other measures are presented in support of the construct validity of the subtests, nor factor analytic data to support their uniqueness. There are probably no more than two different abilities that are measured by the test. Three of the subtests could be said to measure abstract verbal ability. If any subtest can be considered unique, it would be the Memory subtest. This subtest, however, would be improved by a closer correspondence with theory.

What then does the TCS measure? The best answer is that it measures *developed abilities*, defined by Anastasi (1984) as ''. . . skills acquired through years of training and practice with verbal and numerical material'' (p.132). Users of the TCS therefore, should ignore the subtest scale scores in favor of the overall Cognitive Skills Index. But for the user who needs a single measure of abstract, acquired, school-related ability that can be administered to a group in a short time, the Test of Cognitive Skills is highly recommended.

References

Anastasi, A. (1984). Aptitude and achievement tests: The curious case of the indestructible strawperson. In B. S. Plake (Ed.), *Social and technical issues in testing: Implications for test construction and usage* (pp. 129-140). Hillsdale, NJ: Lawrence Erlbaum Associates, Inc.

Brown, F. G. (1980). *Guidelines for test use: A commentary of the standards for educational and psychological tests.* Ames, IA: National Council on Measurement in Education.

Hambleton, R. K. (1983). *Applications of item response theory.* Vancouver, British Columbia: Educational Research Institute of British Columbia.

Lennon, R. T. (1980). The anatomy of a scholastic aptitude test. *NCME Measurement in Education, 11*(2), 1-9.

Lord, F. M. (1980). *Applications of item response theory to practical testing problems.* Hillsdale, NJ: Lawrence Erlbaum Associates, Inc.

Paivio, A. (1970). *Imagery and verbal processes.* New York: Holt, Rinehart & Winston.

Sternberg, R. J. (1977). *Intelligence, information processing, and analogical reasoning: The componential analysis of human abilities.* Hillsdale, NJ: Lawrence Erlbaum Associates, Inc.

Wikoff, R. L., & Parolini, R. J. (1982). Prediction of the WISC-R full scale IQ from the SFTAA. *Journal of Clinical Psychology, 38*(2), 387-388.

Wittrock, M. C. (1977). The generative processes of memory. In M. C. Wittrock (Ed.), *The human brain* (pp. 153-184). Englewood Cliffs, NJ: Prentice-Hall, Inc.

Robert G. Harrington, Ph.D.
Assistant Professor in Educational Psychology and Research,
University of Kansas, Lawrence, Kansas.

TEST OF NONVERBAL INTELLIGENCE

Linda Brown, Rita J. Sherbenou, and Susan K. Johnsen.
Austin, Texas: PRO-ED.

Introduction

The Test of Nonverbal Intelligence (TONI; Brown, Sherbenou, & Johnsen, 1982) was designed to be a nonbiased test of intellectual ability for use with handicapped or minority populations who may require language-free testing formats. The TONI is a nationally standardized, individually administered measure of cognitive ability designed for subjects who range in age from 5-0 through 85-11 years. There are two equivalent forms, A and B. Problem-solving is the basis for all TONI items.

Although it is true that there is a wide variety of intelligence tests from which an examiner may choose, most of these share one common limitation. Because the test directions or response formats are verbally loaded they may be biased against nonreaders, poor writers, language impaired, mentally retarded, learning disabled, deaf, nonEnglish speakers, and culturally different individuals. These subjects require a test that is more performance-oriented, that is entirely free of listening, speaking, reading, and writing.

Bias against social, ethnic, socioeconomic, and linguistic minorities may be minimized when tests require less knowledge of language symbols, especially language symbols common only to the predominant white, middle-class culture. The term Sattler (1982) coined to refer to tests that do not require any culturally specific language knowledge is "culturally reduced." Culturally reduced testing may be a viable alternative to the so-called culture-fair and culture-specific tests (Arvey, 1972).

According to Jensen (1980) culturally reduced tests differ from traditional intelligence tests in several important ways. Culturally reduced tests employ performance rather than paper-and-pencil language-based tasks. Items should assess reasoning or problem solving because most factual content is so culturally based. These problems should be novel so that test items will not be biased by the content of previously learned information. Furthermore, pantomimed directions should replace oral or written directions. Sample items should serve as examples to ensure that the subject fully comprehends the directions. Untimed items should replace timed items. Items should be composed of abstract content instead of culturally loaded pictures or passages. When currently popular measures of intelligence, including the Culture Fair Intelligence Test (Cattell, 1950), Leiter International Performance Scales (Leiter, 1948), Otis-Lennon Mental Ability Test

(Otis & Lennon, 1970), Progressive Matrices (Raven, 1938), Slosson Intelligence Test for Children and Adults-Revised (Slosson, 1981), Stanford-Binet Intelligence Test (Terman & Merrill, 1962), and Wechsler Intelligence Scale for Children-Revised (Wechsler, 1974), were compared against Jensen's guidelines none of the tests met all of the criteria. Consequently, the authors of the TONI believed there was a need for such a culturally reduced test.

The construction of the TONI began by reviewing the contents and formats employed in other nonverbal and performance tests of intelligence. Items from the Raven's Progressive Matrices, the performance subtests of the Wechsler Scales, and the Leiter International Performance Scale served as models. The theoretical background for the TONI was derived from Guilford's (1956) Structure of Intellect model, Gagne's learning theory (1959), and researchers who have studied different facets of problem solving (Bourne 1963, 1967; Bourne & Guy, 1968a, 1968b, Glucksberg, 1964; Dominowski 1966).

After this thorough review of nonverbal intelligence test items and research in problem solving, 307 items consisting of abstract/figural problem-solving tasks were devised. None of the abstract/figural designs or shapes were symbolic or had any inherent meaning. These items were critically reviewed by both potential users of the TONI and technical experts including university professors, graduate students, school psychologists, psychometrists, special education teachers, and other professionals. The 183 items that remained after review were subjected to statistical analysis for their item-discriminating power and item difficulty.

Discriminating power was estimated by means of a point-biserial correlation. Only items that correlated with the total score in the .30 to .80 range were retained. This range was chosen because it ensured that all of the coefficients would be sufficiently large to justify the assumption that all of the items are making a significant contribution to the total test score. Items with coefficients above .80 were eliminated because they were duplicative and would not contribute anything unique to the total test score. Items were also analyzed for item difficulty. Only those items that were answered correctly by approximately 15 to 85% of the people tested during item analysis were retained. The estimates of item-discriminating power and item difficulty were based on a sample of 322 subjects grouped into eight age or grade intervals (students in Kindergarten, Grades 1, 3, 5, 7, 9, young adults aged 18-35 years, and older adults aged 65-85 years). Two sets of 50 items that met the item-discrimination and item-difficulty criteria were assigned to the parallel Forms A and B of the TONI. The item-discriminating power and item-difficulty levels were found to be approximately equal on both forms. These item analysis procedures were replicated on a sample drawn from the TONI standardization population. One hundred subjects were randomly selected from each of four age intervals (6-7 years, 13-14 years, 35-40 years, and 60-65 years). The median item correlations at the four age intervals ranged from .33 to .45 for Form A and from .32 to .47 for Form B.

The authors refer to the TONI as a "language free measure of cognitive ability" (Brown, Sherbenou, & Johnsen, 1982, p. 2). The test instructions are pantomimed by the examiner and the subject answers by pointing to one of four possible responses. The TONI covers the kindergarten- to adult-age range of 5-0 through 85-11 years. Each of the two equivalent forms of the TONI, Form A and Form B, contains 50 items sequenced hierarchically in order of difficulty. The TONI is untimed but requires about 15 minutes for most subjects to complete. Six preliminary training items are administered prior to each of the six testing formats.

All 50 nonverbal problems on the TONI require examinees to identify the most salient relationships among several abstract figures. Each item consists of at least three abstract figure drawings in which one of the figures is missing. The subject is asked to complete the set. Either four or six response alternatives are displayed below each stimulus item. By identifying the correct relationship between the figures the subject can select the appropriate response from among the several options. This may be accomplished by examining the similarities and differences among the figures in the set and in the response alternatives. Figures may be related by one or more rules. Each item has a new rule or set of rules operating. The many possible relationships between figures are defined by shape, position, direction or contiguity, shading, size or length, movement, and pattern within the figure. The TONI items were designed according to five rules: Simple Matching, Analogies, Classification, Intersections, and Progressions. With Simple Matching the stimulus figures are all the same. The subject must select the figural response that is identical or matches the stimulus figures.

With Analogies a relationship between two or more figures is presented in a row or column. The examinee must identify this relationship and select an analogous response to complement the figures in another row or column. These analogous relationships may vary in five different ways:

1. *Matching.* Because there are no differences between the figures in one of the rows or columns the examinee must find the item that matches exactly the figure(s) in the remaining row or column.
2. *Addition.* The characteristics of figures in one row or column change by adding new attributes or additional figures. The examinee must find the item response that represents an analogous addition to the item(s) in the remaining row or column.
3. *Subtraction.* Stimulus figures change by subtracting one or more attributes. The examinee must complete the remaining row or column by choosing the response item that subtracts some figural attribute in an analogous manner.
4. *Alteration.* One or more of the attributes of the stimulus figures is changed or altered. The examinee must select the item response that represents an analogous figural alternation.
5. *Progressions.* The examinee must find the item response that represents the progressive change that continues between or among figures.

With Classification the figure in the stimulus item is a member of one of the sets of figures in the response alternatives. With Intersections a new figure is formed by joining parts of figures in the rows and columns and with Progressions the same change continues between or among figures.

Because Forms A and B are equivalent, examiners may administer either form and expect to get similar results. Practically speaking, Form A should be administered to a subject first as a pretest. Form B could be administered as a posttest to evaluate the effectiveness of an intervention, as a reevaluation for continued program eligibility, or to overcome any forms of test contamination such as test-wise behavior. Because the reliability coefficients associated with ages five and six are borderline (coefficients alpha of .78 each and Kuder-Richardson coefficients in the .60s) the developers of the TONI recommend that the alternate form also be administered to young children in this age range. If the results of Form B agree with those of Form A, the examiner may be more assured of the reliability of those test scores.

The answer sheets for Form A and Form B are not interchangeable. It is very important that the examiner has the correct one. On the front of both Form A and Form B protocols there is space for identifying information (i.e., examiner's name, subject's name, school, grade, address, chronological age, and date tested) and questions about the conditions under which the TONI was administered. The questions deal with whether the test was administered individually or in a group, whether the examiner was experienced with the TONI, whether there were any departures from standardized administration procedures, the physical test conditions, and any salient test behaviors observed. The front of the TONI answer sheet also has space for a description of other relevant test data as well as the test profile. The examiner may plot the TONI Quotient for Form A and Form B so that comparisons in performance may be made. In addition, there is a chart for profiling the standard scores of other measures of intelligence, language, or achievement. In this way direct comparisons may be made between a child's performance on the TONI and various other tests. On the back side of the TONI answer sheet there is a paragraph of instructions for test administration and a list of the response options for each of the 50 items. The correct response is circled for the scoring convenience of the examiner. Arrows point to the items that represent suggested starting points for children of varying ages.

Practical Applications/Uses

Ethnic minority group children are not "culturally handicapped," "culturally disadvantaged," or "culturally deprived" simply because they have values, customs, patterns of thought, or languages that differ significantly from those of the white, middle-class majority of society in which they live (Sattler, 1982). These terms are degrading and reveal a value system that is tolerant of the cultural patterns of the majority group only. Cultural variability may be quite adaptive for minority groups whose living environments differ substantially from those of the dominant culture (Barnes, 1971). These cultural variables are powerful forces that shape the child's attitudes toward the test situation, including the test materials, the examiner, and the reasons for the assessment. Another minority group whose special circumstances would invalidate most standardized assessments of intelligence includes handicapped children. Children who have impaired hearing, vision, speech, motor skills, or multiple handicaps present deficits that may require adaptations in administration procedures or scoring criteria.

Psychological examiners have used various approaches to deal with the assessment challenges presented by ethnic minority children and handicapped individuals. Some examiners have dealt with this problem by simply modifying standard procedures to meet the needs of the ethnic minority or handicapped person. Based on their own clinical judgments they may decide to pantomime responses, supply multiple-choice responses, assist the examinee with motor responses, allow pointing to answers, or enlarge the test materials (Harrington, 1979). The dilemma is that such nonstandardized modifications in test administration as these may distort any norm-referenced comparisons with the standardization sample. On the other hand, when modifications are not made the verbal item content may be biased against ethnic minorities and the response requirements may not be fair to the handicapped individual. Consequently, the test may not reflect the examinee's intelligence. Rather, it may reflect impaired sensory processing, limited manual or speaking skills (Sullivan, 1978), or the cultural diversity of the examinee's background (Flaugher, 1978).

The problem-solving format of the TONI has reduced the cultural loading commonly found in the major standardized intelligence tests. In addition, the nonverbal item content and pointing response adaptation has made the TONI a much fairer measure of intellectual ability for ethnic minorities and handicapped individuals than many other verbally loaded measures.

One of the major criteria for admission into school-based special education programs has been the IQ score on an intelligence test. Eligibility for educational programs for the mentally retarded, learning disabled, and gifted is based in part on IQ test results. The TONI might be used as a primary measure of intelligence for admission into any of these programs. Preferably, the TONI could be used to complement and confirm the results derived from some other major intelligence test such as the Wechsler Intelligence Scale for Children-Revised (1974).

An IQ test score is one of the requirements for some college programs and many vocational training programs. Counseling psychologists and industrial psychologists may find the TONI useful as one source for predicting occupational performance as well as academic success. Clinical psychologists and rehabilitation counselors working in clinics, mental health agencies, or hospitals may find the TONI useful in psychodiagnostic assessment and treatment planning. However, one caveat regarding the use of the TONI is in order. The TONI should never be used to profile cognitive strengths and weaknesses. There are no subtest scores on the TONI and research has not substantiated the validity of clinically interpreted profiles for learning disabled, developmentally delayed, or psychopathologically disordered individuals.

The TONI may be given individually or in small groups up to five subjects. The authors suggest that the TONI may be administered by classroom teachers, special education personnel, psychologists, psychometrists, educational diagnosticians or anyone else qualified to administer intelligence tests according to local and state regulations. The TONI should be administered in an environment that is private, well lit, comfortable, and free from distractions. The fact that the TONI is a nonverbal measure should not deter the examiner from interacting with the examinee to establish rapport, to explain the purpose of the test, and to answer any questions the subject might have. After the testing has begun the examiner should refrain completely from talking with the examinee. Praise and encouragement for hard work should be expressed through facial expressions or gestures rather than verbal reinforcement, but no gestures or expressions should be made that communicate the accuracy of the subject's response.

To begin testing, the examiner should place the Picture Book in the subject's visual plane and administer the six training items, none of which are scored or recorded. They are intended to give subjects practice with the nonverbal testing format and with the item configurations they will encounter throughout the test. Each training item is administered by gesturing through the sequence of the stimulus and stopping at the empty square in the stimulus pattern. Subsequently the examiner looks quizzically at the subject, points to the first response choice, points to the empty square in the stimulus, and then nods "yes" or "no" depending on whether the response is correct or incorrect. Subjects may join in this training exercise by pointing to the correct response for each of the remaining stimulus items. After all six practice items have been administered the examinee should be ready to respond to the items in the Picture Book that correspond with the form of the TONI being given; however, the six practice items may be repeated if the subject does not appear to understand what to do after the training-item demonstration.

The starting point for testing will vary depending on the age and suspected ability level of the examinee. For example, testing should begin with the first item if the subject is very young or if previous testing has shown retarded intellectual ability. In the examiner's manual there is a table of suggested starting points corresponding to various age ranges. In any case, the examiner should begin at a point where the subject will be successful.

The actual test items are administered in exactly the same manner as the six practice items. The subject chooses from among the line of response choices by pointing. The TONI is not timed. If subjects do not respond after 30 seconds, some nonverbal prompt should be administered to encourage them to make a choice. This action is intended to keep the test moving. Responses given much after 30 seconds are probably guesses. Subjects' responses are recorded on the back of the one-page answer sheet by placing an "x" over the number of the response given by the subject. The response is considered correct if it matches the response number in boldface type and circled. The examiner places a "+" (correct) or "0" (incorrect) on the line to the left of the item depending on whether the subject's response is correct or not.

Most subjects will not be administered all 50 items of the TONI. Instead, the examiner tries to find a basal of five consecutive correct responses in a row. Because the test items are arranged in an ascending order of difficulty the examiner should move to successively easier (lower numbered) items if the basal rule of five consecutive correct responses is not achieved. After finding the basal, the testing continues until three out of five items are missed and the ceiling rule has been met.

To expedite the testing process trained and experienced examiners may administer the TONI to groups of two to five subjects. The examiner has the option to administer training items individually or to the entire group. Examinees should respond individually, in turn, by pointing to actual test item responses. Basal and ceiling rules remain unchanged under group administration. Every other subject should be administered an alternate form of the TONI so that examinees are not solving the same items simultaneously.

To score the TONI, the number of the basal item is entered in the Scoring Summary area on the front side of the answer sheet. The basal item is the item just below the subject's first error. Next, a line is drawn underneath the subject's last error. This is the third incorrect response in five items. The total raw score is the sum of the number of correct responses (+ s) that were made between the basal item and the last error. This raw score can be converted to a TONI Quotient and percentile rank for either Form A or B by referring to the correct conversion table in the manual. The examiner should note that the columns containing the TONI Quotients for five- and six-year-old subjects have been shaded to remind examiners that the reliability coefficients at these age levels are borderline.

To the extent that the TONI has no subtests and renders only a TONI Quotient and a percentile rank the interpretation of the TONI is limited. The TONI Quotient is a deviation standard score based on a distribution with a mean of 100 and a standard deviation of 15. Consequently, TONI Quotients from 85 to 115 should be considered in the normal range. Scores in the normal range are plotted in the unshaded portion of the TONI Profile. High or low scores outside the normal range are plotted in the shaded areas. A table of standard error of measurements is given in the examiner's manual so that the TONI Quotient will not be interpreted as a single point score. The percentile rank can be used effectively to communicate an individual's relative position in the normative group.

Examiners may wish to compare standard scores from other tests with the TONI Quotients. A table is provided to convert standard scores from other commonly used distributions into the distribution used by the TONI. These standard scores may be plotted and compared on the same profile as the TONI Quotient. No person should be diagnosed as mentally retarded based on a low TONI Quotient alone. Other explanations, such as test anxiety, lack of motivation, poor vision or hearing, or inattention, should be investigated. Other intelligence, adaptive behavior, and achievement test scores must also be considered before arriving at such a diagnosis. In other words, multiple methods and multiple sources should be considered before arriving at a final diagnosis. The examiner should also be suspicious when the TONI scores are normal or above average and the comparative scores on other language loaded tests are below average because this discrepancy may be symptomatic of a language delay or reflective of the subject's ethnic minority status. By carefully studying the subject's case history and comparing the test results on the TONI with those of other tests the examiner should be able to discern whether the discrepancy is intellectually based or language based. Local and specialized norms for individuals in specific subgroups, such as mentally retarded or learning disabled, could be very helpful for program planning purposes. In any case, examiners should be careful to state explicitly whether national or local norms were applied in their interpretations.

Technical Aspects

The TONI was standardized on 1,929 subjects ranging in age from 5-0 through 85-11. The sample was further stratified on the basis of sex (47% male, 53% female); race (77% Caucasian, 14% Negroid, 9% Mongolian); ethnicity (6% American, 8% Hispanic, 86% other); domicile (17% urban, 61% suburban, 22% rural); grade in school (for child subjects only; Kindergarten through high school); parental educational/occupational attainment (for child subjects only) and current educational/occupational attainment (for adult subjects only); and four geographic regions including 28 states. The authors report that these demographic characteristics approximate the proportions reported in the 1980 U.S. Census (Statistical Abstract for the United States, 1980). Subjects suspected of impaired intellectual ability were excluded from the standardization group. Most subjects were administered both Forms A and B in immediate succession and in a randomized order. All examiners were trained by the test authors.

TONI Quotients were derived from the cumulative frequencies of raw scores at every six-month age interval from 5-18 years, every one-year interval from 19-24 years, and every five-year interval from 25-85 years. A test for significant mean differences among these groups made it necessary to report normative data for only ten chronological age intervals for Form A and nine intervals for Form B.

In order to establish the internal consistency of the TONI both coefficient alpha and the Kuder-Richardson Formula 21 were each calculated for 100 subjects at four age intervals (6-7 years, 13-14 years, 35-40 years, and 60-65 years). All but two coefficients for these four age ranges round to or exceed .90. The coefficients for the youngest age group for both Forms A and B round to .80.

Another measure of test consistency is the standard error of measurement, which establishes the range within which an individual's true test score probably lies. The standard error of measurement for the TONI Quotient ranges from ± 5 to ± 9 for both Forms A and B. The largest standard error of measurement is at the youngest age levels between ages 5 and 6 years. This means that the TONI is more unreliable at the earliest age levels and has the smallest standard error measurement after age 15. The coefficient alpha for the total group of 400 subjects on both Forms A and B is .96. The Kuder-Richardson 21 coefficients for both Forms A and B ranged from .60 to .90. Only the coefficients calculated for the five- and six-year-olds failed to reach the .80 criterion. The results of the coefficient alpha and the Kuder-Richardson 21 coefficient show strong evidence for the internal consistency of the TONI at most ages.

The Pearson Product moment coefficients of correlation were calculated to establish the alternate forms reliability of the TONI. During the standardization of the TONI 98% of the subjects (1,888) were administered successively both Forms A and B in random order. All of the coefficients at each of the age intervals for which normative data are reported were in the .80 to .95 range except for a .78 coefficient in the 8-6 to 10-11 years interval. These high correlations between alternate forms suggest that the two forms are essentially equivalent.

In order to establish the internal consistency and alternate forms reliability of the TONI with sensory and intellectually impaired individuals the TONI was administered to ten educable mentally retarded students (mean age = 11-5 years); 30 deaf students (mean age = 16-1 years); and two groups of learning disabled students, eleven with a mean age of 9-5 years and sixteen with a mean age of 12-1 years. All of the Kuder-Richardson 21 coefficients for Forms A and B for these groups rounded to at least .80 and two of them exceeded .90. The Pearson Product moment correlations ranged from .81 to .95.

In part, the content validity of the TONI was ensured through the careful development and selection of test items. To determine concurrent validity TONI scores for Forms A and B were correlated with performance on several measures of intelligence and achievement, including the Raven (1938) Progressive Matrices, the Leiter International Performance Scale (Leiter, 1948), the Wechsler Intelligence Scale for Children-Revised (WISCR; Wechsler, 1974), the Otis-Lennon Mental Ability Test (Otis & Lennon, 1970), the Iowa Tests of Basic Skills (ITBS) (Lindquist & Hieronymous, 1956), the SRA Achievement Series (Naslund, Thorpe, & Lefever, 1978), and the Stanford Achievement Test (SAT; Madden & Gardner, 1972). In all, the results of eight small sample size concurrent validity studies are reported: three with normal subjects, two with deaf subjects, two with learning disabled subjects, and one with mentally retarded subjects.

The results of these concurrent validity studies conducted with various populations show that the correlations between the TONI and these various measures of intelligence and achievement ranged between .46 to .95 depending on the criterion measure. The TONI appears to be related more strongly to intelligence than to achievement, and to language-free or composite measures of intelligence than to verbal measures.

Because the TONI, which is supposed to measure intelligence, correlates with known measures of ability, it can be concluded that the test's construct validity has been partially established. To empirically test the construct validity the TONI was administered to a class of ten mentally retarded students with a mean age of 11-4 years and a mean Full Scale IQ of 60.9 on the WISC-R. This sample was matched on the basis of sex and chronological age to a random sample of normal subjects from the same community. The retarded students had mean TONI raw scores of 5.6 and 6.5 on Form A and B, respectively. The means for the matched normals were 23.4 and 23.5. The t-tests conducted between the Form A and Form B means for these two groups were both significant beyond the .001 level. In conclusion, the research reported here tends to support the reliability and validity of the TONI.

Critique

One of the greatest problems in psychological assessment is posed by examinees whose culturally different backgrounds, physical handicaps, or language difficulties make it impossible to administer to them in a standardized manner one of the more verbally loaded measures of intelligence. In response to this need the TONI represents a relatively new language-free performance measure of intelligence and reasoning. It is a compact, easily administered, time-efficient test requiring no extra equipment other than the examiner's manual and scoring sheet provided in the test kit. The examiner's directions are completely pantomimed and the multiple-choice response format permits the examinee to respond nonverbally. The TONI provides unscored practice exercises to ensure that the examinee understands the task. Other current measures of intelligence employ this same item format to ensure that directions are clearly understood. Because there are two equivalent forms of the TONI it may be very useful as a pre- and post-measure or for reevaluations required by PL 94:142. The parallel forms should reduce the probability that test-wise behavior will confound and reduce the reliability of the retested TONI Quotient. In addition, when using the TONI, children may be monitored over an extended period of time because the norms range from 5-0 through 85-11 years.

Standardization and norming have been areas of weakness for other specialized measures of intelligence. Often, regional norms have been reported the representativeness of which for other locales has been unknown. Other drawbacks include a small sample size or no control for demographic variables. In contrast, the TONI was standardized on a large, nationally representative population of 1,929 subjects from 28 states. Furthermore, the sample was stratified based on eleven important demographic variables similar to those used to standardize the Wechsler Scales. To some extent, these standardization procedures should have increased the representativeness of the TONI norms. The percentage of the sample represented by subjects in the 21-0 to 85-11 year range is small, however. This situation is apt to make TONI Quotients in this age range less representative. TONI Quotients are standard scores identical to the distribution on the Wechsler Scales, which are familiar to many examiners. For this reason, comparisons with the Wechsler Scales and other tests should be facilitated.

The TONI appears to be a highly reliable test at most age levels with normal students, and with populations of retarded, learning disabled, and deaf students. Internal consistency and alternate forms reliability coefficients are in the .80s and .90s at most ages. Alpha coefficients and standard error of measurements in the 5- and 6-year-old range are the least reliable of all age intervals. The concurrent validity of the TONI was established by correlating performance on the TONI with performance on other measures of intelligence and achievement. In a study of the test's construct validity or diagnostic utility, the TONI accurately discriminated among groups of retarded and normal subjects. The problem with these two validity studies is that they are based on extremely limited sample sizes and sample characteristics. Further validity studies using more representative sampling procedures should be conducted with the TONI to corroborate the tentative validity results reported in the examiner's manual.

The TONI assesses only a single component of intelligence, problem solving. It is not a global intelligence measure. Consequently, there are no profile scores on the TONI. The authors are very careful to point out certain ethical considerations that follow from these structural limitations of the test. Like other intelligence tests, the TONI should never be used solely to diagnose mental retardation or giftedness. Instead, the TONI could serve as an excellent nonverbal comparison to other verbally loaded measures of intelligence, achievement, and adaptive behavior. In addition, potential examiners should be cautioned against using the results of the TONI for instructional programming purposes. The TONI has no items that directly assess school achievement or a set of prerequisite learning skills. Criterion-referenced tests and achievement tests serve these purposes much better. Preferably, examiners should have training and experience in intellectual assessment before administering, scoring, and interpreting the TONI. To reduce the amount of time spent in testing examiners may opt to administer the TONI in small groups of up to five individuals. There are some potential problems with this group administration option, however. Examinees may distract each other during testing, or the examiner may have difficulty in keeping track of individual subject's pointing responses. There is also the opportunity for copying responses. Simply alternating the two forms of the TONI, as the authors suggest, may not be sufficient to alleviate this potential problem.

In conclusion, the Test of Nonverbal Intelligence has great potential as a supplemental test of nonverbal intelligence to other formal intellectual and achievement measures. As a culturally reduced test the TONI should provide the opportunity for examiners to evaluate language delayed, mentally retarded, learning disabled, deaf, or culturally different individuals in a more nonbiased manner than other measures of intellectual ability have allowed in the past.

References

Arvey, R. D. (1972). Some comments on culture fair tests. *Personnel Psychology, 25,* 433-448.

Barnes, E. J. (1971, September). The utilization of behavioral and social sciences in minority grant education: Some critical implications. In W. R. Rhine (Chair), *Ethnic minority issues on the utilization of behavioral and social science in a pluralistic society.* Symposium conducted at the meeting of the American Psychological Association, Washington, DC.

Bourne, L. E. (1963). Some factors affecting strategies used in problems of concept formation. *American Journal of Psychology, 75,* 229-238.

Bourne, L. E. (1967). Learning and utilization of conceptual rules. In B. Kleinmuntz (Ed.), *Memory and the structure of concepts.* New York: Wiley.

Bourne, L. E., & Guy, D. E. (1968a). Learning conceptual rules: I. Some inter-rule transfer effects. *Journal of Experimental Psychology, 75,* 423-429.

Bourne, L. E., & Guy, D. E. (1968b). Learning conceptual rules: II. The role of positive and negative instances. *Journal of Experimental Psychology, 77,* 488-494.

Brown, L., Sherbenou, R. J., & Johnsen, S. K. (1982). *The Test of Nonverbal Intelligence (TONI).* Austin, TX: PRO-ED.

Cattell, R. B. (1950). *Culture Fair Intelligence Test.* Champaign, IL: Institute for Personality and Ability Testing.

Dominowski, R. L. (1966). Problem solving as a function of relative frequency of correct responses. *Psychonomic Science, 5,* 107-111.

Flaugher, R. L. (1978). The many definitions of test bias. *American Psychologist, 33,* 671-679.

Gagne, R. M. (1959). Problem solving and thinking. *Annual Review of Psychology, 10,* 147-172.

Glucksberg, S. (1964). Functional fixedness: Problem solution as a function of observing responses. *Psychonomic Science, 1,* 117-118.

Guilford, J. P. (1956). The structure of intellect. *Psychological Bulletin, 53,* 267-293.

Harrington, R. G. (1979). A review of Sattler's modifications of standard intelligence tests for use with handicapped children. *School Psychology Digest, 8,* 296-302.

Jensen, A. (1980). *Bias in mental testing.* New York: Free Press.

Leiter, R. G. (1948). *Leiter International Performance Scale.* Chicago: Stoelting Co.

Lindquist, E. F., & Hieronymous, A. N. (1956). *Iowa Tests of Basic Skills.* Boston: Houghton Mifflin.

Madden, R., & Gardner, E. F. (1972). *Stanford Achievement Tests.* New York: The Psychological Corporation.

Naslund, R. A., Thorpe, L. P., & Lefever, D. W. (1978). *SRA Achievement Series.* Chicago: Science Research Associates.

Otis, A. S., & Lennon, R. T. (1970). *The Otis-Lennon Mental Ability Test.* New York: The Psychological Corporation.

Raven, J. C. (1938). *Standard Progressive Matrices.* London: Leives.

Sattler, J. M. (1982). *Assessment of children's intelligence and special abilities* (2nd ed.). Boston: Allyn & Bacon.

Slosson, R. L. (1981). *Slosson Intelligence Test for Children and Adults-Revised.* New York: Slosson Educational Publications.

Statistical Abstract for the United States (1980). Washington, DC: U.S. Department of Commerce, Bureau of the Census.

Sullivan, P. M. (1978). *A comparison of administration modifications on the WISC-R performance scale with different categories of deaf children.* Unpublished doctoral dissertation, The University of Iowa, Iowa City.

Terman, L. M., & Merrill, M. A. (1962). *Stanford-Binet Intelligence Scale Form L-M.* Boston: Houghton Mifflin.

Wechsler, D. (1974). *Manual for the Wechsler Intelligence Scale for Children-Revised.* New York: The Psychological Corporation.

Richard M. Ryan, Ph.D.

*Assistant Professor of Psychology, University of Rochester, Rochester,
New York.*

THEMATIC APPERCEPTION TEST

*Henry A. Murray. Cambridge, Massachusetts: Harvard
University Press.*

Introduction

The Thematic Apperception Test (TAT) is, along with the Rorschach, among the
most widely used, researched, and taught projective tests in existence (Wade,
Baker, Morton, & Baker, 1978). It is also among the most controversial devices,
with proponents citing its manifold clinical uses and long history of provocative
and sometimes impressive research findings, and critics describing it as a psychometrician's quicksand (Varble, 1971; Entiwisle, 1972; McClelland, 1980). What
becomes evident following any comprehensive review is that both views have
some validity. Used in theoretically appropriate contexts and with regard to
relevant criteria, the TAT can demonstrate remarkable sensitivity and utility.
Nonetheless, when subjected to the criteria developed for and appropriate to
many objective test instruments, the TAT provides little firm ground upon which
the traditional psychometrician could stand.

The TAT is now at its golden anniversary, being introduced in 1935 by Morgan
and Murray with only minor changes since that inception. It consists of a series of
pictures of relatively ambiguous scenes to which subjects are requested to make
up stories or fantasies concerning what is, has, and is going to happen, along with
a description of the thoughts and feelings of the various characters depicted. The
test protocol thus provides the examiner with a rich source of data, based on the
subject's perceptions and imagination, for use in the understanding of the subject's current needs, motives, emotions, and conflicts, both conscious and uncon-
cious (Murray, 1943). The data from the TAT can be scored according to a variety of
existing quantitative systems. However, more commonly in clinical use the stories
are interpreted in accord with general principles of inference derived from psychodynamic theory. Its use in clinical assessment is generally part of a larger
battery of tests and interview data, which provide the background and convergent
information necessary for appropriate interpretation.

As a research device, the TAT can be best understood as a method of eliciting a
sample of perceptual and verbal material in response to a set of standard stimuli,
which can lend itself to a plethora of empirical uses. It can be rated on nearly any
clearly defined dimension or criterion, content based or formal in character, that
can be reliably assessed. Its status then, both as a clinical and research instrument,
is based primarily on its capacity to elicit an abundant, complex, albeit somewhat
variable, response from varied subjects to a common situation. Accordingly, the
strength of the "test" is no better than the properties of the chosen scoring system

799

or the interpretive skills of the examiner in dealing with the material this situation generates. In this sense the TAT is more a method than a "test."

Aside from its own specific properties and popularity, the TAT is also important as a projective paradigm. Since its release 50 years ago, the technique of using relatively ambiguous pictures to elicit free response stories has been widely emulated. Close relatives include the Children's Apperception Test (CAT) and the Senior Apperception Test (SAT) (Bellak, 1975), but its lineage can also be traced to a still growing extended family that includes the Blacky Pictures Test (Blum, 1950), the Rosenzweig Picture Frustration Study (Rosenzweig, 1976), the Michigan Pictures Test-Revised (Hutt, 1980), the Tasks of Emotional Development (TED), (Cohen & Weil, 1975), the Symonds (1948), the Picture Arrangement Test (PAT) (Tomkins & Miner, 1957), and undoubtedly numerous others. Although these descendants may have applications to specific populations or may "pull" for issues and themes not covered by the TAT, they all rely to some extent on the assumptive basis of their originator. Before explicating the specific applications and scoring systems of the TAT, the projective assumptions that underlie it and all of its imitators should be presented.

The major uses and interpretation of the TAT are based on several key interrelated principles herein subsumed under the general rubric of the projective hypothesis or viewpoint. The projective viewpoint is widespread among practicing clinicians and personality psychologists and is intimately interwoven with psychodynamic theory, yet it has never fully achieved acceptance with mainstream academic psychology (Karon, 1981). Indeed projective psychology has often been described as dissident, or a "psychology of protest" (Abt, 1952) with respect to more behavioral or traditional scientific approaches, embracing values and beliefs not shared by that wider community (Dana, 1982). This has undoubtedly influenced the selection of individuals who comfortably employ a technique like the TAT.

Projective psychology assumes as a starting point that individuals' perceptions or behavior cannot be understood merely as an outcome of impinging, objectively describable stimuli. Rather, that which determines psychological and behavioral processes is assumed to be at least in part an outcome of subjective interpretation of what the environment affords. Perception is conceived as an active, constructive, and selective process, the organization of which is influenced by the person's unique capacities and history, and more importantly by current drives or needs that energize such processes. In short, perception is never neutral but rather selective and motivated.

Without doubt, however, projective psychology recognizes that strong situational determinants lead predictably to similar perceptual and behavioral responses across most subjects. Skinner (1957) called such potent situational determinants "mands." However, most situations in life are more equivocal and subject to multiple meanings, a fact that leads to individual differences in responses of all kinds. Indeed the more ambiguous the situation, the more a subject's own current needs, motives, or propensities are likely to play a role in determining its meaning and the actions that occur with respect to it.

The rationale of projective tests follows from this reasoning. By providing relatively ambiguous stimuli along with minimal constraints or structuring of the response that follows, the assumption is that a person's needs, motives, sentiments, and interests can be allowed maximal play in the formation of a response. Perceptions or responses elicited in the projective situation are thus evaluated in terms of the underlying dynamic processes in the subject's "inner world" that are assumed to have shaped them. Projective tests are thus of most significant value when used in the assessment of motives, needs, and other organizing influences on perception and behavior.

Nonetheless, the emphasis is on the *relative* ambiguity of the stimuli and nonstructuring of response in projective methods because a wide variety of research has shown that even projective stimuli mand or "pull" for certain types of responses (Peterson & Schilling, 1983) and the testing situation always places some constraints upon response. Card pull and response structuring are a recognized and important element in projective test construction and scoring, and in the TAT in particular.

Test Description: The TAT materials consist of 30 pictures with a variety of subject matters and themes portrayed. The majority of the cards depict life situations involving one or more persons, based on the assumption that this facilitates the subject's projection of motives, emotions and attitudes. Each card is coded on the reverse side of the picture with numbers and letters to designate the order of administration and to whom it should be administered, i.e., whether it is appropriate to adult males (M), adult females (F), boys (B), girls (G), or some combination. Thus, for example, the code 3BM is designed for use with boys and adult males, whereas 3GF would be used with either girls or adult females. Ten cards merely have a number without letter codes, indicating their appropriateness for subjects of all ages and both gender. Using this coding system there is a series of 20 sequentially arranged cards appropriate for use with any given group of subjects.

Murray (1943) originally advocated that subjects receive all 20 cards divided over two sessions. In actual practice, however, few examiners administer all 20 cards. Generally, both clinicians and researchers select some smaller subset of cards ranging from 6-10 in number. Some authors have identified subsets of cards that they advocate for use with all subjects, such as Arnold (1962). In her "story sequence analysis" method she recommended 13 cards (1, 2, 3BM, 4MF, 6BM, 7BM, 8BM, 10, 11, 13MF, 14, 16, and 20) regardless of the subject's gender. Dana (1956) also selected a subset of cards (2, 3GF, 4, 6GF, and 7GF for females; and 2, 3BM, 4 6BM, and 7BM for males) on which he collected extensive normative data. Finally, the popular Menninger Institute method employs the following sequence: 1, 5, 15, 3BM, 14, 10, 7GF, 13MF, 18GF, and 12M.

The most common practice, however, particularly in clinical applications, is to preselect cards that elicit themes that are thought to be pertinent to a given examinee's conflicts or concerns. Such selection, of course, will vary from person to person and depends on what is called the "pull" of the card (i.e., the properties of the card that tend to evoke particular affective and/or thematic responses across subjects). Presumably it is the manner in which subjects respond or adjust to the pull of each card that provides the information about their own idiosyncratic motives, conflicts, and capacities.

A number of investigators have researched the particular properties of the cards with regard to pull or response, eliciting properties using normative analyses of content or themes (Eron, 1950; Murstein, 1963; Campus, 1976), formal characteristics (Dana 1955, 1956), or semantic differential techniques (Goldfried & Zax, 1965). Murstein (1963) has gone so far as to state that the "stimulus is by far the most important determinant of a TAT response" (p. 195). Although not everyone would agree with this point, it nonetheless behooves the examiner to be familiar with the properties of the cards and the typical responses they elicit. What follows is a list of the 31 cards (30 pictures and 1 blank), along with a brief description of their features and more suggestions as to typical themes and issues they elicit. The interested examiner should beware that this list of themes is in no way intended to be exhaustive. The card description is based on Murray's (1943) original test manual.

Card 1: A young boy is contemplating a violin which rests on a table in front of him. Common themes and issues: needs for achievement; autonomy, particularly with respect to parents and/or authorities; self- versus other-motivation.

Card 2: Country scene—in the foreground is a young woman with books in her hand; in the background a man is working in the fields and an older woman is looking on. Common themes and issues: family relations; separation and individuation; achievement values and aspirations; pregnancy issues.

Card 3BM: On the floor against a couch is the huddled form of a boy with his head bowed on his right arm. Beside him on the floor is a revolver. Common themes and issues: depression, helplessness, suicide; guilt; impulse control; handling of aggression.

Card 3GF: A young woman is standing with downcast head, her face covered with her right hand. Her left arm is stretched forward against a wooden door. Common themes and issues: depression; loss; suicide; guilt.

Card 4: A woman is clutching the shoulders of a man whose face and body are averted as if he were trying to pull away from her. Common themes and issues: male-female relationships; sexuality; infidelity; interpersonal control, dominance, and conflict.

Card 5: A middle-aged woman is standing on the threshold of a half-opened door, looking into a room. Common themes and issues: attitude toward mother or wife; guilt; autonomy issues; fear of intruders; paranoia.

Card 6BM: A short elderly woman stands with her back turned to a tall young man. The latter is looking downward with a perplexed expression. Common themes and issues: mother-son relations; loss and grief; separation-individuation.

Card 6GF: A young woman sitting on the edge of a sofa looks back over her shoulder at an older man with a pipe in his mouth who seems to be addressing her. Common themes and issues: daughter-father or male-female relationships; heterosexual relationships; interpersonal trust; employer-employee relationships.

Card 7BM: A gray-haired man is looking at a younger man who is sullenly staring into space. Common themes and issues: father-son relationships; employer-employee relationships; authority issues.

Card 7GF: An older woman is sitting on a sofa close beside a girl, speaking or reading to her. The girl, who holds a doll in her lap, is looking away. Common themes and issues: mother-daughter relationships; rejection issues; child-rearing attitudes and experiences.

Card 8BM: An adolescent boy looks straight out of the picture. The barrel of a rifle is visible at one side, and in the background is the dim scene of a surgical operation, like a reverie-image. Common themes and issues: aspirations and achievement; handling of aggression; guilt; fears of being harmed; oedipal issues.

Card 8GF: A young woman sits with her chin in her hand, looking off into space. Common themes and issues: because of card ambiguity it elicits very diverse themes, aspirations; sense of future possibilities often noted.

Card 9BM: Four men in overalls are lying on the grass, taking it easy. Common themes and issues: homosexuality; male-male relationships; work attitudes; social prejudice.

Card 9GF: A young woman with a magazine and a purse in her hand looks from behind a tree at another young woman in a party dress running along a beach. Common themes and issues: female-female relationships; rivalry; jealousy; sexual attack; trust versus suspicion; suicide.

Card 10: A young woman's head rests against a man's shoulder. Common themes and issues: marital or parents' relationships; intimacy; loss or grief.

Card 11: A road skirts a deep chasm between high cliffs. On the road in the distance are obscure figures. Protruding from the rocky wall on one side is the long head and neck of a dragon. Common themes and issues: unknown, threatening forces; attack and defense; aggression. (Good card for assessing imaginative ability.)

Card 12M: A young man is lying on a couch with his eyes closed. leaning over him is the gaunt form of an elderly man, his hand stretched out above the face of the reclining figure. Common themes and issues: health; homosexuality; father-son relationships; issues of control; response to psychotherapy.

Card 12F: The portrait of a young woman. A weird old woman with a shawl over her head is grimacing in the background. Common themes and issues: mother or mother-in-law relationships; guilt and superego conflicts; good and evil.

Card 12BG: A rowboat is drawn up on the bank of a woodland stream. There are no human figures in the picture. Common themes and issues: loneliness; nature; peace; imaginal capacities; suicide.

Card 13MF: A young man is standing with downcast head buried in his arm. Behand him is the figure of a woman lying in bed. Common themes and issues: sexual conflict and attitudes; heterosexual relationships; guilt; handling of provocative stimulus; aggression.

Card 13B: A little boy is sitting on the doorstep of a log cabin. Common themes and issues: loneliness; abandonment; childhood memories. (Stories are extremely diverse due to ambiguity of picture.)

Card 13G: A little girl is climbing a winding flight of stairs. Common themes and issues: childhood memories; loneliness. (Themes extremely varied due to ambiguity of picture.)

Card 14: The silhouette of a man (or woman) against a bright window. The rest of the picture is totally black. Common themes and issues: wishes and aspirations; depression; suicide; loneliness; burglary; intrapsychic concerns.

Card 15: A gaunt man with clenched hands is standing among gravestones.

Common themes and issues: death; religion; fantasy; aggression.

Card 16: Blank card. Common themes and issues: extremely varied—handling of unstructured situation; imaginal capacities; optimism versus pessimism.

Card 17BM: A naked man is clinging to a rope. He is in the act of climbing up or down. Common themes and issues: achievement and aspirations; homosexuality; optimism and pessimism; danger, escape, competitiveness.

Card 17GF: A bridge spans over water. A female figure leans over the railing. In the background are tall buildings and small figures of men. Common themes and issues: loneliness; suicide; intrapsychic concerns.

Card 18BM: A man is clutched from behind by three hands. The figures of his antagonists are invisible. Common themes and issues: alcoholism, drunkenness; homosexuality; aggression; paranoia; helplessness.

Card 18GF: A woman has her hands squeezed around the throat of another woman, whom she appears to be pushing backward across the banister of a stairway. Common themes and issues: aggression, particularly mother-daughter; rivalry; jealousy; conflict.

Card 19: A weird picture of cloud formations overhanging a snow-covered cabin in the country. Common themes and issues: highly varied; imaginal capacities.

Card 20: The dimly illuminated figure of a man (or woman) in the dead of night leaning against a lamppost. Common themes and issues: loneliness; fears; aggression.

Administration: In addition to a selection of cards for the subject, the examiner should come prepared with a stopwatch, pencils, and paper. The stopwatch is used to time response latency, and the pencils and paper are used for response recording. Some examiners prefer an audio recording device. Nonetheless, paper and pencils should be available to note any specific behavioral or emotional reactions of the subject not accessible through the voice recording.

The single most important consideration in TAT administration is the creation of a psychological atmosphere in which the examiner feels relaxed, comfortable, and freely available to respond to the situation. Examiner rigidity or lack of friendliness or evaluative attitude is likely to result in constriction or discouragement of the subject, an unwanted situational contribution to the results. A quite, comfortable physical setting is most suitable for the session. Murray advocated that when possible the examinee be seated with his or her back to the examiner, presumably to facilitate free responding. However, many test users find that this standard arrangement is somewhat unnatural and instead sit across from or adjacent to the subject. The particulars of the seating arrangement are less important than maximizing rapport and freedom of response.

Appropriate subjects are those who range in age from 4 through adult. However, since projective story tasks more pertinent to childhood issues are available, the TAT is most widely used for subjects who are late adolescents or older.

Instructional sets have been varied by many examiners; thus, in actual practice there is not one standard phrasing. However, it is very important to introduce the following elements: 1) the subject is to make up a dramatic or imaginative story; 2) the story should include a description of what is occurring in the picture, what led up to it, and what will occur; and 3) the story should include something about what the various characters are thinking and feeling. Murray's (1943) manual used the following set for adults:

> I am going to show you some pictures, one at a time; and your task will be to make up as dramatic a story as you can for each. Tell what has led up to the event shown in the picture, describe what is happening at the moment, what the characters are feeling and thinking; and then give the outcome. Speak your thoughts as they come to your mind. Do you understand? Since you have fifty minutes for ten pictures, you can devote about five minutes to each story. Here is the first picture. (p. 3)

Murray's instructions also included a statement that this was "a test of imagination, one form of intelligence" (p. 3). However, because such a statement can create an ego-involved approach to the task (Ryan, 1982) it is not advocated by the present author. Murray also had a separate set of instructions for children:

> I have some pictures here that I am going to show you, and for each picture I want you to make up a story. Tell what has happened before and what is happening now. Say what the people are feeling and thinking and how it will come out. You can make up any kind of story you please. Do you understand? Well, then, here is the first picture. You have five minutes to make up a story. See how well you can do. (p. 4)

At times subjects may need these instructions repeated, in full or in part, particularly if the examiner is interested in obtaining a complete story with all the elements for each picture. In any case, it is noteworthy when subjects, once having grasped the task, omit certain elements either consistently or in response to certain cards.

After the initial instructions are presented, the examiner hands the first card of the selected series to the subject. The examiner then begins timing, recording the number of seconds that pass from the presentation of the card to the point at which the subject actually begins the true response. Some comments, exclamations, or halting verbalizations given by the subject may not be the beginning of the story, although they should be noted. The measure of time from card presentation to response is called the *response latency*, and is useful in gauging the subject's handling of the specific card. For example, very long response latencies may reflect a struggle with conflictual material. On the other hand, extremely short responses may suggest an impulsive or perhaps counter-phobic approach to the card material.

The examiner should record all of the subject's verbalizations, including spontaneous verbalizations, extra-test comments, utterings, laughter, etc., as well as the story response itself. In addition, it is extremely helpful to note specific behavioral and affective reactions such as fidgeting, facial expressions, sighs, gestures, etc., as these may reflect aspects of the subject's psychological response.

The examiner should interfere with a subject's responses as little as possible. However, at times it may be important to remind subjects about parts of the tasks being omitted, or to repeat something they miss. If the subject asks for more detailed instructions as to what to do, or seeks feedback or input from the examiner, it is best to respond openly but noncommitally, such as stating "You may make it anything you please." Discussion is to be avoided. Occasionally certain subjects, particularly children, may require encouragement, but this should be applied judiciously.

Following the administration of all cards, many examiners like to obtain further information from the subject about specific responses, a procedure often called the *inquiry*. This may be introduced by saying "I have a few more questions I'd like to ask," or alternatively by providing a more elaborate rationale concerning one's interest in the factors that enter into imaginal construction as Murray did. In any case, the inquiry should be accomplished in a way that minimizes evaluation apprehension. Typical foci of the inquiry are the subject's possible sources for the themes that emerged, associations to the cards or stories, or emotional reactions to particular stimuli. Other examiners have asked subjects to recall their most and least favorite cards or stories. This is especially useful if a day or more has passed since the actual administration. Finally the inquiry may be useful in "testing the limits" of certain responses. Thus the examiner can inquire about aspects of the pictures that may have been conspicuously omitted or distorted in the stories, or encourage elaborations to themes or stories that were particularly barren or sparse.

Murray's Theory and Its Relation to the TAT Interpretation: The assumptions associated with the projective hypothesis are given perhaps their most elegant expression in the personality theory of Murray (1938), whose constructs and formulations formed the basis through which the TAT was originally developed and interpreted. Murray articulated a dialectical theory of behavior that considers both the psychobiological and environmental determinants of human action. He provided a system that describes both how people are influenced by external forces and how they select and organize their own actions based on current needs and values.

The two central constructs in his psychology were those of *needs* and *press*, both of which the TAT was initially developed to assess. According to Murray, needs represent a force or energy that "organizes perception, apperception, intellectualization, connotation and action" (1938, p. 123). Needs play a role in the selection of those aspects of the world that are perceived and what meaning is given to them. Furthermore, they energize behavior in the direction of their satisfaction. Needs can be classified as either primary or biological (e.g., hunger, thirst, sex), or secondary or psychogenic (e.g., achievement, affliction, autonomy, dominance). Specific needs can be more or less dominant at any given time, or alternatively weak. They can also conflict, fuse, or become subsidiary to one another. Needs can also either arise spontaneously or be evoked by certain environmental circumstances. In any case, needs represent the most important internal determinants of behavior.

In contrast, press refers to the power of events in the environment to affect or influence a person. Murray described two kinds of press, which he designated as "Alpha" and "Beta." Alpha press is the influence on the person of objective or "real" external forces. Beta press concerns the subjective components of those forces, or pushes and pulls, that the individual perceives to be affecting him or her in the world. What is forceful and salient to one individual is not necessarily so for another.

Needs and press interact to form *thema*, dynamic combinations or "molor units" that reflect significant patterns of behavior (Maddi & Costa, 1972). Thema may be discreet or complex and can vary in importance. Fantasy productions will display various thema since here, in the subjects's verbal behavior, needs and press of the stimulus will combine to produce characteristic reactions.

This skeletal presentation of Murray's theory is introduced merely to illustrate how individuals' behavior (and TAT stories) can be conceptualized within a framework that includes consideration of needs, press, and thema. These bare bones, however, fail to capture the real body of the theory, which is indeed intricate and comprehensive. Nonetheless, it provides description of some of the major dimensions upon which a subject's TAT stories can be evaluated.

In interpreting a TAT protocol the initial task is to identify in each story the protagonist, who Murray called the *hero*. It is assumed that, in developing their fantasies, subjects identify with the hero and are therefore likely to project onto this figure needs, motives, beliefs, or emotions that are actually the subjects' own. At times subjects may identify with more than one figure, in which case attributes of other figures might be considered.

The next step is to analyze and quantify the needs that the hero expresses or exhibits. For this purpose Murray developed a list of 36 needs, both primary and secondary, that are rated by the examiner on a scale from 1-5 in terms of the intensity and centrality of their expression within the story. A similar procedure is used for rating press as revealed by the stories. Press includes such forces as physical dangers, interpersonal rejections, deaths, and other significant forces in the environment that may affect the hero.

Needs and press then must be put together in a meaningful way that corresponds to the consideration of thema and story outcomes. For instance, does the hero achieve success or failure? Does he or she do right or wrong? Does the hero engage in or flee from relationships? Does he or she fall into depression or turn to optimism in reaction to adversity? What interests or endeavors does the hero typically form in the force of needs or press?

From both these quantitative and qualitative considerations interpretation follows. Here, undoubtedly, the examiner's theoretical bias plays a significant role in the organization and integration of the data into some useful formulation, as well as the use to which that formulation will be put. Useful guidelines for using Murray's system are provided by several sources, the most up-to-date and comprehensive of which is offered by Stein (1981).

Although Murray's own "personological" theory undoubtedly spawned the development of the instrument and his scoring system, soon after its release a variety of researchers and clinicians used the TAT method as a way of studying their own specific interests or followed divergent pursuits. Some of these resulted in quantitative systems, others in qualitative ones, and many, like Murray's own, combined elements of both. In addition, some systems are oriented primarily toward the scoring or interpretation of the stories' content, while others focus on formal aspects (i.e., the manner in which the story is constructed or its form). Among some of the more noteworthy of these various approaches are those presented by Eron (1950); Dana (1955, 1982); McClelland et al. (1953); Veroff (1958); Arnold (1962); Cramer (1983); Bellak (1975); Bunin (1978); Rapaport, Gill, and

Schafer (1968); and Wyatt (1947). Some of these will receive further elaboration later in this review.

Practical Applications/Uses

Clinical use: Despite the fact that the clinical use of the TAT appears in many contexts to be essentially ad hoc and idiosyncratic, the vast literature pertaining to its interpretations contains a fairly consistent core of strategies and lore. Although not intended in any way to be exhaustive or authoritative, what follows is a distillation of some of these common themas of the interpretive literature. There is no replacement for direct contact with the empirical and clinical literat::re in the topic. For heuristic purposes, *formal* considerations, and interpretation of *content* will be examined separately here, although the two often overlap. Formal analyses are those that stem from the study of *how* a subject constructs or presents his or her responses; content analyses emerge from the study of *what* the subject provides (Holt, 1958).

TAT stories are, before all else, samples of the subject's verbal behavior. As such they can be used to assess aspects of the subject's language fluency, degree of concreteness versus abstractness, coherence of thought, and intellectual capacities. Assessing such formal aspects is often a useful starting point for interpretation.

There are three levels of possible responses to the card stimuli that can be used as gauges for the examinee's current functional capacities. The most primitive style of response is one of *enumeration,* in which the subject simply lists or names various elements or characters in the picture without elaborations or connections between them. A "story" is not developed. For instance, a subject might say, in response to Card 1, "A boy, a violin. Nothing else in the picture." Somewhat more complex is a *descriptive* style of response, which occurs when the subject describes the card and even what may be occurring, but does not complete a story or elaborate beyond what is explicitly presented. Elements may be linked together, but there is no attempt to move far beyond the stimulus characteristics per se. Finally, and most usually, subjects will offer an *interpretive* response to the card, incorporating the stimulus elements into a fantasy or story that extends well beyond the presented elements into a rich network of projections.

Adult subjects who, if not neurologically impaired, merely enumerate or describe the explicit elements of the cards may be markedly defensive or constricted, which prevents them from more freely responding to the evocative material at hand. Such a situation, although minimal in terms of interpretive possibilities, is helpful in determining the person's functional level. Intrepretive responses, on the other hand, are most common and more useful to the examiner because as they afford more complex dynamic interferences and interpretations.

Also noteworthy in formal approaches is the subject's level of fluency and productivity. Fluency can be related to aspects of intelligence, social background, and developmental level. Productivity is a useful variable in considering the energy and inner resources available to the test taker. Depressed subjects, or those who are markedly constricted or guarded for other reasons, often provide sparse or impoverished records. Finally, the degree to which stories have manifest internal coherence or consistency can be an important issue and help in the assessment of the integrity and control of thought processes.

Another level of formal investigation involves examining the degree to which the subject has given each of the requested elements of the story (i.e., has described the situation, what preceded and followed it, and the thoughts and feelings of the characters). According to Rapaport et at. (1968) the failure to provide specific elements may result from the fact that what comes to the subject's consciousness is conflictual and therefore suppressed, or perhaps repressed altogether. At any rate, the general issue of the way in which the subject complies with the task instruction is seen frequently as having dynamic significance.

Formal analyses have also been directed to more microscopic levels, as in examining linguistic characteristics such as number and type of verbs used relative to other elements (Henry, 1956; Wyatt, 1947). A related technique of considerable clinical interest was suggested by Hutt (1980) with reference to another projective test (MPT-R) in which stories are evaluated for the direction of forces depicted. A story is rated as *centifugal* when the hero acts upon his world and as *centripetal* when the hero is acted upon. Hutt reports evidence suggesting that this direction of forces construct can be useful for assessing adjustment levels.

Despite the fact that formal considerations bear upon interpretation, unquestionably the TAT is most often interpreted primarily in terms of the content of the responses. The central consideration of content scoring harks back to Murray's theory and its "hero" assumption. The hero is the protagonist of the subject's story and it is assumed that this is the character with whom the subject most clearly identifies. Accordingly, the hero's attributes, needs, strivings, and feelings are often interpreted as having significance in the storyteller's own life. Conversely, those thoughts, feelings, or actions that the hero avoids or denies may represent areas of conflict for the subject. For example, a depressed and potentially self-destructive client gave the following response to Card 3BM:

> Looks like . . . I can't tell if it's a girl or boy. Could be either. I guess it doesn't matter. This person just had a hard physical workout. I guess it's a her. She's just tired. No trauma happened or anything. She was sitting around a table with friends and she got real tired. She's not in a health danger or anything. These are her keys. Her friends drag her back to her room and put her to bed. She's O.K. the next day. No trauma. She's tired physically, not mentally.

Note particularly the repetitive denial of danger or trauma. However, later in the TAT series, in response to the blank card (16), the same subject told a story of a young man, traumatized at school, who takes his car down to the river:

> He sees the bridge, he's really down. He remembers that he's heard stories about people jumping off and killing themselves. He could never understand why they did that. Now he understands, he jumps and dies . . . he should have waited 'cause things always get better sometime. But he didn't wait, he died.

This rather dramatic case example illustrates one way in which the hero assumption operates. Impulses of the characters are assumed to be impulses of the storyteller. Additionally, impulses, actions, or emotions that are repeatedly denied or otherwise defended against are seen as conflict areas even if not directly or literally expressed. The verbal material is interpreted in accord with general principles of influence drawn from psychodynamic theory. Such interpretation needs to be tempered by an appropriate hypothesis-testing framework, such as that outlined by Deinhardt (1983).

A question that follows from these considerations is the problem of levels of prediction (Karon, 1981). For instance if the hero "thinks" about doing something versus actually doing something versus denying that something is done, does this suggest differing predictions about the subject's own propensities? Tomkins (1947) argued, for example, that story behavior predicts subject's behavior, character's thoughts predict subject's thoughts, and manifest defenses of the characters predict manifest defenses of the subject. Others have argued that all of these levels should be used only to index the subject's motives rather than to predict behavior. Research by Kagan and Leaser (1961) suggested that responses to earlier cards in the series are more highly correlated with overt behavior, and stories later in the series less so. Needless to say, predictions of behavior from the TAT are risky and should be backed up by convergent data from other methods. The TAT is most appropriate for looking at psychological processes that may or may not have direct behavioral correlates.

Using the hero assumption, one can form hypotheses by fully assessing the appropriate story characters. It might be important to ask, for example: How adequately does the hero deal with the situation at hand? Is he she active or passive? What coping mechanisms does he or she employ? What types of outcomes are expected and achieved? What is the nature of the interpersonal relations depicted? etc. Through such a procedure one tries to gain a description of the *lebenswelt* of the hero and, by implication, of the subject. For the most part the validity of this description derived by the interpreter will require outside confirmation or support.

In addition to the hero assumption, a second central aspect of content interpretation involves consideration of the stimulus pull of the cards. As previously noted each card has a very definite content upon which subjects elaborate. Some aspects of a story will then have close correspondence to the stimulus materials and others will reflect more subjective, interpretive elements. Bellak (1975) labels these subjective components the *apperceptive distortion*, which is the dynamically significant part of the protocol. The concept of "distortion" is not meant to suggest pathology, but rather merely a departure from the objectively given. The interpretive activity of sorting out the apperceptive distortion from the more directly stimulus-bound material was once described by Murray as "separating the wheat from the chaff," the wheat having the most value in evaluating the subject's inner processes. This sorting process on the part of the examiner requires great familiarity with the literature on card pull and personal experience with the test.

A number of excellent articles exist that pertain to clinical interpretation. Among the foremost are the psychoanalytic treatments of Rapaport, Gill, and Schafer (1968), the ego-analytic approach of Bellak (1975), and the personological approach by Stein (1981). These and other approaches to clinical interpretation undoubtedly have many pitfalls due to their ideographic assumptions and personalized style of application. As Rapaport et al. (1968) state:

These techniques are not hard and fast rules like those of scoring other tests, they are rather like viewpoints for looking upon the TAT stories that must become ingrained in the examiner, so that he can use them flexibly and judiciously (p. 490).

Research use: The TAT method has been used for a variety of research purposes. In these cases data collected through standard or only slightly modified procedures are subjected to analyses or ratings tailored to detect specific variables or dimensions that can be reliably assessed. Data pertaining to the reliability and validity of these analyses vary from case to case and system to system; thus no attempt will be made here to present such data. Rather, an overview of some fo the more prominent systems is presented.

McClelland and Atkinson have provided what is perhaps the most famous and well-researched method of scoring the TAT for empirical use. Together with Clark and Lowell they published a book in 1953 entitled *The Achievement Motive,* which outlined a theory and measurement strategy for the study of achievement motives and other dimensions of motivation. They developed a scoring system with excellent reliability, but which takes considerable training and experience to master. McClelland (1980) has recently presented an elegant argument for the validity of his approach, as well as theoretical justification for gauging validity issues on criteria more appropriate to projective (or, as he calls them "operant") techniques than those traditionally applied to structured, "respondent," measures.

May (1966) developed a formal approach to the TAT that he used to measure aspects of the subject's gender identity. This approach assesses what he termed the Deprivation-Enhancement pattern of the stories. Men tend to give stories that begin with enhancement (e.g., success, fame, happiness) and end with deprivation (e.g., disaster, failure, unhappiness), whereas the tendency of women is to develop stories that move in the opposite direction. He has a detailed manual used to score such patterns, which has good interrater reliability. A number of studies have had success in employing this approach to the study of gender identity in adult and child subjects.

Cramer (1983) has recently developed a manual for the assessment of defenses from TAT stories. Her scoring system reliably identifies three major categories of defenses—denial, projection, and identification. She has also demonstrated with her system that these three defenses show a definite developmental course, with denial being prominent in young children, projection more prominent in late childhood and early adolescence, and identification more characteristic in late adolescence. Gender differences are also apparent.

Sutton and Swensen (1983) have provided evidence that the TAT can be reliably scored for the subject's level of ego development using priniciples derived from Loevinger and Wessler's (1970) manual for scoring sentence completion tests. Concurrent validity for their technique with Loevinger's sentence completion technique is impressive.

Technical Aspects

These few examples of empirical uses for the TAT are not meant to be exhaustive, as numerous other scoring systems exist. They do, however, illustrate that the TAT method can be used for special purposes and can provide credible, sometimes impressive, results. It also should suggest that summary conclusions about *the* reliability or *the* validity of the TAT are necessarily overgeneralizations. One must speak more specifically about the properties of specific approaches. It also lends more credence to the view that the TAT is not a test but rather a method, one with considerable adaptability and generative capacities.

The data that emerge from the story production procedure are varied and intricate, and thus lend themselves to many analytic techniques. The usefulness of the data is thus equivalent to the validity of any given scoring system that the examiner chooses to apply, or alternatively to the skill of the examiner in interpreting the complex products of the TAT situation. Several of the existing scoring systems have demonstrable reliability and construct validity, while most interpretive methods and lore have not been adequately tested or researched.

Critique

The existing literature on the TAT is voluminous. However, comprehensive reviews appear periodically that can help the test user to orient to various TAT scoring, interpretive, or empirical uses. Some of the more authoritative reviews include Varble (1971), Vane (1981); Stein (1978; 1981); Dana (1982) and Deinhardt (1983). In addition, several excellent papers exist on projective theory and TAT theory in particular. These include Abt (1952), Rabin (1981), McClelland (1980), and Bellak (1975).

The proliferation of systems of approach to material elicited with the TAT method attests to its flexibility and richness. One of the TAT's major assets is that it can be subjected to so many constructs and techniques; however, this is also a significant liability in many respects. Practitioners interpreting the TAT are likely to use different systems, an idiosyncratic combination of systems, or no system at all. This is the bane of the psychometrician, and it also suggests that in common usage the interpretation of the TAT is based on strategies of unknown and untested reliability and validity, a potentially dangerous outcome. That this is a reality rather than speculation is attested to by the results of a recent survey (Wade & Baker, 1977) that revealed that 81.5% of projective test users employ "personalized" procedures for interpretation. The impact of this upon the effectiveness and value of these tests is presently unknown.

References

Abt, L. E. (1952). A theory of projective psychology. In L. E. Abt & L. Bellak (Eds.), *Projective psychology* (pp. 33-66). New York: Alfred A. Knopf.

Arnold, M. B. (1962). *Story sequence analysis.* New York: Columbia University Press.

Bellak, L. (1975). *The T.A.T., C.A.T. and S.A.T. in clinical use* (3rd ed.). New York: Grune & Stratton.

Blum, G. S. (1950). *The Blacky Pictures.* Cleveland: The Psychological Corporation.

Bunin, A. I. (1978). *Structural analysis of the TAT.* Unpublished manuscript, Florida State University, Talahasee.

Campus, N. (1976). A measure of needs to assess the stimulus characteristics of TAT cards. *Journal of Personality, 40,* 248-258.

Cohen, H., & Weil, G. R. (1975). *Tasks of emotional development.* Brookline, MA: TED Assoc.

Cramer, P. (1983, August). *Defense mechanisms: A developmental study.* Paper presented at the annual meeting of The American Psychological Association, Anaheim, CA.

Dana, R. H. (1955). Selection of abbreviated TAT sets. *Journal of Clinical Psychology, 11,* 401-403.

Dana, R. H. (1956). Selections of abbreviated TAT sets. *Journal of Clinical Psychology, 12,* 36-40.

Dana, R. H. (1982). *A human science model for personality assessment with projective techniques.* Springfield, IL: Charles C. Thomas.

Deinhardt, C. L. (1983). *Personality assessment and psychological interpretation.* Springfield, IL: Charles C. Thomas.

Entiwisle, D. R. (1972). To dispel fantasies about fantasy-based measures of achievement motivation. *Psychological Bulletin, 77,* 377-391.

Eron, L. D. (1950). A normative study of the Thematic Apperception Test. *Psychological Monographs, 69.*

Goldfried, M. R., & Zax, M. (1965). The stimulus value of the TAT. *Journal of projective Techniques, 29,* 46-58.

Henry, W. E. (1956). *The analysis of fantasy: The thematic apperception technique in the study of personality.* New York: John Wiley.

Holt, R. R. (1958). Formal aspects of the TAT: A neglected resource. *Journal of Projective Techniques, 22,* 163-172.

Hutt, M. L. (1980). *The Michigan Picture Test-Revised.* New York: Grune & Stratton.

Kagan, J., & Leaser, G. (1961). *Contemporary issues in Thematic Apperception methods.* Springfield, IL: Charles C. Thomas.

Karon, B. P. (1981). The Thematic Apperception Test (TAT). In A. I. Rabin (Ed.), *Assessment with projective techniques* (pp. 85-120). New York: Springer Publishing Co.

Loevinger, J., & Wessler, R. (1970). *Measuring ego development Vol. 1.* San Francisco: Jossey-Bass.

McClelland, D. C. (1980). Motive dispositions: The merits of operant and respondent measures. In L. Wheeler (Ed.), *Review of personality and social psychology* (pp. 10-41). Beverly Hills, CA: Sage Publications.

McClelland, D. C., Atkinson, J. W., Clark, R. A., & Lowell, E. L. (1953). *The achievement motive.* Englewood Cliffs, NJ: Prentice-Hall.

Maddi, S. R., & Costa, P. T. (1972). *Humanism in personology.* Chicago: Aldine Publishing Co.

May, R. (1966). Sex differences in fantasy patterns. *Journal of Projective Techniques and Personality Assessment, 30,* 576-586.

Morgan, C. D., & Murray, H. A. (1935). A method for investigating phantasies: The Thematic Apperception Test. *Archives Neurology and Psychiatry, 34,* 289-306.

Murray, H. A. (1938). *Explorations in personality.* New York: Oxford University Press.

Murray, H. A. (1943). *Thematic Apperception Test-Manual.* Cambridge: Harvard University.

Murstein, B. I. (1963). *Theory and research in projective techniques (emphasizing the TAT).* New York: John Wiley.

Perterson, C. A., & Schilling, K. M. (1983). Card pull in projective testing. *Journal of Personality Assessment, 47,* 265-275.

Rabin, A. I. (Ed.) (1981). *Assessment with projective techniques: A concise introduction.* New York: Springer Publishing Company.

Rapaport, D., Gill, M. M., & Schafer, R. (1968). *Diagnostic psychological testing.* New York: International Universities Press.

Rosenzweig, S. (1976). *Manual for the Rosenzweig Picture-Frustration Study, Adolescent Form.* St. Louis, MO: Roma House.

Ryan, R. M. (1982). Control and information in the intrapersonal sphere: An extension of cognitive evaluation theory. *Journal of Personality and Social Psychology, 43,* 450-461.

Skinner, B. F. (1957). *Verbal behavior.* New York: Appleton-Century-Crofts.

Stein, M. I. (1978). The Thematic Apperception Test and related methods. In B. B. Wolman

(Ed.), *Clinical diagnosis of mental disorders: A handbook* (pp. 179-236). New York: Plenum Publishing Corp.

Stein, M. I. (1981). *Thematic Apperception Test* (2nd ed.). Springfield, IL: Charles C. Thomas.

Sutton, P. M., & Swensen, C. H. (1983). The reliability and concurrent validity of alternative methods for assessing ego development. *Journal of Personality Assessment, 47,* 468-475.

Symonds, P. M. (1948). *Symonds Picture-Story Test.* New York: Columbia University, Bureau of Publications.

Tomkins, S. S. (1947). *The Thematic Apperception Test.* New York: Grune & Stratton.

Tomkins, S. S., & Miller, J. B. (1957). *The Tomkins-Horn Picture Arrangement Test.* New York: Springer Publishing Company.

Vane, J. R. (1981). The Thematic Apperception Test: A review. *Clinical Psychology Review, 1,* 319-336.

Varble, D. L. (1971). Current status of The Thematic Apperception Test. In McReynolds (Ed.), *Advances in psychological assessment* (pp. 216-235). Palo Alto, CA: Science & Behavior Books.

Veroff, J. (1958). A scoring manual for the power motive. In J. W. Atkinson (Ed.), *Motives of fantasy, action and society.* Princeton, NJ: VanNostrand.

Wade, T. C., & Baker, T. B. (1977). Opinions and use of psychological tests. *American Psychologist, 32,* 874-882.

Wade, T. C., Baker, T. B., Morton, T. L., & Baker, L. J. (1978). The status of psychological testing in clinical psychology: Relationships between test use and professional activities and orientation. *Journal of Personality Assessment, 42,* 3-10.

Wyatt, F. (1947). The scoring and analysis of The Thematic Apperception Test. *Journal of Psychology, 24,* 319-330.

Christopher Hertzog, Ph.D.
*Assistant Professor of Human Development, Department of
Individual and Family Studies, Pennsylvania State University,
University Park, Pennsylvania.*

THURSTONE TEMPERAMENT SCHEDULE

*L. L. Thurstone and Thelma G. Thurstone. Chicago, Illinois:
Science Research Associates, Inc.*

Introduction

The Thurstone Temperament Schedule (TTS) is an instrument assessing multiple dimensions of personality hypothesized to exist in normal, well adjusted individuals. It does not attempt to assess personality attributes associated with psychosis or neurosis (e.g., degree of conflict, insecurity, or maladjustment); instead, it seeks to assess normative styles of behavior or temperament (e.g., activity, vigor, impulsivity).

The Thurstone Temperament Schedule, first published in 1950, was developed by L. L. Thurstone, who is perhaps best known for his pioneering work in psychometric intelligence, and Thelma G. Thurstone. The instrument, developed during L. L. Thurstone's tenure as a professor of psychology at the University of Chicago, grew out of an older personality instrument developed by J. P. Guilford in the early 1930s (Guildford & Guilford, 1936, 1939a, 1939b). A complete description of the dimensions of personality studied may be found in Thurstone (1951). By reanalyzing a correlation matrix of the thirteen Guilford factors originally collected by Lovel (1945) the TTS's authors identified seven factors that form the basis of the Thurstone Temperament Schedule. The Guilford items that attempted to assess abnormal or psychiatric personality attributes were omitted from the item pool and supplemented by personality items obtained from other instruments available in the late 1940s. A 320-item pool was then administered to 198 adults. These data were used to identify the 20 most discriminating items for each of the seven factors resulting in the final 140 item schedule.

Subsequent samples used college freshmen (694 men, 161 women), high-school students (419 men, 504 women), and adult office workers (540 men, 496 women) from the Chicago area to establish gender-segregated norms for the seven factors. A second edition was published in 1953 (Thurstone & Thurstone, 1953); separate percentile norms for the high-school, college, and office-worker populations and extensive reliability and validity analyses are reported in the 1953 manual, but no differences between editions are reported or discussed. And no other forms of the test are available.

The 140 items consist of short questions about behavioral temperament. Respondents indicate whether a sentence accurately describes their own behaviors by checking one of three boxes: "yes," "no," or"?" (undecided). Items are spaced appropriately on the form for ease of reading and appear to minimize the chance of mismatching item descriptors with responses. The schedule is self-administered and can easily be used in a group testing format.

The seven areas of temperament or personality examined by the TTS are as follows:

Active: The tendency to work or move rapidly;

Vigorous: The degree of energy and preference for physical activity;

Impulsive: The tendency to act or decide quickly;

Dominant: Tendency to exert leadership and be involved in decision process;

Stable: Disposed toward even-tempered demeanor;

Sociable: The tendency to be cooperative, agreeable, and favorably disposed toward social situations; and

Reflective: Degree to which the individual prefers meditative, reflective, and abstract thinking.

Some of these factors are highly intercorrelated. For example, all factorial validity studies of the TTS reported a correlation of more than .5 between Sociable and Dominant.

Practical Applications/Uses

The primary use of the TTS designated by the publisher is appraisal and selection (e.g., by personnel officers). As noted by other reviewers of the instrument (e.g., Eysenck, 1953), the TTS has limitations for this purpose, given its modest reliability (see below) and its unknown relationship to other personality instruments more commonly used today for personality assessment. A similar problem would be encountered in using the TTS for personality research.

Theoretically, the TTS, designed to be a measure of personality attributes in normal samples, would be appropriate for any application measuring personality. In practice, however, the test is dated and has not achieved widespread use. The seven factors, appear to be similar to the personality dimensions tapped by the more recent 16PF and the revised Guilford-Zimmerman instruments, and in the domain of personality both Cattell's 16 PF and the revised Guilford-Zimmerman instrument are more apt to be used to measure nonpathological personality dimensions. The test has not been used for other purposes, such as assessing vocational preferences or making clinical judgements, either. Clinicians would probably employ the MMPI in mental health situations, but the instrument might be more useful to researchers than psychologists or educators in the field.

The schedule was developed using data from high-school and college samples in the Chicago area. Some of the validation studies involved use of young and middle-aged workers. The instrument does appear to be appropriate for use in young adult and adolescent populations, but its validity in specialized subpopulations (e.g., the elderly) is unknown.

The instrument is self-administered without time limits and is reported to take between 15-20 minutes to complete the 140 items. More time would clearly be required in special populations (e.g., the elderly). Directions are brief and readily understood, making the test easily adaptable to group assessment sessions. However, the test booklets are not reusable.

The answers are recorded directly onto a carbon, "self-scoring" pad that is simple to use. Responses in a particular direction (labeled, surprisingly, as "correct" in the examiner's manual) will show up on the carboned surface. The score for each subscale is obtained by totalling the number of responses for each scale. Interpretation of the TTS requires a high degree of familiarity with test theory and assessment of individual test profiles. Indeed, SRA indicates that use of the test is restricted to persons obtaining application approval, based on the criterion of prior training in personality assessment. Interpretation of the scores is made on the basis of comparing objective scores to adult norms. Extensive adult norms (tabulated separately by gender) are in the examiner manual. The scoring sheet contains a profile of adult norms that can immediately be used to evaluate the response profile. However, an open question is whether these norms, developed in the early 1950s, apply today.

Technical Aspects

The manual is exemplary in providing information on the validity and reliability of the schedule, but, unfortunately, the reliability is modest for certain subscales. Reliabilities were calculated both by the split-half and test-retest approaches. The most reliable subscale, Dominant, has a reliability of approximately .8 (averaged over a number of samples). Split-half methods yield substantially lower reliability estimates than the test-retest method for the Active, Vigorous, and Impulsive scales (e.g., Active has a median split-half reliability, across samples, of .48, but a test-retest coefficient of .78 in an adult male sample). These findings call into question the factorial homogeneity of the items for these scales, although homogeneity per se is not a required feature of personality scales. The Stable dimension has a reliability in the low .6 range, irrespective of method. It appears that the reliability of most of the subscales falls somewhere in the .7 range.

Validation studies include reports of high point-biserial correlations of the different subscales with employer ratings (high/low) of these dimensions, suggesting convergence validity of the TTS with an alternative measure of employee personality. Several validation studies in employment settings are reported in the manual. The degree of predictive validity of the TTS for employee performance varied markedly across these studies. In one study of office workers, the TTS yielded poor predictive validity as acknowledged by the tests' authors. "The failure of the *schedule* [TTS] scores to discriminate between good and poor office workers seems to indicate that the temperament characteristics leading to success or failure vary from job to job" (Thurstone & Thurstone, 1953, p. 11). In other studies more encouraging results were found with the Vigorous and Dominant subscales modestly predicting managerial performance in several settings. However, on balance the predictive validity of the TTS for personnel performance is unimpressive.

Critique

The Thurstone Temperament Schedule is an instrument that is dated in light of more recent advances in the measurement of psychometric personality. The examiner's manual, for example, provides extensive information on the intercorrelation of the TTS with the early Guilford scales and with psychometric measures of intelligence. Today, one would prefer to see correlations of the TTS with the newer measures of personality (e.g., the 16PF, the Guilford-Zimmerman, the Eysenck scales) before opting for its use. The reliability of many of the scales is modest, and the adult norms may be to an unknown degree invalid due to cohort differences in personality. In the 4th and 5th *Mental Measurements Yearbooks* the TTS was criticized on various grounds. Eysenck (1953), for example, questioned the high correlations among the temperament subscales. This criticism seems less telling today, given more recent work showing that second-order personality factors (e.g., neuroticism, extroversion) have been identified in similar personality batteries. All the reviews however, agreed on the limited utility of the TTS in the absence of better validity studies on its practical applications. This criticism is even more appropos today in light of the limited use the TTS has received. This reviewer can see no justification for use of the TTS in lieu of other multidimensional personality scales that have been more widely validated and used in recent times.

References

Eysenck, H. J. (1953). [Review of Thurstone Temperament Schedule.] In O. K. Buros (Ed.), *The fourth mental measurements yearbook* (93). Highland Park, NJ: The Grypon Press.

Guilford, J. P., & Guilford, R. B. (1936). Personality factors S, E, and M and their measurements. *Journal of Psychology, 2,* 107-127.

Guilford, J. P., & Guilford, R. B. (1939a). Personality factors D, T, R, and A. *Journal of Abnormal and Social Psychology, 34,* 21-36.

Guilford, J. P., & Guilford, R. B. (1939b). Personality factors N and GD. *Journal of Abnormal and Social Psychology, 34,* 239-248.

Harsh, C. M. (1953). [Review of Thurstone Temperament Schedule.] In O. K. Buros (Ed.), *The fourth mental measurements yearbook* (93). Highland Park, NJ: The Gryphon Press.

Lovell, C. (1945). A study of factor structure of thirteen personality variables. *Educational and Psychological Measurement, 5,* 335-350.

Ryans, G. G. (1953). [Review of Thurstone Temperament Schedule.] In O. K. Buros (Ed.), *The fourth mental measurements yearbook* (93). Highland Park, NJ: The Gryphon Press.

Thurstone, L. L. (1951). The dimensions of temperament. *Psychometrika, 16,* 11-20.

Thurstone, L. L., & Thurstone, T. G. (1953). *Examiner manual for the Thurstone Temperament Schedule* (2nd ed.). Chicago: Science Research Associates.

Van Steenberg, N. J. (1959). [Review of Thurstone Temperament Schedule.] In O. K. Buros (Ed.), *The fifth mental measurements yearbook* (118). Highland Park, NJ: The Gryphon Press.

Forrest G. Umberger, Ph.D.
Associate Professor of Communication Disorders, Department of Special Education, Georgia State University, Atlanta, Georgia.

THE WESTERN APHASIA BATTERY

Andrew Kertesz. New York, New York: Grune & Stratton, Inc.

Introduction

The Western Aphasia Battery (WAB) is a test of language functioning designed for research and clinical use. The instrument assesses seven areas of language functioning: content, fluency, auditory comprehension, repetition and naming, reading, writing, and calculation. The WAB also tests nonverbal skills such as drawing, block design, and praxis (testing skilled or practiced movements).

Employing taxonomic principles of classification, patients can be numerically classified according to their performance on the subtests into the following aphasia categories: Global, Motor (Brocha's), Isolation, Sensory (Wernicke's), Transcortical Motor, Transcortical Sensory, Conduction, and Anomic. Classification serves as a baseline for research, diagnosis, and prognosis.

Spontaneous speech, comprehension, repetition, and naming comprise the oral language subtests and are used to determine the severity and type of aphasia. The summary of the oral language subtest scores provides an Aphasia Quotient (AQ), which is a measurement of the severity of language impairment. Additional tests—reading, writing, praxis, drawing, block design, calculation, and Raven's Progressive Matrices—can be scored to provide a Performance Quotient (PQ). The AQ combined with the PQ provides a Cortical Quotient (CQ), which indicates more than language functioning because it includes other aspects of higher cortical functioning, such as constructional tasks.

The test is easily administered with some training, and most aphasic adults can complete the oral portion in one hour. The administration can be split into two sessions if necessary.

The author of the WAB, Andrew Kertesz, M.D., holds a professorship in the Department of Clinical Neurological Sciences at the University of Western Ontario and heads the Department of Clinical Neurological Sciences at St. Joseph's Hospital in London, Canada.

In an effort to reliably quantify the classification of certain groups of aphasic patients observed in clinical practice, Kertesz and Poole (1974) drew from their extensive experience with aphasic phenomena and from reviews of a number of existing aphasia examinations to report on a taxonomic standardization of the test. In this standardization the results of only the oral language subtests were reported for 150 patients and 59 controls. The first standardization appeared again in 1979 (Kertesz) and included the additional subtests on reading, writing, praxis, and construction. The same publication contained the second standardization of the

WAB, employing 215 aphasics and 63 controls. The WAB was published for clinical and research purposes in 1982 (Kertesz).

The physical contents of the WAB include a test manual, test booklets, and fifty-seven 8"x5" cards with pictured objects, forms, letters, numbers, colors, words, sentence completion tasks, written commands, and calculation problems. Materials for test administration that are not supplied include 20 test objects (e.g., screwdriver, matches, comb, etc.), a stopwatch, 4 Koh's blocks from the Weschler Adult Intelligence Scale (WAIS), and the Raven's Coloured Progressive Matrices test. Although these last two items are administered in conjunction with the test, they must be obtained separately.

The Raven's Coloured Progressive Matrices consist of three sets of 12 problems, each of which has 6 figures from which a selection can easily be made. This test can be given without verbal instructions and assesses the degree to which a person can think clearly or the level to which their intellectual functions have deteriorated.

Koh's blocks are employed by requiring the subject to arrange them to match four predetermined patterns. This task is less dependent on logical reasoning and more on perception of spatial orientation.

The test manual contains an introduction to the test, including a table listing the criteria for taxonomic classification. Standardization procedures are provided with correlation coefficients for the subtests of the test's old and new versions. The remainder of the manual contains instructions for test-scoring and calculation of the Aphasia Quotient.

The test booklet consists of space for recording patient data and findings such as handedness, presence and degree of hemiplegia, hemianopsia, sensory loss and investigations (e.g., E.E.G., C.T. Scan, etc.); specific instructions for administering and scoring the subtests; and a summary score sheet where individual subtest scores are transferred and totaled to derive the Aphasia and Cortical Quotients. The materials and tasks are designed to allow the examiner to make a judgment on how well an aphasic patient performs on the following parameters: spontaneous speech, auditory verbal comprehension, repetition, naming, reading, writing, apraxia, and constructional visuospatial and calculation tasks.

The examiner's participation in this battery requires considerable involvement not only in quantifying responses, but in some instances making professional judgments as to the quality of the responses. Some of the examiner's tasks include presenting objects in particular order or sequence, providing auditory stimuli, and eliciting responses from the patient with tasks of increasing length and complexity. The examiner is encouraged to audiotape portions of the examination in order to make judgments on fluency and preserve sections for future analysis.

Test responses are recorded in a booklet by the examiner. Scoring for each of the test sections vary and include recording speech by note-taking and audio-taping, checking appropriate boxes, checking off instructions followed, filling in responses to sentence completion tasks, and recording yes-no responses. Scoring directions are given for all modes of responding whether the judgment is on a qualitative or quantitative basis. Also included is a score sheet where all the subtest scores can be assembled under the following headings: Spontaneous Speech, Comprehension, Repetition, Naming, Reading and Writing, Praxis, and

Construction. Aphasia and Cortical Quotients are easily obtained by adding and dividing the scores as instructed.

Practical Applications/Uses

The WAB is intended to measure the clinical differences found in aphasics, classify this population according to taxonomic principles, evaluate the main clinical aspects of language function and nonverbal skills; and assess the patients' ability to think clearly or the degree to which their intellectual functions have deteriorated.

The test would be most useful to speech-language pathologists and professionals dealing primarily with the evaluation of language deficits encountered in patients with aphasia. The taxonomic classification would allow the clinician to base therapy goals and activities on known characteristics of behavior and recovery associated with each classification. Test-retest results would provide information related to the recovery process and therapy effectiveness.

According to Kertesz and Poole (1974), research is providing evidence for distinct localization of the lesions in each of the subgroups, suggesting that the taxonomic classification of the WAB could, at some future time, be a diagnostic tool for the neurologist.

Most aphasic patients are evaluated in the hospital, rehabilitation center, or nursing home when they show evidence of awareness of their surroundings. At this time the patient is usually able to sit up and the test can be administered, preferably, with the patient sitting across from the examiner at a table. However, the test can be administered at bedside.

In most cases the examiner will be a speech-language pathologist with training and experience in evaluating and treating speech and language disorders related to aphasia; however, other professionals interested in assessing the language capabilities of aphasics may have sufficient experience to administer the test. In either case the examiner must be familiar with the phenomena associated with aphasia and how deficits in various components of language will be manifested.

The test's use is to provide a practical classification of the patient according to a taxonomic table (Kertesz, 1979). The Aphasia Quotient is useful in distinguishing between aphasic and nonaphasic, brain-damaged patients. The patient most likely to be evaluated on the instrument will be one who has had a cerebral insult related to ischemia, trauma, or hemorrhage resulting in suspected language impairment or aphasia. However, cognitive functioning measures of this test can also be used for nonaphasic, brain-damaged populations (e.g., for severe deficits in which IQ testing is inappropriate).

The WAB is administered individually. Test administration procedures and scoring criteria are clearly delineated and defined in the test manual and booklet; with some practice and experience the test is very manageable and not difficult to administer. The oral language subtest can be completed in an hour and can be given in sections on consecutive days. The entire battery may take longer than one session depending on the patient's endurance level.

The test is divided into 8 sections and the sequence can be altered to fit the individual needs of the patient. The oral language section is an independent unit and provides the AQ. Those subtests measuring various functions of cognition are optional and are not included in calculating the AQ.

Scoring instructions accompany each subtest in the test booklet and scoring is carried out by the examiner during the test administration. The examiner scores the patient's performance numerically on a variety of tasks according to a pre-determined scoring criteria. The score for a given item may reflect the completeness or quality of the task, degree of assistance required by the patient, the number of items identified, or simply the indication of yes or no.

Subtest scores are totaled and divided by predetermined numbers to derive the AQ, CQ, or aphasia classification according to the results of the four subtests: Fluency, Comprehension, Repetition, and Naming.

Extreme care must be taken in scoring fluency in the Spontaneous Speech section of the oral language subtests in order to differentiate nonfluent from fluent aphasics. Scoring this section requires experience in recognizing and differentiating aphasic speech production errors. Although the scoring may be considered quantifiable, it requires subjective judgments from speech recorded on paper and tape.

Although numerical scores are assigned to specific behaviors, clinical judgment is required in many instances in the determination of a score. For example, ". . . fluent recurrent utterances or mumbling, very low volume jargon" requires the examiner to make a judgment as to what is considered a ". . . very low volume jargon."

The interpretation of the test results is not difficult but does require a knowledge and understanding of language, particularly as it is manifested in various forms of aphasia and brain damage without accompanying aphasia. The individual routinely trained and most likely to treat and evaluate aphasic language disorders with a battery of this type would be a speech-language pathologist although disciplines closely associated with treating aphasics could certainly prepare themselves to give the battery.

Technical Aspects

Extensive standardization was carried out on the previous version (1977) of the WAB (Kertesz, 1979, Shewan & Kertesz, 1980). For this reason the present version (1982) was compared to the earlier test. No substantial differences were found between the new version and the previously standardized version of the test. Therefore the present review of the reliability and validity characteristics of the WAB will be based on the most recent available report (Shewan & Kertesz, 1980).

The standardization population consisted of a sample of 150 aphasic adults and three groups of control subjects. The control sample was made up of 21 nonbrain-damaged, neurological patients with spinal cord disease, peripheral neuropathy, tics, etc., 17 nondominant hemispheric-lesion patients, and 21 diffusely brain-damaged, subcortically damaged, or dominant-hemisphere-damaged, but none exhibiting clinically evident aphasia. The criteria for selecting the adult aphasics included the ". . . presence of paraphasia, word-finding difficulty, and comprehension disturbance with a focal central-nervous-system lesion in the absence of confusion, dementia, or psychosis" (Shewan & Kertesz, 1980, p. 310).

The aphasic and control groups were basically comparable for age, number of years of education, language backgrounds, and general socioeconomic factors. Intellectual functioning for both samples was judged to be the same as measured by the Raven's Coloured Progressive Matrices. Male and female subjects were represented in both groups with the majority of subjects being male.

Internal consistency refers to the consistency of results obtained throughout a single test administration. The subject sample consisted of 140 aphasic subjects who had received the complete WAB. A coefficient of 0.905 using a random-half correlation procedure indicates high internal consistency.

The WAB contains a number of components that are combined to yield a composite score. To determine if the composite score reflects each of the components, Bentler's (1972) coefficient theta (Θ) was administered yielding a coefficient of 0.974 indicating high internal consistency.

Correlations on the subtests were satisfactory and reflected the relationships expected between related language behaviors and activities that are less dependent on language.

Test-retest reliability refers to the predictive value of a test from one administration to the next. Stability of the WAB test score was obtained using 38 aphasic subjects who were stable at the initial testing. Pearson product-moment correlation coefficients for each of the subtests contributing to and included the AQ were above 0.880 and were significant at the 0.001 level. The remainder of the subtests with the exception of praxis were at or above the 0.900 level. These results provide strong evidence that the WAB is stable over time. Individual subtests were also examined for mean change and revealed less than 10% variation.

The consistency of a judge's rating of the same performance on two different occasions is particularly important on the WAB inasmuch as the scoring includes many judgments that extend beyond a simple plus-minus dichotomy. To check intrajudge reliability ten videotaped administrations of the WAB were viewed and scored by three judges on two occasions. Correlations for each judge were in the 0.9 range and significant at the 0.001 level of confidence.

To assess the level of agreement among judges evaluating the same test administration, eight judges scored videotaped WAB test administrations to 10 aphasic patients. Pearson product-moment correlation coefficients for all subtests were above 0.900 for all eight judges indicating good interjudge reliability.

Face validity is simply a judgment as to whether the content of the test is relevant to its stated purpose (Freeman, 1962). The WAB tests all language modalities that other tests of aphasia assess and therefore satisfies face validity.

Inasmuch as the WAB is a modification of the Boston Diagnostic Aphasia Examination (BDAE), many of the items are similar to those of the BDAE. Subsequently many of the areas tested in the WAB are similar to the test items in many of the current batteries. One way to assess whether the WAB measures the aphasic patient's communicative ability would be to see how well it correlates with the recently developed Communicative Activity in Daily Living (Holland, 1977). The BDAE correlates at the 0.84 level with the Communicative Activity in Daily Living instrument, and although a similar correlation has not been conducted with the WAB, we can probably assume that the WAB will correlate positively as well because it is similar in many ways to the BDAE. For these reasons it appears that the WAB meets subjective criteria for content validity.

To determine the degree to which the WAB measures the construct it claims to measure 15 patients, who had been given the WAB and the Neurosensory Center Comprehensive Examination for Aphasia (NCCEA), were identified. Pearson product-moment correlation coefficients were computed for corresponding sub-tests from both batteries. The resulting correlations ranged from 0.817 to 0.919 and were significant at the 0.01 level.

Construct validity was also checked by factor analysis (Kertesz & Phipps, 1977) and by verifying that the test does differentiate between normal and aphasic performances (Shewan & Kertesz, 1980).

Critique

The WAB is not just another aphasia battery among many. It is a unique instrument that will provide useful information to the clinician and researcher. It is unique in that it takes a taxonomic approach to aphasia classification and by doing so provides a differential diagnosis relevant to initiating and planning a language intervention program based on the known major differences between classifications of aphasia. It also provides additional information regarding the patient's cognitive and intellectual functioning often neglected by other tests.

The test can be given in a relatively short period of time or broken into sections and administered over a number of days. Although some expertise in speech and language pathology is required, the test does not require additional extensive training to master the administration procedures. It is easy to score with some practice.

Researchers and clinicians who are interested in neuroanatomical correlations and want a more objective measure to replace arbitrary clinical impressions will find the WAB to be one of the more useful instruments available.

References

This list includes text citations as well as a suggested additional reading.

Bentler, P. M. (1972). A lower-bound method for the dimension-free measurement of internal consistency. *Social Sciences Research, 1,* 343-357.

Freeman, F. S. (1962). *Theory and practice of psychological testing* (3rd ed.). New York: Holt, Rinehart and Winston.

Gray, L., Hoyt, P., Hogil, S., & Lefkowitz, N. (1977). A comparison of clinical tests of yes/no questions in aphasia. *Clinical Aphasiology Conference Proceedings* (pp. 265-269).

Kertesz, A. (1979). *Aphasia and associated disorders: Taxonomy, localization and recovery.* New York: Grune & Stratton Inc.

Kertesz, A. (1982). *Western Aphasia Battery.* New York: Grune & Stratton, Inc.

Kertesz, A., & Phipps, J. B. (1977). Numerical taxonomy of aphasia. *Brain Language, 4,* 1-10.

Kertesz, A., & Phipps, J. (1980). The numerical taxonomy of acute and chronic aphasic syndromes. *Psychological Research, 41,* 179-198.

Kertesz, A., & Poole, E. (1974). The aphasia quotient: The taxonomic approach to measurement of aphasic disability. *Canadian Journal of Neurological Sciences, 1,* 7-16.

Sanders, S. B., & Davis, G. A. (1978). A comparison of the Porch Index of Communicative

Ability and the Western Aphasia Battery. *Clinical Aphasiology Conference Proceedings* (pp. 117-126).

Shewan, C. M., & Kertesz, A. (1980). Reliability and validity characteristics of the Western Aphasia Battery (WAB). *Journal of Speech and Hearing Disorders, 45,* 308-324.

Zaidel, E. (1981). Reading by the disconnected right hemisphere: An aphasiological prospective. In Y. Zotterman (Ed.), *WennerGren Symposium on Dyslexia* London: Plenum Press.

Ronald R. Holden, Ph.D.

Assistant Professor of Psychology, Queen's University, Kingston, Canada.

WESTERN PERSONALITY INVENTORY

Morse P. Manson. Los Angeles, California: Western Psychological Services.

Introduction

The Western Personality Inventory (Manson, 1963) is a structured, self-report, yes-no, psychological test designed to diagnose the presence and degree of alcoholism in adults. However, rather than being a single psychological instrument, the Western Personality Inventory is actually composed of two, much older, formerly separate tests; the Manson Evaluation developed in 1948, and the Alcadd Test constructed in 1949.

More specifically, the Manson Evaluation was introduced by Dr. Morse P. Manson as a brief, objective, paper-and-pencil test to be used 1) to screen for individuals who were formerly alcoholic, 2) to identify nonalcoholics who demonstrate personality traits that are characteristically similar to alcoholics, and 3) to explore personality areas associated with alcoholism. The focus of this test is on personality characteristics associated with alcoholism, rather than actual drinking behavior, per se. Originally, the Manson Evaluation had its roots in clinical observation (Manson, 1948). Approximately 1,800 characteristics, symptoms, descriptions, and manifestations related to behavior, personality, attitudes, preferences, health, development, and other relevant areas served as a starting point. Interviews with alcoholics from a variety of settings, social case histories, other personality tests, and relevant published literature then served as sources for the production of test items. Initially, 470 test items were generated and compiled into a preliminary inventory that was administered to a sample of 283 subjects composed of both alcoholics (N = 157) and nonalcoholics (N = 126). The 114 items that best discriminated between alcoholics and nonalcoholics were retained. Then, using a new sample composed of 268 alcoholics and 303 nonalcoholics, further item selection procedures reduced the pool of 114 items to a final instrument consisting of 72 yes-no questions.

Although an overall total score is generated by the Manson Evaluation, Manson decided that subsets of items should be grouped together because they probed common personality traits. Therefore, based on subjective analysis, seven subscales were developed for this test. These seven subscales assess three psychoneurotic traits (Anxiety, Depressive Fluctuations, and Emotional Sensitivity) and four psychopathic characteristics (Resentfulness, Incompleteness, Aloneness, and Interpersonal Relations).

Normative data for 571 cases are available in the 1963 manual. Norms are

826

provided separately for alcoholics and nonalcoholics and for males and females.

The second part of the Western Personality is the Alcadd Test, also developed by Dr. Morse P. Manson (1949c). This test is also a short, objective, self-report instrument and is designed 1) to quantify alcoholic addiction, 2) to identify specific areas of dysfunctioning in alcoholics, and 3) to offer insight concerning the psychodynamics of alcohol addiction. This part of the Western Personality Inventory differs from the Manson Evaluation in that the Alcadd Test contains items that directly refer to drinking and drinking behaviors. The origins of the Alcadd Test are in clinical and experimental experience. Observations of alcoholics in a variety of settings led to the formulation of a preliminary questionnaire composed of 160 test items. This initial inventory was administered to a sample comprised of 123 alcoholics, 119 social drinkers, and 40 abstainers. Based on the ability of test items to discriminate between nonalcoholics (i.e., social drinkers plus abstainers) and alcoholics, the pool of 160 test items was reduced to 60 yes-no questions. It should be noted, however, that although only 60 items are scored, 65 items appear on the test.

As well as a total scale for the Alcadd Test, Manson subjectively grouped together items measuring common characteristics. Therefore, the Alcadd Test also yields scores on five "traits" often found in alcoholics; Regularity of Drinking, Preference for Drinking over other Activities, Lack of Controlled Drinking, Rationalization of Drinking, and Excessive Emotionality.

The 1963 manual supplies normative data for 282 cases. These data are presented separately for alcoholics, social drinkers, and abstainers, and for males and females.

Practical Applications/Uses

The Western Personality Inventory comprises 137 yes-no questions. Its primary purpose is to assist in the identification of alcoholics or potential alcoholics prior to employment, training, military service, or hospitalization. Toward this goal, the Western Personality Inventory is designed to assess *both* alcohol-related personality dimensions and actual drinking behavior.

The entire inventory is available as a hand-scorable six-page questionnaire on which test items are presented. The test can be self-administered, although the examiner may read the test instructions to ensure understanding. No indication should be given by the examiner as to the purpose or use of the test. This test is designed to be used with adults and the level of reading difficulty does not appear to be problematic. The test manual consists of four pages: two primarily devoted to the Manson Evaluation and two dealing with the Alcadd Test.

The Western Personality Inventory is intended to be useful to individuals working with alcoholics or potential alcoholics. The entire test can be completed in 15 to 35 minutes. Administration of the inventory can involve either group or individual testing. The manual does not make explicit the qualifications of the test examiner; however, the straightforwardness of administration should allow any responsible individual to be an appropriate proctor. The scoring key for the test is provided in the manual. Instructions for scoring are easily learned and, once mastered, test scoring requires approximately six minutes. Because of the simplicity of the scoring system, no computerized scoring is offered. Interpretation of test scores is in comparison to the original norms for the Manson Evaluation and the Alcadd Test. Interpretation of test results would best be carried out by a professional (e.g., a psychologist) with training in testing. Although total scores on the main subcomponents (i.e., the Manson Evaluation and the Alcadd Test) of the Western Personality Inventory are directly interpreted with respect to critical scores derived from normative alcoholic and nonalcoholic groups, trait scores are interpreted by "glancing" at profile similarities between an individual's psychograph and the profiles of alcoholic and nonalcoholic normative groups.

Technical Aspects

The psychometric characteristics of the Western Personality Inventory have not been studied thoroughly. For the total scale on the Manson Evaluation, the test manual reports substantial Spearman-Brown corrected, split-half reliabilities (i.e., internal consistencies) of .94 for both males and females. Equally impressive total scale reliabilities on the Alcadd Test are .92 and .96 for males and females, respectively. It should be noted, however, that these reported reliabilities may be spuriously high because they are calculated using the same subjects that were used to select test items. Furthermore, these reliabilities may or may not be inflated by response styles related to social desirability and acquiescence. For example, on the entire Western Personality Inventory, only 21 of the 132 scored items are keyed "no." All other items are keyed "yes," thus yielding an inventory that in terms of keying is unbalanced. Consequently, response styles related to "yea-saying," "nay-saying," or response perseveration may artificially increase estimates of scale content reliability. No other types of reliability (e.g., parallel forms, test-retest) are reported for the total scales on the Western Personality Inventory. Furthermore, no reliability information of any sort is reported for the trait scales on the inventory.

With respect to validity, the manual reports a number of methods of validity determination; however, these are not all independent. Only the classification efficiency (alcoholics vs. nonalcoholics) is of prime importance. Using the normative data sample of 571 cases, total scores on the Manson Evaluation have led to correct diagnoses of 79% of male alcoholics, 79% of male nonalcoholics, 80% of female alcoholics, and 86% of female nonalcoholics. Using the Alcadd Test total scores with its normative sample of 282 cases, correct diagnoses were found for 96% of male alcoholics, 93% of male nonalcoholics, 97% of female alcoholics, and 97% of female nonalcoholics. No validity data are presented on the combined use of the Manson Evaluation and the Alcadd Test. Trait scale validities are not reported in the manual either. Although the total scales' diagnostic efficiencies may seem commendable, these may be spuriously high. For both the Manson Evaluation and the Alcadd Test, diagnostic validities were determined using the same groups of subjects that were used during the stages of item selection for the tests. Thus diagnostic results, as reported in the manual, are *not* cross-validated data and may be speciously inflated.

From a factor analytic perspective, no data are cited concerning the basic structure of the Western Personality Inventory. Whether the subjective grouping of items into trait scales has any empirical support remains unexplored. Trait scale intercorrelations have yet to be determined. Even the statistical relationship between the Manson Evaluation and the Alcadd Test, although available else-where (e.g., a correlation of .85 as reported by Clark, 1958), is not described in the manual.

Other research exists concerning the utility of the Western Personality Inventory, in particular, the Manson Evaluation. Manson (1949 a,b) relates the total scale of the Manson Evaluation to the Psychopathic Deviate Scale of the Minnesota Multiphasic Personality Inventory (correlations of .62 and .54 for males and females, respectively) and to the Cornell Selectee Index, Form N (correlations of .80 and .77 for males and females, respectively). Murphy (1956) provides a cross-validation of diagnostic efficiency for both the Manson Evaluation (77% hit rate) and the Alcadd Test (95% hit rate). Gibbins, Smart, and Seeley (1959) have severely criticized the Manson Evaluation on the grounds that the groups used in the test standardization were not comparable. Gibbins, et al. (p. 361) state, "This seems to eliminate most of the situations in which the use of the test for diagnostic purposes would make any sense." Gubernachuk and Brockman (1976) indicate that the Manson Evaluation could not distinguish between male heroin addicts and alcoholics nor among female heroin addicts, alcoholics, and criminals. Although this may be taken as support for the test's evaluation of a psychopathic personality, it does not support the discriminant validity of the Manson Evaluation for the detection of "alcoholism," per se. Finally, Fowler and Bernard (1965) argue that the Alcadd Test's original norms for alcoholics are inappropriate and biased because these scores are based on a sample largely comprised of self-disclosing members of Alcoholics Anonymous.

Critique

The original intent of the Western Personality Inventory appears to have a great deal of merit. The assessment of both a domain of actual drinking behavior and a field of related personality is a laudable approach. Despite this initial positive characteristic, however, the Western Personality Inventory would seem to be an anachronism. Theories and typologies of alcoholism (e.g., Cox, 1979; Morey, Skinner, & Blashfield, 1984) have surpassed Manson's earlier formulations of three decades ago. Psychometrically, the instrument appears to be of questionable status. Norms are over 35-years-old and appear based on atypical alcoholics. Although total scale scores have some reliability and validity, these results have not been demonstrated to be independent of response styles. Dissimulation may also be a problem for this inventory, particularly given its focus on alcoholism. As is, the Western Personality Inventory possesses no validity indices that could warn of attempts to fake on the apart of test respondents. Finally, at a structural level, no empirical support exists for the subjective development of the trait scales on this test. Future statistical analysis may or may not support the legitimacy of these arbitrary scales. Overall, therefore, the current clinical and research usefulness of the Western Personality Inventory appears to be extremely limited.

References

Clark, J. W. (1958). *Personality syndromes in chronic alcoholism: A factorial study.* Unpublished doctoral dissertation, Queen's University, Kingston, Canada.

Cox, W. M. (1979). The alcoholic personality: A review of the evidence. In B. A. Maher (Ed.), *Progress in experimental personality research: Vol. 9* (pp. 89-148). New York: Academic Press.

Fowler, R. D., & Bernard, J. L. (1965). Alternative norms for the Alcadd based on outpatient alcoholics. *Journal of Clinical Psychology, 21,* 29-33.

Gibbons, R. J., Smart, R. G., & Seeley, J. R. (1959). A critique of the Manson Evaluation test. *Quarterly Journal of Studies on Alcohol, 20,* 357-361.

Gubernachuk, E., & Brockman, L. M. (1976). The Manson Evaluation as an indicator of heroin independence. *British Journal of Addictions, 71,* 353-358.

Manson, M. P. (1948). A psychometric differentiation of alcoholics from nonalcoholics. *Quarterly Journal of Studies on Alcohol, 9,* 175-206.

Manson, M. P. (1949a). A psychometric analysis of psychoneurotic and psychosomatic characteristics of alcoholics. *Journal of Clinical Psychology, 5,* 77-83.

Manson, M. P. (1949b). A psychometric analysis of psychopathic characteristics of alcoholics. *Journal of Consulting Psychology, 13,* 111-118.

Manson, M. P. (1949c). A psychometric determination of alcoholic addiction. *American Journal of Psychiatry, 106,* 199-205.

Manson, M. P. (1963). *The Western Personality Inventory manual.* Los Angeles: Western Psychological Services.

Morey, L. C., Skinner, H. A., & Blashfield, R. K. (1984). A typology of alcohol abusers: Correlates and implications. *Journal of Abnormal Psychology, 93,* 408-417.

Murphy, D. G. (1956). The revalidation of diagnostic tests for alcohol addiction. *Journal of Consulting Psychology, 20,* 301-304.

G. Beverly Wells, Ph.D.
Professor and Coordinator of Graduate Studies, Department of Communicative Disorders, University of Southwestern Louisiana, Lafayette, Louisiana.

THE WORD TEST

Carol Jorgensen, Mark Barrett, Rosemary Huisingh, and Linda Zachman. Moline, Illinois: LinguiSystems, Inc.

Introduction

The WORD Test is designed to assess the expressive vocabulary and semantics of children, ages 7-12 years. The semantic items are sampled in six categories, ranging from vocabulary definitions to semantic absurdities.

The authors of The WORD Test are all ASHA certified speech language pathologists, who spent two years developing this standardized testing instrument to assess vocabulary and semantics. In addition to The WORD Test, the authors, Carol Jorgensen, Mark Barrett, Rosemary Huisingh, and Linda Zachman, have coauthored The Test of Problem Solving, The Oral Language Sentence Imitation Screening Test, The Oral Language Sentence Imitation Diagnostic Inventory, Teaching Vocabulary, Manual of Exercises for Expressive Reasoning, MEER Images, and Situational Language: A Pragmatic Approach to Problem Solving.

The test is published by Linguisystems where Jorgensen is director of special projects; Barrett is chief financial officer; Huisingh is director of creative writing; and Zachman is chief executive officer. Each of the authors has a special interest area within the broad area of language development and disorders. Barrett is also director of the Bi-State Speech and Language Clinic in Moline, Illinois.

The normative population included 270 subjects from 74 Milwaukee public schools. The subjects, randomly selected according to race, sex, age, and school, within the age range of 7-12 years, were administered the test items by trained speech-language pathologists.

The test materials consist of an examiner's manual and test forms. The manual contains administration protocol, statistical and normative analyses, tables with age equivalents, percentile ranks, standard score values, and data on reliability and correlation. The test forms provide space for identifying information and raw scores, age equivalents, percentile ranks, and standard scores for individual task levels. It also provides graphs for the examiner to plot the age equivalency profile and the standard score profile. Each form also contains the stimulus items, lists of acceptable responses, and places to circle or write in the actual responses.

The subject's semantic skills are assessed through the following six categories of test items:

Association: The ability to discriminate a word that does not belong in a group of words;

Synonyms: The ability to provide a word that has the same meaning as the stimulus word;

Semantic Absurdities: The ability to understand why a given sentence is incorrect;

Antonyms: The ability to provide a word that has the opposite meaning of the stimulus word;

Definitions: The ability to explain the meaning of a stimulus word;

Multiple Definitions: The ability to provide more than one meaning for each stimulus word.

The test is individually administered and not suitable for group use. All test categories are presented orally by the examiner. It is designed for older children, ages 7-12 years, with the level of test difficulty corresponding to the normative age group. The vocabulary for the test items was derived from the general reading vocabulary of elementary schools in Iowa.

Practical Applications/Uses

The WORD Test is a practical, useful test for the speech-language pathologist to obtain a comprehensive analysis of an older child's linguistic strengths and weaknesses with respect to vocabulary and semantics. This test is useful for speech-language pathologists regardless of job setting. Other trained professionals who work with the communicatively handicapped may benefit from this type of assessment if the communicative disorder present is language-related. The authors indicate that it can be administered to the learning disabled, mentally disabled, and other exceptional children, as well as to the language disabled. The test is designed to comprehensively examine the older child's ability to recognize and express the critical semantic elements in the reading vocabulary of children ages 7 to 12 years. The test may also be used to obtain a semantic analysis of the language of children and adults, older than the normative population, whose functional language is within the range of this test. This test would not be appropriate for children whose functional language was lower than that typical of the 7 year old, nor would it be appropriate for the deaf individual, since the test is designed to be presented auditorally.

The test may be used in any setting but is designed to be administered to one child at a time. Although designed specifically to meet the needs of speech-language pathologists, it may also be administered by other trained professionals, such as psychologists, teachers of the learning disabled, and special education consultants. The WORD Test, however, should be administered in a one-on-one situation by trained professionals.

The test is highly portable, relatively inexpensive, and easy to administer. It is untimed and administration takes approximately thirty minutes and may be given in more than one testing session. Scoring is by hand and simplified by the inclusion of acceptable and unacceptable responses for each item. Responses are scored as either 0, 1, or 2. All tasks except one require only a 0 or 1 score (incorrect/correct). The Associations task requires a correct reason as well as a correct choice, resulting in a score of 2. However, it is recommended that the examiner keep the manual open to the scoring standards section, in which a complete listing of correct and incorrect responses may be found.

The testing ceiling for each task is easily and quickly identifiable; it is reached when the subject gives three consecutive incorrect responses. The scoring system also facilitates speedy and easy compilation of test scores. The instructions for scoring are presented clearly and are simple and straightforward. A trained professional should be able to score this test easily.

Interpretaion is based on objective scores, raw score totals for each task, and a total raw score for the entire test. The raw scores are then converted to age equivalents, percentiles, and standard scores. This data is provided in tables included in the manual. A professional trained in tests and measurements will have no difficulty interpreting the test results.

Technical Aspects

Standard errors of measurement, split-half coefficients, and reliability coefficients based on item difficulty, using the Kuder-Richardson formula, KR 20, were used to determine the reliability of The WORD Test. The standard error of measurement indicates the degree of variability that would take place in repeated assessments of a single individual. Split-half coefficients and reliability coefficients indicate the degree to which the individuals tested would maintain their same relative standing if examined again and again. The measures indicate high reliability for each task and for the overall test scores. The 7 years, 0 months to 7 years, 11 months group have a lower reliability on the Antonyms task (.67 and .69) than do the remainder of the age levels (overall reliability coefficients range from .80 to .85). This information is found in the test manual.

The normative population included relatively equal numbers of males and females. Races represented in this population included Caucasians, blacks, and a group labeled, "Hispanics and others." The number of subjects in the black and Hispanic and others groups was considerably lower tha the number of Caucasians. Generalization of the consistency of performance of nonCaucasian groups, then, should be made with caution.

Content validity (whether the construction of the test really represents the skills and abilities the test was designed to measure) was determined by comparison with other tests that were already available, such as the Test of Language Development and the Illinois Test of Psycholinguistic Abilities. The authors also tried to assess areas not included in tests that were available at that time, but were recognized by authorities as being important aspects of semantics, such as Task F, Multiple Definitions.

The empirical validity was determined by measuring internal consistency. The authors selected as final test items those which met the criteria of increasing scores with increasing age and significant discrimination, as revealed by the results of the Chi Square Test. The authors also computed correlations between each item and task scores. The results appear in tables in the manual and reveal satisfactory degrees of discrimination across age groups. Additionally, tables are presented which reveal task intercorrelations and correlations between the tasks and the total test for each age level. The results imply that a common dimension is present in the separate tasks, while each task assesses a unique feature of that common dimension. However, factor analytic studies need to be completed to provide definitive evidence. Estimates of predictive and concurrent validity have not yet been determined for The WORD Test.

Critique

The WORD Test is an up-to-date test of semantics, which provides the speech-language pathologist with a comprehensive analysis of the individual's strengths and weaknesses in understanding the use of vocabulary and semantics. It was specifically developed for use with children ages 7 to 12 years. However, it can be used with older individuals if their functional language is within the test norms. The test is portable, relatively inexpensive, and simple to administer. The scoring and interpretation are practical and easy for trained professionals.

It provides two important features not present in many of the available tests of vocabulary and semantics. One feature is the number of specific areas assessed by the test in a short period of time; most similar tests require greater administration time or lack the comprehensiveness of this one. The other feature it provides is the additional verification of the subjects' correct responses, which is built into the structure of the test. For example, in the Association task, guessing is compensated for by requiring subjects to explain their reasoning in addition to discriminating an inappropriate word within a group of words.

The WORD Test's assessment of semantics provides the speech-language pathologist with a comprehensive analysis of the subject's language within a short period of time and requires only a limited amount of materials. It also enables the speech-language pathologist to devise a more individualized therapy plan.

References

This list includes text citations as well as suggested additional reading.

Allen, H. B. (Ed.), (1964). *Readings in applied English linguistics.* New York: Appleton-Century-Crofts.

Jorgensen, C., Barrett, M., Huisingh, R., & Zachman, L. (1981). *The WORD Test.* Moline, IL: LinguiSystems, Inc.

Lehmann, W. (1972). *Descriptive linguistics: An introduction.* New York: Random House, Inc.

Lucas, E. (1980). *Semantic and pragmatic language disorders: Assessment and remediation.* Rockville, MD: Aspen Systems Corp.

Schwabel, M., & Raph, J. (1973). *Piaget in the classroom.* New York: Basic Books, Inc.

Smart, M., & Smart, R. (1973). *Adolescents development and relationships.* New York: Macmillan Publishing Co.

Brian Bolton, Ph.D.

Professor, Arkansas Rehabilitation Research and Training Center, University of Arkansas, Fayetteville, Arkansas.

WORK VALUES INVENTORY

Donald E. Super. Chicago, Illinois: The Riverside Publishing Company.

Introduction

The Work Values Inventory (WVI; Super, 1968) was developed to measure the goals that motivate people to work. Values are defined as desirable ends or objectives that people seek in their behavior. Work values refer to those goal-directed motives that influence vocational choice, career development, and occupational adjustment. The WVI measures the entire range of values that are intrinsic and extrinsic to work. It is suitable for use with males and females at all educational and intelligence levels beginning with entry into junior high school.

Donald Super received an M.A. from Oxford, specializing in philosophy, politics, and economics, and a Ph.D. in applied psychology from Columbia University. His lengthy academic career, spent almost entirely at Columbia, has focused on vocational guidance, career development, and occupational psychology. Super's extensive contributions were recognized in 1983 by the American Psychological Association when he received its Distinguished Scientific Award for the Applications of Psychology. He is best known for his publications resulting from the Career Pattern Study and, more recently, the Work Importance Study.

Research on the WVI began in 1951 in conjunction with the Career Pattern Study. The current form, which consists of 45 items rated by the respondent using a standard 5-point Likert format, was preceded by two earlier forms and numerous psychometric studies. The 15 work values were originally identified through a comprehensive literature review, which included Spranger's (1928) theory and research by Centers (1948), Ginzberg, Ginzberg, Axelrad, and Herma (1951), and Hoppock (1935). The development and refinement of WVI items encompassed analysis of interviews with and essays by junior high school students, card sorting and labelling experiments with young adults, and internal consistency statistical analyses. Forced-choice, rank order, and ratings on a 4-point scale were tried before the present 5-point rating format was selected (Super, 1970; 1973).

In order to communicate the direct relevance of work values to the concerns of vocational guidance and occupational psychology, Super (1973, pp. 189-191; 1984) carefully distinguishes among four constructs: personality traits, values, interests, and needs. These important distinctions can be summarized in a series of brief propositions:

1. Traits, values, and interests derive from needs. A need is a lack of something that, if present, would contribute to the well-being of the individual

835

and is accompanied by a drive to do something about it (see Bolton 1980a, for a discussion of needs).

2. The need to have, do, or be leads to action, and action leads to modes of behavior or traits that seek objectives formulated in generic terms (values) or in specific terms (interests).

3. Traits are ways of acting to meet a need in a given situation; values are objectives that one seeks to attain to satisfy a need; interests are the specific activities through which values can be attained and needs met.

4. Assessments of needs and traits may help us to understand the make-up of people, but they do not help us to predict occupational behavior; it is therefore to values and interests that counselors must look if they want to assess employment-related motivation and behavior.

The WVI is a self-report inventory consisting of 45 brief statements that refer to various aspects and benefits of work. Representative examples* are "Gain prestige in your field," "Make your own decisions," "Feel you have helped another person," and "Have a supervisor who is considerate." The respondent judges the importance of each statement using a standard set of five characterizations ranging from "Very Important" to "Unimportant." The *Work Values Inventory Manual* (Super, 1970) contains detailed information about administration, score interpretation, norms, and technical information for the WVI, which is suitable for use with adolescents and adults who have sixth-grade reading competence.

The 15 work values that are measured by the WVI are briefly described as follows (manual, pp. 8-10):

1. *Altruism* (Al): present in work that enables one to contribute to the welfare of others.

2. *Esthetic* (Es): inherent in work that permits one to make beautiful things and contribute beauty to the world.

3. *Creativity* (Cr): associated with work that permits one to invent new things, design new products, or develop new ideas.

4. *Intellectual Stimulation* (IS): associated with work that provides opportunity for independent thinking and for learning how and why things work.

5. *Achievement* (Ac): associated with work that gives one a feeling of accomplishment in doing a job well.

6. *Independence* (In): associated with work that permits one to work in his or her own way as fast or as slowly as desired.

7. *Prestige* (Pr): associated with work that gives one standing in the eyes of others and evokes respect.

8. *Management* (Ma): associated with work that permits one to plan and lay out work for others to do.

9. *Economic Returns* (ER): associated with work which pays well and enables one to have the things he or she wants.

10. *Security* (Se): associated with work that provides one with the certainty of having a job even in hard times.

---

*These items (#6, 21, 30, and 43) are from the Work Values Inventory, copyright © 1970, and are reproduced with the permission of The Riverside Publishing Company, 8420 Bryn Mawr Avenue, Chicago, IL 60631.

11. *Surroundings* (Su): associated with work that is carried out under pleasant conditions—not too hot, cold, noisy, dirty, etc.

12. *Supervisory Relations* (SR): associated with work that is carried out under a supervisor who is fair and with whom one can get along.

13. *Associates* (As): characterized by work which brings one into contact with compatible fellow workers.

14. *Way of Life* (WL): associated with the kind of work that permits one to live the kind of life he or she chooses and to be the type of person he or she wishes to be.

15. *Variety* (Va): associated with work that provides an opportunity to do different types of jobs.

Practical Applications/Uses

The WVI was designed for use in vocational and career counseling with students in junior and senior high schools, vocational-technical schools, and colleges, and clients of community employment agencies. It may also be appropriately used in personnel selection and development programs; however, these applications must recognize that responses to the instrument are subject to social desirability by individuals who are motivated to answer in culturally approved ways. Knowledge of the value structure of a student or client in vocational counseling or an applicant or employee in business and industry is important in helping to clarify career goals and judge the appropriateness of various types of training and employment.

As stated previously, the WVI is suitable for use with almost all persons from junior high school to retirement age. Although the language level of the WVI items is easily within the functioning capability of the typical sixth-grader, and the directions and response format are simple to understand, oral administration would be entirely appropriate for poor readers. It would be a very simple task for the examiner to prepare an audio-tape cassette to facilitate WVI administration to persons with poor reading skills or to visually impaired examinees.

The directions for administering the WVI are presented in detail in the manual (pp. 5-7). The WVI can be easily administered to groups of examinees in school classrooms, personnel offices, or almost any other convenient setting. It can be administered by teachers, psychometric technicians, or other trained personnel under the supervision of a psychological or educational examiner or a vocational guidance counselor. Except for the possibility of reading difficulty for a small segment of the respondent population, users of the WVI should not anticipate problems with test administration; most examinees complete it in 10 to 15 minutes.

The WVI may be either machine-scored or hand-scored. Each of the 15 values is scored by summing the numerical equivalent of the five response characterizations (i.e., Very Important = 5; Important = 4; Moderately Important = 3; Of Little Importance = 2; Unimportant = 1) for the three statements that measure that work value. The manual contains the scoring key that lists the three items that are scored on each of the 15 work value scales. The publisher offers a machine scoring service that generates individual demographic data (name, sex, and date), raw scores for each of the 15 scales, and grade percentile ranks for each raw score. At the time of this writing the cost was about $1.00 per WVI protocol.

Three approaches to the WVI's interpretation—the individualized, the normative, and predictive strategies—are available to the user of the instrument. The simplest strategy, the individualized, involves the identification of the three work scales on which the respondent scored highest (i.e., judged to be most important). The identification process entails reviewing the 15 raw scores (ranging from 3 to 15) and noting the three highest scores. This *intra*-individual interpretive procedure assumes that the 15 triples of statements have equal stimulus properties within the domain of measured work values.

By selecting the three work values with the highest scores the counselor and examinee can focus their attention on those motivational elements that have the greatest salience for the examinee. Another assumption underlying this interpretive strategy is that the highest triad will result in a relatively unique or individualized picture of the respondent's work value preferences. An evaluation of this assumption using a large sample of physically disabled vocational rehabilitation clients revealed that no single triad accounted for as much as 10% of the WVI response patterns and that the twelve most common triads accounted for fewer than one-half of the clients' WVI response patterns (Bolton, 1980b). Thus, it may be concluded that the highest-triad interpretive strategy produces a relatively unique piece of information about the vocational motivation of physically disabled adults.

The normative strategy involves the use of appropriate normative data to convert the respondent's profile of raw scores to a corresponding set of derived scores (i.e., percentile equivalents). The purpose of the normative comparison is to determine the examinee's salient work values relative to other persons. The resulting *inter*-individual interpretation assumes that the normative data provide a suitable comparison for the examinee population with which the instrument is being used. The manual (pp. 12-25) presents excellent normative data for junior and senior high school students, with separate conversion tables for each combination of grade-level and sex for grades 7-12. However, because the normative data was collected in spring, 1968 there may be some question as to its suitability for use in the 1980s. In a study that compared the work values of undergraduate college students in 1970, 1976, 1978, and 1980, it was observed that work valuation increased during the decade, especially for females (Staats, 1981).

Because the oldest normative samples in the manual are twelfth-grade boys and girls the use of the normative interpretation with college students and other adult populations may be questionable. Zaccaria, Jacobs, Creaser, and Klehr (1972) compared the WVI profiles of a large sample of college-bound seniors with the seniors-in-general normative samples in the manual (pp. 24-25) and found that the college-bound students scored lower on most of the work value scales. In contrast to this finding, Bolton (1980b) concluded that the WVI seniors-in-general standardization sample provides an appropriate base for the normative interpretation of WVI scores of physically disabled adults.

The predictive strategy uses the occupational reinforcer patterns (ORPs) for 148 diverse occupations that were developed to operationalize the Minnesota Theory of Work Adjustment (MTWA: Dawis, 1976). The ORPs are descriptions of the 148 occupations in terms of differential patterns of reinforcers that the work environments provide. The MTWA maintains that job satisfaction is a function of the correspondence between the employee's needs or work values and the reinforcers available in the work situation.

To identify those occupations that match a respondent's profile of work values, it is first necessary to convert the WVI scales into parallel ORP dimensions; this translation can be accomplished using a table developed by Zytowski (1973, p. 13). The next step is to compare the respondent's WVI-ORP profile to each of the 12 occupational clusters in the handbook assembled by Rosen, Weiss, Hendel, Dawis, and Lofquist (1972, pp. 154-177). A reasonably accurate comparison can be obtained by using the three highest and three lowest values from the WVI-ORP profile. Each of the 12 clusters contains about a dozen specific occupations that the examinee can explore in conjunction with the vocational counseling process. If a more detailed search is preferred, each of the 148 occupations have been ranked on each of the 21 ORP dimensions (Rosen et al., 1972, pp. 188-271).

The advantage of the predictive occupational strategy over the individualized and normative strategies is that it translates the profile of work values directly into potential occupations that are identified in terms of their capacities to satisfy the examinee's motivational pattern. It should also be mentioned that the detailed WVI scale descriptions which are given in the manual (pp. 8-10) and are essential to the individualized and normative interpretive strategies, are based partly on research investigations that used earlier forms of the WVI. In particular, the correlations with other instruments (p. 37) and the occupational comparisons (pp. 46-48) should be regarded with caution.

Technical Aspects

Test-retest reliabilities for the 15 scales of the WVI for a sample of 99 tenth-grade students with a 2-week interval between administrations are (manual, p. 27) Al(.83), Es(.84), Cr(.84), IS(.81), Ac(.83), In(.83), Pr(.76), Ma(.84), ER(.88), Se(.87), Su(.82), SR(.83), As(.74), WL(.80), and Va(.82). The median reliability is .83 with a range from .74 to .88, coefficients that are consistent with the careful development of the WVI and supportive of the use of the WVI with individual cases. It should be noted, however, that Zaccaria et al. (1972) obtained a median test-retest reliability of only .62 with a range from .48 to .74 for 97 college-bound seniors who were retested after about two months.

Several lines of evidence suggest that the WVI is a valid measure of work values. The foundation of the validity of the WVI is Super's (1973) careful conceptual delineation of the construct of values summarized earlier. A substantial indication of the WVI's content validity was provided by a comparison of six independently developed systems of work values (including the WVI) by Zytowski (1970); the author concluded that 12 to 15 value categories spanned the domain of work values. Following a different strategy, Gable and Pruzek (1971) statistically analyzed the 45 WVI items and concluded that the 15 scales represent discriminable value dimensions.

A factor analysis of the 45 WVI items for a large sample of physically disabled adults who were applicants for vocational rehabilitation services resulted in five higher-order dimensions of work values that were similar to five second-order value factors of the Minnesota Importance Questionnaire (MIQ: Lofquist &

Dawis, 1978). This convergence of independently derived value structures supports the construct of both instruments. The second-order WVI factors are as follows (Bolton, 1980c):

1. *Stimulating Work.* The items that define this dimension come from three primary value scales: Intellectual Stimulation (IS), Variety (Va), and Creativity (Cr). The item content reflects a common core of need for challenging and meaningful work. (MIQ: Achievement)
2. *Interpersonal Satisfaction.* The three best definers of this factor are from the Altruism (Al) scale, with lower-loading items from the Associates (As) and Achievement (Ac) scales. The items suggest a clear people orientation in this dimension; what is valued is helping others, being with others, and doing worthwhile work. (MIQ: Altruism)
3. *Economic Security.* The five highest-loading items are from the Economic Return (ER) and Security (Se) subscales and reflect financial concerns and job security. (MIQ: Safety)
4. *Responsible Autonomy.* Five of the six significant items that define this factor are from the Management (Ma) and Independence (In) subscales. These items express the need to function autonomously and, at the same time, exercise authority and supervise the work of others. (MIQ: Autonomy)
5. *Comfortable Existence.* The five highest-loading items are from the Surroundings (Su) and Way of Life (WL) subscales and indicate a central concern with a pleasant environment, both work and nonwork. (MIQ: Comfort)

The second-order factors as well as the WVI primary scales are essentially independent of respondents' age, education, and intelligence, findings supportive of Super's (1970; 1973) claim that the WVI is a wide-range values inventory suitable for use with almost all segments of the adolescent and adult population. However, there is consistent evidence of sex differences on some scales (e.g., females typically score higher on Altruism while males score higher on Economic Returns) and several studies have reported numerous sex differences on the WVI (e.g., Drummond, McIntire, & Skaggs, 1978; Hesketh, 1982; and Thomas, 1974). Hence, normative interpretations of WVI profiles should be based on separate norms for males and females.

The construct validity of the WVI has been extended by the results of some three dozen investigations reported in the psychological literature since 1970. Although it is obviously not feasible to review all of these studies here, several with findings directly relevant to the validity of the WVI are briefly summarized: 1) The WVI was independent of job knowledge for undergraduate students who were seeking career counseling, and the process of occupational exploration did not necessarily change students' values (Sampson & Loesch, 1981); 2) Several WVI scales were associated with greater reliance on the "planning style" of career decision-making for undergraduate students—use of the "intuitive style" or the "dependent style" was negatively correlated with some WVI scales (Lunneborg, 1978); 3) College students who were vocationally undecided scored lower on intrinsic WVI scales than did occupationally committed students (Greenhaus & Simon, 1977); 4) Intrinsic work values were associated with vocational maturity for vocational-technical students, whereas extrinsic values were not (Gade & Peterson, 1977; see also

Miller, 1974); 5) Among community college students, viewing one's chosen occupation as ideal was related to its perceived capacity to satisfy intrinsic work values (Greenhaus & Simon, 1976); 6) Self-estimate ability of work values did not increase with age for high school students, as Super's hypothesis of increased clarification of vocational concept would predict (Tierney & Herman, 1973; see also Tiedman, 1973; and Brown, Fulkerson, Vedder, & Ware, 1983); and 7) Several WVI scales were negatively correlated with a semantic differential measure of self-meaning for high school students (Pallone, Rickard, Hurley, & Tirman, 1970).

The WVI has also been used in several other investigations of vocationally related topics, e.g., value fulfillment and job satisfaction (Butler, 1983), work value changes among student nurses (Dietrich, 1977), participative management in a developing country (Ejiogu, 1983), Super's self-concept theory of career development (Kidd, 1984), career orientation of college women (Richardson, 1974), and long-term effects of developmental counseling (Wearne & Powell, 1977).

Critique

In addition to Super's Work Values Inventory (WVI), five instruments for assessing work values have been developed for use in vocational counseling settings since 1950: the Occupational Attitude Rating Scales (OARS; Hammond, 1954), the Vocational Values Inventory (VVI; Stefflre, 1959), the Minnesota Importance Questionnaire (MIQ; Gay, Weiss, Hendel, Dawis, & Lofquist, 1971), the Survey of Work Values (SWV; Wollack, Goodale, Wijtinrg, & Smith, 1971), and the Ohio Work Values Inventory (OWVI; Hales & Fenner, 1975). Of these six instruments, Super's WVI and the MIQ stand apart for their excellent psychometric foundations and their continuing use in research studies.

However, the forced-choice response format of the MIQ, as well as its length (four times as long as the WVI) and complicated scoring procedure, render it cumbersome for both respondents and counselors. A short version of the MIQ, which requires the respondent to rank five stimulus statements within each of 21 sets, is also available (Rounds & Dawis, 1976), but the ranking format also introduces problems, e.g., some individuals have trouble comparing five statements simultaneously. Because of its simple format, easy administration, face validity, and extensive research base, the WVI is the best all-around work values assessment instrument.

Despite this favorable evaluation, the WVI possesses several limitations and deficiencies, which deserve the attention of the author and publisher: 1) The WVI manual should be thoroughly revised and brought up to date by incorporating the results of research studies conducted since 1970. 2) Normative data for post-secondary students and employed adults in various occupations should be presented in appropriate tables. The manual (p. 8) indicates that this information was being collected 15 years ago. 3) The results of occupational validity studies using the current form of the WVI should replace findings based on earlier WVI forms in the interpretive descriptions of the 15 work value scales. The manual (p. 43) states that predictive validity data was also being collected. 4) Additional reliability studies should be conducted using college students and adults; the reliability evidence for a published instrument should not be limited to one modest sample of tenth-grade students.

References

Bolton, B. (1980a). Rehabilitation needs. In R. Woody (Ed.), *Encyclopedia of clinical assessment* (Vol. 2). San Francisco: Jossey-Bass.

Bolton, B. (1980b). The assessment of vocational motivation of physically disabled clients. *Journal of Applied Rehabilitation Counseling, 11*(1), 28-31.

Bolton, B. (1980c). Second-order dimensions of the Work Values Inventory (WVI). *Journal of Vocational Behavior, 17,* 33-40.

Brown, D., Fulkerson, K. F. Vedder, M., & Ware, W. B. (1983). Self-estimate ability in black and white 8th-, 10th- and 12th-grade males and females. *Vocational Guidance Quarterly, 32,* 21-28.

Butler, J. K. (1983). Value importance as a moderator of the value fulfillment-job satisfaction relationship: Group differences. *Journal of Applied Psychology, 63,* 420-428.

Centers, R. (1948). Motivational aspects of occupational stratification. *Journal of Social Psychology, 28,* 187-217.

Dawis, R. V. (1976). The Minnesota theory of work adjustment. In B. Bolton (Ed.), *Handbook of measurement and evaluation in rehabilitation.* Baltimore: University Park Press.

Dietrich, M. C. (1977). Work values evolution in a baccalaureate student nurse population. *Journal of Vocational Behavior, 10,* 25-34.

Drummond, R. J., McIntire, W. G., & Skaggs, C. T. (1978). The relationship of work to occupational level in young adult workers. *Journal of Employment Counseling, 15,* 117-121.

Ejiogu, A. M. (1983). Participative management in a developing economy. *Journal of Applied Behavioral Science, 19,* 239-247.

Gable, R. K., & Pruzek, R. M. (1971). Super's Work Values Inventory: Two multivariate studies of interitem relationships. *The Journal of Experimental Education, 40,* 41-50.

Gade, E. M., & Peterson, G. (1977). Intrinsic and extrinsic work values and the vocational maturity of vocational-technical students. *Vocational Guidance Quarterly, 26,* 125-130.

Gay, E. G., Weiss, D. J., Hendel, D. D., Dawis, R. V., & Lofquist, L. H. (1971). *Manual for the Minnesota Importance Questionnaire* (Monograph 28). Minneapolis: University of Minnesota, Vocational Psychology Research.

Ginzberg, E., Ginzberg, S., Axelrad, S., & Herma, J. (1951). *Occupational choice.* New York: Columbia University Press.

Greenhaus, J. H., & Simon, W. E. (1976). Self-esteem, career salience, and the choice of an ideal occupation. *Journal of Vocational Behavior, 10,* 104-110.

Greenhaus, J. H., & Simon, W. E. (1977). Career salience, work values, and vocational indecision. *Journal of Vocational Behavior, 10,* 104-110.

Hales, L. W., & Fenner, B. J. (1975). Measuring the work values of children: The Ohio Work Values Inventory. *Measurement and evaluation in guidance, 8,* 20-25.

Hammond, M. (1954). Occupational Attitude Rating Scales. *Personnel and Guidance Journal, 32,* 470-474.

Hesketh, B. (1982). Work values of a group of potential school leavers in two New Zealand high schools. *New Zealand Journal of Educational Studies, 17,* 68-73.

Hoppock, R. (1935). *Job satisfaction.* New York: Harper & Row.

Kidd, J. M. (1984). The relationship of self and occupational concepts to the occupational preferences of adolescents. *Journal of Vocational Behavior, 24,* 48-65.

Lofquist, L. H, & Dawis, R. V. (1978). Values as second-order needs in the Theory of Work Adjustment. *Journal of Vocational Behavior, 12,* 12-19.

Lunneborg, P. W. (1978). Sex and career decision-making styles. *Journal of Counseling Psychology, 25*(4), 299-305.

Miller, M. F. (1974). Relationship of vocational maturity to work values. *Journal of Vocational Behavior, 5*, 367-371.

Pallone, N. J., Rickard, F. S., Hurley, R. B., & Tirman, R. J. (1970). Work values and self-meaning. *Journal of Counseling Psychology, 17*, 376-377.

Richardson, M. S. (1974). The dimensions of career and work orientation in college women. *Journal of Vocational Behavior, 5*, 161-172.

Rosen, S. D., Weiss, D. J., Hendel, D. D., Dawis, R. V., & Lofquist, L. H. (1972). *Occupational reinforcer patterns* (2nd vol.) (Monograph 29). Minneapolis: University of Minnesota, Vocational Psychology Research.

Rounds, J. B., & Dawis, R. V. (1976). *Comparison of multiple rank order and paired comparison scaling techniques* (Research Rep.). Minneapolis: University of Minnesota, Vocational Psychology Research.

Sampson, J. P., & Loesch, L. C. (1981). Relationships among work values and job knowledge. *Vocational Guidance Quarterly, 29*, 229-235.

Spranger, E. (1928). *Types of men* (trans. by P.J.W. Pigors). Halle: Niemeyer.

Staats, S. (1981). Work Values Inventory scores from 1970 to 1980. *Perceptual & Motor Skills, 53*, 113-114.

Stefflre, B. (1959). Concurrent validities of the Vocational Values Inventory. *Journal of Educational Research, 52*, 339-341.

Super, D. E. (1968). *Work Values Inventory.* Chicago: Riverside Publishing Company.

Super, D. E. (1970). *Work Values Inventory Manual.* Chicago: Riverside Publishing Company.

Super, D. E. (1963). The Work Values Inventory. In D. G. Zytowski (Ed.), *Contemporary approaches to interest measurement.* Minneapolis: University of Minnesota Press.

Super, D. E. (1984). Perspectives on the meaning and value of work. In N. C. Gysbers (Ed.), *Designing careers: Counseling to enhance education, work, and leisure.* San Francisco: Jossey-Bass.

Thomas, H. B. (1974). The effects of social position, race, and sex on work values of ninth-grade students. *Journal of Vocational Behavior, 4*, 357-364.

Tiedeman, D. V. (1973). Comment on self-estimate ability in adolescence. *Journal of Counseling Psychology, 20*, 298-302.

Tierney, R. J., & Herman, A. (191973). Self-estimate ability in adolescence. *Journal of Counseling Psychology, 20*, 298-302.

Wearne, T. D., & Powell, J. C. (1977). The differential long-term effects of client-centered, developmental counseling with individuals and group. *Canadian Counsellor, 11*(2), 83-92.

Wollack, S., Goodale, J. G., Wijting, J. P., & Smith, P. C. (1971). Development of the Survey of Work Values. *Journal of Applied Psychology, 55*, 331-338.

Zaccaria, L., Jacobs, M., Creaser, J., & Klehr, H. (1972). Work values of college-bound students. *Psychological Reports, 31*, 567-569.

Zytowski, D. G. (1970). The concept of work values. *Vocational Guidance Quarterly, 18*, 176-186.

Zytowski, D. G. (Ed.). (1973). *Contemporary approaches to interest measurement.* Minneapolis: University of Minnesota Press.

INDEX OF TEST TITLES

INDEX OF TEST PUBLISHERS

Academic Therapy Publications, 20 Commercial Boulevard, Novato, California 94947; (415)883-3314—[II:621]

American College Testing Program, (The), 2201 North Dodge Street, P.O. Box 168, Iowa City, Iowa 52243; (319)337-1000—[I:11]

American Guidance Service, Publisher's Building, Circle Pines, Minnesota 55014; (800)328-2560, in Minnesota (612)786-4343—[I:322, 393, 712, 715]

American Orthopsychiatric Association, Inc., (The), 1775 Broadway, New York, New York 10019; (212)586-5690—[I:90]

ASIEP Education Company, 3216 N.E. 27th, Portland, Oregon 97212; (503) 281-4115—[I:75; II:441]

Associated Services for the Blind (ASB), 919 Walnut Street, Philadelphia, Pennsylvania 19107; (215)627-0600—[II:12]

Behavior Science Systems, Inc., Box 1108, Minneapolis, Minnesota 55440; no business phone—[II:472]

Bruce, (Martin M.), Ph.D., Publishers, 50 Larchwood Road, Larchmont, New York 10538; (914)834-1555—[I:70]

Center for Child Development and Education, College of Education, University of Arkansas at Little Rock, 33rd and University, Little Rock, Arkansas 72204; (501)569-3422—[II:337]

Center for Cognitive Therapy, 133 South 36th Street, Room 602, Philadelphia, Pennsylvania 19104; (215)898-4100—[II:83]

Center for Epidemiologic Studies, Department of Health and Human Services, 5600 Fishers Lane, Rockville, Maryland 20857; (301)443-4513—[II:144]

Clinical Psychometric Research, 1228 Wine Spring Lane, Towson, Maryland 21204; (301)321-6165—[II:32]

Communication Research Associates, Inc., P.O. Box 11012, Salt Lake City, Utah 84147; (801)292-3880—[I:707]

Communication Skill Builders, Inc., 3130 N. Dodge Blvd., P.O. Box 42050, Tucson, Arizona 85733; (602)323-7500—[II:191, 562]

Consulting Psychologists Press, Inc., 577 College Avenue, P.O. Box 60070, Palo Alto, California 94306; (415)857-1444—[I:34, 41, 146, 226, 259, 284, 380, 482, 623, 626, 663, 673; II:23, 56, 113, 263, 293, 509, 594, 697, 729]

C.P.S. Inc., Box 83, Larchmont, New York 10538; no business phone—[I:185]

Creative Learning Press, Inc., P.O. Box 320, Mansfield Center, Connecticut 06250; (203)423-8120—[II:402]

CTB/McGraw-Hill, Publishers Test Service, Del Monte Research Park, 2500 Garden Road, Monterey, California 93940; (800)538-9547, in California (800)682-9222, or (408)649-8400—[I:3, 164, 578; II:517, 584, 780]

Delis, (Dean), Ph.D., 3753 Canyon Way, Martinez, California 94553—[I:158]

Devereaux Foundation Press, (The), 19 South Waterloo Road, Box 400, Devon, Pennsylvania 19333; (215)964-3000—[II:231]

Diagnostic Specialists, Inc., 1170 North 660 West, Orem, Utah 84057; (801)224-8492—[II:95]

DLM Teaching Resources, P.O. Box 4000, One DLM Park, Allen, Texas 75002; (800)527-4747, in Texas (800)442-4711—[II:72]

D.O.K. Publishers, Inc., 71 Radcliffe Road, Buffalo, New York 14214; (716) 837-3391—[II:211]

Educational and Industrial Testing Service (EdITS), P.O. Box 7234, San Diego, California 92107; (619)222-1666—[I:279, 522, 555; II:3, 104, 258]

Educational Assessment Service, Inc., Route One, Box 139-A, Watertown, Wisconsin 53094; (414)261-1118—[II:332]

Elbern Publications, P.O. Box 09497, Columbus, Ohio 43209; (614)235-2643— [II:627]

Essay Press, P.O. Box 2323, La Jolla, California 92307;(619)565-6603—[II:646]

Evaluation Research Associates, P.O. Box 6503, Teall Station, Syracuse, New York 13217; (315)422-0064—[II:551]

Foundation for Knowledge in Development, (The), KID Technology, 11715 East 51st Avenue, Denver, Colorado 80239; (303)373-1916—[I:443]

Grune & Stratton, Inc., 111 Fifth Avenue, New York, New York 10003; (212) 741-6800—[I:189; II:819]

Halgren Tests, 873 Persimmon Avenue, Sunnyvale, California 94807; (408)738-1342—[I:549]

Harvard University Press, 79 Garden Street, Cambridge, Massachusetts 02138; (617)495-2600—[II:799]

Humanics Limited, 1182 W. Peachtree Street NE, Suite 201, Atlanta, Georgia 30309; (602)323-7500—[II:161, 426]

Industrial Psychology Incorporated (IPI), 515 Madison Avenue, New York, New York 10022; (212)355-5330—[II:363]

Institute for Personality and Ability Testing, Inc. (IPAT), P.O. Box 188, 1602 Coronado Drive, Champaign, Illinois 61820; (217)352-4739—[I:195, 202, 214, 233, 377; II:357]

Institute for Psycho-Imagination Therapy, c/o Joseph Shorr, Ph.D., 111 North La Cienega Boulevard #108, Beverly Hills, California 90211; (213)652-2922—[I:593]

Institute of Psychological Research, Inc., 34, Fleury Street West, Montreal, Quebec, Canada H3L 1S9; (514)382-3000—[II:530]

Jastak Associates, Inc., 1526 Gilpin, Wilmington, Delaware 19806; (302)652-4990— [I:758, 762]

Ladoca Publishing Foundation, Laradon Hall Training and Residential Center, East 51st Avenue & Lincoln Street, Denver, Colorado 80216; (303)629-6379— [I:239]

Lake, (David S.), Publishers, 19 Davis Drive, Belmont, California 94002; (415)592-7810—[II:241]

Lewis, (H.K.), & Co. Ltd., 136 Gower Street, London, England WC1E 6BS; (01)387-4282—[I:47, 206, 595]

LinguiSystems, Inc., Suite 806, 1630 Fifth Avenue, Moline, Illinois 61265; (800)ALL-TIME, in Illinois (309)762-5112—[II:831]

Marathon Consulting and Press, P.O. Box 09189, 575 Enfield Road, Columbus, Ohio 43209-0189; (614)237-5267—[II:138, 535]

Merrill, (Charles E.), Publishing Company, 1300 Alum Creek Drive, Box 508, Columbus, Ohio 43216; (614)258-8441—[I:125; II:35]

NCS Professional Assessment Services, P.O. Box 1416, Minneapolis, Minnesota 55440; (800)328-6759, in Minnesota (612)933-2800—[I:455, 466, 660; II:128]

Nelson Canada, 1120 Birchmount Road, Scarborough, Ontario M1K 5G4, Canada; (416)752-9100—[II:350]

Neuropsychology Laboratory, University of Wisconsin, University Hospitals, Madison, Wisconsin 53711; no business phone—[I:478]

NFER-Nelson Publishing Company Ltd., Darville House, 2 Oxford Road East, Windsor, Berkshire SL4 1DF, England; (07535)58961—[I:51, 130; II:88, 169, 388, 642]

Pediatric Psychology Press, 2915 Idlewood Drive, Charlottesville, Virginia 22901; (804)973-5680—[I:504]

PRO-ED, 5341 Industrial Oaks Boulevard, Austin, Texas 78735; (512)892-3142—[I:688; II:223, 235, 787]

Programs for Education, Inc., Dept. W-16, 82 Park Avenue, Flemington, New Jersey 08822; (212)689-3911—[II:310, 314, 681]

Psychodynamic Instruments, c/o Gerald Blum, Dept. of Psychology, University of California, Santa Barbara, California 93106; no business phone—[I:99]

Psychological Assessment and Services, Inc., P.O. Box 1031, Iowa City, Iowa 52240; no business phone—[I:473]

Psychological Assessment Resources, Inc., P.O. Box 98, Odessa, Florida 33556; (813)977-3395—[I:113, 491; II:288]

Psychological Corporation, (The), A Subsidiary of Harcourt Brace Jovanovich, Inc., 7500 Old Oak Boulevard, Cleveland, Ohio 44130; (216)234-5300—[I:47, 106, 117, 206, 252, 295, 328, 494, 499, 595, 608, 614, 648, 720, 728, 740, 750; II:16, 63, 175, 182, 319, 326, 436, 446, 463, 495, 579, 653]

Psychological Publications, Inc., 5300 Hollywood Boulevard, Los Angeles, California 90027; (213)465-4163—[I:654]

Psychological Services, Inc., 3450 Wilshire Boulevard, Suite 1200, Los Angeles, California 90010; (213)738-1132—[I:266]

Psychological Test Specialists, Box 9229, Missoula, Montana 59805; no business phone—[I:530; II:299, 376, 451, 603]

Psychologists and Educators, Inc., 211 West State Street, Jacksonville, Illinois 62650; (217)243-2135—[I:568]

Reid Psychological Systems, 233 North Michigan Avenue, Chicago, Illinois 60601; (312)938-9200—[I:631]

Reitan Neuropsychology Laboratory, 1338 East Edison Street, Tucson, Arizona 85719; (602)795-3717—[I:305, 536; II:637]

Research Psychologists Press, Inc., 1110 Military Street, P.O. Box 984, Port Huron, Michigan 48061-0984; (800)265-1285, in Michigan (313)982-4556—[II:369, 501]

Riverside Publishing Company, (The), 8420 Bryn Mawr Avenue, Chicago, Illinois 60631; (800)323-9540, in Alaska, Hawaii, or Illinois call collect (312)693-0040—

[I:421, 603, 641; II:416, 674, 835]

Rocky Mountain Behavioral Science Institute, Inc. (RMBSI), P.O. Box 1066, Fort Collins, Colorado 80522; no business phone—[I:436, 682]

Roll, (Samuel), Ph.D., 1100 Alvarado N.E., Suite C, Albuquerque, New Mexico 87110; no business phone—[II:559]

Scholastic Testing Service, Inc. (STS), 480 Meyer Road, P.O. Box 1056, Bensenville, Illinois 60106; (312)766-7150—[I:300; II:45]

Science Research Associates, Inc. (SRA), 155 North Wacker Drive, Chicago, Illinois 60606; (312)904-7000, —[I:29, 364, 406; II:198, 204, 275, 282, 395, 759, 773, 815]

Slosson Educational Publications, Inc., P.O. Box 280, East Aurora, New York 14052; (800) 828-4800, in New York (716)652-0930—[II:40]

Special Child Publications (SCP), P.O. Box 33548, Seattle, Washington 98133; (206)771-5711—[II:216]

Stanford University Press, Stanford, California 94305; (415)497-9434—[II:737]

Stoelting Company, 1350 S. Kostner Avenue, Chicago, Illinois 60623; (312) 522-4500—[I:274, 288, 411; II:255, 347, 383, 392, 411, 457, 491, 751]

Teachers College Press, Teachers College, Columbia University, 1234 Amsterdam Avenue, New York, New York 10027; (212)678-3929—[II:244, 303]

Test Analysis and Development Corporation, 2400 Park Lane Drive, Boulder, Colorado 80301; (303)666-8651—[II:707]

United States Department of Defense, Testing Directorate, Headquarters, Military Enlistment Processing Command, Attn: MEPCT, Fort Sheridan, Illinois 60037; (312)926-4111—[I:61]

United States Department of Labor, Division of Testing, Employment and Training Administration, Washington, D.C. 20213; (202)376-6270—[I:83]

University Associates, Inc., Learning Resources Corporation, 8517 Production Avenue, P.O. Box 26240, San Diego, California 92121; (619)578-5900—[I:559; II:765]

University of Illinois Press, 54 E. Gregory Drive, Box 5081, Station A, Champaign, Illinois 61820; institutions (800)233-4175, individuals (800)638-3030, or (217)333-0950—[I:354; II:543]

University of Minnesota Press, 2037 University Avenue S.E., Minneapolis, Minnesota 55414; (612)373-3266. Tests are distributed by NCS Professional Assessment Services, P.O. Box 1416 Minneapolis, Minnesota 55440; (800)328-6759, in Minnesota (612)933-2800—[I:466]

University of Vermont, College of Medicine, Department of Psychiatry, Section of Child, Adolescent, and Family Psychiatry, 1 South Prospect Street, Burlington, Vermont 05401; (802)656-4563—[I:168]

University of Washington Press, P.O. Box 85569, 4045 Brooklyn Avenue N.E., Seattle, Washington 98105; (206)543-4050, business department (206) 543-8870—[II:661, 714]

Valett, (Robert E.), Department of Advanced Studies, California State University at Fresno, Fresno, California 93740; no business phone—[II:68]

Vocational Psychology Research, University of Minnesota, Elliott Hall, 75 East

INDEX OF TEST AUTHORS/REVIEWERS

ABOUT THE EDITORS

Daniel J. Keyser, Ph.D. A graduate of the University of Kansas (1974), the University of Missouri (1965) and the University of Wisconsin (1959), Dr. Keyser has worked in drug and alcohol rehabilitation and psychiatric settings, and has taught undergraduate psychology at Rockhurst College for 15 years. He is presently employed by the Veterans Administration Hospital in Kansas City as a medical psychologist. Dr. Keyser specializes in behavioral medicine—biofeedback, pain control, stress management, terminal care support, habit management, and wellness maintenance. He also has a private clinical practice in Raytown, Missouri. Dr. Keyser co-edited *Tests* and *Tests:Supplement*, and has made significant contributions to computerized psychological testing. He is currently chairman of the board of Test Corporation of America.

Richard C. Sweetland, Ph.D. A graduate of Baylor University (1953), The University of Texas (1959), and Utah State University (1968), Dr. Sweetland completed postdoctoral training in psychoanalytically oriented clinical psychology at the Topeka State Hospital in conjunction with the training program of the Menninger Foundation in 1969. Following appointments in child psychology at the University of Kansas Medical Center and in neuropsychology at the Kansas City Veterans Administration Hospital, he entered the practice of psychotherapy in the Kansas City area. In addition to his clinical work in neuropsychology and psychoanalytic psychotherapy, Dr. Sweetland has been extensively involved in the development of computerized psychological testing. Dr. Sweetland co-edited *Tests* and *Tests:Supplement*. He is currently president of Test Corporation of America.